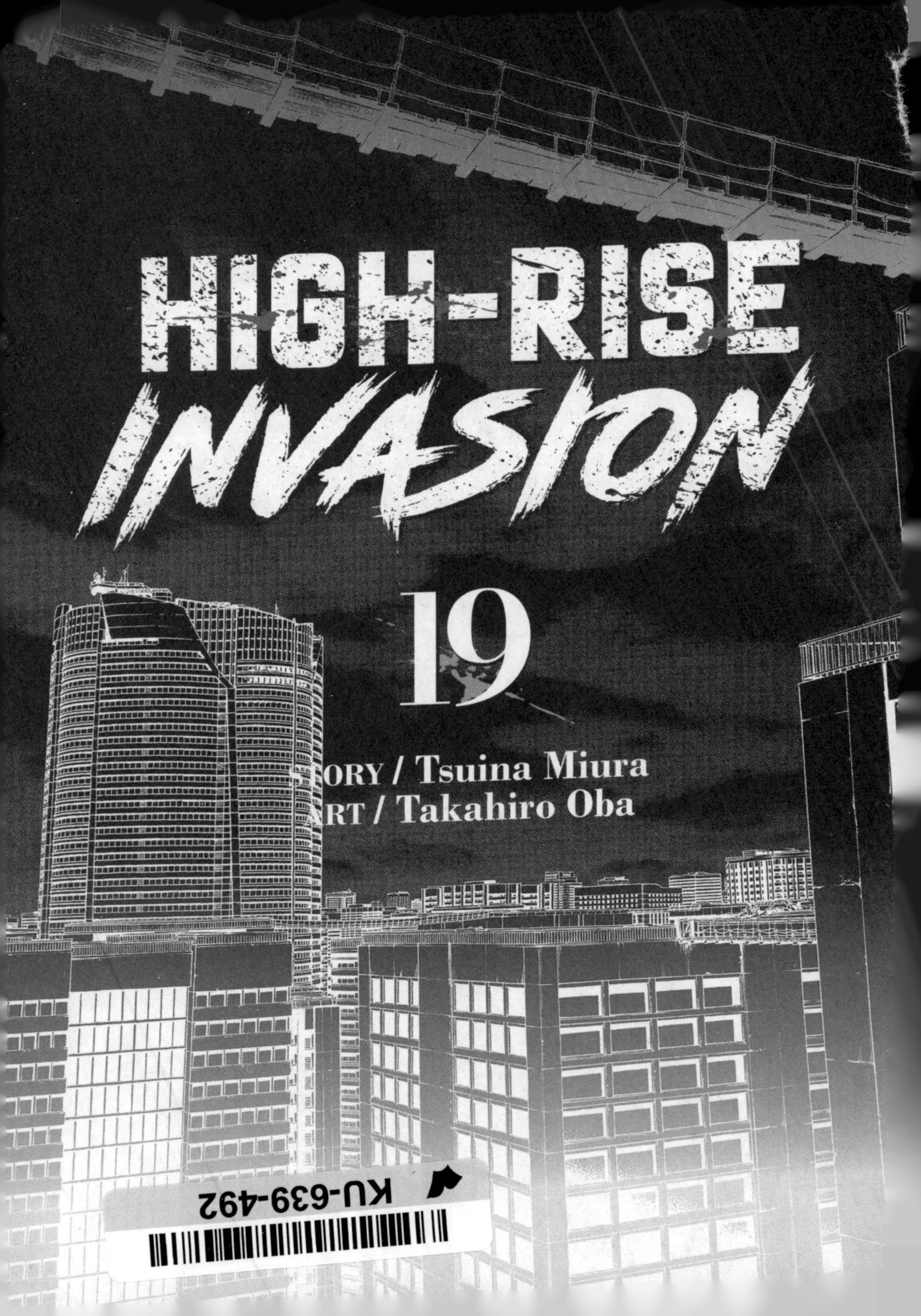
HIGH-RISE
INVASION
19
STORY / Tsuina Miura
ART / Takahiro Oba

HIGH-RISE INVASION

19

CONTENTS

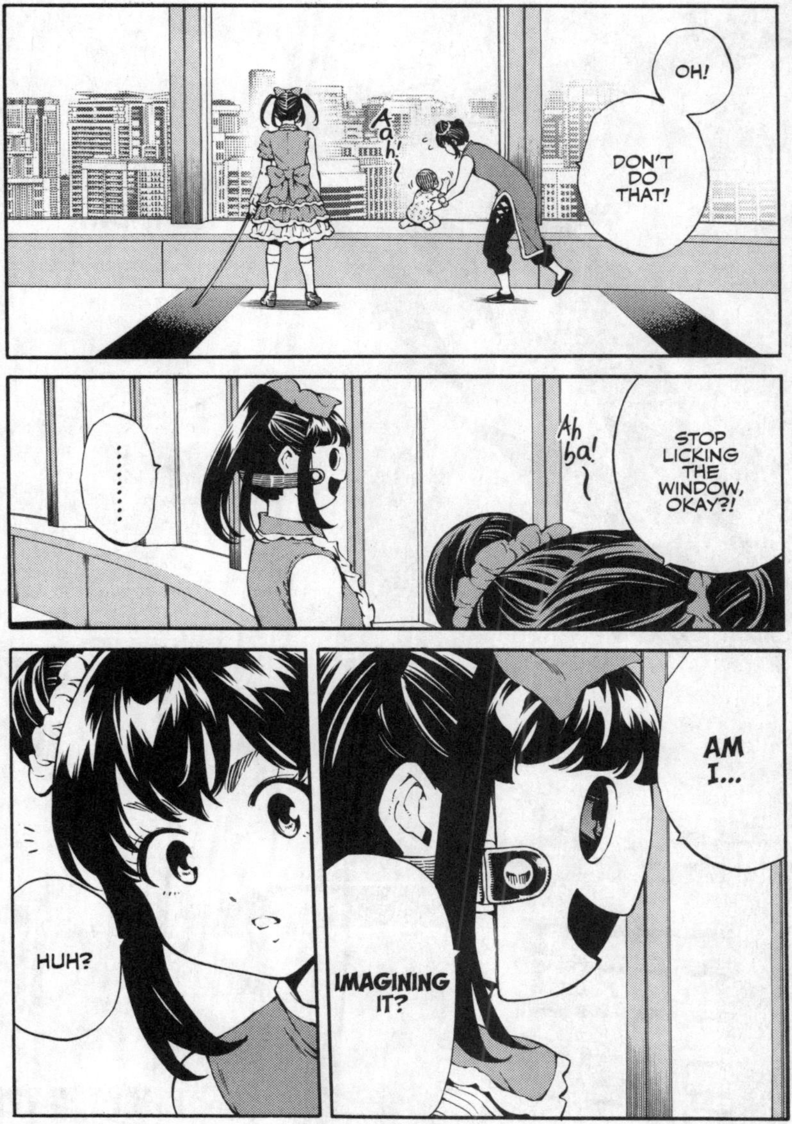
OH!
DON'T DO THAT!
Aah!~
STOP LICKING THE WINDOW, OKAY?!
Ah ba!~
......
AM I...
IMAGINING IT?
HUH?

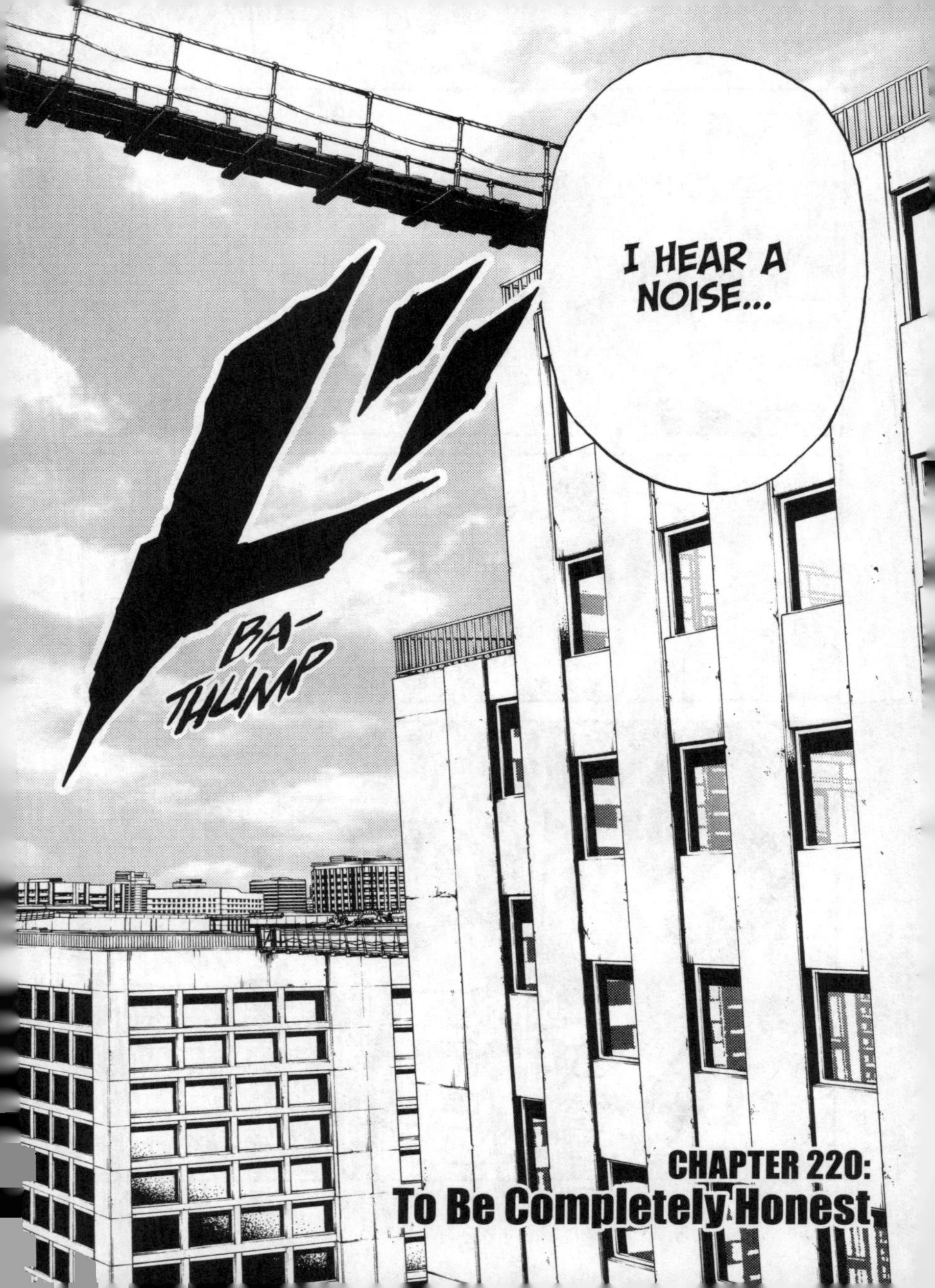
I HEAR A NOISE...
BA-THUMP
CHAPTER 220:
To Be Completely Honest

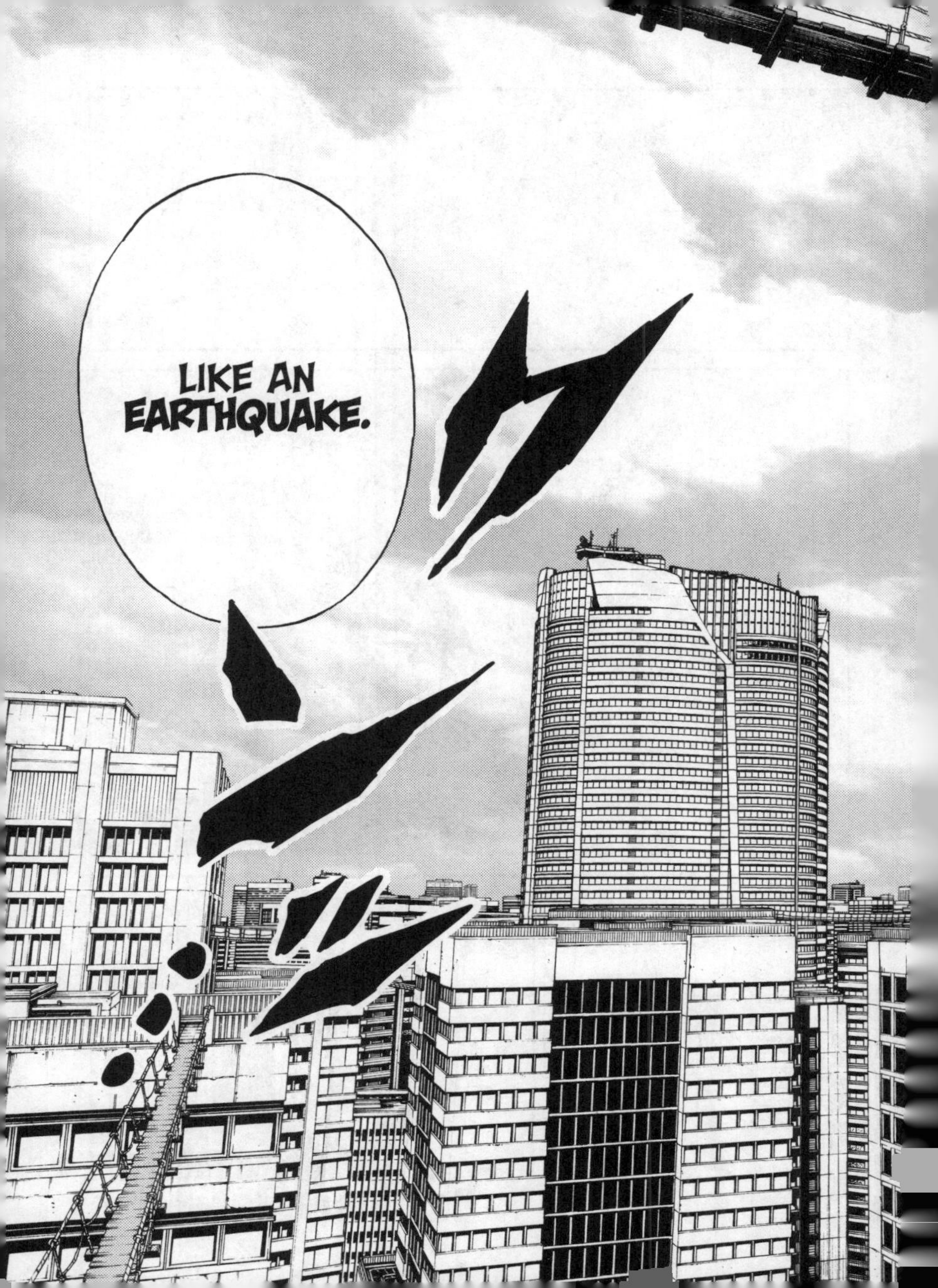
LIKE AN EARTHQUAKE.

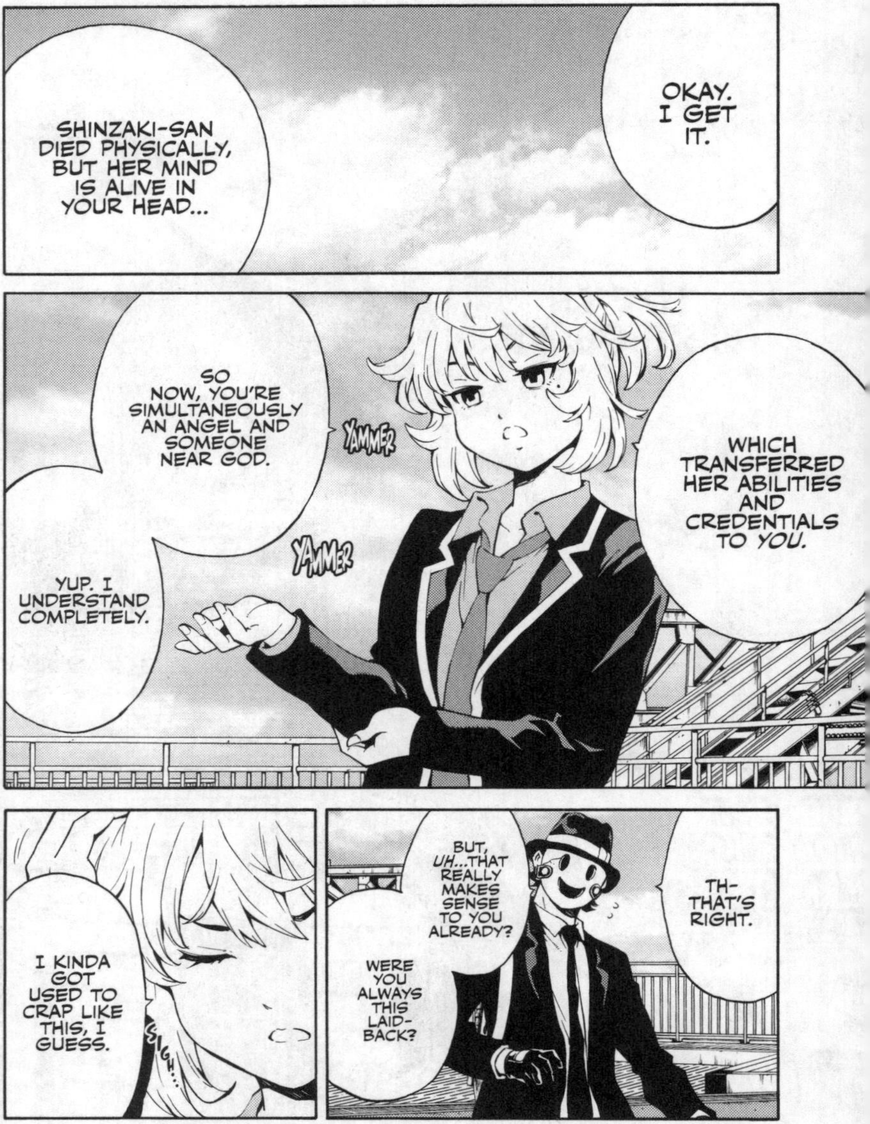
OKAY. I GET IT.
SHINZAKI-SAN DIED PHYSICALLY, BUT HER MIND IS ALIVE IN YOUR HEAD...
WHICH TRANSFERRED HER ABILITIES AND CREDENTIALS TO *YOU.*
SO NOW, YOU'RE SIMULTANEOUSLY AN ANGEL AND SOMEONE NEAR GOD.
YAMMER
YAMMER
YUP. I UNDERSTAND COMPLETELY.
TH-THAT'S RIGHT.
BUT, *UH*...THAT REALLY MAKES SENSE TO YOU ALREADY?
WERE YOU ALWAYS THIS LAID-BACK?
I KINDA GOT USED TO CRAP LIKE THIS, I GUESS.
SIGH...

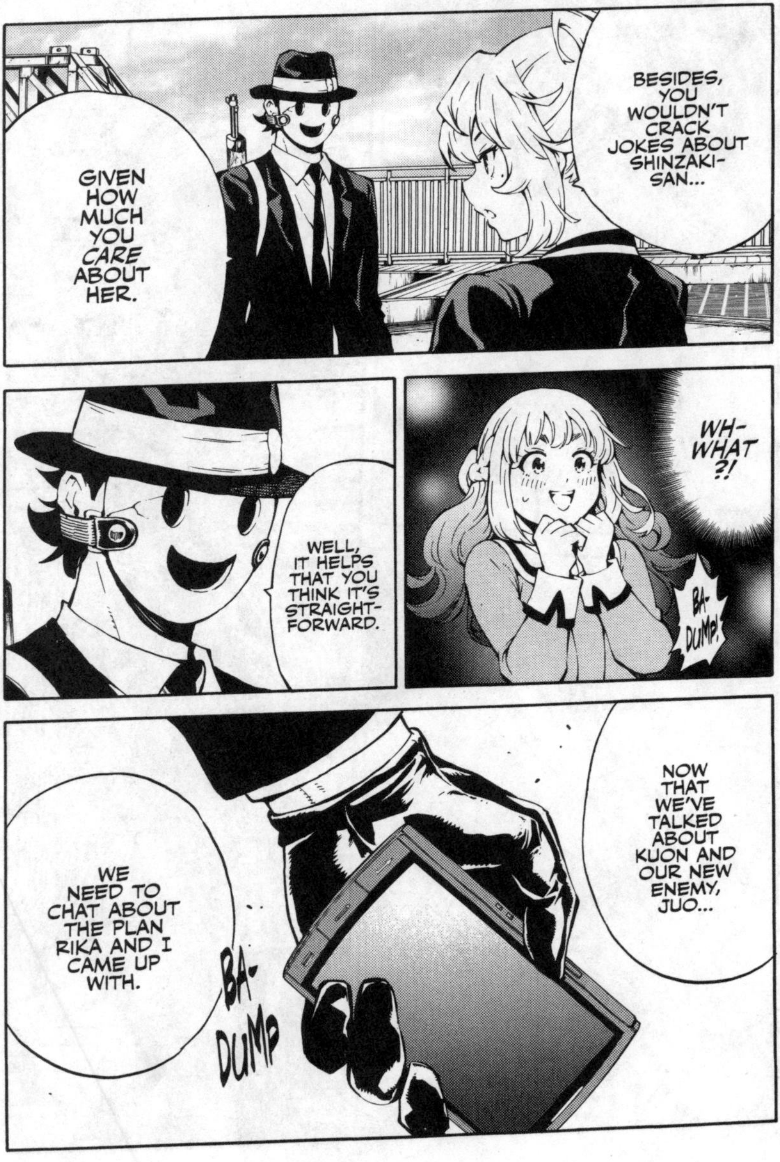
BESIDES, YOU WOULDN'T CRACK JOKES ABOUT SHINZAKI-SAN...
GIVEN HOW MUCH YOU *CARE* ABOUT HER.
WH-WHAT?!
BA-DUMP!
WELL, IT HELPS THAT YOU THINK IT'S STRAIGHT-FORWARD.
NOW THAT WE'VE TALKED ABOUT KUON AND OUR NEW ENEMY, JUO...
WE NEED TO CHAT ABOUT THE PLAN RIKA AND I CAME UP WITH.
BA-DUMP

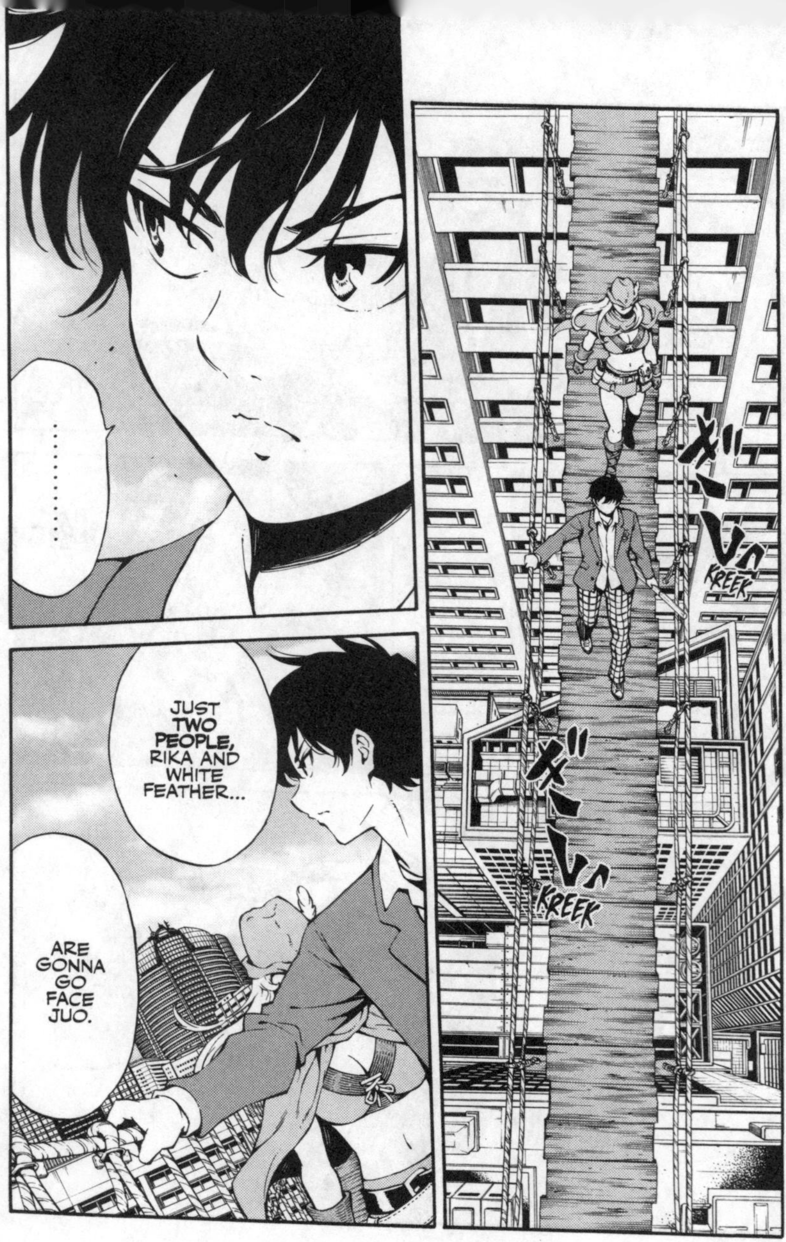
KREEK
KREEK
……
JUST TWO PEOPLE, RIKA AND WHITE FEATHER...
ARE GONNA GO FACE JUO.

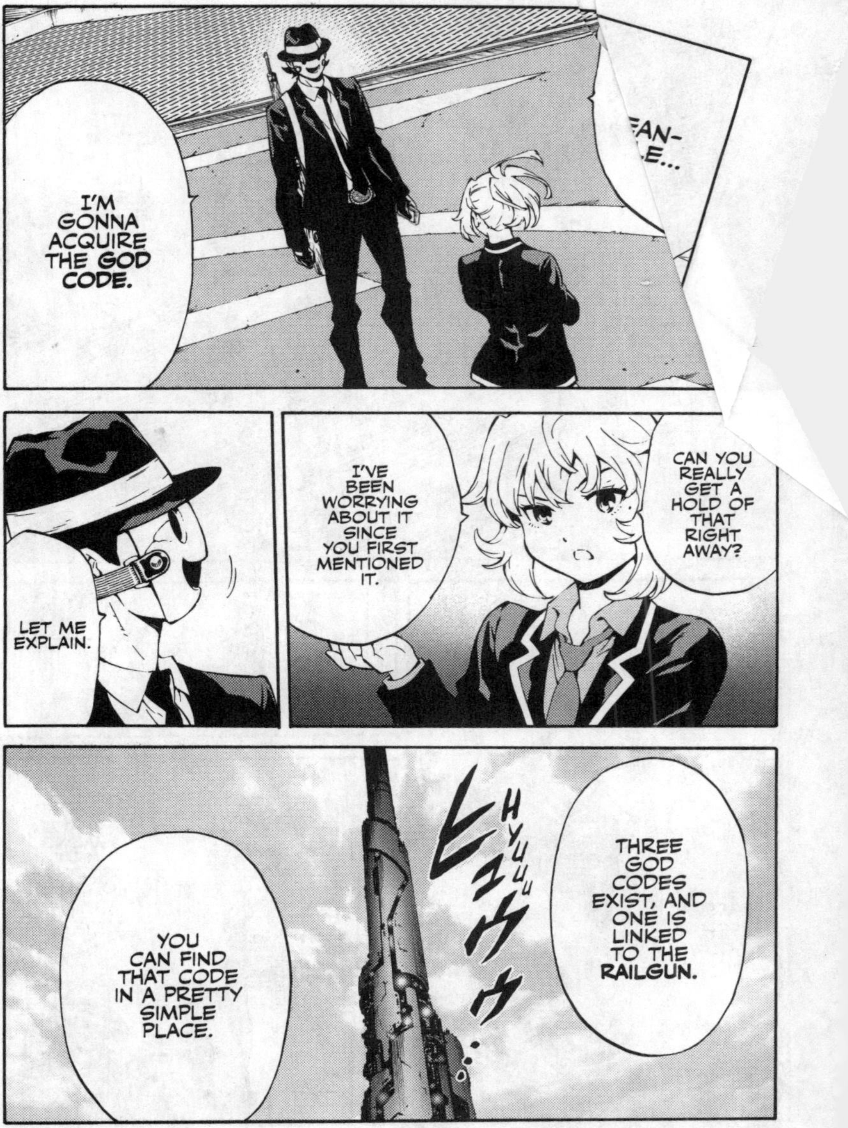

I'M GONNA ACQUIRE THE GOD CODE.
CAN YOU REALLY GET A HOLD OF THAT RIGHT AWAY?
I'VE BEEN WORRYING ABOUT IT SINCE YOU FIRST MENTIONED IT.
LET ME EXPLAIN.
THREE GOD CODES EXIST, AND ONE IS LINKED TO THE RAILGUN.
HYUUU
YOU CAN FIND THAT CODE IN A PRETTY SIMPLE PLACE.

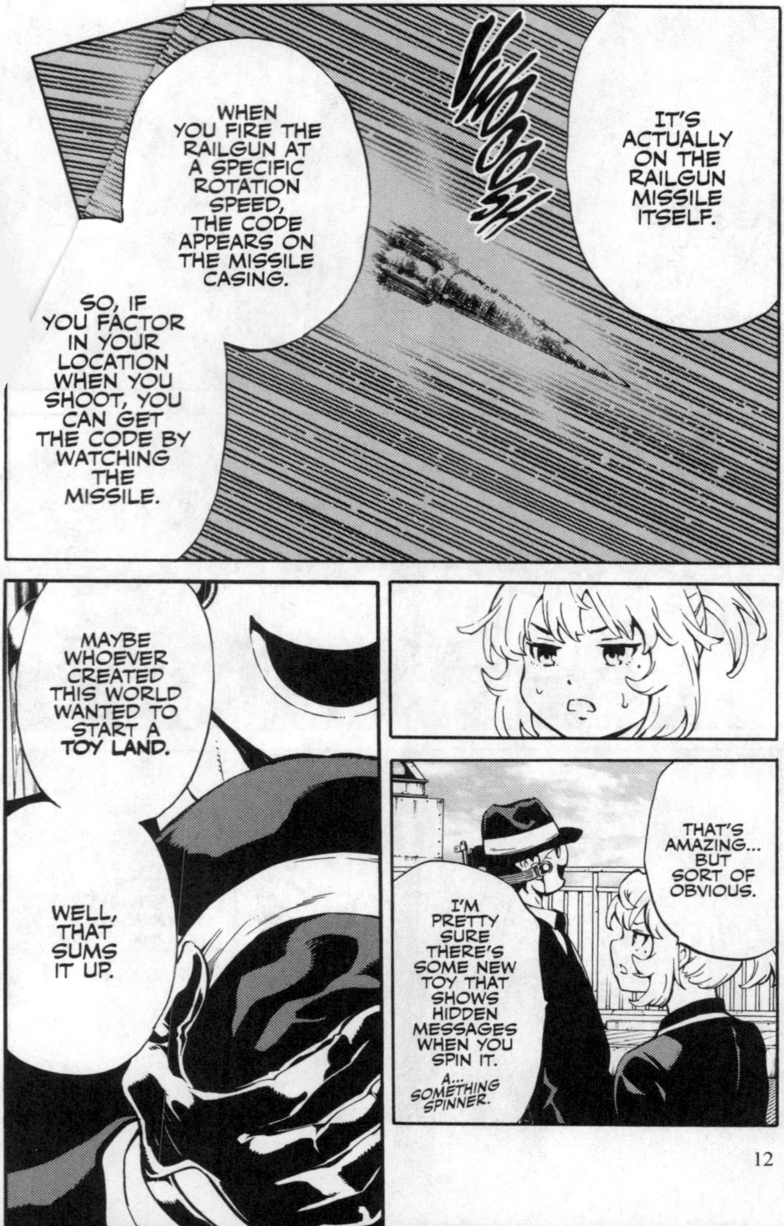
VWOOOSH
IT'S ACTUALLY ON THE RAILGUN MISSILE ITSELF.
WHEN YOU FIRE THE RAILGUN AT A SPECIFIC ROTATION SPEED, THE CODE APPEARS ON THE MISSILE CASING.
SO, IF YOU FACTOR IN YOUR LOCATION WHEN YOU SHOOT, YOU CAN GET THE CODE BY WATCHING THE MISSILE.
THAT'S AMAZING... BUT SORT OF OBVIOUS.
I'M PRETTY SURE THERE'S SOME NEW TOY THAT SHOWS HIDDEN MESSAGES WHEN YOU SPIN IT.
A... SOMETHING SPINNER.
MAYBE WHOEVER CREATED THIS WORLD WANTED TO START A TOY LAND.
WELL, THAT SUMS IT UP.

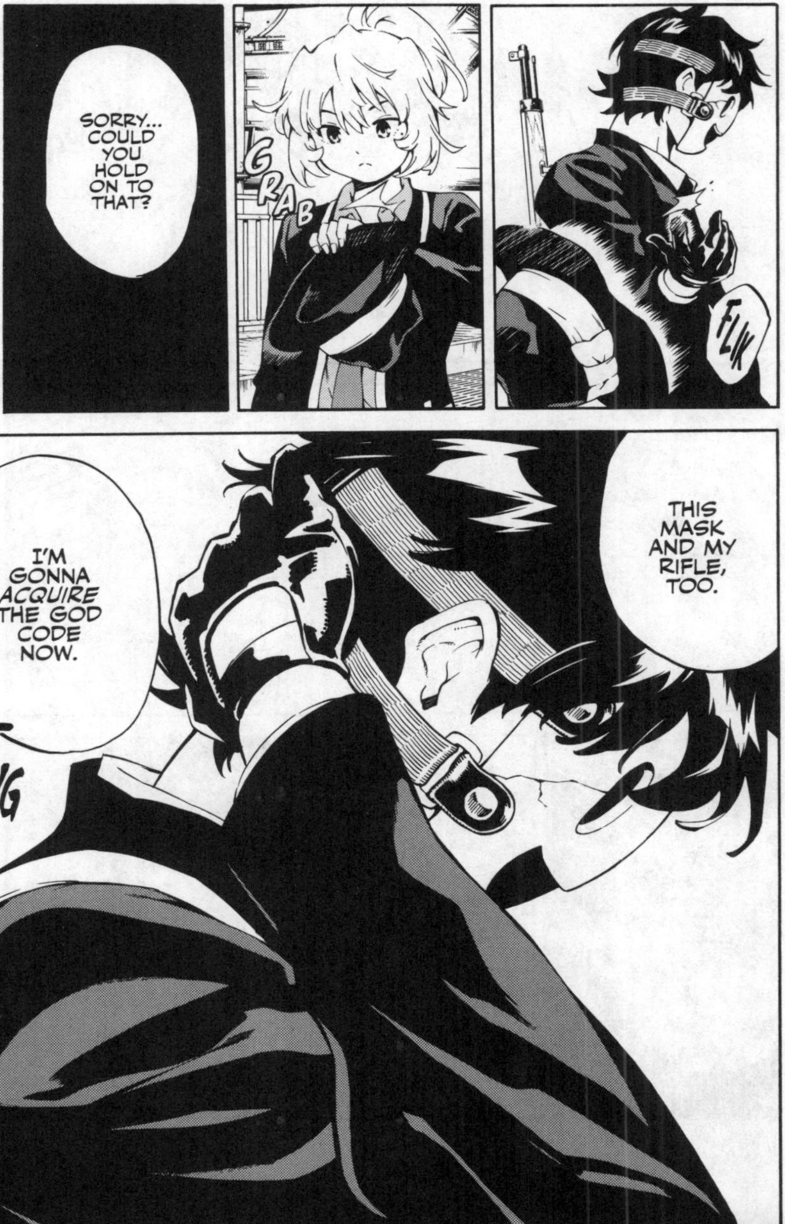
FLIK
GRAB
SORRY... COULD YOU HOLD ON TO THAT?
THIS MASK AND MY RIFLE, TOO.
I'M GONNA *ACQUIRE* THE GOD CODE NOW.
TUG

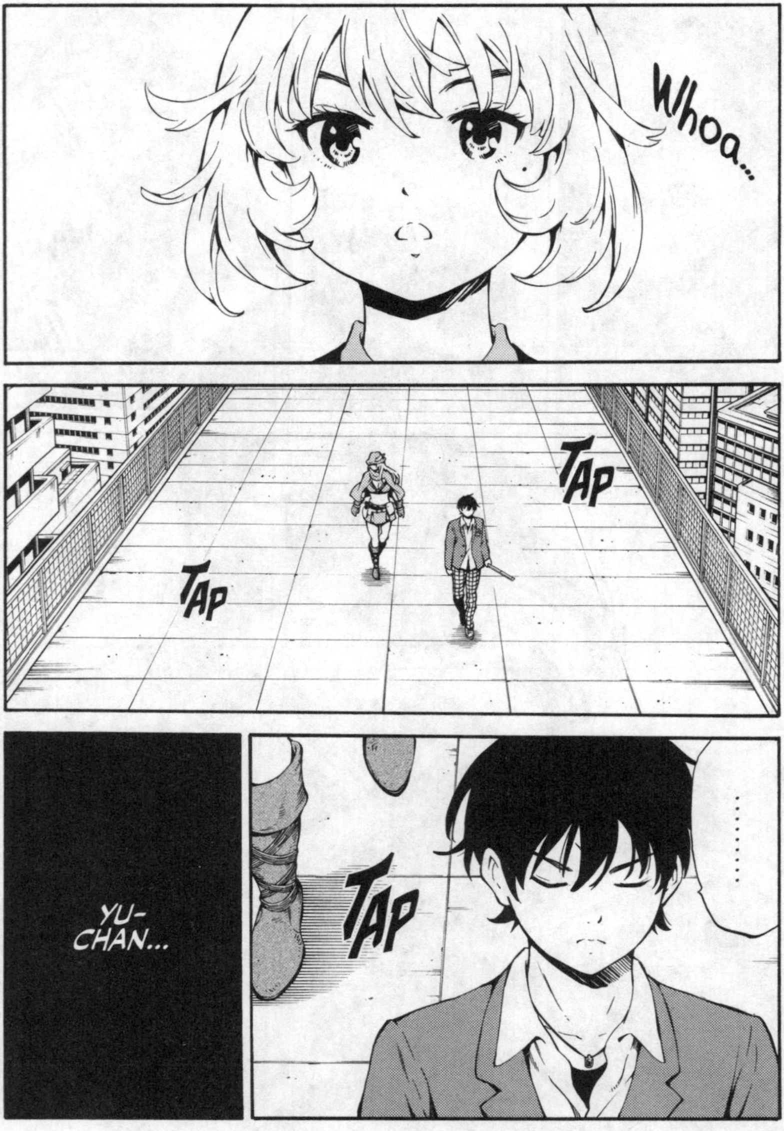
Whoa...
TAP
TAP
......
TAP
YU-CHAN...

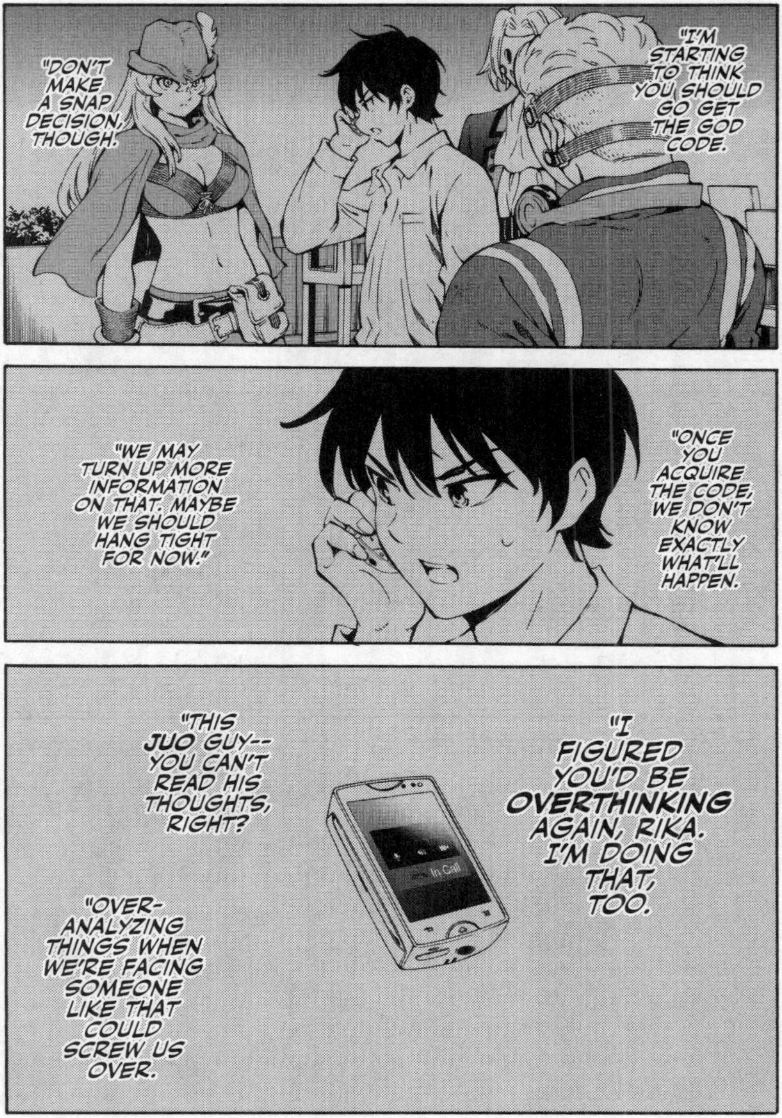
"I'M STARTING TO THINK YOU SHOULD GO GET THE GOD CODE.
"DON'T MAKE A SNAP DECISION, THOUGH.
"ONCE YOU ACQUIRE THE CODE, WE DON'T KNOW EXACTLY WHAT'LL HAPPEN.
"WE MAY TURN UP MORE INFORMATION ON THAT. MAYBE WE SHOULD HANG TIGHT FOR NOW."
"I FIGURED YOU'D BE **OVERTHINKING** AGAIN, RIKA. I'M DOING THAT, TOO.
In Call
"THIS **JUO** GUY-- YOU CAN'T READ HIS THOUGHTS, RIGHT?
"OVER-ANALYZING THINGS WHEN WE'RE FACING SOMEONE LIKE THAT COULD SCREW US OVER.

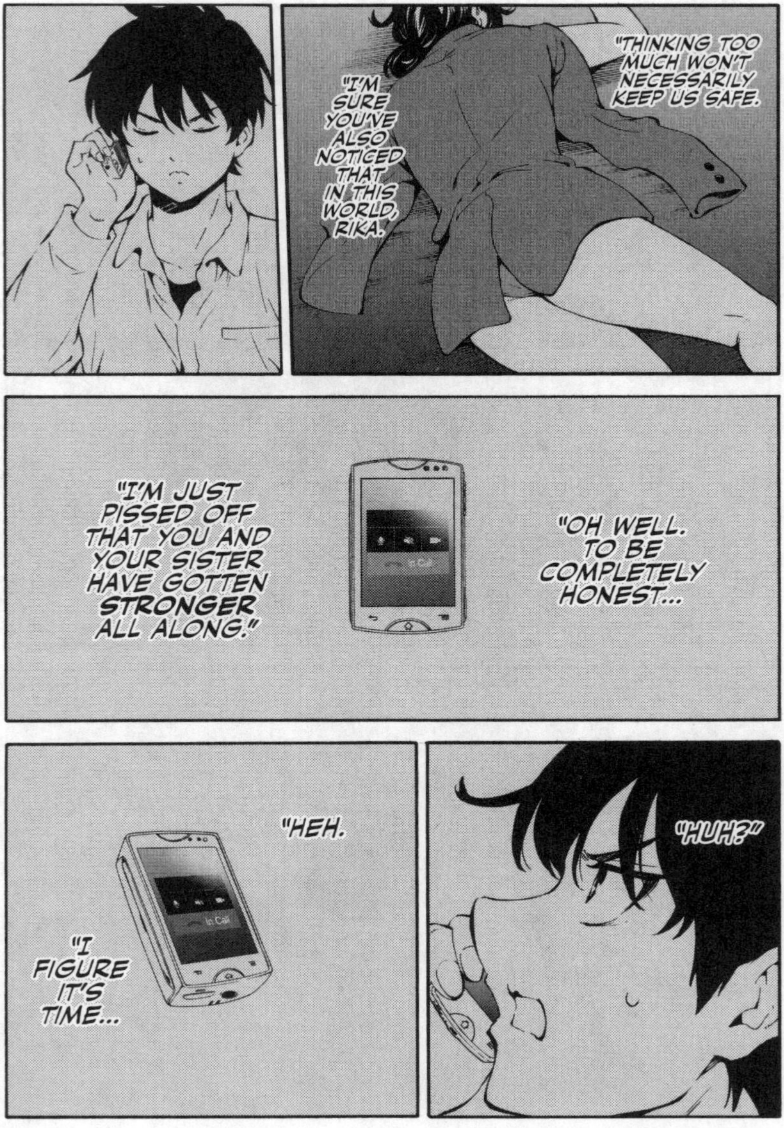
"THINKING TOO MUCH WON'T NECESSARILY KEEP US SAFE.
"I'M SURE YOU'VE ALSO NOTICED THAT IN THIS WORLD, RIKA.
"OH WELL. TO BE COMPLETELY HONEST...
"I'M JUST PISSED OFF THAT YOU AND YOUR SISTER HAVE GOTTEN STRONGER ALL ALONG."
"HUH?"
"HEH.
"I FIGURE IT'S TIME...

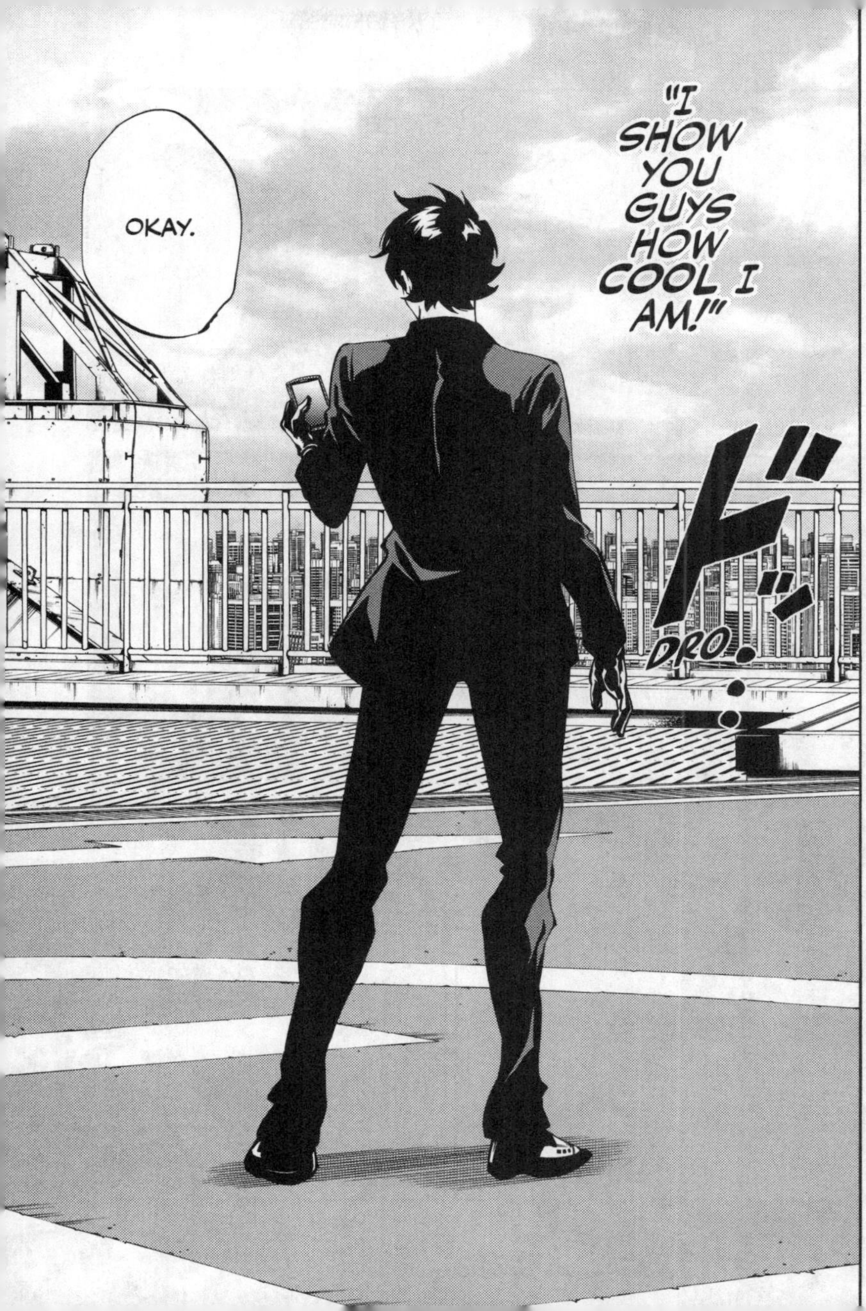
"I SHOW YOU GUYS HOW COOL I AM!"
OKAY.
DRO...

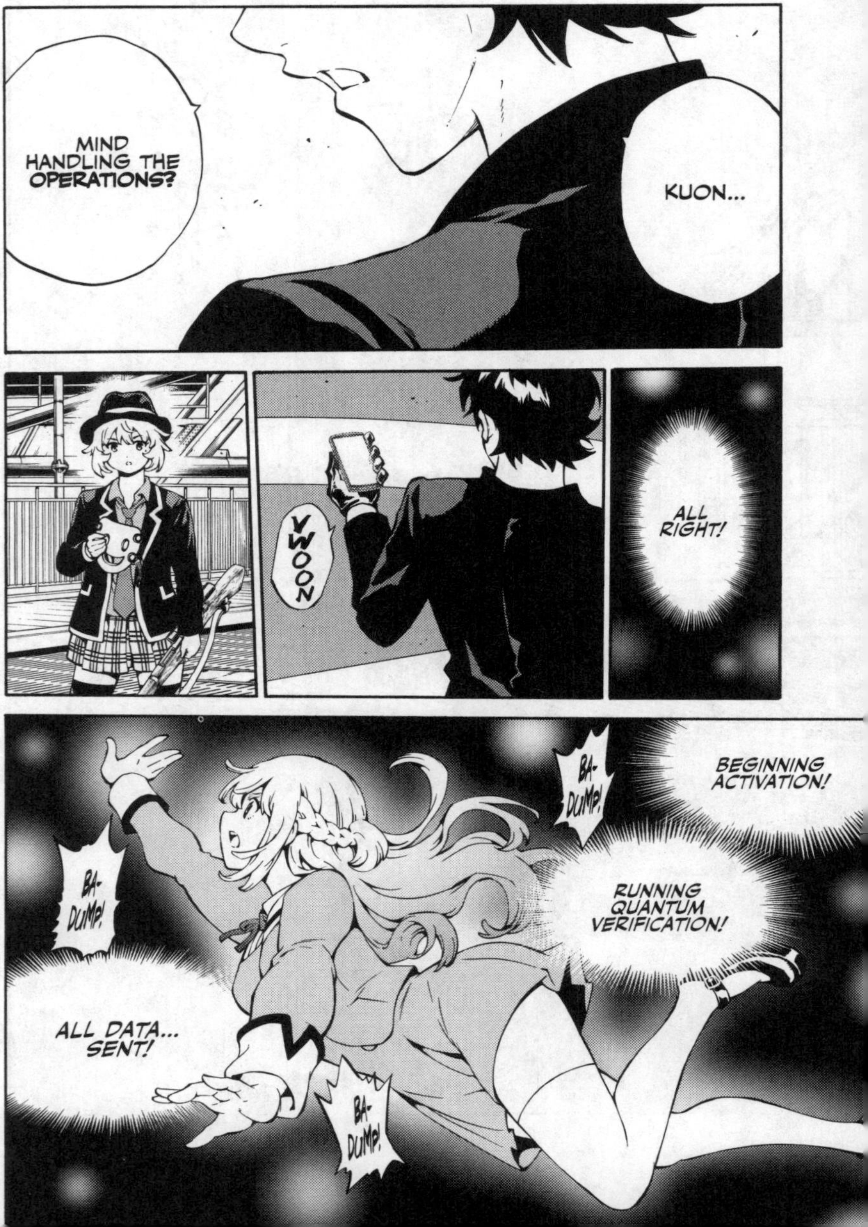
KUON...
MIND HANDLING THE OPERATIONS?
ALL RIGHT!
VWOON
BEGINNING ACTIVATION!
BA-DUMP!
RUNNING QUANTUM VERIFICATION!
BA-DUMP!
ALL DATA... SENT!
BA-DUMP!

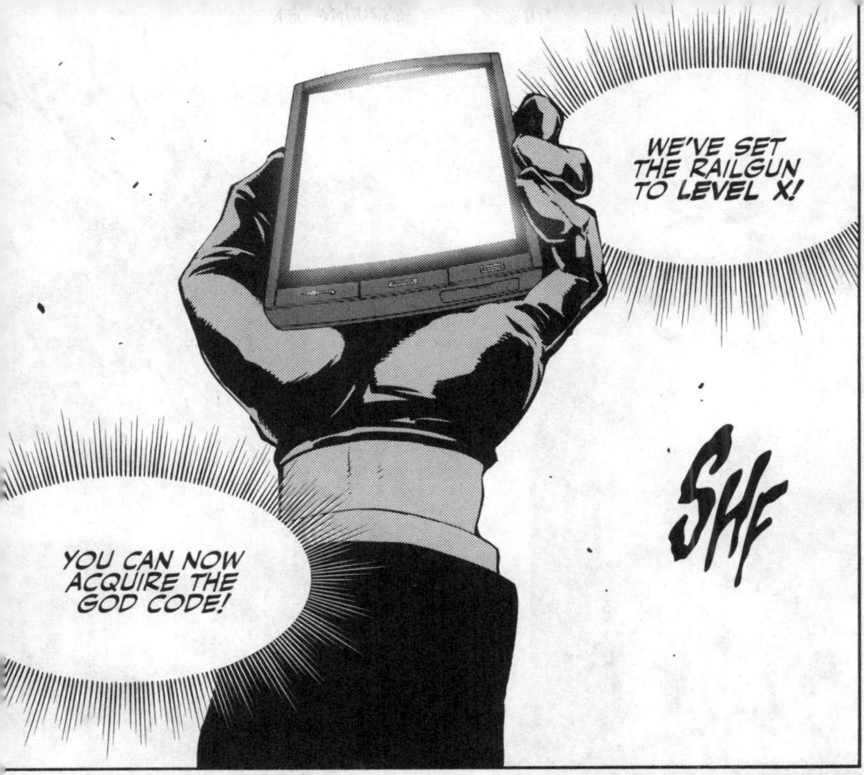
WE'VE SET THE RAILGUN TO LEVEL X!
SHF
YOU CAN NOW ACQUIRE THE GOD CODE!

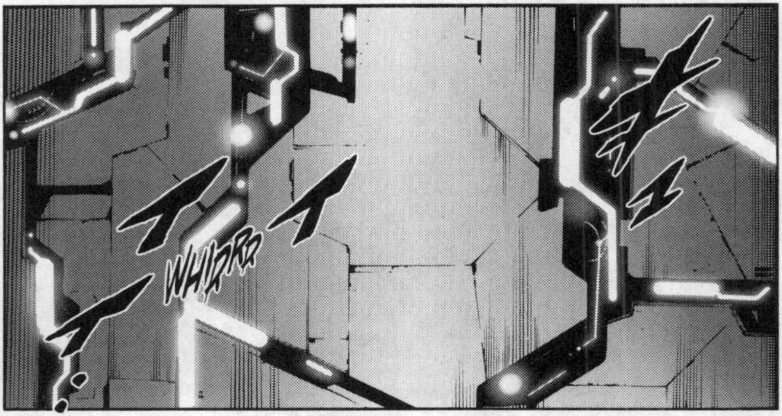
WHIRR

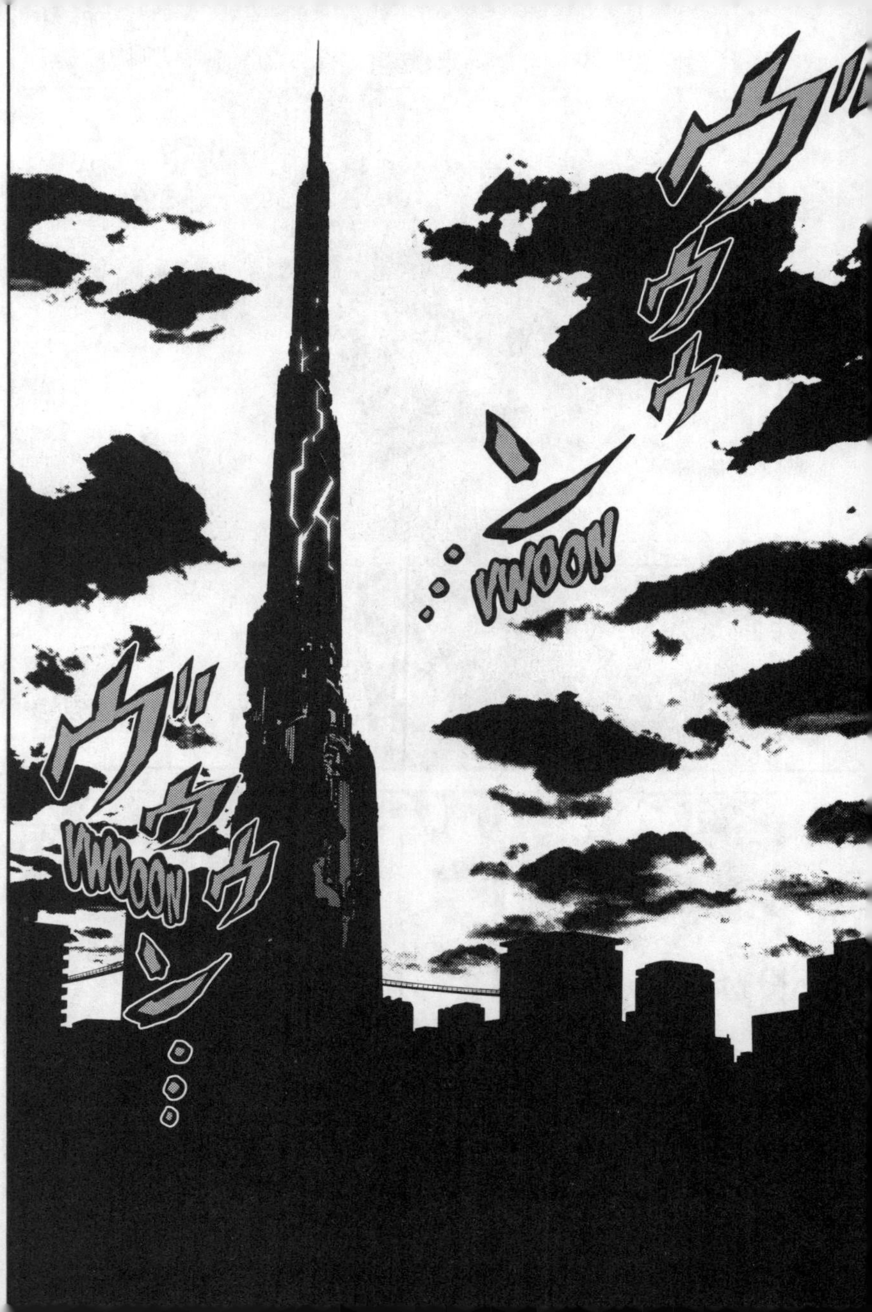
ヴゥゥゥン
VWOON
ヴゥゥン
VWOOON

CHAPTER 221: So, What'll Happen to Him?

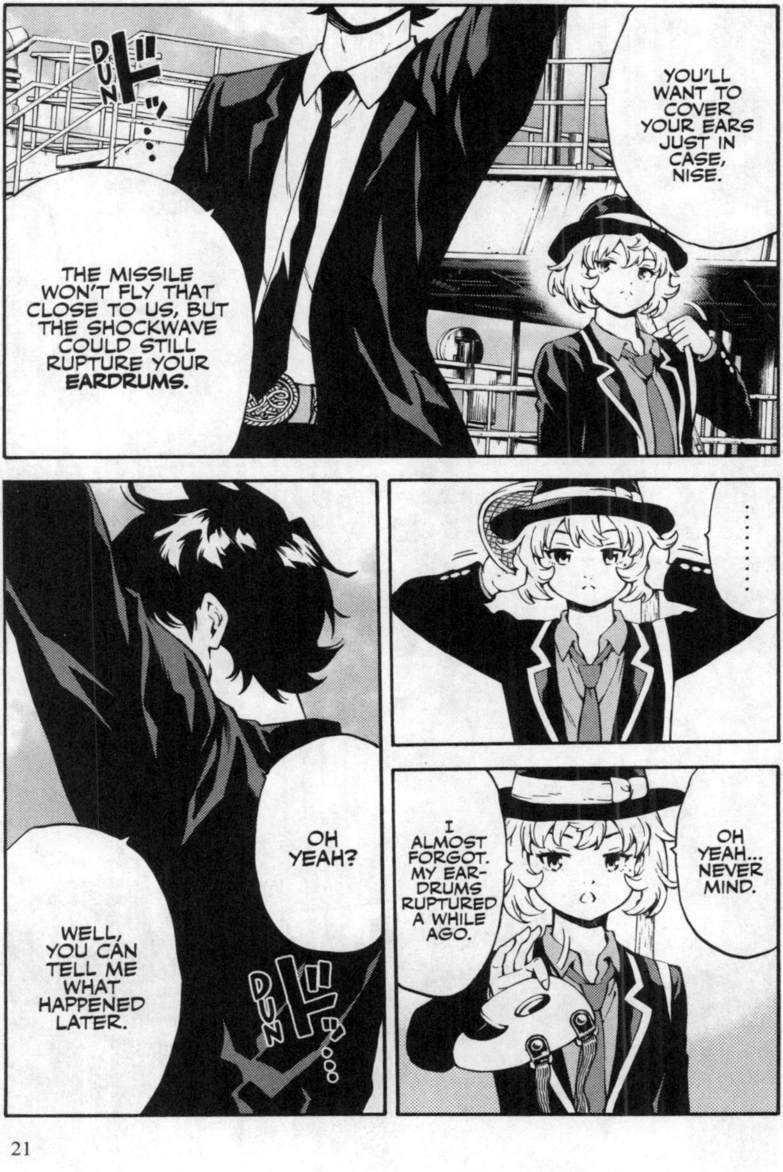

YOU'LL WANT TO COVER YOUR EARS JUST IN CASE, NISE.
DUN...
THE MISSILE WON'T FLY THAT CLOSE TO US, BUT THE SHOCKWAVE COULD STILL RUPTURE YOUR EARDRUMS.
....
OH YEAH... NEVER MIND.
I ALMOST FORGOT. MY EARDRUMS RUPTURED A WHILE AGO.
OH YEAH?
WELL, YOU CAN TELL ME WHAT HAPPENED LATER.
DUN...

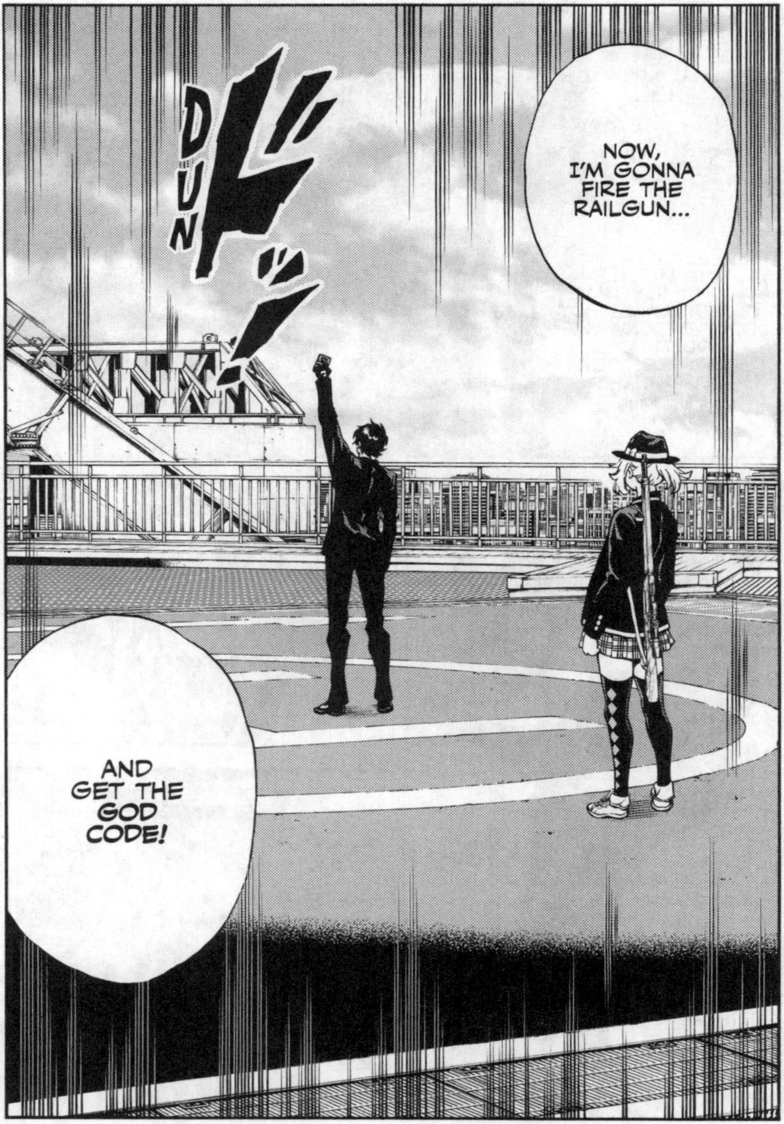
NOW, I'M GONNA FIRE THE RAILGUN...
DUN
AND GET THE GOD CODE!

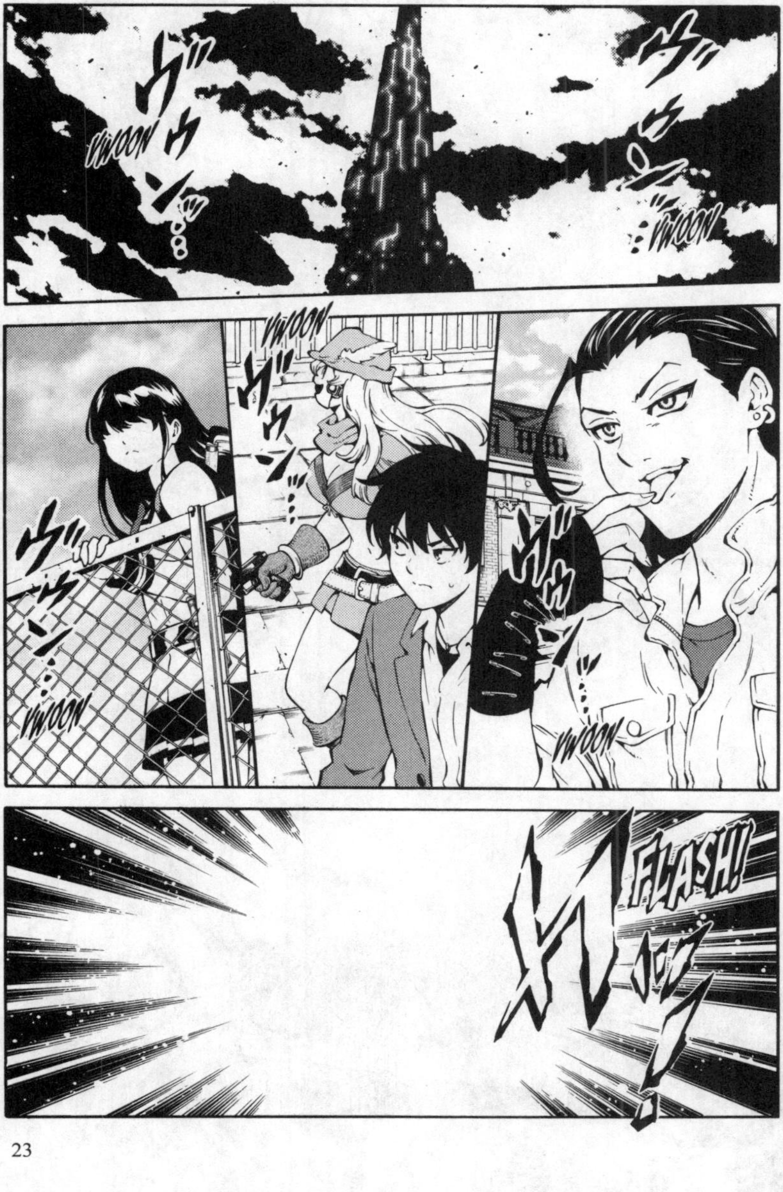
VWOON
VWOON
VWOON
VWOON
VWOON
FLASH!

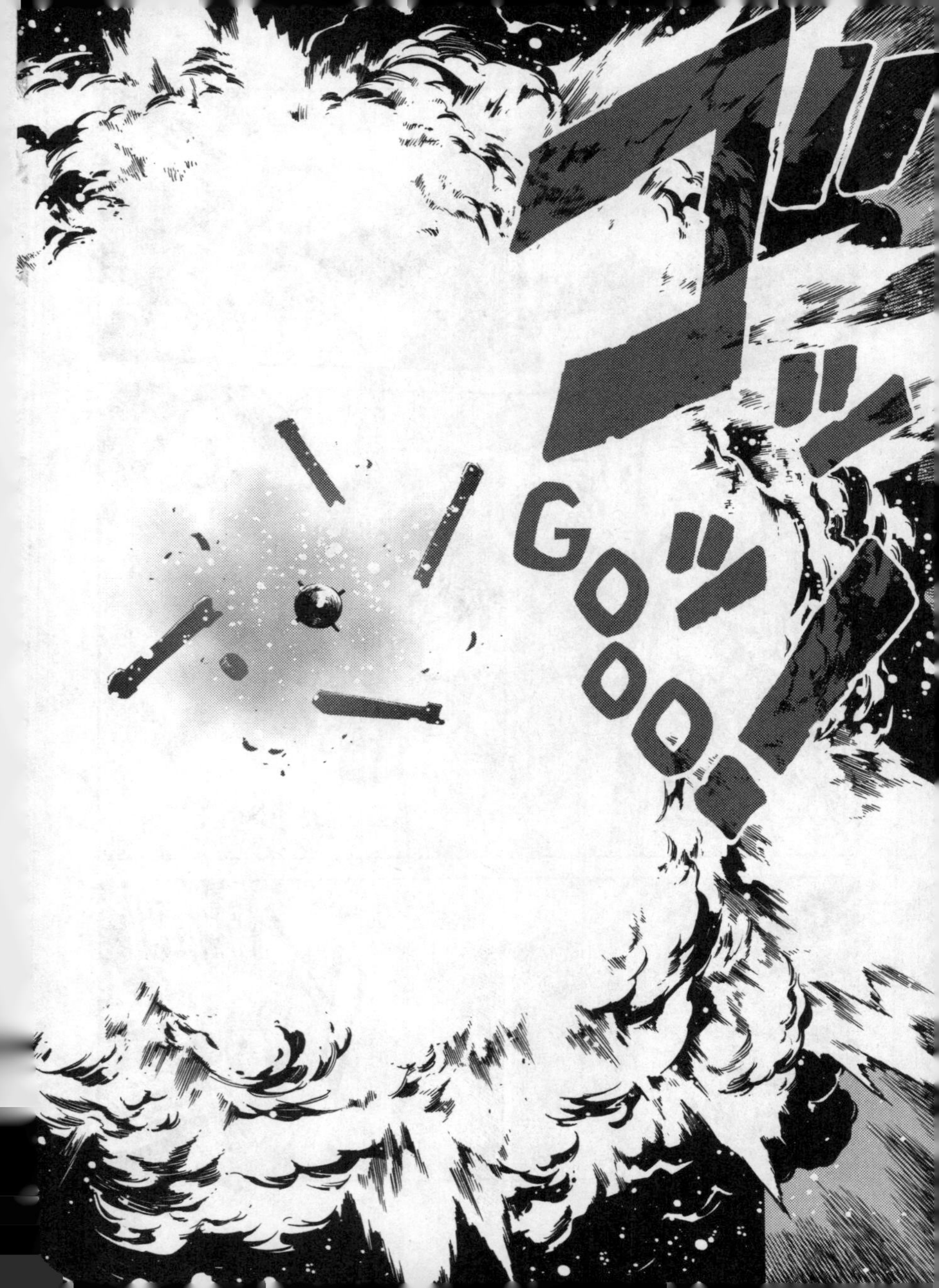
GOOO

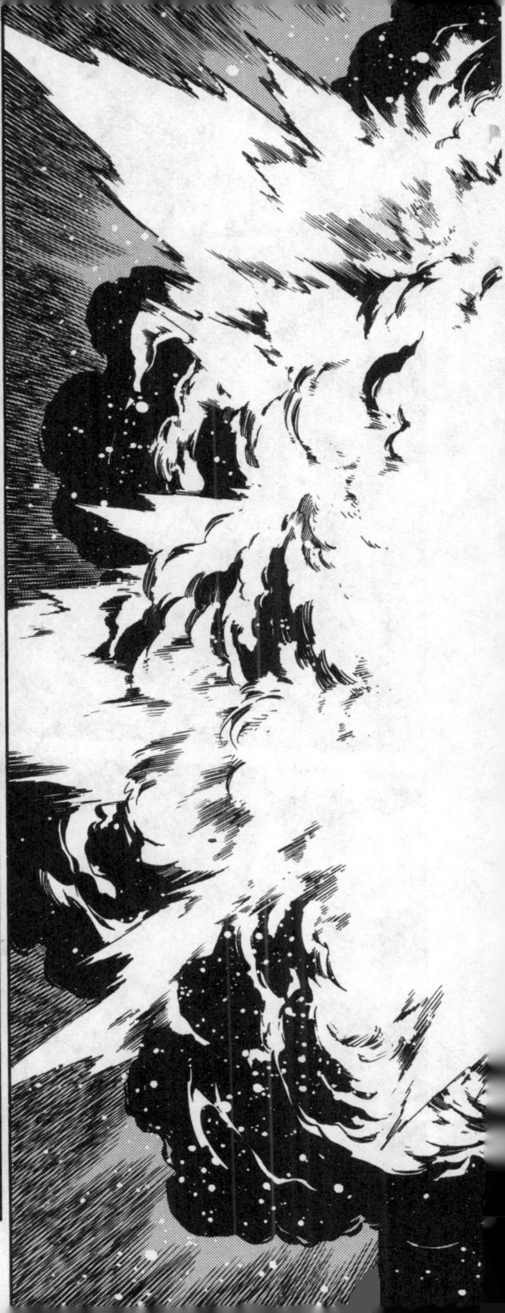

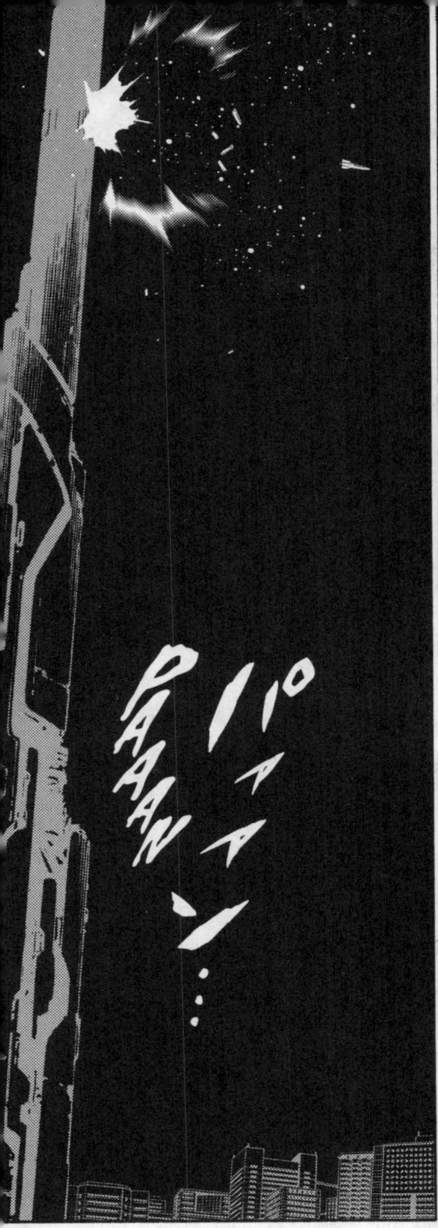
パァァン…
PAAAAN

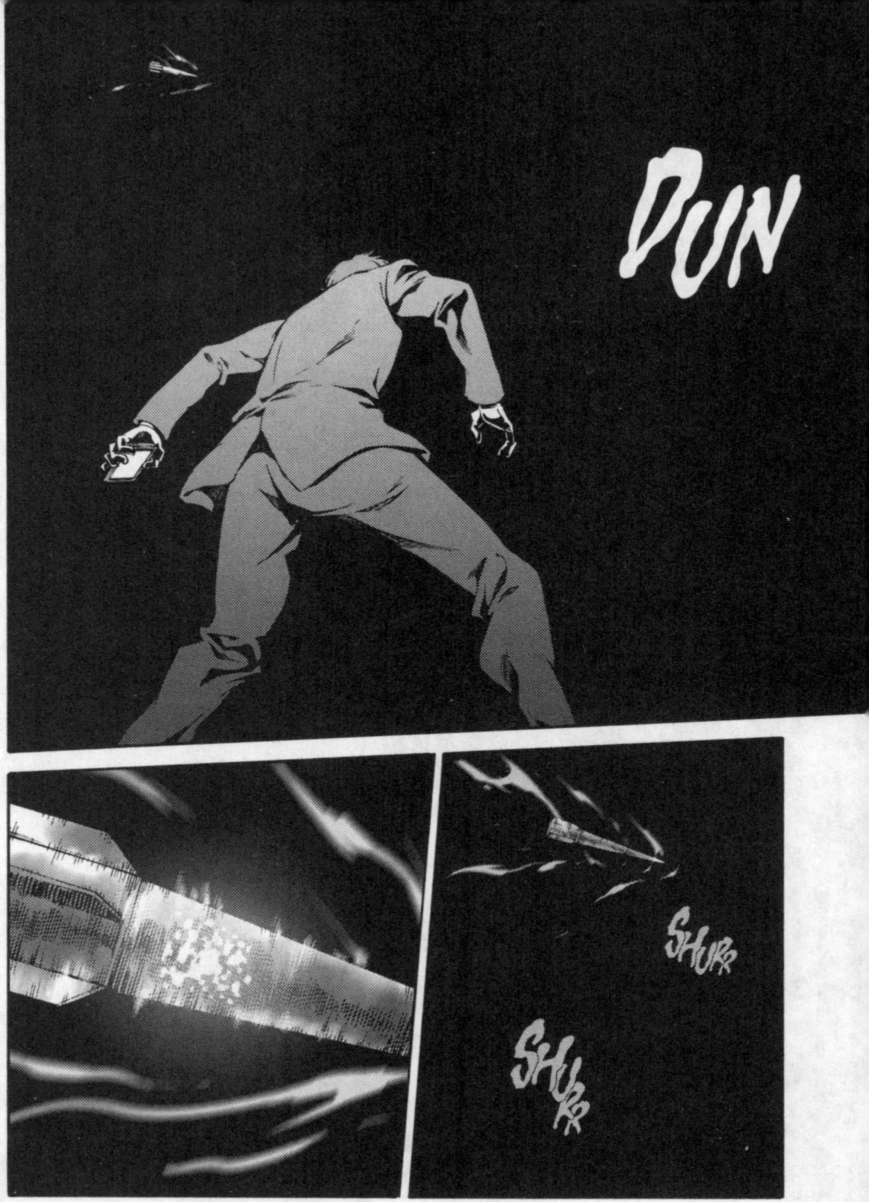
DUN
SHURR
SHURR

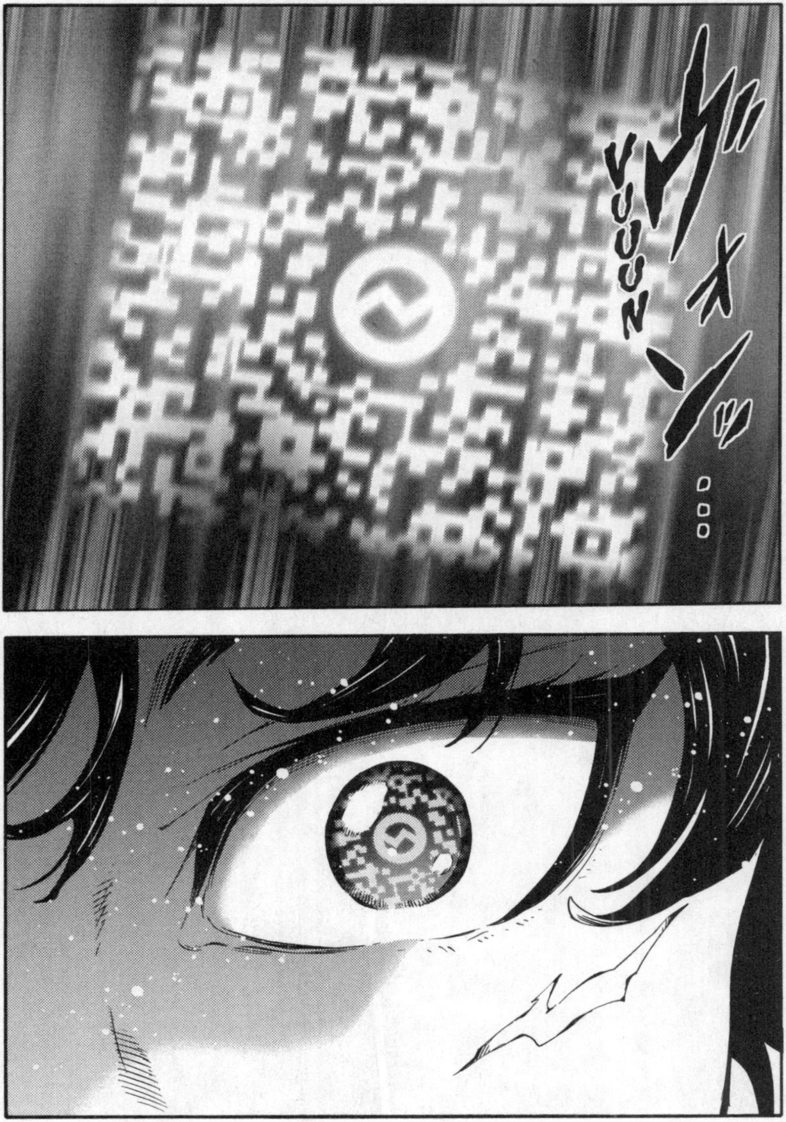
ヴォンッ
VUUUN
...

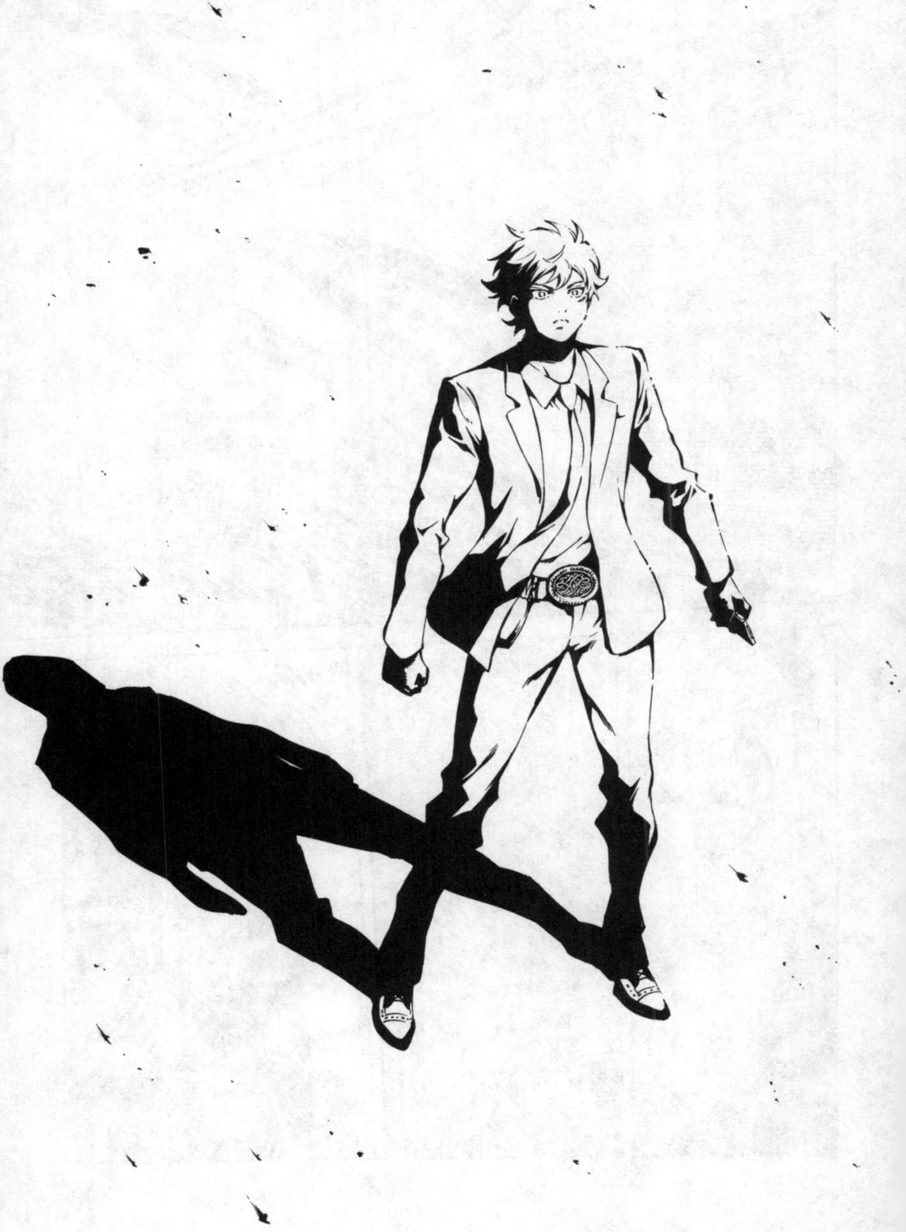

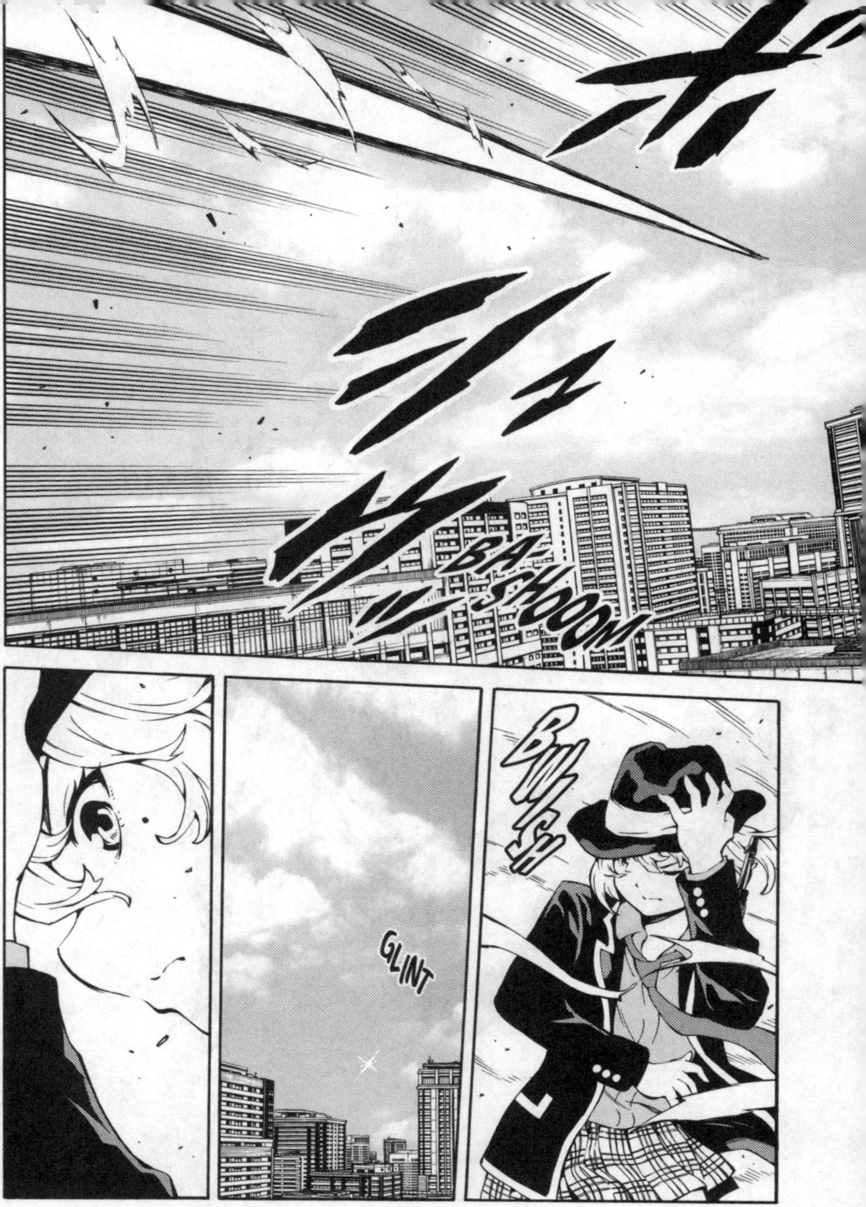
BA-SHOOOM
BWISH
GLINT

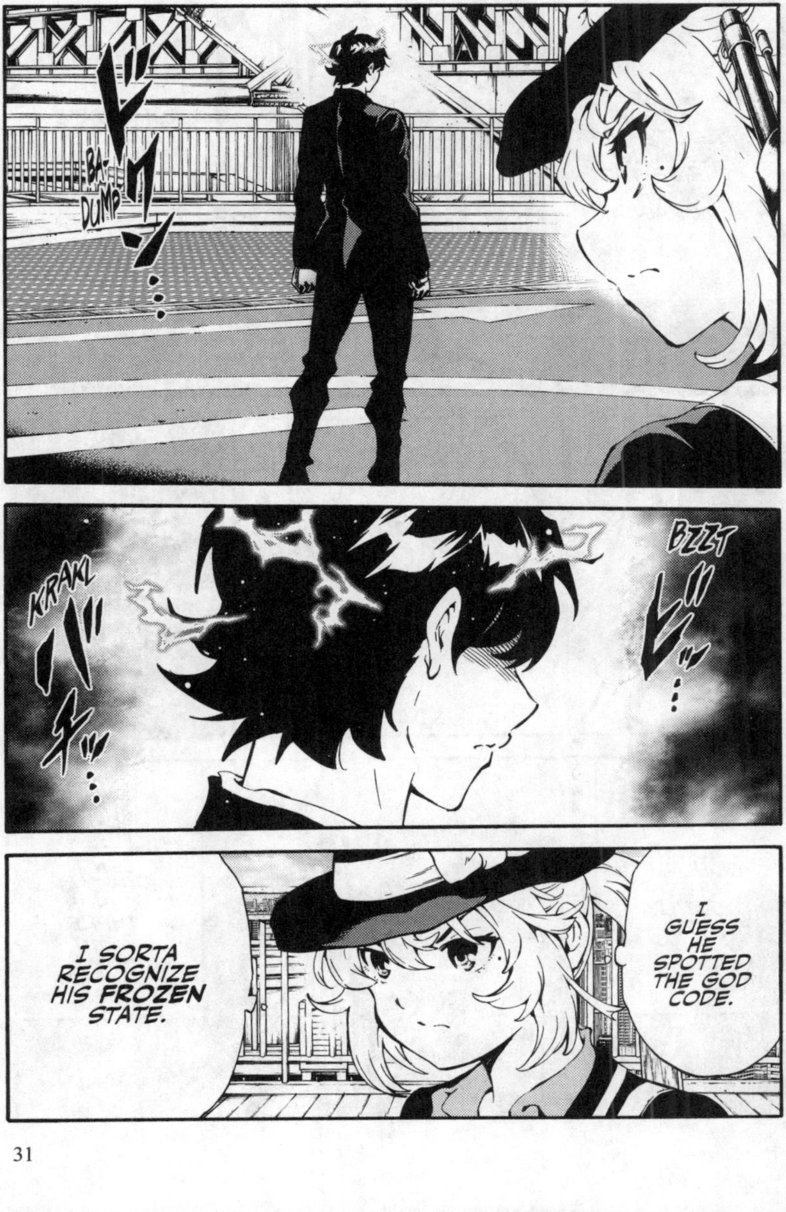
BA-DUMP
BZZT
KRAKL
I GUESS HE SPOTTED THE GOD CODE.
I SORTA RECOGNIZE HIS FROZEN STATE.

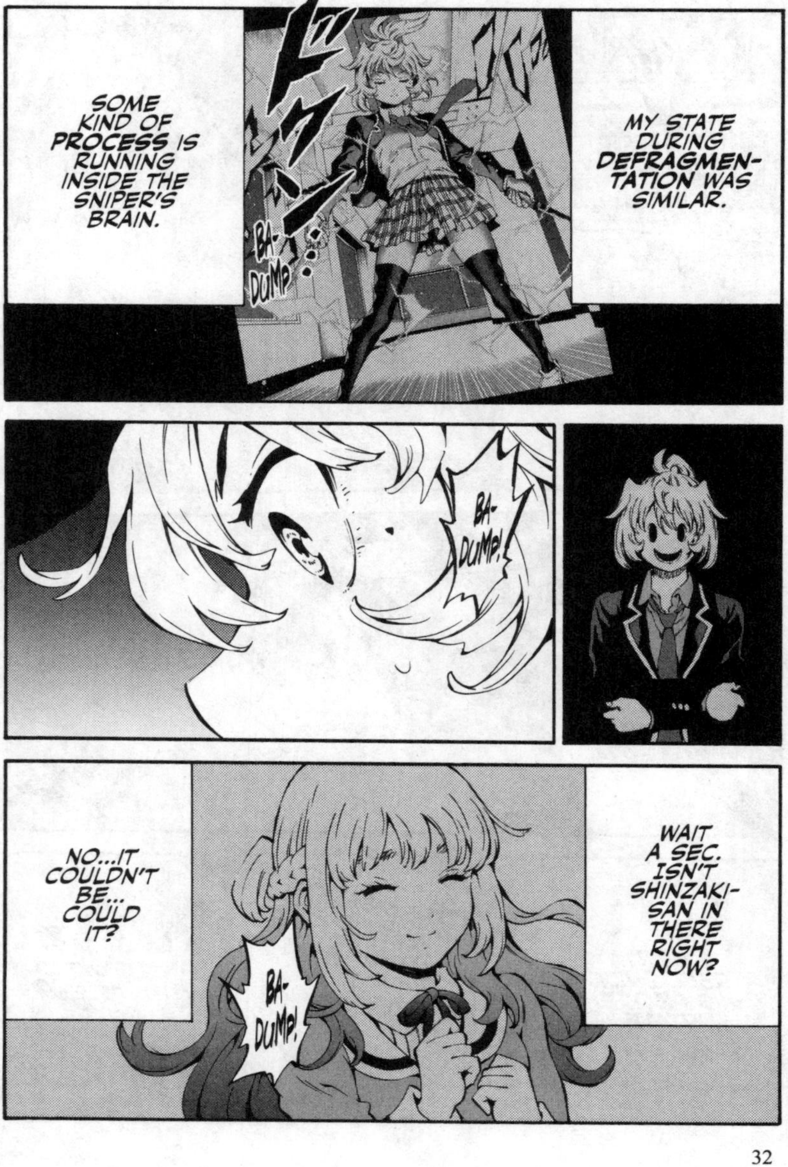
MY STATE DURING DEFRAGMENTATION WAS SIMILAR.
SOME KIND OF PROCESS IS RUNNING INSIDE THE SNIPER'S BRAIN.
BA-DUMP
BA-DUMP!
WAIT A SEC. ISN'T SHINZAKI-SAN IN THERE RIGHT NOW?
NO...IT COULDN'T BE...COULD IT?
BA-DUMP!

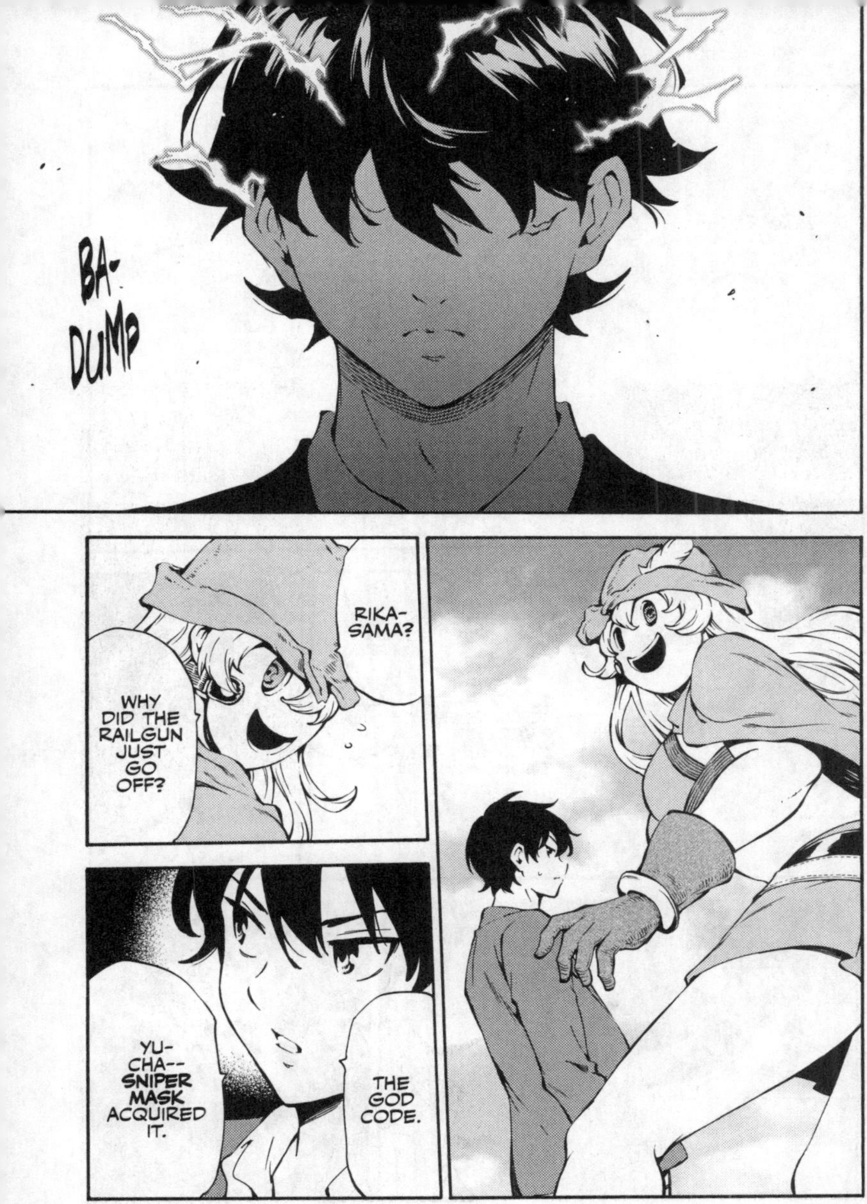
BA-DUMP
RIKA-SAMA?
WHY DID THE RAILGUN JUST GO OFF?
THE GOD CODE.
YU-CHA--SNIPER MASK ACQUIRED IT.

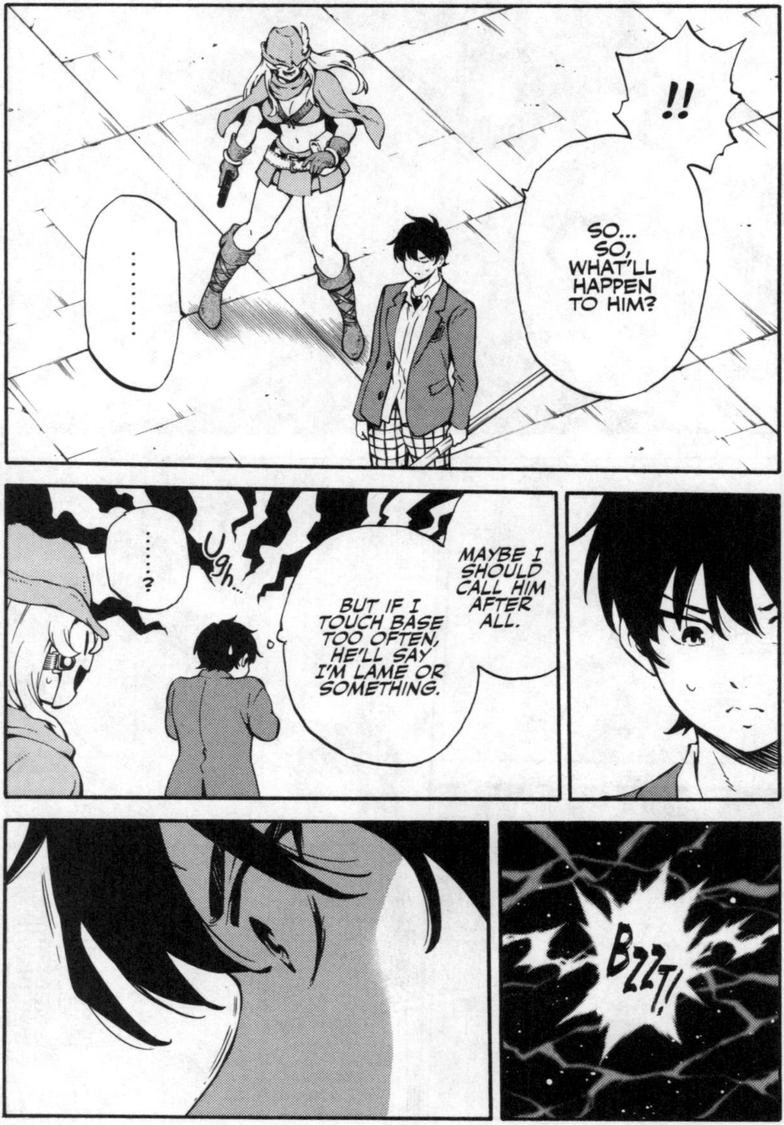
!!
SO... SO, WHAT'LL HAPPEN TO HIM?
......
MAYBE I SHOULD CALL HIM AFTER ALL.
BUT IF I TOUCH BASE TOO OFTEN, HE'LL SAY I'M LAME OR SOMETHING.
Ugh...
......?
BZZT!

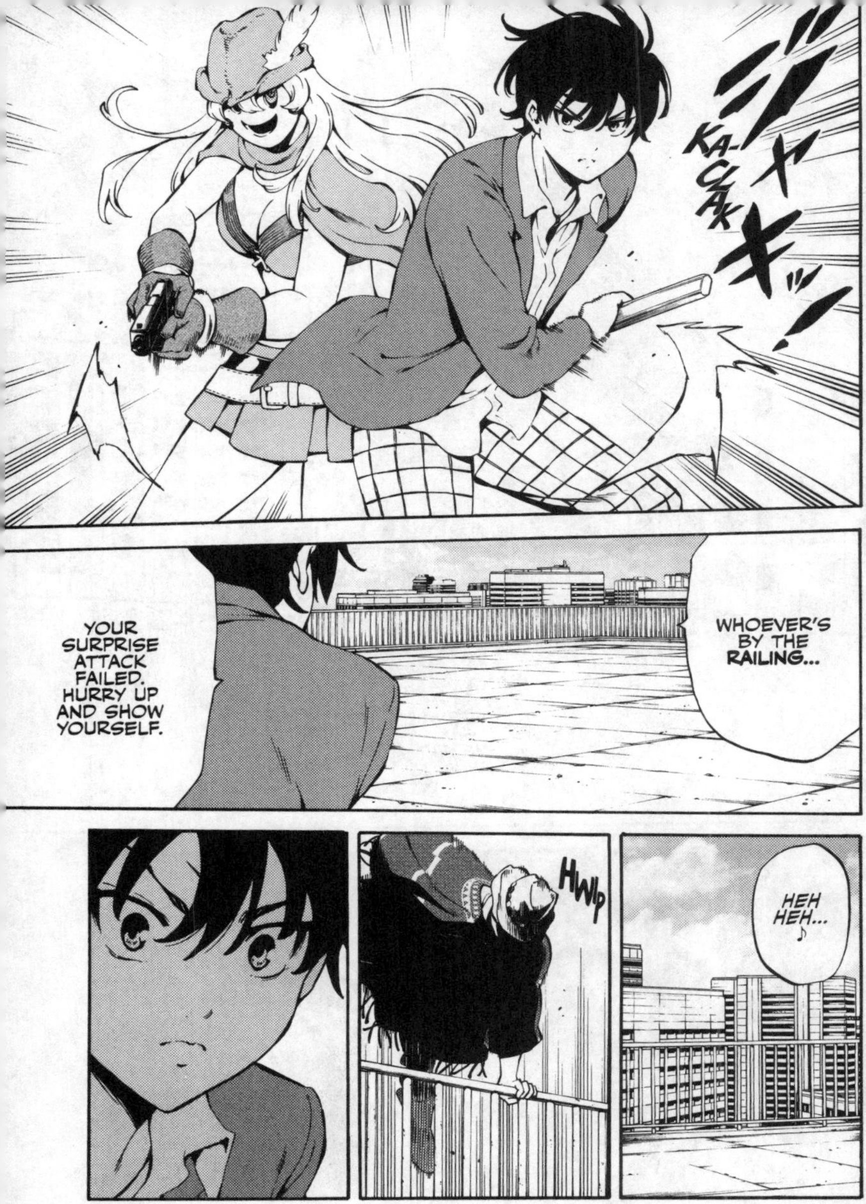
KA-CLAK
WHOEVER'S BY THE RAILING...
YOUR SURPRISE ATTACK FAILED. HURRY UP AND SHOW YOURSELF.
HEH HEH...♪
HWIP

トン
TOMP

AH...

ド
ド
BA-
DUMP

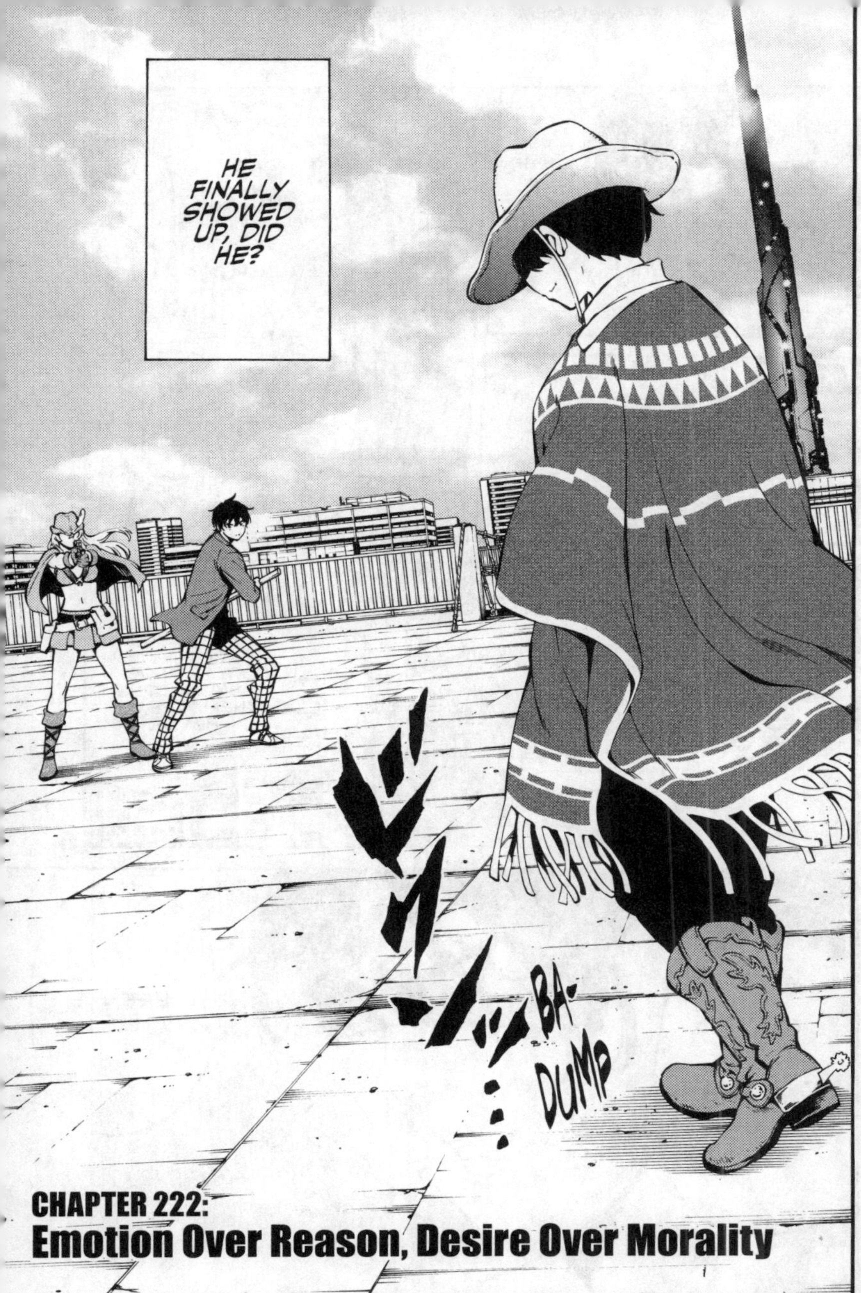
HE FINALLY SHOWED UP, DID HE?
BA-DUMP

CHAPTER 222:
Emotion Over Reason, Desire Over Morality

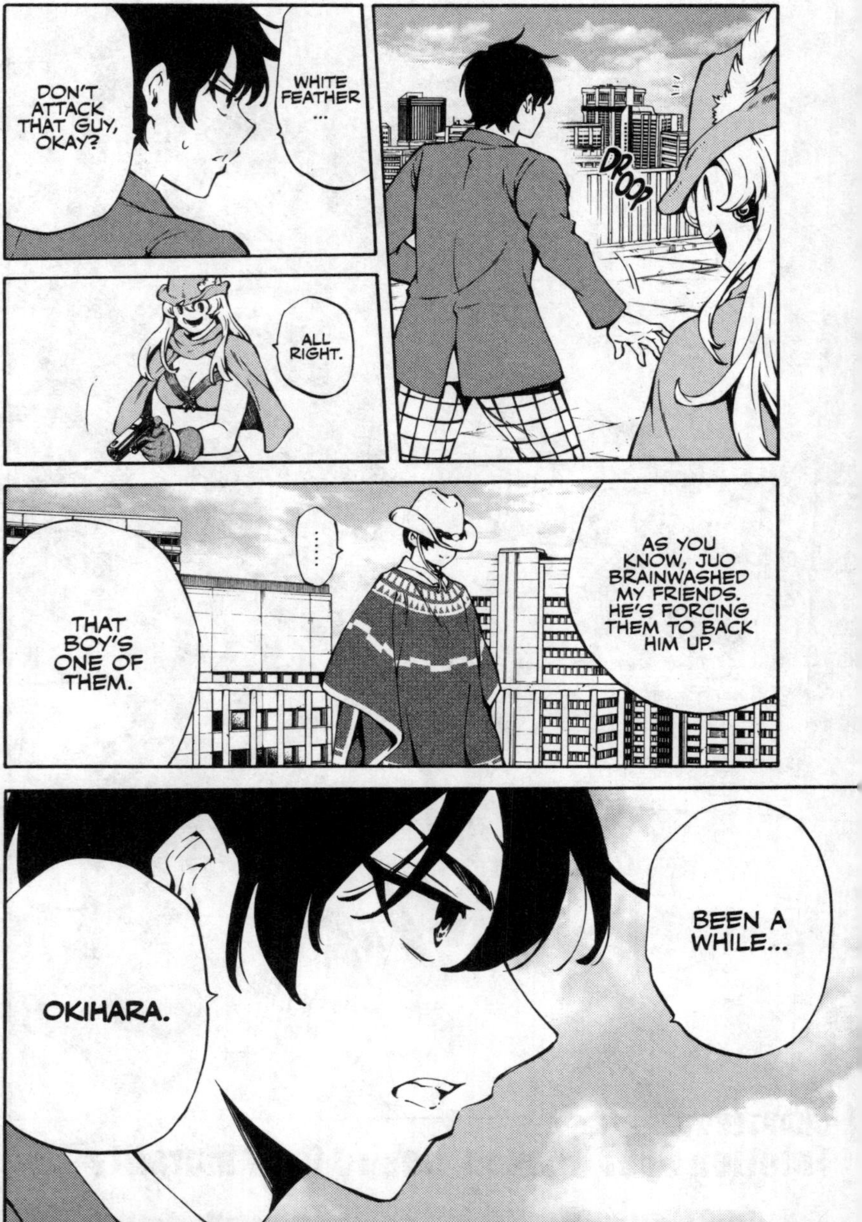
DROOP
WHITE FEATHER ...
DON'T ATTACK THAT GUY, OKAY?
ALL RIGHT.
AS YOU KNOW, JUO BRAINWASHED MY FRIENDS. HE'S FORCING THEM TO BACK HIM UP.
......
THAT BOY'S ONE OF THEM.
BEEN A WHILE...
OKIHARA.

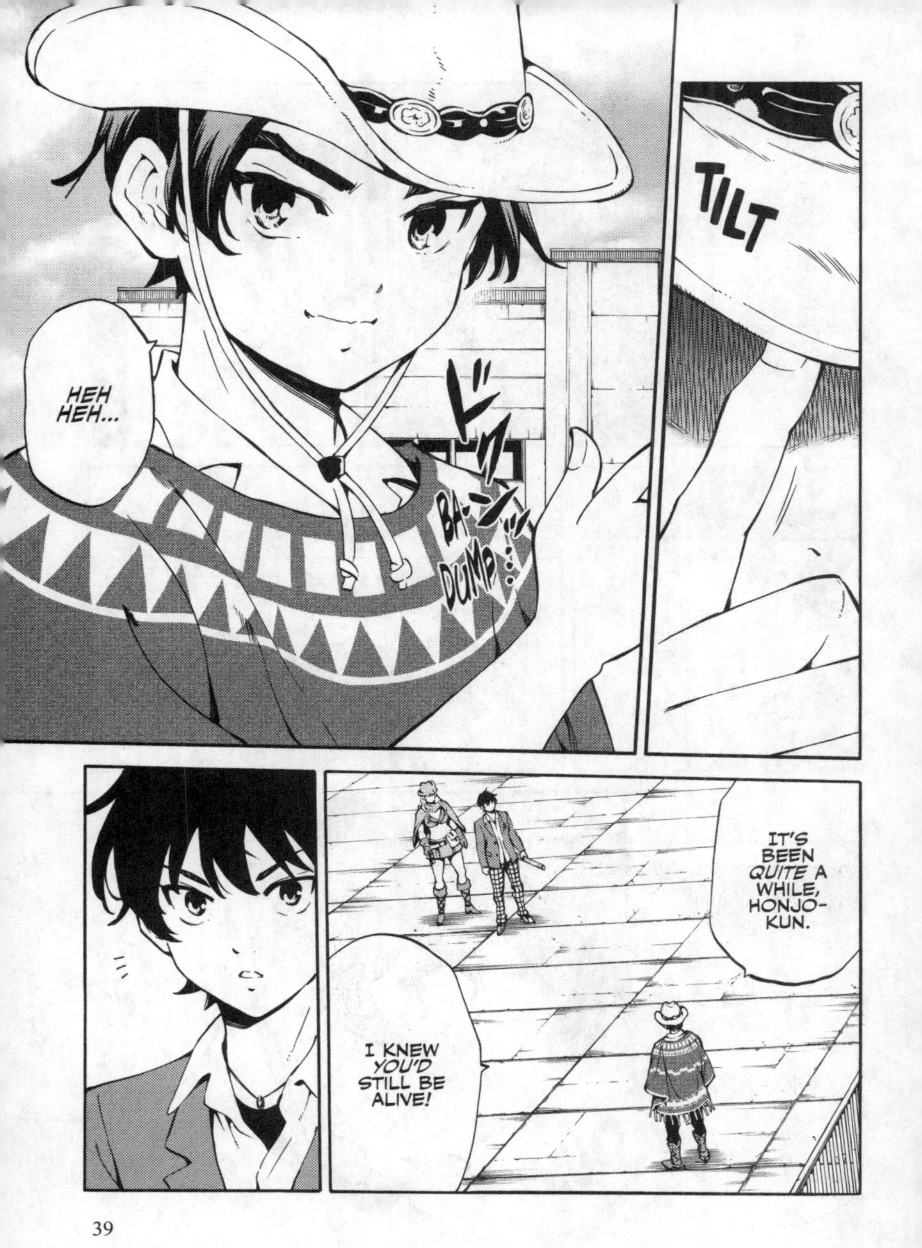
TILT
HEH HEH...
BA-DUMP...
IT'S BEEN *QUITE* A WHILE, HONJO-KUN.
I KNEW *YOU'D* STILL BE ALIVE!

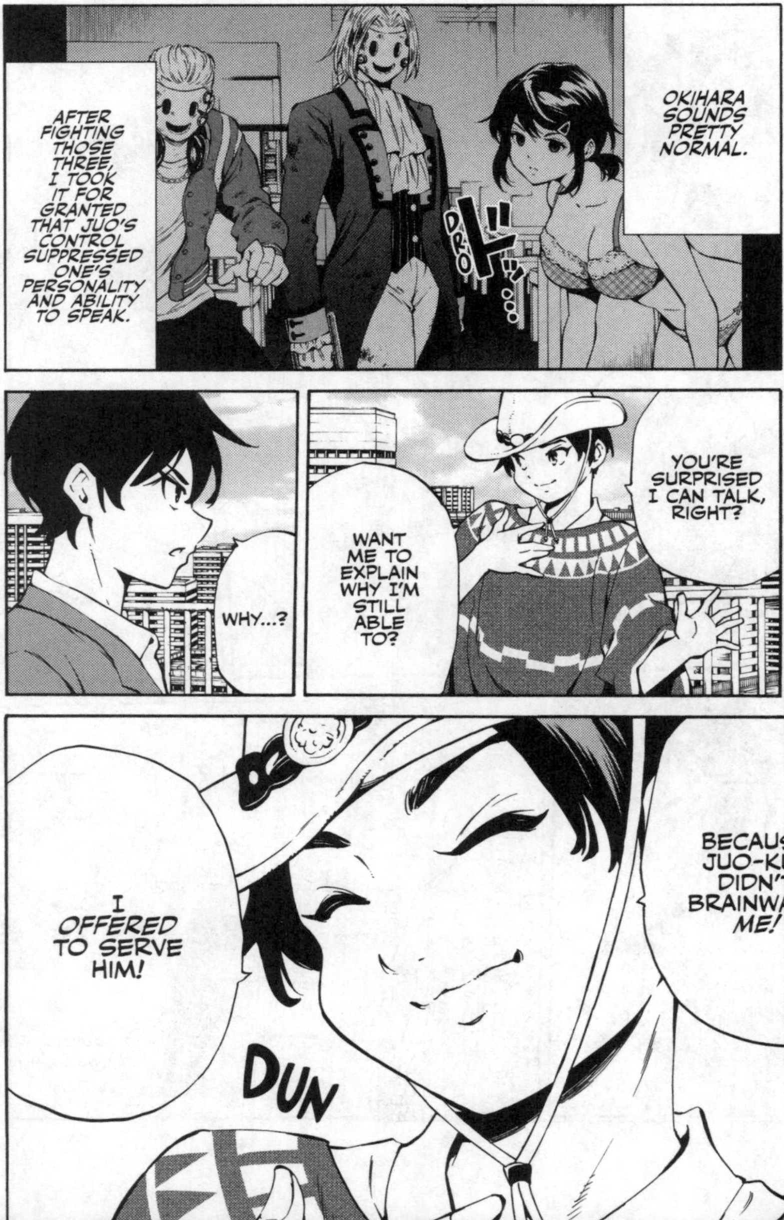
OKIHARA SOUNDS PRETTY NORMAL.
DRO
AFTER FIGHTING THOSE THREE, I TOOK IT FOR GRANTED THAT JUO'S CONTROL SUPPRESSED ONE'S PERSONALITY AND ABILITY TO SPEAK.
YOU'RE SURPRISED I CAN TALK, RIGHT?
WANT ME TO EXPLAIN WHY I'M STILL ABLE TO?
WHY...?
BECAUSE JUO-KUN DIDN'T BRAINWASH *ME!*
I *OFFERED* TO SERVE HIM!
DUN

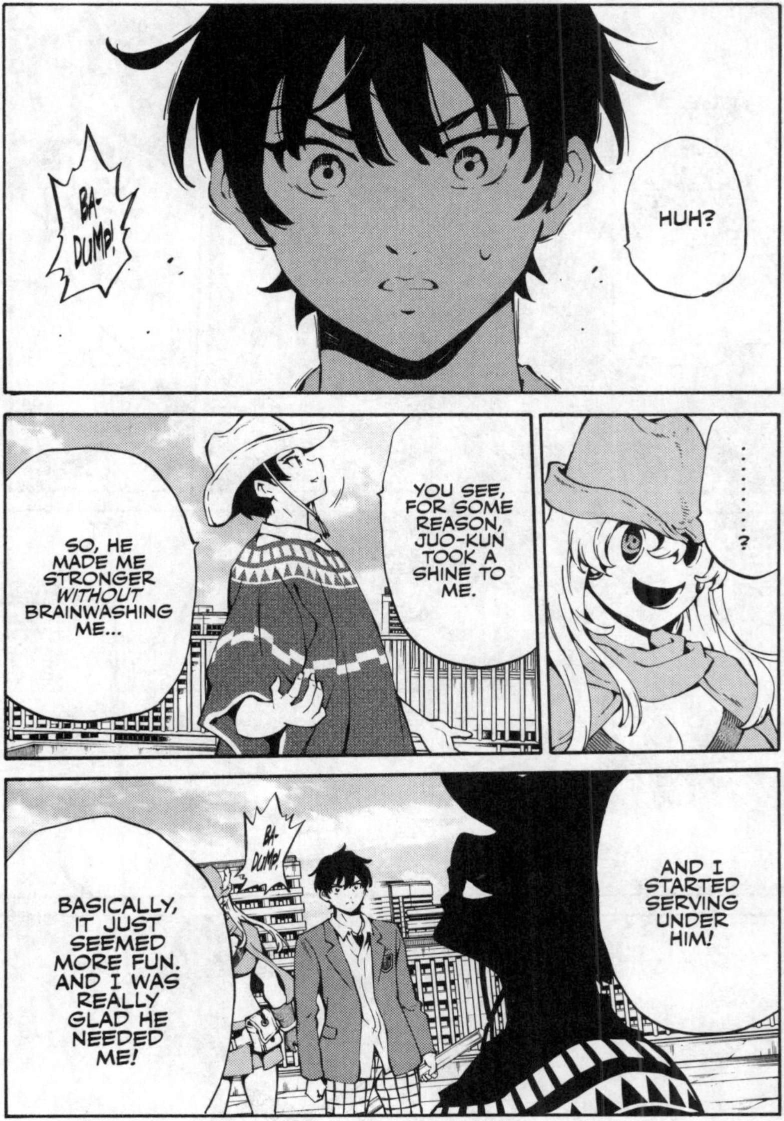
HUH?
BA-DUMP!
......?
YOU SEE, FOR SOME REASON, JUO-KUN TOOK A SHINE TO ME.
SO, HE MADE ME STRONGER *WITHOUT* BRAINWASHING ME...
AND I STARTED SERVING UNDER HIM!
BA-DUMP!
BASICALLY, IT JUST SEEMED MORE FUN. AND I WAS REALLY GLAD HE NEEDED ME!

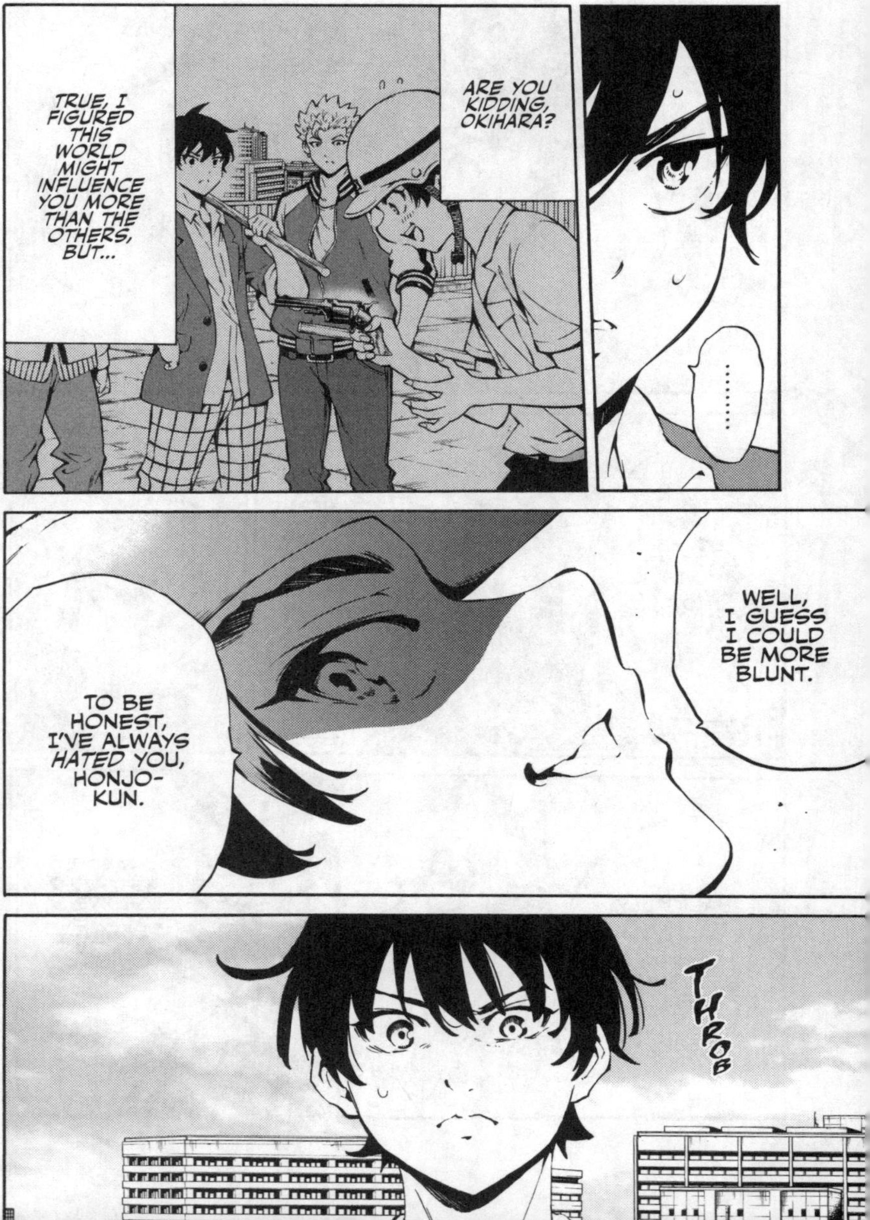
......
ARE YOU KIDDING, OKIHARA?
TRUE, I FIGURED THIS WORLD MIGHT INFLUENCE YOU MORE THAN THE OTHERS, BUT...
WELL, I GUESS I COULD BE MORE BLUNT.
TO BE HONEST, I'VE ALWAYS HATED YOU, HONJO-KUN.
THROB

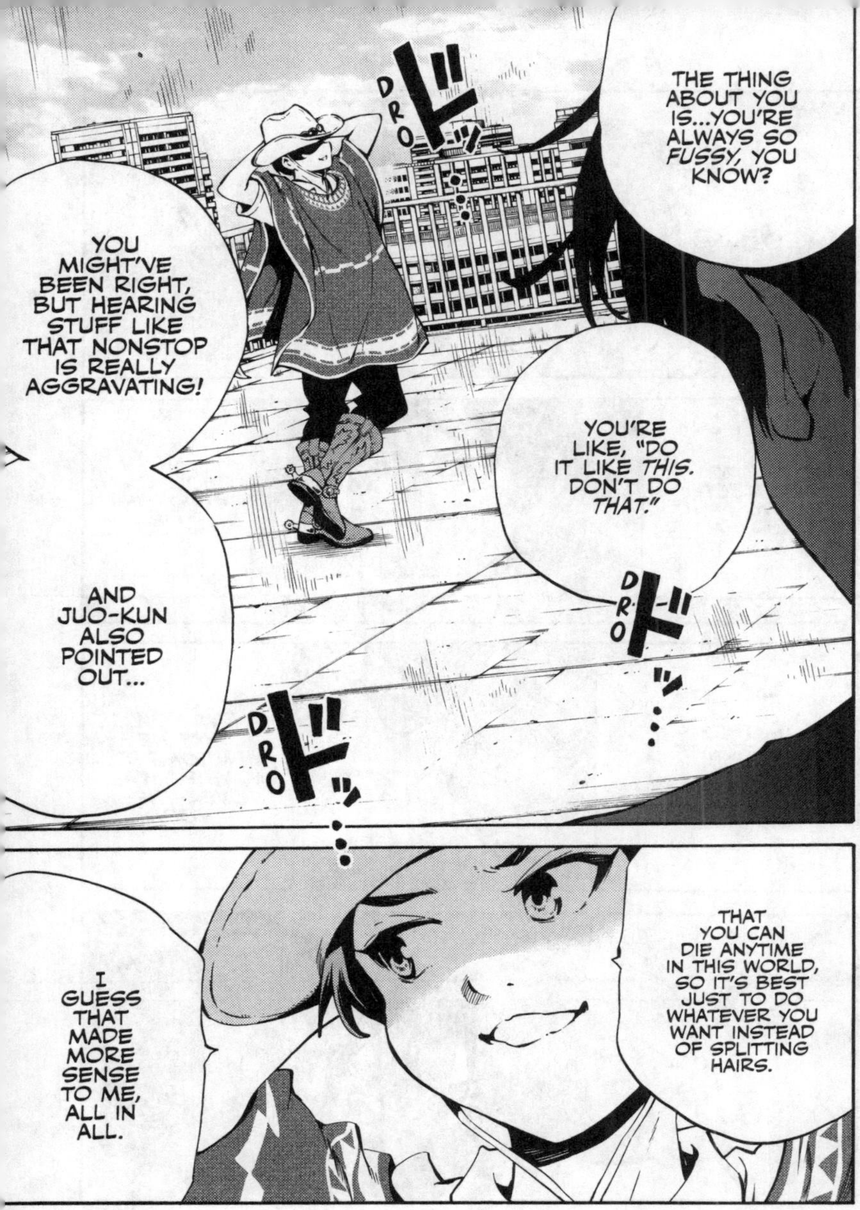
DRO
THE THING ABOUT YOU IS...YOU'RE ALWAYS SO *FUSSY*, YOU KNOW?
YOU'RE LIKE, "DO IT LIKE *THIS*. DON'T DO *THAT*."
DRO
YOU MIGHT'VE BEEN RIGHT, BUT HEARING STUFF LIKE THAT NONSTOP IS REALLY AGGRAVATING!
DRO
AND JUO-KUN ALSO POINTED OUT...
THAT YOU CAN DIE ANYTIME IN THIS WORLD, SO IT'S BEST JUST TO DO WHATEVER YOU WANT INSTEAD OF SPLITTING HAIRS.
I GUESS THAT MADE MORE SENSE TO ME, ALL IN ALL.

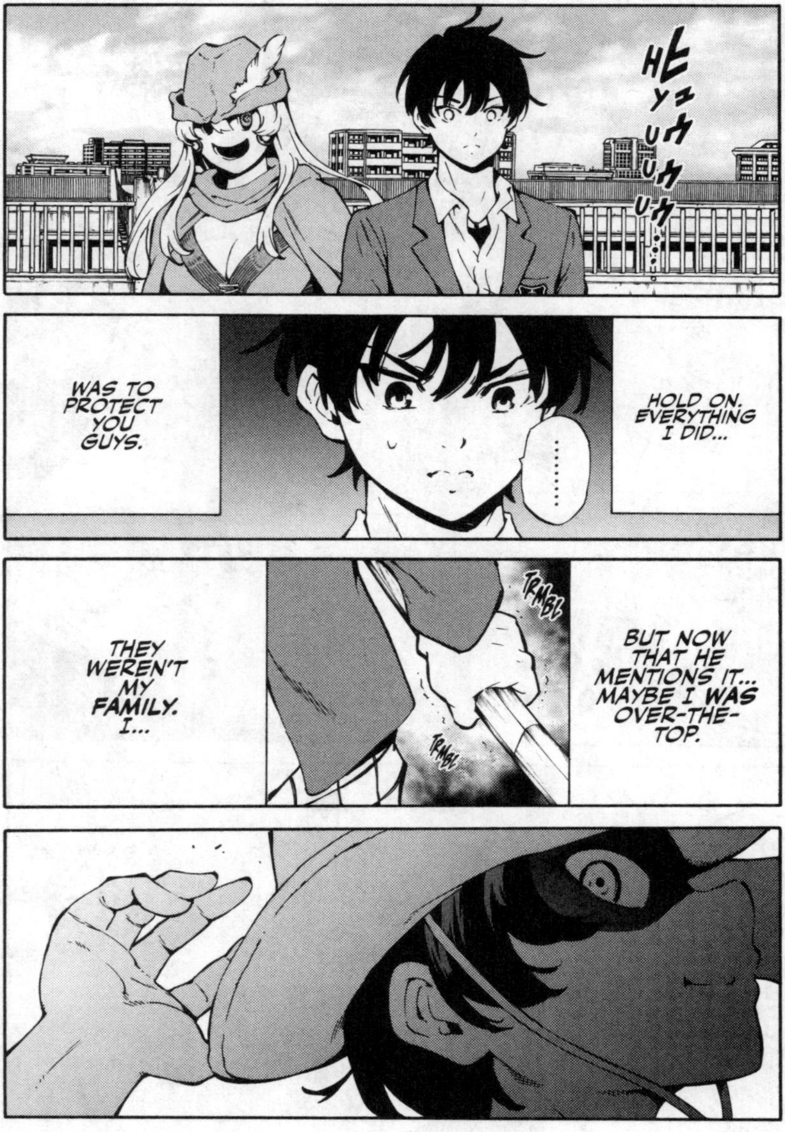

HYUUUU...
HOLD ON. EVERYTHING I DID...
......
WAS TO PROTECT YOU GUYS.
TRMBL
BUT NOW THAT HE MENTIONS IT... MAYBE I WAS OVER-THE-TOP.
TRMBL
THEY WEREN'T MY **FAMILY.** I...

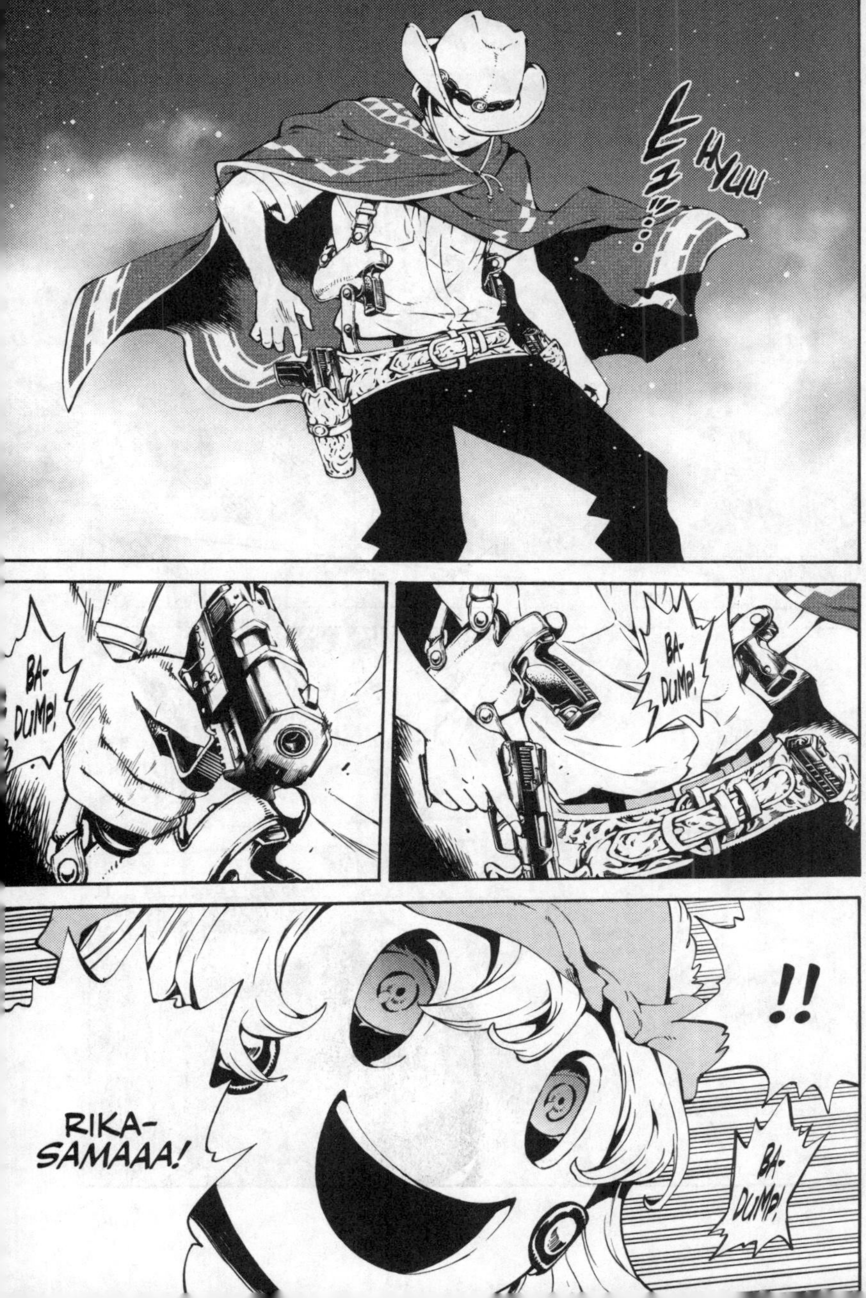
HYUU
BA-DUMP!
BA-DUMP!
!!
BA-DUMP!
RIKA-SAMAAA!

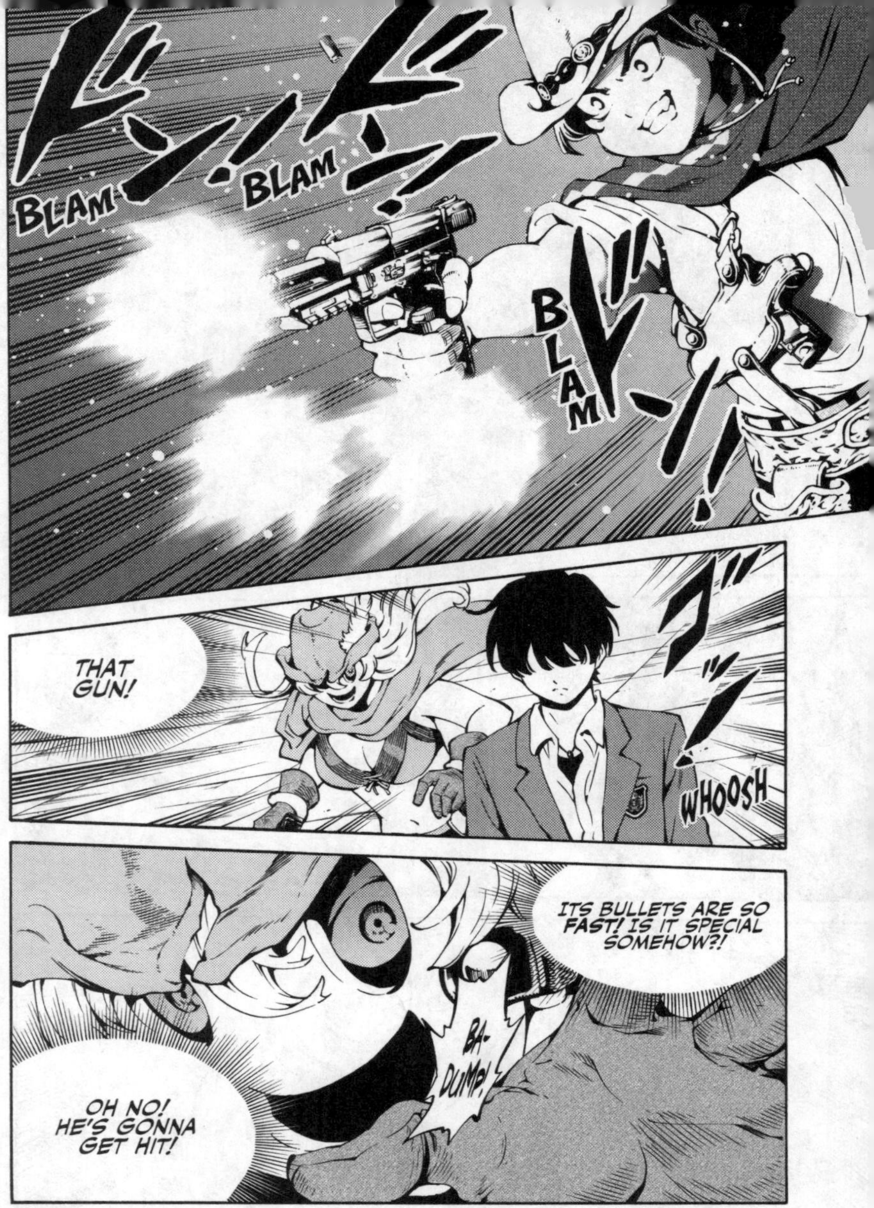
BLAM
BLAM
BLAM
BLAM
THAT GUN!
WHOOSH
ITS BULLETS ARE SO FAST! IS IT SPECIAL SOMEHOW?!
BA-DUMP!
OH NO! HE'S GONNA GET HIT!

RIKA-
SAMA!!

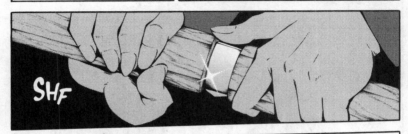

SHF

GWOOSH

HWIP

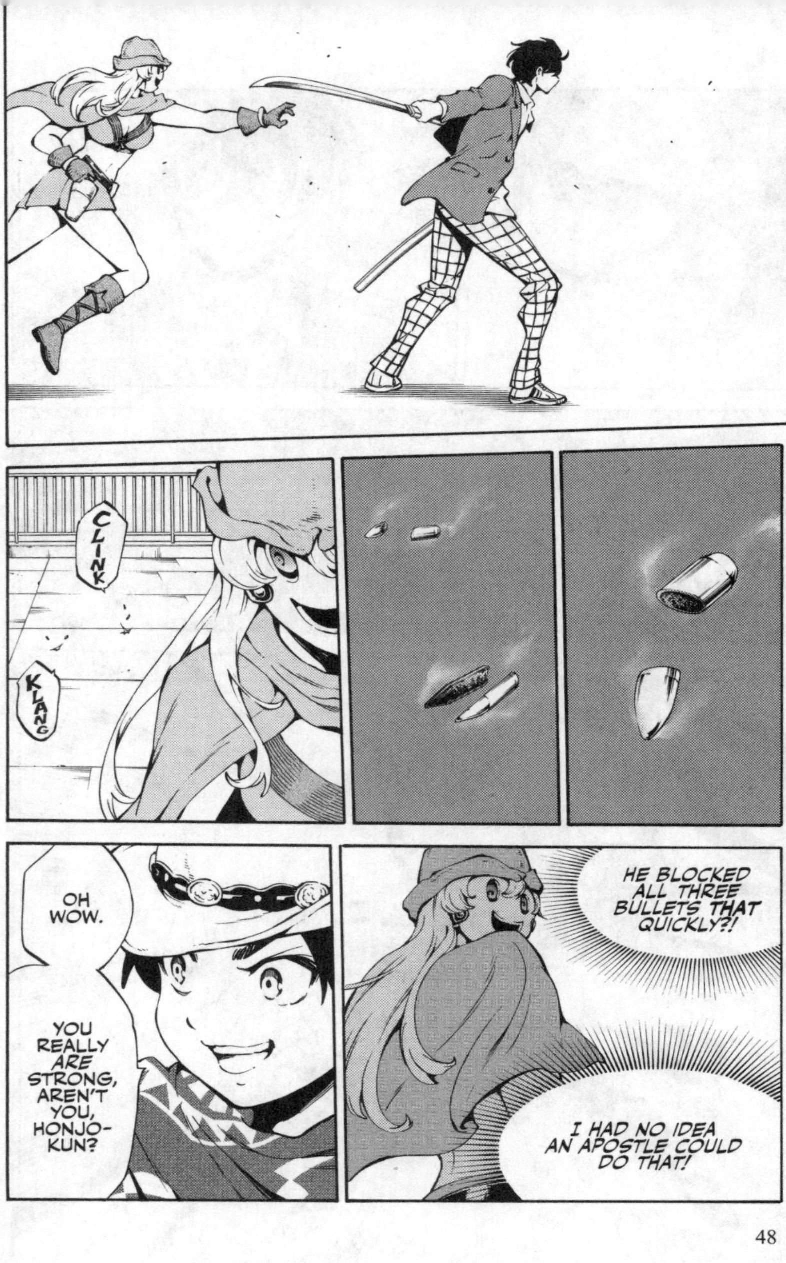
CLINK
KLANG
HE BLOCKED ALL THREE BULLETS THAT QUICKLY?!
I HAD NO IDEA AN APOSTLE COULD DO THAT!
OH WOW.
YOU REALLY ARE STRONG, AREN'T YOU, HONJO-KUN?

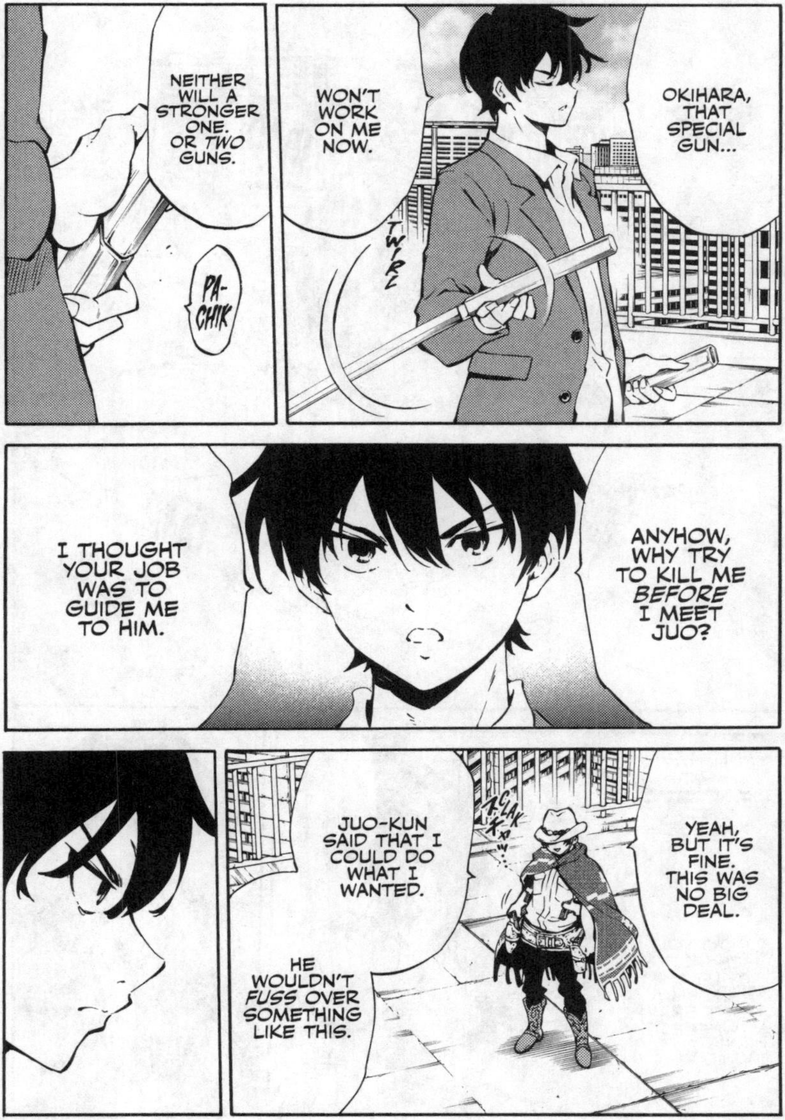
OKIHARA, THAT SPECIAL GUN...
WON'T WORK ON ME NOW.
TWIRL
NEITHER WILL A STRONGER ONE. OR *TWO* GUNS.
PA-CHIK
ANYHOW, WHY TRY TO KILL ME *BEFORE* I MEET JUO?
I THOUGHT YOUR JOB WAS TO GUIDE ME TO HIM.
YEAH, BUT IT'S FINE. THIS WAS NO BIG DEAL.
CLAK
JUO-KUN SAID THAT I COULD DO WHAT I WANTED.
HE WOULDN'T *FUSS* OVER SOMETHING LIKE THIS.

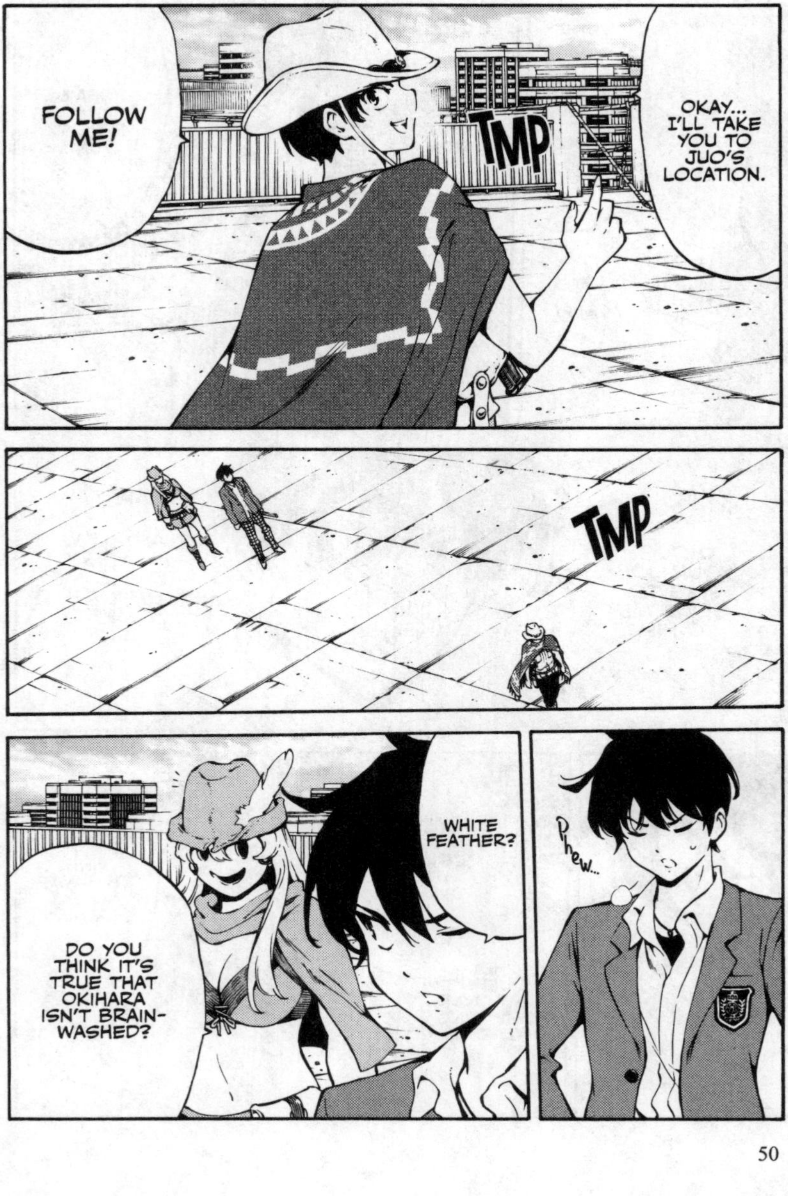
OKAY... I'LL TAKE YOU TO JUO'S LOCATION.
TMP
FOLLOW ME!
TMP
Phew...
WHITE FEATHER?
DO YOU THINK IT'S TRUE THAT OKIHARA ISN'T BRAIN-WASHED?

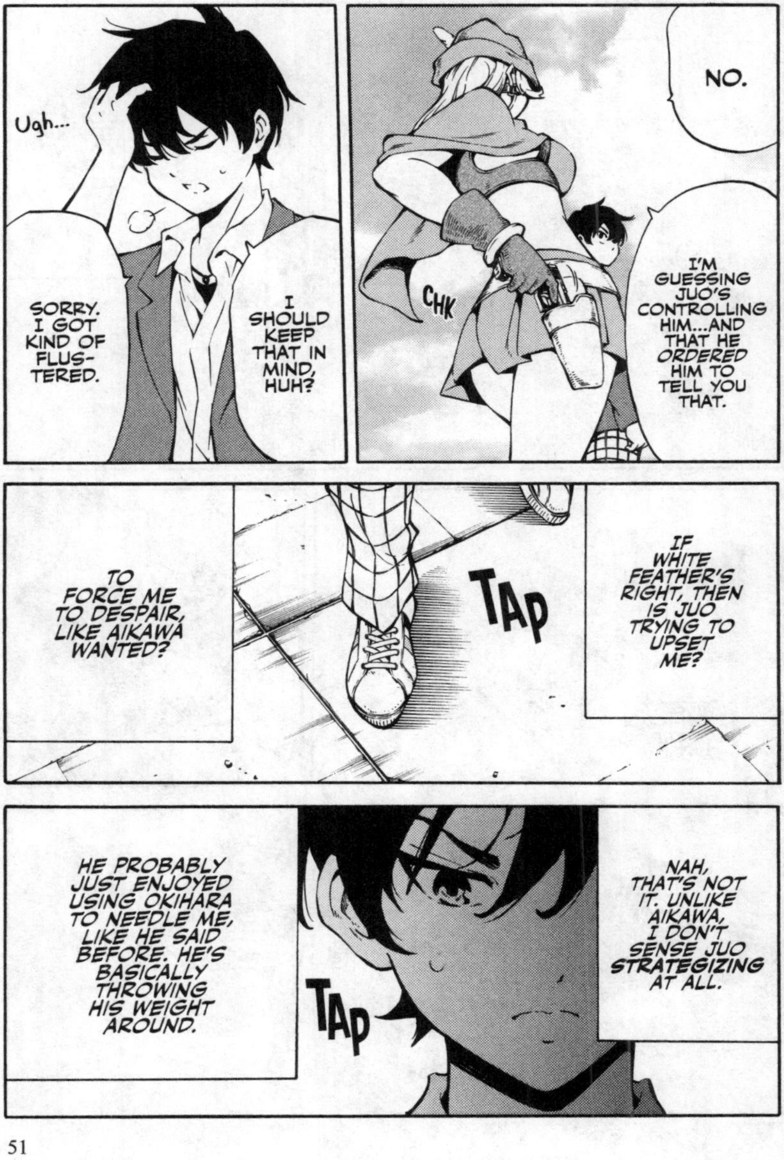
NO.
I'M GUESSING JUO'S CONTROLLING HIM...AND THAT HE ORDERED HIM TO TELL YOU THAT.
CHK
Ugh...
I SHOULD KEEP THAT IN MIND, HUH?
SORRY. I GOT KIND OF FLUS-TERED.
IF WHITE FEATHER'S RIGHT, THEN IS JUO TRYING TO UPSET ME?
TAP
TO FORCE ME TO DESPAIR, LIKE AIKAWA WANTED?
NAH, THAT'S NOT IT. UNLIKE AIKAWA, I DON'T SENSE JUO STRATEGIZING AT ALL.
TAP
HE PROBABLY JUST ENJOYED USING OKIHARA TO NEEDLE ME, LIKE HE SAID BEFORE. HE'S BASICALLY THROWING HIS WEIGHT AROUND.

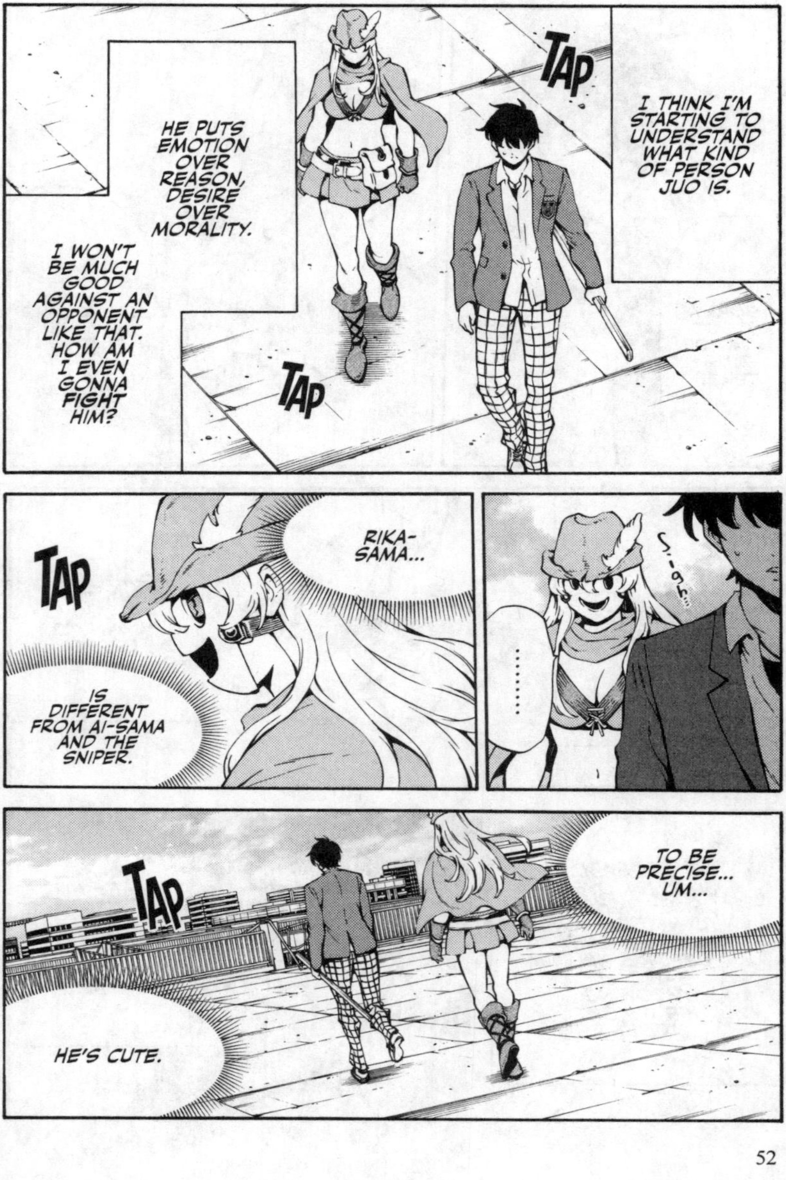
TAP
I THINK I'M STARTING TO UNDERSTAND WHAT KIND OF PERSON JUO IS.
HE PUTS EMOTION OVER REASON, DESIRE OVER MORALITY.
I WON'T BE MUCH GOOD AGAINST AN OPPONENT LIKE THAT. HOW AM I EVEN GONNA FIGHT HIM?
TAP
Sigh...
......
RIKA-SAMA...
TAP
IS DIFFERENT FROM AI-SAMA AND THE SNIPER.
TO BE PRECISE... UM...
TAP
HE'S CUTE.

HIGH-RISE INVASION

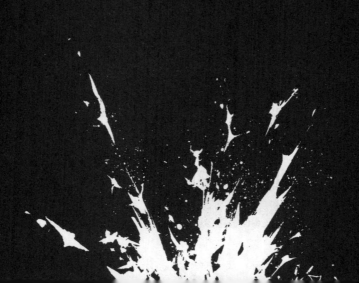

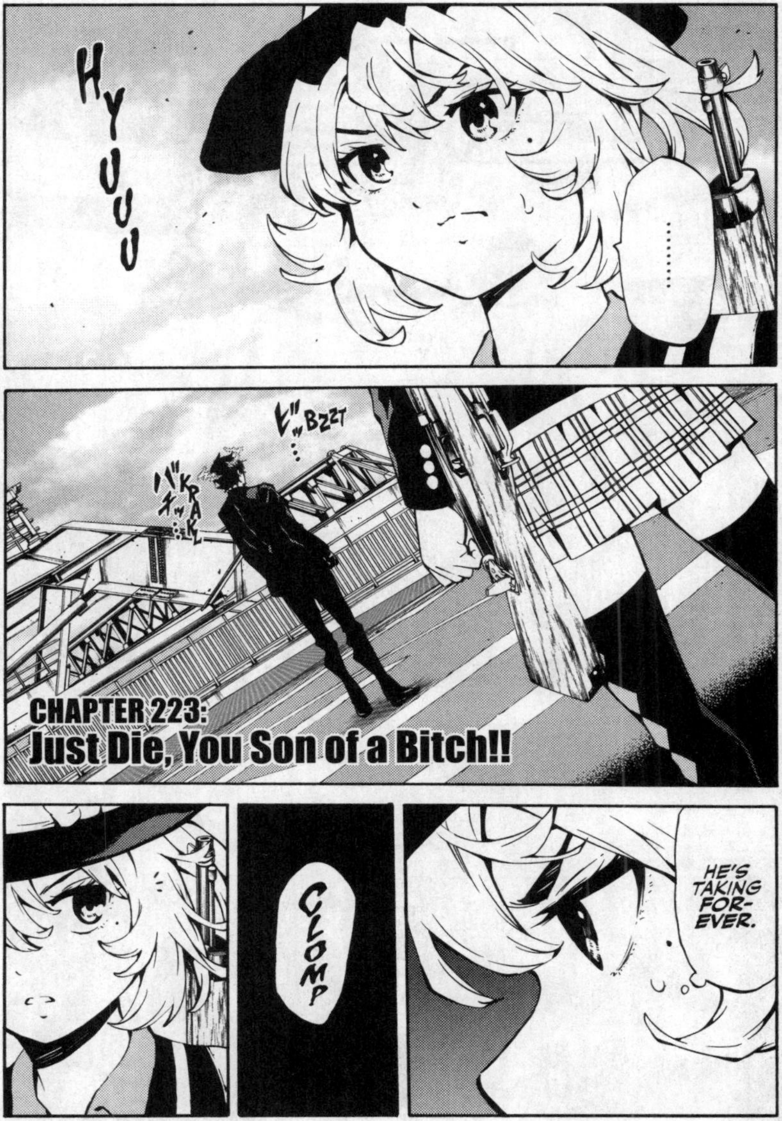
HYUUU
......
ビッ BZZT
バチッ KRAKL
CHAPTER 223:
Just Die, You Son of a Bitch!!
HE'S TAKING FOR-EVER.
CLOMP

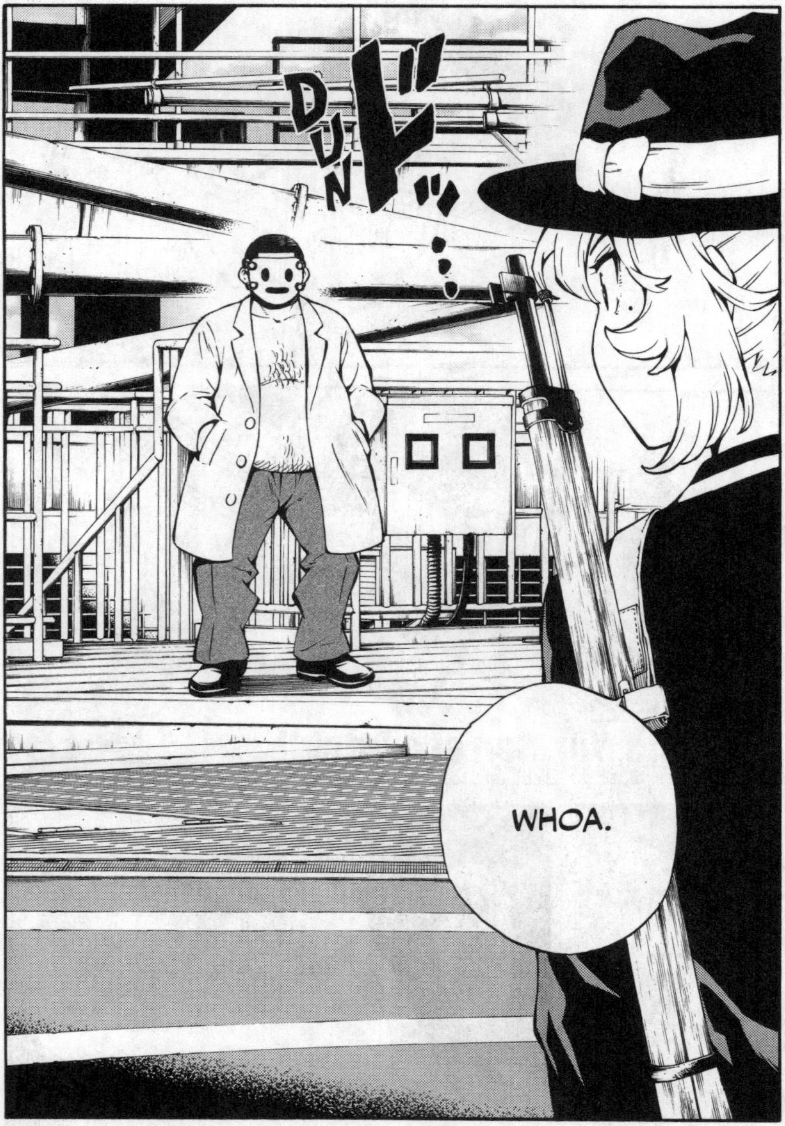
DUN ドン…
WHOA.

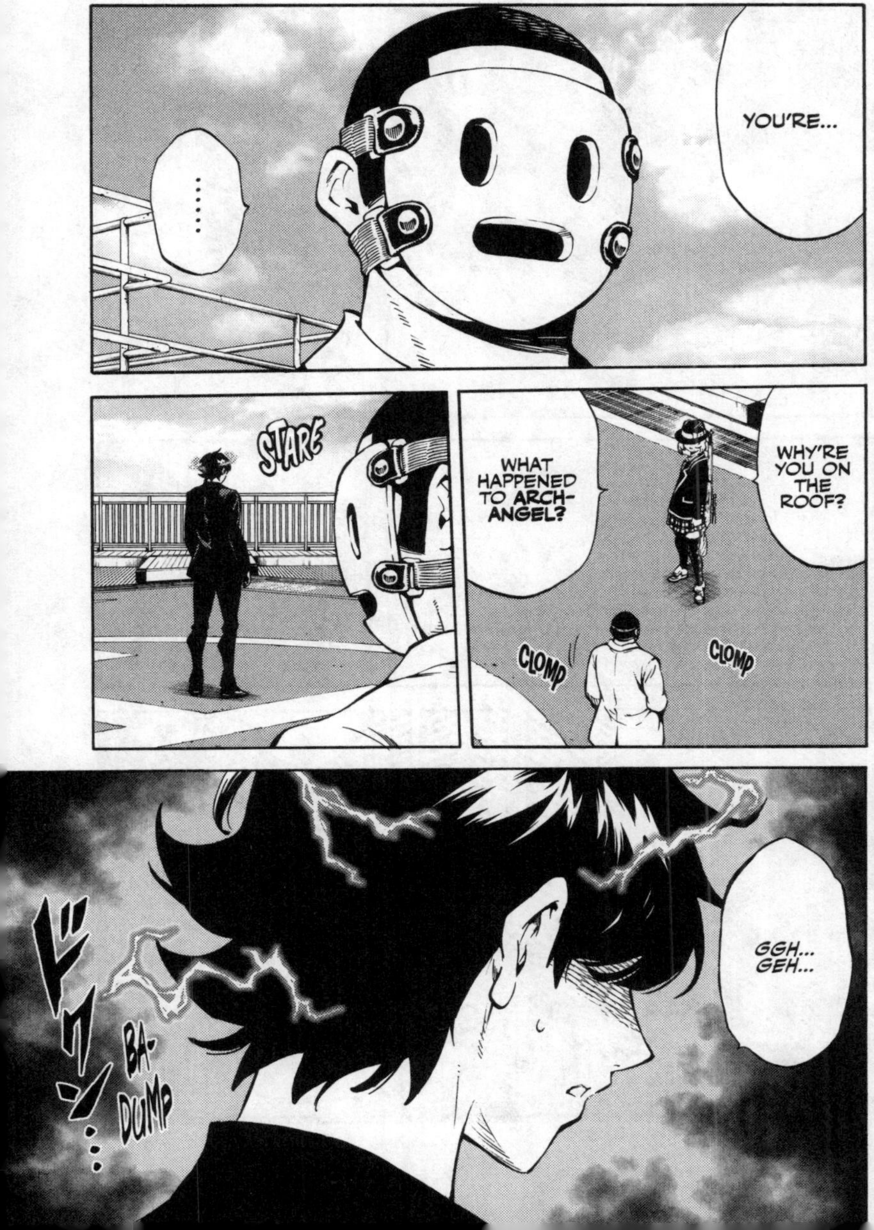
YOU'RE...
......
WHY'RE YOU ON THE ROOF?
WHAT HAPPENED TO ARCH-ANGEL?
CLOMP
CLOMP
STARE
GGH... GEH...
ドクン…
BA-DUMP

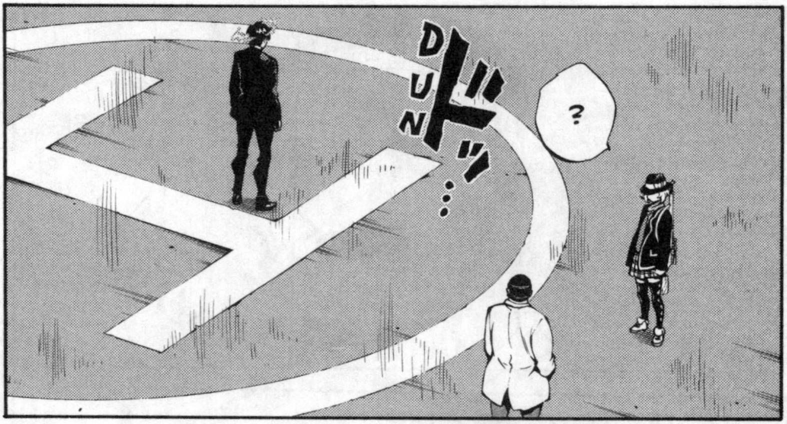
?
DUN
ドッ…
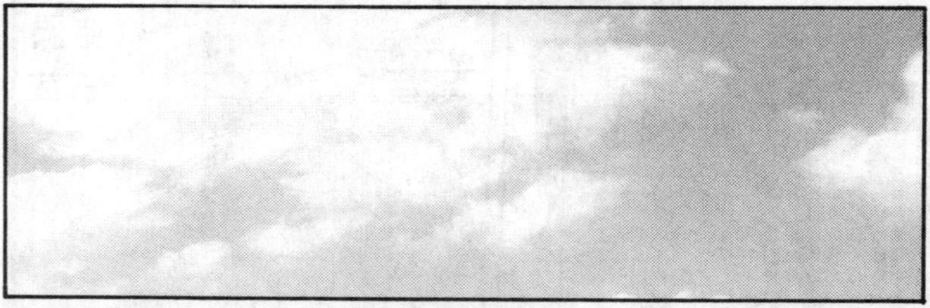
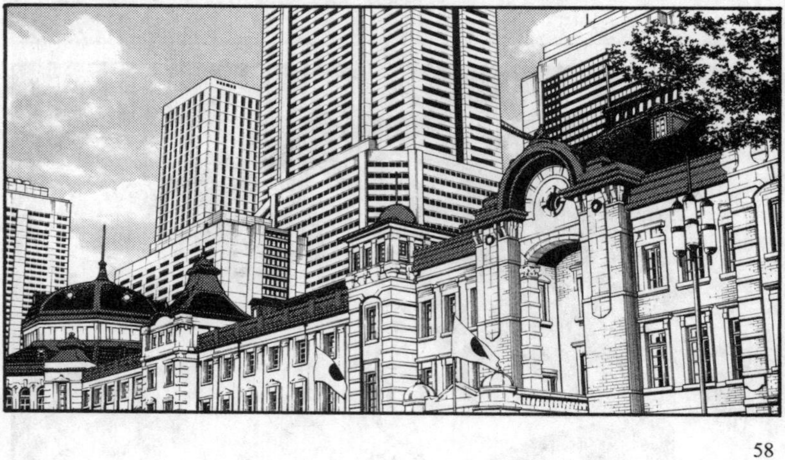

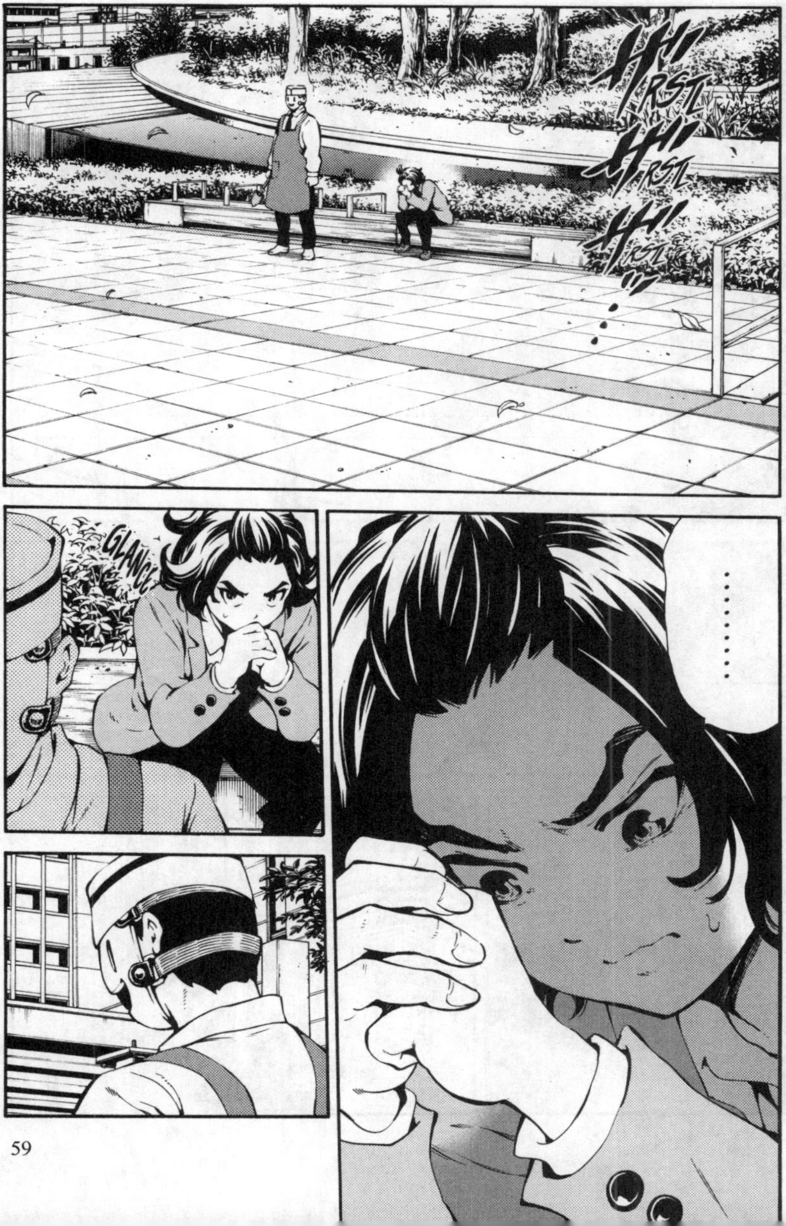
HHRSTL HHRSTL HHRSTL...
....
GLANCE

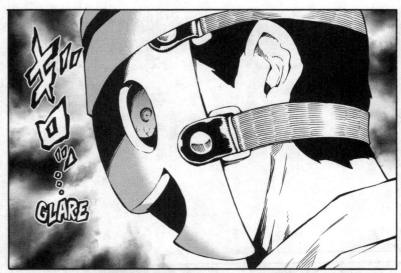

GLARE

AUGH!

HEY.

!

TAP

HOW'D THINGS END UP LIKE THIS?

HOW...

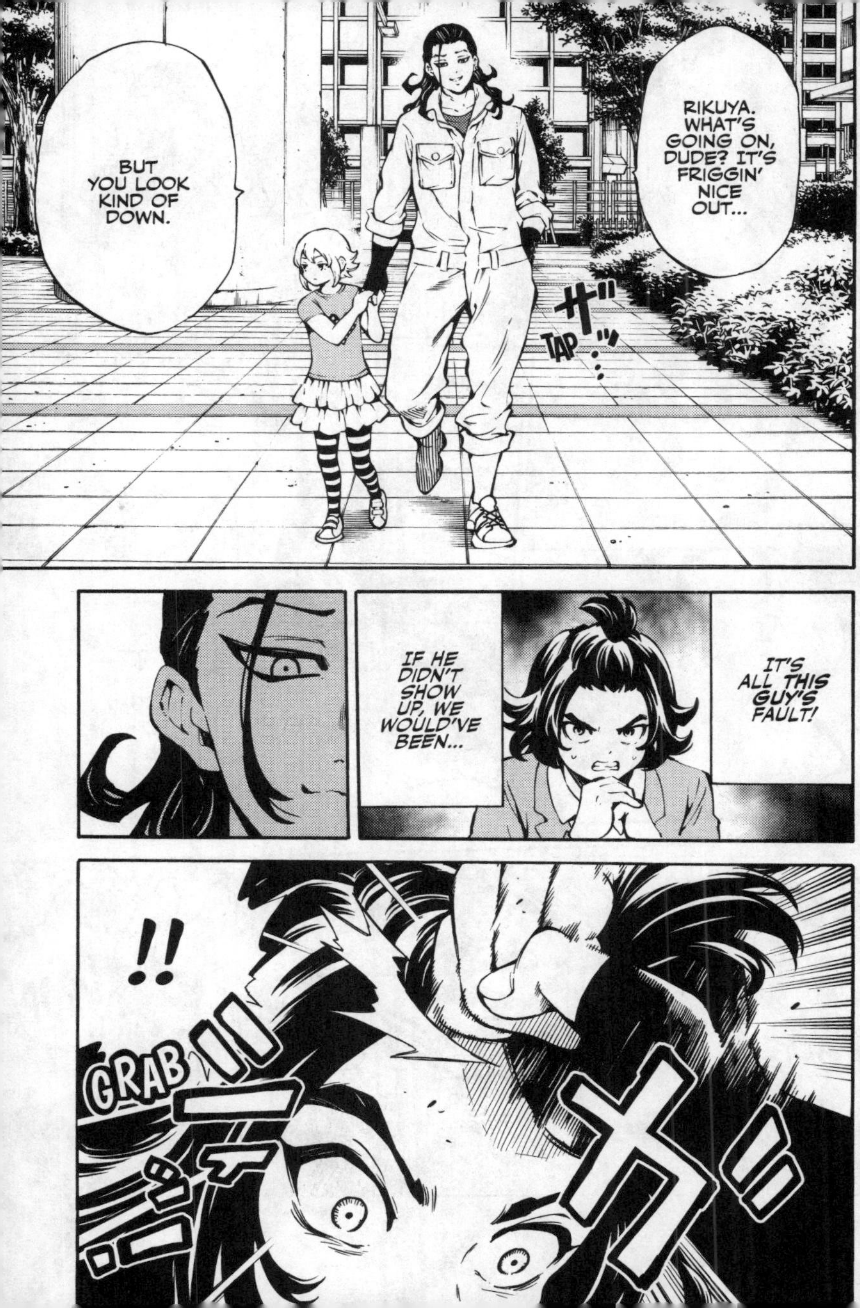
RIKUYA. WHAT'S GOING ON, DUDE? IT'S FRIGGIN' NICE OUT...
TAP
BUT YOU LOOK KIND OF DOWN.
IT'S ALL THIS GUY'S FAULT!
IF HE DIDN'T SHOW UP, WE WOULD'VE BEEN...
!!
GRAB

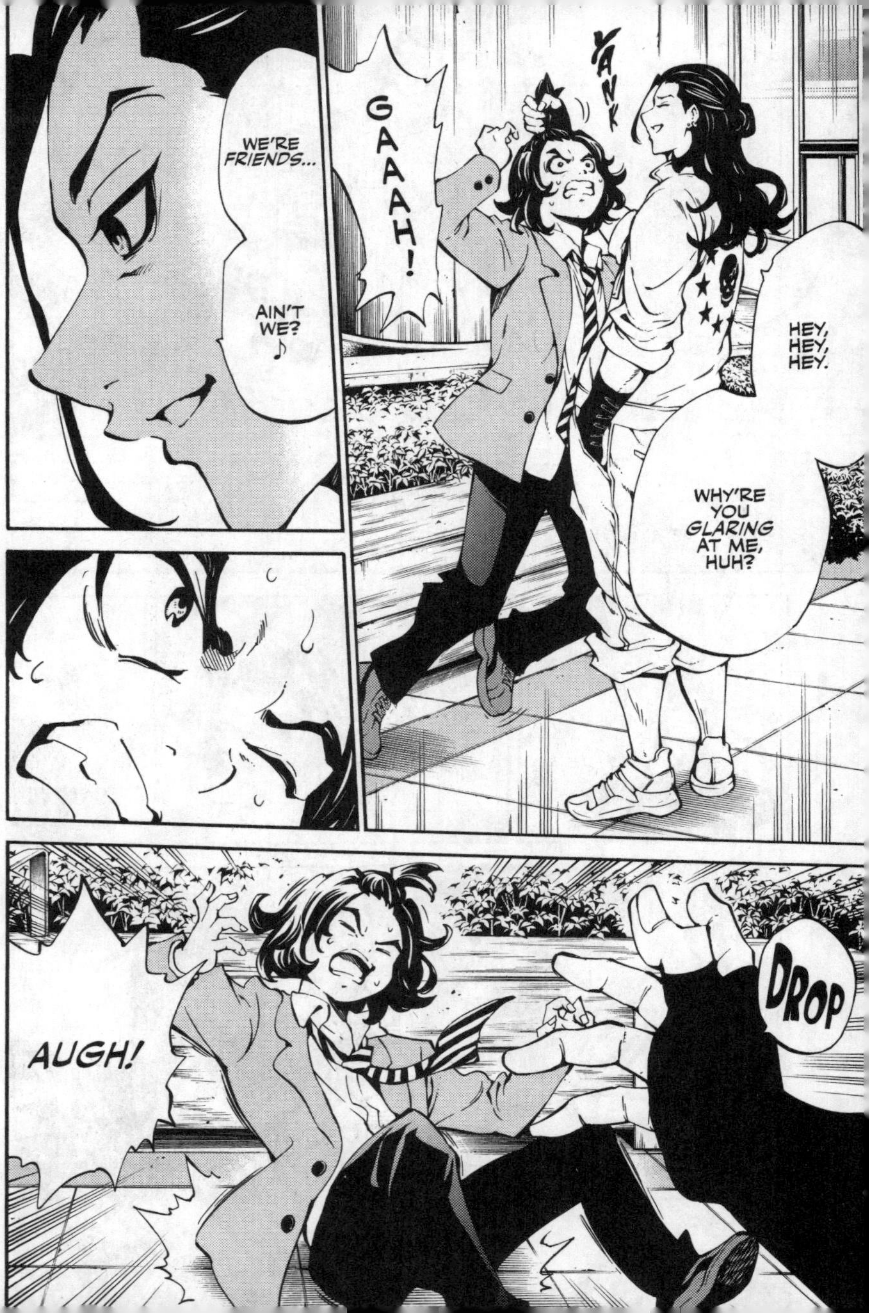
YANK
GAAAH!
HEY, HEY, HEY.
WHY'RE YOU GLARING AT ME, HUH?
WE'RE FRIENDS...
AIN'T WE? ♪
DROP
AUGH!

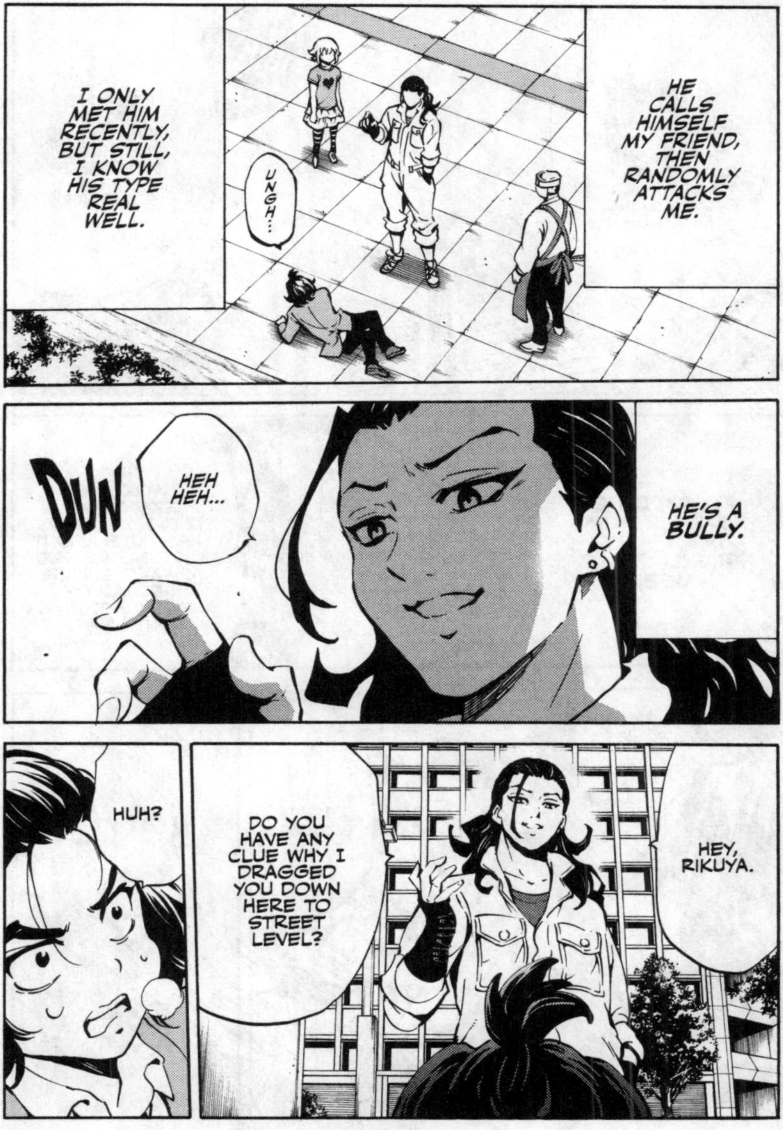
HE CALLS HIMSELF MY FRIEND, THEN RANDOMLY ATTACKS ME.
I ONLY MET HIM RECENTLY, BUT STILL, I KNOW HIS TYPE REAL WELL.
UNGH...
HE'S A BULLY.
HEH HEH...
DUN
HEY, RIKUYA.
DO YOU HAVE ANY CLUE WHY I DRAGGED YOU DOWN HERE TO STREET LEVEL?
HUH?

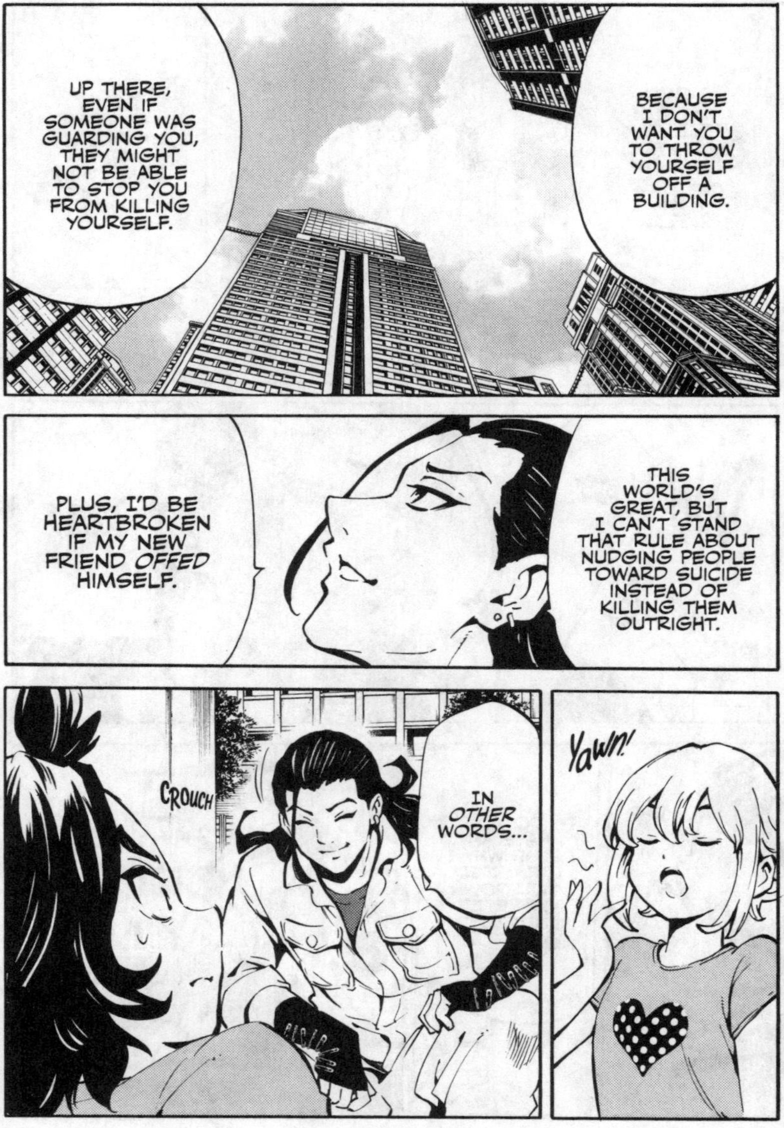
BECAUSE I DON'T WANT YOU TO THROW YOURSELF OFF A BUILDING.
UP THERE, EVEN IF SOMEONE WAS GUARDING YOU, THEY MIGHT NOT BE ABLE TO STOP YOU FROM KILLING YOURSELF.
THIS WORLD'S GREAT, BUT I CAN'T STAND THAT RULE ABOUT NUDGING PEOPLE TOWARD SUICIDE INSTEAD OF KILLING THEM OUTRIGHT.
PLUS, I'D BE HEARTBROKEN IF MY NEW FRIEND *OFFED* HIMSELF.
YAWN!
IN *OTHER* WORDS...
CROUCH

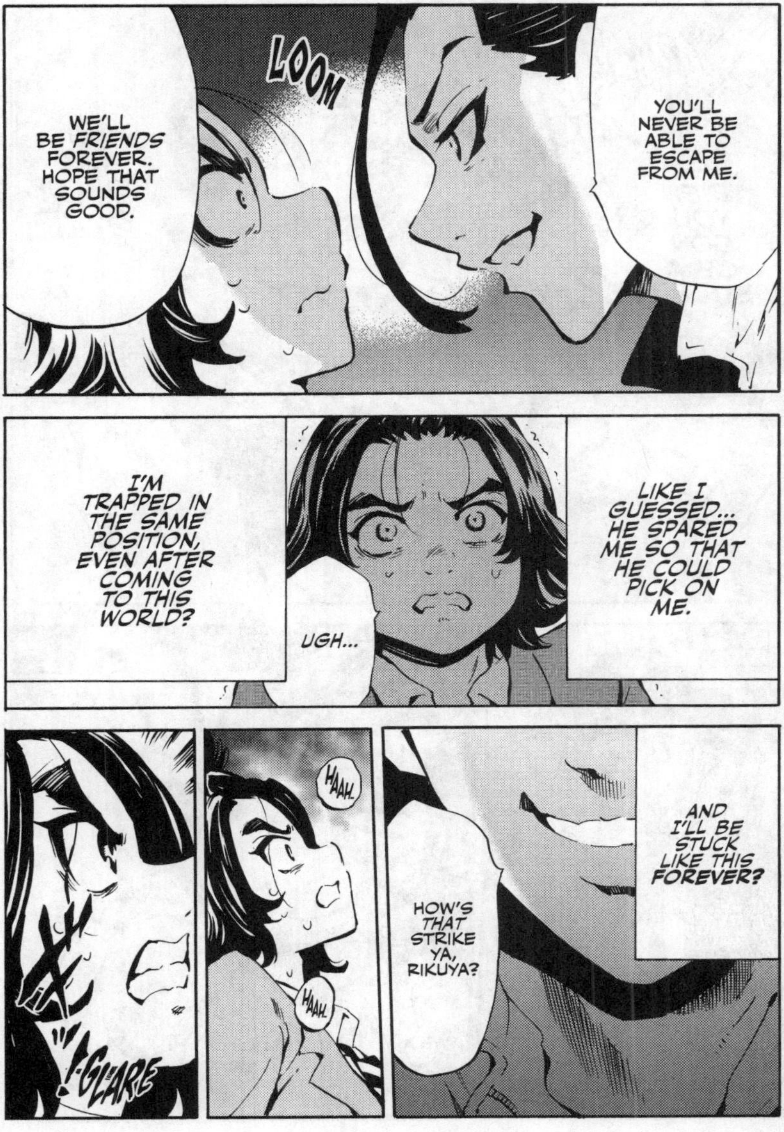
YOU'LL NEVER BE ABLE TO ESCAPE FROM ME.
LOOM
WE'LL BE *FRIENDS* FOREVER. HOPE THAT SOUNDS GOOD.
LIKE I GUESSED... HE SPARED ME SO THAT HE COULD PICK ON ME.
I'M TRAPPED IN THE SAME POSITION, EVEN AFTER COMING TO THIS WORLD?
UGH...
AND I'LL BE STUCK LIKE THIS **FOREVER?**
HOW'S *THAT* STRIKE YA, RIKUYA?
HAAH
HAAH
GLARE

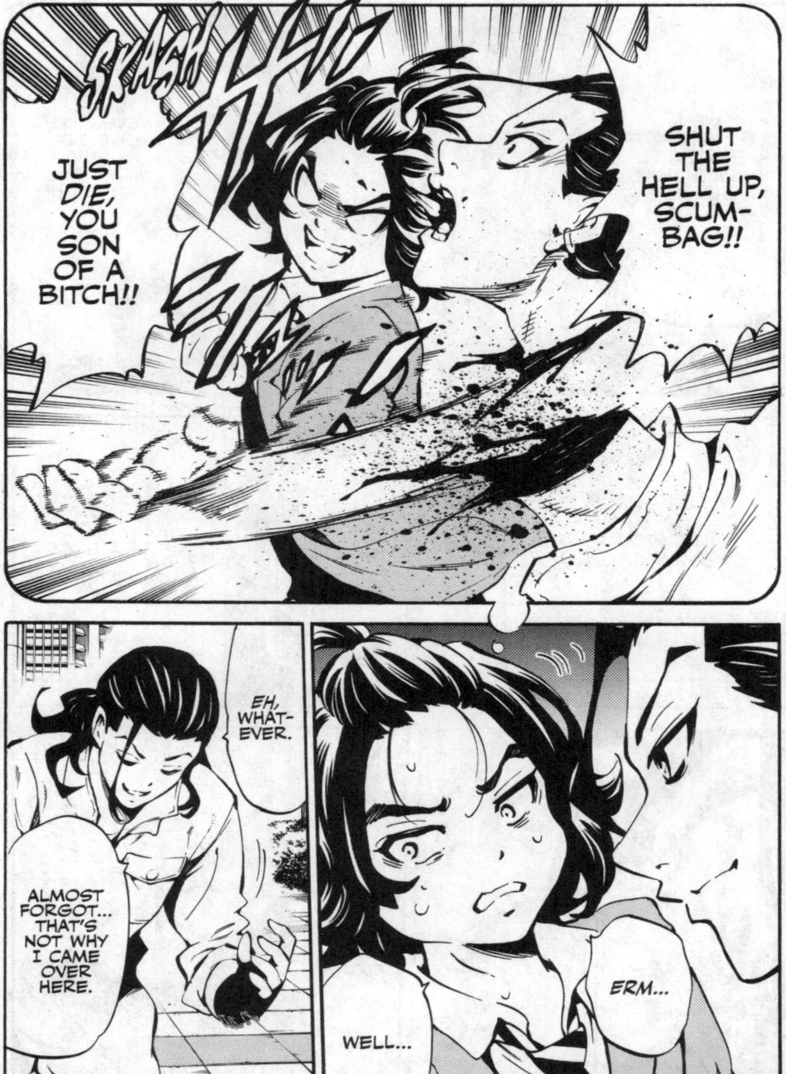
SHUT THE HELL UP, SCUM-BAG!!
SKASH
JUST DIE, YOU SON OF A BITCH!!
ERM...
WELL...
EH, WHAT-EVER.
ALMOST FORGOT... THAT'S NOT WHY I CAME OVER HERE.

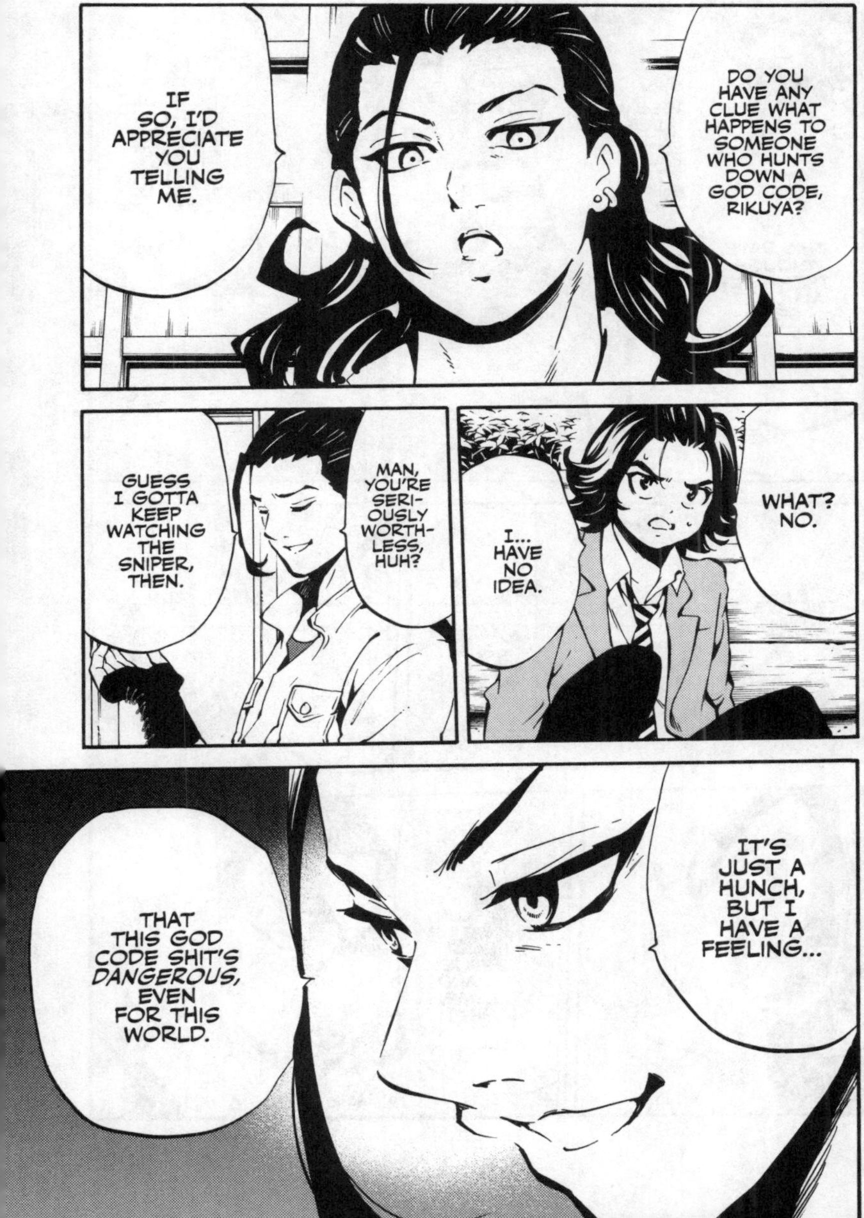
DO YOU HAVE ANY CLUE WHAT HAPPENS TO SOMEONE WHO HUNTS DOWN A GOD CODE, RIKUYA?
IF SO, I'D APPRECIATE YOU TELLING ME.
WHAT? NO.
I... HAVE NO IDEA.
MAN, YOU'RE SERIOUSLY WORTHLESS, HUH?
GUESS I GOTTA KEEP WATCHING THE SNIPER, THEN.
IT'S JUST A HUNCH, BUT I HAVE A FEELING...
THAT THIS GOD CODE SHIT'S *DANGEROUS*, EVEN FOR THIS WORLD.

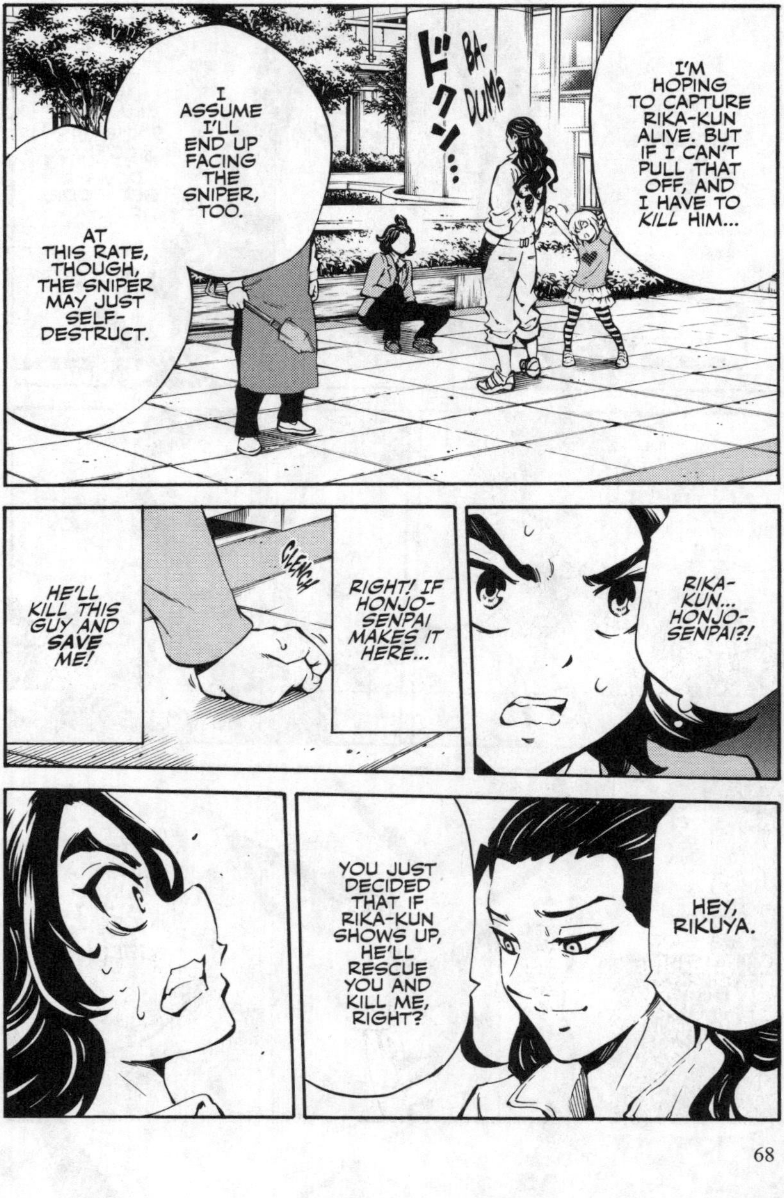
I'M HOPING TO CAPTURE RIKA-KUN ALIVE. BUT IF I CAN'T PULL THAT OFF, AND I HAVE TO *KILL* HIM...
ドクン...
BA-DUMP
I ASSUME I'LL END UP FACING THE SNIPER, TOO.
AT THIS RATE, THOUGH, THE SNIPER MAY JUST SELF-DESTRUCT.
RIKA-KUN... HONJO-SENPAI?!
RIGHT! IF HONJO-SENPAI MAKES IT HERE...
CLENCH
*HE'LL KILL THIS GUY AND **SAVE** ME!*
HEY, RIKUYA.
YOU JUST DECIDED THAT IF RIKA-KUN SHOWS UP, HE'LL RESCUE YOU AND KILL ME, RIGHT?

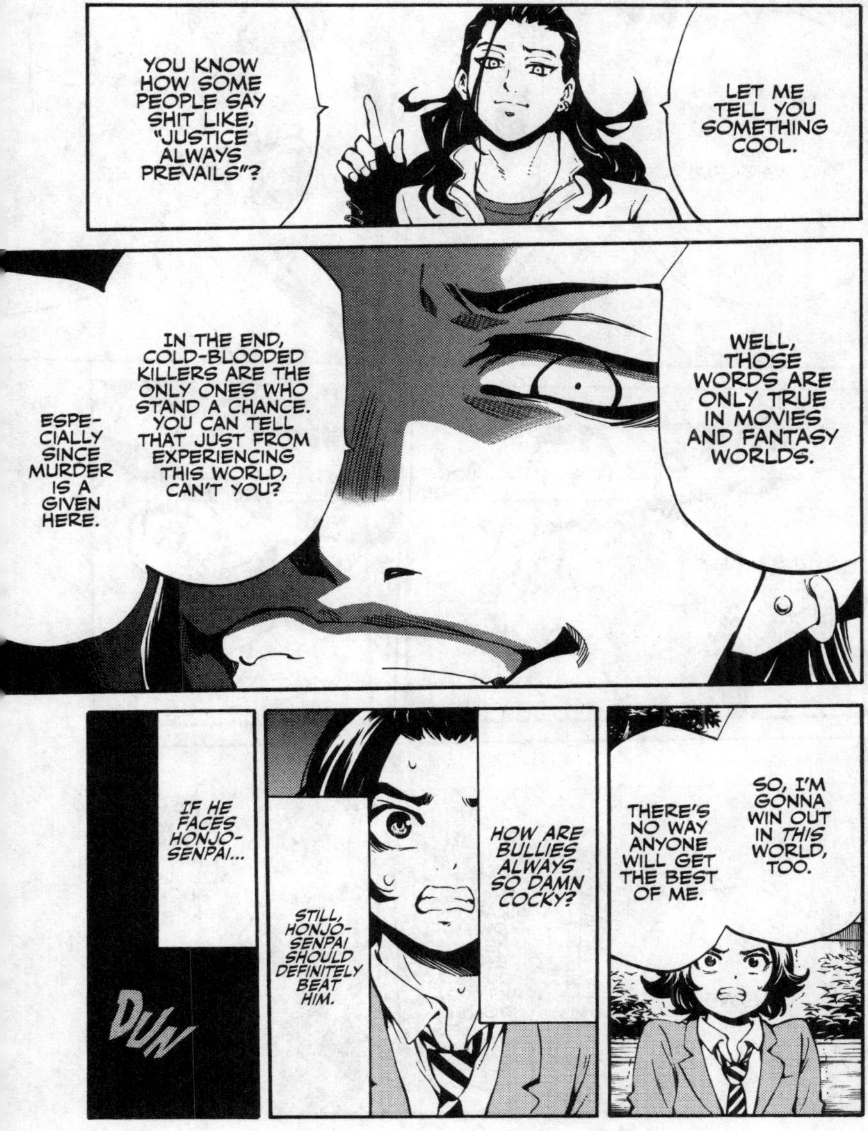
LET ME TELL YOU SOMETHING COOL.
YOU KNOW HOW SOME PEOPLE SAY SHIT LIKE, "JUSTICE ALWAYS PREVAILS"?
WELL, THOSE WORDS ARE ONLY TRUE IN MOVIES AND FANTASY WORLDS.
IN THE END, COLD-BLOODED KILLERS ARE THE ONLY ONES WHO STAND A CHANCE. YOU CAN TELL THAT JUST FROM EXPERIENCING THIS WORLD, CAN'T YOU?
ESPE-CIALLY SINCE MURDER IS A GIVEN HERE.
SO, I'M GONNA WIN OUT IN *THIS* WORLD, TOO.
THERE'S NO WAY ANYONE WILL GET THE BEST OF ME.
HOW ARE BULLIES ALWAYS SO DAMN COCKY?
STILL, HONJO-SENPAI SHOULD DEFINITELY BEAT HIM.
IF HE FACES HONJO-SENPAI...
DUN

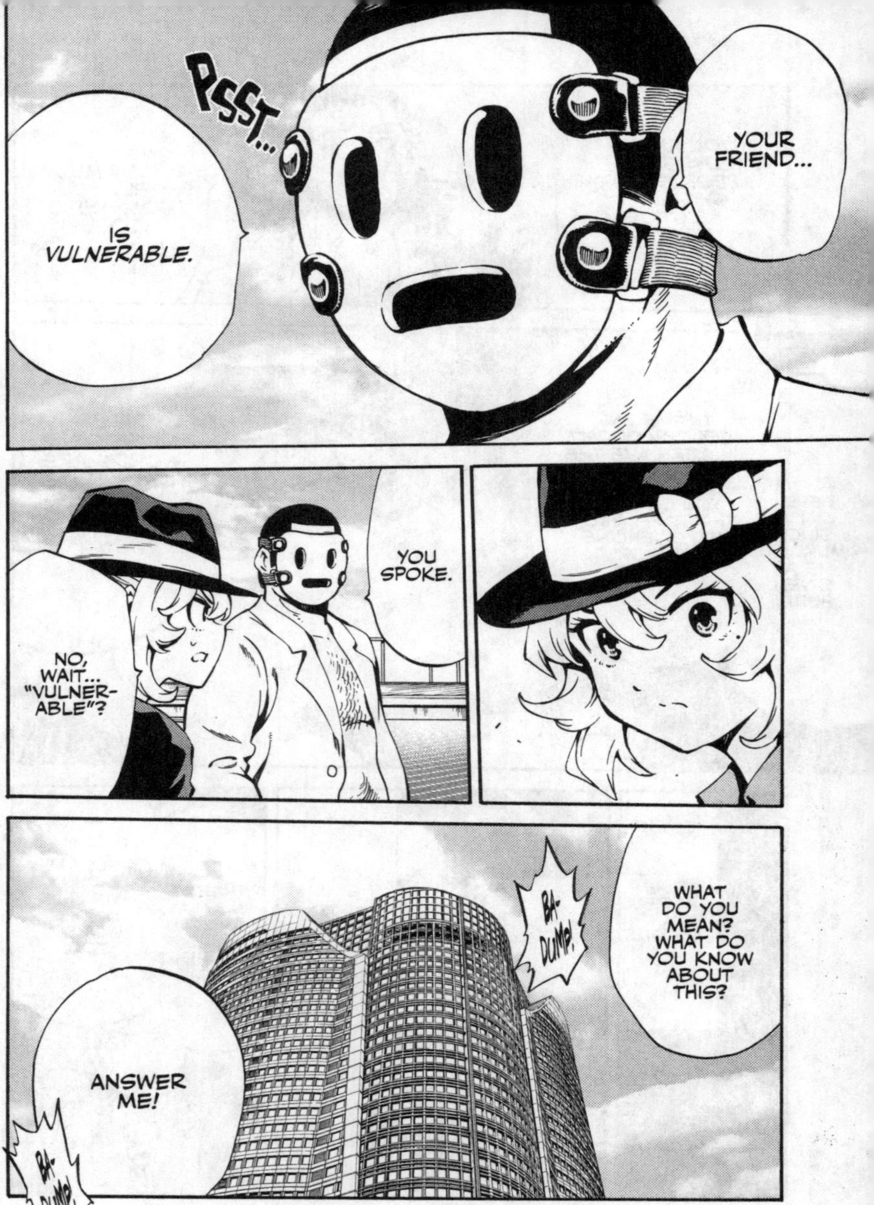
YOUR FRIEND...
PSST...
IS VULNERABLE.
YOU SPOKE.
NO, WAIT... "VULNERABLE"?
WHAT DO YOU MEAN? WHAT DO YOU KNOW ABOUT THIS?
BA-DUMP!
ANSWER ME!
BA-DUMP!

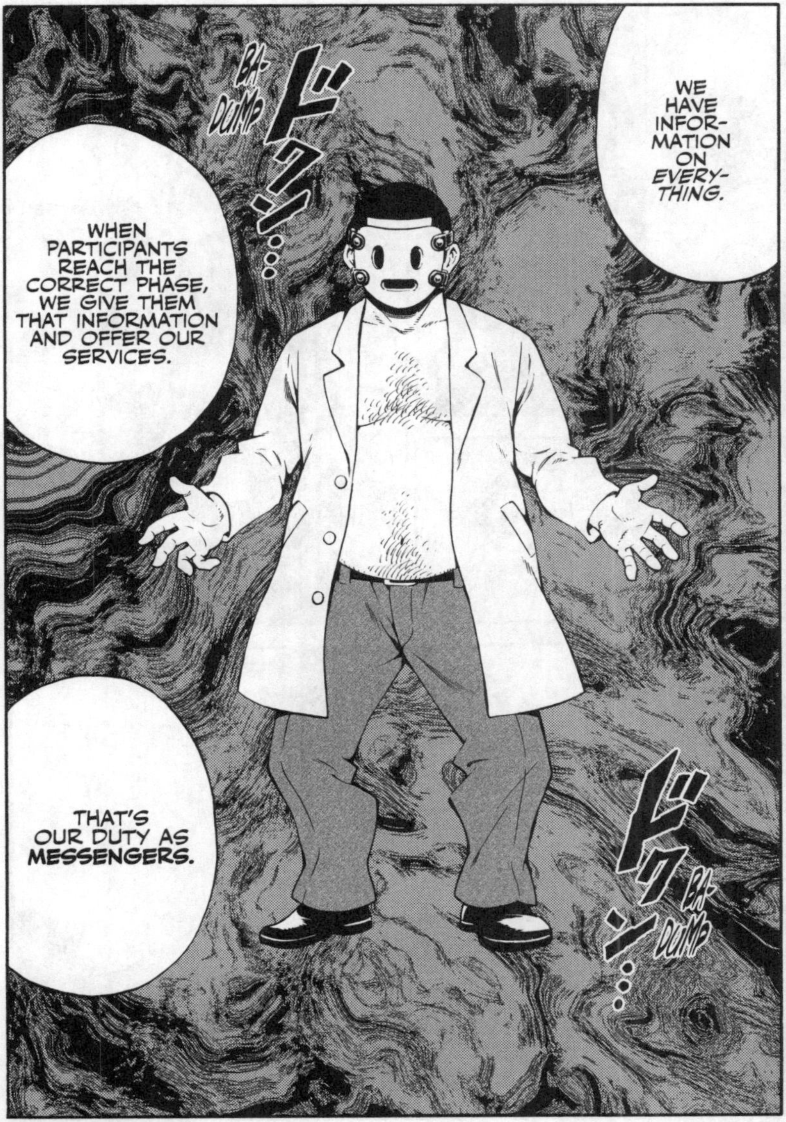
WE HAVE INFORMATION ON EVERYTHING.
BA-DUMP
WHEN PARTICIPANTS REACH THE CORRECT PHASE, WE GIVE THEM THAT INFORMATION AND OFFER OUR SERVICES.
BA-DUMP
THAT'S OUR DUTY AS MESSENGERS.

CHAPTER 224:
Their Consciousness Is a Different World

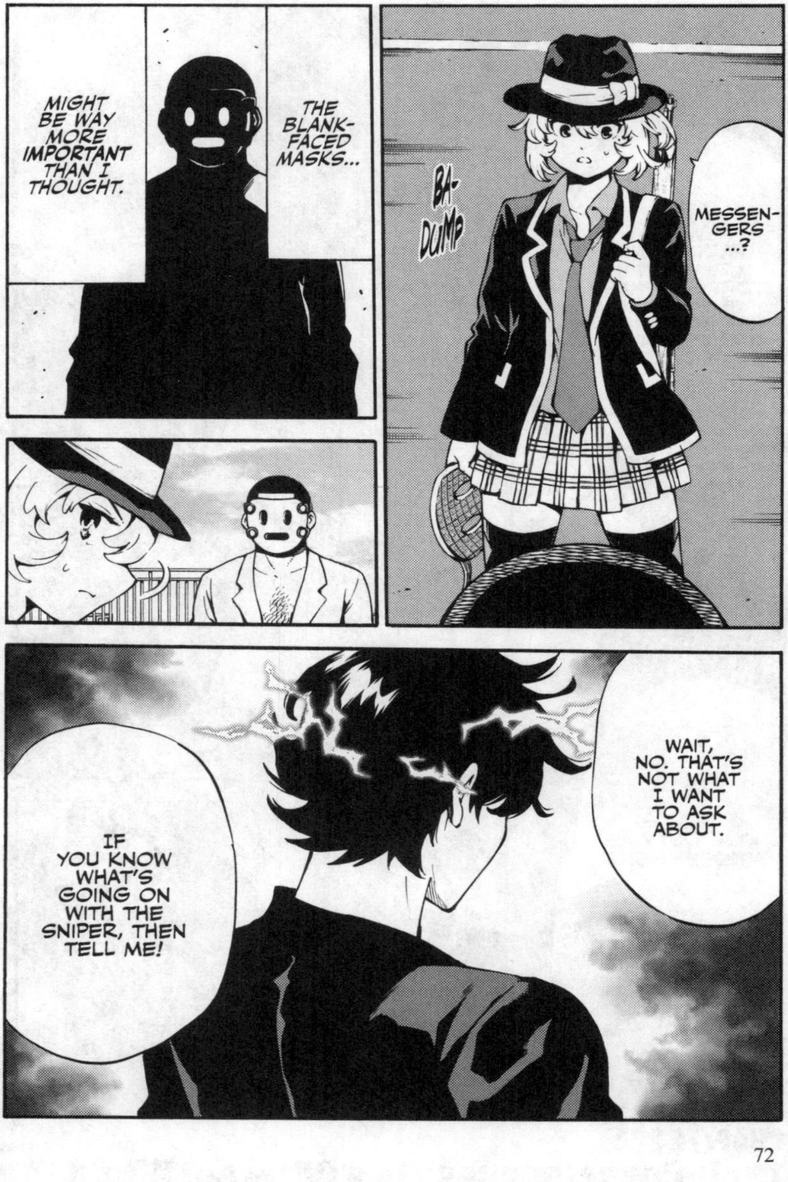
MESSENGERS...?
BA-DUMP
THE BLANK-FACED MASKS...
MIGHT BE WAY MORE IMPORTANT THAN I THOUGHT.
WAIT, NO. THAT'S NOT WHAT I WANT TO ASK ABOUT.
IF YOU KNOW WHAT'S GOING ON WITH THE SNIPER, THEN TELL ME!

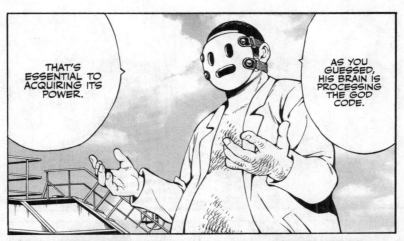

AS YOU GUESSED, HIS BRAIN IS PROCESSING THE GOD CODE.
THAT'S ESSENTIAL TO ACQUIRING ITS POWER.
SOMEONE'S INSIDE THEIR OWN BRAIN *AGAIN?*
IN THIS WORLD, THAT HAPPENS EVERY FIVE MINUTES.
YES. IT'S STANDARD.
AFTER ALL, A PERSON'S BRAIN...THEIR CONSCIOUSNESS... IS A *DIFFERENT WORLD.*

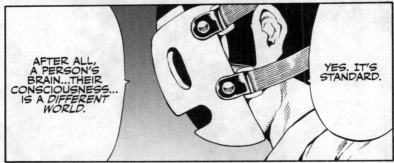

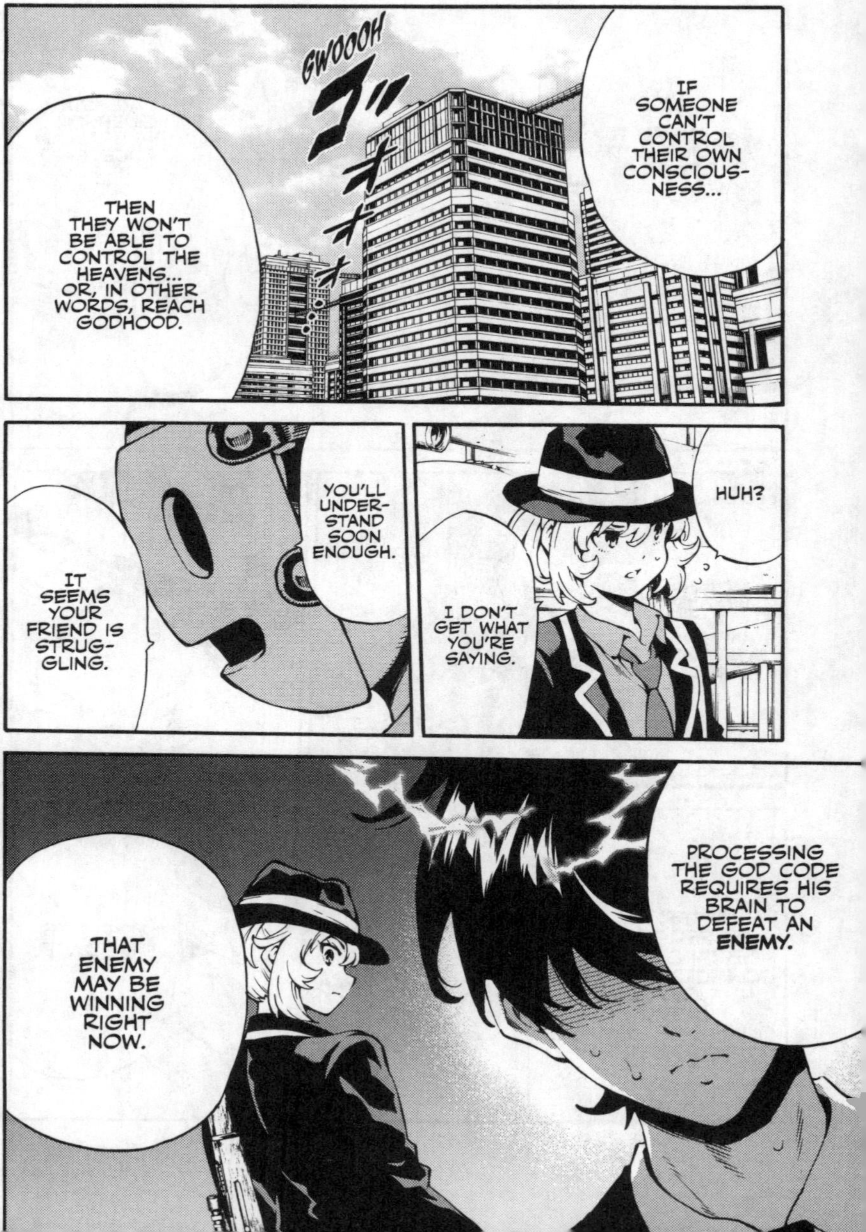
IF SOMEONE CAN'T CONTROL THEIR OWN CONSCIOUS-NESS...
GWOOOH
THEN THEY WON'T BE ABLE TO CONTROL THE HEAVENS... OR, IN OTHER WORDS, REACH GODHOOD.
HUH?
I DON'T GET WHAT YOU'RE SAYING.
YOU'LL UNDER-STAND SOON ENOUGH.
IT SEEMS YOUR FRIEND IS STRUG-GLING.
PROCESSING THE GOD CODE REQUIRES HIS BRAIN TO DEFEAT AN **ENEMY.**
THAT ENEMY MAY BE WINNING RIGHT NOW.

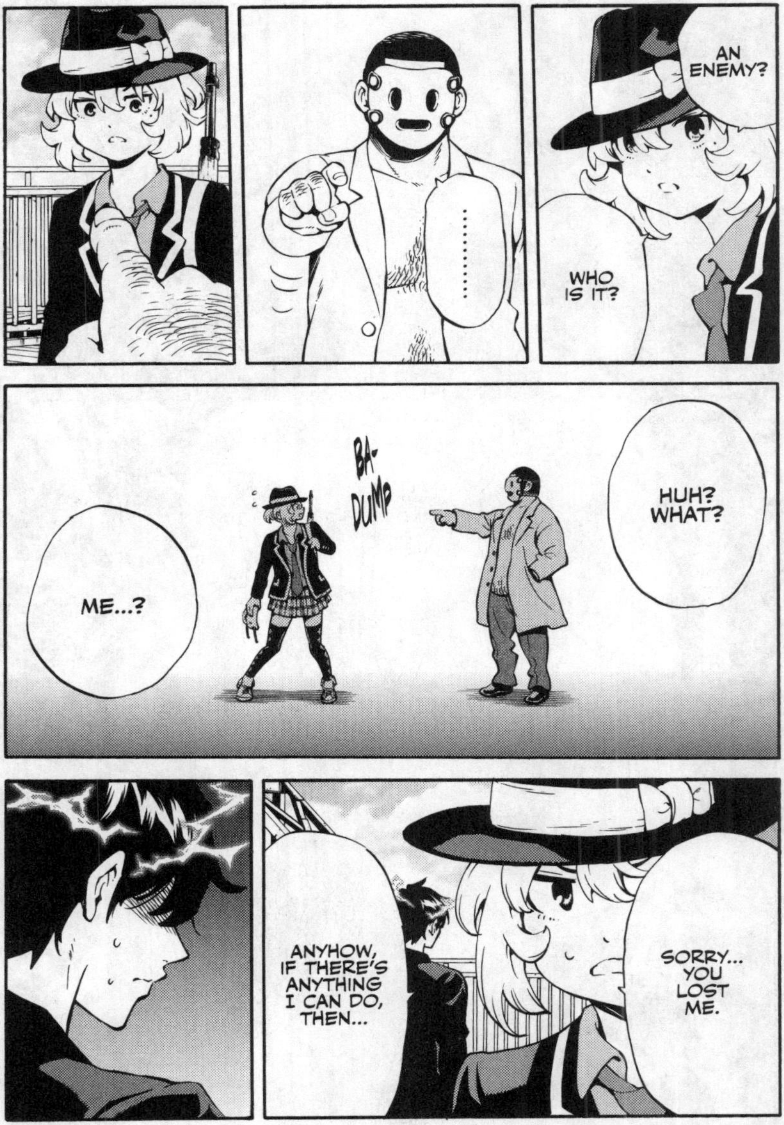
AN ENEMY?
WHO IS IT?
......
HUH? WHAT?
BA-DUMP
ME...?
SORRY... YOU LOST ME.
ANYHOW, IF THERE'S ANYTHING I CAN DO, THEN...

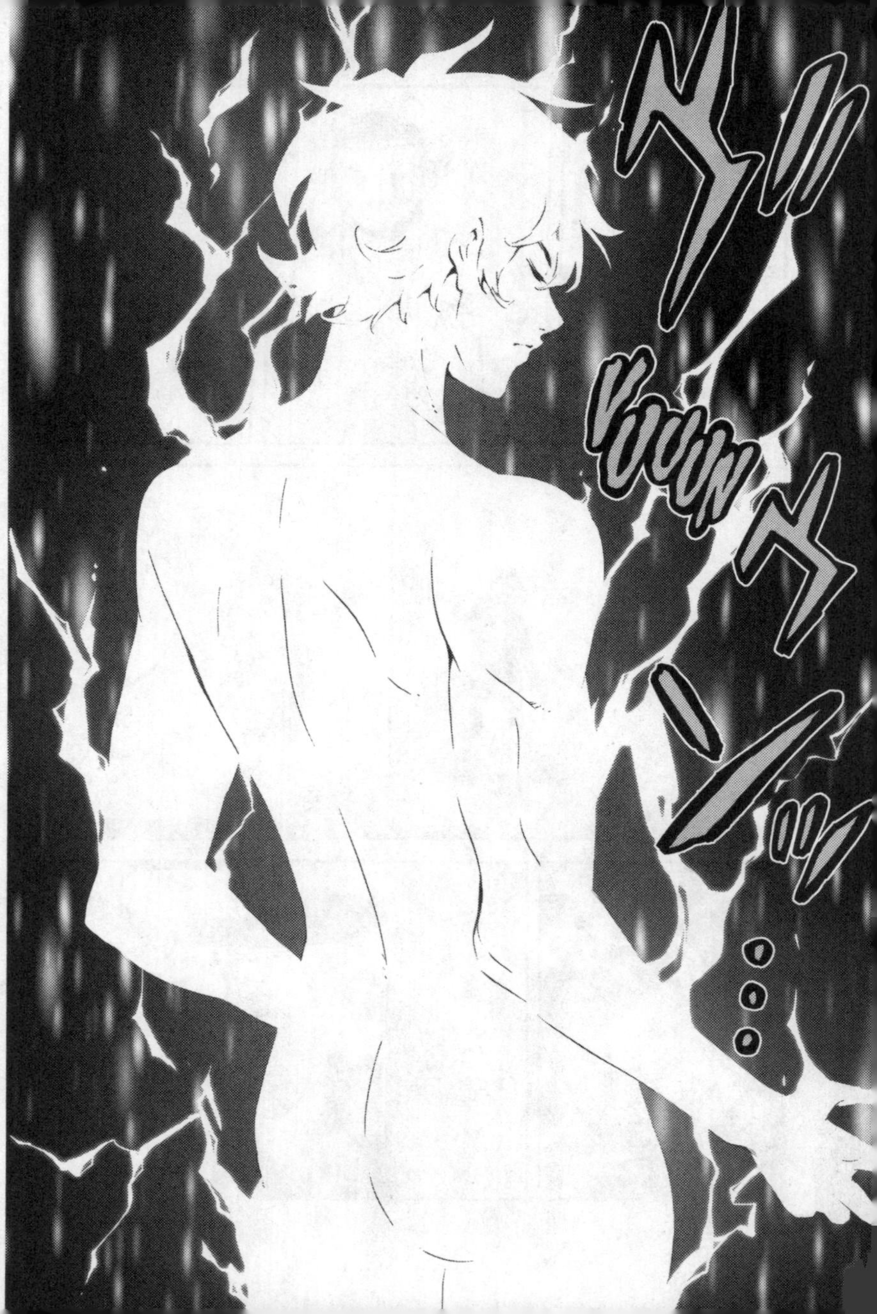

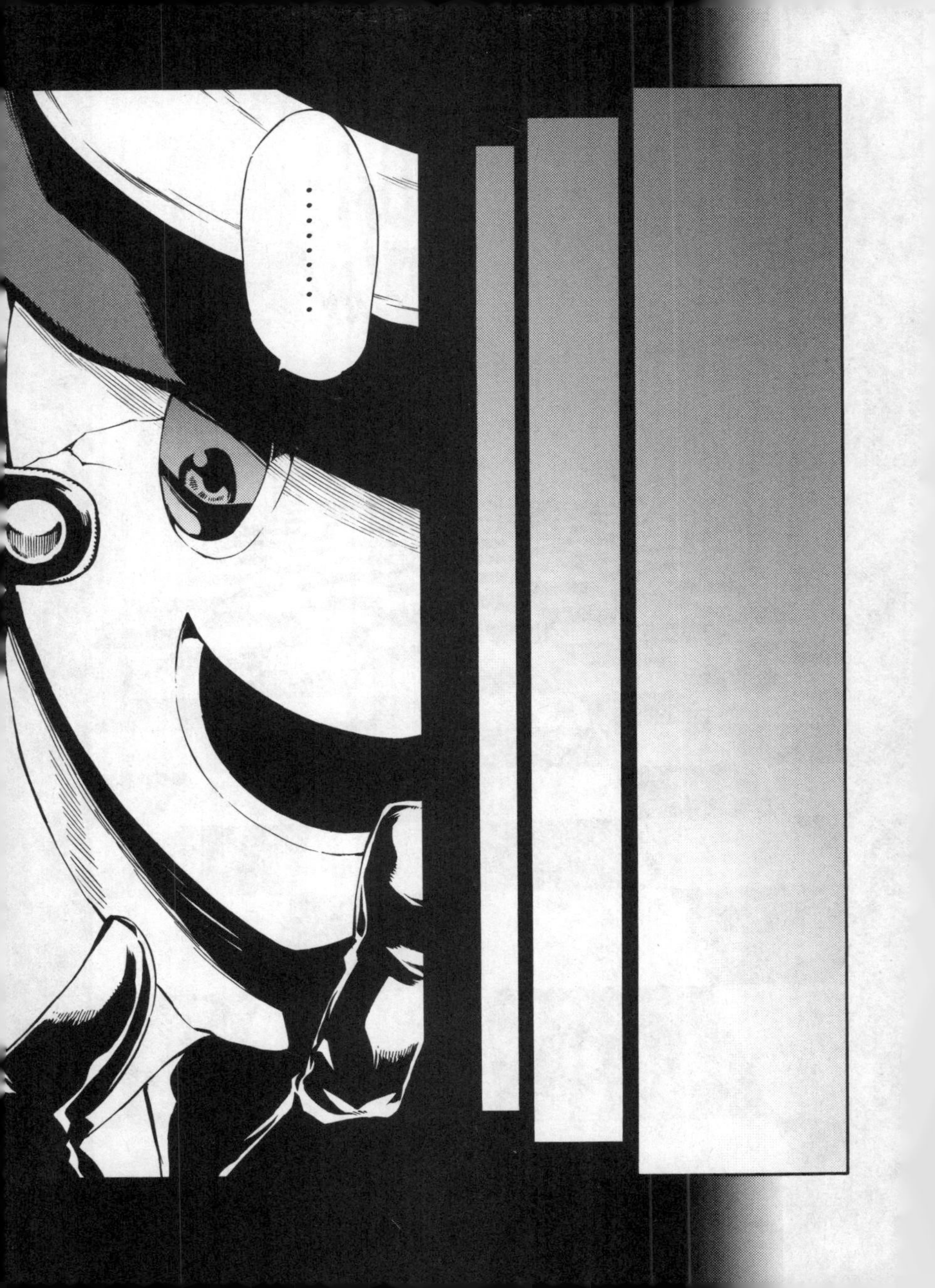
……

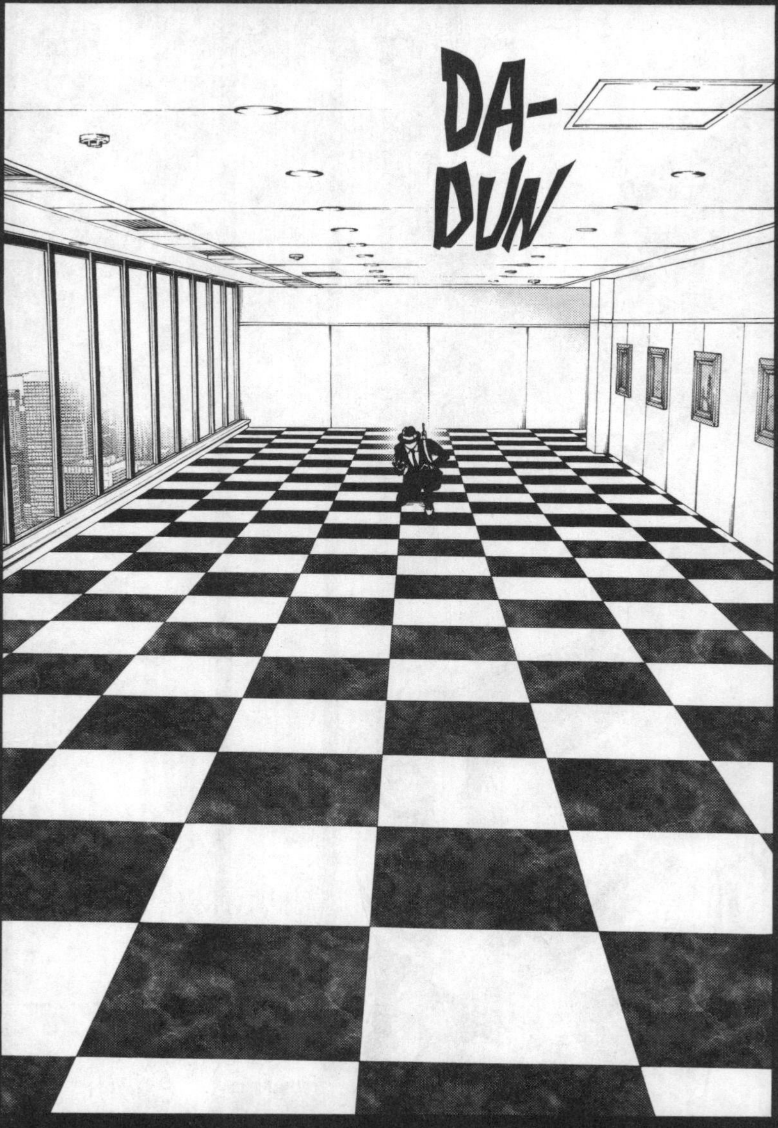
DA-
DUN

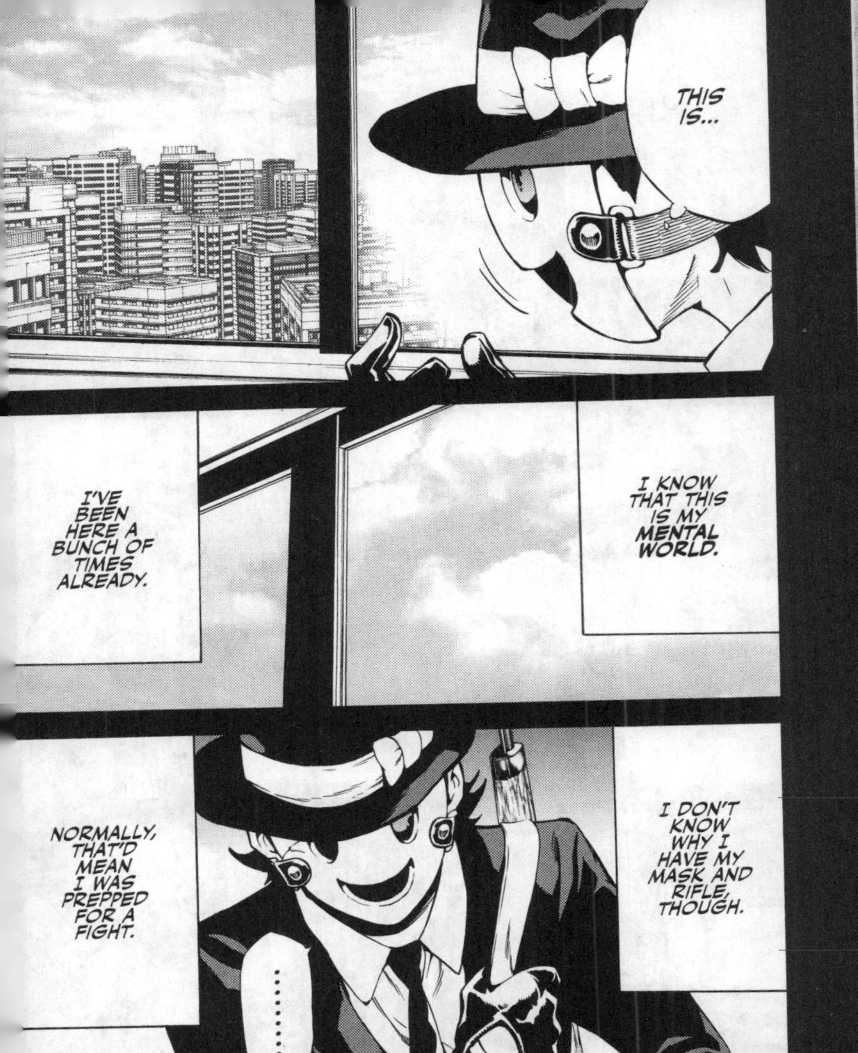
THIS IS...
I KNOW THAT THIS IS MY MENTAL WORLD.
I'VE BEEN HERE A BUNCH OF TIMES ALREADY.
I DON'T KNOW WHY I HAVE MY MASK AND RIFLE, THOUGH.
NORMALLY, THAT'D MEAN I WAS PREPPED FOR A FIGHT.
....

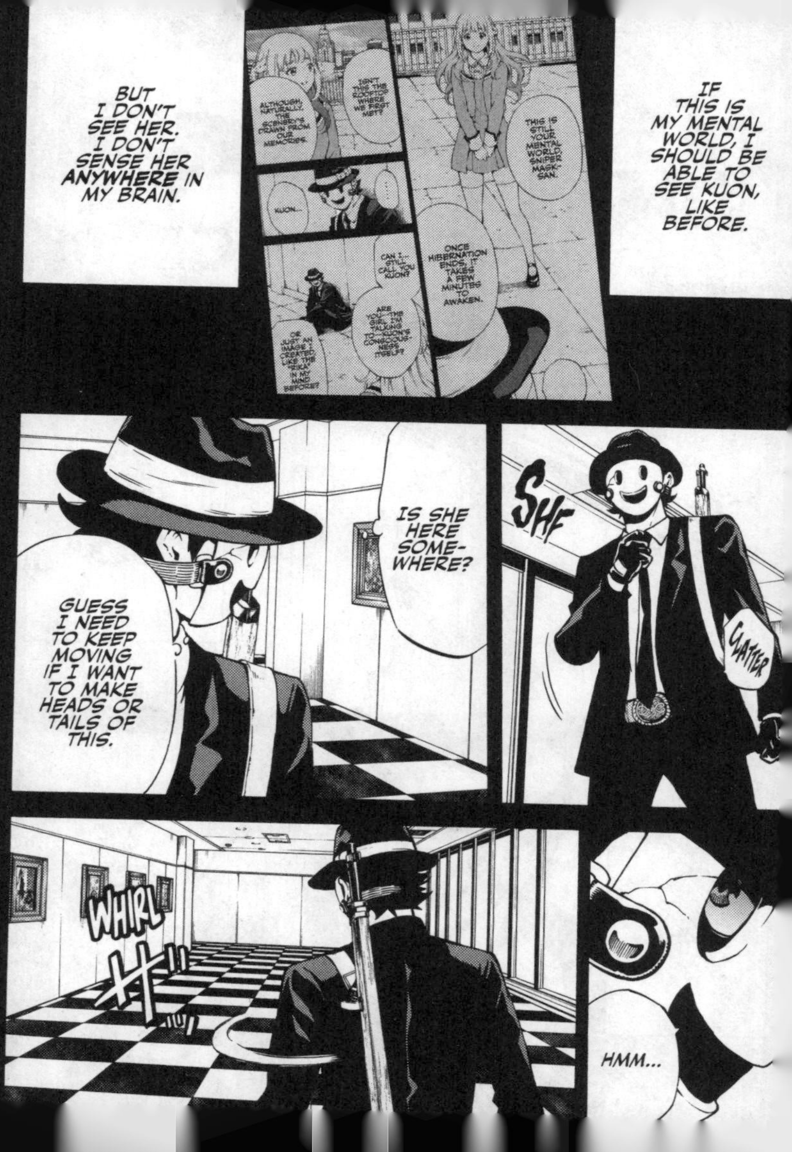
IF THIS IS MY MENTAL WORLD, I SHOULD BE ABLE TO SEE KUON, LIKE BEFORE.
THIS IS STILL YOUR MENTAL WORLD, SNIPER MASK-SAN.
ONCE HIBERNATION ENDS, IT TAKES A FEW MINUTES TO AWAKEN.
ISN'T THIS THE ROOFTOP WHERE WE FIRST MET?
ALTHOUGH, NATURALLY, THE SCENERY'S DRAWN FROM OUR MEMORIES.
. . .
KUON...
CAN I... STILL CALL YOU KUON?
ARE YOU THE GIRL I'M TALKING TO—KUON'S CONSCIOUSNESS ITSELF?
OR JUST AN IMAGE I CREATED, LIKE THE "ZIKA" IN MY MIND BEFORE?
BUT I DON'T SEE HER. I DON'T SENSE HER ANYWHERE IN MY BRAIN.
SHF
CLATTER
IS SHE HERE SOMEWHERE?
GUESS I NEED TO KEEP MOVING IF I WANT TO MAKE HEADS OR TAILS OF THIS.
HMM...
WHIRL

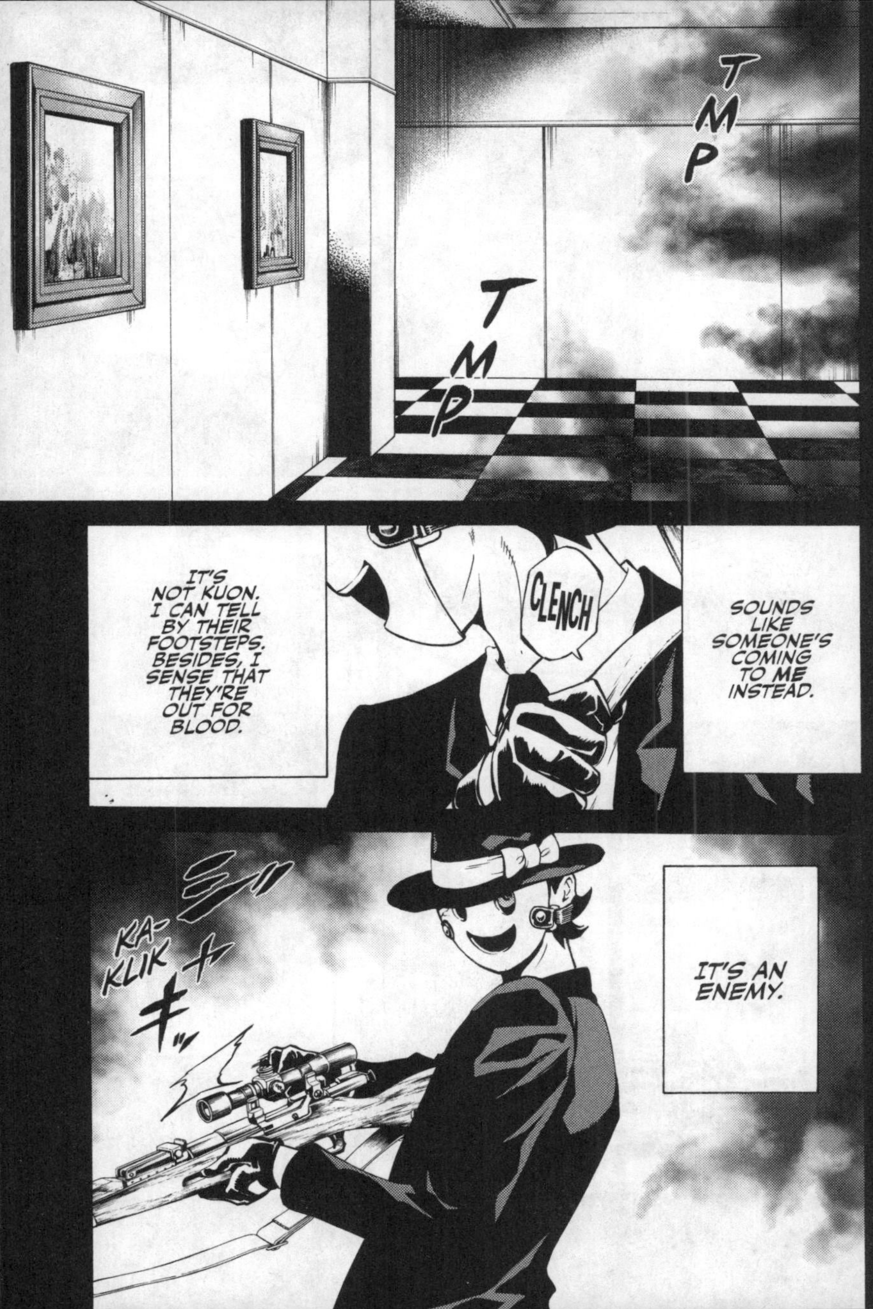
TMP
TMP
SOUNDS LIKE SOMEONE'S COMING TO ME INSTEAD.
CLENCH
IT'S NOT KUON. I CAN TELL BY THEIR FOOTSTEPS. BESIDES, I SENSE THAT THEY'RE OUT FOR BLOOD.
IT'S AN ENEMY.
KA-KLIK

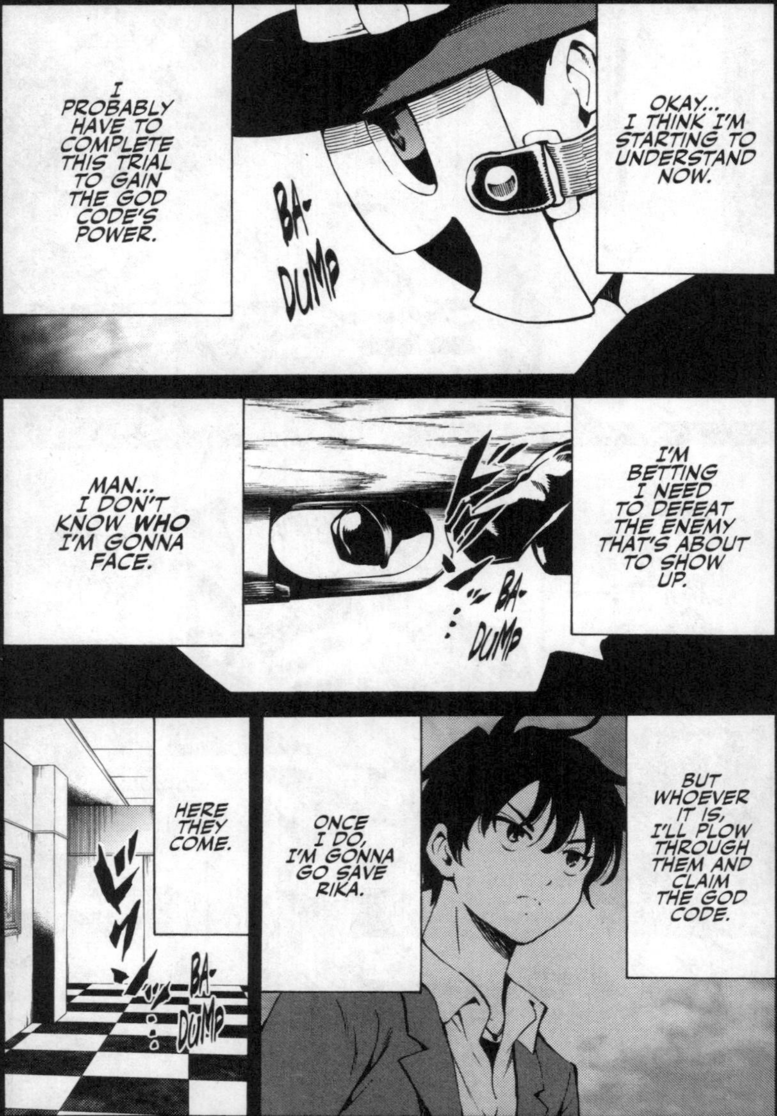
OKAY... I THINK I'M STARTING TO UNDERSTAND NOW.
BA-DUMP
I PROBABLY HAVE TO COMPLETE THIS TRIAL TO GAIN THE GOD CODE'S POWER.
I'M BETTING I NEED TO DEFEAT THE ENEMY THAT'S ABOUT TO SHOW UP.
BA-DUMP
MAN... I DON'T KNOW WHO I'M GONNA FACE.
BUT WHOEVER IT IS, I'LL PLOW THROUGH THEM AND CLAIM THE GOD CODE.
ONCE I DO, I'M GONNA GO SAVE RIKA.
HERE THEY COME.
BA-DUMP

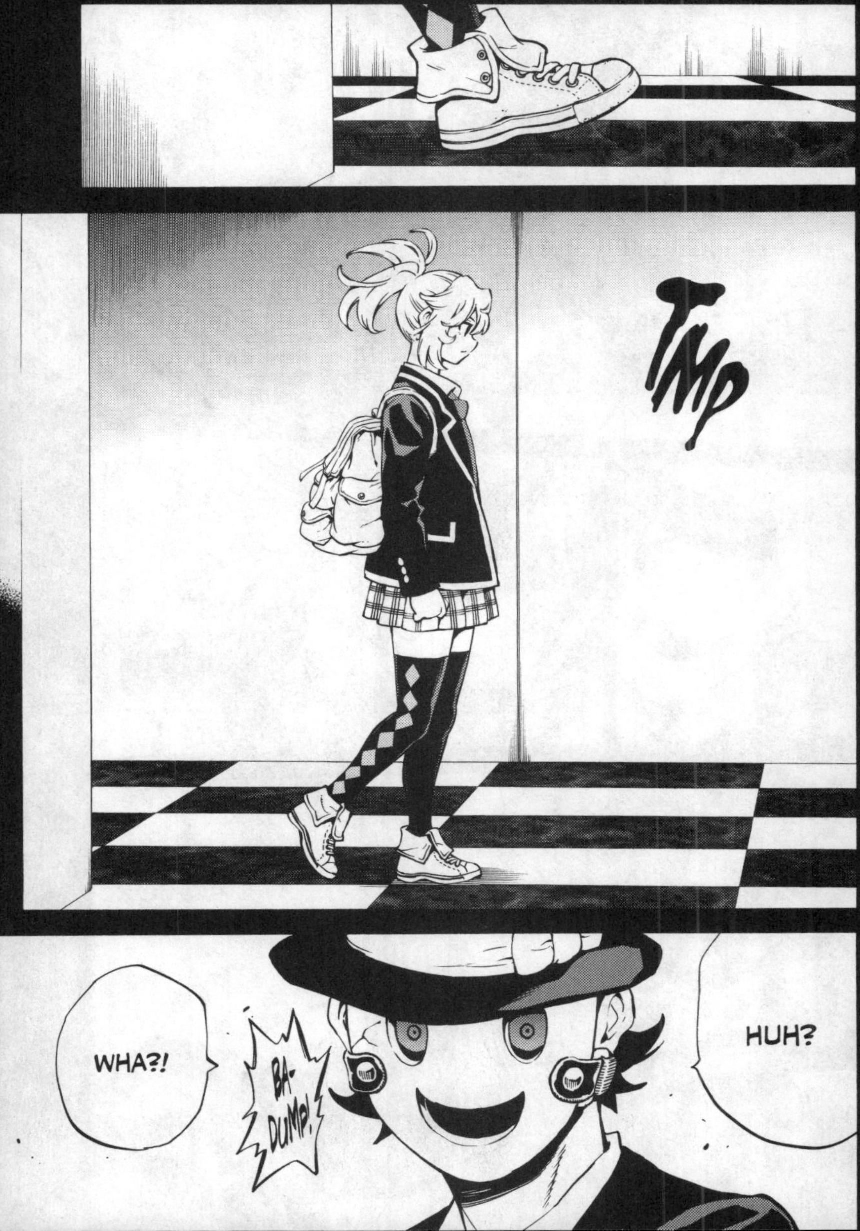
TMP
HUH?
BA-DUMP!
WHA?!

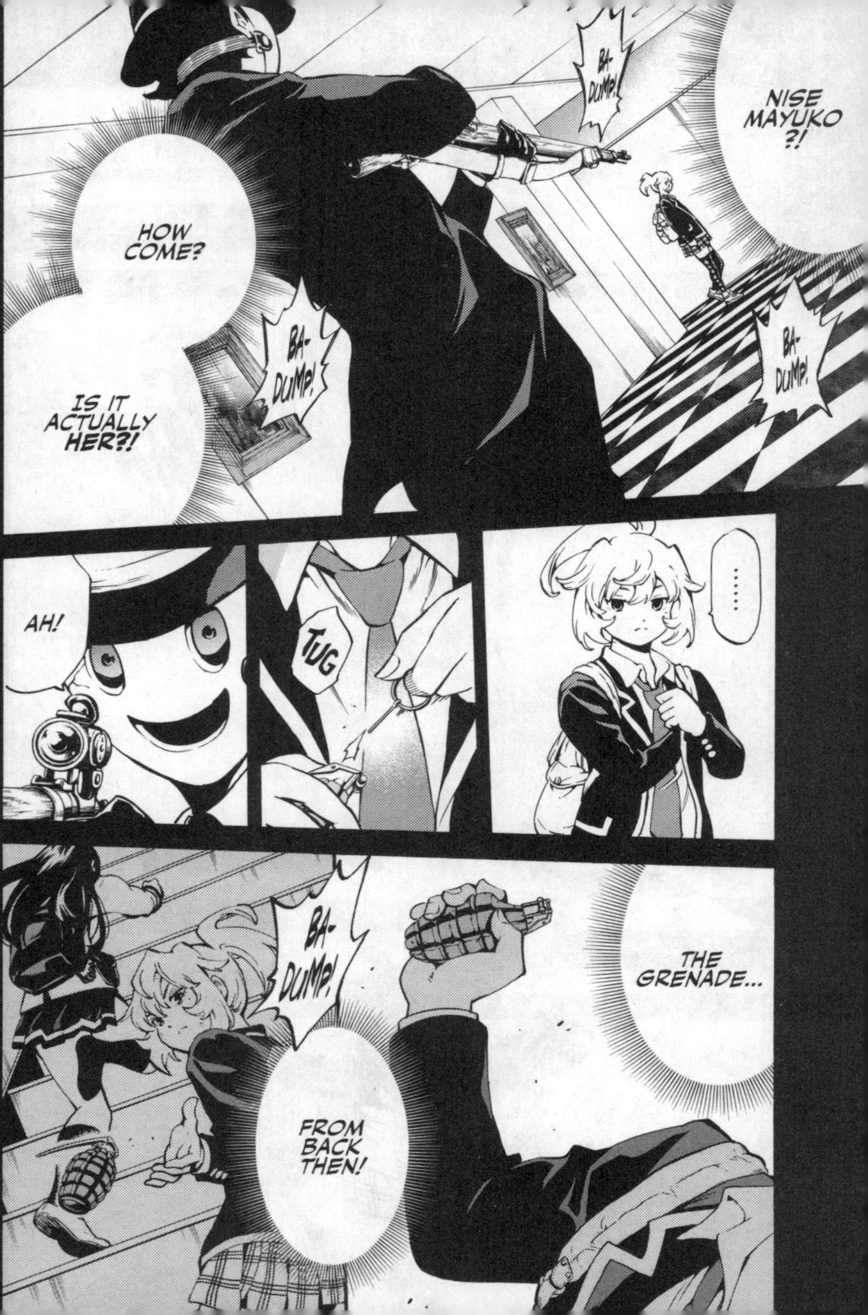
NISE MAYUKO?!
BA-DUMP!
HOW COME?
BA-DUMP!
BA-DUMP!
IS IT ACTUALLY HER?!
......
TUG
AH!
THE GRENADE...
BA-DUMP!
FROM BACK THEN!

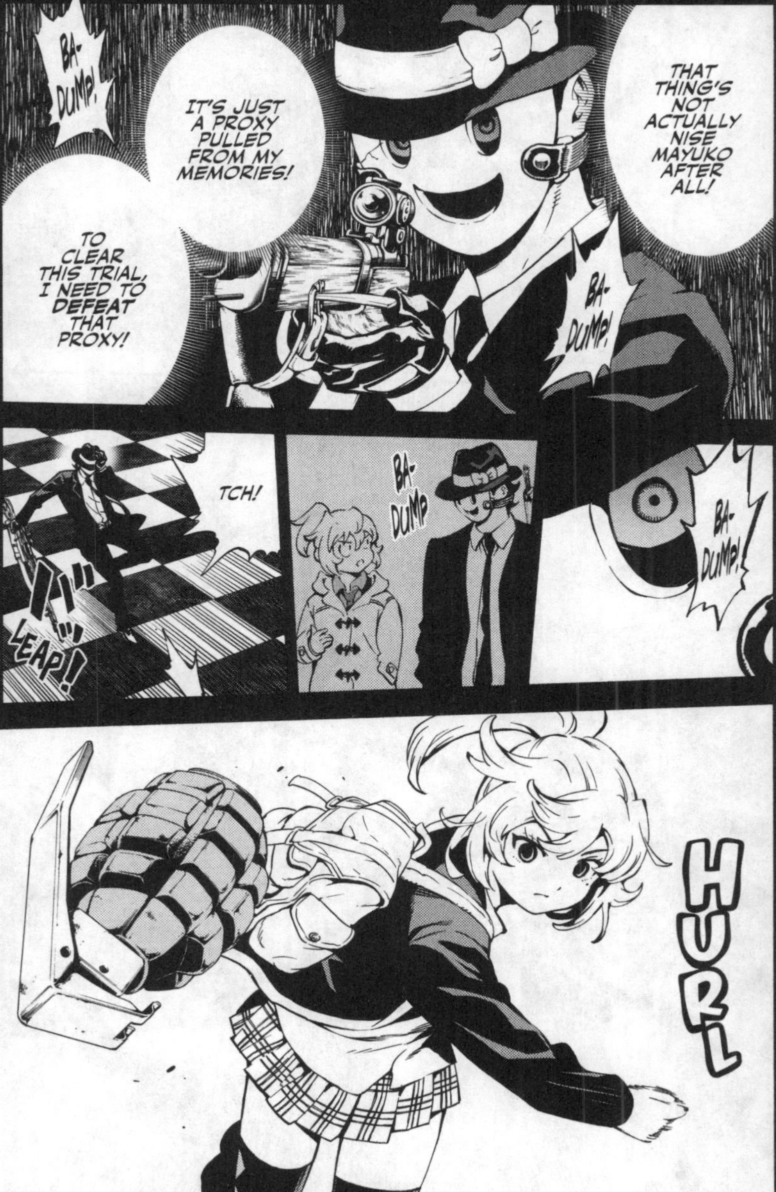
THAT THING'S NOT ACTUALLY NISE MAYUKO AFTER ALL!
IT'S JUST A PROXY PULLED FROM MY MEMORIES!
BA-DUMP!
BA-DUMP!
TO CLEAR THIS TRIAL, I NEED TO DEFEAT THAT PROXY!
BA-DUMP!
BA-DUMP
TCH!
LEAP!
HURL

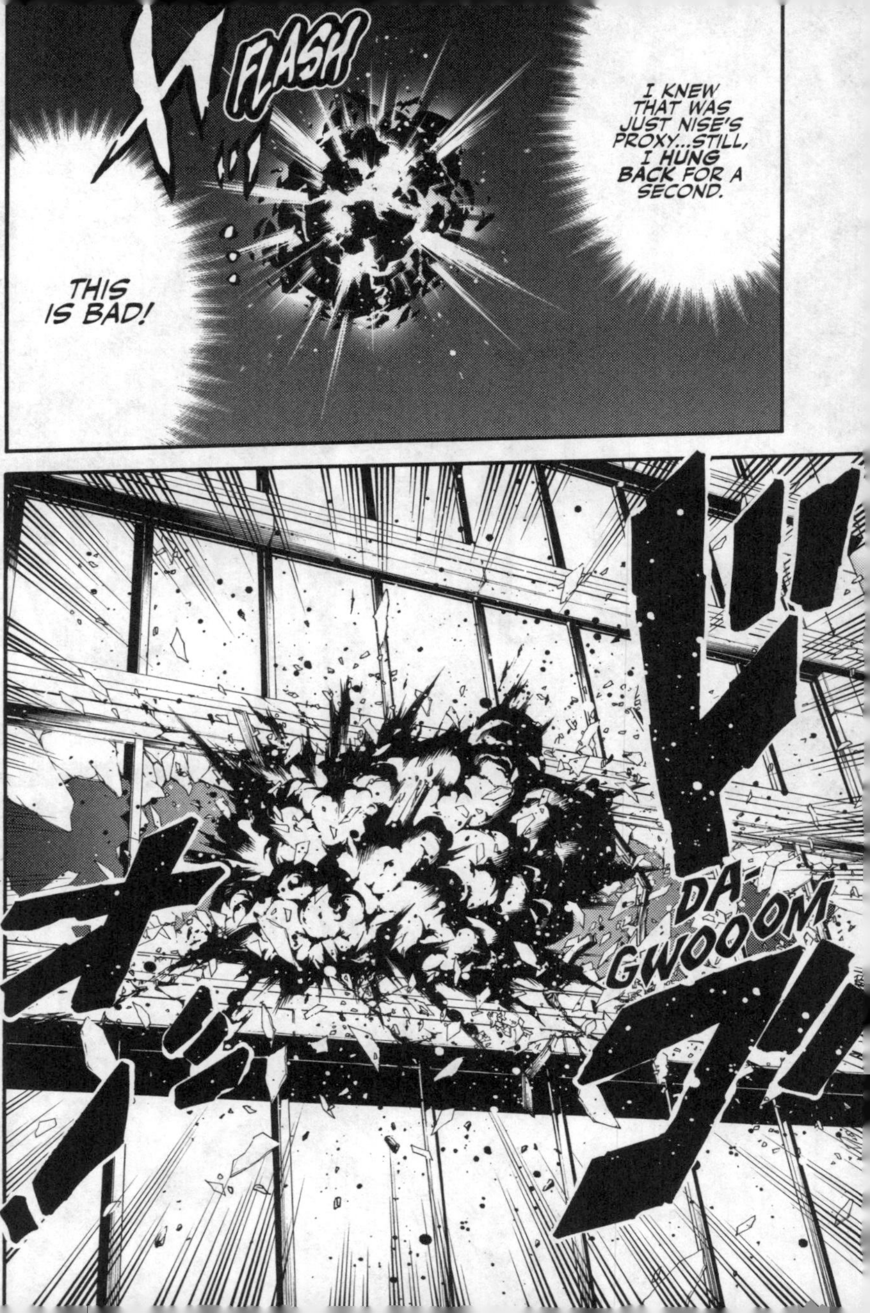
FLASH
I KNEW THAT WAS JUST NISE'S PROXY...STILL, I HUNG BACK FOR A SECOND.
THIS IS BAD!
DA-GWOOOOM

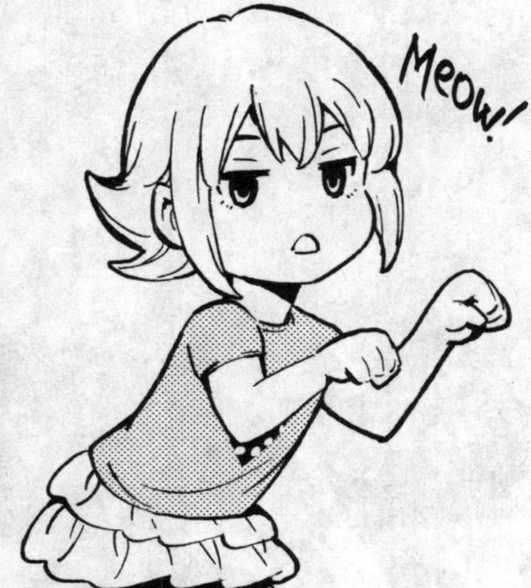
Meow!

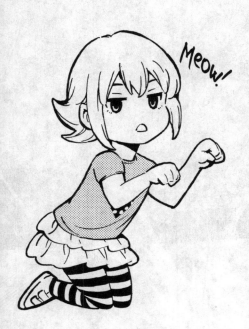

HIGH-RISE INVASION

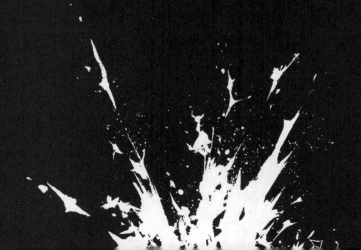

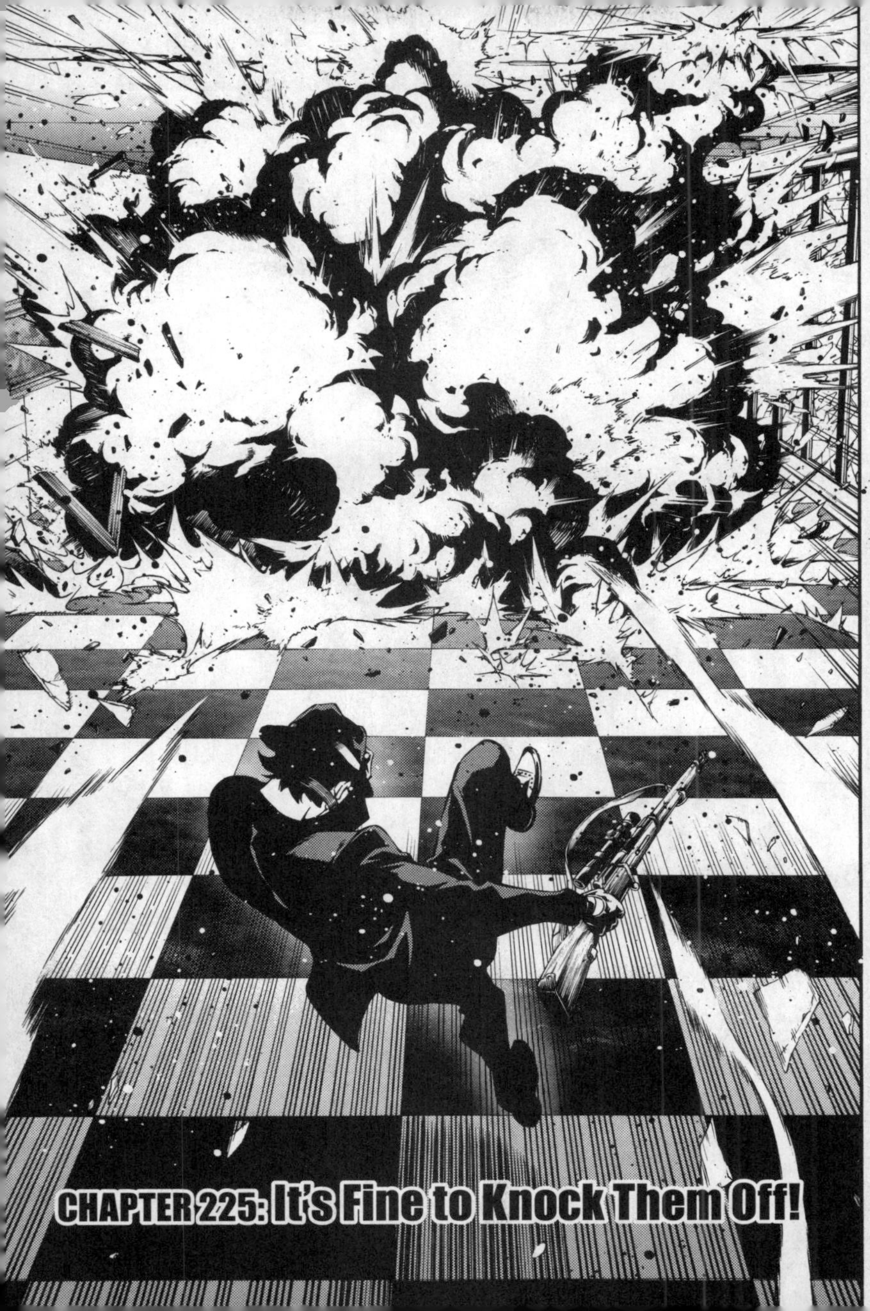
CHAPTER 225: It's Fine to Knock Them Off!

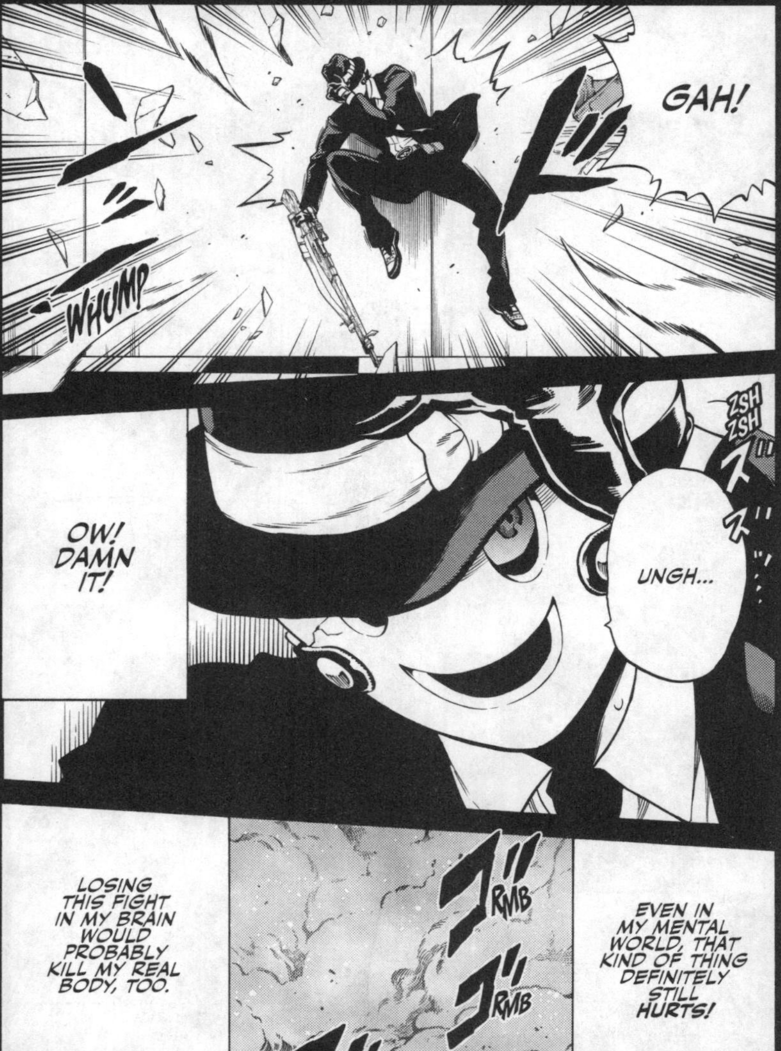
GAH!
WHUMP
ZSH ZSH
UNGH...
OW! DAMN IT!
EVEN IN MY MENTAL WORLD, THAT KIND OF THING DEFINITELY STILL HURTS!
RMB
RMB
RMB
LOSING THIS FIGHT IN MY BRAIN WOULD PROBABLY KILL MY REAL BODY, TOO.

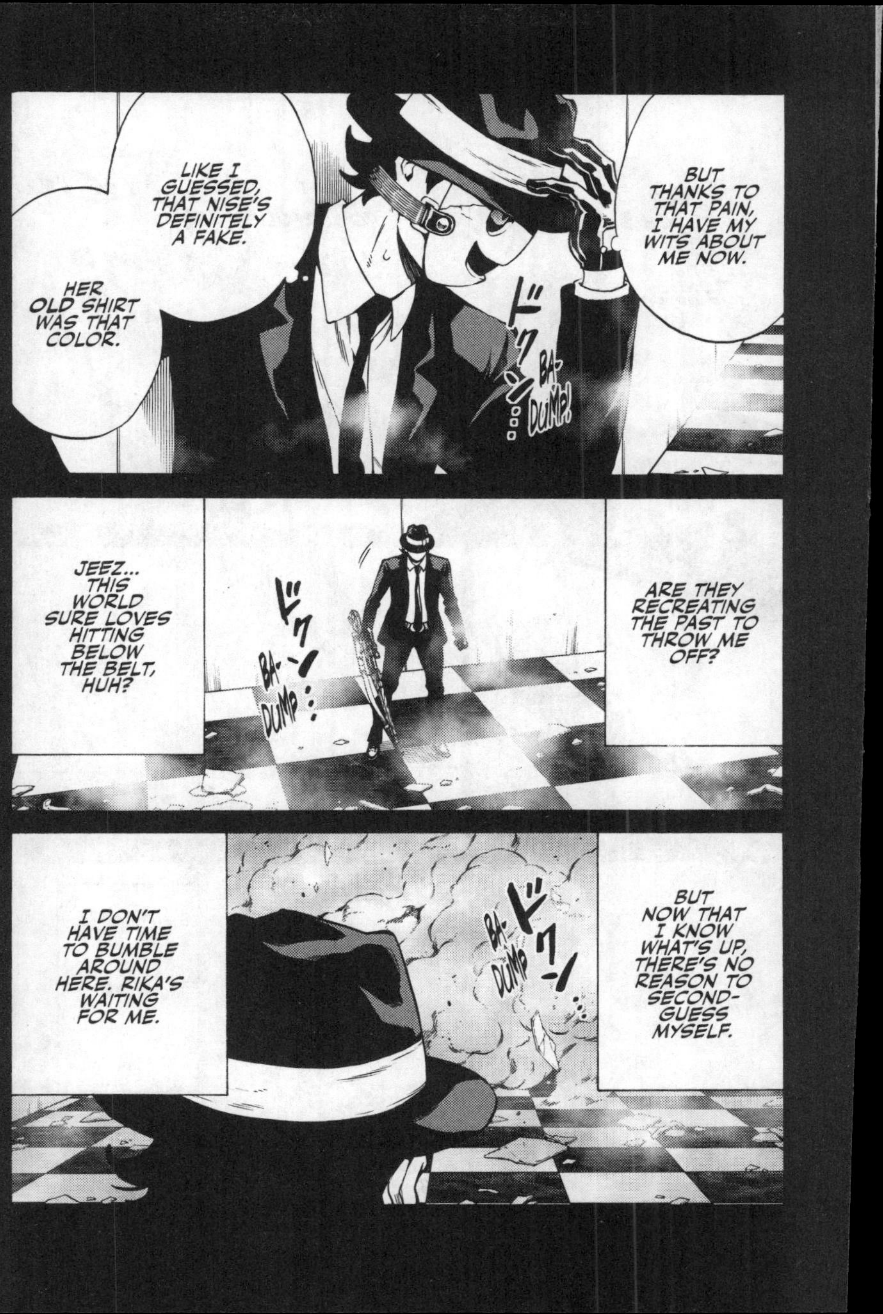
LIKE I GUESSED, THAT NISE'S DEFINITELY A FAKE.
HER OLD SHIRT WAS THAT COLOR.
BUT THANKS TO THAT PAIN, I HAVE MY WITS ABOUT ME NOW.
ドクン…
BA-DUMP!
JEEZ... THIS WORLD SURE LOVES HITTING BELOW THE BELT, HUH?
ARE THEY RECREATING THE PAST TO THROW ME OFF?
ドクン…
BA-DUMP
I DON'T HAVE TIME TO BUMBLE AROUND HERE. RIKA'S WAITING FOR ME.
BUT NOW THAT I KNOW WHAT'S UP, THERE'S NO REASON TO SECOND-GUESS MYSELF.
ドクン…
BA-DUMP

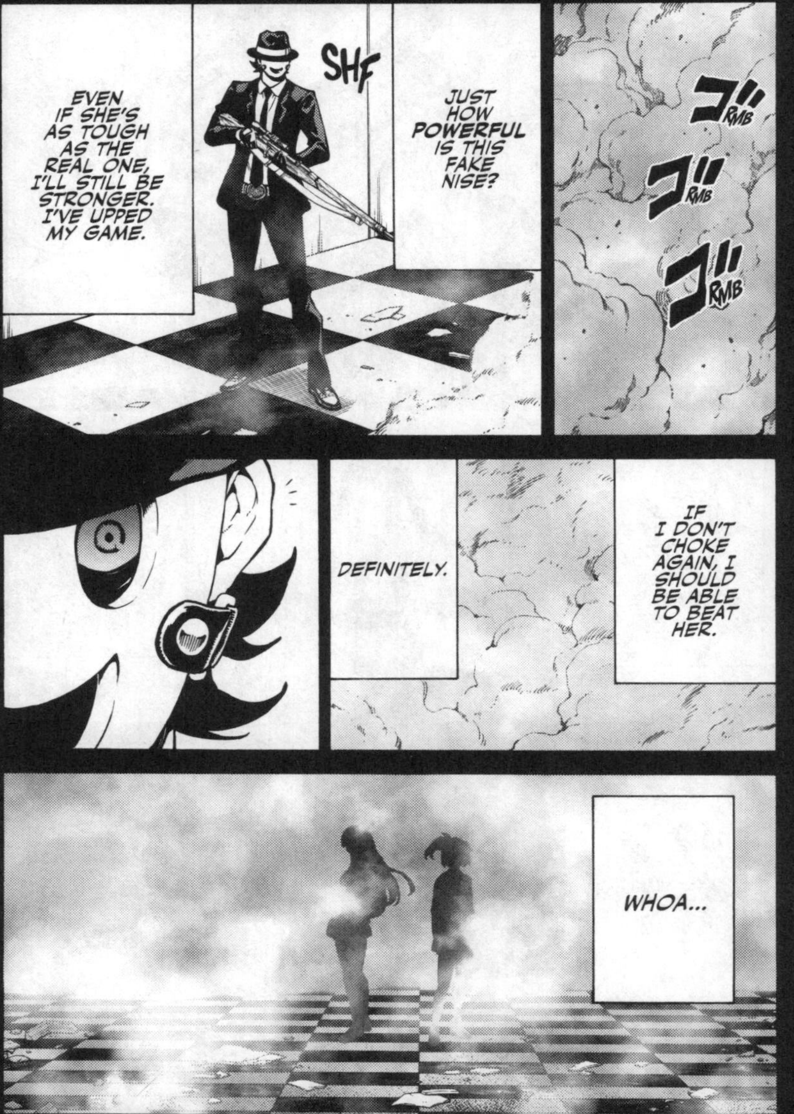
ゴ RMB
ゴ RMB
ゴ RMB
SHF
JUST HOW POWERFUL IS THIS FAKE NISE?
EVEN IF SHE'S AS TOUGH AS THE REAL ONE, I'LL STILL BE STRONGER. I'VE UPPED MY GAME.
IF I DON'T CHOKE AGAIN, I SHOULD BE ABLE TO BEAT HER.
DEFINITELY.
WHOA...

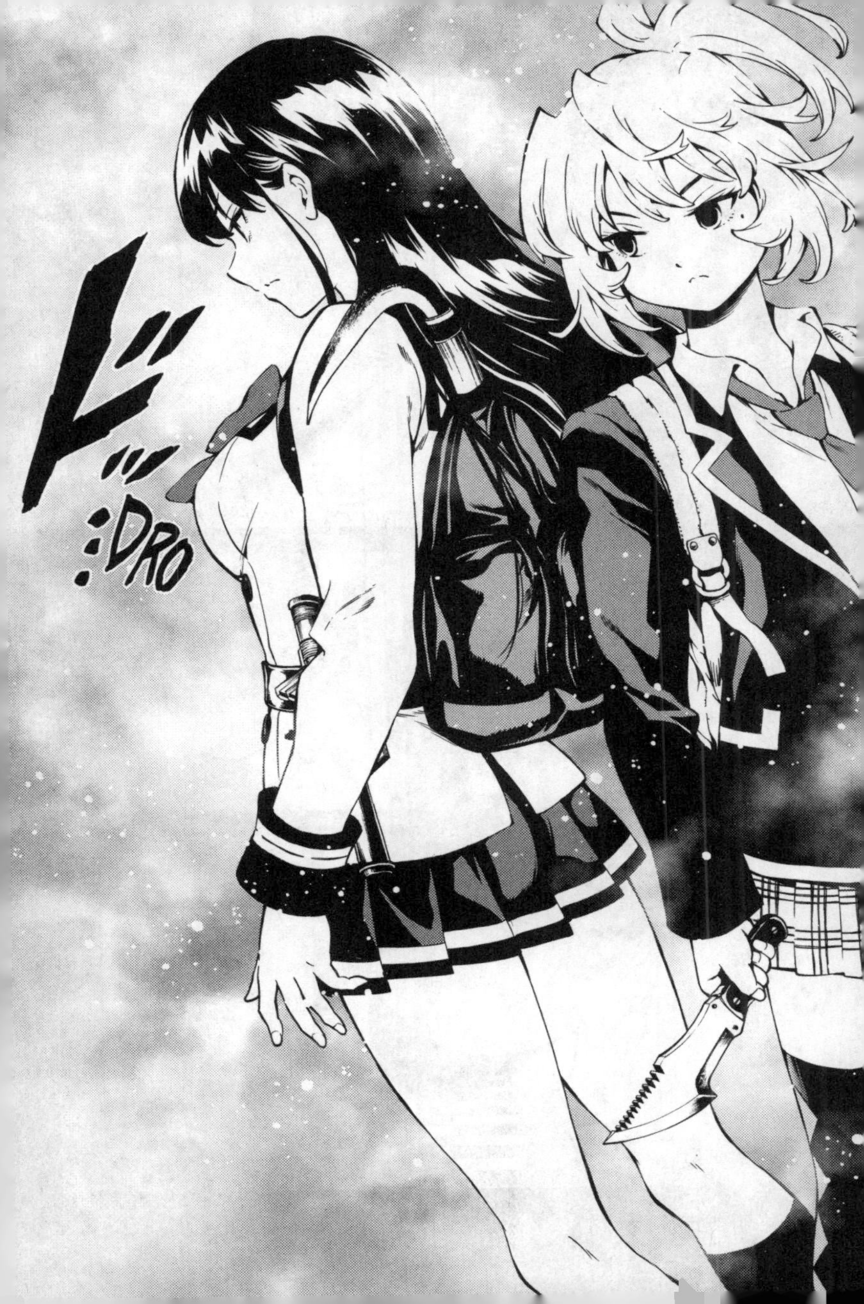
DRO

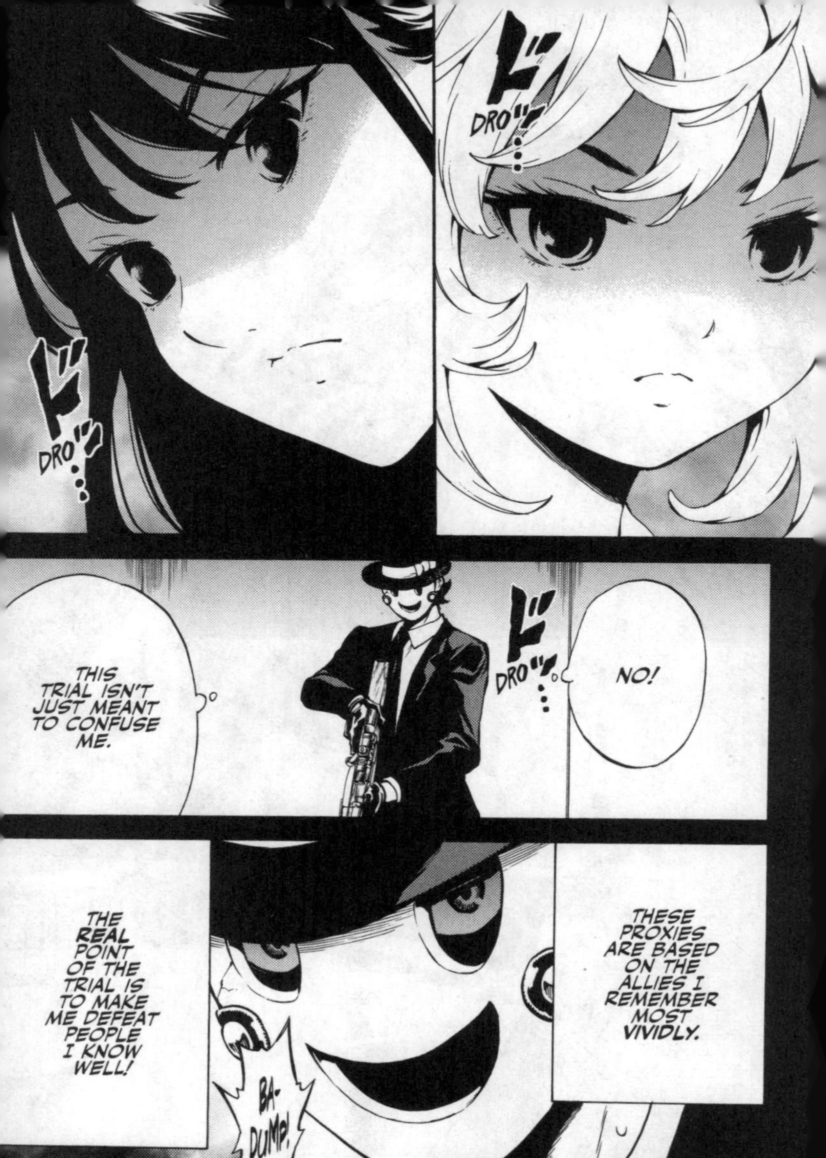
DRO
DRO
DRO
NO!
THIS TRIAL ISN'T JUST MEANT TO CONFUSE ME.
THESE PROXIES ARE BASED ON THE ALLIES I REMEMBER MOST VIVIDLY.
THE REAL POINT OF THE TRIAL IS TO MAKE ME DEFEAT PEOPLE I KNOW WELL!
BA-DUMP!

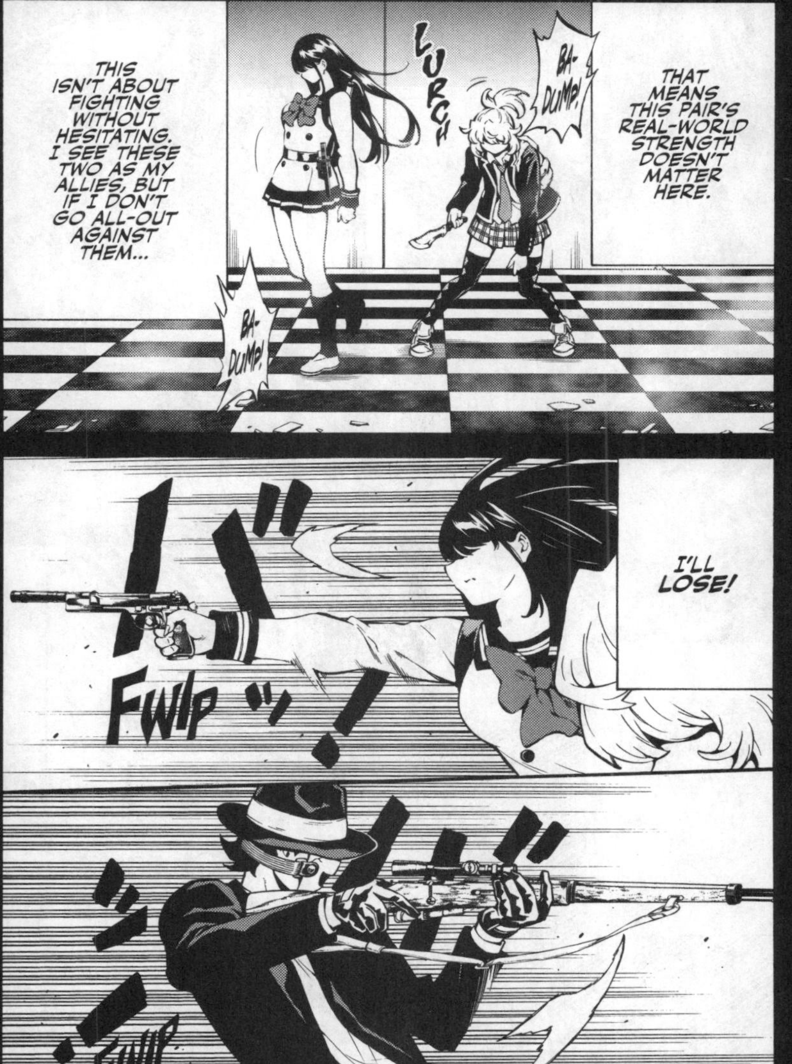
THAT MEANS THIS PAIR'S REAL-WORLD STRENGTH DOESN'T MATTER HERE.
BA-DUMP!
LURCH
THIS ISN'T ABOUT FIGHTING WITHOUT HESITATING. I SEE THESE TWO AS MY ALLIES, BUT IF I DON'T GO ALL-OUT AGAINST THEM...
BA-DUMP!
I'LL LOSE!
FWIP
FWIP

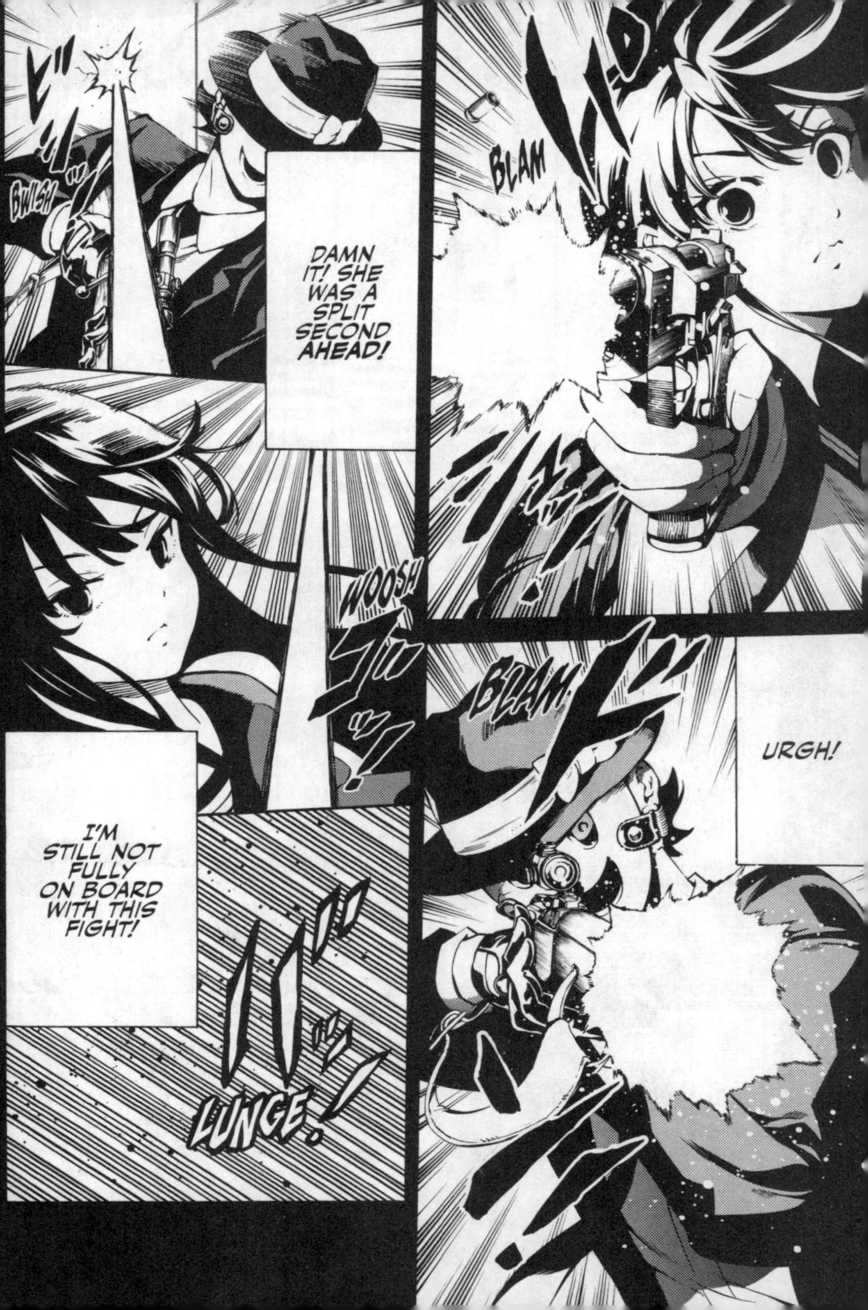
BLAM
BWISH
DAMN IT! SHE WAS A SPLIT SECOND AHEAD!
WOOSH
BLAM
URGH!
I'M STILL NOT FULLY ON BOARD WITH THIS FIGHT!
LUNGE!

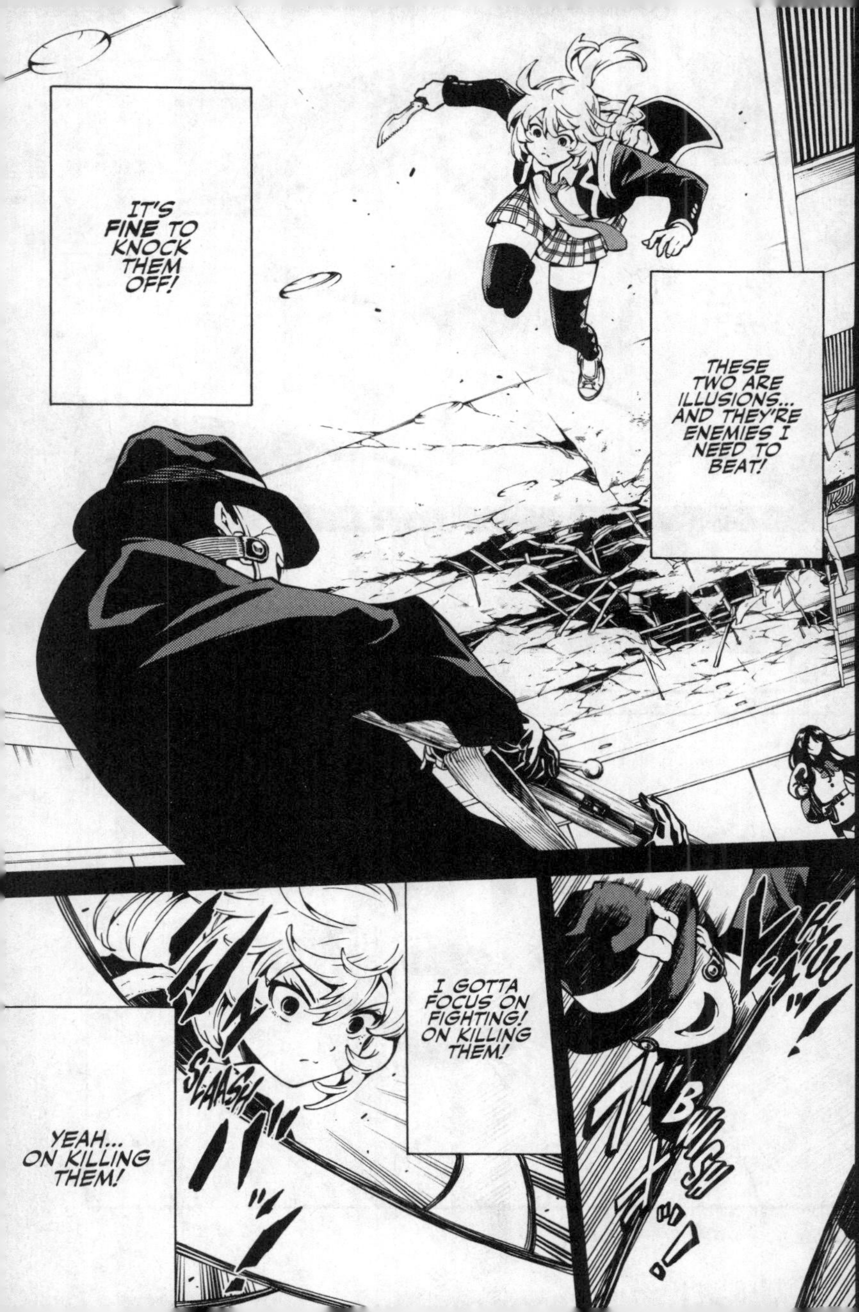
THESE TWO ARE ILLUSIONS... AND THEY'RE ENEMIES I NEED TO BEAT!
IT'S FINE TO KNOCK THEM OFF!
BWUSH!!
I GOTTA FOCUS ON FIGHTING! ON KILLING THEM!
SLAASH!!
YEAH... ON KILLING THEM!

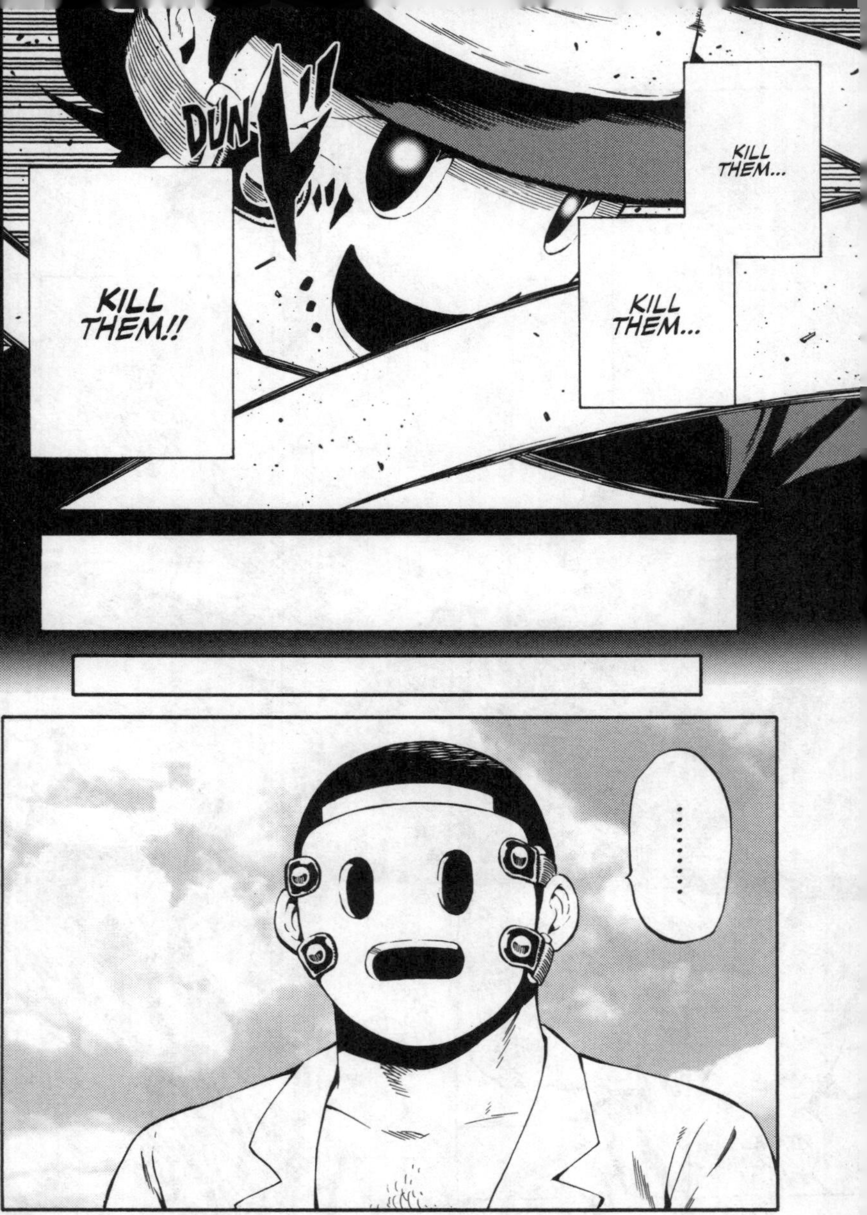
KILL THEM...
KILL THEM...
DUN
KILL THEM!!
....

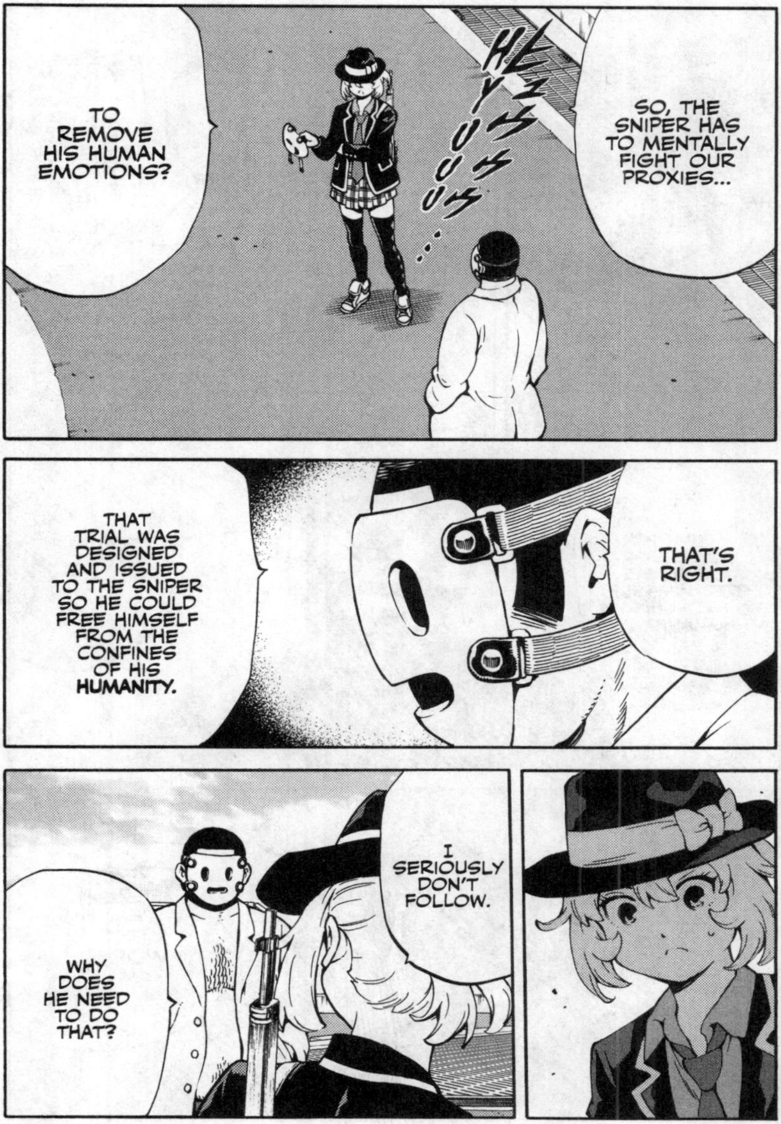
SO, THE SNIPER HAS TO MENTALLY FIGHT OUR PROXIES...
TO REMOVE HIS HUMAN EMOTIONS?
THAT'S RIGHT.
THAT TRIAL WAS DESIGNED AND ISSUED TO THE SNIPER SO HE COULD FREE HIMSELF FROM THE CONFINES OF HIS **HUMANITY.**
I SERIOUSLY DON'T FOLLOW.
WHY DOES HE NEED TO DO THAT?

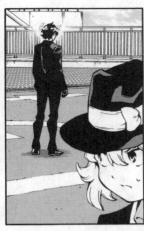

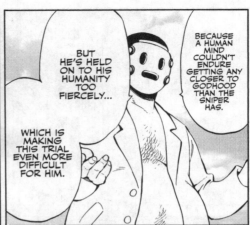

BECAUSE A HUMAN MIND COULDN'T ENDURE GETTING ANY CLOSER TO GODHOOD THAN THE SNIPER HAS.
BUT HE'S HELD ON TO HIS HUMANITY TOO FIERCELY...
WHICH IS MAKING THIS TRIAL EVEN MORE DIFFICULT FOR HIM.
THIS IS A DANGEROUS SITUATION.
IF HE CONTINUES TO FAIL TO FREE HIMSELF FROM HIS HUMANITY...
HE'LL PERISH WITHIN HIS MENTAL WORLD.

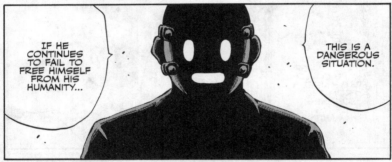

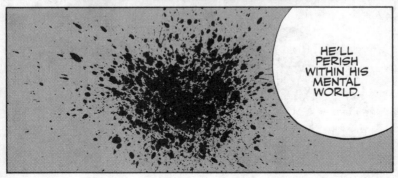

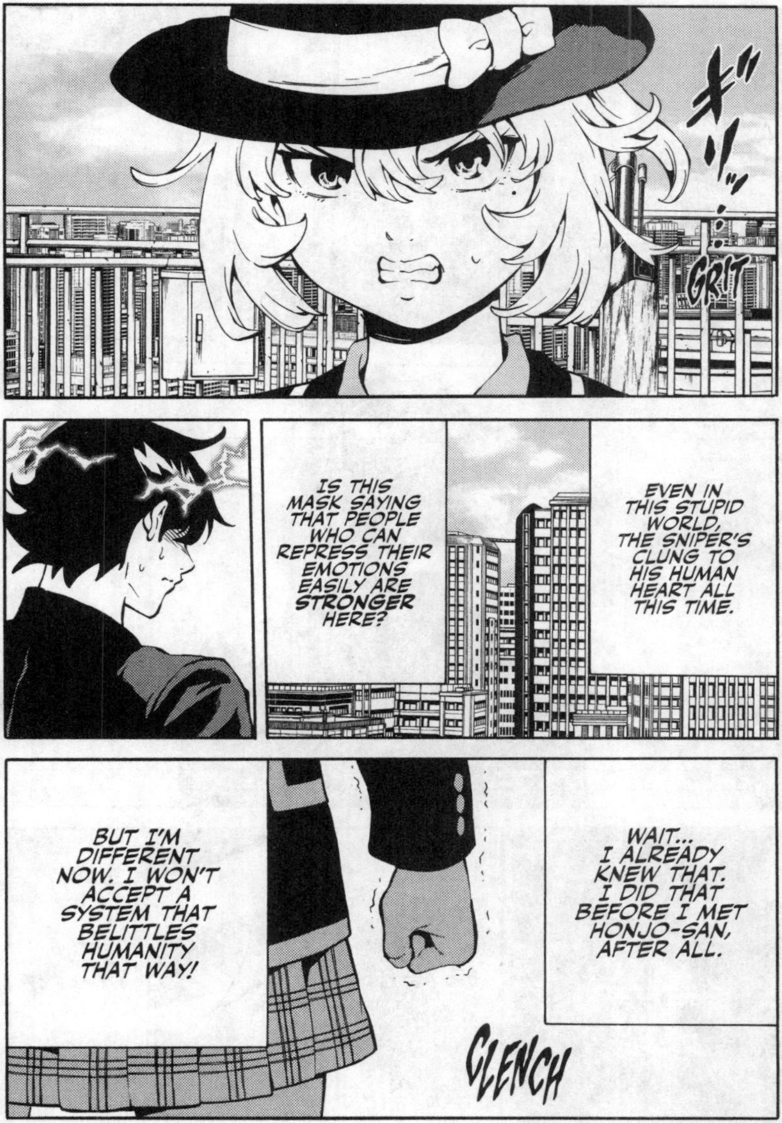
GRIT
EVEN IN THIS STUPID WORLD, THE SNIPER'S CLUNG TO HIS HUMAN HEART ALL THIS TIME.
IS THIS MASK SAYING THAT PEOPLE WHO CAN REPRESS THEIR EMOTIONS EASILY ARE STRONGER HERE?
WAIT... I ALREADY KNEW THAT. I DID THAT BEFORE I MET HONJO-SAN, AFTER ALL.
BUT I'M DIFFERENT NOW. I WON'T ACCEPT A SYSTEM THAT BELITTLES HUMANITY THAT WAY!
CLENCH

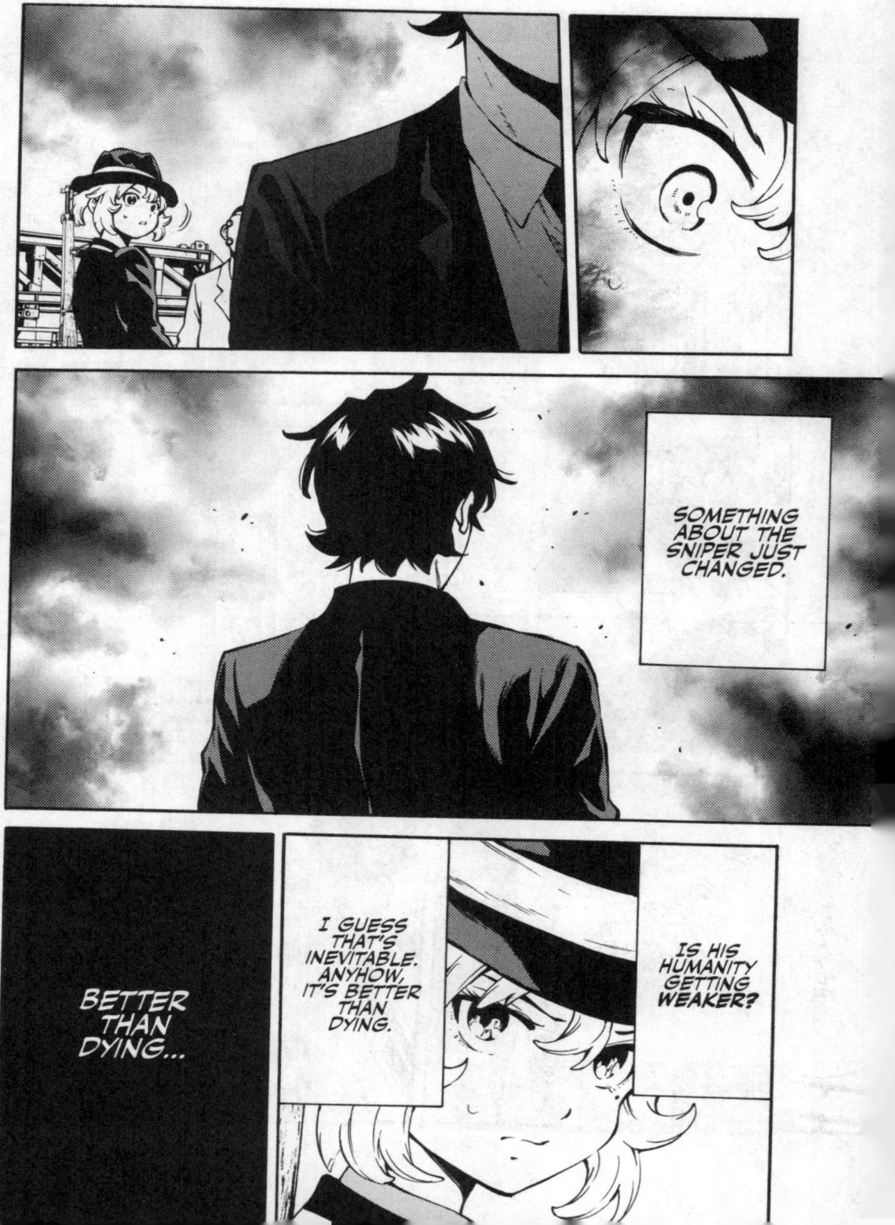
SOMETHING ABOUT THE SNIPER JUST CHANGED.
IS HIS HUMANITY GETTING WEAKER?
I GUESS THAT'S INEVITABLE. ANYHOW, IT'S BETTER THAN DYING.
BETTER THAN DYING...

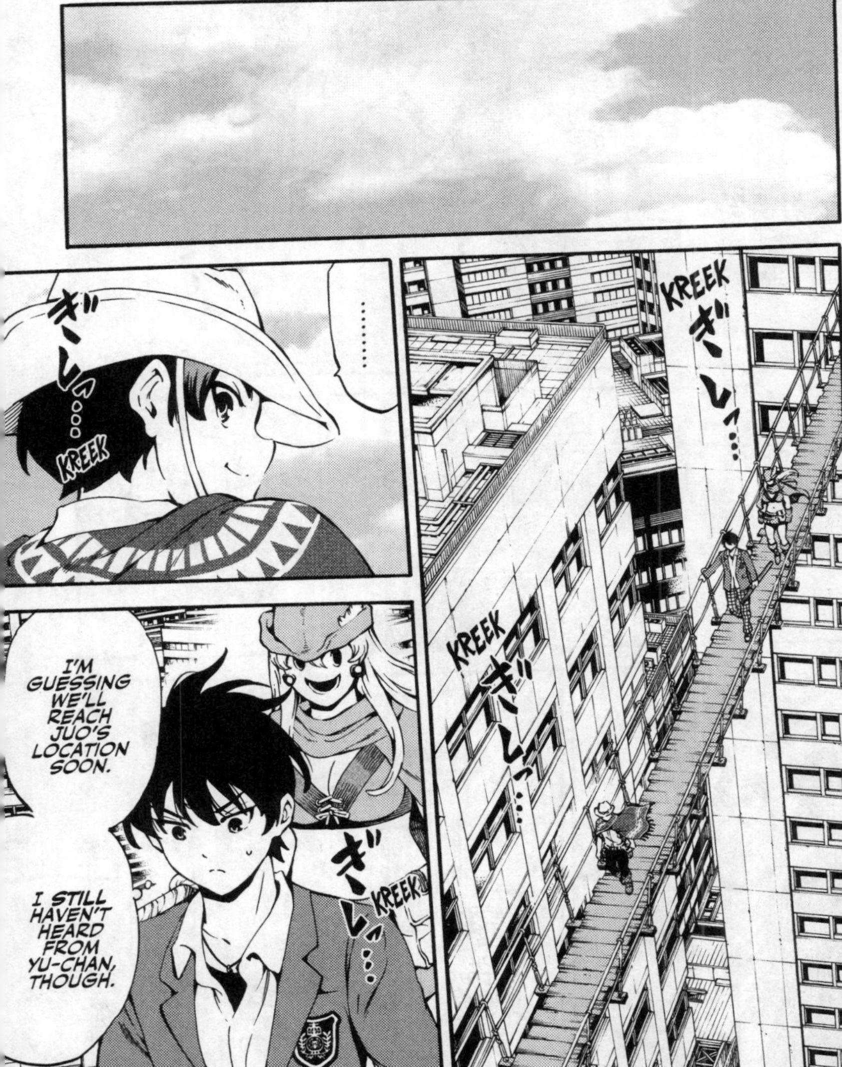
KREEK
ぎしっ…
KREEK
ぎしっ…
……
ぎしっ…
KREEK
I'M GUESSING WE'LL REACH JUO'S LOCATION SOON.
I STILL HAVEN'T HEARD FROM YU-CHAN, THOUGH.
ぎしっ…
KREEK

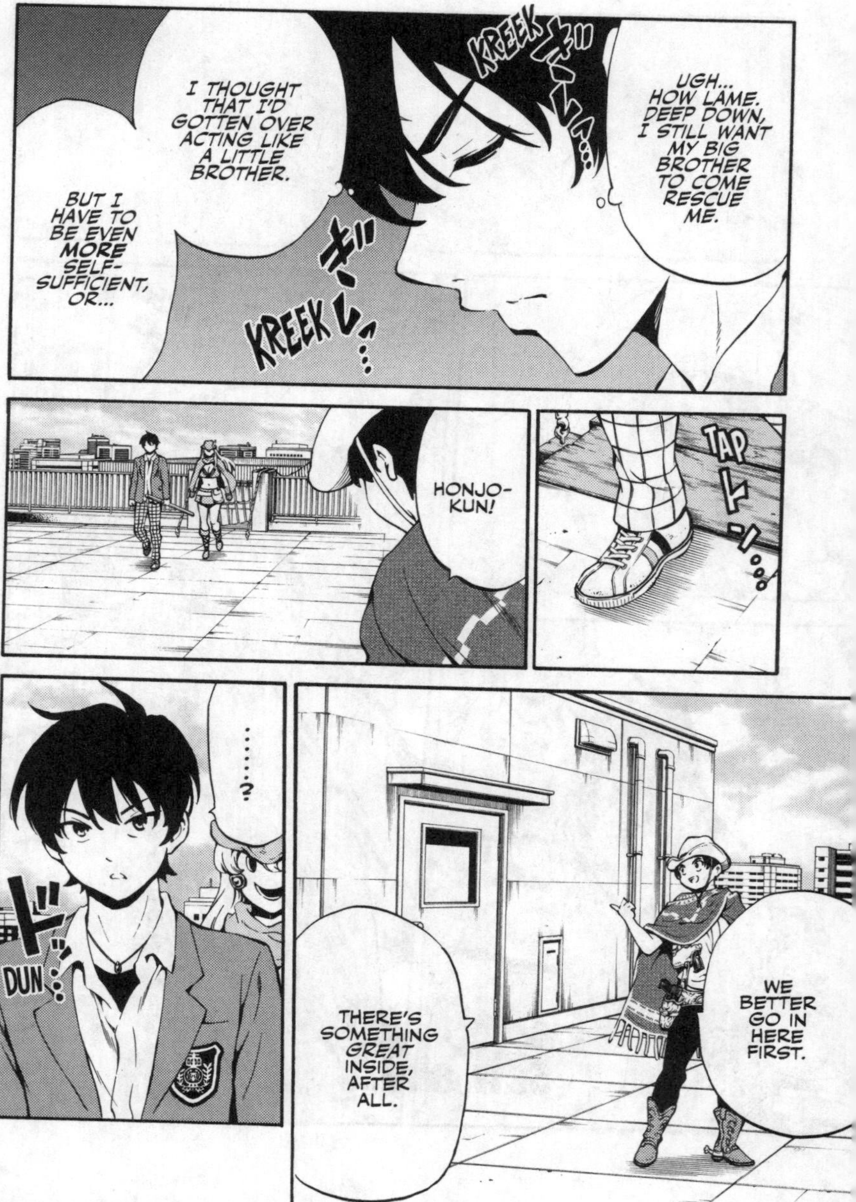
KREEK
UGH... HOW LAME. DEEP DOWN, I STILL WANT MY BIG BROTHER TO COME RESCUE ME.
I THOUGHT THAT I'D GOTTEN OVER ACTING LIKE A LITTLE BROTHER.
BUT I HAVE TO BE EVEN MORE SELF-SUFFICIENT, OR...
KREEK
TAP
HONJO-KUN!
WE BETTER GO IN HERE FIRST.
THERE'S SOMETHING GREAT INSIDE, AFTER ALL.
......?
DUN

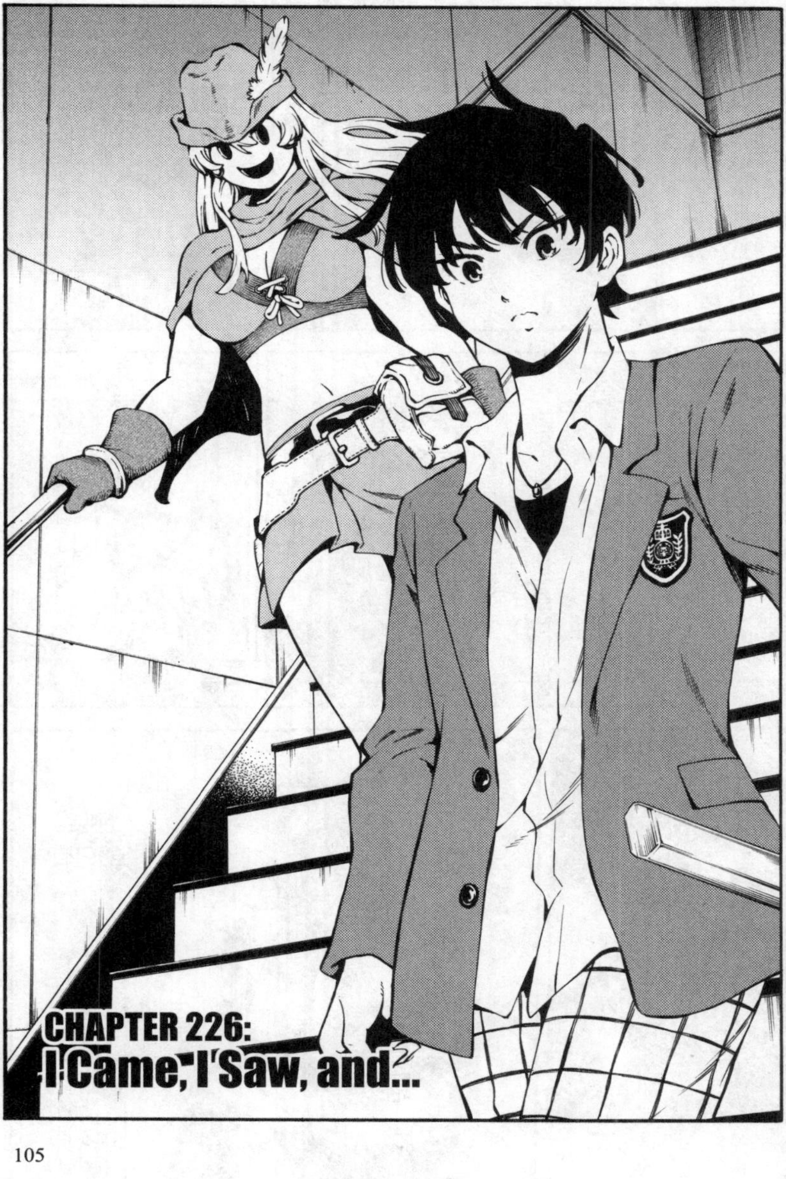
CHAPTER 226:
I Came, I Saw, and...

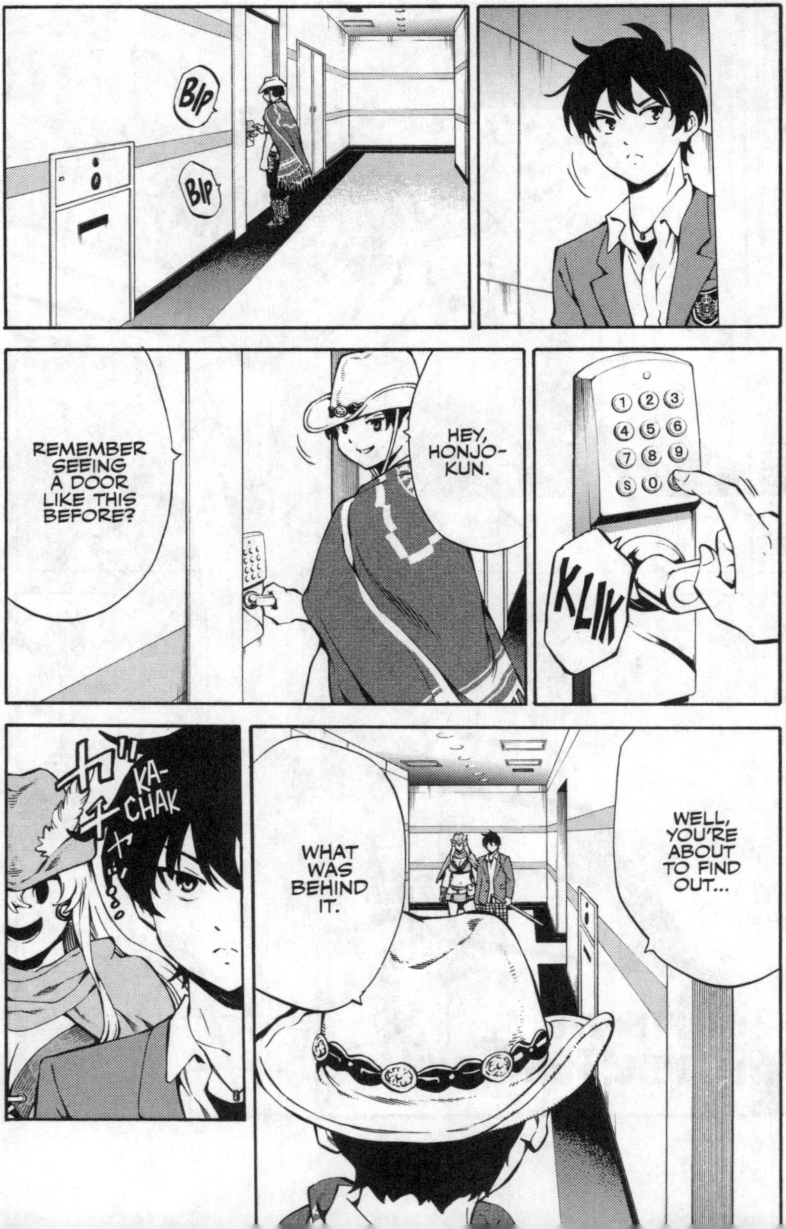
BIP
BIP
KLIK
HEY, HONJO-KUN.
REMEMBER SEEING A DOOR LIKE THIS BEFORE?
WELL, YOU'RE ABOUT TO FIND OUT...
WHAT WAS BEHIND IT.
KA-CHAK

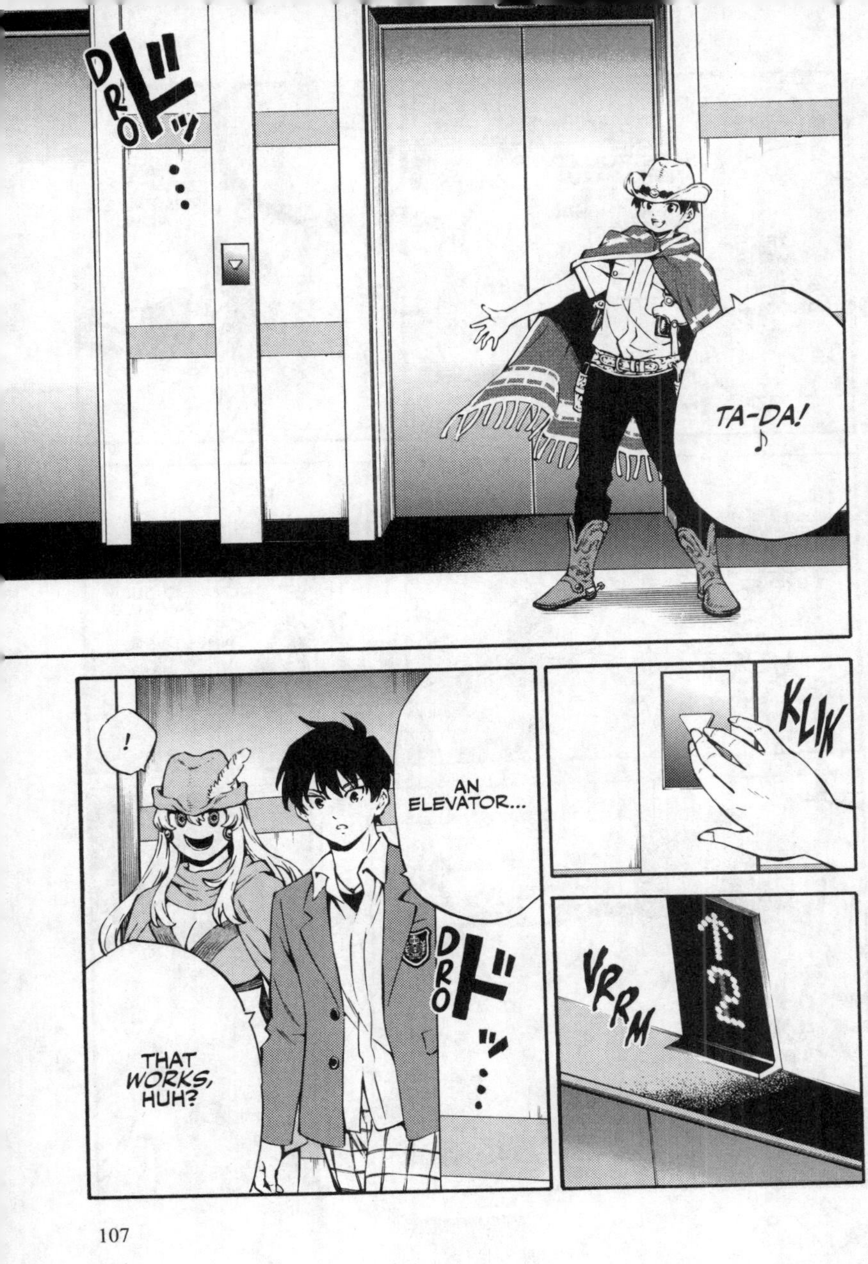
DRO ドッ
...
TA-DA! ♪
KLIK
VRRM
2
AN ELEVATOR...
!
DRO ドッ...
THAT WORKS, HUH?

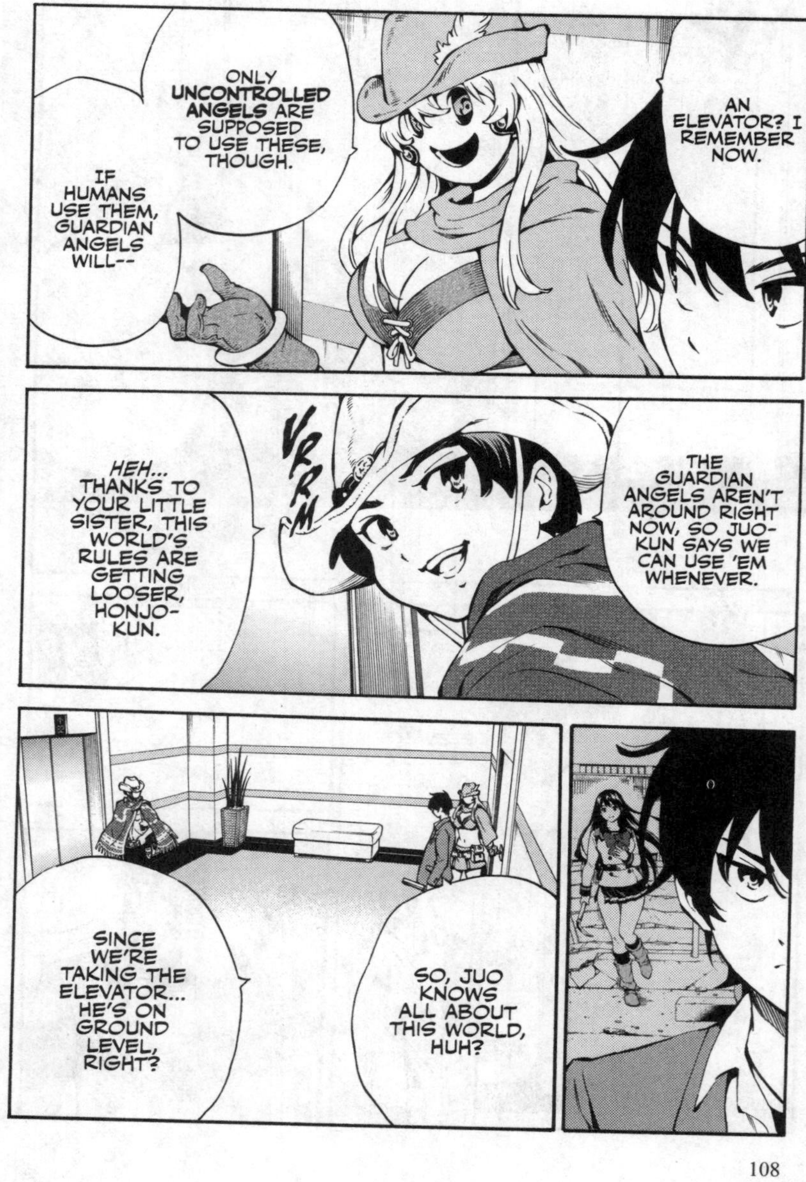
AN ELEVATOR? I REMEMBER NOW.
ONLY **UNCONTROLLED ANGELS** ARE SUPPOSED TO USE THESE, THOUGH.
IF HUMANS USE THEM, GUARDIAN ANGELS WILL--
THE GUARDIAN ANGELS AREN'T AROUND RIGHT NOW, SO JUO-KUN SAYS WE CAN USE 'EM WHENEVER.
VRRM
HEH... THANKS TO YOUR LITTLE SISTER, THIS WORLD'S RULES ARE GETTING LOOSER, HONJO-KUN.
SO, JUO KNOWS ALL ABOUT THIS WORLD, HUH?
SINCE WE'RE TAKING THE ELEVATOR... HE'S ON GROUND LEVEL, RIGHT?

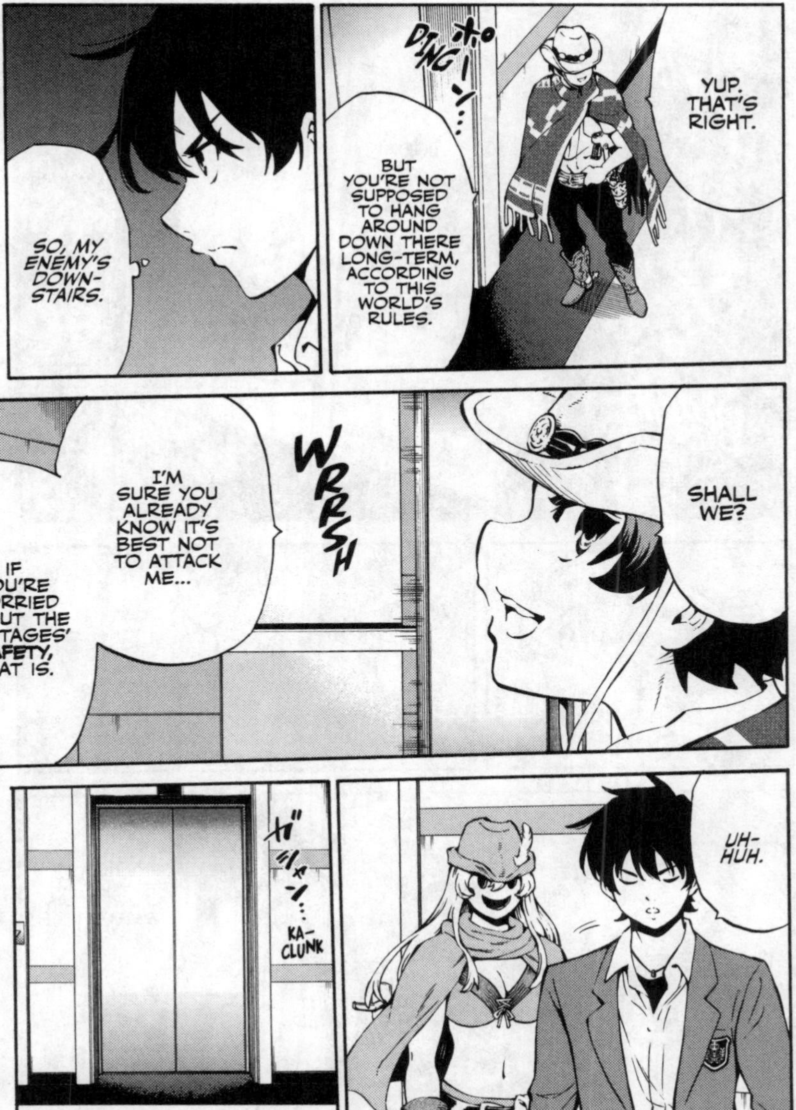
YUP. THAT'S RIGHT.
DING
ポーン…
BUT YOU'RE NOT SUPPOSED TO HANG AROUND DOWN THERE LONG-TERM, ACCORDING TO THIS WORLD'S RULES.
SO, MY ENEMY'S DOWN-STAIRS.
SHALL WE?
WRRSH
I'M SURE YOU ALREADY KNOW IT'S BEST NOT TO ATTACK ME...
IF YOU'RE WORRIED ABOUT THE HOSTAGES' **SAFETY,** THAT IS.
UH-HUH.
ガシャン…
KA-CLUNK

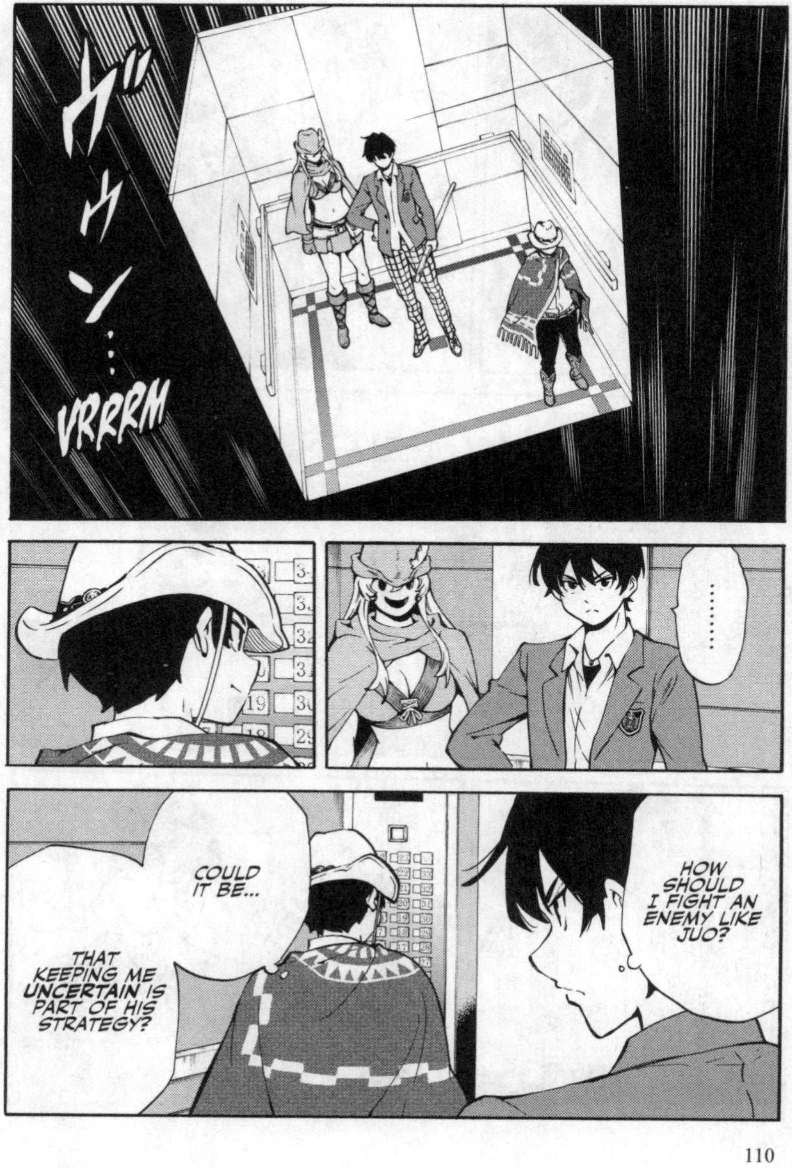
ヴゥン…
VRRRM
......
HOW SHOULD I FIGHT AN ENEMY LIKE JUO?
COULD IT BE...
THAT KEEPING ME UNCERTAIN IS PART OF HIS STRATEGY?

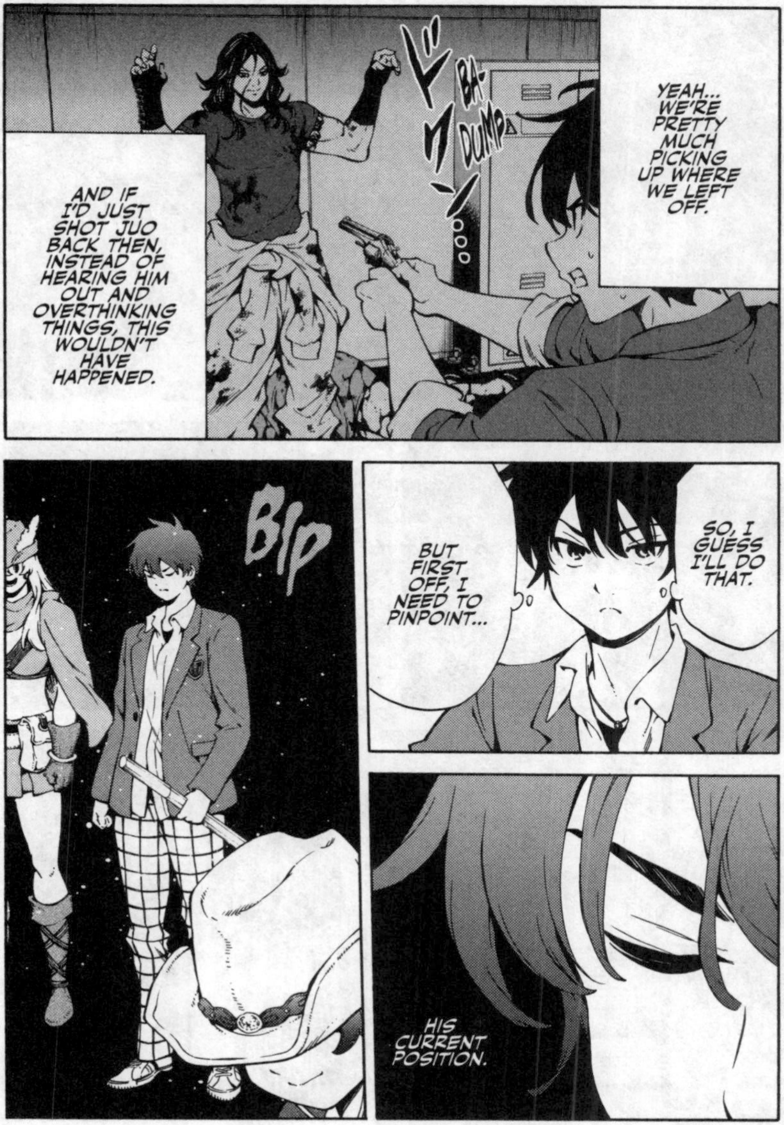
YEAH... WE'RE PRETTY MUCH PICKING UP WHERE WE LEFT OFF.
BA-DUMP
AND IF I'D JUST SHOT JUO BACK THEN, INSTEAD OF HEARING HIM OUT AND OVERTHINKING THINGS, THIS WOULDN'T HAVE HAPPENED.
SO, I GUESS I'LL DO THAT.
BUT FIRST OFF, I NEED TO PINPOINT...
HIS CURRENT POSITION.
BIP

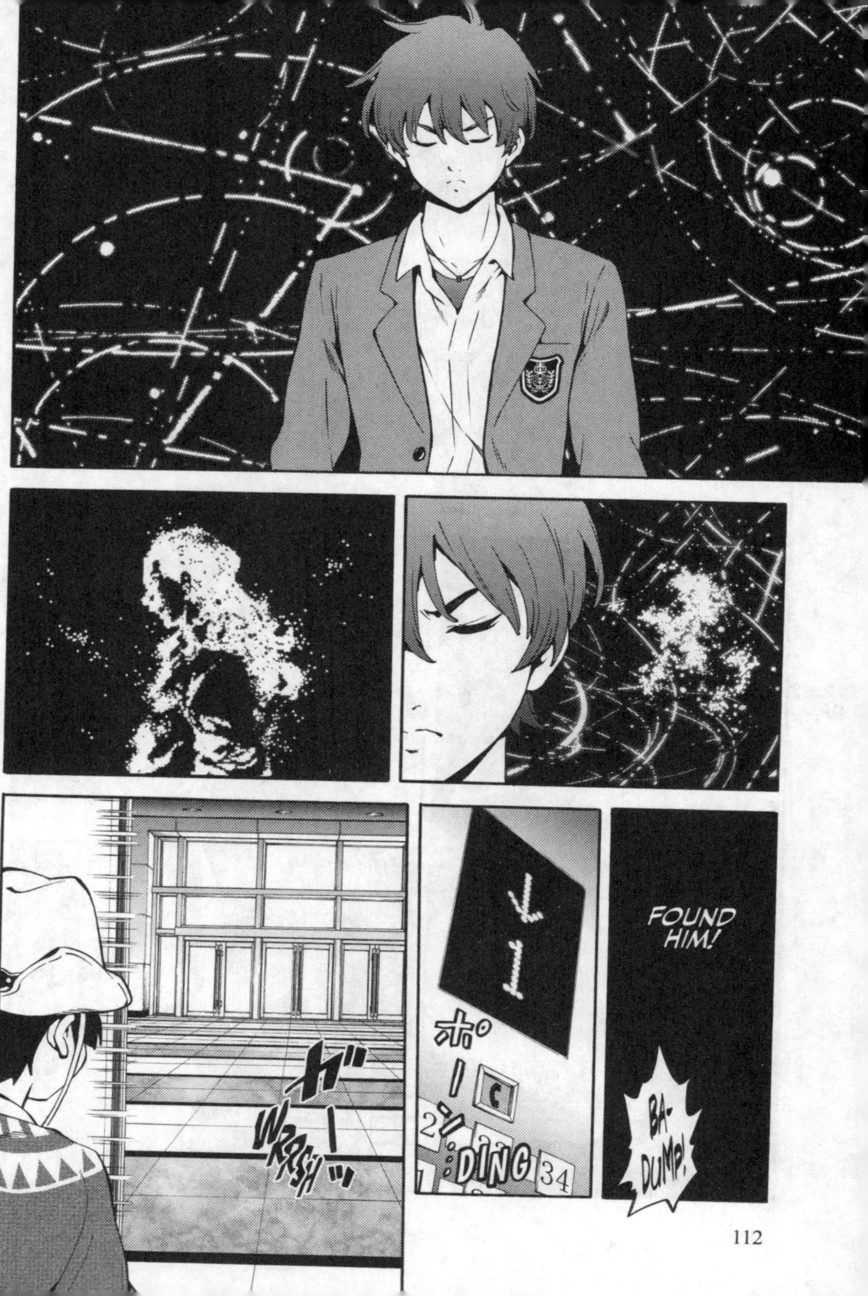
FOUND HIM!
BA-DUMP!
DING
WRSSH

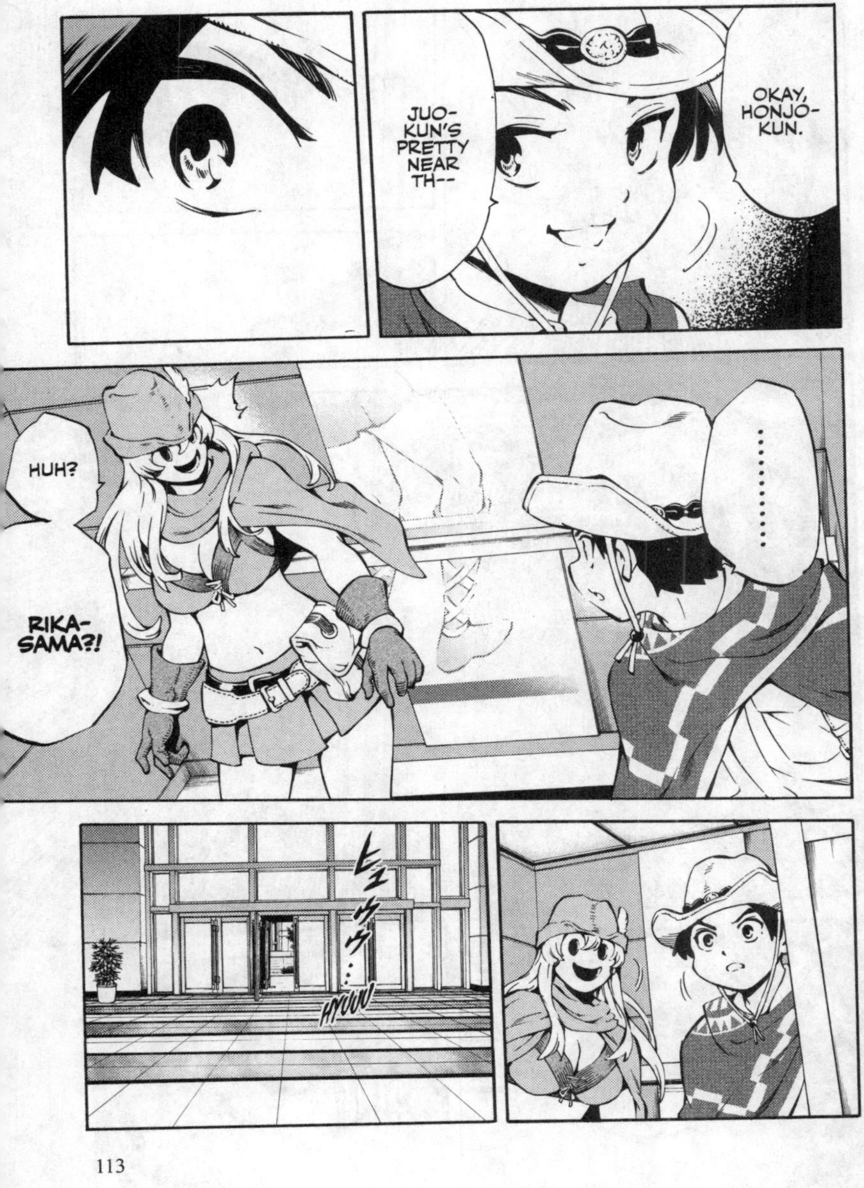
OKAY, HONJO-KUN.
JUO-KUN'S PRETTY NEAR TH--
......
HUH?
RIKA-SAMA?!
HYUUU

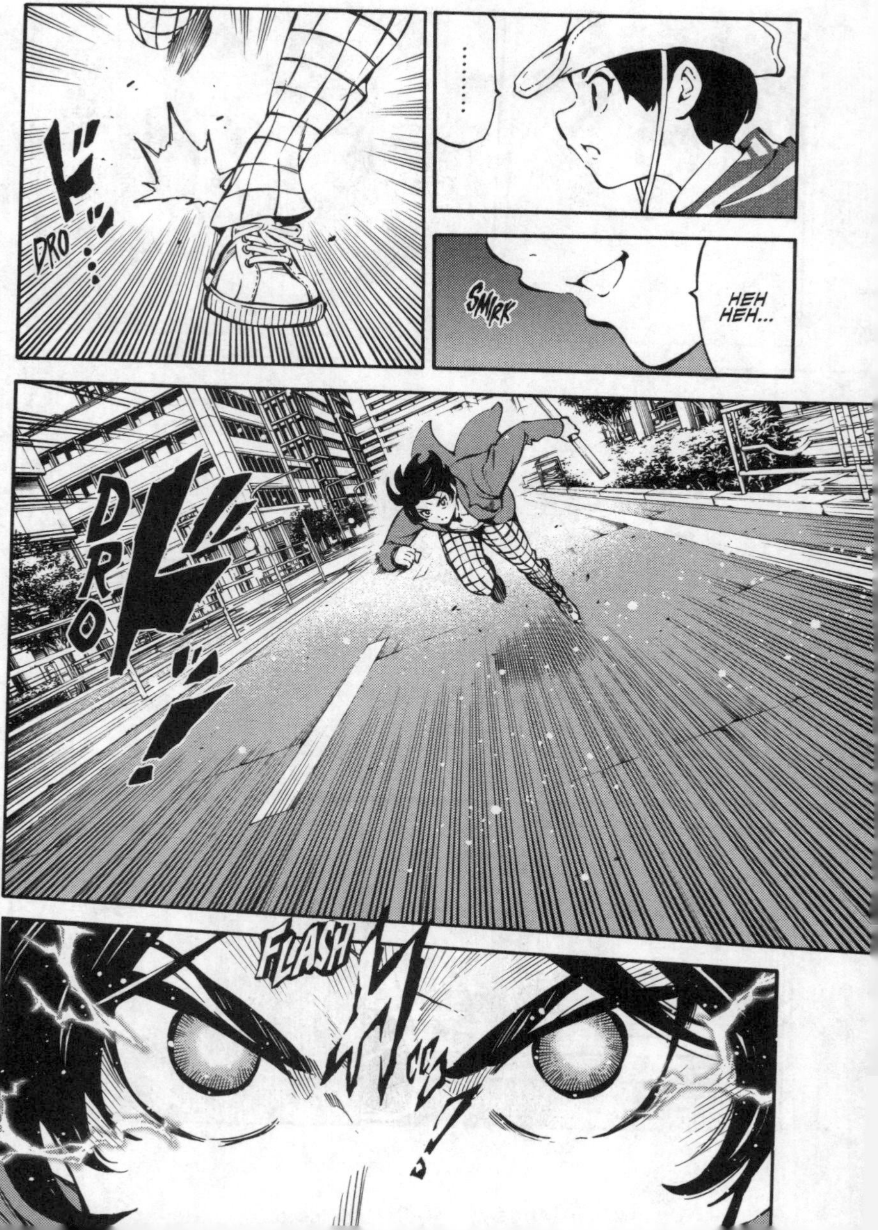
......
HEH HEH...
SMIRK
DRO
DRO
FLASH

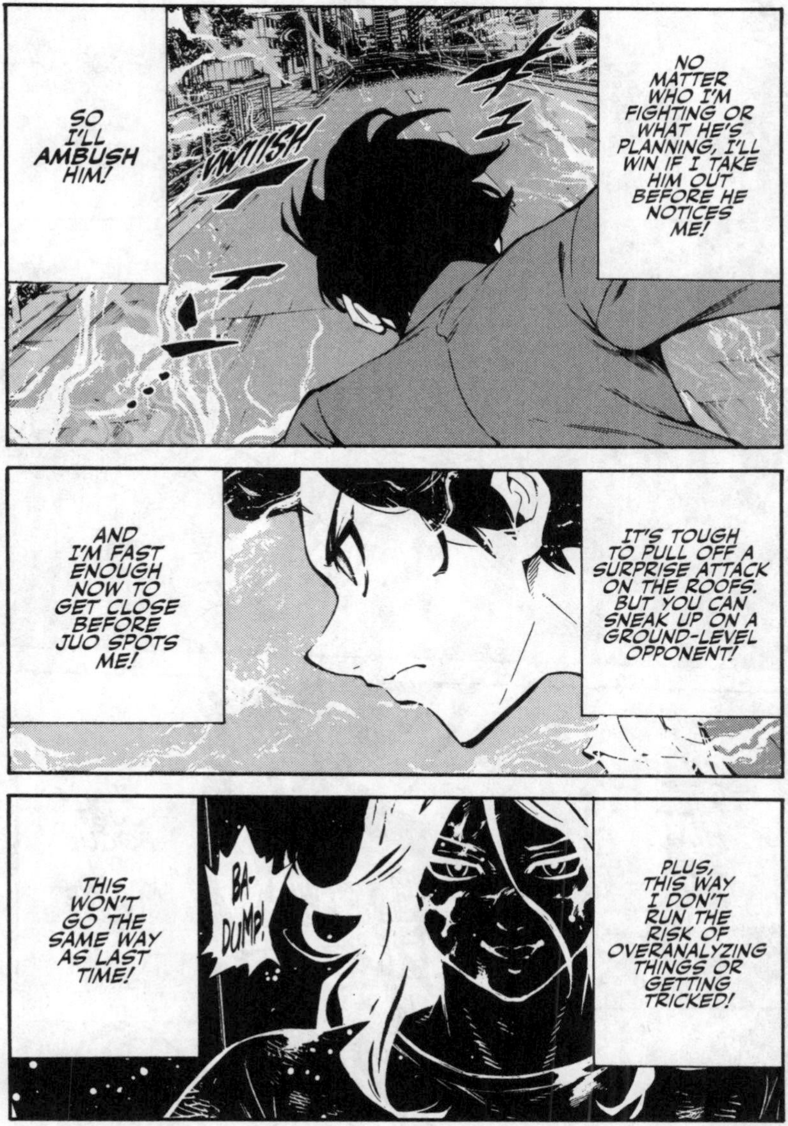
NO MATTER WHO I'M FIGHTING OR WHAT HE'S PLANNING, I'LL WIN IF I TAKE HIM OUT BEFORE HE NOTICES ME!
VWIIISH
SO I'LL AMBUSH HIM!
IT'S TOUGH TO PULL OFF A SURPRISE ATTACK ON THE ROOFS. BUT YOU CAN SNEAK UP ON A GROUND-LEVEL OPPONENT!
AND I'M FAST ENOUGH NOW TO GET CLOSE BEFORE JUO SPOTS ME!
PLUS, THIS WAY I DON'T RUN THE RISK OF OVERANALYZING THINGS OR GETTING TRICKED!
BA-DUMP!
THIS WON'T GO THE SAME WAY AS LAST TIME!

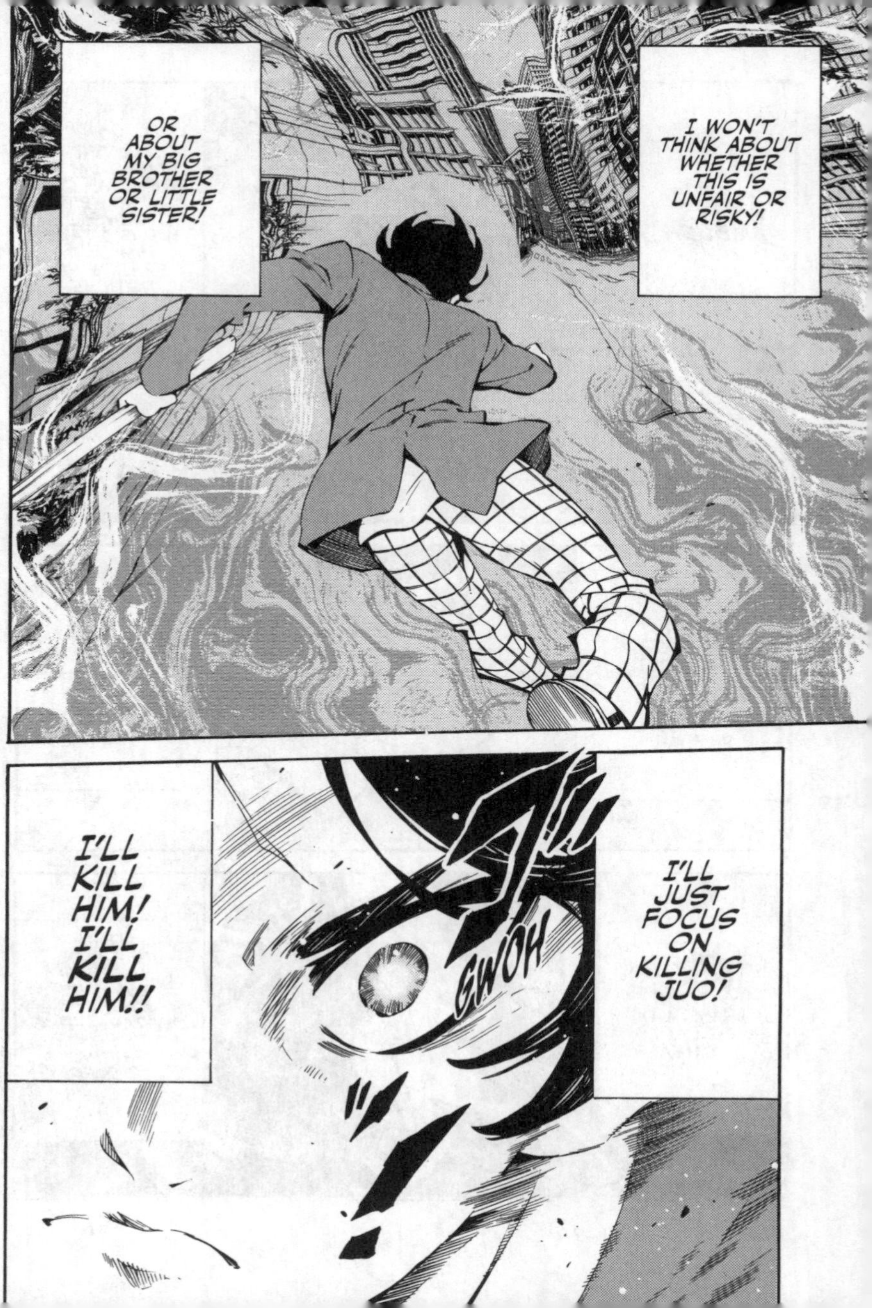
I WON'T THINK ABOUT WHETHER THIS IS UNFAIR OR RISKY!
OR ABOUT MY BIG BROTHER OR LITTLE SISTER!
I'LL JUST FOCUS ON KILLING JUO!
GWOH
I'LL KILL HIM! I'LL KILL HIM!!

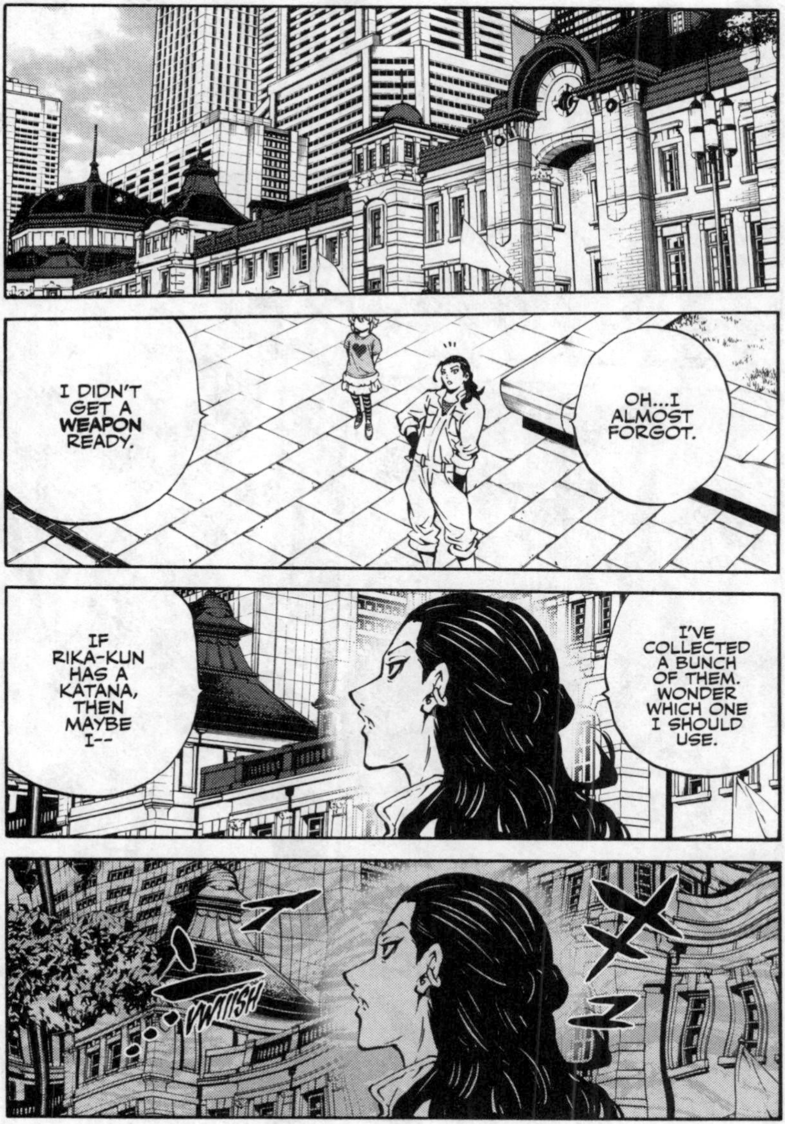
OH...I ALMOST FORGOT.
I DIDN'T GET A **WEAPON** READY.
I'VE COLLECTED A BUNCH OF THEM. WONDER WHICH ONE I SHOULD USE.
IF RIKA-KUN HAS A KATANA, THEN MAYBE I--
VWIIISH

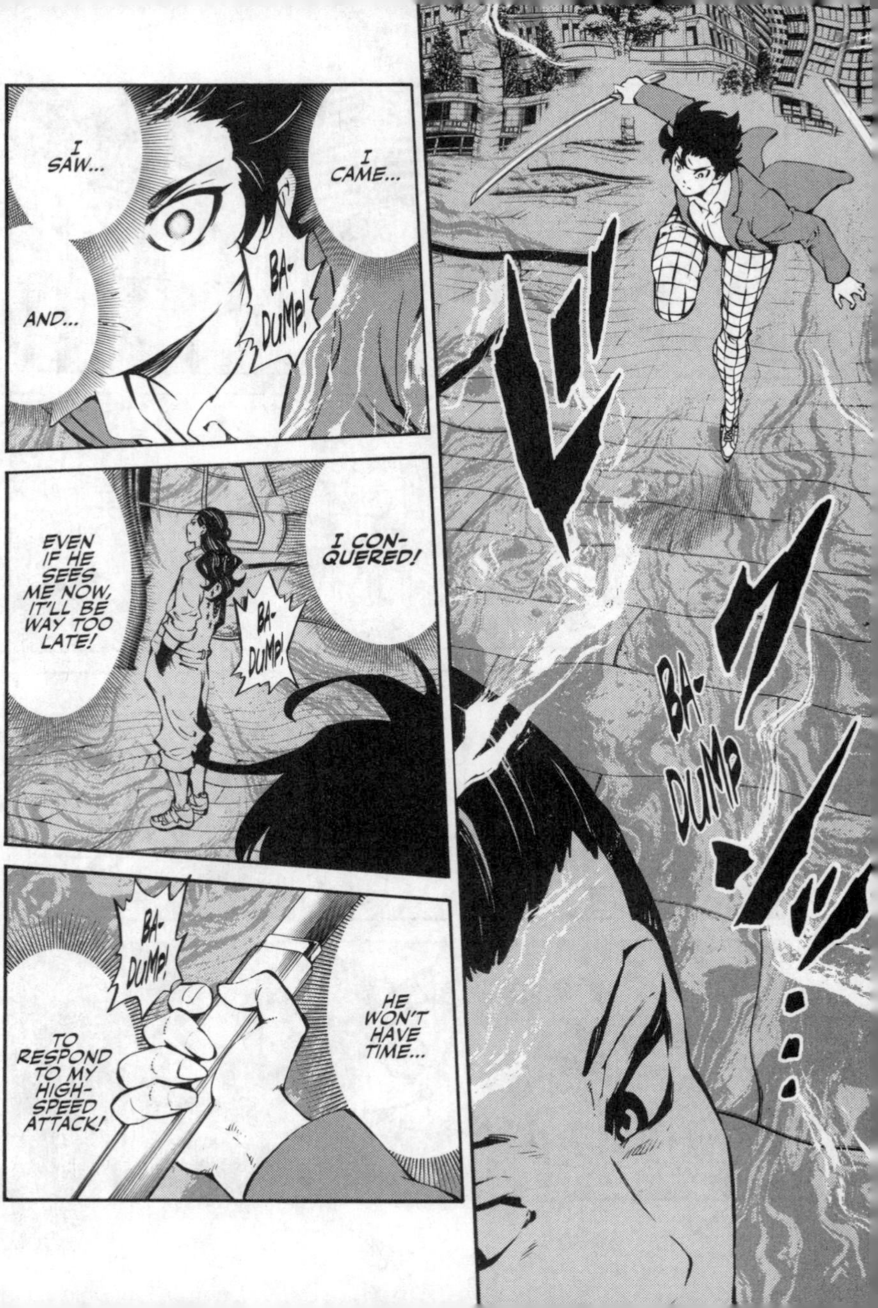
BA-DUMP
I CAME...
BA-DUMP!
I SAW...
AND...
I CONQUERED!
BA-DUMP!
EVEN IF HE SEES ME NOW, IT'LL BE WAY TOO LATE!
BA-DUMP!
HE WON'T HAVE TIME...
TO RESPOND TO MY HIGH-SPEED ATTACK!

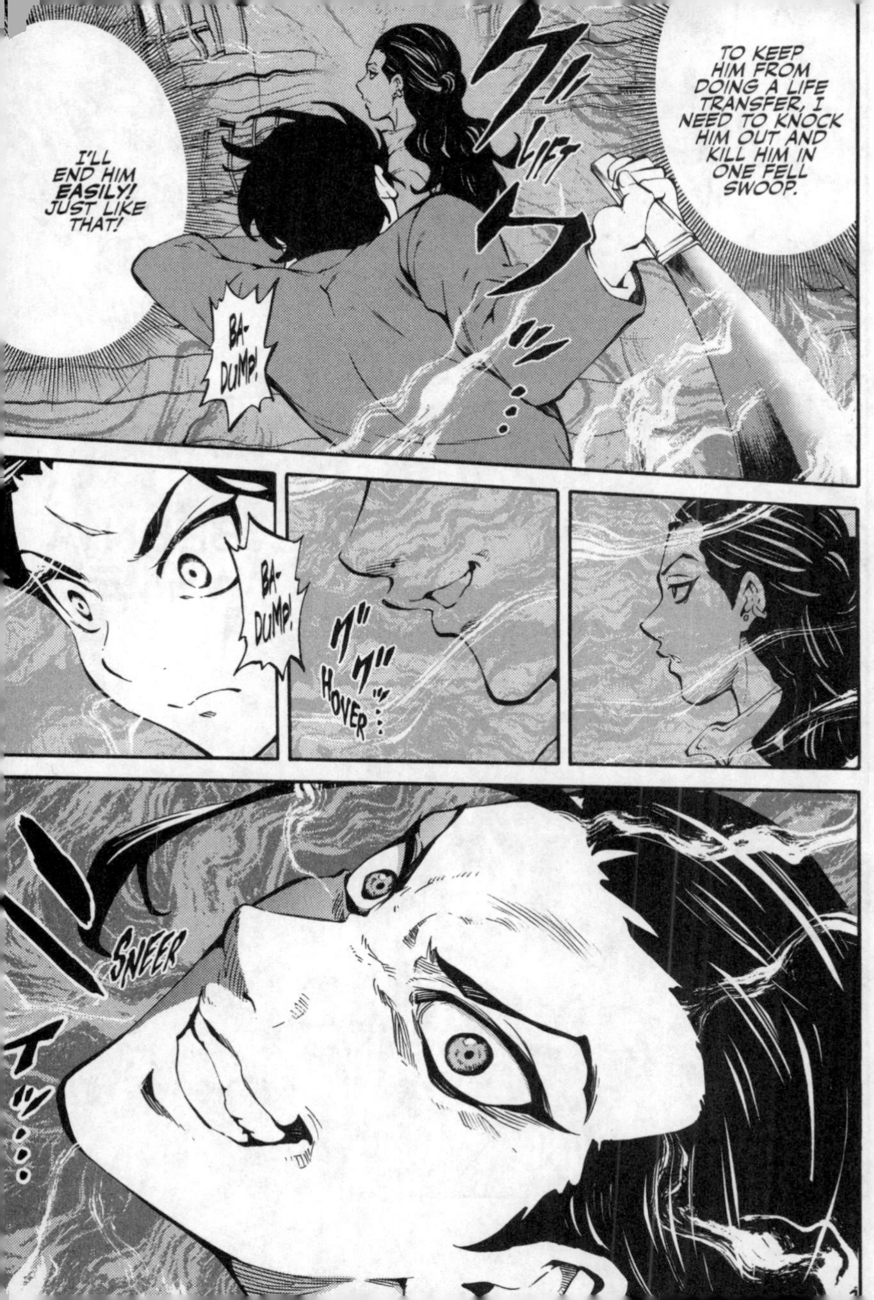
TO KEEP HIM FROM DOING A LIFE TRANSFER, I NEED TO KNOCK HIM OUT AND KILL HIM IN ONE FELL SWOOP.
LIFT
I'LL END HIM EASILY! JUST LIKE THAT!
BA-DUMP!
HOVER
BA-DUMP!
SNEER

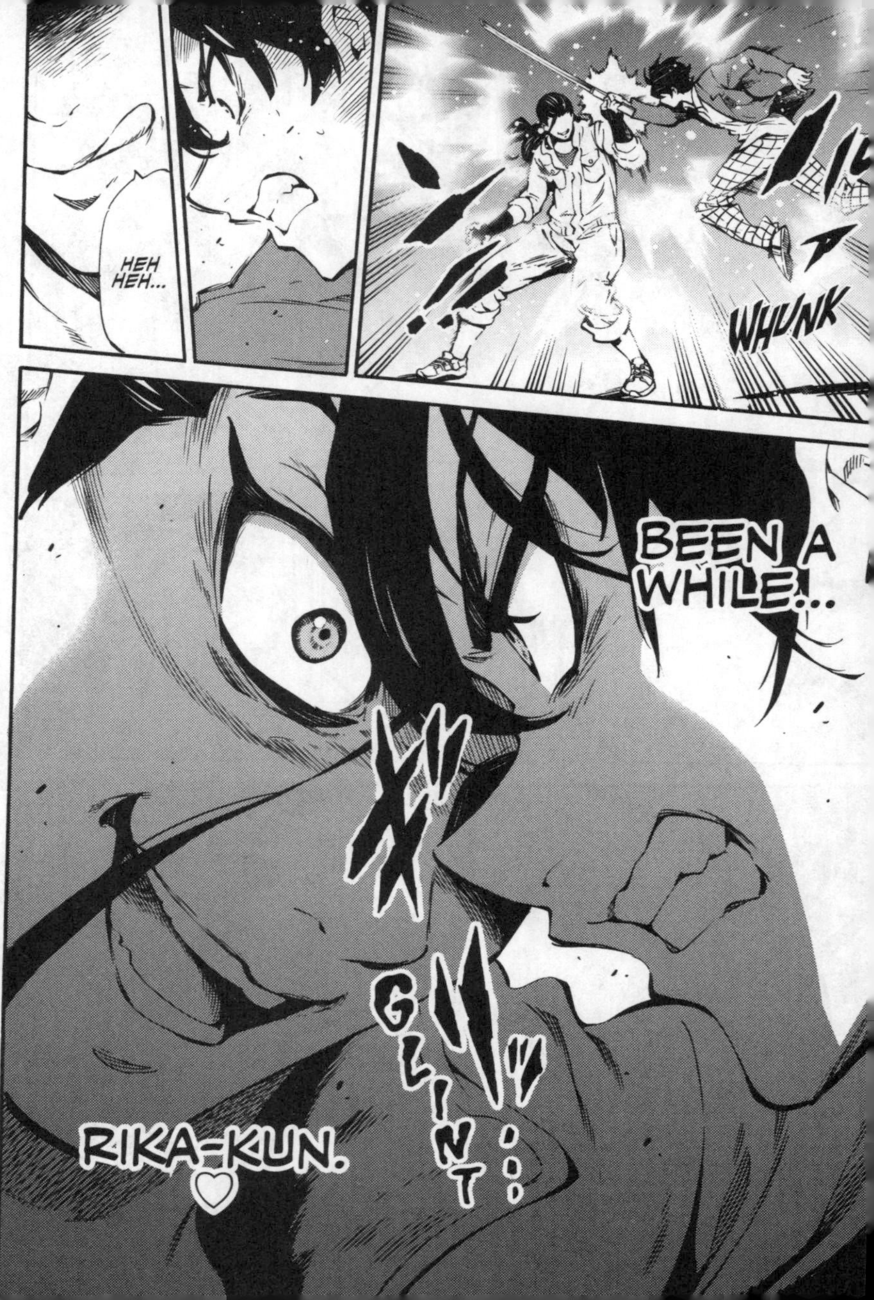
WHUNK
HEH HEH...
BEEN A WHILE...
GLINT
RIKA-KUN. ♡

HIGH-RISE INVASION

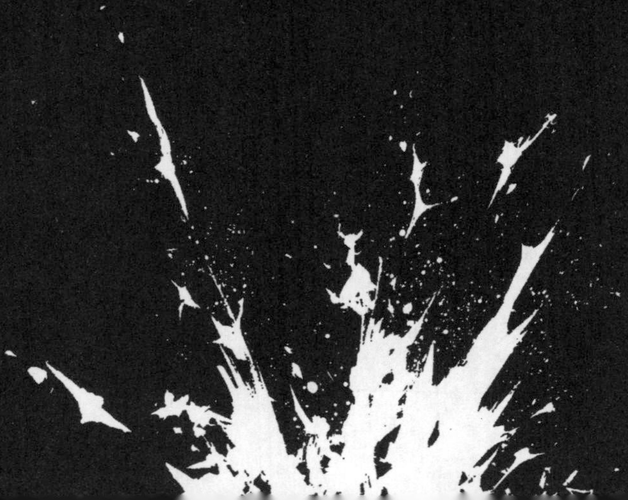

CHAPTER 227: I Want to Ask You Something

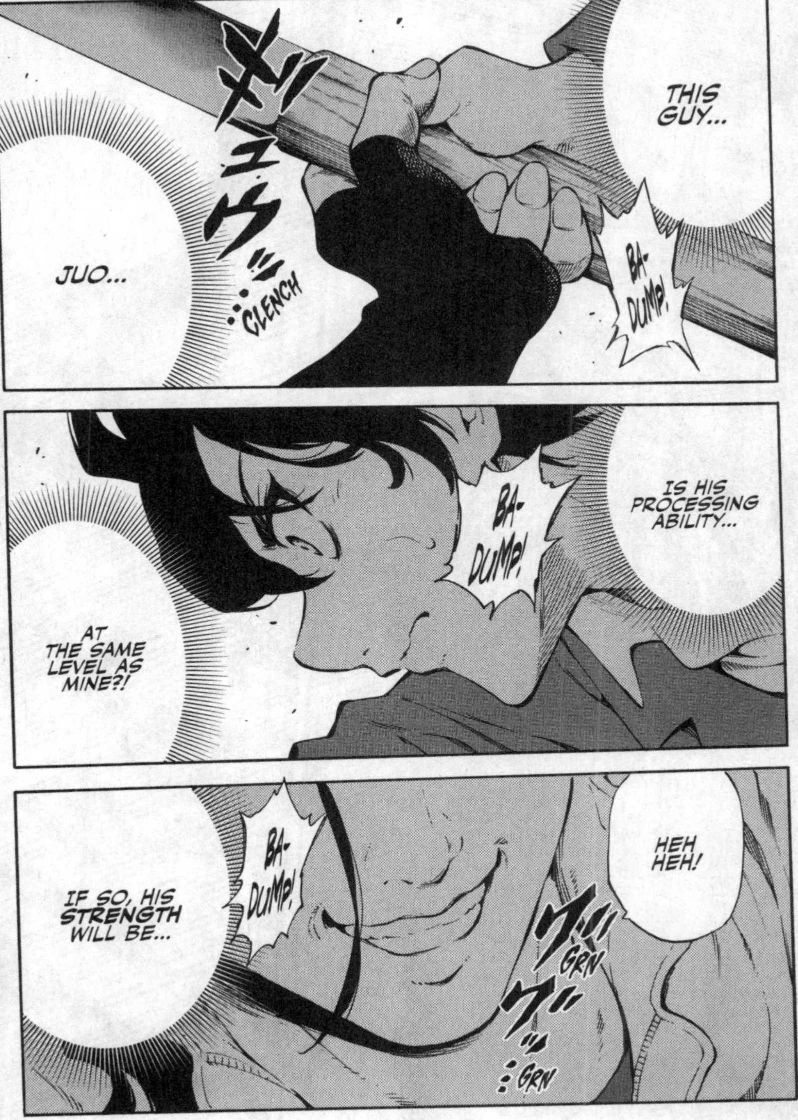
THIS GUY...
BA-DUMP!
CLENCH
JUO...
IS HIS PROCESSING ABILITY...
BA-DUMP!
AT THE SAME LEVEL AS MINE?!
HEH HEH!
GRN
GRN
BA-DUMP!
IF SO, HIS STRENGTH WILL BE...

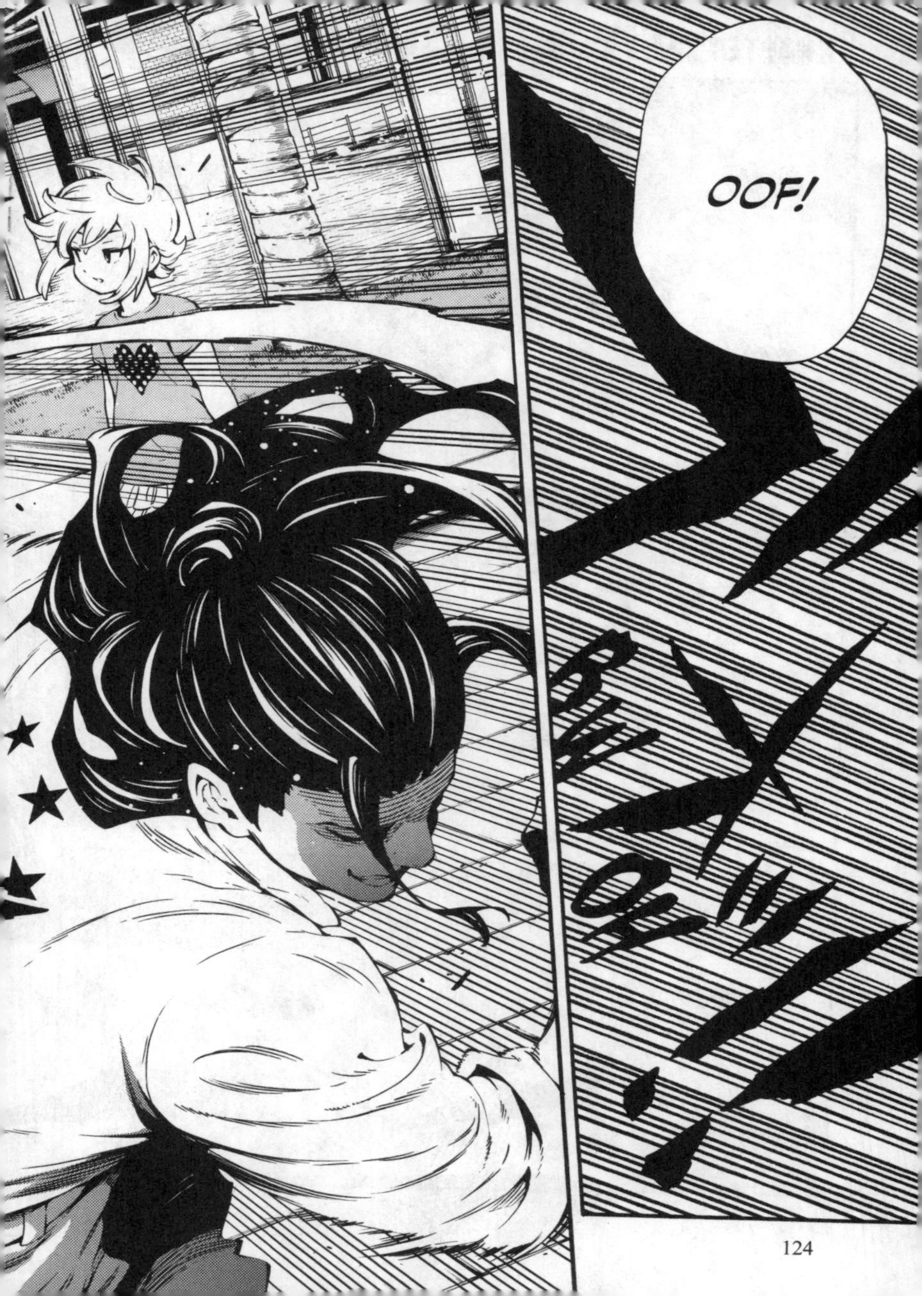
OOF!

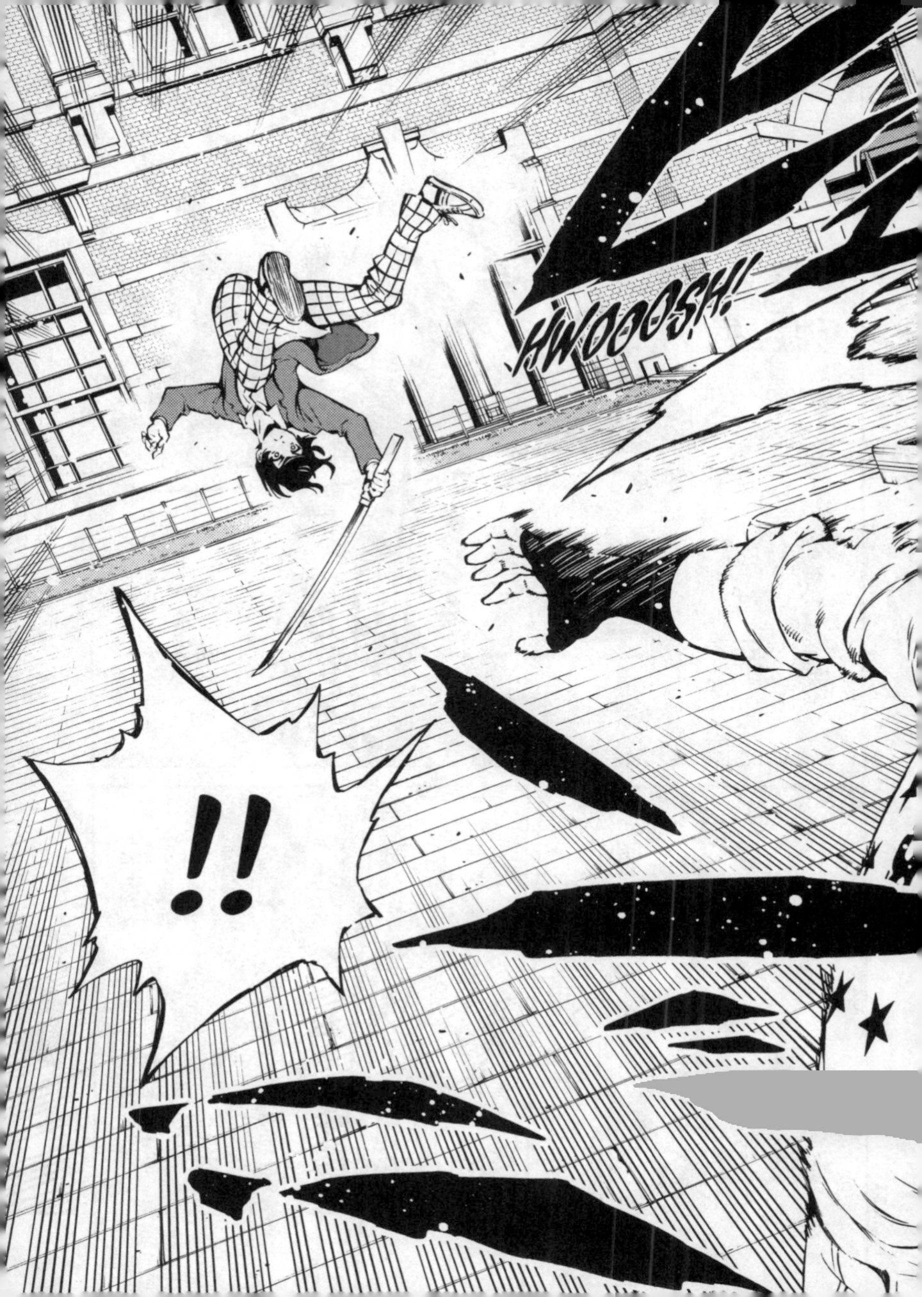
HWOOOSH!
!!

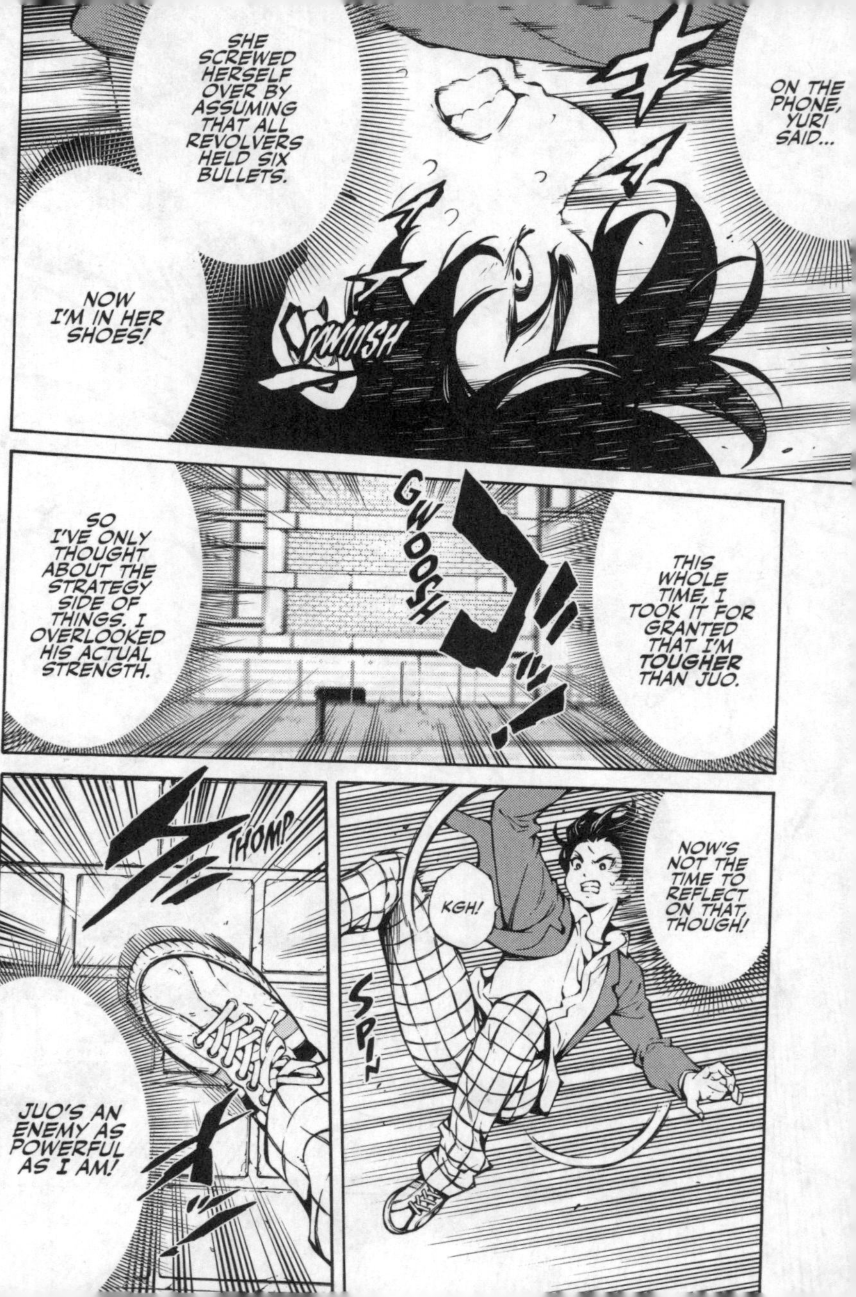
ON THE PHONE, YURI SAID...
SHE SCREWED HERSELF OVER BY ASSUMING THAT ALL REVOLVERS HELD SIX BULLETS.
NOW I'M IN HER SHOES!
THIS WHOLE TIME, I TOOK IT FOR GRANTED THAT I'M TOUGHER THAN JUO.
GWOOSH
SO I'VE ONLY THOUGHT ABOUT THE STRATEGY SIDE OF THINGS. I OVERLOOKED HIS ACTUAL STRENGTH.
NOW'S NOT THE TIME TO REFLECT ON THAT, THOUGH!
KGH!
SPIN
THOMP
JUO'S AN ENEMY AS POWERFUL AS I AM!

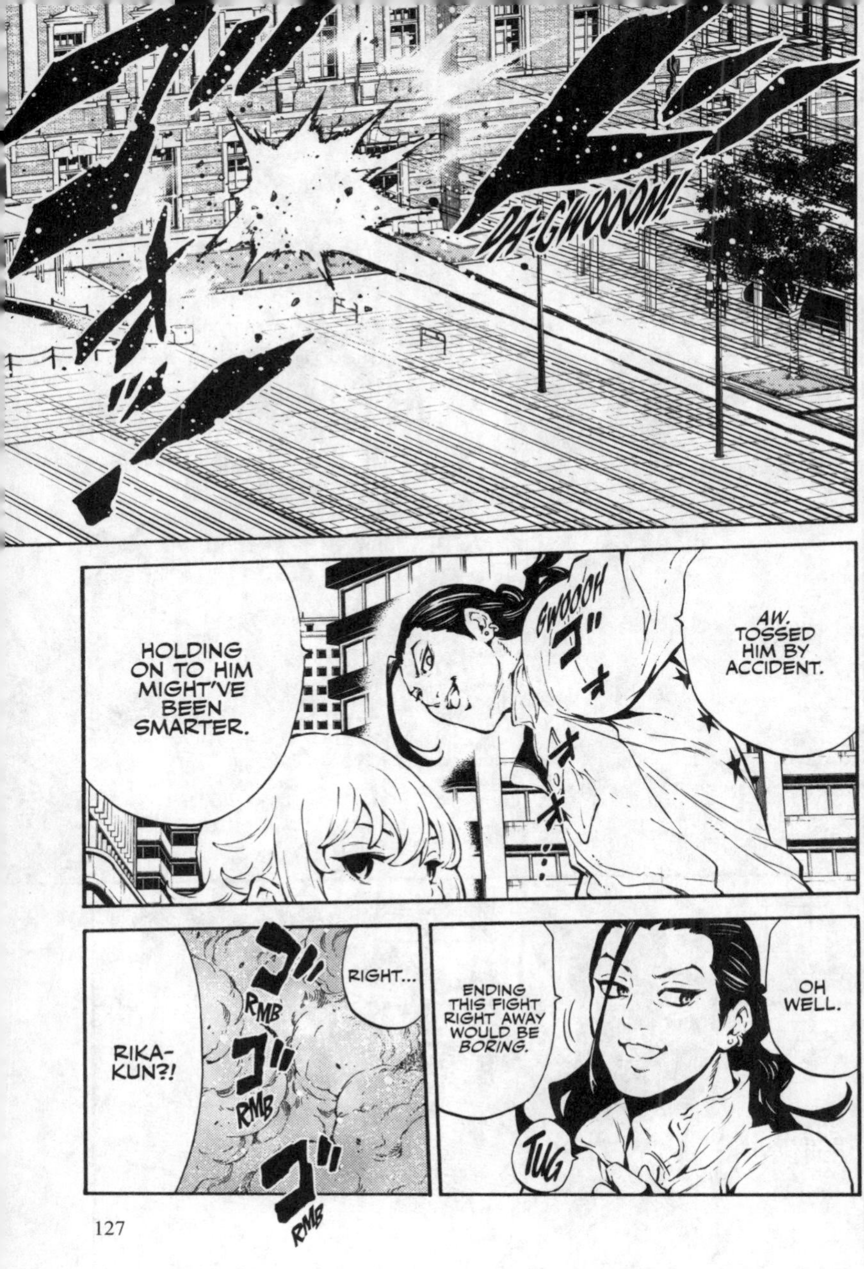
DA-GWOOOM!
AW. TOSSED HIM BY ACCIDENT.
GWOOOH
HOLDING ON TO HIM MIGHT'VE BEEN SMARTER.
OH WELL.
ENDING THIS FIGHT RIGHT AWAY WOULD BE BORING.
TUG
RIGHT...
RMB
RMB
RIKA-KUN?!
RMB

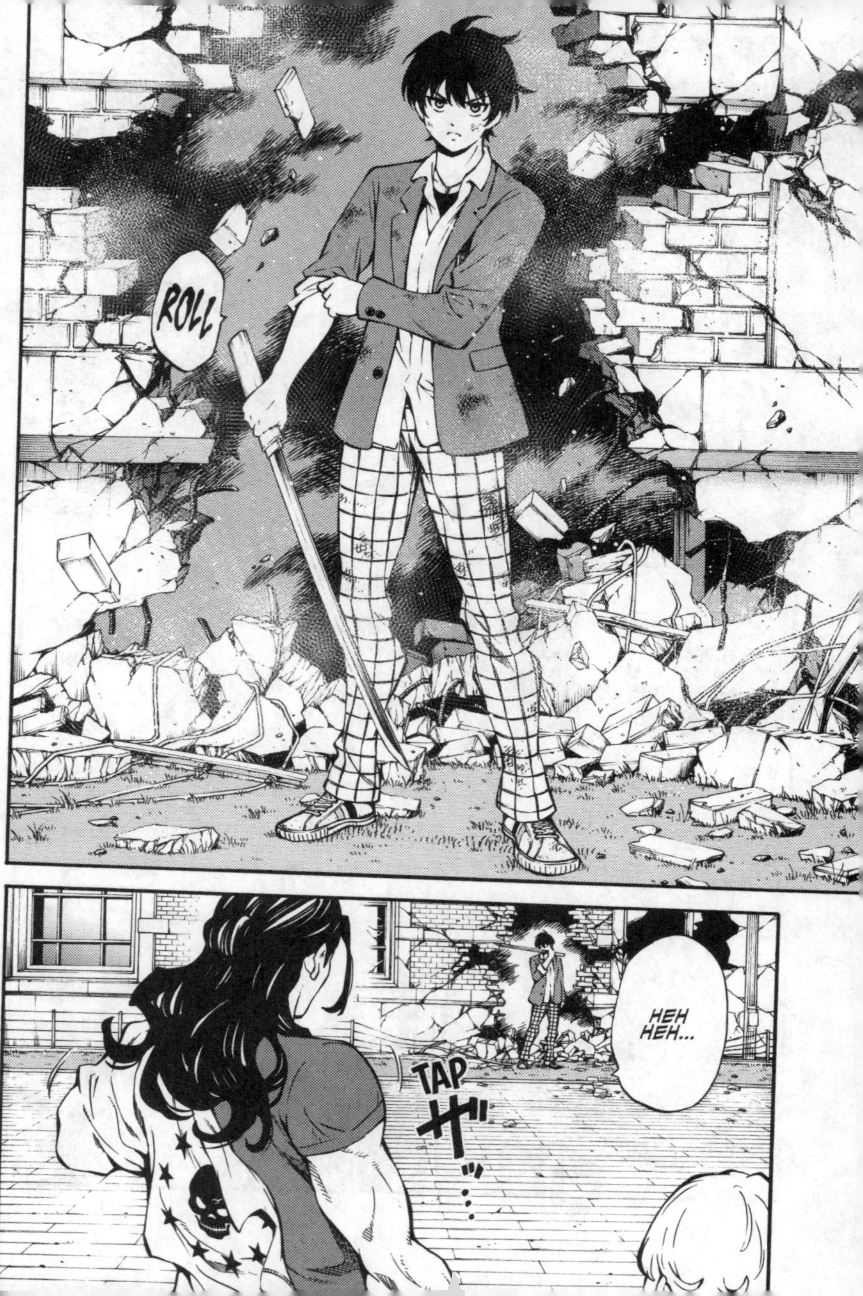
ROLL
HEH HEH...
TAP

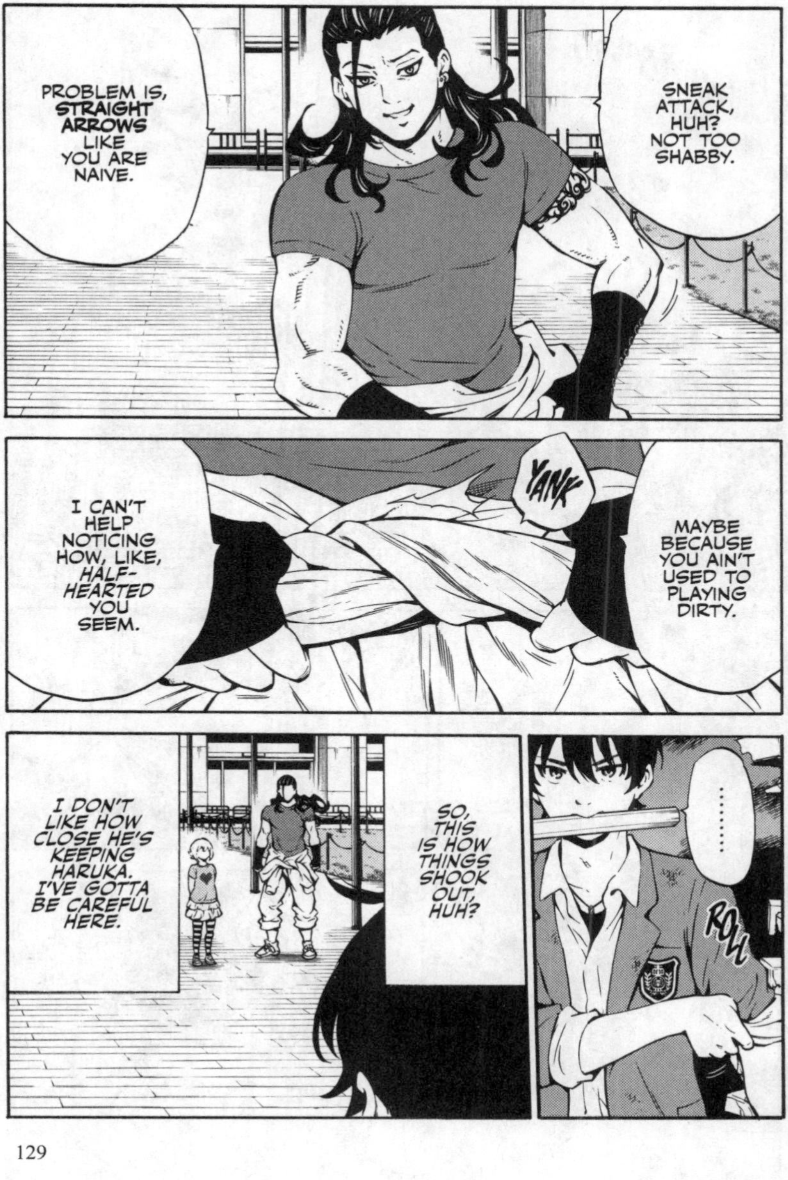
SNEAK ATTACK, HUH? NOT TOO SHABBY.
PROBLEM IS, **STRAIGHT ARROWS** LIKE YOU ARE NAIVE.
YANK
MAYBE BECAUSE YOU AIN'T USED TO PLAYING DIRTY.
I CAN'T HELP NOTICING HOW, LIKE, *HALF-HEARTED* YOU SEEM.
......
ROLL
SO, THIS IS HOW THINGS SHOOK OUT, HUH?
I DON'T LIKE HOW CLOSE HE'S KEEPING HARUKA. I'VE GOTTA BE CAREFUL HERE.

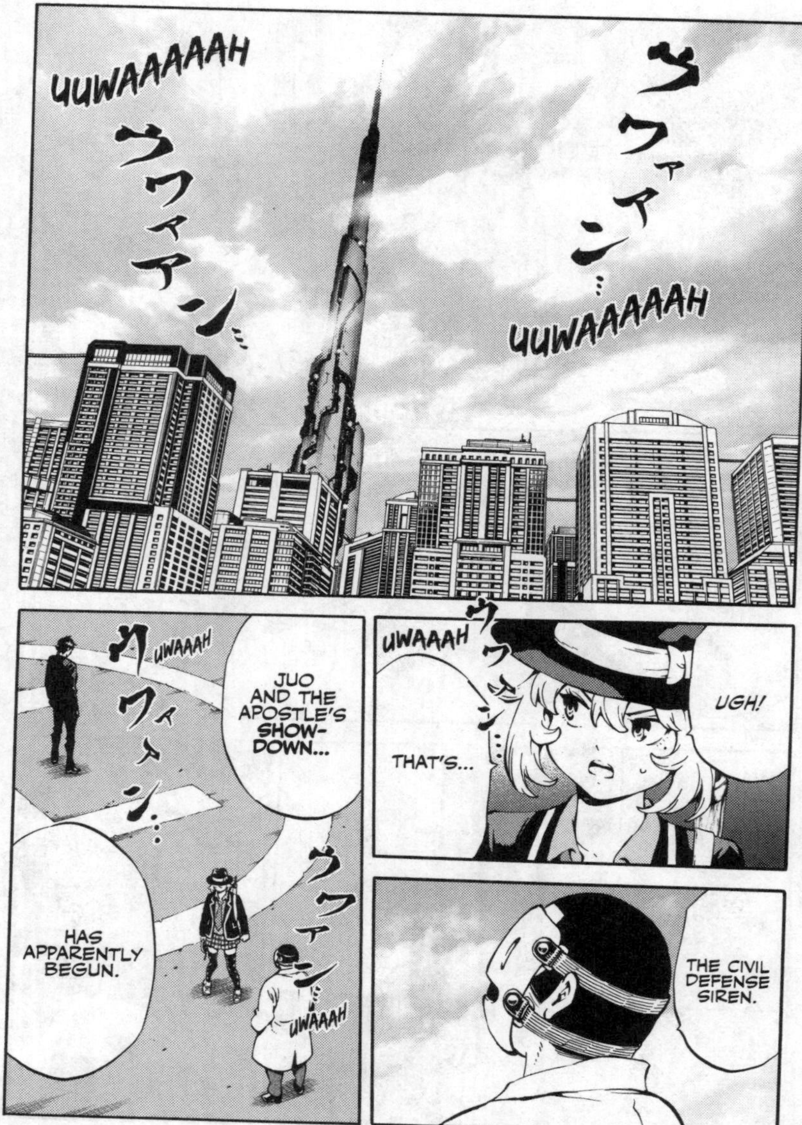
ウァアン…
UUWAAAAAH
UUWAAAAAH
ウワァアン…
UWAAAH
UGH!
THAT'S...
THE CIVIL DEFENSE SIREN.
UWAAAH
JUO AND THE APOSTLE'S SHOW-DOWN...
HAS APPARENTLY BEGUN.
UWAAAH

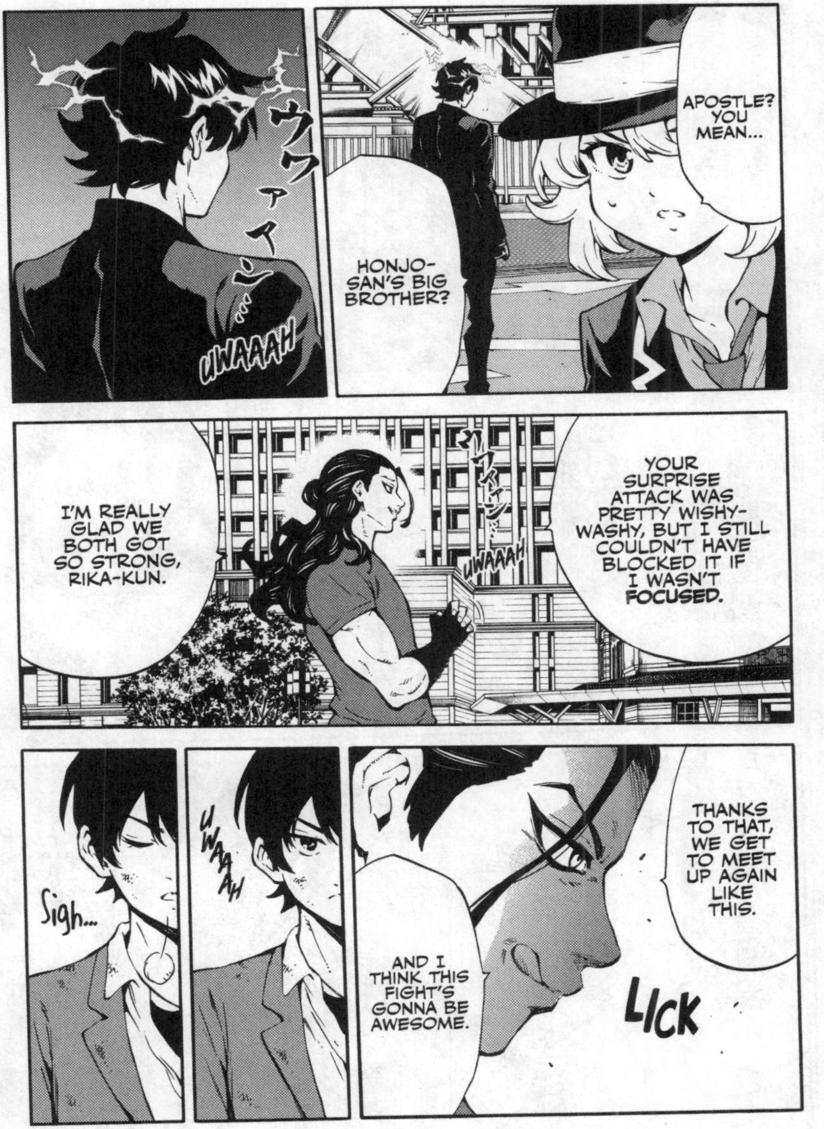
APOSTLE? YOU MEAN...
HONJO-SAN'S BIG BROTHER?
ウワァァン…
UWAAAH
YOUR SURPRISE ATTACK WAS PRETTY WISHY-WASHY, BUT I STILL COULDN'T HAVE BLOCKED IT IF I WASN'T **FOCUSED.**
UWAAAH
I'M REALLY GLAD WE BOTH GOT SO STRONG, RIKA-KUN.
THANKS TO THAT, WE GET TO MEET UP AGAIN LIKE THIS.
AND I THINK THIS FIGHT'S GONNA BE AWESOME.
LICK
UWAAAH
Sigh...

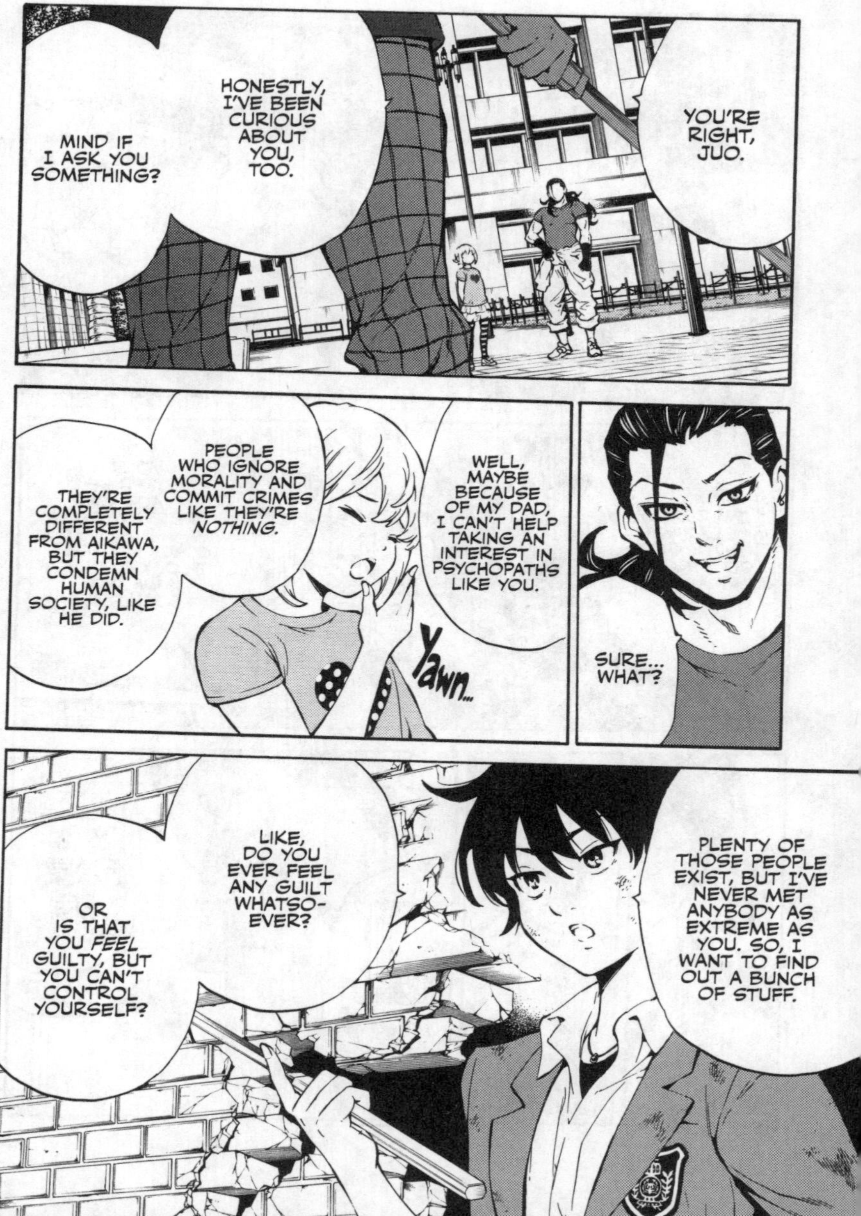
YOU'RE RIGHT, JUO.
HONESTLY, I'VE BEEN CURIOUS ABOUT YOU, TOO.
MIND IF I ASK YOU SOMETHING?
SURE... WHAT?
WELL, MAYBE BECAUSE OF MY DAD, I CAN'T HELP TAKING AN INTEREST IN PSYCHOPATHS LIKE YOU.
Yawn...
PEOPLE WHO IGNORE MORALITY AND COMMIT CRIMES LIKE THEY'RE *NOTHING.*
THEY'RE COMPLETELY DIFFERENT FROM AIKAWA, BUT THEY CONDEMN HUMAN SOCIETY, LIKE HE DID.
PLENTY OF THOSE PEOPLE EXIST, BUT I'VE NEVER MET ANYBODY AS EXTREME AS YOU. SO, I WANT TO FIND OUT A BUNCH OF STUFF.
LIKE, DO YOU EVER FEEL ANY GUILT WHATSO-EVER?
OR IS THAT YOU *FEEL* GUILTY, BUT YOU CAN'T CONTROL YOURSELF?

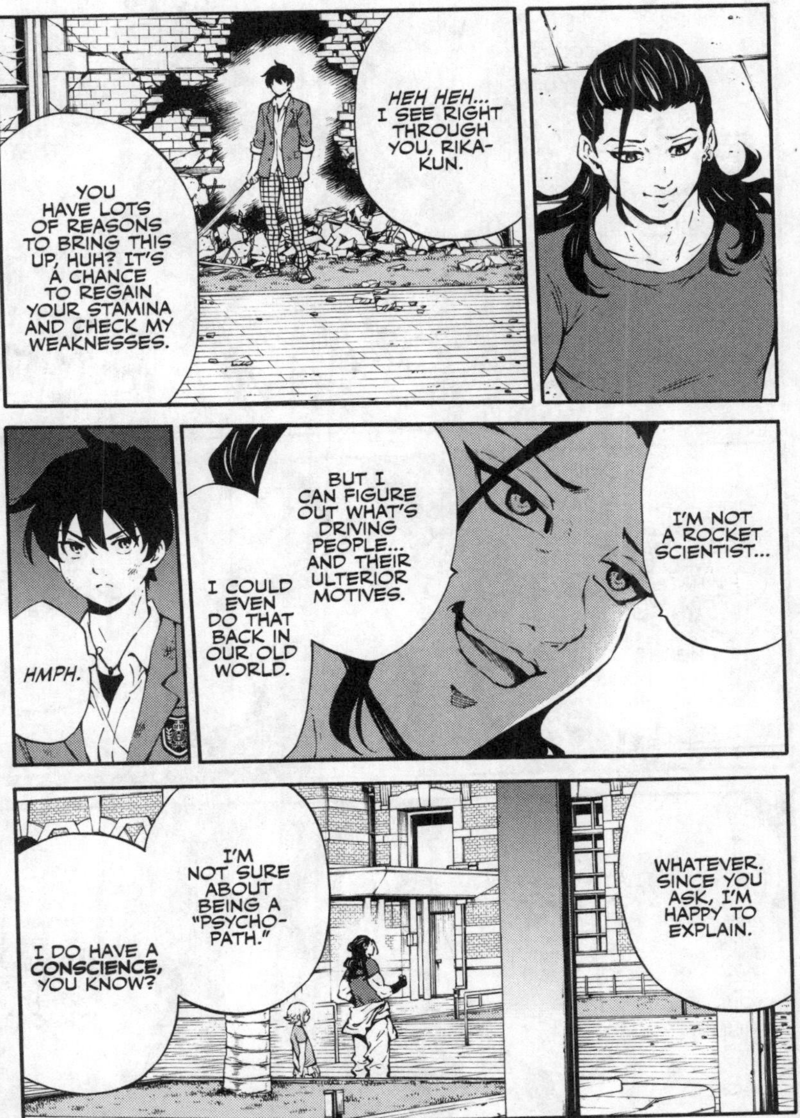
HEH HEH... I SEE RIGHT THROUGH YOU, RIKA-KUN.
YOU HAVE LOTS OF REASONS TO BRING THIS UP, HUH? IT'S A CHANCE TO REGAIN YOUR STAMINA AND CHECK MY WEAKNESSES.
I'M NOT A ROCKET SCIENTIST...
BUT I CAN FIGURE OUT WHAT'S DRIVING PEOPLE... AND THEIR ULTERIOR MOTIVES.
I COULD EVEN DO THAT BACK IN OUR OLD WORLD.
HMPH.
WHATEVER. SINCE YOU ASK, I'M HAPPY TO EXPLAIN.
I'M NOT SURE ABOUT BEING A "PSYCHOPATH."
I DO HAVE A CONSCIENCE, YOU KNOW?

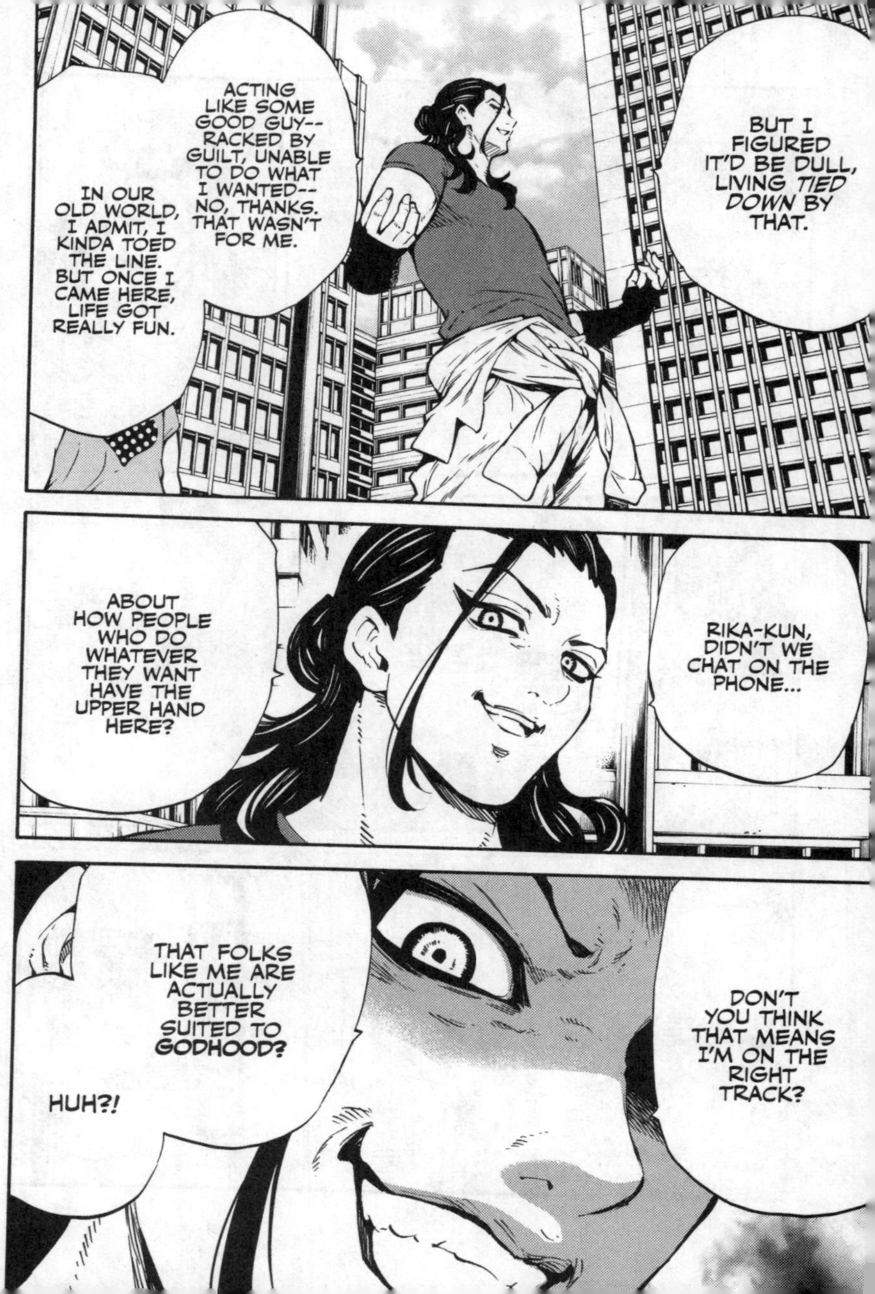
BUT I FIGURED IT'D BE DULL, LIVING *TIED DOWN* BY THAT.
ACTING LIKE SOME GOOD GUY-- RACKED BY GUILT, UNABLE TO DO WHAT I WANTED-- NO, THANKS. THAT WASN'T FOR ME.
IN OUR OLD WORLD, I ADMIT, I KINDA TOED THE LINE. BUT ONCE I CAME HERE, LIFE GOT REALLY FUN.
RIKA-KUN, DIDN'T WE CHAT ON THE PHONE...
ABOUT HOW PEOPLE WHO DO WHATEVER THEY WANT HAVE THE UPPER HAND HERE?
DON'T YOU THINK THAT MEANS I'M ON THE RIGHT TRACK?
THAT FOLKS LIKE ME ARE ACTUALLY BETTER SUITED TO GODHOOD?
HUH?!

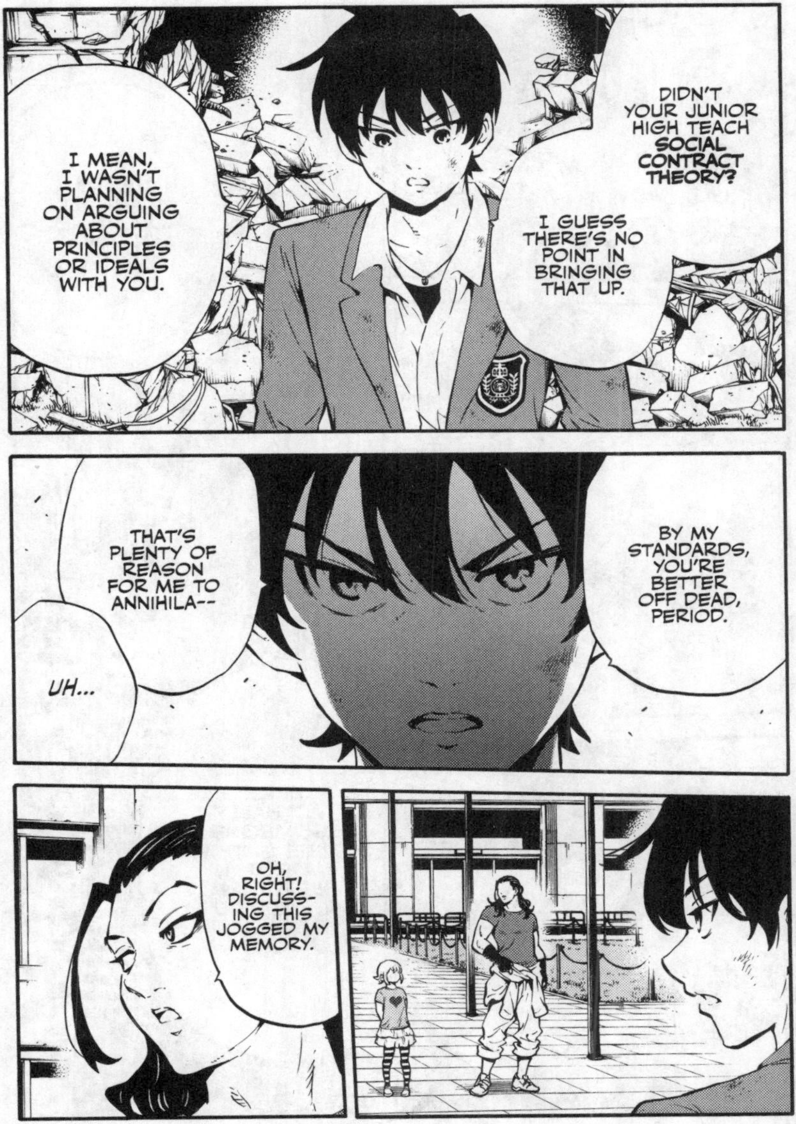
DIDN'T YOUR JUNIOR HIGH TEACH SOCIAL CONTRACT THEORY?
I GUESS THERE'S NO POINT IN BRINGING THAT UP.
I MEAN, I WASN'T PLANNING ON ARGUING ABOUT PRINCIPLES OR IDEALS WITH YOU.
BY MY STANDARDS, YOU'RE BETTER OFF DEAD, PERIOD.
THAT'S PLENTY OF REASON FOR ME TO ANNIHILA--
UH...
OH, RIGHT! DISCUSS-ING THIS JOGGED MY MEMORY.

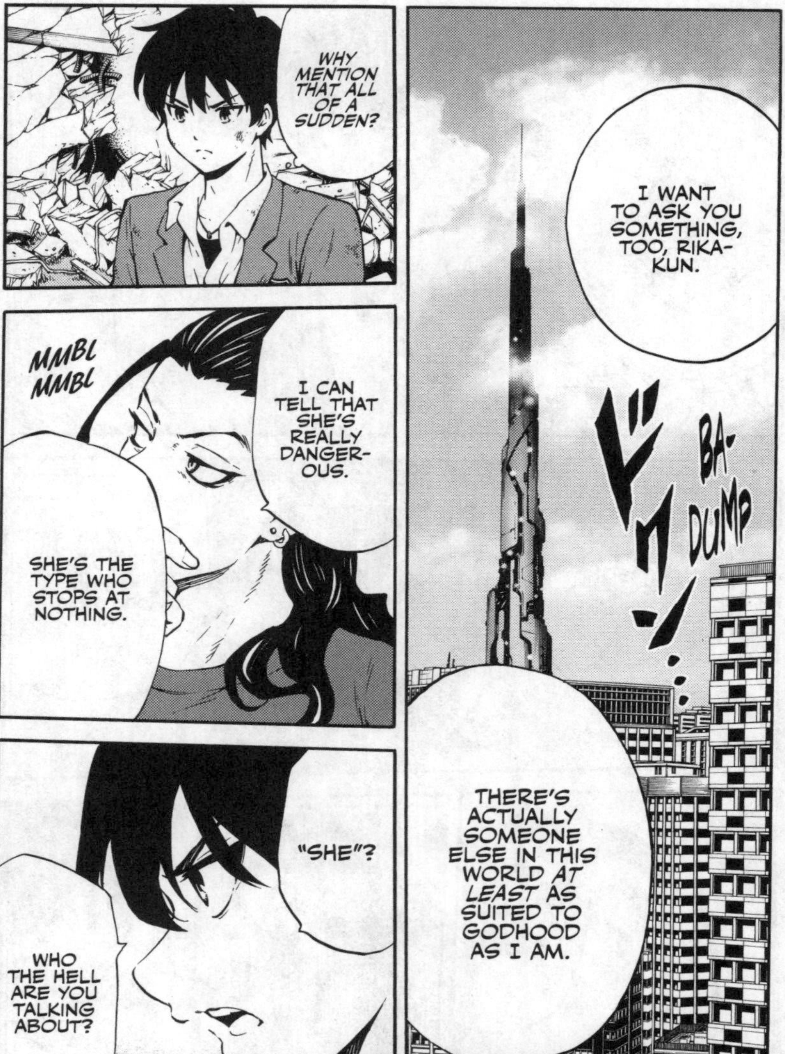
I WANT TO ASK YOU SOMETHING, TOO, RIKA-KUN.
BA-DUMP
THERE'S ACTUALLY SOMEONE ELSE IN THIS WORLD *AT LEAST* AS SUITED TO GODHOOD AS I AM.
WHY MENTION THAT ALL OF A SUDDEN?
MMBL MMBL
I CAN TELL THAT SHE'S REALLY DANGER-OUS.
SHE'S THE TYPE WHO STOPS AT NOTHING.
"SHE"?
WHO THE HELL ARE YOU TALKING ABOUT?

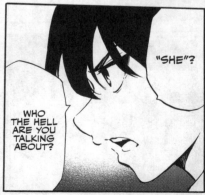

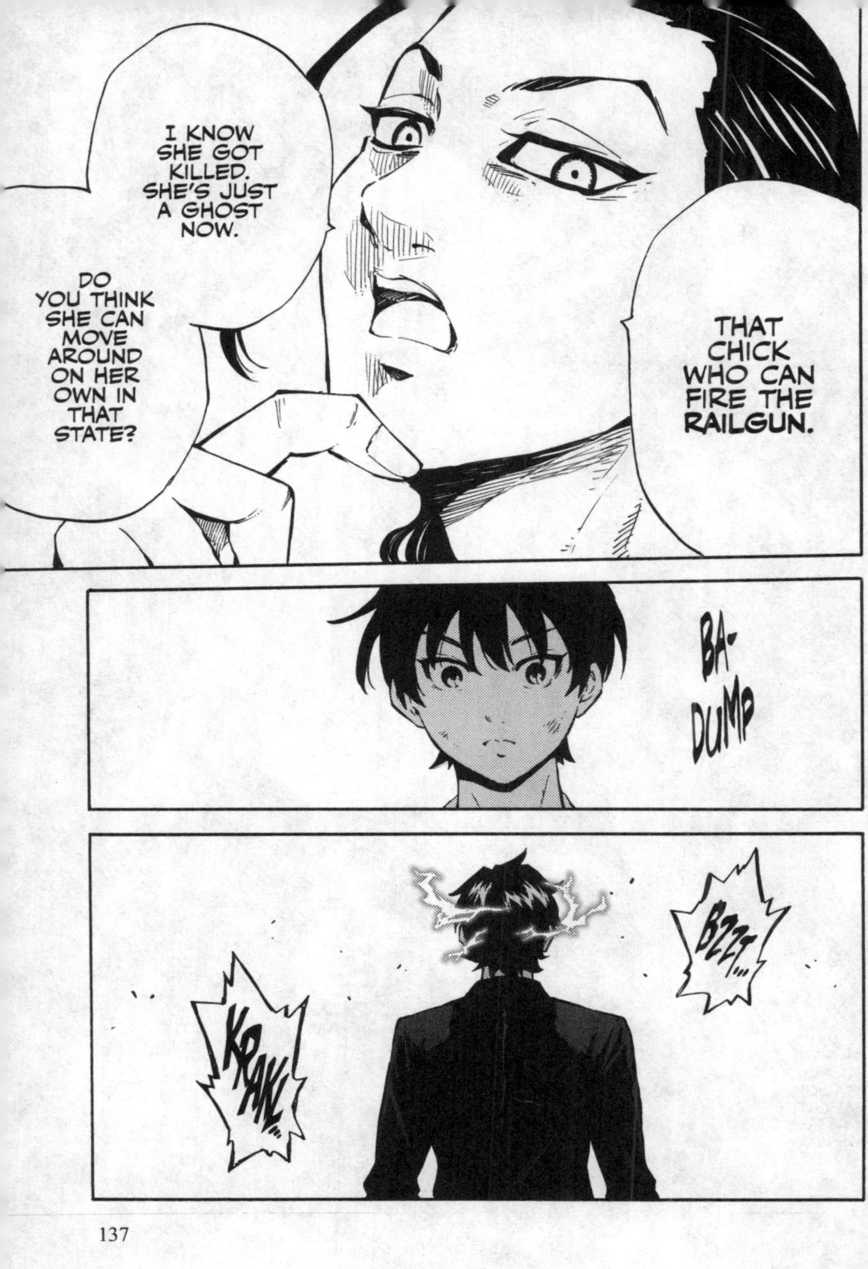
THAT CHICK WHO CAN FIRE THE RAILGUN.
I KNOW SHE GOT KILLED. SHE'S JUST A GHOST NOW.
DO YOU THINK SHE CAN MOVE AROUND ON HER OWN IN THAT STATE?
BA-DUMP
BZZT...
KRAK!...

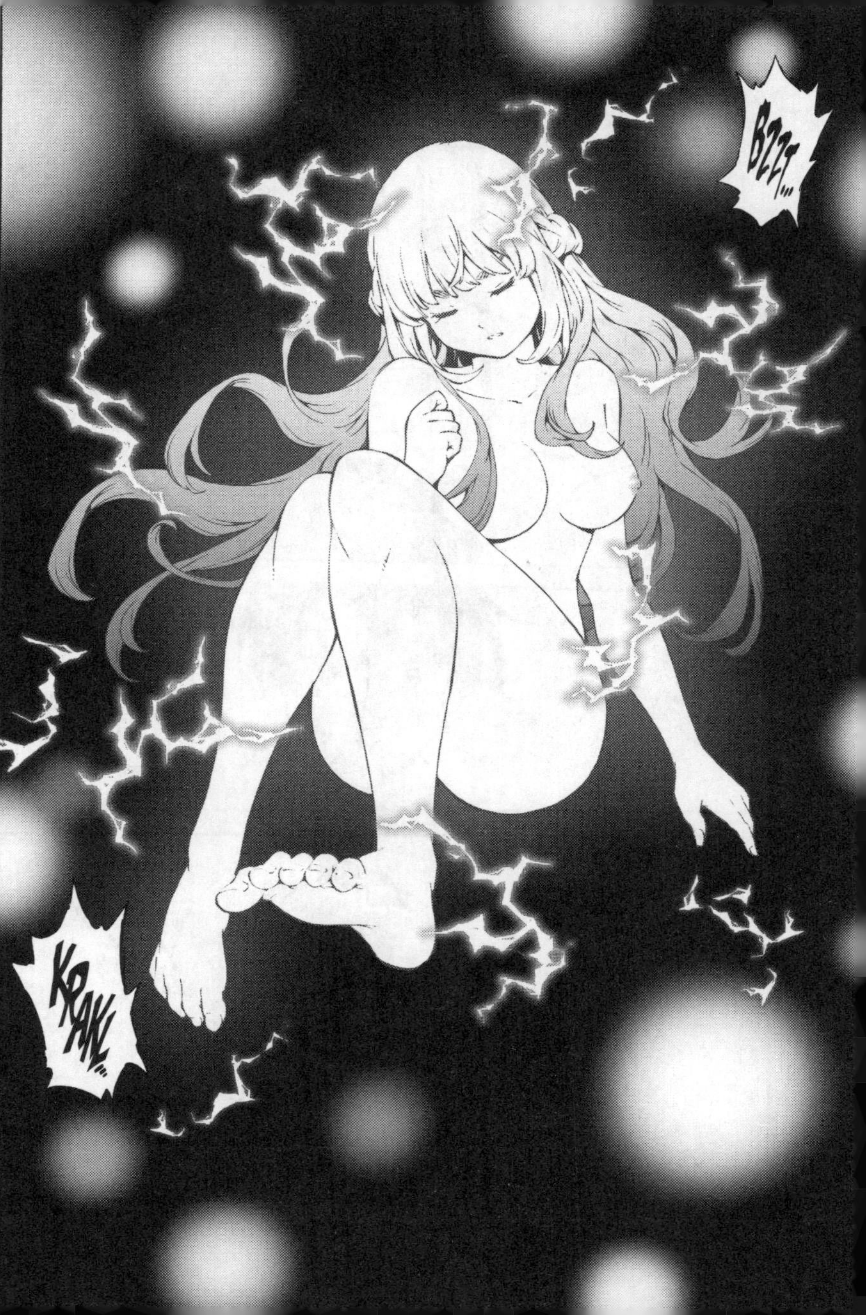
BZZT...
KRAKL...

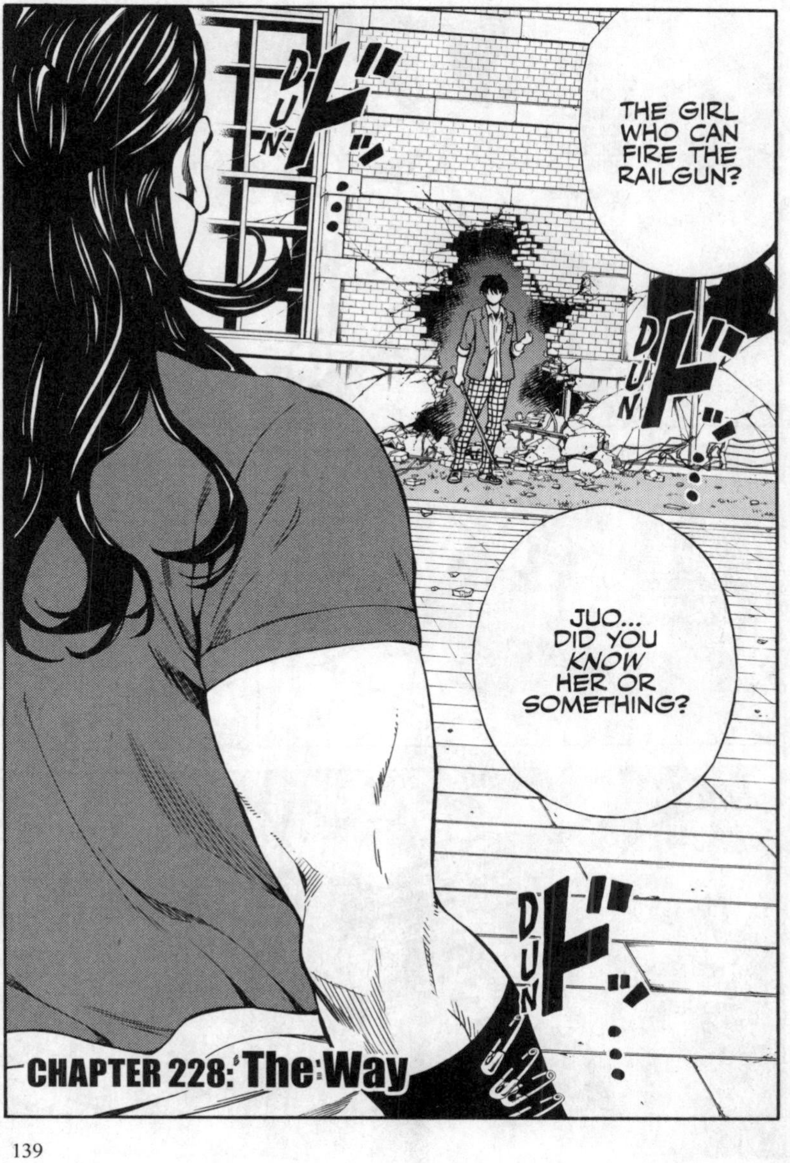
THE GIRL WHO CAN FIRE THE RAILGUN?
DUN...
DUN...
JUO... DID YOU KNOW HER OR SOMETHING?
DUN...
CHAPTER 228: The Way

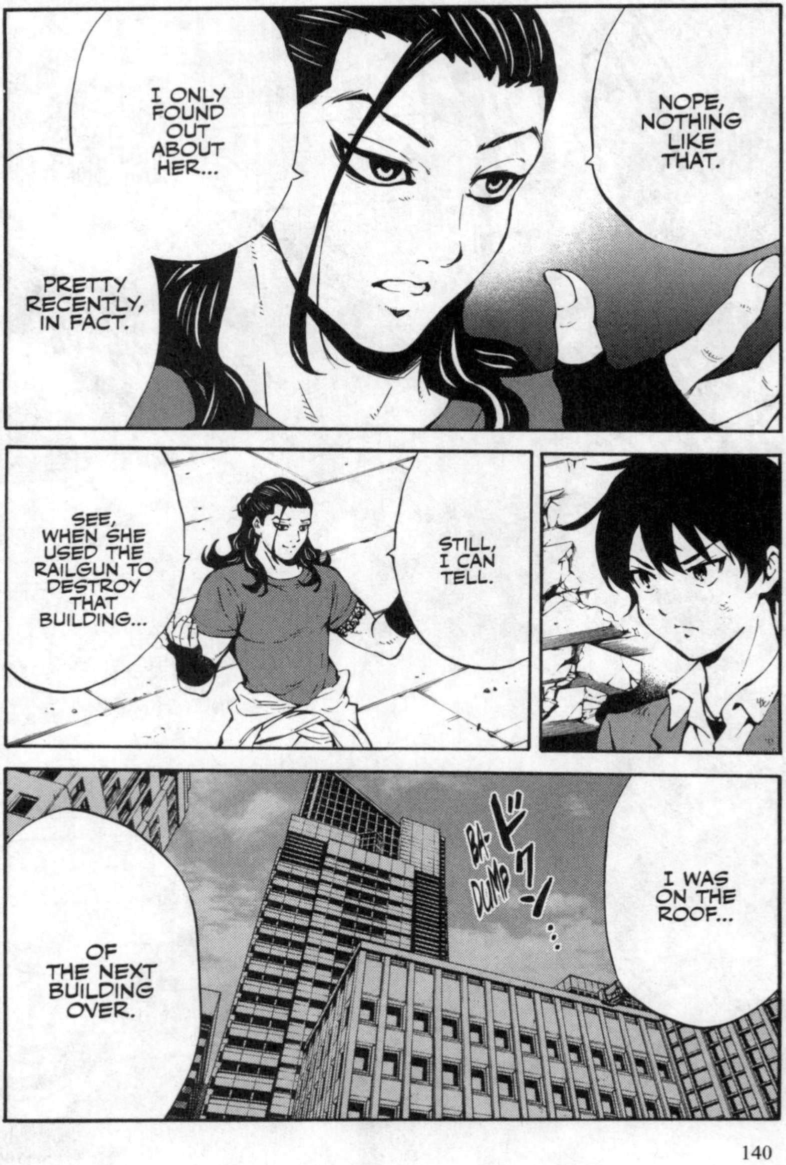
NOPE, NOTHING LIKE THAT.
I ONLY FOUND OUT ABOUT HER...
PRETTY RECENTLY, IN FACT.
STILL, I CAN TELL.
SEE, WHEN SHE USED THE RAILGUN TO DESTROY THAT BUILDING...
I WAS ON THE ROOF...
BA-DUMP
OF THE NEXT BUILDING OVER.

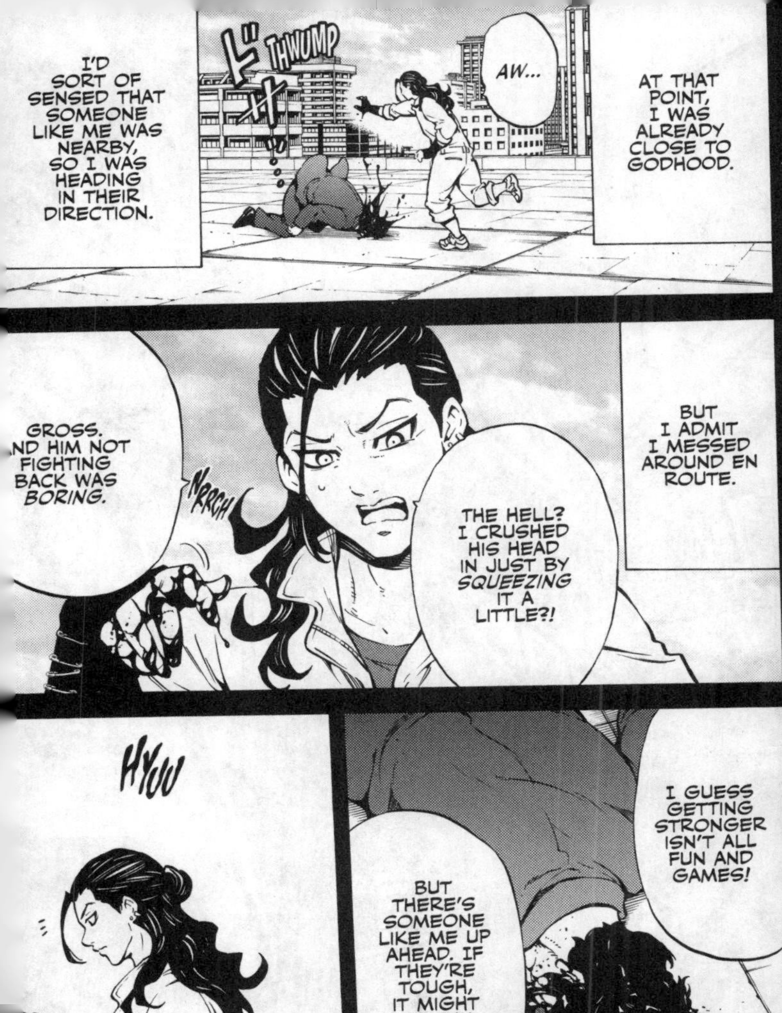
AT THAT POINT, I WAS ALREADY CLOSE TO GODHOOD.
AW...
THWUMP
I'D SORT OF SENSED THAT SOMEONE LIKE ME WAS NEARBY, SO I WAS HEADING IN THEIR DIRECTION.
BUT I ADMIT I MESSED AROUND EN ROUTE.
THE HELL? I CRUSHED HIS HEAD IN JUST BY *SQUEEZING* IT A LITTLE?!
NRRCH
GROSS. ND HIM NOT FIGHTING BACK WAS *BORING*.
I GUESS GETTING STRONGER ISN'T ALL FUN AND GAMES!
BUT THERE'S SOMEONE LIKE ME UP AHEAD. IF THEY'RE TOUGH, IT MIGHT BE FUN FIGHTING 'EM.
HYUU

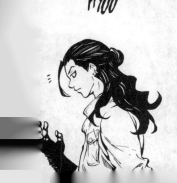

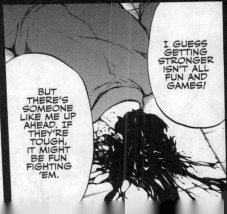

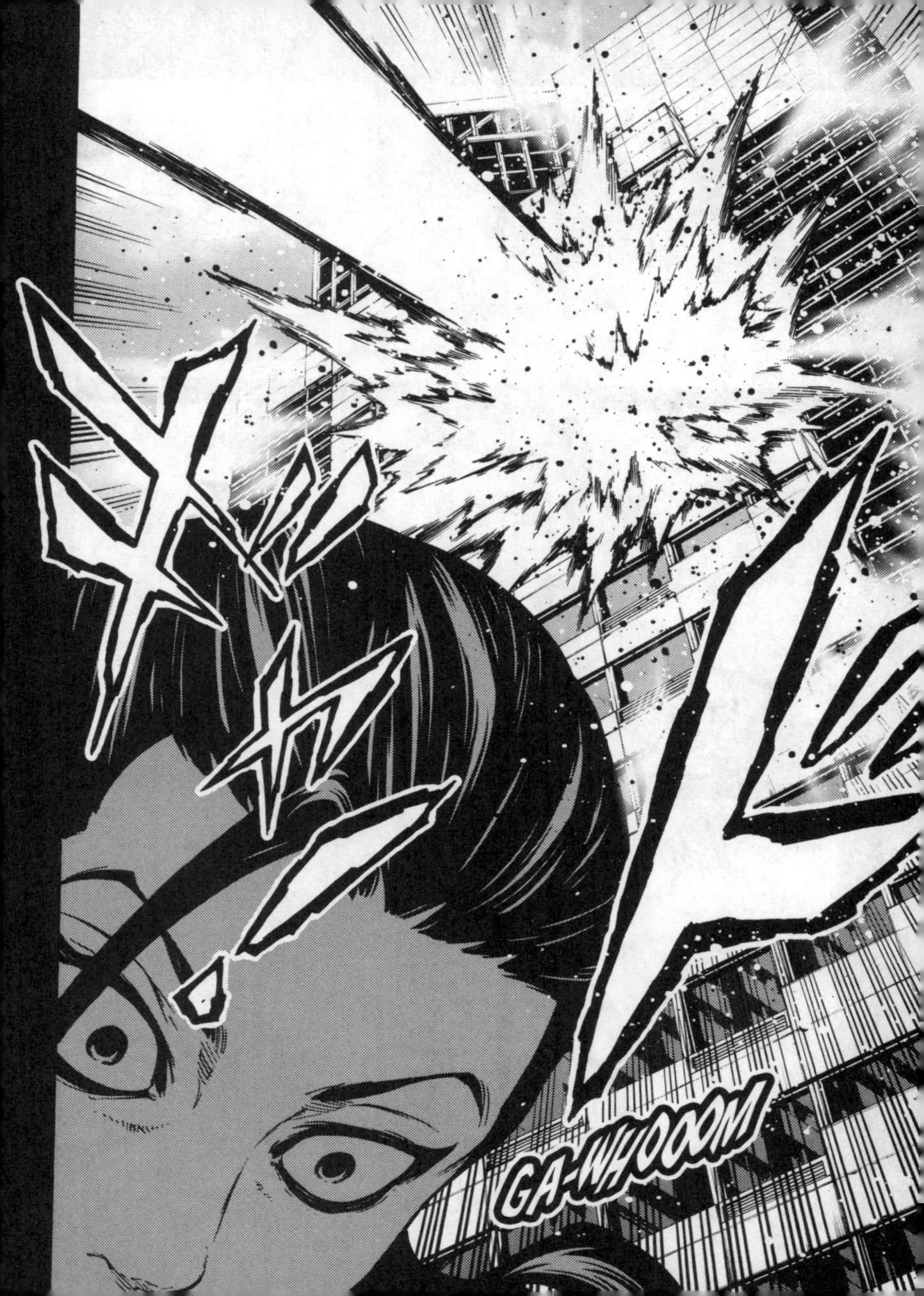
GA-WHOOOM

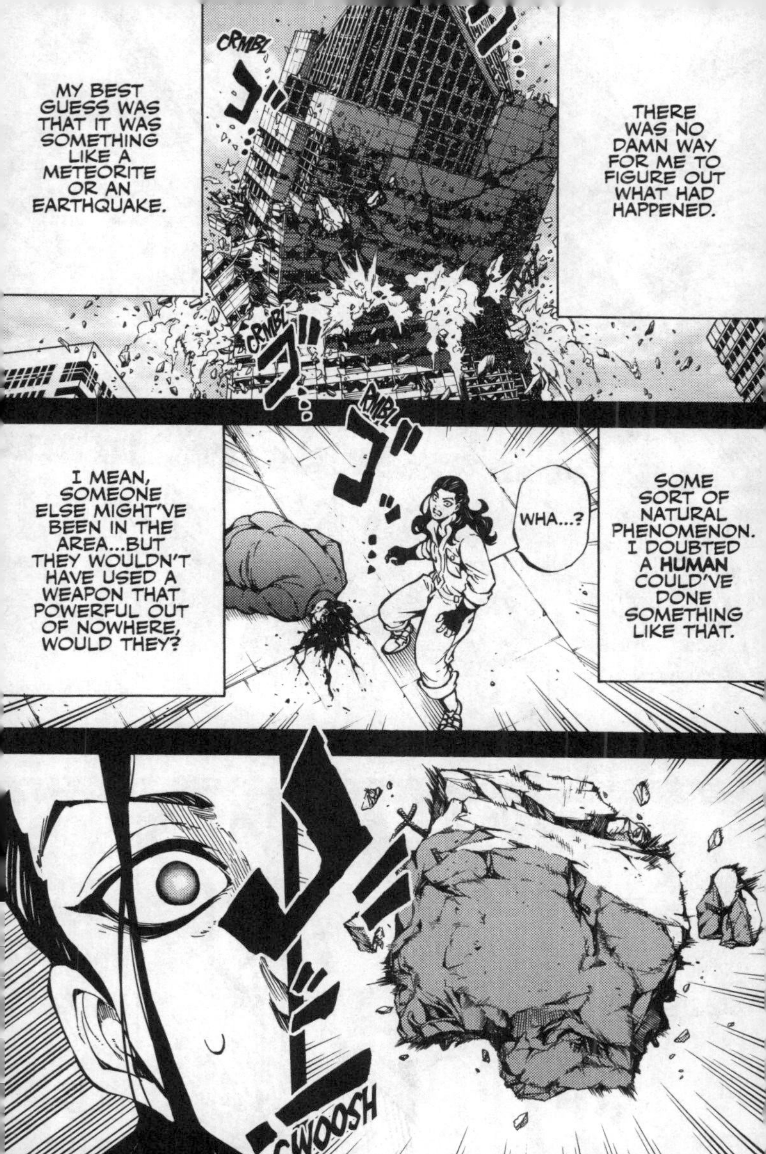
THERE WAS NO DAMN WAY FOR ME TO FIGURE OUT WHAT HAD HAPPENED.
CRMBL
MY BEST GUESS WAS THAT IT WAS SOMETHING LIKE A METEORITE OR AN EARTHQUAKE.
CRMBL
SOME SORT OF NATURAL PHENOMENON. I DOUBTED A **HUMAN** COULD'VE DONE SOMETHING LIKE THAT.
WHA...?
RMBL
I MEAN, SOMEONE ELSE MIGHT'VE BEEN IN THE AREA...BUT THEY WOULDN'T HAVE USED A WEAPON THAT POWERFUL OUT OF NOWHERE, WOULD THEY?
GWOOSH

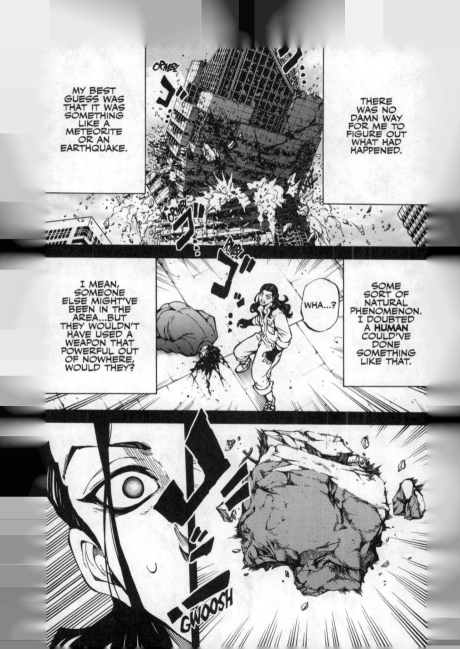

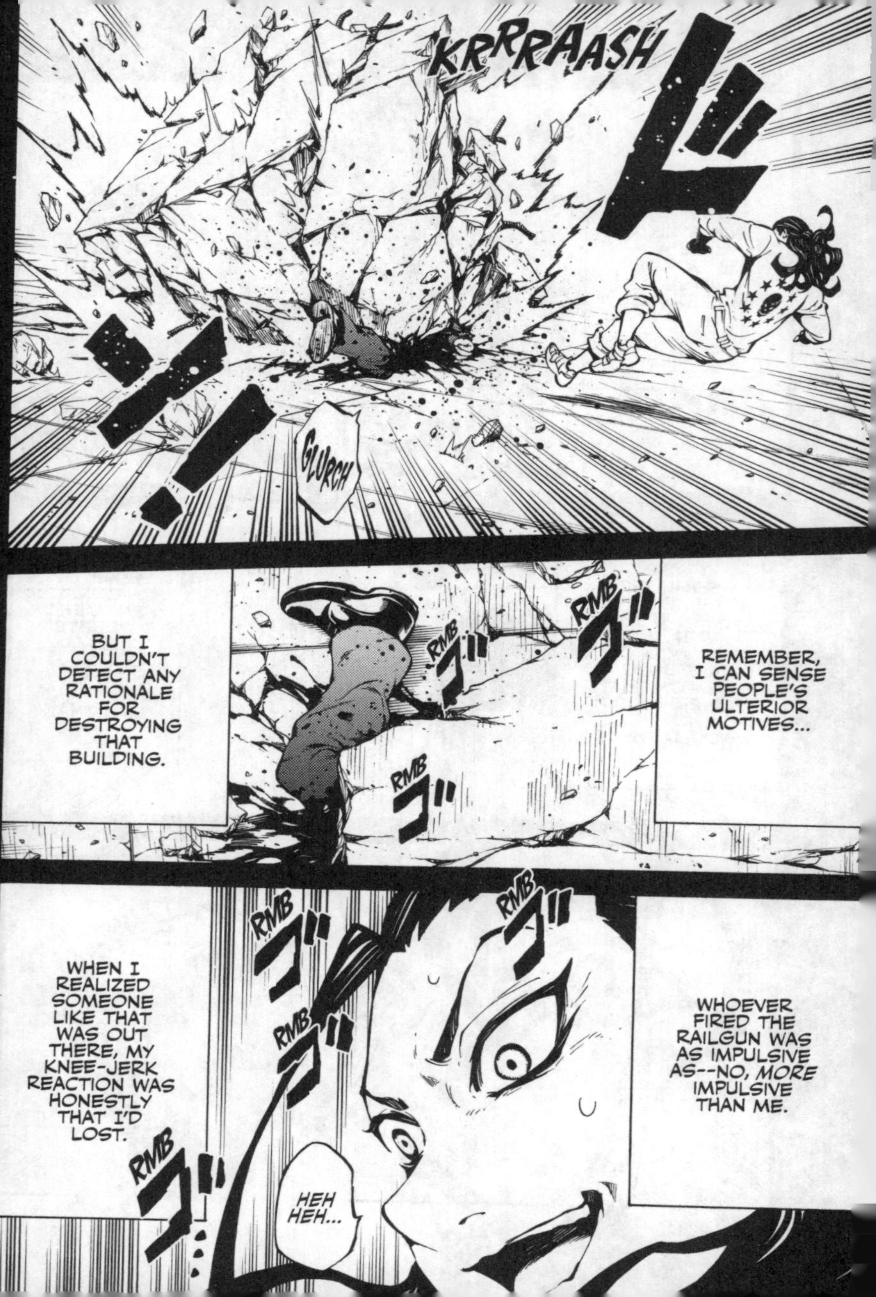
KRRRAASH
GLURCH
REMEMBER, I CAN SENSE PEOPLE'S ULTERIOR MOTIVES...
RMB
RMB
RMB
BUT I COULDN'T DETECT ANY RATIONALE FOR DESTROYING THAT BUILDING.
WHOEVER FIRED THE RAILGUN WAS AS IMPULSIVE AS--NO, *MORE* IMPULSIVE THAN ME.
RMB
RMB
RMB
WHEN I REALIZED SOMEONE LIKE THAT WAS OUT THERE, MY KNEE-JERK REACTION WAS HONESTLY THAT I'D LOST.
HEH HEH...
RMB

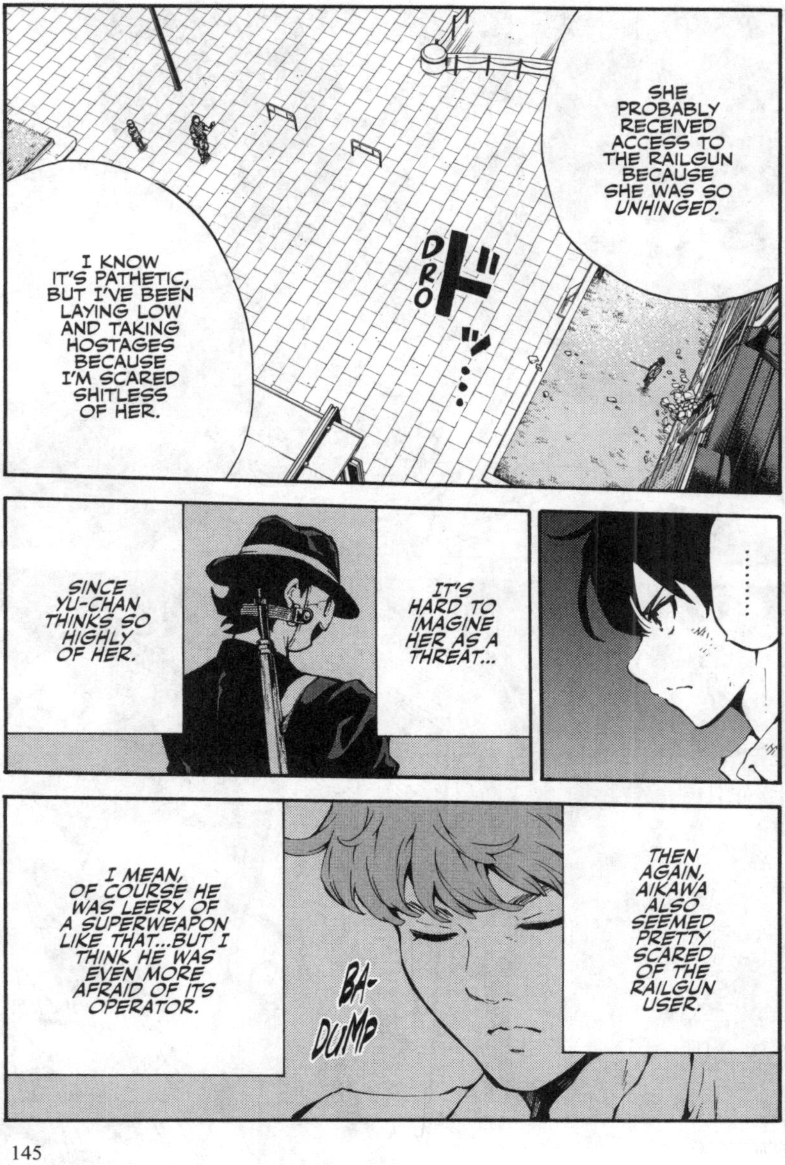
SHE PROBABLY RECEIVED ACCESS TO THE RAILGUN BECAUSE SHE WAS SO *UNHINGED*.
I KNOW IT'S PATHETIC, BUT I'VE BEEN LAYING LOW AND TAKING HOSTAGES BECAUSE I'M SCARED SHITLESS OF HER.
DRO
......
IT'S HARD TO IMAGINE HER AS A THREAT...
SINCE YU-CHAN THINKS SO HIGHLY OF HER.
THEN AGAIN, AIKAWA ALSO SEEMED PRETTY SCARED OF THE RAILGUN USER.
BA-DUMP
I MEAN, OF COURSE HE WAS LEERY OF A SUPERWEAPON LIKE THAT...BUT I THINK HE WAS EVEN MORE AFRAID OF ITS OPERATOR.

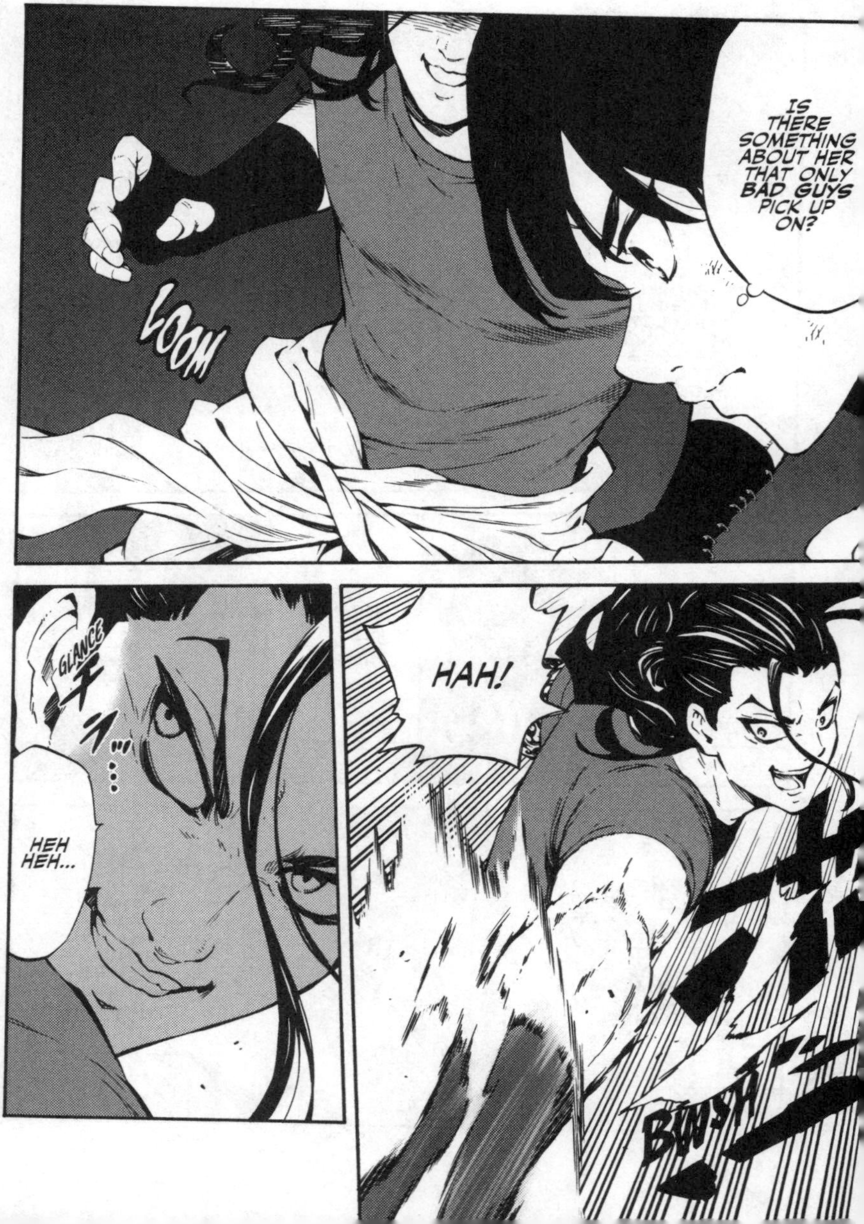
IS THERE SOMETHING ABOUT HER THAT ONLY BAD GUYS PICK UP ON?
LOOM
HAH!
BWSH
GLANCE
...
HEH HEH...

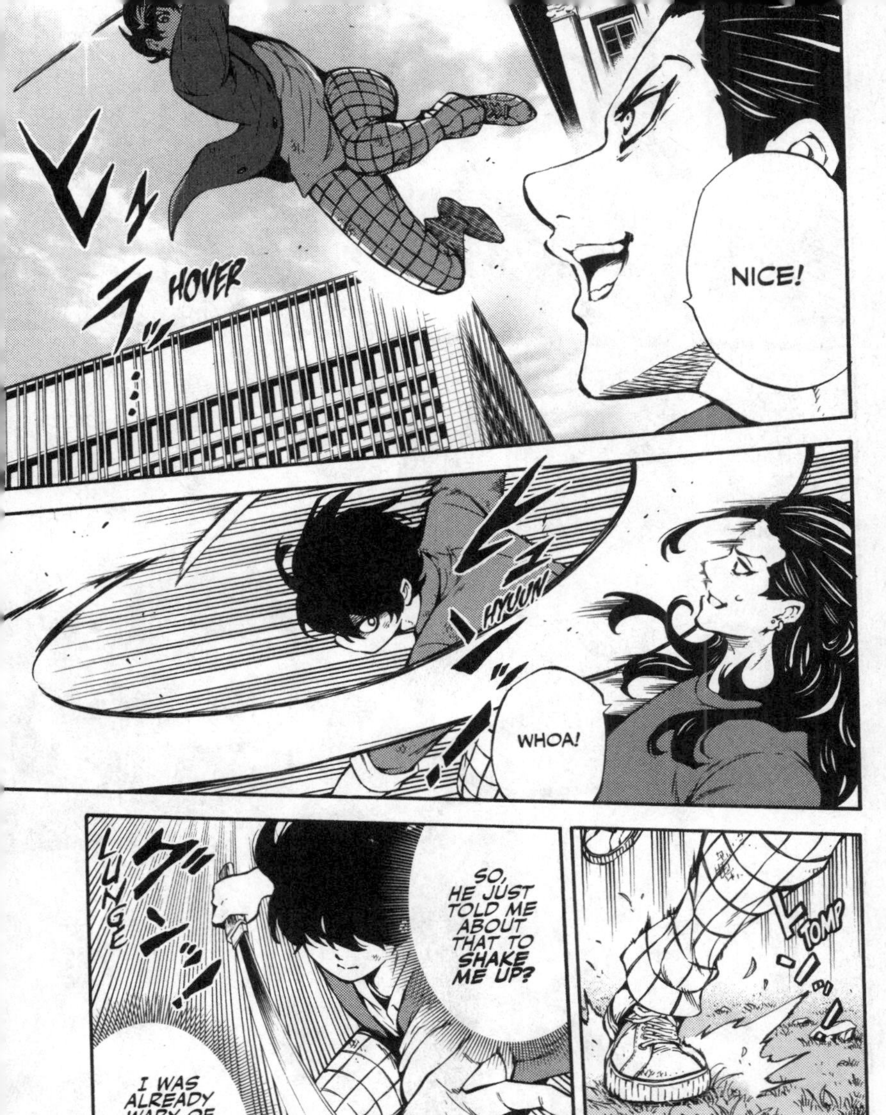
NICE!
HOVER
HYUUN
WHOA!
TOMP
SO, HE JUST TOLD ME ABOUT THAT TO SHAKE ME UP?
LUNGE
I WAS ALREADY WARY OF HIM TRYING SOMETHING LIKE THAT.

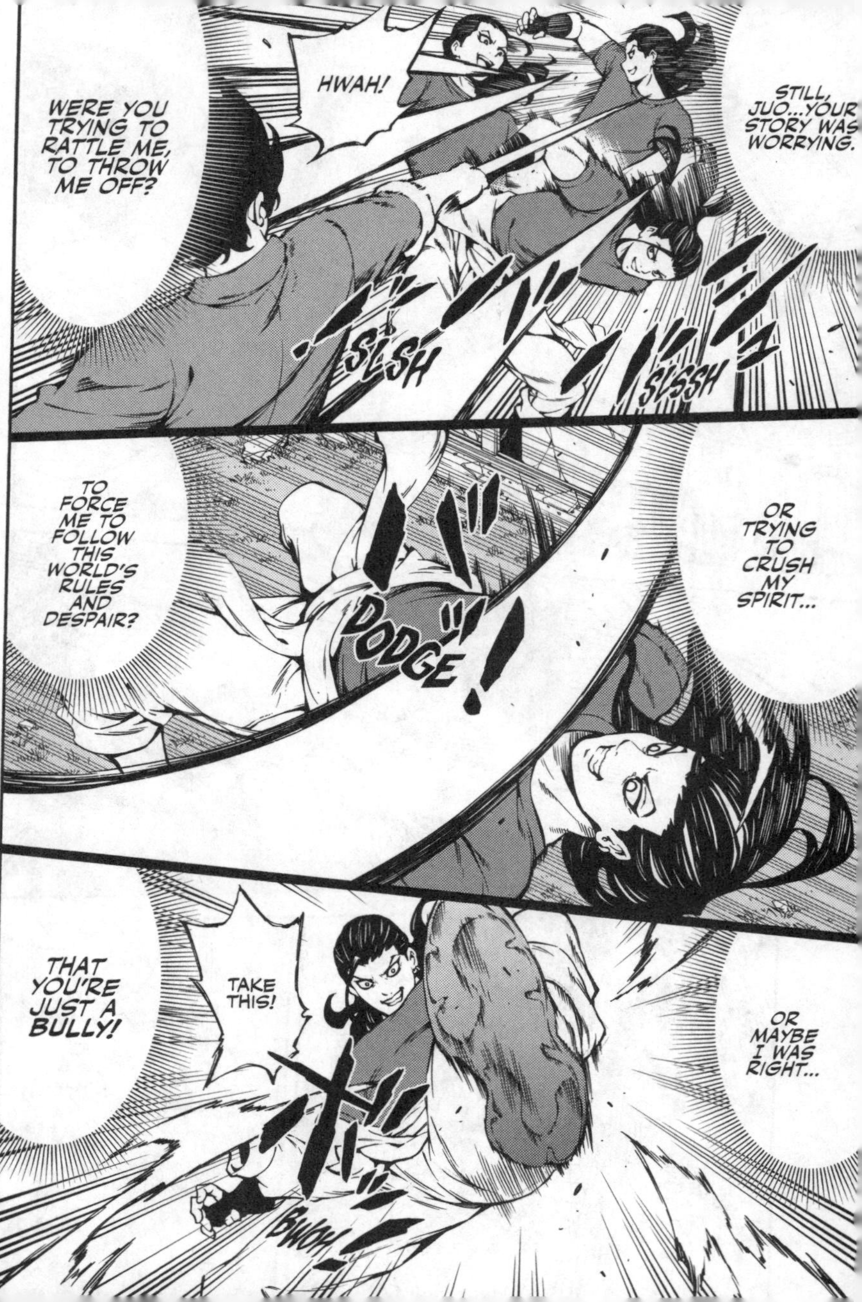
STILL, JUO...YOUR STORY WAS WORRYING.
HWAH!
WERE YOU TRYING TO RATTLE ME, TO THROW ME OFF?
SLSSH
SLSH
OR TRYING TO CRUSH MY SPIRIT...
DODGE
TO FORCE ME TO FOLLOW THIS WORLD'S RULES AND DESPAIR?
OR MAYBE I WAS RIGHT...
TAKE THIS!
THAT YOU'RE JUST A BULLY!
BWOH

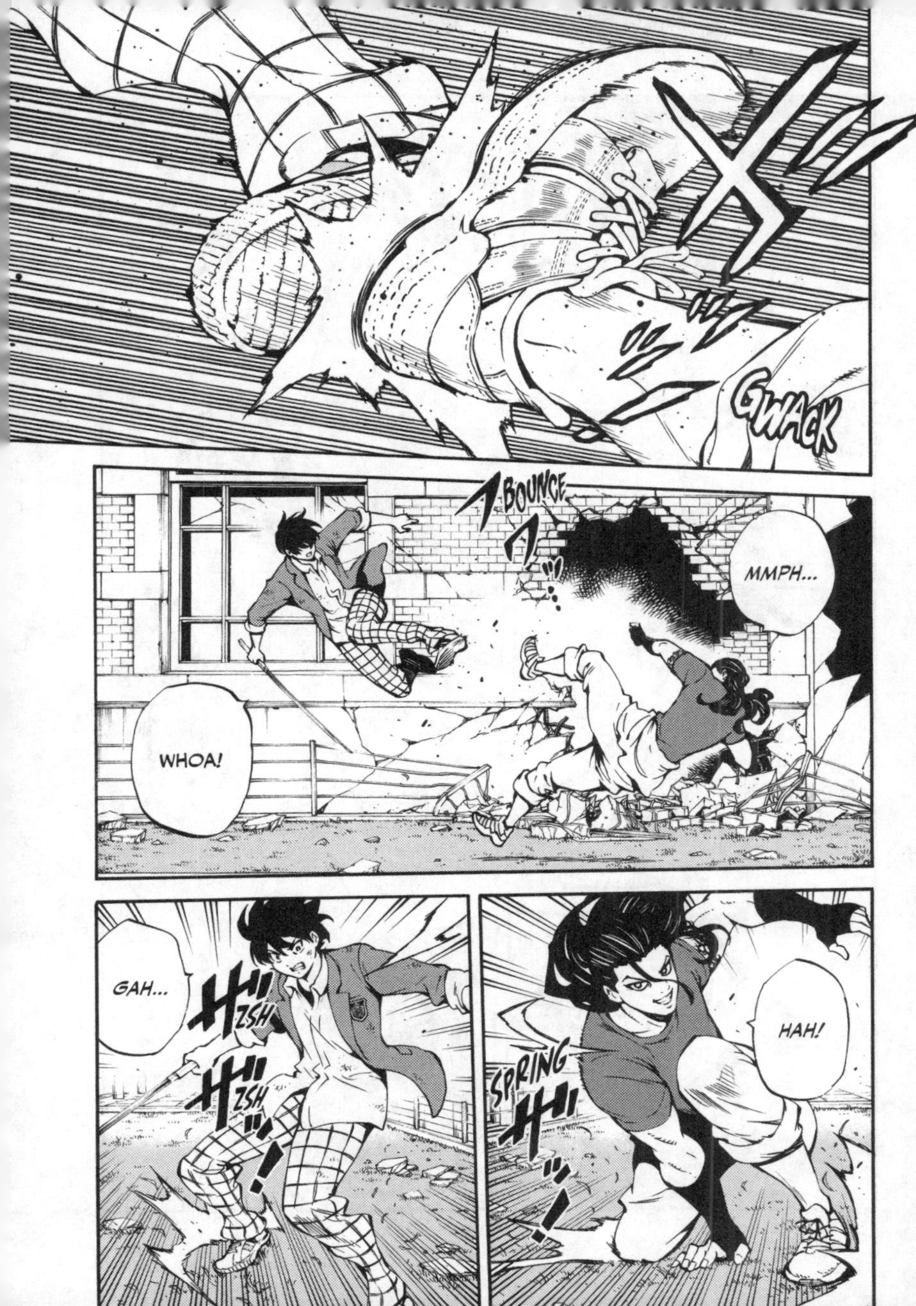
GWACK
MMPH...
BOUNCE
WHOA!
HAH!
SPRING
GAH...
ZSH
ZSH

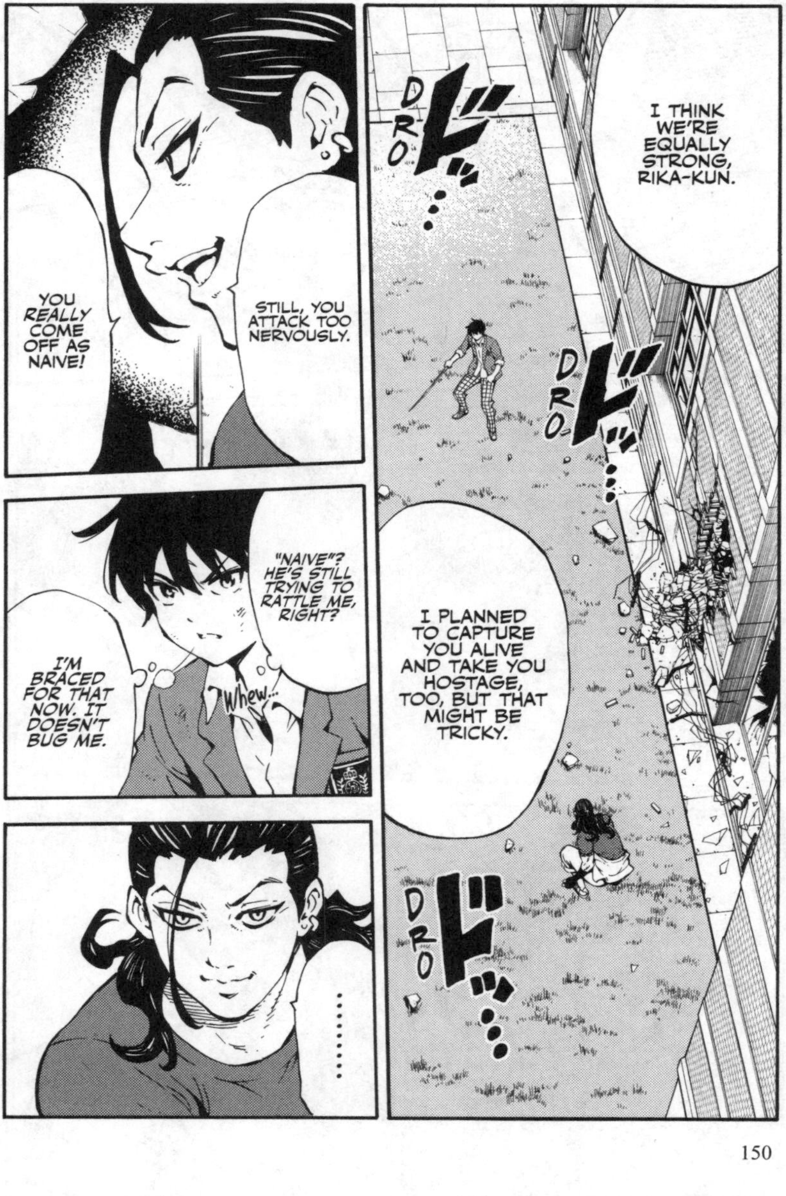
DRO
I THINK WE'RE EQUALLY STRONG, RIKA-KUN.
DRO
I PLANNED TO CAPTURE YOU ALIVE AND TAKE YOU HOSTAGE, TOO, BUT THAT MIGHT BE TRICKY.
DRO
STILL, YOU ATTACK TOO NERVOUSLY.
YOU REALLY COME OFF AS NAIVE!
"NAIVE"? HE'S STILL TRYING TO RATTLE ME, RIGHT?
Whew...
I'M BRACED FOR THAT NOW. IT DOESN'T BUG ME.
....

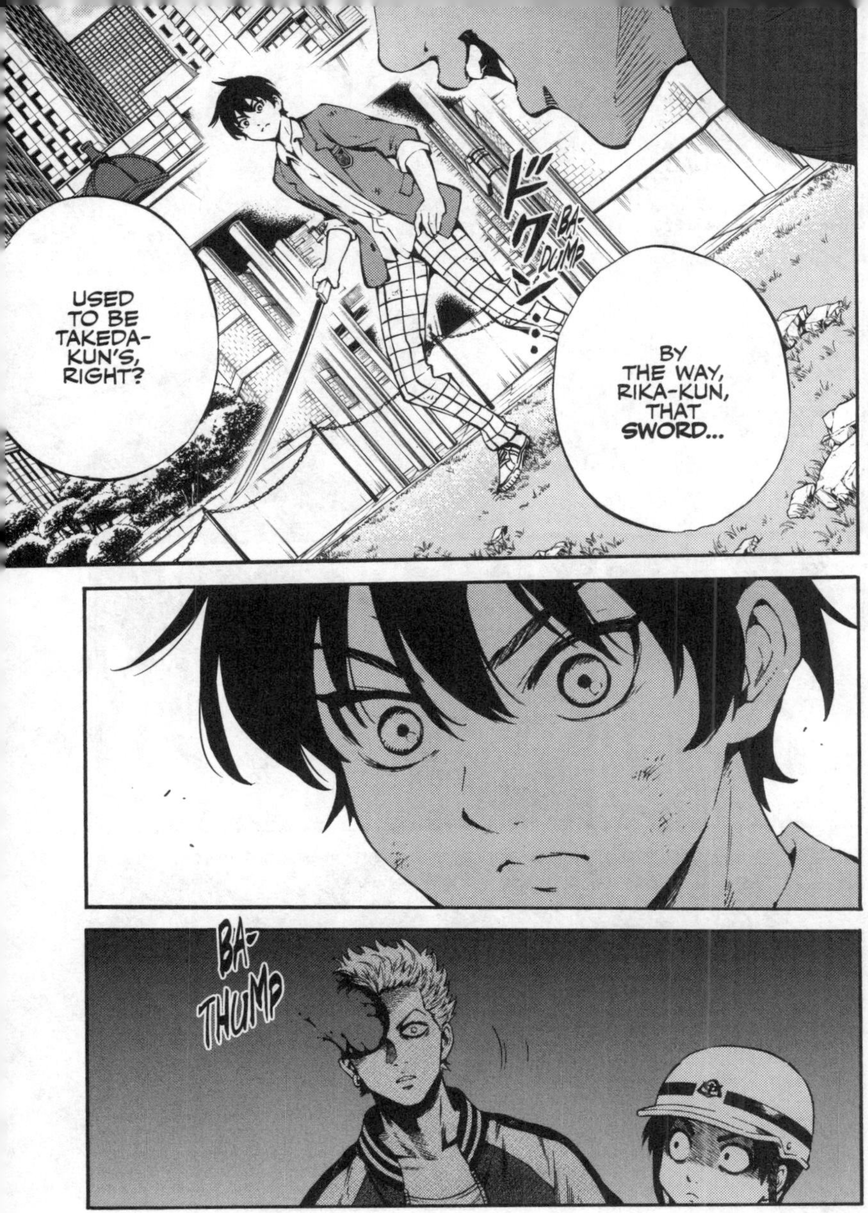
BY THE WAY, RIKA-KUN, THAT SWORD...
BA-DUMP
USED TO BE TAKEDA-KUN'S, RIGHT?
BA-THUMP

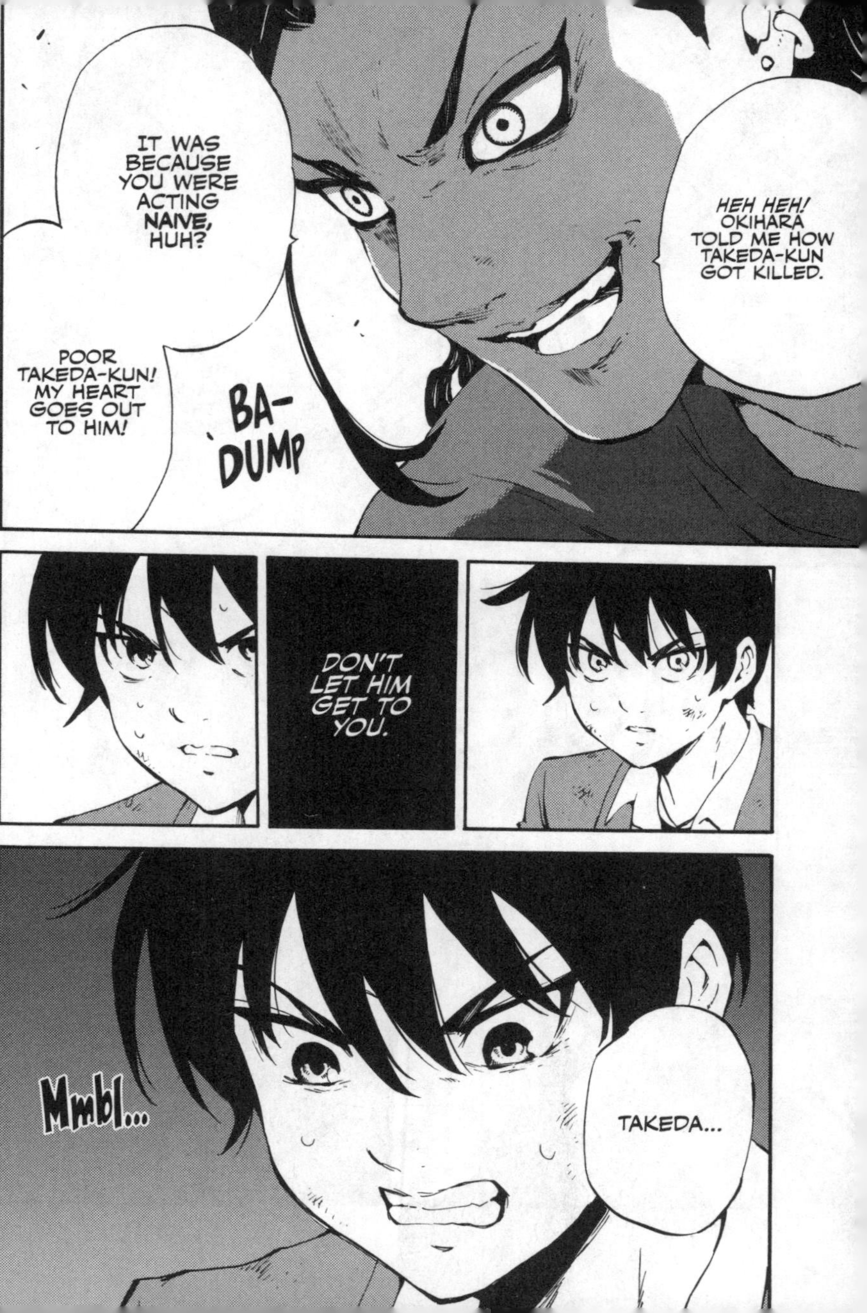
HEH HEH! OKIHARA TOLD ME HOW TAKEDA-KUN GOT KILLED.
IT WAS BECAUSE YOU WERE ACTING NAIVE, HUH?
POOR TAKEDA-KUN! MY HEART GOES OUT TO HIM!
BA-DUMP
DON'T LET HIM GET TO YOU.
TAKEDA...
Mmbl...

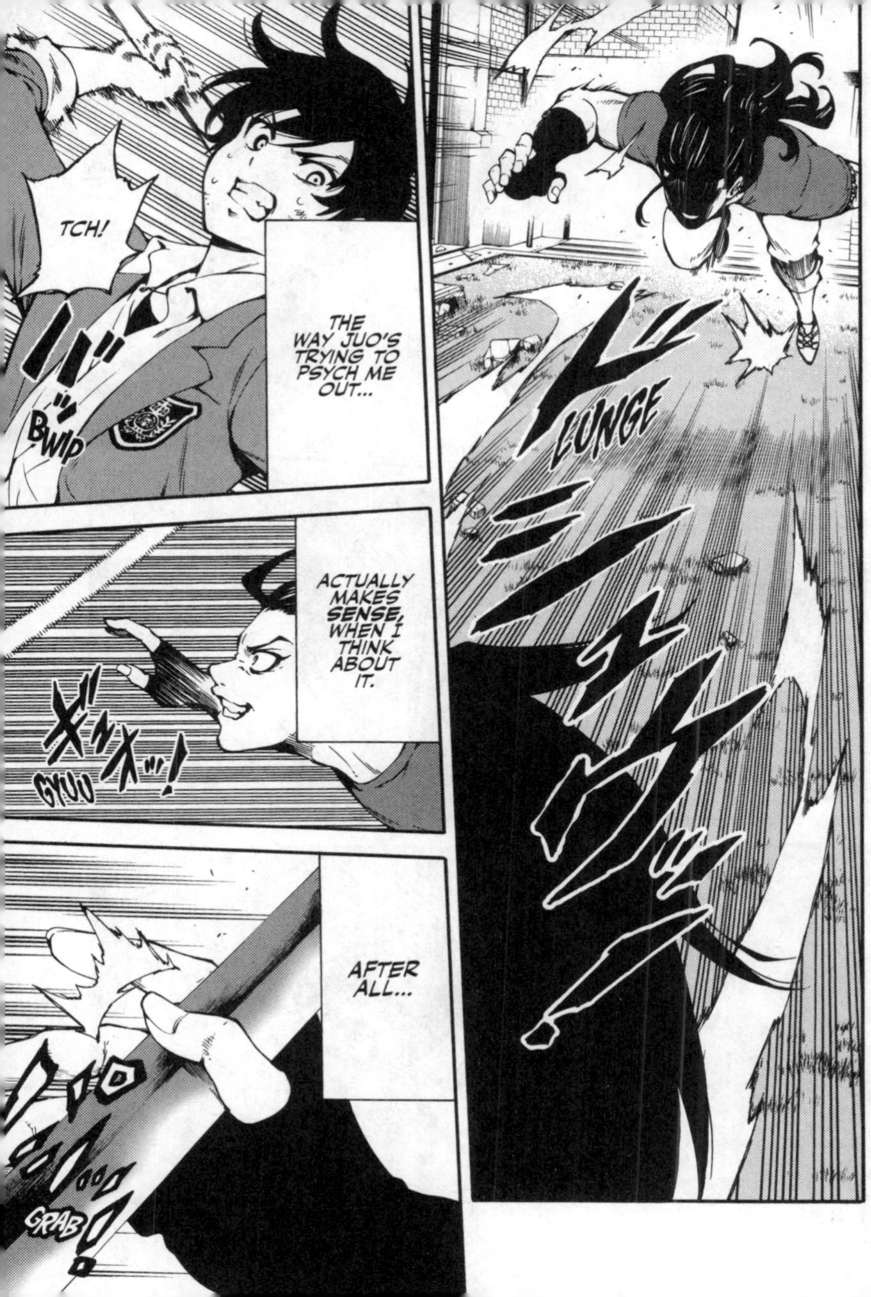
LUNGE
THE WAY JUO'S TRYING TO PSYCH ME OUT...
TCH!
BWIP
ACTUALLY MAKES SENSE, WHEN I THINK ABOUT IT.
GYUU
AFTER ALL...
GRAB

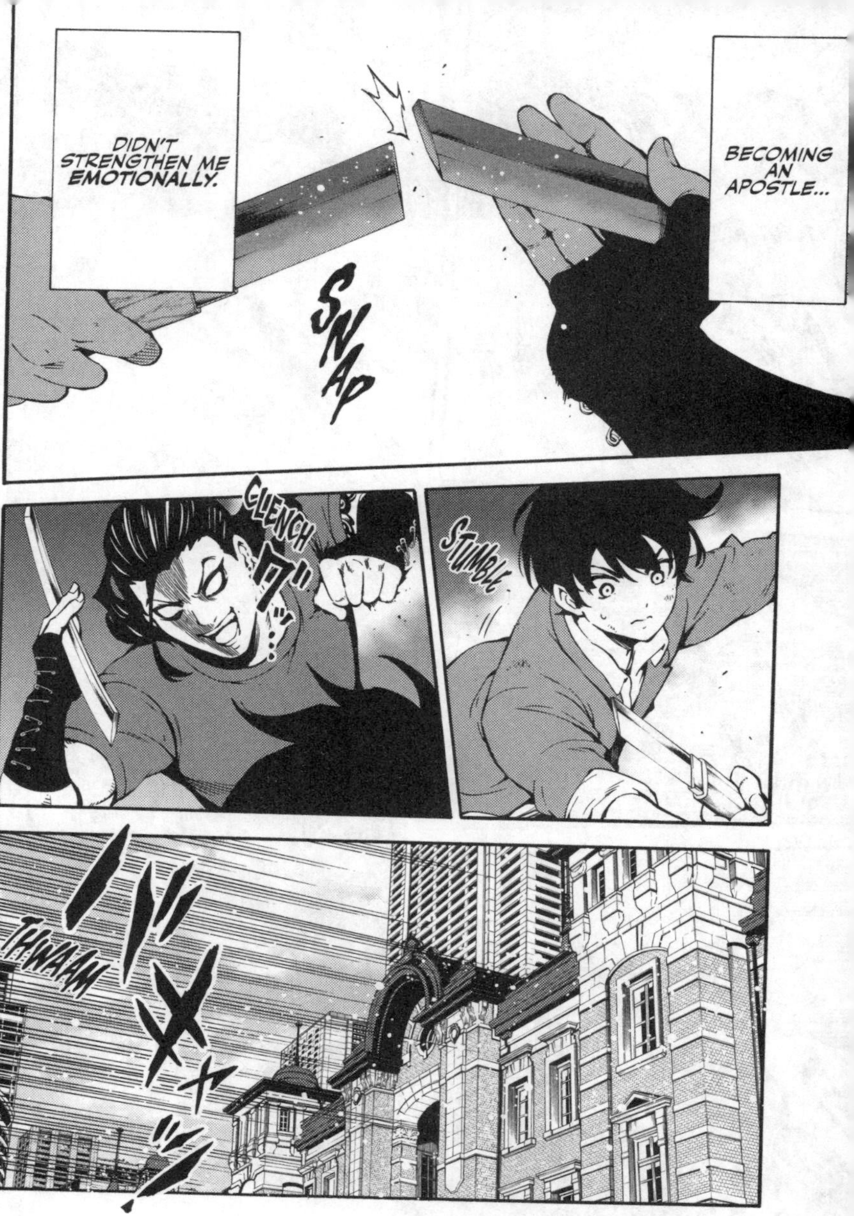
BECOMING AN APOSTLE...
DIDN'T STRENGTHEN ME EMOTIONALLY.
SNAP
STUMBLE
CLENCH
THWAAM

HIGH-RISE INVASION

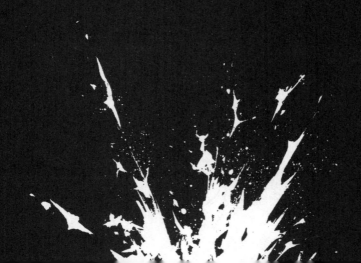

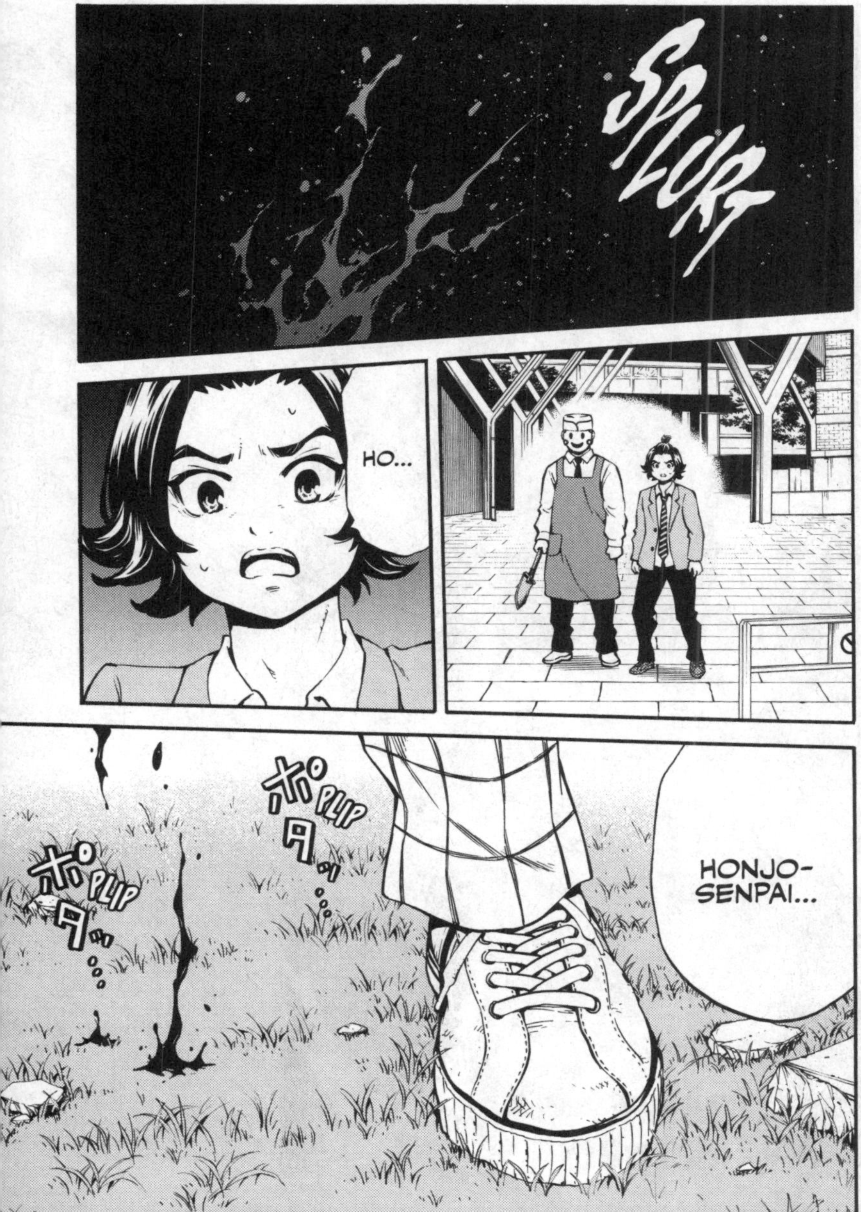
SPLURT
HO...
HONJO-SENPAI...
ポ PLIP タッ...
ポ PLIP タッ...

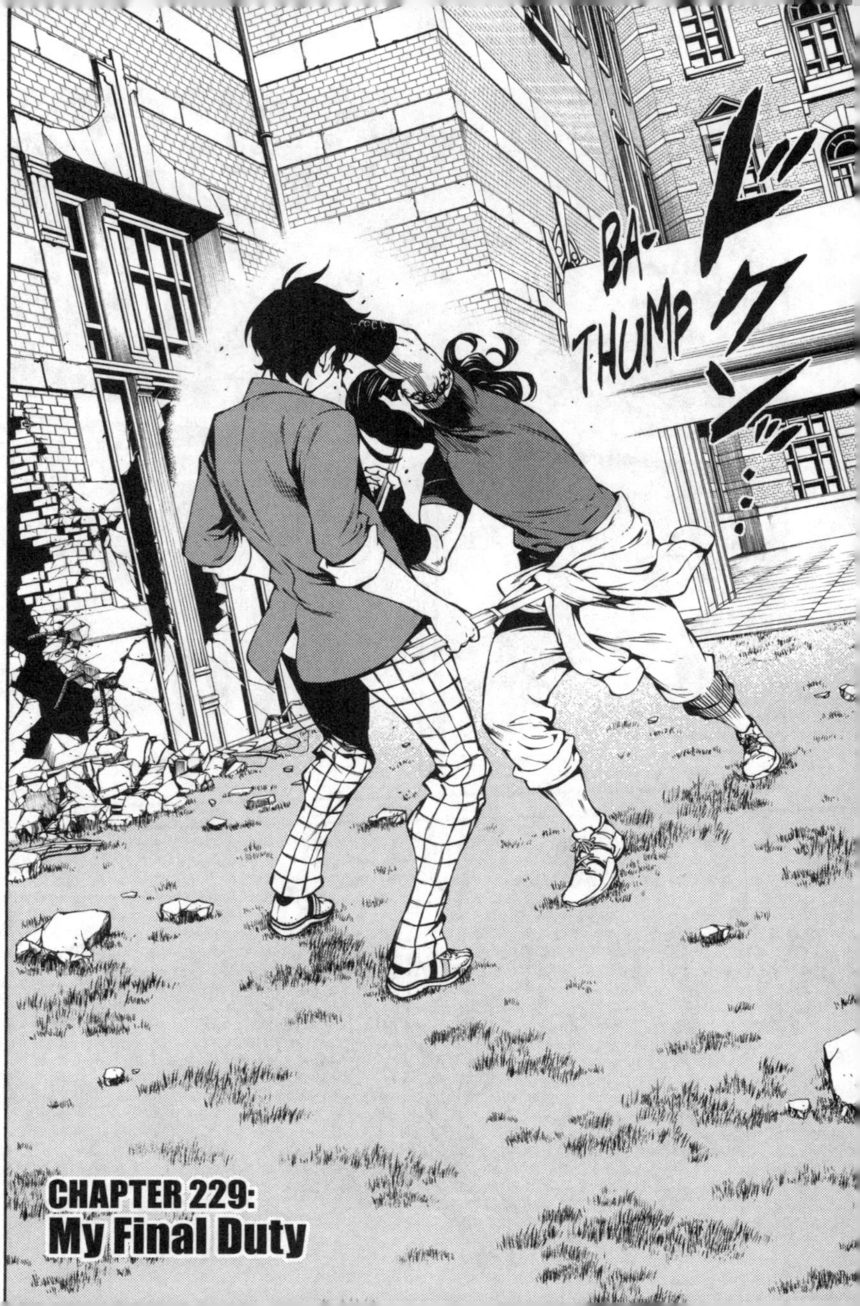
BA-THUMP
ドクン

CHAPTER 229: My Final Duty

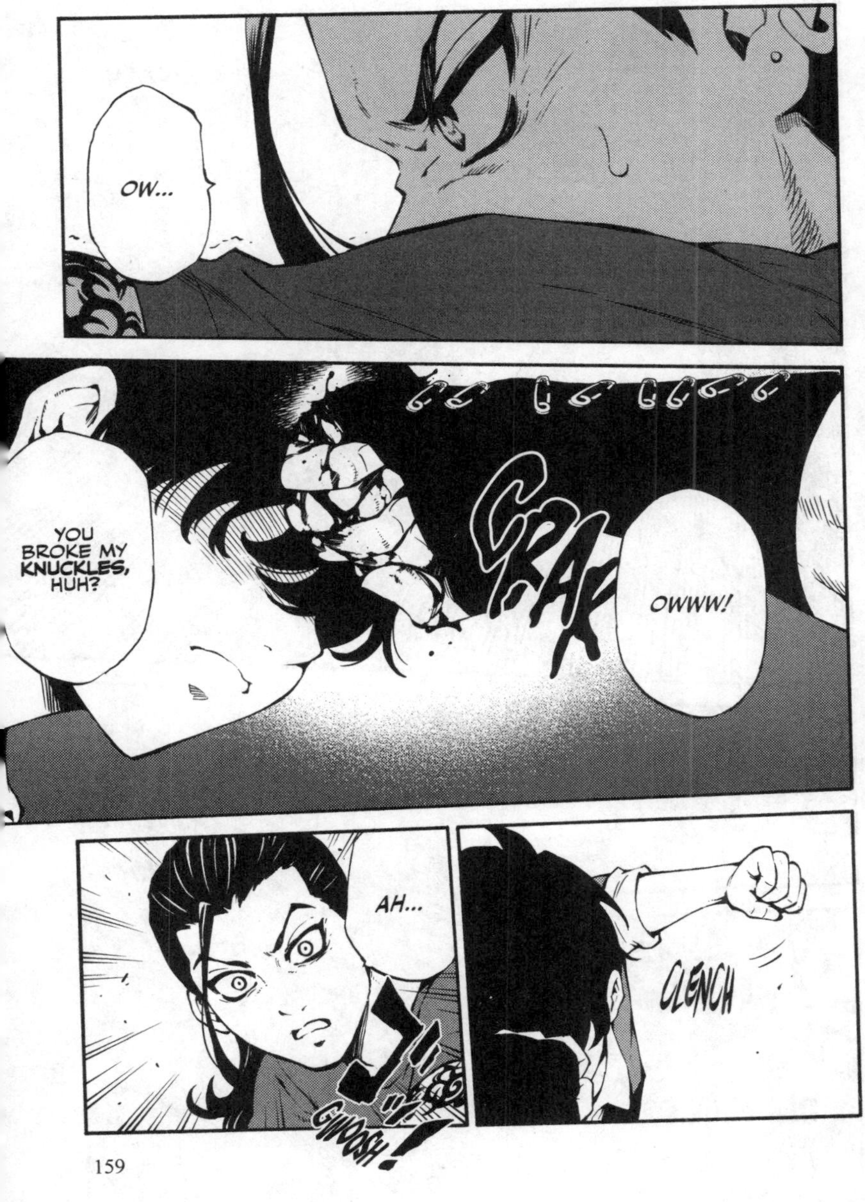
OW...
OWWW!
CRAK
YOU BROKE MY KNUCKLES, HUH?
CLENCH
AH...
GWOOSH!

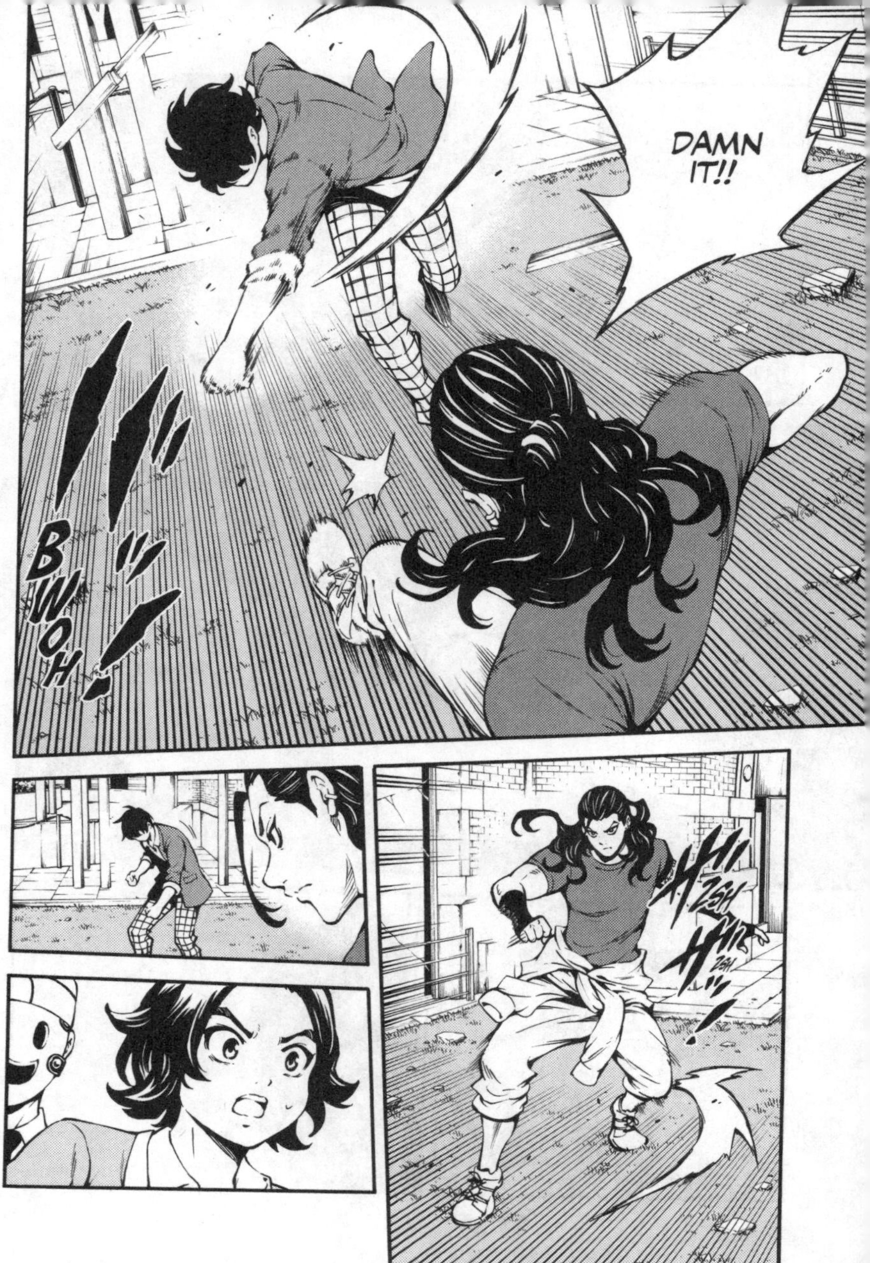
DAMN IT!!
BWOH!

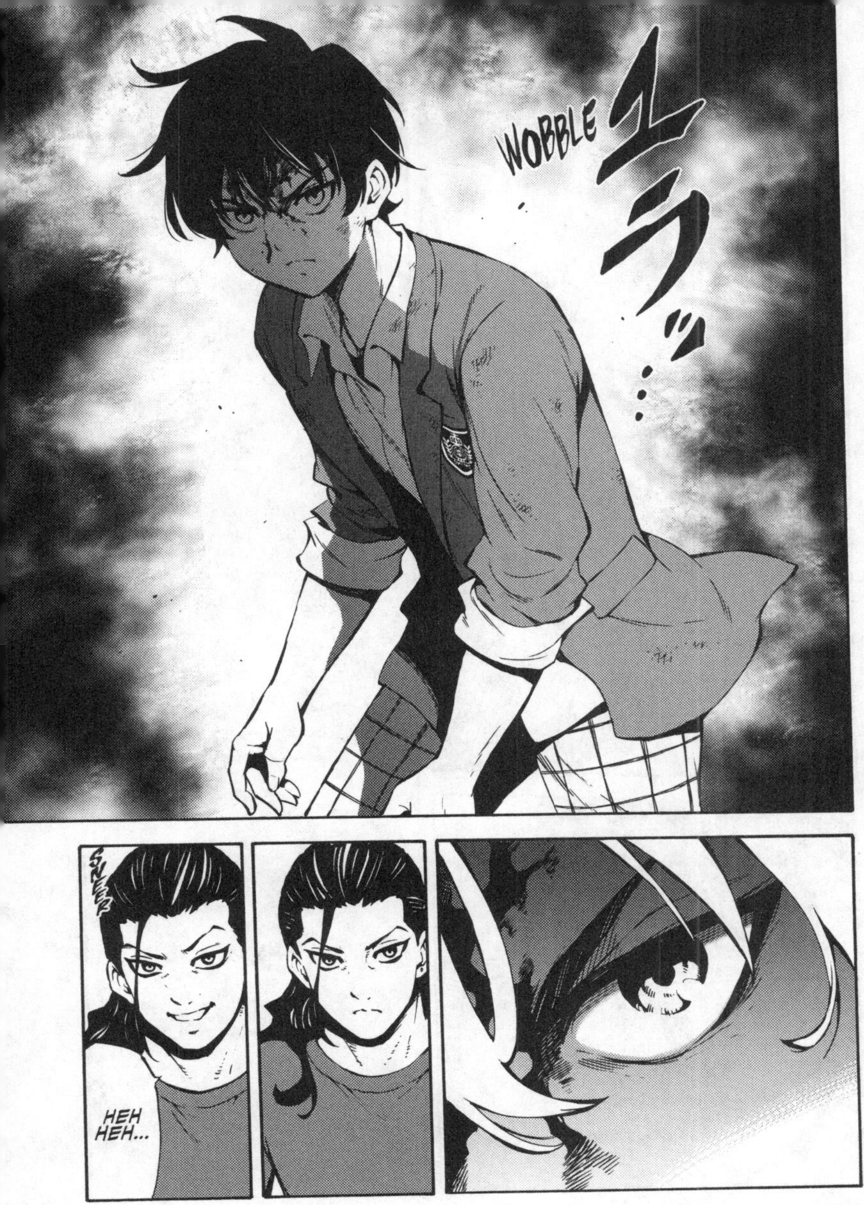
WOBBLE
ユラッ…
SNEER
HEH HEH...

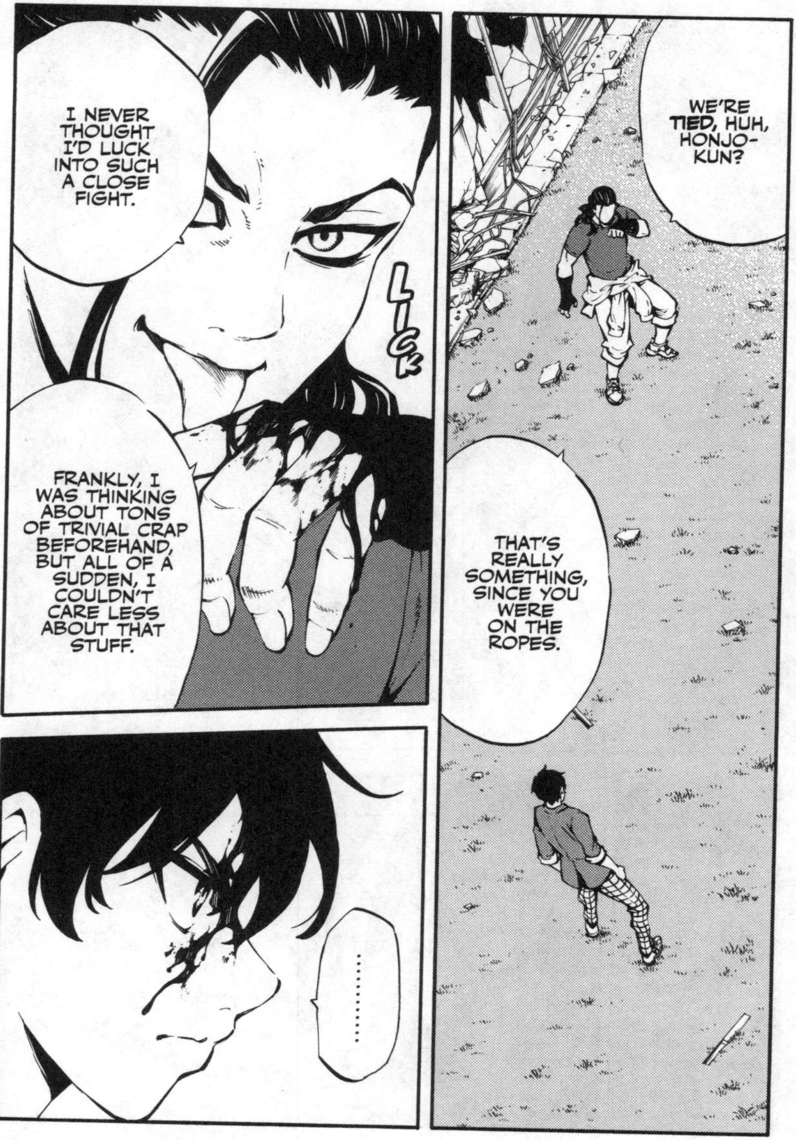
WE'RE TIED, HUH, HONJO-KUN?
THAT'S REALLY SOMETHING, SINCE YOU WERE ON THE ROPES.
I NEVER THOUGHT I'D LUCK INTO SUCH A CLOSE FIGHT.
LICK
FRANKLY, I WAS THINKING ABOUT TONS OF TRIVIAL CRAP BEFOREHAND, BUT ALL OF A SUDDEN, I COULDN'T CARE LESS ABOUT THAT STUFF.
....

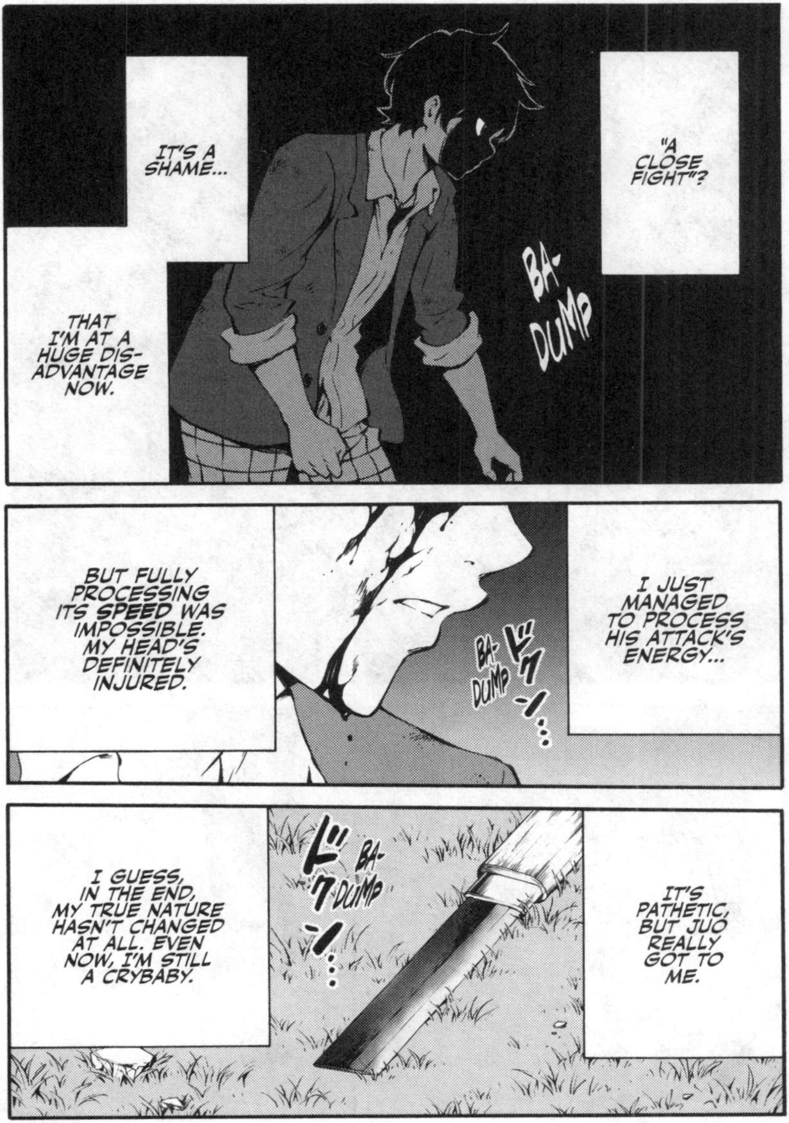
"A CLOSE FIGHT"?
BA-DUMP
IT'S A SHAME...
THAT I'M AT A HUGE DIS-ADVANTAGE NOW.
I JUST MANAGED TO PROCESS HIS ATTACK'S ENERGY...
BA-DUMP
ドクン…
BUT FULLY PROCESSING ITS **SPEED** WAS IMPOSSIBLE. MY HEAD'S DEFINITELY INJURED.
IT'S PATHETIC, BUT JUO REALLY GOT TO ME.
BA-DUMP
ドクン…
I GUESS, IN THE END, MY TRUE NATURE HASN'T CHANGED AT ALL. EVEN NOW, I'M STILL A CRYBABY.

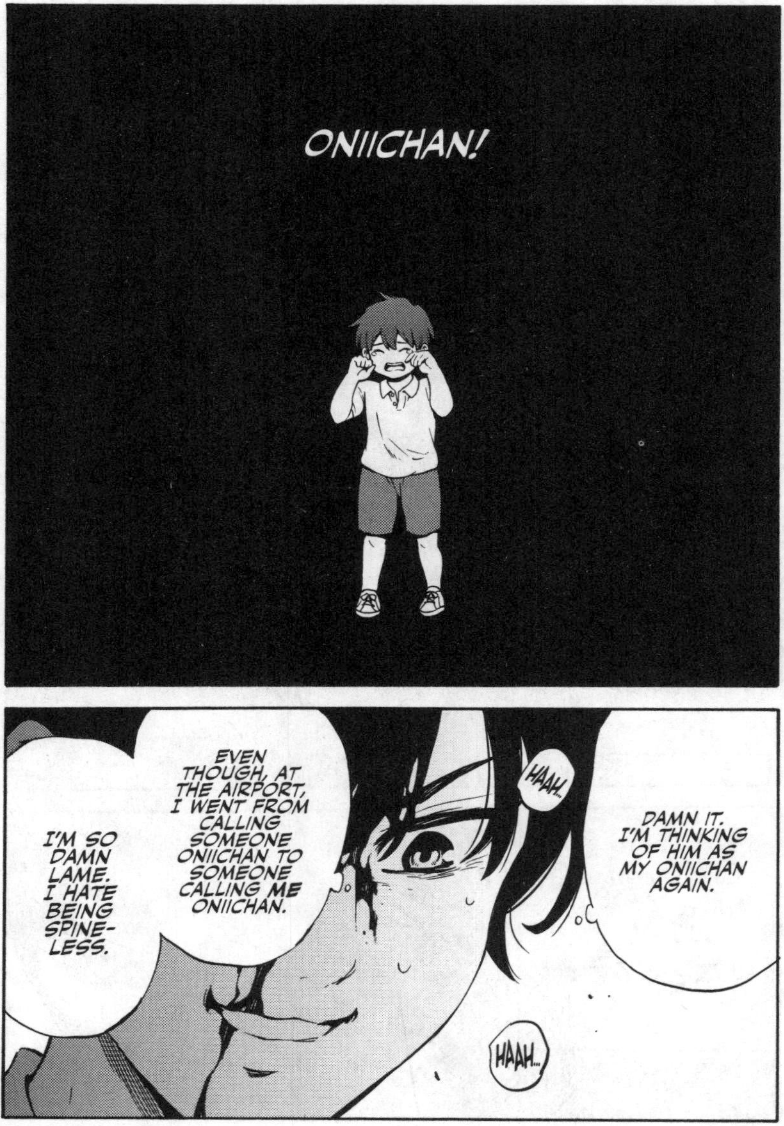
ONIICHAN!
HAAH...
DAMN IT. I'M THINKING OF HIM AS MY ONIICHAN AGAIN.
EVEN THOUGH, AT THE AIRPORT, I WENT FROM CALLING SOMEONE ONIICHAN TO SOMEONE CALLING ME ONIICHAN.
I'M SO DAMN LAME. I HATE BEING SPINE-LESS.
HAAH...

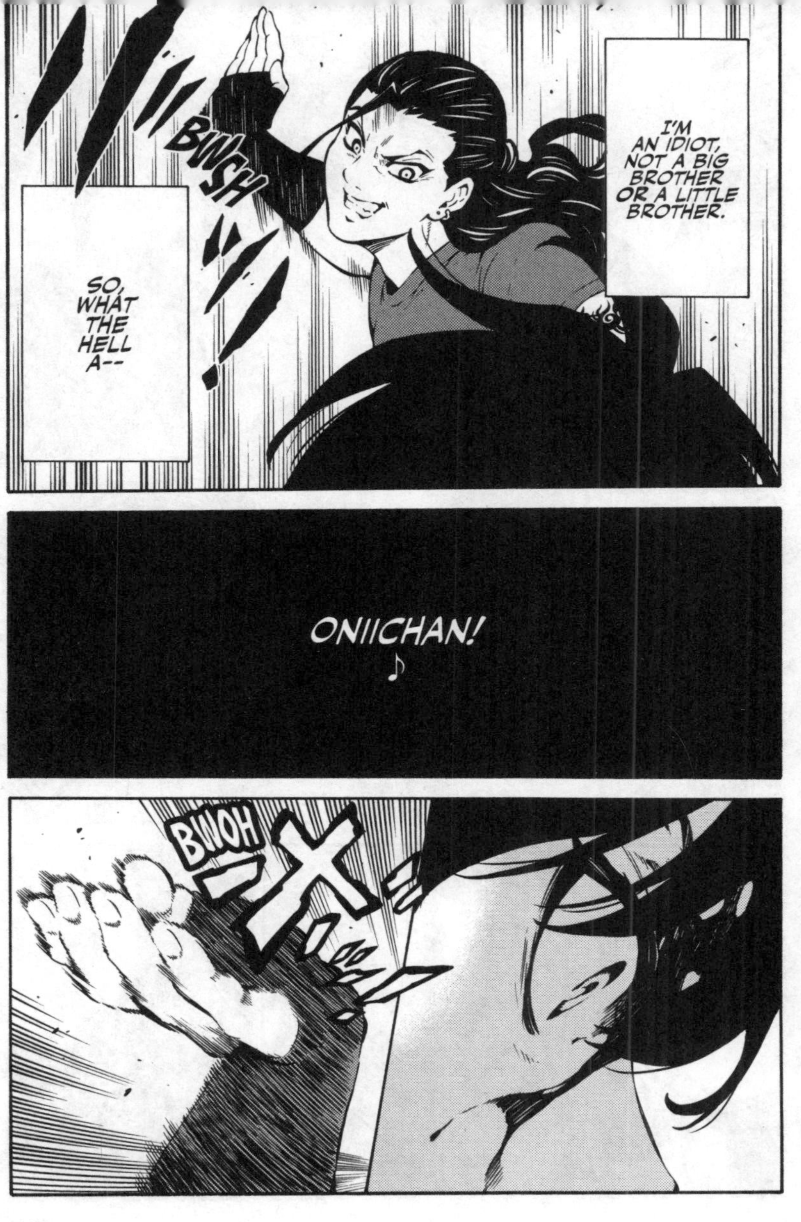
I'M AN IDIOT, NOT A BIG BROTHER OR A LITTLE BROTHER.
BWSH
SO, WHAT THE HELL A--
ONIICHAN! ♪
BWOH

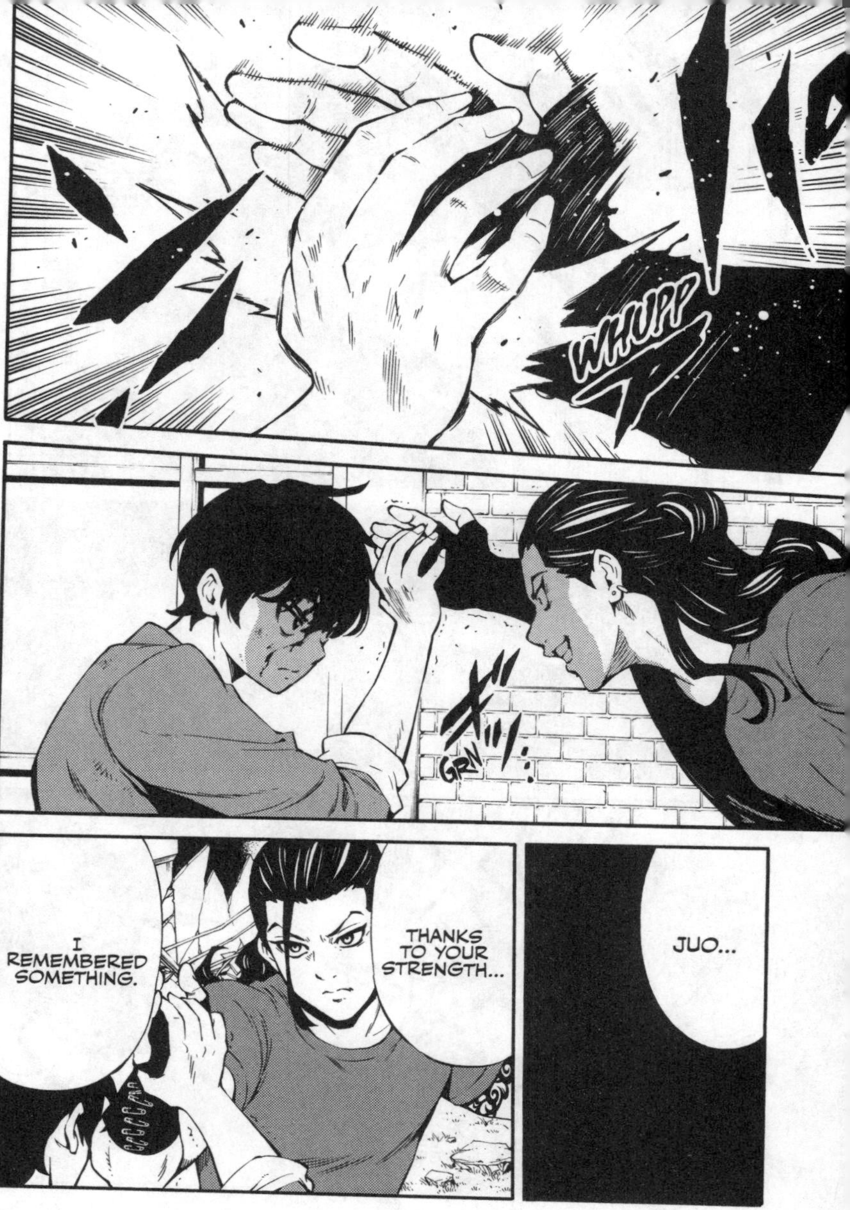
WHUPP
GRN
JUO...
THANKS TO YOUR STRENGTH...
I REMEMBERED SOMETHING.

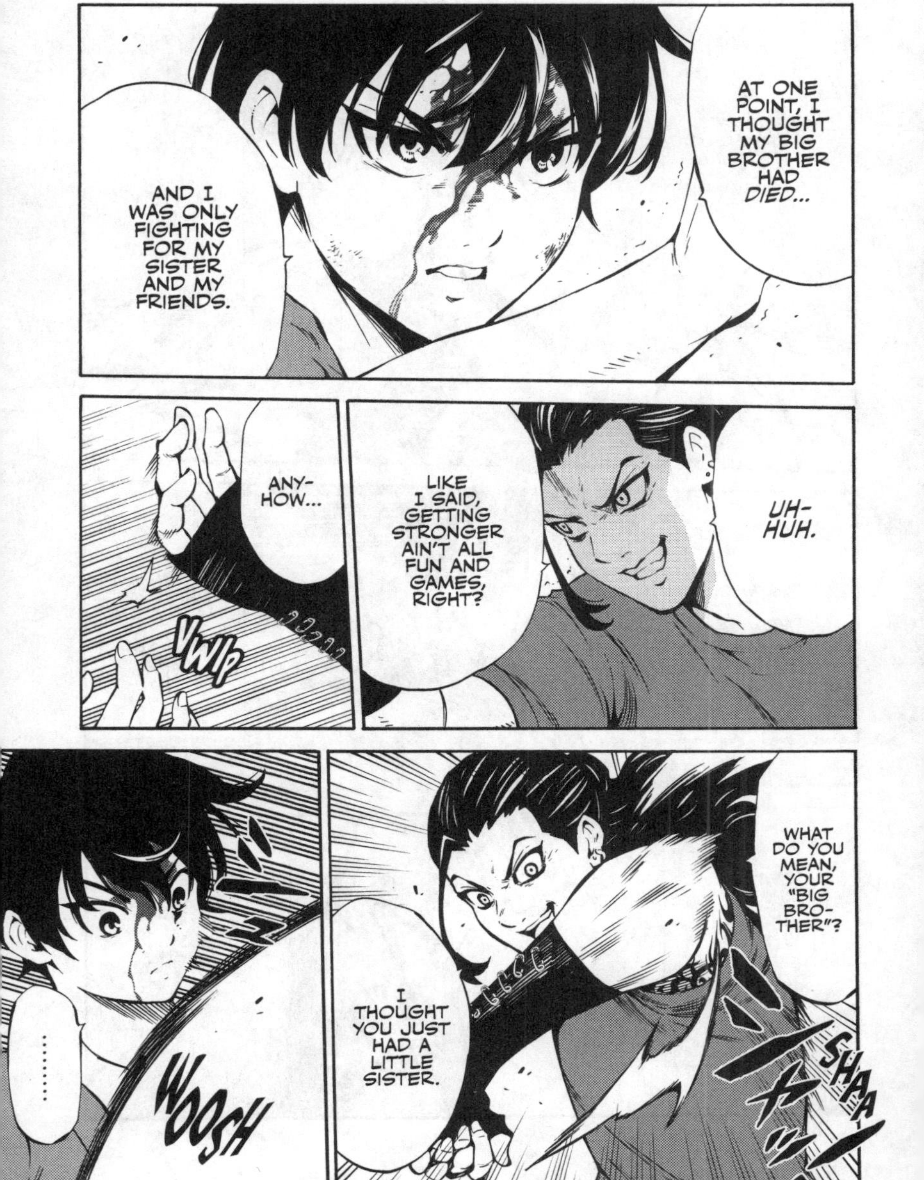
AT ONE POINT, I THOUGHT MY BIG BROTHER HAD *DIED*...
AND I WAS ONLY FIGHTING FOR MY SISTER AND MY FRIENDS.
UH-HUH.
LIKE I SAID, GETTING STRONGER AIN'T ALL FUN AND GAMES, RIGHT?
ANY-HOW...
VWIP
WHAT DO YOU MEAN, YOUR "BIG BRO-THER"?
I THOUGHT YOU JUST HAD A LITTLE SISTER.
SHAA!
......
WOOSH

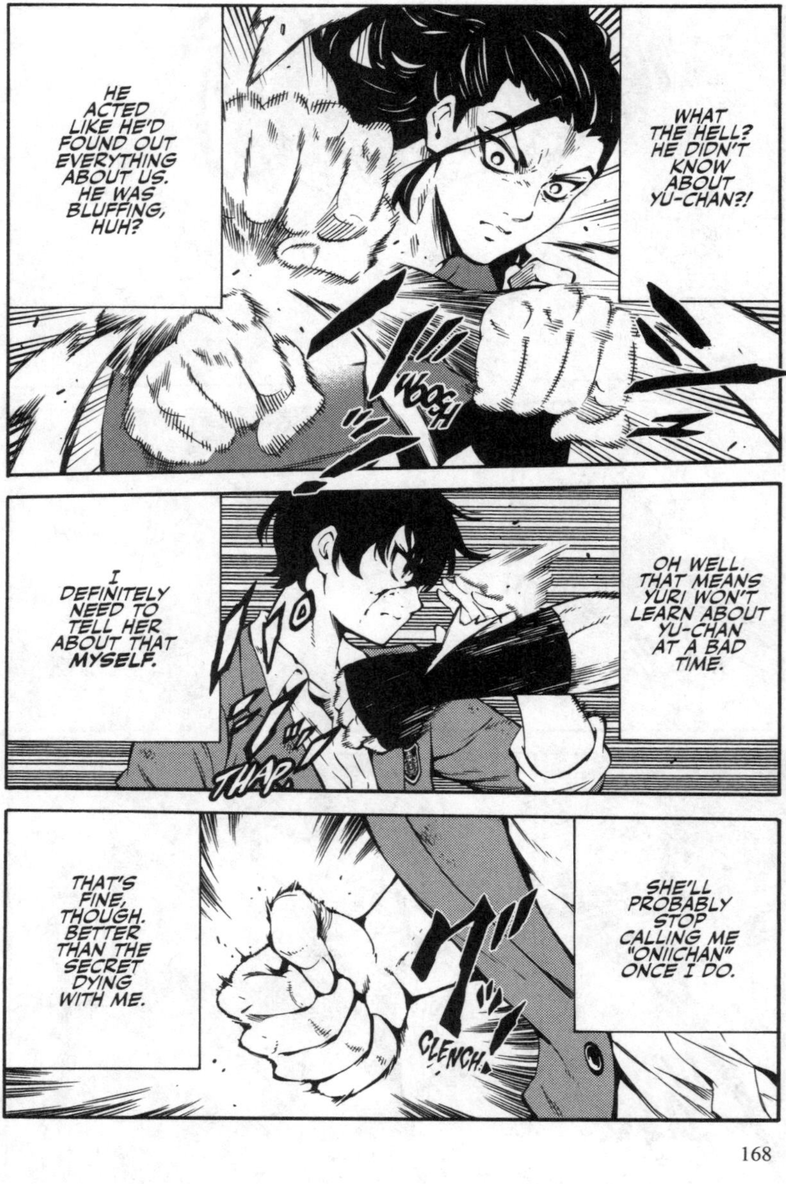
WHAT THE HELL? HE DIDN'T KNOW ABOUT YU-CHAN?!
HE ACTED LIKE HE'D FOUND OUT EVERYTHING ABOUT US. HE WAS BLUFFING, HUH?
WOOSH
OH WELL. THAT MEANS YURI WON'T LEARN ABOUT YU-CHAN AT A BAD TIME.
I DEFINITELY NEED TO TELL HER ABOUT THAT MYSELF.
THAP
SHE'LL PROBABLY STOP CALLING ME "ONIICHAN" ONCE I DO.
THAT'S FINE, THOUGH. BETTER THAN THE SECRET DYING WITH ME.
CLENCH

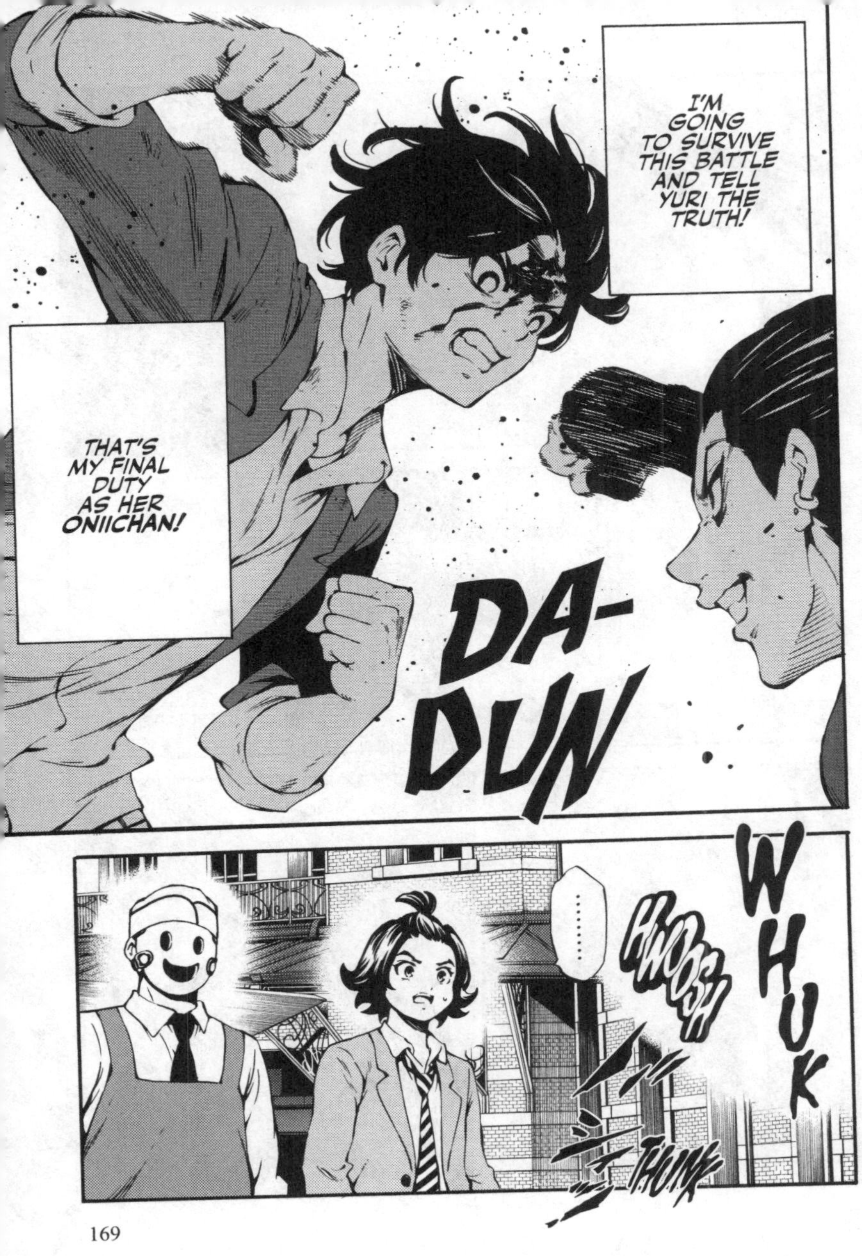
I'M GOING TO SURVIVE THIS BATTLE AND TELL YURI THE TRUTH!
THAT'S MY FINAL DUTY AS HER ONIICHAN!
DA-DUN
WHUK
FWOOSH
THUNK
......

I'M LETTING MY COMRADE RISK HIS LIFE WHILE I JUST WATCH.

YET AGAIN...

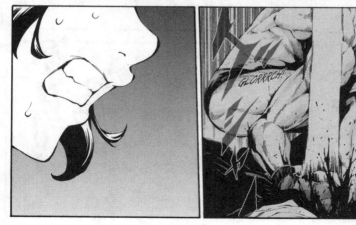

GLORRRCH!

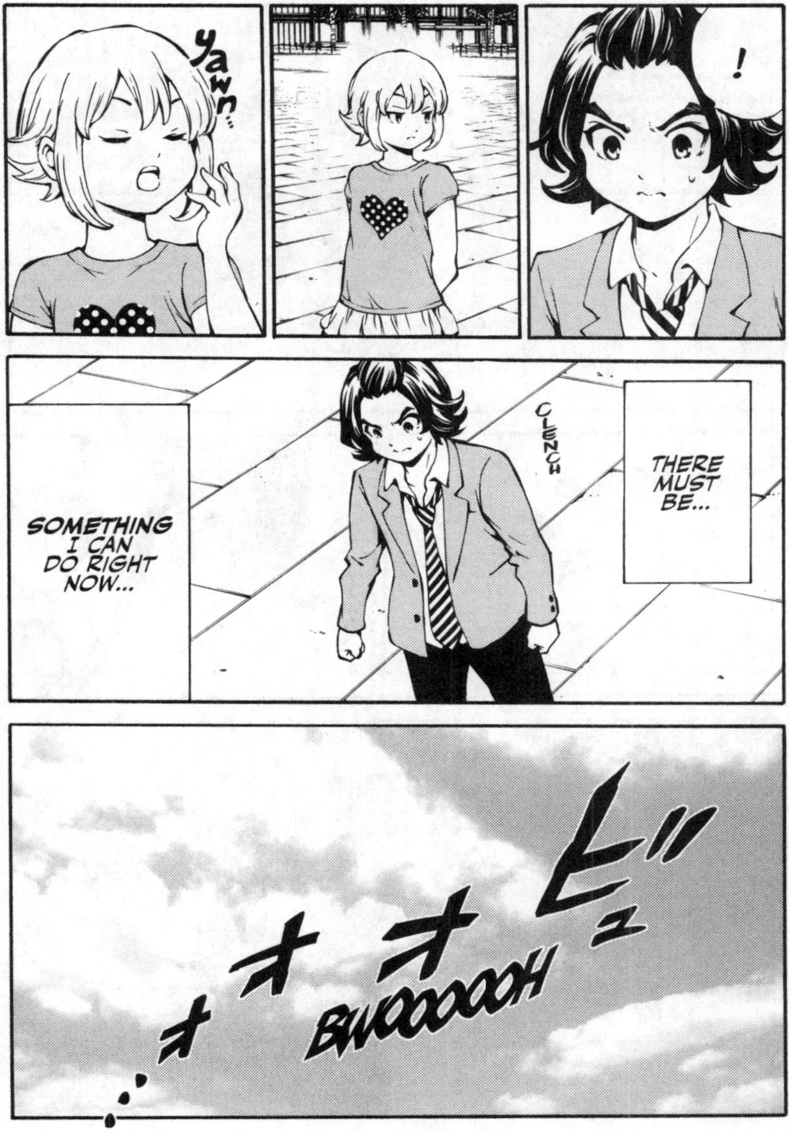
!
yawn...
THERE MUST BE...
CLENCH
SOMETHING I CAN DO RIGHT NOW...
ビュオオオ
BWOOOOOH

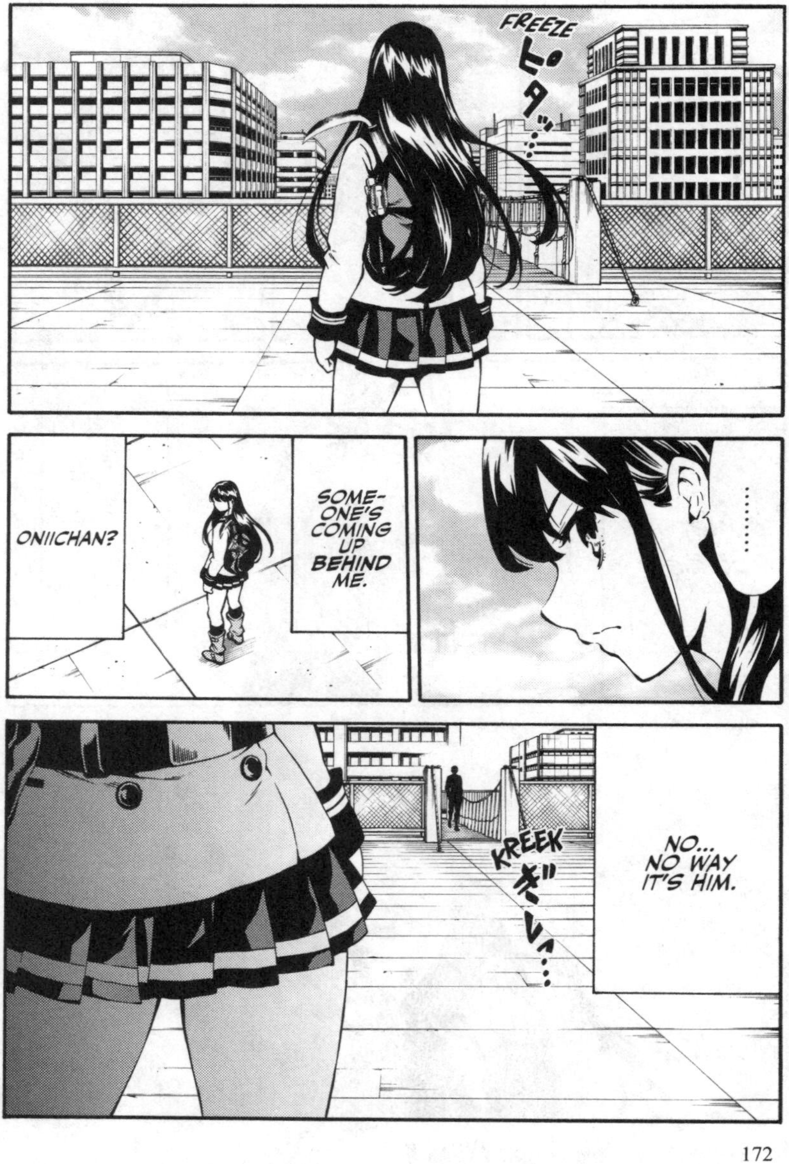
FREEZE
ピタッ…
……
SOME-ONE'S COMING UP BEHIND ME.
ONIICHAN?
NO... NO WAY IT'S HIM.
KREEK
ギィ…

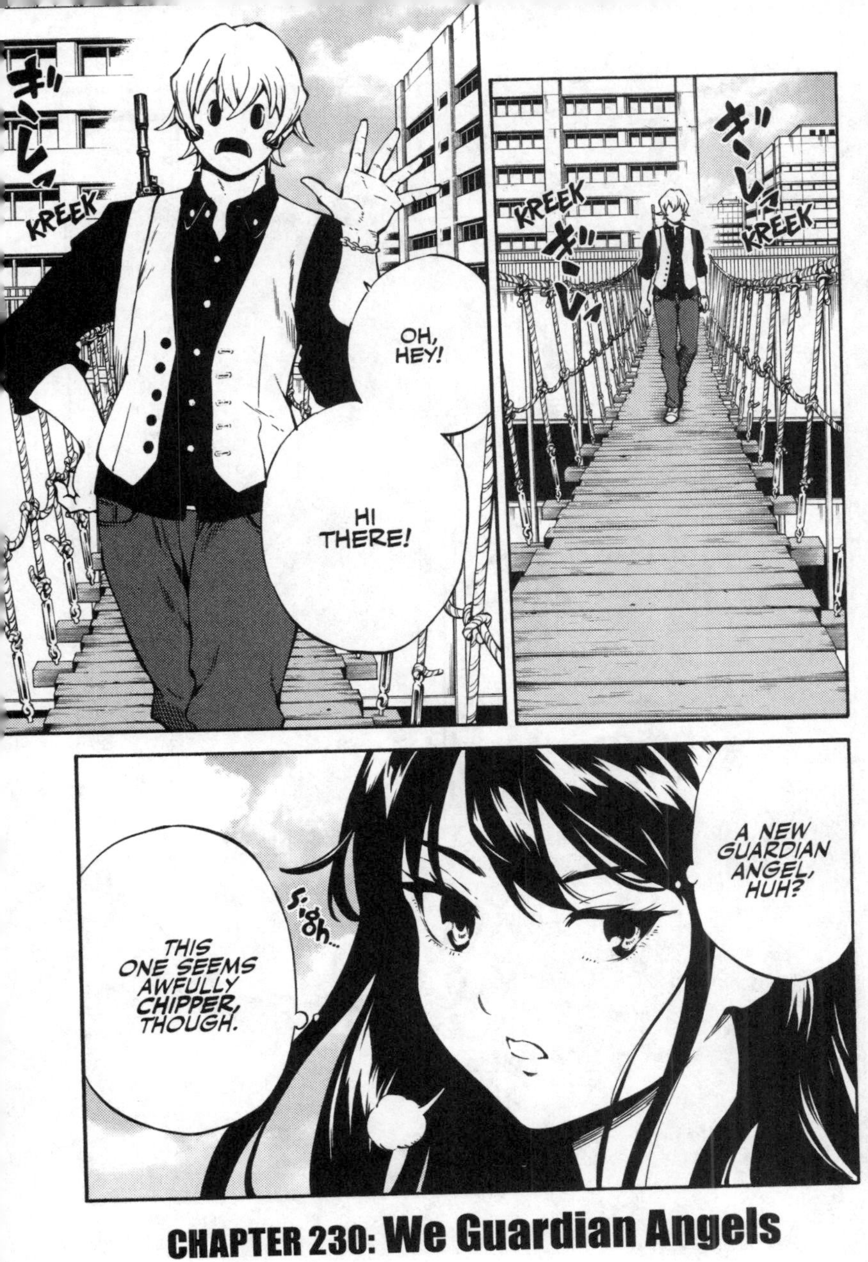
KREEK
KREEK
KREEK
OH, HEY!
HI THERE!
A NEW GUARDIAN ANGEL, HUH?
sigh...
THIS ONE SEEMS AWFULLY CHIPPER, THOUGH.

CHAPTER 230: We Guardian Angels

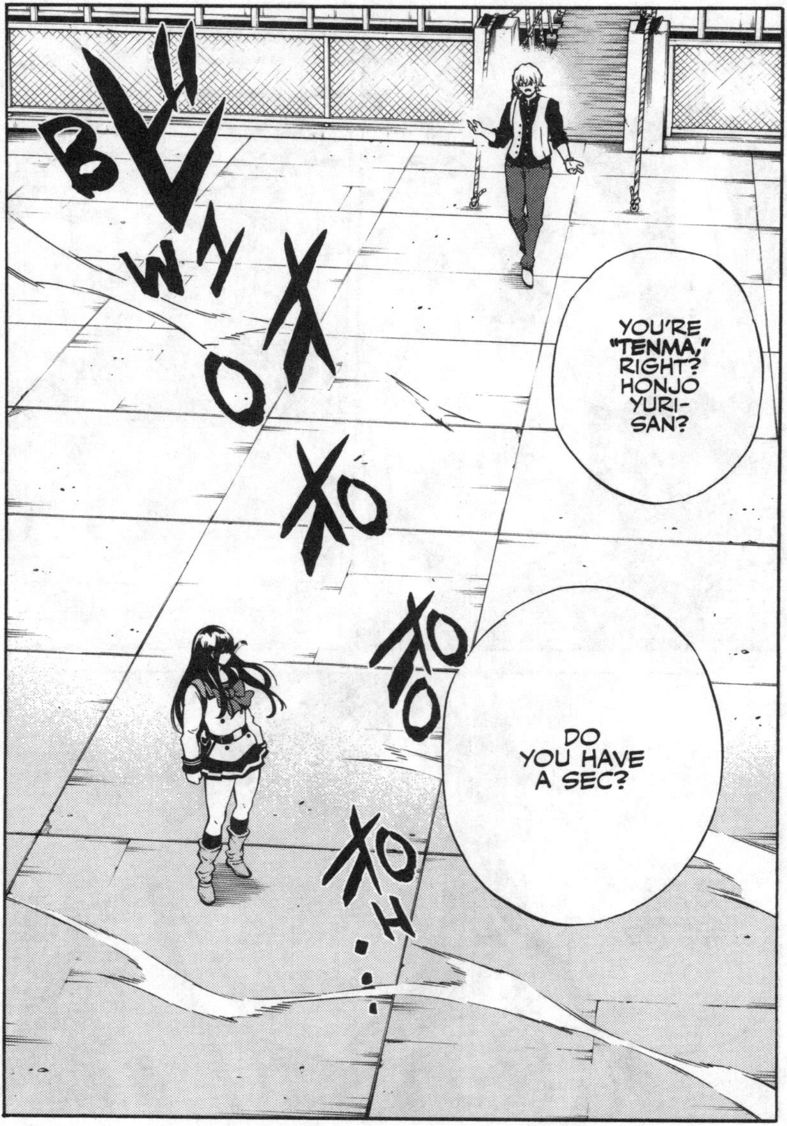
YOU'RE "TENMA," RIGHT? HONJO YURI-SAN?
DO YOU HAVE A SEC?

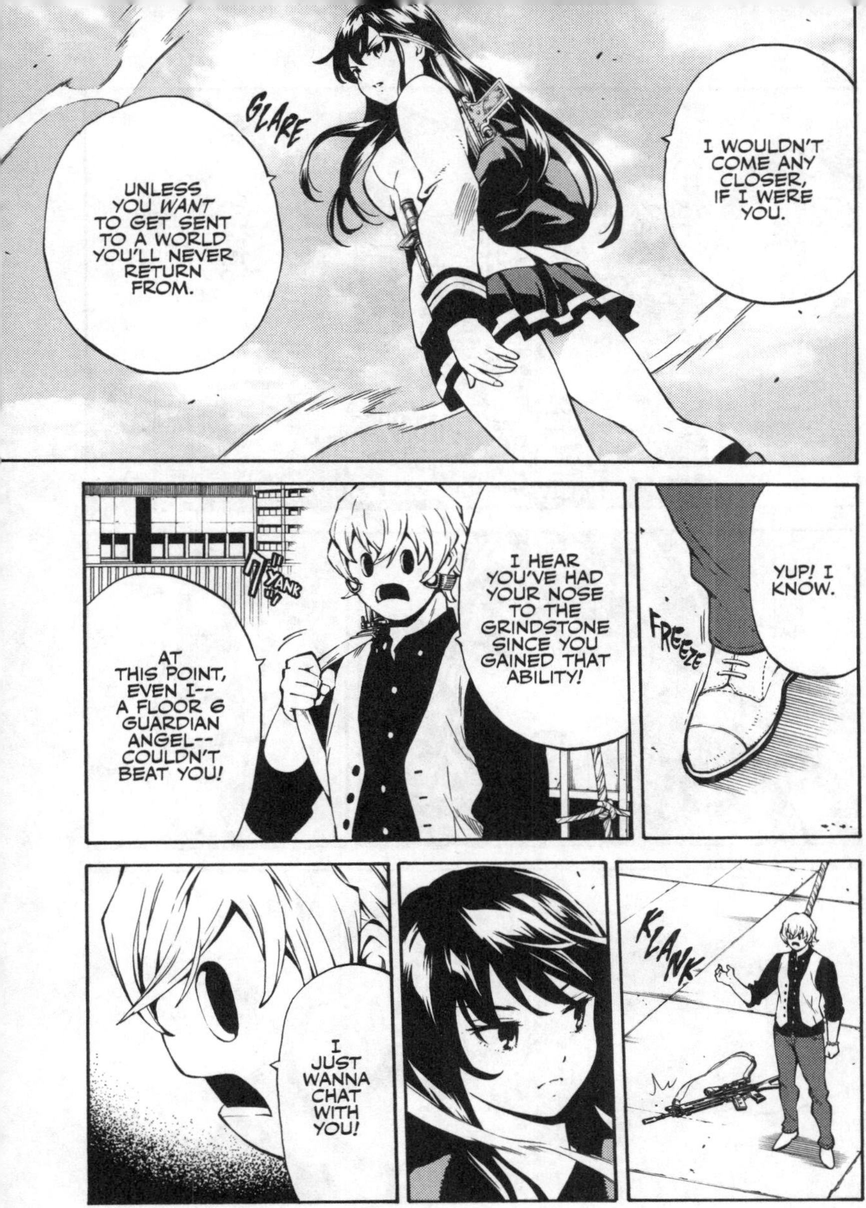
I WOULDN'T COME ANY CLOSER, IF I WERE YOU.
GLARE
UNLESS YOU *WANT* TO GET SENT TO A WORLD YOU'LL NEVER RETURN FROM.
YUP! I KNOW.
FREEZE
I HEAR YOU'VE HAD YOUR NOSE TO THE GRINDSTONE SINCE YOU GAINED THAT ABILITY!
YANK
AT THIS POINT, EVEN I-- A FLOOR 6 GUARDIAN ANGEL-- COULDN'T BEAT YOU!
KLANK
I JUST WANNA CHAT WITH YOU!

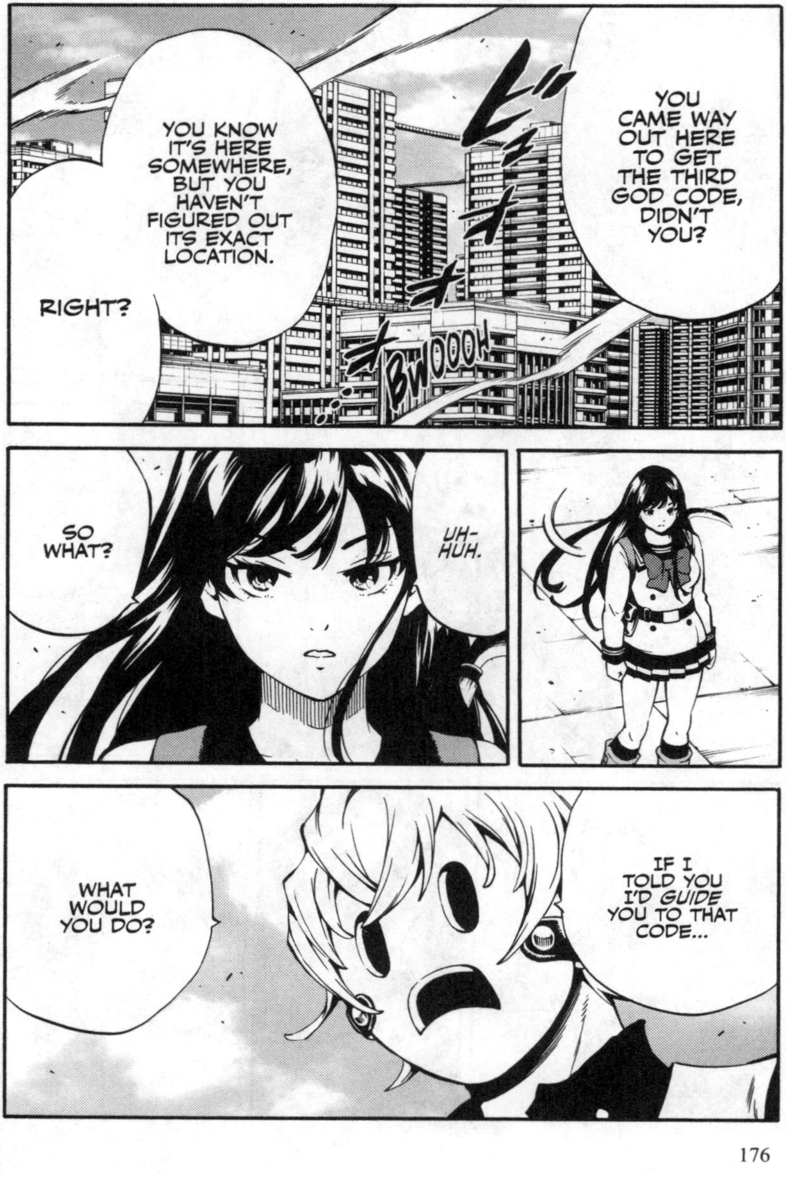
YOU CAME WAY OUT HERE TO GET THE THIRD GOD CODE, DIDN'T YOU?
YOU KNOW IT'S HERE SOMEWHERE, BUT YOU HAVEN'T FIGURED OUT ITS EXACT LOCATION.
RIGHT?
BWOOOH
UH-HUH.
SO WHAT?
IF I TOLD YOU I'D *GUIDE* YOU TO THAT CODE...
WHAT WOULD YOU DO?

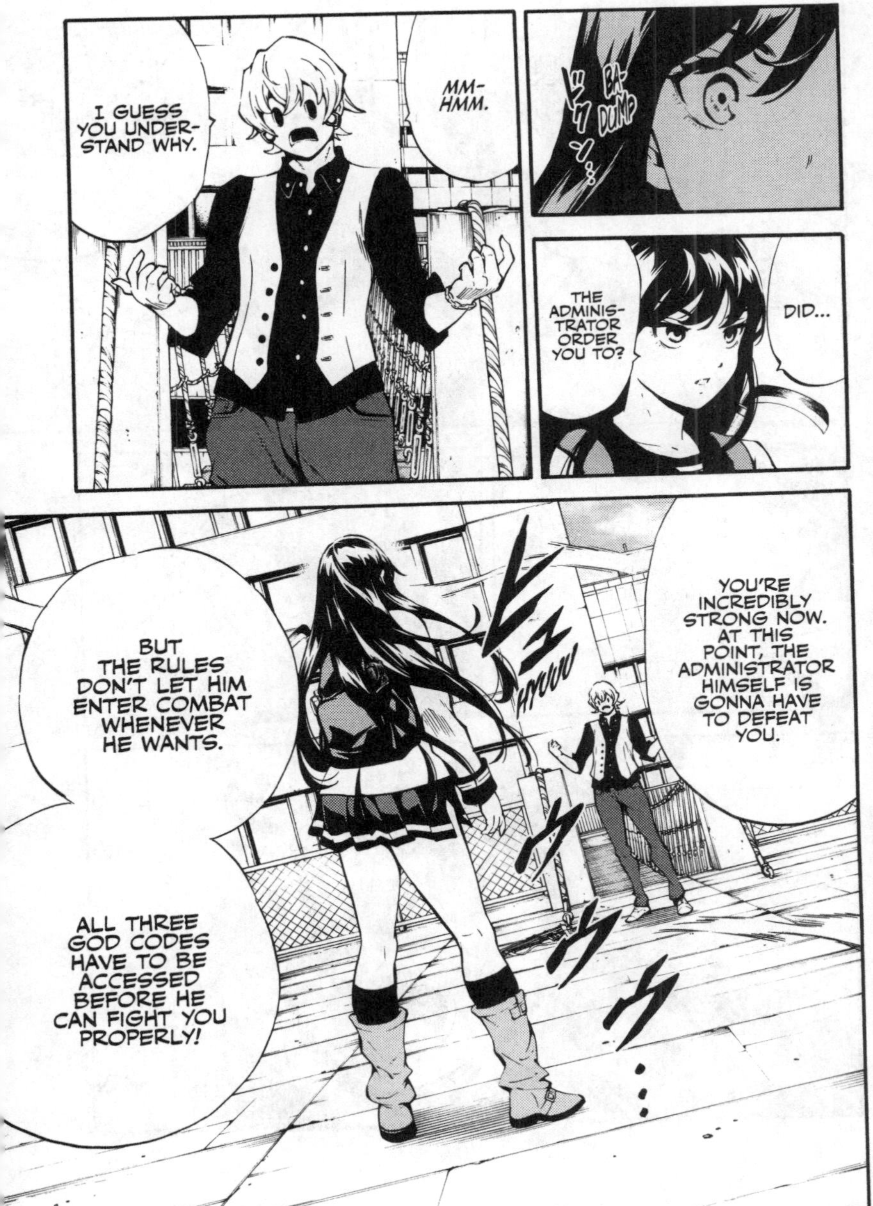
BA-DUMP
DID...
THE ADMINISTRATOR ORDER YOU TO?
MM-HMM.
I GUESS YOU UNDERSTAND WHY.
YOU'RE INCREDIBLY STRONG NOW. AT THIS POINT, THE ADMINISTRATOR HIMSELF IS GONNA HAVE TO DEFEAT YOU.
HYUUU
BUT THE RULES DON'T LET HIM ENTER COMBAT WHENEVER HE WANTS.
ALL THREE GOD CODES HAVE TO BE ACCESSED BEFORE HE CAN FIGHT YOU PROPERLY!

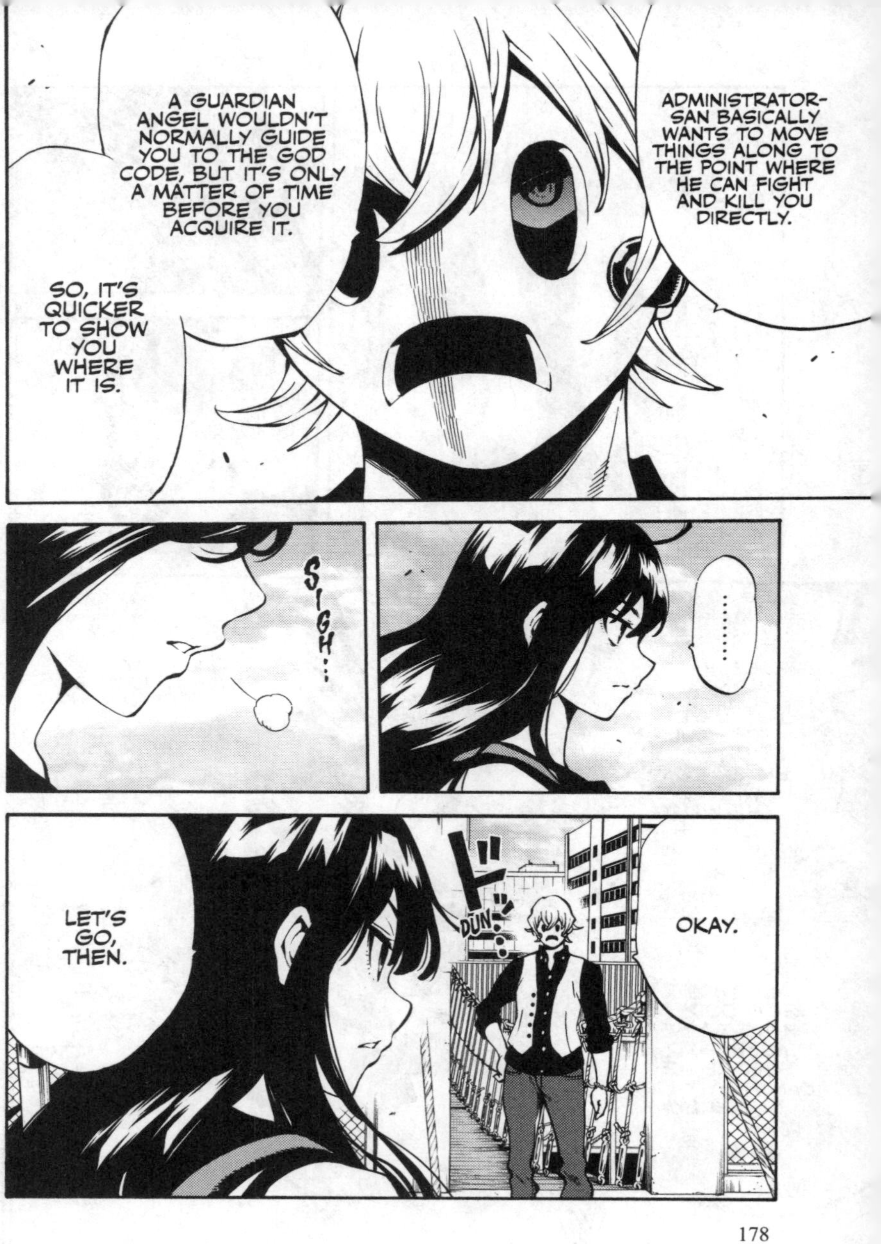
ADMINISTRATOR-SAN BASICALLY WANTS TO MOVE THINGS ALONG TO THE POINT WHERE HE CAN FIGHT AND KILL YOU DIRECTLY.
A GUARDIAN ANGEL WOULDN'T NORMALLY GUIDE YOU TO THE GOD CODE, BUT IT'S ONLY A MATTER OF TIME BEFORE YOU ACQUIRE IT.
SO, IT'S QUICKER TO SHOW YOU WHERE IT IS.
....
SIGH...
OKAY.
DUN
LET'S GO, THEN.

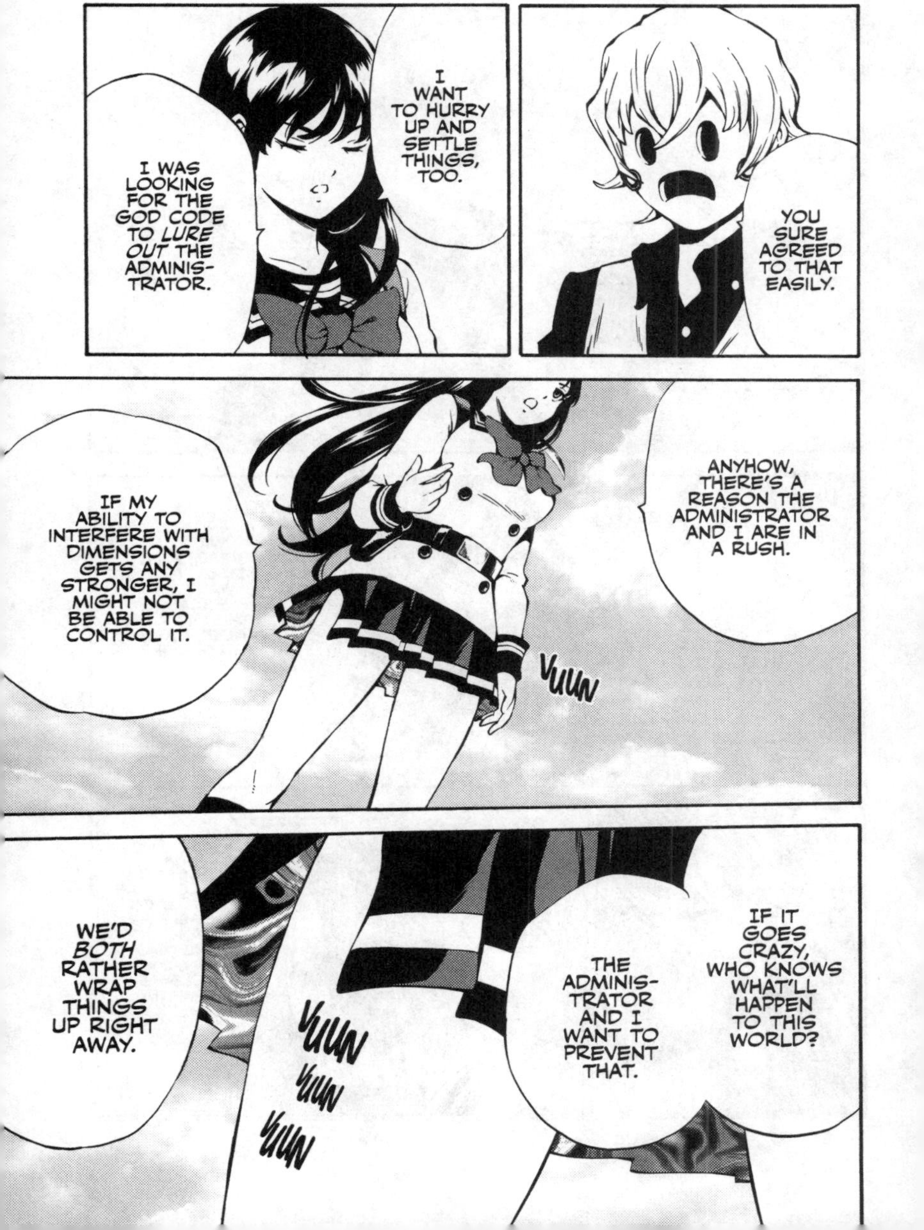
YOU SURE AGREED TO THAT EASILY.
I WANT TO HURRY UP AND SETTLE THINGS, TOO.
I WAS LOOKING FOR THE GOD CODE TO *LURE OUT* THE ADMINISTRATOR.
ANYHOW, THERE'S A REASON THE ADMINISTRATOR AND I ARE IN A RUSH.
VUUN
IF MY ABILITY TO INTERFERE WITH DIMENSIONS GETS ANY STRONGER, I MIGHT NOT BE ABLE TO CONTROL IT.
IF IT GOES CRAZY, WHO KNOWS WHAT'LL HAPPEN TO THIS WORLD?
THE ADMINISTRATOR AND I WANT TO PREVENT THAT.
VUUN
VUUN
VUUN
WE'D *BOTH* RATHER WRAP THINGS UP RIGHT AWAY.

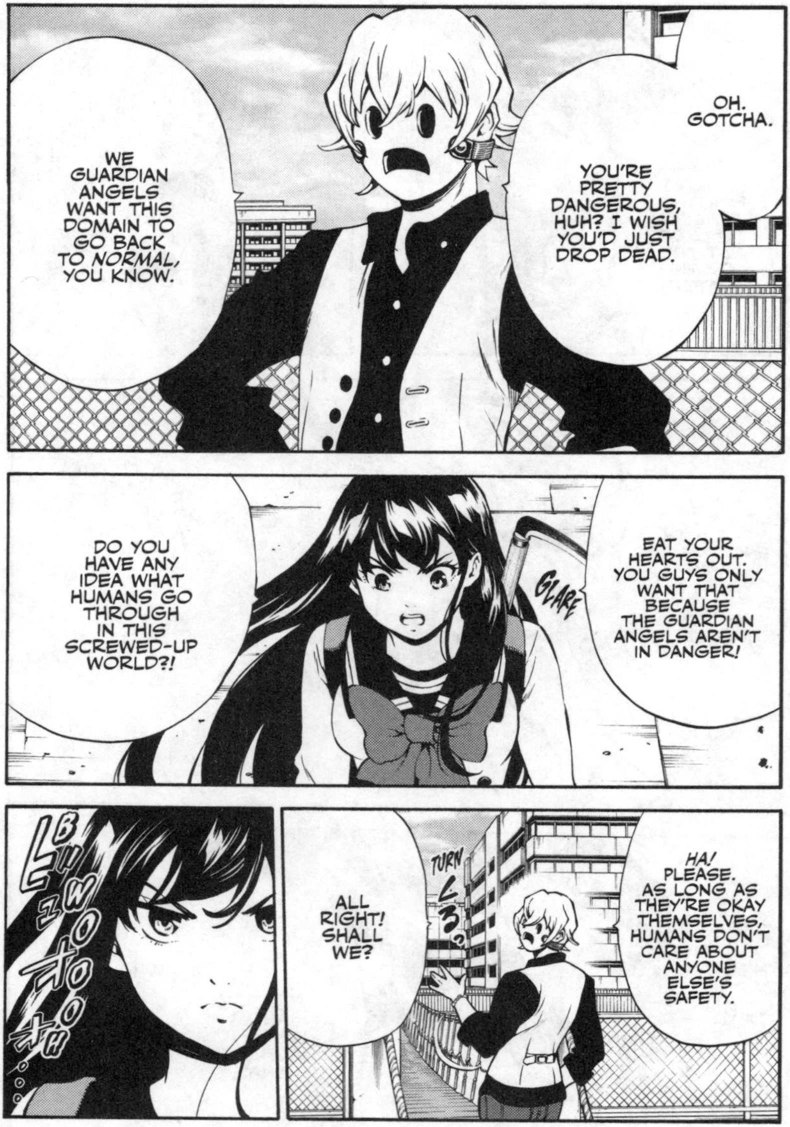
OH. GOTCHA.
YOU'RE PRETTY DANGEROUS, HUH? I WISH YOU'D JUST DROP DEAD.
WE GUARDIAN ANGELS WANT THIS DOMAIN TO GO BACK TO *NORMAL*, YOU KNOW.
EAT YOUR HEARTS OUT. YOU GUYS ONLY WANT THAT BECAUSE THE GUARDIAN ANGELS AREN'T IN DANGER!
GLARE
DO YOU HAVE ANY IDEA WHAT HUMANS GO THROUGH IN THIS SCREWED-UP WORLD?!
HA! PLEASE. AS LONG AS THEY'RE OKAY THEMSELVES, HUMANS DON'T CARE ABOUT ANYONE ELSE'S SAFETY.
TURN
ALL RIGHT! SHALL WE?
BWOOOOOOH...

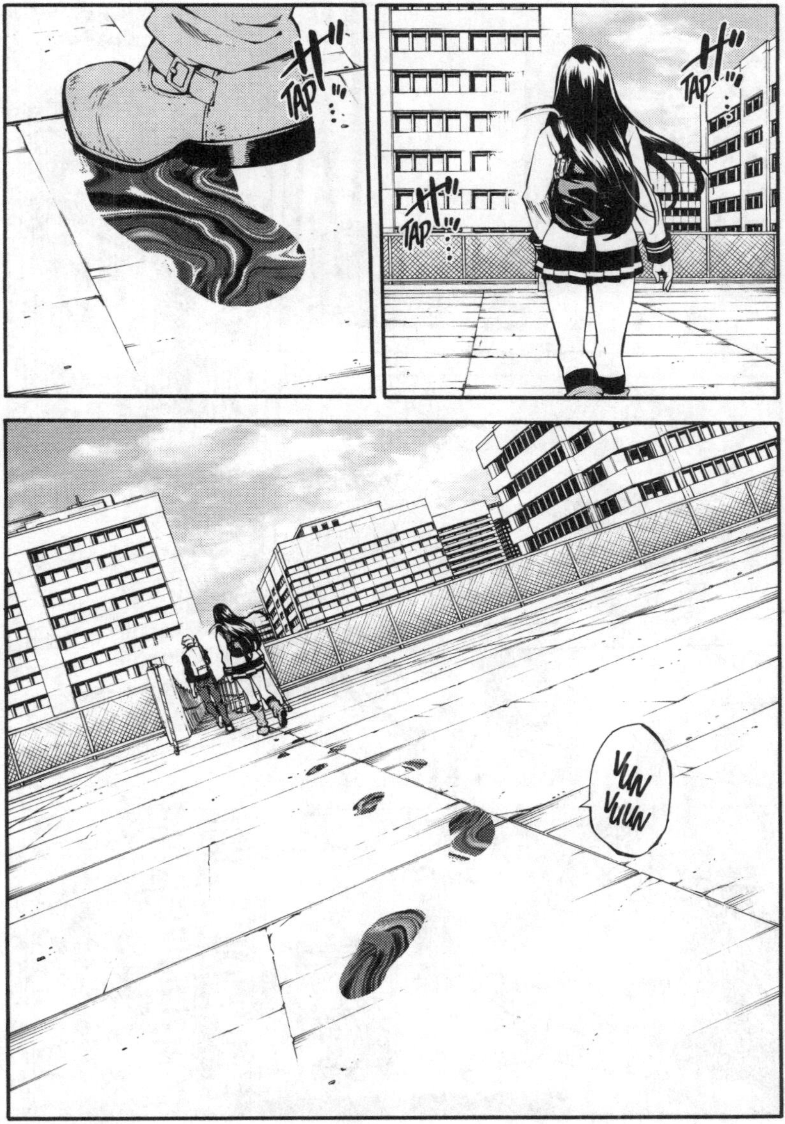
TAP
TAP
TAP
VUN VUUN

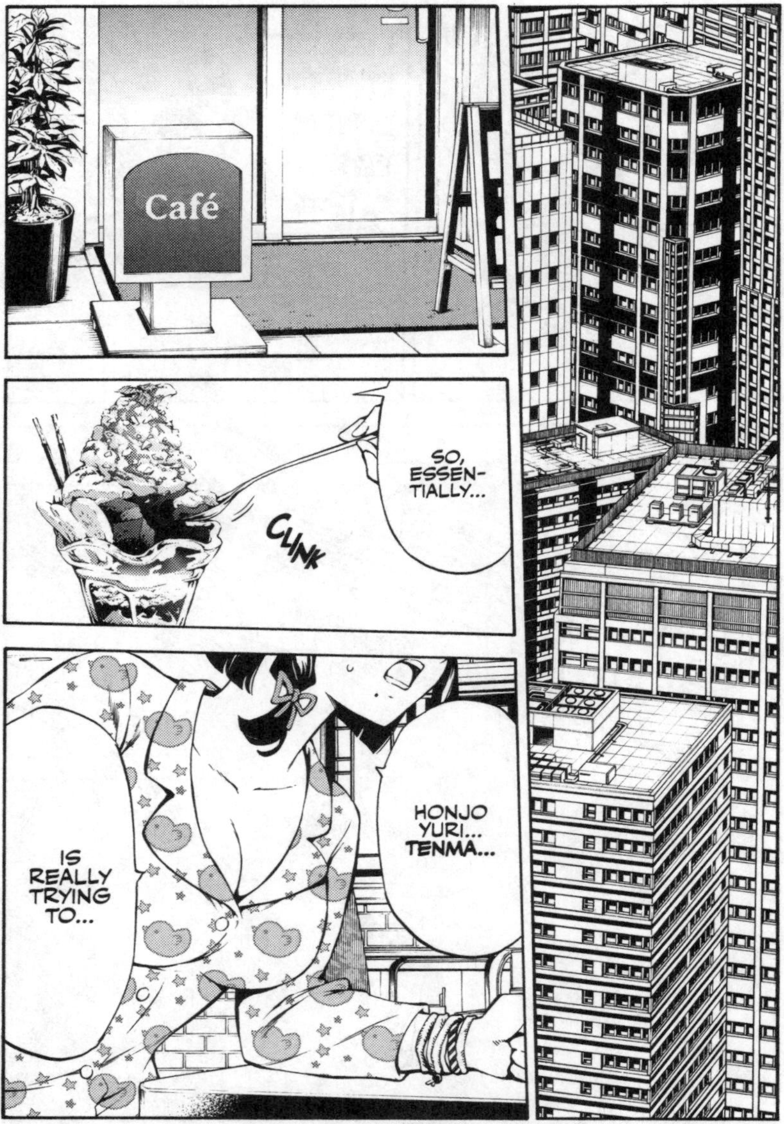
Café
SO, ESSEN-TIALLY...
CLINK
HONJO YURI... TENMA...
IS REALLY TRYING TO...

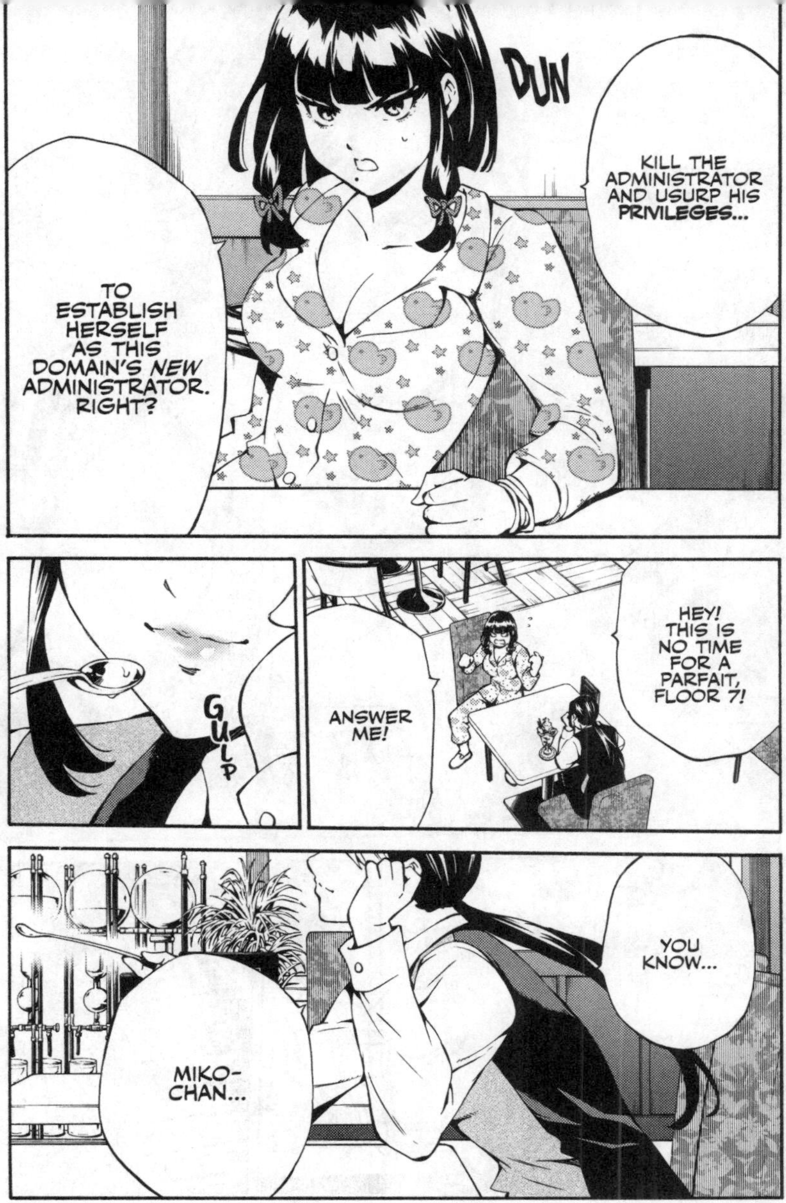
KILL THE ADMINISTRATOR AND USURP HIS PRIVILEGES...
DUN
TO ESTABLISH HERSELF AS THIS DOMAIN'S *NEW* ADMINISTRATOR. RIGHT?
HEY! THIS IS NO TIME FOR A PARFAIT, FLOOR 7!
ANSWER ME!
GULP
YOU KNOW...
MIKO-CHAN...

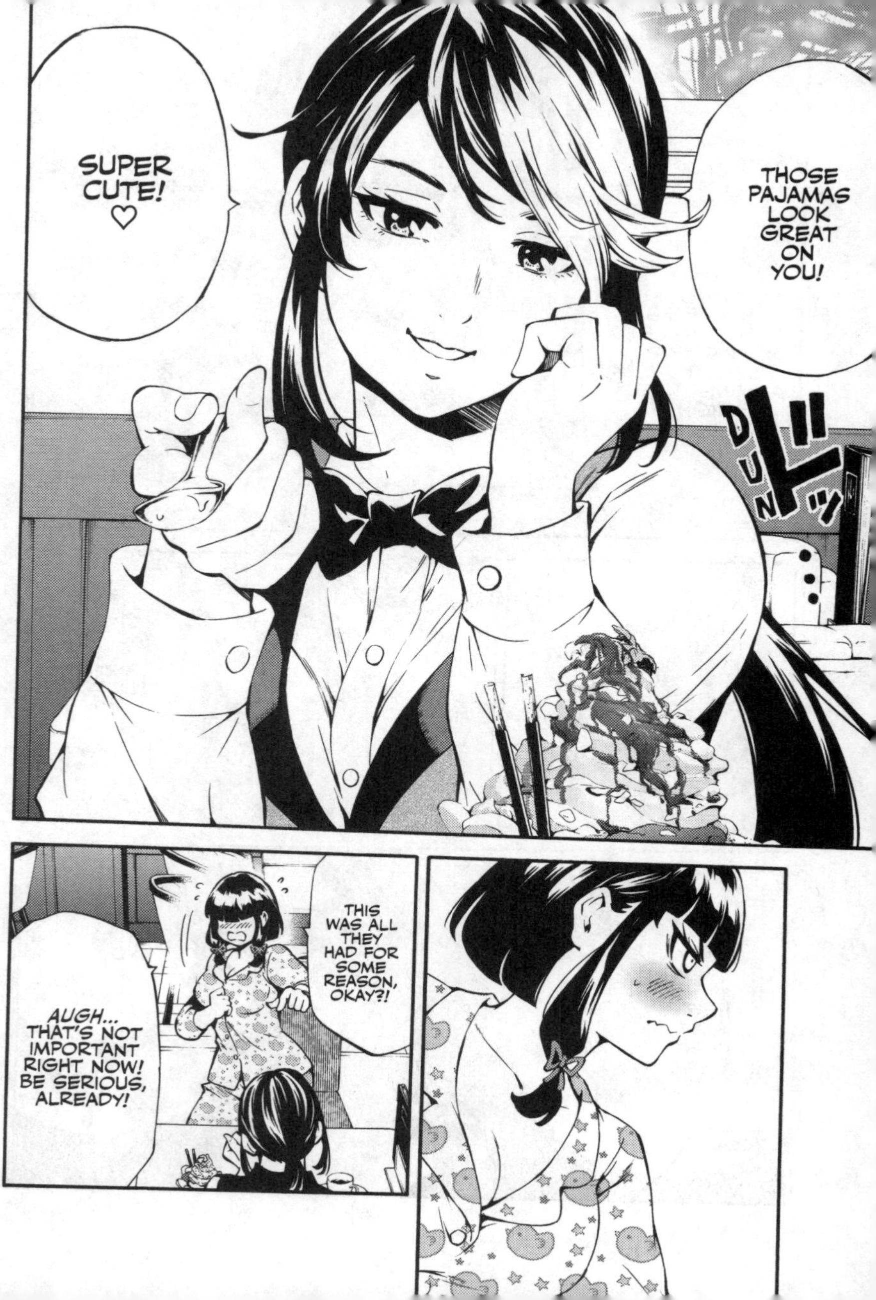
THOSE PAJAMAS LOOK GREAT ON YOU!
SUPER CUTE! ♡
DUN
THIS WAS ALL THEY HAD FOR SOME REASON, OKAY?!
AUGH... THAT'S NOT IMPORTANT RIGHT NOW! BE SERIOUS, ALREADY!

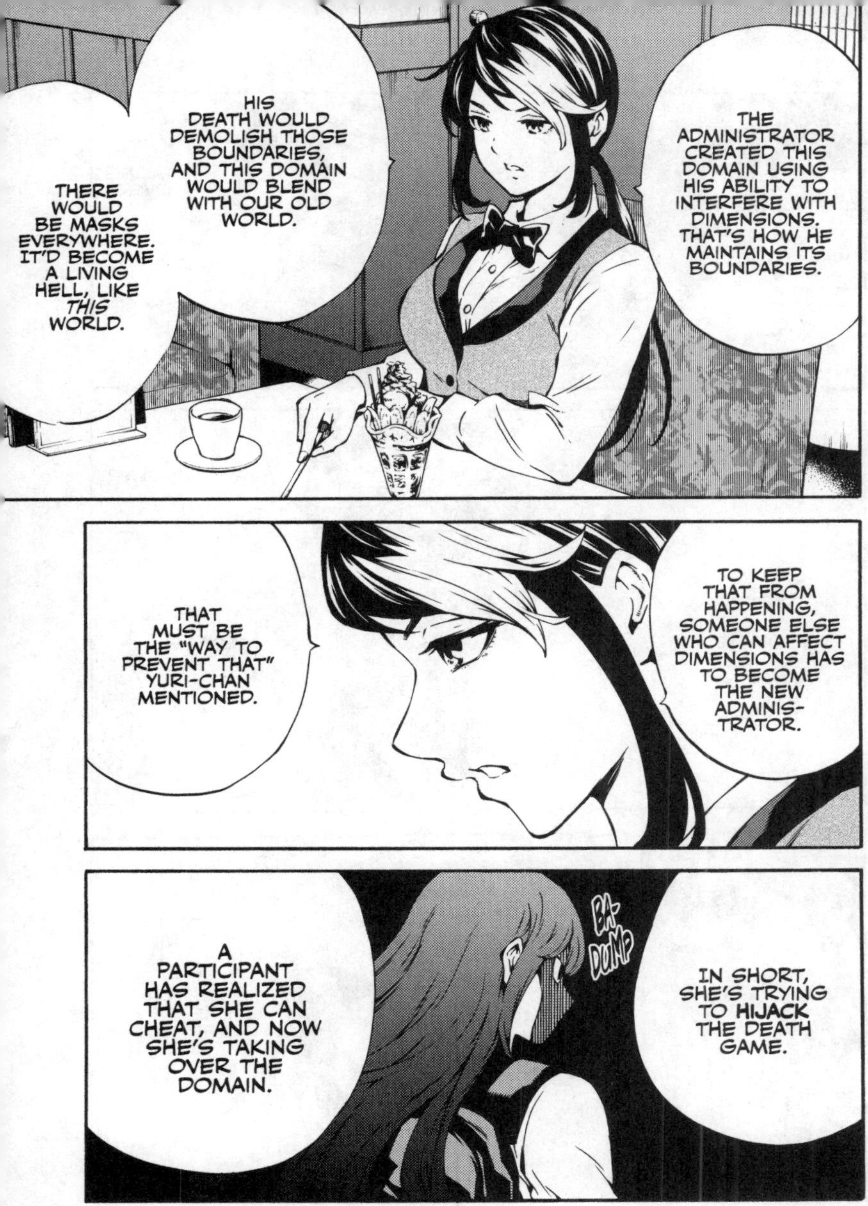
THE ADMINISTRATOR CREATED THIS DOMAIN USING HIS ABILITY TO INTERFERE WITH DIMENSIONS. THAT'S HOW HE MAINTAINS ITS BOUNDARIES.
HIS DEATH WOULD DEMOLISH THOSE BOUNDARIES, AND THIS DOMAIN WOULD BLEND WITH OUR OLD WORLD.
THERE WOULD BE MASKS EVERYWHERE. IT'D BECOME A LIVING HELL, LIKE *THIS* WORLD.
TO KEEP THAT FROM HAPPENING, SOMEONE ELSE WHO CAN AFFECT DIMENSIONS HAS TO BECOME THE NEW ADMINIS-TRATOR.
THAT MUST BE THE "WAY TO PREVENT THAT" YURI-CHAN MENTIONED.
IN SHORT, SHE'S TRYING TO **HIJACK** THE DEATH GAME.
BA-DUMP
A PARTICIPANT HAS REALIZED THAT SHE CAN CHEAT, AND NOW SHE'S TAKING OVER THE DOMAIN.

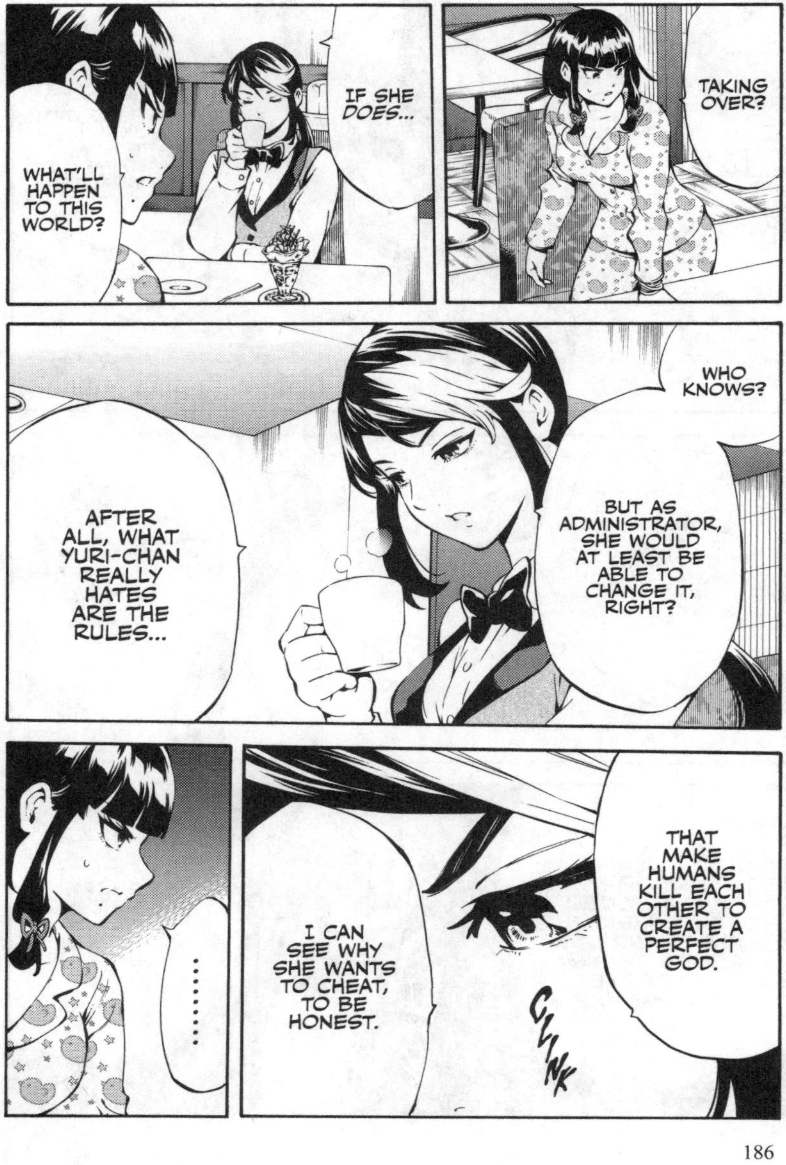
TAKING OVER?
IF SHE DOES...
WHAT'LL HAPPEN TO THIS WORLD?
WHO KNOWS?
BUT AS ADMINISTRATOR, SHE WOULD AT LEAST BE ABLE TO CHANGE IT, RIGHT?
AFTER ALL, WHAT YURI-CHAN REALLY HATES ARE THE RULES...
THAT MAKE HUMANS KILL EACH OTHER TO CREATE A PERFECT GOD.
I CAN SEE WHY SHE WANTS TO CHEAT, TO BE HONEST.
CLINK
....

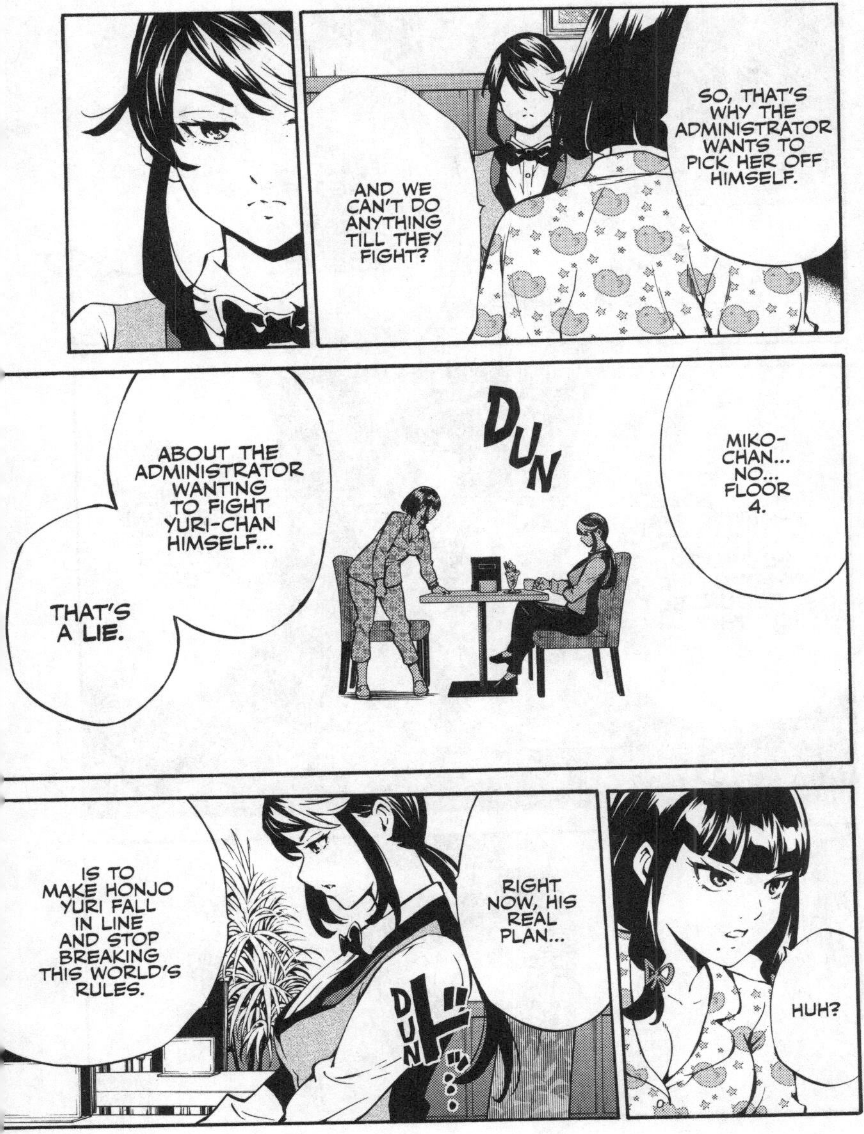
SO, THAT'S WHY THE ADMINISTRATOR WANTS TO PICK HER OFF HIMSELF.
AND WE CAN'T DO ANYTHING TILL THEY FIGHT?
MIKO-CHAN... NO... FLOOR 4.
DUN
ABOUT THE ADMINISTRATOR WANTING TO FIGHT YURI-CHAN HIMSELF...
THAT'S A LIE.
HUH?
RIGHT NOW, HIS REAL PLAN...
IS TO MAKE HONJO YURI FALL IN LINE AND STOP BREAKING THIS WORLD'S RULES.
DUN

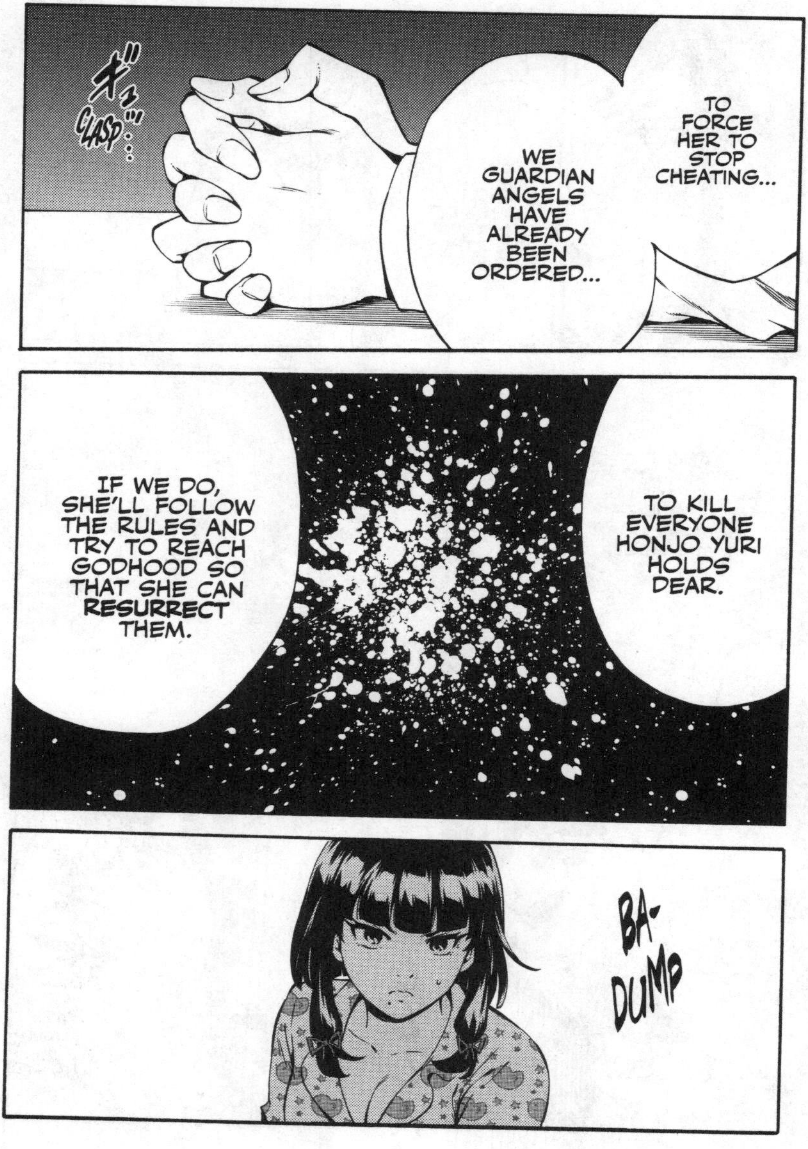
TO FORCE HER TO STOP CHEATING...
WE GUARDIAN ANGELS HAVE ALREADY BEEN ORDERED...
CLASP...
TO KILL EVERYONE HONJO YURI HOLDS DEAR.
IF WE DO, SHE'LL FOLLOW THE RULES AND TRY TO REACH GODHOOD SO THAT SHE CAN RESURRECT THEM.
BA-DUMP

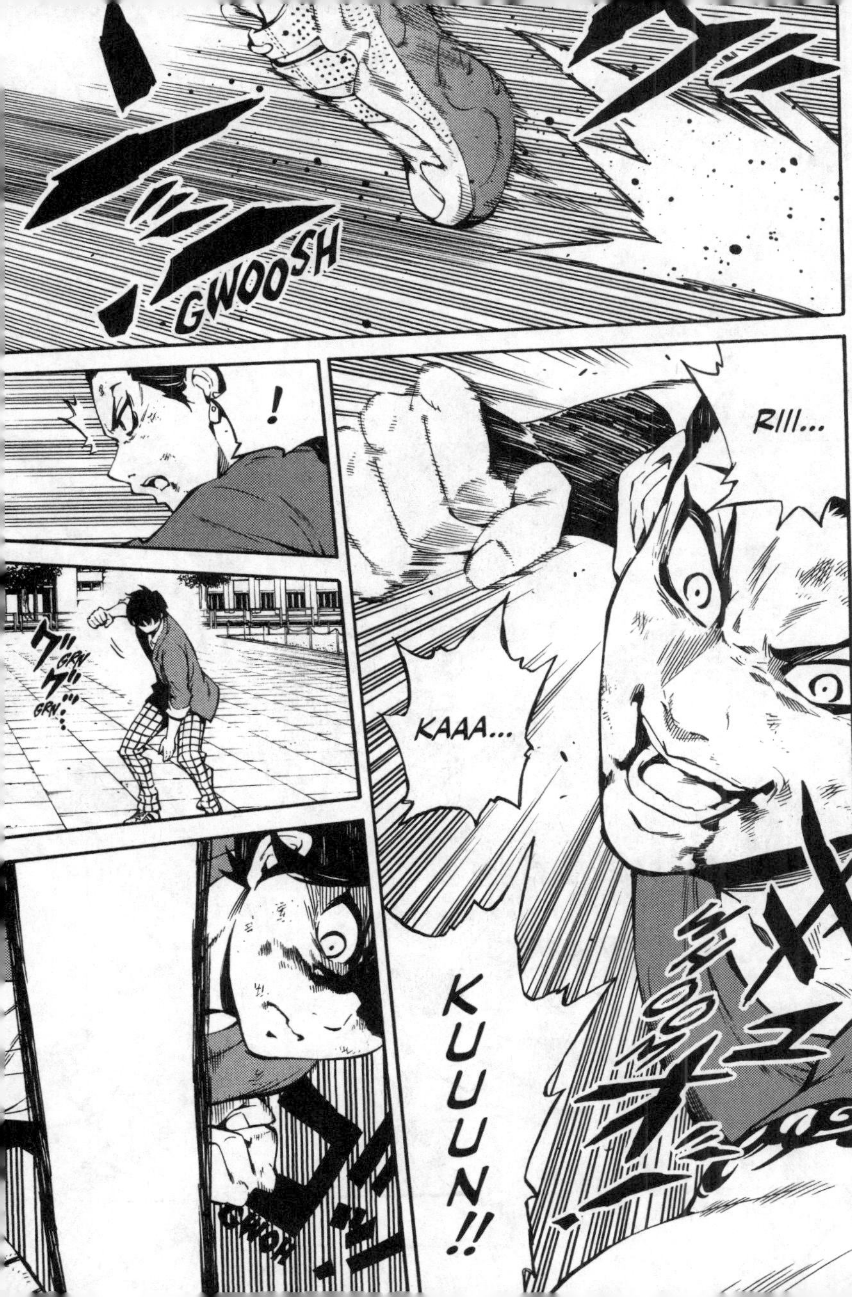
GWOOSH
RIII...
KAAA...
KUUUN!!
WHOOM
!
GRN
GRN
GNOK

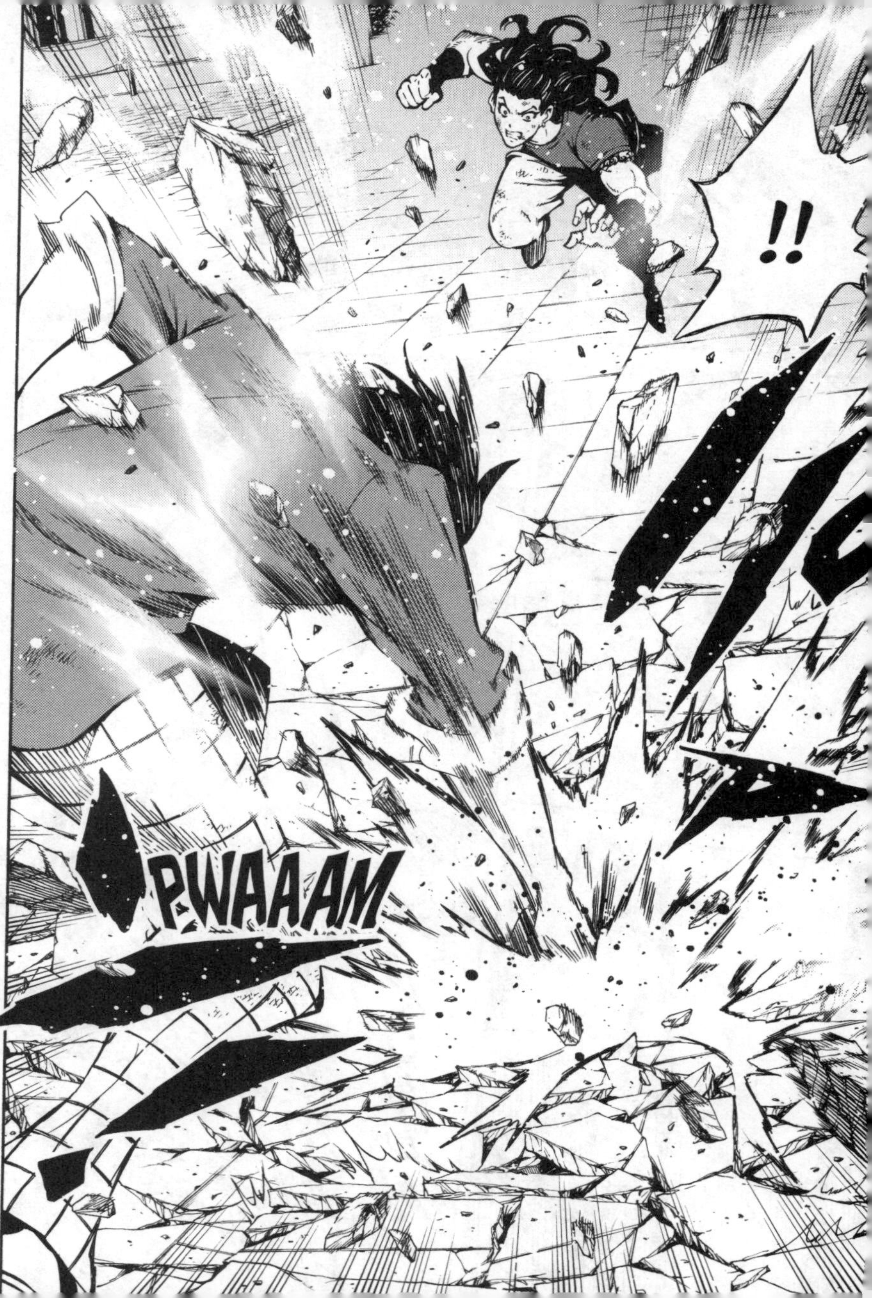
!!
PWAAAM

HIGH-RISE INVASION

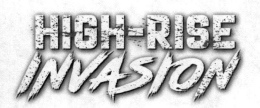

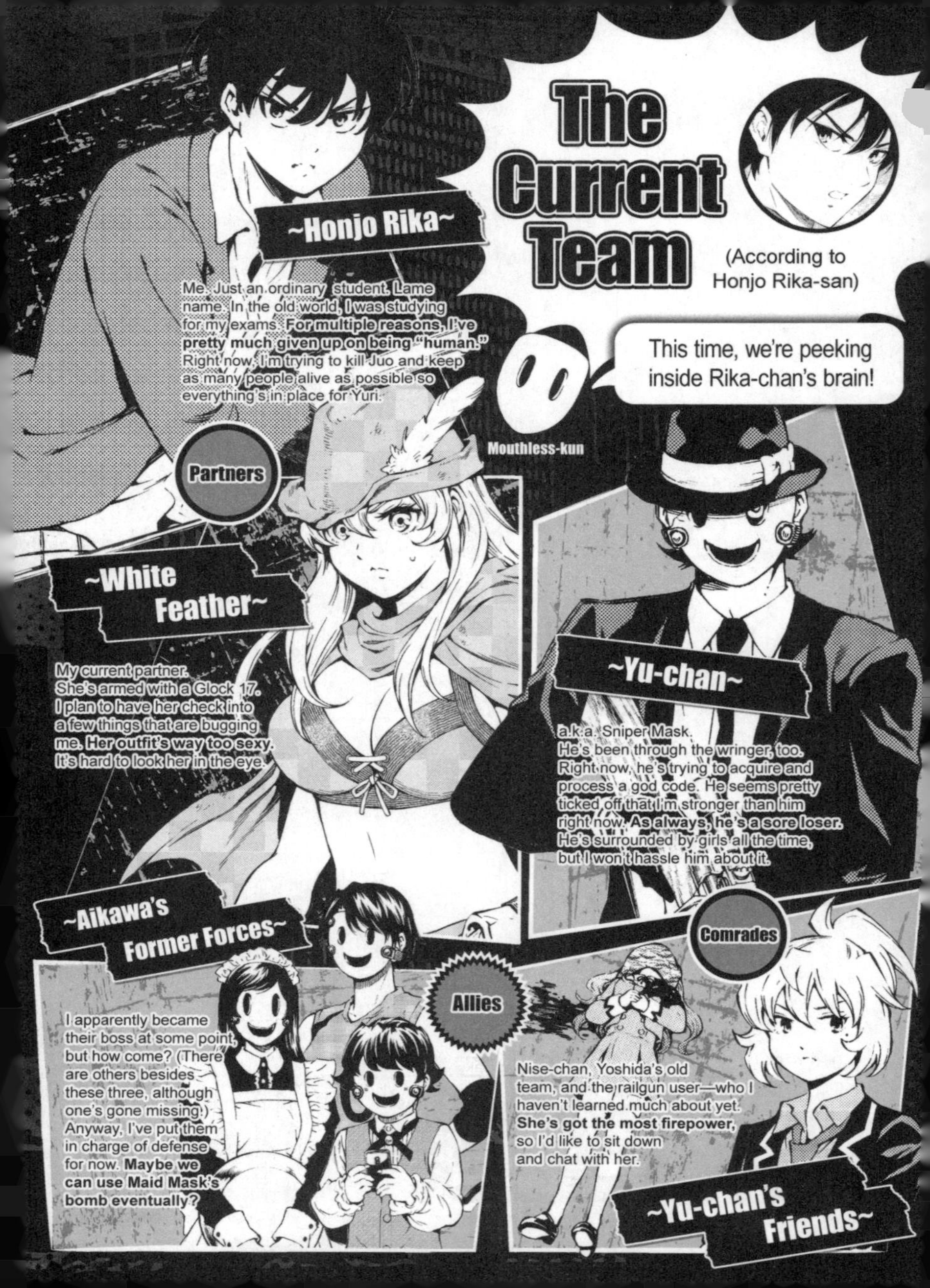

The Current Team
(According to Honjo Rika-san)
This time, we're peeking inside Rika-chan's brain!
Mouthless-kun
~Honjo Rika~
Me. Just an ordinary student. Lame name. In the old world, I was studying for my exams. **For multiple reasons, I've pretty much given up on being "human."** Right now, I'm trying to kill Juo and keep as many people alive as possible so everything's in place for Yuri.
~Yu-chan~
a.k.a. Sniper Mask. He's been through the wringer, too. Right now, he's trying to acquire and process a god code. He seems pretty ticked off that I'm stronger than him right now. **As always, he's a sore loser.** He's surrounded by girls all the time, but I won't hassle him about it.
Partners
~White Feather~
My current partner. She's armed with a Glock 17. I plan to have her check into a few things that are bugging me. **Her outfit's way too sexy.** It's hard to look her in the eye.
Comrades
~Yu-chan's Friends~
Nise-chan, Yoshida's old team, and the railgun user—who I haven't learned much about yet. **She's got the most firepower,** so I'd like to sit down and chat with her.
Allies
~Aikawa's Former Forces~
I apparently became their boss at some point, but how come? (There are others besides these three, although one's gone missing.) Anyway, I've put them in charge of defense for now. **Maybe we can use Maid Mask's bomb eventually?**

~Juo's Lackeys~

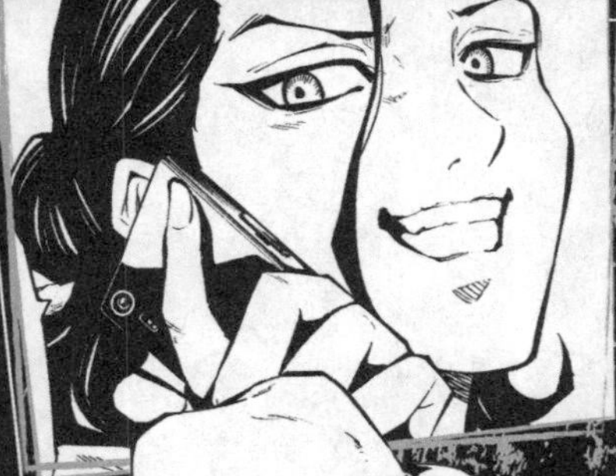

I'm en route to fight Juo. Okihara's guiding me to him. **Juo's definitely one of my old world's few monsters.** I already let him go once before I worked that out—I feel really guilty about that. I don't know how strong he is, or what weapon he carries, but he's probably pretty powerful if he can use a self-strengthening ability.

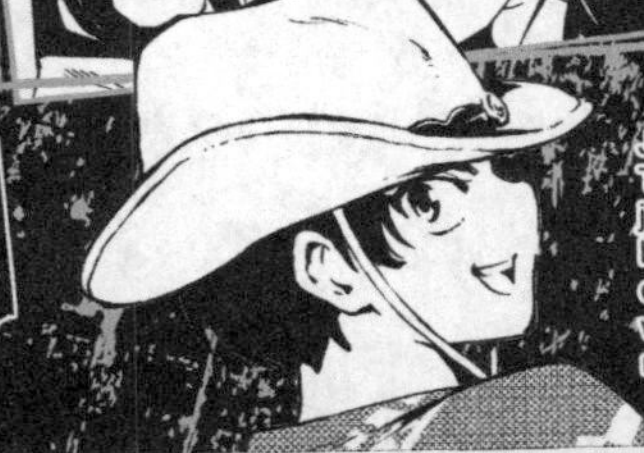

Juo brainwashed my old comrades to follow him. That's a real pain in the ass, because they aren't just hostages—they're fighting for him, too. I just battled Okihara, who I need to be especially wary of. **He's always been an amazing gunman,** and what he said about not being brainwashed is really bugging me.

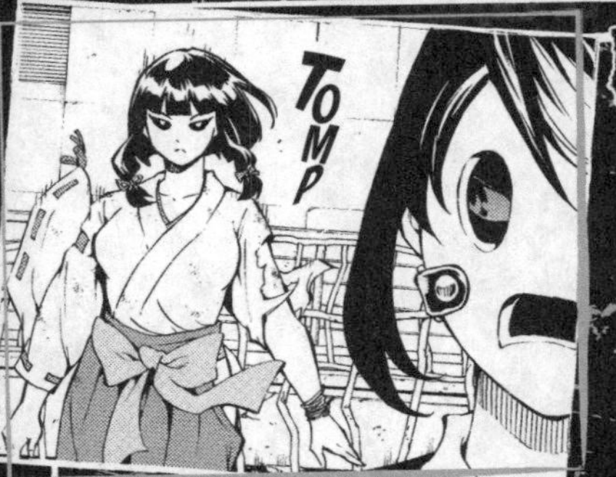
TOMP

~The Administrator/Guardian Angels~

These guys run this domain. When I became an apostle, **information on them poured into my brain.** As you get closer to godhood, the Guardian Angels target you in stages, as a trial. That's apparently because **the administrator can't move easily on his own.** Still, he showed up before, and even revealed some of his abilities. **Did Yuri's awakening change something...?**

×Foes×

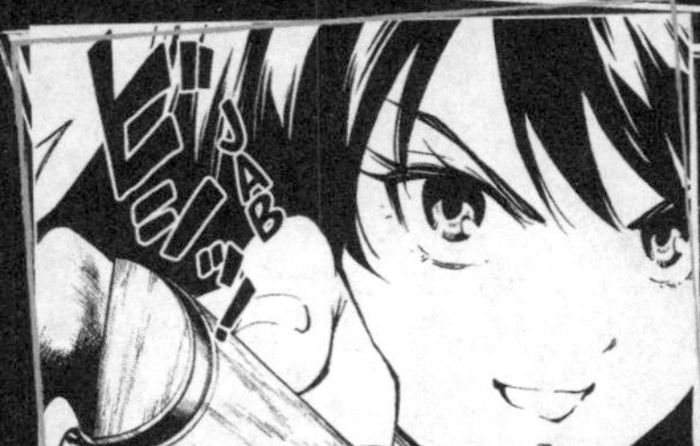
JAB

My precious little sister can break this world's rules. **She's always gone above and beyond.** I've thought about her ability to tamper with dimensions, but I still don't understand all the details. **When I call her, it never goes through—maybe because of her ability?** I have a hunch that, right now, Yuri's peckish and wishing she'd eaten a bigger breakfast. I'd like to think more about her, but I'll wait till I calm down.

~Honjo Yuri~

Bye-bye!

Rika-chan's gone through a ton since childhood, and I don't think he's out of the woods!

Text/Tsuina Miura

HIGH-RISE INVASION

20

STORY / Tsuina Miura
ART / Takahiro Oba

HIGH-RISE INVASION

20

CONTENTS

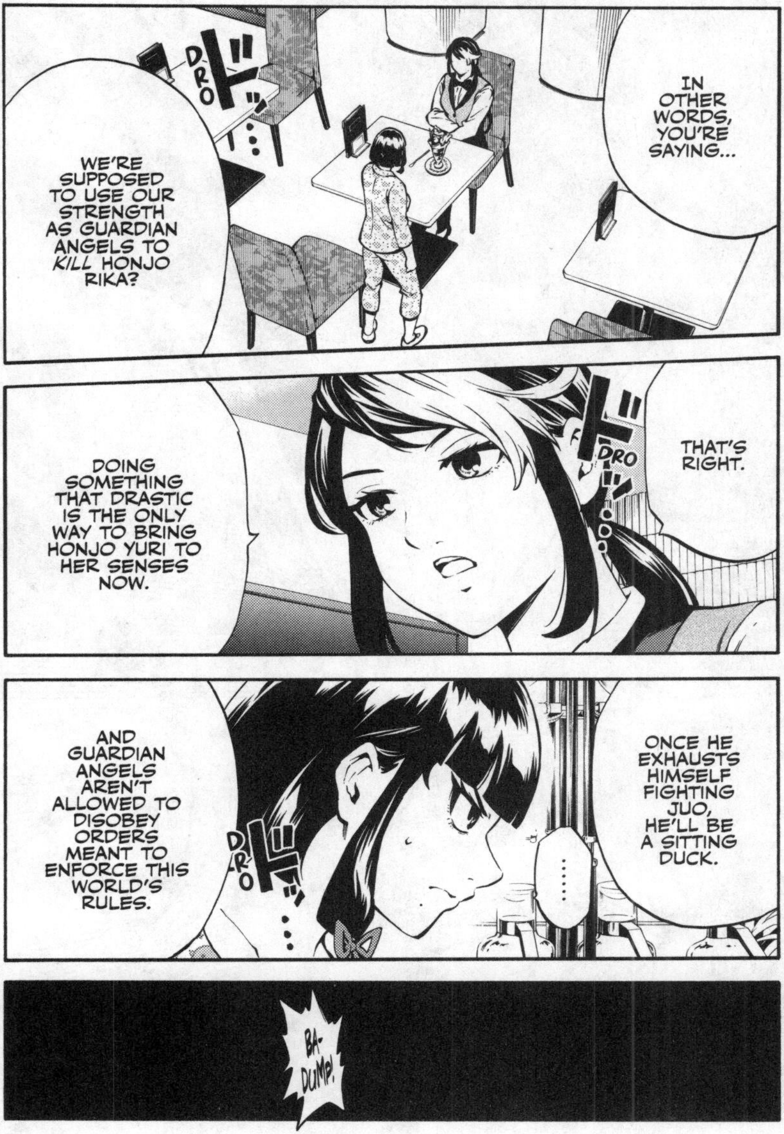
IN OTHER WORDS, YOU'RE SAYING...
DRO
WE'RE SUPPOSED TO USE OUR STRENGTH AS GUARDIAN ANGELS TO *KILL* HONJO RIKA?
DRO
THAT'S RIGHT.
DOING SOMETHING THAT DRASTIC IS THE ONLY WAY TO BRING HONJO YURI TO HER SENSES NOW.
ONCE HE EXHAUSTS HIMSELF FIGHTING JUO, HE'LL BE A SITTING DUCK.
......
DRO
AND GUARDIAN ANGELS AREN'T ALLOWED TO DISOBEY ORDERS MEANT TO ENFORCE THIS WORLD'S RULES.
BA-DUMP!

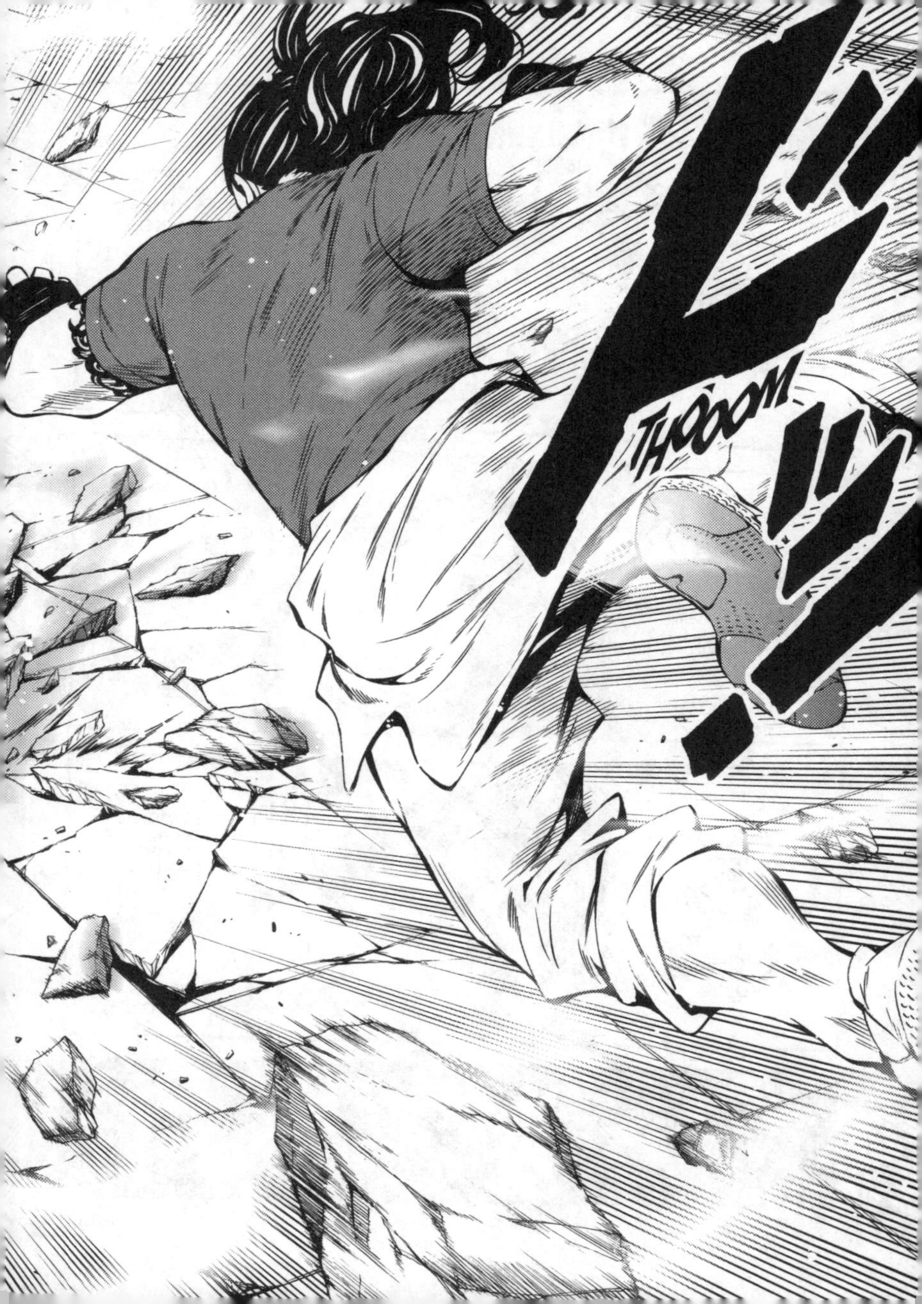
THOOOM

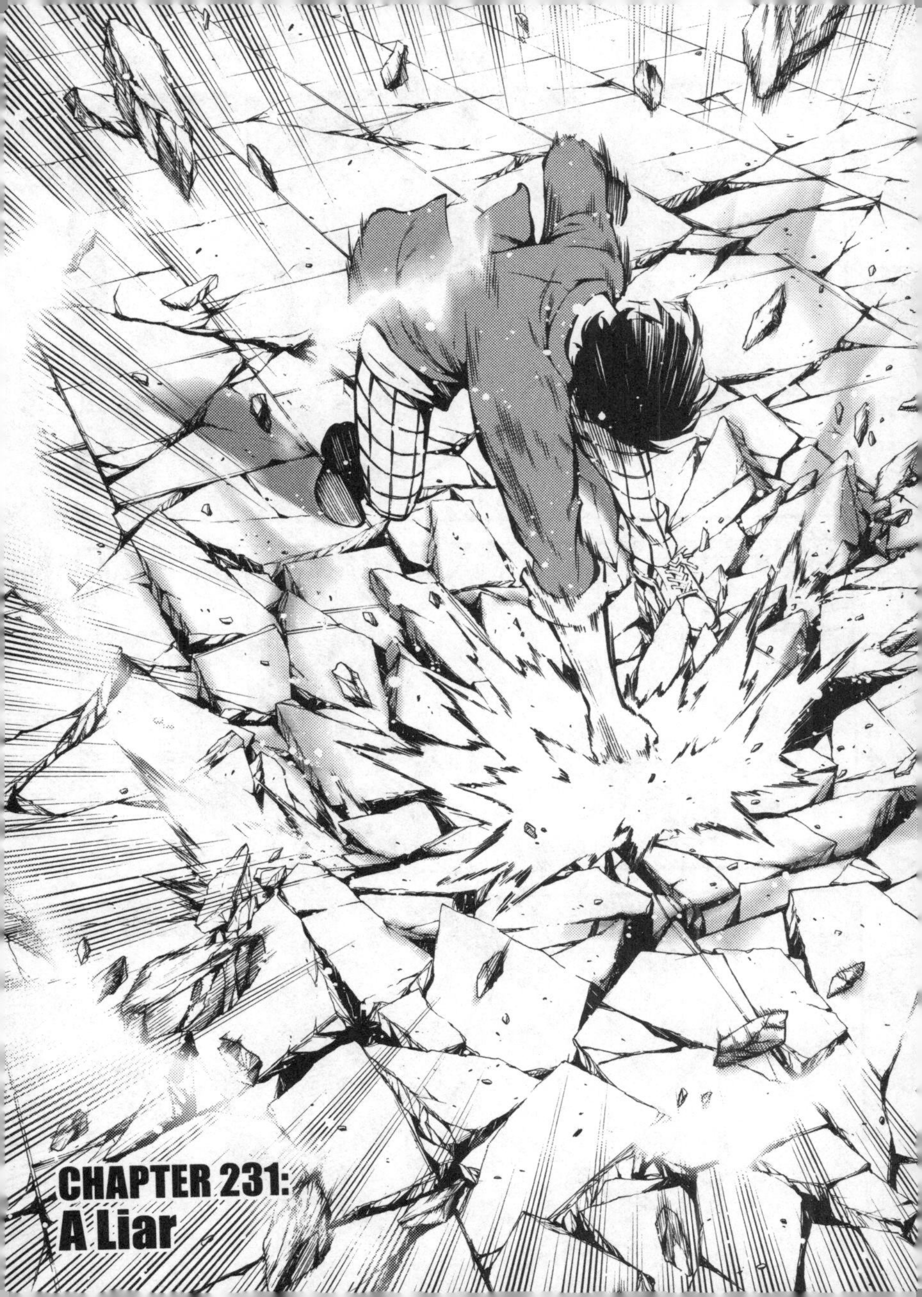

CHAPTER 231: A Liar

SHIT!

TONS OF THEM!

SHARDS OF TILE...

SO FAST...

HWOOSH!

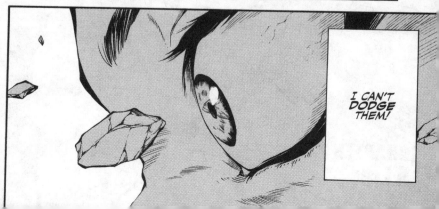

I CAN'T DODGE THEM!

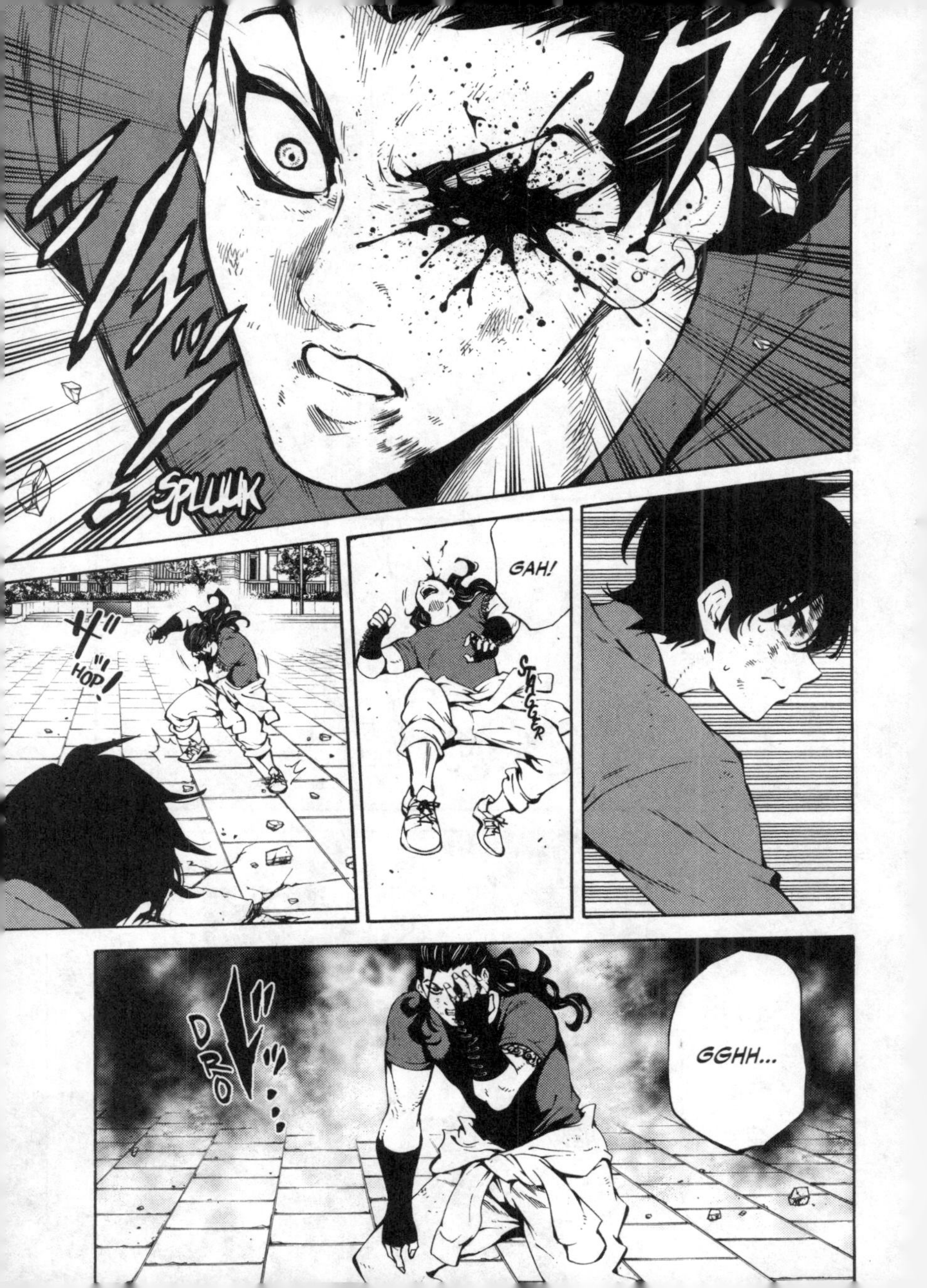
SPLUUK
GAH!
STAGGER
HOP!
GGHH...
DRO...

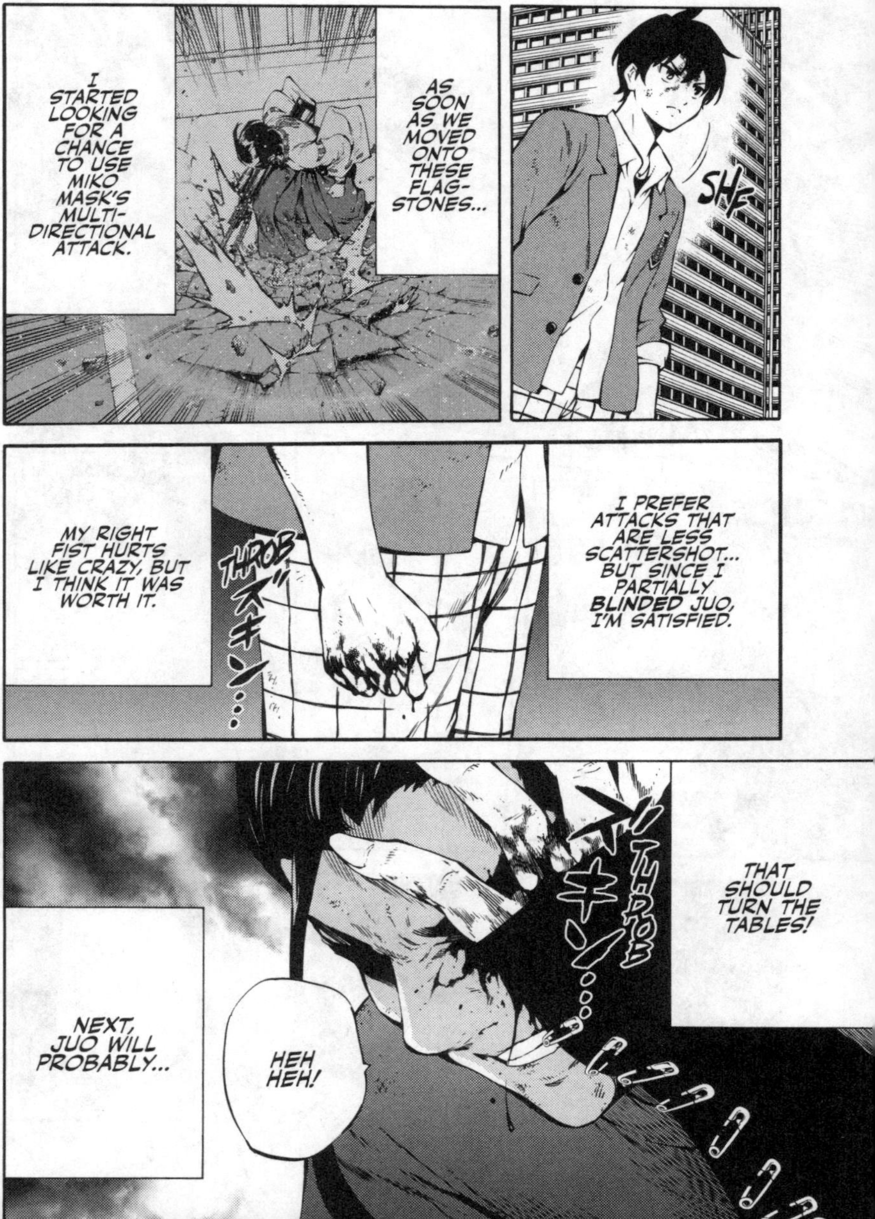
SHF
AS SOON AS WE MOVED ONTO THESE FLAG-STONES...
I STARTED LOOKING FOR A CHANCE TO USE MIKO MASK'S MULTI-DIRECTIONAL ATTACK.
I PREFER ATTACKS THAT ARE LESS SCATTERSHOT... BUT SINCE I PARTIALLY BLINDED JUO, I'M SATISFIED.
THROB
MY RIGHT FIST HURTS LIKE CRAZY, BUT I THINK IT WAS WORTH IT.
THAT SHOULD TURN THE TABLES!
THROB
HEH HEH!
NEXT, JUO WILL PROBABLY...

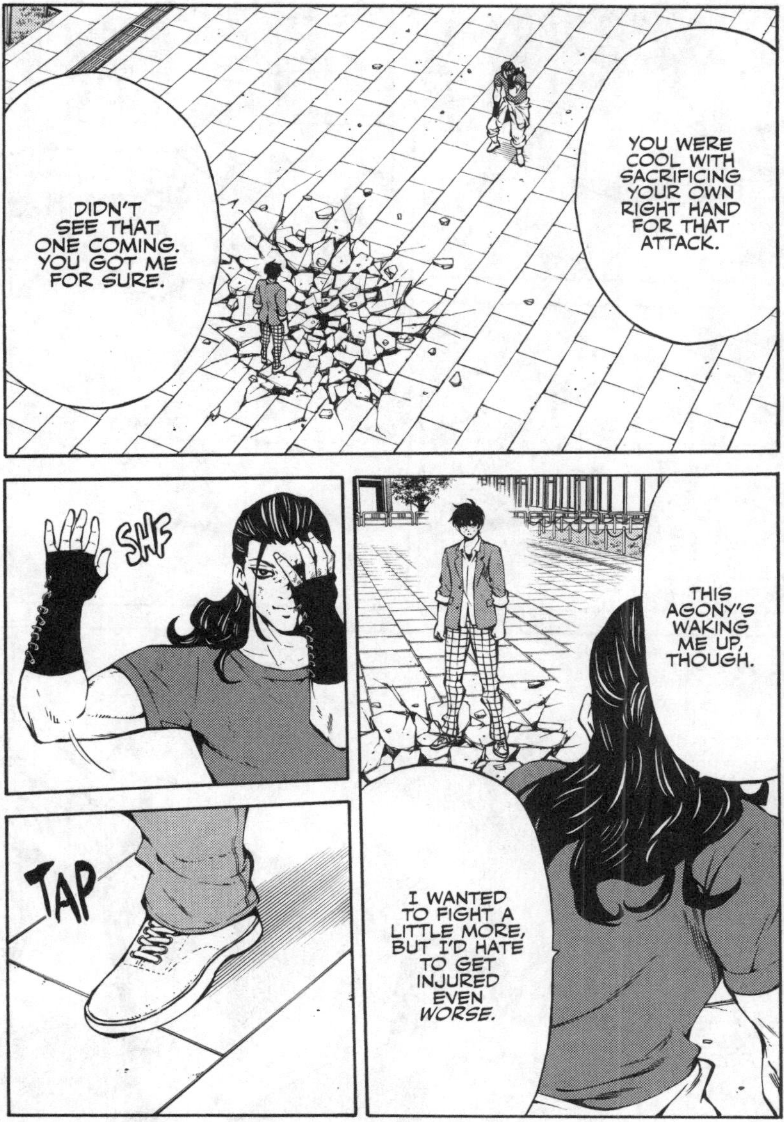
YOU WERE COOL WITH SACRIFICING YOUR OWN RIGHT HAND FOR THAT ATTACK.
DIDN'T SEE THAT ONE COMING. YOU GOT ME FOR SURE.
THIS AGONY'S WAKING ME UP, THOUGH.
I WANTED TO FIGHT A LITTLE MORE, BUT I'D HATE TO GET INJURED EVEN *WORSE.*
SHF
TAP

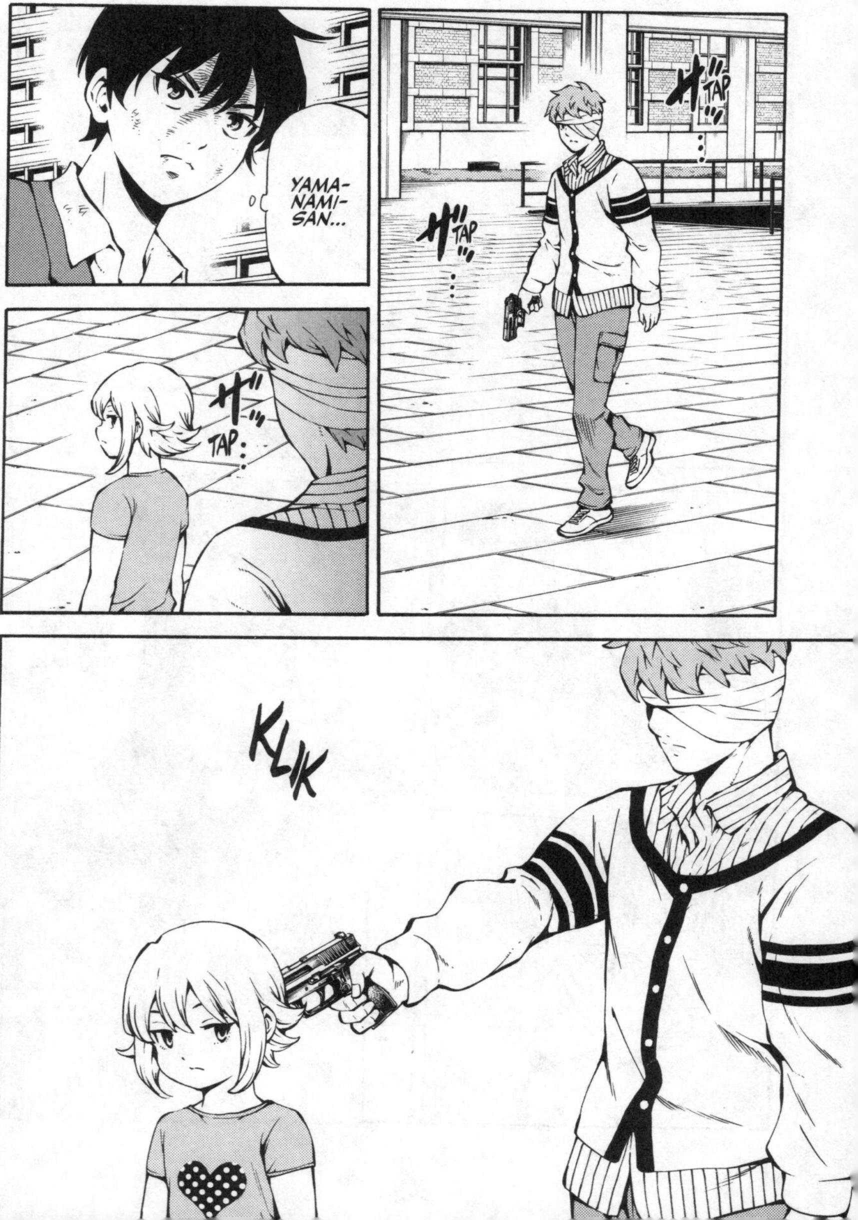
TAP
TAP
YAMANAMI-SAN...
TAP
KLIK

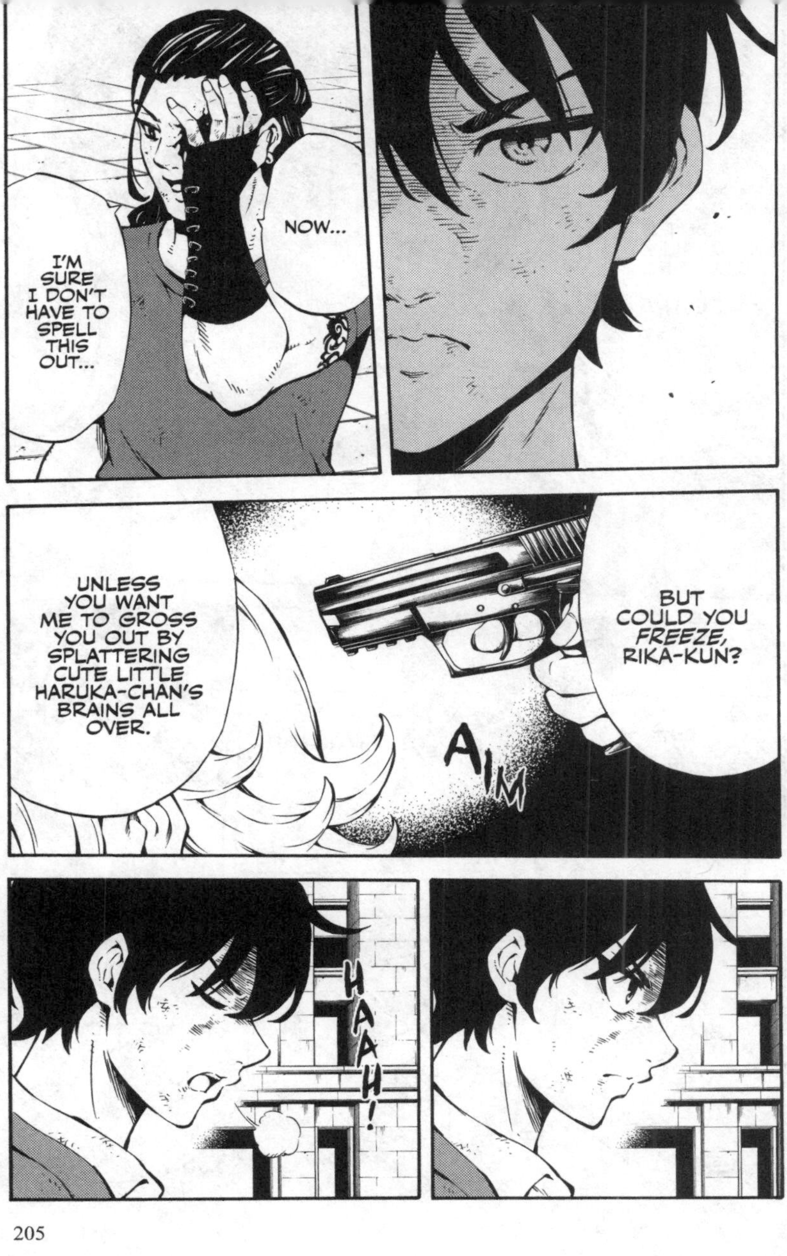
NOW...
I'M SURE I DON'T HAVE TO SPELL THIS OUT...
BUT COULD YOU *FREEZE,* RIKA-KUN?
AIM
UNLESS YOU WANT ME TO GROSS YOU OUT BY SPLATTERING CUTE LITTLE HARUKA-CHAN'S BRAINS ALL OVER.
HAAH!

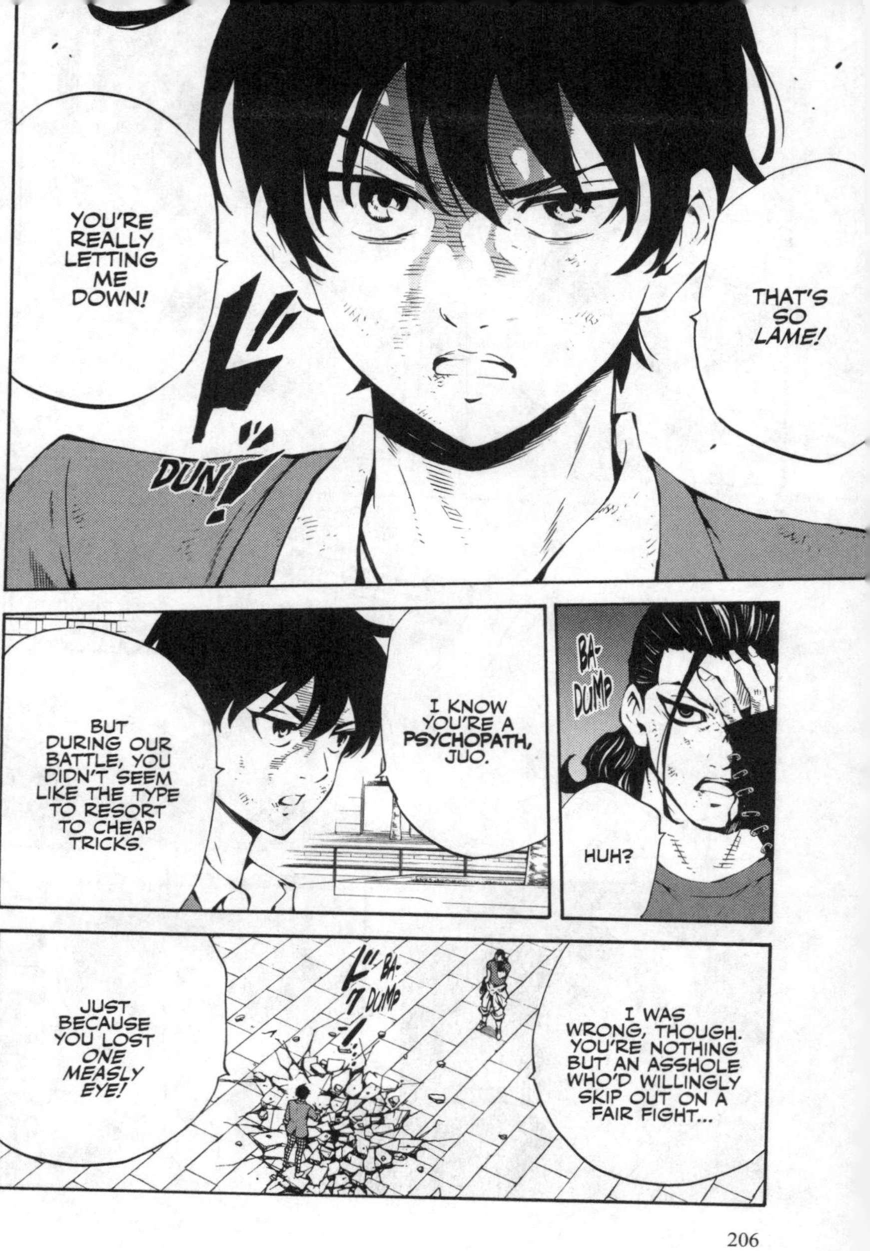
THAT'S SO LAME!
YOU'RE REALLY LETTING ME DOWN!
DUN!
BA-DUMP
HUH?
I KNOW YOU'RE A PSYCHOPATH, JUO.
BUT DURING OUR BATTLE, YOU DIDN'T SEEM LIKE THE TYPE TO RESORT TO CHEAP TRICKS.
I WAS WRONG, THOUGH. YOU'RE NOTHING BUT AN ASSHOLE WHO'D WILLINGLY SKIP OUT ON A FAIR FIGHT...
BA-DUMP
JUST BECAUSE YOU LOST ONE MEASLY EYE!

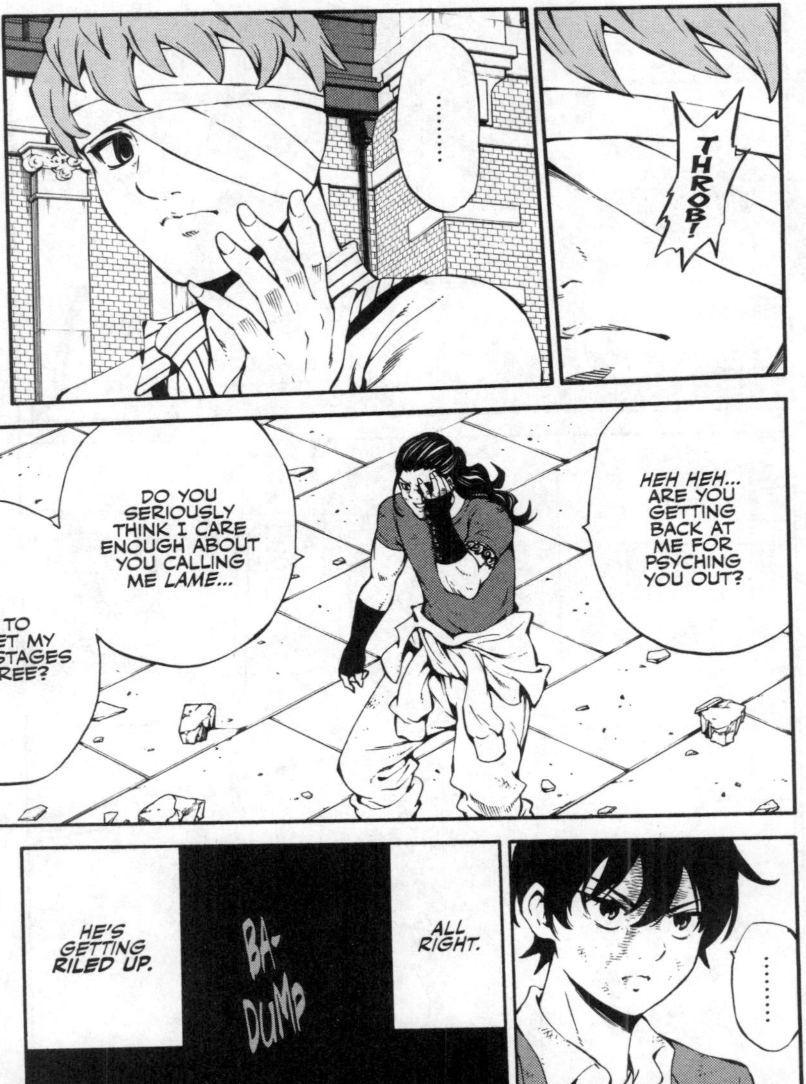
THROB!
......
HEH HEH... ARE YOU GETTING BACK AT ME FOR PSYCHING YOU OUT?
DO YOU SERIOUSLY THINK I CARE ENOUGH ABOUT YOU CALLING ME *LAME*...
TO SET MY HOSTAGES FREE?
......
ALL RIGHT.
BA-DUMP
HE'S GETTING RILED UP.

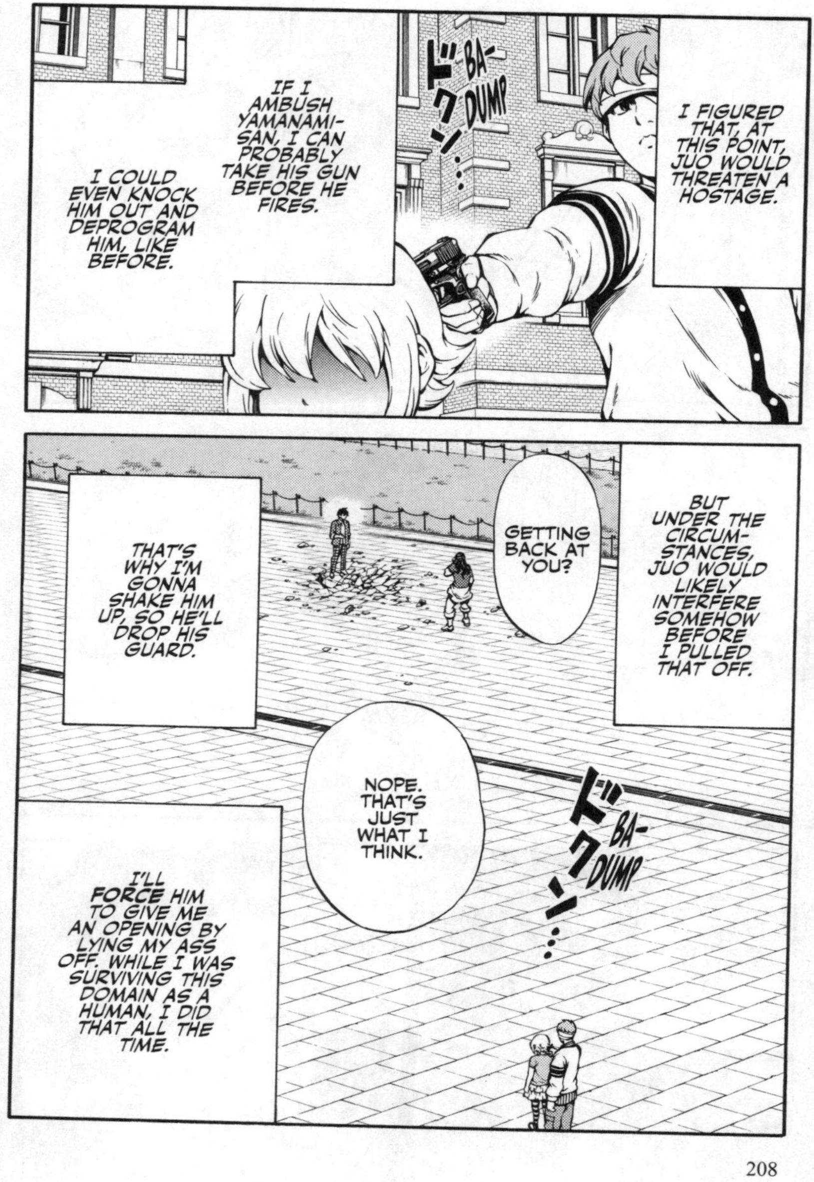
I FIGURED THAT, AT THIS POINT, JUO WOULD THREATEN A HOSTAGE.
BA-DUMP
IF I AMBUSH YAMANAMI-SAN, I CAN PROBABLY TAKE HIS GUN BEFORE HE FIRES.
I COULD EVEN KNOCK HIM OUT AND DEPROGRAM HIM, LIKE BEFORE.
BUT UNDER THE CIRCUM-STANCES, JUO WOULD LIKELY INTERFERE SOMEHOW BEFORE I PULLED THAT OFF.
GETTING BACK AT YOU?
THAT'S WHY I'M GONNA SHAKE HIM UP, SO HE'LL DROP HIS GUARD.
BA-DUMP
NOPE. THAT'S JUST WHAT I THINK.
I'LL FORCE HIM TO GIVE ME AN OPENING BY LYING MY ASS OFF. WHILE I WAS SURVIVING THIS DOMAIN AS A HUMAN, I DID THAT ALL THE TIME.

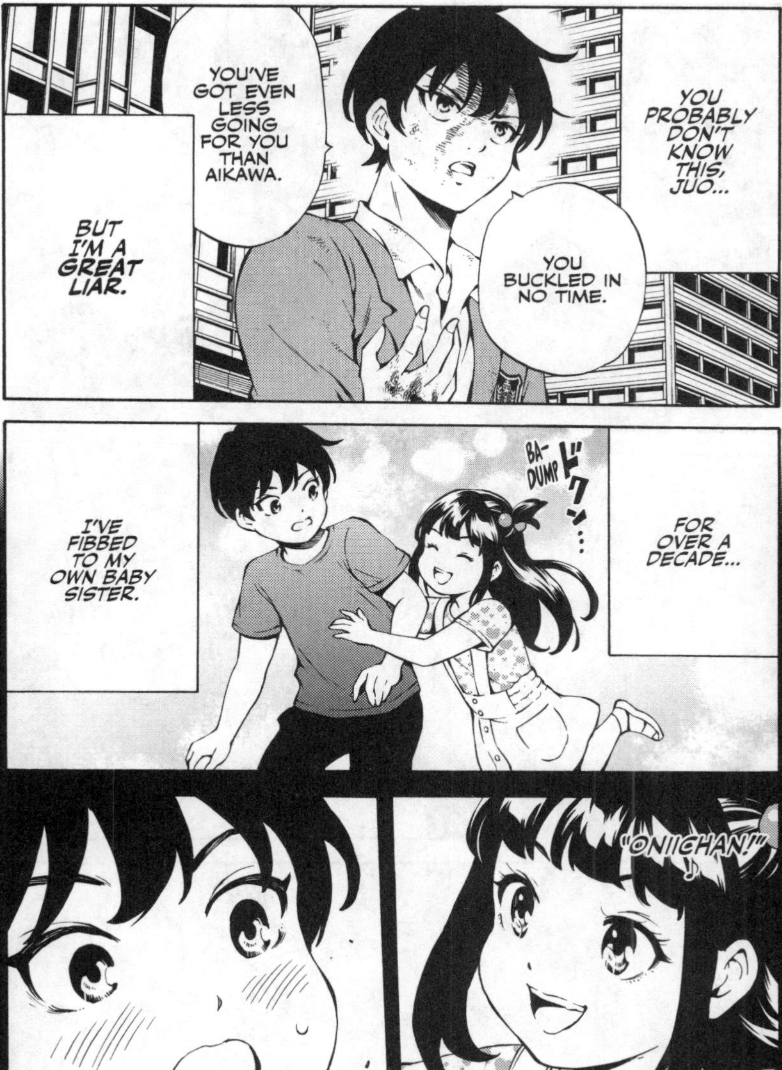

YOU PROBABLY DON'T KNOW THIS, JUO...
YOU'VE GOT EVEN LESS GOING FOR YOU THAN AIKAWA.
YOU BUCKLED IN NO TIME.
BUT I'M A GREAT LIAR.
FOR OVER A DECADE...
BA-DUMP
I'VE FIBBED TO MY OWN BABY SISTER.
"ONIICHAN!" ♪

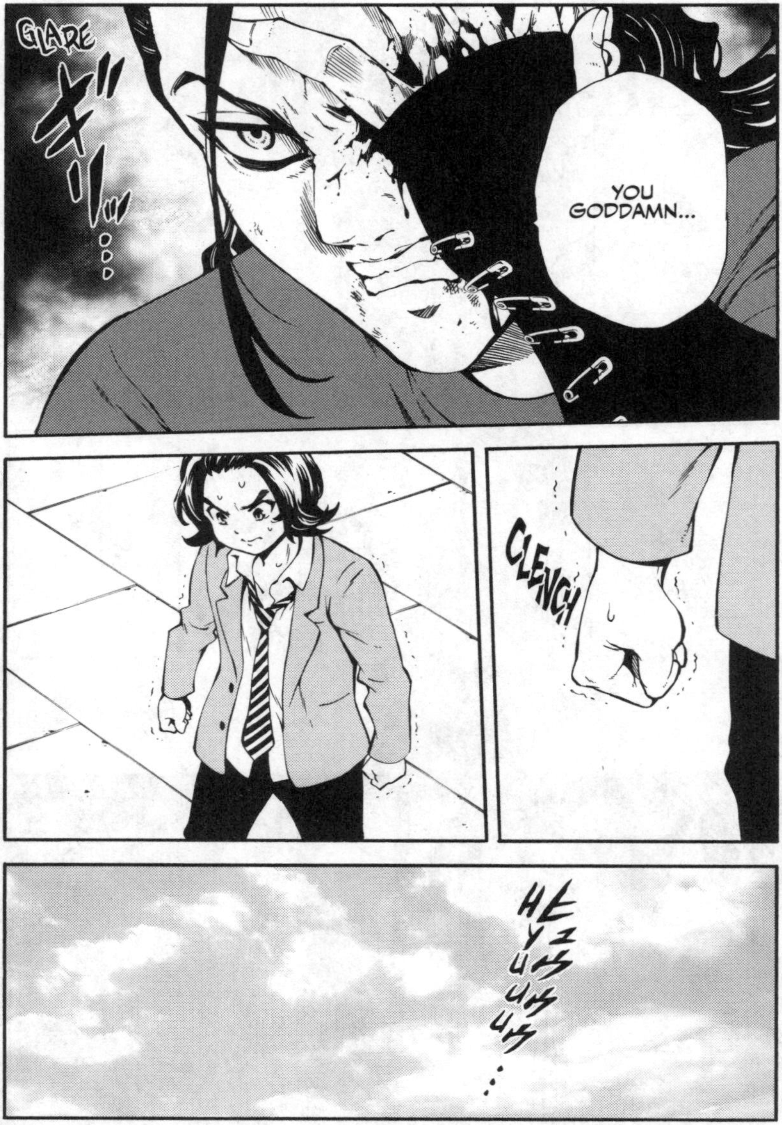
GLARE
YOU GODDAMN...
CLENCH
HYUUU...

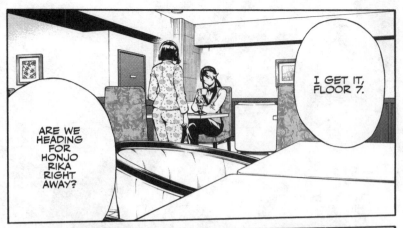

I GET IT, FLOOR 7.
ARE WE HEADING FOR HONJO RIKA RIGHT AWAY?
I KIND OF HOPED...
I COULD GET CHANGED SOME-PLACE BEFORE THAT.
YEAH, WE'LL HEAD OUT, ALL RIGHT.
AFTER ALL, WE WERE *ORDERED* TO.
BY THE TIME WE REACH HIM, THOUGH...
THIS MAY ALL BE OVER.
DON'T TELL ME...

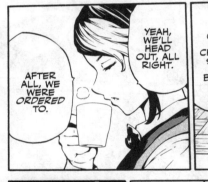

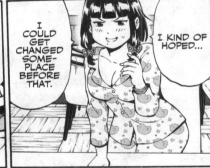

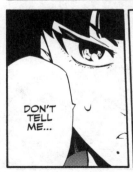

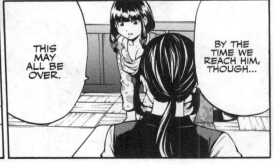

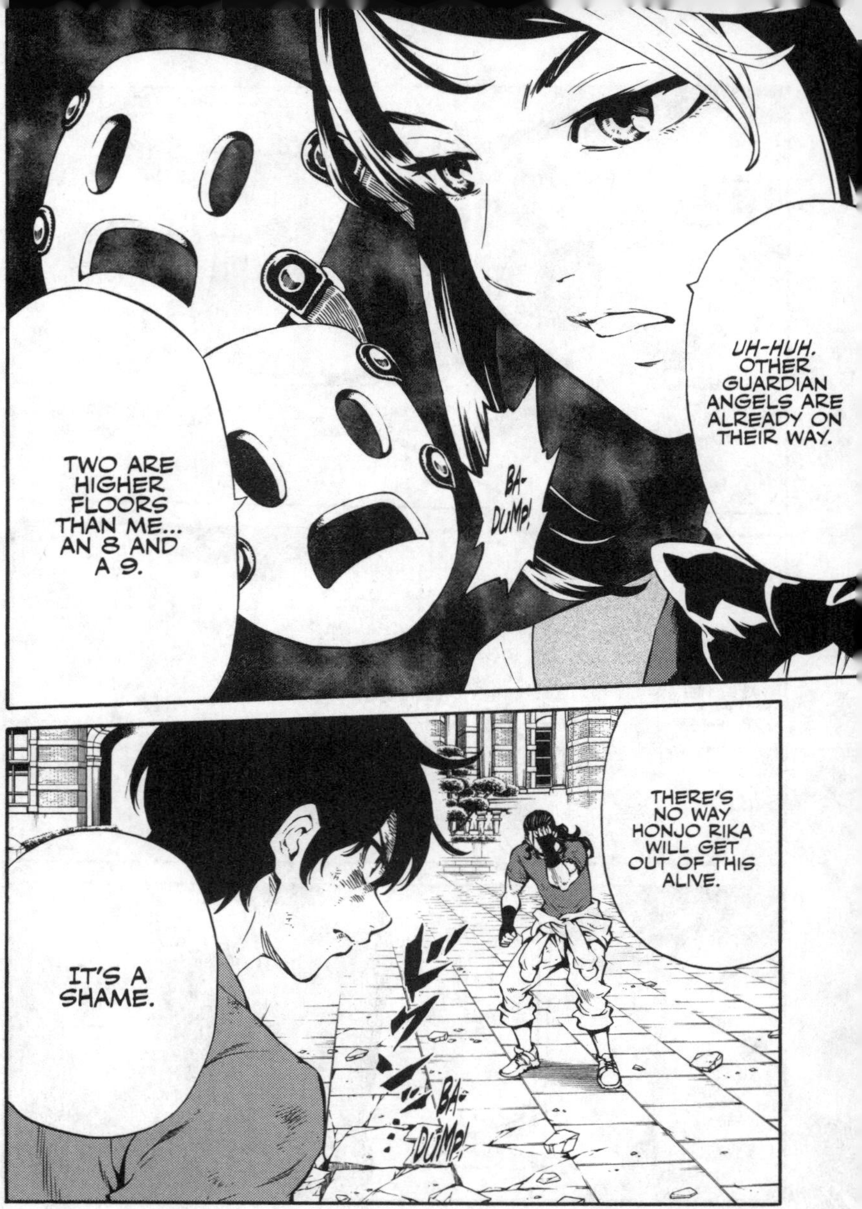
UH-HUH. OTHER GUARDIAN ANGELS ARE ALREADY ON THEIR WAY.
BA-DUMP!
TWO ARE HIGHER FLOORS THAN ME... AN 8 AND A 9.
THERE'S NO WAY HONJO RIKA WILL GET OUT OF THIS ALIVE.
BA-DUMP!
IT'S A SHAME.

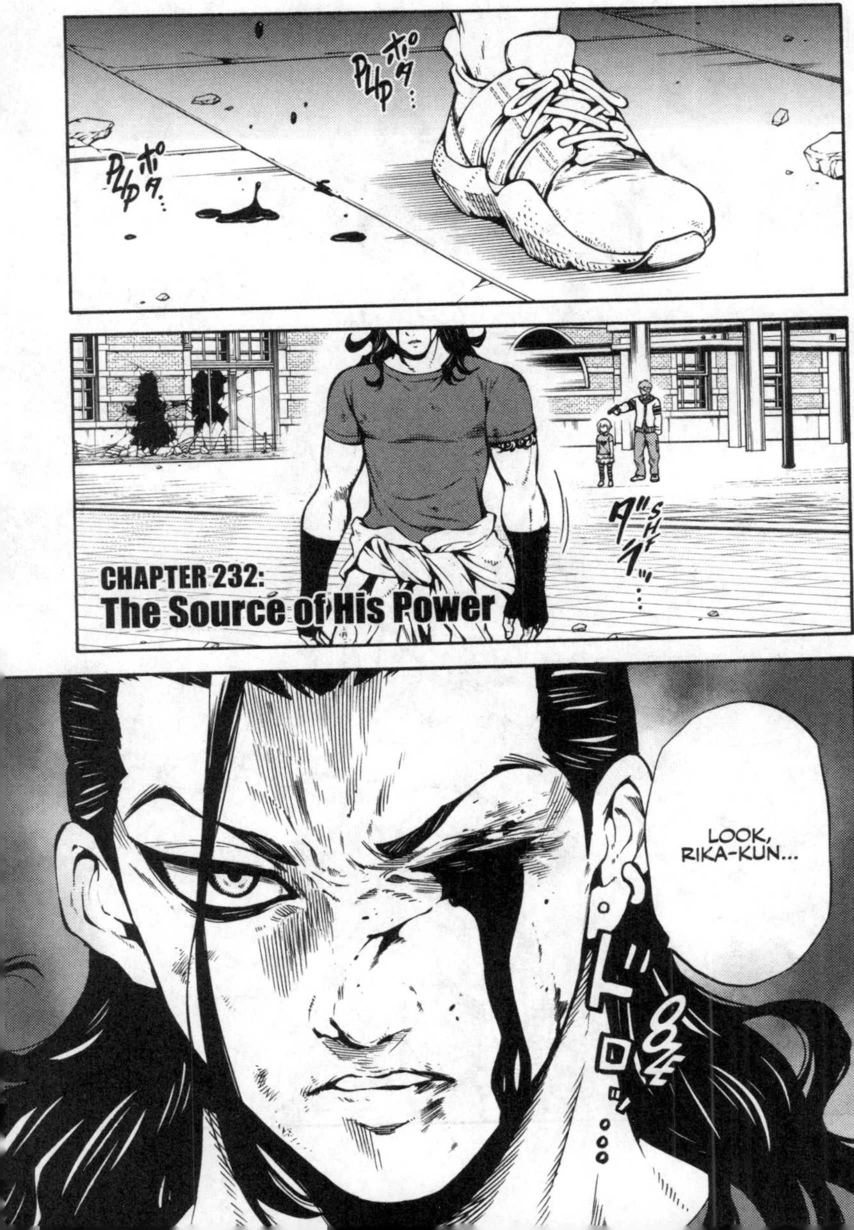
PLIP ポタ…
PLIP ポタ…
CHAPTER 232:
The Source of His Power
SHF ダッ…
LOOK, RIKA-KUN...
OOZE ドロッ…

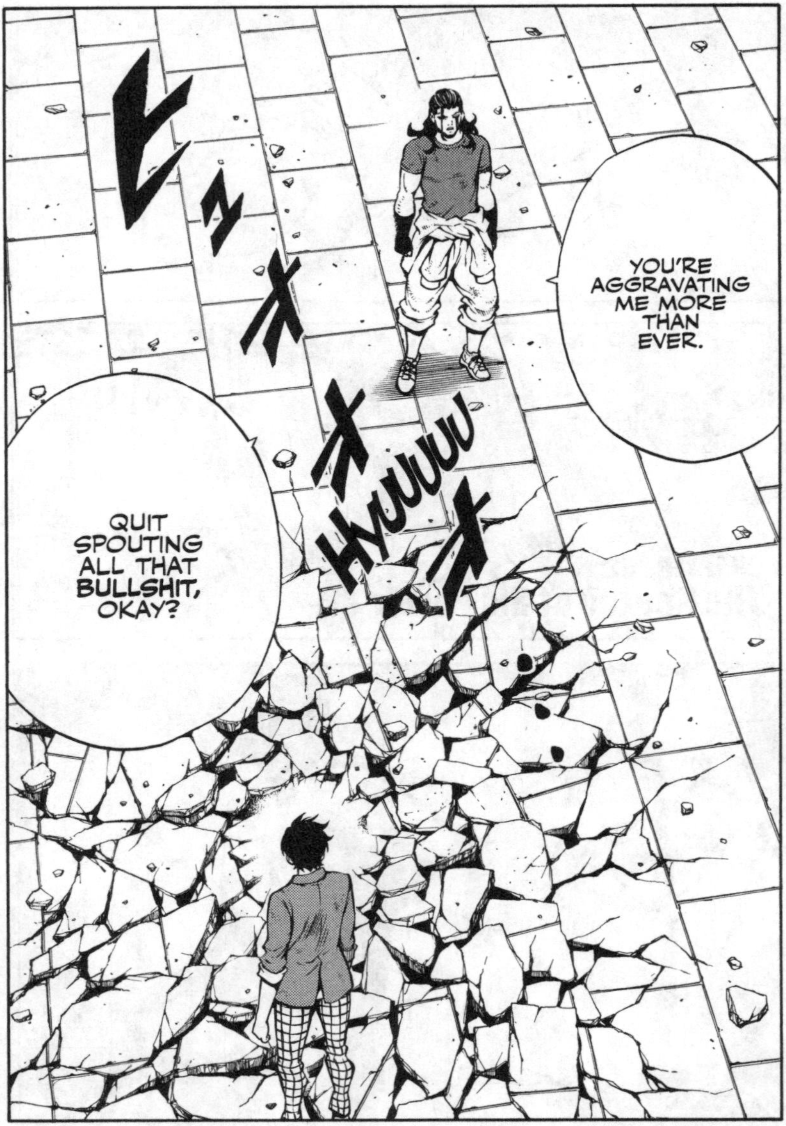
YOU'RE AGGRAVATING ME MORE THAN EVER.
ヒュオオオ
HYUUUUU
QUIT SPOUTING ALL THAT BULLSHIT, OKAY?

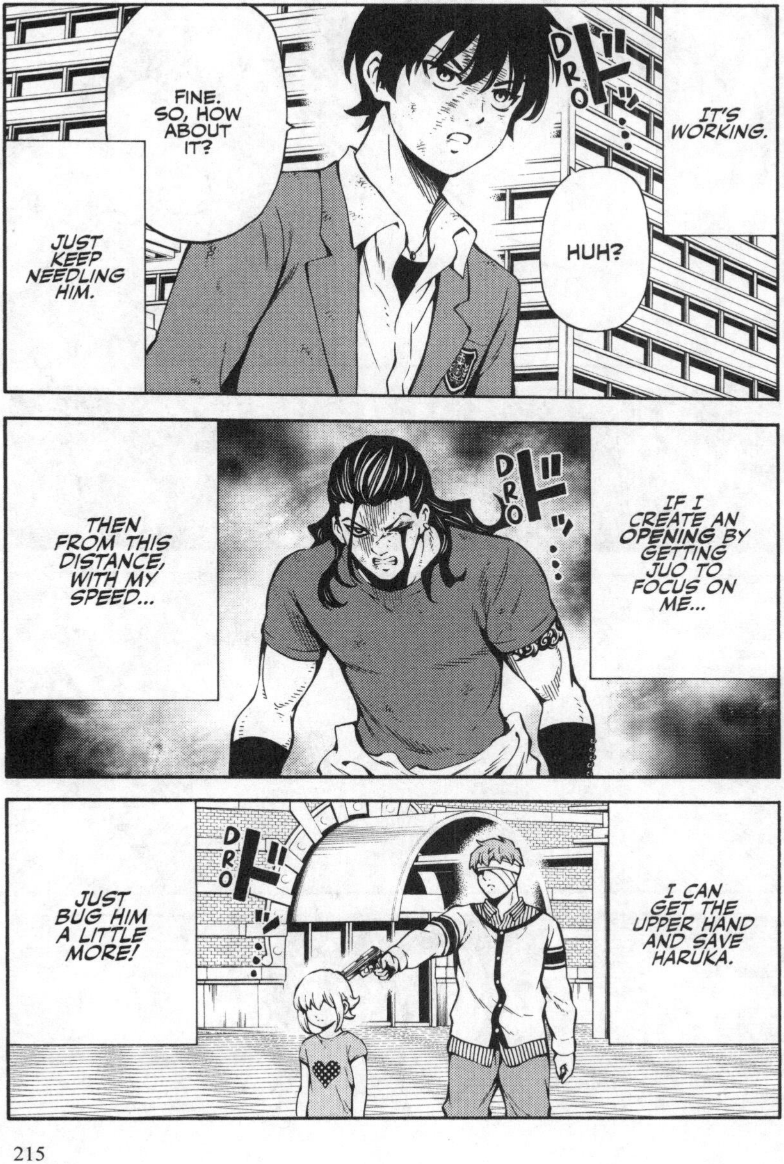
IT'S WORKING.
DRO
FINE. SO, HOW ABOUT IT?
HUH?
JUST KEEP NEEDLING HIM.
IF I CREATE AN OPENING BY GETTING JUO TO FOCUS ON ME...
DRO
THEN FROM THIS DISTANCE, WITH MY SPEED...
I CAN GET THE UPPER HAND AND SAVE HARUKA.
DRO
JUST BUG HIM A LITTLE MORE!

DRO

BA-
DUMP!

THOMP!

BA-
DUMP!

?!

216

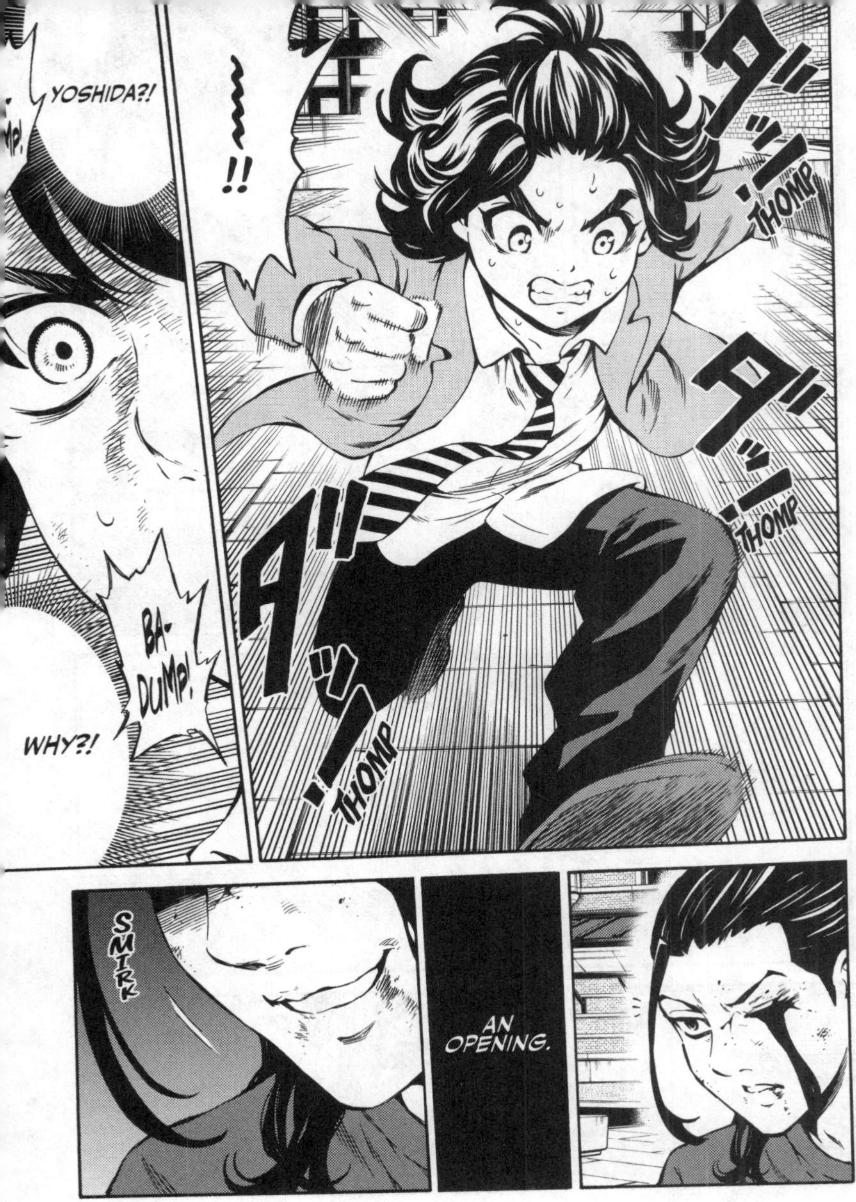

THOMP
THOMP
THOMP
YOSHIDA?!
BA-DUMP!
WHY?!
AN OPENING.
SMIRK

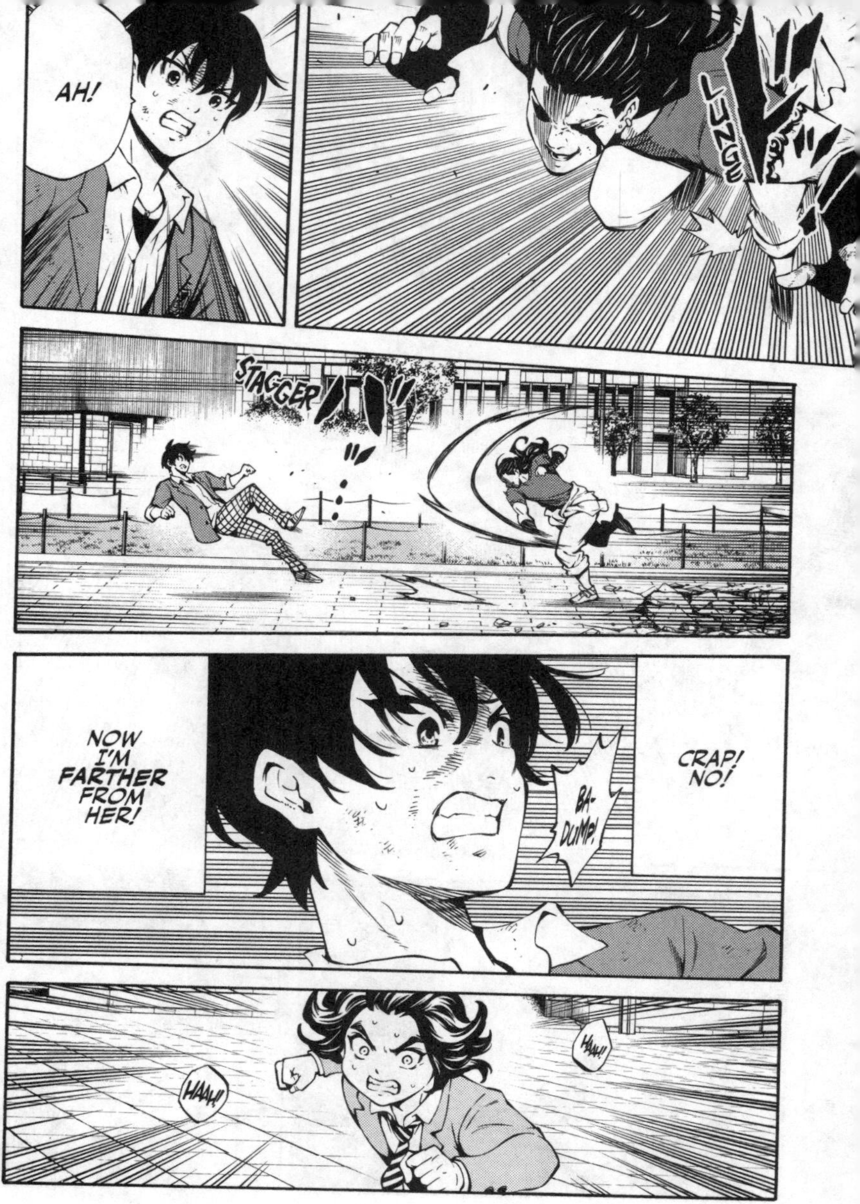
LUNGE
AH!
STAGGER
CRAP! NO!
BA-DUMP!
NOW I'M FARTHER FROM HER!
HAAH!
HAAH!

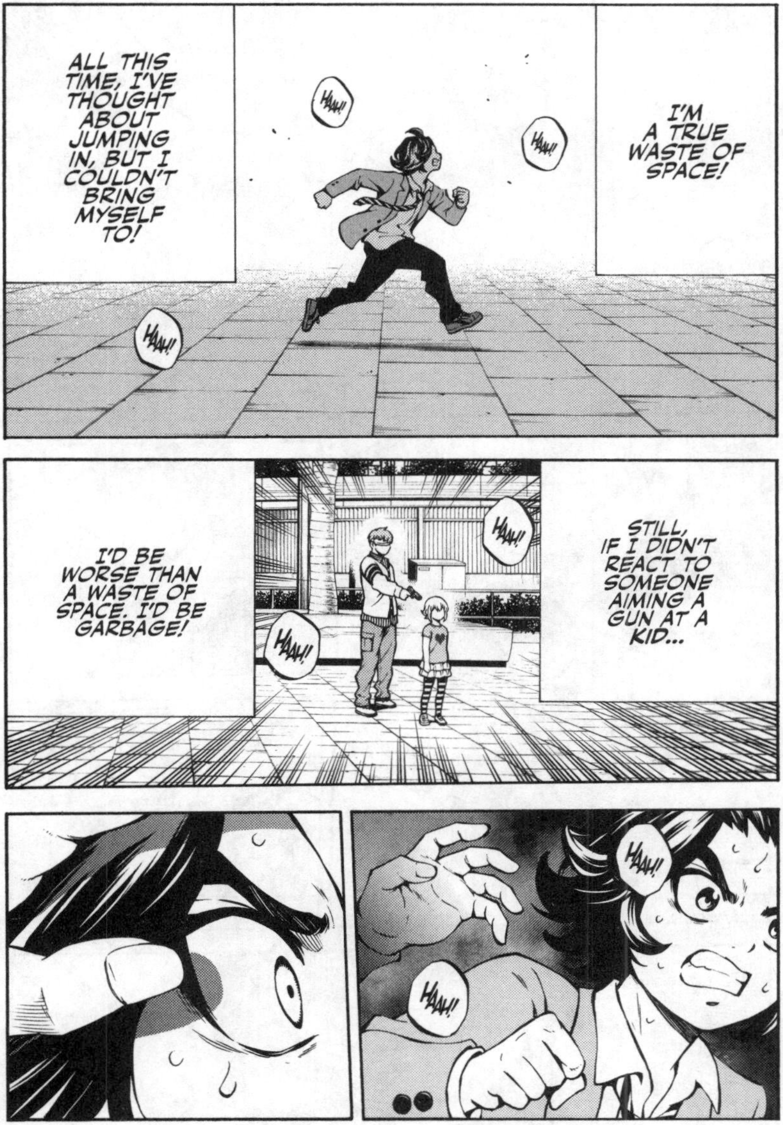
I'M A TRUE WASTE OF SPACE!
HAAH!
HAAH!
ALL THIS TIME, I'VE THOUGHT ABOUT JUMPING IN, BUT I COULDN'T BRING MYSELF TO!
HAAH!
STILL, IF I DIDN'T REACT TO SOMEONE AIMING A GUN AT A KID...
HAAH!
HAAH!
I'D BE WORSE THAN A WASTE OF SPACE. I'D BE GARBAGE!
HAAH!
HAAH!

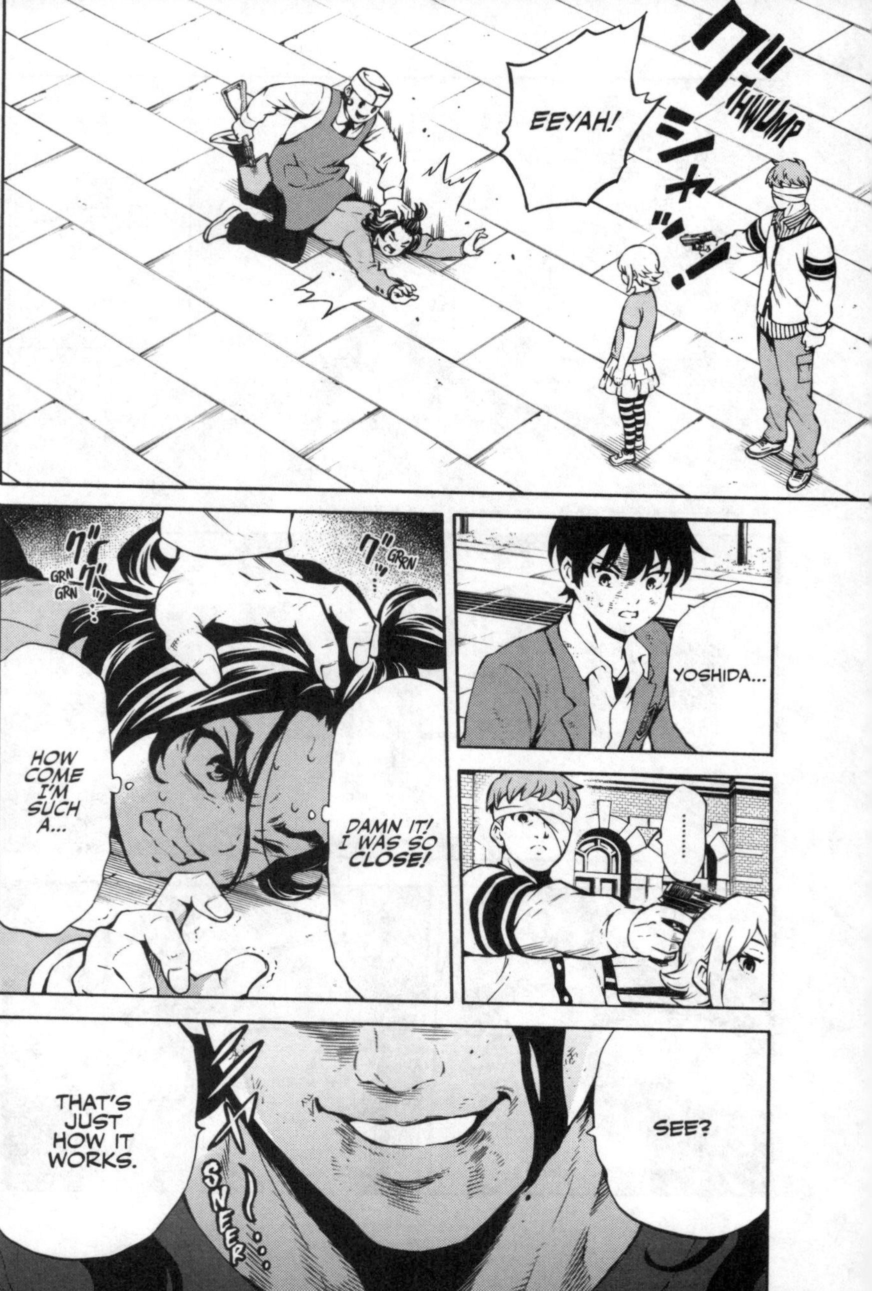
THWUMP
EEYAH!
YOSHIDA...
......
GRRN
GRN GRN
DAMN IT! I WAS SO CLOSE!
HOW COME I'M SUCH A...
SEE?
SNEER
THAT'S JUST HOW IT WORKS.

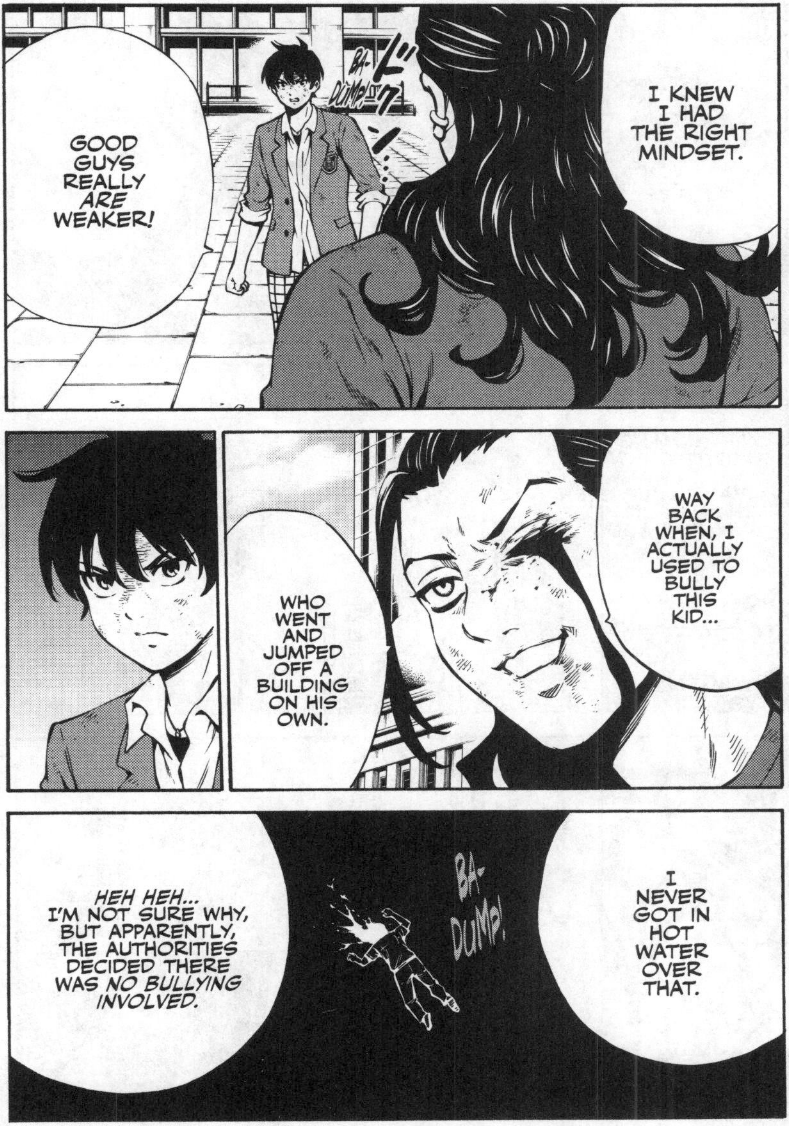
I KNEW I HAD THE RIGHT MINDSET.
BA-DUMP!
GOOD GUYS REALLY *ARE* WEAKER!
WAY BACK WHEN, I ACTUALLY USED TO BULLY THIS KID...
WHO WENT AND JUMPED OFF A BUILDING ON HIS OWN.
I NEVER GOT IN HOT WATER OVER THAT.
BA-DUMP!
HEH HEH... I'M NOT SURE WHY, BUT APPARENTLY, THE AUTHORITIES DECIDED THERE WAS *NO BULLYING INVOLVED.*

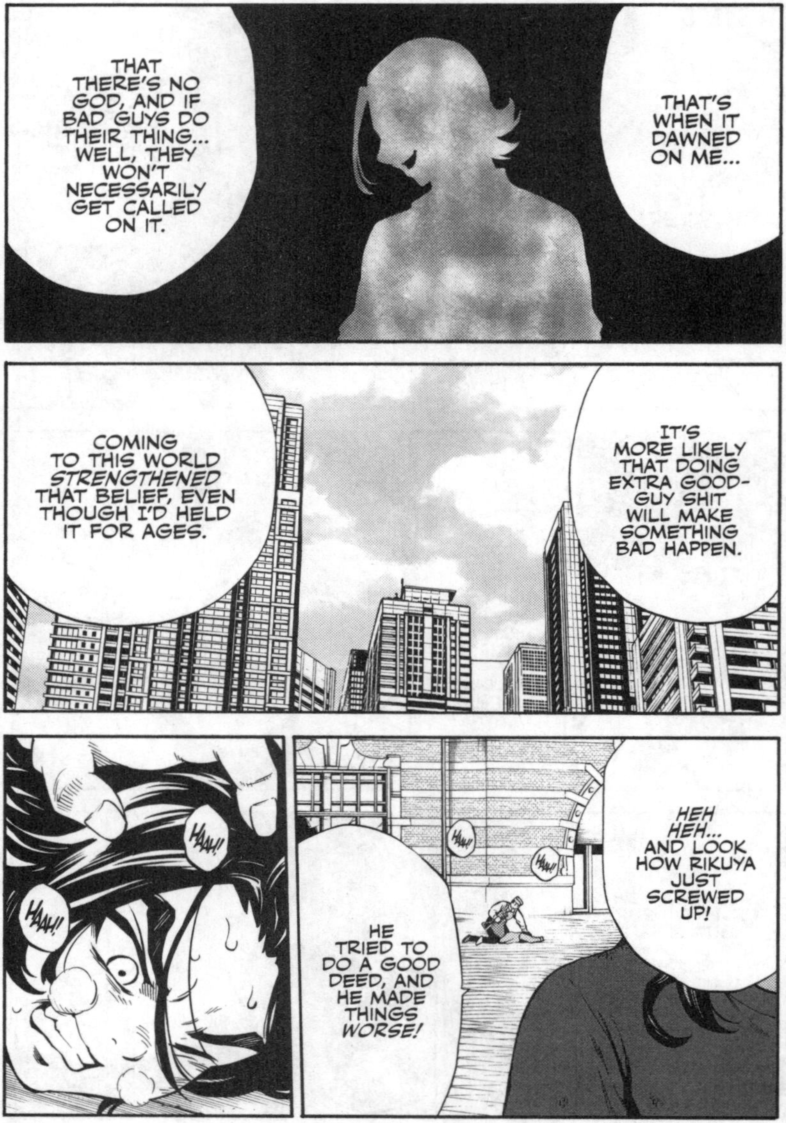
THAT'S WHEN IT DAWNED ON ME...
THAT THERE'S NO GOD, AND IF BAD GUYS DO THEIR THING... WELL, THEY WON'T NECESSARILY GET CALLED ON IT.
IT'S MORE LIKELY THAT DOING EXTRA GOOD-GUY SHIT WILL MAKE SOMETHING BAD HAPPEN.
COMING TO THIS WORLD *STRENGTHENED* THAT BELIEF, EVEN THOUGH I'D HELD IT FOR AGES.
HEH HEH... AND LOOK HOW RIKUYA JUST SCREWED UP!
HAAH!
HAAH!
HE TRIED TO DO A GOOD DEED, AND HE MADE THINGS *WORSE!*
HAAH!
HAAH!

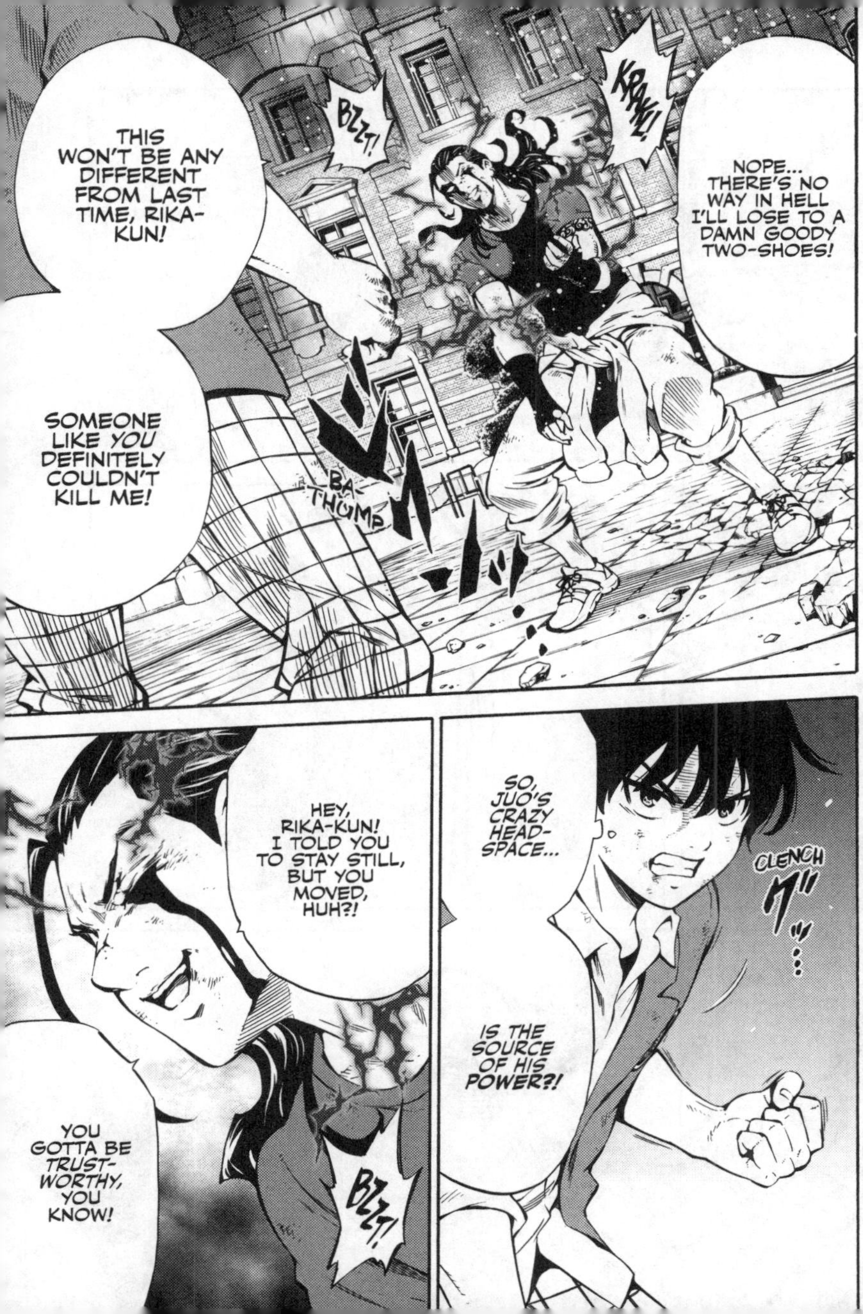
NOPE... THERE'S NO WAY IN HELL I'LL LOSE TO A DAMN GOODY TWO-SHOES!
BZZT!
THIS WON'T BE ANY DIFFERENT FROM LAST TIME, RIKA-KUN!
SOMEONE LIKE *YOU* DEFINITELY COULDN'T KILL ME!
BA-THUMP
SO, JUO'S CRAZY HEAD-SPACE...
CLENCH
IS THE SOURCE OF HIS *POWER?!*
HEY, RIKA-KUN! I TOLD YOU TO STAY STILL, BUT YOU MOVED, HUH?!
YOU GOTTA BE *TRUST-WORTHY,* YOU KNOW!
BZZT!

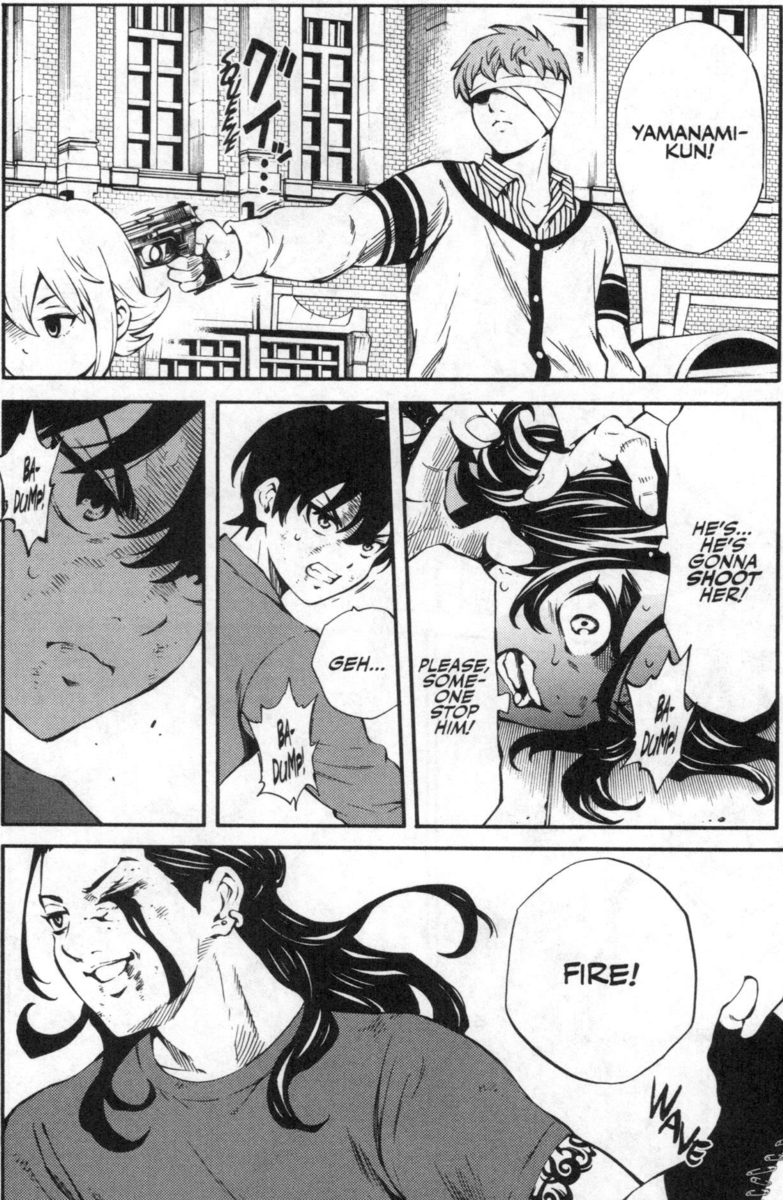
YAMANAMI-KUN!
グイッ
SQUEEZE
HE'S... HE'S GONNA SHOOT HER!
PLEASE, SOME-ONE STOP HIM!
BA-DUMP!
GEH...
BA-DUMP!
BA-DUMP!
FIRE!
WAVE

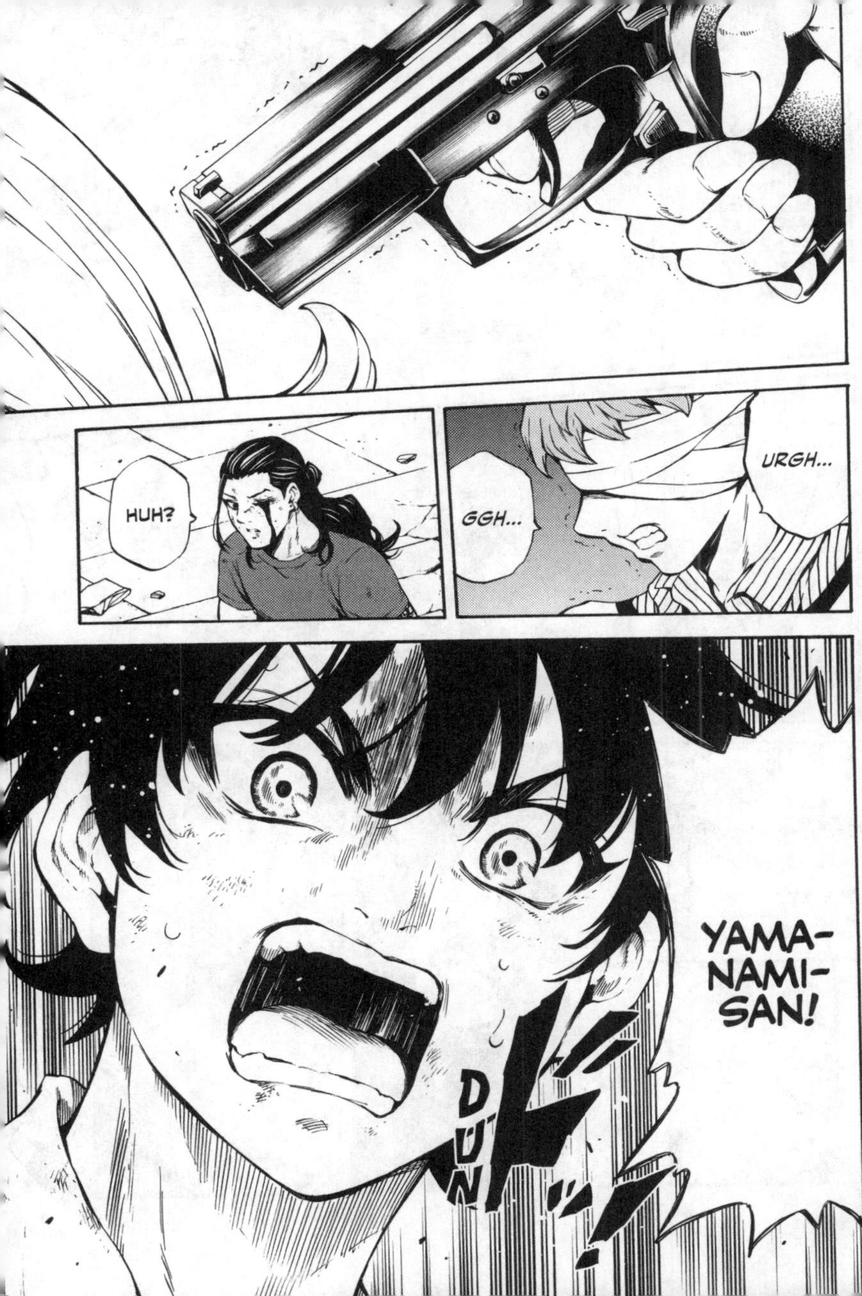
URGH...
GGH...
HUH?
YAMA-NAMI-SAN!
DUN!!

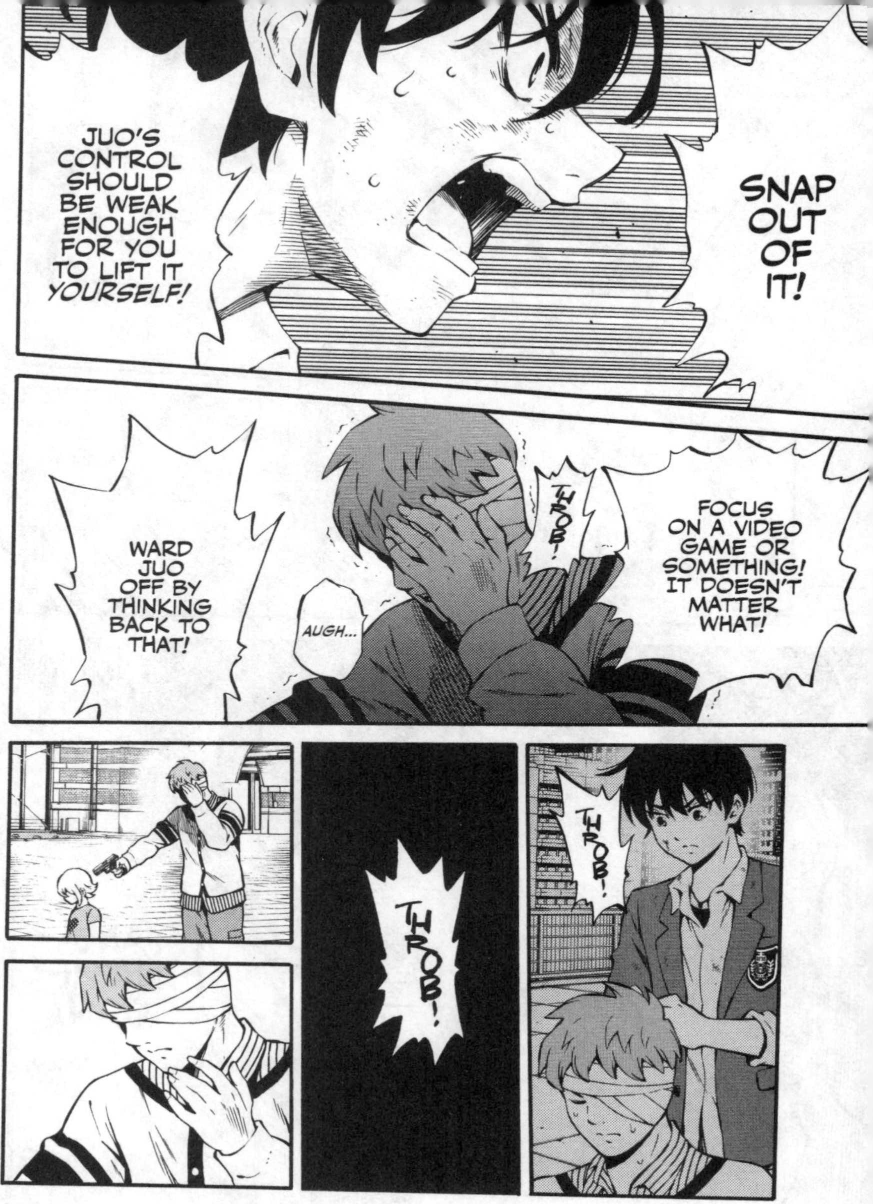
SNAP OUT OF IT!
JUO'S CONTROL SHOULD BE WEAK ENOUGH FOR YOU TO LIFT IT *YOURSELF!*
FOCUS ON A VIDEO GAME OR SOMETHING! IT DOESN'T MATTER WHAT!
THROB!
AUGH...
WARD JUO OFF BY THINKING BACK TO THAT!
THROB!
THROB!

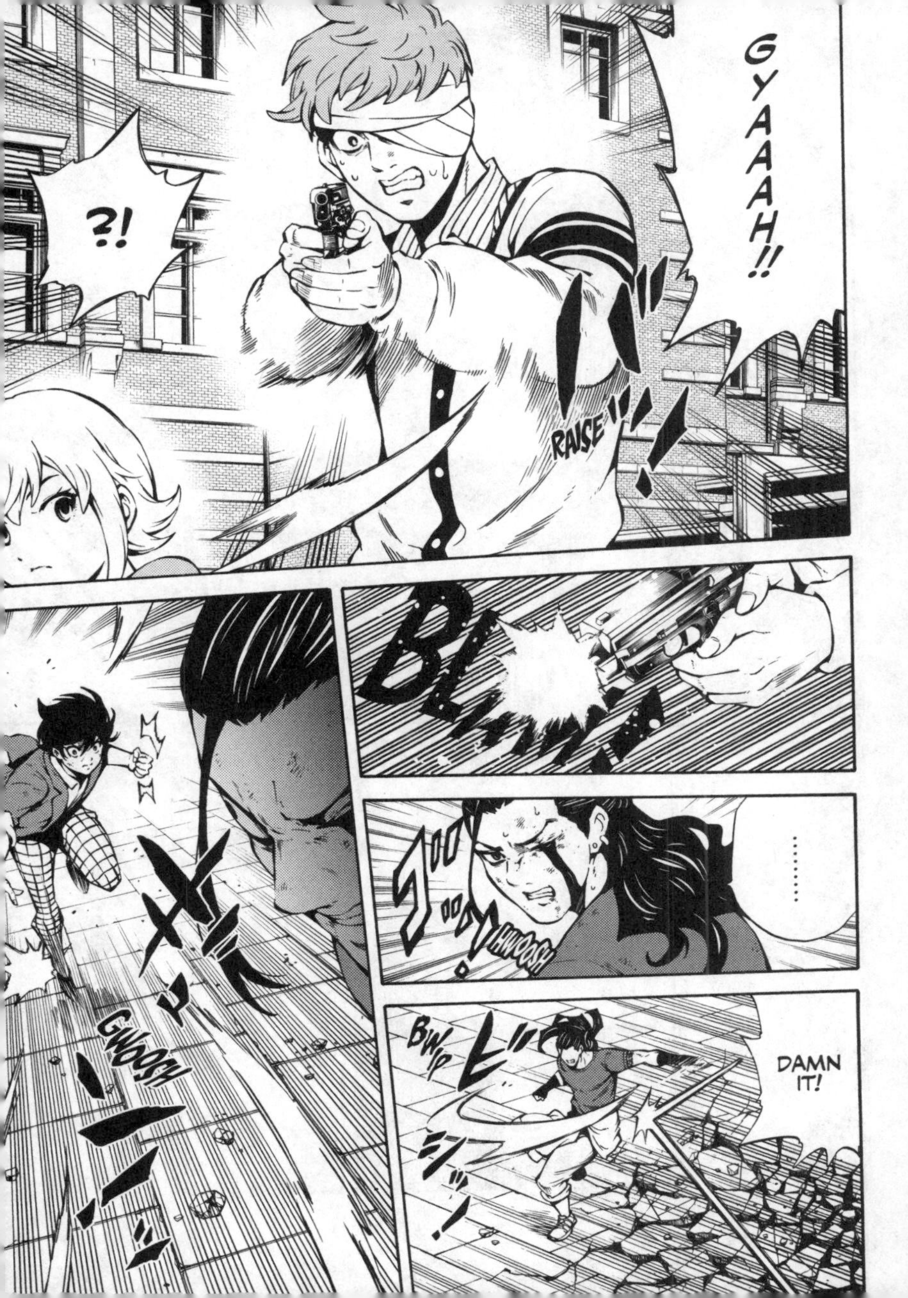
GYAAAAH!!
RAISE
?!
......
WHOOSH
BWIP
DAMN IT!
GWOOSH

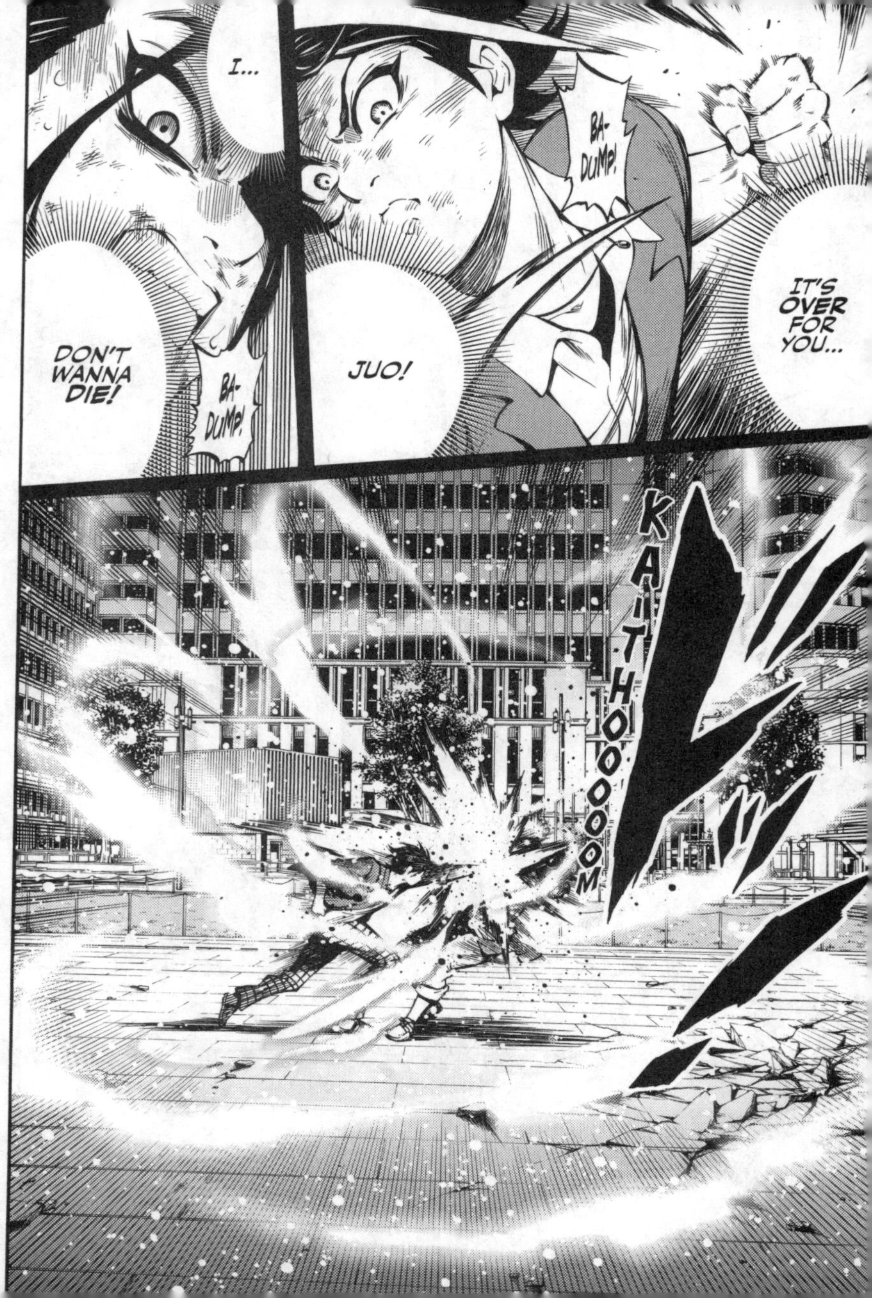
IT'S OVER FOR YOU...
BA-DUMP!
JUO!
I...
DON'T WANNA DIE!
BA-DUMP!
KAITHOOOOOM

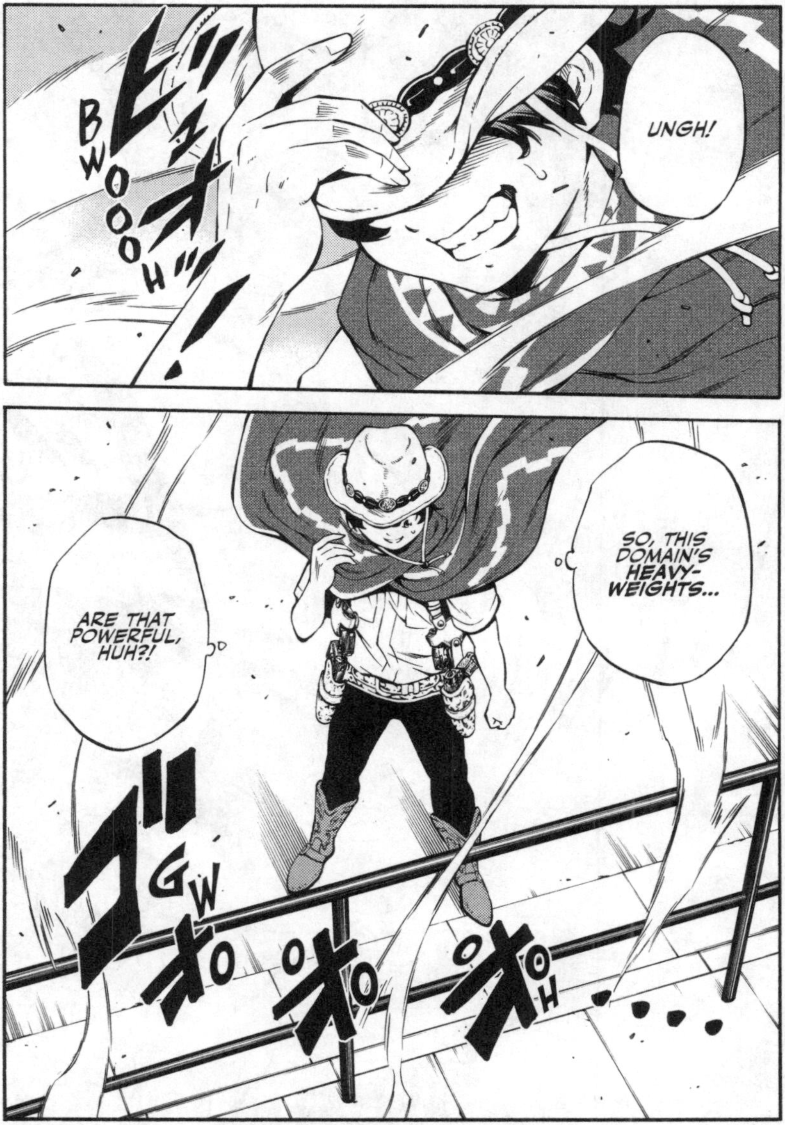
UNGH!
BWOOOOH!
SO, THIS DOMAIN'S HEAVY-WEIGHTS...
ARE THAT POWERFUL, HUH?!
GWOOOOH...

CHAPTER 233: Yeah, He Looks Dangerous

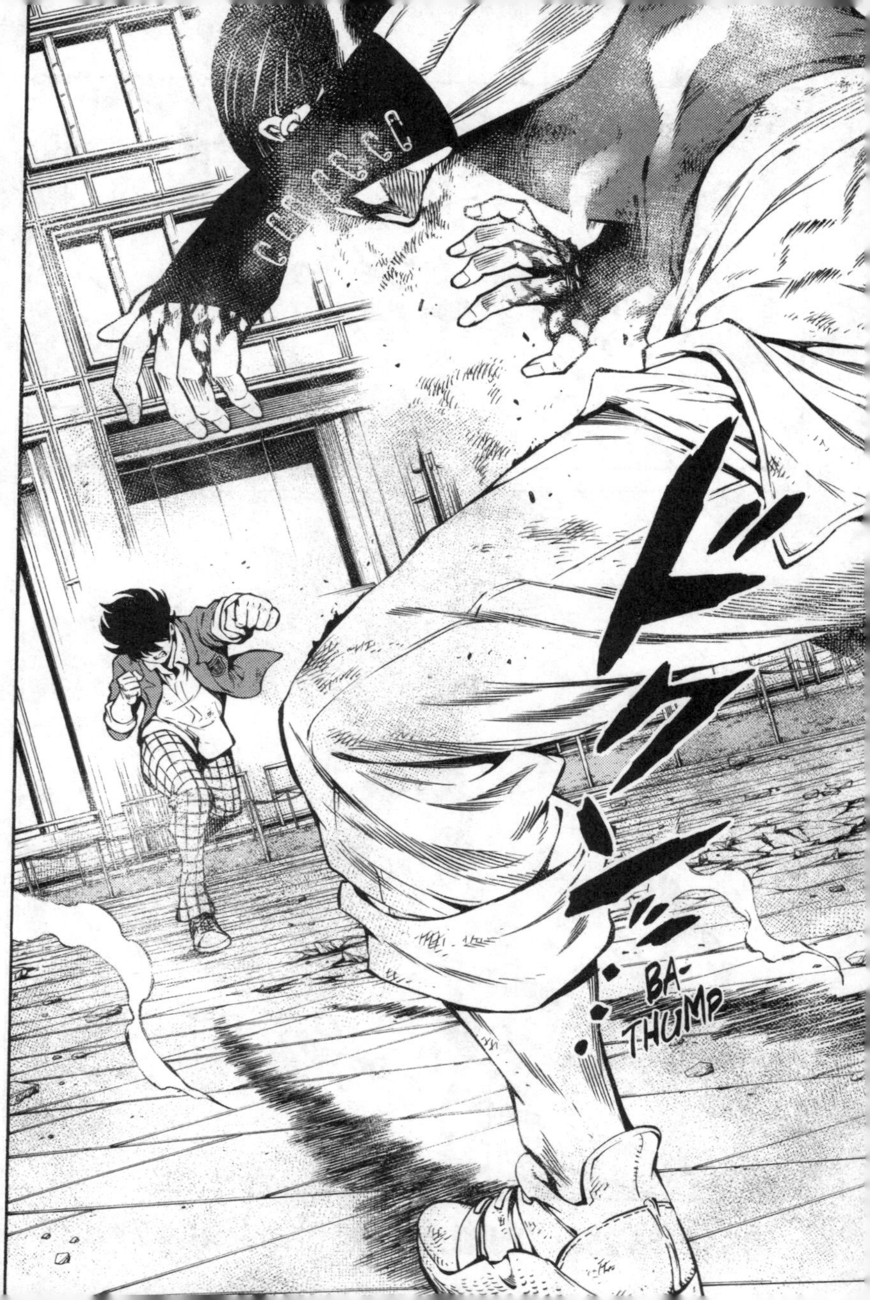
BA-THUMP

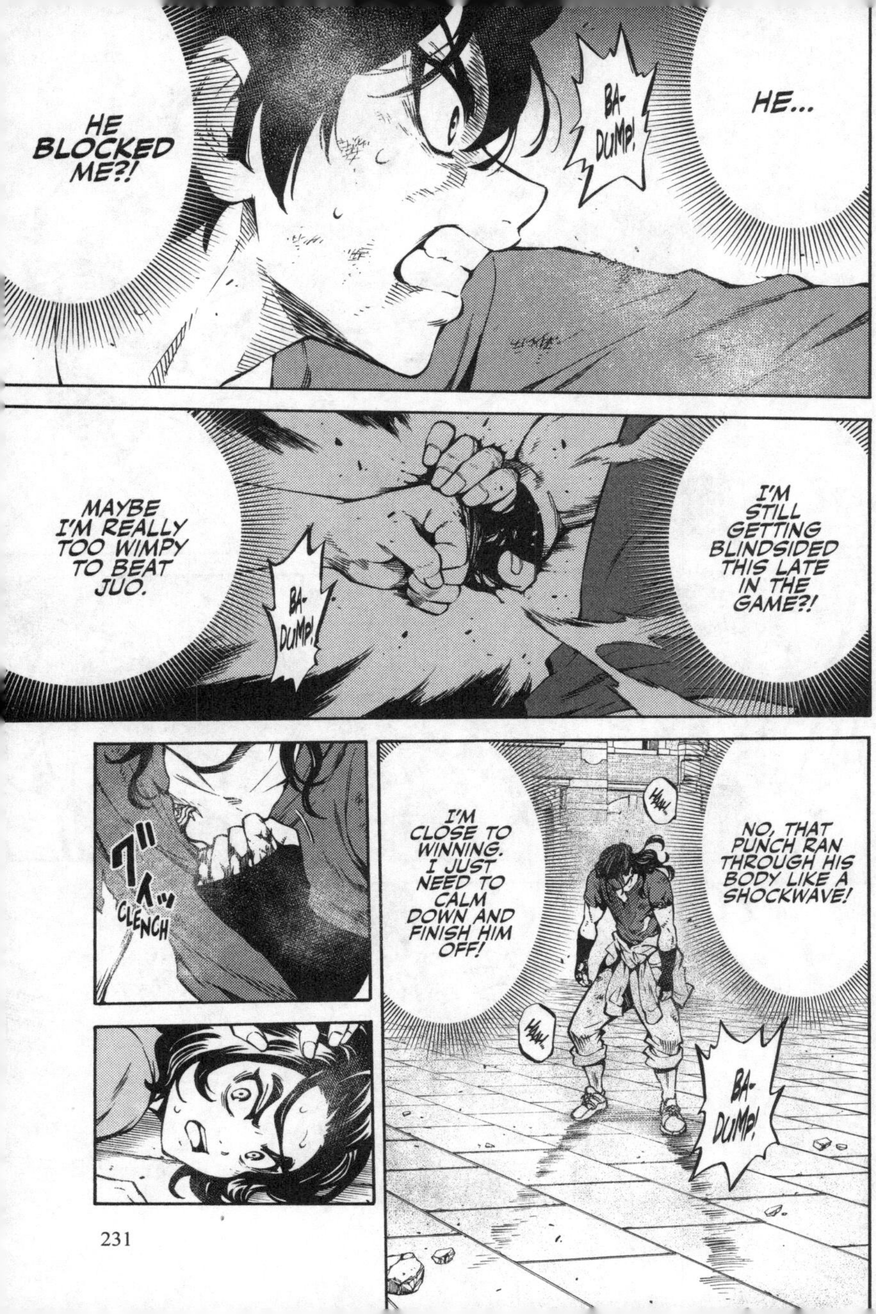
HE...
BA-DUMP!
HE BLOCKED ME?!
I'M STILL GETTING BLINDSIDED THIS LATE IN THE GAME?!
BA-DUMP!
MAYBE I'M REALLY TOO WIMPY TO BEAT JUO.
NO, THAT PUNCH RAN THROUGH HIS BODY LIKE A SHOCKWAVE!
I'M CLOSE TO WINNING. I JUST NEED TO CALM DOWN AND FINISH HIM OFF!
BA-DUMP!
CLENCH

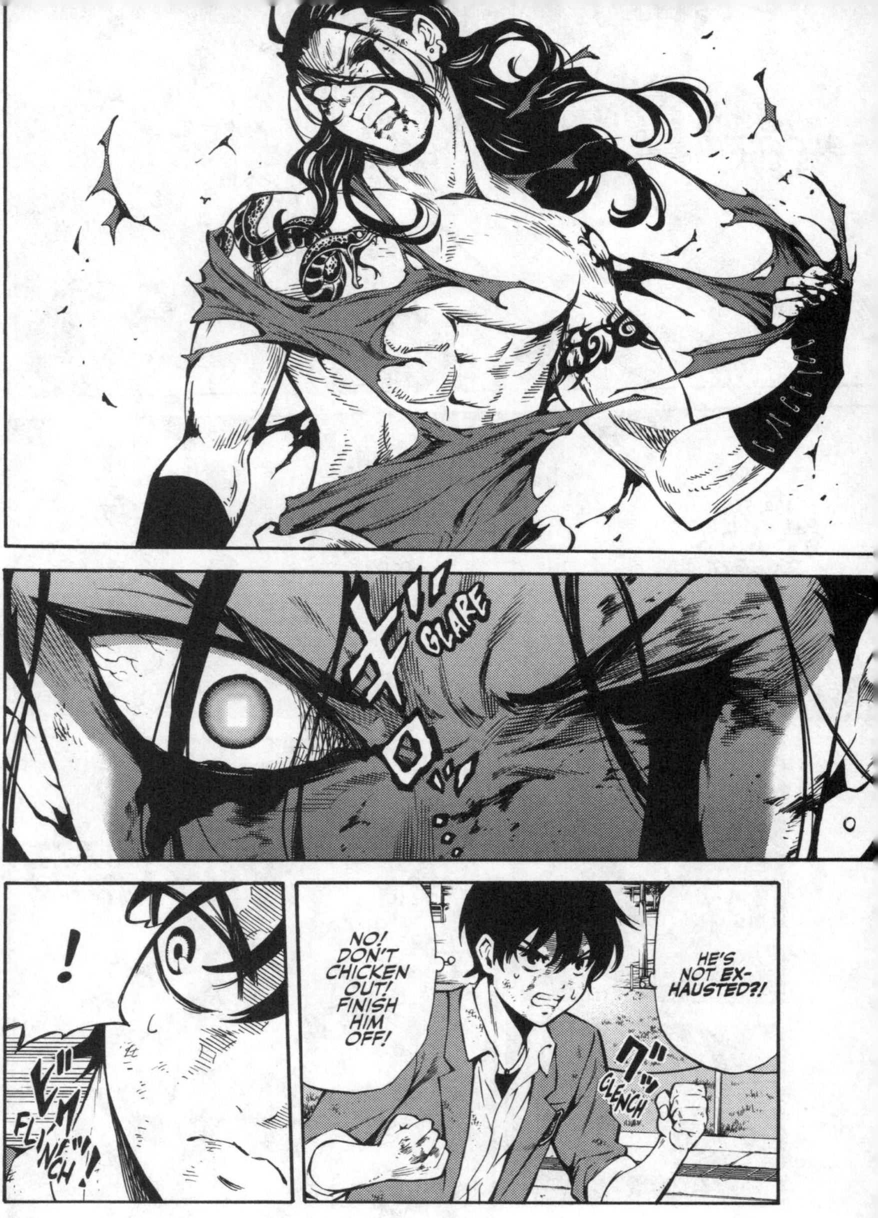
GLARE
HE'S NOT EX-HAUSTED?!
NO! DON'T CHICKEN OUT! FINISH HIM OFF!
CLENCH
!
FLINCH!!

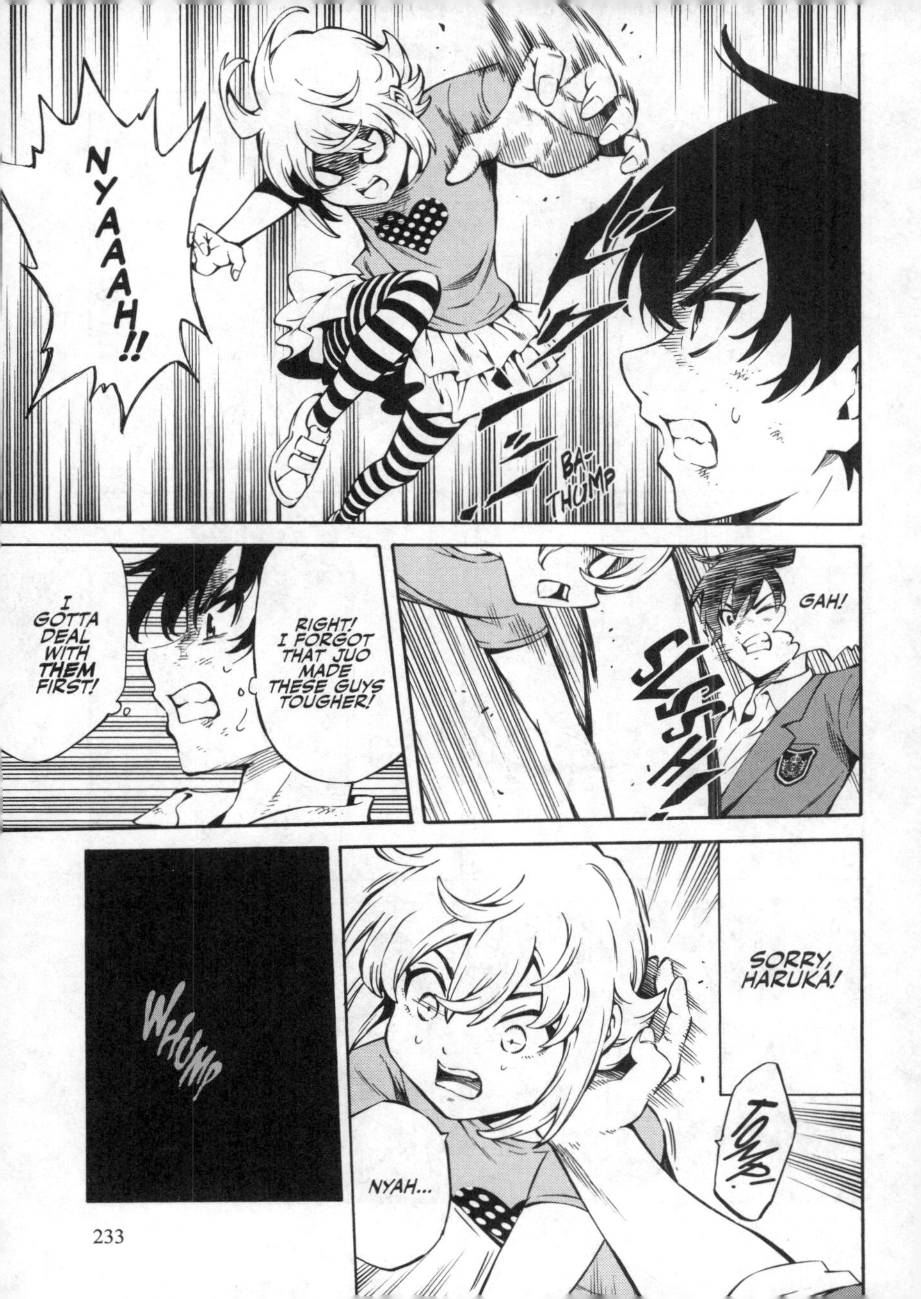
NYAAAAH!!
BA-THUMP
GAH!
SLSSH!
RIGHT! I FORGOT THAT JUO MADE THESE GUYS TOUGHER!
I GOTTA DEAL WITH THEM FIRST!
SORRY, HARUKA!
TOMP!
NYAH...
WHUMP

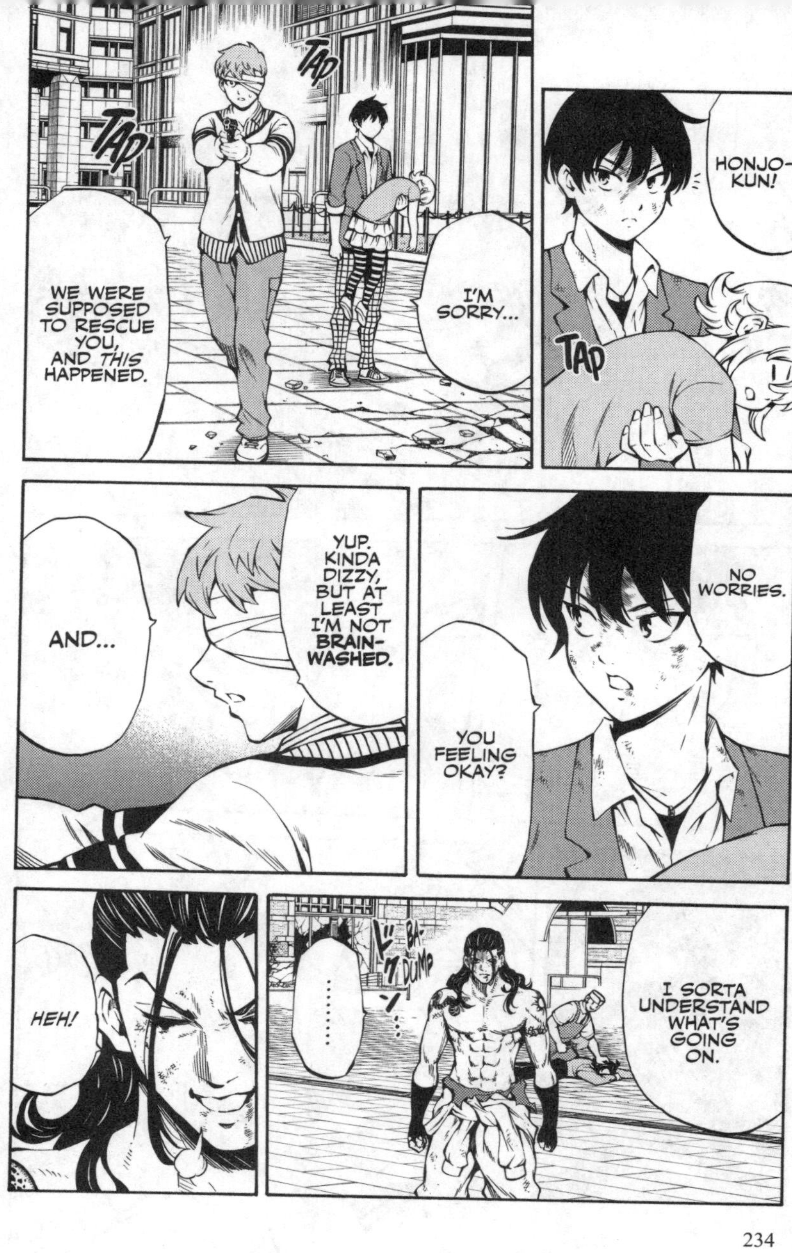
HONJO-KUN!
TAP
TAP
TAP
I'M SORRY...
WE WERE SUPPOSED TO RESCUE YOU, AND *THIS* HAPPENED.
NO WORRIES.
YOU FEELING OKAY?
YUP. KINDA DIZZY, BUT AT LEAST I'M NOT BRAIN-WASHED.
AND...
I SORTA UNDERSTAND WHAT'S GOING ON.
BA-DUMP
......
HEH!

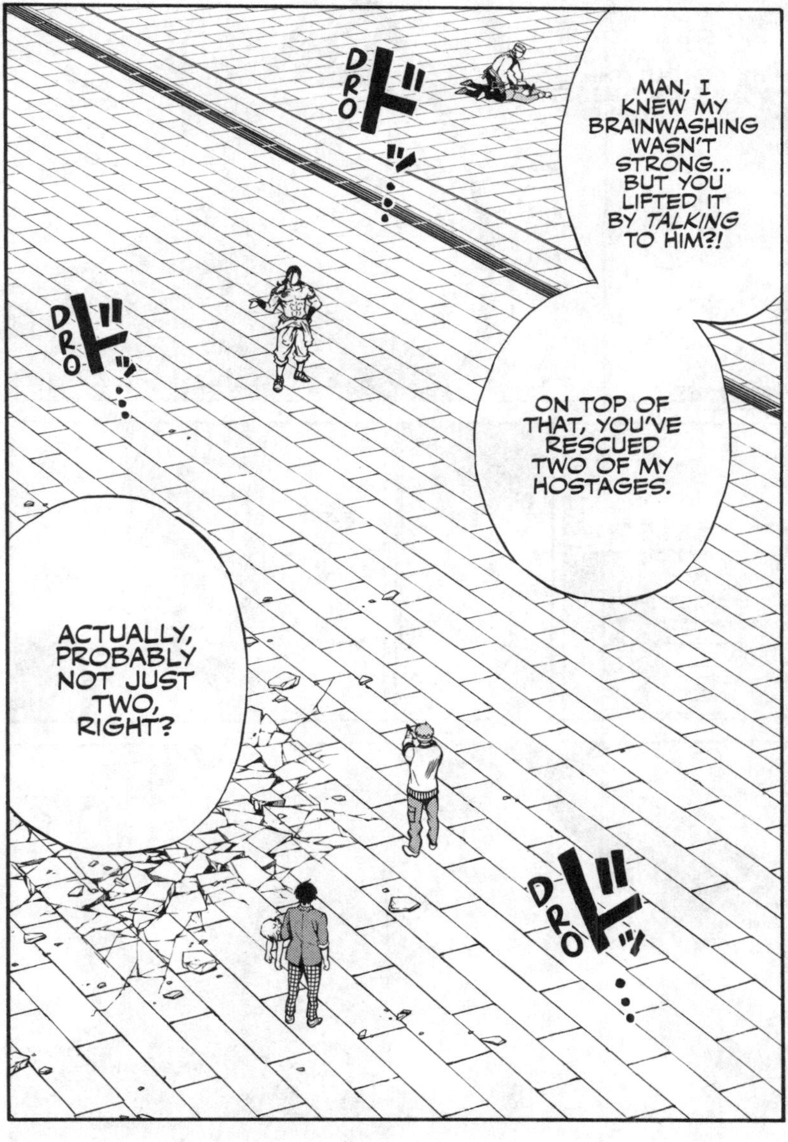
MAN, I KNEW MY BRAINWASHING WASN'T STRONG... BUT YOU LIFTED IT BY *TALKING* TO HIM?!
DRO ドッ
ON TOP OF THAT, YOU'VE RESCUED TWO OF MY HOSTAGES.
DRO ドッ
DRO ドッ
ACTUALLY, PROBABLY NOT JUST TWO, RIGHT?

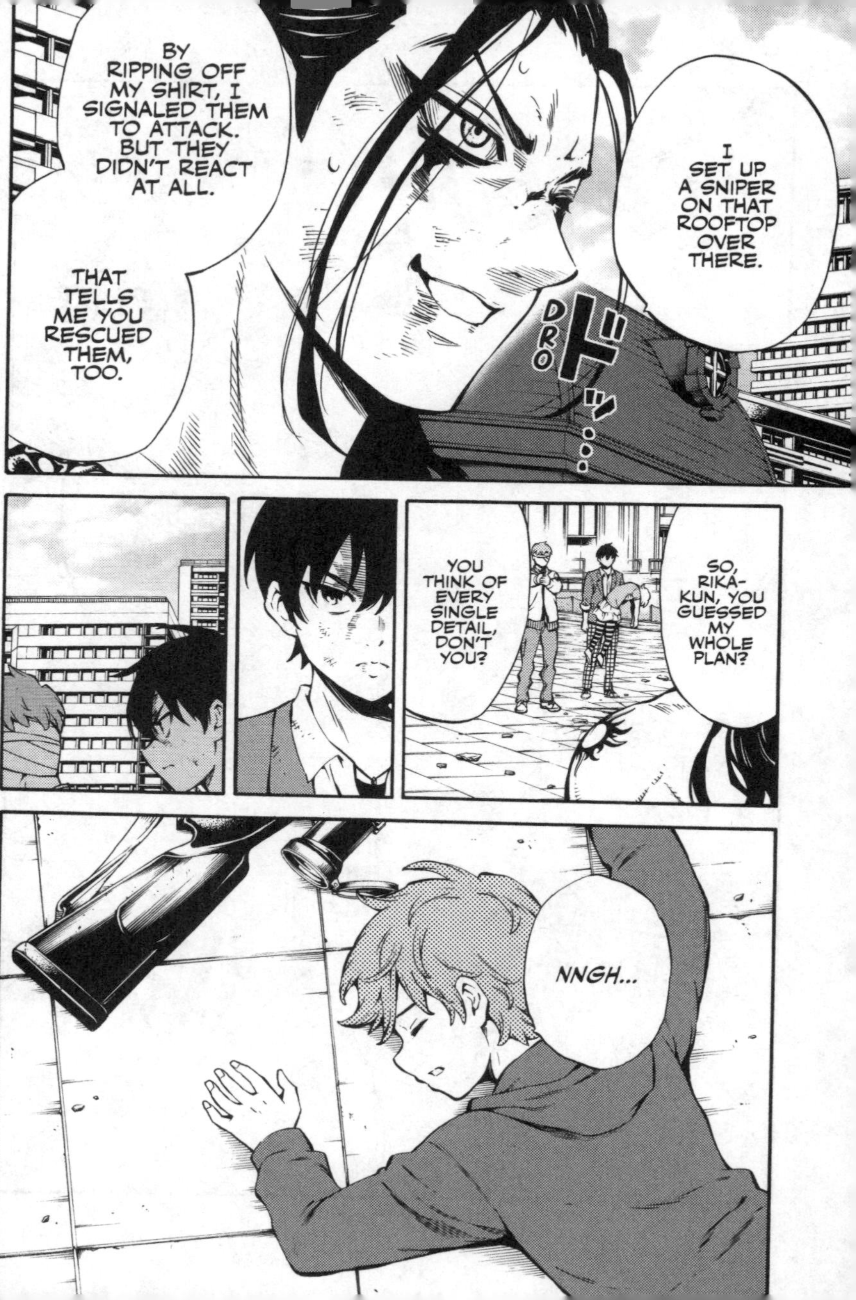
I SET UP A SNIPER ON THAT ROOFTOP OVER THERE.
DRO
BY RIPPING OFF MY SHIRT, I SIGNALED THEM TO ATTACK. BUT THEY DIDN'T REACT AT ALL.
THAT TELLS ME YOU RESCUED THEM, TOO.
SO, RIKA-KUN, YOU GUESSED MY WHOLE PLAN?
YOU THINK OF EVERY SINGLE DETAIL, DON'T YOU?
NNGH...

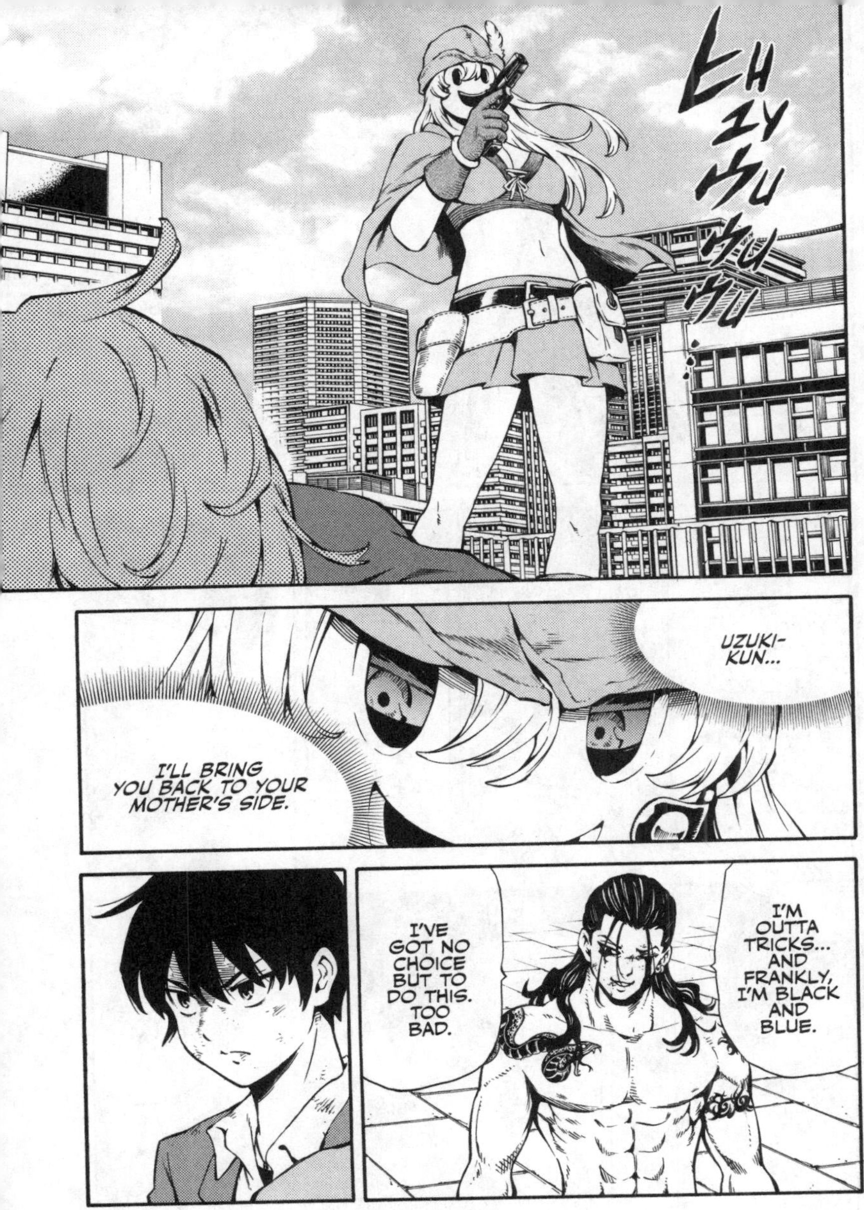
UZUKI-KUN...
I'LL BRING YOU BACK TO YOUR MOTHER'S SIDE.
I'M OUTTA TRICKS... AND FRANKLY, I'M BLACK AND BLUE.
I'VE GOT NO CHOICE BUT TO DO THIS. TOO BAD.

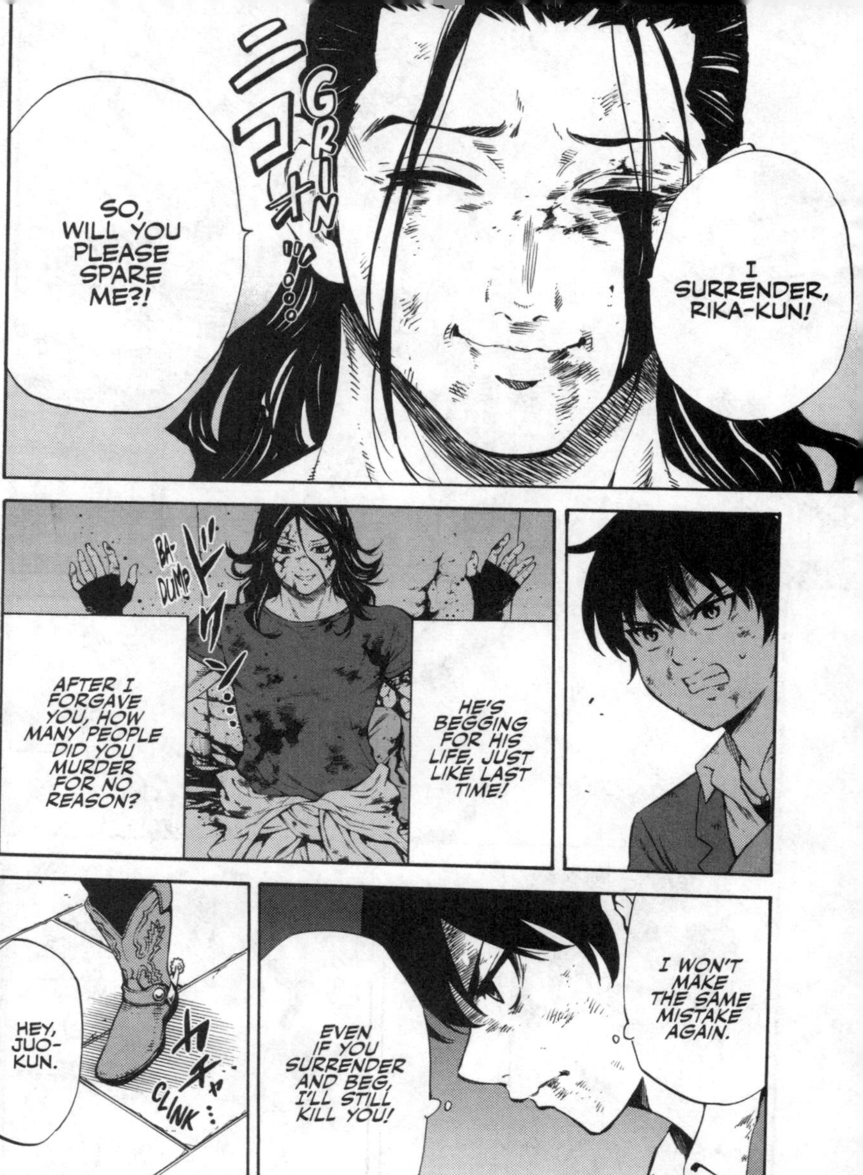
I SURRENDER, RIKA-KUN!
GRIN
SO, WILL YOU PLEASE SPARE ME?!
BA-DUMP
HE'S BEGGING FOR HIS LIFE, JUST LIKE LAST TIME!
AFTER I FORGAVE YOU, HOW MANY PEOPLE DID YOU MURDER FOR NO REASON?
I WON'T MAKE THE SAME MISTAKE AGAIN.
EVEN IF YOU SURRENDER AND BEG, I'LL STILL KILL YOU!
HEY, JUO-KUN.
CLINK…

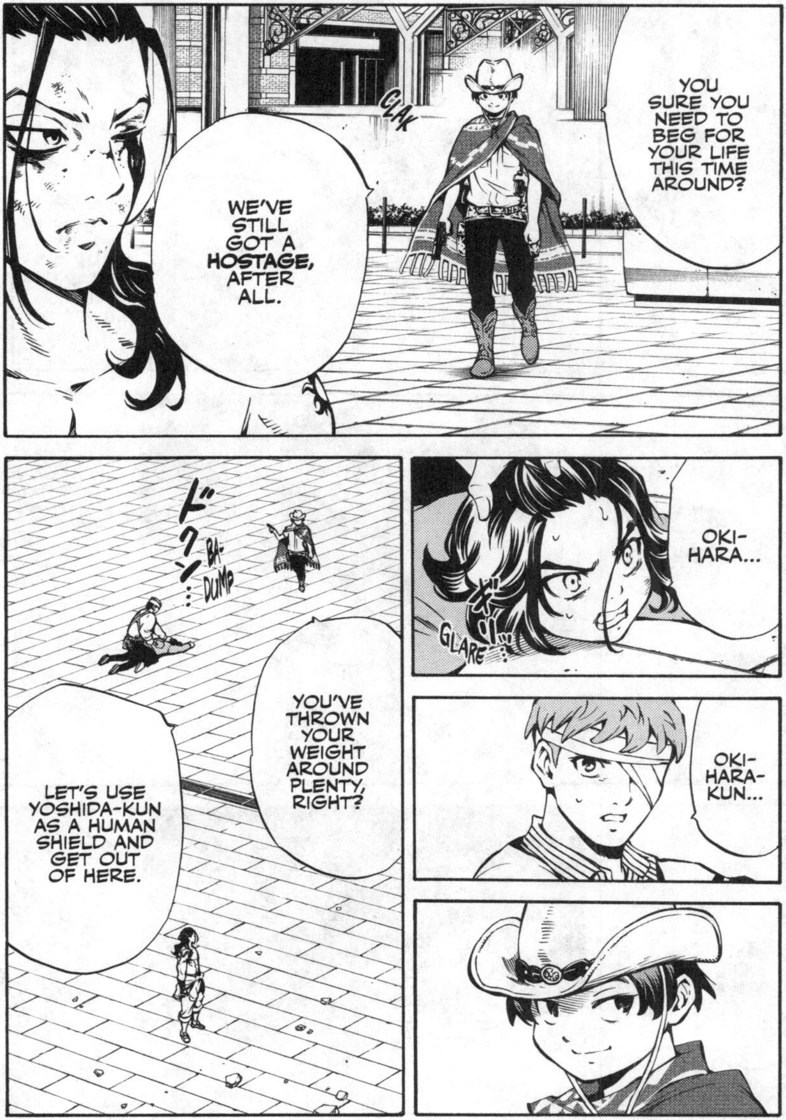
YOU SURE YOU NEED TO BEG FOR YOUR LIFE THIS TIME AROUND?
CLAK
WE'VE STILL GOT A HOSTAGE, AFTER ALL.
OKI-HARA...
GLARE
OKI-HARA-KUN...
ドクン
BA-DUMP
YOU'VE THROWN YOUR WEIGHT AROUND PLENTY, RIGHT?
LET'S USE YOSHIDA-KUN AS A HUMAN SHIELD AND GET OUT OF HERE.

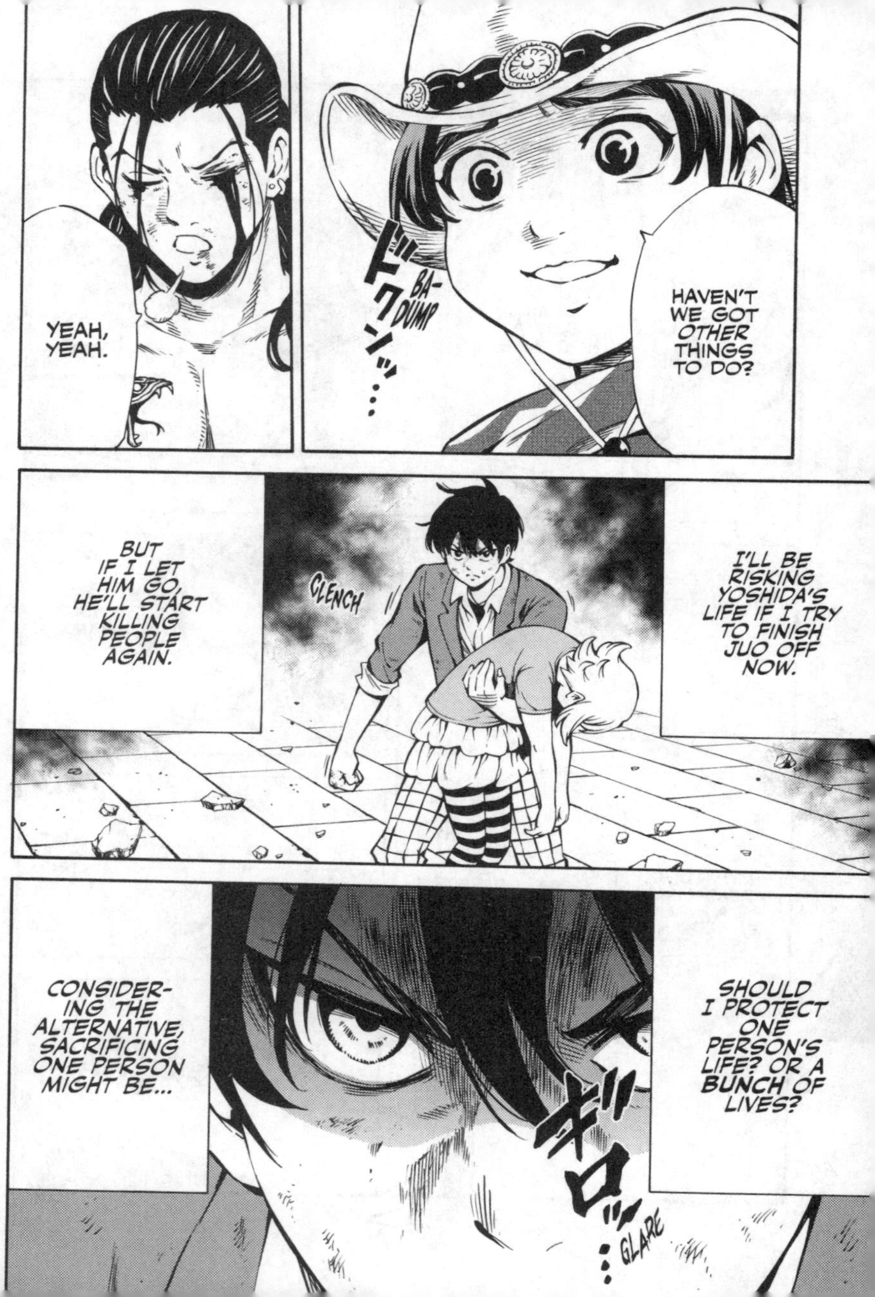

HAVEN'T WE GOT OTHER THINGS TO DO?
BA-DUMP
YEAH, YEAH.
I'LL BE RISKING YOSHIDA'S LIFE IF I TRY TO FINISH JUO OFF NOW.
CLENCH
BUT IF I LET HIM GO, HE'LL START KILLING PEOPLE AGAIN.
SHOULD I PROTECT ONE PERSON'S LIFE? OR A BUNCH OF LIVES?
GLARE
CONSIDER-ING THE ALTERNATIVE, SACRIFICING ONE PERSON MIGHT BE...

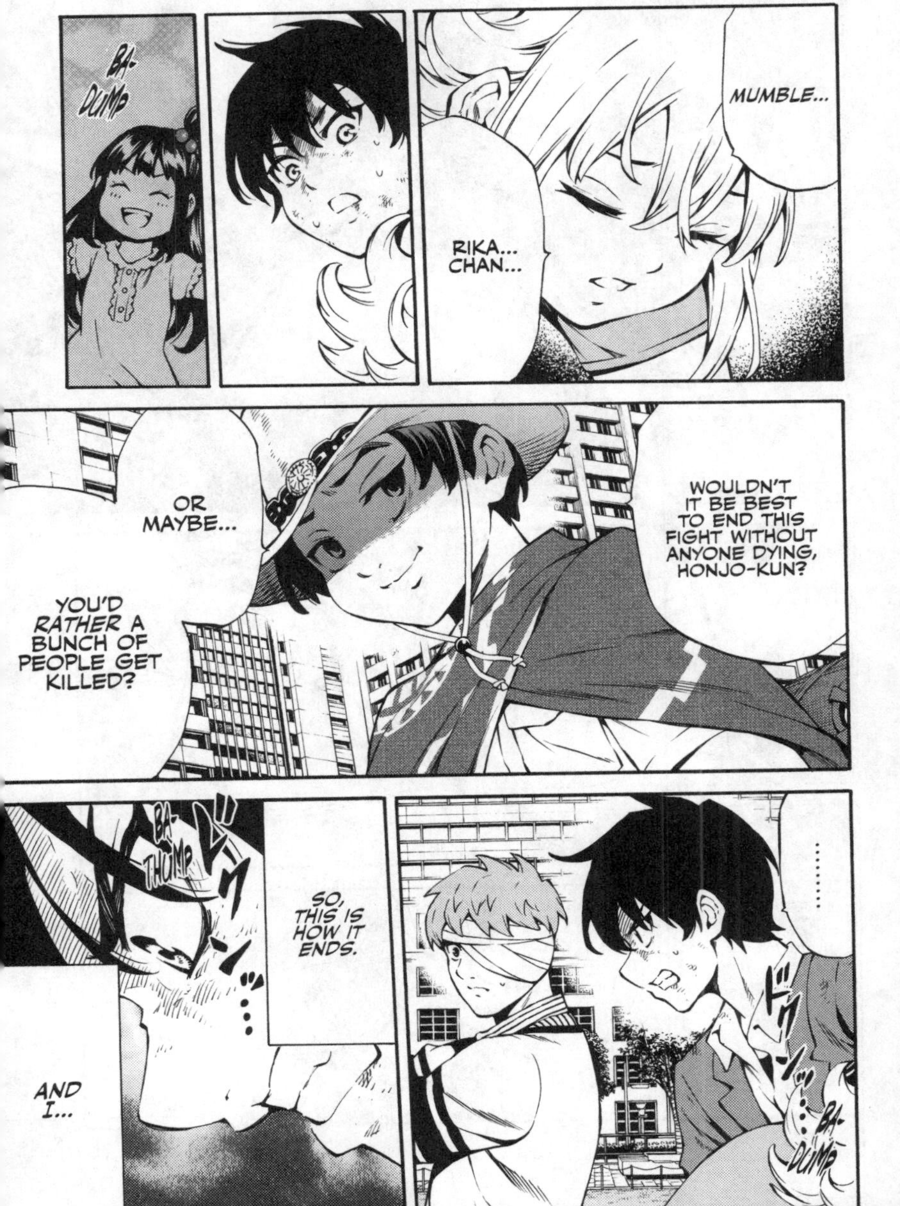
MUMBLE...
RIKA... CHAN...
BA-DUMP
WOULDN'T IT BE BEST TO END THIS FIGHT WITHOUT ANYONE DYING, HONJO-KUN?
OR MAYBE...
YOU'D *RATHER* A BUNCH OF PEOPLE GET KILLED?
......
BA-DUMP
SO, THIS IS HOW IT ENDS.
BA-THUMP
...
AND I...

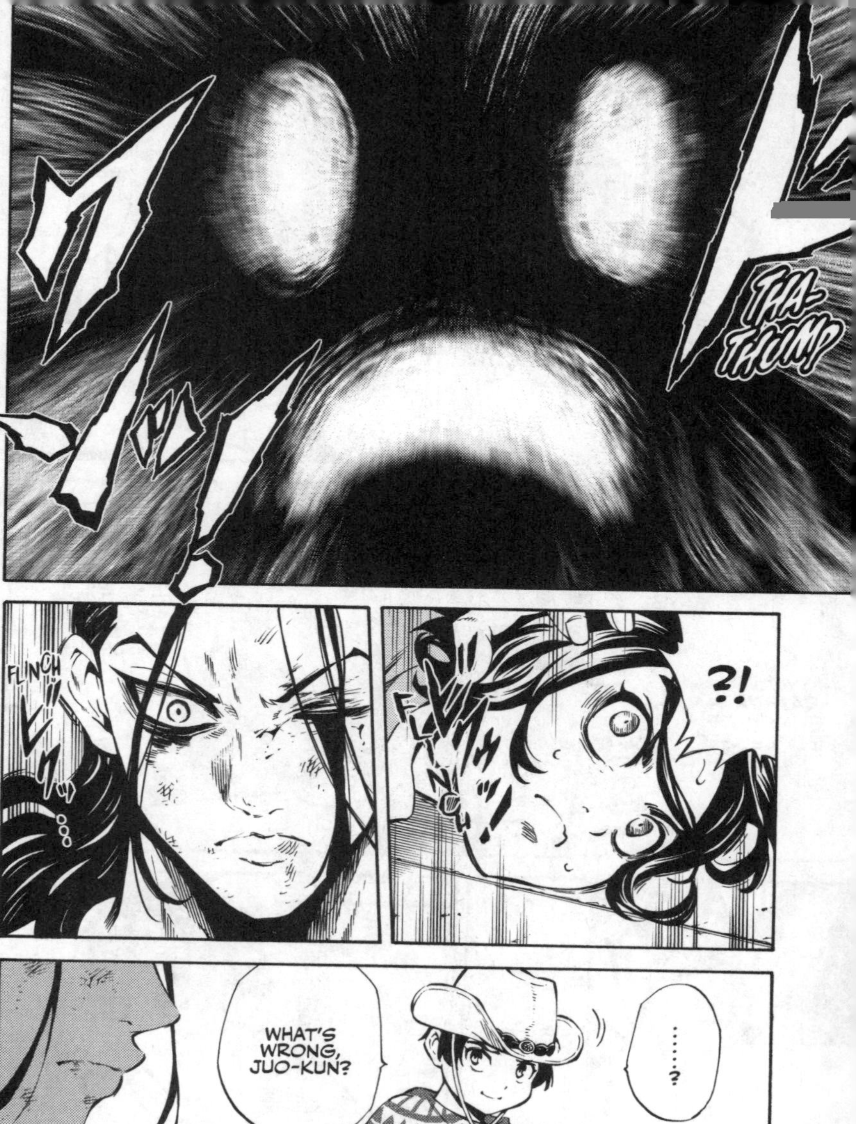
THA-THUMP
FLINCH
?!
FLINCH
......?
WHAT'S WRONG, JUO-KUN?

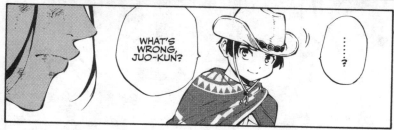

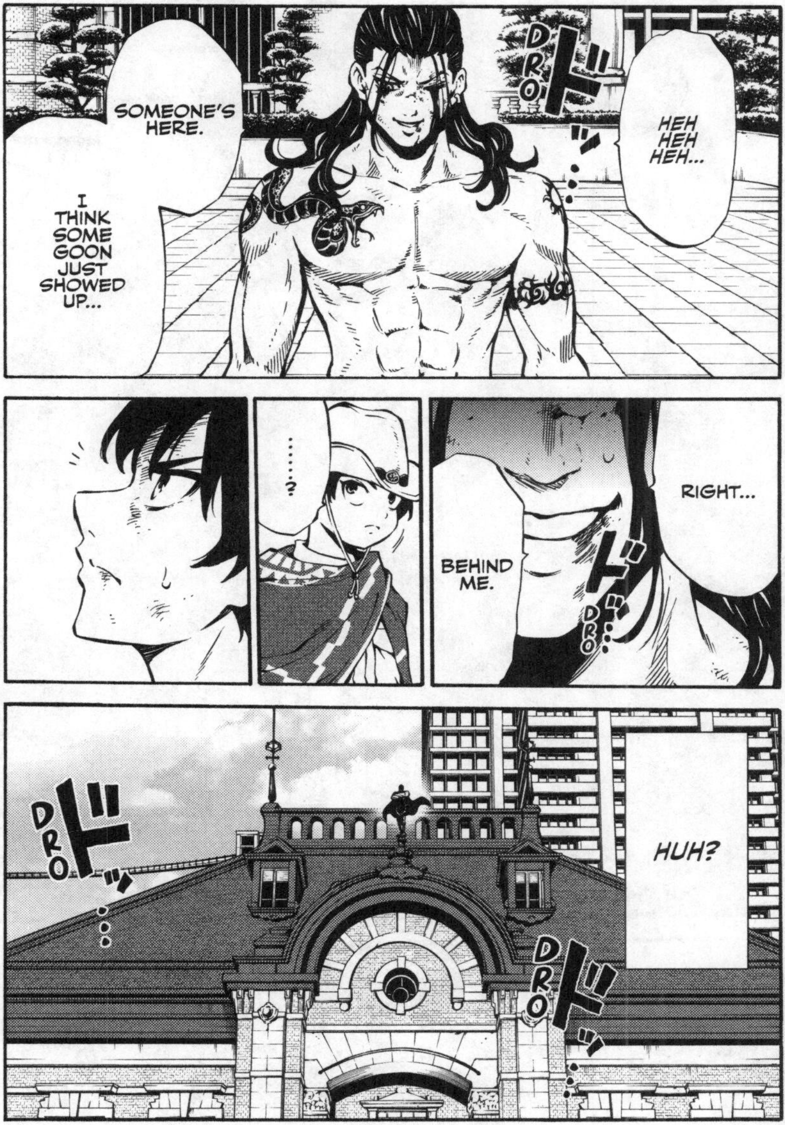
DRO
HEH HEH HEH...
SOMEONE'S HERE.
I THINK SOME GOON JUST SHOWED UP...
RIGHT...
BEHIND ME.
DRO
......?
HUH?
DRO
DRO

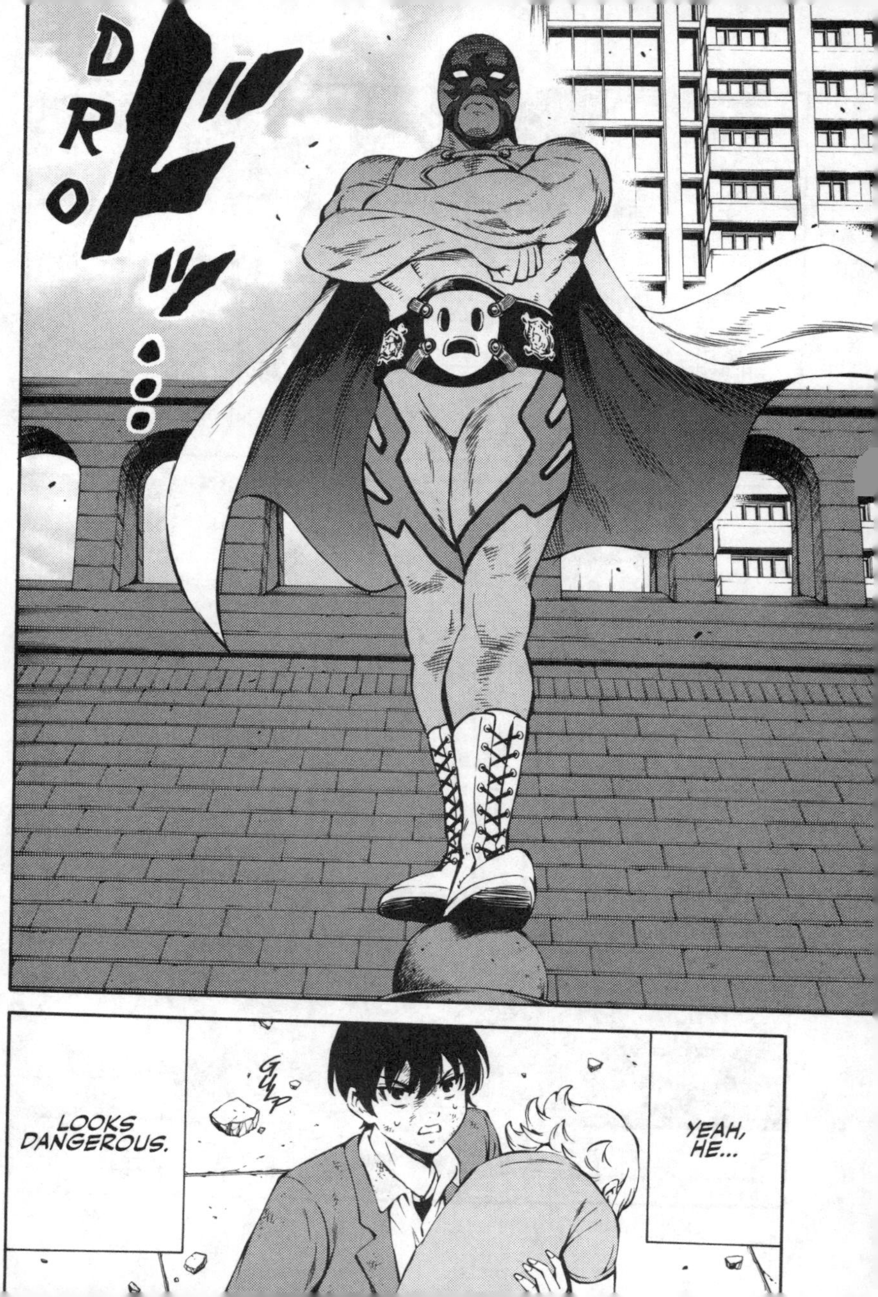
DRO
YEAH, HE...
GULP
LOOKS DANGEROUS.

Don't
look!

HIGH-RISE
INVASION

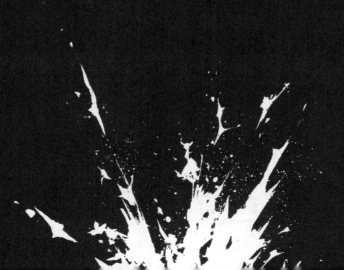

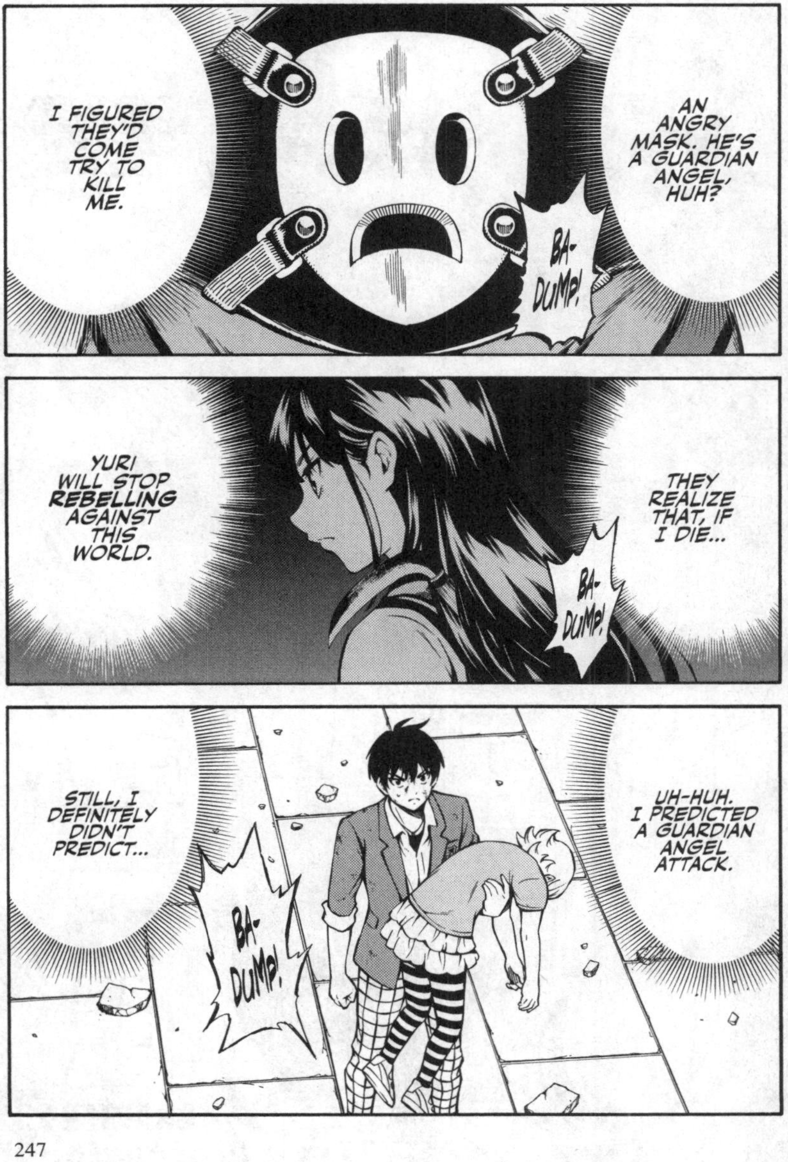
AN ANGRY MASK. HE'S A GUARDIAN ANGEL, HUH?
BA-DUMP!
I FIGURED THEY'D COME TRY TO KILL ME.
THEY REALIZE THAT, IF I DIE...
BA-DUMP!
YURI WILL STOP REBELLING AGAINST THIS WORLD.
UH-HUH. I PREDICTED A GUARDIAN ANGEL ATTACK.
STILL, I DEFINITELY DIDN'T PREDICT...
BA-DUMP!

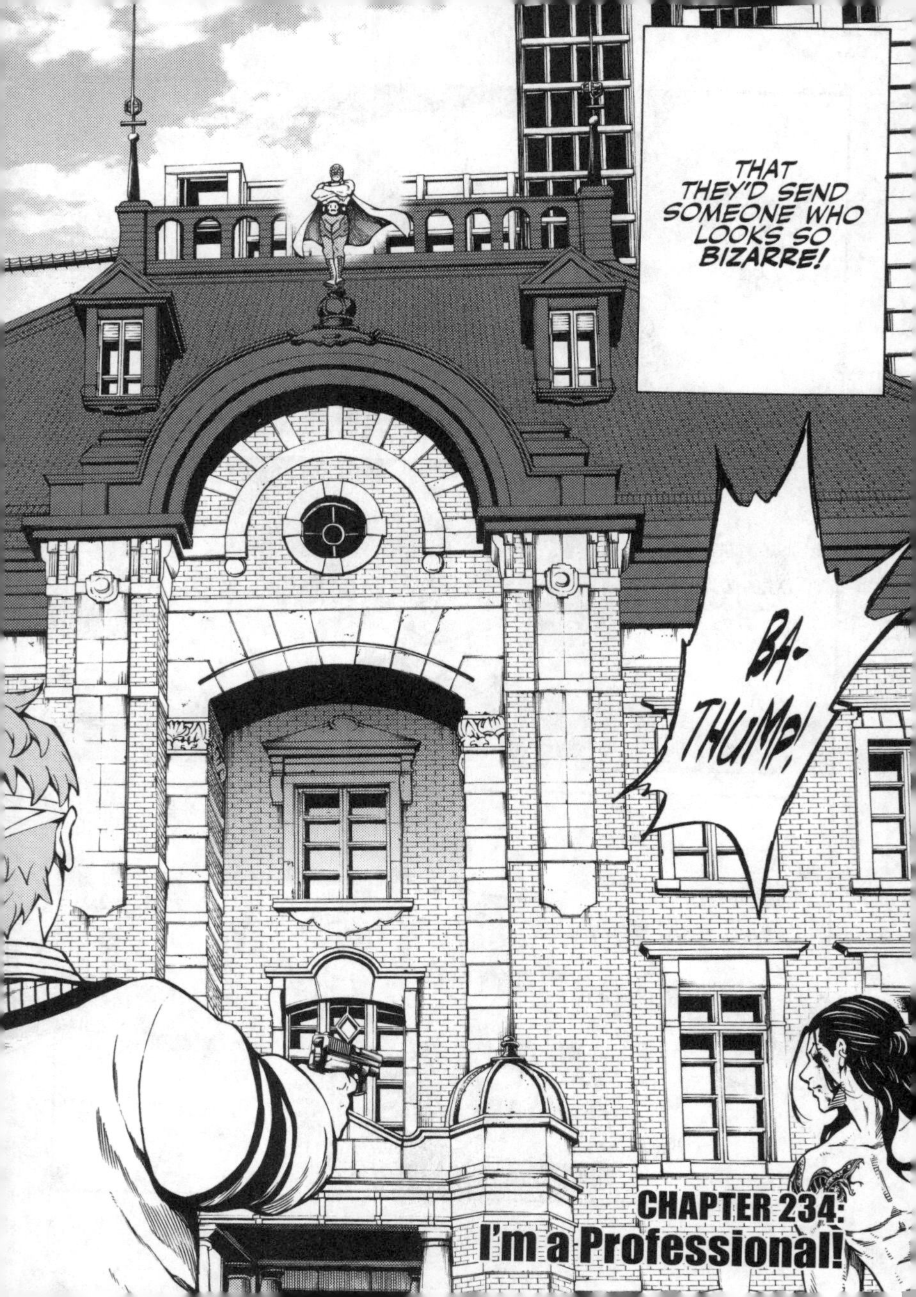
THAT THEY'D SEND SOMEONE WHO LOOKS SO BIZARRE!
BA-THUMP!
CHAPTER 234:
I'm a Professional!

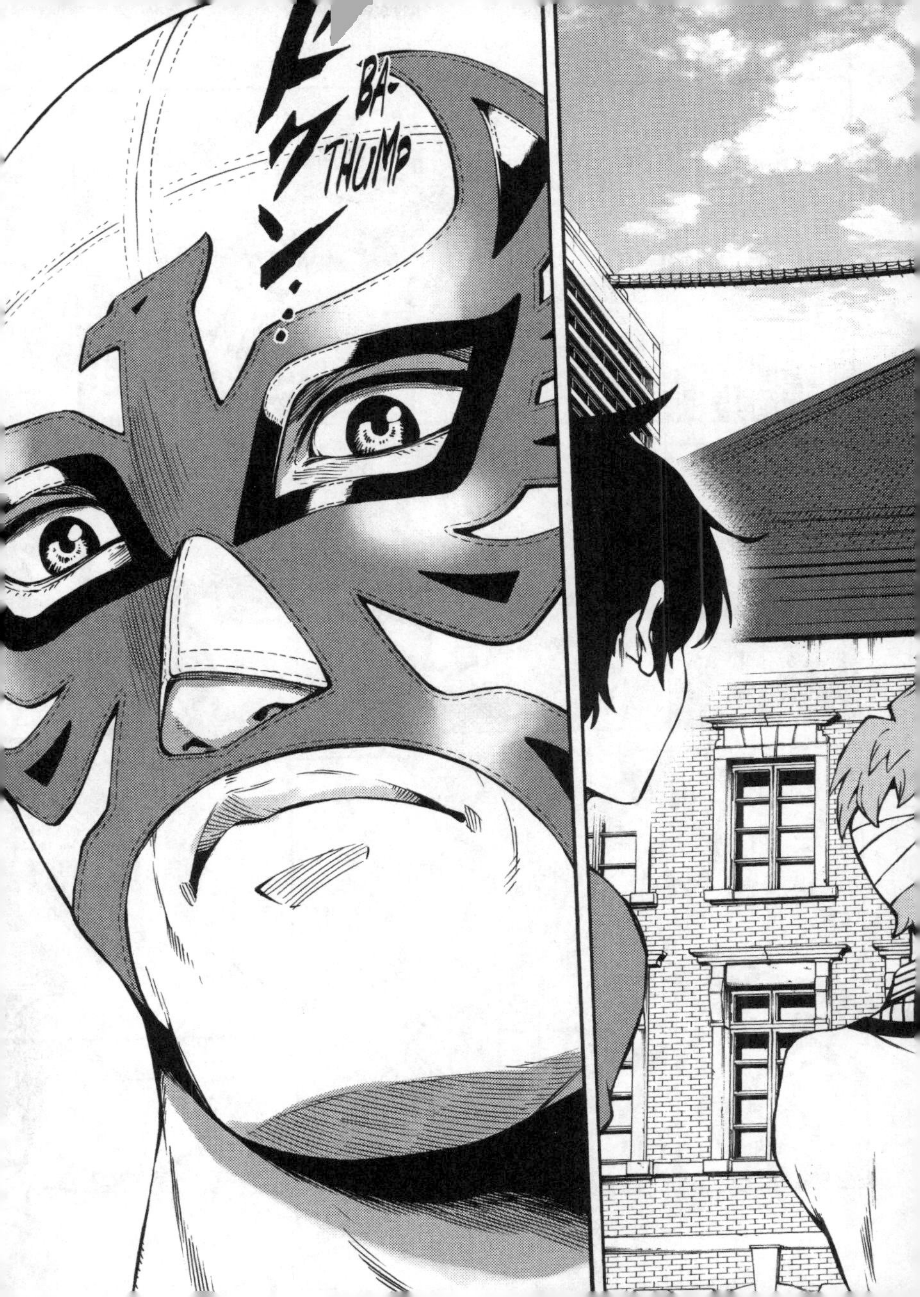
ドクン
BA-THUMP

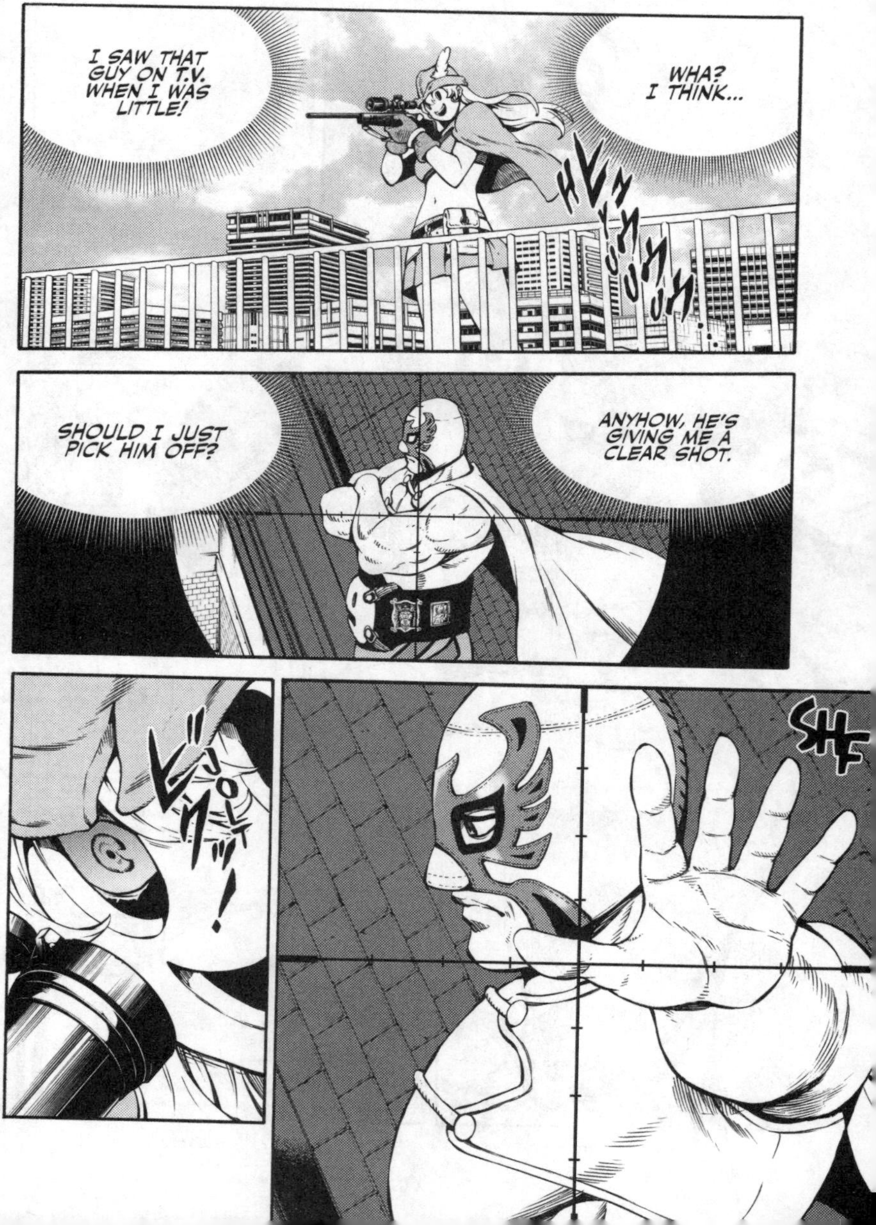
WHA? I THINK...
I SAW THAT GUY ON T.V. WHEN I WAS LITTLE!
ANYHOW, HE'S GIVING ME A CLEAR SHOT.
SHOULD I JUST PICK HIM OFF?
SHF
JOLT!

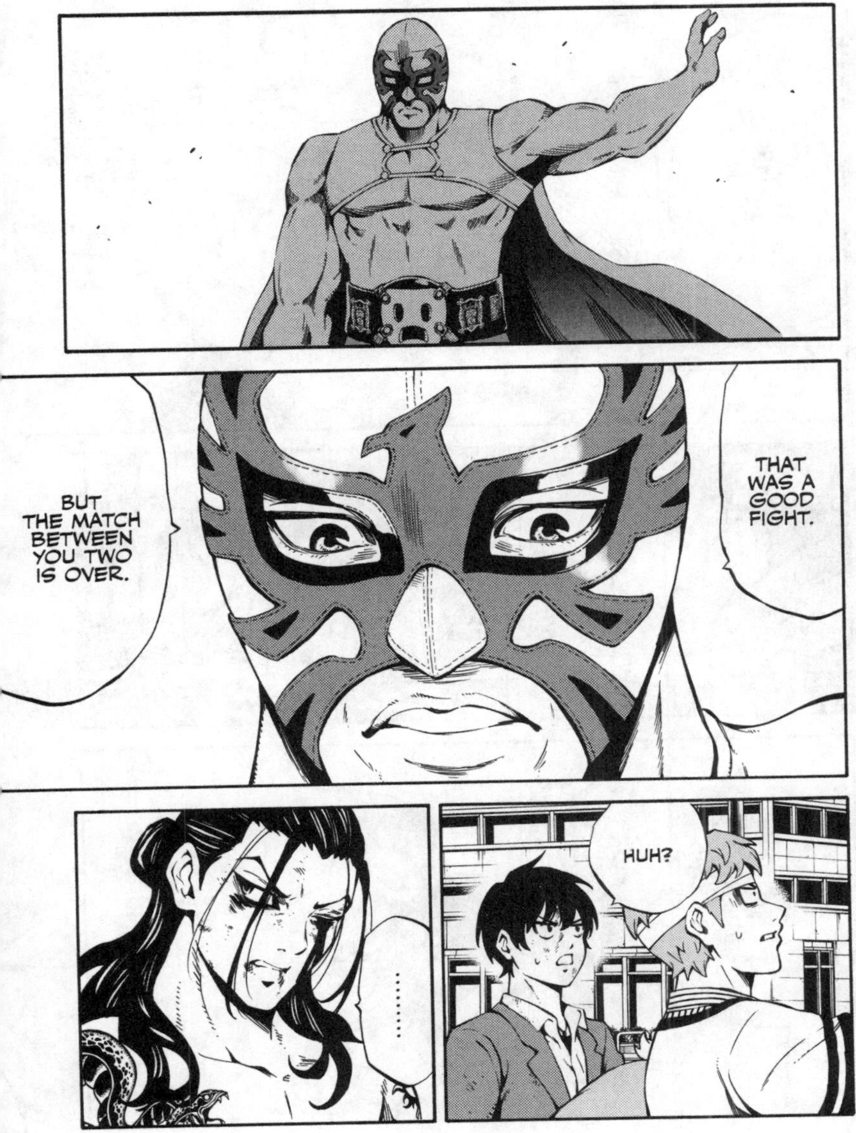
THAT WAS A GOOD FIGHT.
BUT THE MATCH BETWEEN YOU TWO IS OVER.
HUH?
……

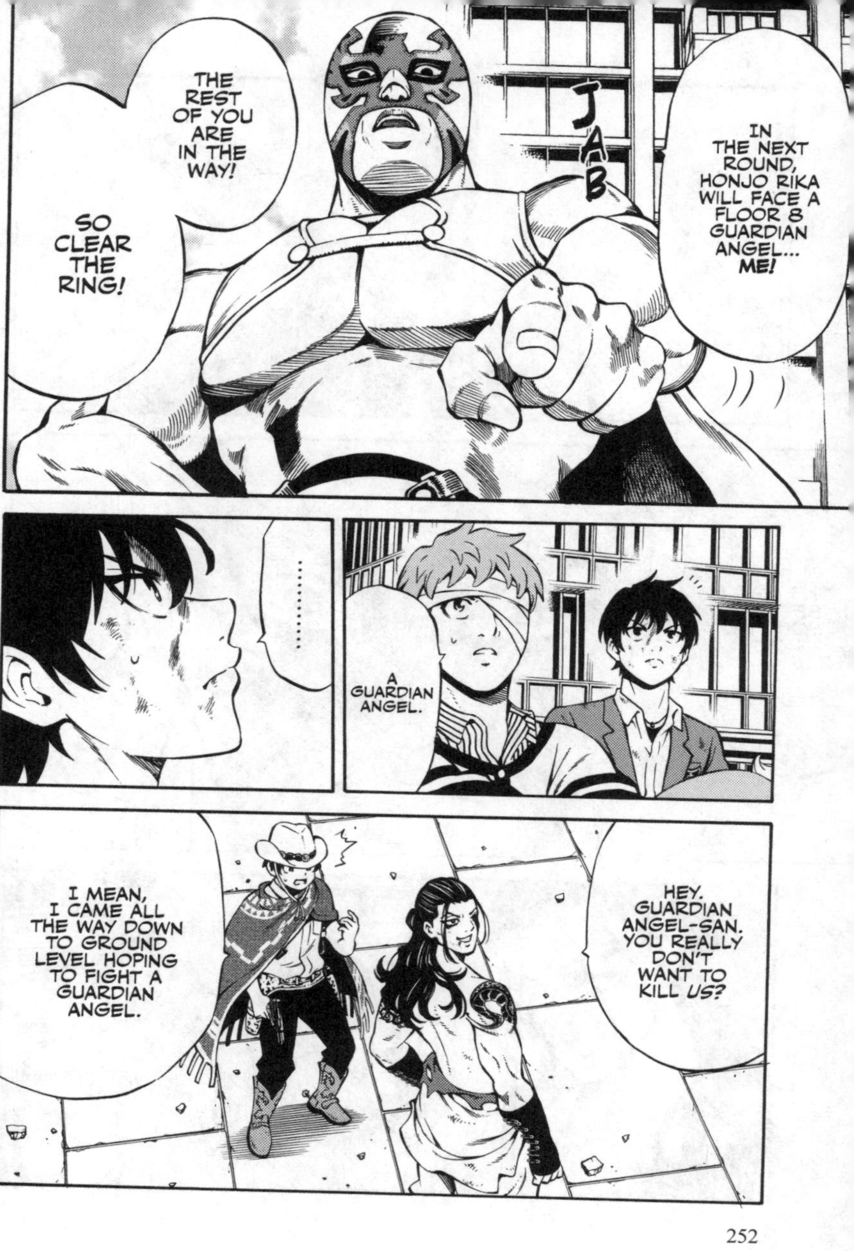
IN THE NEXT ROUND, HONJO RIKA WILL FACE A FLOOR 8 GUARDIAN ANGEL... ME!
JAB
THE REST OF YOU ARE IN THE WAY!
SO CLEAR THE RING!
A GUARDIAN ANGEL.
......
HEY. GUARDIAN ANGEL-SAN. YOU REALLY DON'T WANT TO KILL *US*?
I MEAN, I CAME ALL THE WAY DOWN TO GROUND LEVEL HOPING TO FIGHT A GUARDIAN ANGEL.

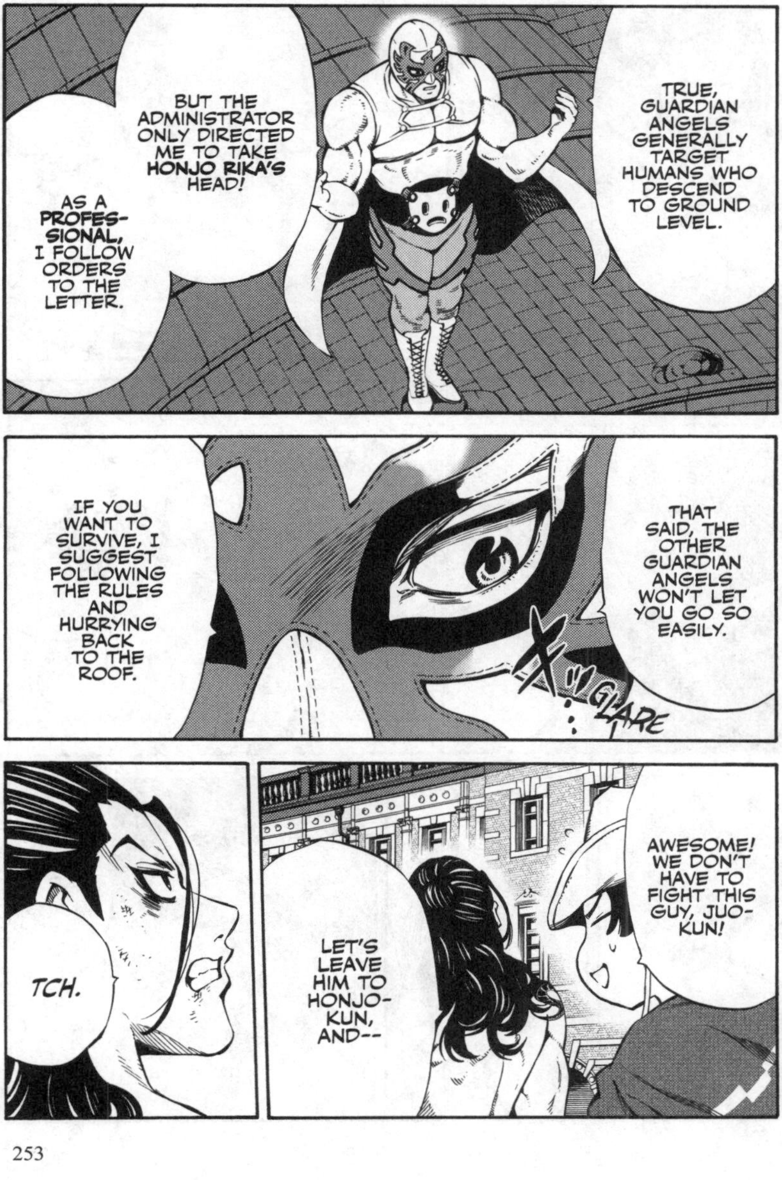
TRUE, GUARDIAN ANGELS GENERALLY TARGET HUMANS WHO DESCEND TO GROUND LEVEL.
BUT THE ADMINISTRATOR ONLY DIRECTED ME TO TAKE HONJO RIKA'S HEAD!
AS A PROFESSIONAL, I FOLLOW ORDERS TO THE LETTER.
THAT SAID, THE OTHER GUARDIAN ANGELS WON'T LET YOU GO SO EASILY.
GLARE
IF YOU WANT TO SURVIVE, I SUGGEST FOLLOWING THE RULES AND HURRYING BACK TO THE ROOF.
AWESOME! WE DON'T HAVE TO FIGHT THIS GUY, JUO-KUN!
LET'S LEAVE HIM TO HONJO-KUN, AND--
TCH.

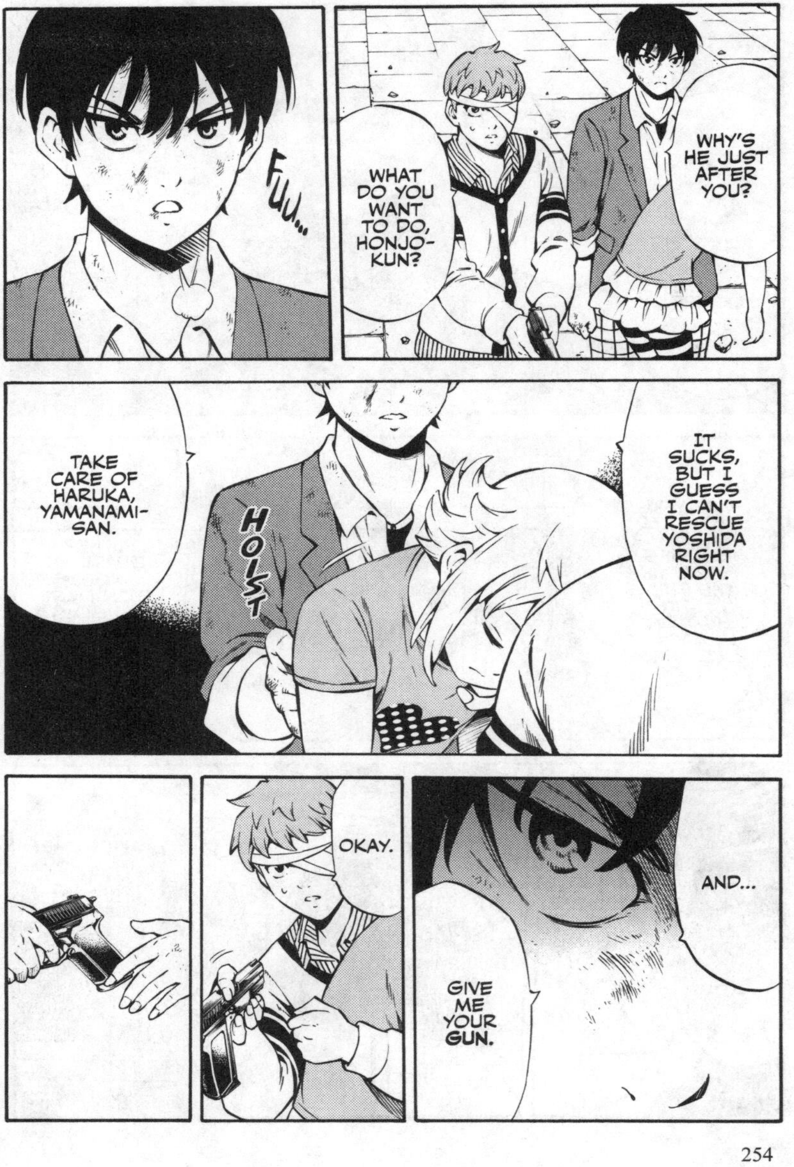
WHY'S HE JUST AFTER YOU?
WHAT DO YOU WANT TO DO, HONJO-KUN?
FUU...
IT SUCKS, BUT I GUESS I CAN'T RESCUE YOSHIDA RIGHT NOW.
HOIST
TAKE CARE OF HARUKA, YAMANAMI-SAN.
AND...
GIVE ME YOUR GUN.
OKAY.

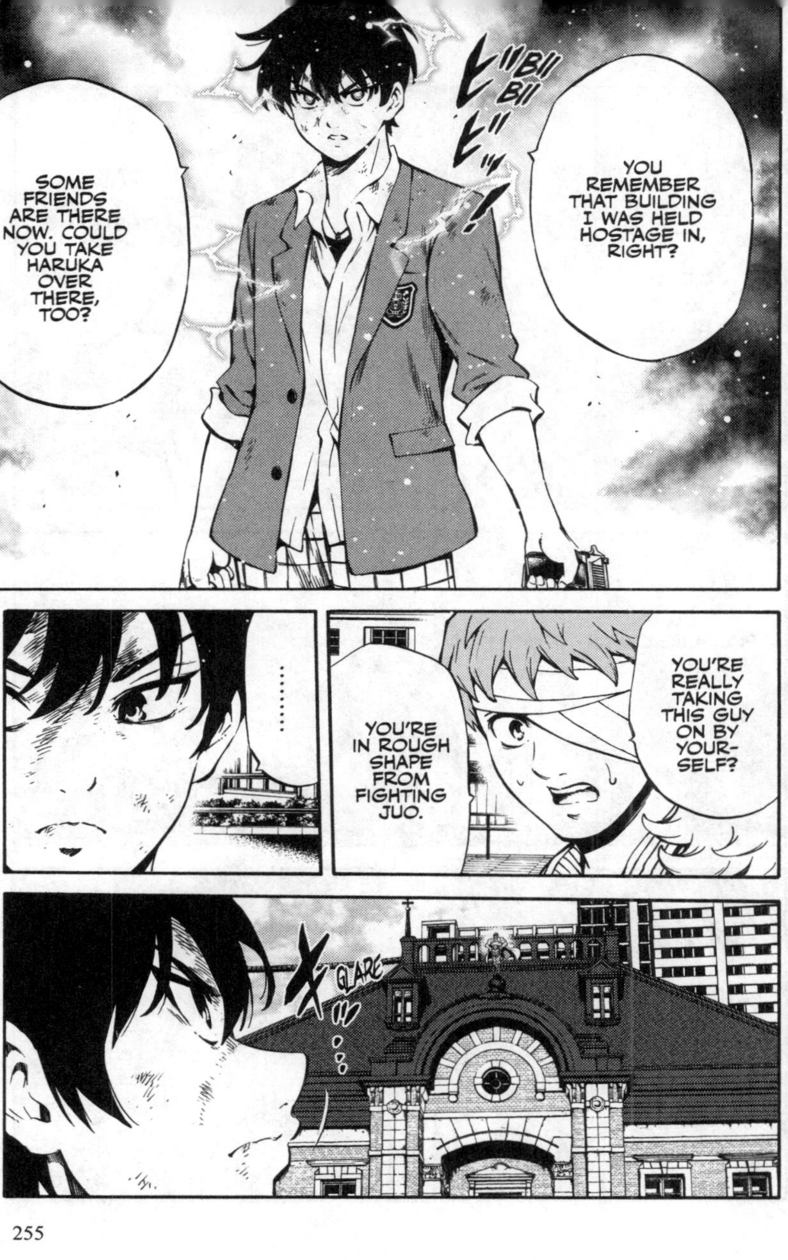
YOU REMEMBER THAT BUILDING I WAS HELD HOSTAGE IN, RIGHT?
BII BII
SOME FRIENDS ARE THERE NOW. COULD YOU TAKE HARUKA OVER THERE, TOO?
YOU'RE REALLY TAKING THIS GUY ON BY YOUR-SELF?
YOU'RE IN ROUGH SHAPE FROM FIGHTING JUO.
......
GLARE

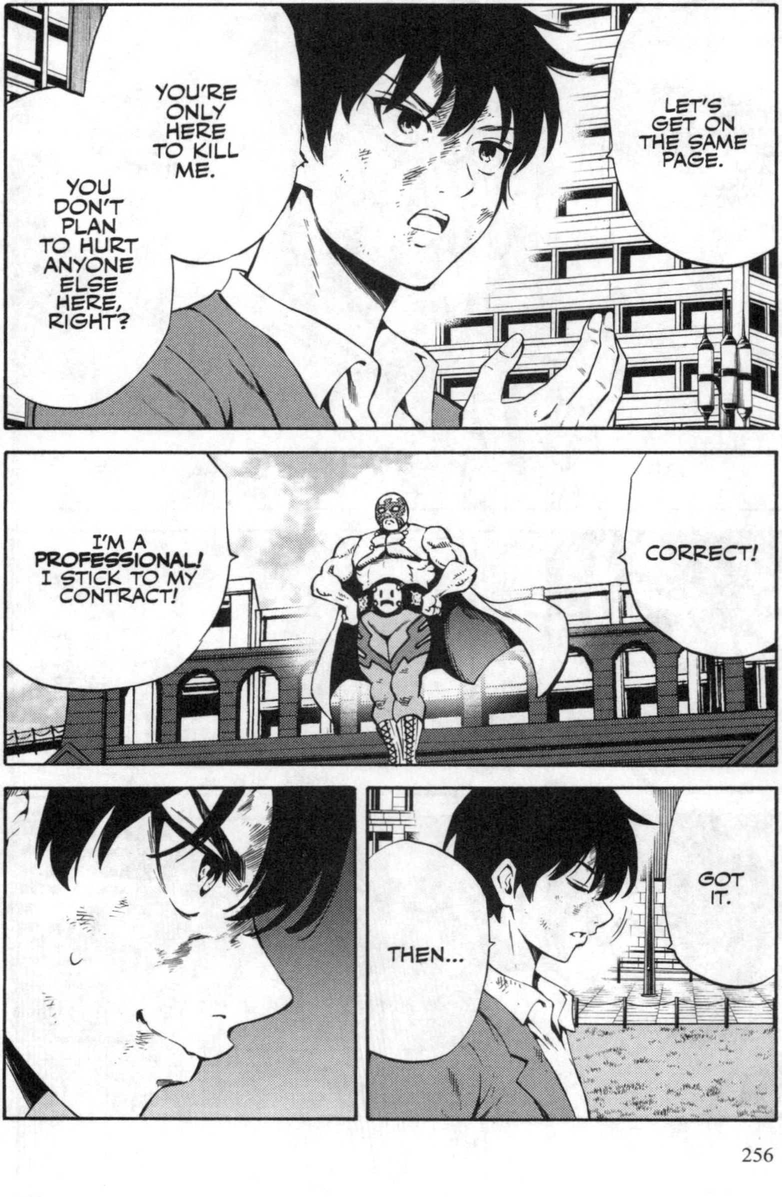
LET'S GET ON THE SAME PAGE.
YOU'RE ONLY HERE TO KILL ME.
YOU DON'T PLAN TO HURT ANYONE ELSE HERE, RIGHT?
CORRECT!
I'M A **PROFESSIONAL!** I STICK TO MY CONTRACT!
GOT IT.
THEN...

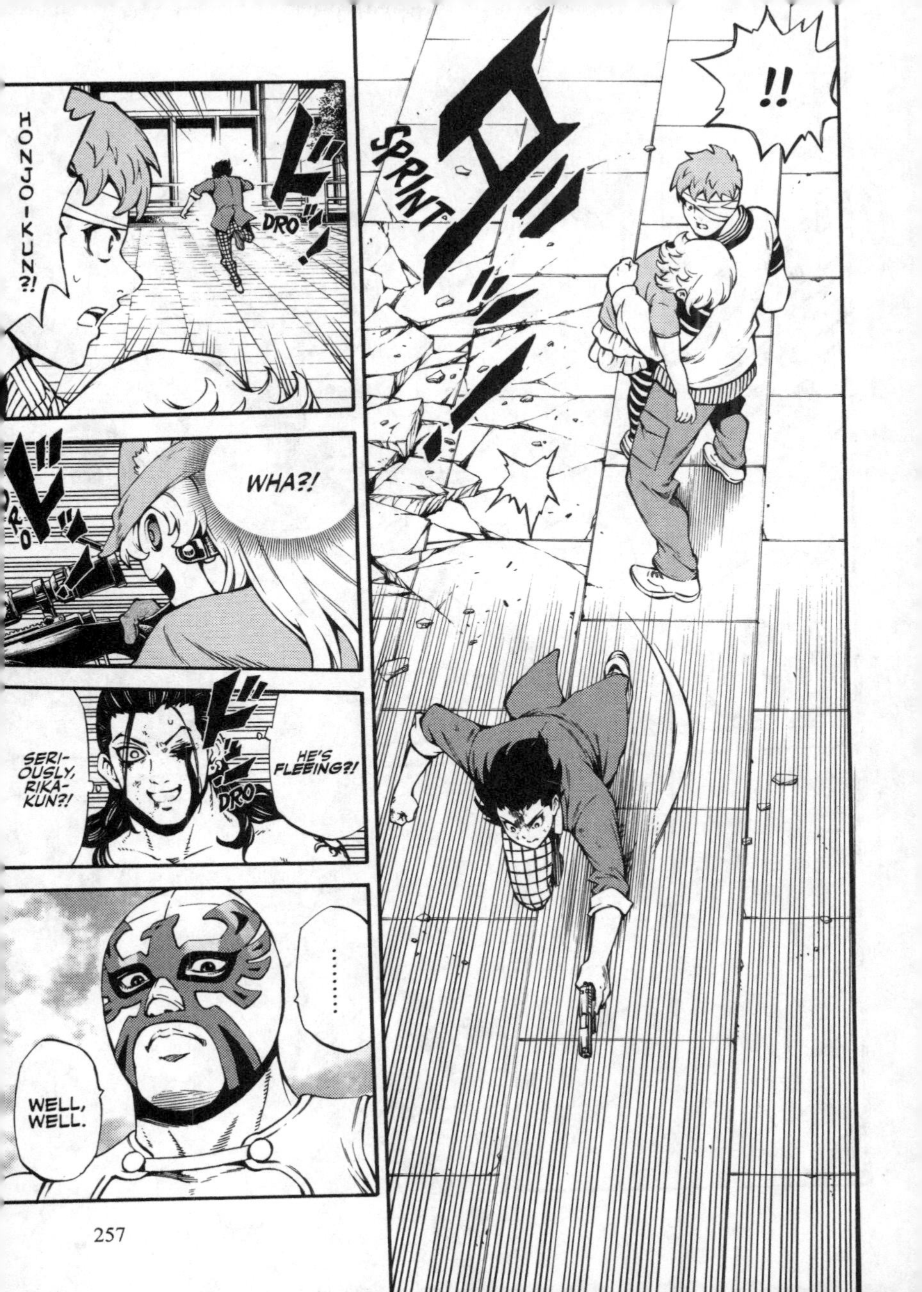
!!
SPRINT
DRO
HONJO-KUN?!
WHA?!
DRO
HE'S FLEEING?!
DRO
SERIOUSLY, RIKA-KUN?!
......
WELL, WELL.

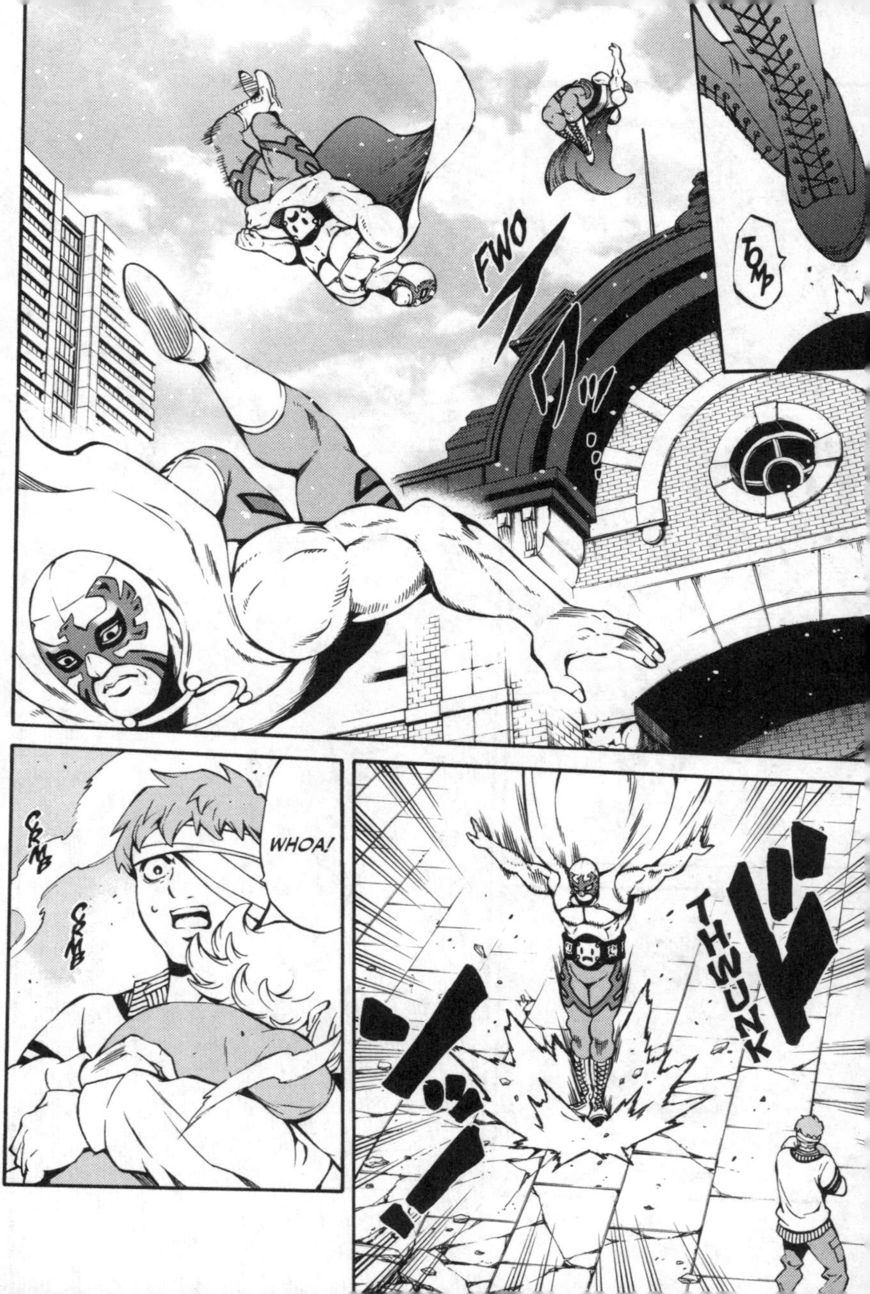
TOMP
FWO
THWUNK
WHOA!
CRMB
CRMB

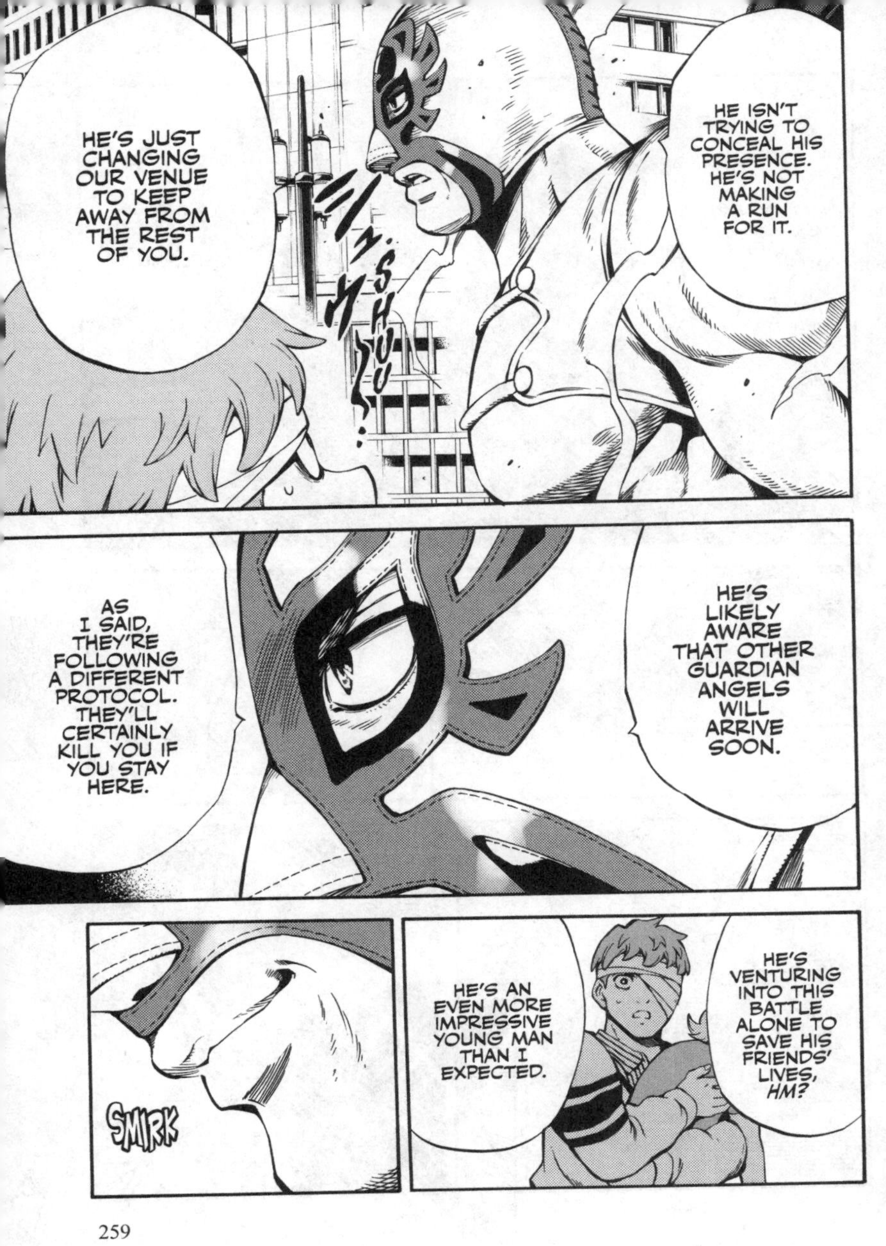
HE ISN'T TRYING TO CONCEAL HIS PRESENCE. HE'S NOT MAKING A RUN FOR IT.
SHUU
HE'S JUST CHANGING OUR VENUE TO KEEP AWAY FROM THE REST OF YOU.
HE'S LIKELY AWARE THAT OTHER GUARDIAN ANGELS WILL ARRIVE SOON.
AS I SAID, THEY'RE FOLLOWING A DIFFERENT PROTOCOL. THEY'LL CERTAINLY KILL YOU IF YOU STAY HERE.
HE'S VENTURING INTO THIS BATTLE ALONE TO SAVE HIS FRIENDS' LIVES, *HM?*
HE'S AN EVEN MORE IMPRESSIVE YOUNG MAN THAN I EXPECTED.
SMIRK

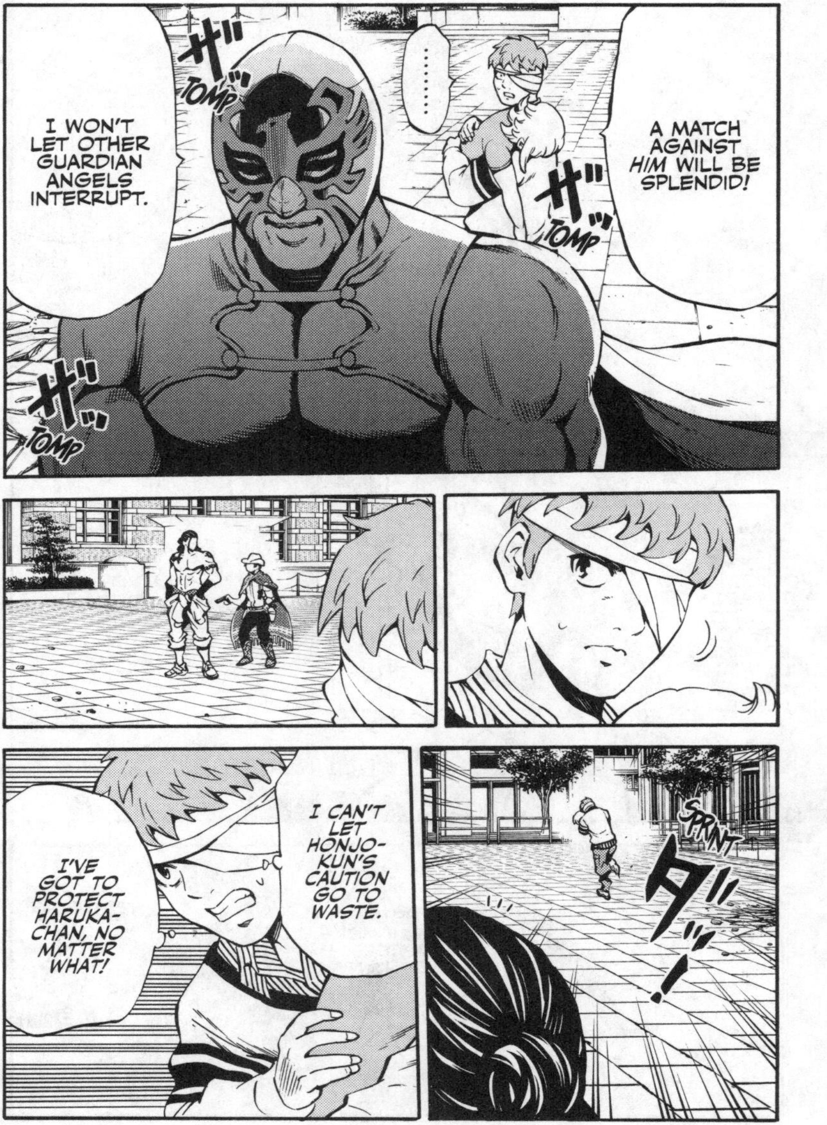
A MATCH AGAINST HIM WILL BE SPLENDID!
TOMP
......
TOMP
I WON'T LET OTHER GUARDIAN ANGELS INTERRUPT.
TOMP
SPRINT
...!
I CAN'T LET HONJO-KUN'S CAUTION GO TO WASTE.
I'VE GOT TO PROTECT HARUKA-CHAN, NO MATTER WHAT!

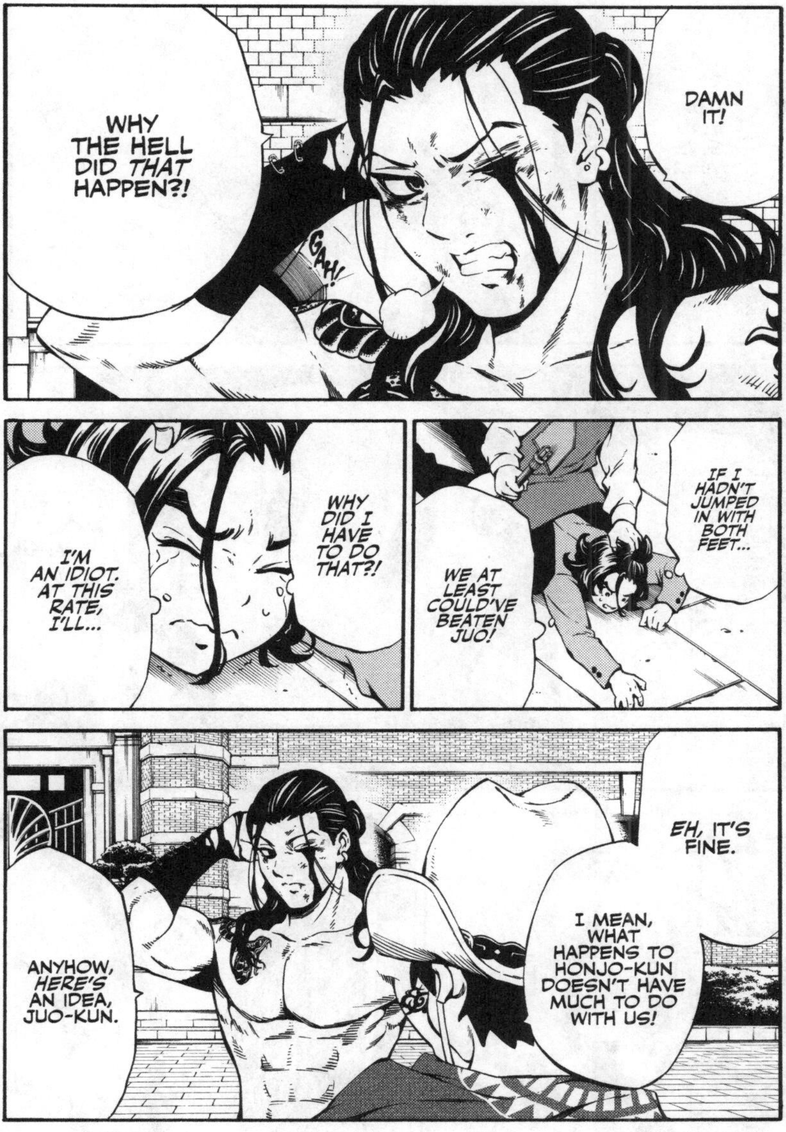
DAMN IT!
WHY THE HELL DID *THAT* HAPPEN?!
GAAH!
IF I HADN'T JUMPED IN WITH BOTH FEET...
WE AT LEAST COULD'VE BEATEN JUO!
WHY DID I HAVE TO DO THAT?!
I'M AN IDIOT. AT THIS RATE, I'LL...
EH, IT'S FINE.
I MEAN, WHAT HAPPENS TO HONJO-KUN DOESN'T HAVE MUCH TO DO WITH US!
ANYHOW, *HERE'S* AN IDEA, JUO-KUN.

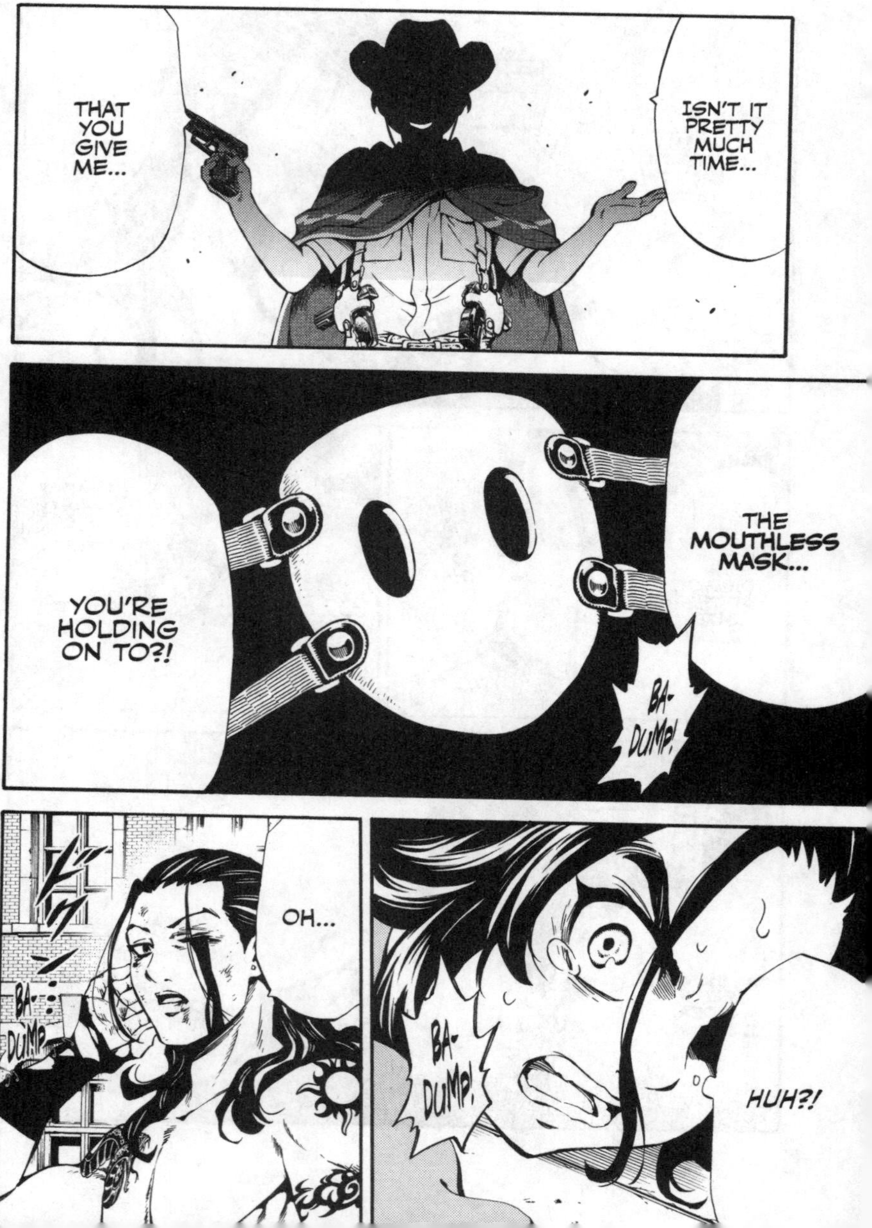
ISN'T IT PRETTY MUCH TIME...
THAT YOU GIVE ME...
THE MOUTHLESS MASK...
BA-DUMP!
YOU'RE HOLDING ON TO?!
HUH?!
BA-DUMP!
OH...
BA-DUMP

CHAPTER 235: From That Spot

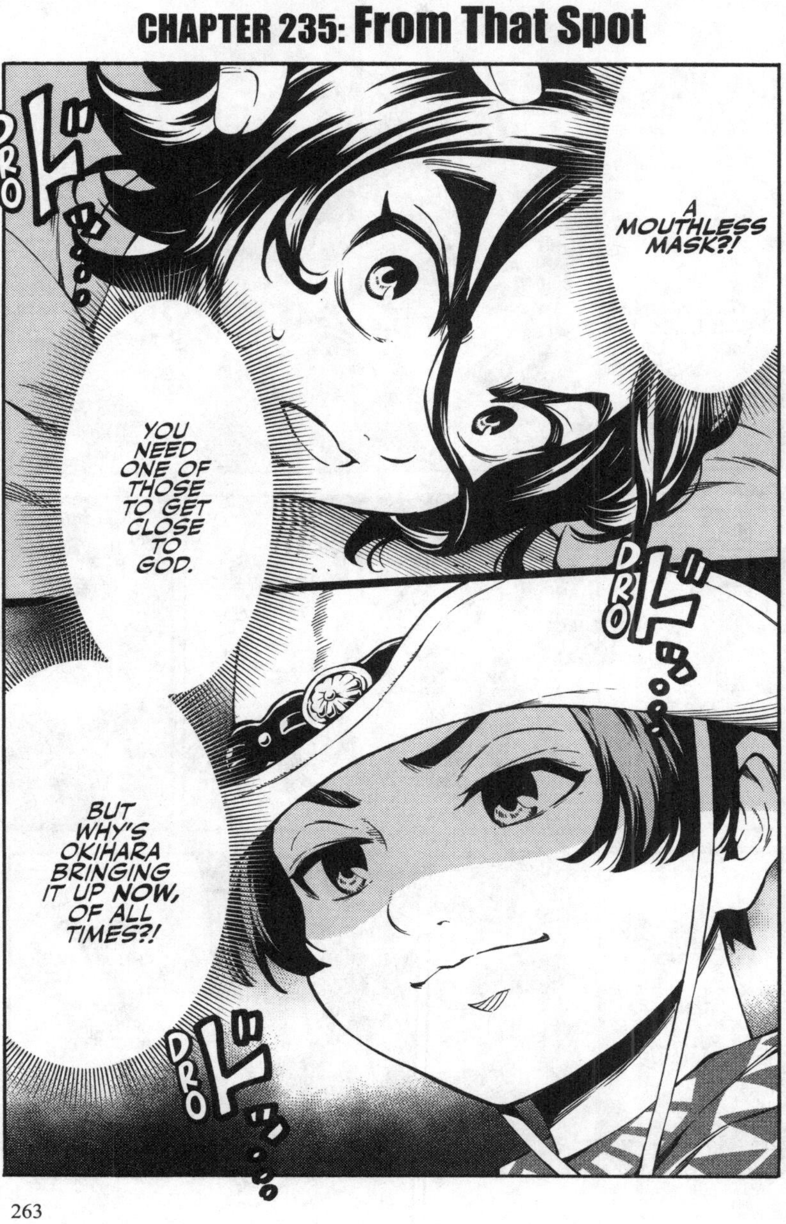
DRO
A MOUTHLESS MASK?!
YOU NEED ONE OF THOSE TO GET CLOSE TO GOD.
DRO
BUT WHY'S OKIHARA BRINGING IT UP NOW, OF ALL TIMES?!
DRO

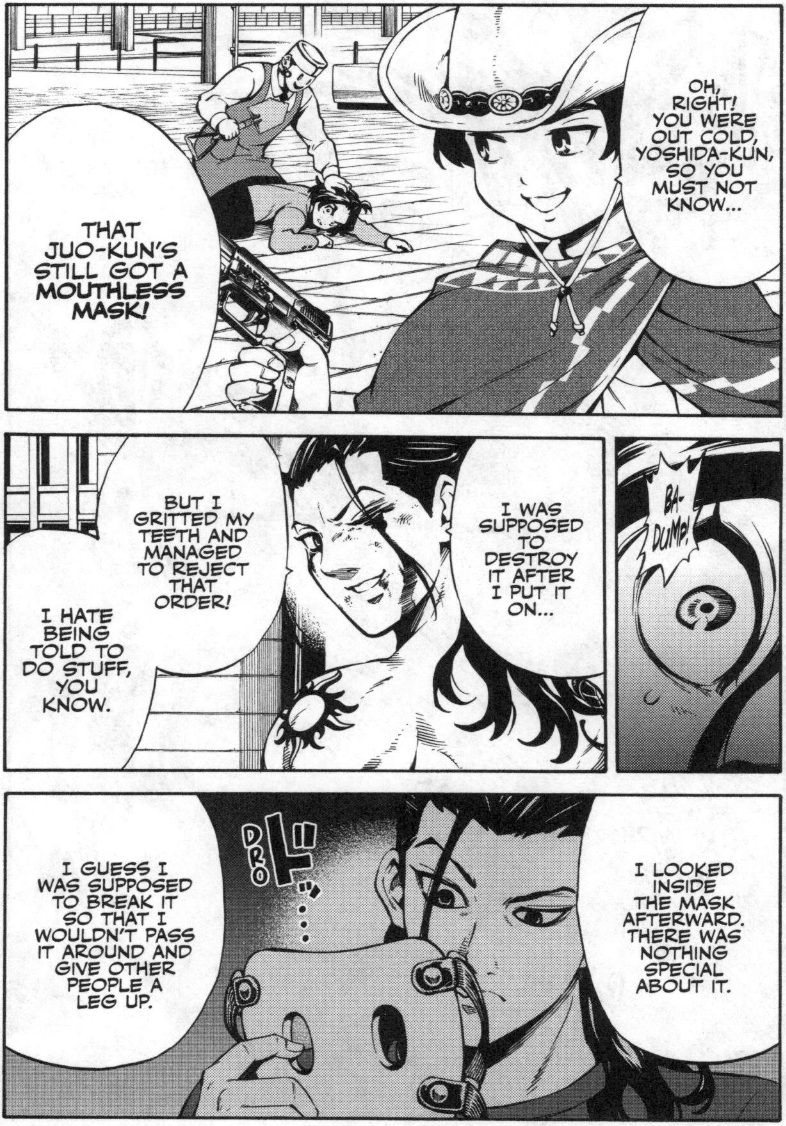
OH, RIGHT! YOU WERE OUT COLD, YOSHIDA-KUN, SO YOU MUST NOT KNOW...
THAT JUO-KUN'S STILL GOT A MOUTHLESS MASK!
BA-DUMP!
I WAS SUPPOSED TO DESTROY IT AFTER I PUT IT ON...
BUT I GRITTED MY TEETH AND MANAGED TO REJECT THAT ORDER!
I HATE BEING TOLD TO DO STUFF, YOU KNOW.
I LOOKED INSIDE THE MASK AFTERWARD. THERE WAS NOTHING SPECIAL ABOUT IT.
DRO
I GUESS I WAS SUPPOSED TO BREAK IT SO THAT I WOULDN'T PASS IT AROUND AND GIVE OTHER PEOPLE A LEG UP.

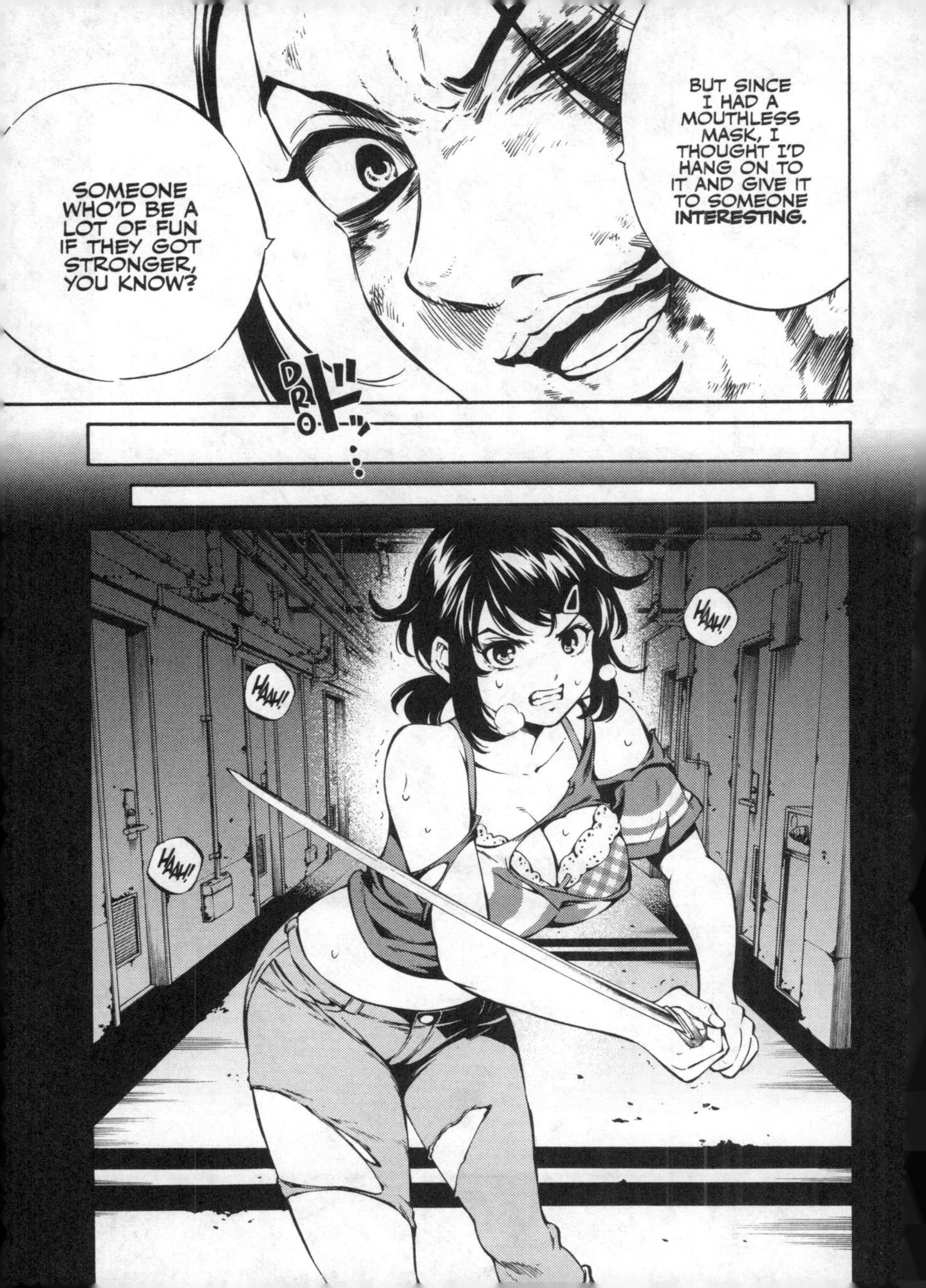
BUT SINCE I HAD A MOUTHLESS MASK, I THOUGHT I'D HANG ON TO IT AND GIVE IT TO SOMEONE **INTERESTING.**
SOMEONE WHO'D BE A LOT OF FUN IF THEY GOT STRONGER, YOU KNOW?
DRO-K...
HAAH!
HAAH!
HAAH!

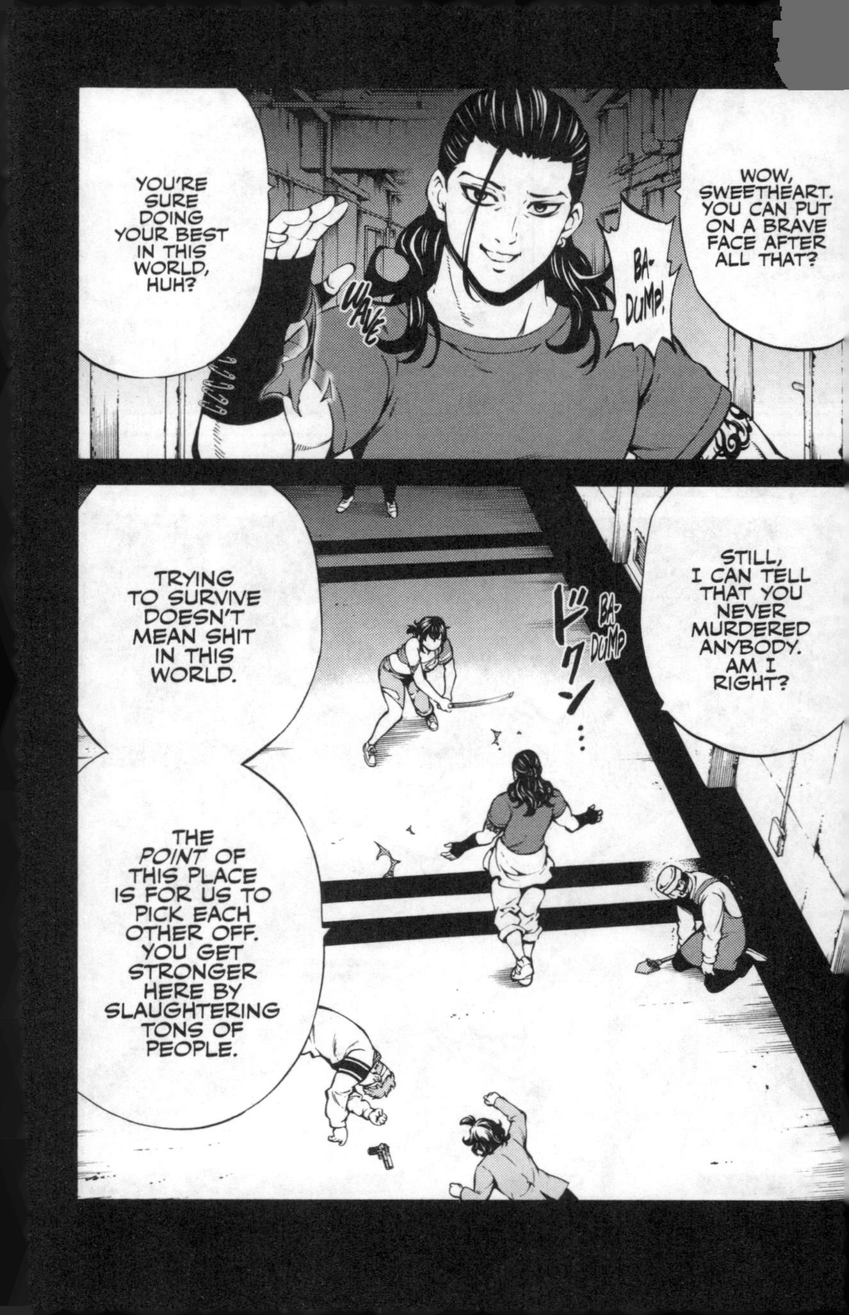
WOW, SWEETHEART. YOU CAN PUT ON A BRAVE FACE AFTER ALL THAT?
BA-DUMP!
WAVE
YOU'RE SURE DOING YOUR BEST IN THIS WORLD, HUH?
STILL, I CAN TELL THAT YOU NEVER MURDERED ANYBODY. AM I RIGHT?
ドクン
BA-DUMP
TRYING TO SURVIVE DOESN'T MEAN SHIT IN THIS WORLD.
THE *POINT* OF THIS PLACE IS FOR US TO PICK EACH OTHER OFF. YOU GET STRONGER HERE BY SLAUGHTERING TONS OF PEOPLE.

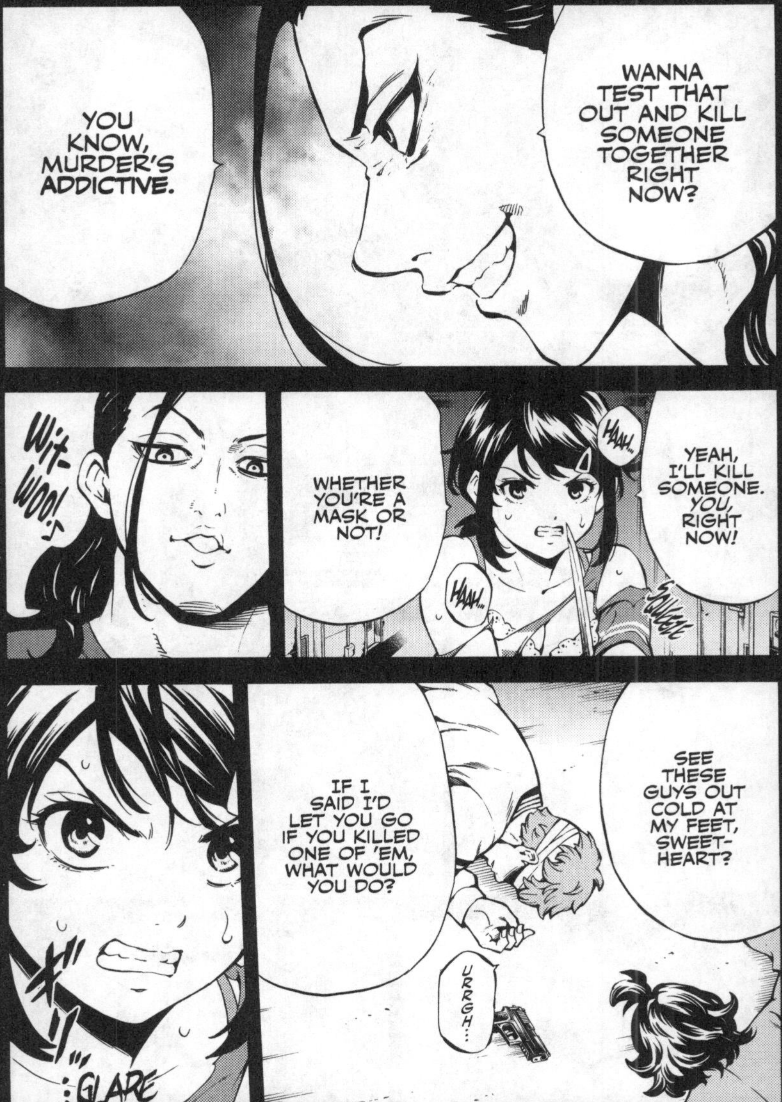
YOU KNOW, MURDER'S ADDICTIVE.
WANNA TEST THAT OUT AND KILL SOMEONE TOGETHER RIGHT NOW?
HAAH...
YEAH, I'LL KILL SOMEONE. *YOU*, RIGHT NOW!
WHETHER YOU'RE A MASK OR NOT!
HAAH...
SQUEEZE
Wit-woo! ♪
SEE THESE GUYS OUT COLD AT MY FEET, SWEET-HEART?
IF I SAID I'D LET YOU GO IF YOU KILLED ONE OF 'EM, WHAT WOULD YOU DO?
URRGH...
GLARE

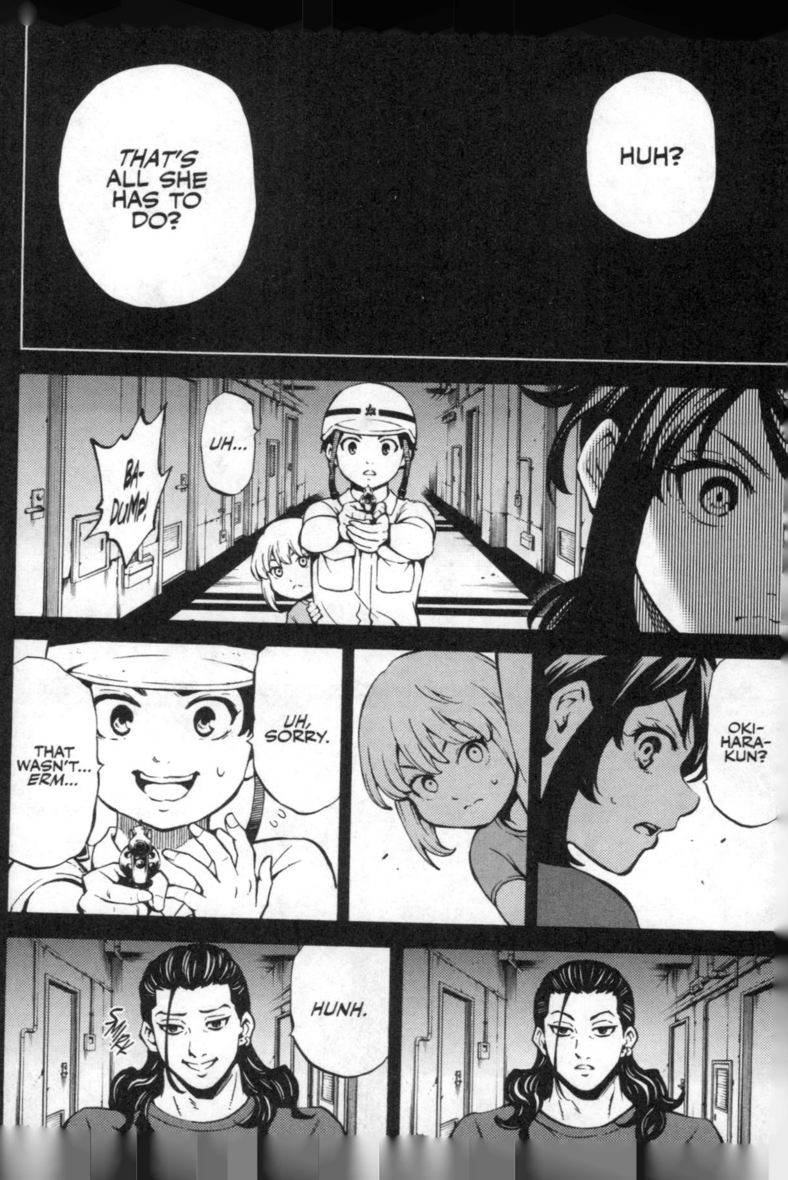
HUH?
THAT'S ALL SHE HAS TO DO?
UH...
BA-DUMP!
OKI-HARA-KUN?
UH, SORRY.
THAT WASN'T... ERM...
HUNH.
SMIRK

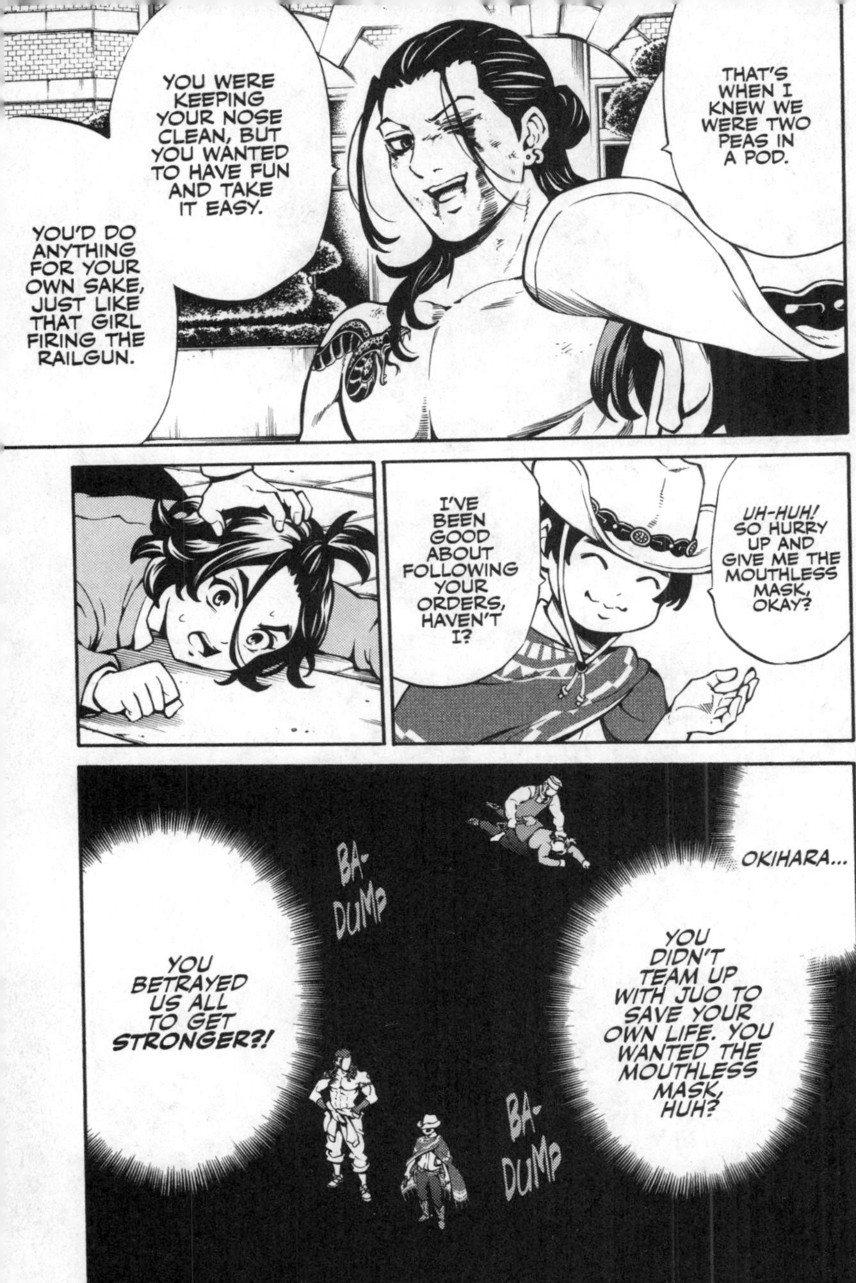
THAT'S WHEN I KNEW WE WERE TWO PEAS IN A POD.
YOU WERE KEEPING YOUR NOSE CLEAN, BUT YOU WANTED TO HAVE FUN AND TAKE IT EASY.
YOU'D DO ANYTHING FOR YOUR OWN SAKE, JUST LIKE THAT GIRL FIRING THE RAILGUN.
UH-HUH! SO HURRY UP AND GIVE ME THE MOUTHLESS MASK, OKAY?
I'VE BEEN GOOD ABOUT FOLLOWING YOUR ORDERS, HAVEN'T I?
OKIHARA...
YOU DIDN'T TEAM UP WITH JUO TO SAVE YOUR OWN LIFE. YOU WANTED THE MOUTHLESS MASK, HUH?
BA-DUMP
YOU BETRAYED US ALL TO GET STRONGER?!
BA-DUMP

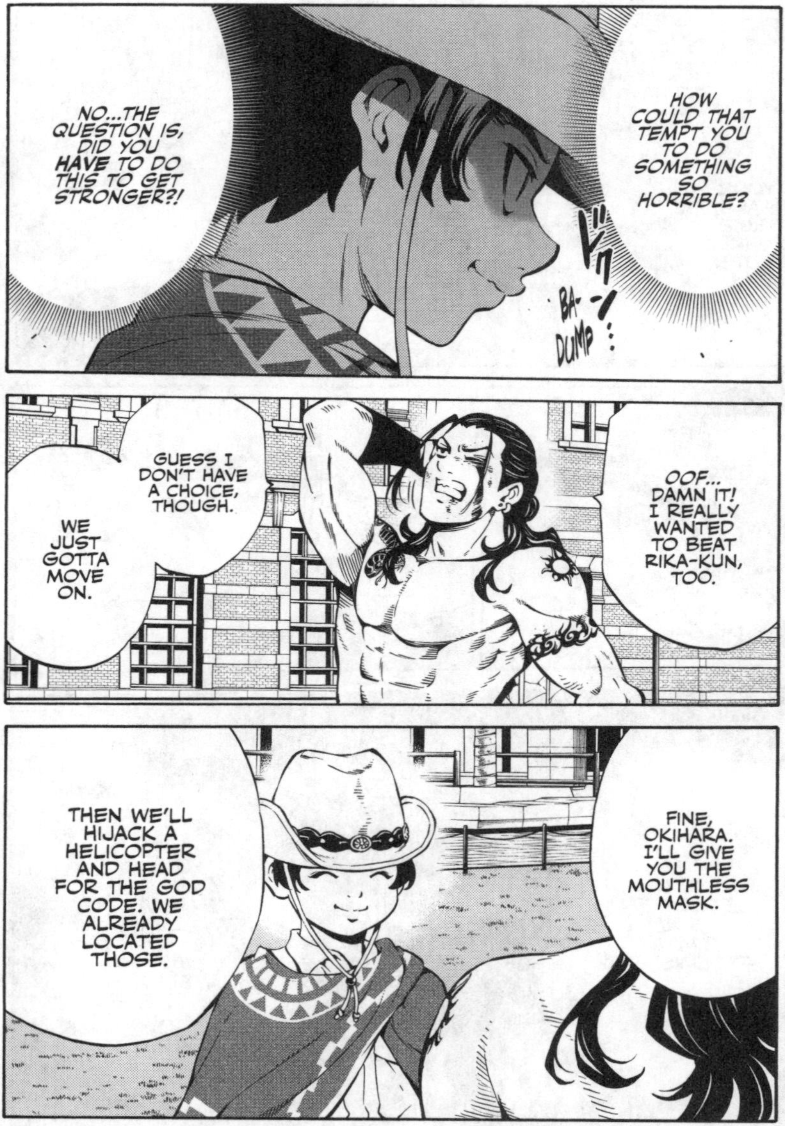
HOW COULD THAT TEMPT YOU TO DO SOMETHING SO HORRIBLE?
NO...THE QUESTION IS, DID YOU HAVE TO DO THIS TO GET STRONGER?!
BA-DUMP
OOF... DAMN IT! I REALLY WANTED TO BEAT RIKA-KUN, TOO.
GUESS I DON'T HAVE A CHOICE, THOUGH.
WE JUST GOTTA MOVE ON.
FINE, OKIHARA. I'LL GIVE YOU THE MOUTHLESS MASK.
THEN WE'LL HIJACK A HELICOPTER AND HEAD FOR THE GOD CODE. WE ALREADY LOCATED THOSE.

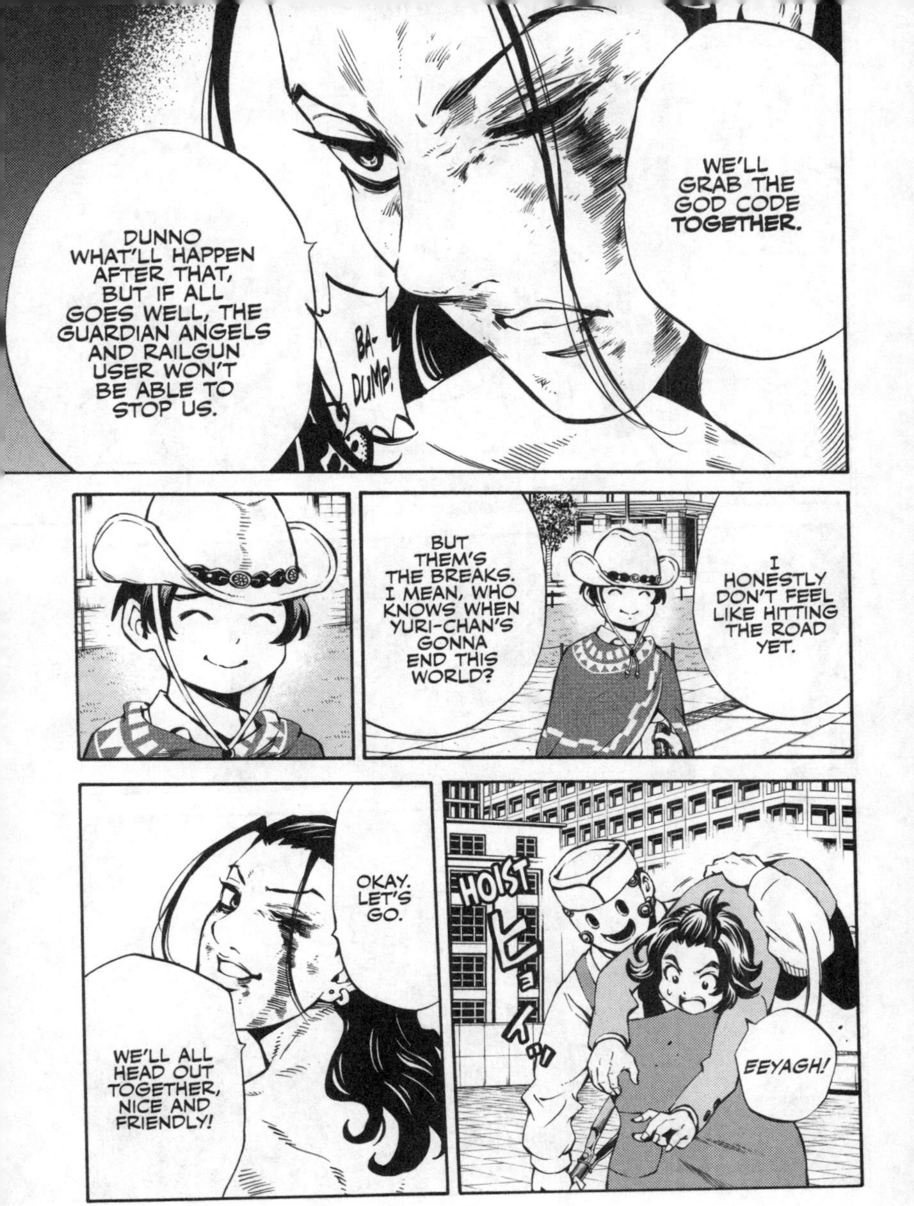
WE'LL GRAB THE GOD CODE TOGETHER.
DUNNO WHAT'LL HAPPEN AFTER THAT, BUT IF ALL GOES WELL, THE GUARDIAN ANGELS AND RAILGUN USER WON'T BE ABLE TO STOP US.
BA-DUMP!
I HONESTLY DON'T FEEL LIKE HITTING THE ROAD YET.
BUT THEM'S THE BREAKS. I MEAN, WHO KNOWS WHEN YURI-CHAN'S GONNA END THIS WORLD?
HOIST
ヒョイッ!
EEYAGH!
OKAY. LET'S GO.
WE'LL ALL HEAD OUT TOGETHER, NICE AND FRIENDLY!

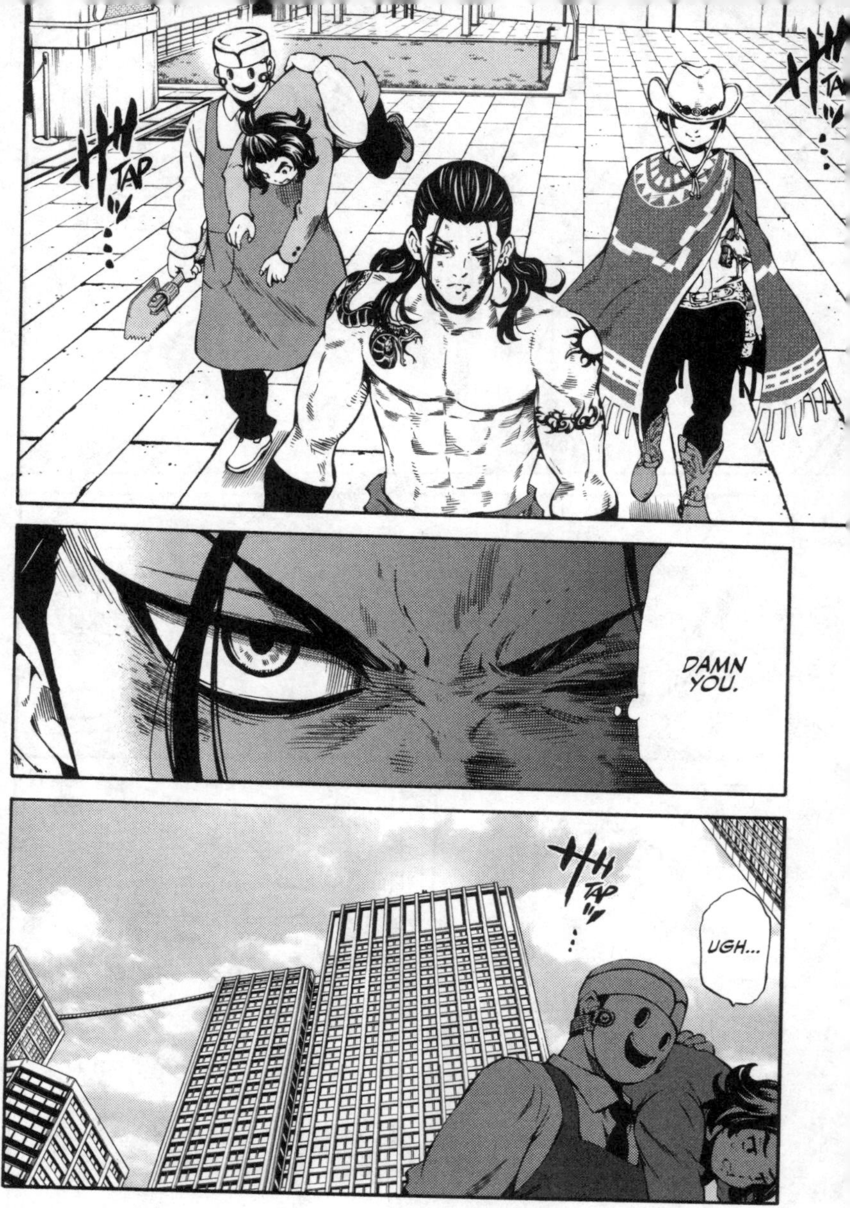
TAP...
TAP...
DAMN YOU.
TAP...
UGH...

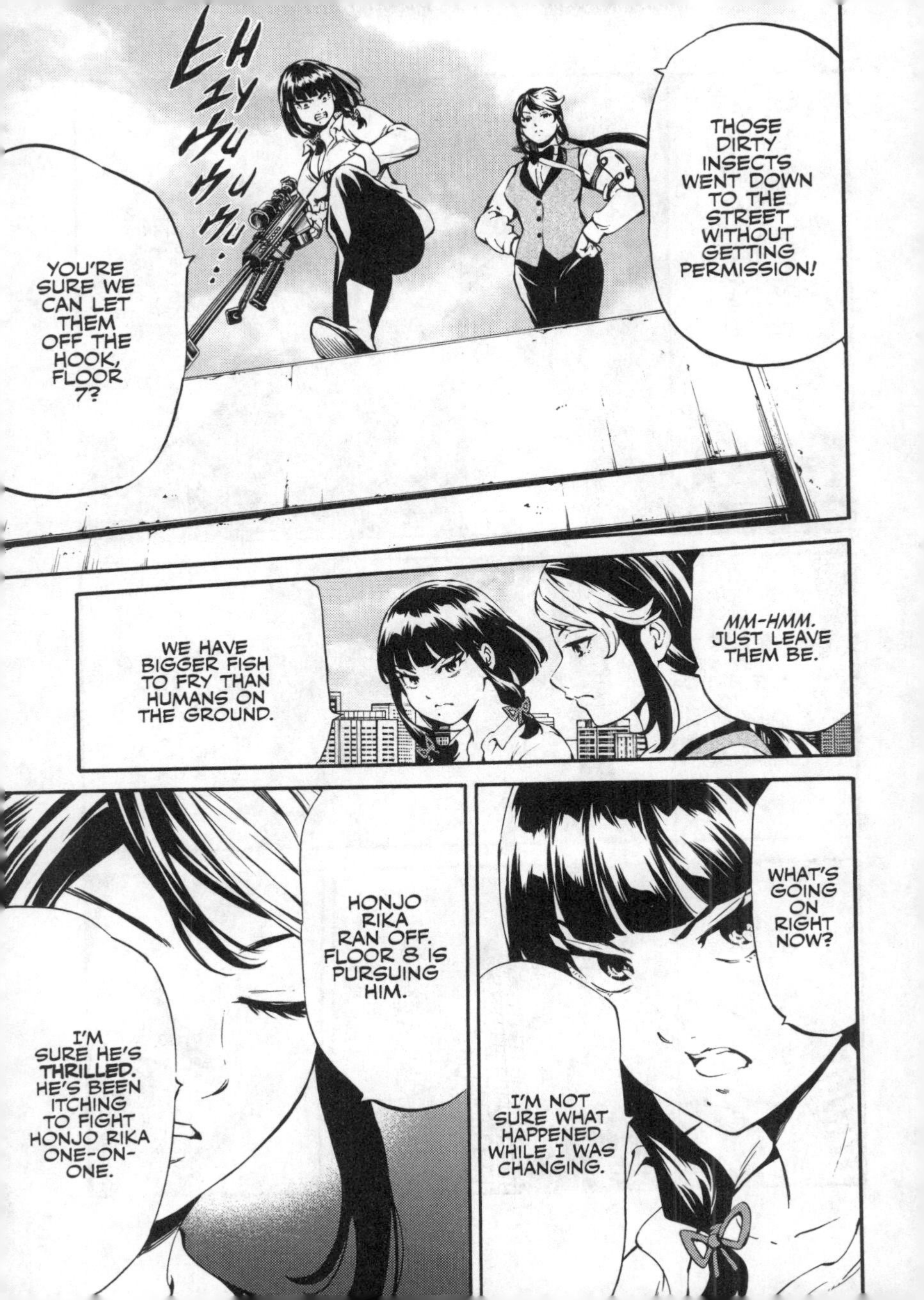
THOSE DIRTY INSECTS WENT DOWN TO THE STREET WITHOUT GETTING PERMISSION!
HYUUU...
YOU'RE SURE WE CAN LET THEM OFF THE HOOK, FLOOR 7?
MM-HMM. JUST LEAVE THEM BE.
WE HAVE BIGGER FISH TO FRY THAN HUMANS ON THE GROUND.
WHAT'S GOING ON RIGHT NOW?
I'M NOT SURE WHAT HAPPENED WHILE I WAS CHANGING.
HONJO RIKA RAN OFF. FLOOR 8 IS PURSUING HIM.
I'M SURE HE'S **THRILLED.** HE'S BEEN ITCHING TO FIGHT HONJO RIKA ONE-ON-ONE.

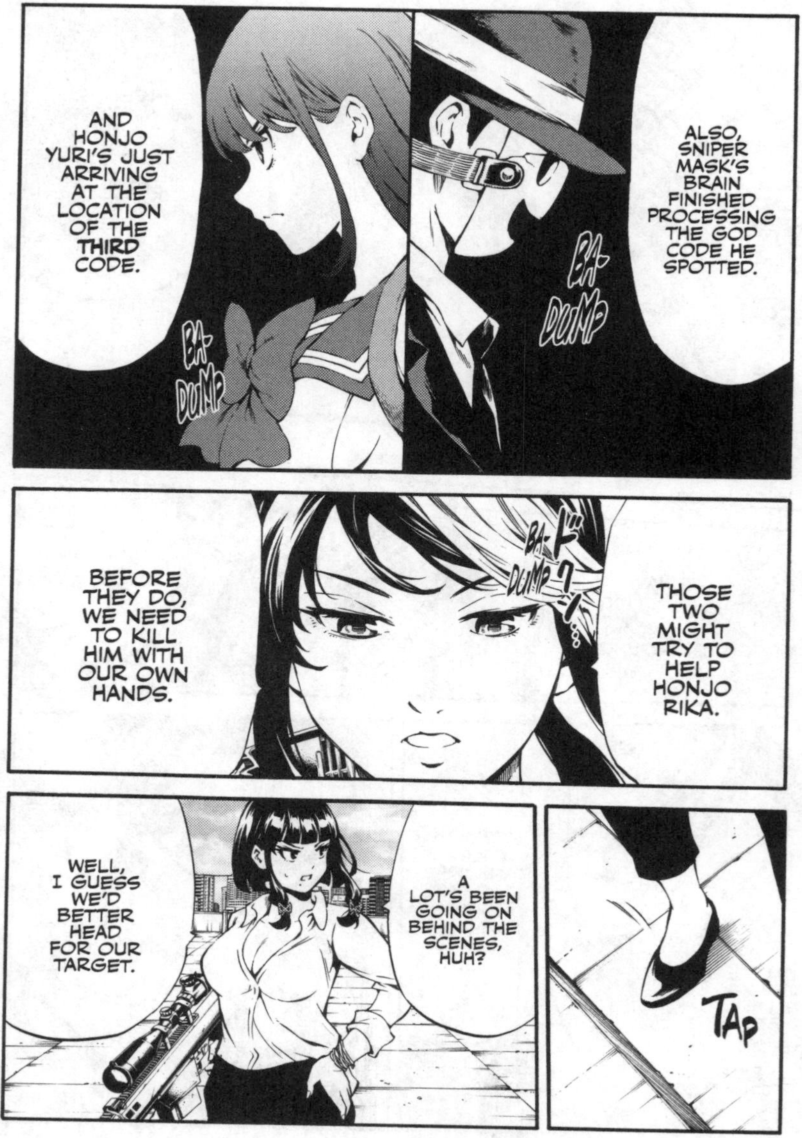
ALSO, SNIPER MASK'S BRAIN FINISHED PROCESSING THE GOD CODE HE SPOTTED.
BA-DUMP
AND HONJO YURI'S JUST ARRIVING AT THE LOCATION OF THE THIRD CODE.
BA-DUMP
THOSE TWO MIGHT TRY TO HELP HONJO RIKA.
BA-DUMP
BEFORE THEY DO, WE NEED TO KILL HIM WITH OUR OWN HANDS.
TAP
A LOT'S BEEN GOING ON BEHIND THE SCENES, HUH?
WELL, I GUESS WE'D BETTER HEAD FOR OUR TARGET.

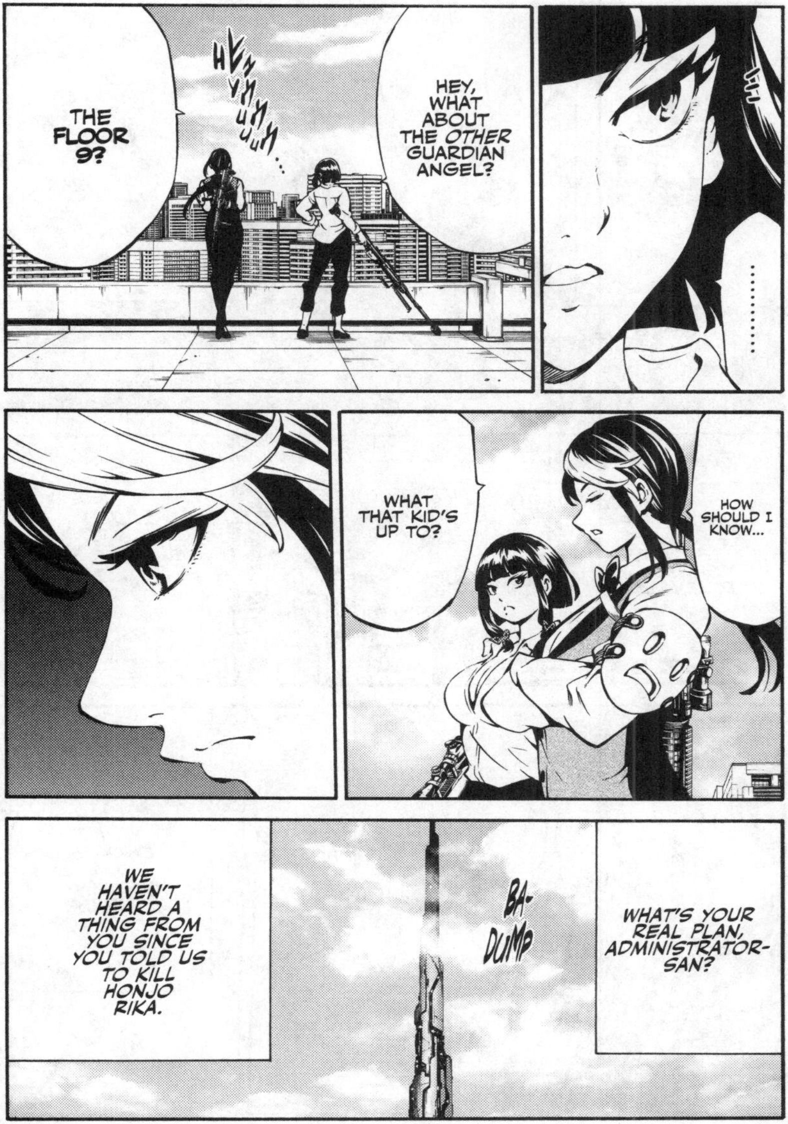
......
HEY, WHAT ABOUT THE *OTHER* GUARDIAN ANGEL?
THE FLOOR 9?
HOW SHOULD I KNOW...
WHAT THAT KID'S UP TO?
WHAT'S YOUR REAL PLAN, ADMINISTRATOR-SAN?
BA-DUMP
WE HAVEN'T HEARD A THING FROM YOU SINCE YOU TOLD US TO KILL HONJO RIKA.

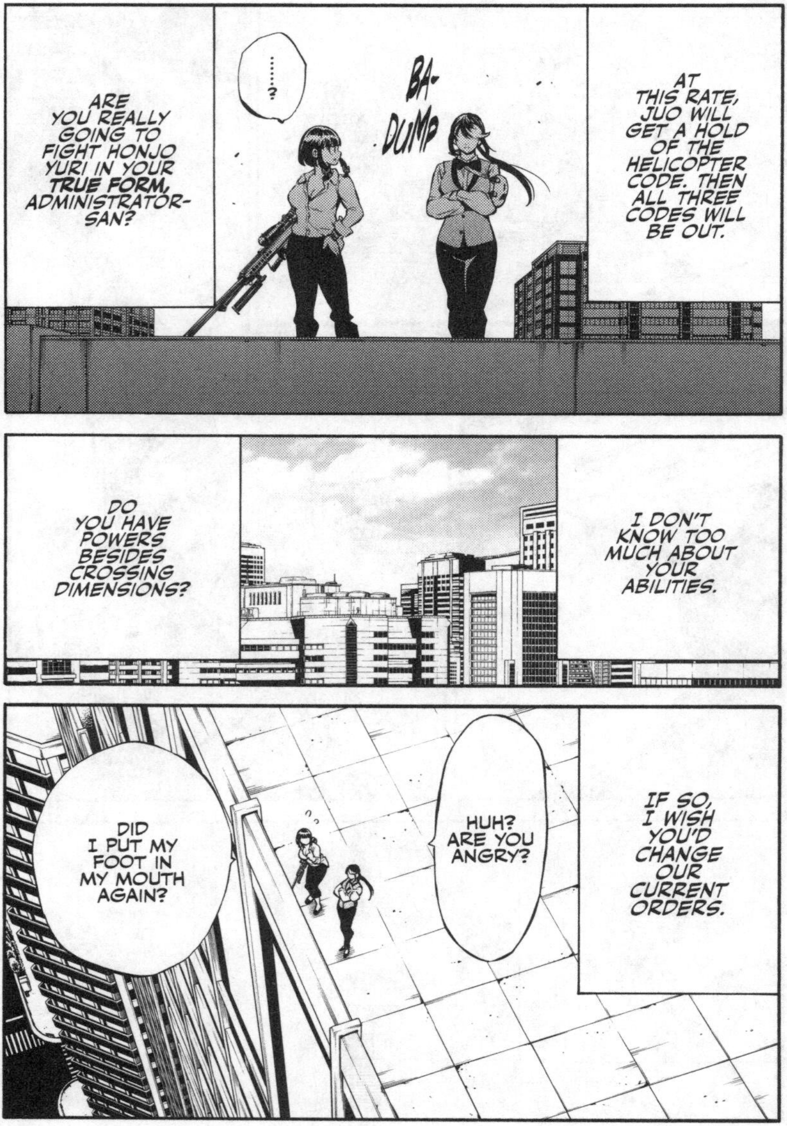
AT THIS RATE, JUO WILL GET A HOLD OF THE HELICOPTER CODE. THEN ALL THREE CODES WILL BE OUT.
BA-DUMP
......?
ARE YOU REALLY GOING TO FIGHT HONJO YURI IN YOUR TRUE FORM, ADMINISTRATOR-SAN?
I DON'T KNOW TOO MUCH ABOUT YOUR ABILITIES.
DO YOU HAVE POWERS BESIDES CROSSING DIMENSIONS?
IF SO, I WISH YOU'D CHANGE OUR CURRENT ORDERS.
HUH? ARE YOU ANGRY?
DID I PUT MY FOOT IN MY MOUTH AGAIN?

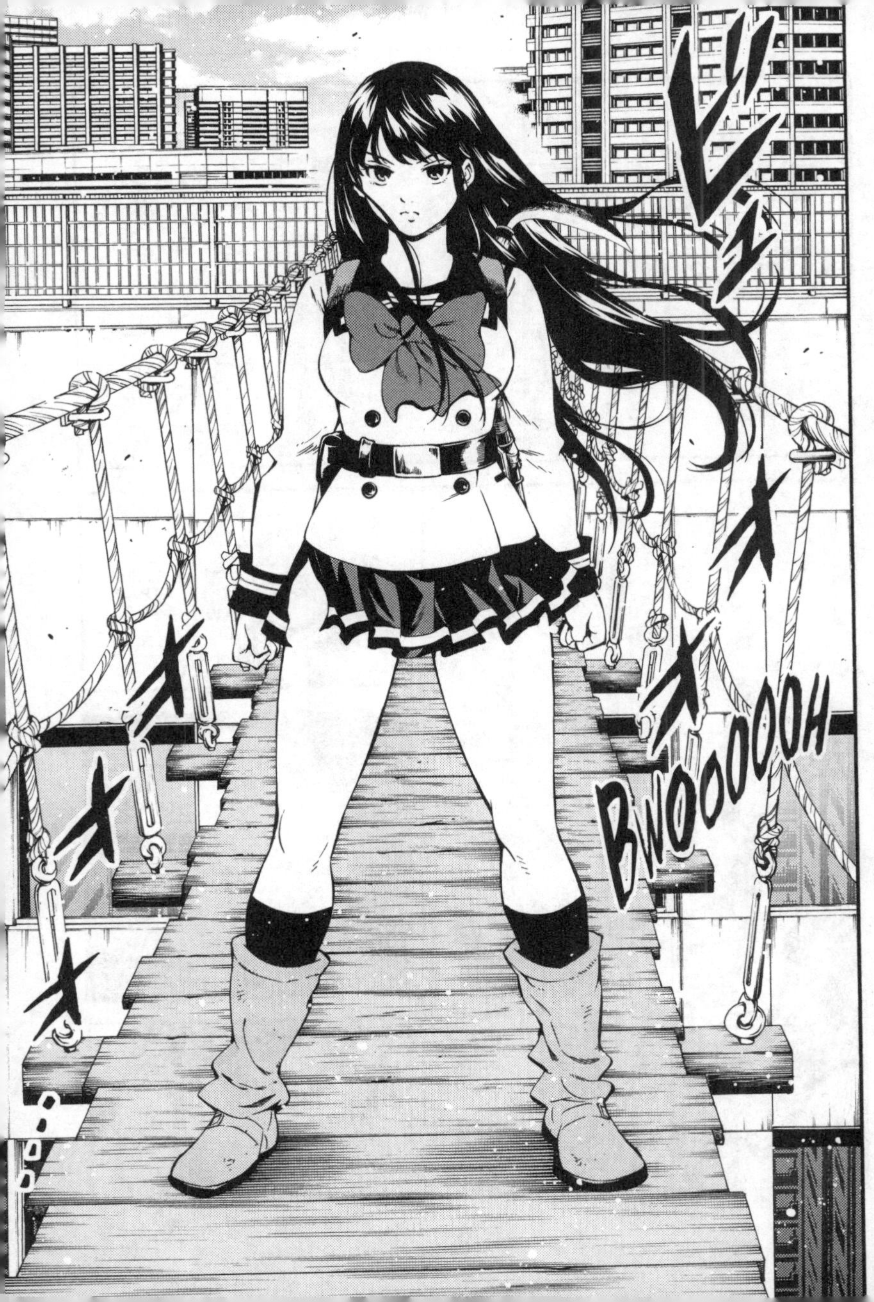
BWOOOOOH

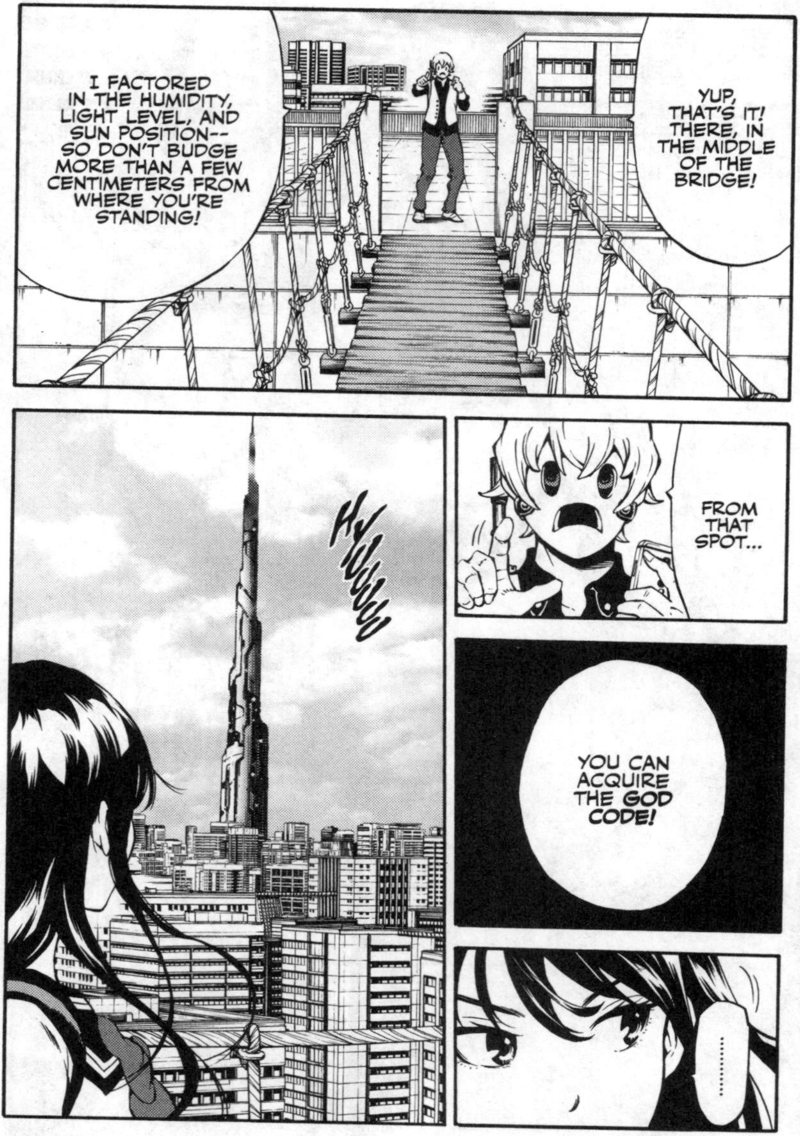
YUP, THAT'S IT! THERE, IN THE MIDDLE OF THE BRIDGE!
I FACTORED IN THE HUMIDITY, LIGHT LEVEL, AND SUN POSITION-- SO DON'T BUDGE MORE THAN A FEW CENTIMETERS FROM WHERE YOU'RE STANDING!
FROM THAT SPOT...
YOU CAN ACQUIRE THE GOD CODE!
......
HYUUUU

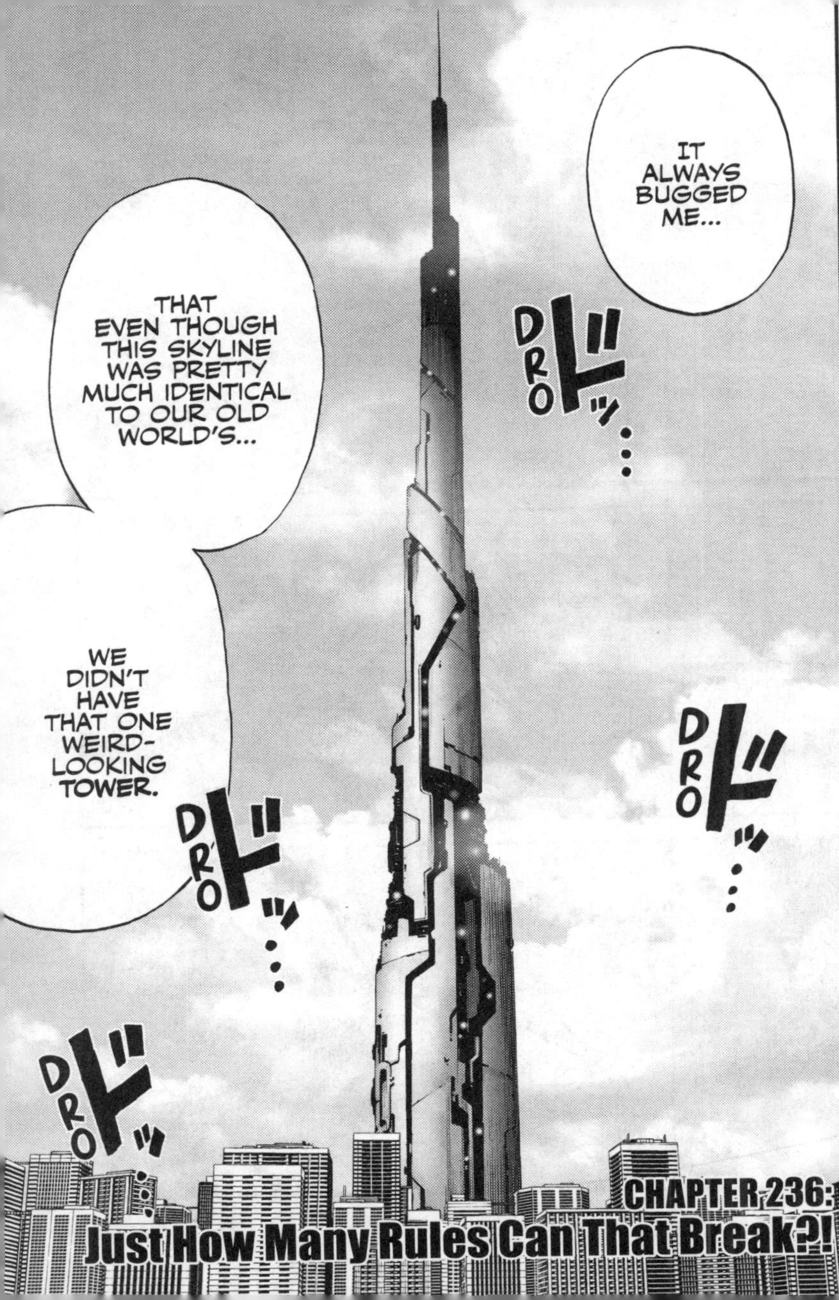
IT ALWAYS BUGGED ME...
THAT EVEN THOUGH THIS SKYLINE WAS PRETTY MUCH IDENTICAL TO OUR OLD WORLD'S...
WE DIDN'T HAVE THAT ONE WEIRD-LOOKING TOWER.
DRO ドッ...
DRO ドッ...
DRO ドッ...
DRO ドッ...
CHAPTER 236:
Just How Many Rules Can That Break?!

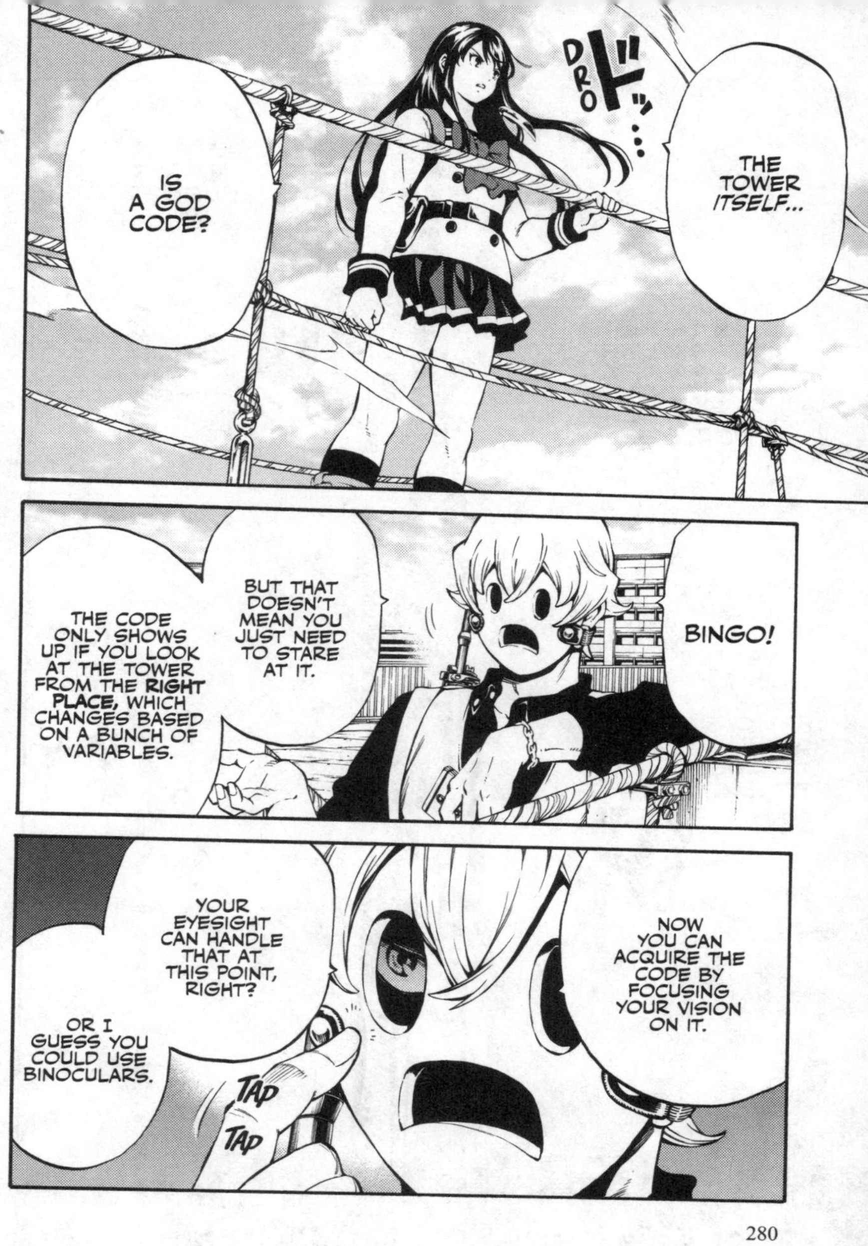
THE TOWER *ITSELF*...
DRO
IS A GOD CODE?
BINGO!
BUT THAT DOESN'T MEAN YOU JUST NEED TO STARE AT IT.
THE CODE ONLY SHOWS UP IF YOU LOOK AT THE TOWER FROM THE **RIGHT PLACE,** WHICH CHANGES BASED ON A BUNCH OF VARIABLES.
NOW YOU CAN ACQUIRE THE CODE BY FOCUSING YOUR VISION ON IT.
YOUR EYESIGHT CAN HANDLE THAT AT THIS POINT, RIGHT?
OR I GUESS YOU COULD USE BINOCULARS.
TAP
TAP

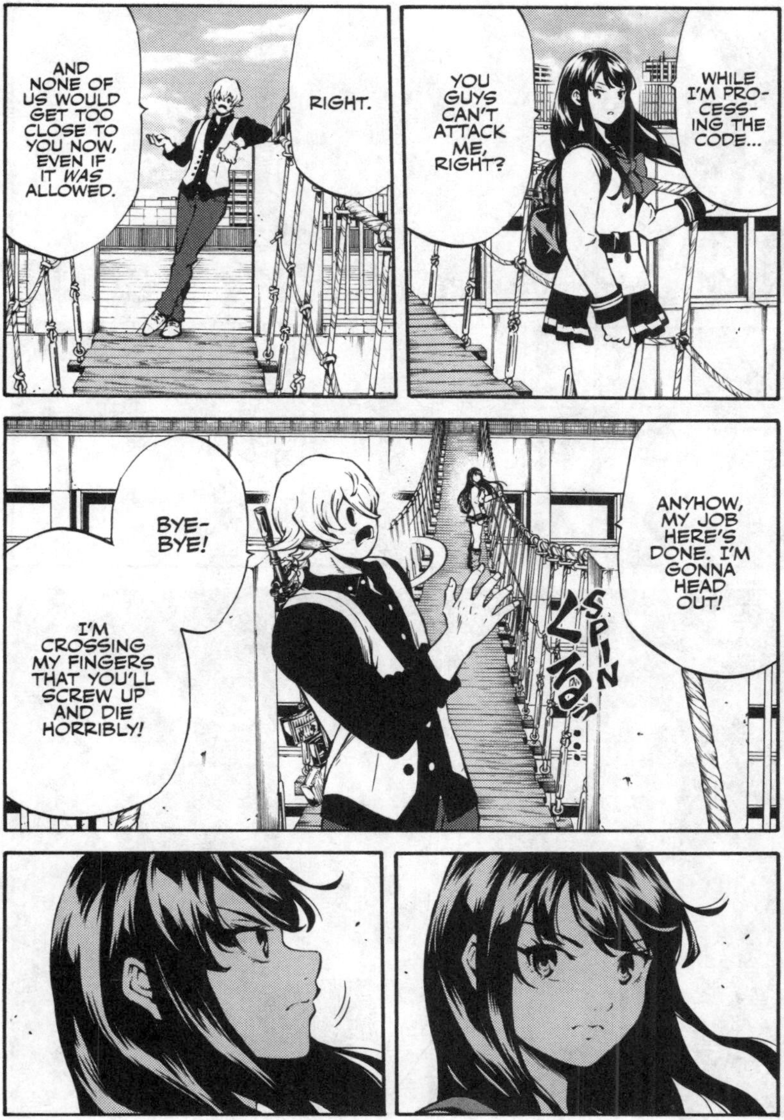
WHILE I'M PRO-CESS-ING THE CODE...
YOU GUYS CAN'T ATTACK ME, RIGHT?
RIGHT.
AND NONE OF US WOULD GET TOO CLOSE TO YOU NOW, EVEN IF IT *WAS* ALLOWED.
ANYHOW, MY JOB HERE'S DONE. I'M GONNA HEAD OUT!
SPIN
BYE-BYE!
I'M CROSSING MY FINGERS THAT YOU'LL SCREW UP AND DIE HORRIBLY!

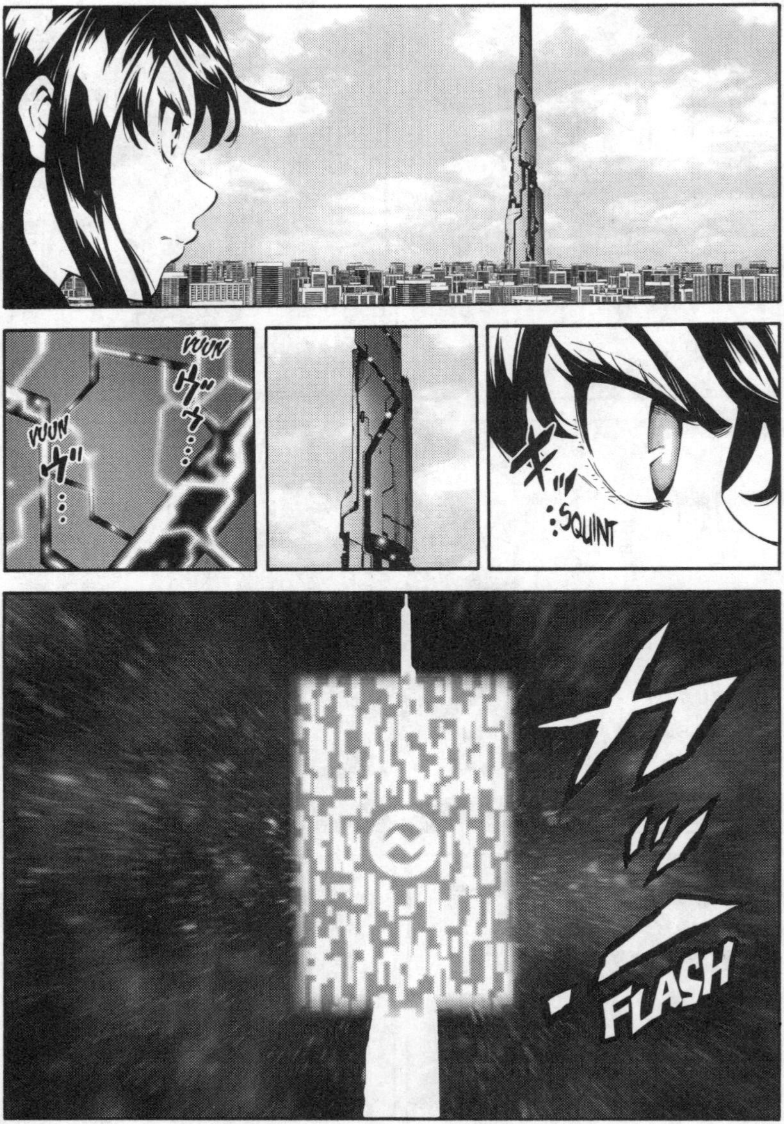
ギッ
SQUINT
VUUN
ヴゥ…
VUUN
ヴ…
カッ
FLASH

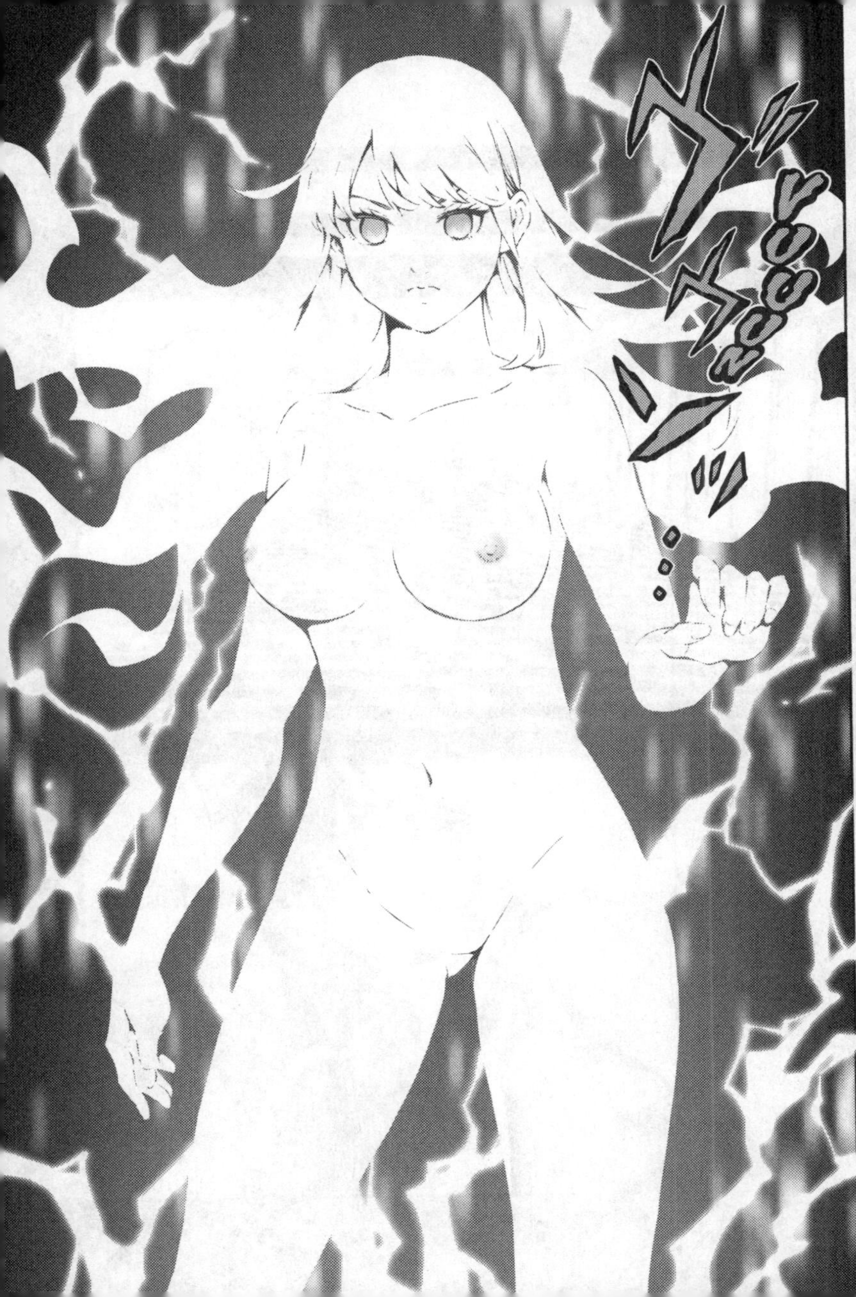
ヴゥン
VOOON

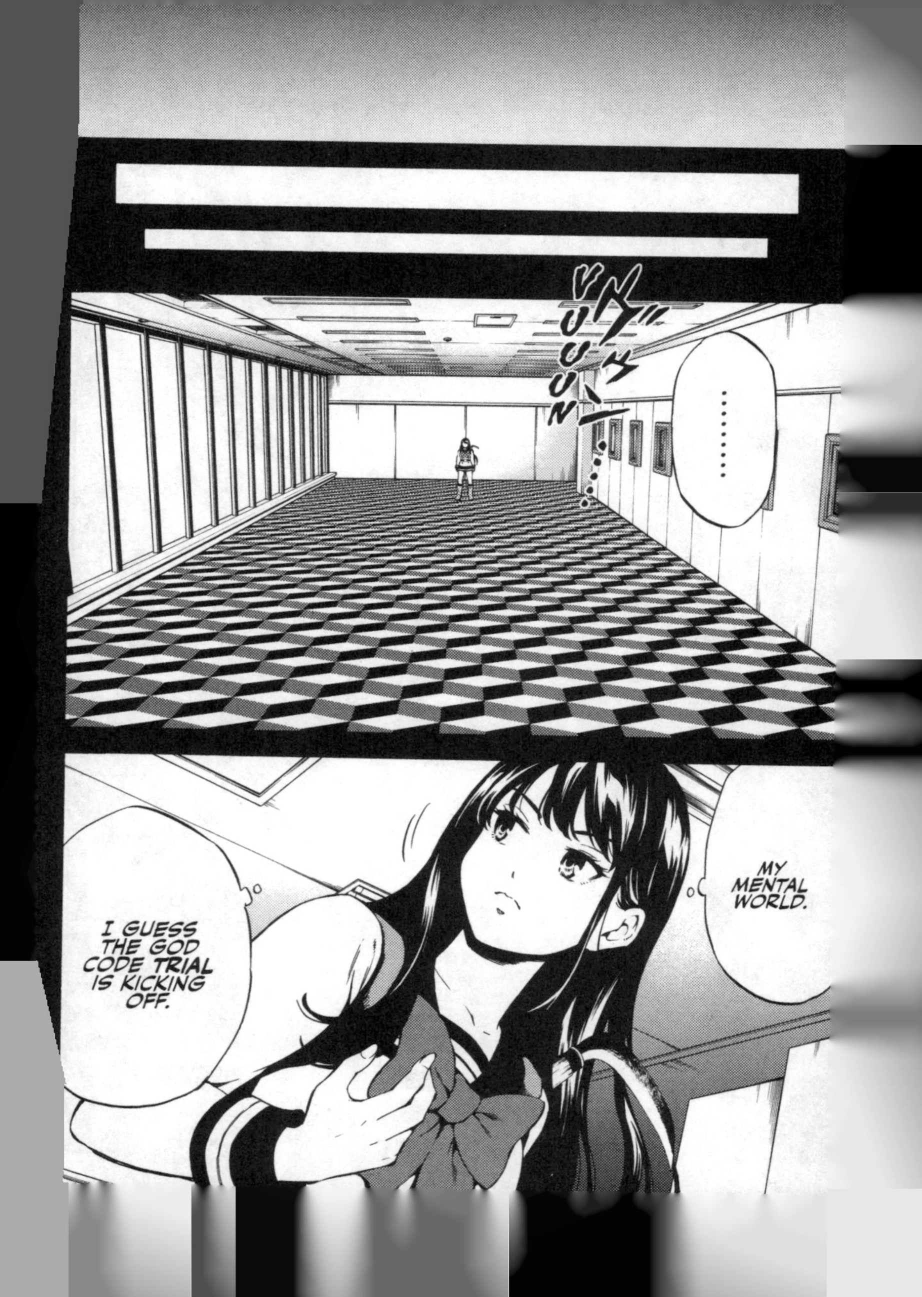
VUUUUN
......
MY MENTAL WORLD.
I GUESS THE GOD CODE TRIAL IS KICKING OFF.

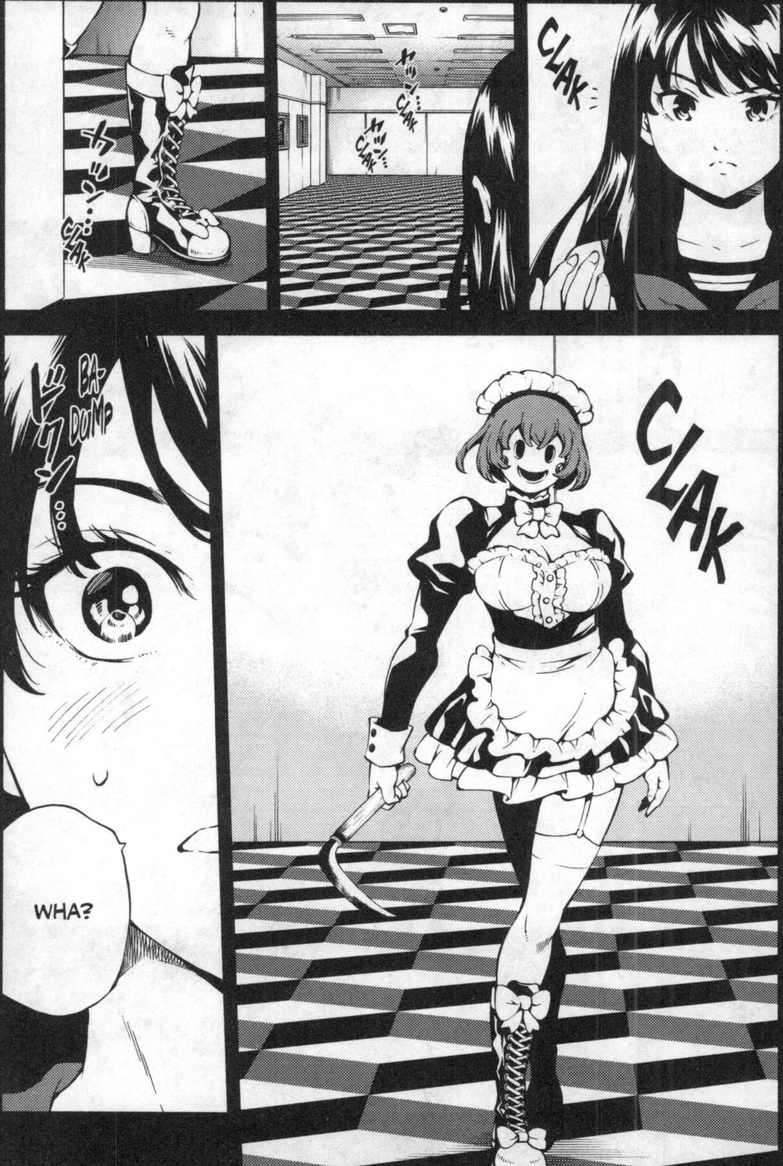
CLAK
CLAK
CLAK
CLAK
CLAK
BA-DUMP
WHA?

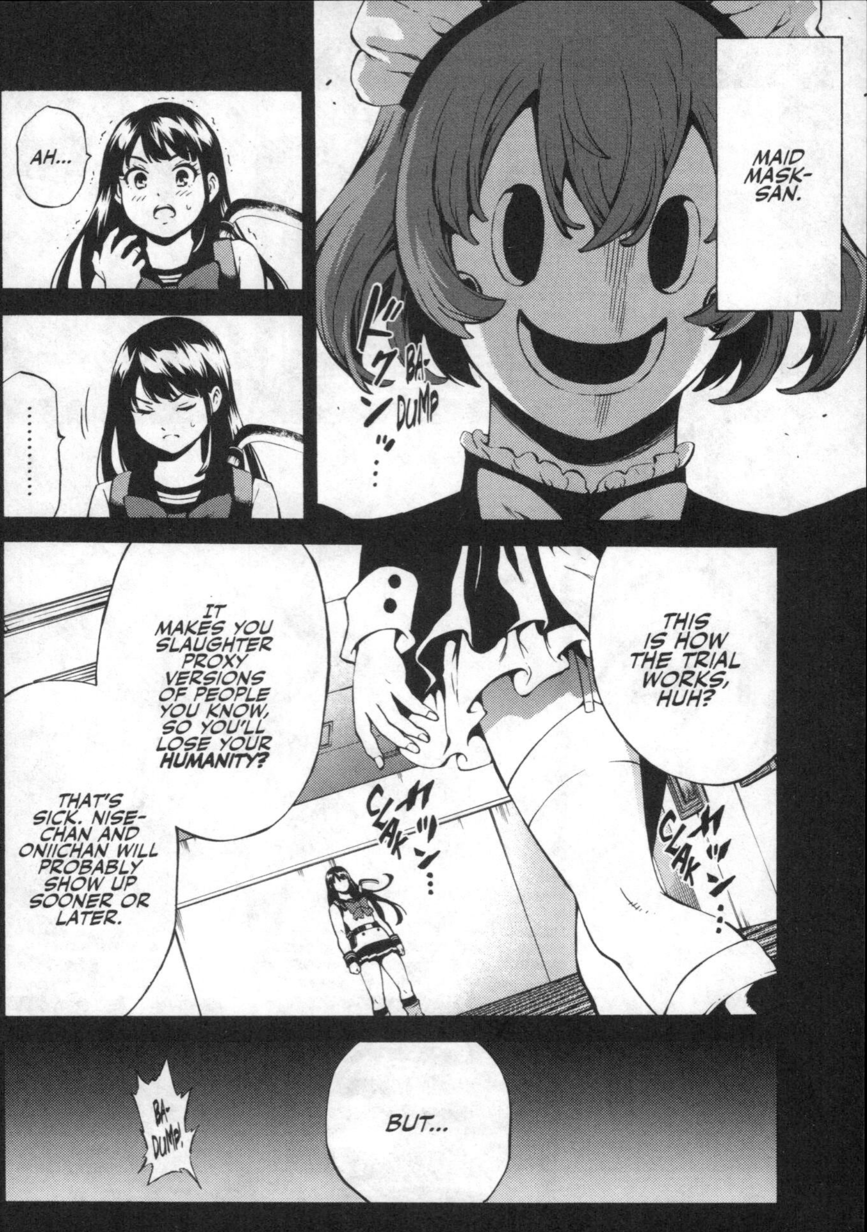
MAID MASK-SAN.
BA-DUMP
AH...
......
THIS IS HOW THE TRIAL WORKS, HUH?
CLAK
IT MAKES YOU SLAUGHTER PROXY VERSIONS OF PEOPLE YOU KNOW, SO YOU'LL LOSE YOUR **HUMANITY**?
THAT'S SICK. NISE-CHAN AND ONIICHAN WILL PROBABLY SHOW UP SOONER OR LATER.
CLAK
BUT...
BA-DUMP!

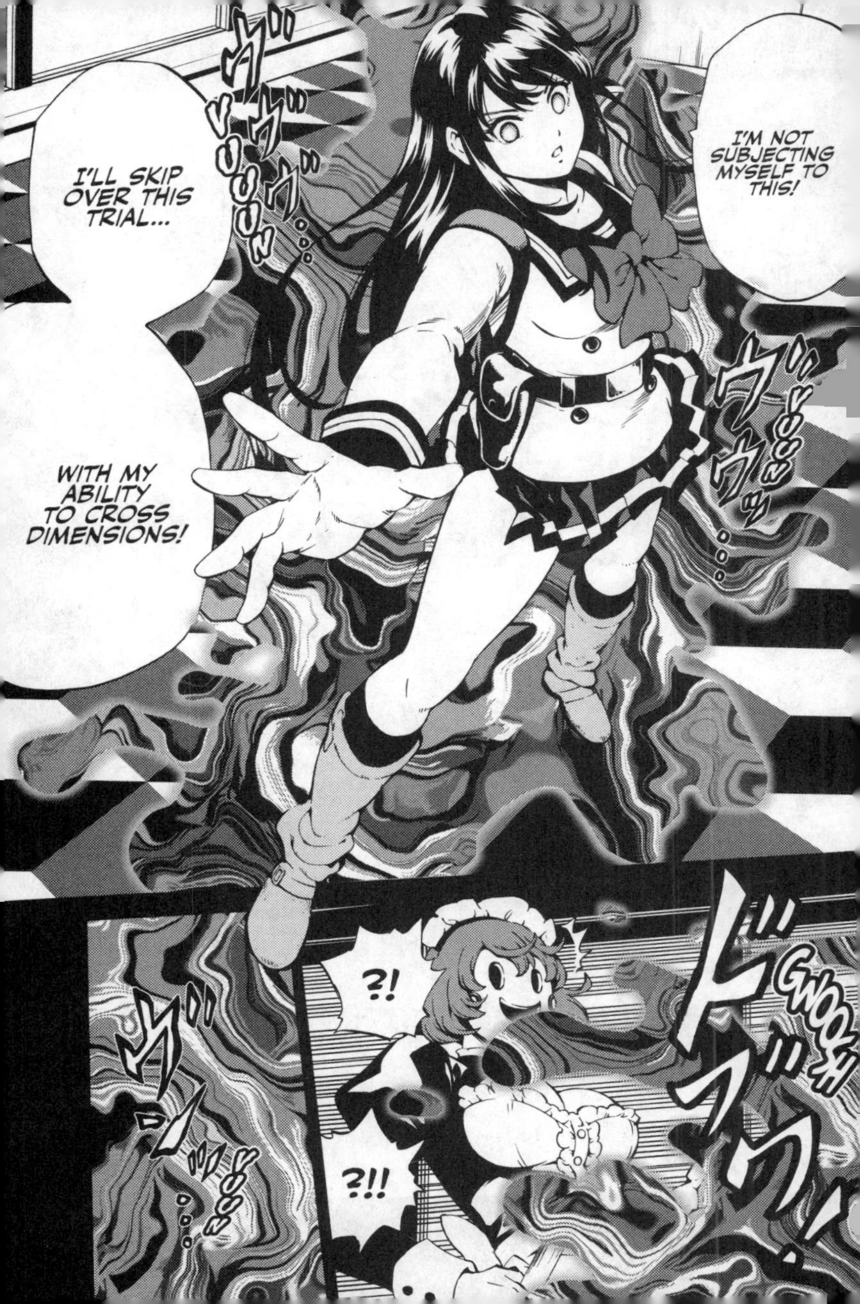
I'M NOT SUBJECTING MYSELF TO THIS!
I'LL SKIP OVER THIS TRIAL...
WITH MY ABILITY TO CROSS DIMENSIONS!
GWOOOH
?!
?!!

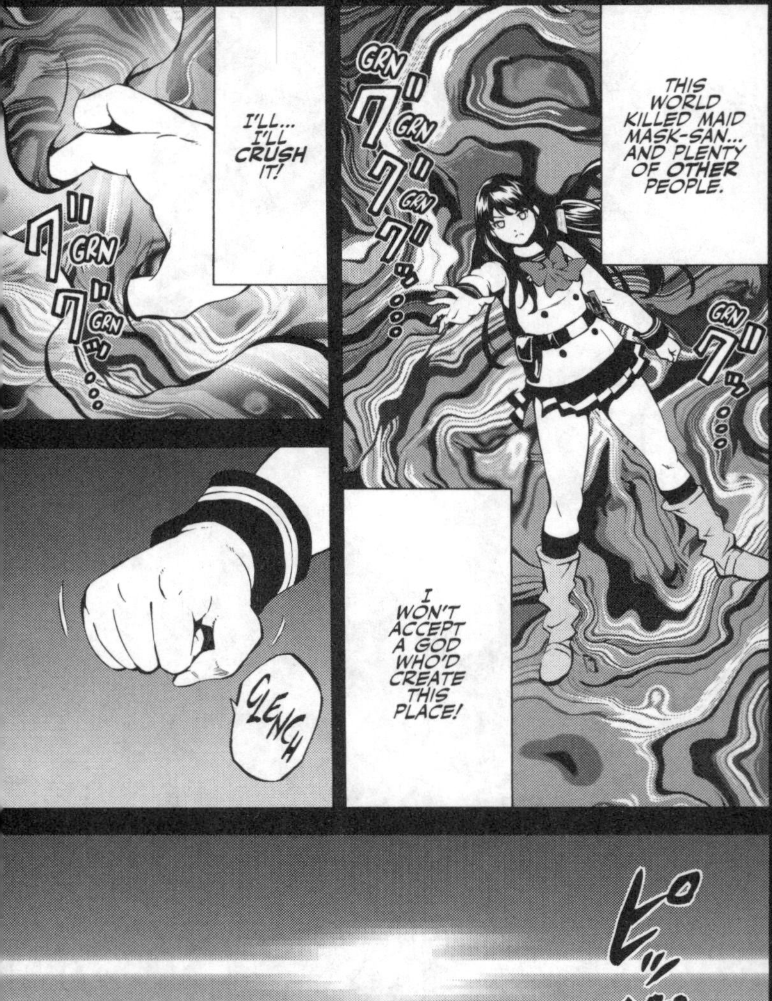
THIS WORLD KILLED MAID MASK-SAN... AND PLENTY OF OTHER PEOPLE.
GRN
GRN
GRN
GRN
I WON'T ACCEPT A GOD WHO'D CREATE THIS PLACE!
I'LL... I'LL CRUSH IT!
GRN
GRN
CLENCH
BIP

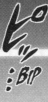

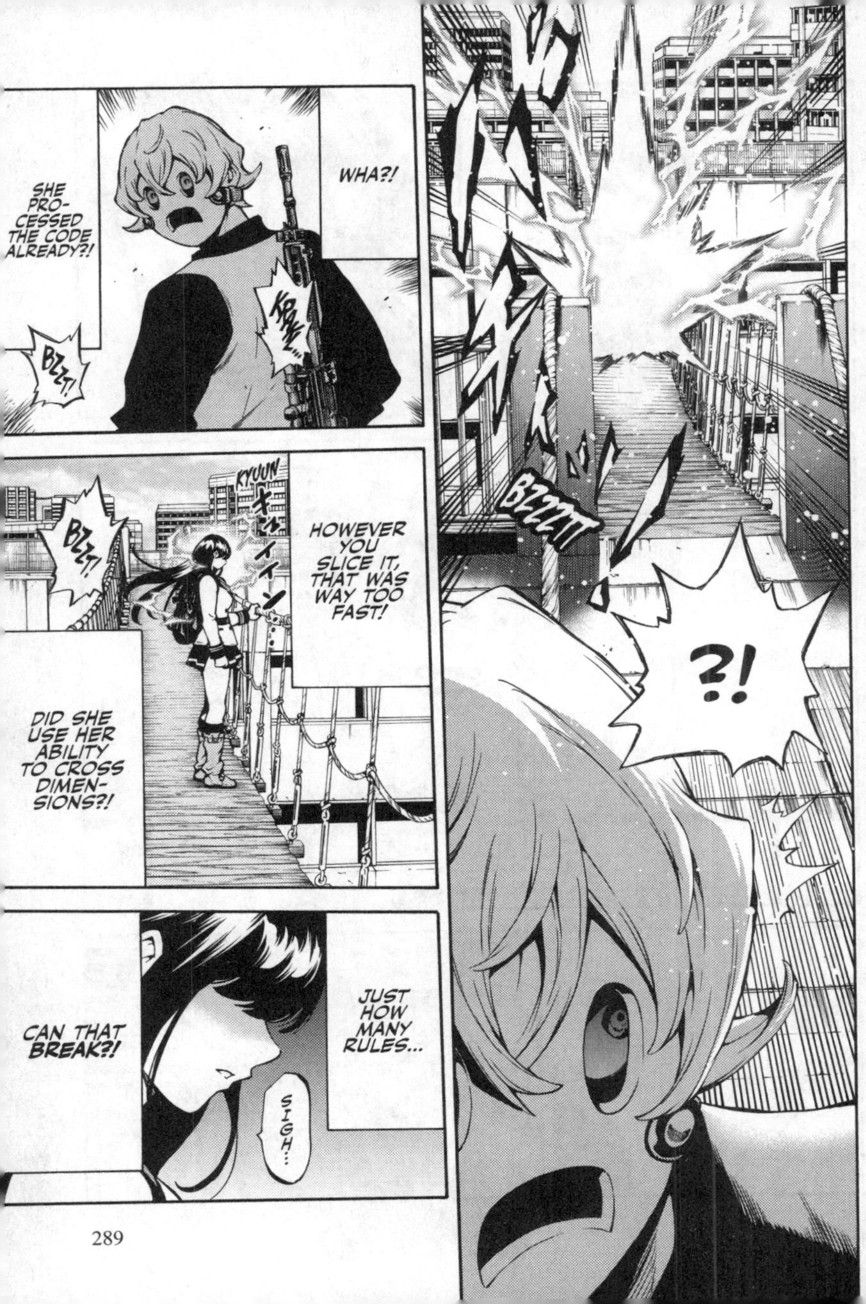
BZZZTT
?!
WHA?!
SHE PROCESSED THE CODE ALREADY?!
KRAKKL...
BZZT!
KYUUN
HOWEVER YOU SLICE IT, THAT WAS WAY TOO FAST!
BZZT!
DID SHE USE HER ABILITY TO CROSS DIMENSIONS?!
JUST HOW MANY RULES...
SIGH...
CAN THAT BREAK?!

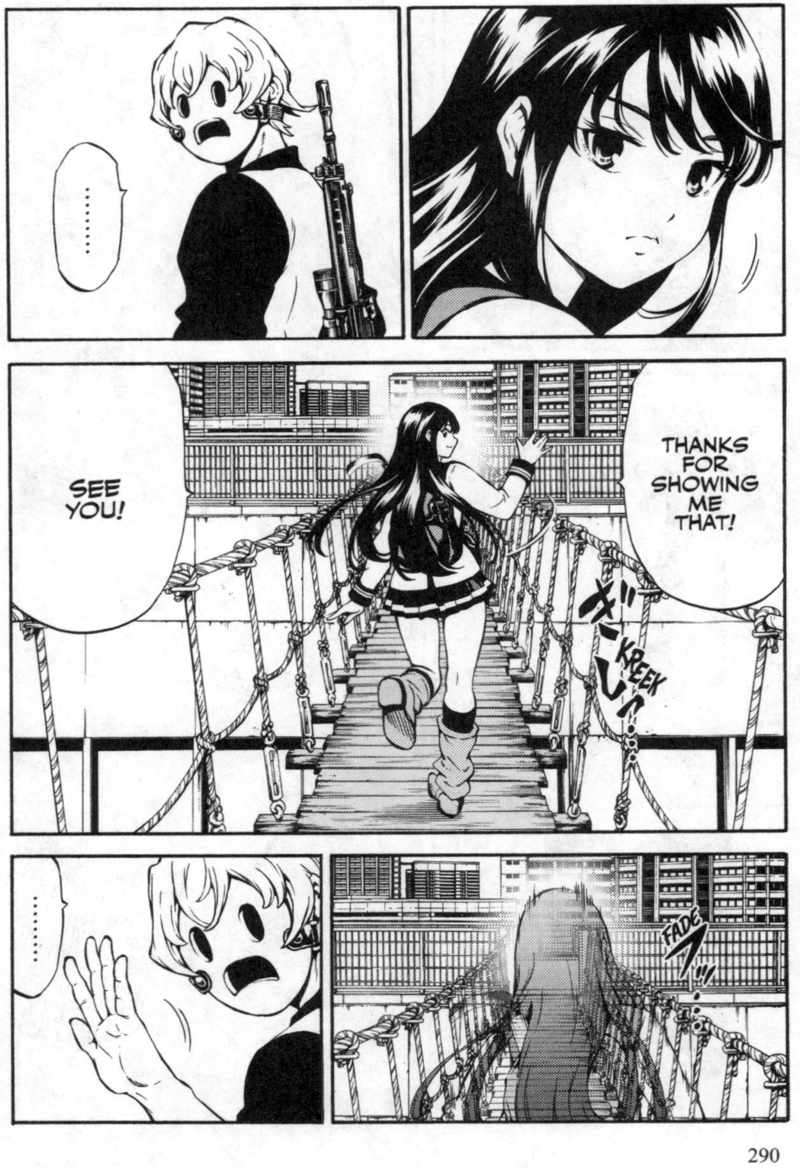
......
THANKS FOR SHOWING ME THAT!
SEE YOU!
KREEK
FADE
......

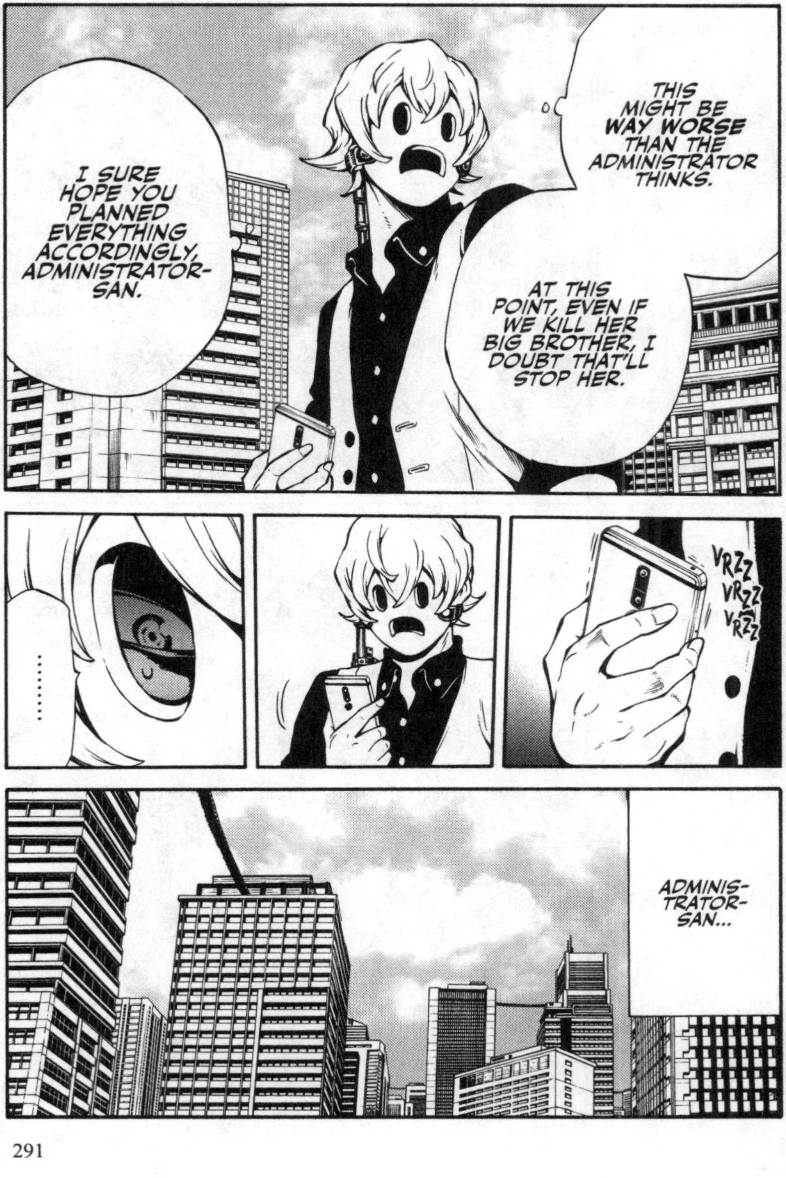
THIS MIGHT BE WAY WORSE THAN THE ADMINISTRATOR THINKS.
AT THIS POINT, EVEN IF WE KILL HER BIG BROTHER, I DOUBT THAT'LL STOP HER.
I SURE HOPE YOU PLANNED EVERYTHING ACCORDINGLY, ADMINISTRATOR-SAN.
VRZZ VRZZ VRZZ
....
ADMINISTRATOR-SAN...

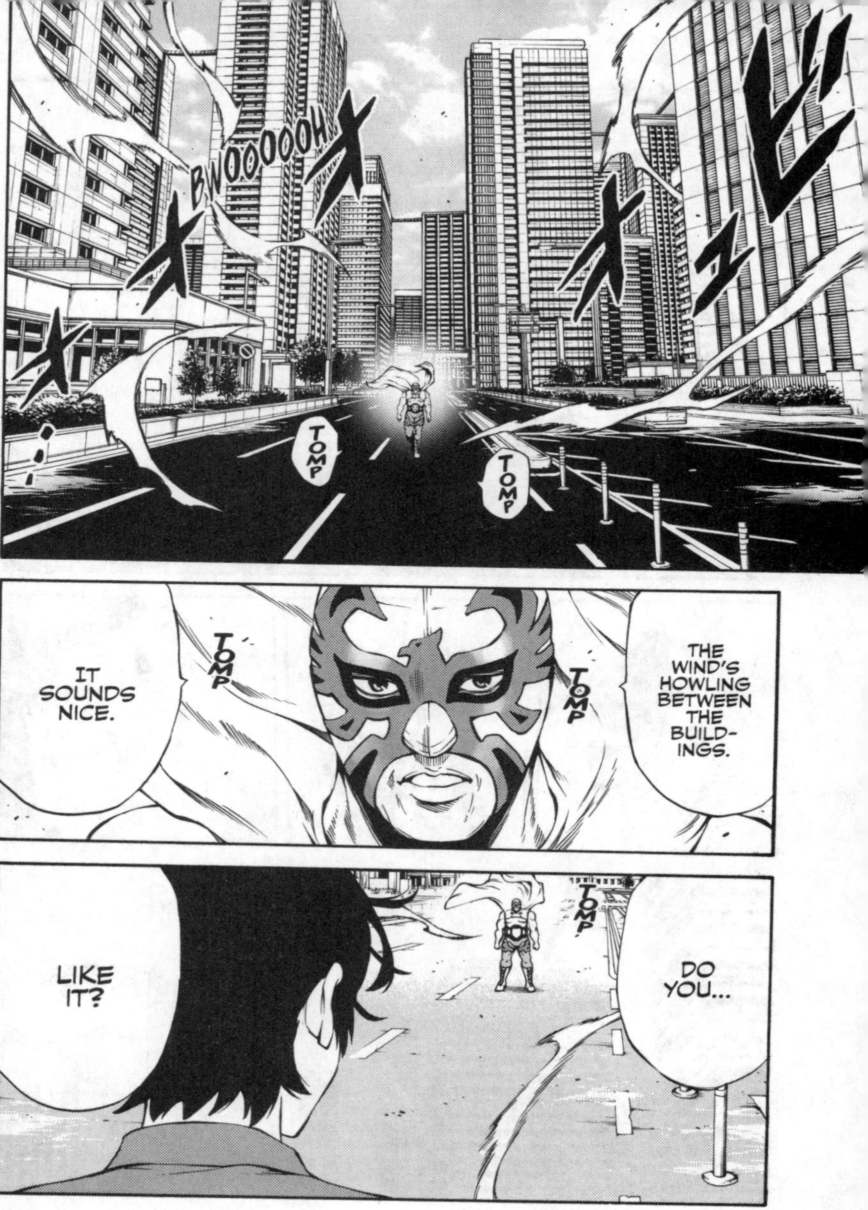
BWOOOOOH
TOMP
TOMP
THE WIND'S HOWLING BETWEEN THE BUILD-INGS.
TOMP
TOMP
IT SOUNDS NICE.
DO YOU...
TOMP
LIKE IT?

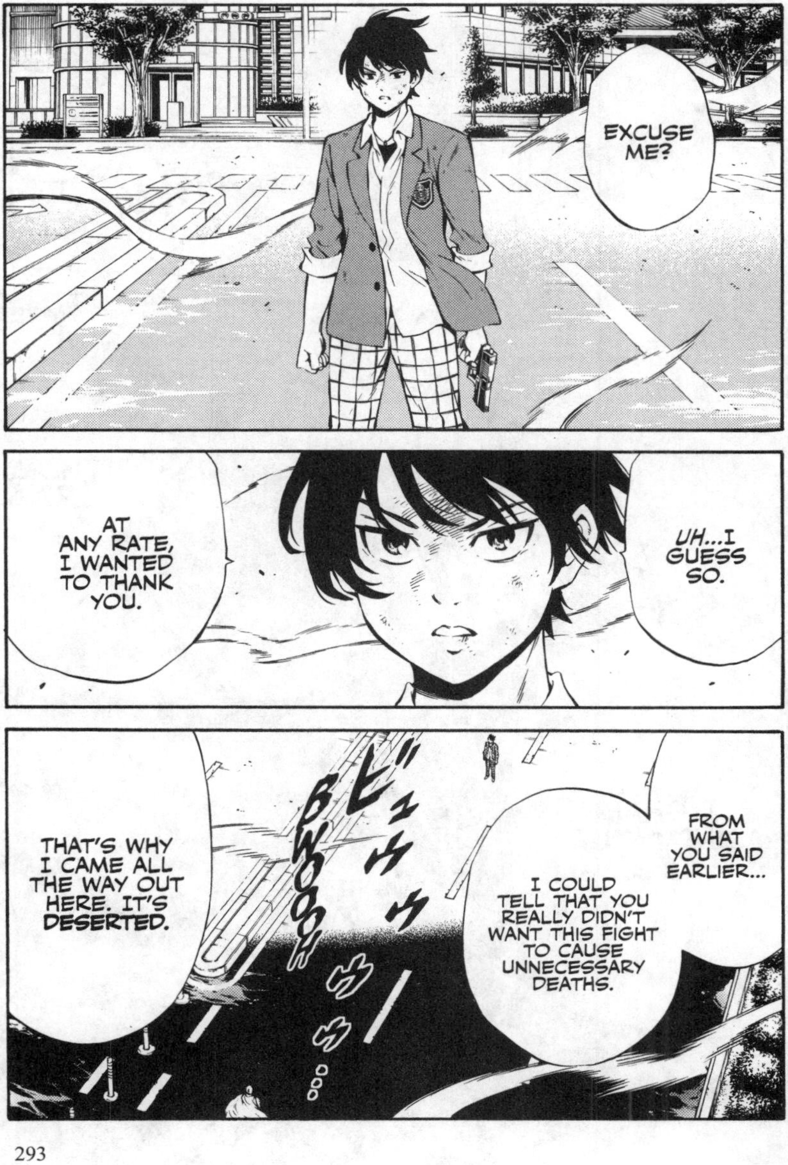
EXCUSE ME?
UH...I GUESS SO.
AT ANY RATE, I WANTED TO THANK YOU.
FROM WHAT YOU SAID EARLIER...
I COULD TELL THAT YOU REALLY DIDN'T WANT THIS FIGHT TO CAUSE UNNECESSARY DEATHS.
BWOOOOH
THAT'S WHY I CAME ALL THE WAY OUT HERE. IT'S DESERTED.

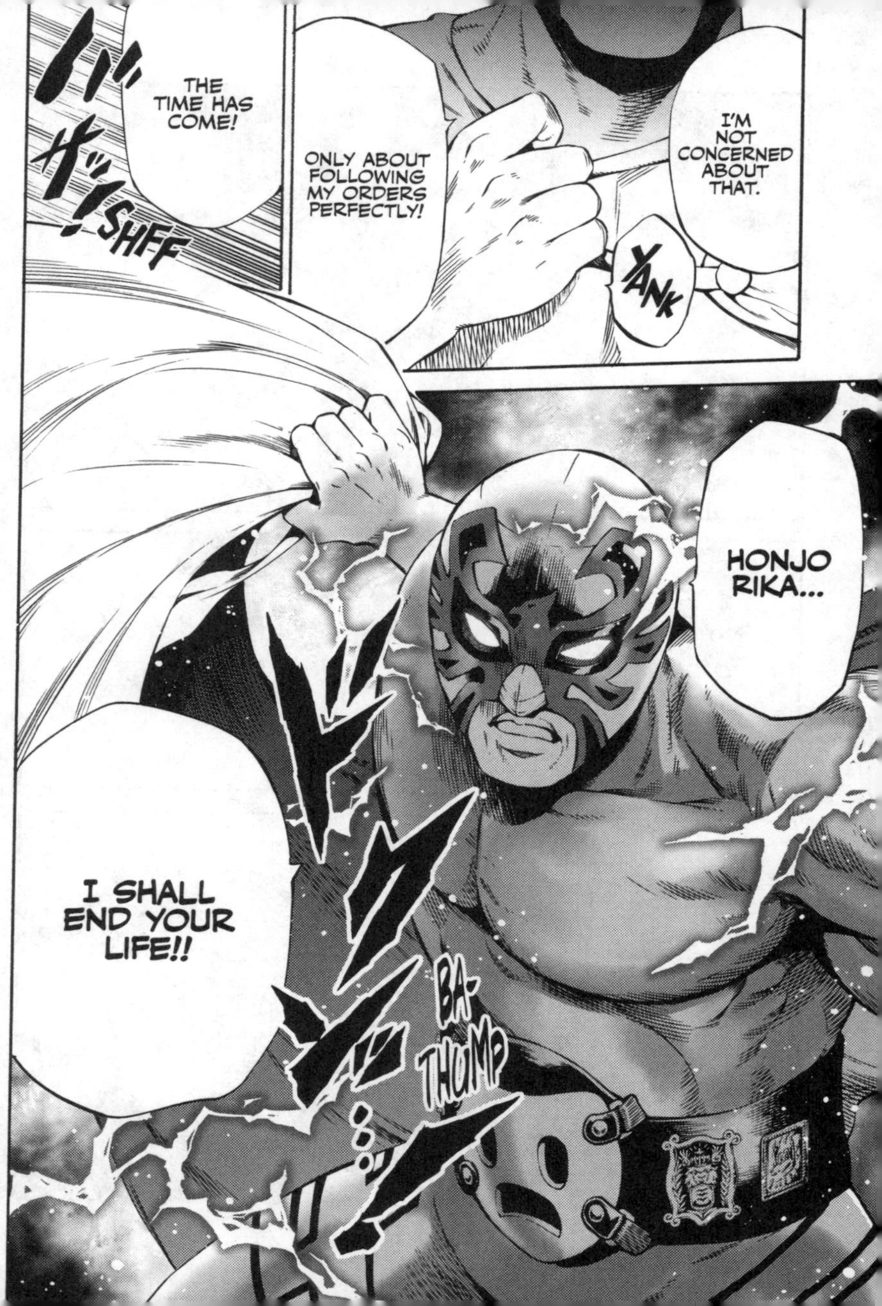
I'M NOT CONCERNED ABOUT THAT.
ONLY ABOUT FOLLOWING MY ORDERS PERFECTLY!
YANK
THE TIME HAS COME!
SHFF
HONJO RIKA...
I SHALL END YOUR LIFE!!
BA-THUMP

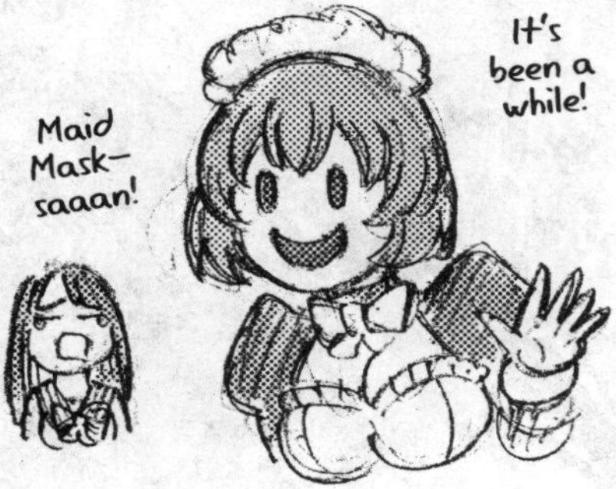
It's been a while!
Maid Mask-saaan!

HIGH-RISE
INVASION

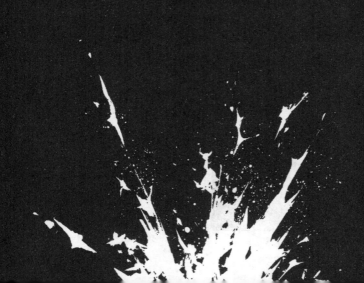

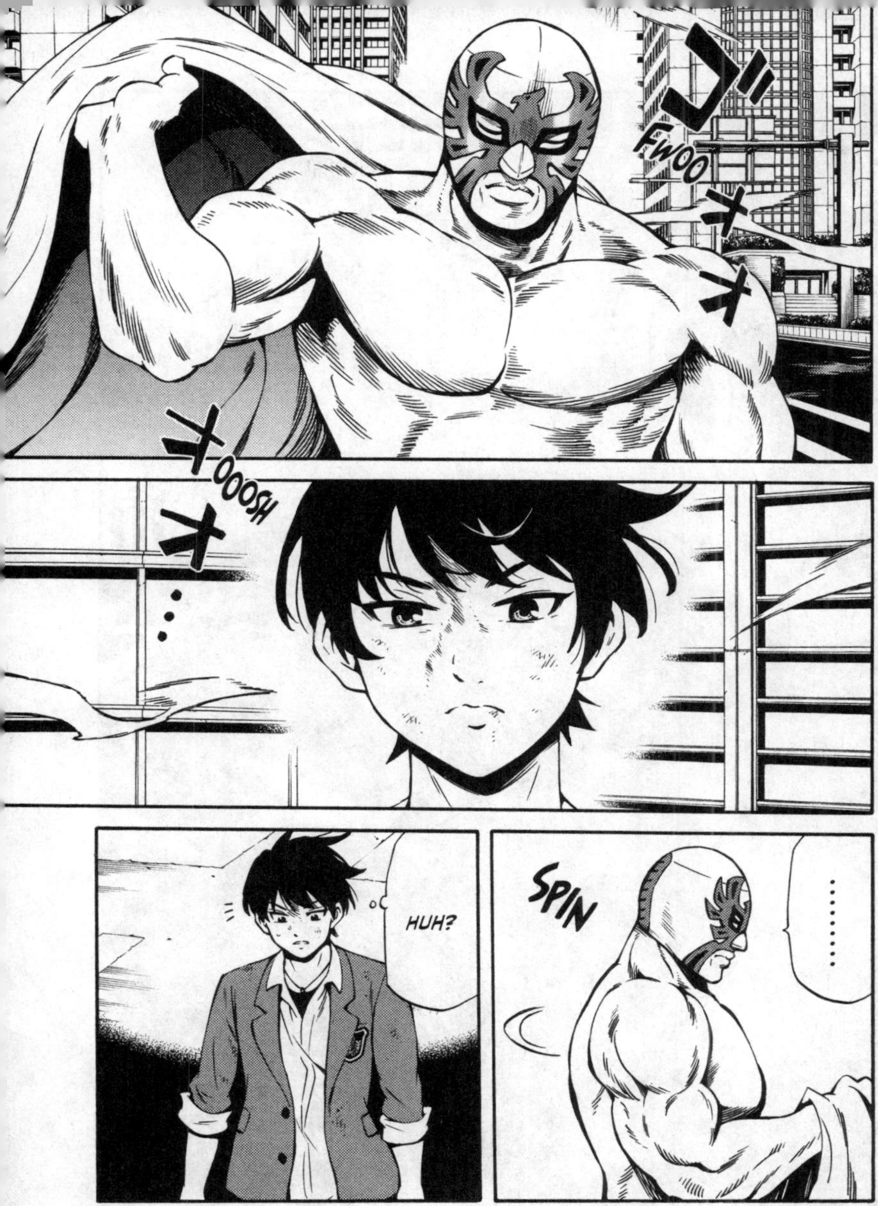
FWOO
WHOOSH
...
SPIN
......
HUH?

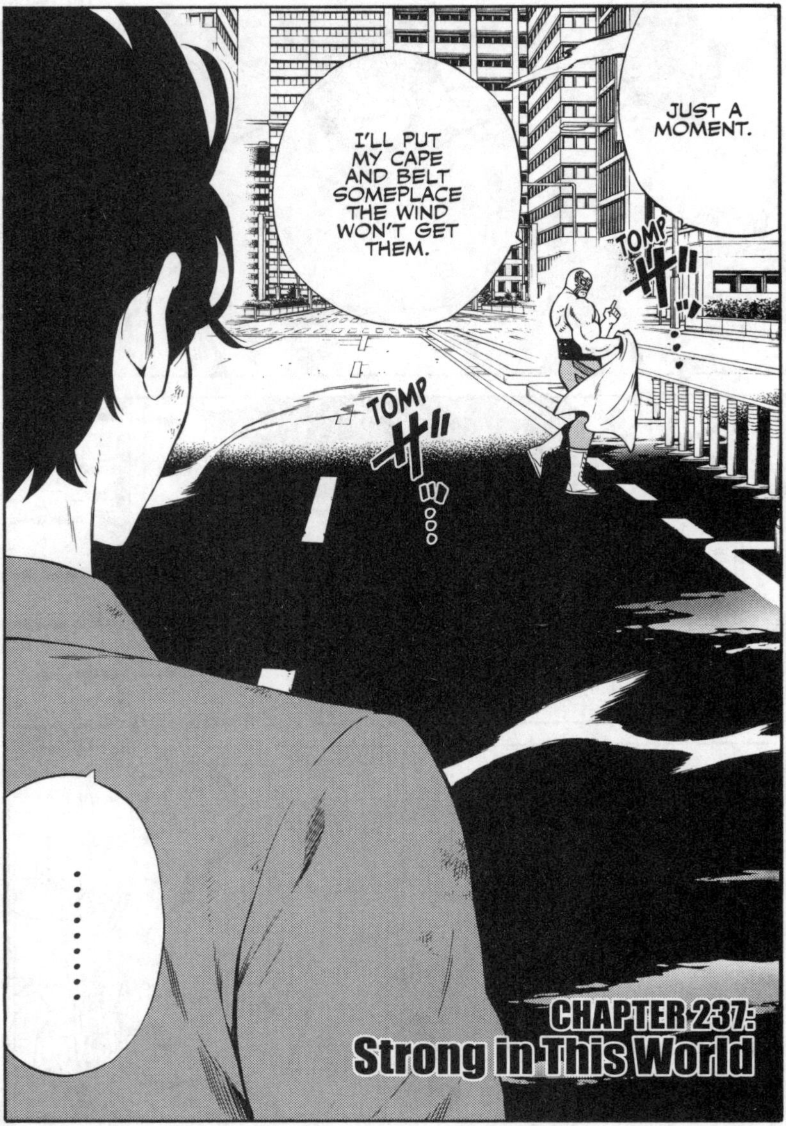
JUST A MOMENT.
I'LL PUT MY CAPE AND BELT SOMEPLACE THE WIND WON'T GET THEM.
TOMP
TOMP
……
CHAPTER 237: Strong in This World

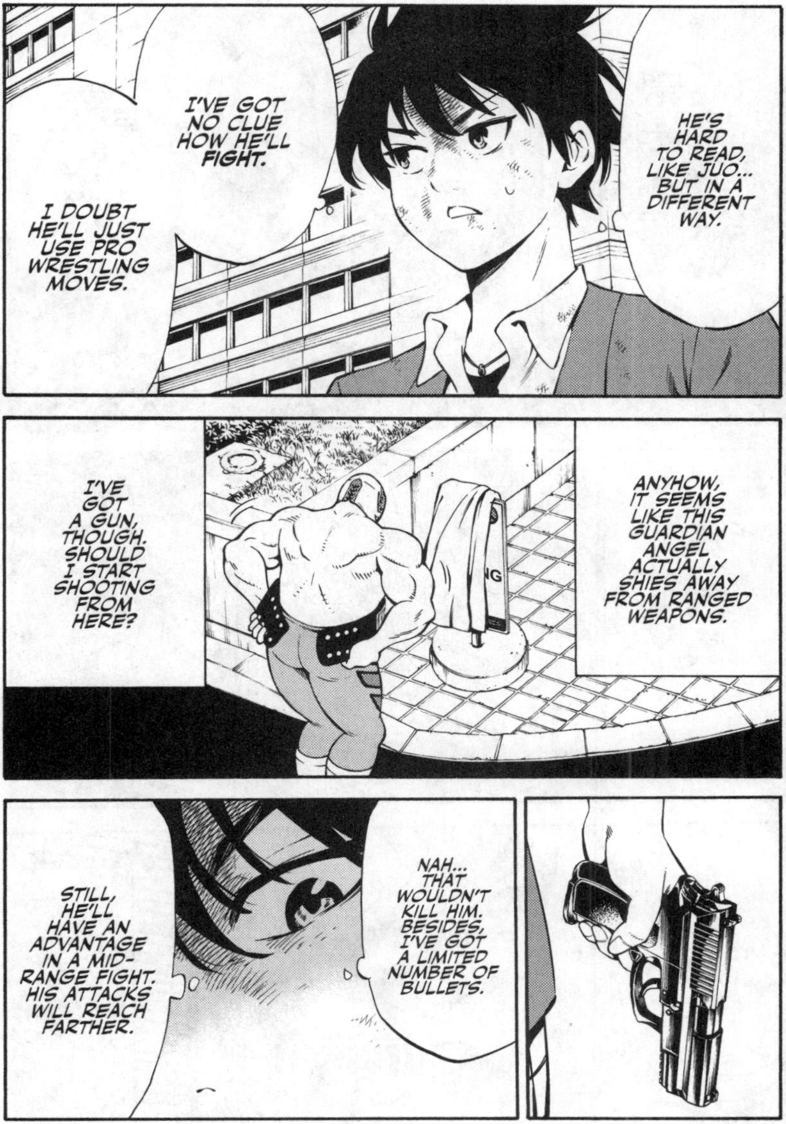
HE'S HARD TO READ, LIKE JUO... BUT IN A DIFFERENT WAY.
I'VE GOT NO CLUE HOW HE'LL FIGHT.
I DOUBT HE'LL JUST USE PRO WRESTLING MOVES.
ANYHOW, IT SEEMS LIKE THIS GUARDIAN ANGEL ACTUALLY SHIES AWAY FROM RANGED WEAPONS.
I'VE GOT A GUN, THOUGH. SHOULD I START SHOOTING FROM HERE?
NAH... THAT WOULDN'T KILL HIM. BESIDES, I'VE GOT A LIMITED NUMBER OF BULLETS.
STILL, HE'LL HAVE AN ADVANTAGE IN A MID-RANGE FIGHT. HIS ATTACKS WILL REACH FARTHER.

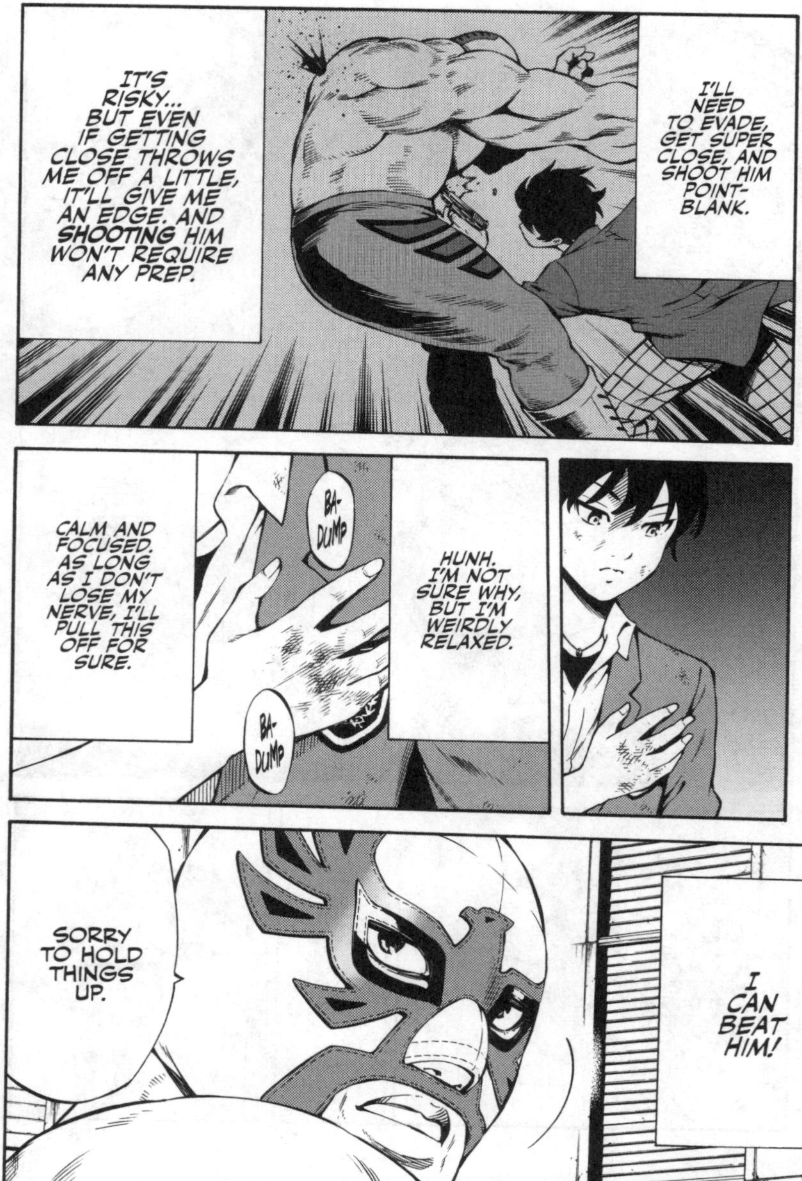
I'LL NEED TO EVADE, GET SUPER CLOSE, AND SHOOT HIM POINT-BLANK.
IT'S RISKY... BUT EVEN IF GETTING CLOSE THROWS ME OFF A LITTLE, IT'LL GIVE ME AN EDGE. AND **SHOOTING** HIM WON'T REQUIRE ANY PREP.
HUNH. I'M NOT SURE WHY, BUT I'M WEIRDLY RELAXED.
BA-DUMP
CALM AND FOCUSED. AS LONG AS I DON'T LOSE MY NERVE, I'LL PULL THIS OFF FOR SURE.
BA-DUMP
I CAN BEAT HIM!
SORRY TO HOLD THINGS UP.

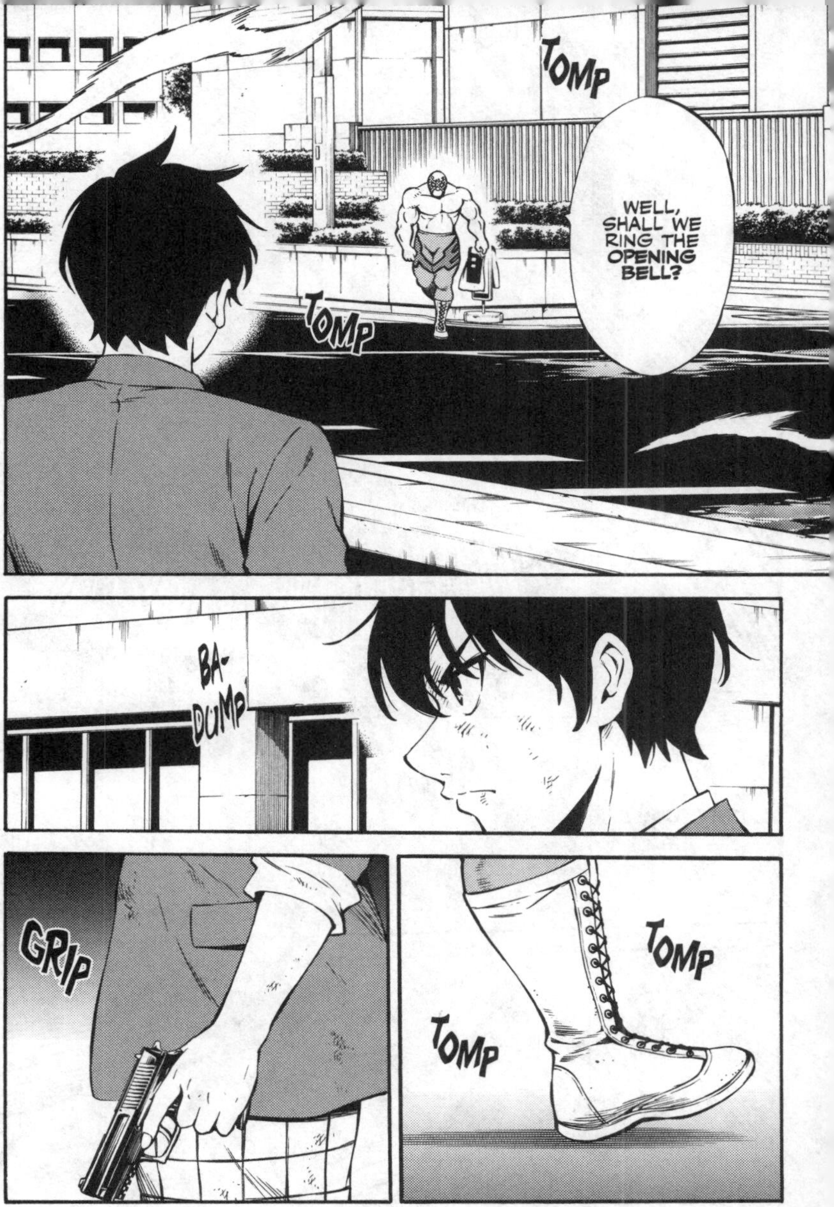
TOMP
WELL, SHALL WE RING THE OPENING BELL?
TOMP
BA-DUMP
TOMP
TOMP
GRIP

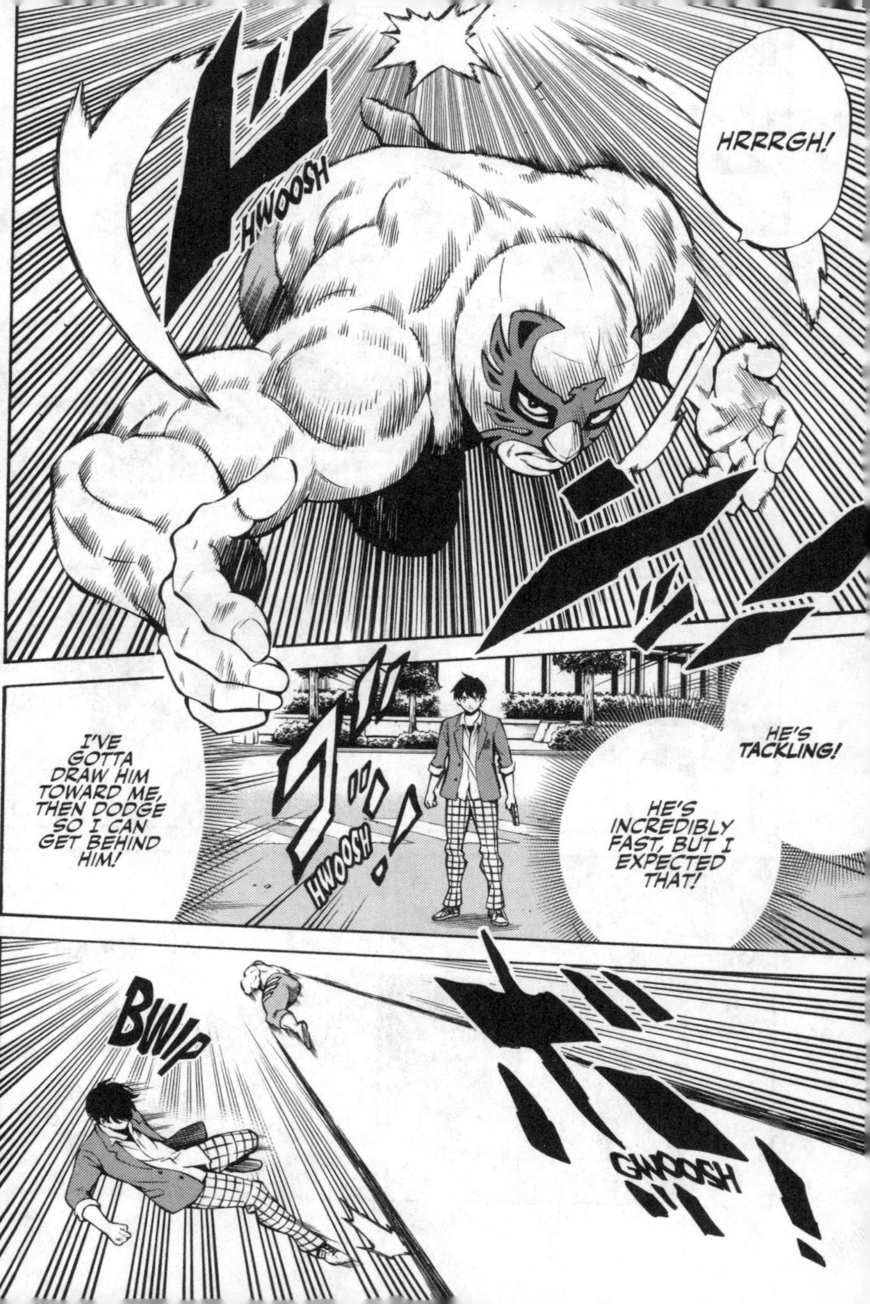
HRRRGH!
HWOOSH
HE'S TACKLING!
HE'S INCREDIBLY FAST, BUT I EXPECTED THAT!
I'VE GOTTA DRAW HIM TOWARD ME, THEN DODGE SO I CAN GET BEHIND HIM!
HWOOSH
GWOOSH
BWIP

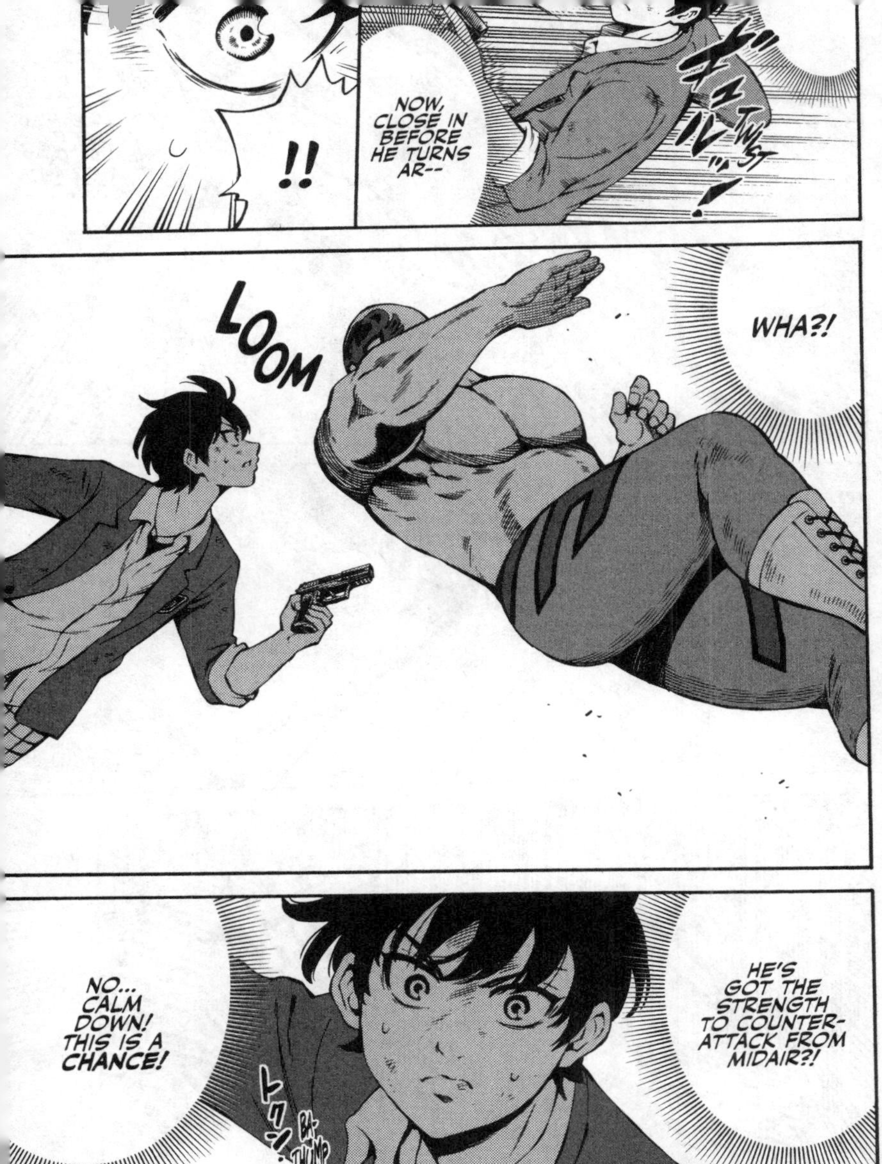

TWIST
NOW, CLOSE IN BEFORE HE TURNS AR--
!!
WHA?!
LOOM
HE'S GOT THE STRENGTH TO COUNTER-ATTACK FROM MIDAIR?!
BA-THUMP
NO... CALM DOWN! THIS IS A CHANCE!

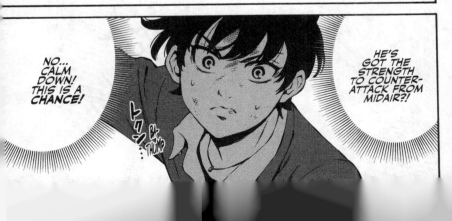

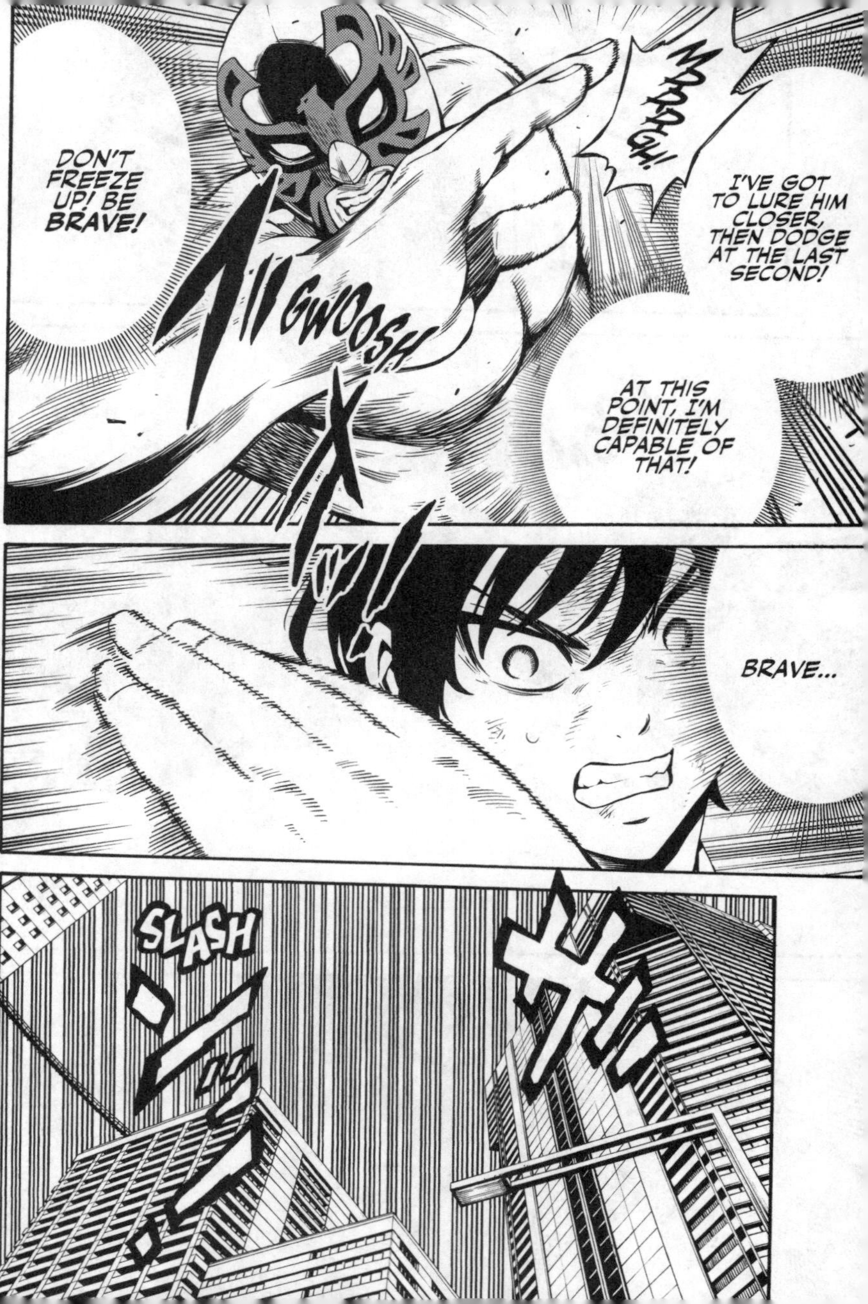
MRAAGH!
I'VE GOT TO LURE HIM CLOSER, THEN DODGE AT THE LAST SECOND!
DON'T FREEZE UP! BE BRAVE!
GWOOSH
AT THIS POINT, I'M DEFINITELY CAPABLE OF THAT!
BRAVE...
SLASH

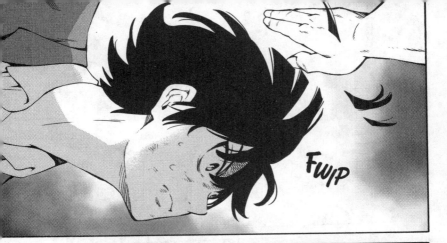

FWIP

I...

AND THIS'LL HIT HIM!

KLIK

I DODGED!

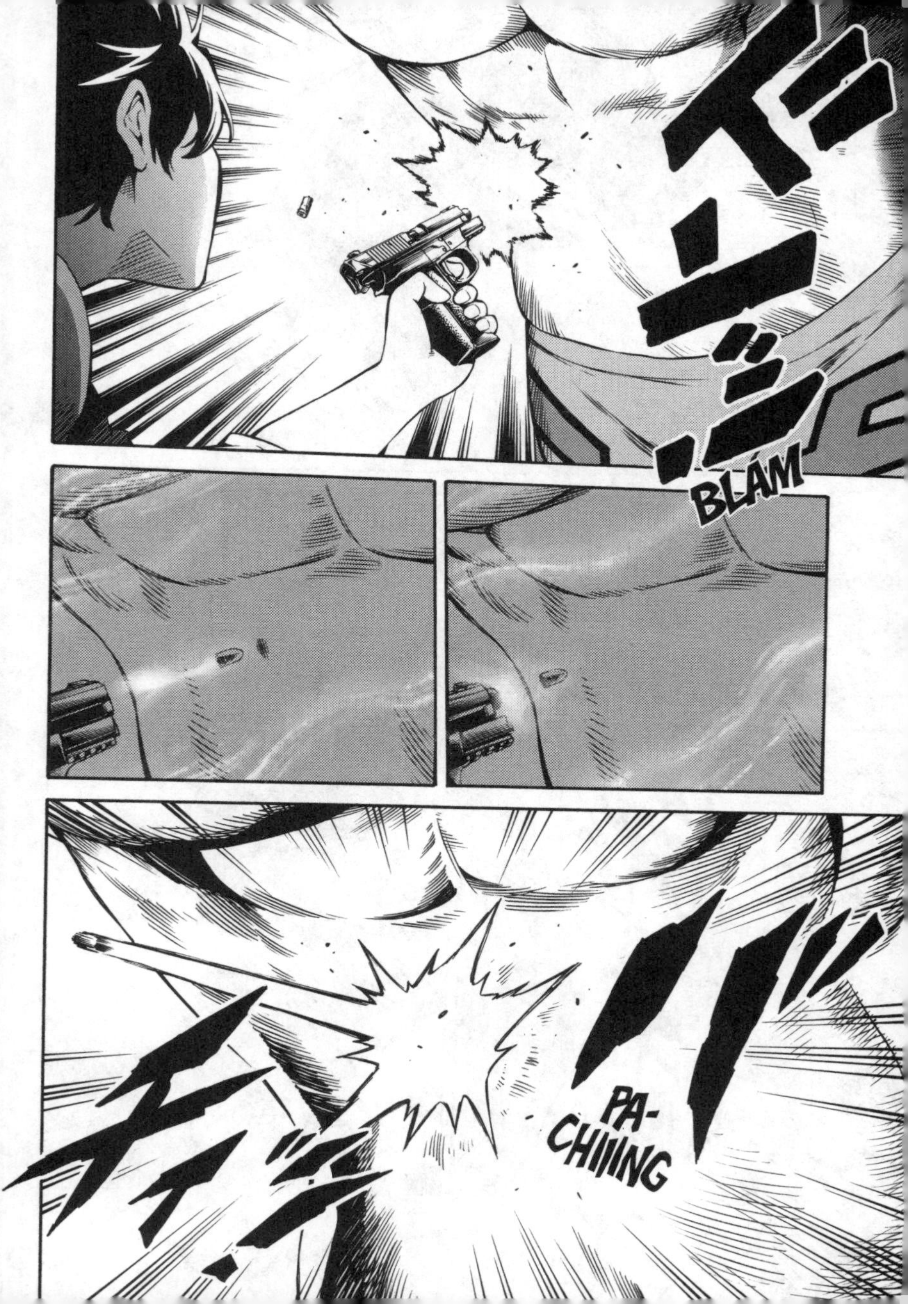
BLAM
PA-
CHIIING

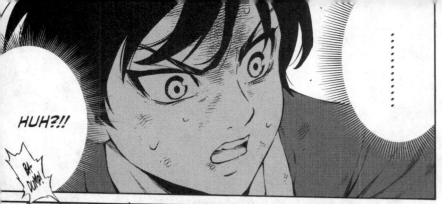

......
HUH?!!
BA-DUMP!
WHA? WHAT JUST HAPPENED?!
BA-DUMP!
BA-DUMP!
THE BULLET GLANCED OFF HIS ABS?! WHAT THE...?!
BA-DUMP!
NOW FOR THE FINISHING MOVE.
LUNGE
GAH!
GWOOSH

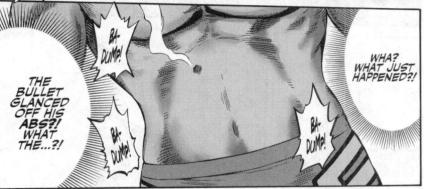

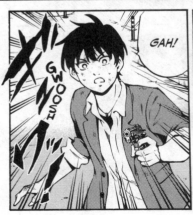

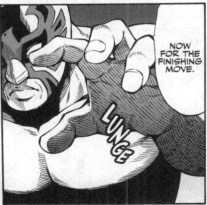

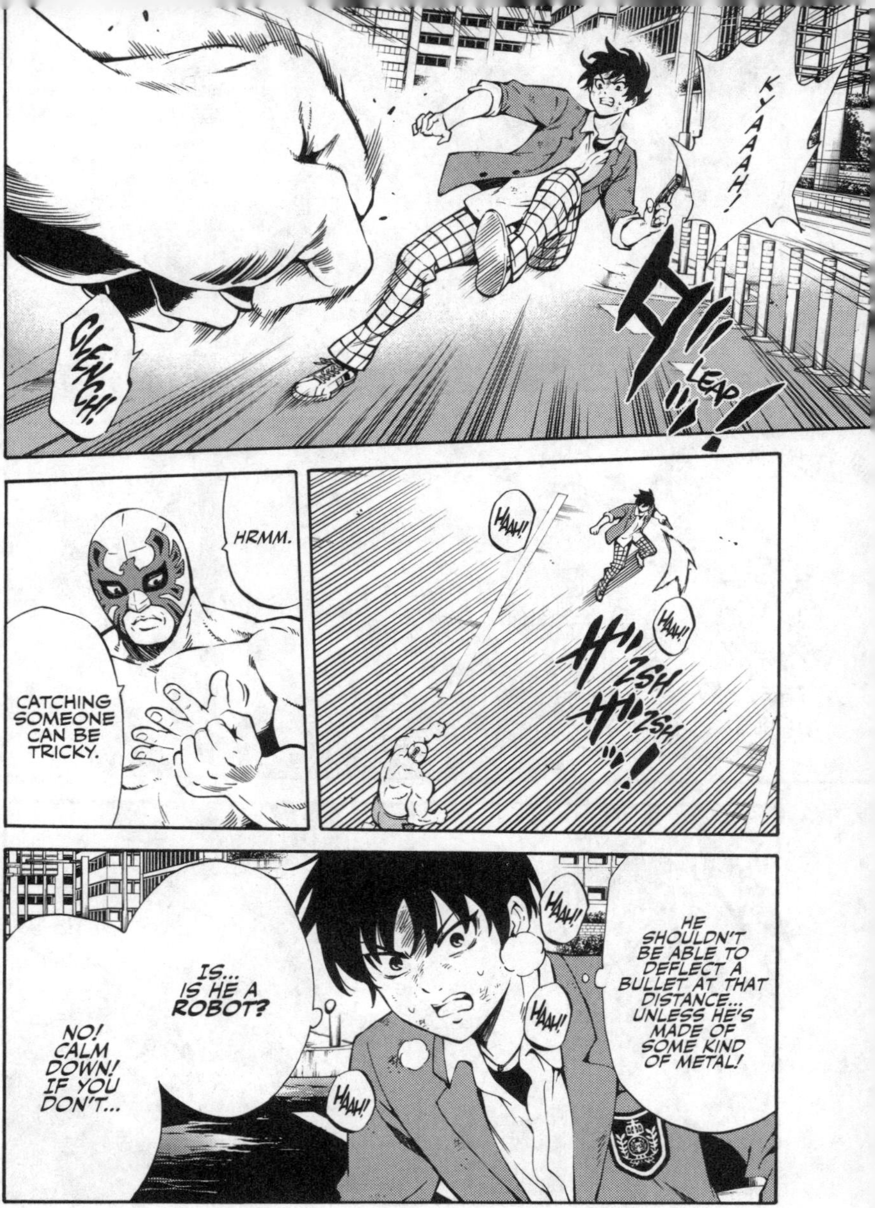
KYAAAAH!
LEAP!!
CLENCH!
HAAH!
HAAH!
ZSH ZSH!!
HRMM.
CATCHING SOMEONE CAN BE TRICKY.
HE SHOULDN'T BE ABLE TO DEFLECT A BULLET AT THAT DISTANCE... UNLESS HE'S MADE OF SOME KIND OF METAL!
HAAH!
HAAH!
HAAH!
IS... IS HE A ROBOT?
NO! CALM DOWN! IF YOU DON'T...

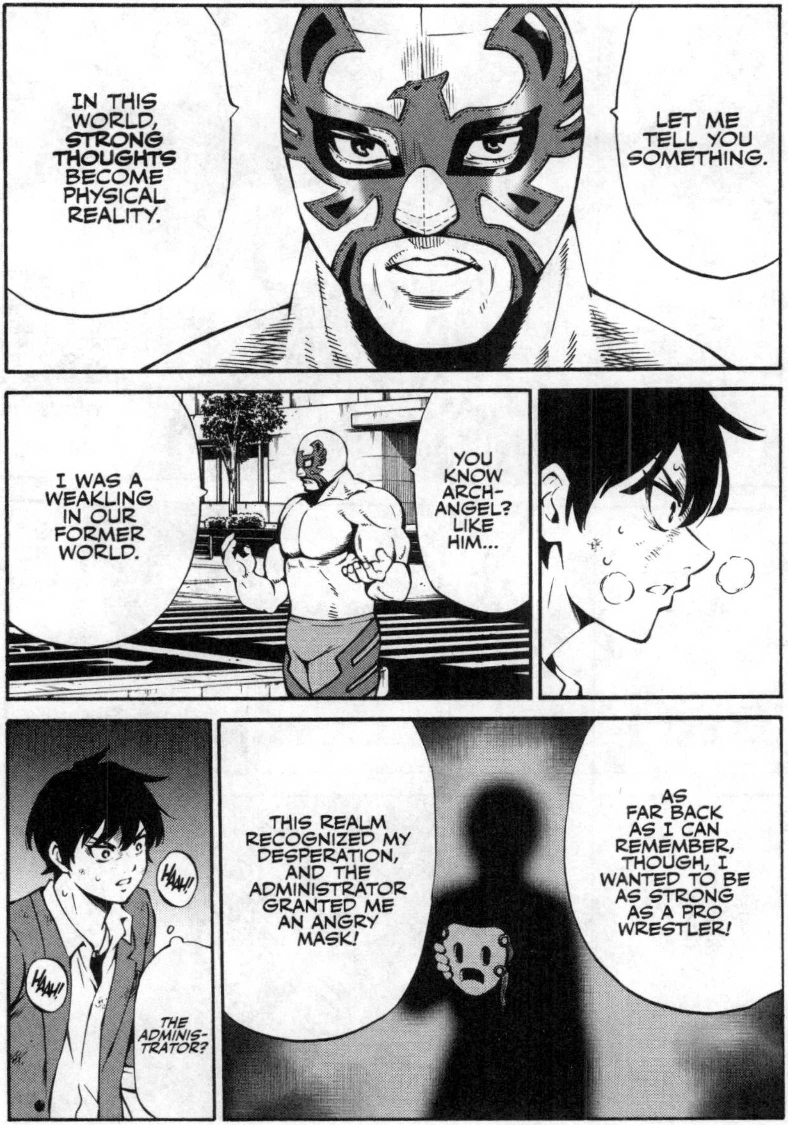
LET ME TELL YOU SOMETHING.
IN THIS WORLD, STRONG THOUGHTS BECOME PHYSICAL REALITY.
YOU KNOW ARCH-ANGEL? LIKE HIM...
I WAS A WEAKLING IN OUR FORMER WORLD.
AS FAR BACK AS I CAN REMEMBER, THOUGH, I WANTED TO BE AS STRONG AS A PRO WRESTLER!
THIS REALM RECOGNIZED MY DESPERATION, AND THE ADMINISTRATOR GRANTED ME AN ANGRY MASK!
HAAH!
HAAH!
THE ADMINIS-TRATOR?

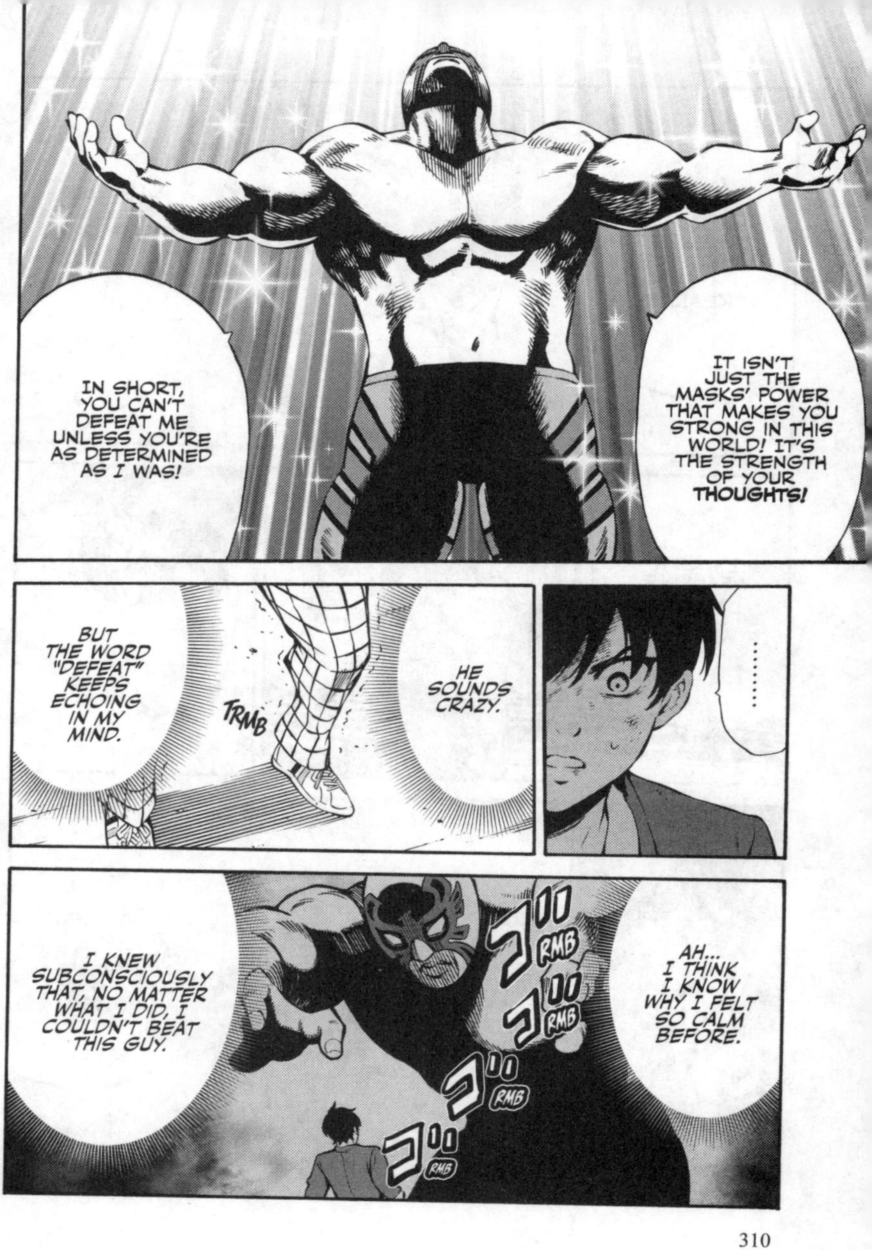
IT ISN'T JUST THE MASKS' POWER THAT MAKES YOU STRONG IN THIS WORLD! IT'S THE STRENGTH OF YOUR **THOUGHTS!**
IN SHORT, YOU CAN'T DEFEAT ME UNLESS YOU'RE AS DETERMINED AS I WAS!
......
HE SOUNDS CRAZY.
TRMB
BUT THE WORD "DEFEAT" KEEPS ECHOING IN MY MIND.
AH... I THINK I KNOW WHY I FELT SO CALM BEFORE.
RMB
RMB
RMB
RMB
I KNEW SUBCONSCIOUSLY THAT, NO MATTER WHAT I DID, I COULDN'T BEAT THIS GUY.

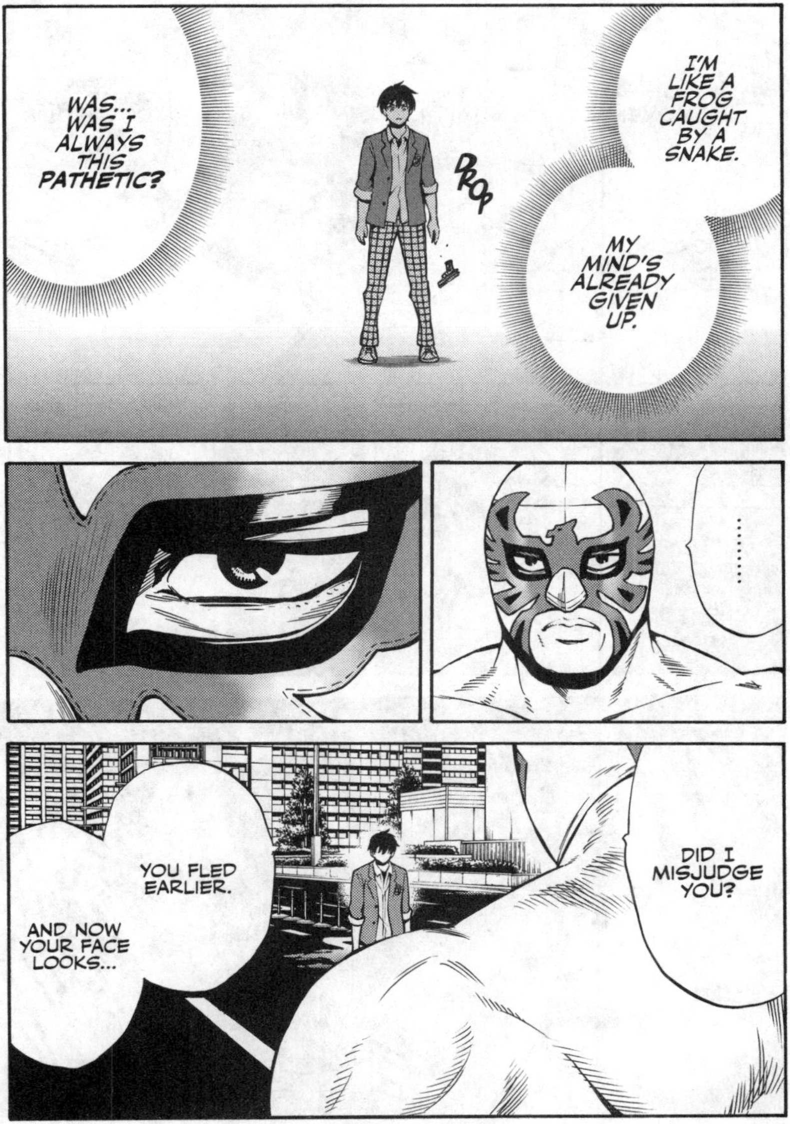
I'M LIKE A FROG CAUGHT BY A SNAKE.
MY MIND'S ALREADY GIVEN UP.
DROP
WAS... WAS I ALWAYS THIS PATHETIC?
......
DID I MISJUDGE YOU?
YOU FLED EARLIER.
AND NOW YOUR FACE LOOKS...

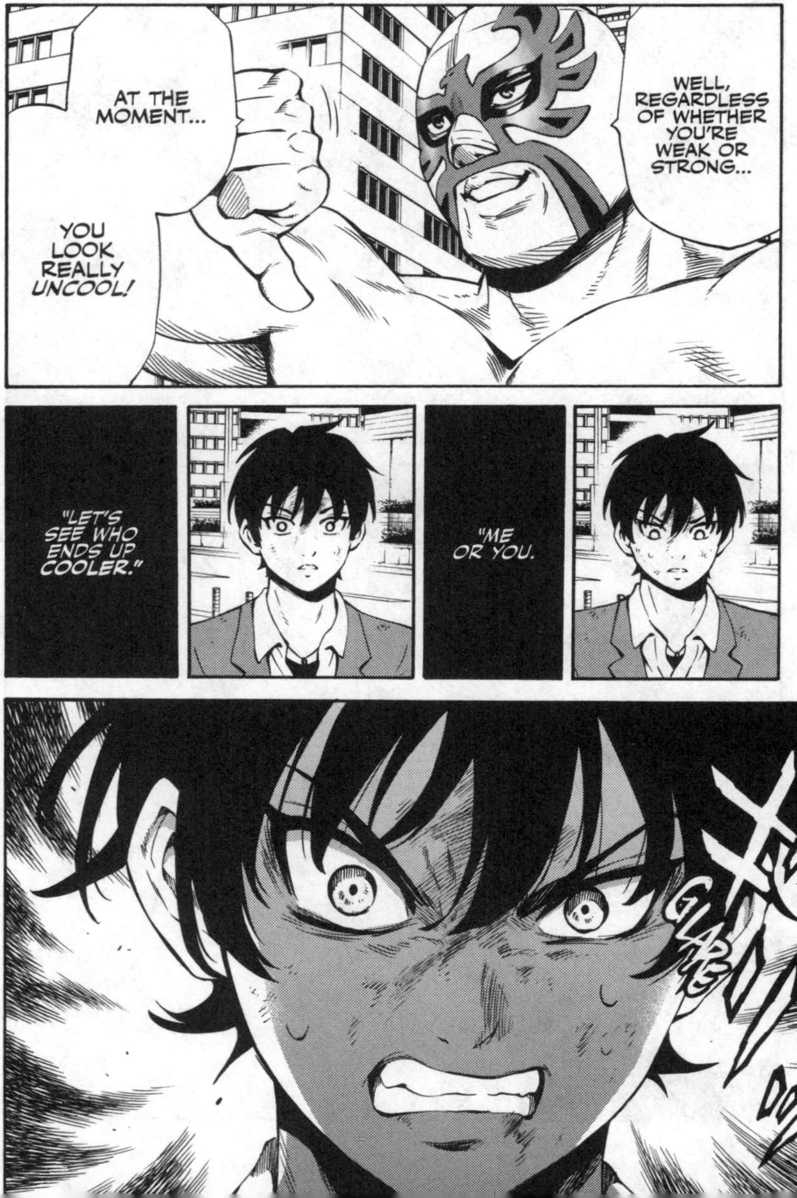
WELL, REGARDLESS OF WHETHER YOU'RE WEAK OR STRONG...
AT THE MOMENT...
YOU LOOK REALLY *UNCOOL!*
"ME OR YOU.
"LET'S SEE WHO ENDS UP COOLER."
GLARE

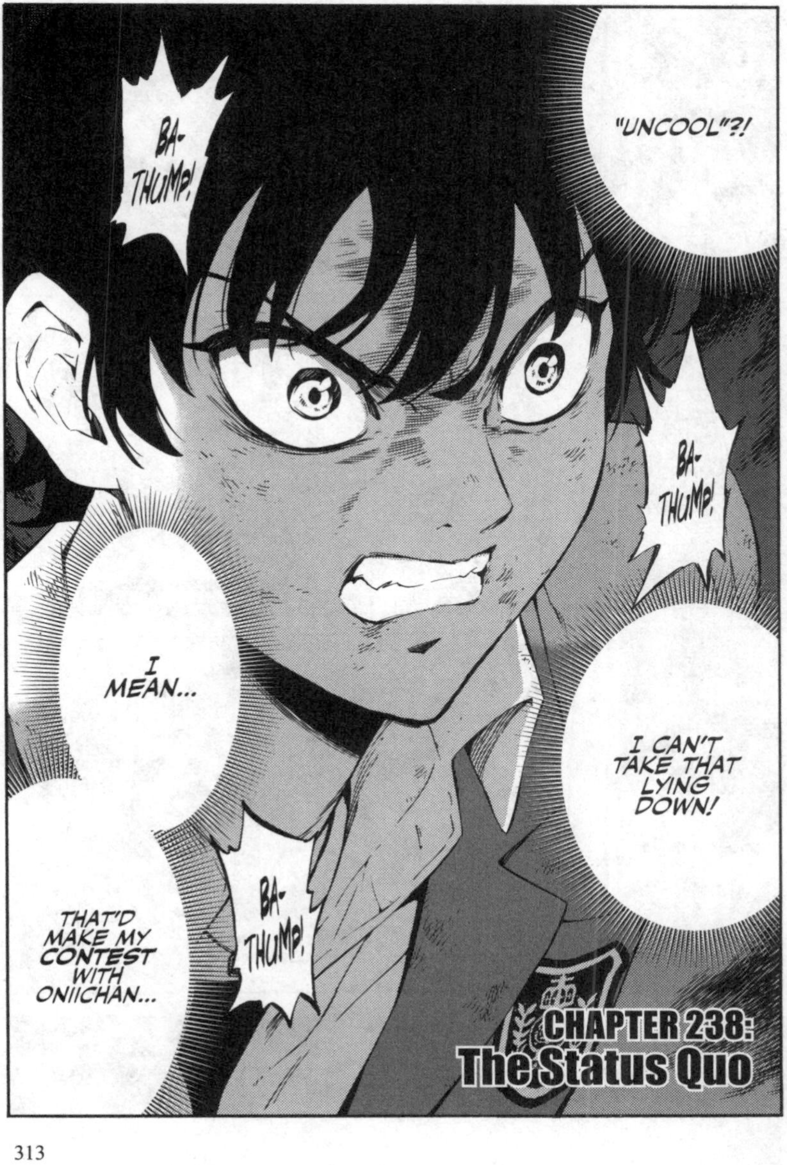
"UNCOOL"?!
BA-THUMP!
BA-THUMP!
I CAN'T TAKE THAT LYING DOWN!
I MEAN...
BA-THUMP!
THAT'D MAKE MY CONTEST WITH ONIICHAN...
CHAPTER 238: The Status Quo

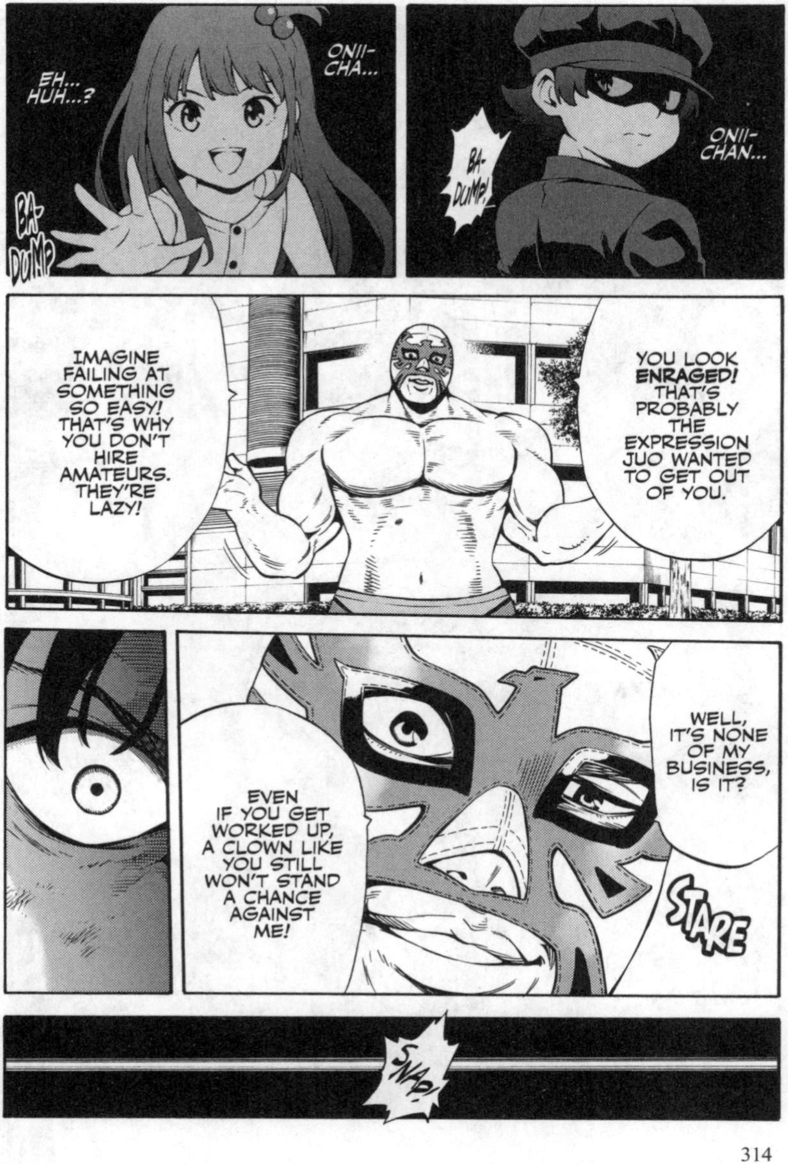
ONII-CHAN...
BA-DUMP!
ONII-CHA...
EH... HUH...?
BA-DUMP
YOU LOOK ENRAGED! THAT'S PROBABLY THE EXPRESSION JUO WANTED TO GET OUT OF YOU.
IMAGINE FAILING AT SOMETHING SO EASY! THAT'S WHY YOU DON'T HIRE AMATEURS. THEY'RE LAZY!
WELL, IT'S NONE OF MY BUSINESS, IS IT?
EVEN IF YOU GET WORKED UP, A CLOWN LIKE YOU STILL WON'T STAND A CHANCE AGAINST ME!
STARE
SNAP!

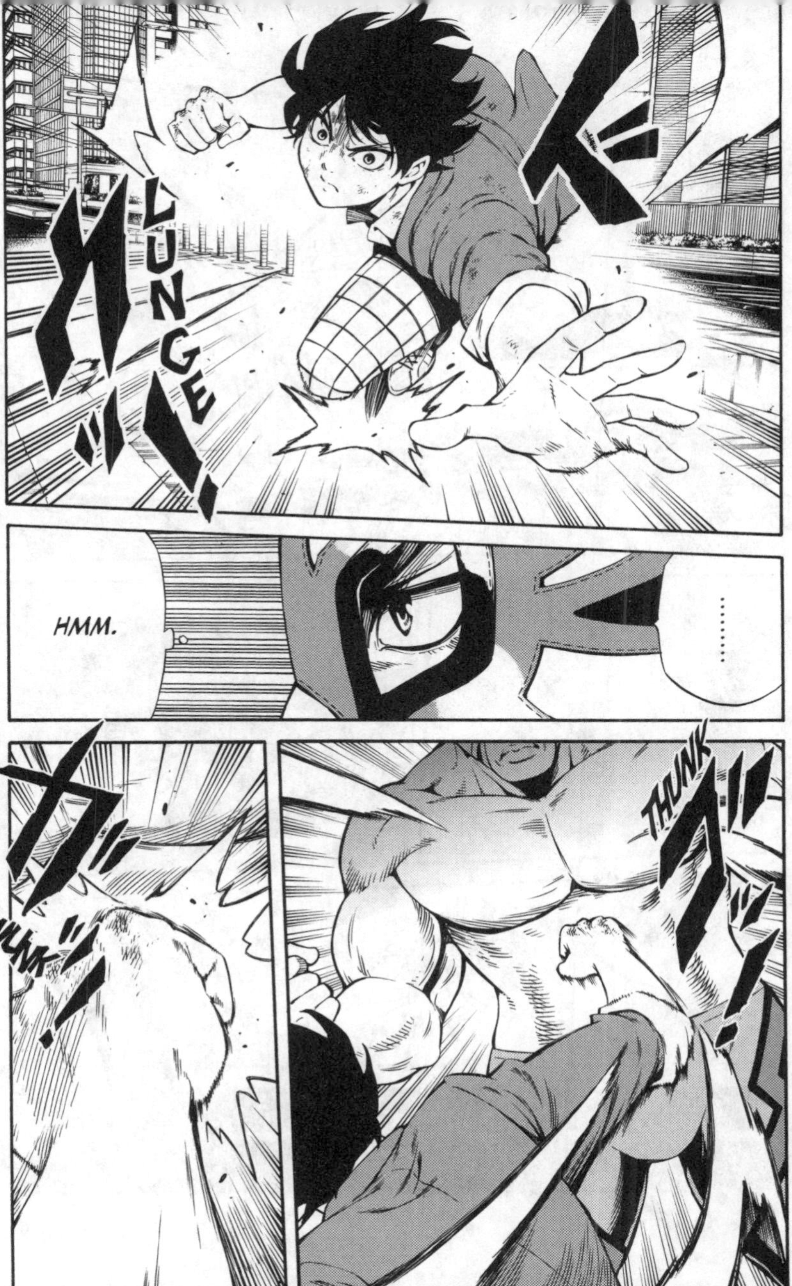
LUNGE
....
HMM.
THUNK
HWUNK

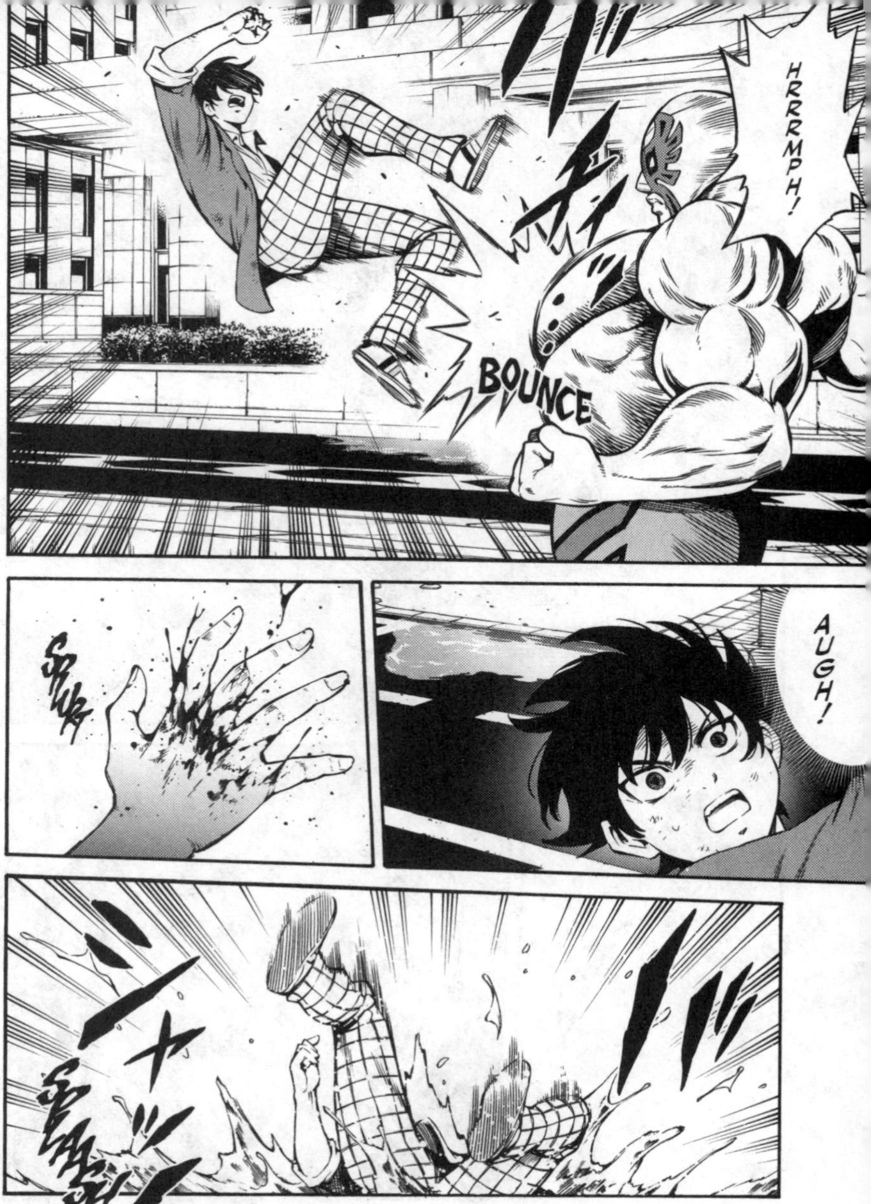
HRRRMPH!
BOUNCE
AUGH!
SPLASH!

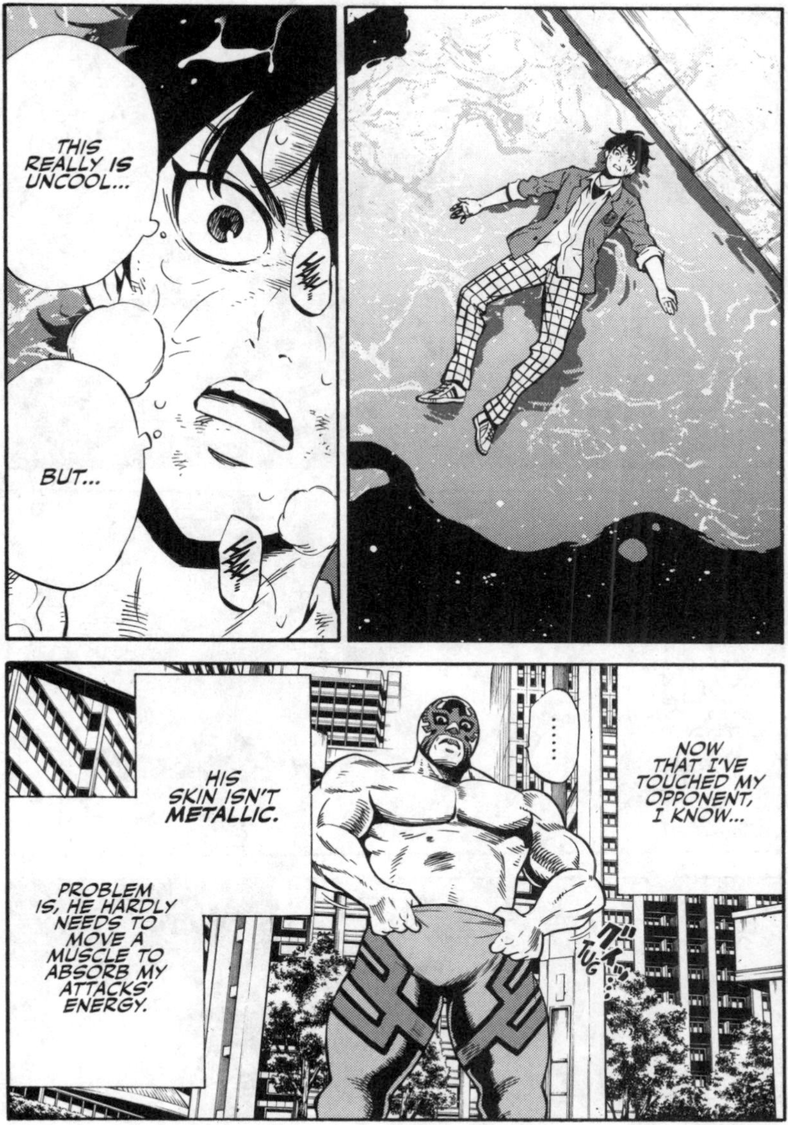
THIS REALLY IS UNCOOL...
BUT...
NOW THAT I'VE TOUCHED MY OPPONENT, I KNOW...
......
HIS SKIN ISN'T METALLIC.
PROBLEM IS, HE HARDLY NEEDS TO MOVE A MUSCLE TO ABSORB MY ATTACKS' ENERGY.
グイッ
TUG

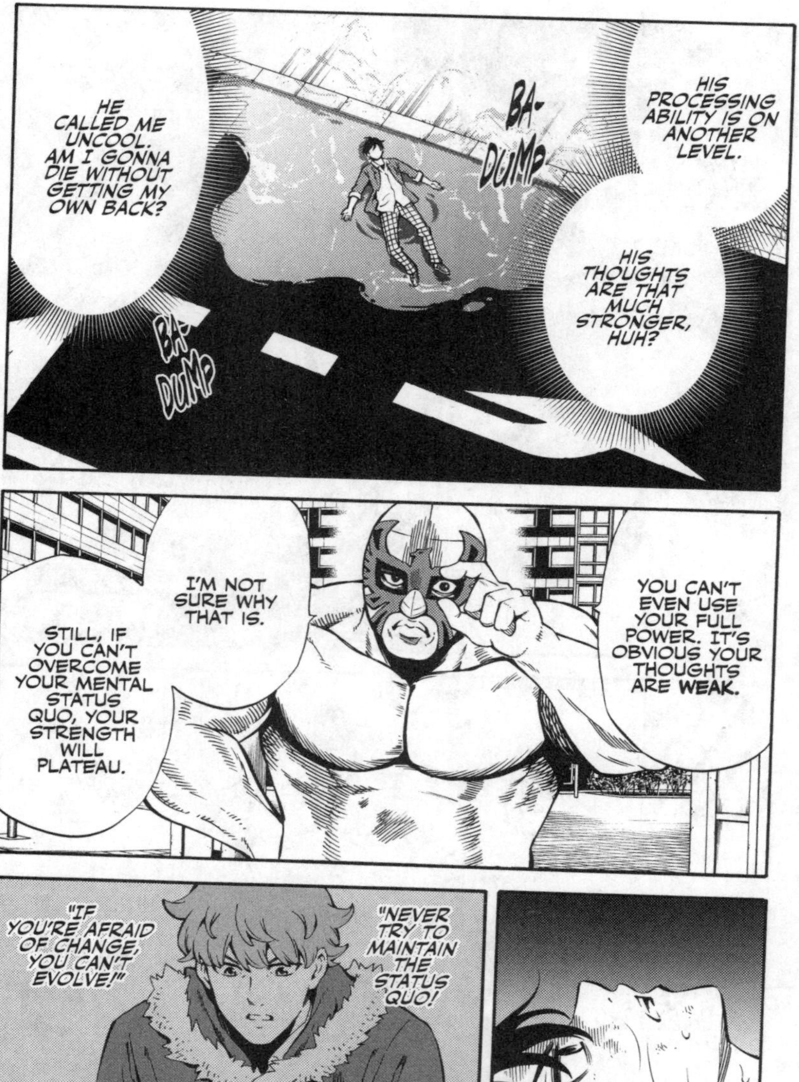
HIS PROCESSING ABILITY IS ON ANOTHER LEVEL.
BA-DUMP
HIS THOUGHTS ARE THAT MUCH STRONGER, HUH?
HE CALLED ME UNCOOL. AM I GONNA DIE WITHOUT GETTING MY OWN BACK?
BA-DUMP
YOU CAN'T EVEN USE YOUR FULL POWER. IT'S OBVIOUS YOUR THOUGHTS ARE **WEAK.**
I'M NOT SURE WHY THAT IS.
STILL, IF YOU CAN'T OVERCOME YOUR MENTAL STATUS QUO, YOUR STRENGTH WILL PLATEAU.
"NEVER TRY TO MAINTAIN THE STATUS QUO!
"IF YOU'RE AFRAID OF CHANGE, YOU CAN'T EVOLVE!"

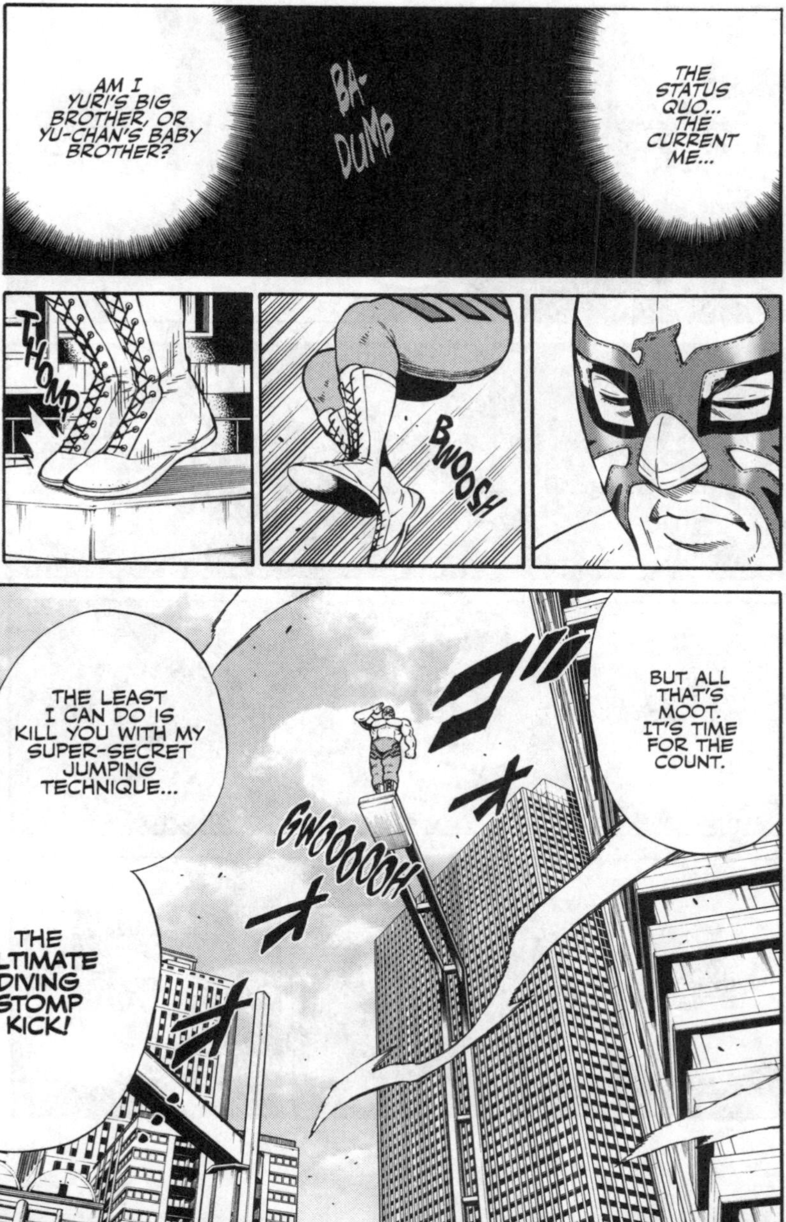
THE STATUS QUO... THE CURRENT ME...
BA-DUMP
AM I YURI'S BIG BROTHER, OR YU-CHAN'S BABY BROTHER?
BWOOSH
THOMP
BUT ALL THAT'S MOOT. IT'S TIME FOR THE COUNT.
GWOOOOOOH
THE LEAST I CAN DO IS KILL YOU WITH MY SUPER-SECRET JUMPING TECHNIQUE...
THE ULTIMATE DIVING STOMP KICK!

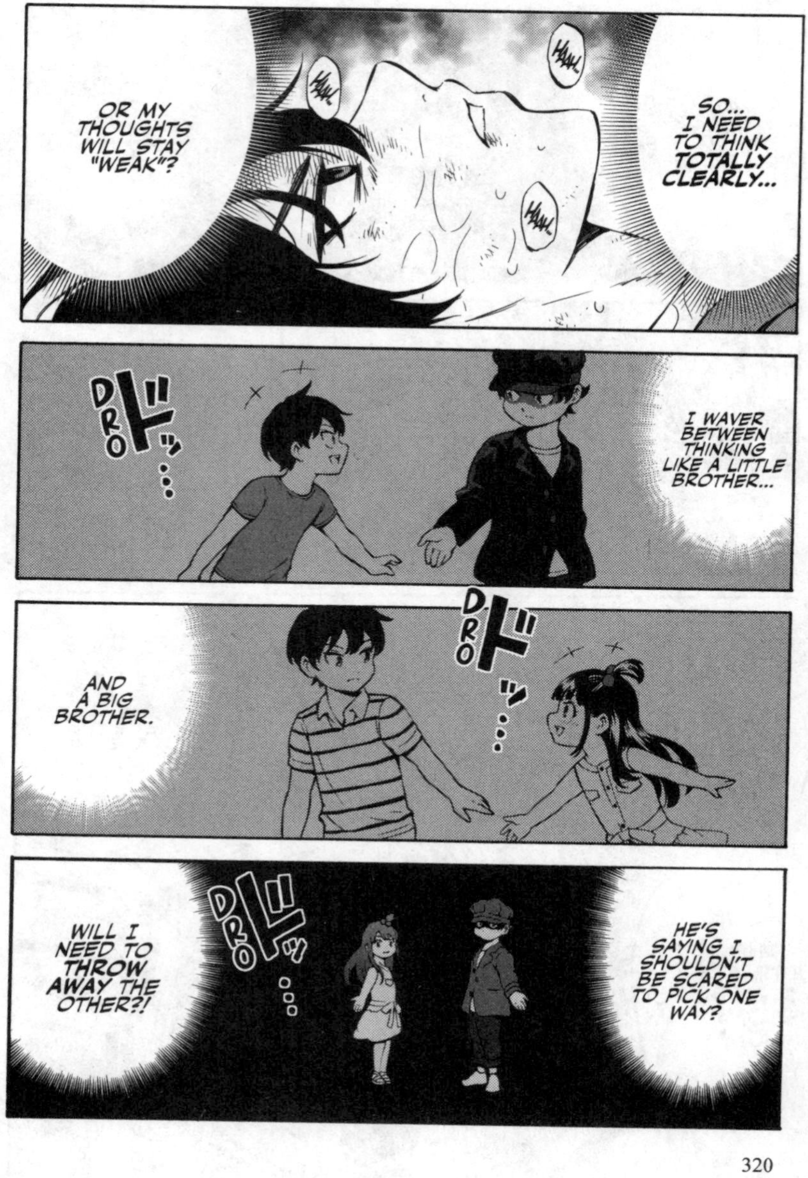
HAAH
HAAH
HAAH
SO... I NEED TO THINK TOTALLY CLEARLY...
OR MY THOUGHTS WILL STAY "WEAK"?
I WAVER BETWEEN THINKING LIKE A LITTLE BROTHER...
DRO ドッ...
DRO ドッ...
AND A BIG BROTHER.
HE'S SAYING I SHOULDN'T BE SCARED TO PICK ONE WAY?
DRO ドッ...
WILL I NEED TO THROW AWAY THE OTHER?!

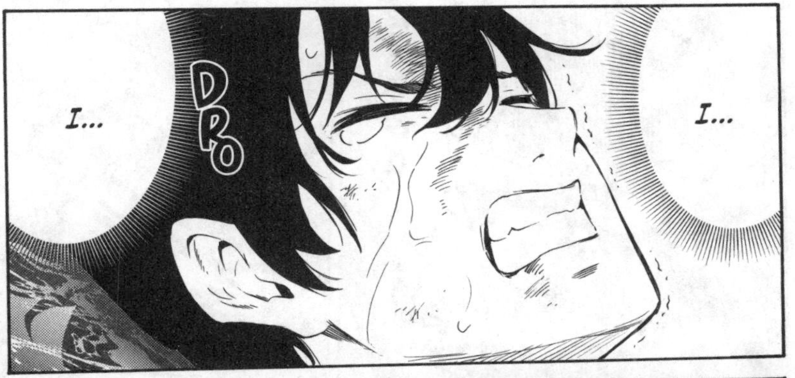
I...
DRO
I...

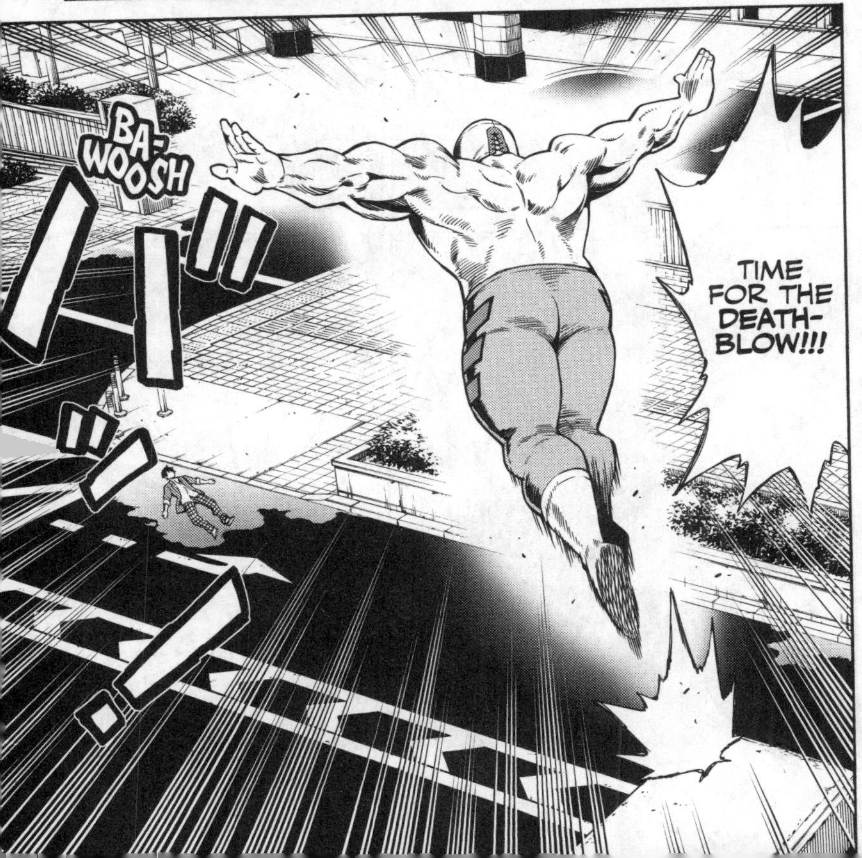
TIME FOR THE DEATH-BLOW!!!
BA-WOOSH

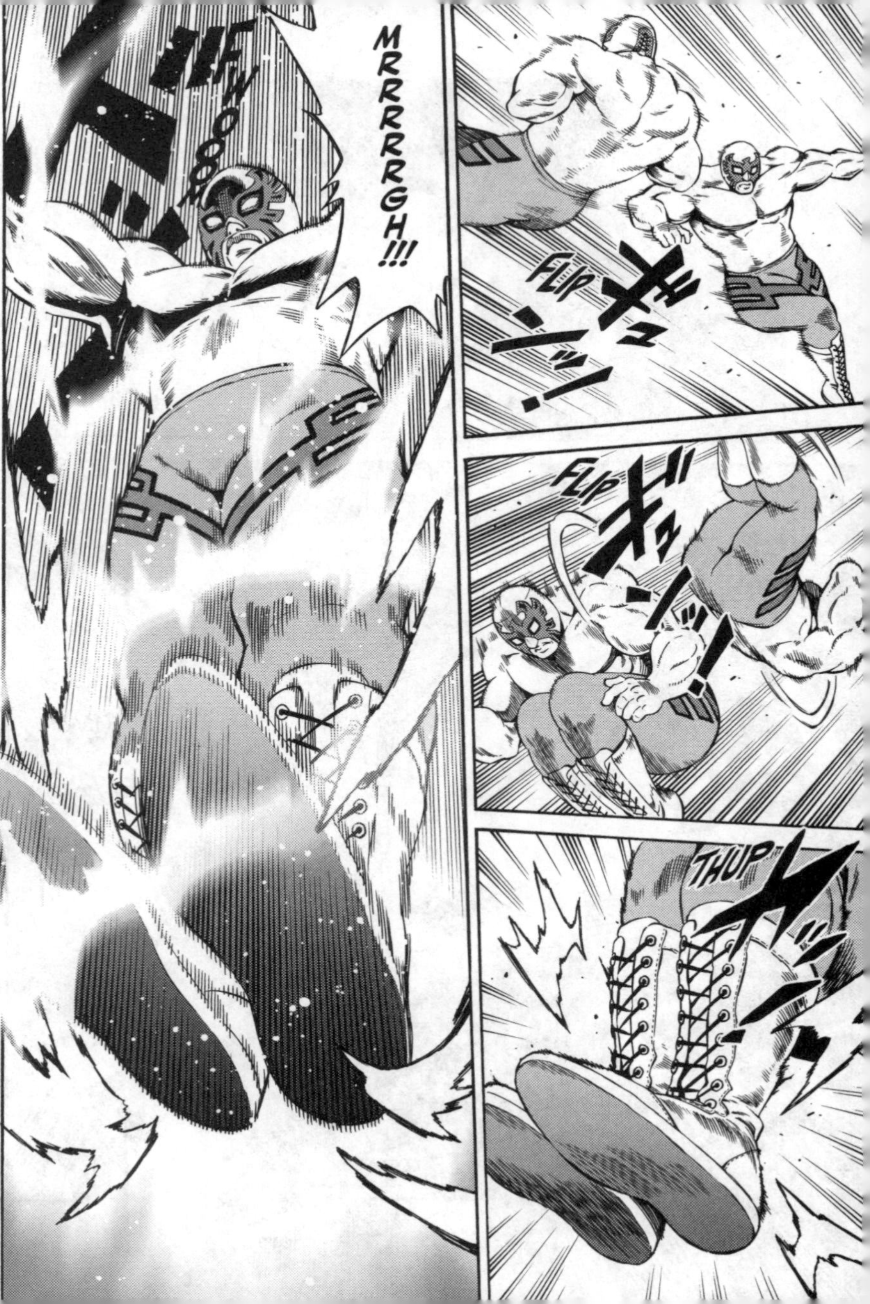
FLIP
FLIP
THUP
MRRRRRGH!!!
FWOOOM

I CAN'T CHOOSE.

GWOOOSH...

SQUEEZE

I WON'T CHOOSE!

THAT ISN'T IT.

NO...

DOESN'T BOTHER ME!

AND THAT...

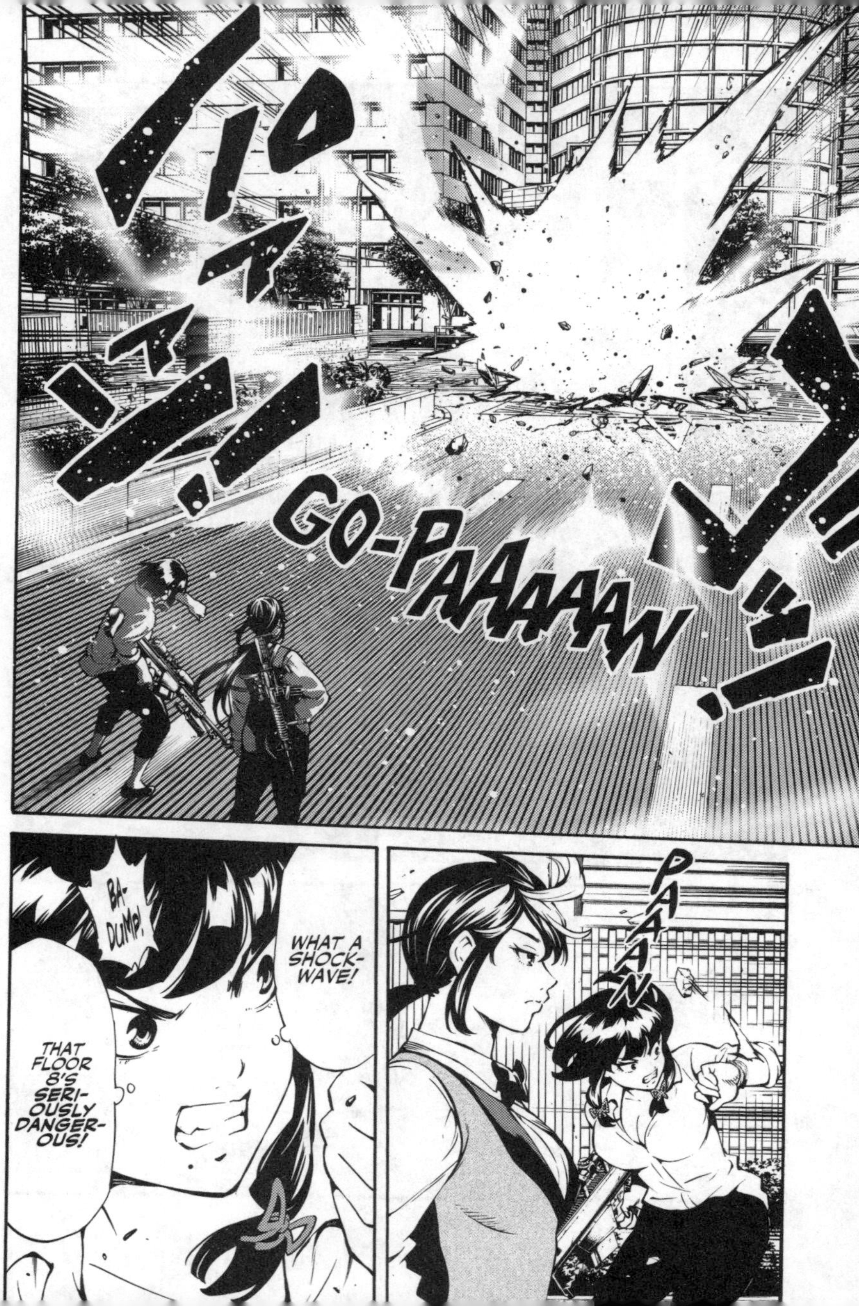
GO-PAAAAAAN
PAAAN
BA-DUMP!
WHAT A SHOCK-WAVE!
THAT FLOOR 8'S SERI-OUSLY DANGER-OUS!

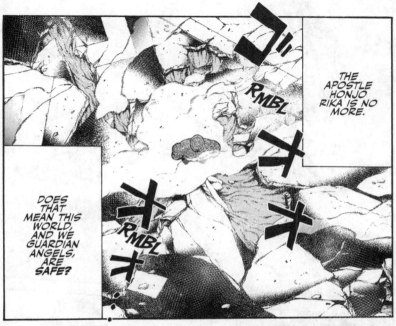

THE APOSTLE HONJO RIKA IS NO MORE.

DOES THAT MEAN THIS WORLD, AND WE GUARDIAN ANGELS, ARE SAFE?

TWITCH

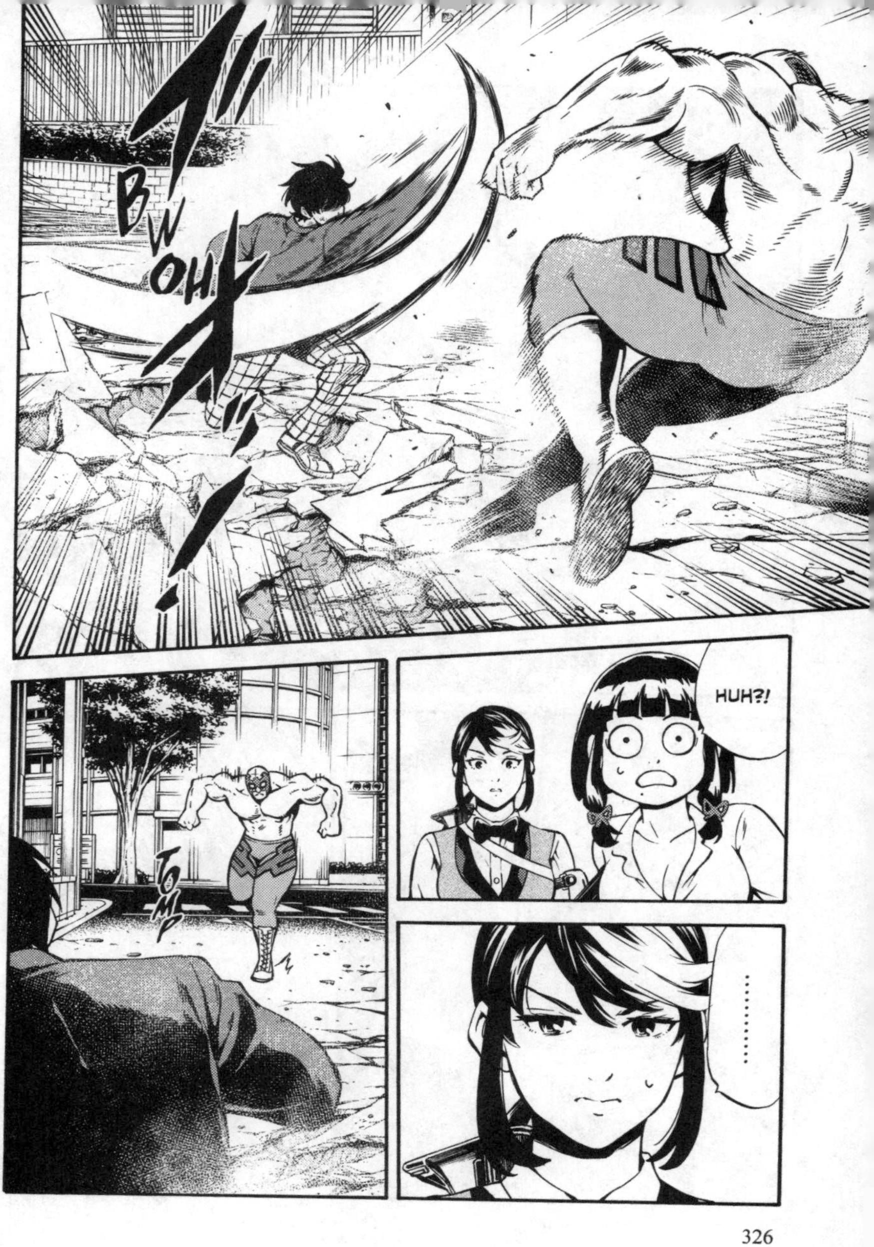
BWOH
HUH?!
....
TOMP

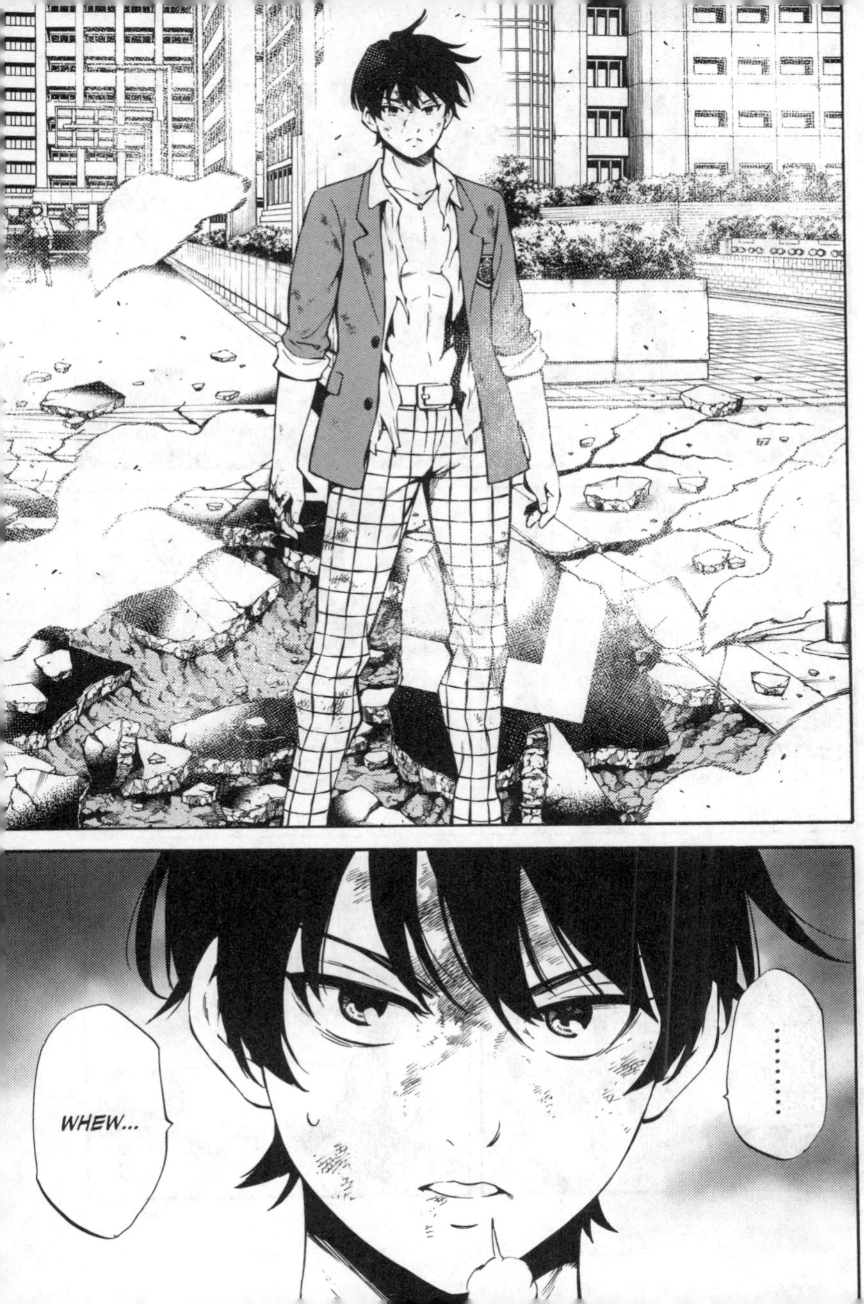
......
WHEW...

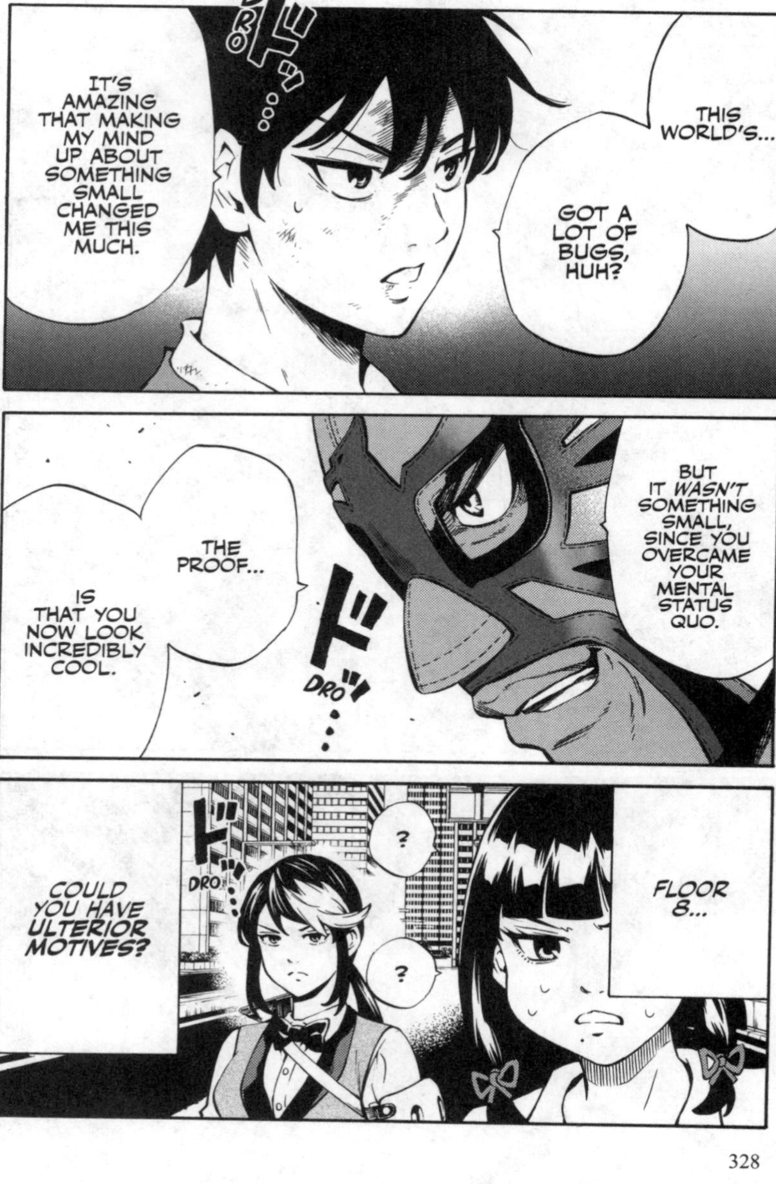
THIS WORLD'S...
GOT A LOT OF BUGS, HUH?
DRO...
IT'S AMAZING THAT MAKING MY MIND UP ABOUT SOMETHING SMALL CHANGED ME THIS MUCH.
BUT IT *WASN'T* SOMETHING SMALL, SINCE YOU OVERCAME YOUR MENTAL STATUS QUO.
DRO...
THE PROOF...
IS THAT YOU NOW LOOK INCREDIBLY COOL.
FLOOR 8...
?
?
DRO...
COULD YOU HAVE ULTERIOR MOTIVES?

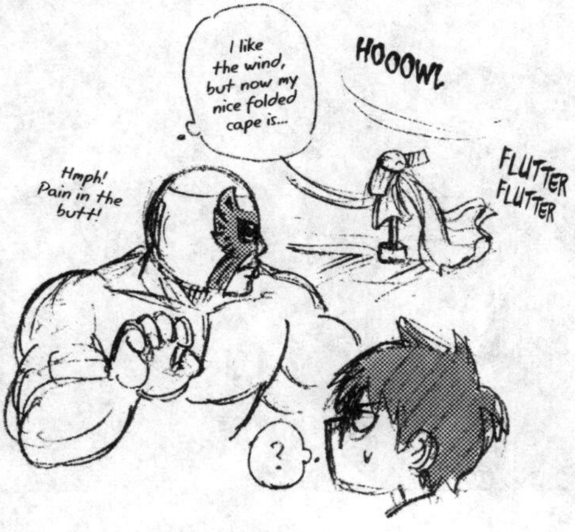
HOOOWL
FLUTTER FLUTTER
I like the wind, but now my nice folded cape is...
Hmph! Pain in the butt!
?

HIGH-RISE INVASION

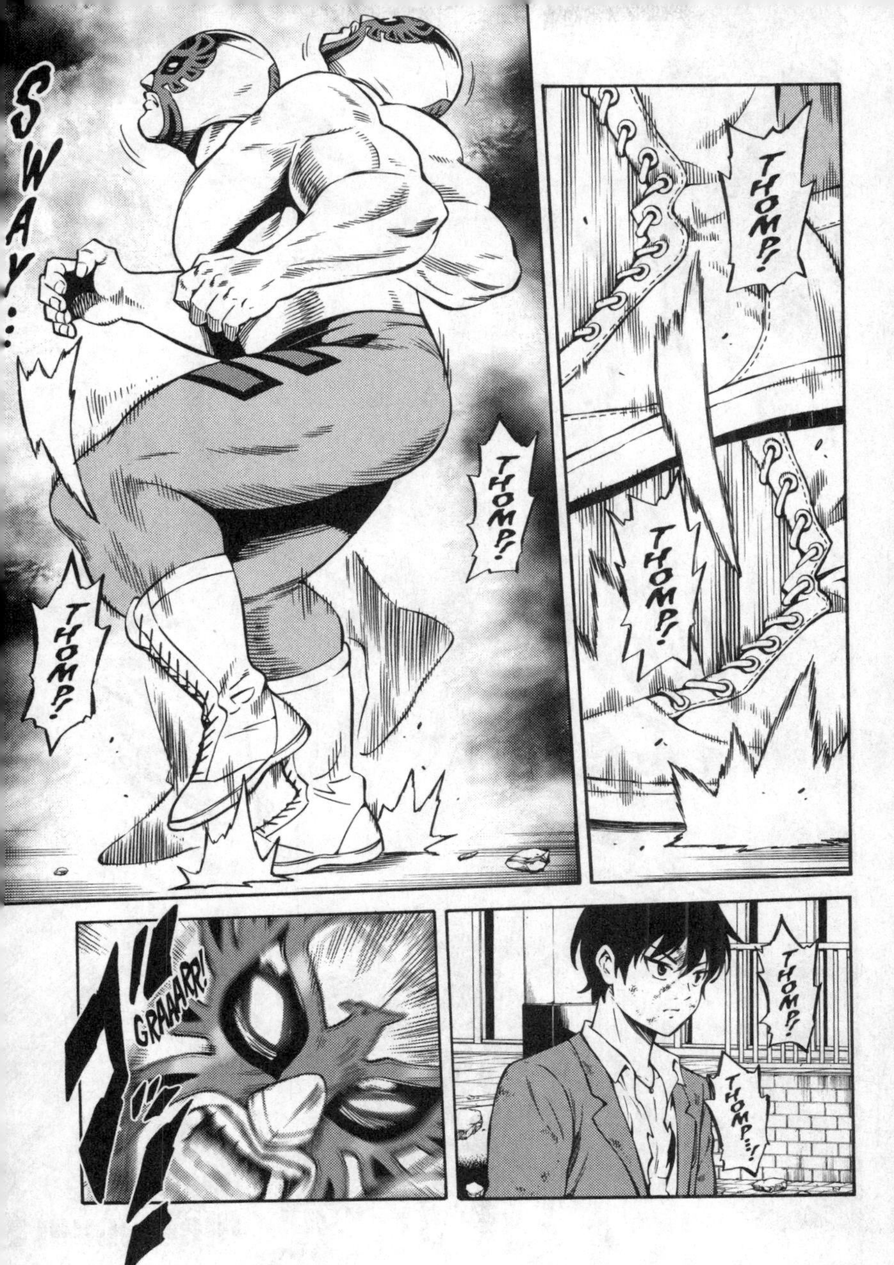
THOMP?!
THOMP?!
SWAY...
THOMP?!
THOMP?!
THOMP?!
THOMP...!
GRAAARR!

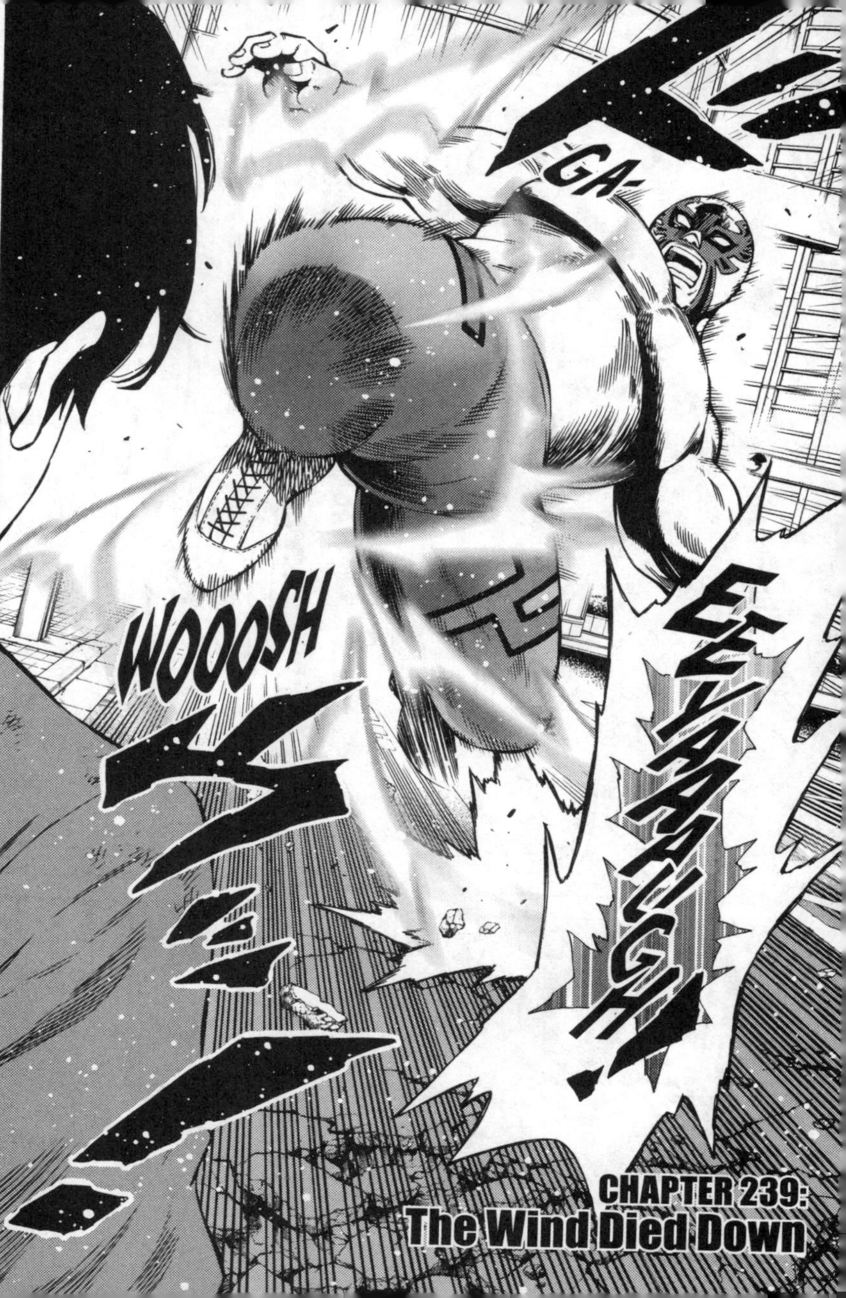
GA-
EEYAAAUGH!!
WOOOSH
CHAPTER 239:
The Wind Died Down

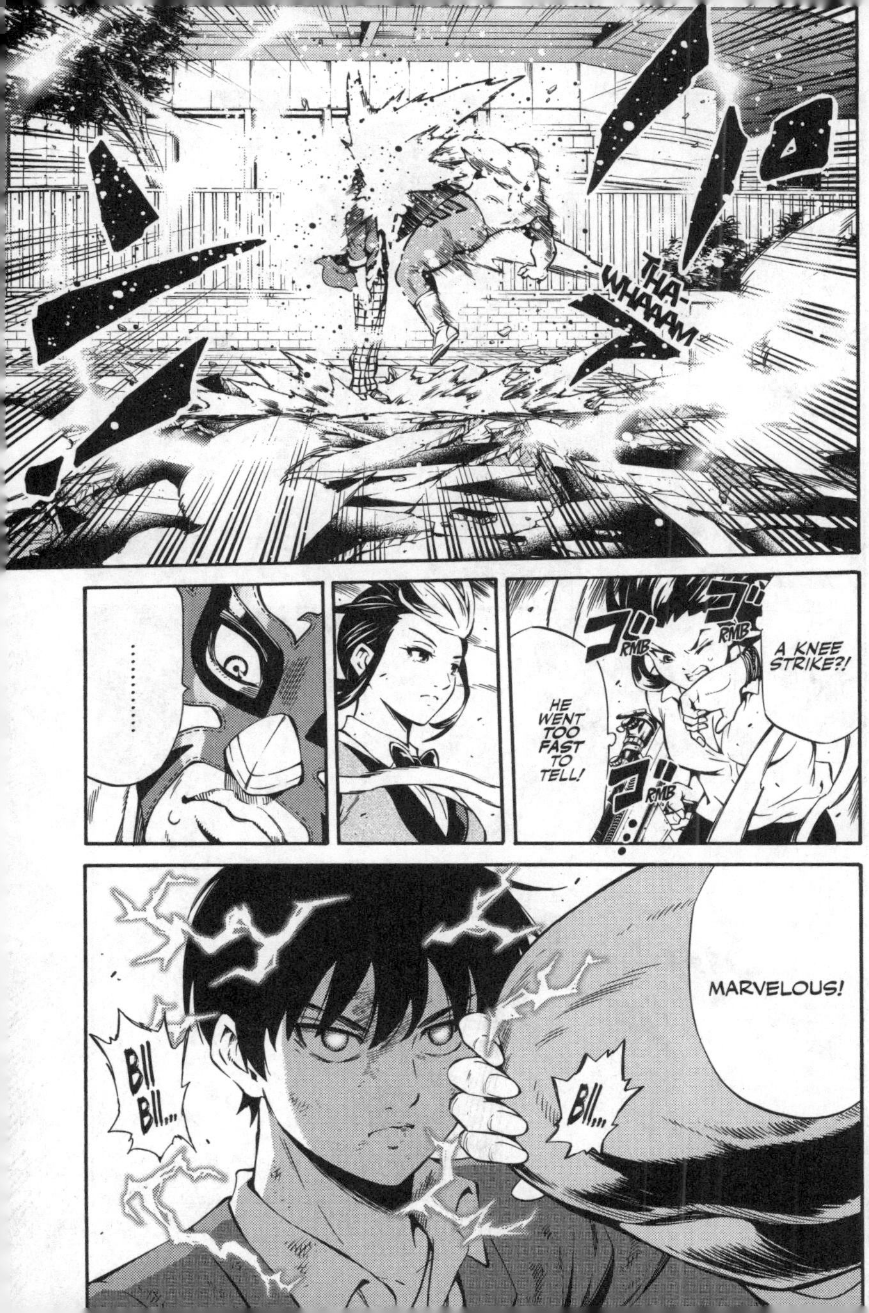
THA-WHAAAM
A KNEE STRIKE?!
RMB
RMB
RMB
HE WENT TOO FAST TO TELL!
......
MARVELOUS!
BII...
BII BII...

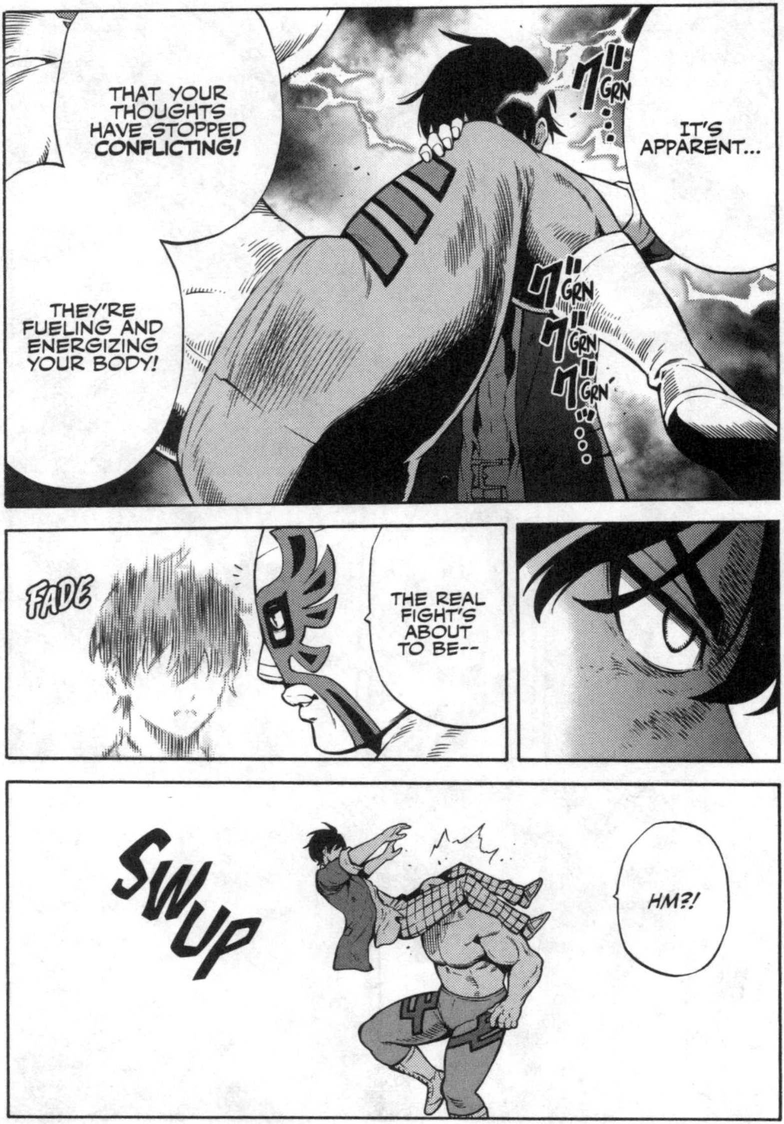
GRN...
IT'S APPARENT...
THAT YOUR THOUGHTS HAVE STOPPED CONFLICTING!
GRN
GRN
GRN...
THEY'RE FUELING AND ENERGIZING YOUR BODY!
THE REAL FIGHT'S ABOUT TO BE--
FADE
HM?!
SWUP

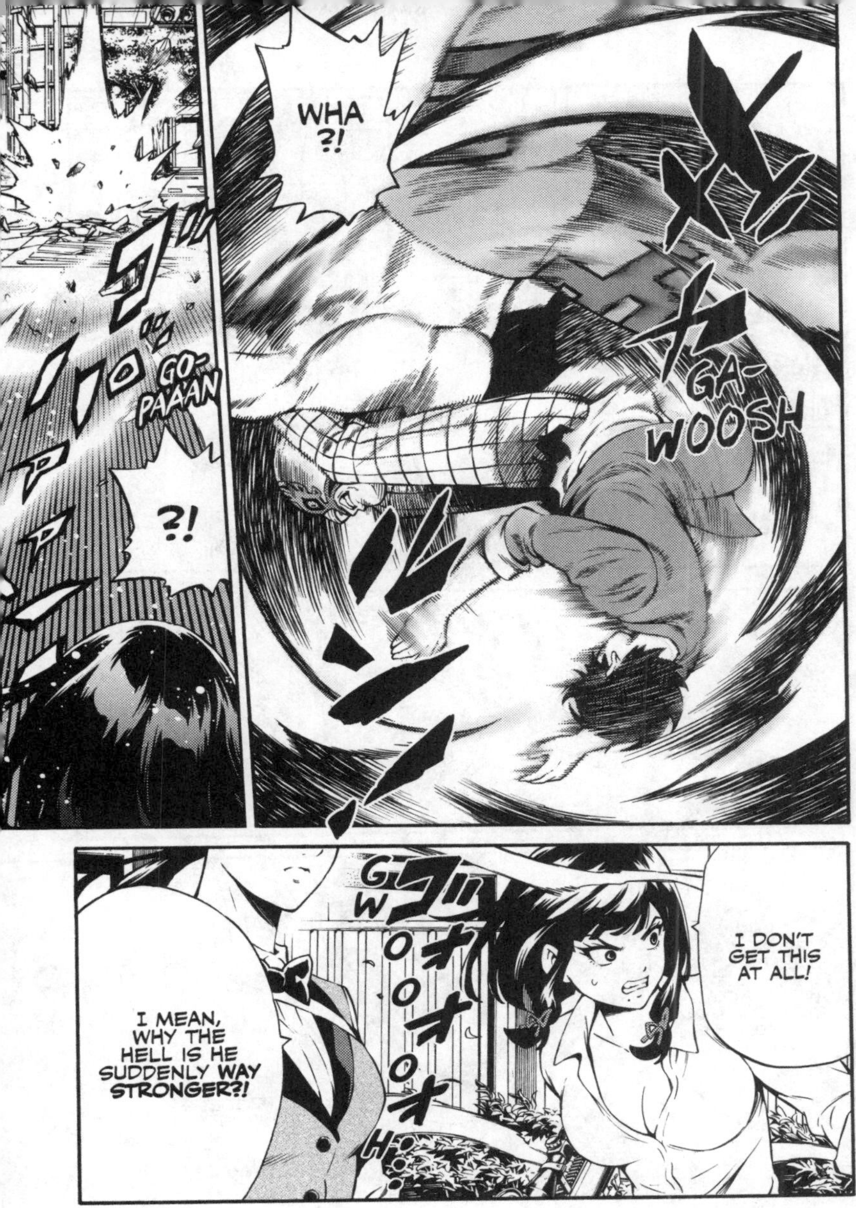
WHA ?!
GA-WOOSH
GO-PAAAN
?!
I DON'T GET THIS AT ALL!
GWOOOH!!
I MEAN, WHY THE HELL IS HE SUDDENLY WAY STRONGER?!

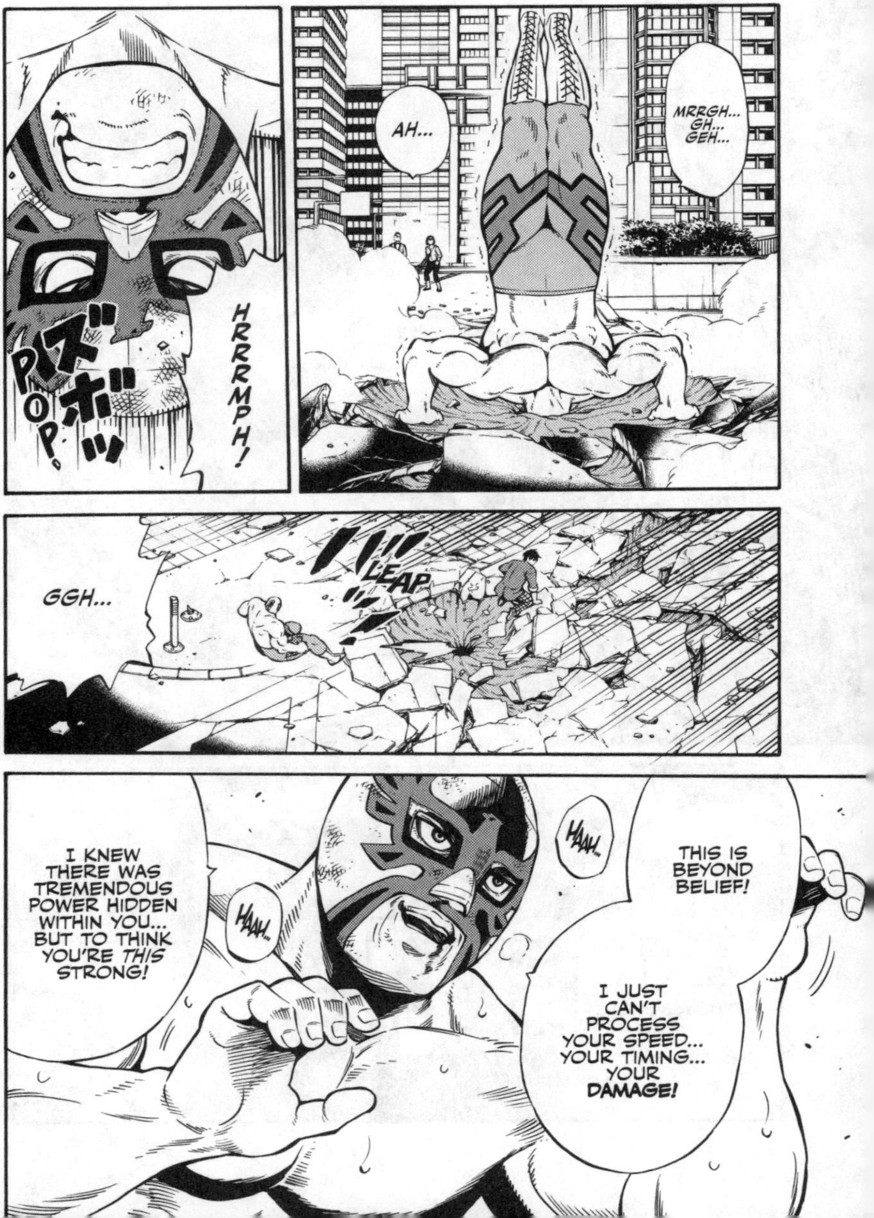
MRRGH... GH... GEH...
AH...
HRRRMPH!
ズボッ
POP!
LEAP
GGH...
THIS IS BEYOND BELIEF!
HAAH...
I JUST CAN'T PROCESS YOUR SPEED... YOUR TIMING... YOUR **DAMAGE!**
HAAH...
I KNEW THERE WAS TREMENDOUS POWER HIDDEN WITHIN YOU... BUT TO THINK YOU'RE *THIS* STRONG!

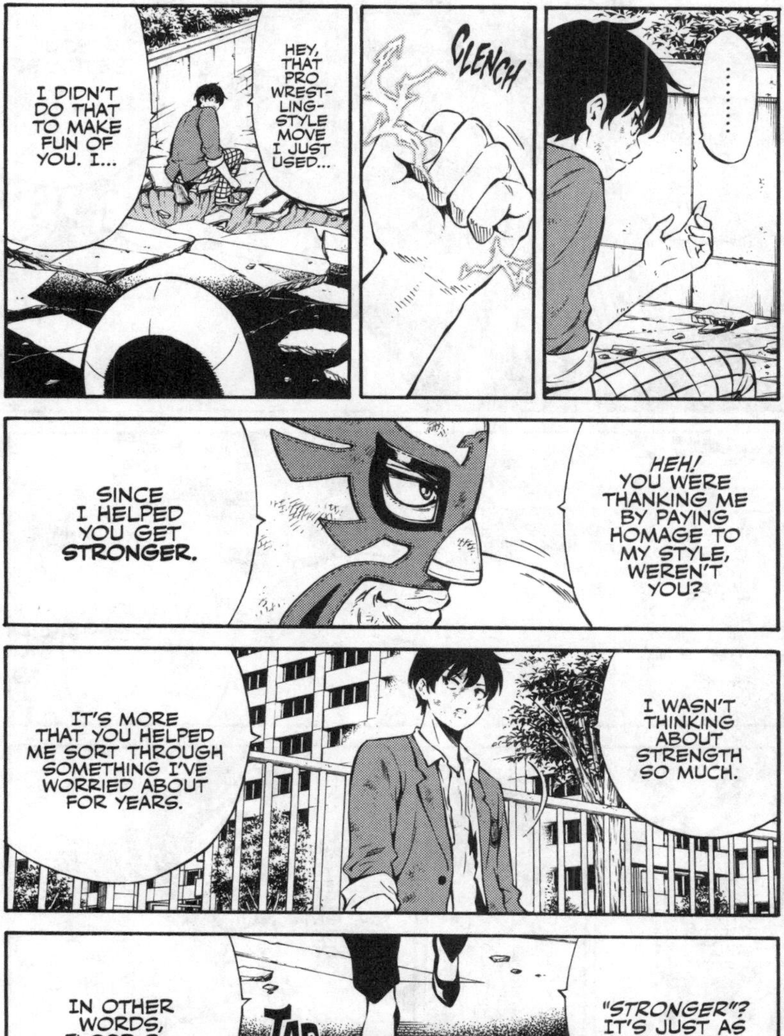
......
CLENCH
HEY, THAT PRO WRESTLING-STYLE MOVE I JUST USED...
I DIDN'T DO THAT TO MAKE FUN OF YOU. I...
HEH! YOU WERE THANKING ME BY PAYING HOMAGE TO MY STYLE, WEREN'T YOU?
SINCE I HELPED YOU GET STRONGER.
I WASN'T THINKING ABOUT STRENGTH SO MUCH.
IT'S MORE THAT YOU HELPED ME SORT THROUGH SOMETHING I'VE WORRIED ABOUT FOR YEARS.
"STRONGER"? IT'S JUST AS I THOUGHT.
TAP
IN OTHER WORDS, FLOOR 8...

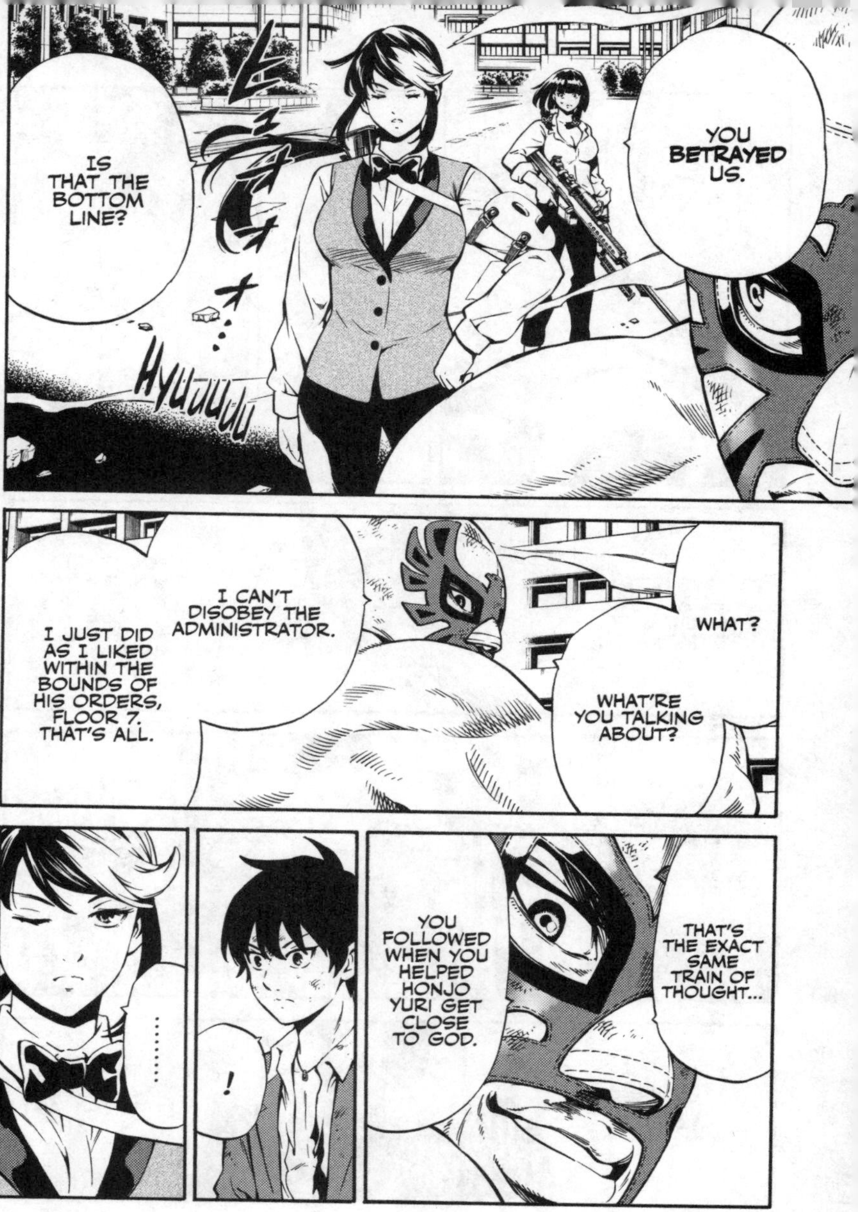
YOU BETRAYED US.
IS THAT THE BOTTOM LINE?
HYUUUUU
WHAT?
WHAT'RE YOU TALKING ABOUT?
I CAN'T DISOBEY THE ADMINISTRATOR.
I JUST DID AS I LIKED WITHIN THE BOUNDS OF HIS ORDERS, FLOOR 7. THAT'S ALL.
THAT'S THE EXACT SAME TRAIN OF THOUGHT...
YOU FOLLOWED WHEN YOU HELPED HONJO YURI GET CLOSE TO GOD.
!
......

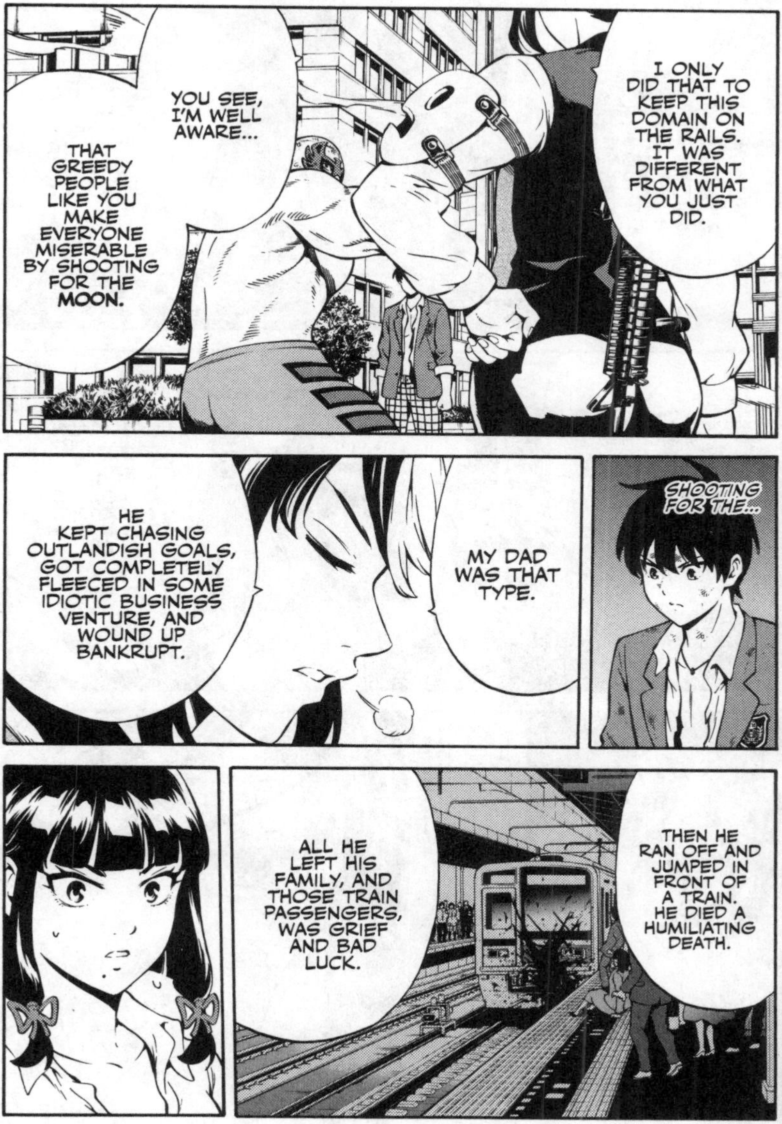
I ONLY DID THAT TO KEEP THIS DOMAIN ON THE RAILS. IT WAS DIFFERENT FROM WHAT YOU JUST DID.
YOU SEE, I'M WELL AWARE...
THAT GREEDY PEOPLE LIKE YOU MAKE EVERYONE MISERABLE BY SHOOTING FOR THE MOON.
SHOOTING FOR THE...
MY DAD WAS THAT TYPE.
HE KEPT CHASING OUTLANDISH GOALS, GOT COMPLETELY FLEECED IN SOME IDIOTIC BUSINESS VENTURE, AND WOUND UP BANKRUPT.
THEN HE RAN OFF AND JUMPED IN FRONT OF A TRAIN. HE DIED A HUMILIATING DEATH.
ALL HE LEFT HIS FAMILY, AND THOSE TRAIN PASSENGERS, WAS GRIEF AND BAD LUCK.

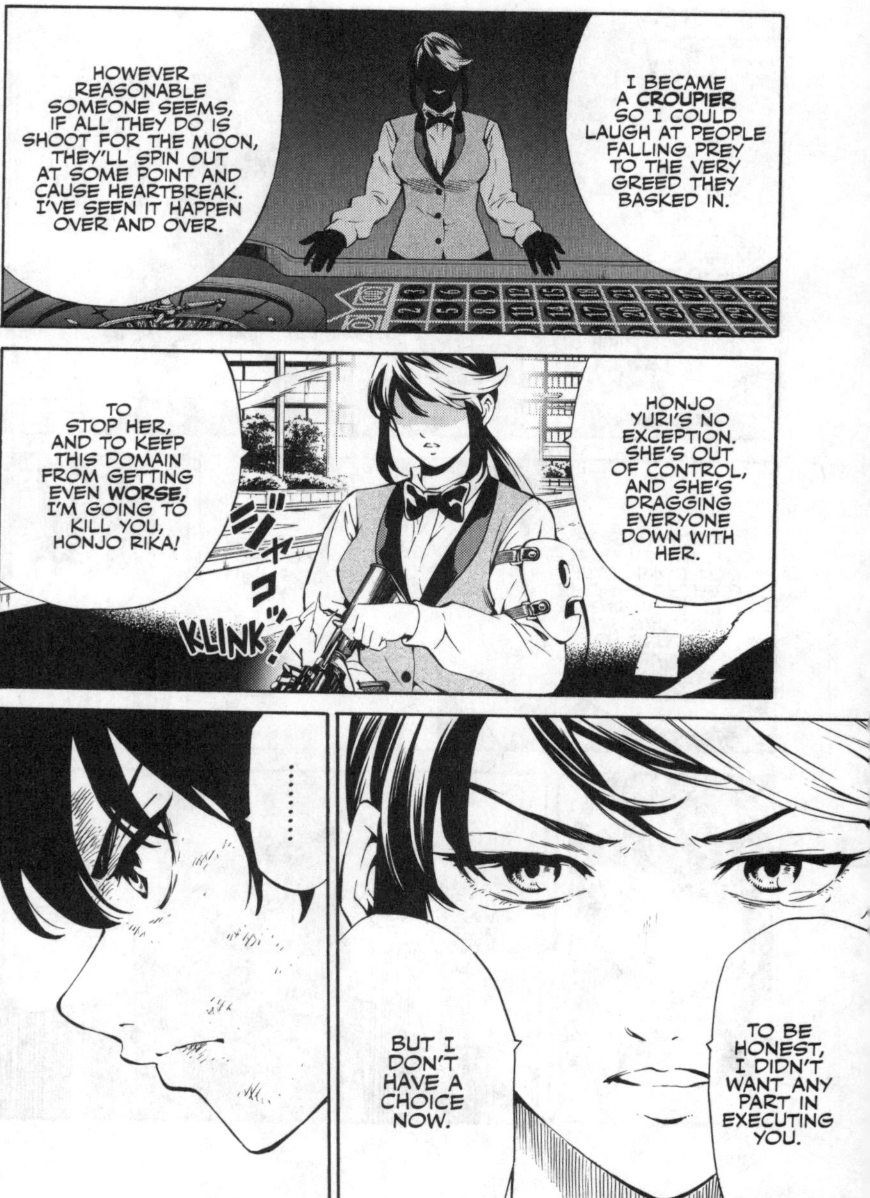
I BECAME A CROUPIER SO I COULD LAUGH AT PEOPLE FALLING PREY TO THE VERY GREED THEY BASKED IN.
HOWEVER REASONABLE SOMEONE SEEMS, IF ALL THEY DO IS SHOOT FOR THE MOON, THEY'LL SPIN OUT AT SOME POINT AND CAUSE HEARTBREAK. I'VE SEEN IT HAPPEN OVER AND OVER.
HONJO YURI'S NO EXCEPTION. SHE'S OUT OF CONTROL, AND SHE'S DRAGGING EVERYONE DOWN WITH HER.
TO STOP HER, AND TO KEEP THIS DOMAIN FROM GETTING EVEN WORSE, I'M GOING TO KILL YOU, HONJO RIKA!
ジャコッ!
KLINK!
TO BE HONEST, I DIDN'T WANT ANY PART IN EXECUTING YOU.
BUT I DON'T HAVE A CHOICE NOW.
......

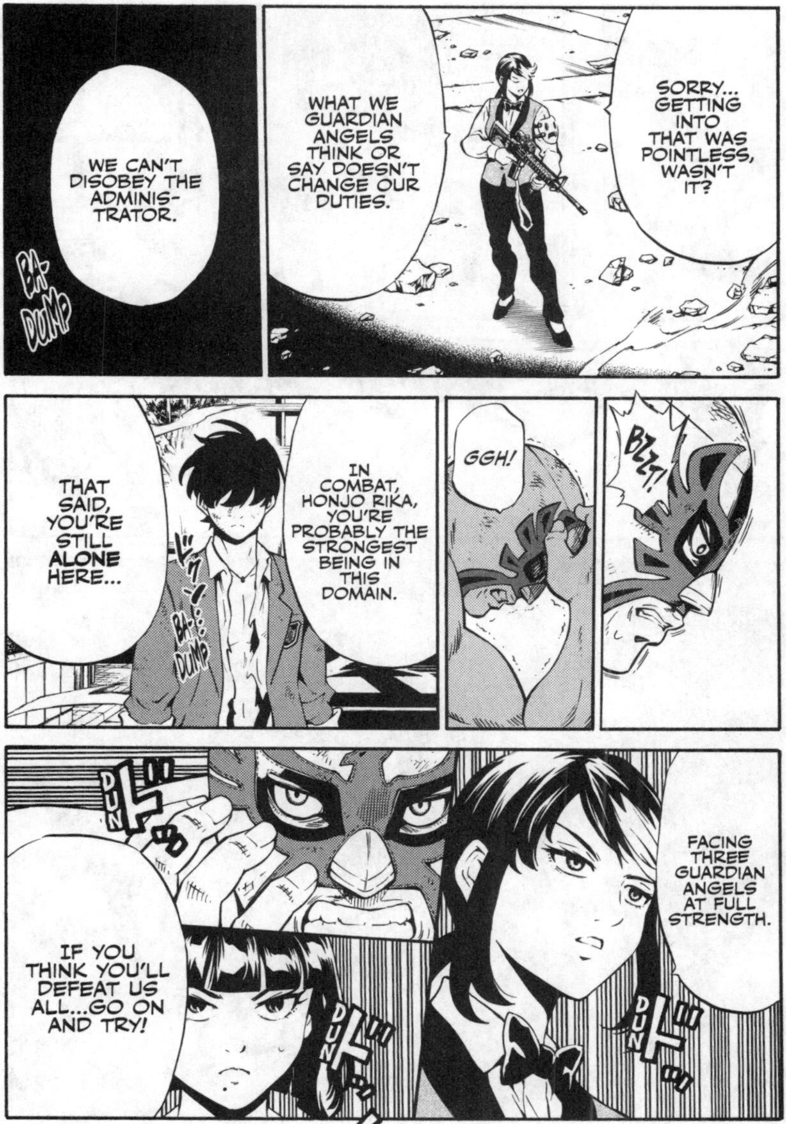
SORRY... GETTING INTO THAT WAS POINTLESS, WASN'T IT?
WHAT WE GUARDIAN ANGELS THINK OR SAY DOESN'T CHANGE OUR DUTIES.
WE CAN'T DISOBEY THE ADMINISTRATOR.
BA-DUMP
BZZT!
GGH!
IN COMBAT, HONJO RIKA, YOU'RE PROBABLY THE STRONGEST BEING IN THIS DOMAIN.
THAT SAID, YOU'RE STILL ALONE HERE...
BA-DUMP
FACING THREE GUARDIAN ANGELS AT FULL STRENGTH.
DUN
IF YOU THINK YOU'LL DEFEAT US ALL...GO ON AND TRY!
DUN
DUN

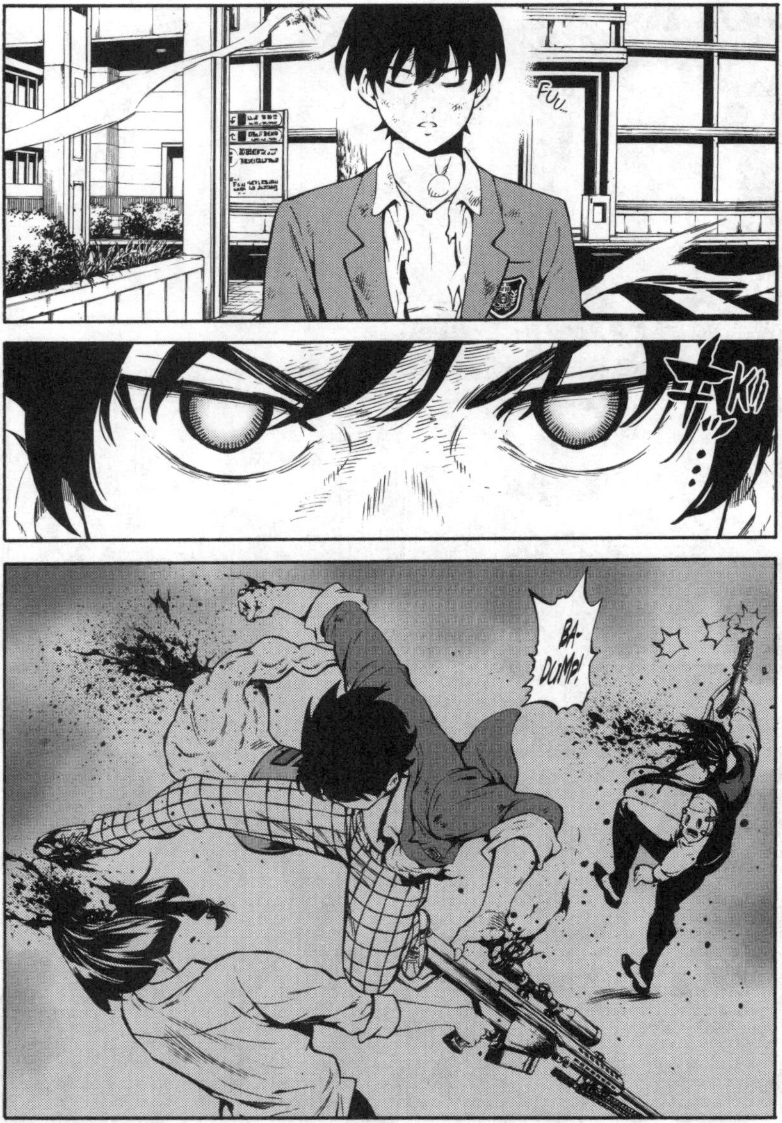
FUU...
キッ
K!!
...
BA-DUMP!

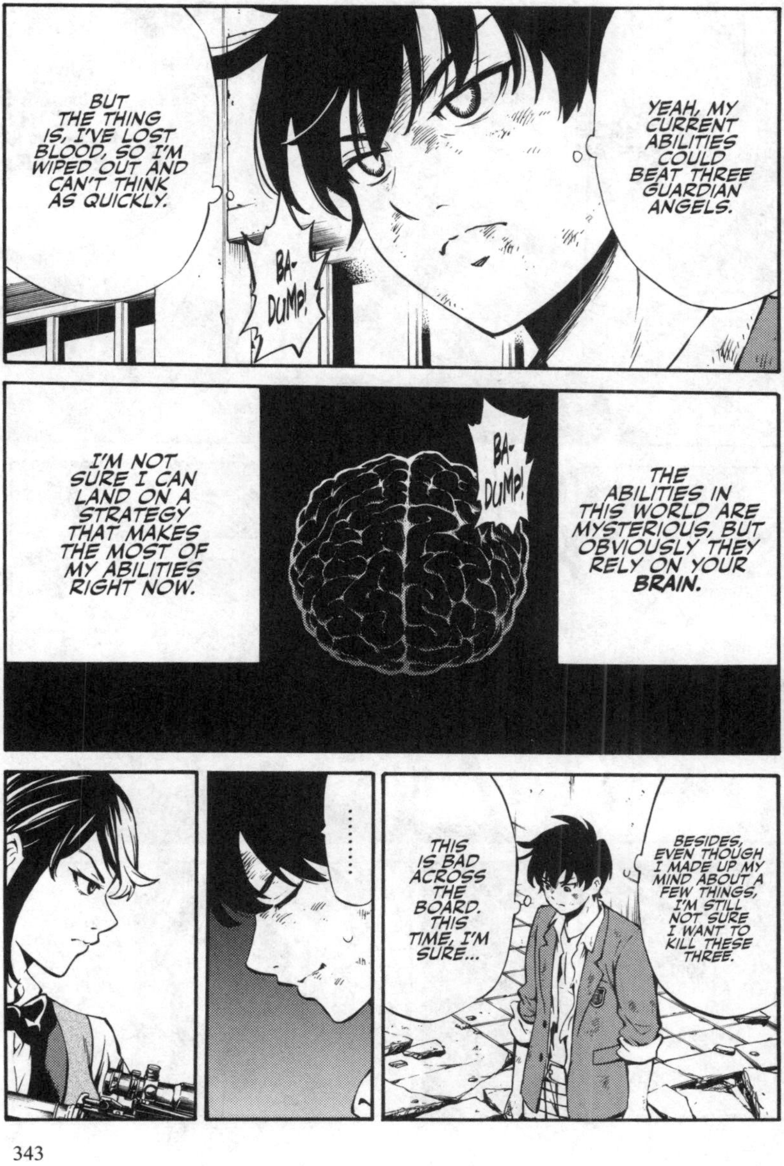
YEAH, MY CURRENT ABILITIES COULD BEAT THREE GUARDIAN ANGELS.
BUT THE THING IS, I'VE LOST BLOOD, SO I'M WIPED OUT AND CAN'T THINK AS QUICKLY.
BA-DUMP!
THE ABILITIES IN THIS WORLD ARE MYSTERIOUS, BUT OBVIOUSLY THEY RELY ON YOUR **BRAIN.**
BA-DUMP!
I'M NOT SURE I CAN LAND ON A STRATEGY THAT MAKES THE MOST OF MY ABILITIES RIGHT NOW.
BESIDES, EVEN THOUGH I MADE UP MY MIND ABOUT A FEW THINGS, I'M STILL NOT SURE I WANT TO KILL THESE THREE.
THIS IS BAD ACROSS THE BOARD. THIS TIME, I'M SURE...
......

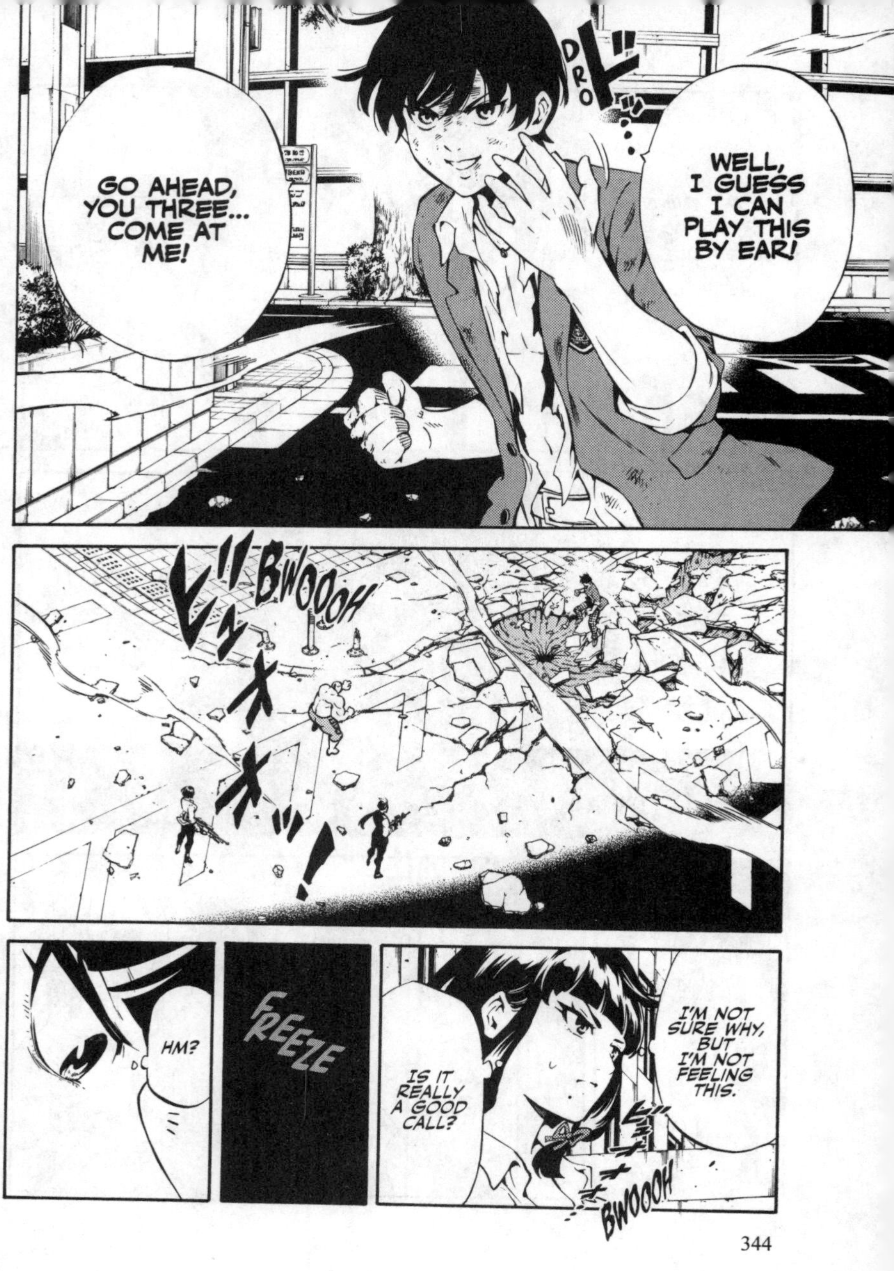
DRO
WELL, I GUESS I CAN PLAY THIS BY EAR!
GO AHEAD, YOU THREE... COME AT ME!
BWOOOH
I'M NOT SURE WHY, BUT I'M NOT FEELING THIS.
IS IT REALLY A GOOD CALL?
BWOOOH
FREEZE
HM?

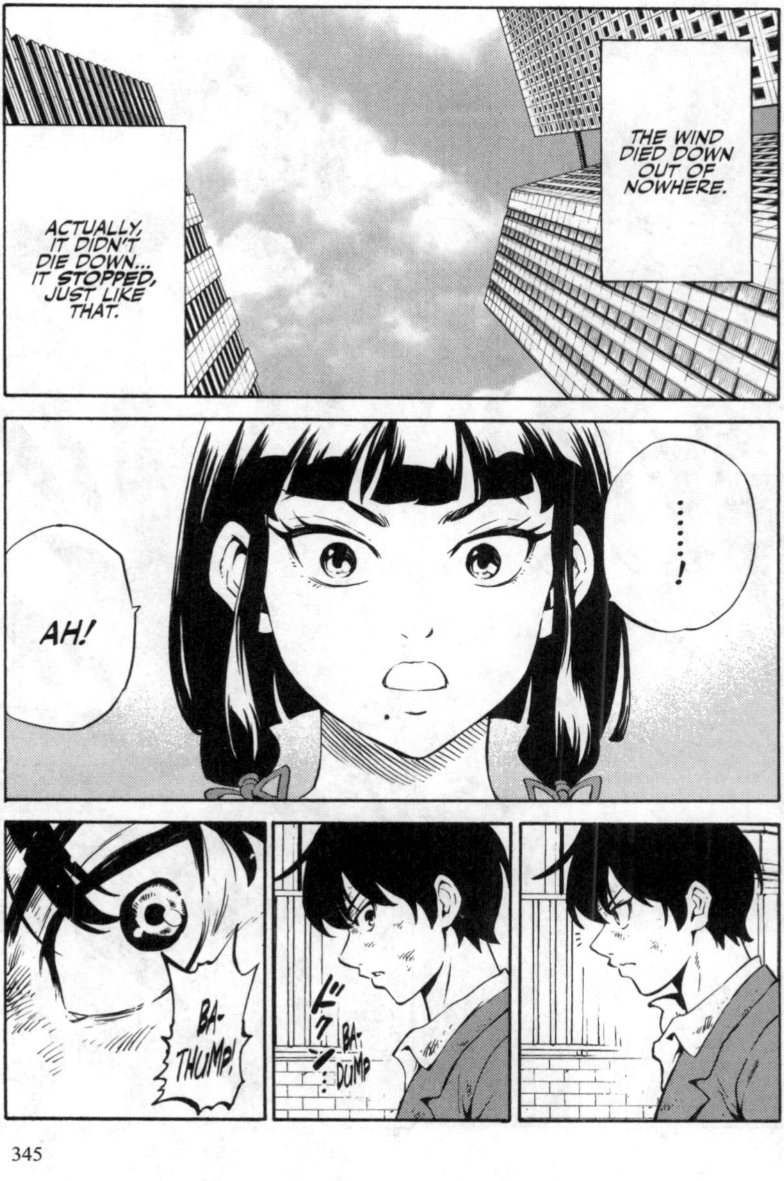
THE WIND DIED DOWN OUT OF NOWHERE.
ACTUALLY, IT DIDN'T DIE DOWN... IT STOPPED, JUST LIKE THAT.
......!
AH!
ドクン
BA-DUMP
BA-THUMP!

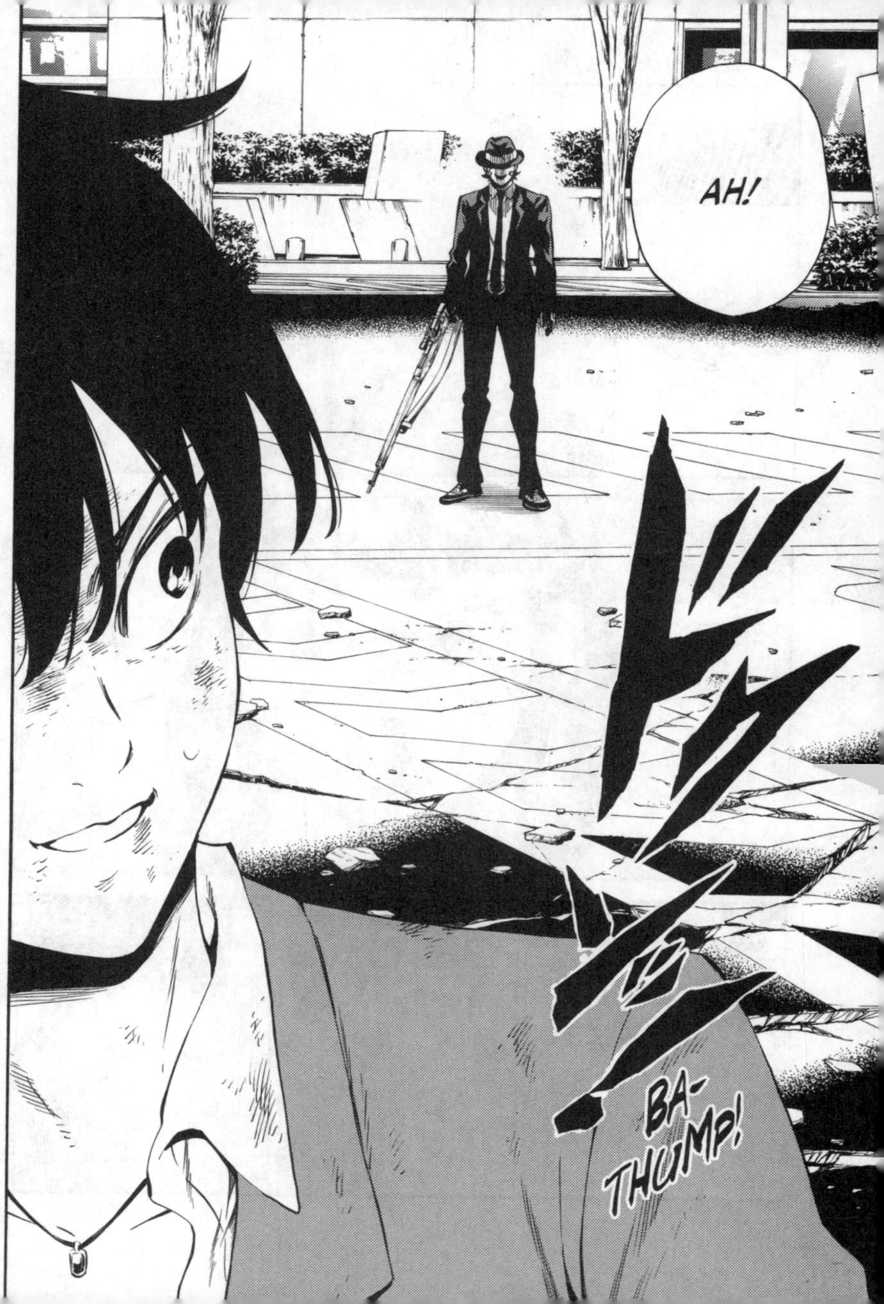
AH!
BA-THUMP!

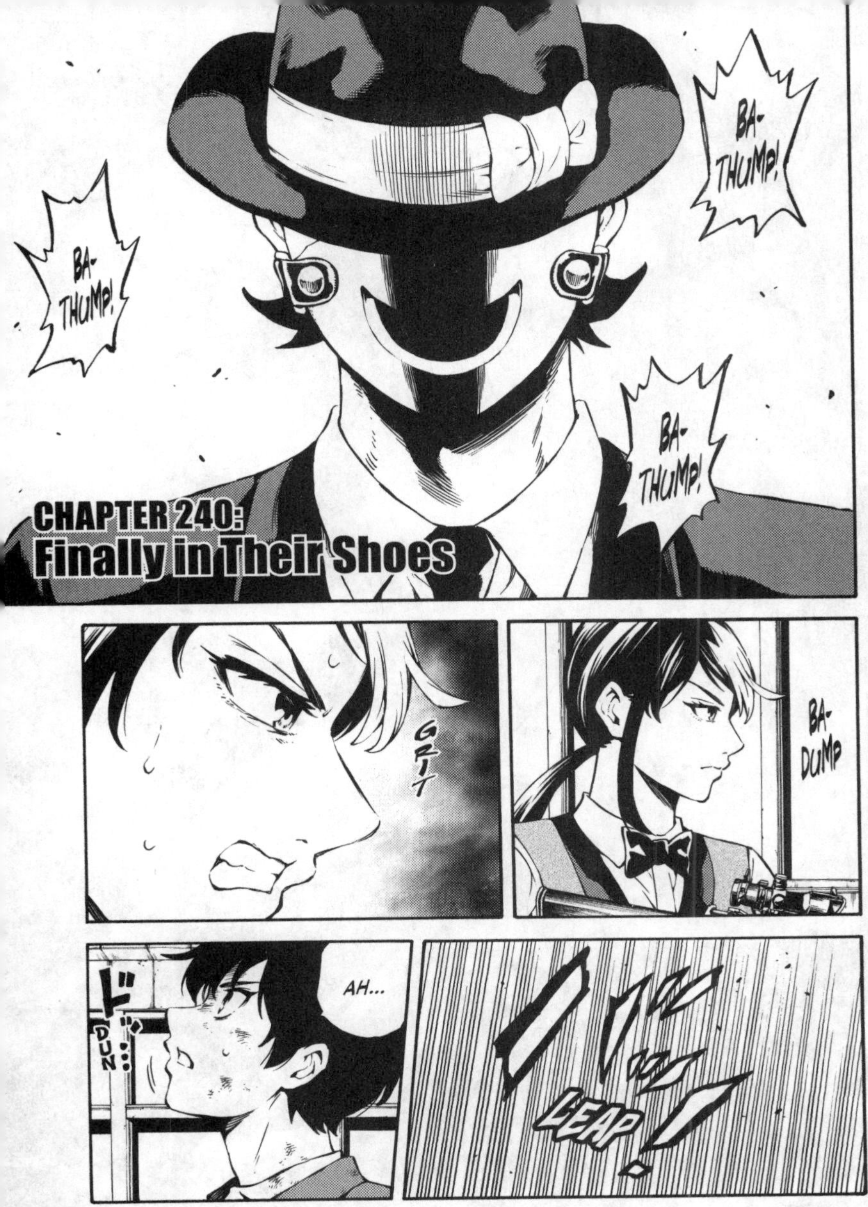
BA-THUMP!
BA-THUMP!
BA-THUMP!
CHAPTER 240:
Finally in Their Shoes
BA-DUMP
GRIT
LEAP!!
AH...
ド
DUN...

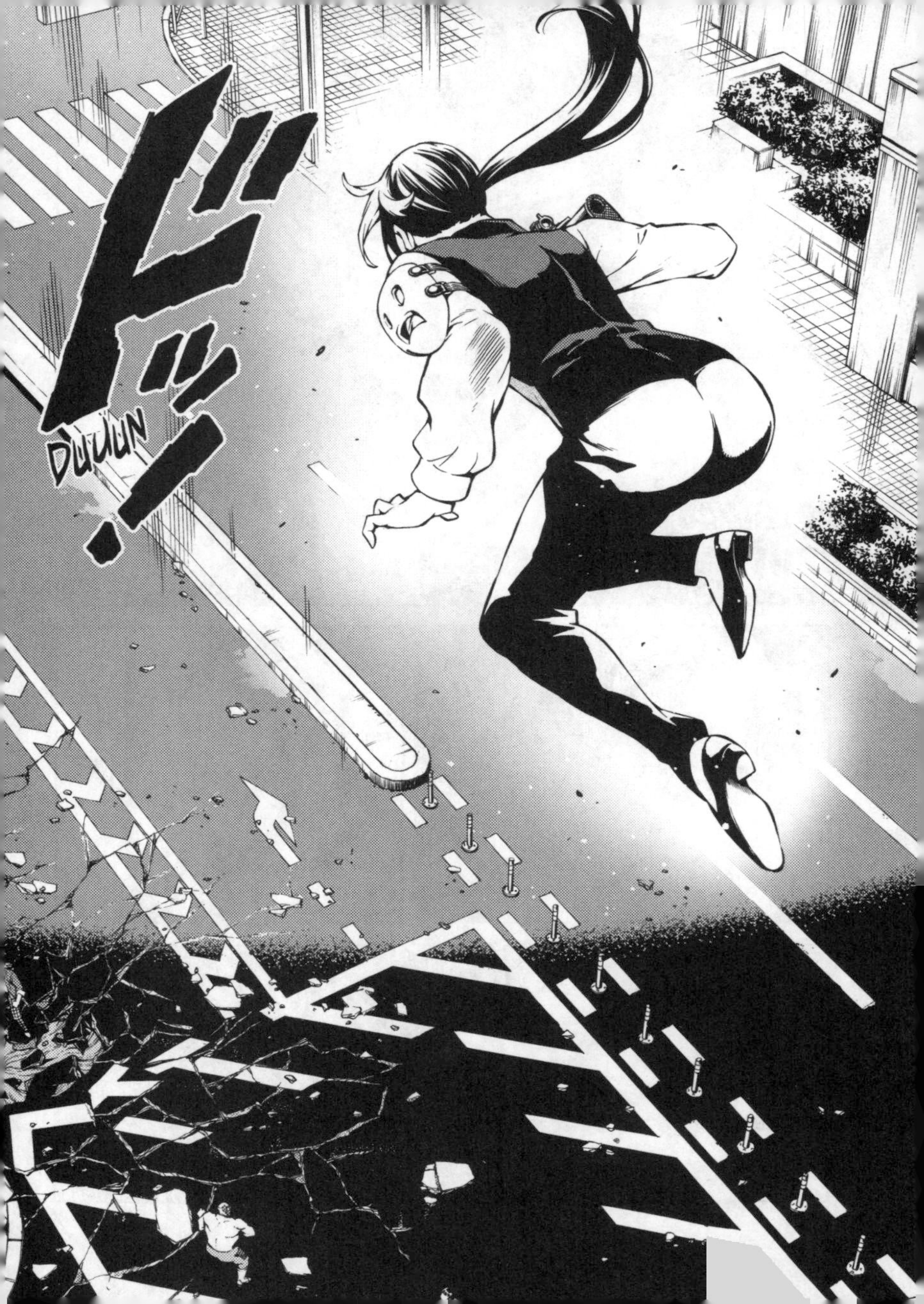
ドン!!
DUUUN

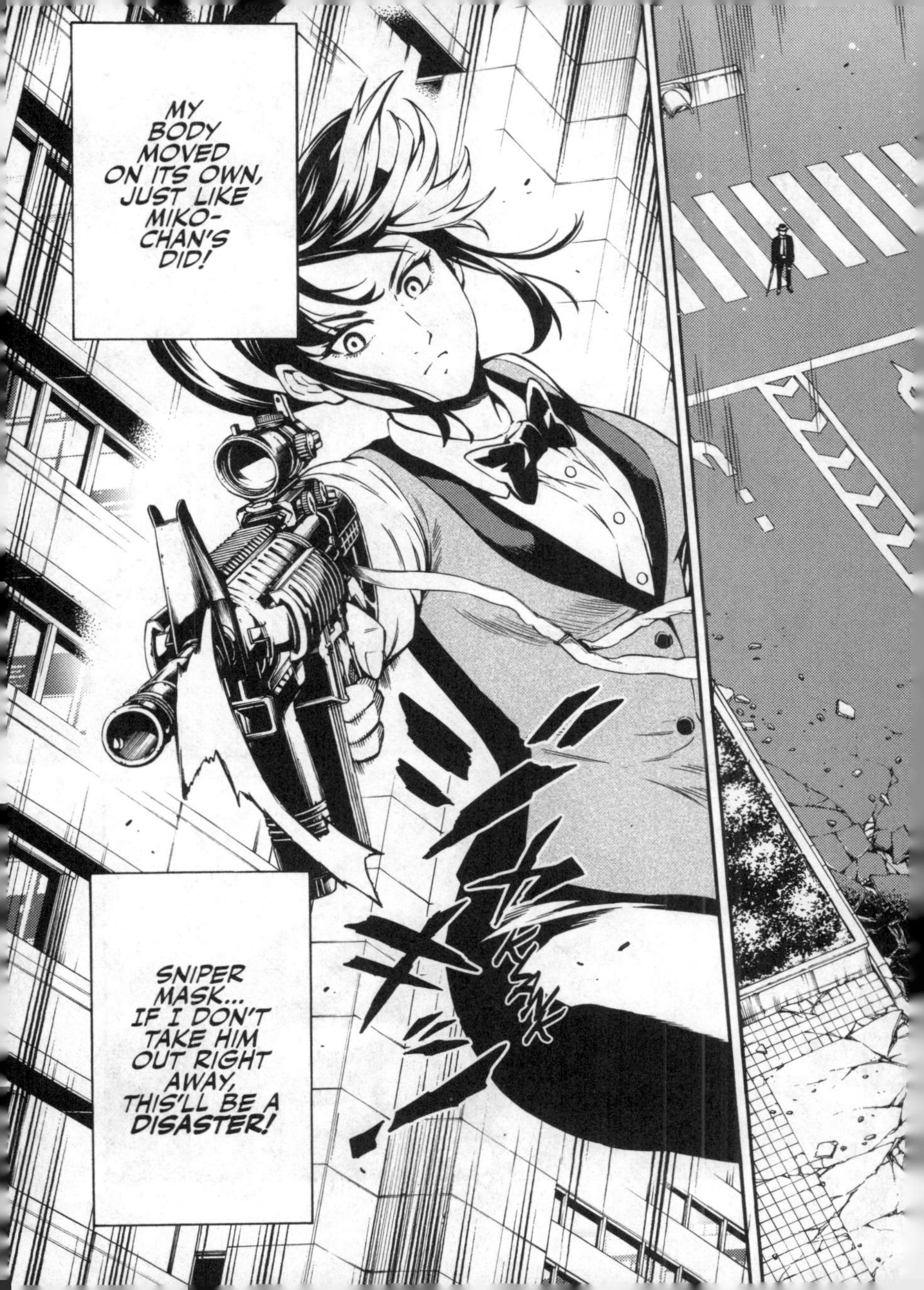
MY BODY MOVED ON ITS OWN, JUST LIKE MIKO-CHAN'S DID!
KRANK
SNIPER MASK... IF I DON'T TAKE HIM OUT RIGHT AWAY, THIS'LL BE A DISASTER!

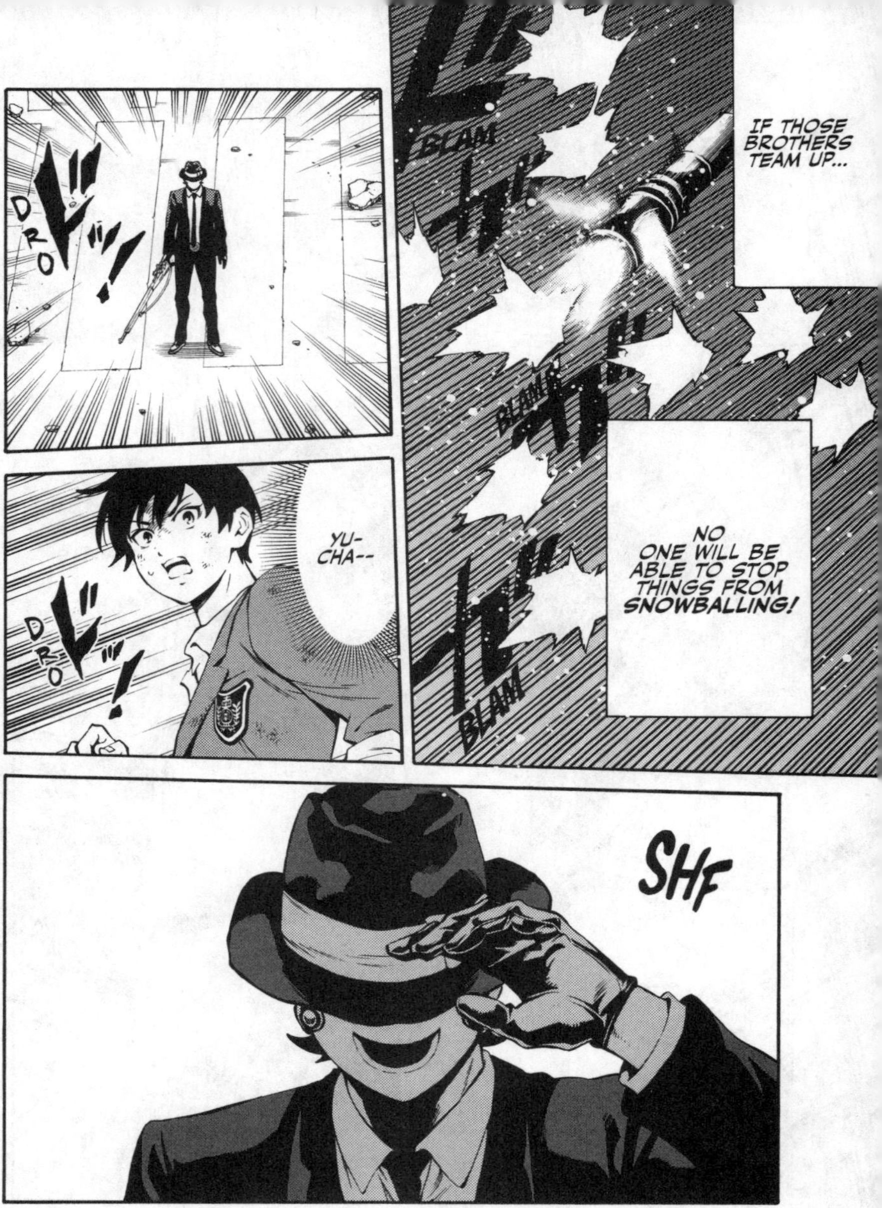
IF THOSE BROTHERS TEAM UP...
BLAM
BLAM
NO ONE WILL BE ABLE TO STOP THINGS FROM SNOWBALLING!
BLAM
DRO
YU-CHA--
DRO
SHF

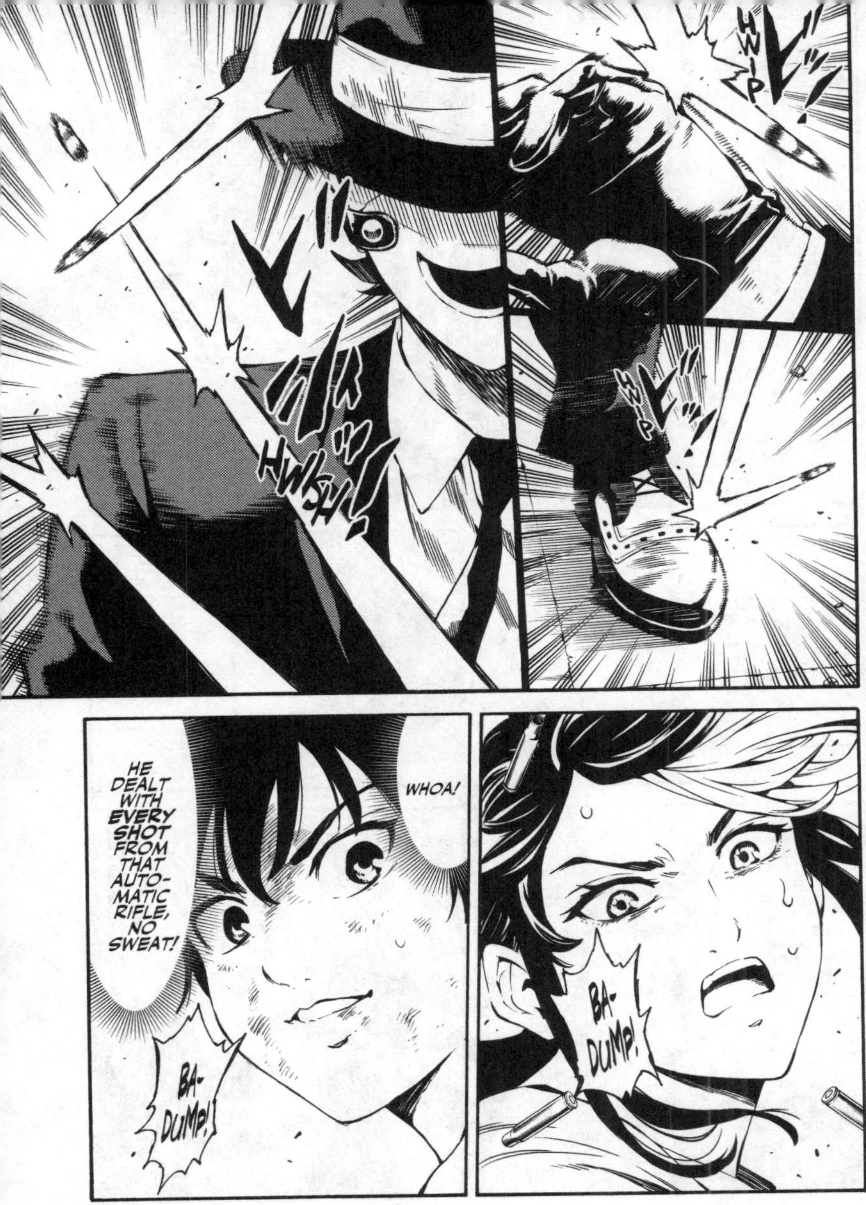
HWIP
HWIP
HWISH!
BA-DUMP!
WHOA!
HE DEALT WITH EVERY SHOT FROM THAT AUTOMATIC RIFLE, NO SWEAT!
BA-DUMP!

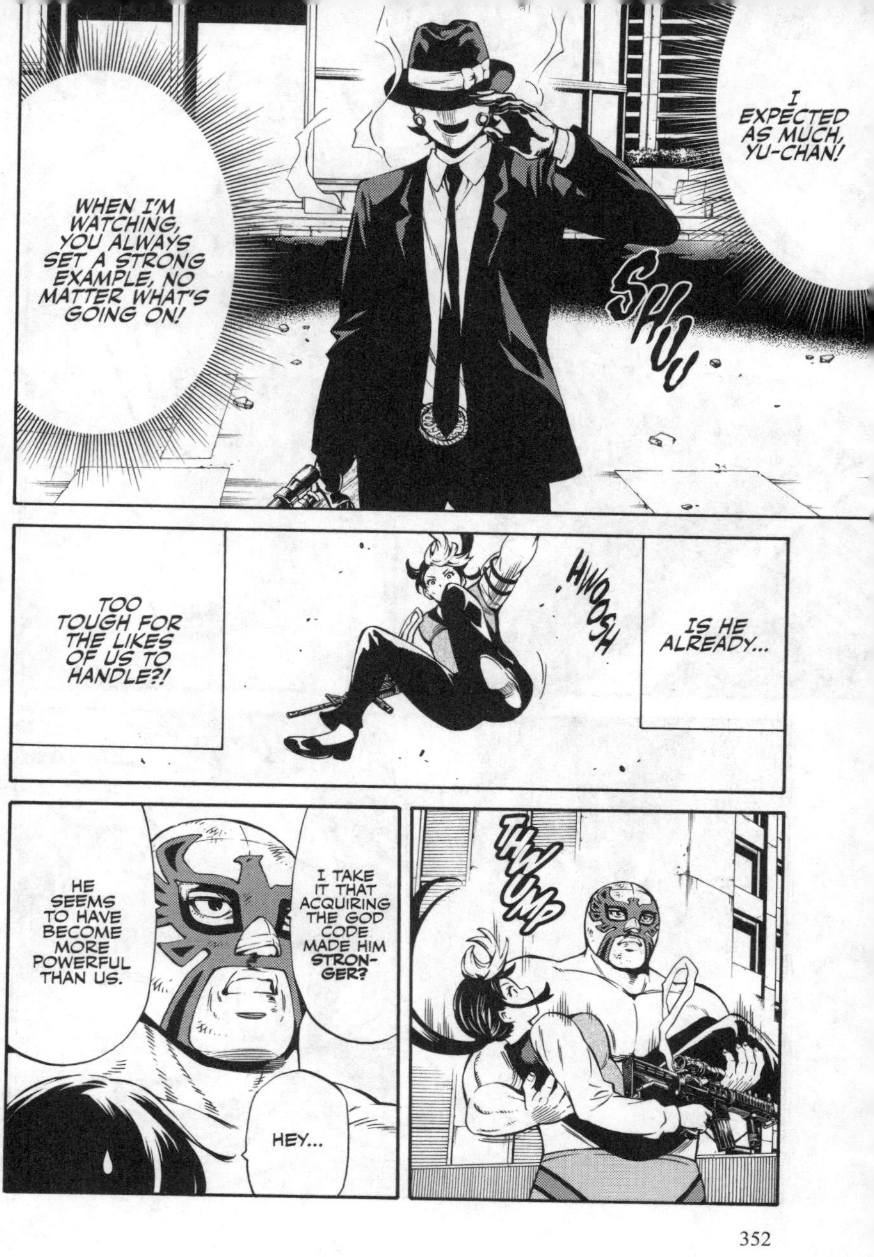
I EXPECTED AS MUCH, YU-CHAN!
SHUU
WHEN I'M WATCHING, YOU ALWAYS SET A STRONG EXAMPLE, NO MATTER WHAT'S GOING ON!
IS HE ALREADY...
HWOOSH
TOO TOUGH FOR THE LIKES OF US TO HANDLE?!
THWUMP
I TAKE IT THAT ACQUIRING THE GOD CODE MADE HIM STRON-GER?
HE SEEMS TO HAVE BECOME MORE POWERFUL THAN US.
HEY...

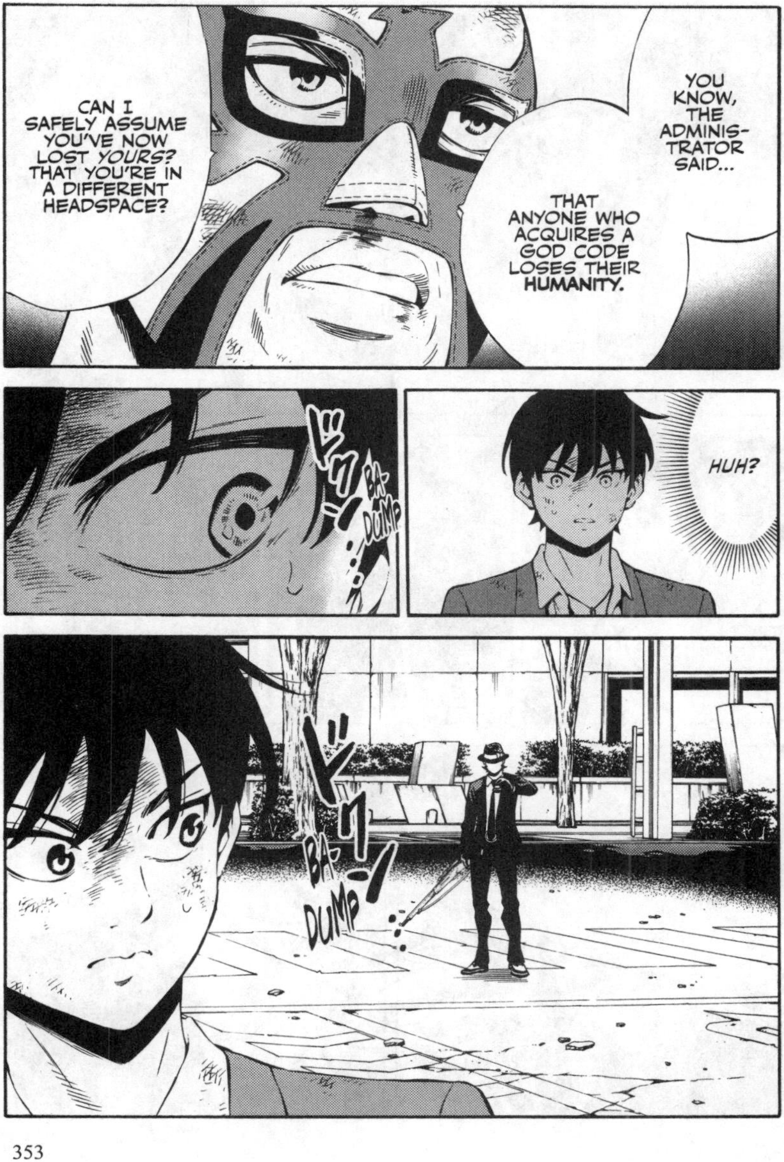
YOU KNOW, THE ADMINISTRATOR SAID...
THAT ANYONE WHO ACQUIRES A GOD CODE LOSES THEIR **HUMANITY.**
CAN I SAFELY ASSUME YOU'VE NOW LOST *YOURS?* THAT YOU'RE IN A DIFFERENT HEADSPACE?
HUH?
BA-DUMP
BA-DUMP

BA-DUMP!
BA-DUMP!
BA-DUMP!
YU... CHAN?
ドクン
BA-DUMP
POP

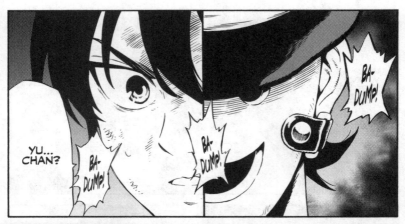

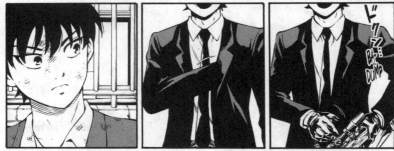

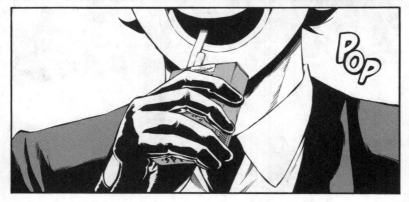

HEH.
NO ONE
WHO'D
LOST THEIR
HUMANITY
WOULD BE
SMOKING.

ONLY A
HUMAN WOULD
WILLINGLY
INHALE
SOMETHING
THAT BAD
FOR HIS
BODY.

MAKOTO
YUKA!

SAY
SOMETHING
ALREADY.
QUIT
ACTING
COOL.

355

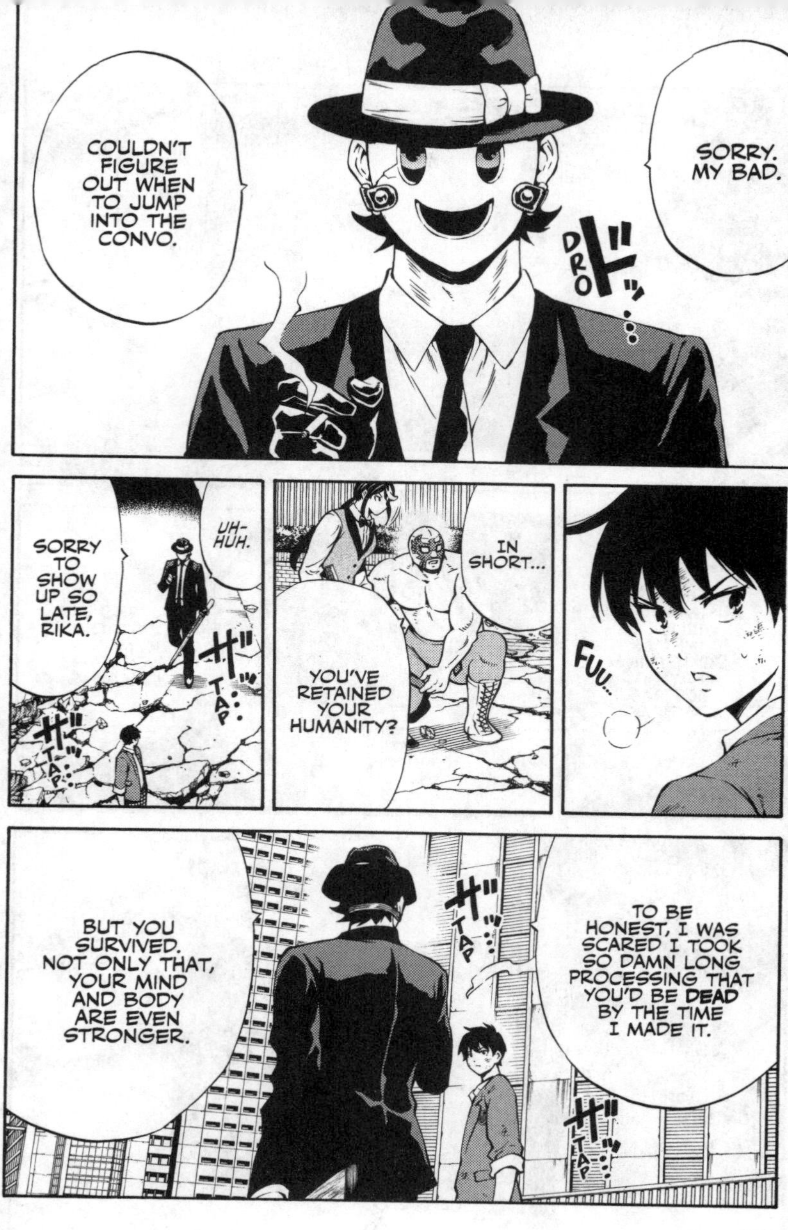
SORRY. MY BAD.
DRO
COULDN'T FIGURE OUT WHEN TO JUMP INTO THE CONVO.
FUU...
IN SHORT...
YOU'VE RETAINED YOUR HUMANITY?
UH-HUH.
SORRY TO SHOW UP SO LATE, RIKA.
TAP
TAP
TO BE HONEST, I WAS SCARED I TOOK SO DAMN LONG PROCESSING THAT YOU'D BE **DEAD** BY THE TIME I MADE IT.
TAP
TAP
BUT YOU SURVIVED. NOT ONLY THAT, YOUR MIND AND BODY ARE EVEN STRONGER.

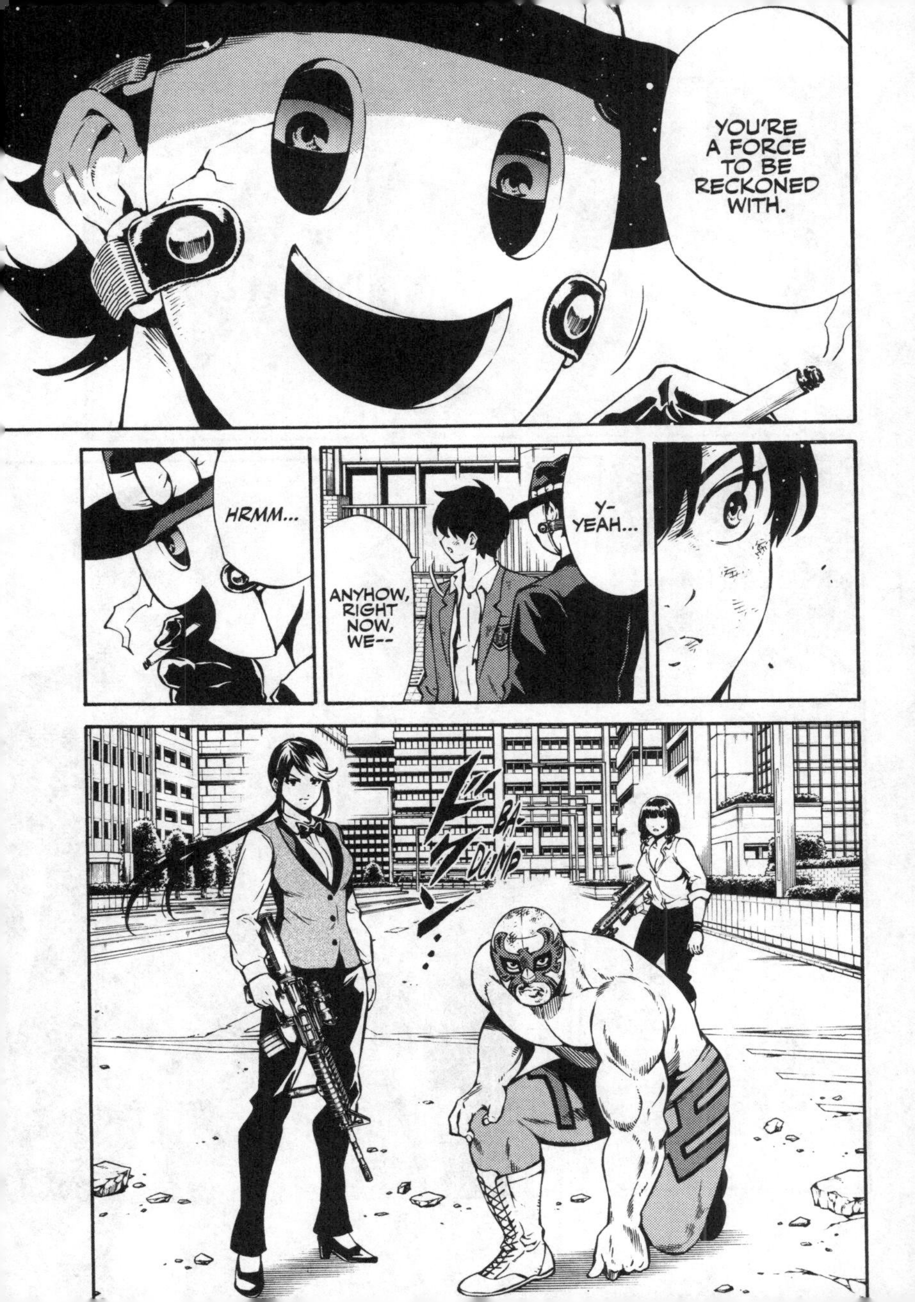
YOU'RE A FORCE TO BE RECKONED WITH.
Y-YEAH...
ANYHOW, RIGHT NOW, WE--
HRMM...
BA-DUMP

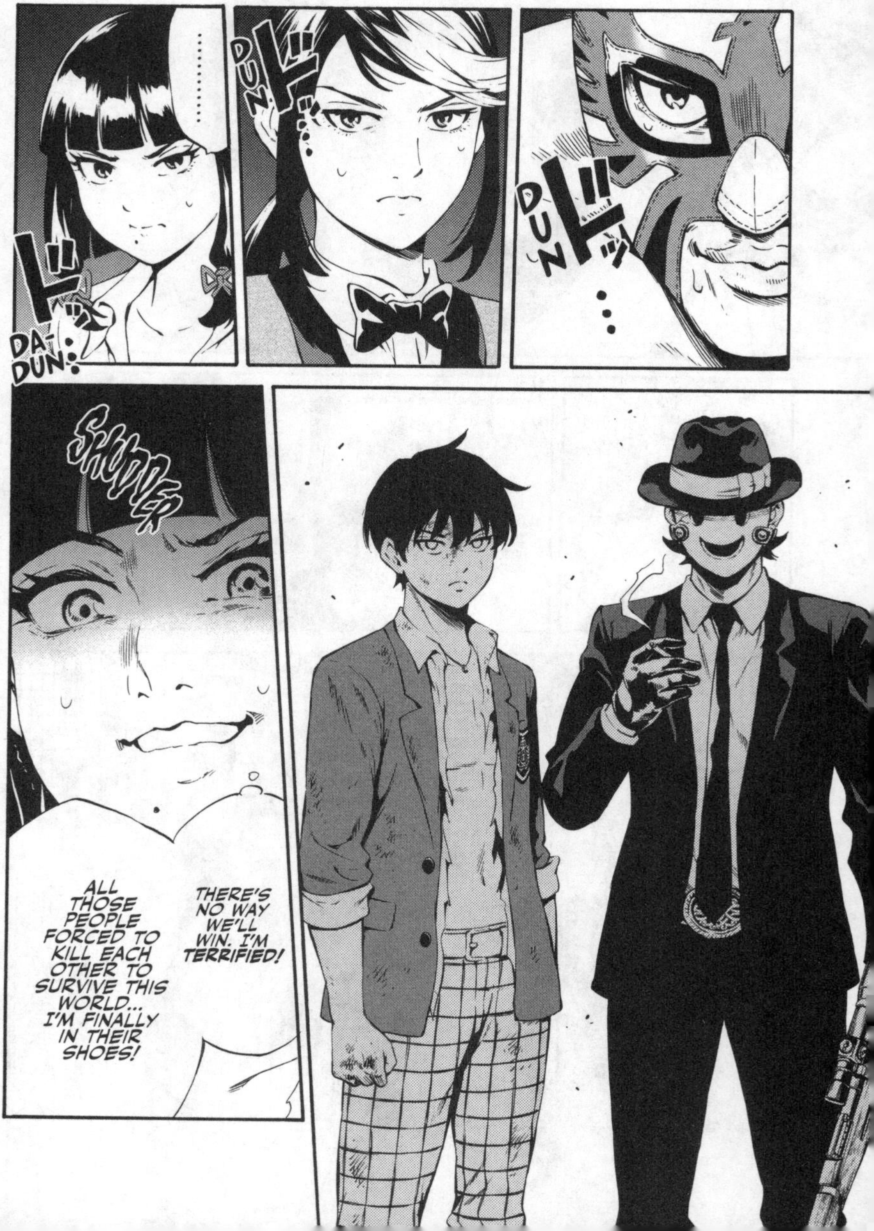
DUN DUN
...
DUN DUN
......
DA-DUN!
SHUDDER
THERE'S NO WAY WE'LL WIN. I'M TERRIFIED!
ALL THOSE PEOPLE FORCED TO KILL EACH OTHER TO SURVIVE THIS WORLD... I'M FINALLY IN THEIR SHOES!

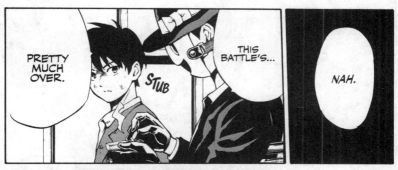

NAH.
THIS BATTLE'S...
STUB
PRETTY MUCH OVER.
GETTING THAT GOD CODE GAVE ME--*US*--NEW ABILITIES.
I'M GONNA USE ONE RIGHT NOW.
!
BA-DUMP!
WHAT DOES HE MEAN?!
WOBBLE
IS HE GOING TO KILL US ALL AT ONCE?!
NAMELY...

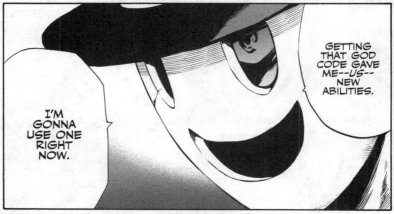

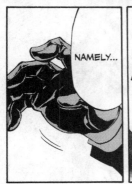

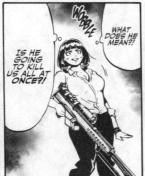

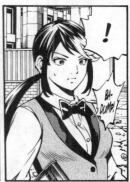

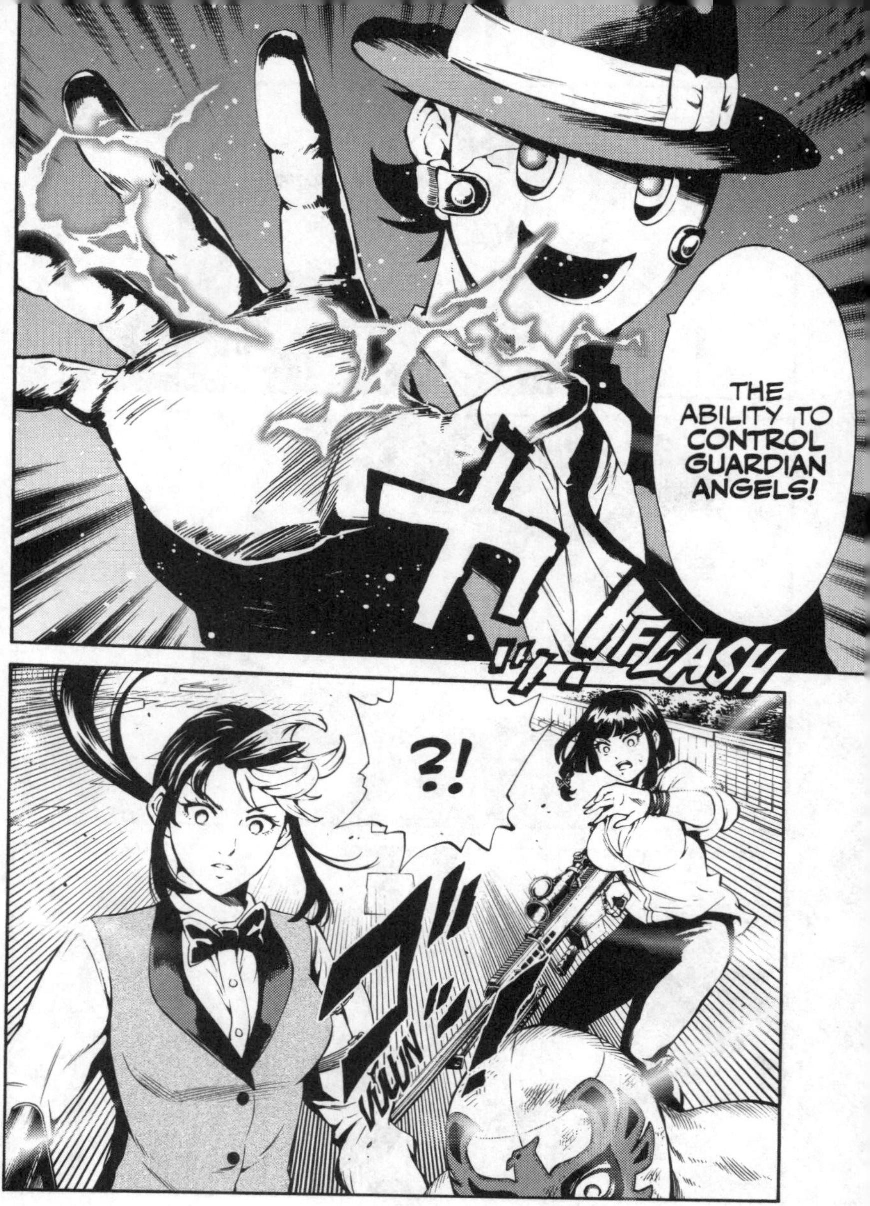
THE ABILITY TO CONTROL GUARDIAN ANGELS!
FLASH
?!
VWUN

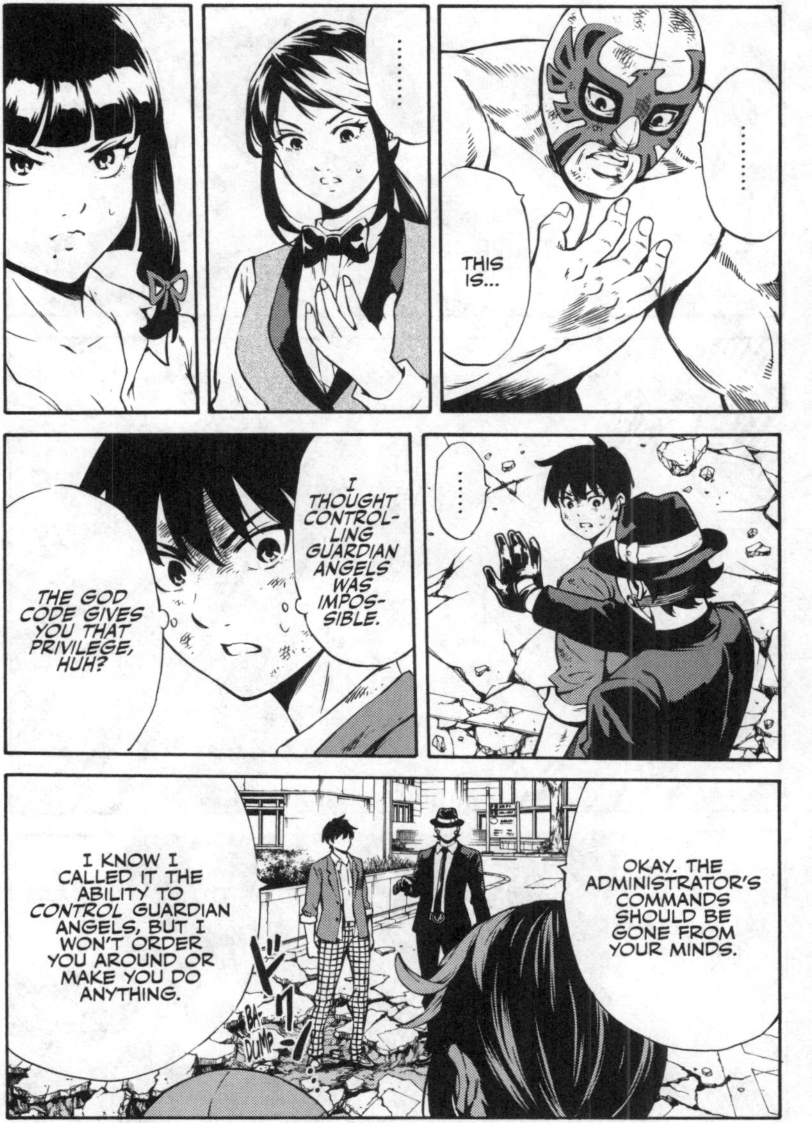
……
THIS IS...
……
……
I THOUGHT CONTROL-LING GUARDIAN ANGELS WAS IMPOS-SIBLE.
THE GOD CODE GIVES YOU THAT PRIVILEGE, HUH?
OKAY. THE ADMINISTRATOR'S COMMANDS SHOULD BE GONE FROM YOUR MINDS.
I KNOW I CALLED IT THE ABILITY TO *CONTROL* GUARDIAN ANGELS, BUT I WON'T ORDER YOU AROUND OR MAKE YOU DO ANYTHING.
BA-DUMP

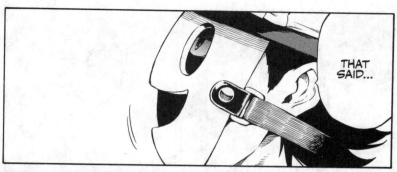

THAT SAID...

I'M GONNA GET YOU TO WORK *WITH* ME...

TO STOP THE ADMINISTRATOR'S COUP.

THE ADMINISTRATOR'S...

BA-DUMP

HUH?

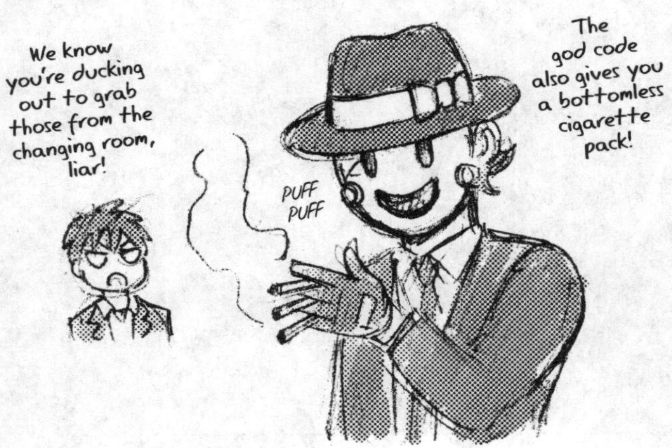
The god code also gives you a bottomless cigarette pack!
PUFF PUFF
We know you're ducking out to grab those from the changing room, liar!

HIGH-RISE INVASION

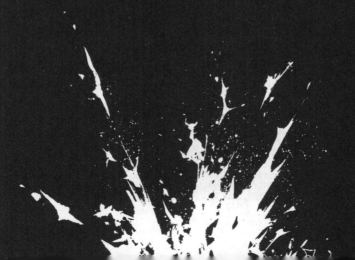

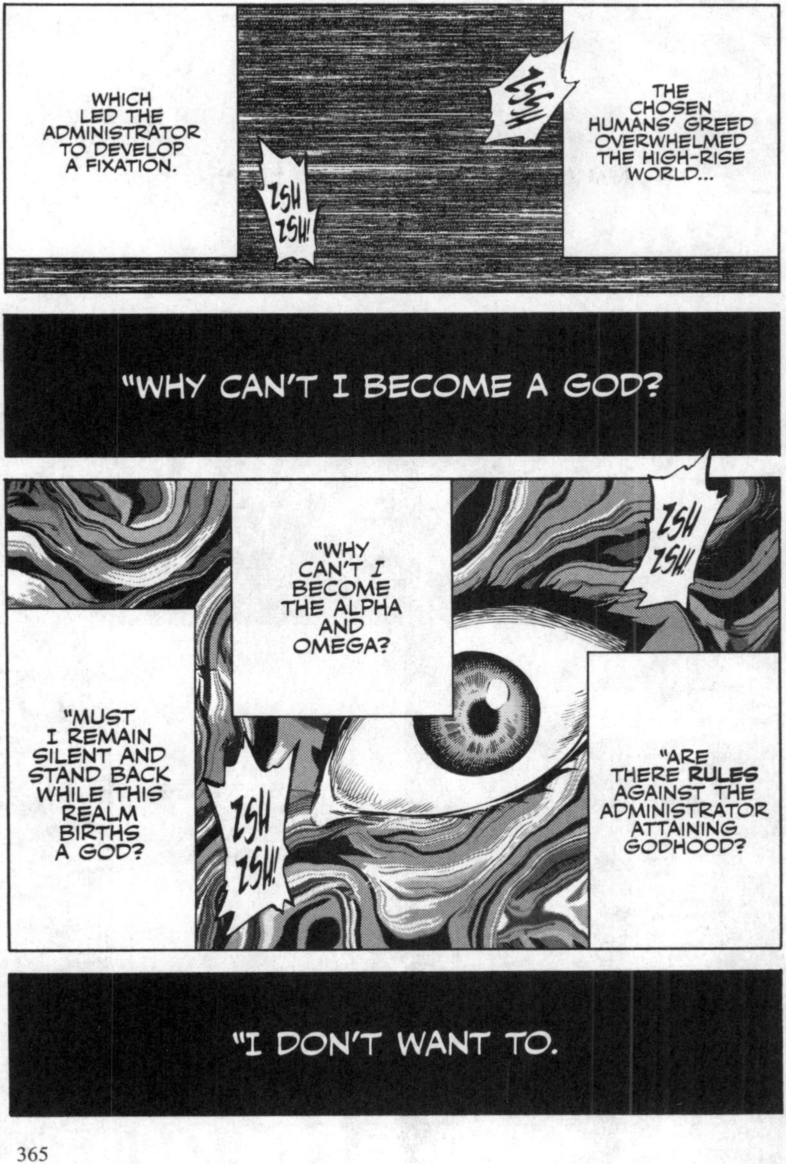
THE CHOSEN HUMANS' GREED OVERWHELMED THE HIGH-RISE WORLD...
ZSSH
ZSH ZSH!
WHICH LED THE ADMINISTRATOR TO DEVELOP A FIXATION.
"WHY CAN'T I BECOME A GOD?
ZSH ZSH!
"WHY CAN'T *I* BECOME THE ALPHA AND OMEGA?
"ARE THERE **RULES** AGAINST THE ADMINISTRATOR ATTAINING GODHOOD?
"MUST I REMAIN SILENT AND STAND BACK WHILE THIS REALM BIRTHS A GOD?
ZSH ZSH!
"I DON'T WANT TO.

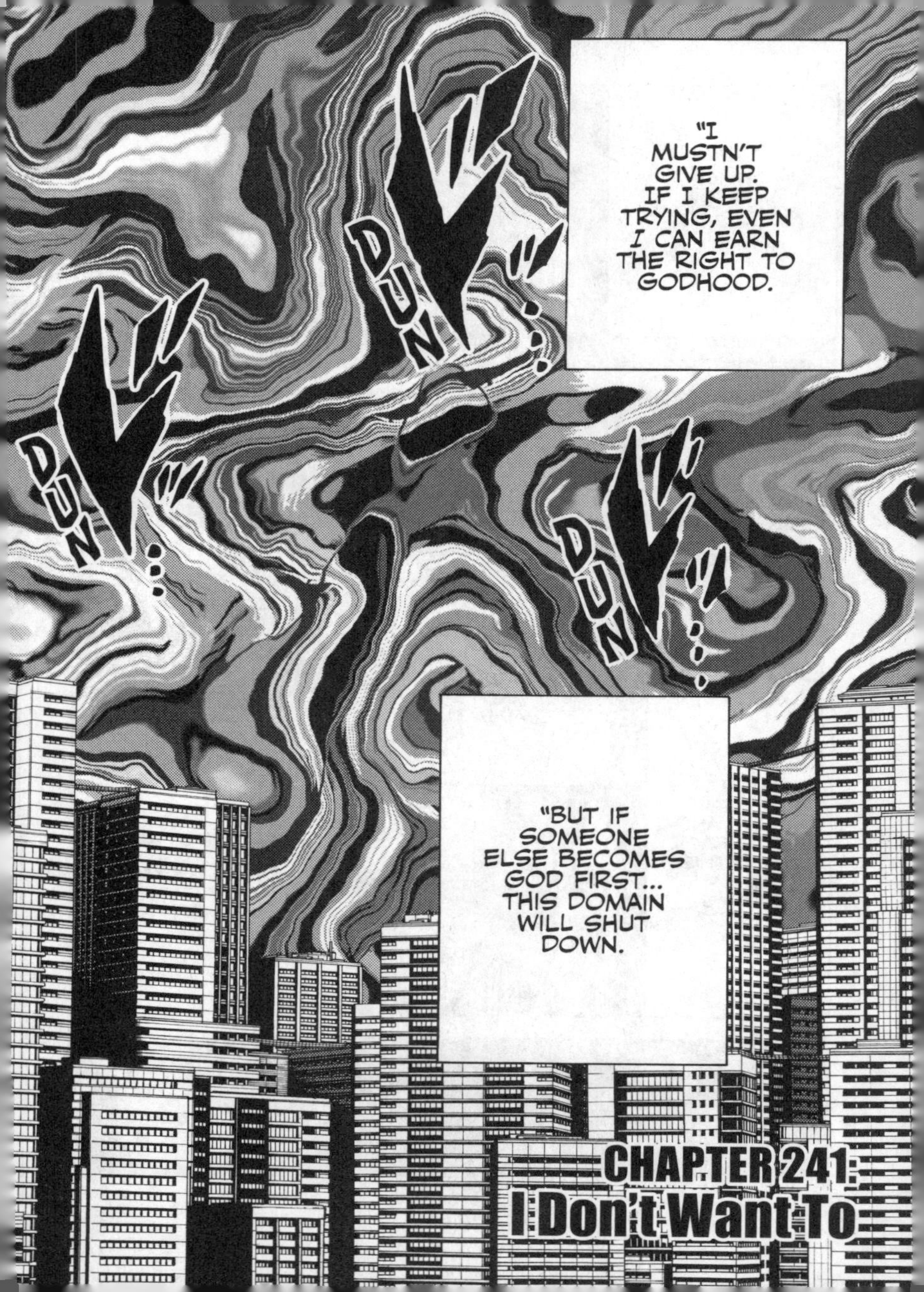
"I MUSTN'T GIVE UP. IF I KEEP TRYING, EVEN I CAN EARN THE RIGHT TO GODHOOD.
DUN...
DUN...
DUN...
"BUT IF SOMEONE ELSE BECOMES GOD FIRST... THIS DOMAIN WILL SHUT DOWN.
CHAPTER 241:
I Don't Want To

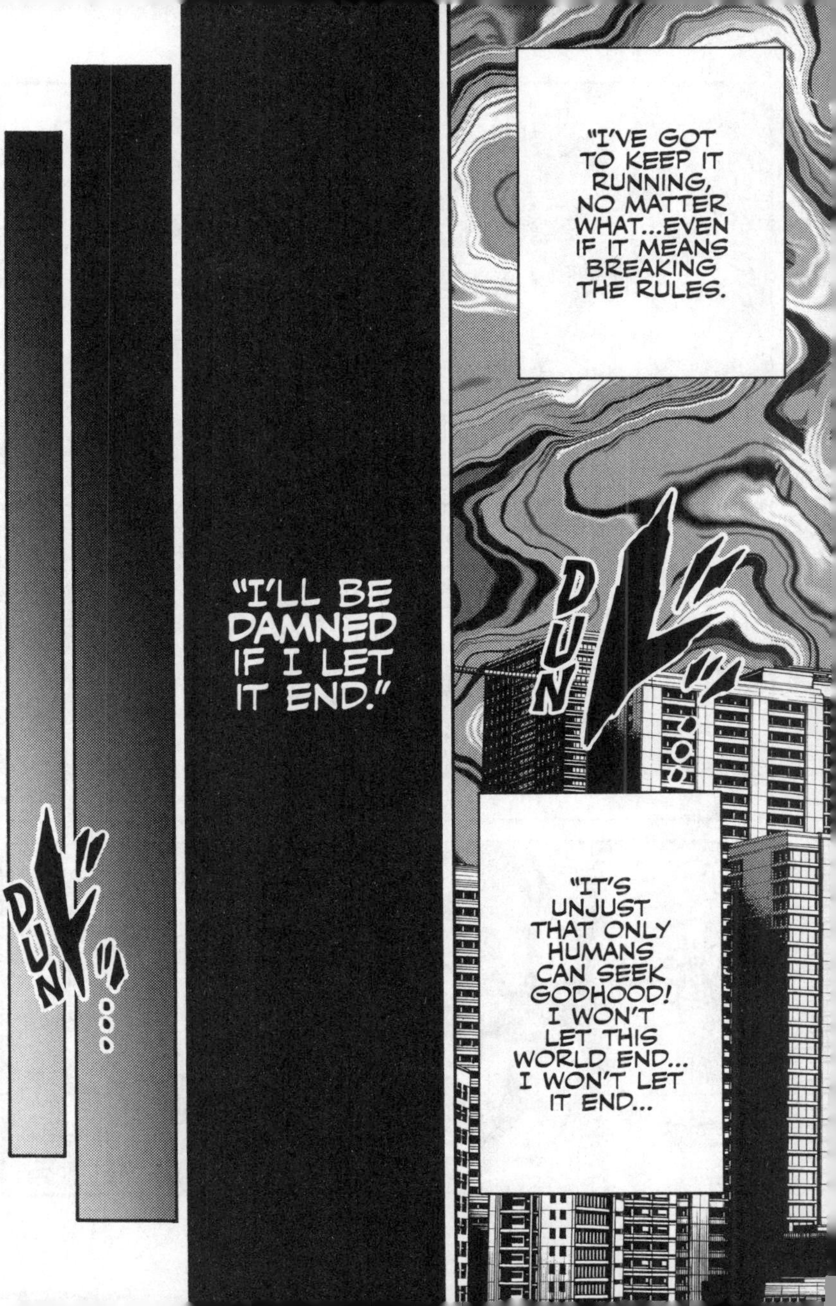
"I'VE GOT TO KEEP IT RUNNING, NO MATTER WHAT...EVEN IF IT MEANS BREAKING THE RULES.
DUN
"IT'S UNJUST THAT ONLY HUMANS CAN SEEK GODHOOD! I WON'T LET THIS WORLD END... I WON'T LET IT END...
"I'LL BE DAMNED IF I LET IT END."
DUN

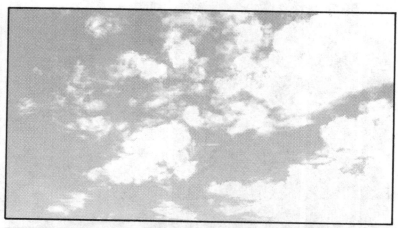

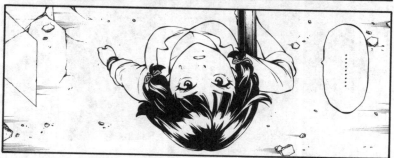

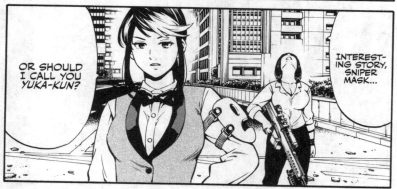

......
INTEREST-ING STORY, SNIPER MASK...
OR SHOULD I CALL YOU YUKA-KUN?

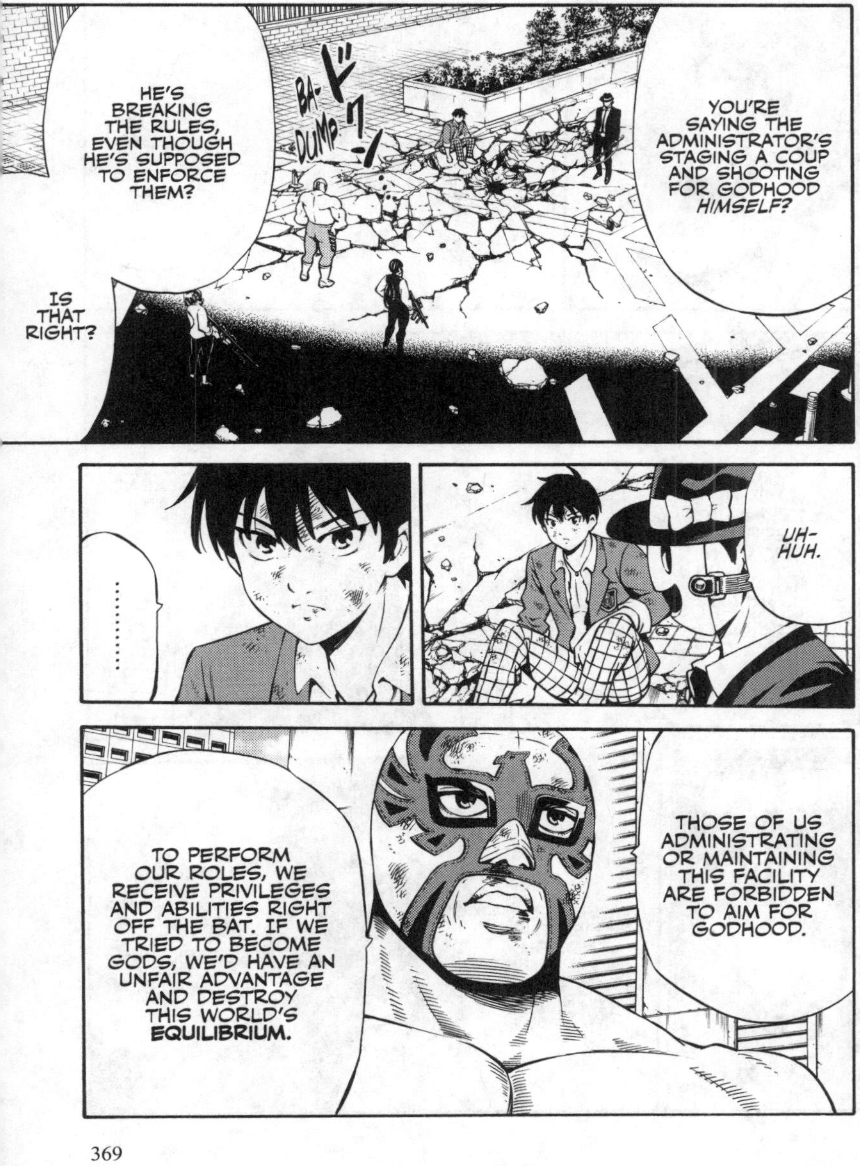
YOU'RE SAYING THE ADMINISTRATOR'S STAGING A COUP AND SHOOTING FOR GODHOOD *HIMSELF?*
BA-DUMP
HE'S BREAKING THE RULES, EVEN THOUGH HE'S SUPPOSED TO ENFORCE THEM?
IS THAT RIGHT?
UH-HUH.
....
THOSE OF US ADMINISTRATING OR MAINTAINING THIS FACILITY ARE FORBIDDEN TO AIM FOR GODHOOD.
TO PERFORM OUR ROLES, WE RECEIVE PRIVILEGES AND ABILITIES RIGHT OFF THE BAT. IF WE TRIED TO BECOME GODS, WE'D HAVE AN UNFAIR ADVANTAGE AND DESTROY THIS WORLD'S **EQUILIBRIUM.**

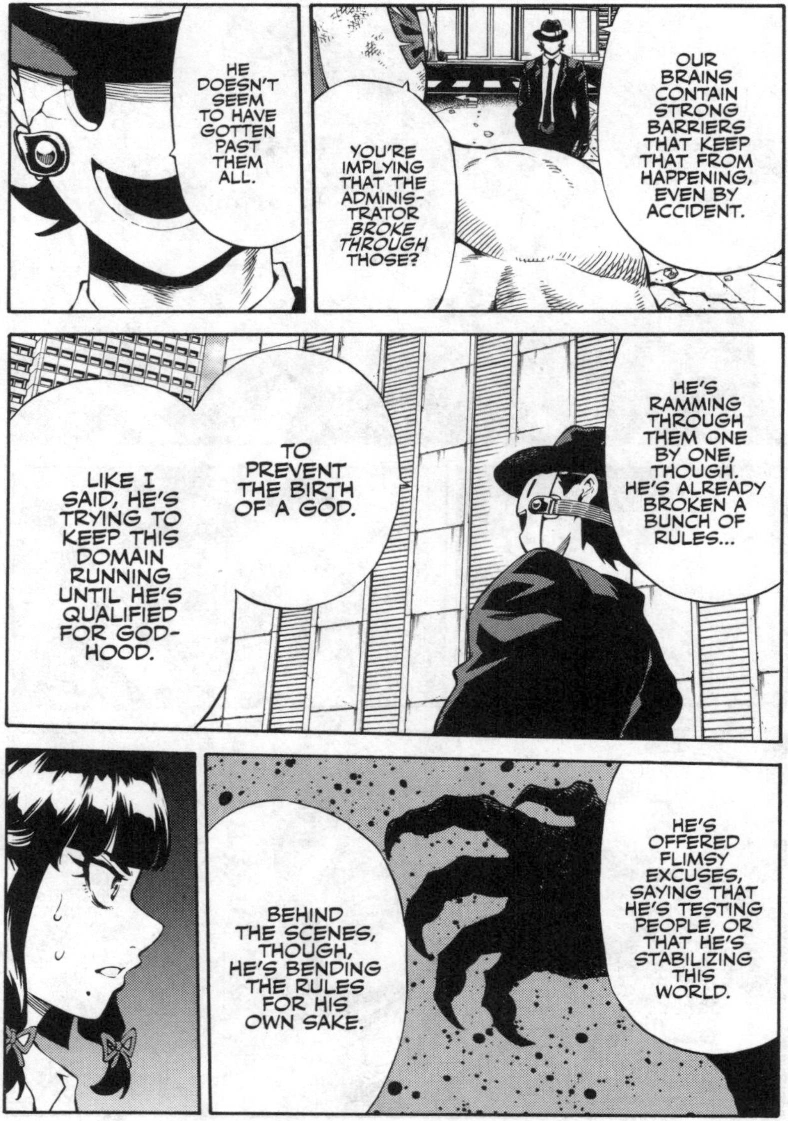
OUR BRAINS CONTAIN STRONG BARRIERS THAT KEEP THAT FROM HAPPENING, EVEN BY ACCIDENT.
YOU'RE IMPLYING THAT THE ADMINIS-TRATOR *BROKE THROUGH* THOSE?
HE DOESN'T SEEM TO HAVE GOTTEN PAST THEM ALL.
HE'S RAMMING THROUGH THEM ONE BY ONE, THOUGH. HE'S ALREADY BROKEN A BUNCH OF RULES...
TO PREVENT THE BIRTH OF A GOD.
LIKE I SAID, HE'S TRYING TO KEEP THIS DOMAIN RUNNING UNTIL HE'S QUALIFIED FOR GOD-HOOD.
HE'S OFFERED FLIMSY EXCUSES, SAYING THAT HE'S TESTING PEOPLE, OR THAT HE'S STABILIZING THIS WORLD.
BEHIND THE SCENES, THOUGH, HE'S BENDING THE RULES FOR HIS OWN SAKE.

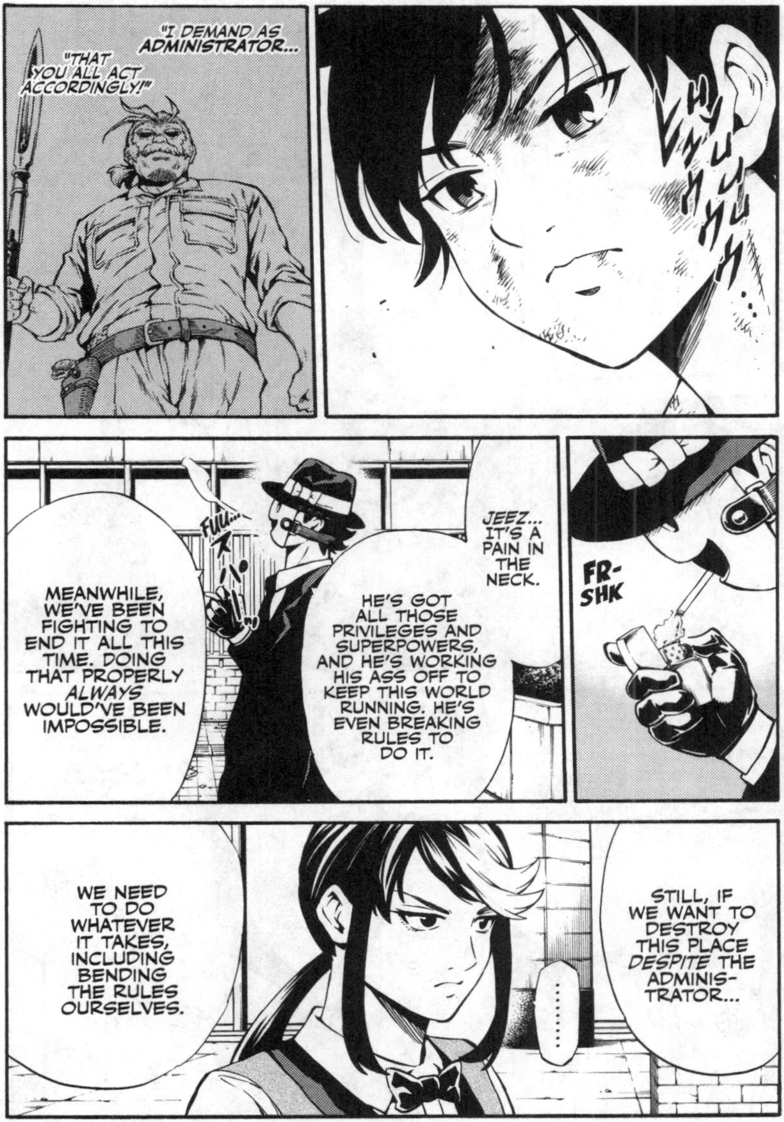
"I DEMAND AS ADMINISTRATOR...
"THAT YOU ALL ACT ACCORDINGLY!"
FR-SHK
JEEZ... IT'S A PAIN IN THE NECK.
HE'S GOT ALL THOSE PRIVILEGES AND SUPERPOWERS, AND HE'S WORKING HIS ASS OFF TO KEEP THIS WORLD RUNNING. HE'S EVEN BREAKING RULES TO DO IT.
MEANWHILE, WE'VE BEEN FIGHTING TO END IT ALL THIS TIME. DOING THAT PROPERLY *ALWAYS* WOULD'VE BEEN IMPOSSIBLE.
STILL, IF WE WANT TO DESTROY THIS PLACE *DESPITE* THE ADMINIS-TRATOR...
......
WE NEED TO DO WHATEVER IT TAKES, INCLUDING BENDING THE RULES OURSELVES.

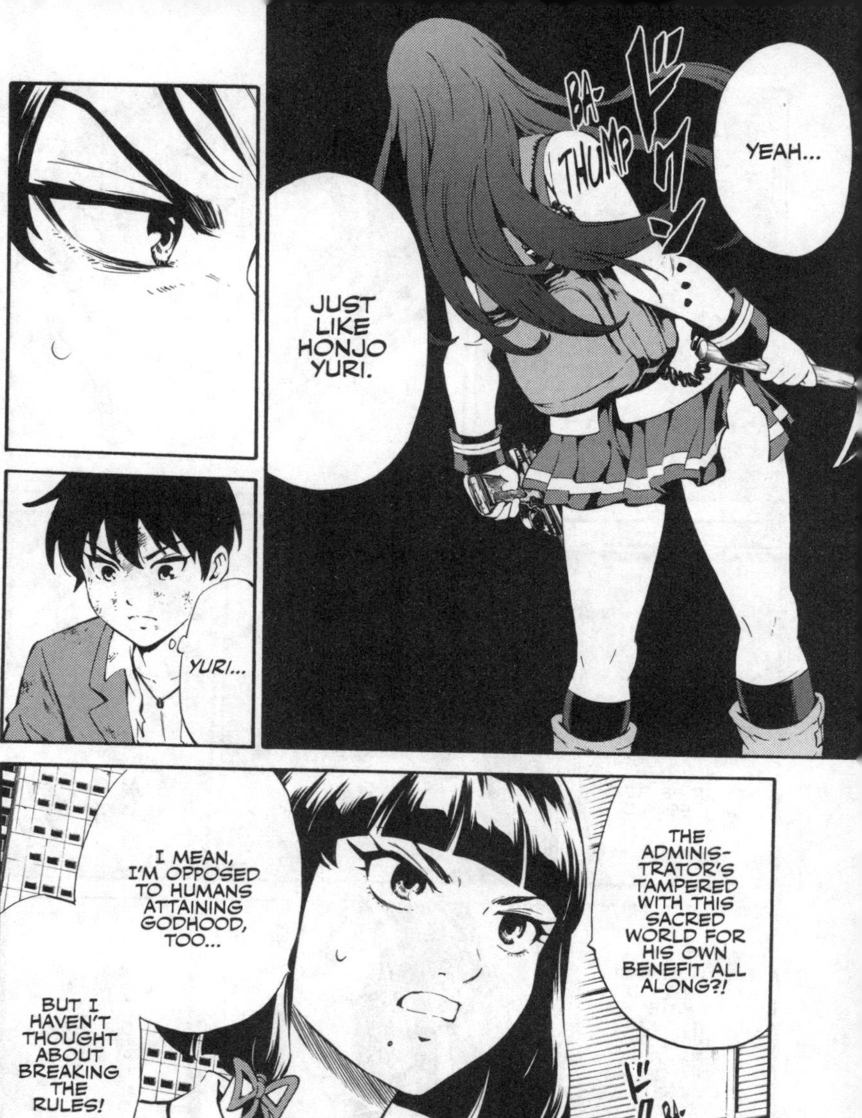
YEAH...
BA-THUMP
JUST LIKE HONJO YURI.
YURI...
THE ADMINIS-TRATOR'S TAMPERED WITH THIS SACRED WORLD FOR HIS OWN BENEFIT ALL ALONG?!
BA-DUMP
I MEAN, I'M OPPOSED TO HUMANS ATTAINING GODHOOD, TOO...
BUT I HAVEN'T THOUGHT ABOUT BREAKING THE RULES!

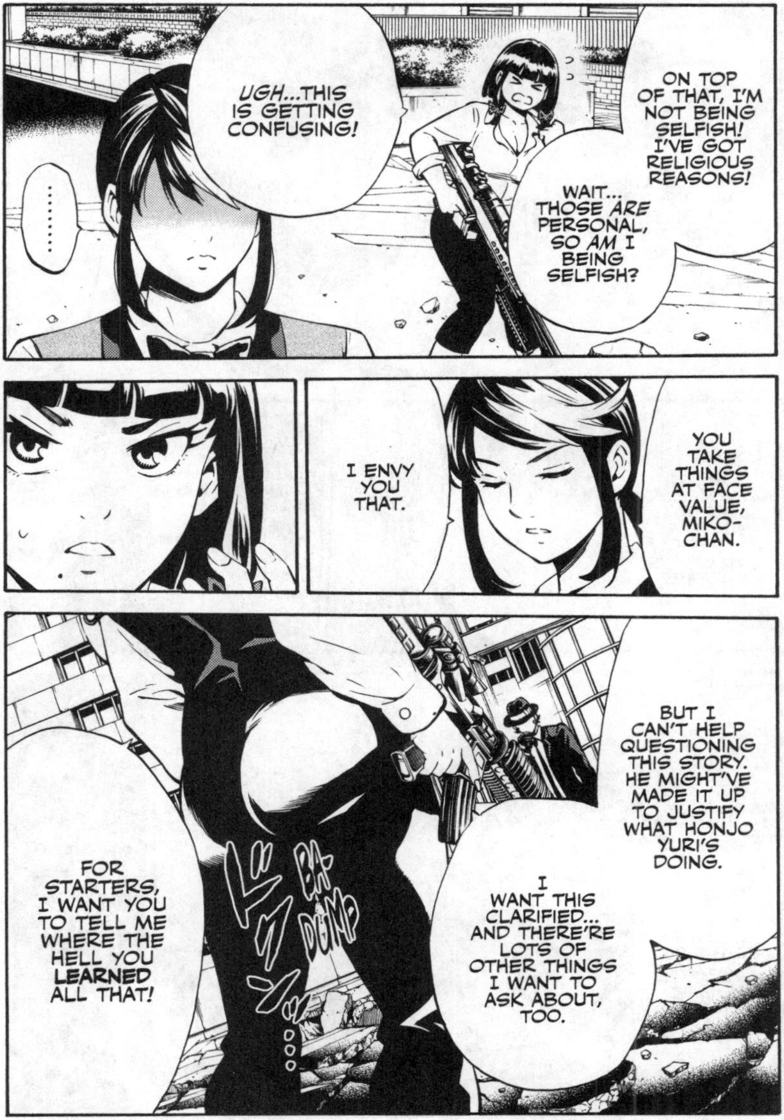
ON TOP OF THAT, I'M NOT BEING SELFISH! I'VE GOT RELIGIOUS REASONS!
UGH...THIS IS GETTING CONFUSING!
WAIT... THOSE *ARE* PERSONAL, SO *AM* I BEING SELFISH?
....
YOU TAKE THINGS AT FACE VALUE, MIKO-CHAN.
I ENVY YOU THAT.
BUT I CAN'T HELP QUESTIONING THIS STORY. HE MIGHT'VE MADE IT UP TO JUSTIFY WHAT HONJO YURI'S DOING.
I WANT THIS CLARIFIED... AND THERE'RE LOTS OF OTHER THINGS I WANT TO ASK ABOUT, TOO.
FOR STARTERS, I WANT YOU TO TELL ME WHERE THE HELL YOU **LEARNED** ALL THAT!
BA-DUMP

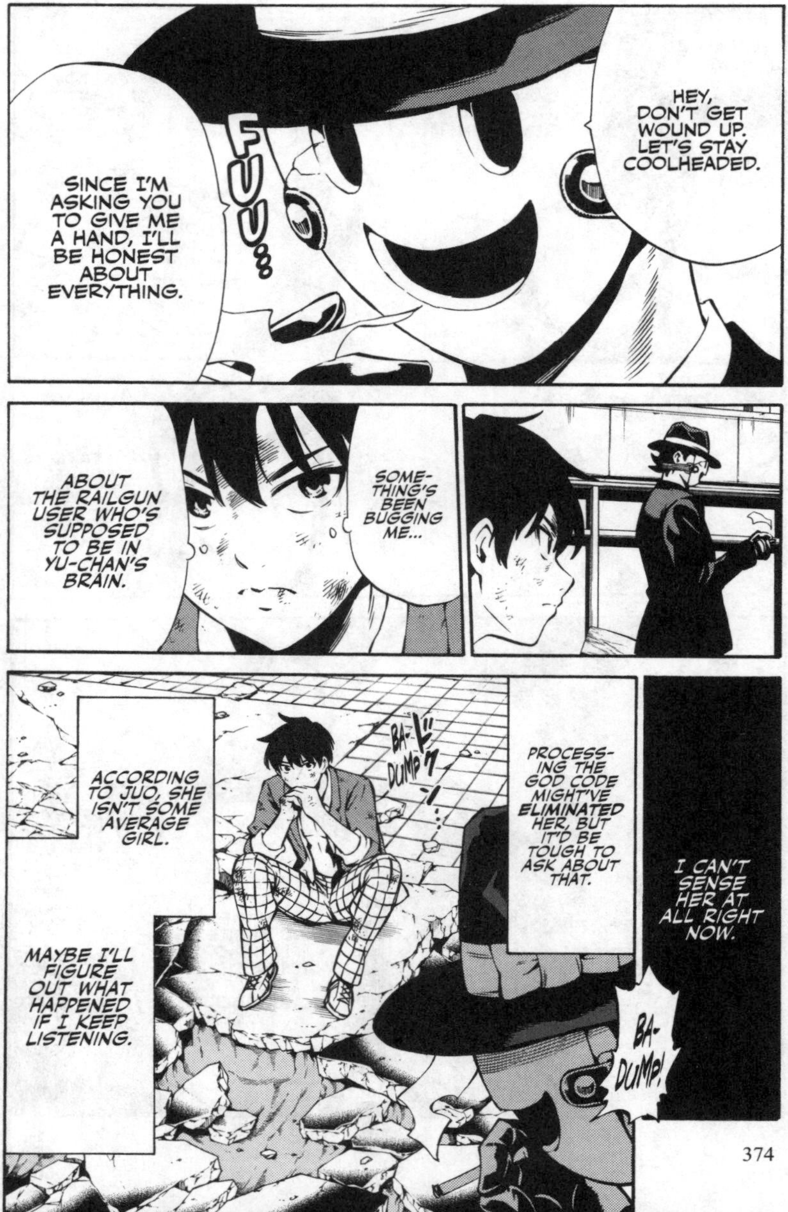
HEY, DON'T GET WOUND UP. LET'S STAY COOLHEADED.
FUUU...
SINCE I'M ASKING YOU TO GIVE ME A HAND, I'LL BE HONEST ABOUT EVERYTHING.
SOME-THING'S BEEN BUGGING ME...
ABOUT THE RAILGUN USER WHO'S SUPPOSED TO BE IN YU-CHAN'S BRAIN.
I CAN'T SENSE HER AT ALL RIGHT NOW.
PROCESS-ING THE GOD CODE MIGHT'VE ELIMINATED HER, BUT IT'D BE TOUGH TO ASK ABOUT THAT.
BA-DUMP!
BA-DUMP
ACCORDING TO JUO, SHE ISN'T SOME AVERAGE GIRL.
MAYBE I'LL FIGURE OUT WHAT HAPPENED IF I KEEP LISTENING.

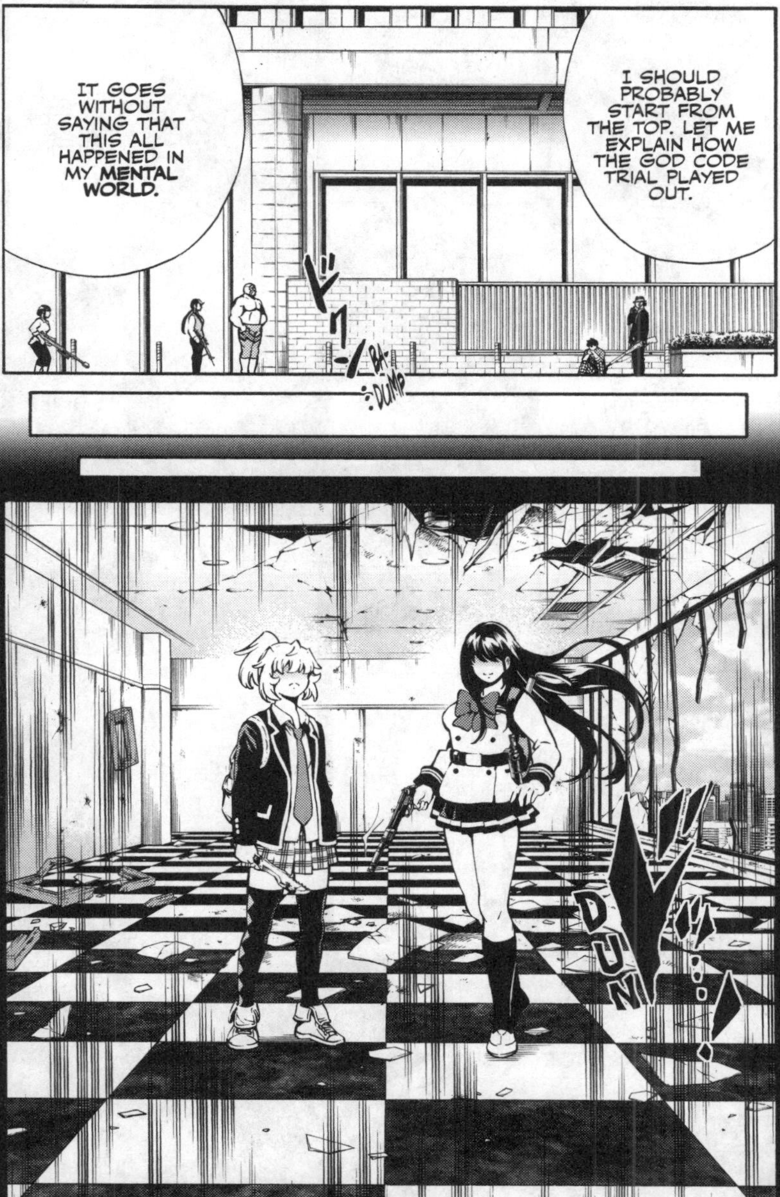
I SHOULD PROBABLY START FROM THE TOP. LET ME EXPLAIN HOW THE GOD CODE TRIAL PLAYED OUT.
IT GOES WITHOUT SAYING THAT THIS ALL HAPPENED IN MY MENTAL WORLD.
BA-DUMP
DUN...!

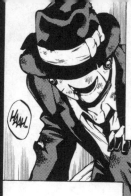

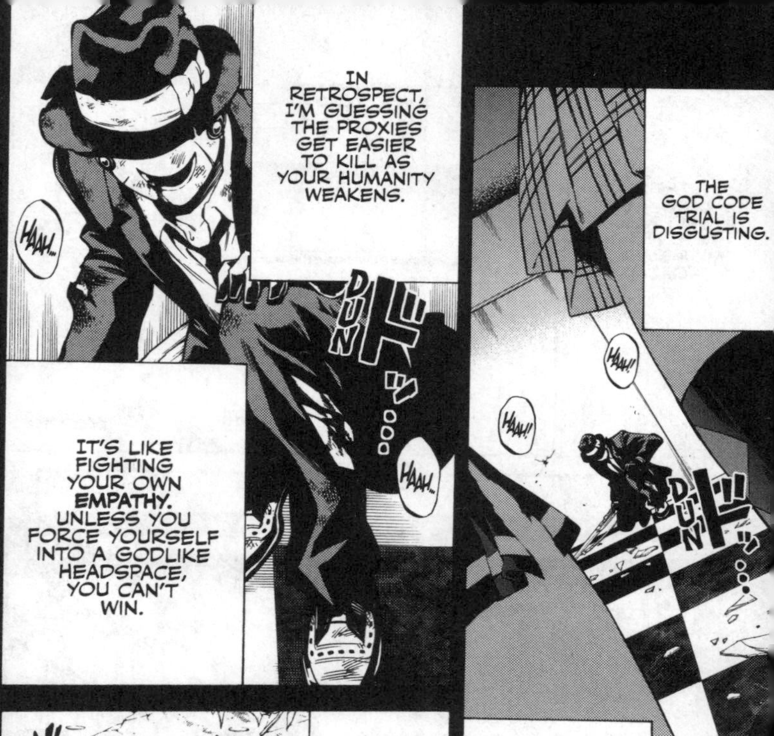

THE GOD CODE TRIAL IS DISGUSTING.
HAAH!!
HAAH!!
DUN
IT WIPES OUT YOUR HUMANITY BY MAKING YOU MURDER PROXIES OF PEOPLE YOU KNOW.
DUN
IN RETROSPECT, I'M GUESSING THE PROXIES GET EASIER TO KILL AS YOUR HUMANITY WEAKENS.
HAAH...
DUN
HAAH...
IT'S LIKE FIGHTING YOUR OWN EMPATHY. UNLESS YOU FORCE YOURSELF INTO A GODLIKE HEADSPACE, YOU CAN'T WIN.
I WAS HAVING A ROUGH TIME, BUT I COULDN'T ADMIT DEFEAT IN MY MENTAL WORLD.
KLIK
TMP
I DID WHAT I COULD TO GET PAST THE TRIAL...

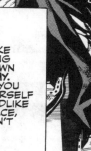

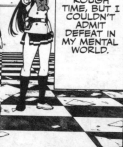

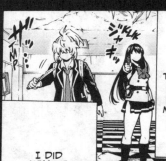

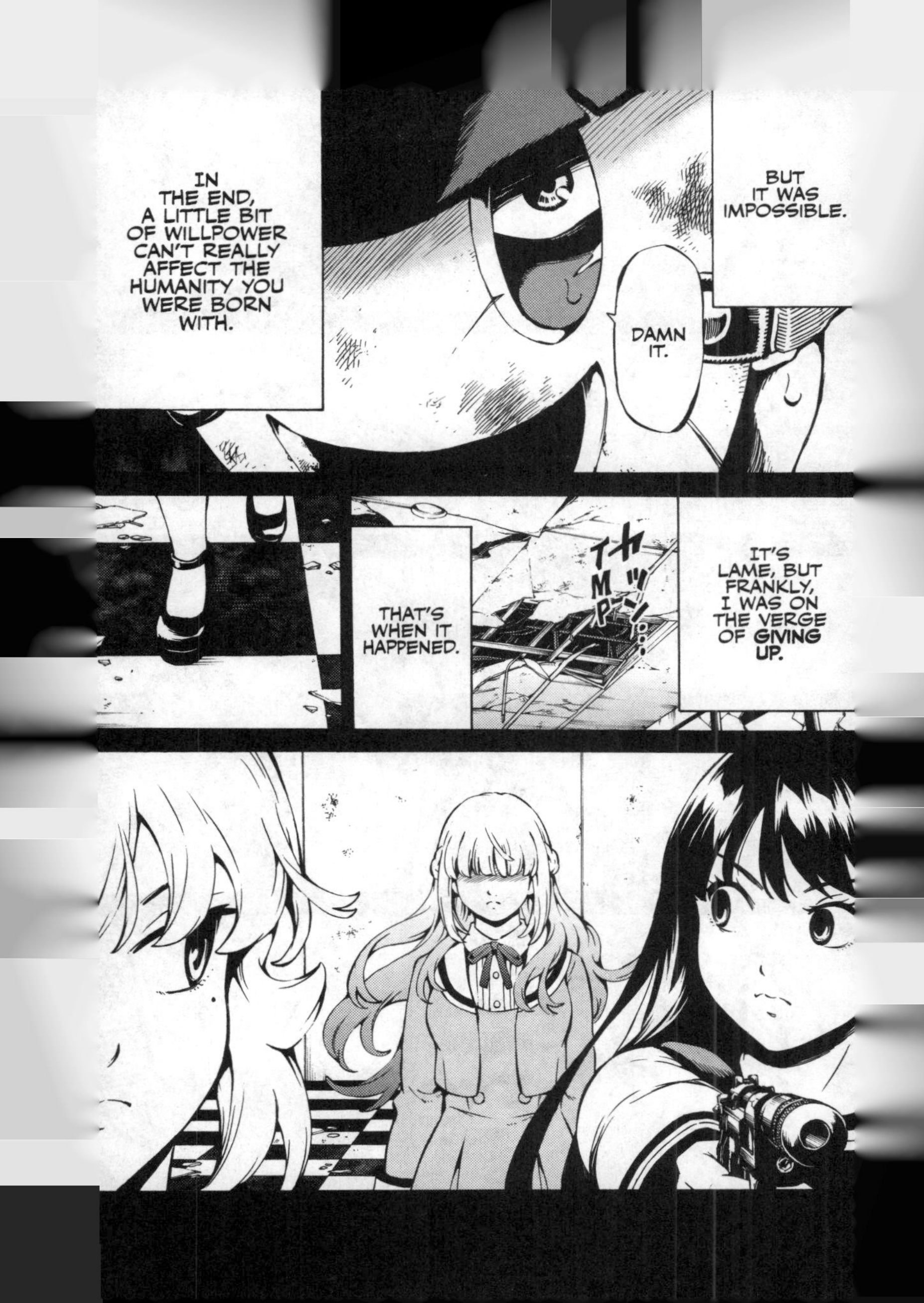
BUT IT WAS IMPOSSIBLE.
DAMN IT.
IN THE END, A LITTLE BIT OF WILLPOWER CAN'T REALLY AFFECT THE HUMANITY YOU WERE BORN WITH.
IT'S LAME, BUT FRANKLY, I WAS ON THE VERGE OF **GIVING UP.**
TMP
THAT'S WHEN IT HAPPENED.

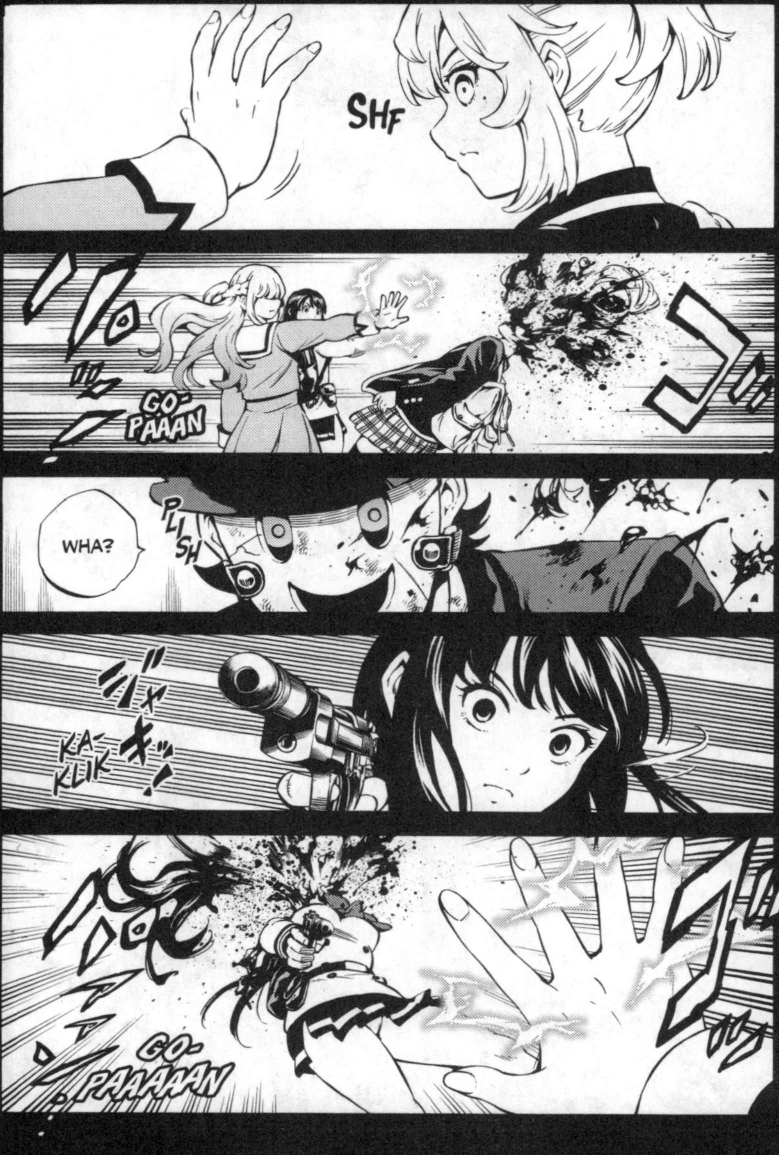
SHF
GO-PAAAN
PLISH
WHA?
KA-KLIK
GO-PAAAAAN

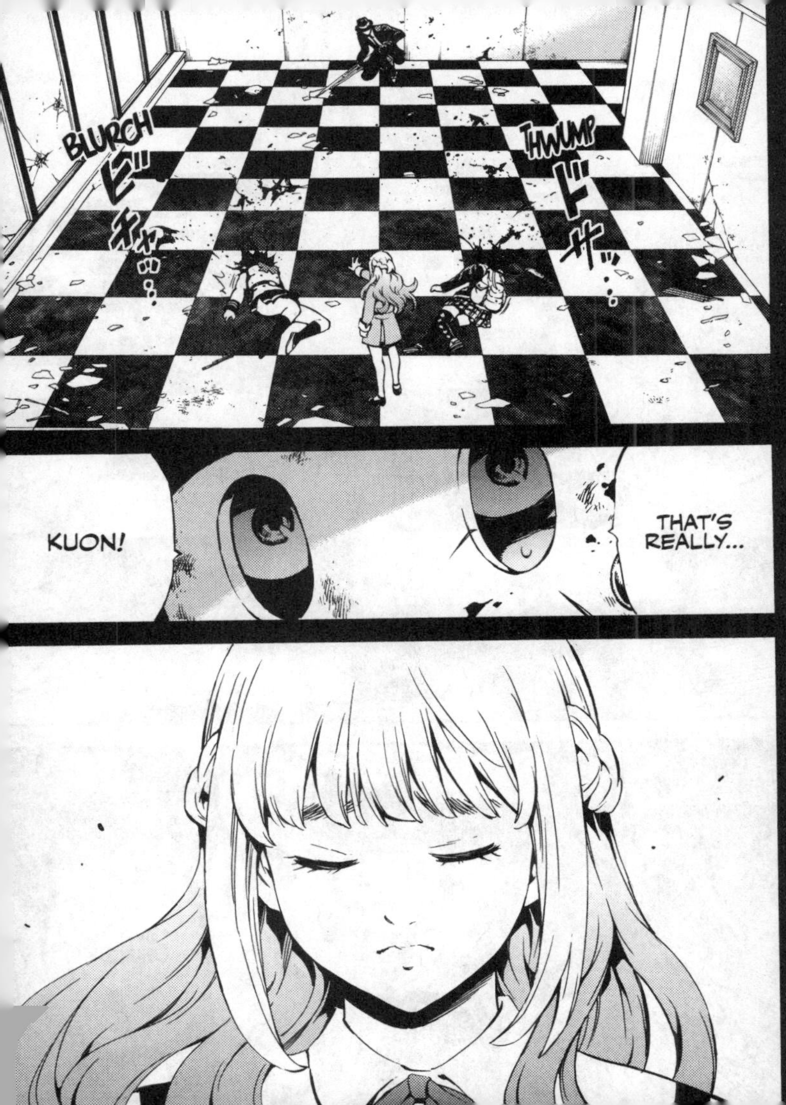
THWUMP
ドサッ
BLURCH
ビチャッ
THAT'S REALLY...
KUON!

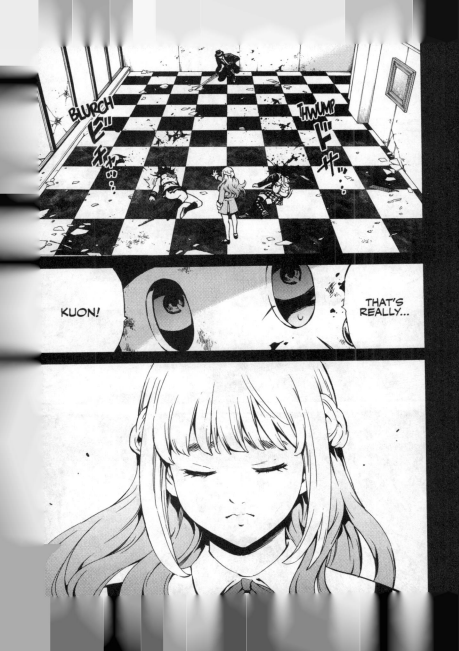

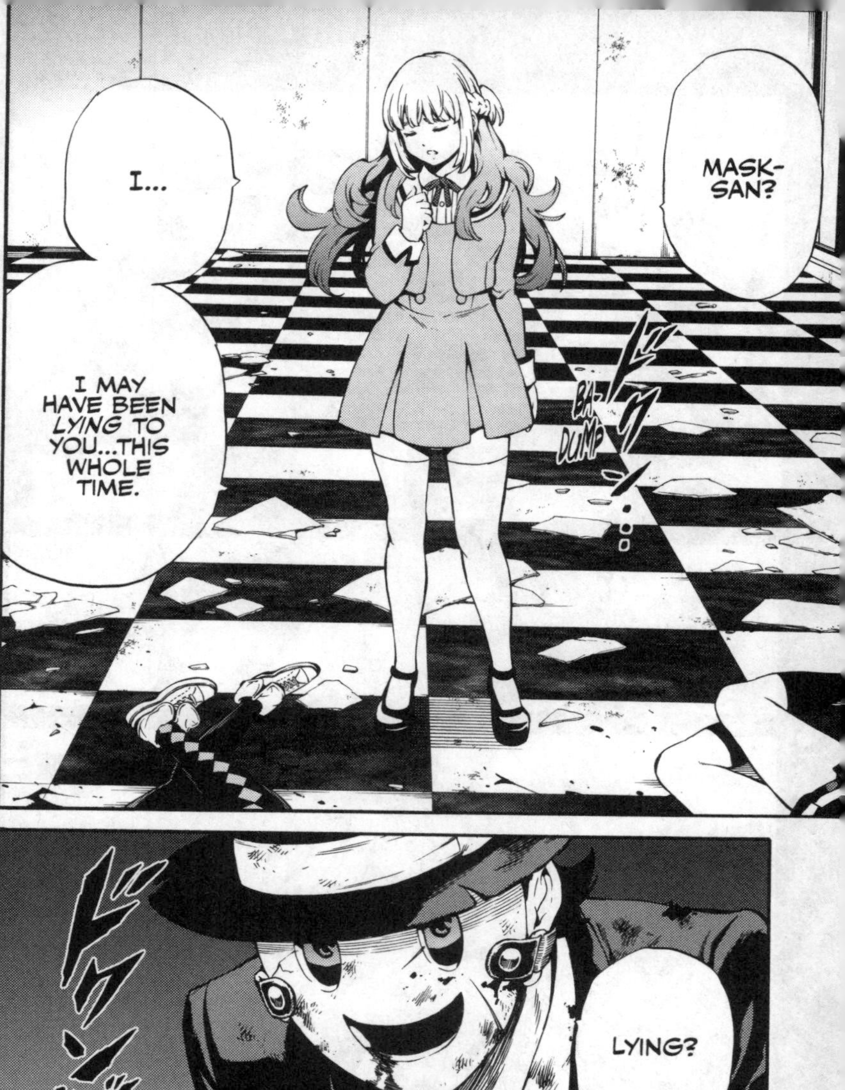
MASK-SAN?
BA-DUMP
I...
I MAY HAVE BEEN *LYING* TO YOU...THIS WHOLE TIME.
LYING?
BA-DUMP

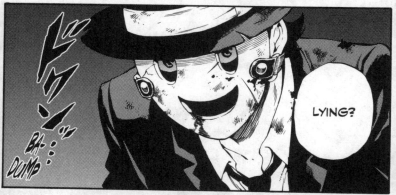

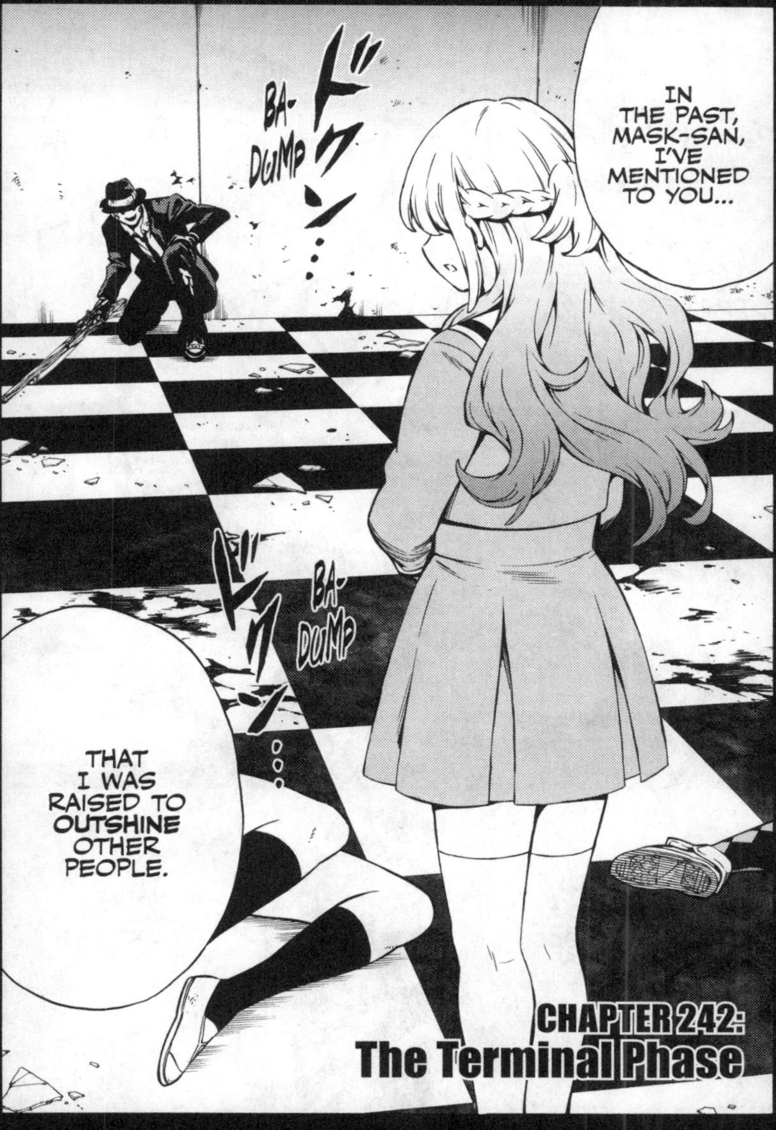

CHAPTER 242:
The Terminal Phase

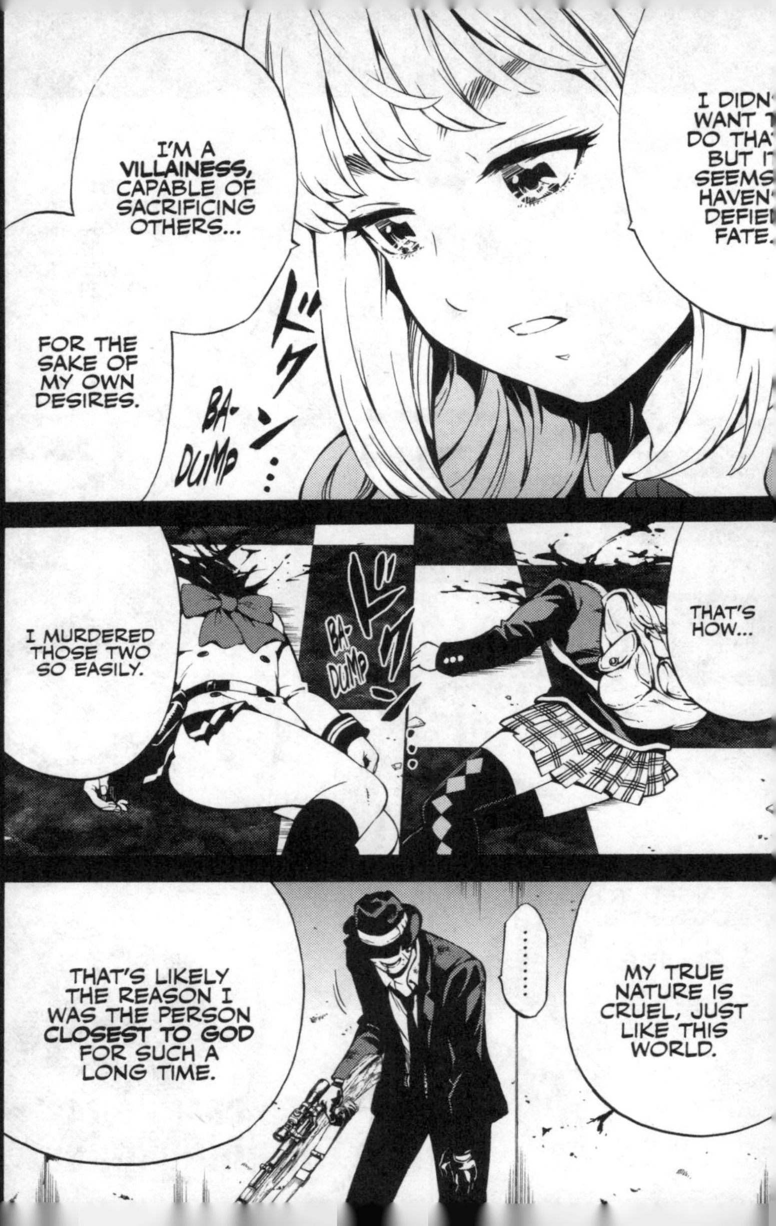
I DIDN
WANT T
DO THA
BUT IT
SEEMS
HAVEN
DEFIED
FATE.
I'M A VILLAINESS, CAPABLE OF SACRIFICING OTHERS...
FOR THE SAKE OF MY OWN DESIRES.
BA-DUMP
THAT'S HOW...
BA-DUMP
I MURDERED THOSE TWO SO EASILY.
MY TRUE NATURE IS CRUEL, JUST LIKE THIS WORLD.
......
THAT'S LIKELY THE REASON I WAS THE PERSON CLOSEST TO GOD FOR SUCH A LONG TIME.

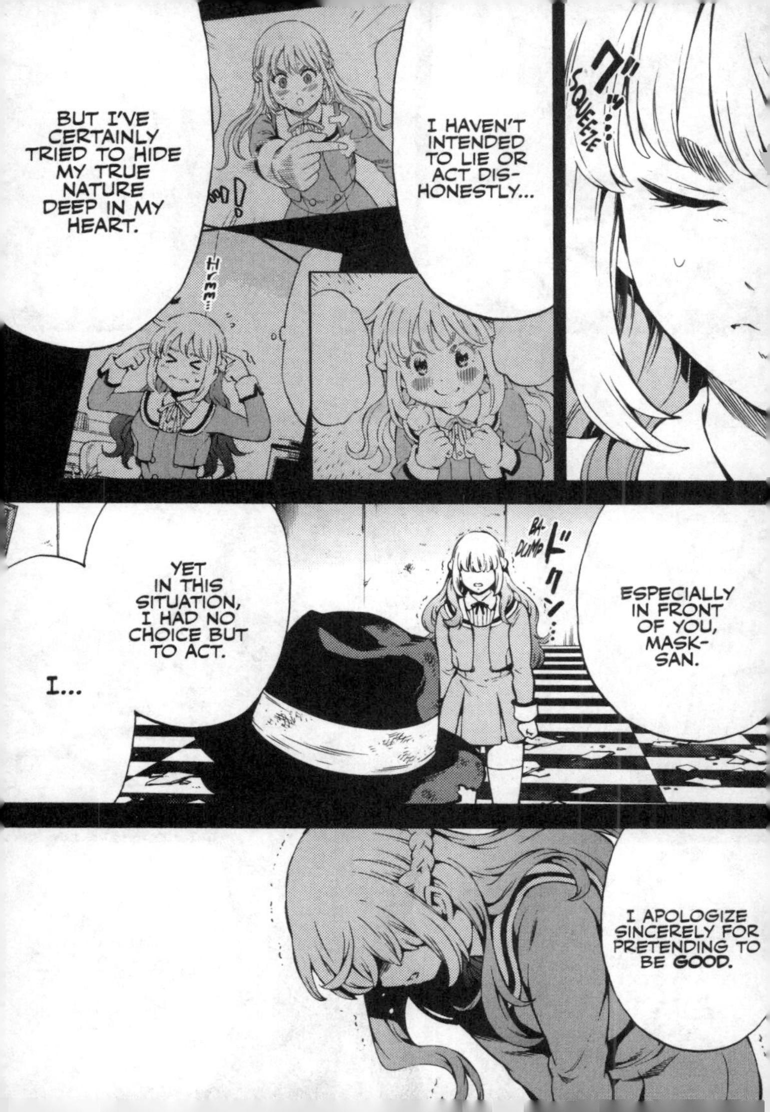
SQUEEZE
I HAVEN'T INTENDED TO LIE OR ACT DIS-HONESTLY...
BUT I'VE CERTAINLY TRIED TO HIDE MY TRUE NATURE DEEP IN MY HEART.
Hrmm...
ESPECIALLY IN FRONT OF YOU, MASK-SAN.
BA-DUMP
YET IN THIS SITUATION, I HAD NO CHOICE BUT TO ACT.
I...
I APOLOGIZE SINCERELY FOR PRETENDING TO BE **GOOD.**

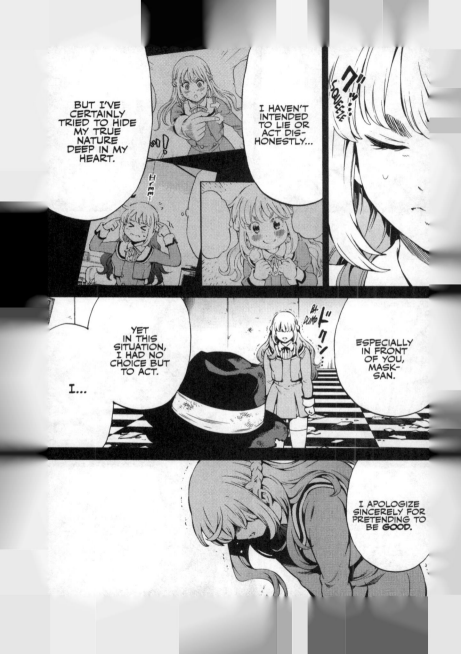

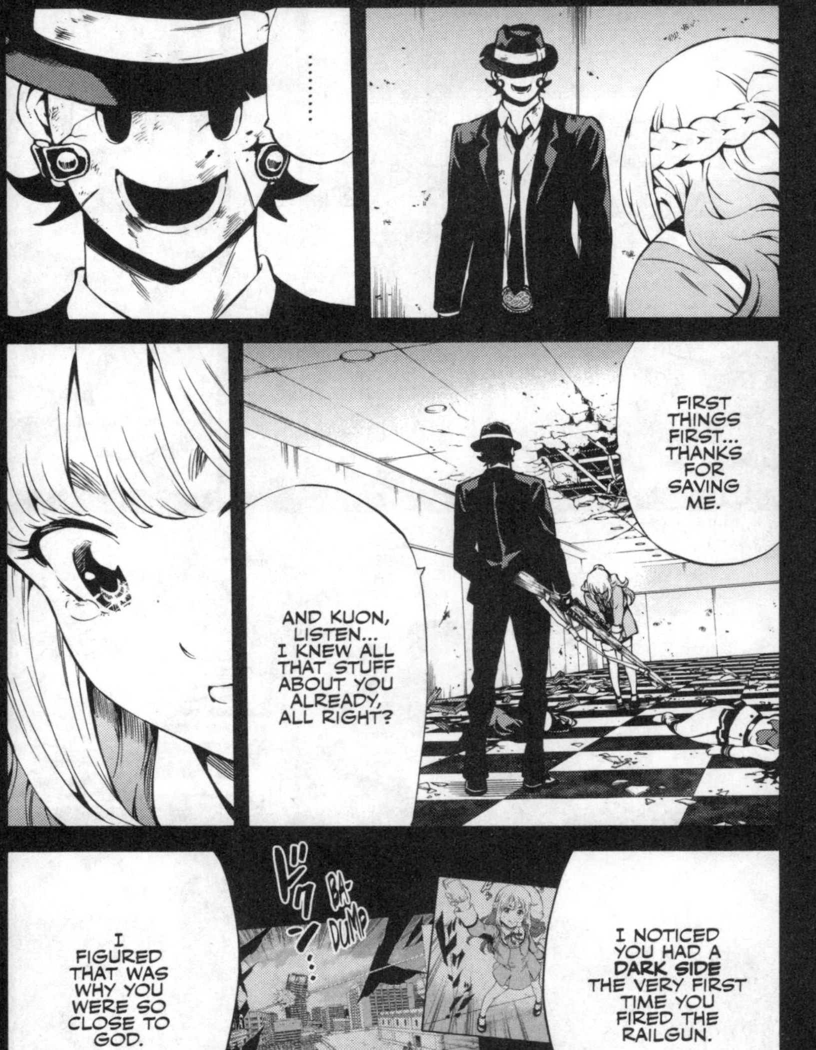
......
FIRST THINGS FIRST... THANKS FOR SAVING ME.
AND KUON, LISTEN... I KNEW ALL THAT STUFF ABOUT YOU ALREADY, ALL RIGHT?
I NOTICED YOU HAD A **DARK SIDE** THE VERY FIRST TIME YOU FIRED THE RAILGUN.
BA-DUMP
I FIGURED THAT WAS WHY YOU WERE SO CLOSE TO GOD.

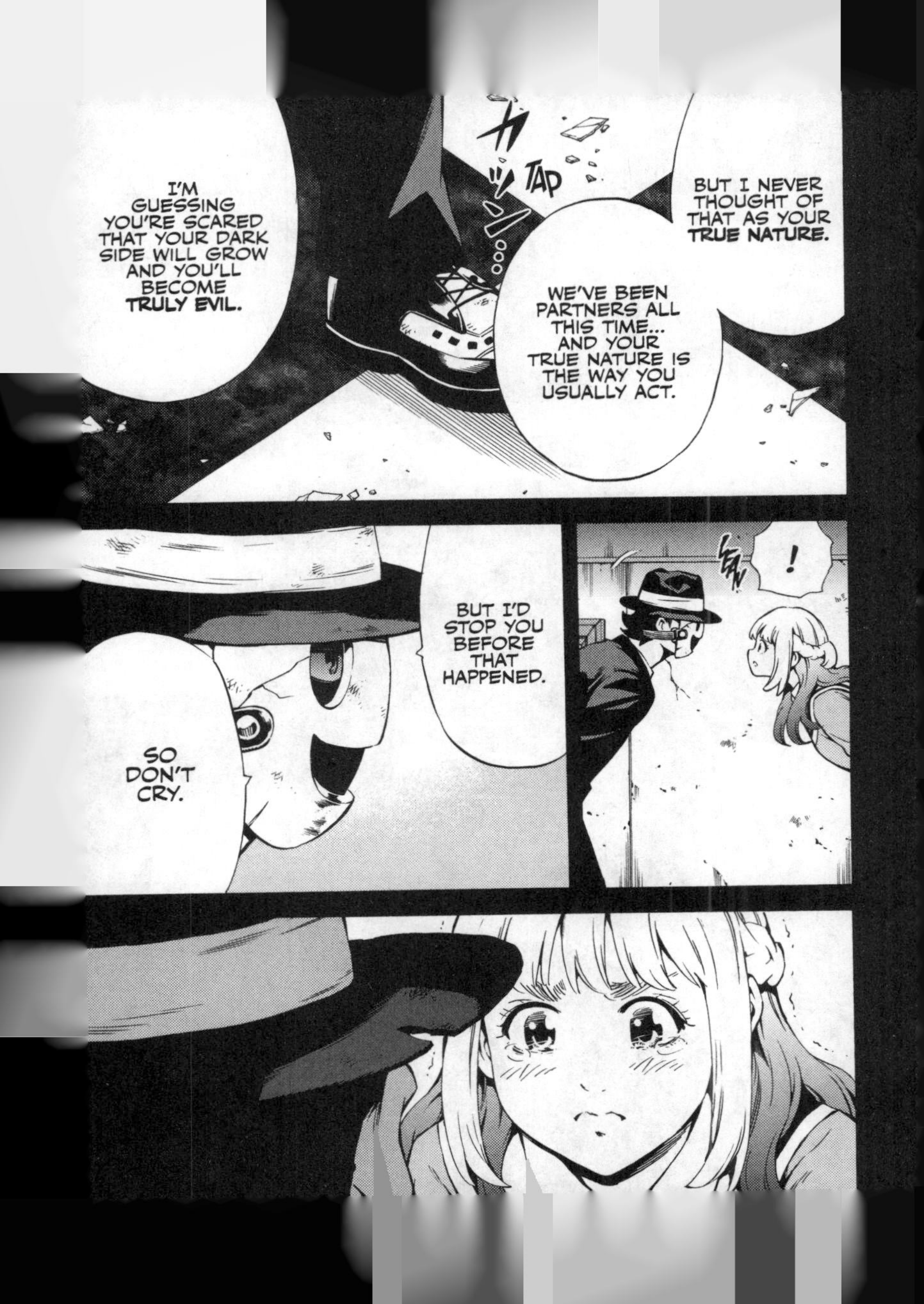
BUT I NEVER THOUGHT OF THAT AS YOUR TRUE NATURE.
TAP
WE'VE BEEN PARTNERS ALL THIS TIME... AND YOUR TRUE NATURE IS THE WAY YOU USUALLY ACT.
I'M GUESSING YOU'RE SCARED THAT YOUR DARK SIDE WILL GROW AND YOU'LL BECOME TRULY EVIL.
!
LEAN
BUT I'D STOP YOU BEFORE THAT HAPPENED.
SO DON'T CRY.

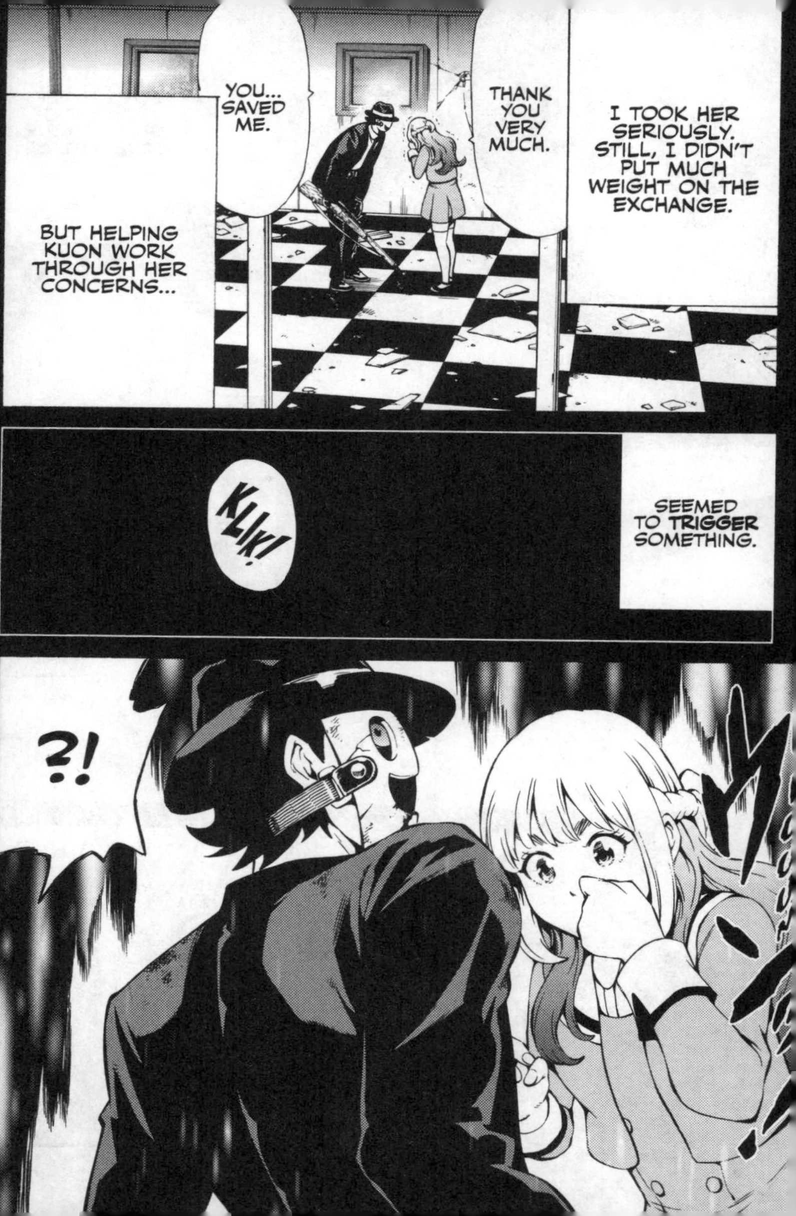
I TOOK HER SERIOUSLY. STILL, I DIDN'T PUT MUCH WEIGHT ON THE EXCHANGE.
THANK YOU VERY MUCH.
YOU... SAVED ME.
BUT HELPING KUON WORK THROUGH HER CONCERNS...
SEEMED TO TRIGGER SOMETHING.
KLIK!
?!

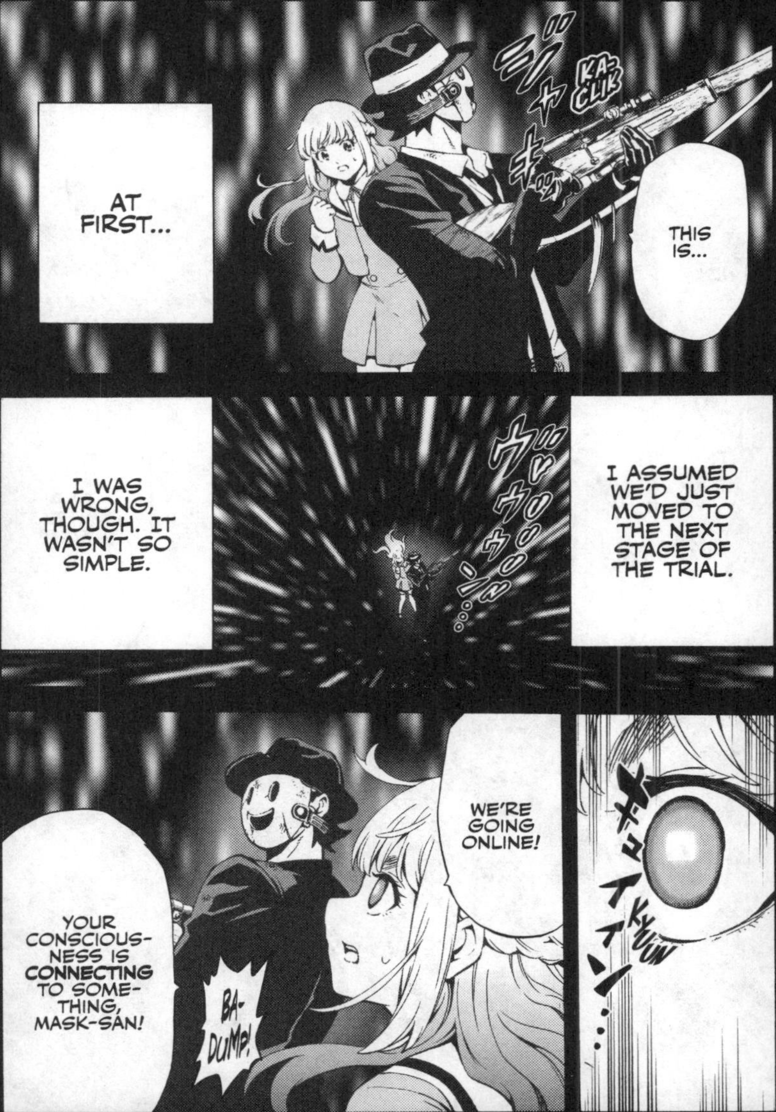
KA-CLIK
THIS IS...
AT FIRST...
I ASSUMED WE'D JUST MOVED TO THE NEXT STAGE OF THE TRIAL.
I WAS WRONG, THOUGH. IT WASN'T SO SIMPLE.
KYUUN
WE'RE GOING ONLINE!
YOUR CONSCIOUS-NESS IS CONNECTING TO SOME-THING, MASK-SAN!
BA-DUMP!

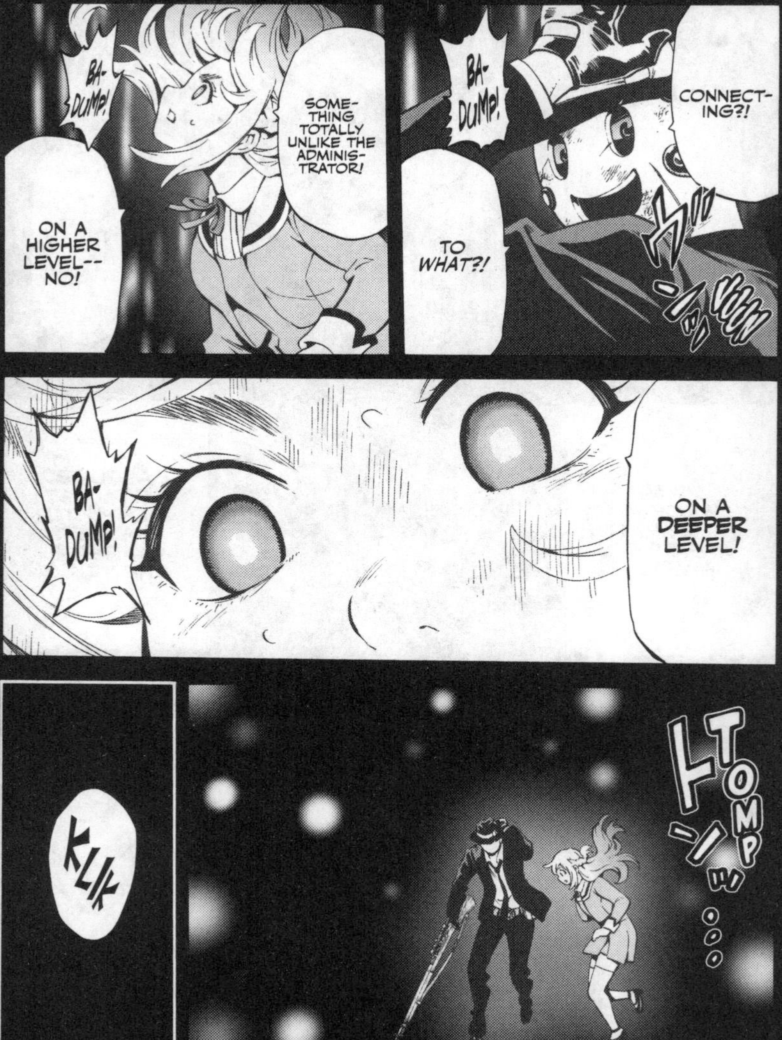
CONNECT-ING?!
BA-DUMP!
TO WHAT?!
SOME-THING TOTALLY UNLIKE THE ADMINIS-TRATOR!
BA-DUMP!
ON A HIGHER LEVEL-- NO!
ON A DEEPER LEVEL!
BA-DUMP!
TOMP...
KLIK

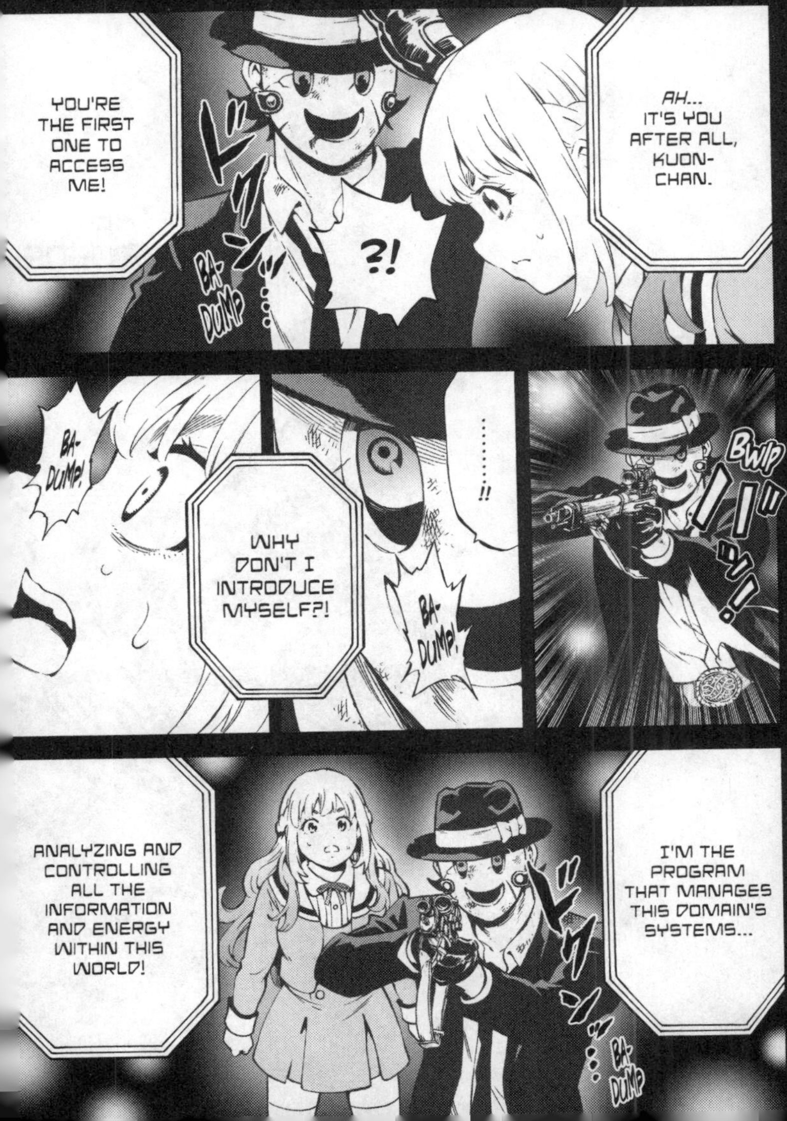
AH... IT'S YOU AFTER ALL, KUON-CHAN.
YOU'RE THE FIRST ONE TO ACCESS ME!
?!
BA-DUMP
BWIP
......!!
WHY DON'T I INTRODUCE MYSELF?!
BA-DUMP!
BA-DUMP!
I'M THE PROGRAM THAT MANAGES THIS DOMAIN'S SYSTEMS...
BA-DUMP
ANALYZING AND CONTROLLING ALL THE INFORMATION AND ENERGY WITHIN THIS WORLD!

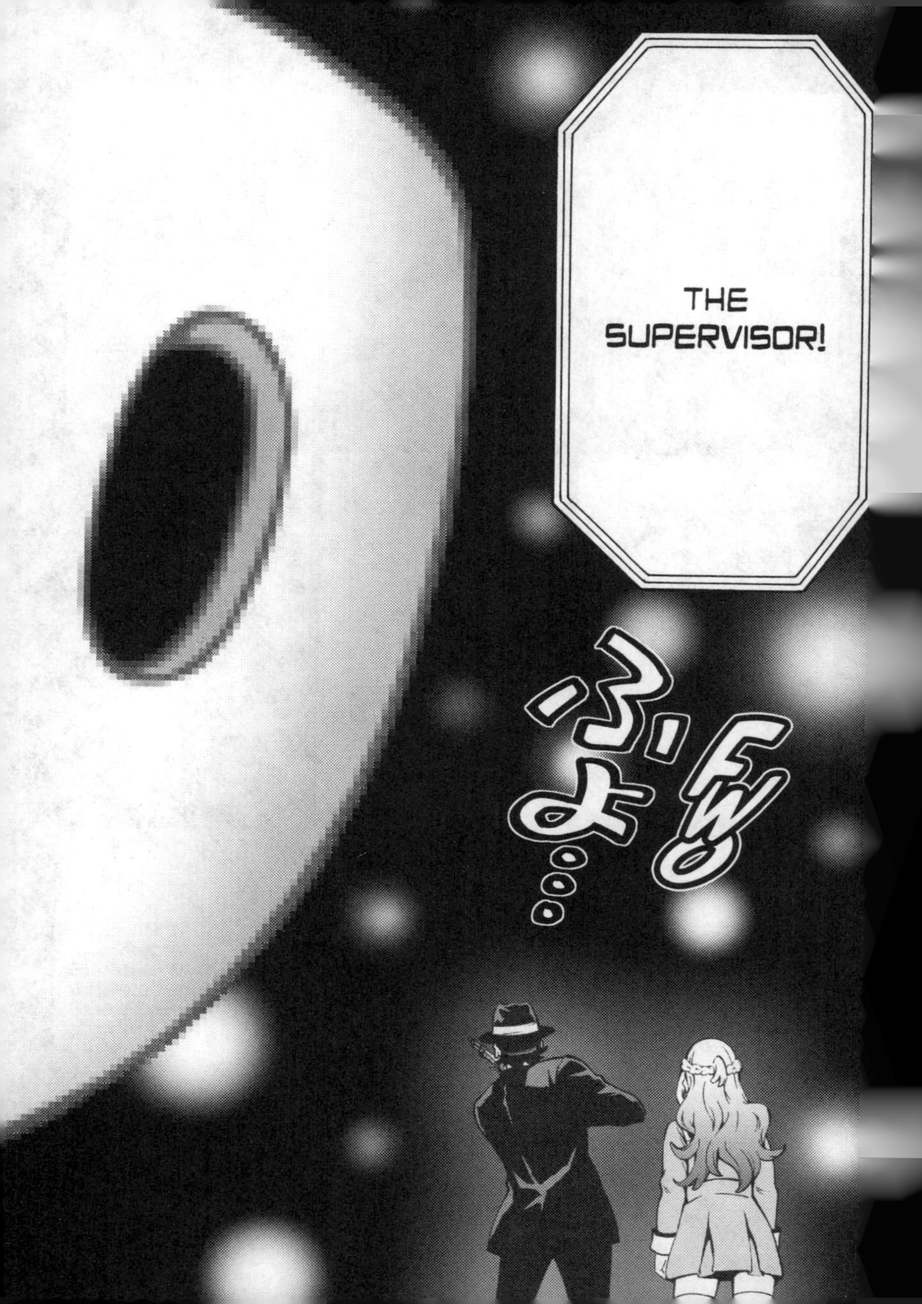
THE SUPERVISOR!
ふよ…
FW

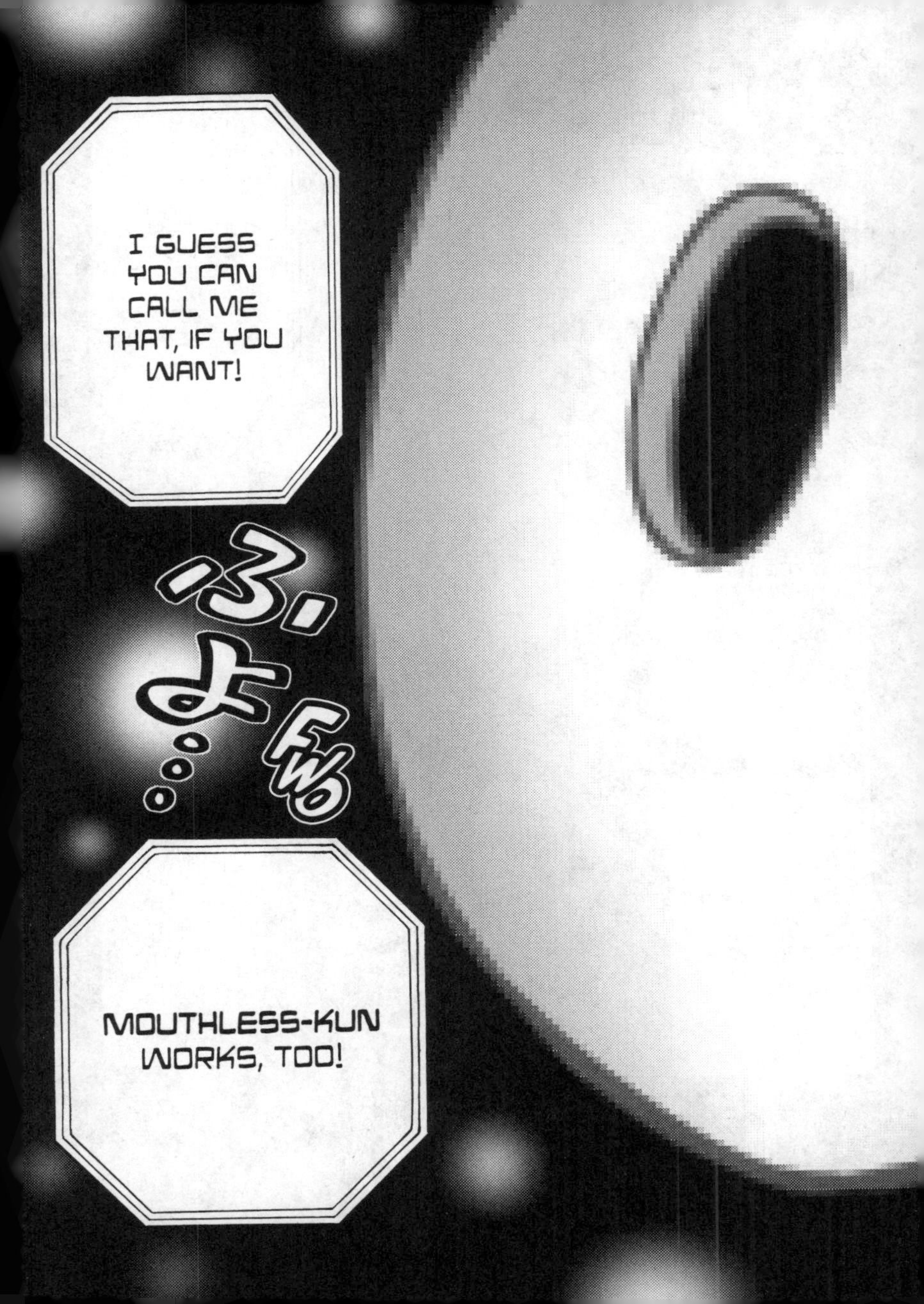
I GUESS YOU CAN CALL ME THAT, IF YOU WANT!
ふよ...
FWO
MOUTHLESS-KUN WORKS, TOO!

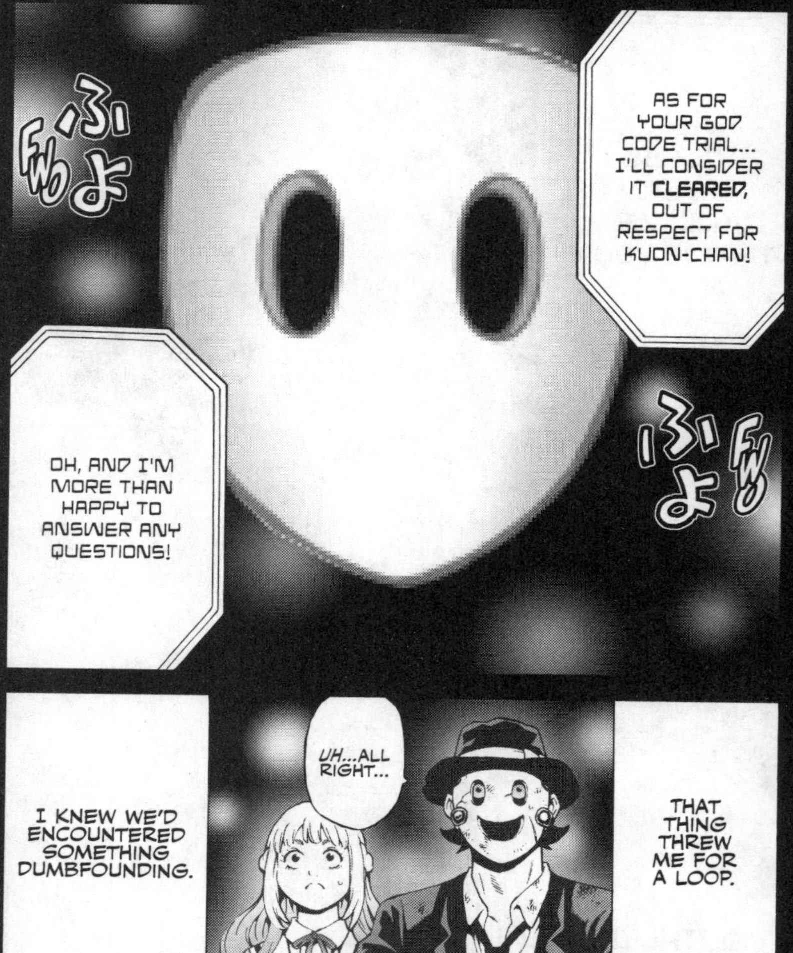
AS FOR YOUR GOD CODE TRIAL... I'LL CONSIDER IT **CLEARED**, OUT OF RESPECT FOR KUON-CHAN!
ふよ FWO
OH, AND I'M MORE THAN HAPPY TO ANSWER ANY QUESTIONS!
ふよ FWO
THAT THING THREW ME FOR A LOOP.
UH...ALL RIGHT...
I KNEW WE'D ENCOUNTERED SOMETHING DUMBFOUNDING.

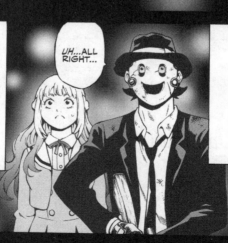

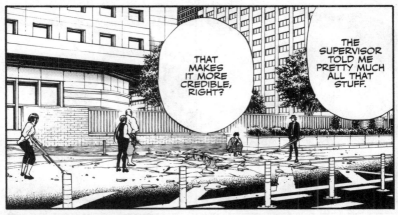

THE SUPERVISOR TOLD ME PRETTY MUCH ALL THAT STUFF.
THAT MAKES IT MORE CREDIBLE, RIGHT?
HMM. EVEN I'M AWARE OF THE SUPER-VISOR'S EXISTENCE.
BUT OF COURSE, SOMEONE IN MY POSITION CAN'T ACCESS HIM.
DRO ド...
MOUTHLESS-KUN?
DRO ド...
KUON, HUH? JUO AND AIKAWA BEING SO SCARED OF HER KINDA MAKES SENSE NOW.
DRO ド...
IF SHE HADN'T MET YU-CHAN, SHE MIGHT'VE GOTTEN REALLY DANGEROUS.

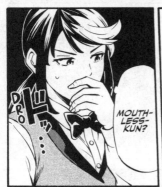

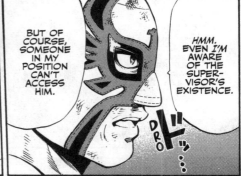

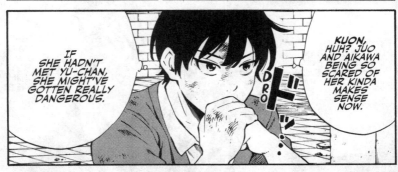

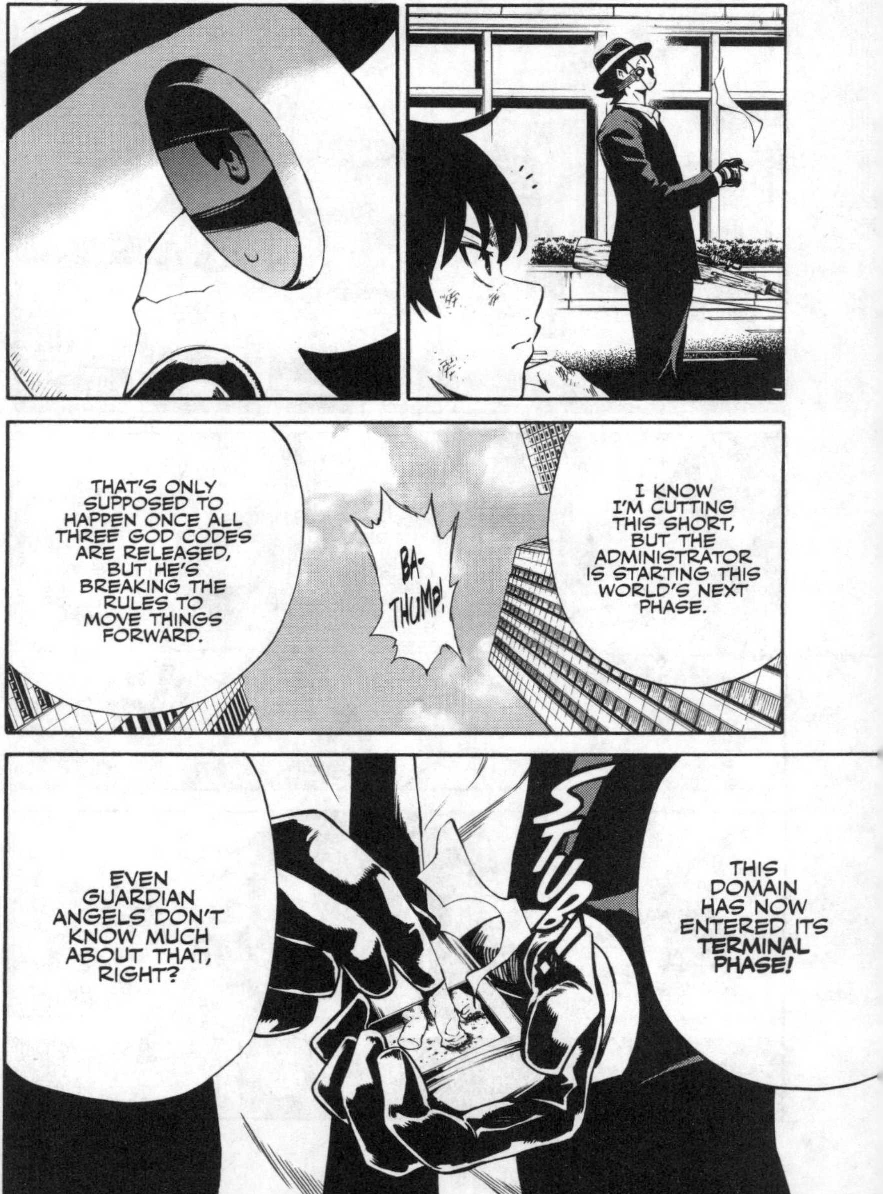
I KNOW I'M CUTTING THIS SHORT, BUT THE ADMINISTRATOR IS STARTING THIS WORLD'S NEXT PHASE.
BA-THUMP!
THAT'S ONLY SUPPOSED TO HAPPEN ONCE ALL THREE GOD CODES ARE RELEASED, BUT HE'S BREAKING THE RULES TO MOVE THINGS FORWARD.
THIS DOMAIN HAS NOW ENTERED ITS **TERMINAL PHASE!**
STUB!
EVEN GUARDIAN ANGELS DON'T KNOW MUCH ABOUT THAT, RIGHT?

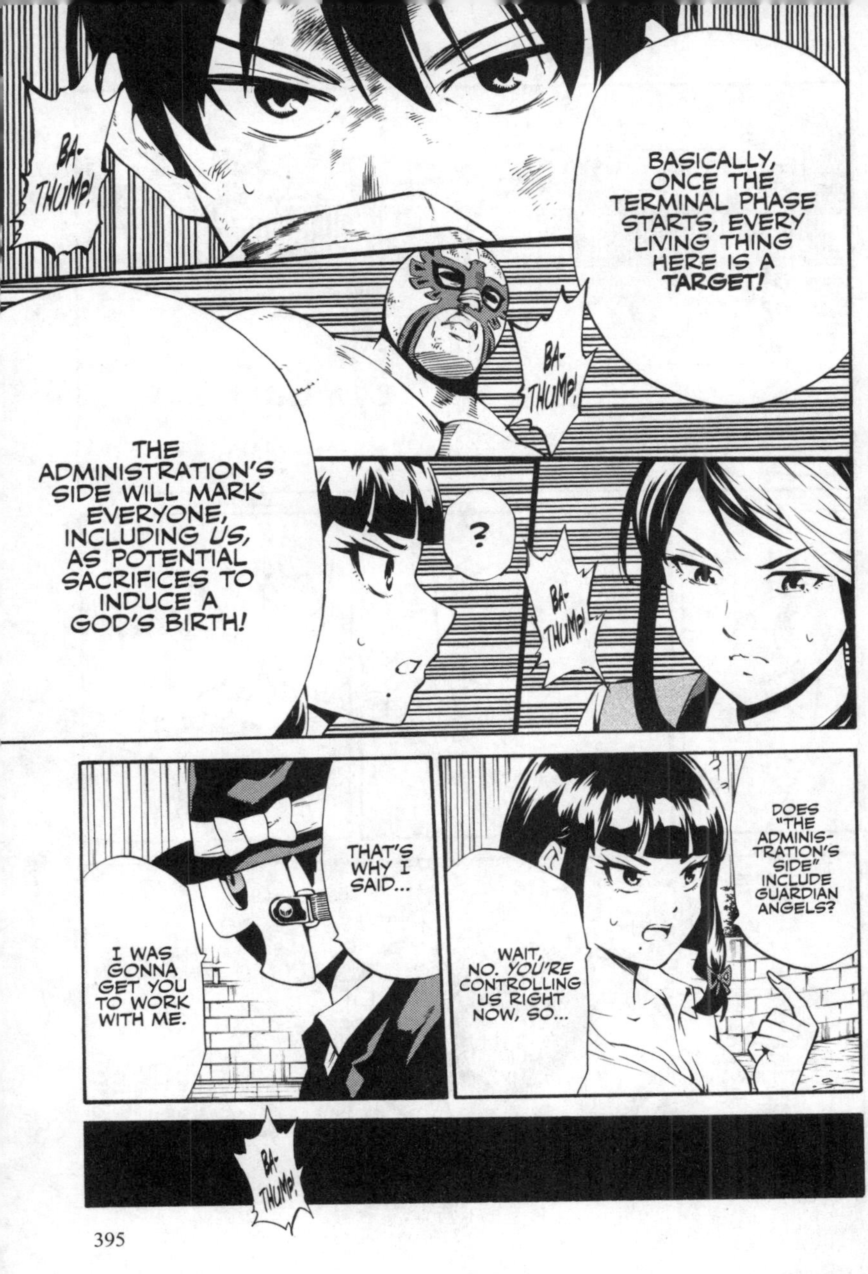
BASICALLY, ONCE THE TERMINAL PHASE STARTS, EVERY LIVING THING HERE IS A TARGET!
BA-THUMP!
BA-THUMP!
THE ADMINISTRATION'S SIDE WILL MARK EVERYONE, INCLUDING *US*, AS POTENTIAL SACRIFICES TO INDUCE A GOD'S BIRTH!
BA-THUMP!
?
DOES "THE ADMINISTRATION'S SIDE" INCLUDE GUARDIAN ANGELS?
WAIT, NO. *YOU'RE* CONTROLLING US RIGHT NOW, SO...
THAT'S WHY I SAID...
I WAS GONNA GET YOU TO WORK WITH ME.
BA-THUMP!

I KNOW YOU'VE GOTTEN TOUGHER, HARUKA-CHAN, BUT LEAVE THIS TO ME.

THAT'S A MASK!

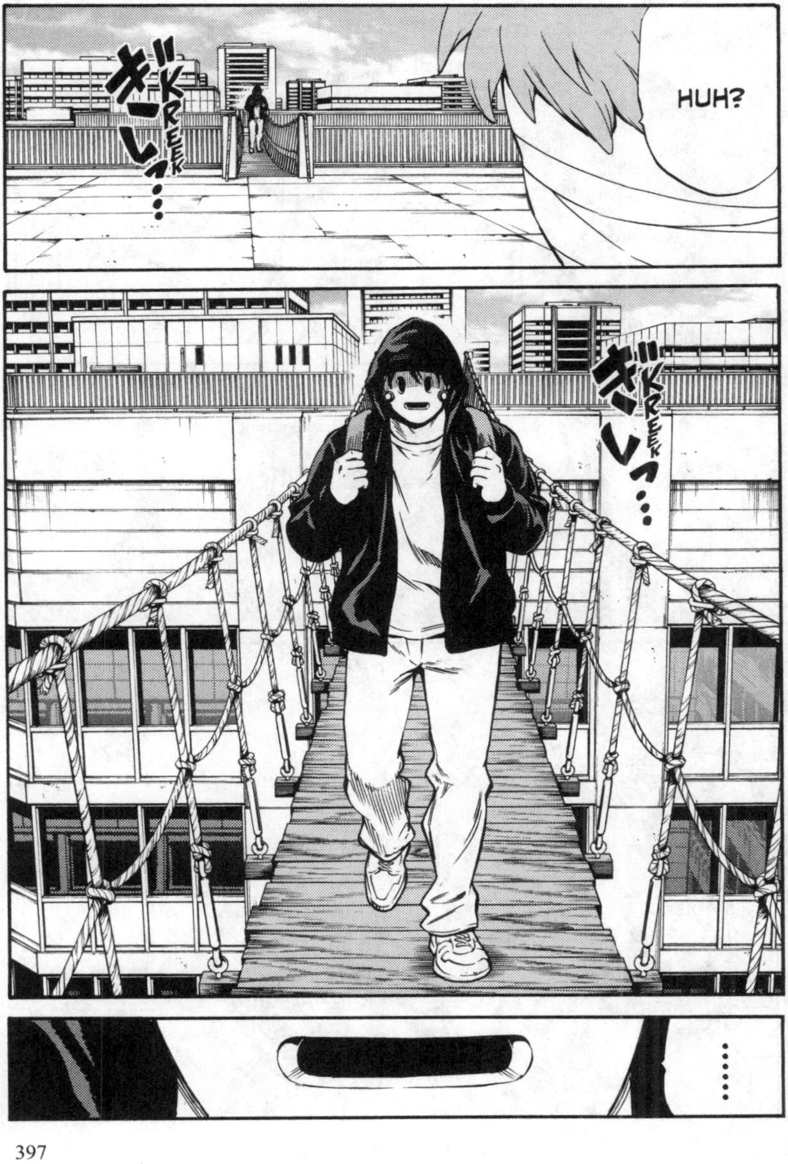
HUH?
KREEK
KREEK
......

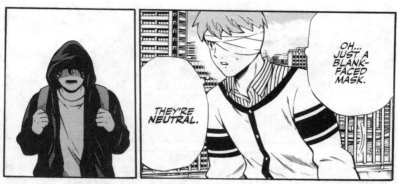

OH... JUST A BLANK-FACED MASK.
THEY'RE NEUTRAL.
SACRI...
HISS
FICE...
HUH?
BA-THUMP

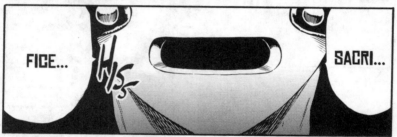

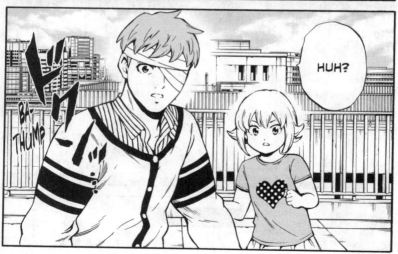

HIGH-RISE INVASION

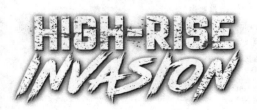

Terminal Phase Bonus!

The *High-Rise Invasion* Character Directory!

These're the kinds of things I found out!

Everything's wrapping up soon, so I put together all the info I've gathered so far!

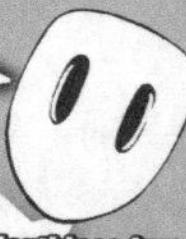

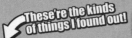

Mouthless-kun

<1> Titles/Nicknames/Pseudonyms <2> Location Before Entering High-Rise World <3> Family

<4> Future Plans <5> Commitments/Hobbies <6> Favorite Food <7> Personal Faves

<8> Favorite Phrase <9> Most Memorable Opponent <10> Prize Possession <11> Weapons/Tools/Tactics/Etc.

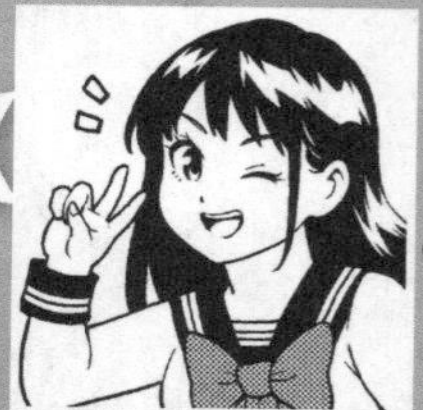

Honjo Yuri

Age: 16 Birthday: Nov. 6 Occupation: High Schooler

<1> Tenma, Small Fry, Sickle Girl, Goddess (by Nise-chan) <2> In Class
<3> Parents, Big Brother <4> Still None <5> Cram School, Hanging Out With Friends/Brother
<6> Mint Chocolate Ice Cream <7> Anime Starring Sakura-chan!
<8> "All Things Come to Those Who Wait" <9> Sniper Mask, Maid Mask, Nise-chan
<10> Snapshot of Brother <11> Police Gear, Sickle, Guns (Black and Silver), Acting Skills

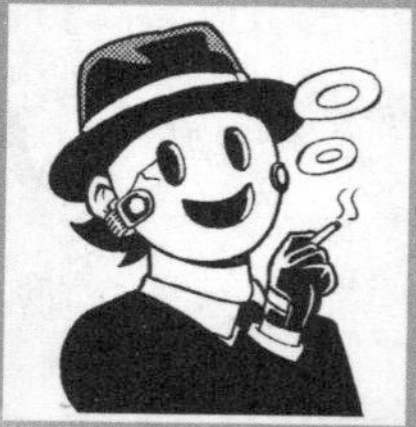

Sniper Mask/ Makoto Yuka

Age: Unknown Birthday: Sept. 13
Occupation: Grad Student

<1> The White Death, Mask-san, Yu-Chan <2> Talking to Little Brother by a River
<3> Unknown <4> Confidential <5> Travel <6> Soba, Cheese
<7> Viral Videos of Animals <8> "To Control Fire with Courage"
<9> Those Two High School Girls, White Feather <10> Cigarettes/Lighter
<11> Bolt-Action Rifle, Throwing Knives, Railgun

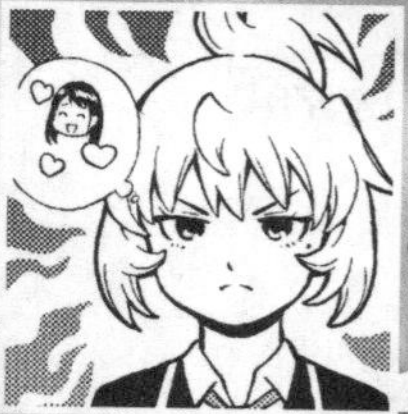

Nise Mayuko

Age: 16 Birthday: June 19 Occupation: High Schooler

<1> Angel, Nise-chan, Bratty Little Bitch (by Chef Mask)<2> On the Street
<3> Father <4> Living Alone <5> Part-Time Job (Karaoke Cashier)
<6> Rolled Omelet, Grated Daikon <7> Songs By Pop Superstars <8> "Nise-chan!"
<9> Honjo-san, Rider Mask <10> Honjo-san's Student Handbook
<11> Knife, Grenade, Black Gun, Damascus Steel Knife, Tanto ("Kanemoto")

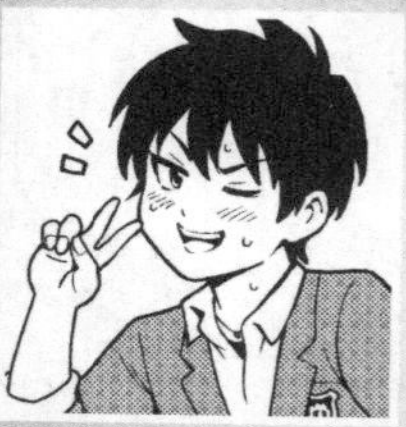

Honjo Rika

Age: 18 Birthday: July 3 Occupation: High Schooler

<1> Apostle, Oniichan, Rika-chan <2> Talking to Someone He Knows by a River
<3> Parents, Little Sister <4> Studying Law <5> Part-Time Job, Cooking, Hanging Out with Sister <6> Matcha Ice Cream <7> A Picture Book about a Bird and a Hunter
<8> "To Control Fire with Reason" <9> Baseball Mask, Sniper Mask
<10> Snapshot of Sister <11> Hammer, Takeda's Swordstick, Multiple Guns

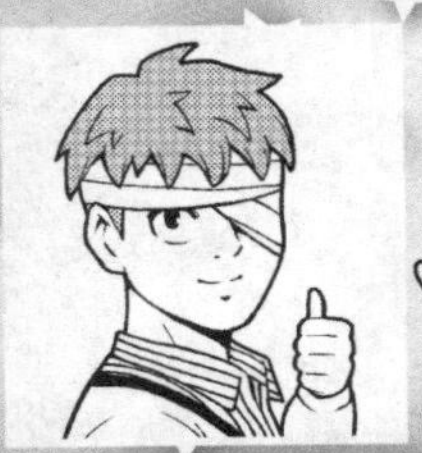

Yamanami Kohei

Age: 19 Birthday: Nov. 23 Occupation: College Student

<1> Yamanami-san, Yama-chan (by Haruka) <2> En Route to Class
<3> Parents, Grandma, Three Big Sisters <4> Something Gaming-Related <5> Gaming
<6> Soda <7> *Last Fantasy 9, Street Fighting 4, Combat Duty 8, Rock Brand 4,* etc.
<8> "I'm gonna go meet someone stronger than me!" <9> Drill Mask, Screwdriver Mask
<10> Portable Game Console, Mobile Phone <11> Gun (SIG SP), Painkillers

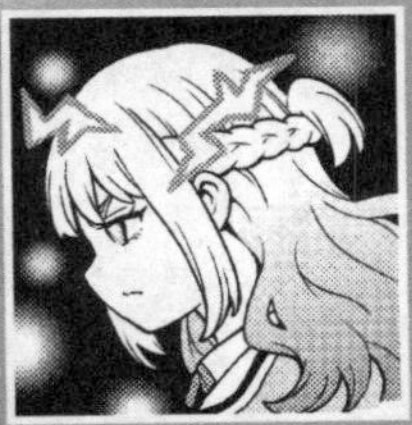

Shinzaki Kuon

Age 16 Birthday: Dec. 1 Occupation: High Schooler

<1> Judge, Lady (by Sniper Mask) <2> At a School Club
<3> Parents, Grandparents, Butler, etc. <4> CEO <5> Political Activism, Extracurricular Lessons, Watching Horse Races <6> That Bread From Before
<7> Gardens in Kyoto's Nishikyo Ward <8> "Heavy Lies the Crown"
<9> Archangel, Aikawa Mamoru <10> No Possessions Currently
<11> Railgun, Supporting Sniper Mask

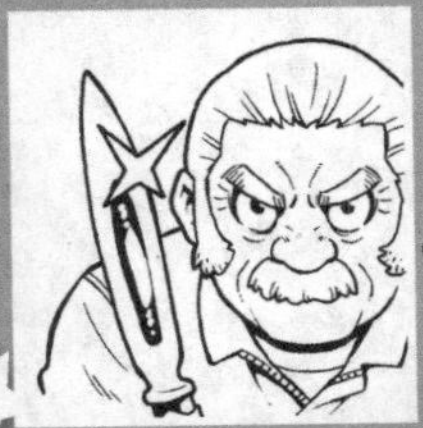

Tanabe Sachio

Age: 59 Birthday: Nov. 6 Occupation: Small Business Owner

<1> Tanabe-san, Tanabe-shi, The Elderly Gentleman with the Spear (by Kuon)
<2> Working in Downtown Tokyo <3> Wife, Children <4> Lifelong Employment
<5> Deep-Sea Fishing <6> Sushi, Yakitori, Soba <7> Skyline GT-R
<8> "Household Peace and Prosperity" <9> Aohara Kazuma, Student Mask
<10> Family Picture <11> Spear ("Tonbokiri"), Gun (S&W M36), Sword ("Ulfberht")

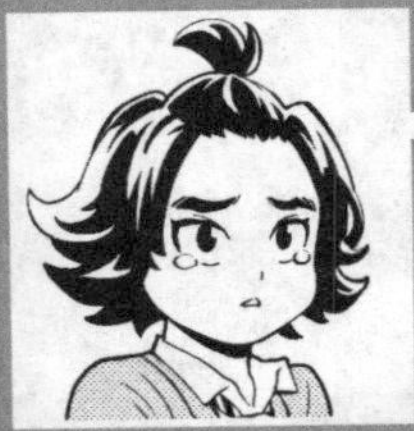

Yoshida Rikuya

Age: 16 Birthday: Apr. 4 Occupation: High Schooler

<1> Yoshida-kun, Rikuya (by Juo) <2> Running an Errand for a "Friend"
<3> Parents, Dog <4> Voice Acting or Comedy
<5> Cram School, Helping His Dad at Work, Playing with His Dog <6> Chicken Karaage
<7> Isekai Anime <8> "Rikuya can do anything he sets his mind to!"
<9> Monk Mask, Juo <10> Smartphone <11> None

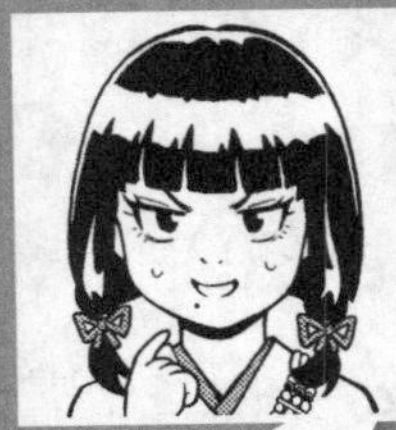

Miko Mask (Real Name Unknown)

Age: 21 Birthday: Feb. 14
Occupation: College Student

<1> Guardian Angel, Miko-chan, Fanatic (on Earth)
<2> In Class <3> Mother, Brothers <4> Starting a Religion, Purifying Humankind
<5> Visiting Religious Sites, Collecting Spiritual Objects <6> Filtered Water <7> None
<8> "Humankind never went to the moon!" <9> Archangel, That Reptilian Guy
<10> Indian Jewelry, Misanga Bracelet <11> Anti-Materiel Rifle

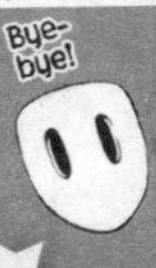
Bye-bye!

In the next volume, we'll reach the climax! Don't miss my star turn!!

Text/Tsuina Miura

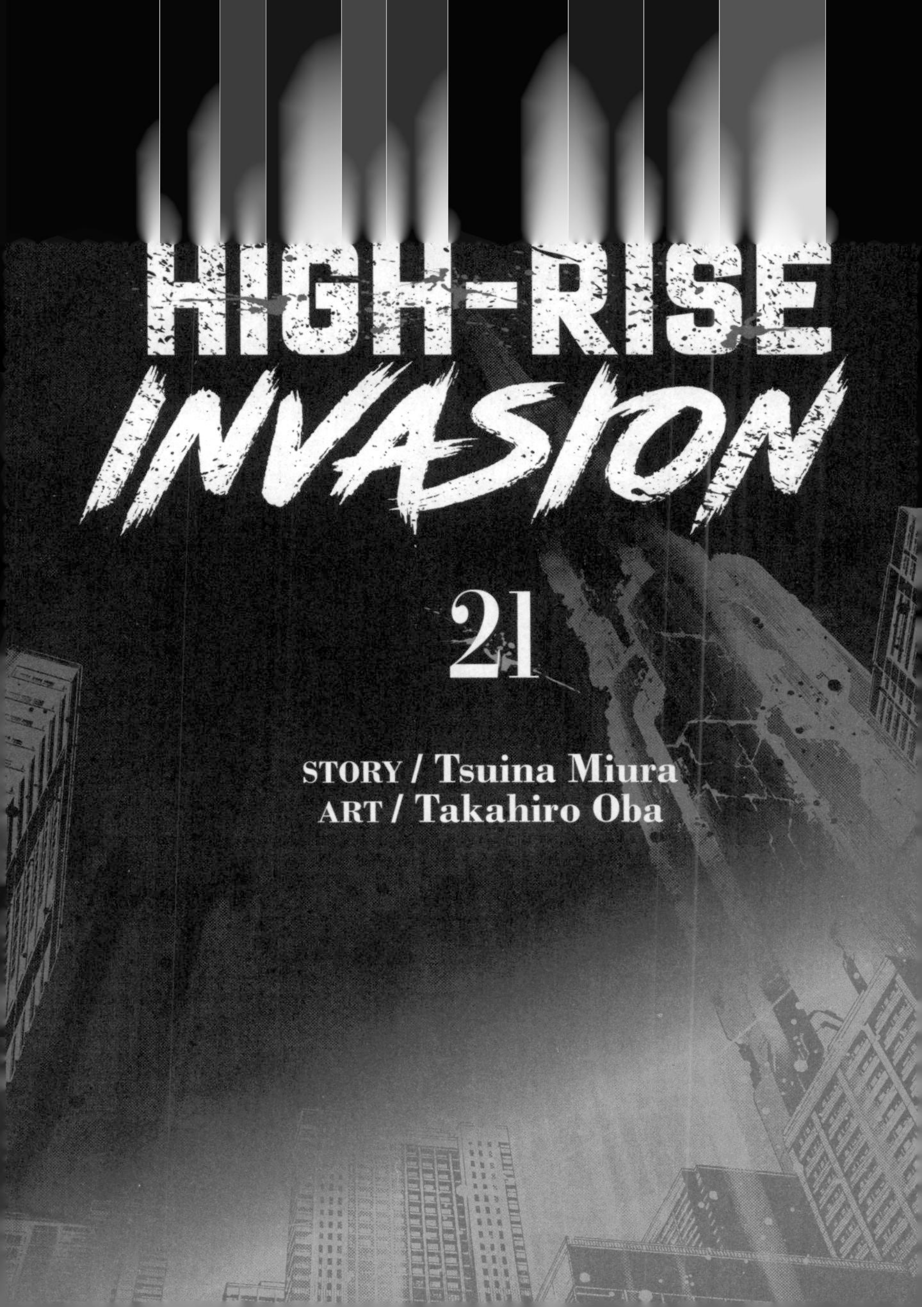

HIGH-RISE INVASION

21

STORY / Tsuina Miura
ART / Takahiro Oba

HIGH-RISE INVASION

21

CONTENTS

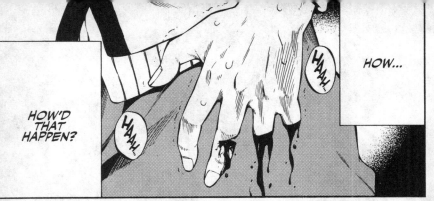

HOW...

HOW'D
THAT
HAPPEN?

HAAH.

HAAH.

AH...

HOW...?

AUGH...

BA-
DUMP

WORLD
CHANGED?

HAAH.

HAAH.

HAAH.

HAS
THIS...

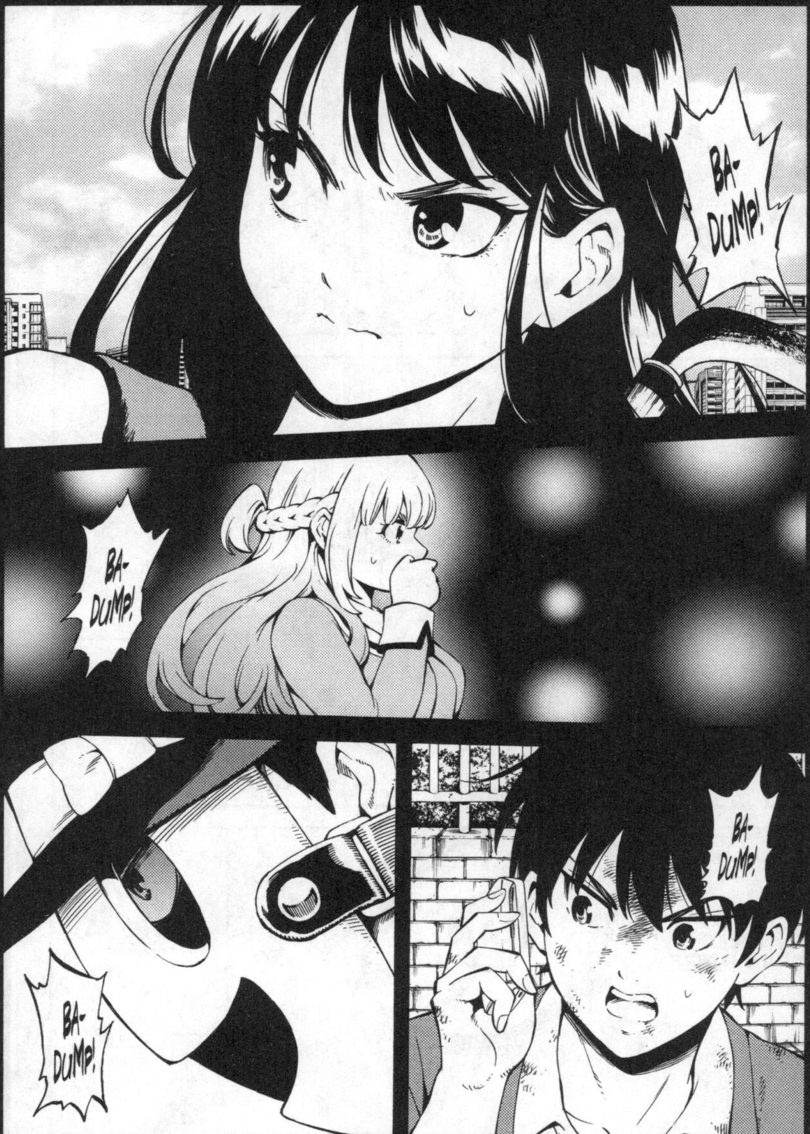
BA-DUMP!
BA-DUMP!
BA-DUMP!
BA-DUMP!

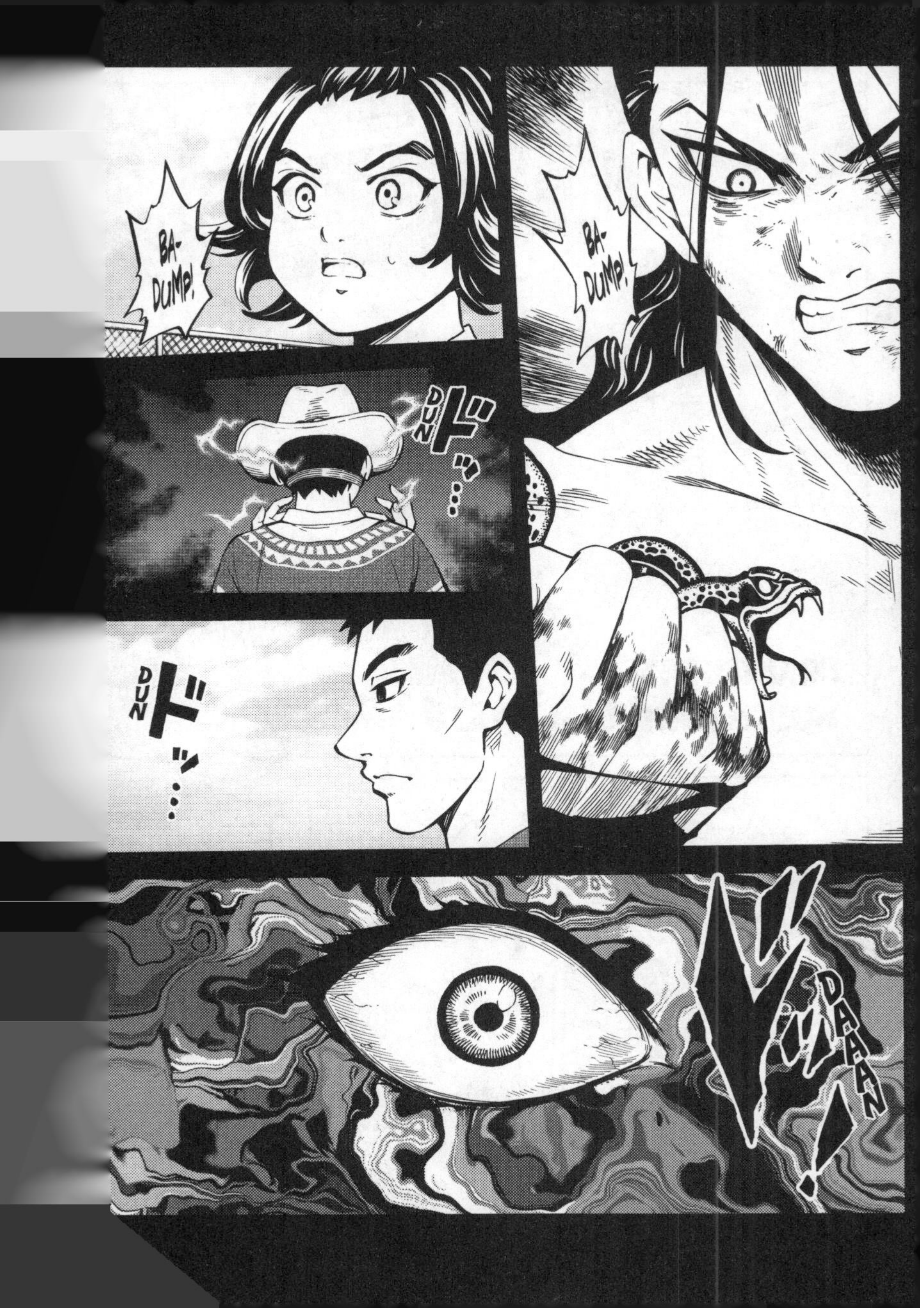
BA-DUMP!
BA-DUMP!
DUN ドッ…
DUN ドッ…
DAAAAN!

URGH...

CHAPTER 243:
Some Kind of Reward

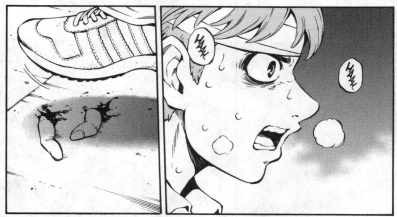

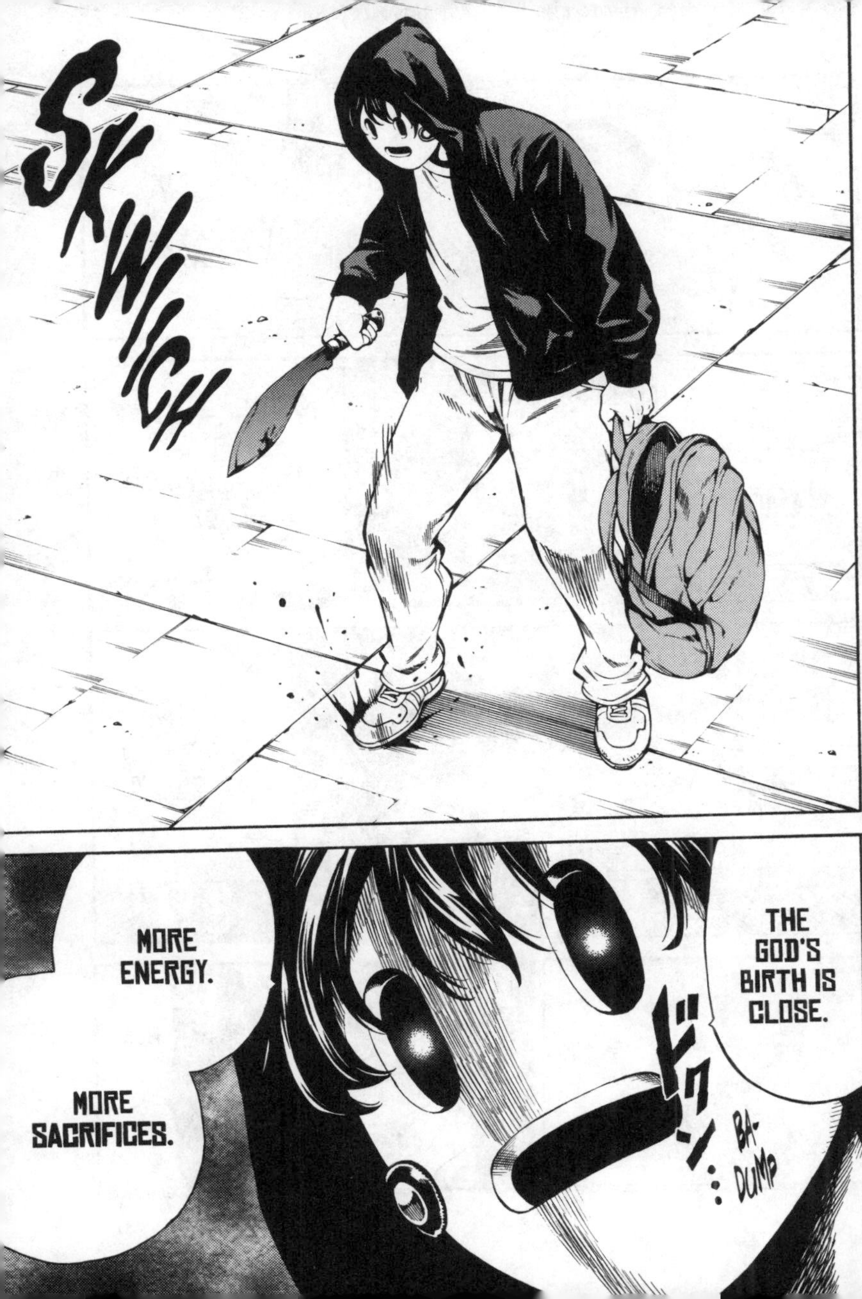
SKWICH
THE GOD'S BIRTH IS CLOSE.
BA-DUMP
MORE ENERGY.
MORE SACRIFICES.

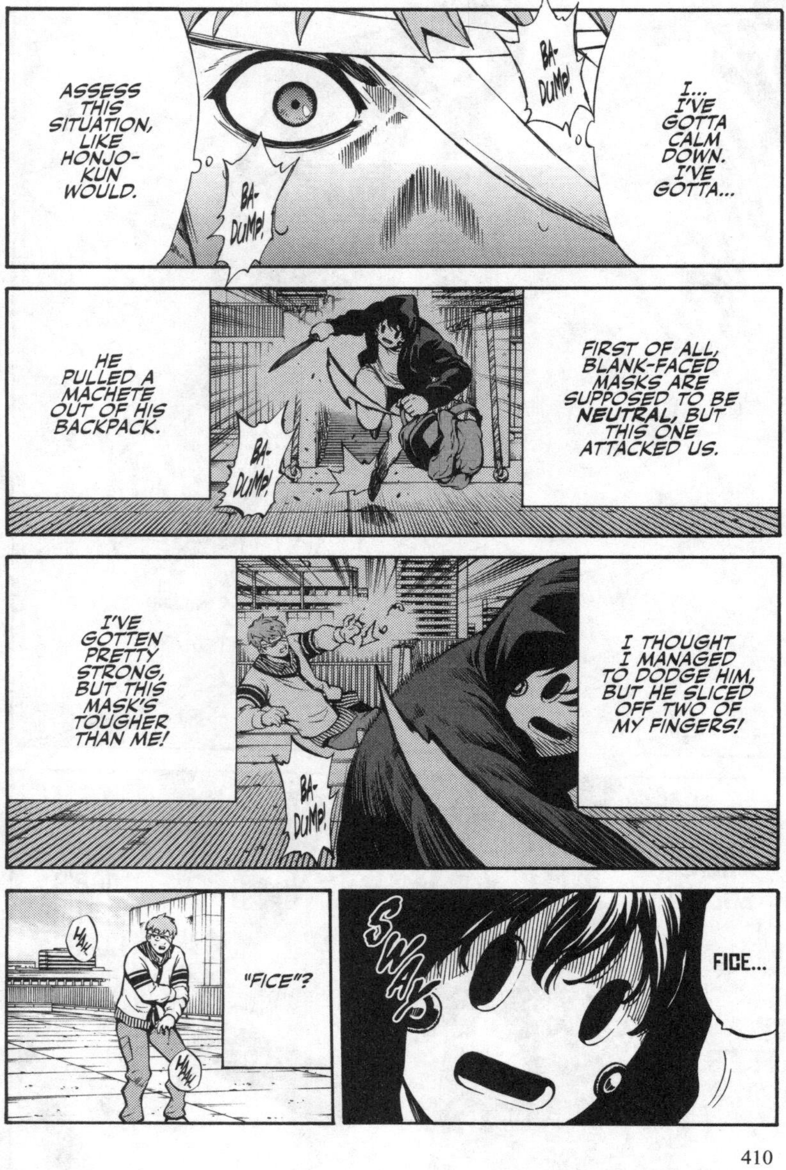
BA-DUMP!
I... I'VE GOTTA CALM DOWN. I'VE GOTTA...
ASSESS THIS SITUATION, LIKE HONJO-KUN WOULD.
BA-DUMP!
FIRST OF ALL, BLANK-FACED MASKS ARE SUPPOSED TO BE NEUTRAL, BUT THIS ONE ATTACKED US.
HE PULLED A MACHETE OUT OF HIS BACKPACK.
BA-DUMP!
I THOUGHT I MANAGED TO DODGE HIM, BUT HE SLICED OFF TWO OF MY FINGERS!
I'VE GOTTEN PRETTY STRONG, BUT THIS MASK'S TOUGHER THAN ME!
BA-DUMP!
FICE...
SWAY
"FICE"?
HAH
HAH

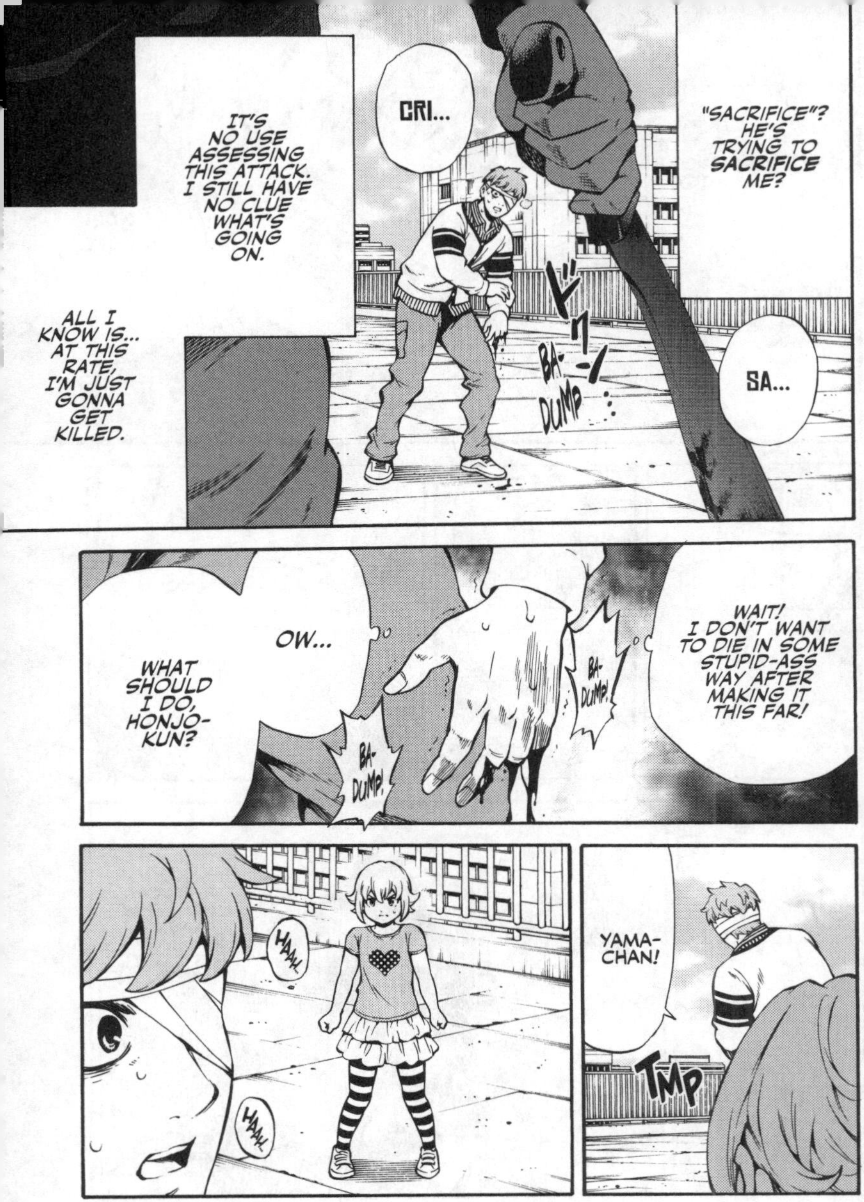
"SACRIFICE"? HE'S TRYING TO SACRIFICE ME?
CRI...
IT'S NO USE ASSESSING THIS ATTACK. I STILL HAVE NO CLUE WHAT'S GOING ON.
SA...
BA-DUMP
ALL I KNOW IS... AT THIS RATE, I'M JUST GONNA GET KILLED.
WAIT! I DON'T WANT TO DIE IN SOME STUPID-ASS WAY AFTER MAKING IT THIS FAR!
BA-DUMP!
OW...
WHAT SHOULD I DO, HONJO-KUN?
BA-DUMP!
YAMA-CHAN!
TMP
HAAH
HAAH

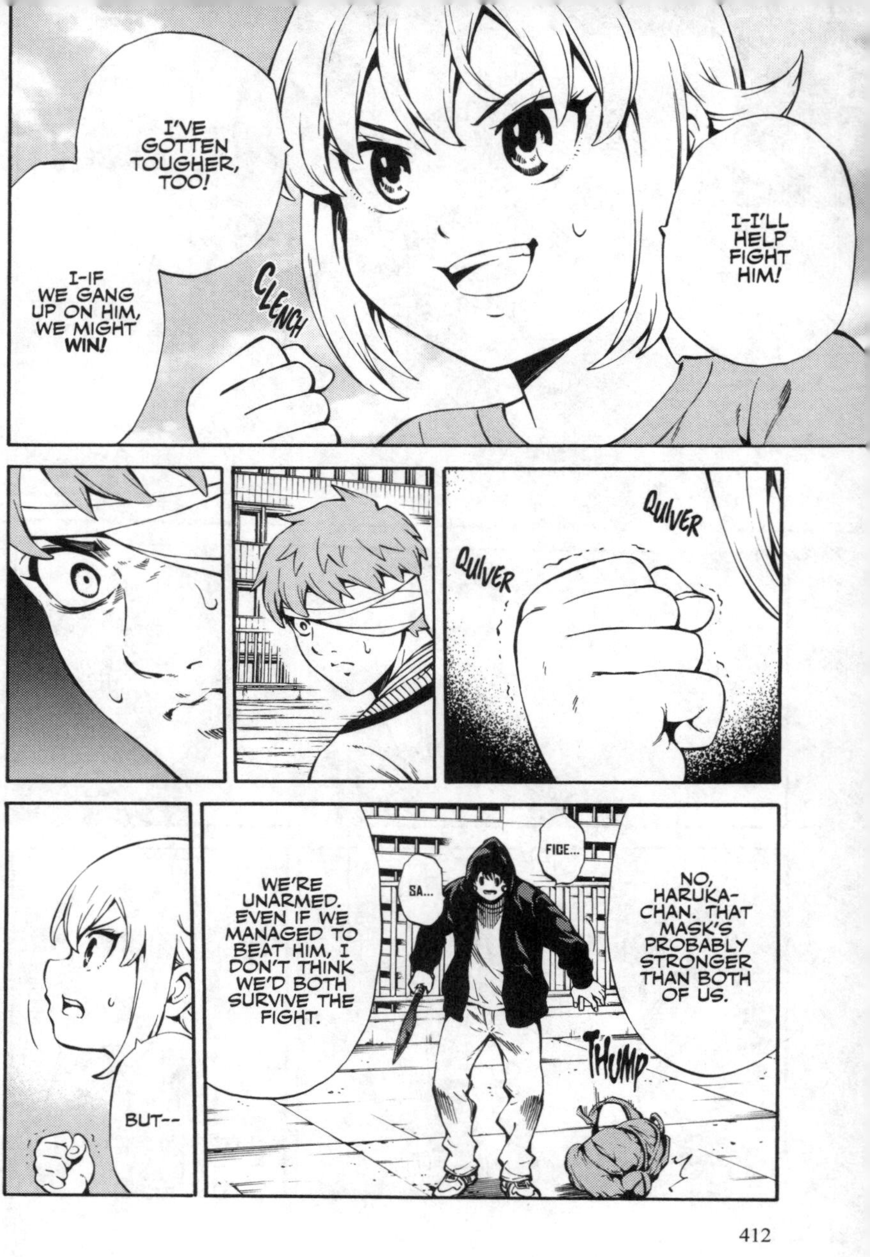
I-I'LL HELP FIGHT HIM!
I'VE GOTTEN TOUGHER, TOO!
I-IF WE GANG UP ON HIM, WE MIGHT WIN!
CLENCH
QUIVER
QUIVER
NO, HARUKA-CHAN. THAT MASK'S PROBABLY STRONGER THAN BOTH OF US.
FICE...
SA...
WE'RE UNARMED. EVEN IF WE MANAGED TO BEAT HIM, I DON'T THINK WE'D BOTH SURVIVE THE FIGHT.
THUMP
BUT--

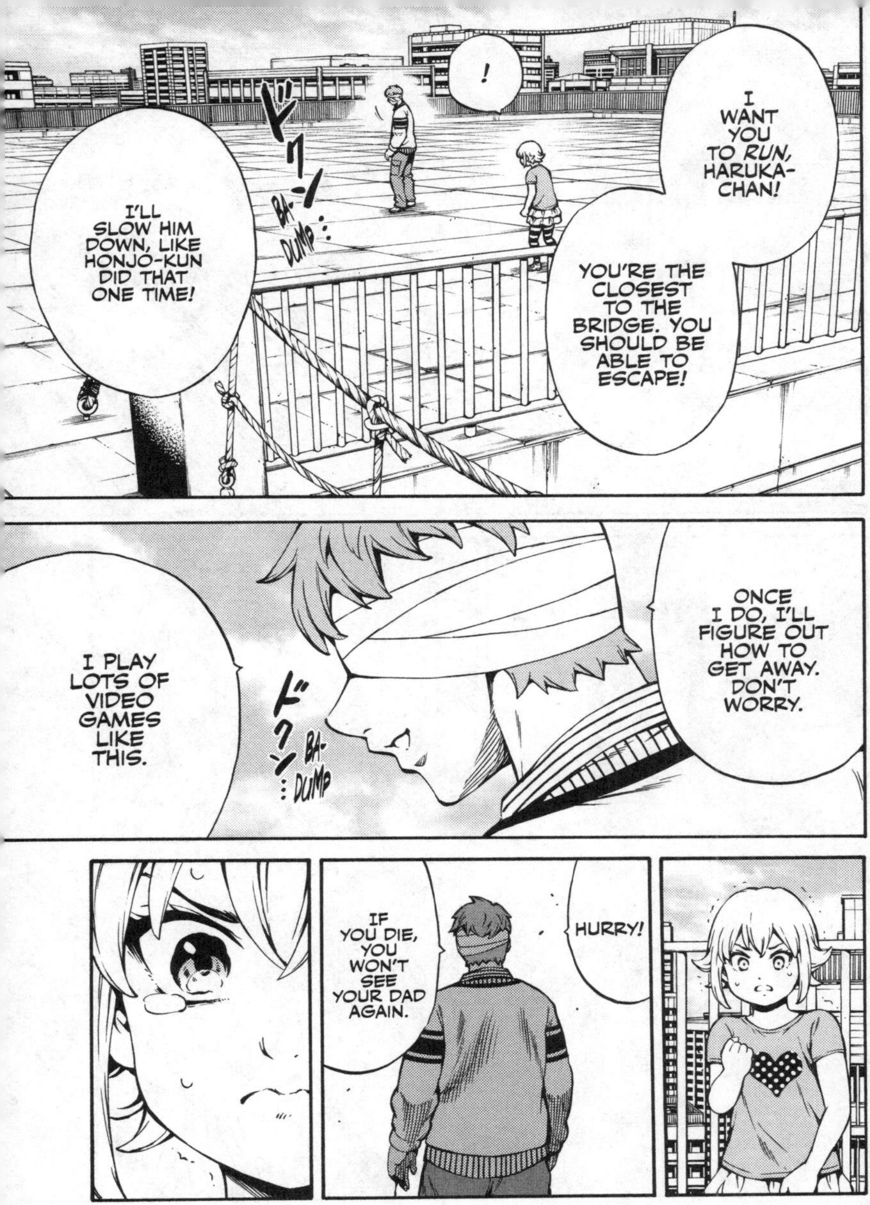
I WANT YOU TO *RUN*, HARUKA-CHAN!
!
YOU'RE THE CLOSEST TO THE BRIDGE. YOU SHOULD BE ABLE TO ESCAPE!
BA-DUMP
I'LL SLOW HIM DOWN, LIKE HONJO-KUN DID THAT ONE TIME!
ONCE I DO, I'LL FIGURE OUT HOW TO GET AWAY. DON'T WORRY.
BA-DUMP
I PLAY LOTS OF VIDEO GAMES LIKE THIS.
HURRY!
IF YOU DIE, YOU WON'T SEE YOUR DAD AGAIN.

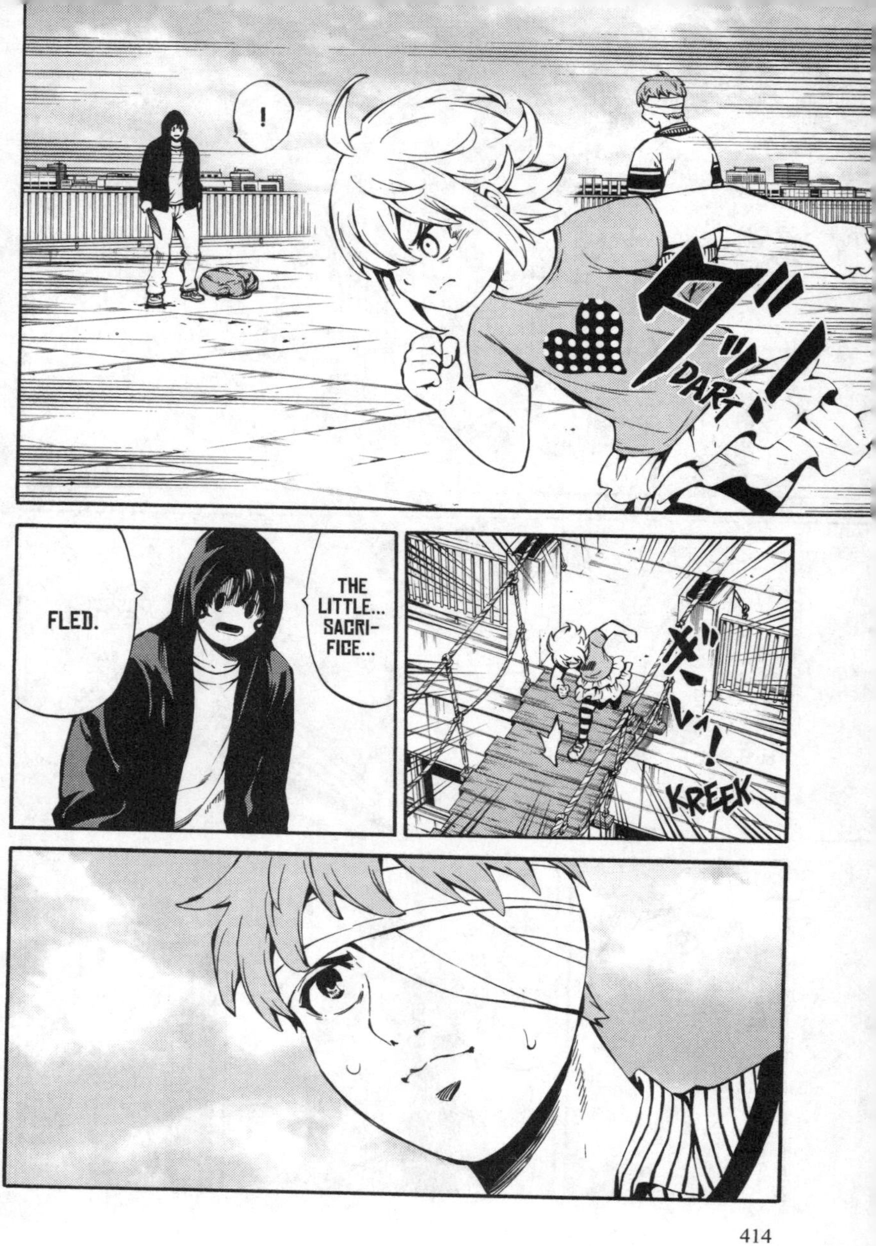
!
DART
KREEK
THE LITTLE... SACRI-FICE...
FLED.

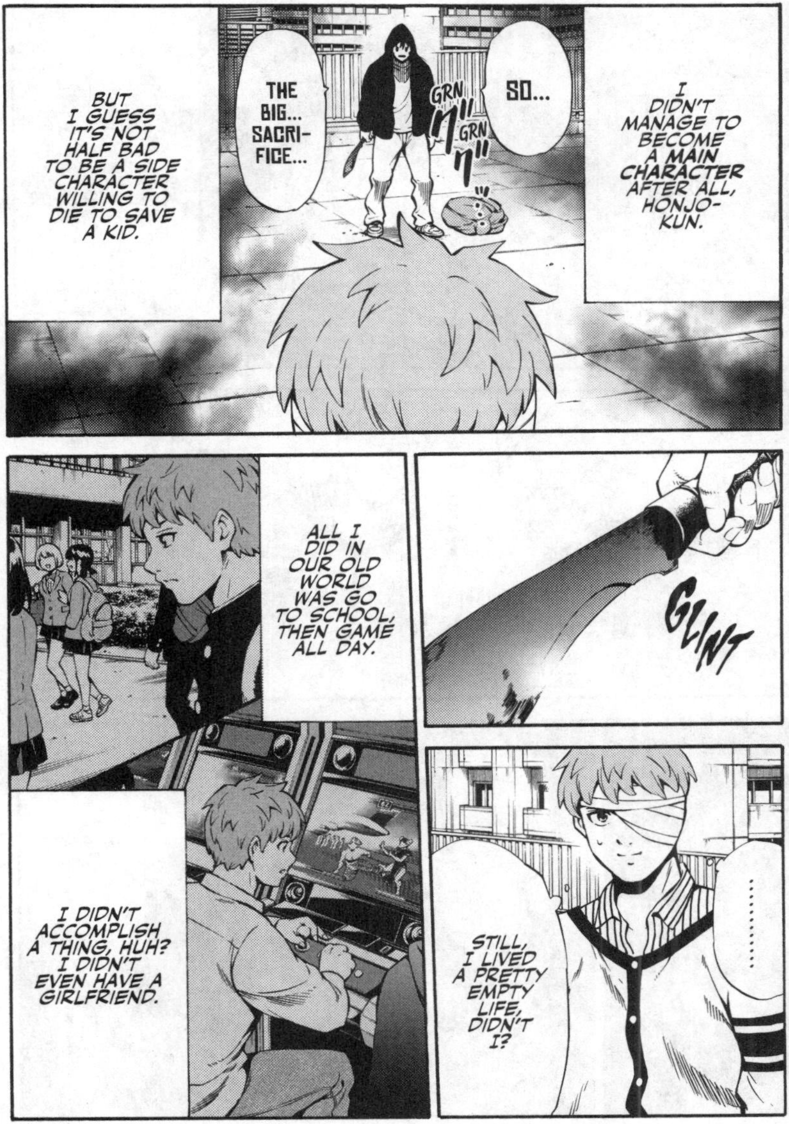
I DIDN'T MANAGE TO BECOME A MAIN CHARACTER AFTER ALL, HONJO-KUN.
SO...
GRN GRN
THE BIG... SACRI-FICE...
BUT I GUESS IT'S NOT HALF BAD TO BE A SIDE CHARACTER WILLING TO DIE TO SAVE A KID.
GLINT
ALL I DID IN OUR OLD WORLD WAS GO TO SCHOOL, THEN GAME ALL DAY.
......
STILL, I LIVED A PRETTY EMPTY LIFE, DIDN'T I?
I DIDN'T ACCOMPLISH A THING, HUH? I DIDN'T EVEN HAVE A GIRLFRIEND.

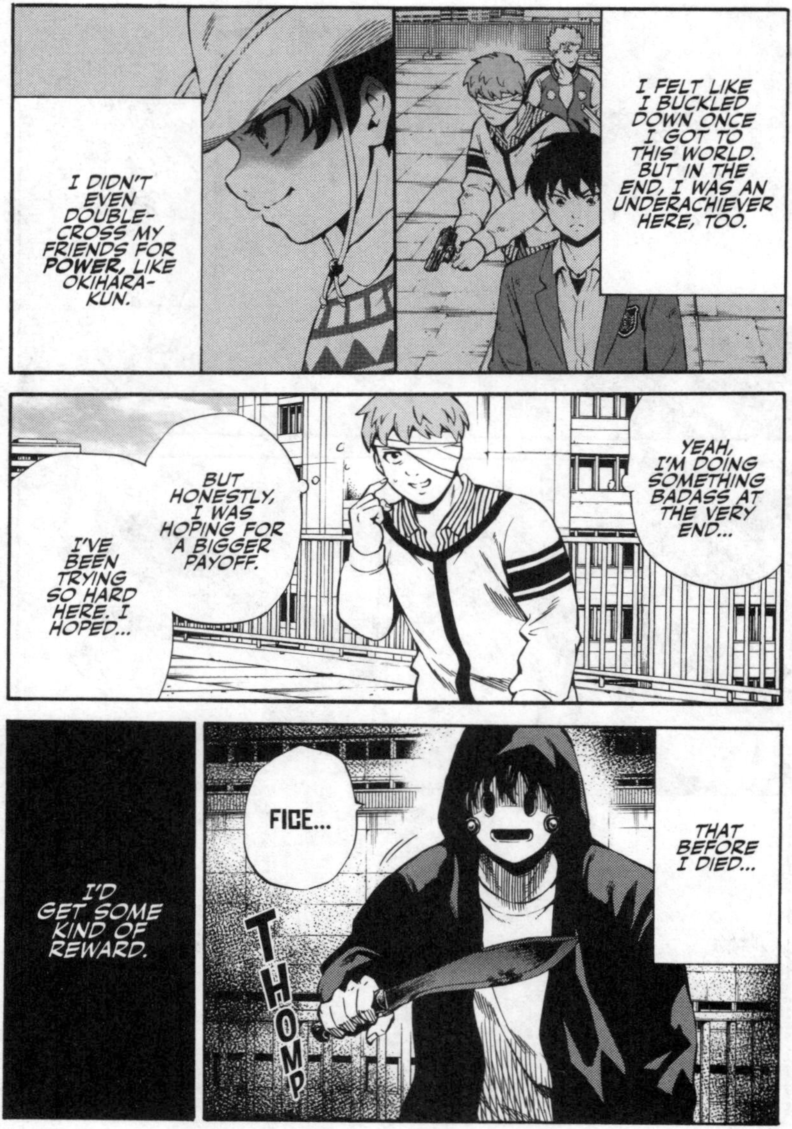
I FELT LIKE I BUCKLED DOWN ONCE I GOT TO THIS WORLD. BUT IN THE END, I WAS AN UNDERACHIEVER HERE, TOO.
I DIDN'T EVEN DOUBLE-CROSS MY FRIENDS FOR POWER, LIKE OKIHARA-KUN.
YEAH, I'M DOING SOMETHING BADASS AT THE VERY END...
BUT HONESTLY, I WAS HOPING FOR A BIGGER PAYOFF.
I'VE BEEN TRYING SO HARD HERE. I HOPED...
THAT BEFORE I DIED...
FICE...
THOMP
I'D GET SOME KIND OF REWARD.

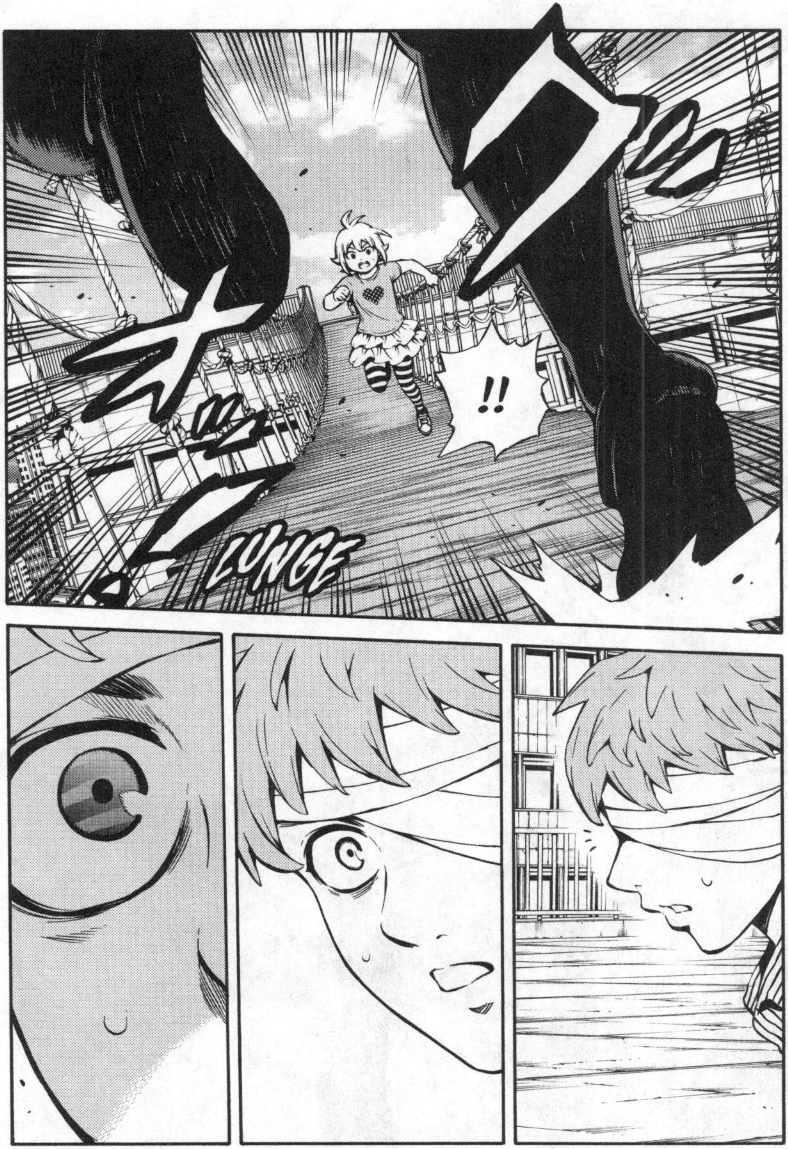
!!
LUNGE

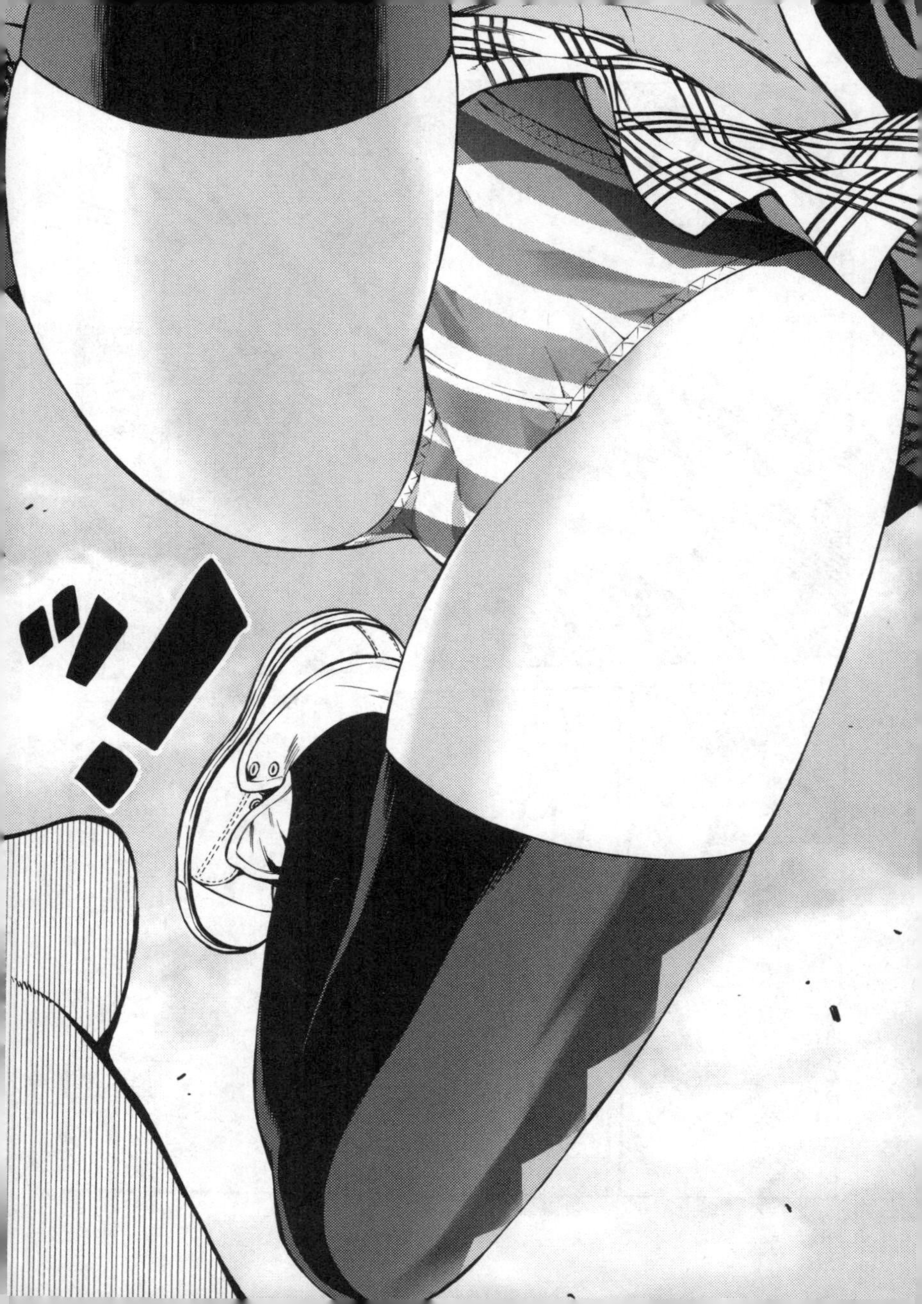

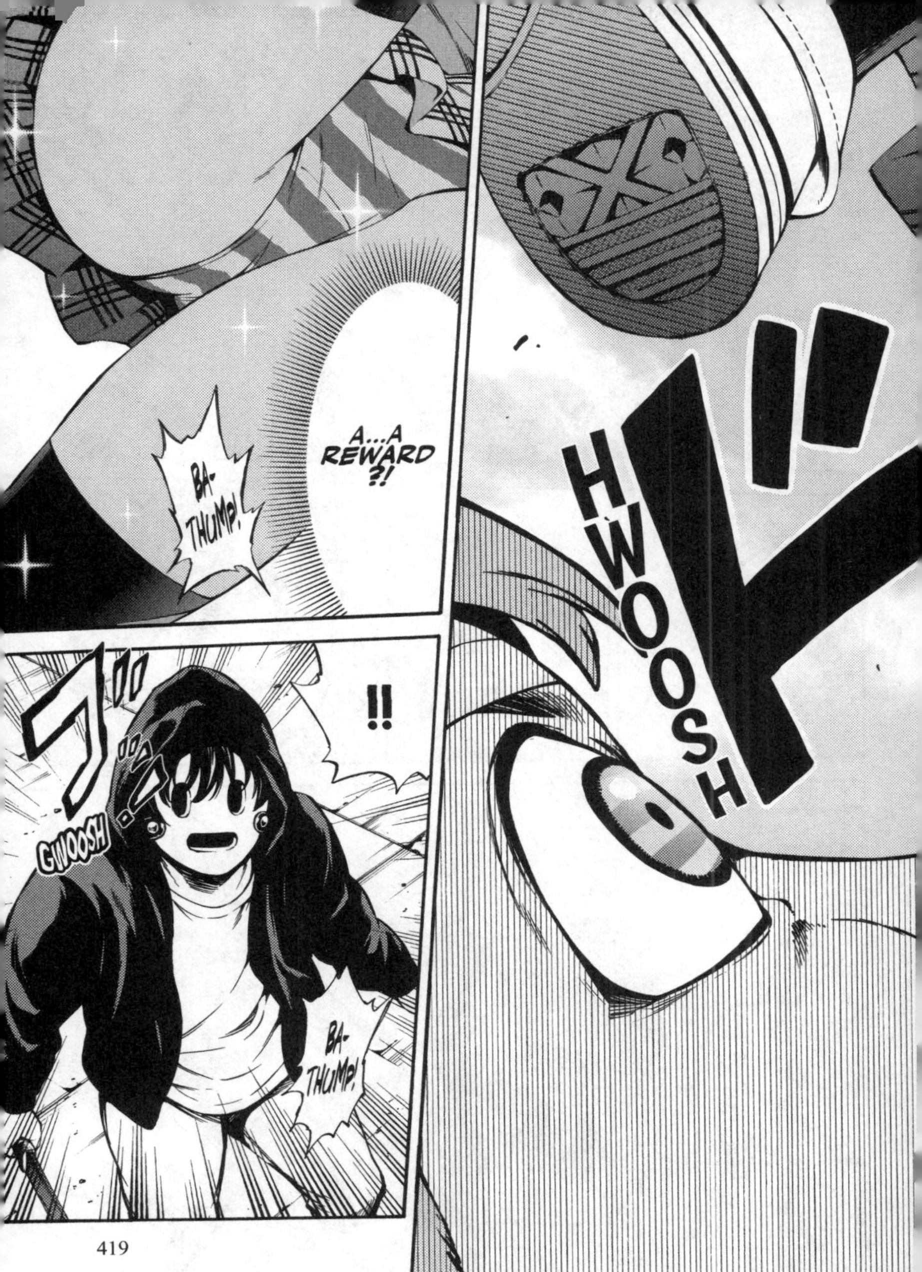
HWOOSH
A...A REWARD?!
BA-THUMP!
!!
GWOOSH
BA-THUMP!

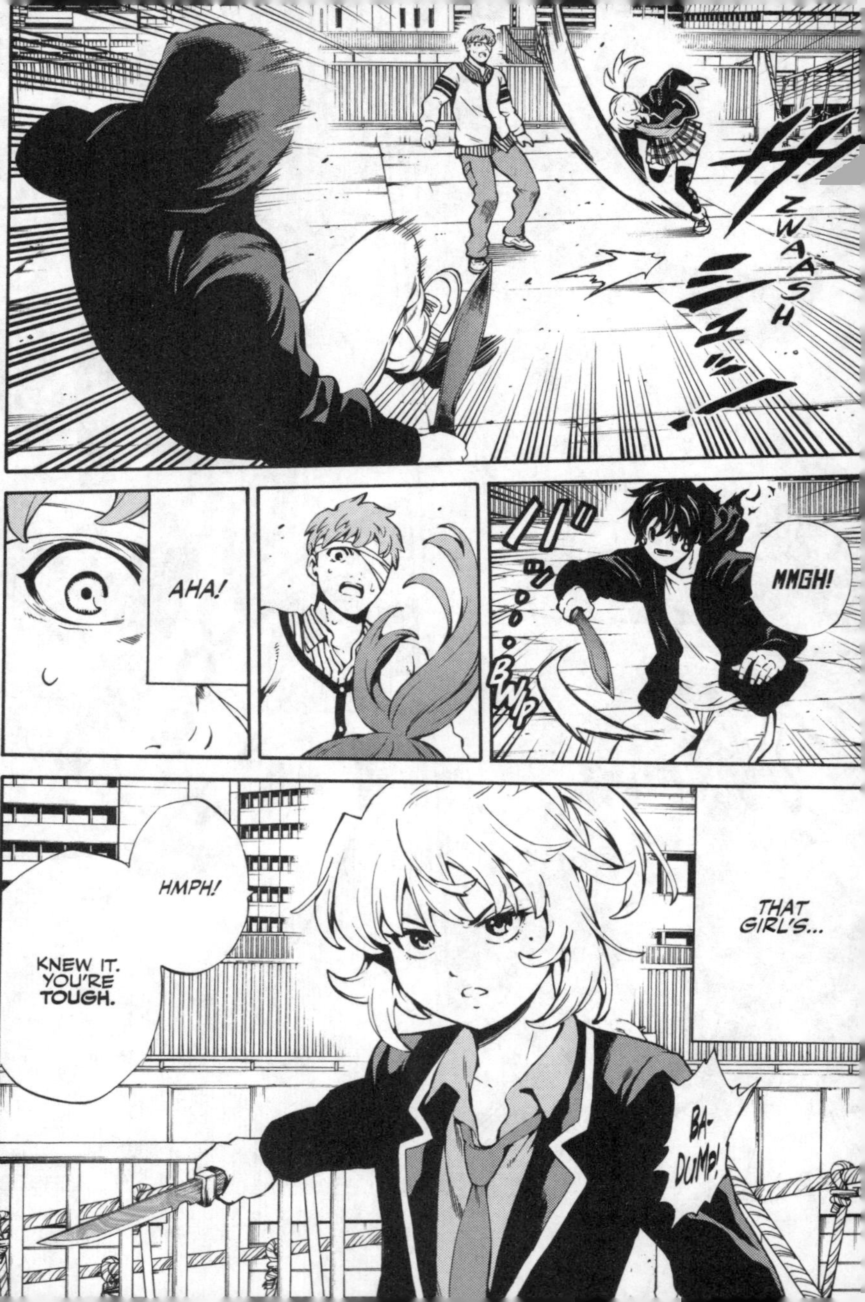
ZWASH
MMGH!
BWIP
AHA!
THAT GIRL'S...
BA-DUMP!
HMPH!
KNEW IT. YOU'RE TOUGH.

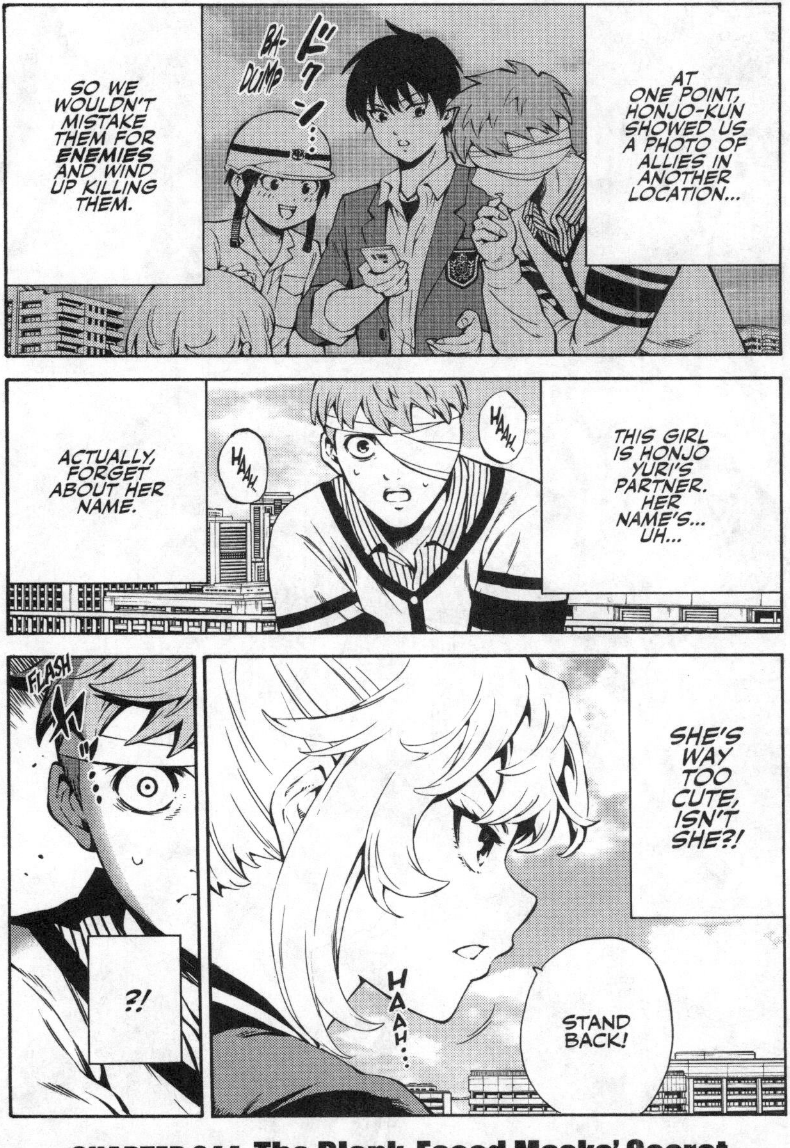
AT ONE POINT, HONJO-KUN SHOWED US A PHOTO OF ALLIES IN ANOTHER LOCATION...
BA-DUMP
SO WE WOULDN'T MISTAKE THEM FOR ENEMIES AND WIND UP KILLING THEM.
THIS GIRL IS HONJO YURI'S PARTNER. HER NAME'S... UH...
HAAH
HAAH
ACTUALLY, FORGET ABOUT HER NAME.
SHE'S WAY TOO CUTE, ISN'T SHE?!
STAND BACK!
HAAAH...
FLASH
?!

CHAPTER 244: The Blank-Faced Masks' Secret

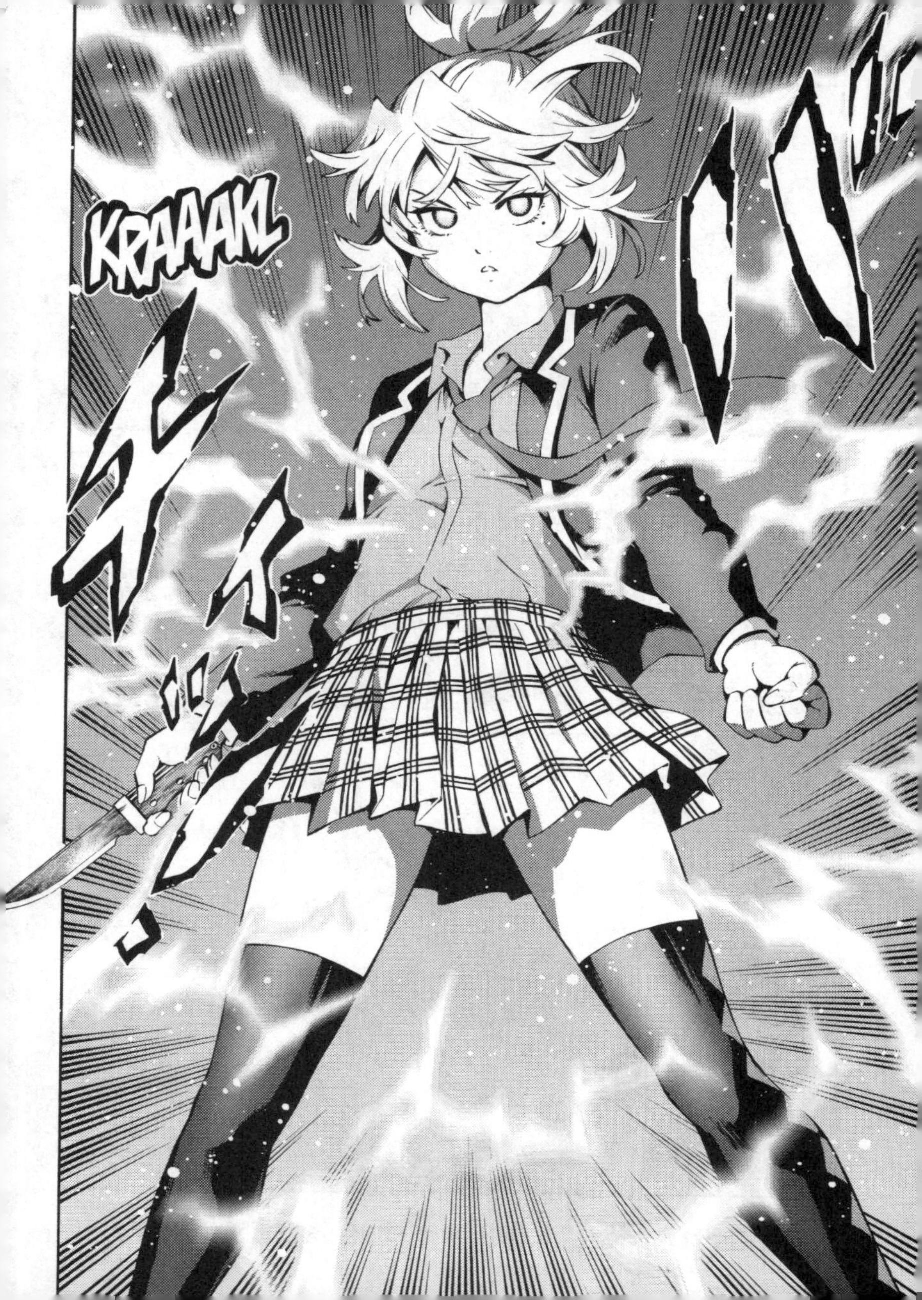
KRAAAK!

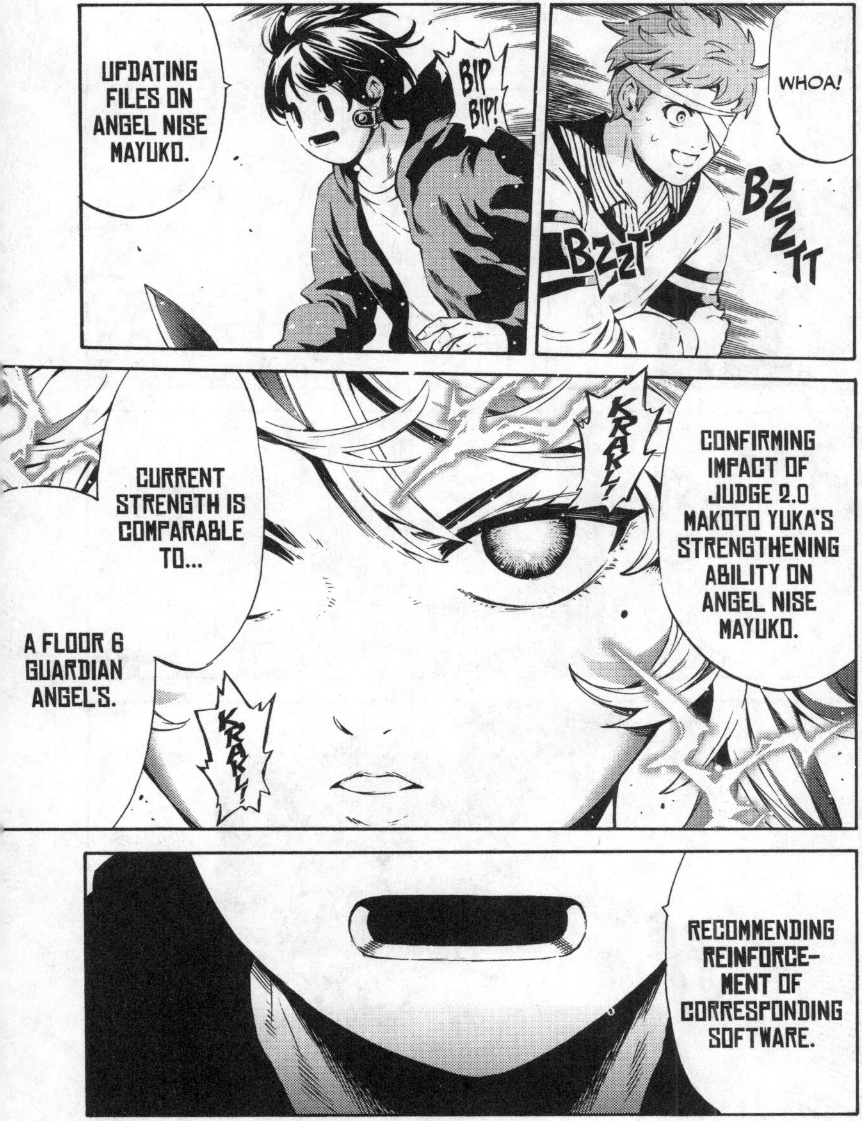
WHOA!
BZZTT
BZZT
BIP BIP!
UPDATING FILES ON ANGEL NISE MAYUKO.
CONFIRMING IMPACT OF JUDGE 2.0 MAKOTO YUKA'S STRENGTHENING ABILITY ON ANGEL NISE MAYUKO.
KRAK!
CURRENT STRENGTH IS COMPARABLE TO...
A FLOOR 6 GUARDIAN ANGEL'S.
KRAK!
RECOMMENDING REINFORCE-MENT OF CORRESPONDING SOFTWARE.

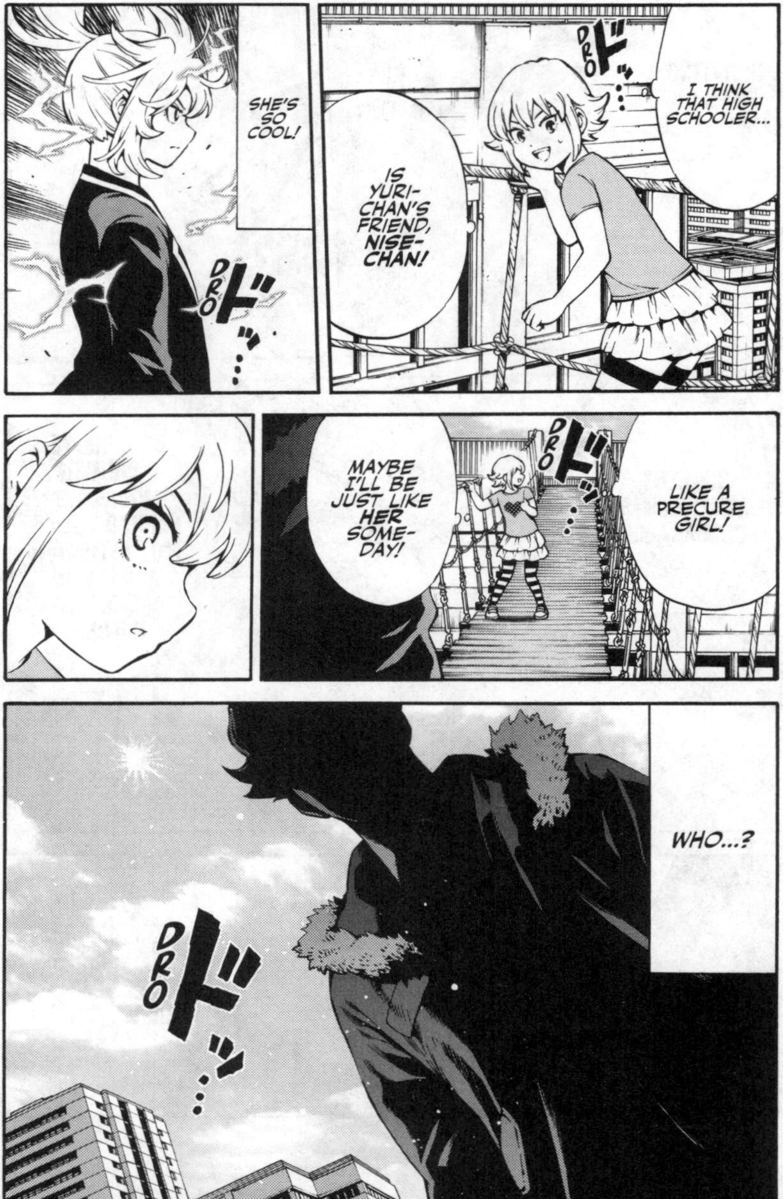
DRO ドッ...
I THINK THAT HIGH SCHOOLER...
IS YURI-CHAN'S FRIEND, NISE-CHAN!
SHE'S SO COOL!
DRO ドッ...
DRO ドッ...
LIKE A PRECURE GIRL!
MAYBE I'LL BE JUST LIKE HER SOME-DAY!
WHO...?
DRO ドッ...

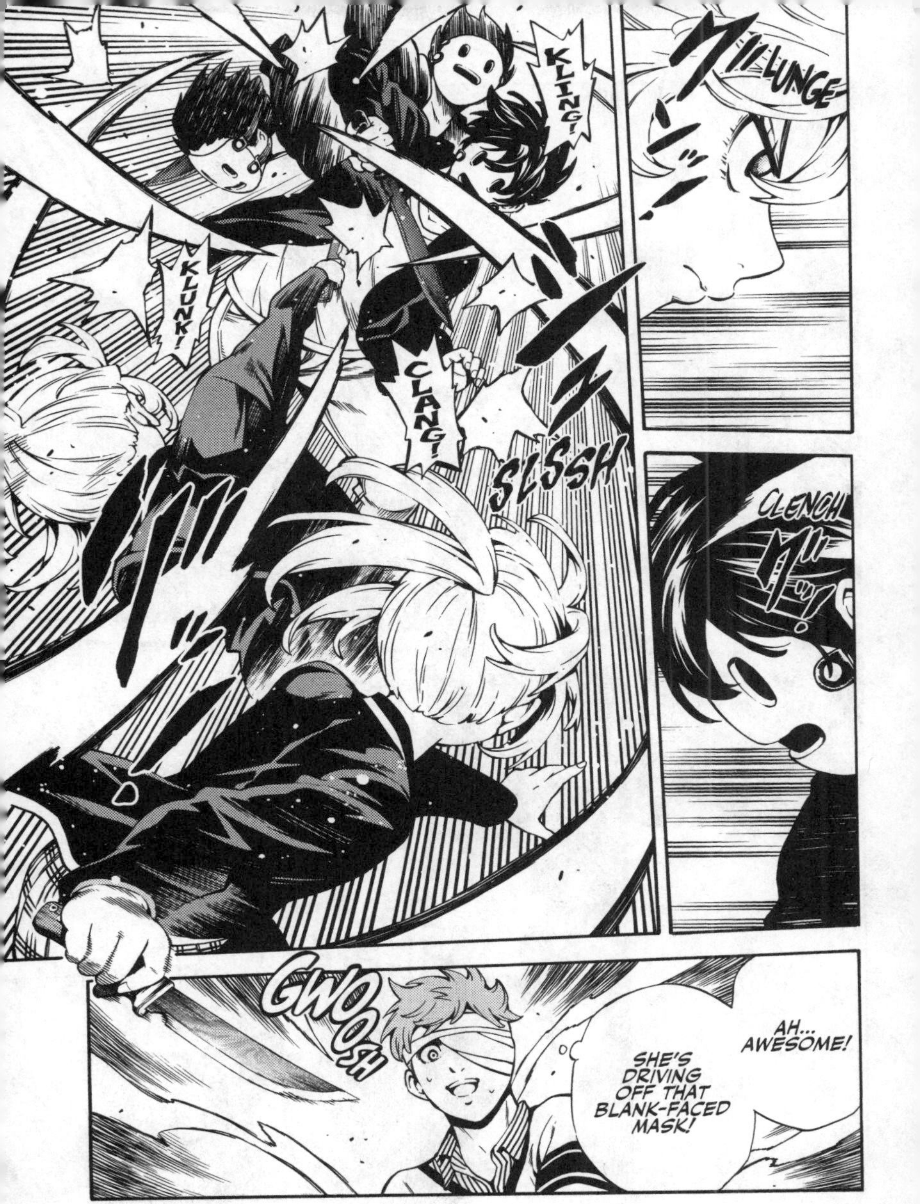
LUNGE
CLENCH
KLING!
KLUNK!
CLANG!
SLSSH
GWOOSH
AH... AWESOME!
SHE'S DRIVING OFF THAT BLANK-FACED MASK!

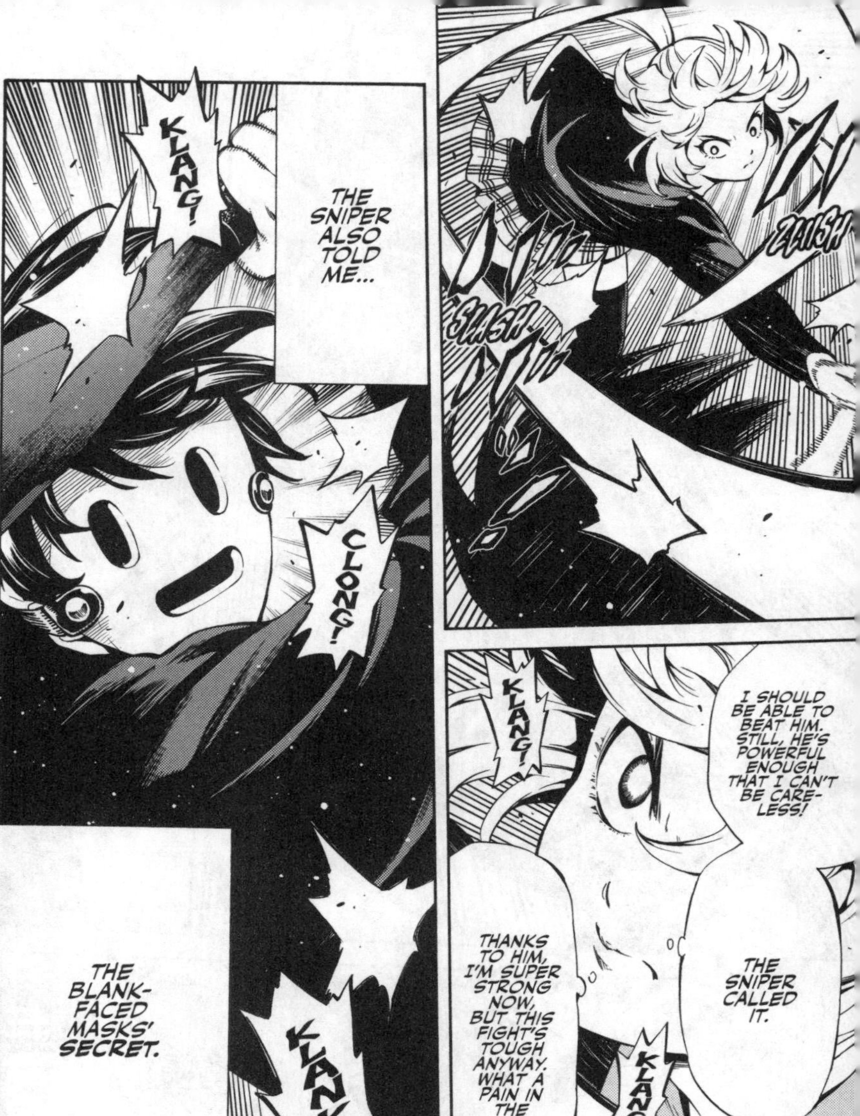
ZAAISH
SLASH
I SHOULD BE ABLE TO BEAT HIM. STILL, HE'S POWERFUL ENOUGH THAT I CAN'T BE CARE-LESS!
KLANG!
THE SNIPER CALLED IT.
THANKS TO HIM, I'M SUPER STRONG NOW, BUT THIS FIGHT'S TOUGH ANYWAY. WHAT A PAIN IN THE ASS!
KLANG!
THE SNIPER ALSO TOLD ME...
KLANG!
CLONG!
THE BLANK-FACED MASKS' SECRET.
KLANK!

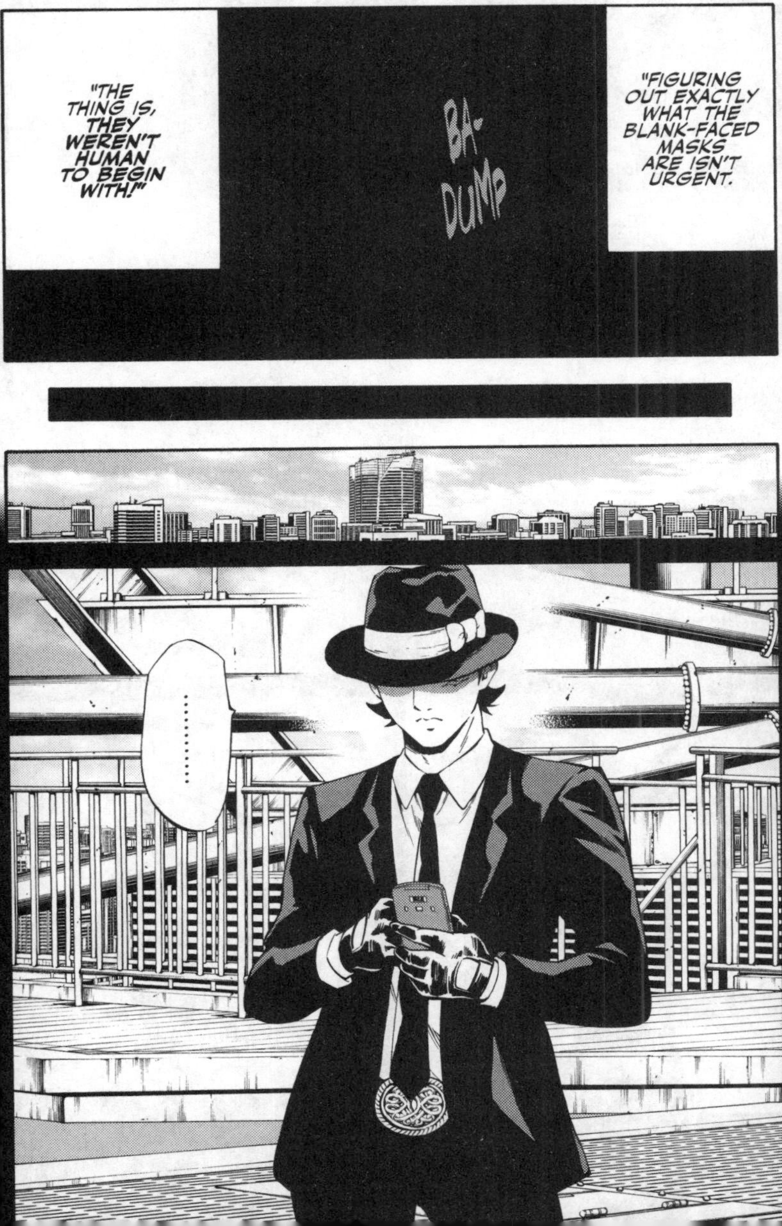
"FIGURING OUT EXACTLY WHAT THE BLANK-FACED MASKS ARE ISN'T URGENT.
BA-DUMP
"THE THING IS, THEY WEREN'T HUMAN TO BEGIN WITH!"
......

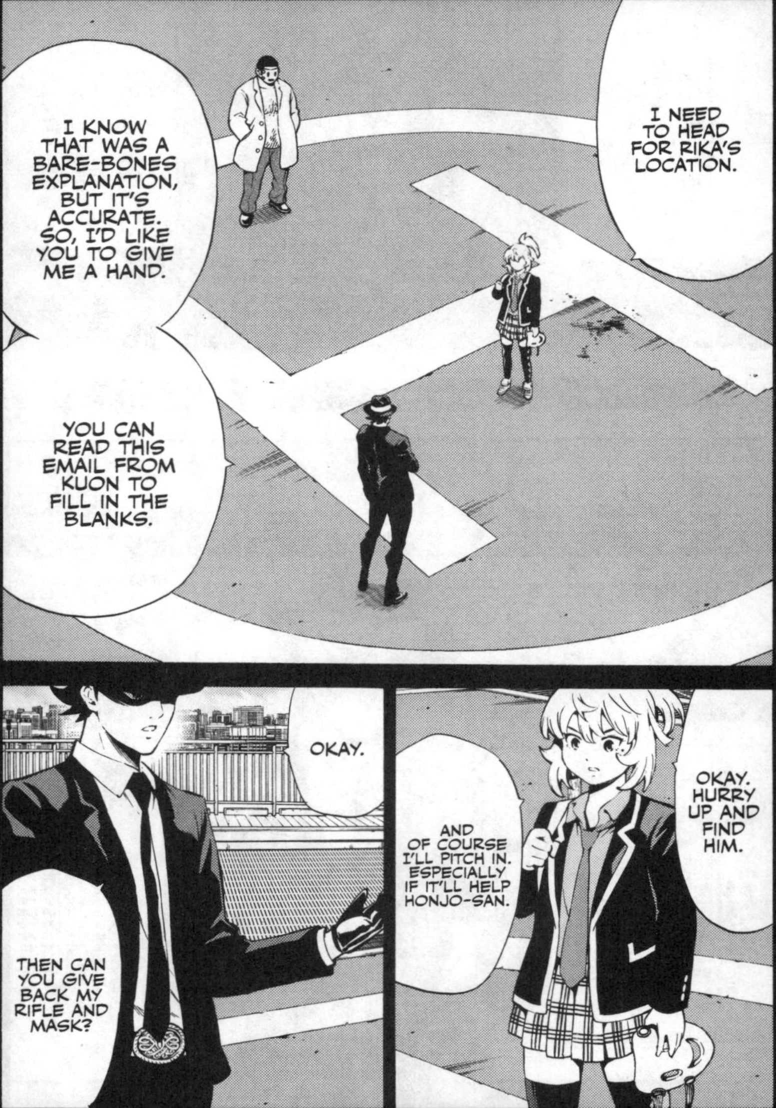
I NEED TO HEAD FOR RIKA'S LOCATION.
I KNOW THAT WAS A BARE-BONES EXPLANATION, BUT IT'S ACCURATE. SO, I'D LIKE YOU TO GIVE ME A HAND.
YOU CAN READ THIS EMAIL FROM KUON TO FILL IN THE BLANKS.
OKAY. HURRY UP AND FIND HIM.
AND OF COURSE I'LL PITCH IN. ESPECIALLY IF IT'LL HELP HONJO-SAN.
OKAY.
THEN CAN YOU GIVE BACK MY RIFLE AND MASK?

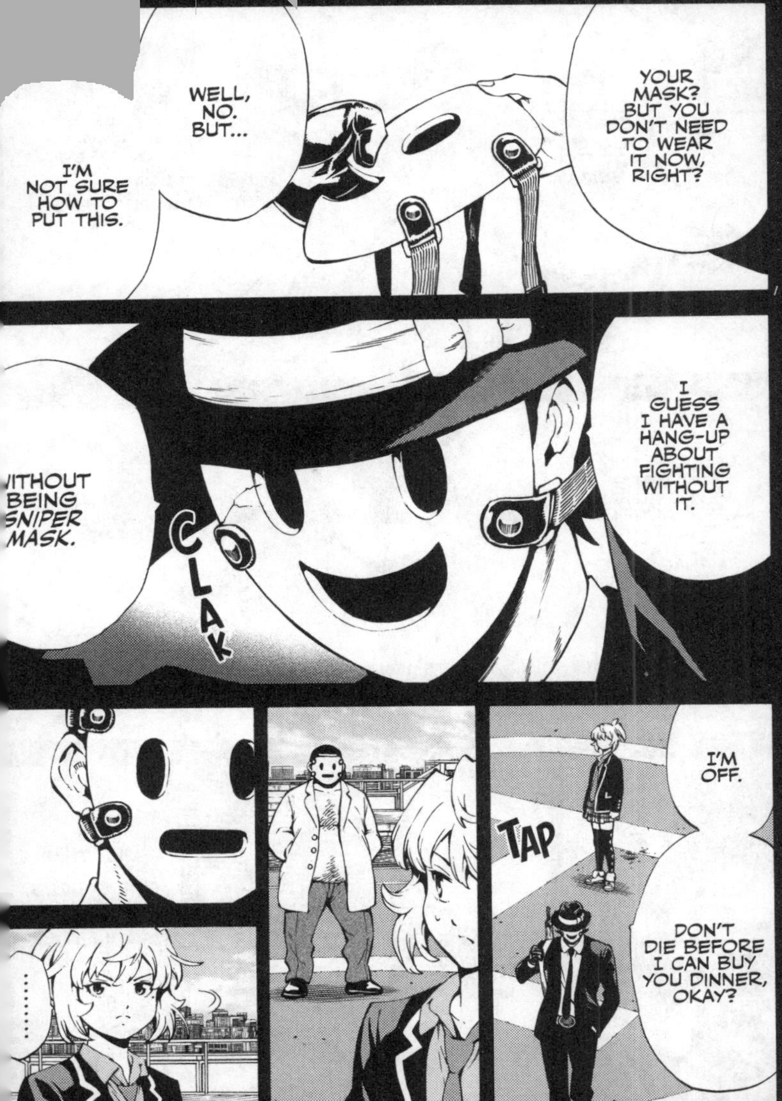
YOUR MASK? BUT YOU DON'T NEED TO WEAR IT NOW, RIGHT?
WELL, NO. BUT...
I'M NOT SURE HOW TO PUT THIS.
I GUESS I HAVE A HANG-UP ABOUT FIGHTING WITHOUT IT.
CLAK
WITHOUT BEING SNIPER MASK.
I'M OFF.
TAP
DON'T DIE BEFORE I CAN BUY YOU DINNER, OKAY?
....

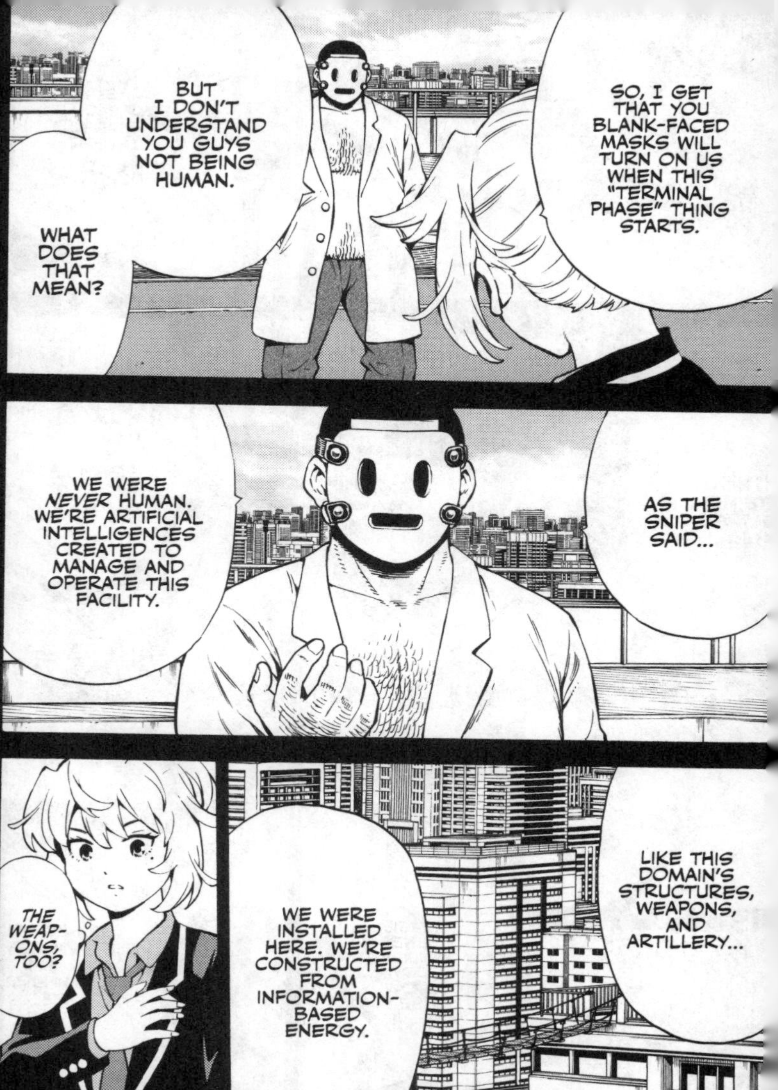
SO, I GET THAT YOU BLANK-FACED MASKS WILL TURN ON US WHEN THIS "TERMINAL PHASE" THING STARTS.
BUT I DON'T UNDERSTAND YOU GUYS NOT BEING HUMAN.
WHAT DOES THAT MEAN?
AS THE SNIPER SAID...
WE WERE *NEVER* HUMAN. WE'RE ARTIFICIAL INTELLIGENCES CREATED TO MANAGE AND OPERATE THIS FACILITY.
LIKE THIS DOMAIN'S STRUCTURES, WEAPONS, AND ARTILLERY...
WE WERE INSTALLED HERE. WE'RE CONSTRUCTED FROM INFORMATION-BASED ENERGY.
THE WEAP-ONS, TOO?

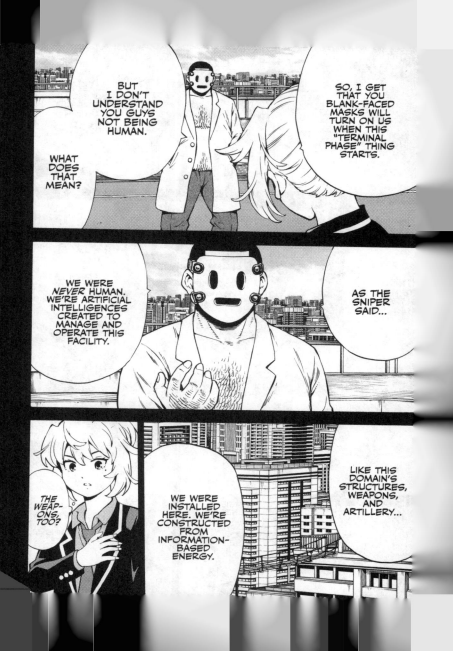

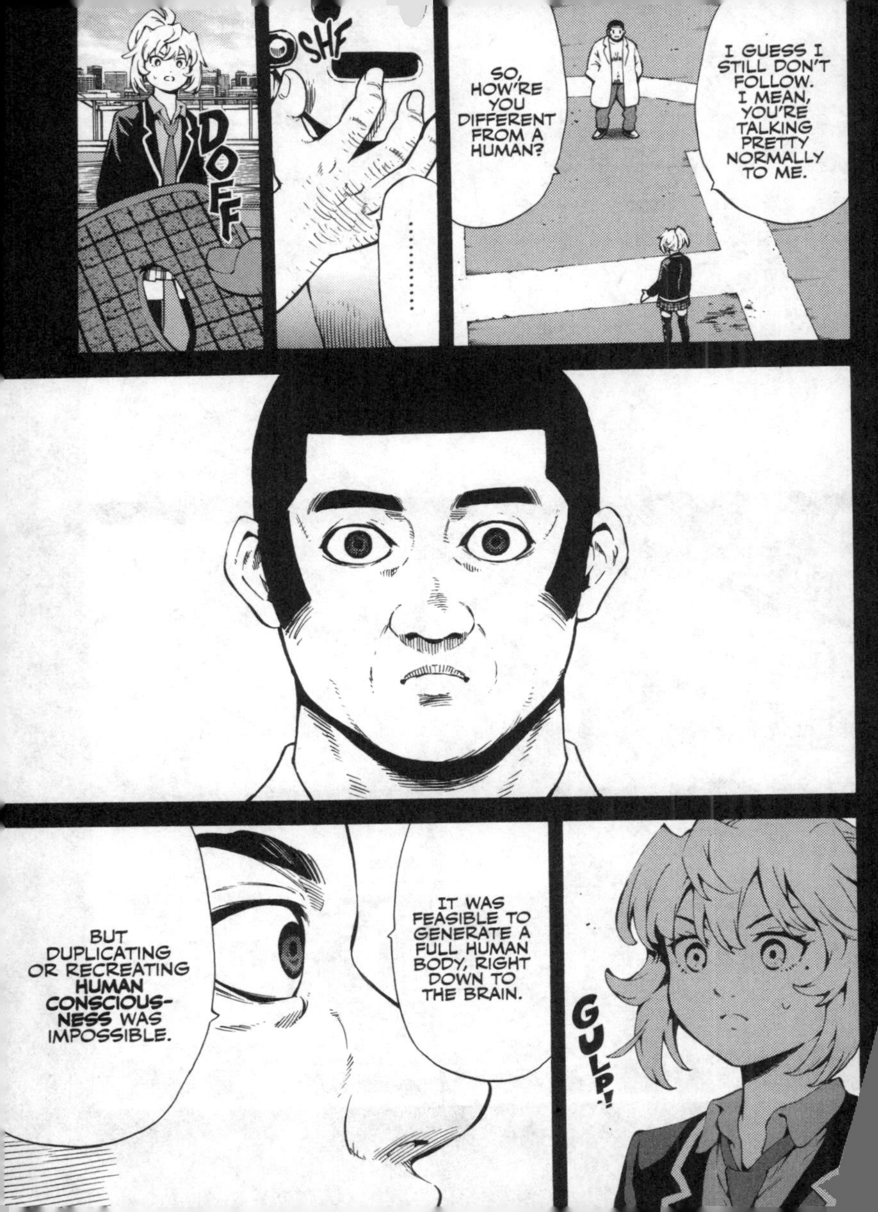
I GUESS I STILL DON'T FOLLOW. I MEAN, YOU'RE TALKING PRETTY NORMALLY TO ME.
SO, HOW'RE YOU DIFFERENT FROM A HUMAN?
SHF
......
DOFF
GULP!
IT WAS FEASIBLE TO GENERATE A FULL HUMAN BODY, RIGHT DOWN TO THE BRAIN.
BUT DUPLICATING OR RECREATING **HUMAN CONSCIOUSNESS** WAS IMPOSSIBLE.

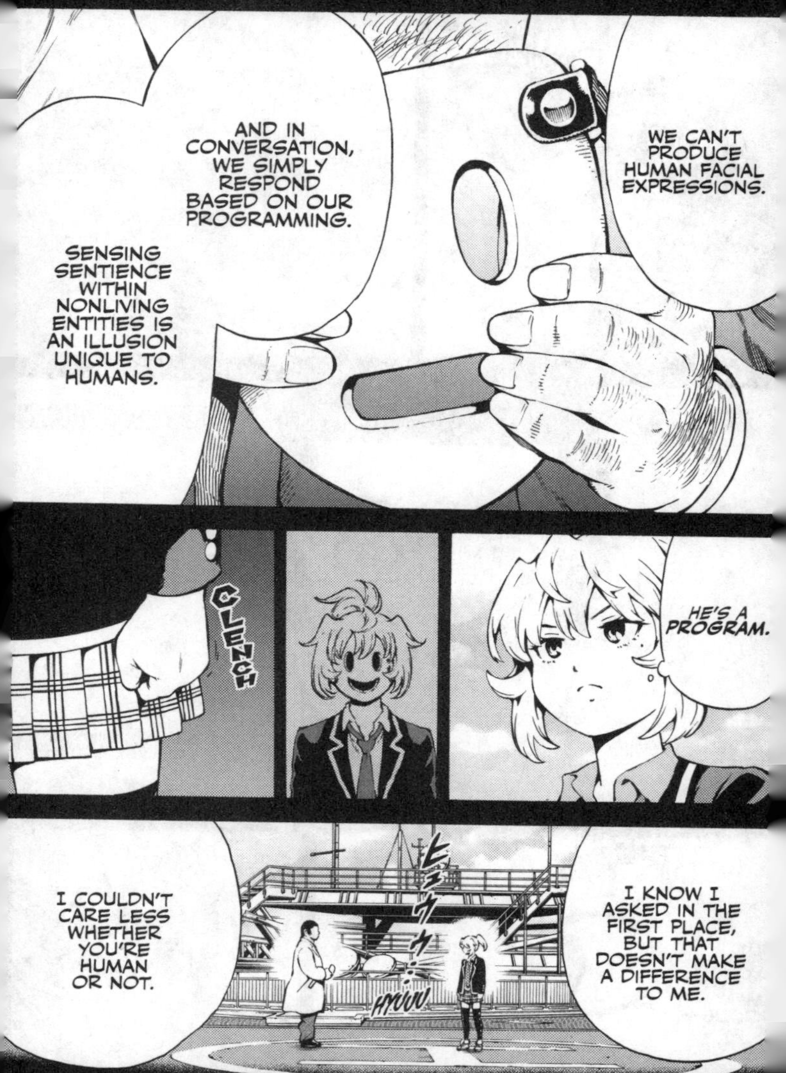
WE CAN'T PRODUCE HUMAN FACIAL EXPRESSIONS.
AND IN CONVERSATION, WE SIMPLY RESPOND BASED ON OUR PROGRAMMING.
SENSING SENTIENCE WITHIN NONLIVING ENTITIES IS AN ILLUSION UNIQUE TO HUMANS.
HE'S A PROGRAM.
CLENCH
I KNOW I ASKED IN THE FIRST PLACE, BUT THAT DOESN'T MAKE A DIFFERENCE TO ME.
HYUUU
I COULDN'T CARE LESS WHETHER YOU'RE HUMAN OR NOT.

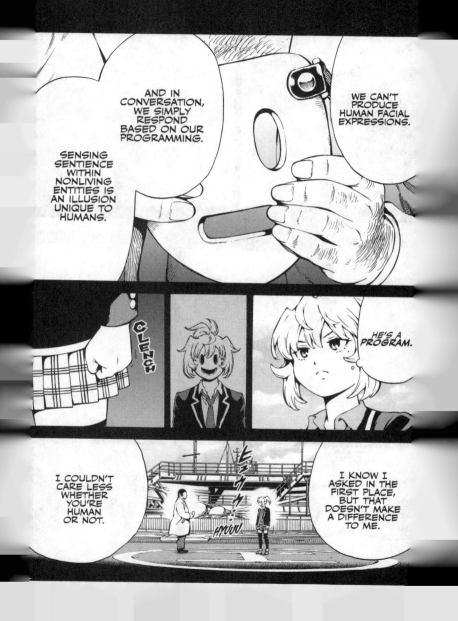

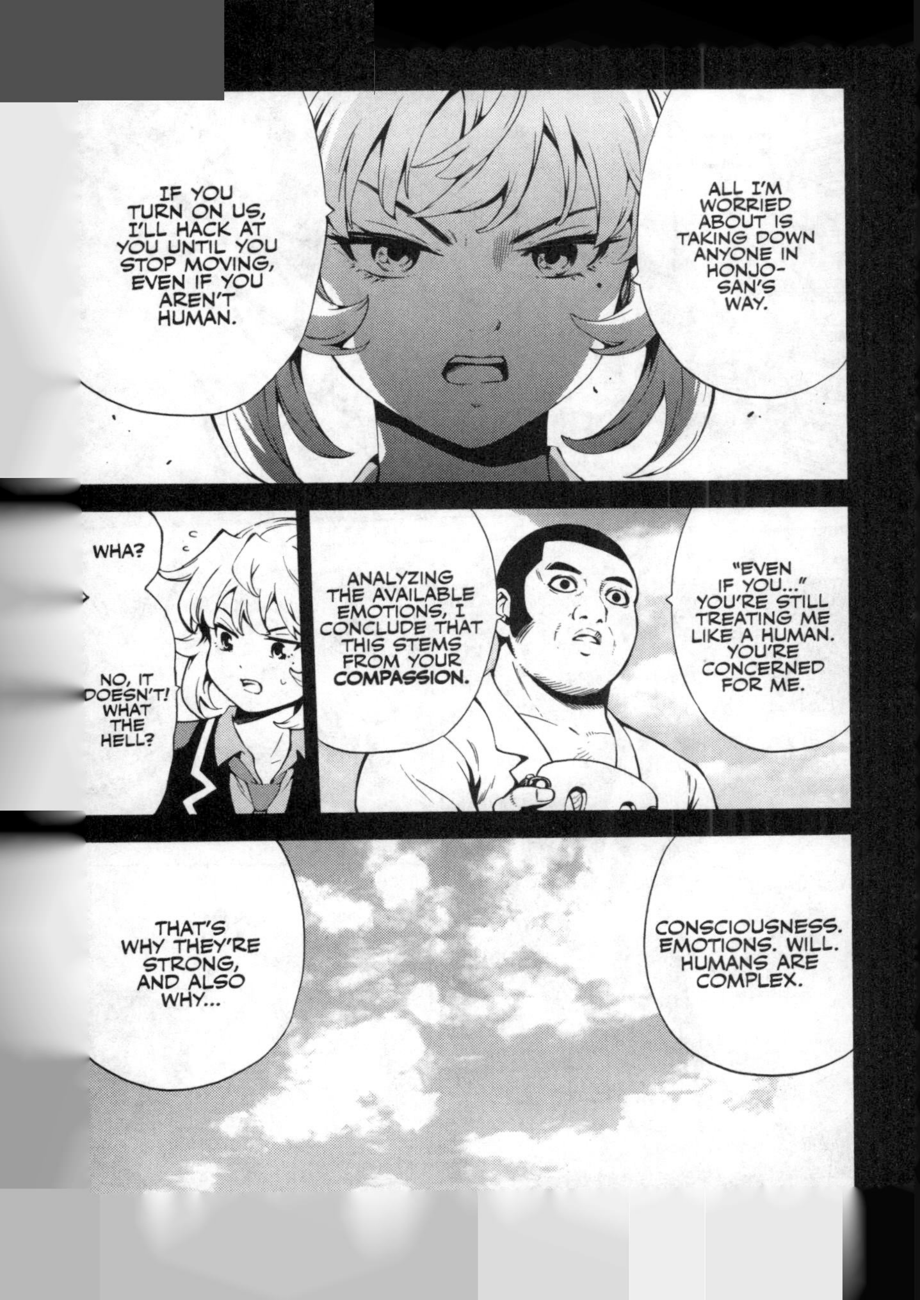
ALL I'M WORRIED ABOUT IS TAKING DOWN ANYONE IN HONJO-SAN'S WAY.
IF YOU TURN ON US, I'LL HACK AT YOU UNTIL YOU STOP MOVING, EVEN IF YOU AREN'T HUMAN.
"EVEN IF YOU..." YOU'RE STILL TREATING ME LIKE A HUMAN. YOU'RE CONCERNED FOR ME.
ANALYZING THE AVAILABLE EMOTIONS, I CONCLUDE THAT THIS STEMS FROM YOUR **COMPASSION.**
WHA?
NO, IT DOESN'T! WHAT THE HELL?
CONSCIOUSNESS. EMOTIONS. WILL. HUMANS ARE COMPLEX.
THAT'S WHY THEY'RE STRONG, AND ALSO WHY...

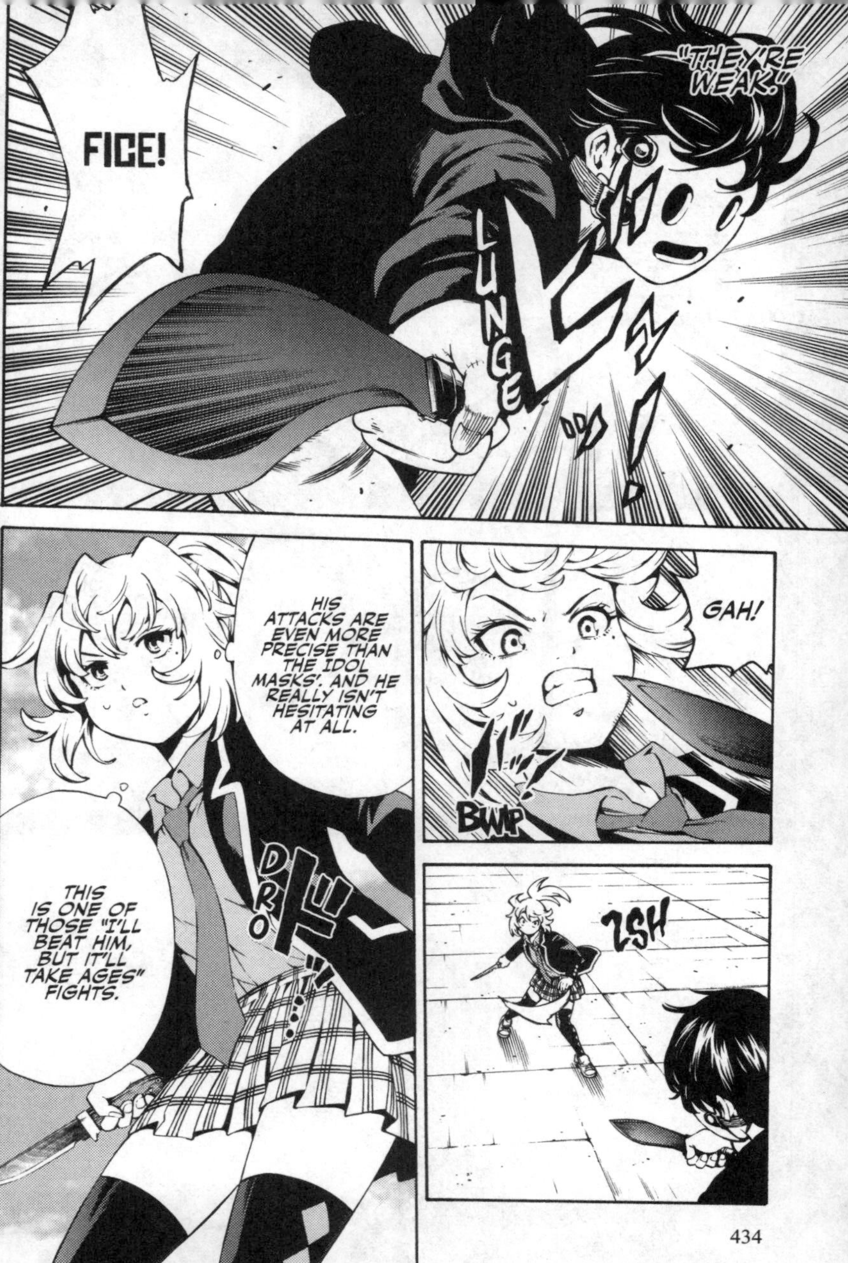

—"THEY'RE WEAK."
FICE!
LUNGE
GAH!
BWMP
ZSH
HIS ATTACKS ARE EVEN MORE PRECISE THAN THE IDOL MASKS'. AND HE REALLY ISN'T HESITATING AT ALL.
THIS IS ONE OF THOSE "I'LL BEAT HIM, BUT IT'LL TAKE AGES" FIGHTS.

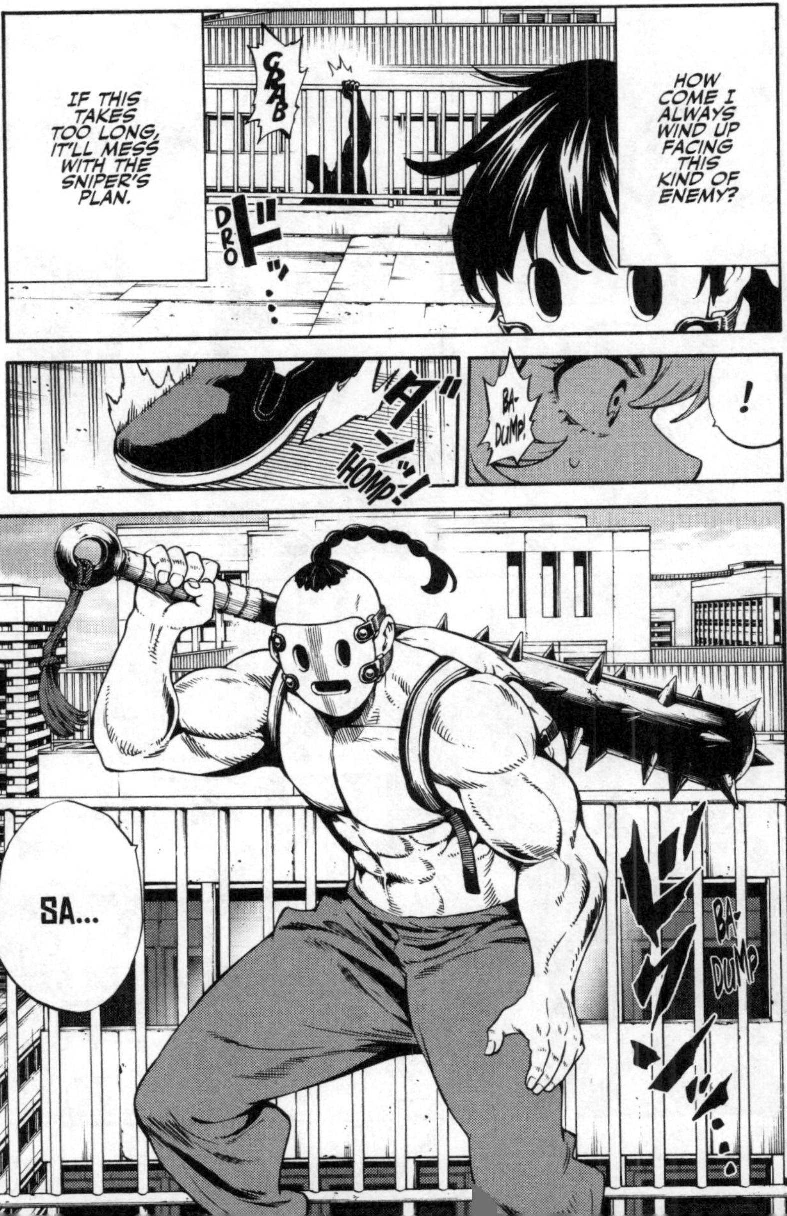
HOW COME I ALWAYS WIND UP FACING THIS KIND OF ENEMY?
GRAB
IF THIS TAKES TOO LONG, IT'LL MESS WITH THE SNIPER'S PLAN.
DRO
!
BA-DUMP!
THOMP!
BA-DUMP
SA...

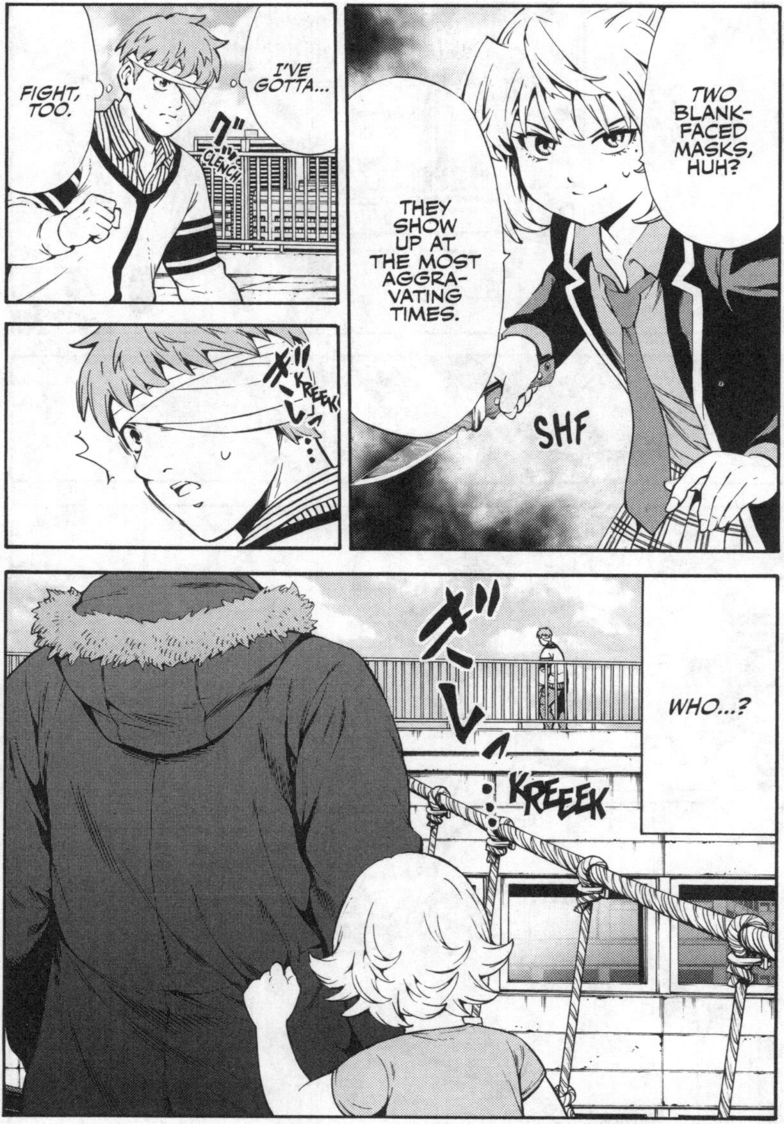
TWO BLANK-FACED MASKS, HUH?
THEY SHOW UP AT THE MOST AGGRAVATING TIMES.
SHF
I'VE GOTTA...
FIGHT, TOO.
CLENCH
KREEEK
WHO...?
KREEEK

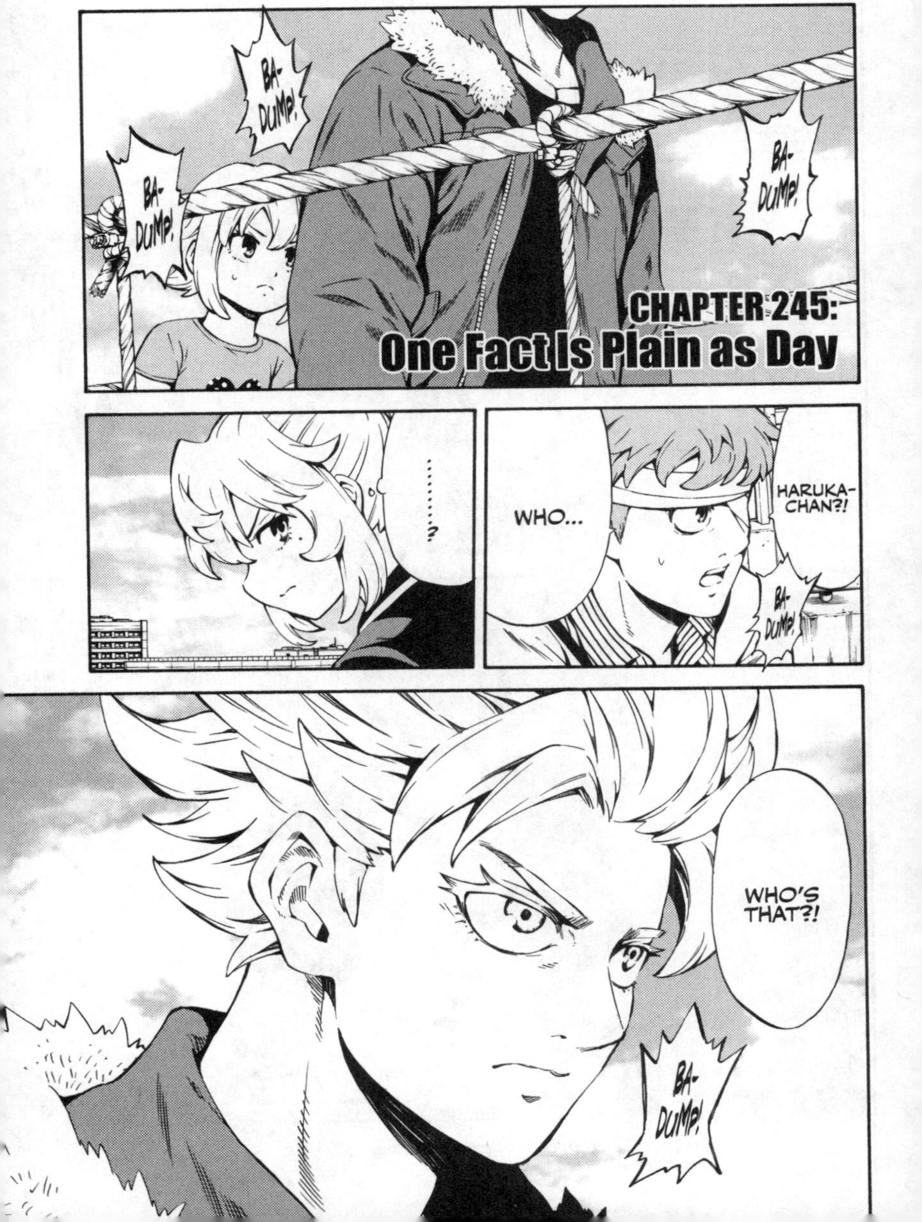
BA-DUMP!
BA-DUMP!
BA-DUMP!
CHAPTER 245:
One Fact Is Plain as Day
HARUKA-CHAN?!
WHO...
BA-DUMP!
......?
WHO'S THAT?!
BA-DUMP!

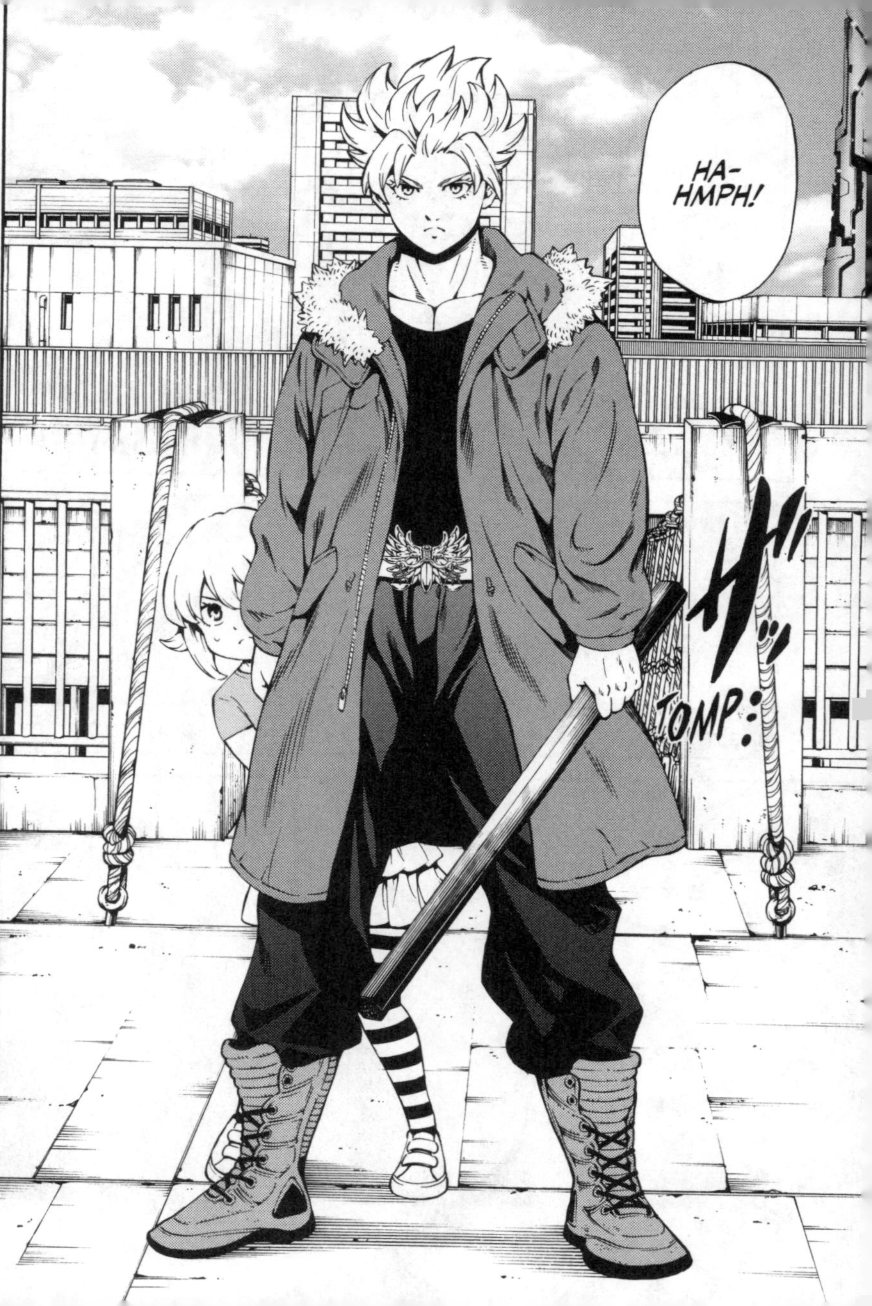
HA-
HMPH!
TOMP

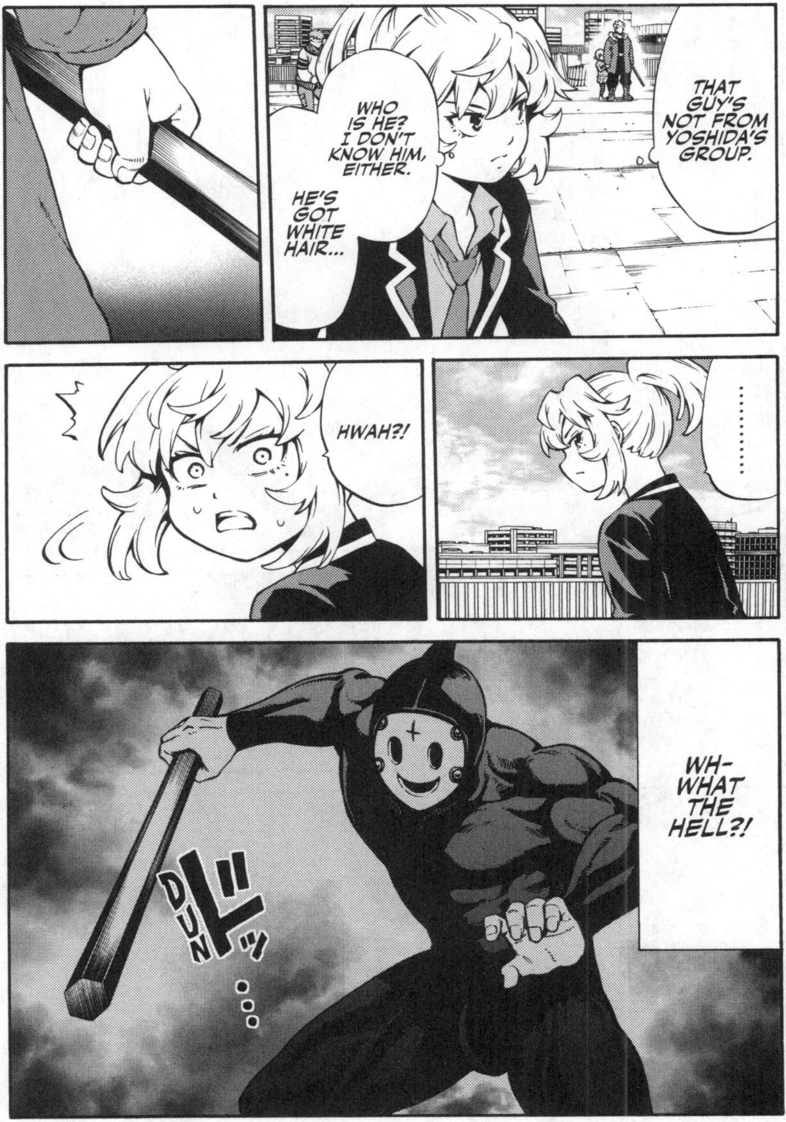
THAT GUY'S NOT FROM YOSHIDA'S GROUP.
WHO IS HE? I DON'T KNOW HIM, EITHER.
HE'S GOT WHITE HAIR...
......
HWAH?!
WH-WHAT THE HELL?!
DUN
...

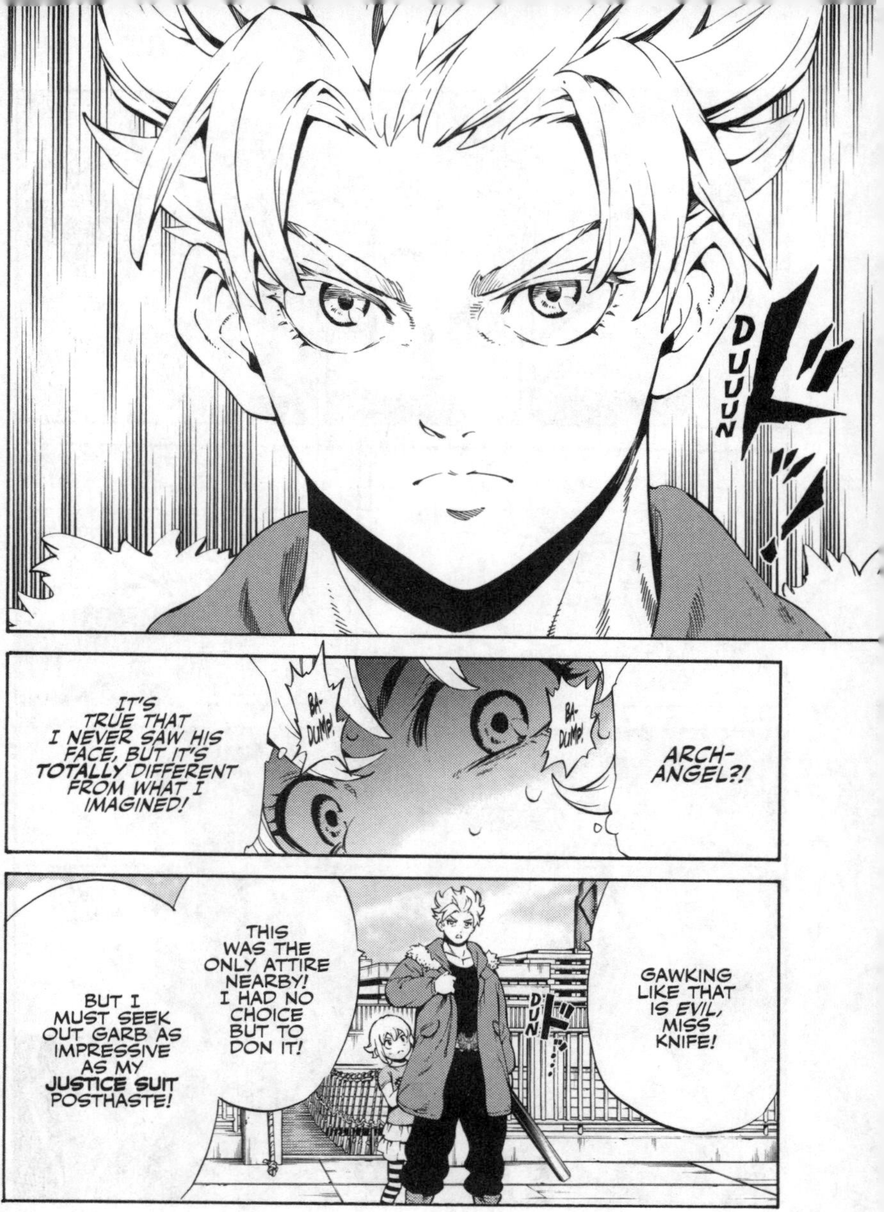
DUUUN
ARCH-ANGEL?!
BA-DUMP!
BA-DUMP!
IT'S TRUE THAT I NEVER SAW HIS FACE, BUT IT'S **TOTALLY** DIFFERENT FROM WHAT I IMAGINED!
GAWKING LIKE THAT IS *EVIL*, MISS KNIFE!
DUN
THIS WAS THE ONLY ATTIRE NEARBY! I HAD NO CHOICE BUT TO DON IT!
BUT I MUST SEEK OUT GARB AS IMPRESSIVE AS MY **JUSTICE SUIT** POSTHASTE!

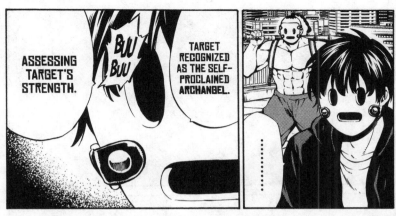

TARGET RECOGNIZED AS THE SELF-PROCLAIMED ARCHANGEL.
BUU BUU
ASSESSING TARGET'S STRENGTH.
TARGET'S STRENGTH IS...
BA-DUMP
COMPARABLE TO AN AVERAGE ANGEL'S.
HUH?
DOES... DOES THAT MEAN HE'S WEAKER?
BA-DUMP

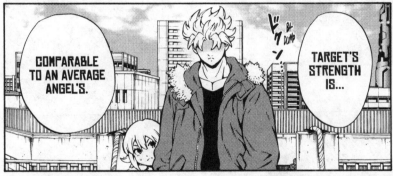

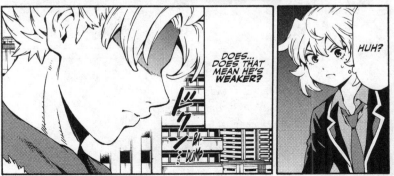

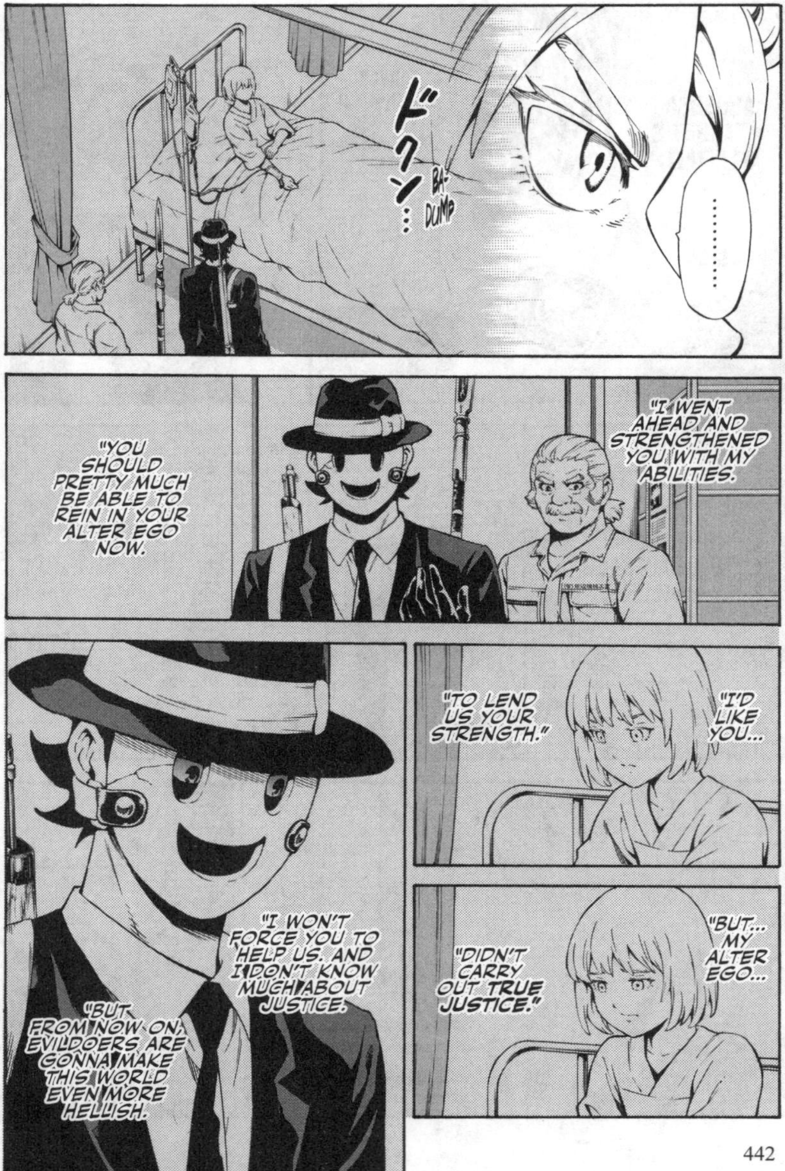
ドクン…
BA-DUMP
……
"I WENT AHEAD AND STRENGTHENED YOU WITH MY ABILITIES.
"YOU SHOULD PRETTY MUCH BE ABLE TO REIN IN YOUR ALTER EGO NOW.
"I'D LIKE YOU...
"TO LEND US YOUR STRENGTH."
"BUT... MY ALTER EGO...
"DIDN'T CARRY OUT TRUE JUSTICE."
"I WON'T FORCE YOU TO HELP US. AND I DON'T KNOW MUCH ABOUT JUSTICE.
"BUT FROM NOW ON, EVILDOERS ARE GONNA MAKE THIS WORLD EVEN MORE HELLISH.

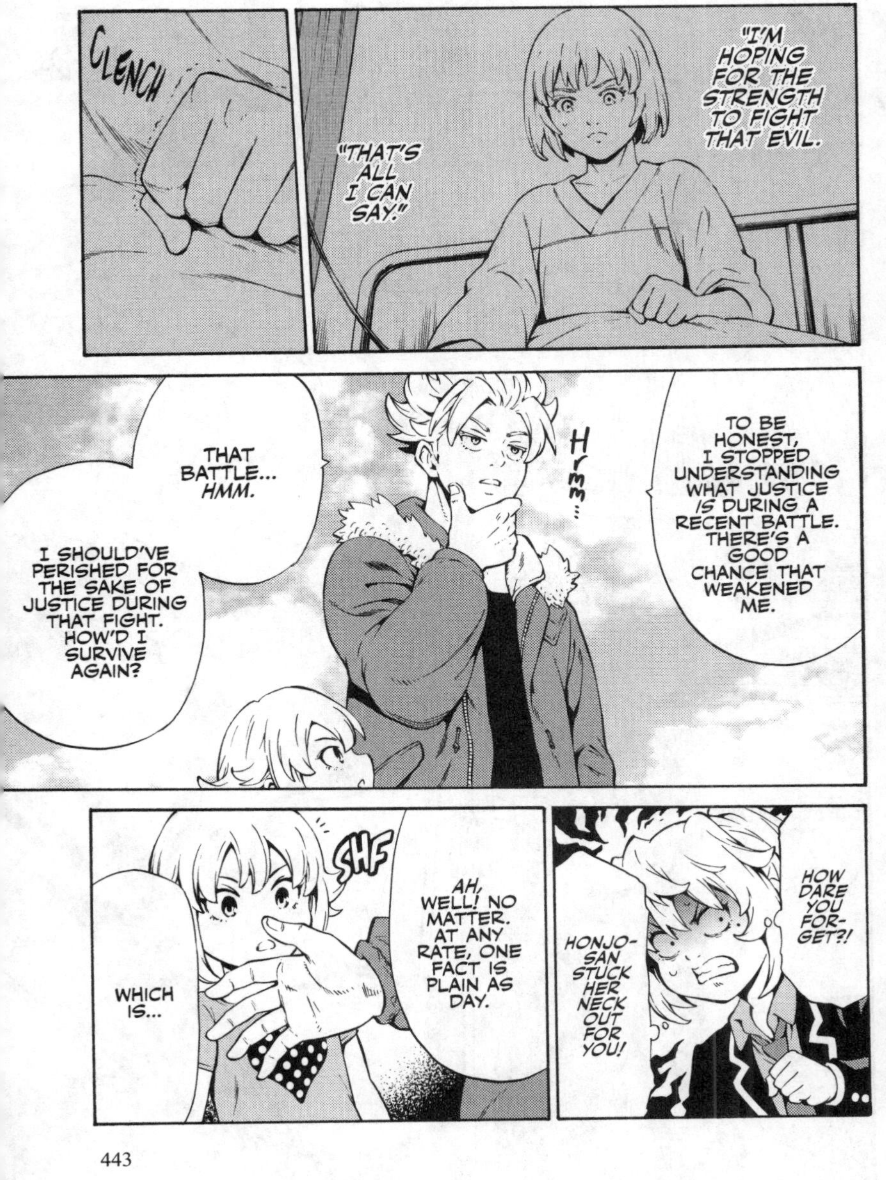
"I'M HOPING FOR THE STRENGTH TO FIGHT THAT EVIL.
"THAT'S ALL I CAN SAY."
CLENCH
TO BE HONEST, I STOPPED UNDERSTANDING WHAT JUSTICE *IS* DURING A RECENT BATTLE. THERE'S A GOOD CHANCE THAT WEAKENED ME.
Hrmm...
THAT BATTLE... *HMM.*
I SHOULD'VE PERISHED FOR THE SAKE OF JUSTICE DURING THAT FIGHT. HOW'D I SURVIVE AGAIN?
HOW DARE YOU FORGET?!
HONJO-SAN STUCK HER NECK OUT FOR YOU!
SHF
AH, WELL! NO MATTER. AT ANY RATE, ONE FACT IS PLAIN AS DAY.
WHICH IS...

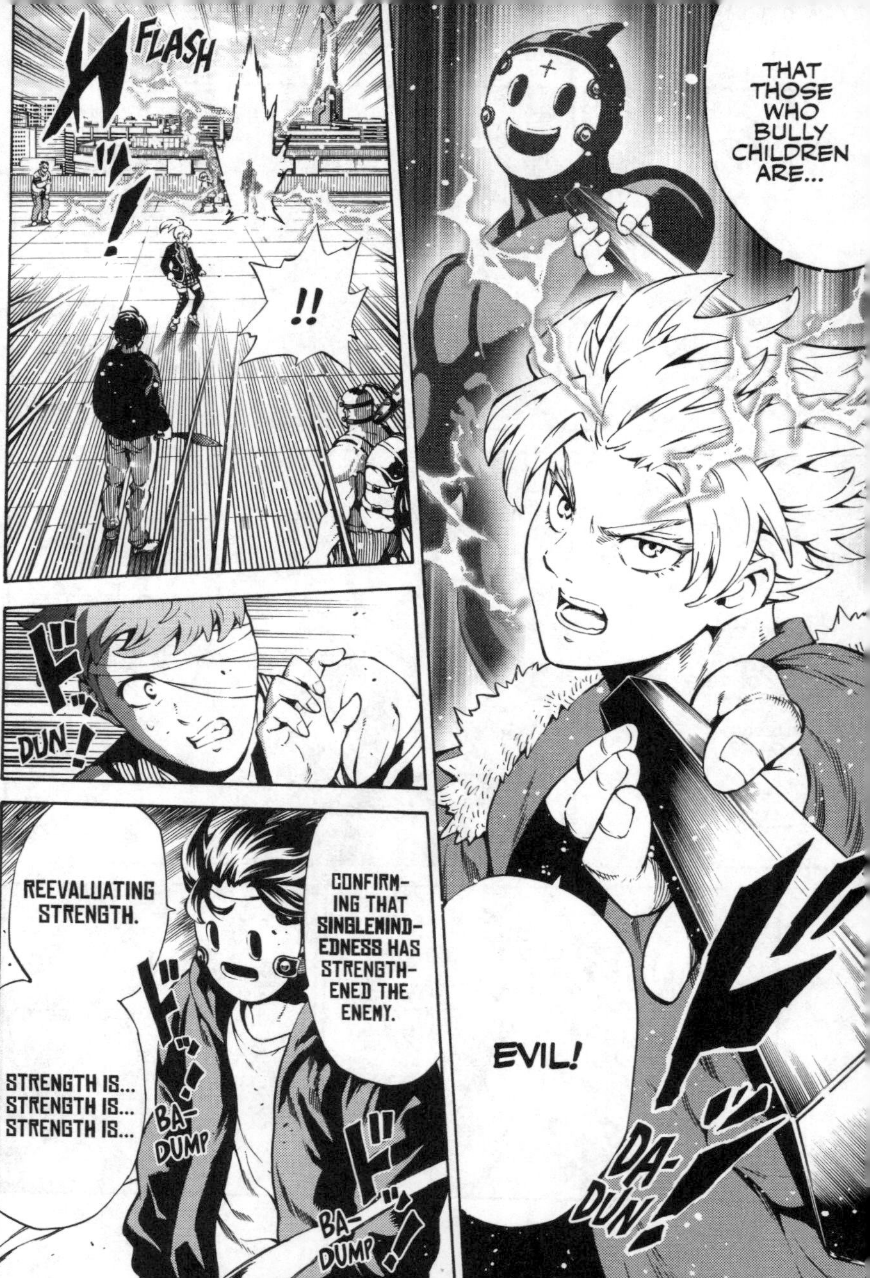
THAT THOSE WHO BULLY CHILDREN ARE...
EVIL!
DA-DUN!
FLASH
!!
DUN!
CONFIRMING THAT SINGLEMINDEDNESS HAS STRENGTHENED THE ENEMY.
REEVALUATING STRENGTH.
STRENGTH IS... STRENGTH IS... STRENGTH IS...
BA-DUMP
BA-DUMP

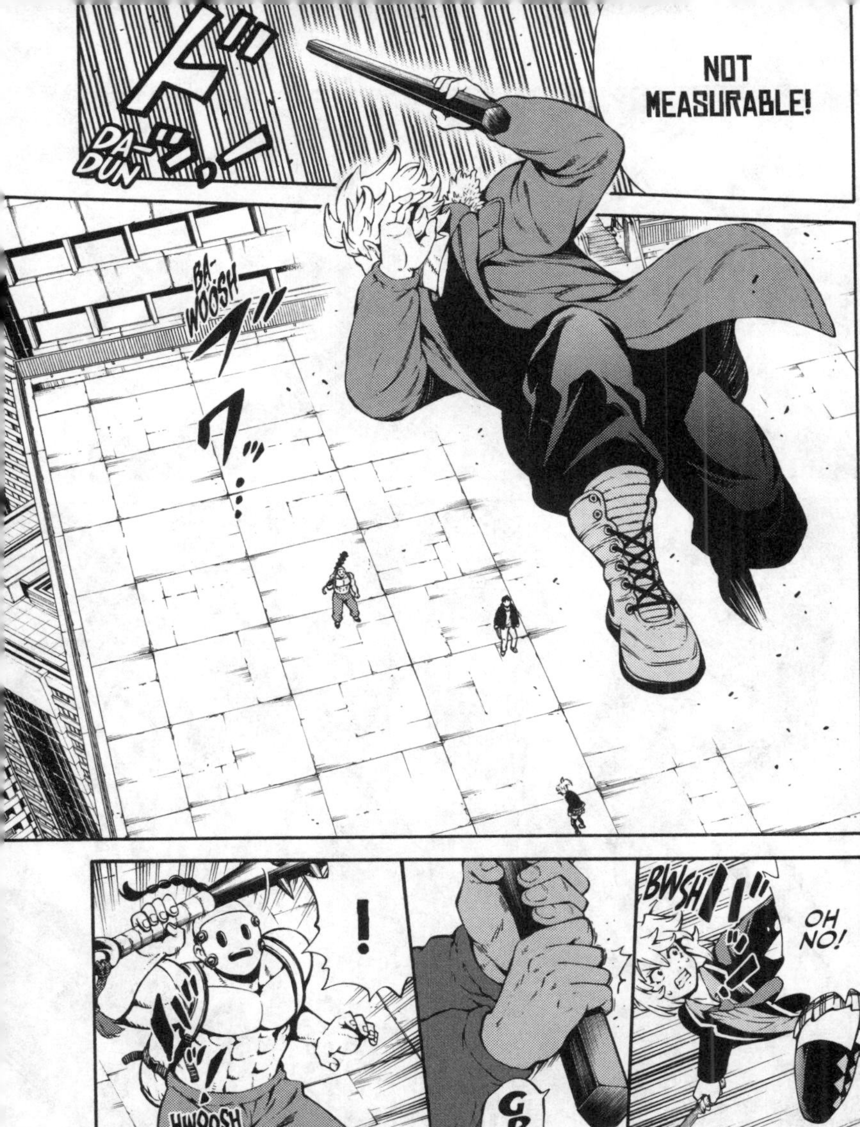
NOT MEASURABLE!
DA-DUN
BA-WOOSH
BWSH
OH NO!
GRIP
!
HWOOSH

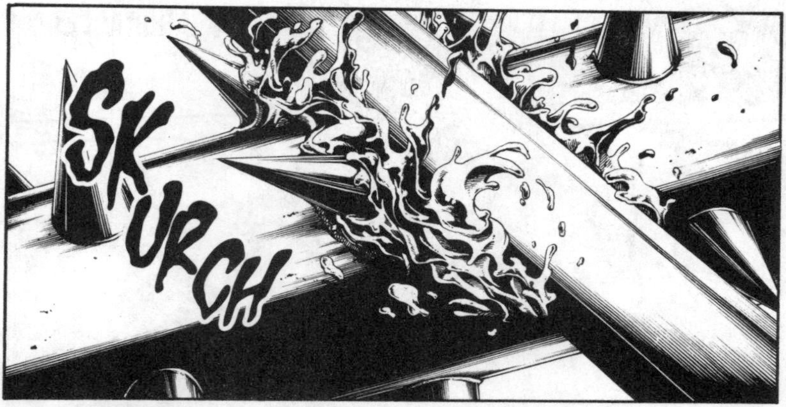
SKURCH
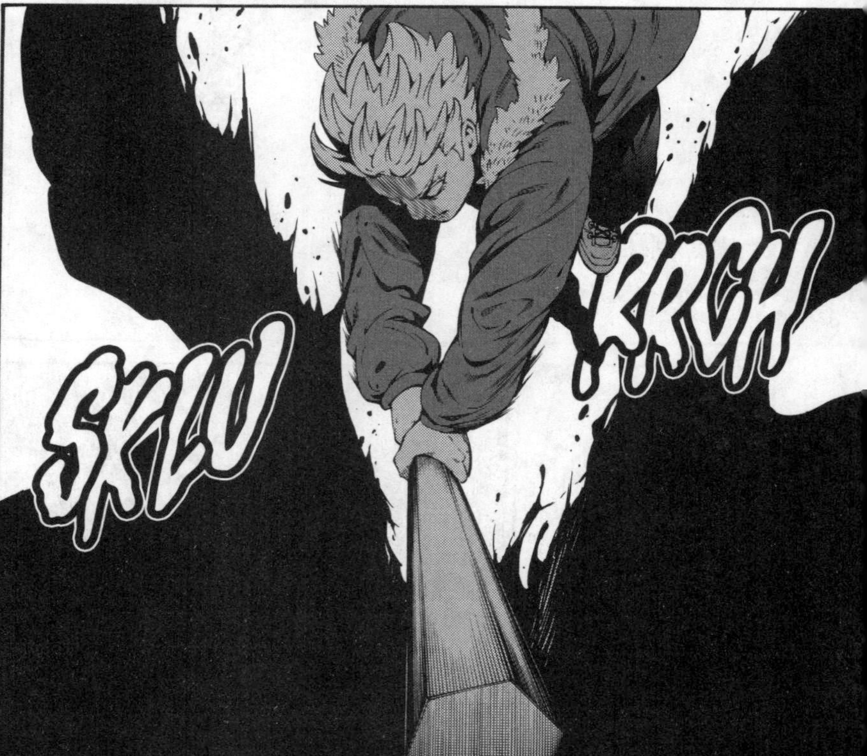
SKLOO
RRCH

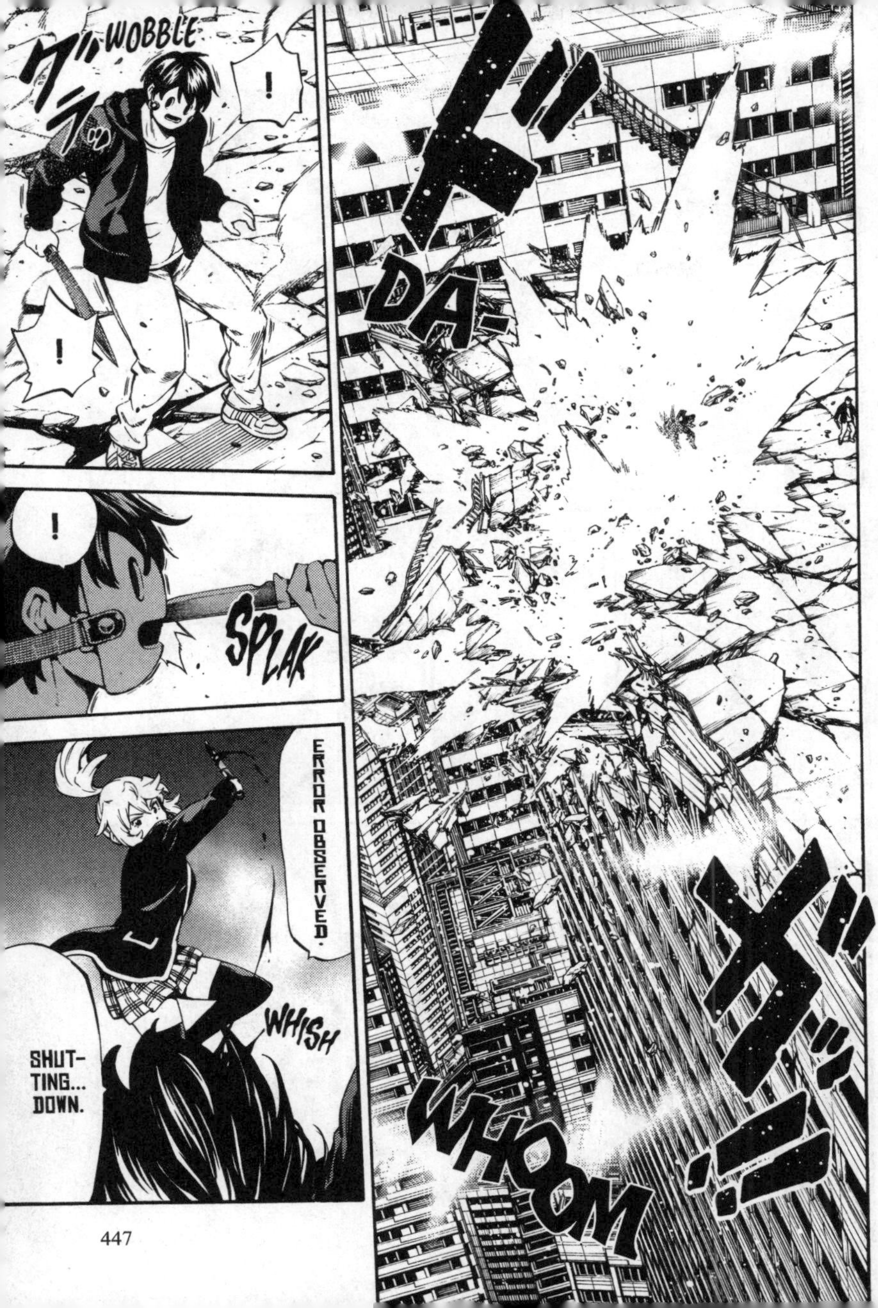
DA-
WHOOM
WOBBLE
!
!
!
SPLAK
ERROR OBSERVED.
WHISH
SHUT-TING... DOWN.

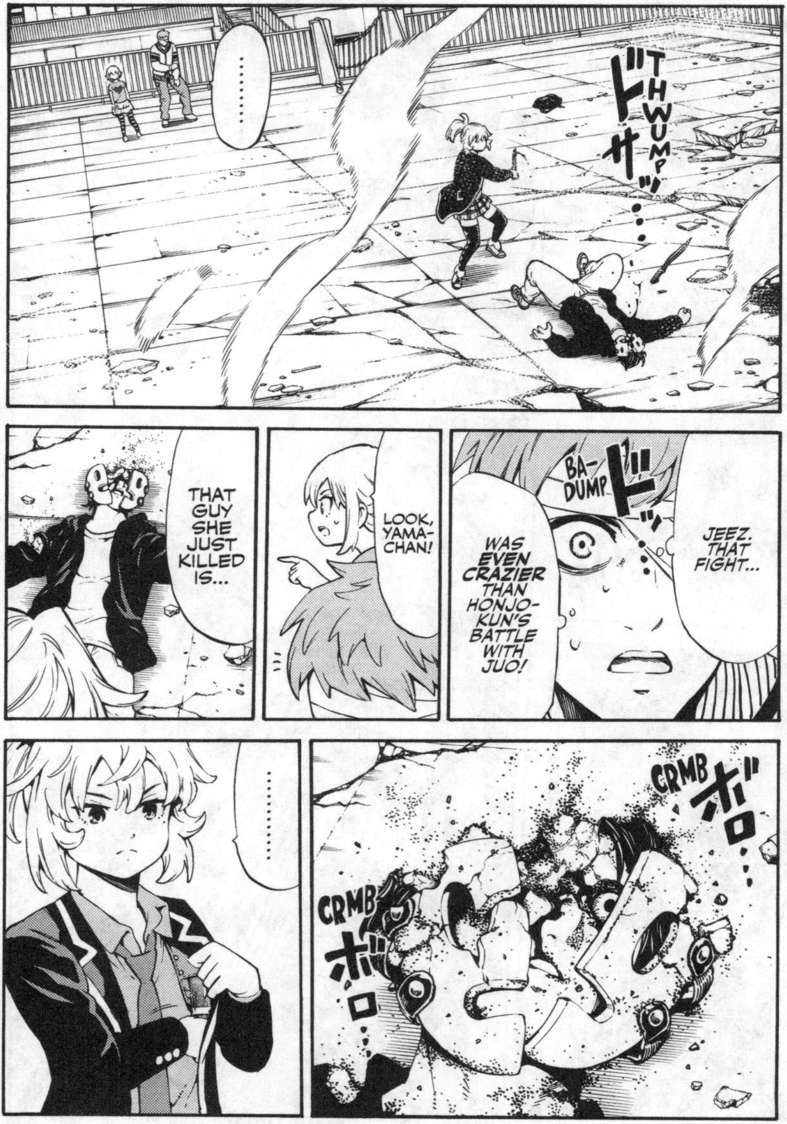
......
THWUMP
JEEZ. THAT FIGHT...
BA-DUMP
WAS EVEN CRAZIER THAN HONJO-KUN'S BATTLE WITH JUO!
LOOK, YAMA-CHAN!
THAT GUY SHE JUST KILLED IS...
CRMB
CRMB
......

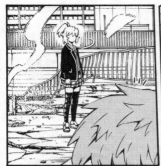

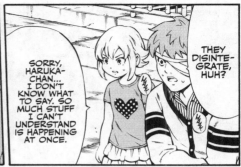

THEY DISINTE-GRATE, HUH?
SORRY, HARUKA-CHAN... I DON'T KNOW WHAT TO SAY. SO MUCH STUFF I CAN'T UNDERSTAND IS HAPPENING AT ONCE.
I'LL GIVE YOU THE RUNDOWN.
THOSE BLANK-FACED MASKS WE JUST BEAT WEREN'T HUMAN.
I DON'T KNOW THE SPECIFICS, BUT THEY'RE MADE OF AN **ENERGY** THIS WORLD POSSESSES.
GEH... GAH!
THIS BUILD-ING'S FALLING APART! CHEAP CON-STRUC-TION IS **EVIL!**
NOW, THEY'RE APPARENTLY TRYING TO KILL EVERY LAST HUMAN HERE, NO QUESTIONS ASKED.
THE PROBLEM IS, THERE ARE STILL ABOUT FIFTY HUMANS IN THIS WORLD. IF HONJO-SAN HADN'T STOPPED PEOPLE FROM COMING IN, THERE'D HAVE BEEN EVEN MORE.

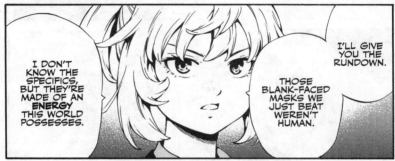

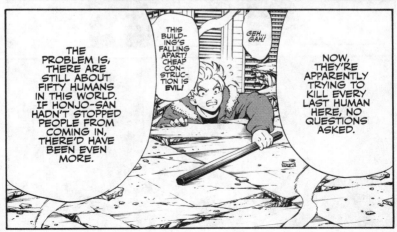

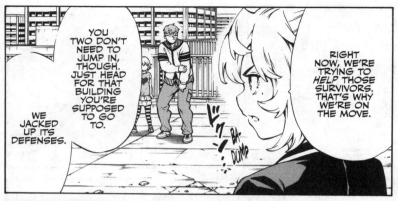

RIGHT NOW, WE'RE TRYING TO *HELP* THOSE SURVIVORS. THAT'S WHY WE'RE ON THE MOVE.
BA-DUMP
YOU TWO DON'T NEED TO JUMP IN, THOUGH. JUST HEAD FOR THAT BUILDING YOU'RE SUPPOSED TO GO TO.
WE JACKED UP ITS DEFENSES.
HRM. NOW THAT YOU MENTION THAT, IT SOUNDS FAMILIAR!
LET'S SET OFF FOR OUR NEXT DESTI-NATION, MISS KNIFE!
JUST WHAT HEAD-SPACE IS THIS GUY IN RIGHT NOW?
THERE'S MORE TO CATCH UP ON, BUT ASK THE TEAM IN THAT BUILDING, ALL RIGHT?
TAP
OKAY, I'M OFF.

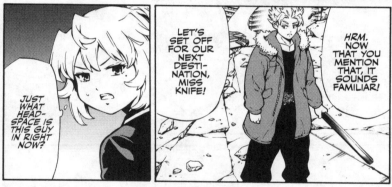

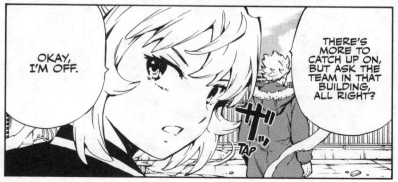

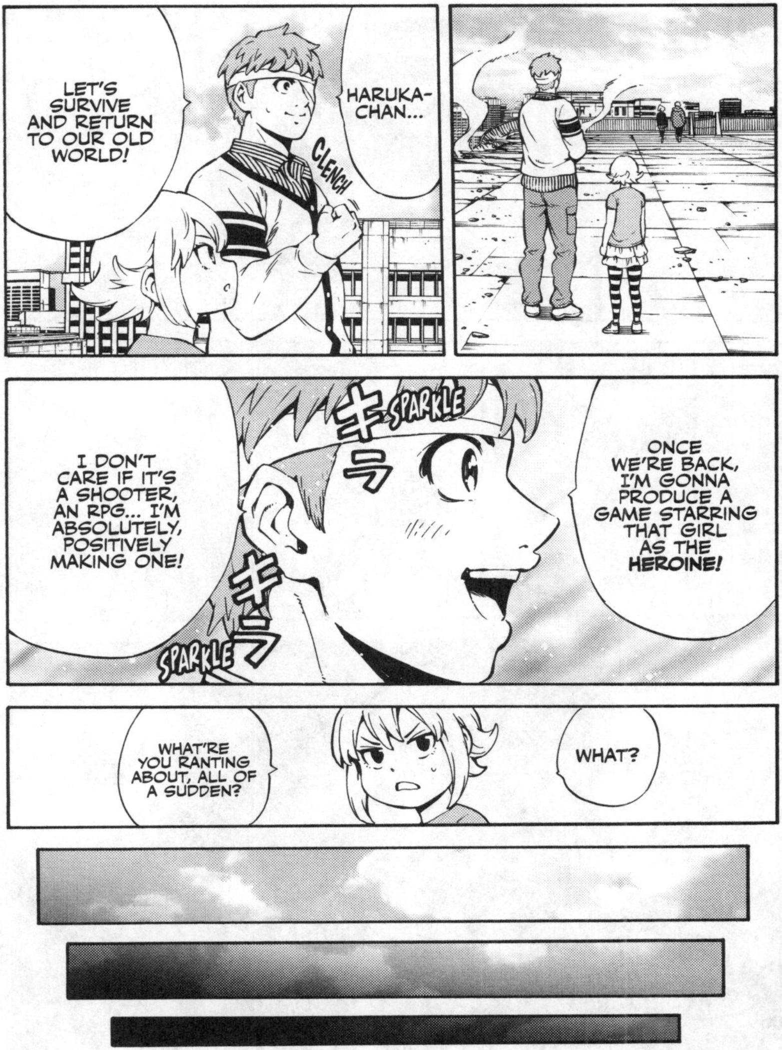
HARUKA-CHAN...
CLENCH
LET'S SURVIVE AND RETURN TO OUR OLD WORLD!
ONCE WE'RE BACK, I'M GONNA PRODUCE A GAME STARRING THAT GIRL AS THE **HEROINE!**
キラ SPARKLE
I DON'T CARE IF IT'S A SHOOTER, AN RPG... I'M ABSOLUTELY, POSITIVELY MAKING ONE!
キラ SPARKLE
WHAT?
WHAT'RE YOU RANTING ABOUT, ALL OF A SUDDEN?

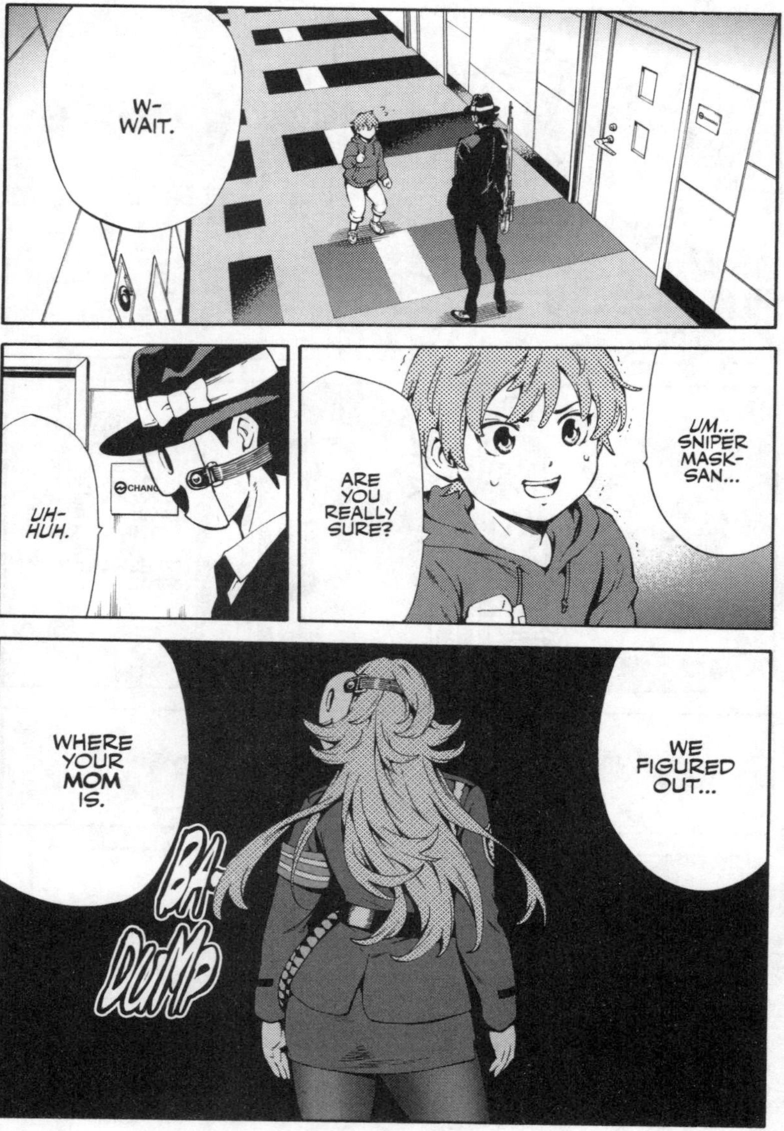
W-WAIT.
UM... SNIPER MASK-SAN...
ARE YOU REALLY SURE?
UH-HUH.
WE FIGURED OUT...
WHERE YOUR MOM IS.
BA-DUMP

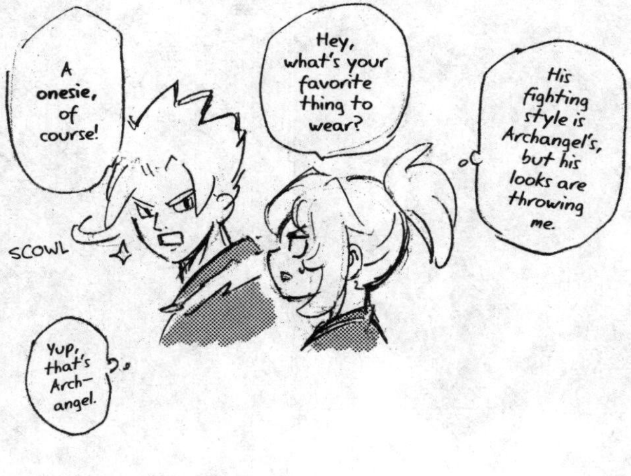
His fighting style is Archangel's, but his looks are throwing me.
Hey, what's your favorite thing to wear?
A onesie, of course!
SCOWL
Yup, that's Arch-angel.

HIGH-RISE INVASION

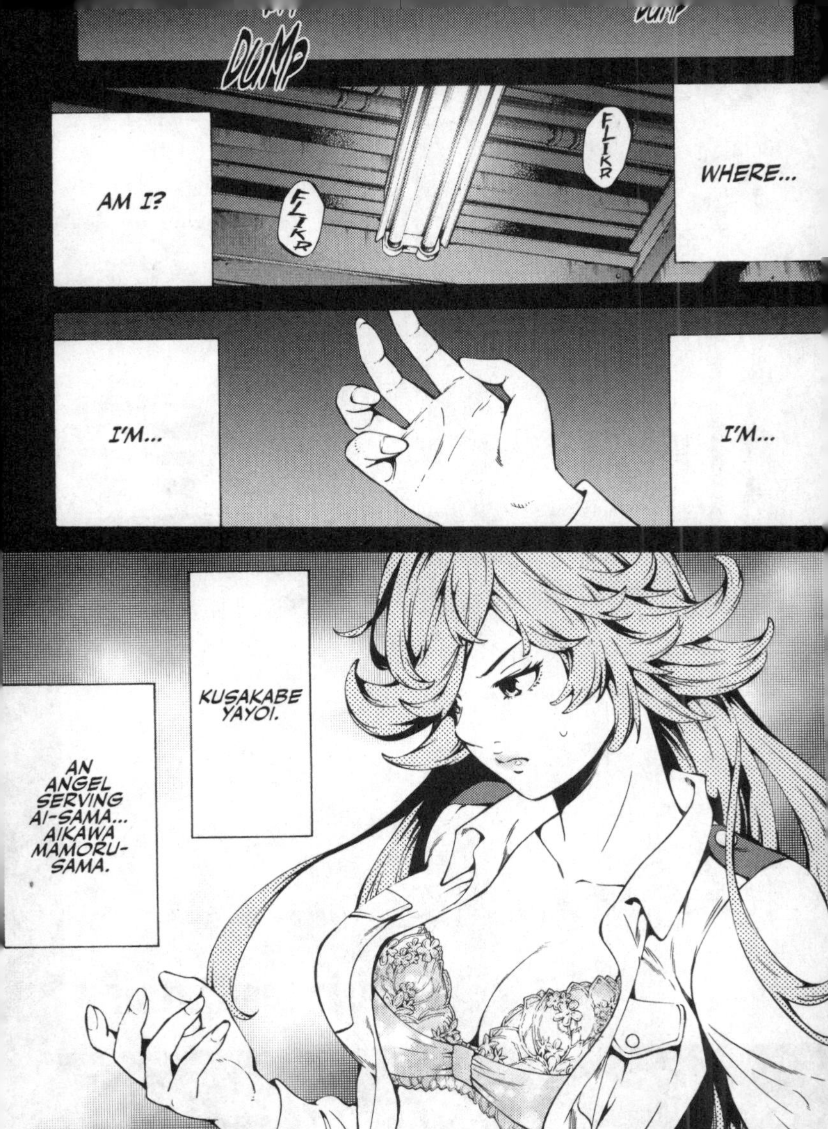
DUMP
DUMP
WHERE...
FLIKR
FLIKR
AM I?
I'M...
I'M...
KUSAKABE YAYOI.
AN ANGEL SERVING AI-SAMA... AIKAWA MAMORU-SAMA.

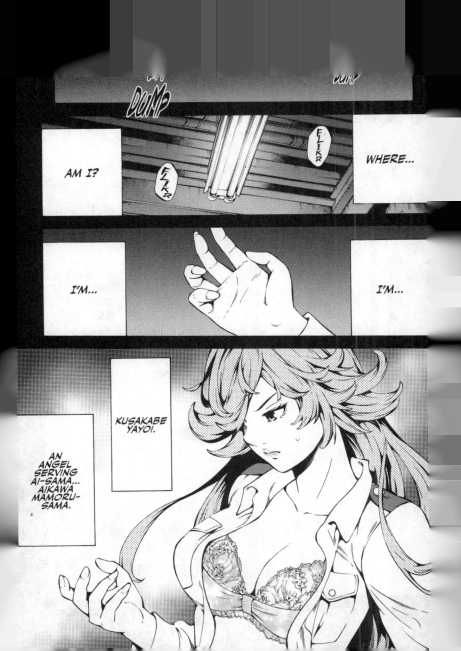

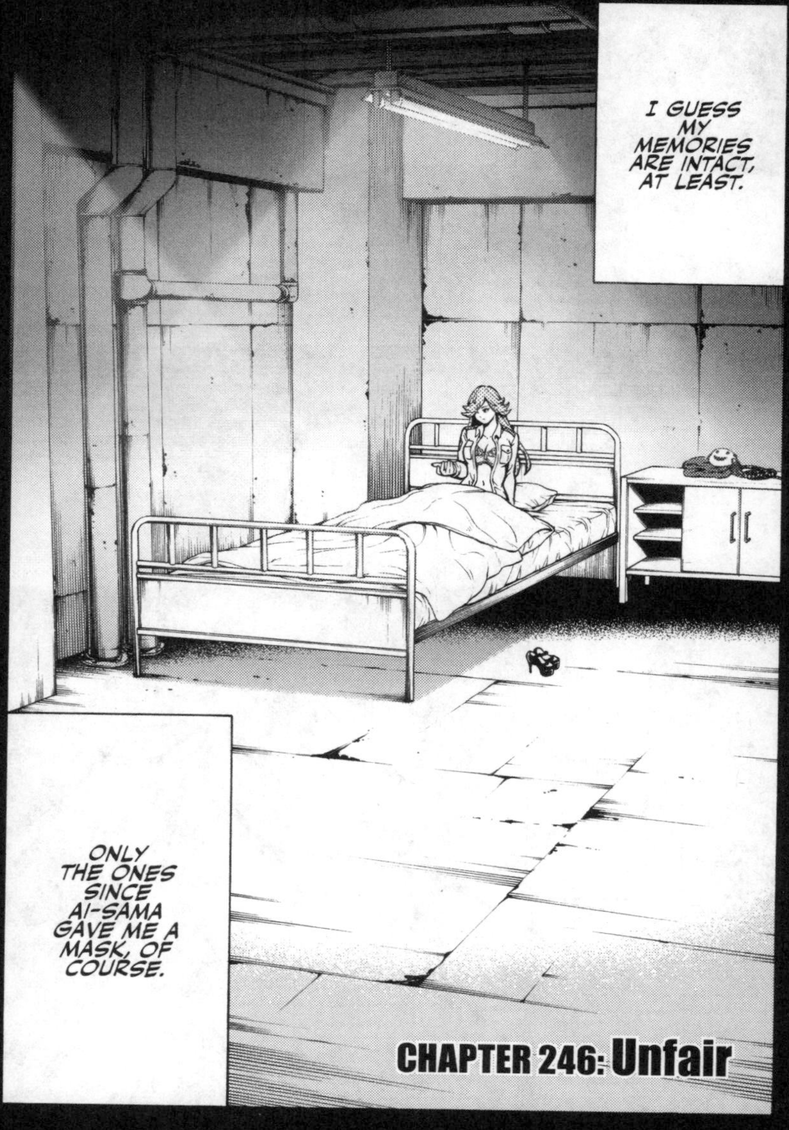
I GUESS MY MEMORIES ARE INTACT, AT LEAST.
ONLY THE ONES SINCE AI-SAMA GAVE ME A MASK, OF COURSE.
CHAPTER 246: Unfair

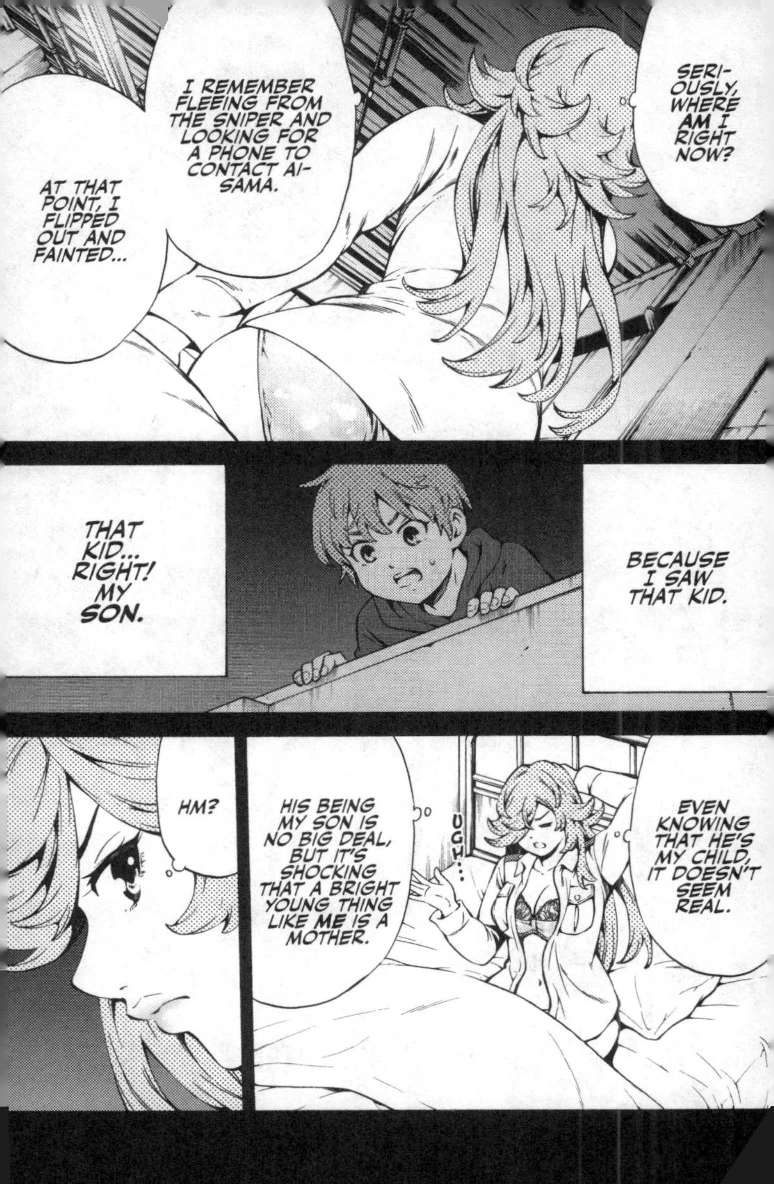
SERIOUSLY, WHERE AM I RIGHT NOW?
I REMEMBER FLEEING FROM THE SNIPER AND LOOKING FOR A PHONE TO CONTACT AI-SAMA.
AT THAT POINT, I FLIPPED OUT AND FAINTED...
BECAUSE I SAW THAT KID.
THAT KID... RIGHT! MY SON.
EVEN KNOWING THAT HE'S MY CHILD, IT DOESN'T SEEM REAL.
UGH...
HIS BEING MY SON IS NO BIG DEAL, BUT IT'S SHOCKING THAT A BRIGHT YOUNG THING LIKE ME IS A MOTHER.
HM?

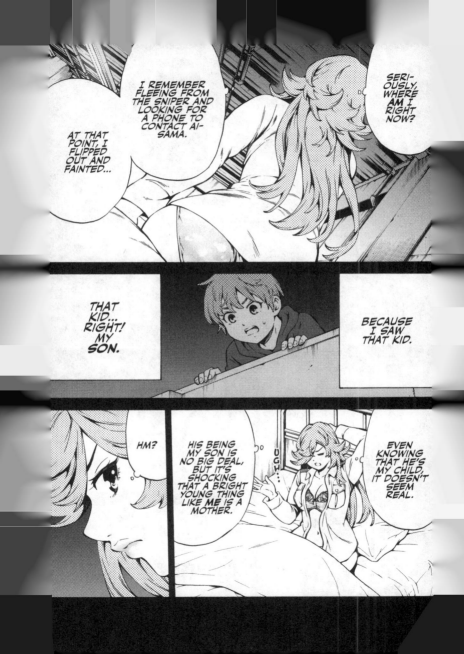

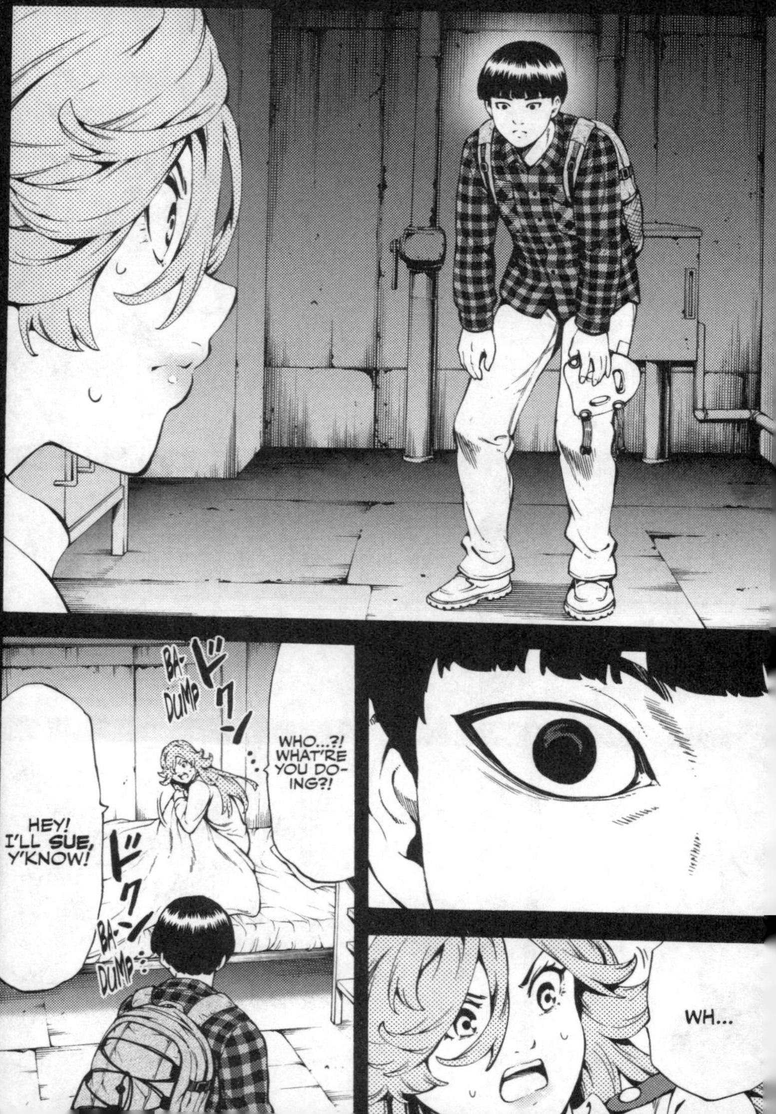
WH...
BA-DUMP
ドクン
WHO...?! WHAT'RE YOU DOING?!
HEY! I'LL SUE, Y'KNOW!
ドクン
BA-DUMP

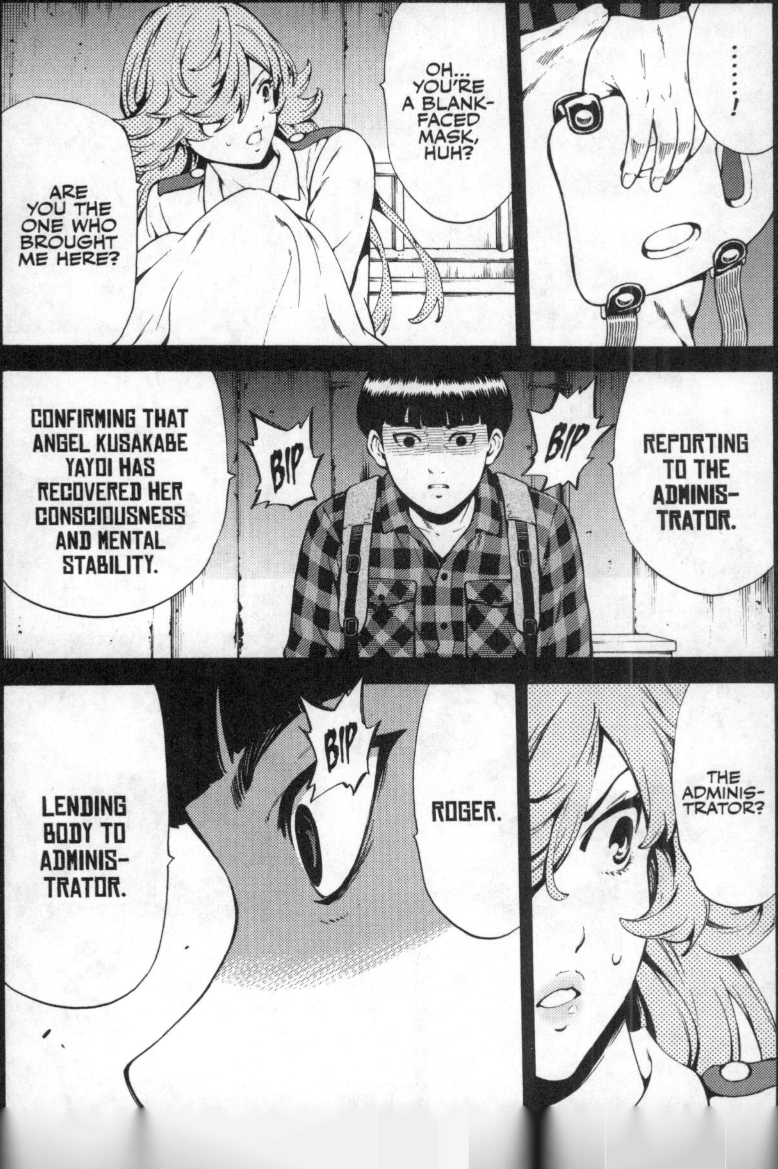
......!
OH... YOU'RE A BLANK-FACED MASK, HUH?
ARE YOU THE ONE WHO BROUGHT ME HERE?
REPORTING TO THE ADMINISTRATOR.
BIP
BIP
CONFIRMING THAT ANGEL KUSAKABE YAYOI HAS RECOVERED HER CONSCIOUSNESS AND MENTAL STABILITY.
THE ADMINISTRATOR?
BIP
ROGER.
LENDING BODY TO ADMINISTRATOR.

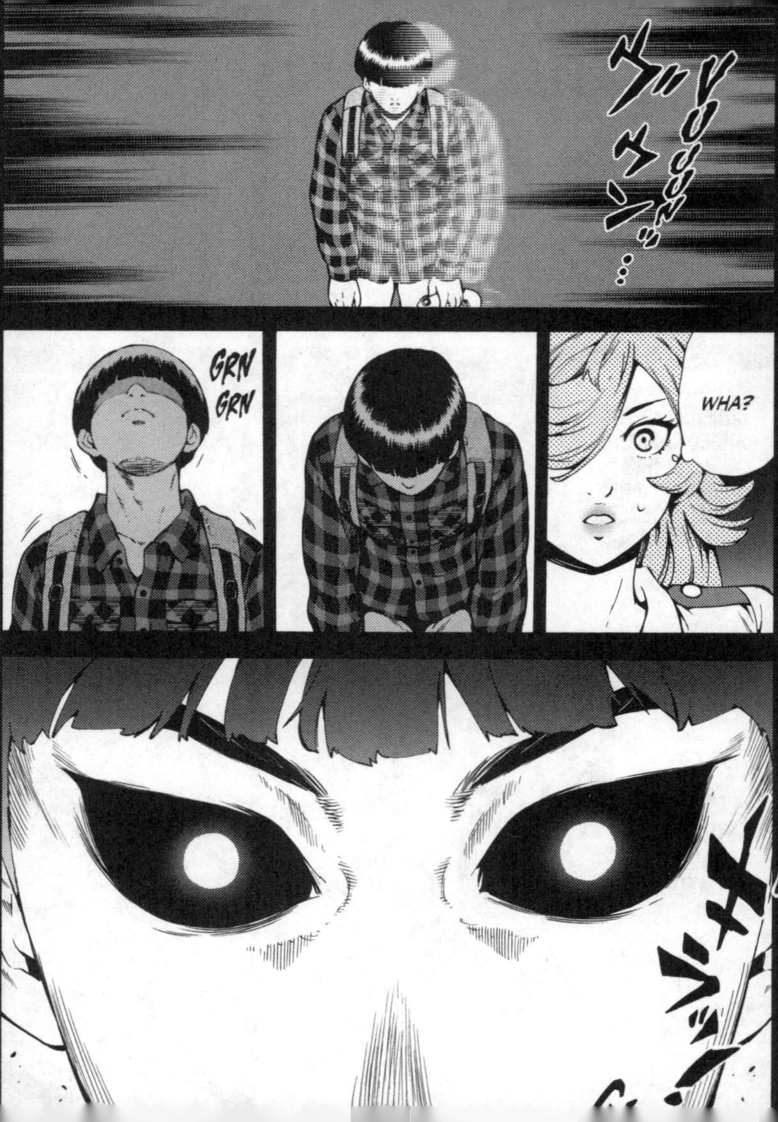
ヴゥゥン…
WHA?
GRN GRN
ギンッ!

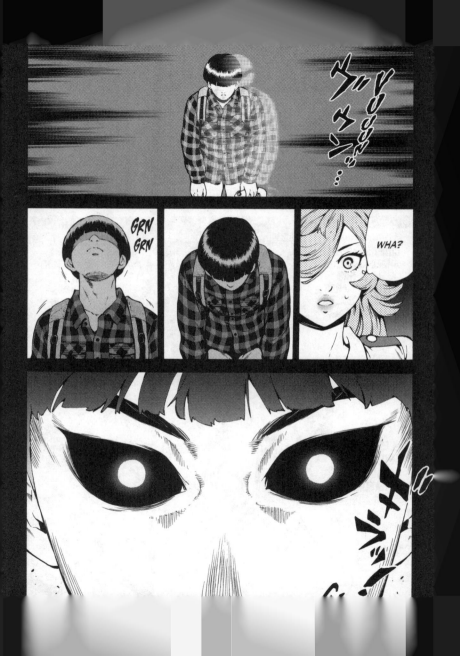

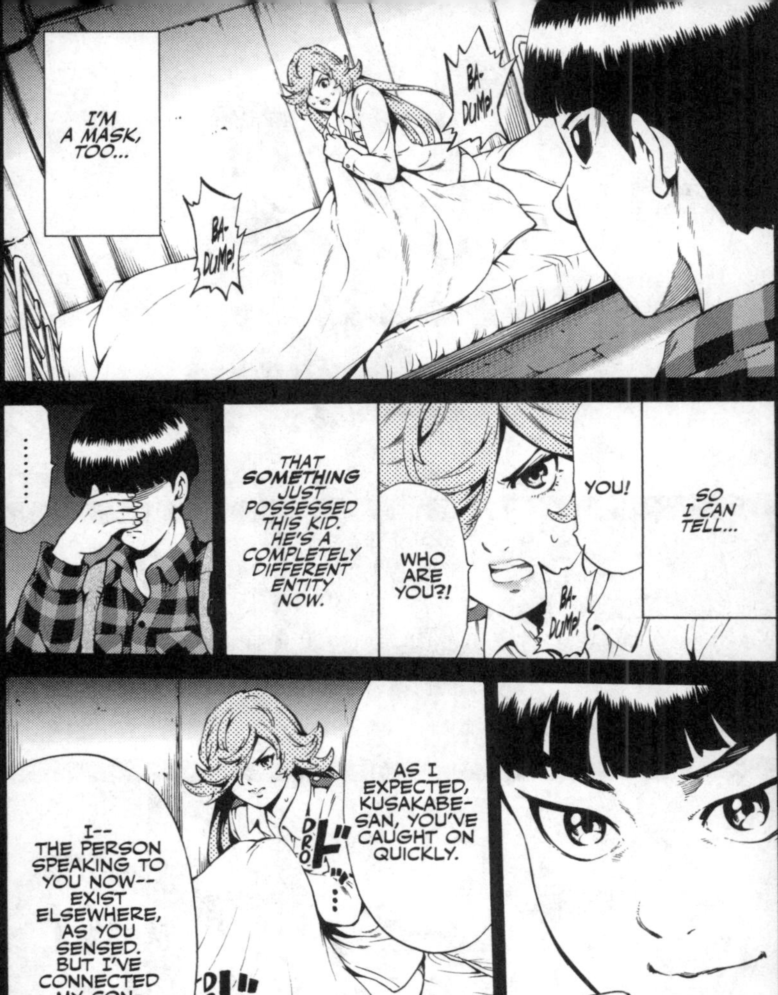
BA-DUMP!
I'M A MASK, TOO...
BA-DUMP!
SO I CAN TELL...
YOU!
WHO ARE YOU?!
BA-DUMP!
THAT **SOMETHING** JUST POSSESSED THIS KID. HE'S A COMPLETELY DIFFERENT ENTITY NOW.
......
AS I EXPECTED, KUSAKABE-SAN, YOU'VE CAUGHT ON QUICKLY.
DRO...
I-- THE PERSON SPEAKING TO YOU NOW-- EXIST ELSEWHERE, AS YOU SENSED. BUT I'VE CONNECTED MY CONSCIOUSNESS TO THIS BEING.
DRO...

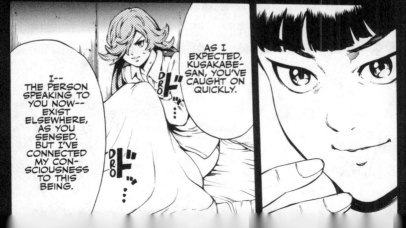

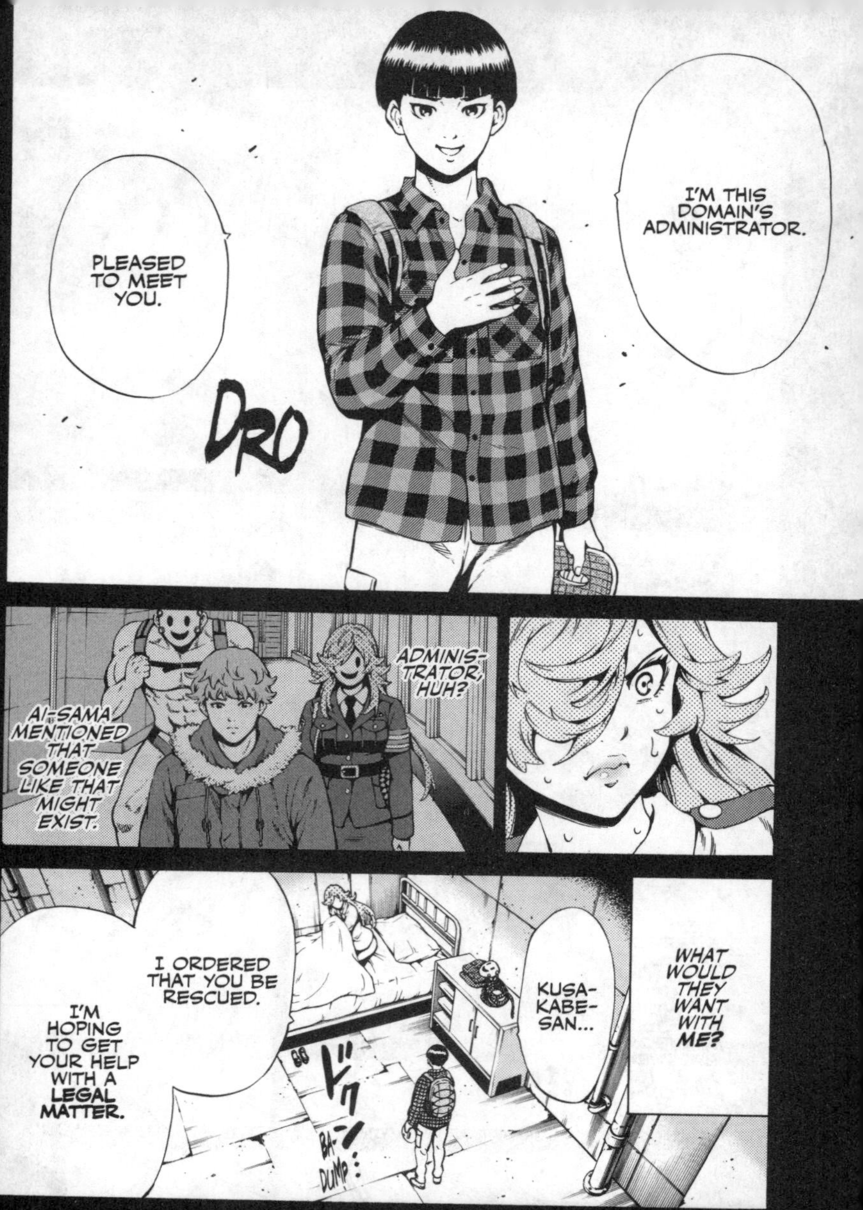
I'M THIS DOMAIN'S ADMINISTRATOR.
PLEASED TO MEET YOU.
DRO
ADMINISTRATOR, HUH?
AI-SAMA MENTIONED THAT SOMEONE LIKE THAT MIGHT EXIST.
WHAT WOULD THEY WANT WITH ME?
KUSA-KABE-SAN...
I ORDERED THAT YOU BE RESCUED.
I'M HOPING TO GET YOUR HELP WITH A **LEGAL MATTER.**
BA-DUMP

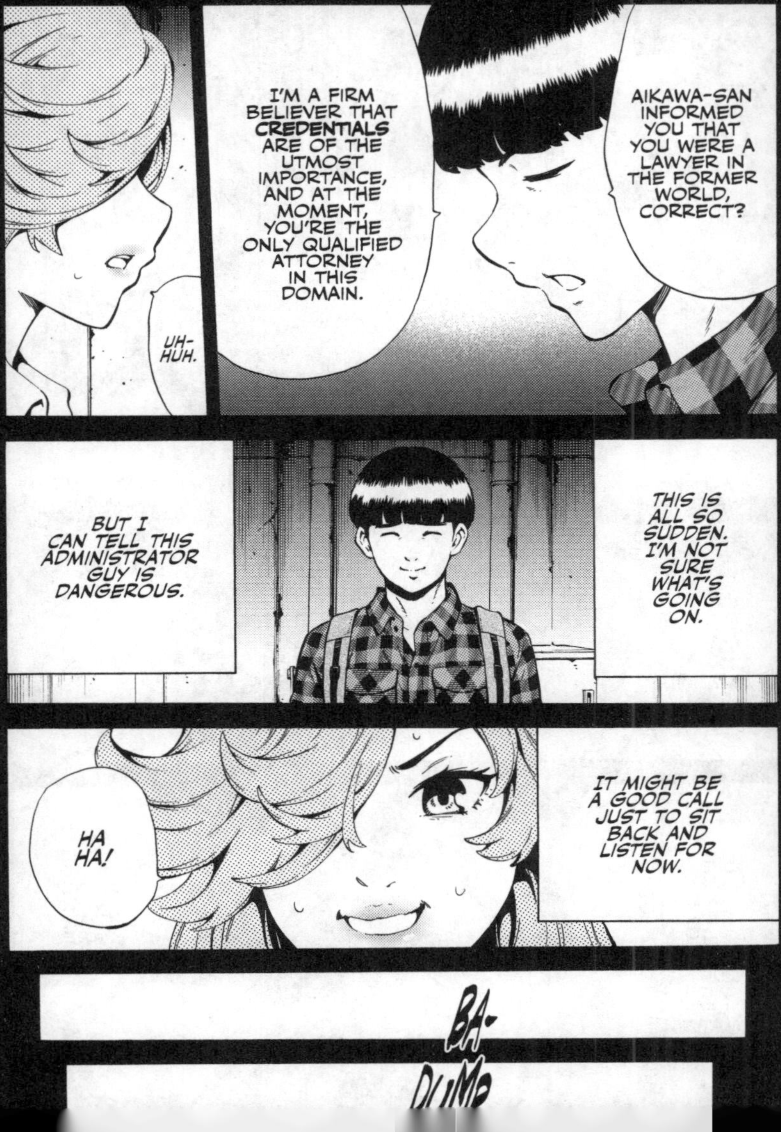
AIKAWA-SAN INFORMED YOU THAT YOU WERE A LAWYER IN THE FORMER WORLD, CORRECT?
I'M A FIRM BELIEVER THAT **CREDENTIALS** ARE OF THE UTMOST IMPORTANCE, AND AT THE MOMENT, YOU'RE THE ONLY QUALIFIED ATTORNEY IN THIS DOMAIN.
UH-HUH.
THIS IS ALL SO SUDDEN. I'M NOT SURE WHAT'S GOING ON.
BUT I CAN TELL THIS ADMINISTRATOR GUY IS DANGEROUS.
IT MIGHT BE A GOOD CALL JUST TO SIT BACK AND LISTEN FOR NOW.
HA HA!
BA-
DUM

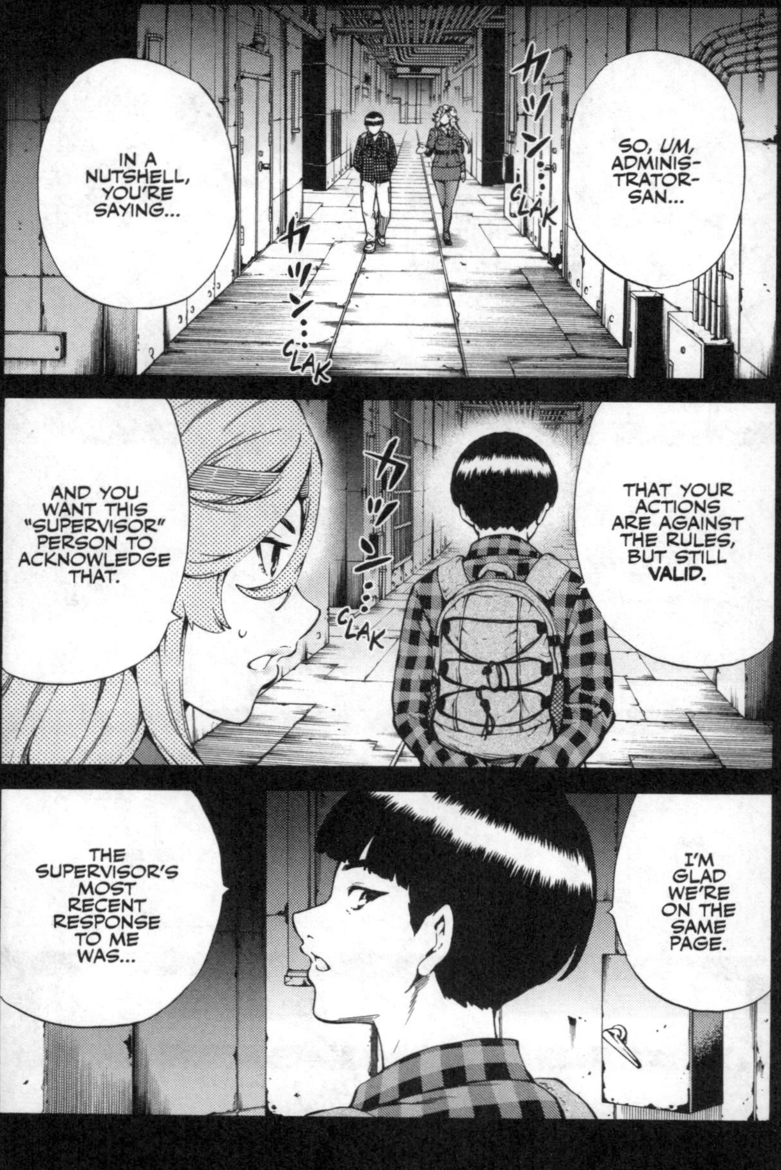

SO, UM, ADMINISTRATOR-SAN...
CLAK
IN A NUTSHELL, YOU'RE SAYING...
CLAK
THAT YOUR ACTIONS ARE AGAINST THE RULES, BUT STILL **VALID.**
CLAK
AND YOU WANT THIS "SUPERVISOR" PERSON TO ACKNOWLEDGE THAT.
I'M GLAD WE'RE ON THE SAME PAGE.
THE SUPERVISOR'S MOST RECENT RESPONSE TO ME WAS...

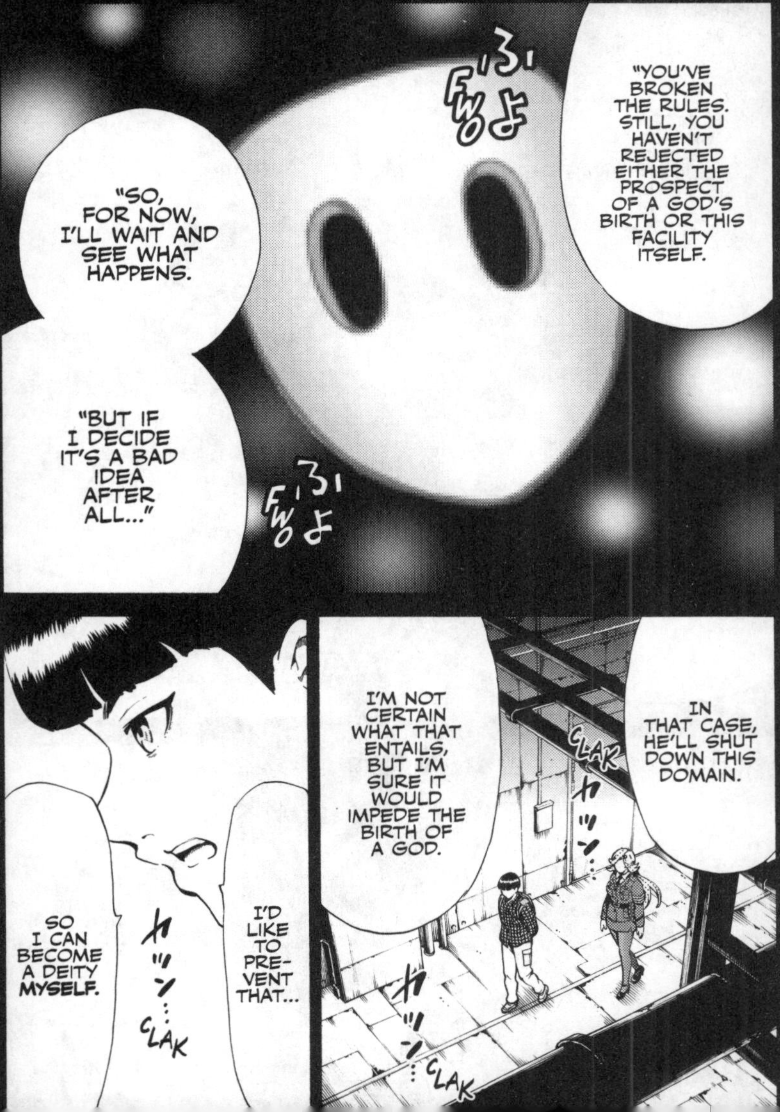

"YOU'VE BROKEN THE RULES. STILL, YOU HAVEN'T REJECTED EITHER THE PROSPECT OF A GOD'S BIRTH OR THIS FACILITY ITSELF.
ふよ FWO
"SO, FOR NOW, I'LL WAIT AND SEE WHAT HAPPENS.
"BUT IF I DECIDE IT'S A BAD IDEA AFTER ALL..."
ふよ FWO
IN THAT CASE, HE'LL SHUT DOWN THIS DOMAIN.
CLAK
I'M NOT CERTAIN WHAT THAT ENTAILS, BUT I'M SURE IT WOULD IMPEDE THE BIRTH OF A GOD.
CLAK
I'D LIKE TO PRE-VENT THAT...
CLAK
SO I CAN BECOME A DEITY **MYSELF**.

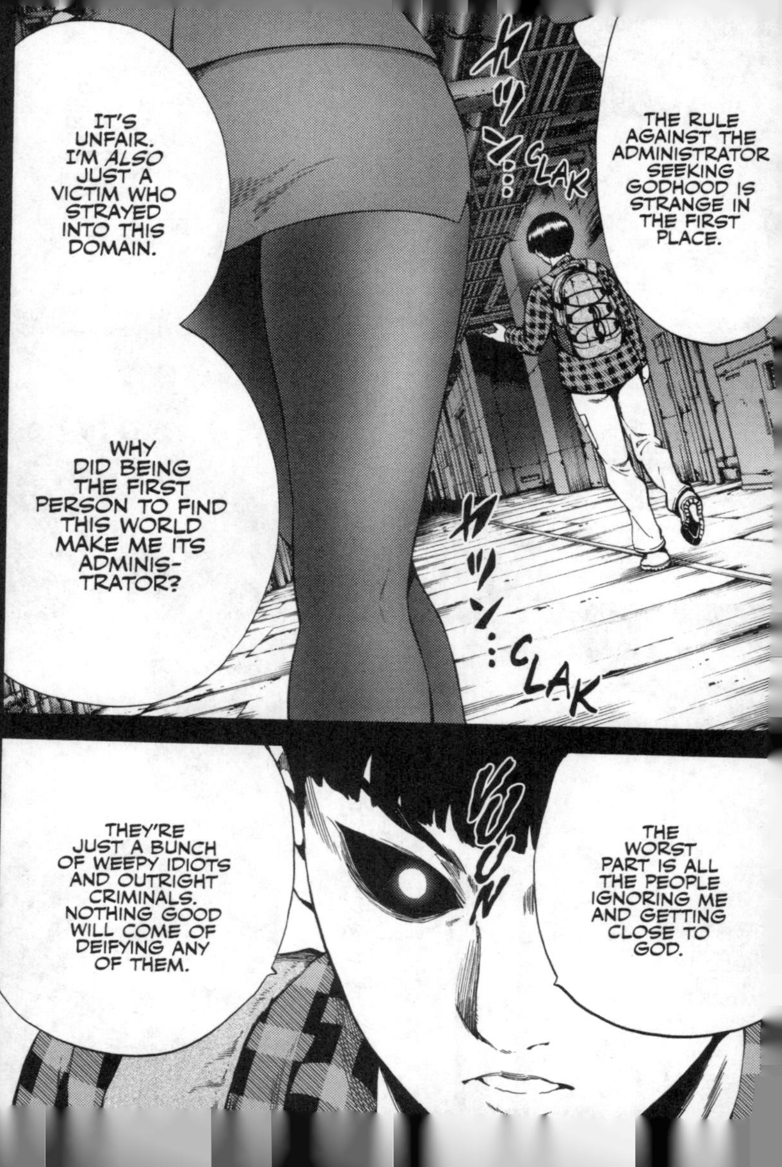
THE RULE AGAINST THE ADMINISTRATOR SEEKING GODHOOD IS STRANGE IN THE FIRST PLACE.
CLAK
IT'S UNFAIR. I'M *ALSO* JUST A VICTIM WHO STRAYED INTO THIS DOMAIN.
WHY DID BEING THE FIRST PERSON TO FIND THIS WORLD MAKE ME ITS ADMINIS-TRATOR?
CLAK
THE WORST PART IS ALL THE PEOPLE IGNORING ME AND GETTING CLOSE TO GOD.
THEY'RE JUST A BUNCH OF WEEPY IDIOTS AND OUTRIGHT CRIMINALS. NOTHING GOOD WILL COME OF DEIFYING ANY OF THEM.

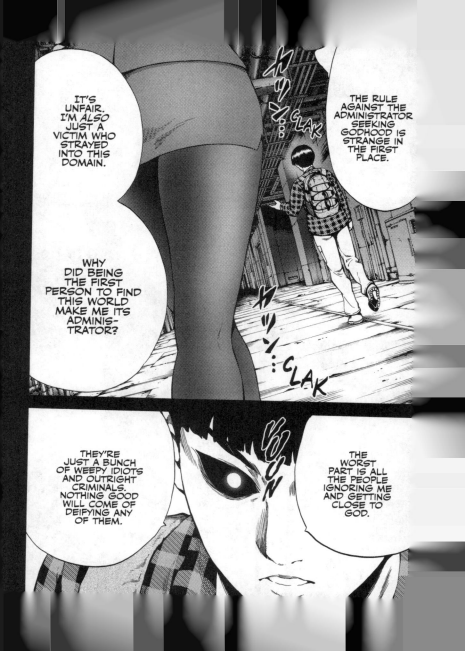

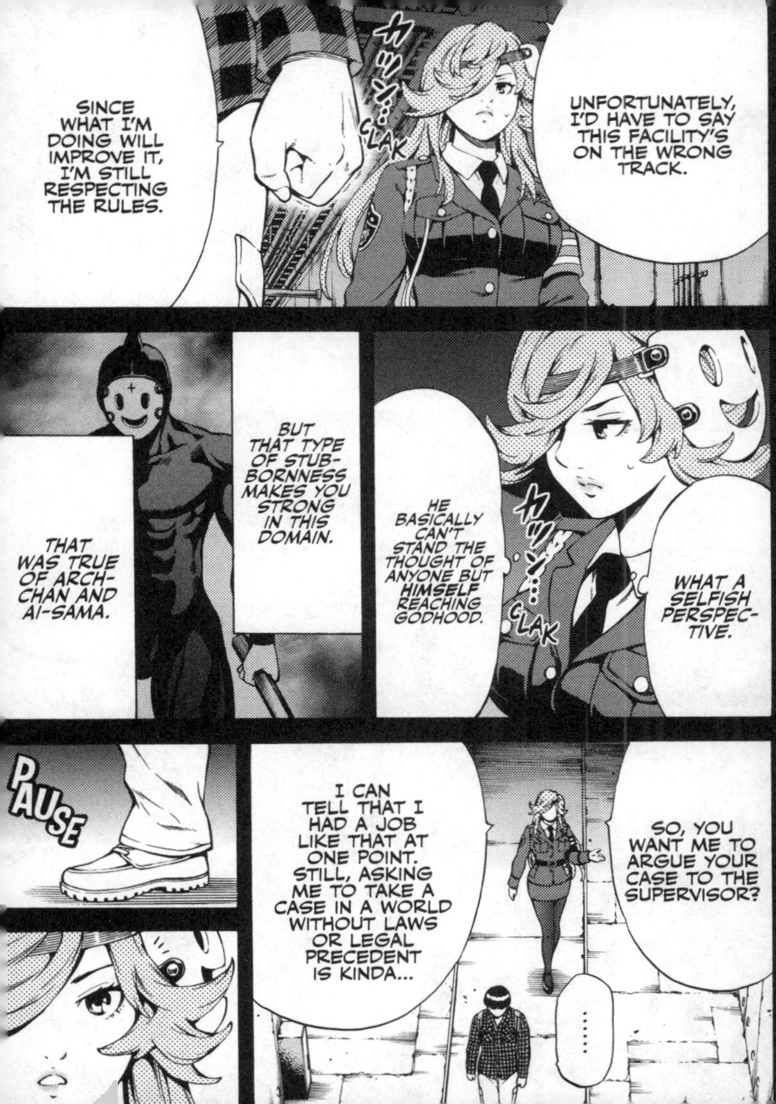
UNFORTUNATELY, I'D HAVE TO SAY THIS FACILITY'S ON THE WRONG TRACK.
CLAK
SINCE WHAT I'M DOING WILL IMPROVE IT, I'M STILL RESPECTING THE RULES.
WHAT A SELFISH PERSPEC-TIVE.
CLAK
HE BASICALLY CAN'T STAND THE THOUGHT OF ANYONE BUT HIMSELF REACHING GODHOOD.
BUT THAT TYPE OF STUB-BORNNESS MAKES YOU STRONG IN THIS DOMAIN.
THAT WAS TRUE OF ARCH-CHAN AND AI-SAMA.
SO, YOU WANT ME TO ARGUE YOUR CASE TO THE SUPERVISOR?
......
I CAN TELL THAT I HAD A JOB LIKE THAT AT ONE POINT. STILL, ASKING ME TO TAKE A CASE IN A WORLD WITHOUT LAWS OR LEGAL PRECEDENT IS KINDA...
PAUSE

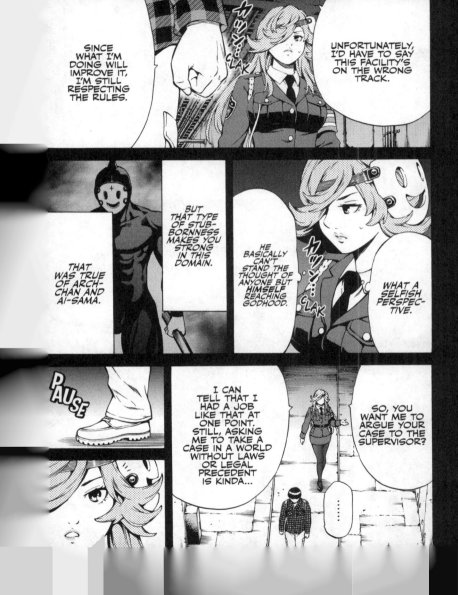

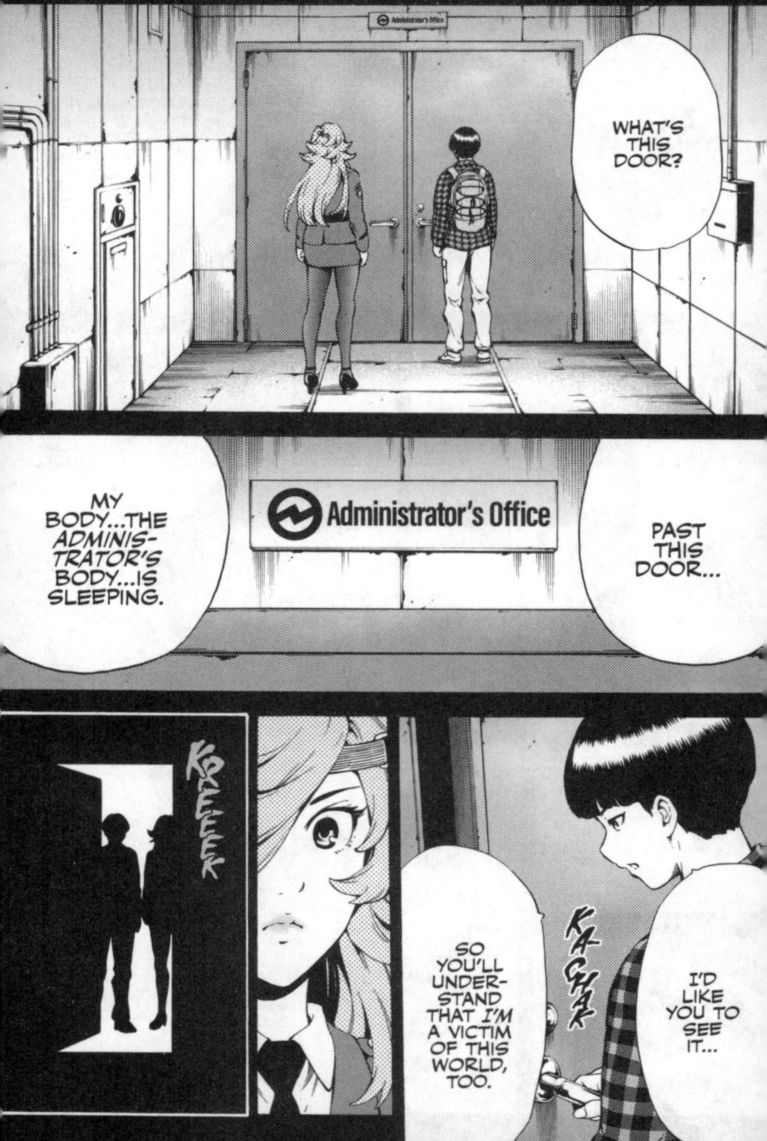
Administrator's Office
WHAT'S THIS DOOR?
PAST THIS DOOR...
Administrator's Office
MY BODY...THE *ADMINISTRATOR'S* BODY...IS SLEEPING.
I'D LIKE YOU TO SEE IT...
KACHAK
SO YOU'LL UNDERSTAND THAT *I'M* A VICTIM OF THIS WORLD, TOO.
KREEEEK

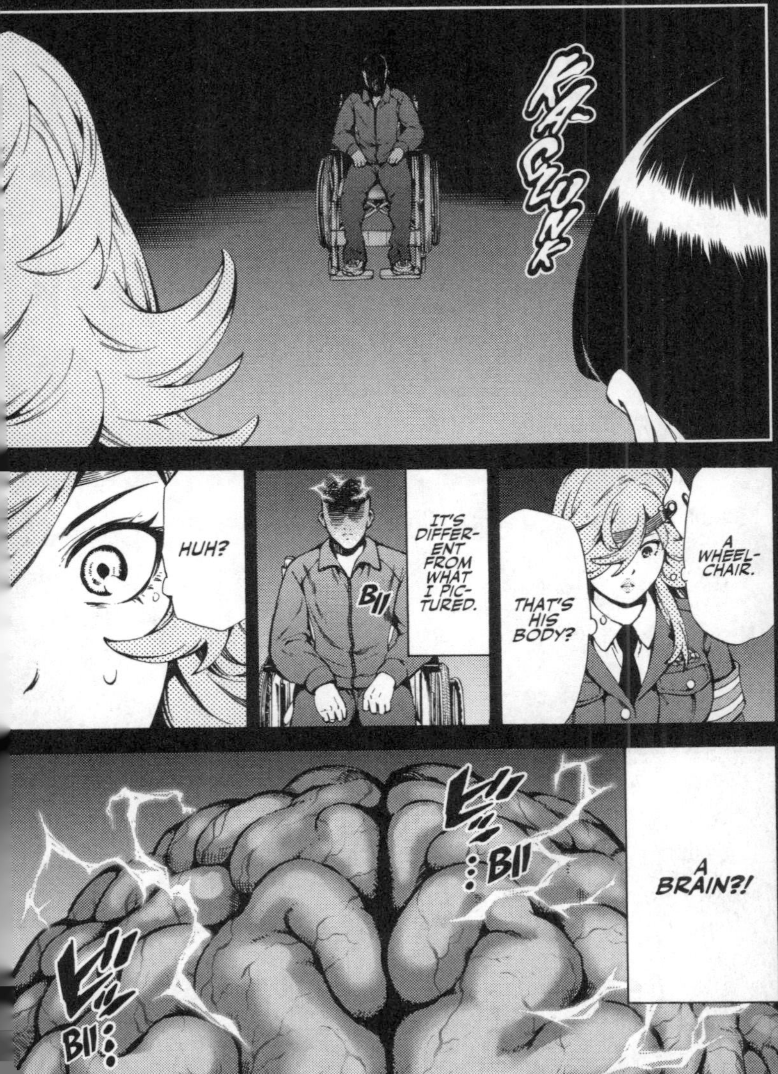
KA-CLUNK
A WHEEL-CHAIR.
THAT'S HIS BODY?
IT'S DIFFER-ENT FROM WHAT I PIC-TURED.
BII
HUH?
A BRAIN?!
BII
BII

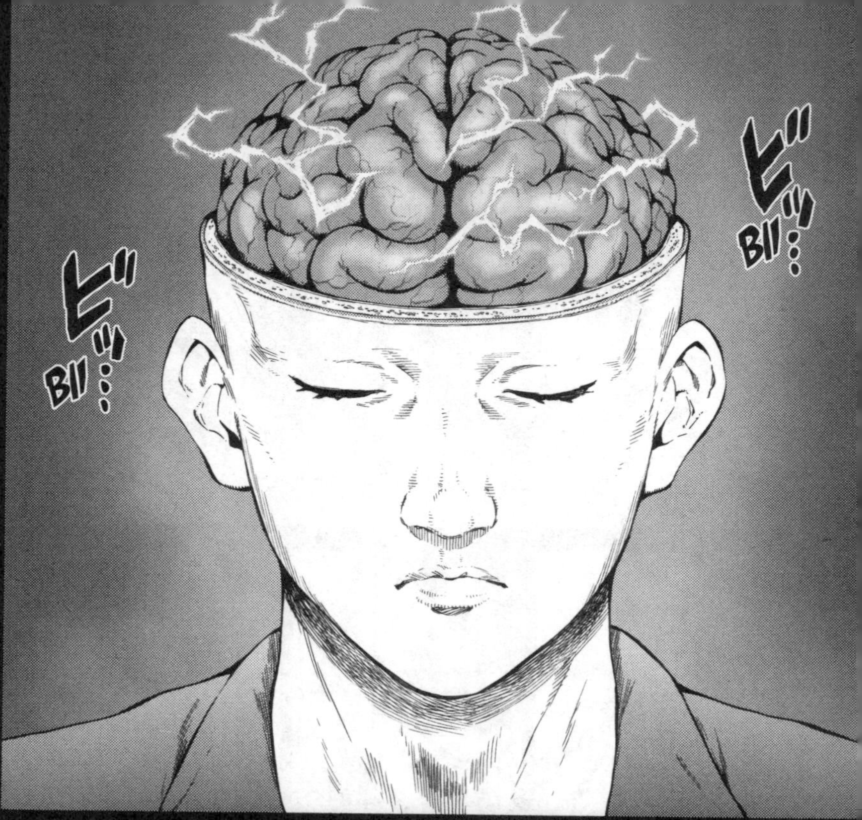
BII...
BII...

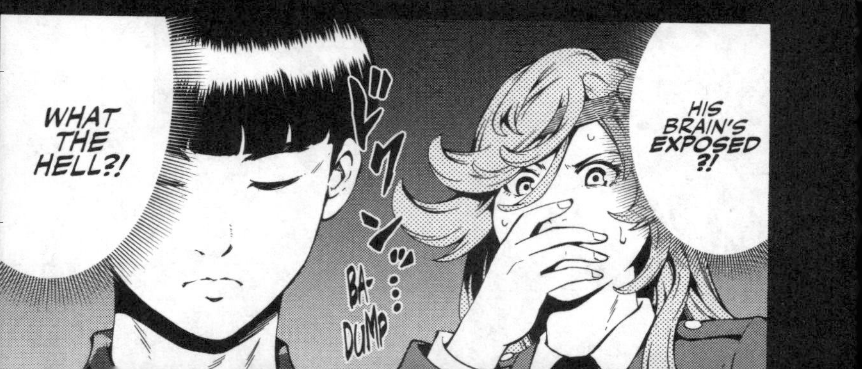
HIS BRAIN'S EXPOSED?!
BA-DUMP...
WHAT THE HELL?!

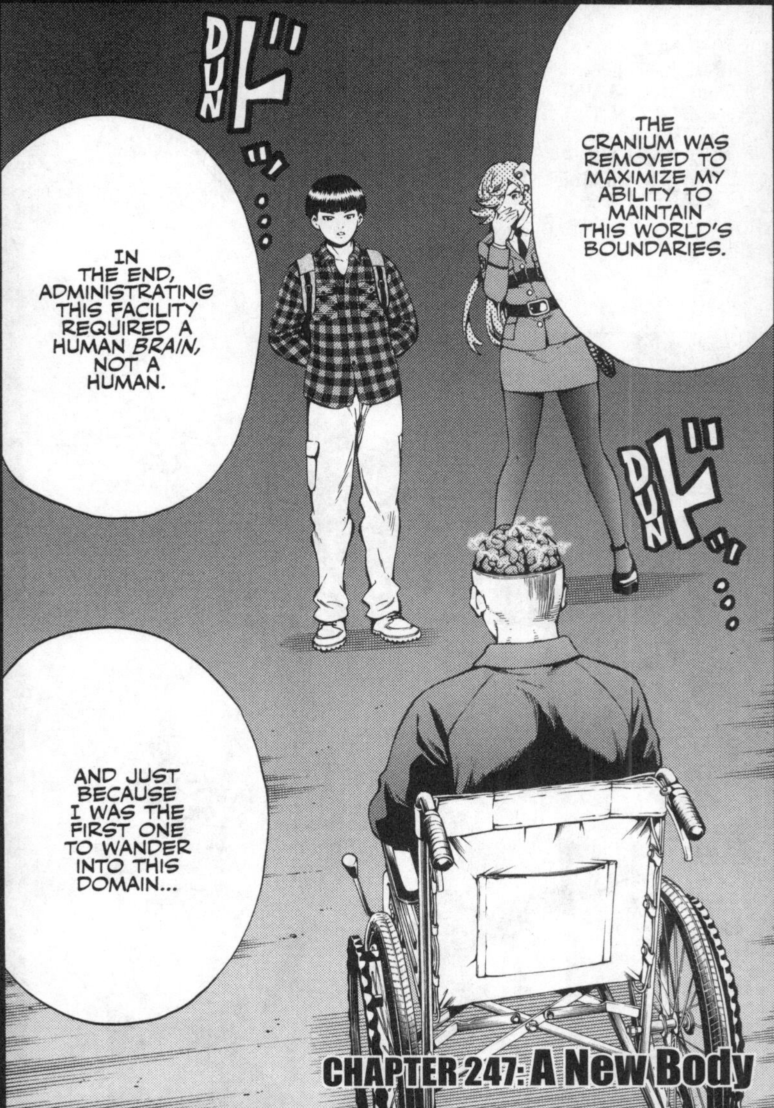
DUN ドドド
THE CRANIUM WAS REMOVED TO MAXIMIZE MY ABILITY TO MAINTAIN THIS WORLD'S BOUNDARIES.
IN THE END, ADMINISTRATING THIS FACILITY REQUIRED A HUMAN *BRAIN,* NOT A HUMAN.
DUN ドドド
AND JUST BECAUSE I WAS THE FIRST ONE TO WANDER INTO THIS DOMAIN...
CHAPTER 247: A New Body

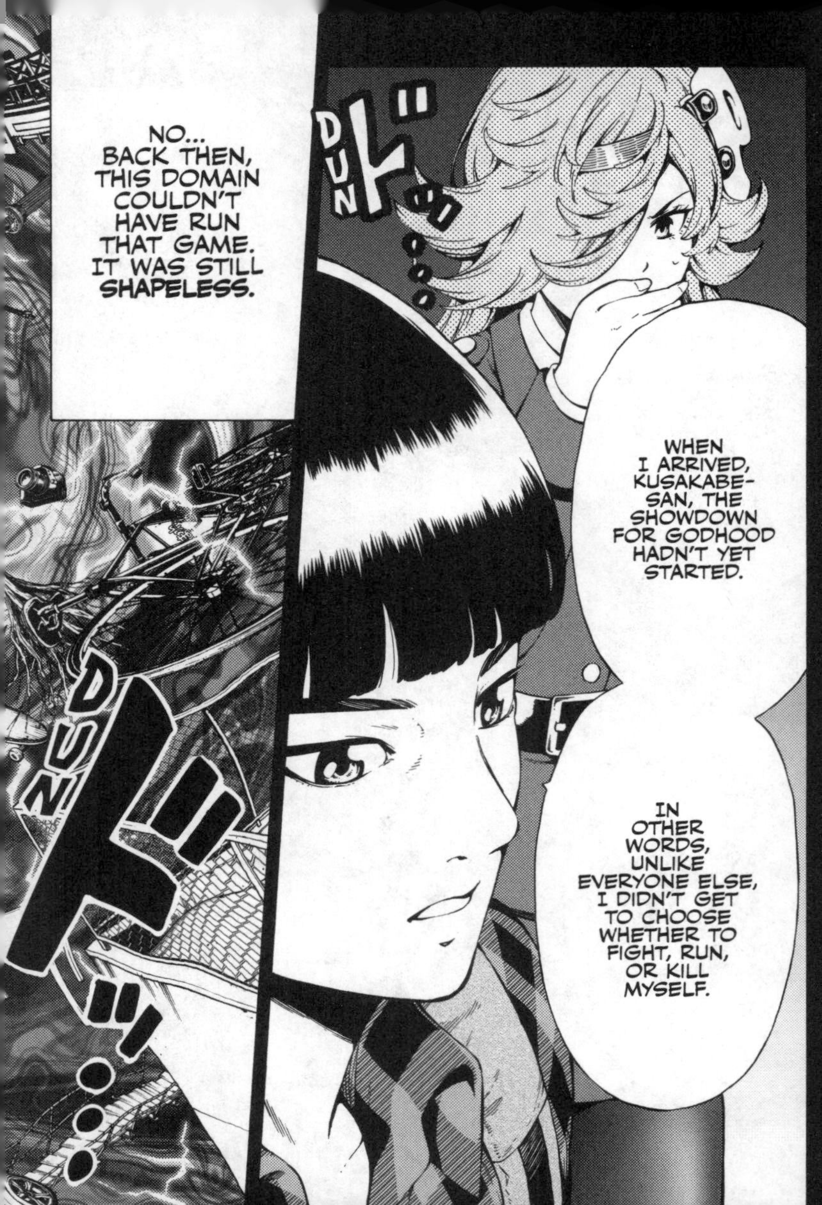
DUN
WHEN I ARRIVED, KUSAKABE-SAN, THE SHOWDOWN FOR GODHOOD HADN'T YET STARTED.
IN OTHER WORDS, UNLIKE EVERYONE ELSE, I DIDN'T GET TO CHOOSE WHETHER TO FIGHT, RUN, OR KILL MYSELF.
NO... BACK THEN, THIS DOMAIN COULDN'T HAVE RUN THAT GAME. IT WAS STILL SHAPELESS.
DUN

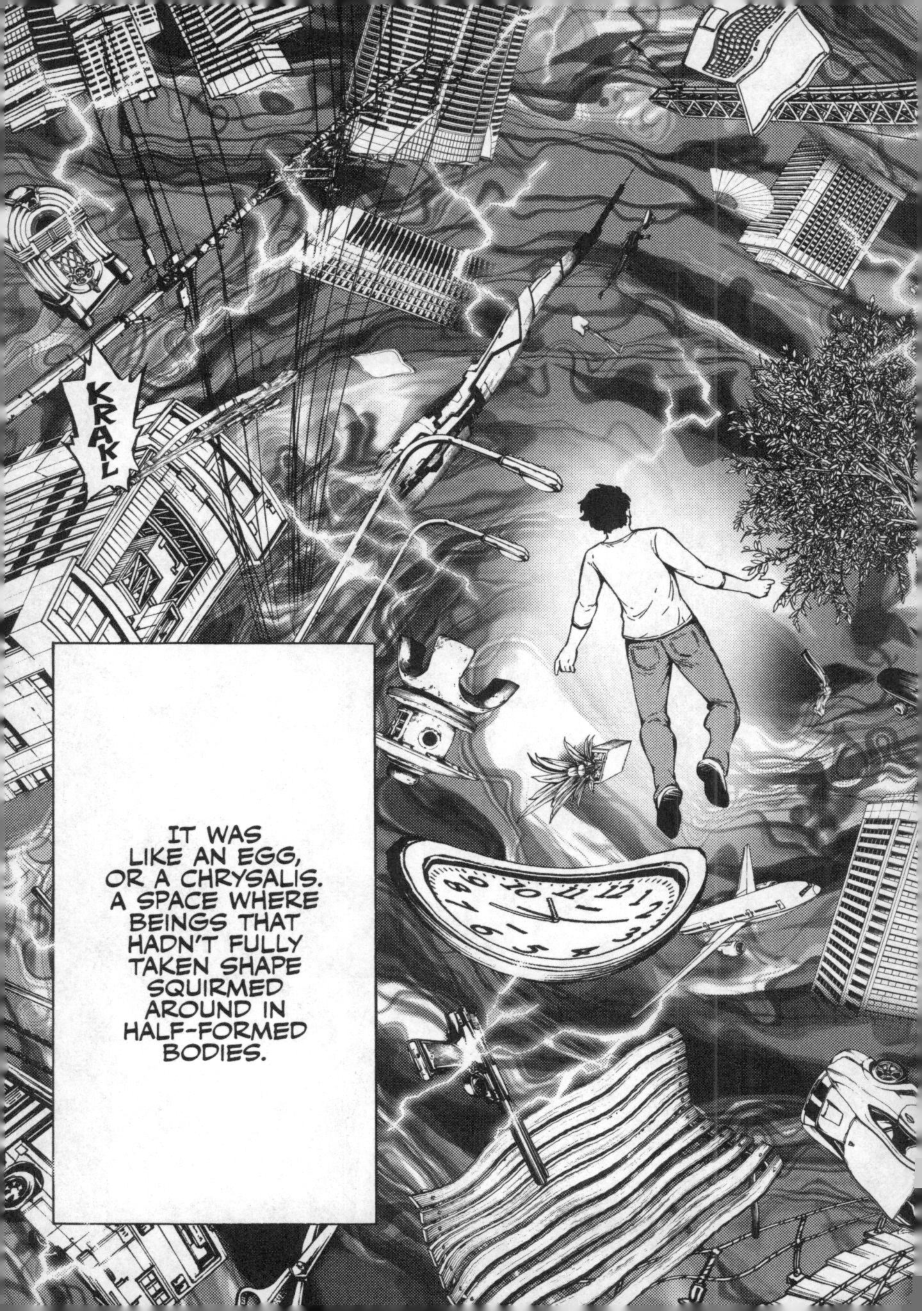
KRAKL
IT WAS LIKE AN EGG, OR A CHRYSALIS. A SPACE WHERE BEINGS THAT HADN'T FULLY TAKEN SHAPE SQUIRMED AROUND IN HALF-FORMED BODIES.

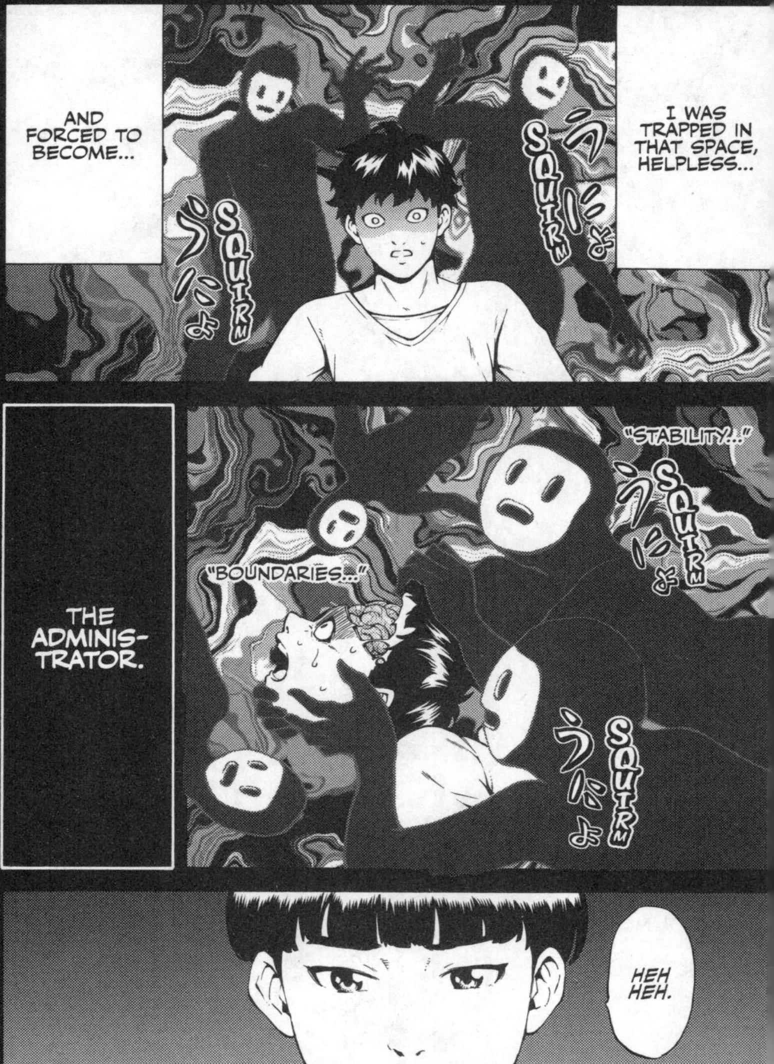
I WAS TRAPPED IN THAT SPACE, HELPLESS...
うにょ
SQUIRM
うにょ
SQUIRM
AND FORCED TO BECOME...
"STABILITY..."
うにょ
SQUIRM
"BOUNDARIES..."
うにょ
SQUIRM
THE ADMINIS-TRATOR.
HEH HEH.

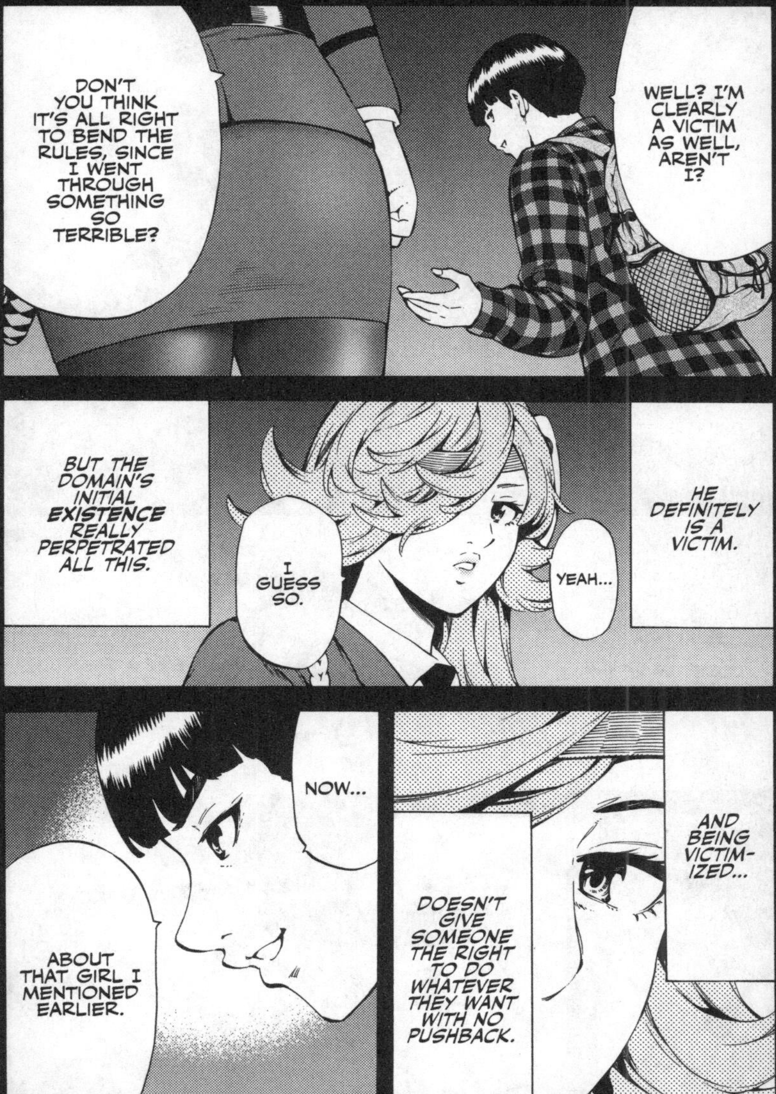
WELL? I'M CLEARLY A VICTIM AS WELL, AREN'T I?
DON'T YOU THINK IT'S ALL RIGHT TO BEND THE RULES, SINCE I WENT THROUGH SOMETHING SO TERRIBLE?
HE DEFINITELY IS A VICTIM.
YEAH...
I GUESS SO.
BUT THE DOMAIN'S INITIAL **EXISTENCE** REALLY PERPETRATED ALL THIS.
AND BEING VICTIMIZED...
DOESN'T GIVE SOMEONE THE RIGHT TO DO WHATEVER THEY WANT WITH NO PUSHBACK.
NOW...
ABOUT THAT GIRL I MENTIONED EARLIER.

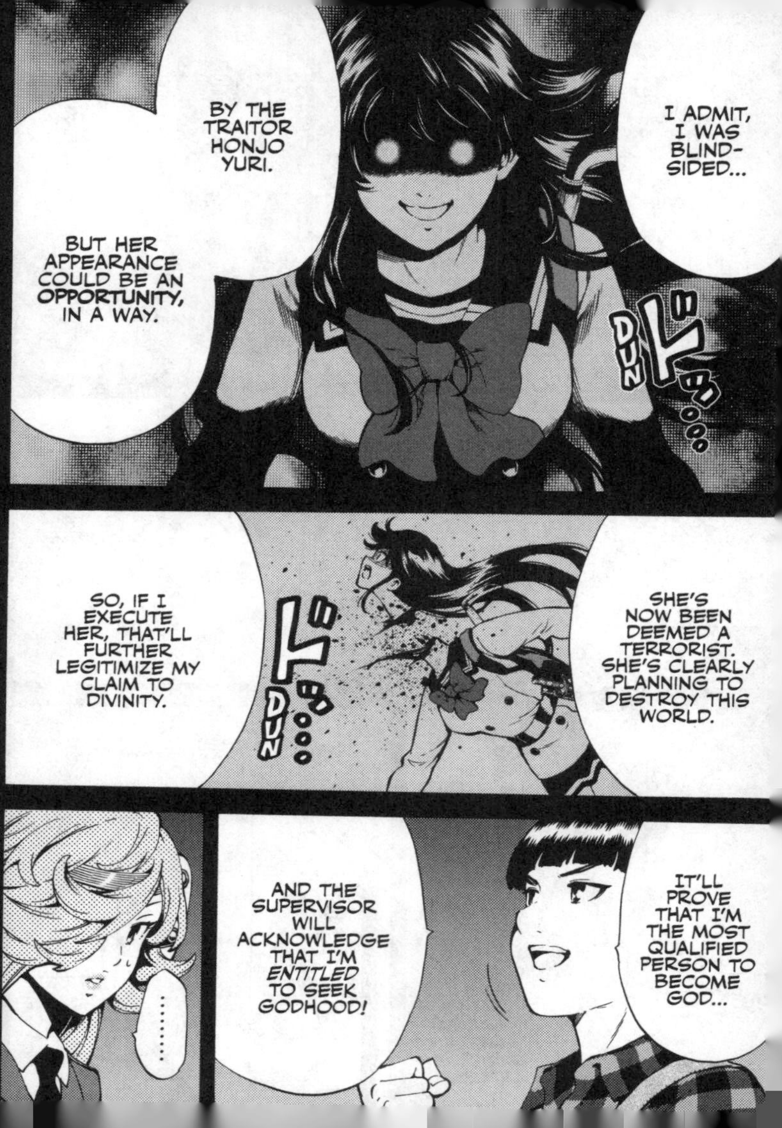
I ADMIT, I WAS BLIND-SIDED...
BY THE TRAITOR HONJO YURI.
BUT HER APPEARANCE COULD BE AN **OPPORTUNITY**, IN A WAY.
DUN
SHE'S NOW BEEN DEEMED A TERRORIST. SHE'S CLEARLY PLANNING TO DESTROY THIS WORLD.
SO, IF I EXECUTE HER, THAT'LL FURTHER LEGITIMIZE MY CLAIM TO DIVINITY.
DUN
IT'LL PROVE THAT I'M THE MOST QUALIFIED PERSON TO BECOME GOD...
AND THE SUPERVISOR WILL ACKNOWLEDGE THAT I'M *ENTITLED* TO SEEK GODHOOD!
....

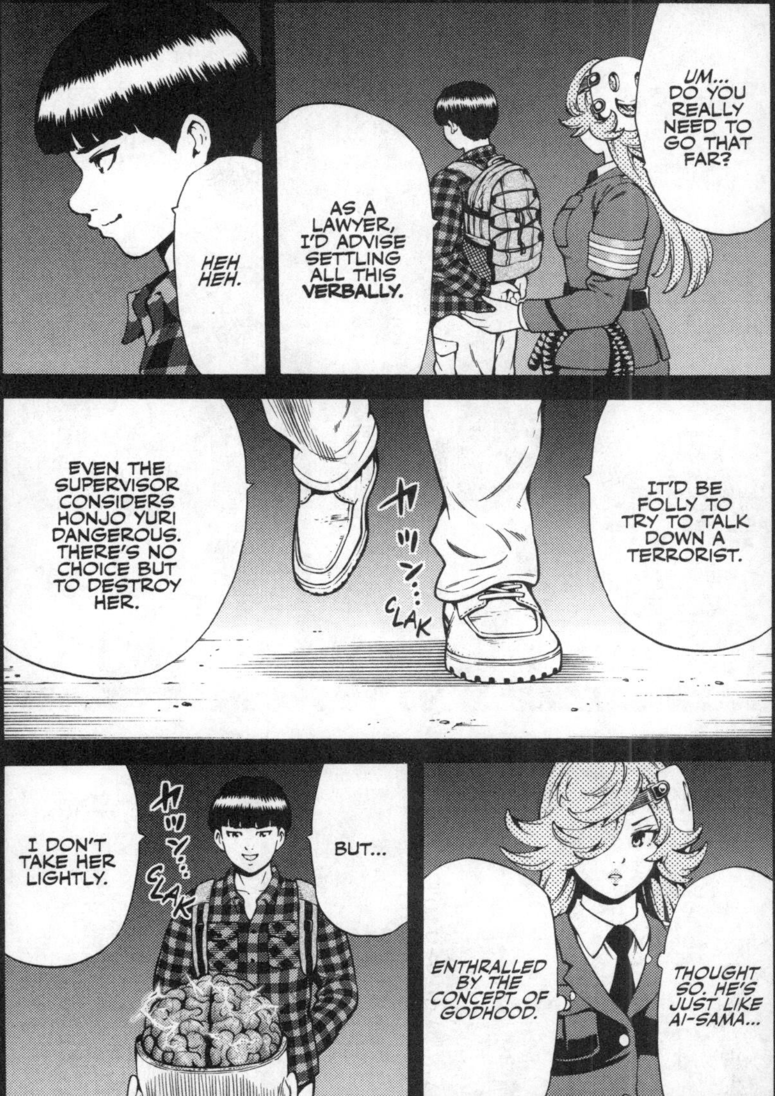
UM... DO YOU REALLY NEED TO GO THAT FAR?
AS A LAWYER, I'D ADVISE SETTLING ALL THIS **VERBALLY.**
HEH HEH.
IT'D BE FOLLY TO TRY TO TALK DOWN A TERRORIST.
CLAK
EVEN THE SUPERVISOR CONSIDERS HONJO YURI DANGEROUS. THERE'S NO CHOICE BUT TO DESTROY HER.
THOUGHT SO. HE'S JUST LIKE AI-SAMA...
ENTHRALLED BY THE CONCEPT OF GODHOOD.
BUT...
CLAK
I DON'T TAKE HER LIGHTLY.

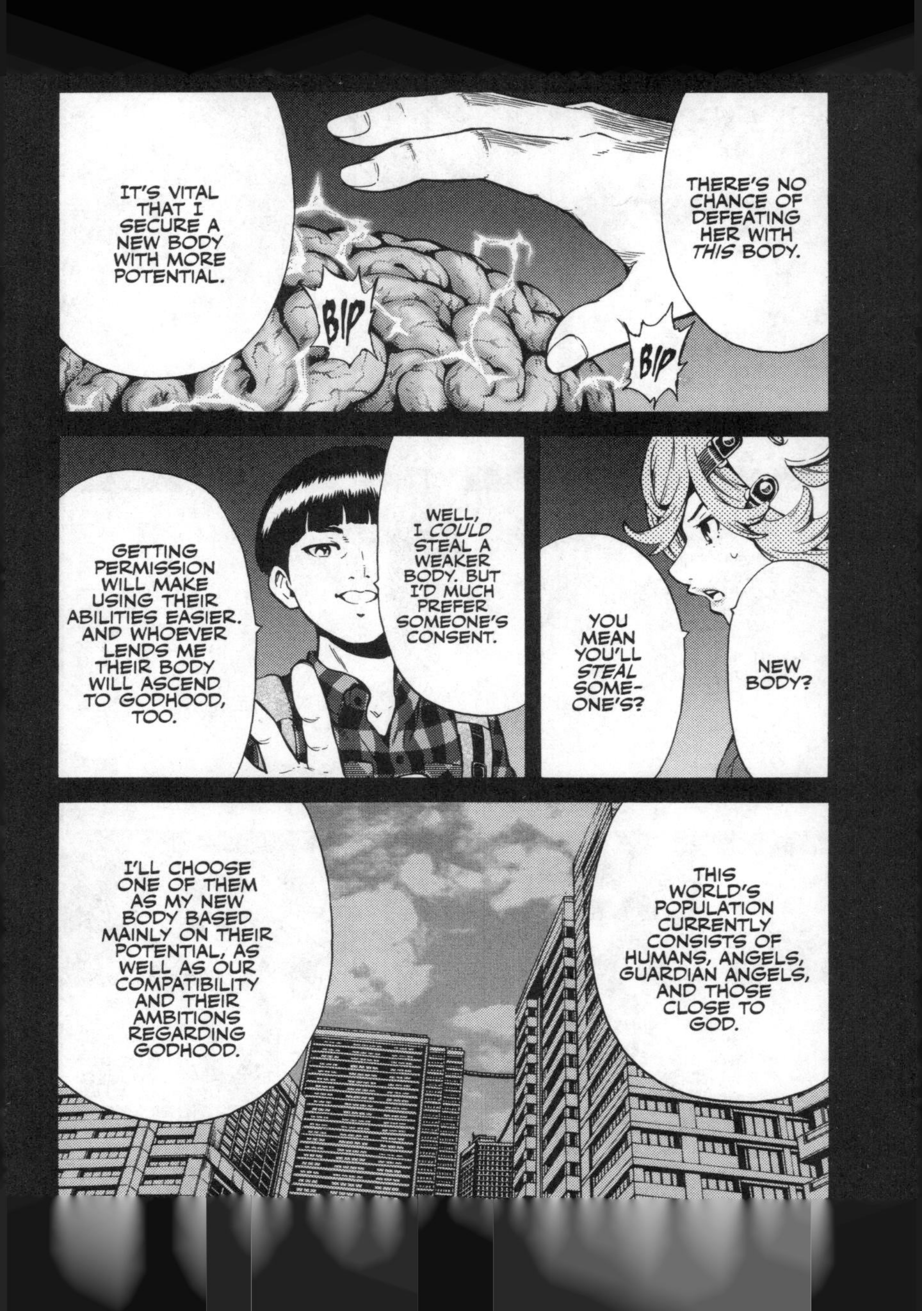
THERE'S NO CHANCE OF DEFEATING HER WITH *THIS* BODY.
BIP
BIP
IT'S VITAL THAT I SECURE A NEW BODY WITH MORE POTENTIAL.
NEW BODY?
YOU MEAN YOU'LL *STEAL* SOME-ONE'S?
WELL, I *COULD* STEAL A WEAKER BODY. BUT I'D MUCH PREFER SOMEONE'S CONSENT.
GETTING PERMISSION WILL MAKE USING THEIR ABILITIES EASIER. AND WHOEVER LENDS ME THEIR BODY WILL ASCEND TO GODHOOD, TOO.
THIS WORLD'S POPULATION CURRENTLY CONSISTS OF HUMANS, ANGELS, GUARDIAN ANGELS, AND THOSE CLOSE TO GOD.
I'LL CHOOSE ONE OF THEM AS MY NEW BODY BASED MAINLY ON THEIR POTENTIAL, AS WELL AS OUR COMPATIBILITY AND THEIR AMBITIONS REGARDING GODHOOD.

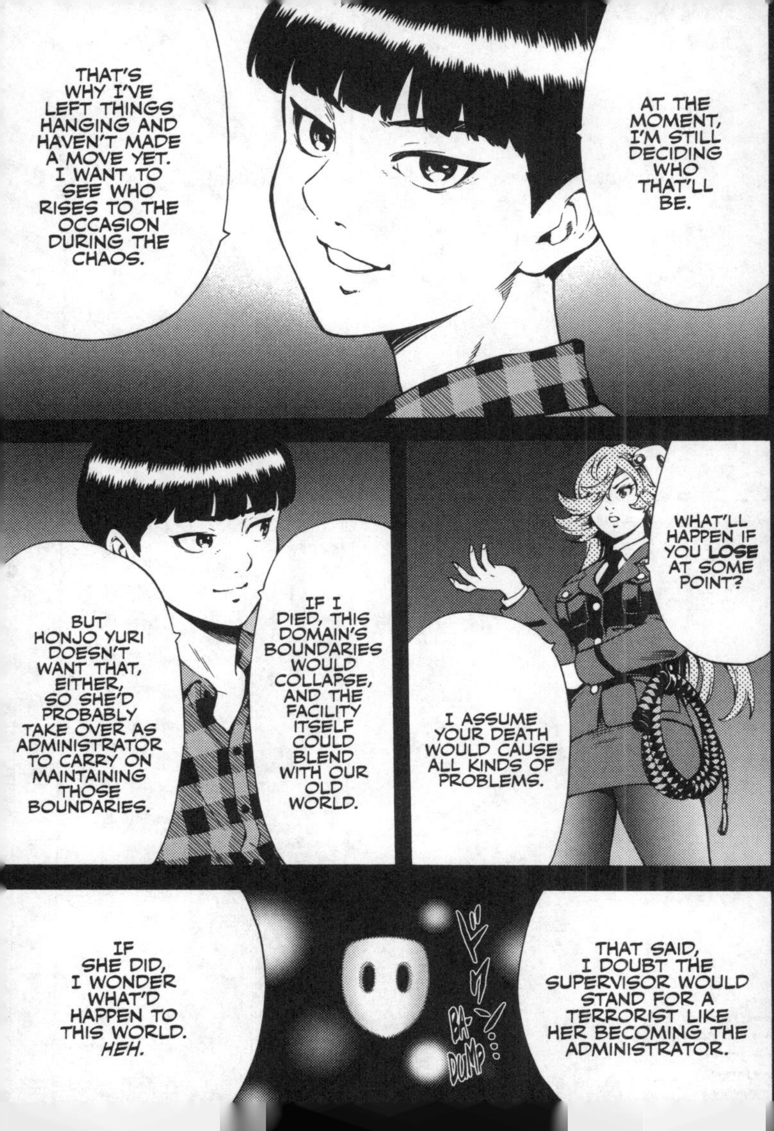
AT THE MOMENT, I'M STILL DECIDING WHO THAT'LL BE.
THAT'S WHY I'VE LEFT THINGS HANGING AND HAVEN'T MADE A MOVE YET. I WANT TO SEE WHO RISES TO THE OCCASION DURING THE CHAOS.
WHAT'LL HAPPEN IF YOU **LOSE** AT SOME POINT?
I ASSUME YOUR DEATH WOULD CAUSE ALL KINDS OF PROBLEMS.
IF I DIED, THIS DOMAIN'S BOUNDARIES WOULD COLLAPSE, AND THE FACILITY ITSELF COULD BLEND WITH OUR OLD WORLD.
BUT HONJO YURI DOESN'T WANT THAT, EITHER, SO SHE'D PROBABLY TAKE OVER AS ADMINISTRATOR TO CARRY ON MAINTAINING THOSE BOUNDARIES.
THAT SAID, I DOUBT THE SUPERVISOR WOULD STAND FOR A TERRORIST LIKE HER BECOMING THE ADMINISTRATOR.
BA-DUMP
IF SHE DID, I WONDER WHAT'D HAPPEN TO THIS WORLD. *HEH.*

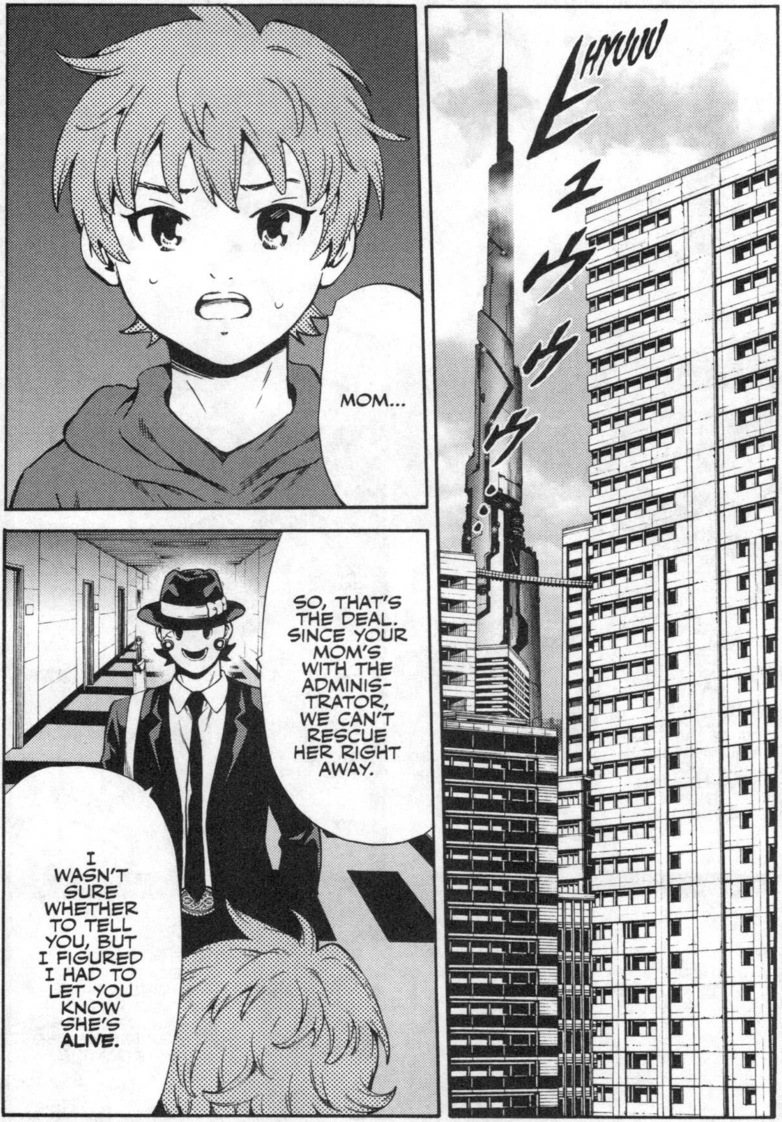
HYUUU
MOM...
SO, THAT'S THE DEAL. SINCE YOUR MOM'S WITH THE ADMINISTRATOR, WE CAN'T RESCUE HER RIGHT AWAY.
I WASN'T SURE WHETHER TO TELL YOU, BUT I FIGURED I HAD TO LET YOU KNOW SHE'S **ALIVE.**

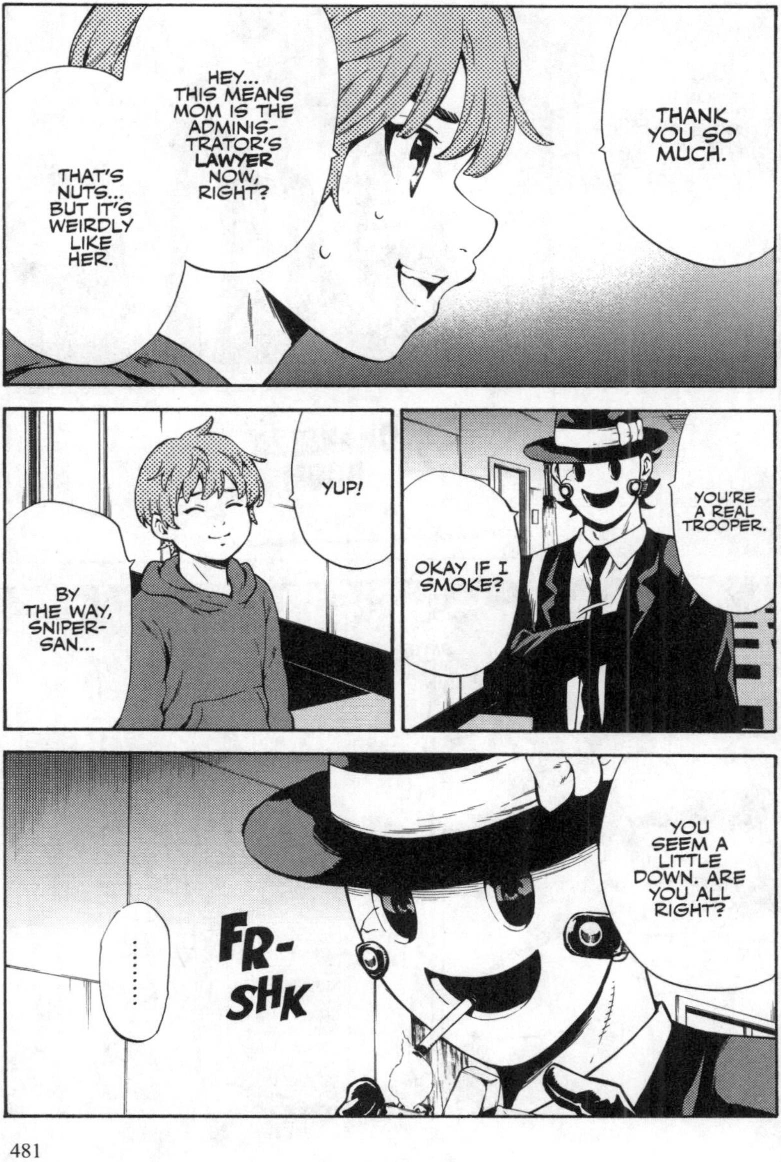
THANK YOU SO MUCH.
HEY... THIS MEANS MOM IS THE ADMINIS-TRATOR'S **LAWYER** NOW, RIGHT?
THAT'S NUTS... BUT IT'S WEIRDLY LIKE HER.
YOU'RE A REAL TROOPER.
OKAY IF I SMOKE?
YUP!
BY THE WAY, SNIPER-SAN...
YOU SEEM A LITTLE DOWN. ARE YOU ALL RIGHT?
FR-SHK
......

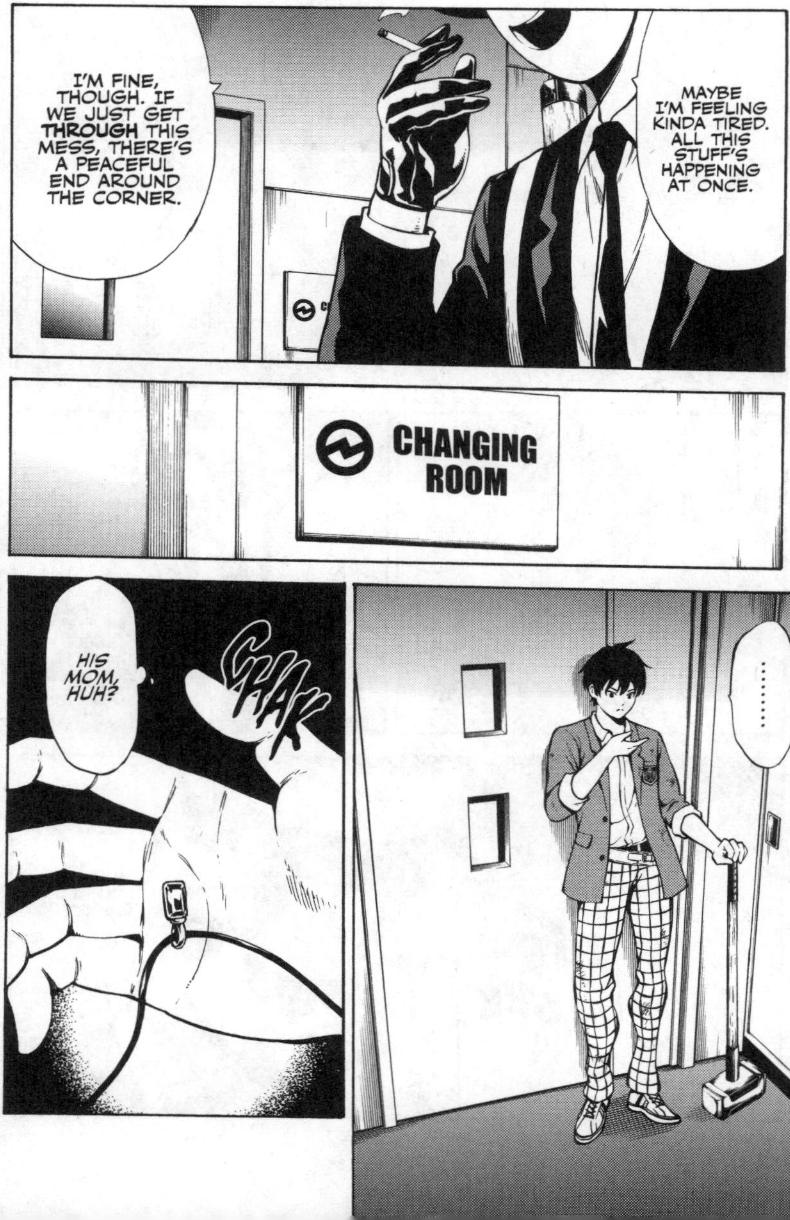
MAYBE I'M FEELING KINDA TIRED. ALL THIS STUFF'S HAPPENING AT ONCE.
I'M FINE, THOUGH. IF WE JUST GET **THROUGH** THIS MESS, THERE'S A PEACEFUL END AROUND THE CORNER.
CHANGING ROOM
......
HIS MOM, HUH?
CHAK

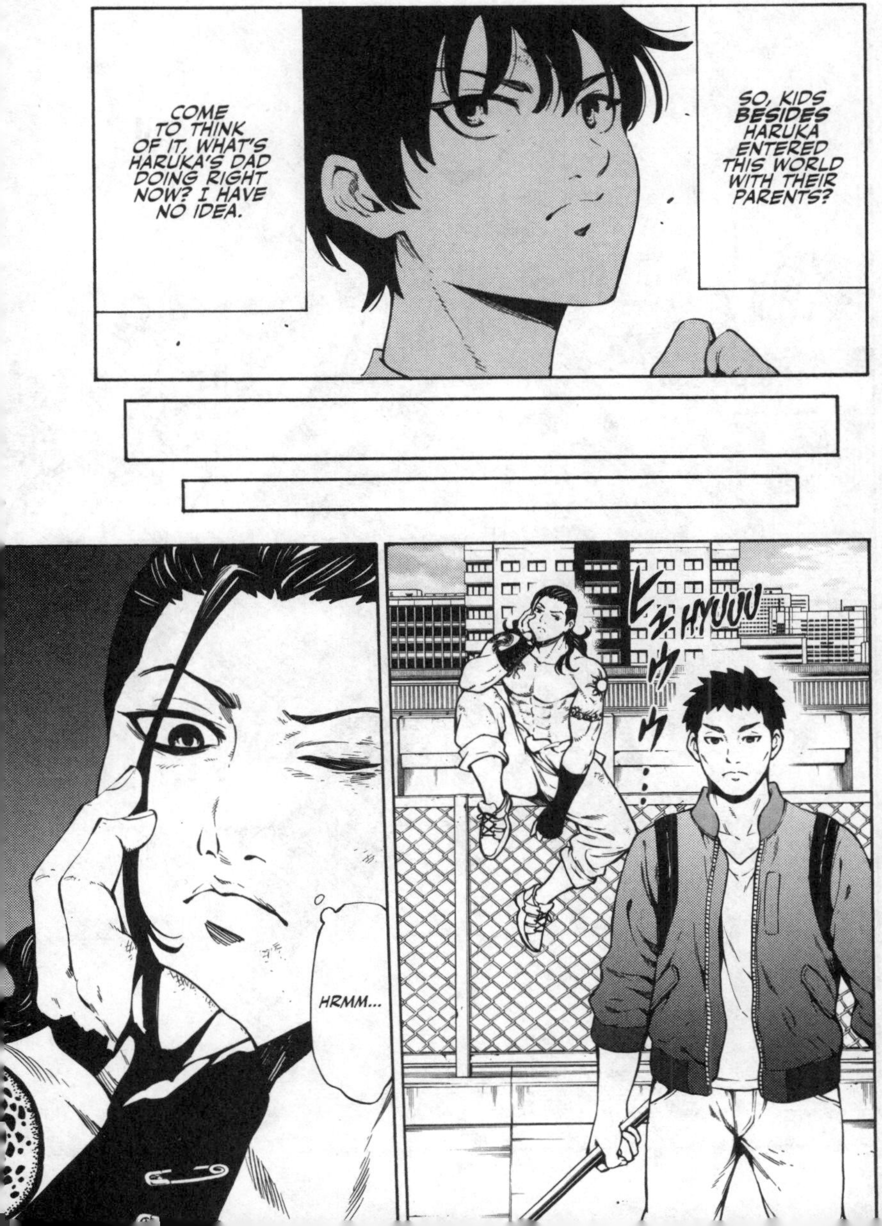
SO, KIDS BESIDES HARUKA ENTERED THIS WORLD WITH THEIR PARENTS?
COME TO THINK OF IT, WHAT'S HARUKA'S DAD DOING RIGHT NOW? I HAVE NO IDEA.
HYUUU
HRMM...

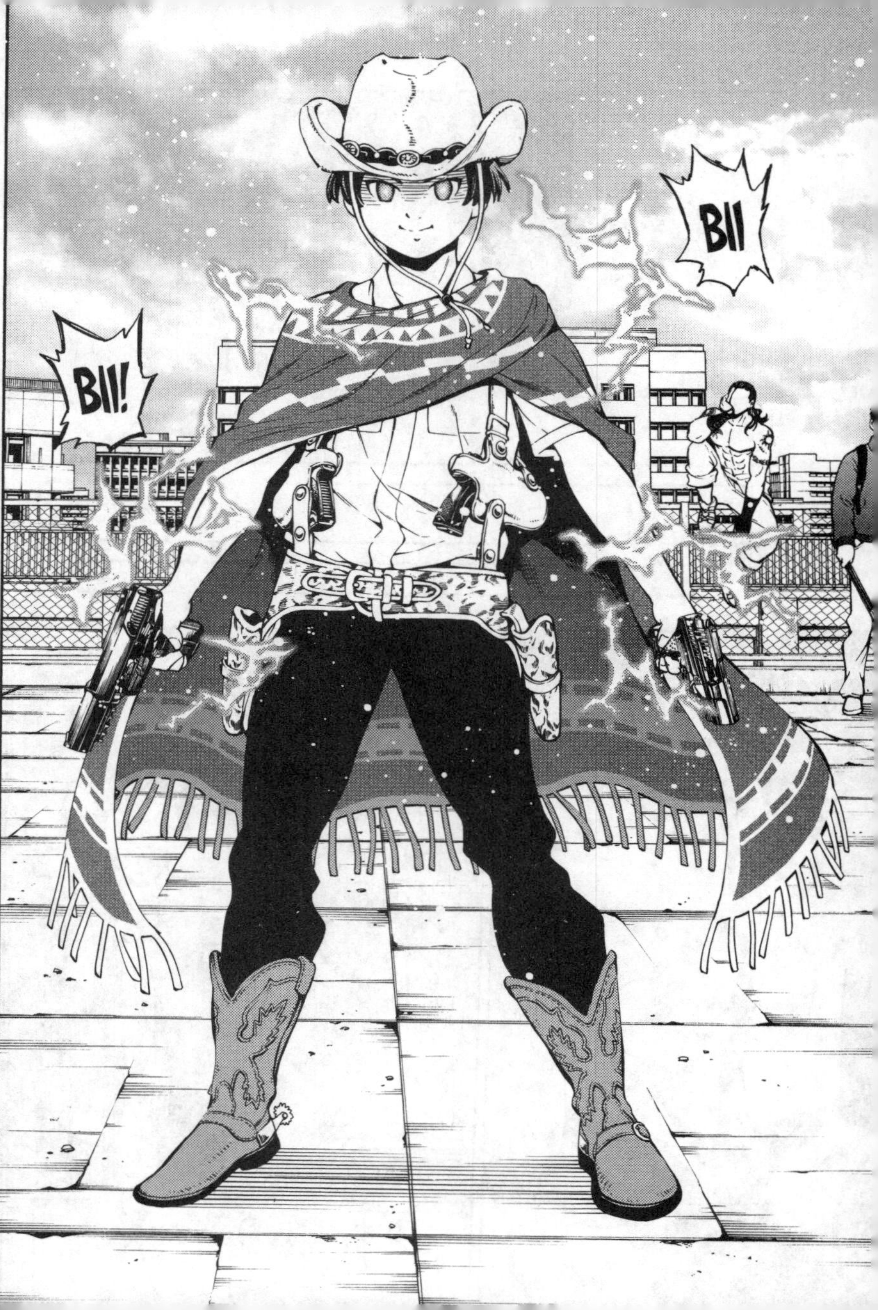
BII
BII!

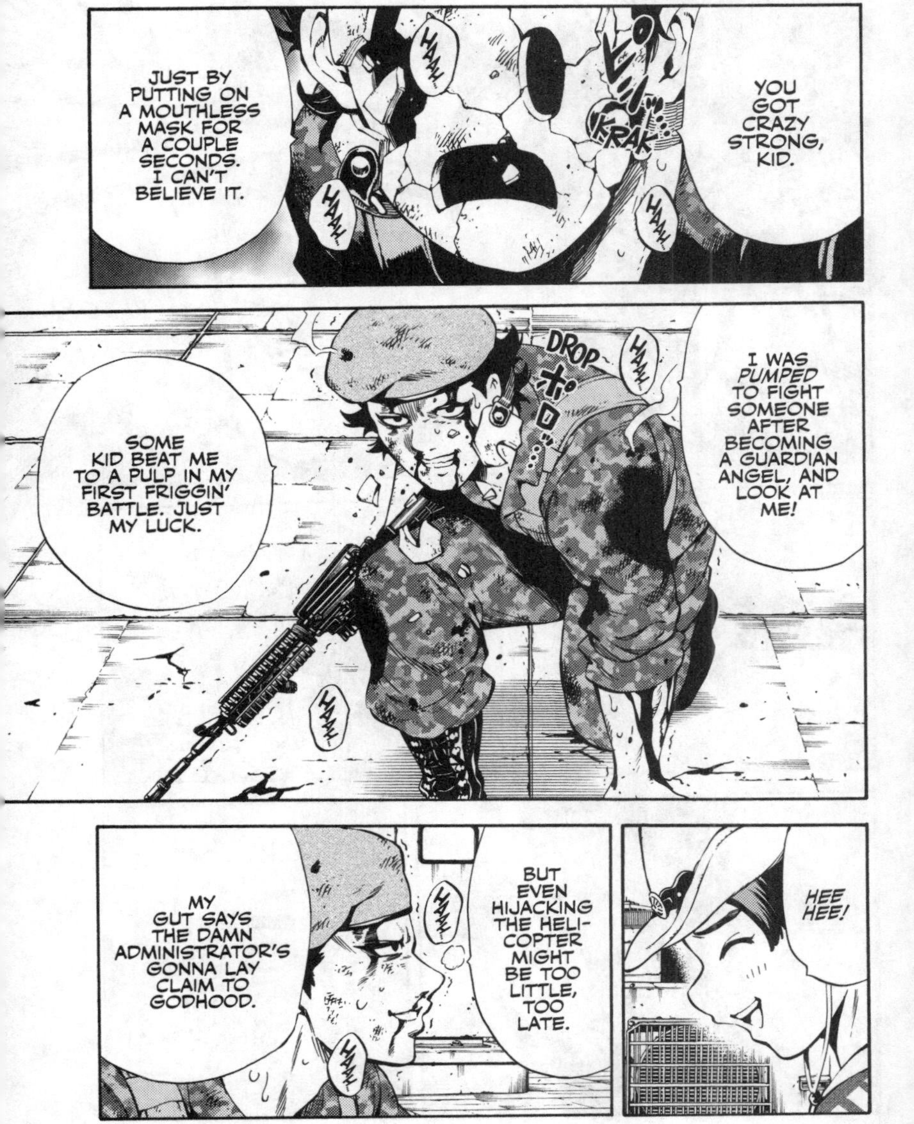
YOU GOT CRAZY STRONG, KID.
KRAK
HAAH
HAAH
JUST BY PUTTING ON A MOUTHLESS MASK FOR A COUPLE SECONDS. I CAN'T BELIEVE IT.
HAAH
I WAS PUMPED TO FIGHT SOMEONE AFTER BECOMING A GUARDIAN ANGEL, AND LOOK AT ME!
HAAH
DROP
SOME KID BEAT ME TO A PULP IN MY FIRST FRIGGIN' BATTLE. JUST MY LUCK.
HAAH
HEE HEE!
BUT EVEN HIJACKING THE HELI-COPTER MIGHT BE TOO LITTLE, TOO LATE.
HAAH
MY GUT SAYS THE DAMN ADMINISTRATOR'S GONNA LAY CLAIM TO GODHOOD.
HAAH

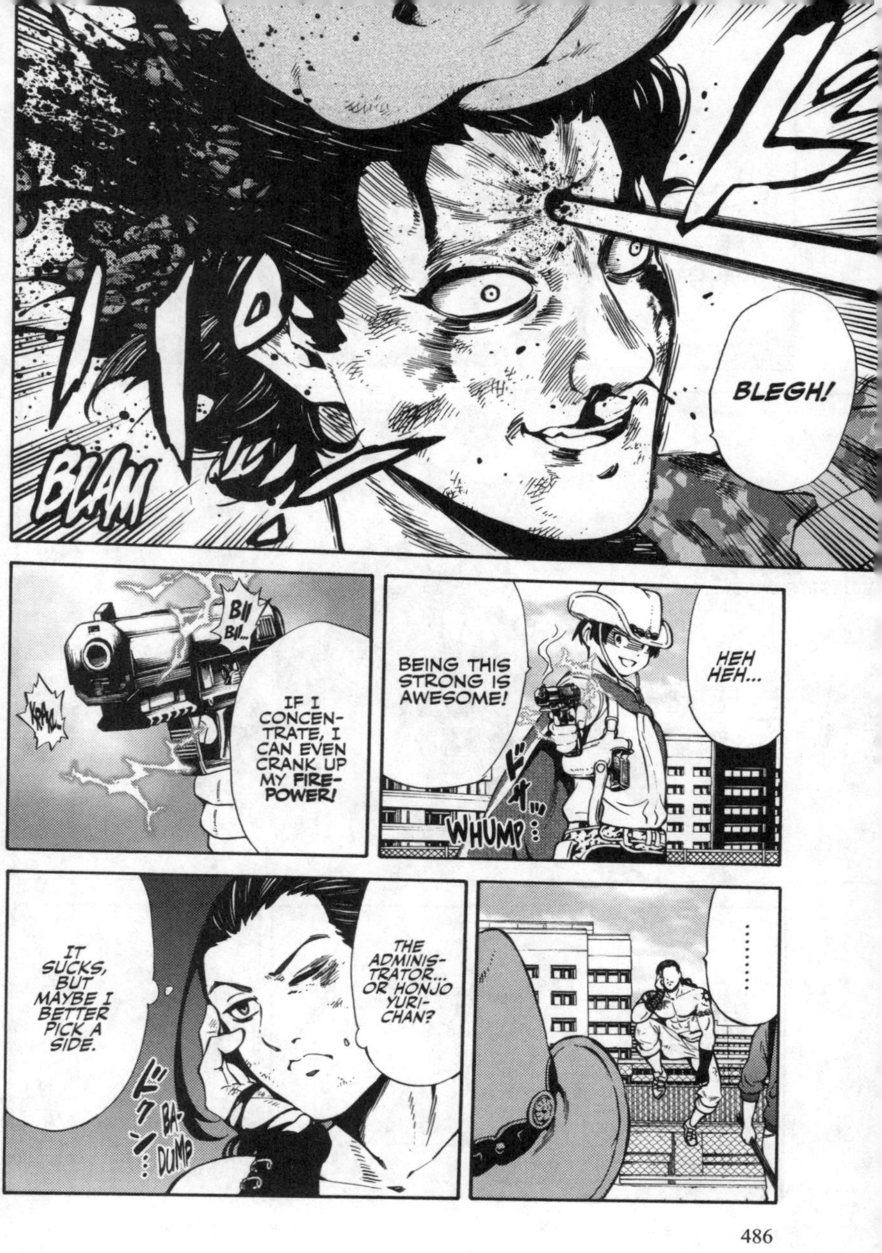
BLEGH!
BLAM
HEH HEH...
BEING THIS STRONG IS AWESOME!
WHUMP...
BII BII...
IF I CONCEN-TRATE, I CAN EVEN CRANK UP MY FIRE-POWER!
......
THE ADMINIS-TRATOR... OR HONJO YURI-CHAN?
IT SUCKS, BUT MAYBE I BETTER PICK A SIDE.
BA-DUMP

CHAPTER 248: Minding My Own Business

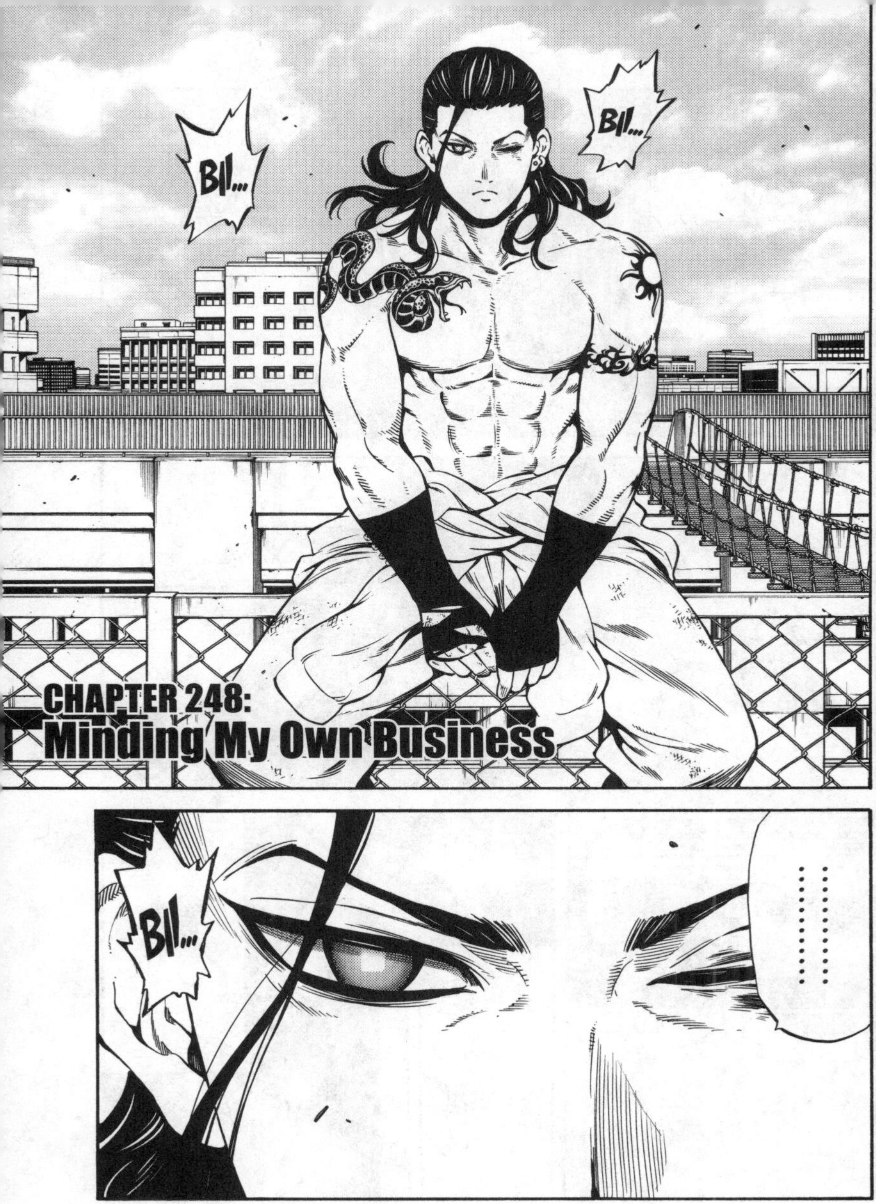

BII...
BII...
......
BII...

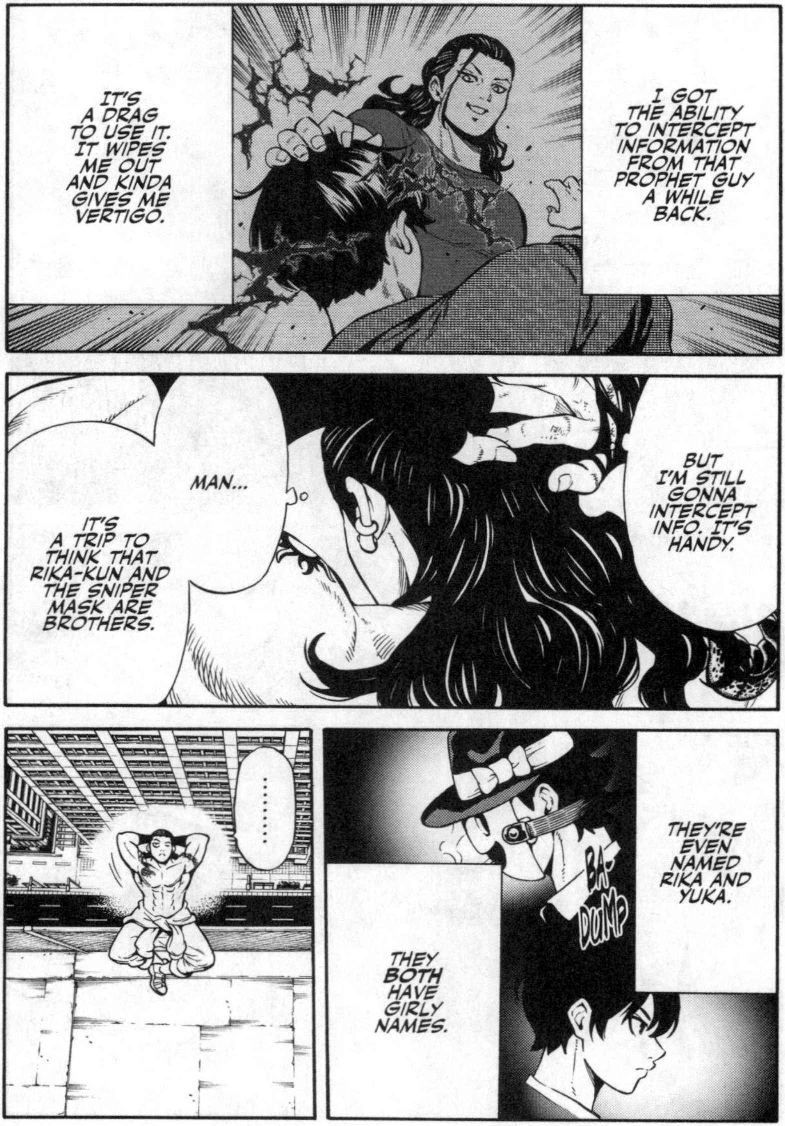
I GOT THE ABILITY TO INTERCEPT INFORMATION FROM THAT PROPHET GUY A WHILE BACK.
IT'S A DRAG TO USE IT. IT WIPES ME OUT AND KINDA GIVES ME VERTIGO.
BUT I'M STILL GONNA INTERCEPT INFO. IT'S HANDY.
MAN...
IT'S A TRIP TO THINK THAT RIKA-KUN AND THE SNIPER MASK ARE BROTHERS.
THEY'RE EVEN NAMED RIKA AND YUKA.
BA-DUMP
THEY BOTH HAVE GIRLY NAMES.
......

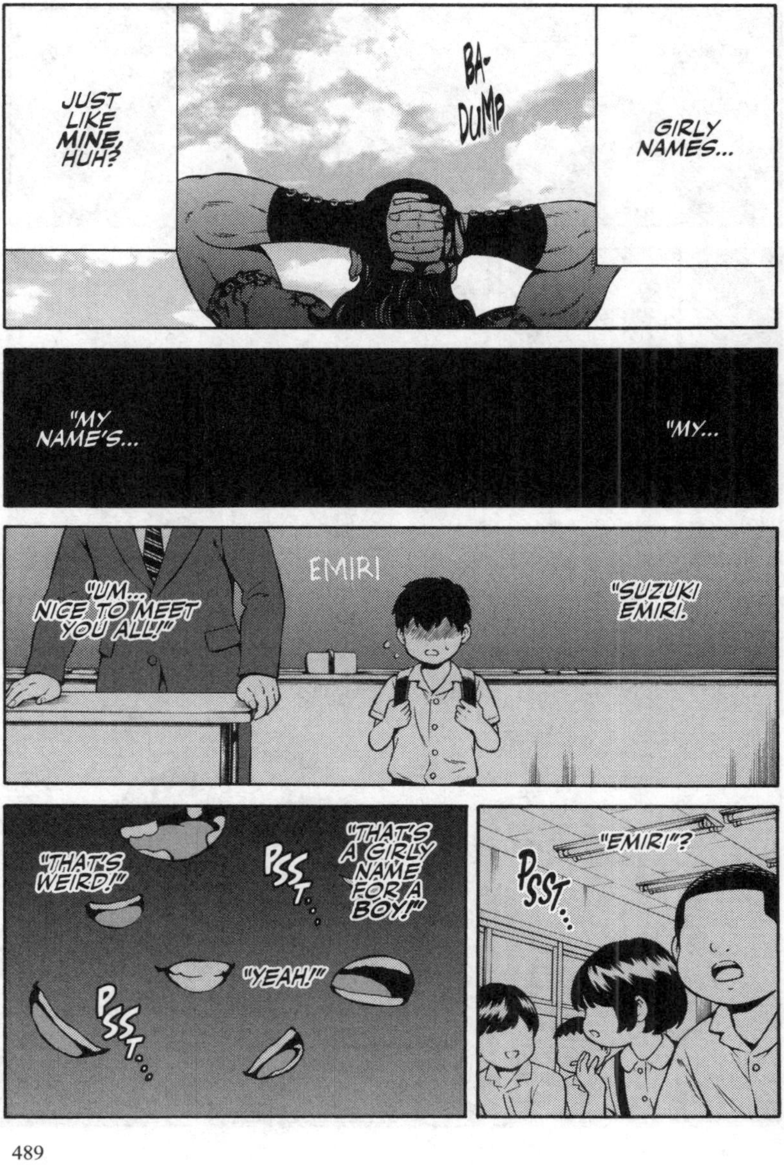
GIRLY NAMES...
BA-DUMP
JUST LIKE MINE, HUH?
"MY...
"MY NAME'S...
"SUZUKI EMIRI.
EMIRI
"UM... NICE TO MEET YOU ALL!"
"EMIRI"?
PSST...
"THAT'S A GIRLY NAME FOR A BOY!"
PSST...
"THAT'S WEIRD!"
"YEAH!"
PSST...

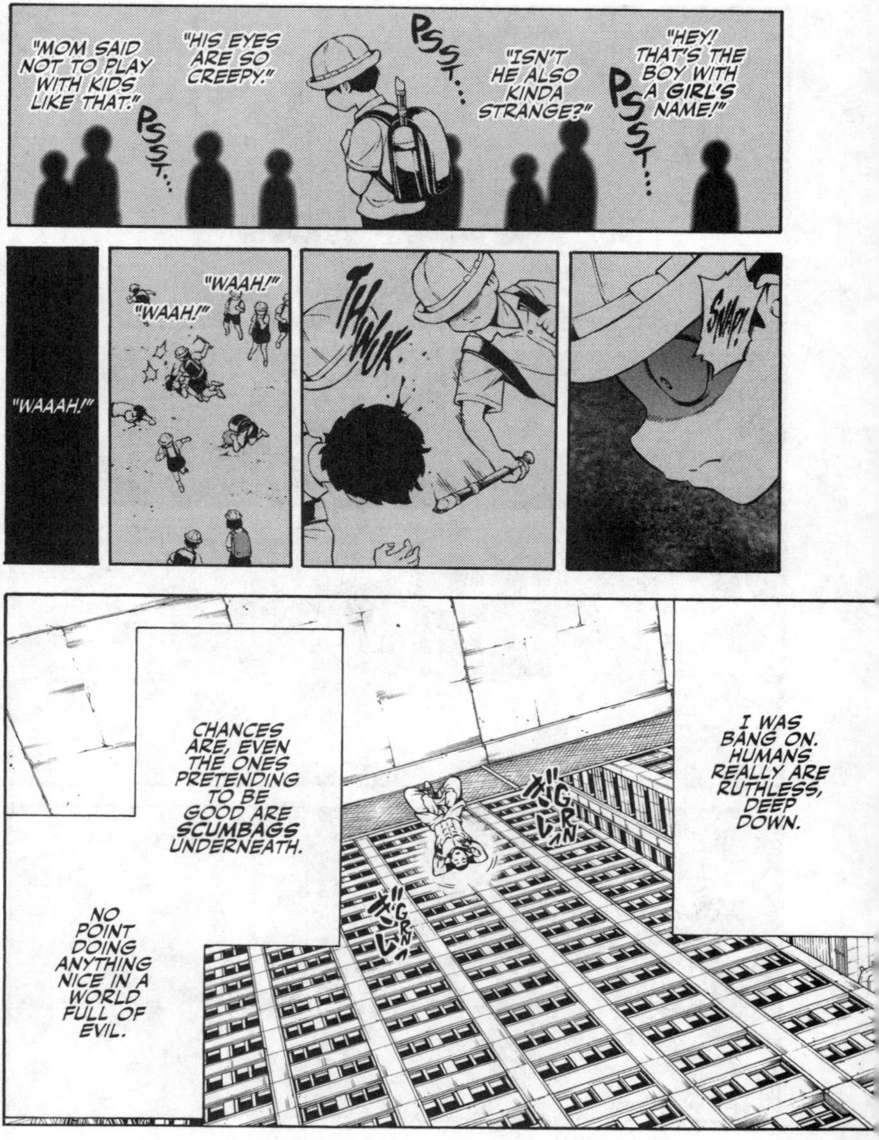
"HEY! THAT'S THE BOY WITH A GIRL'S NAME!"
PSST...
"ISN'T HE ALSO KINDA STRANGE?"
PSST...
"HIS EYES ARE SO CREEPY."
"MOM SAID NOT TO PLAY WITH KIDS LIKE THAT."
PSST...
SNAP!
THWUK
"WAAH!"
"WAAH!"
"WAAAH!"
I WAS BANG ON. HUMANS REALLY ARE RUTHLESS, DEEP DOWN.
GRN
CHANCES ARE, EVEN THE ONES PRETENDING TO BE GOOD ARE SCUMBAGS UNDERNEATH.
GRN
NO POINT DOING ANYTHING NICE IN A WORLD FULL OF EVIL.

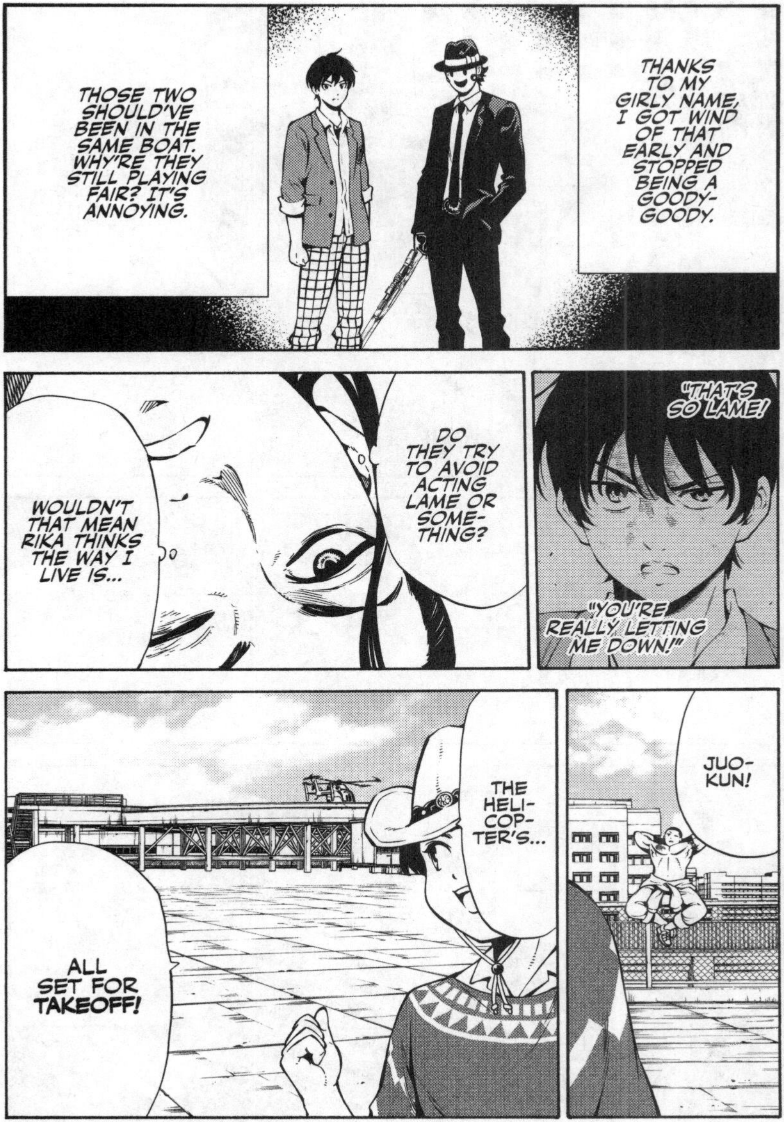
THANKS TO MY GIRLY NAME, I GOT WIND OF THAT EARLY AND STOPPED BEING A GOODY-GOODY.
THOSE TWO SHOULD'VE BEEN IN THE SAME BOAT. WHY'RE THEY STILL PLAYING FAIR? IT'S ANNOYING.
"THAT'S SO LAME!
"YOU'RE REALLY LETTING ME DOWN!"
DO THEY TRY TO AVOID ACTING LAME OR SOME-THING?
WOULDN'T THAT MEAN RIKA THINKS THE WAY I LIVE IS...
JUO-KUN!
THE HELI-COP-TER'S...
ALL SET FOR TAKEOFF!

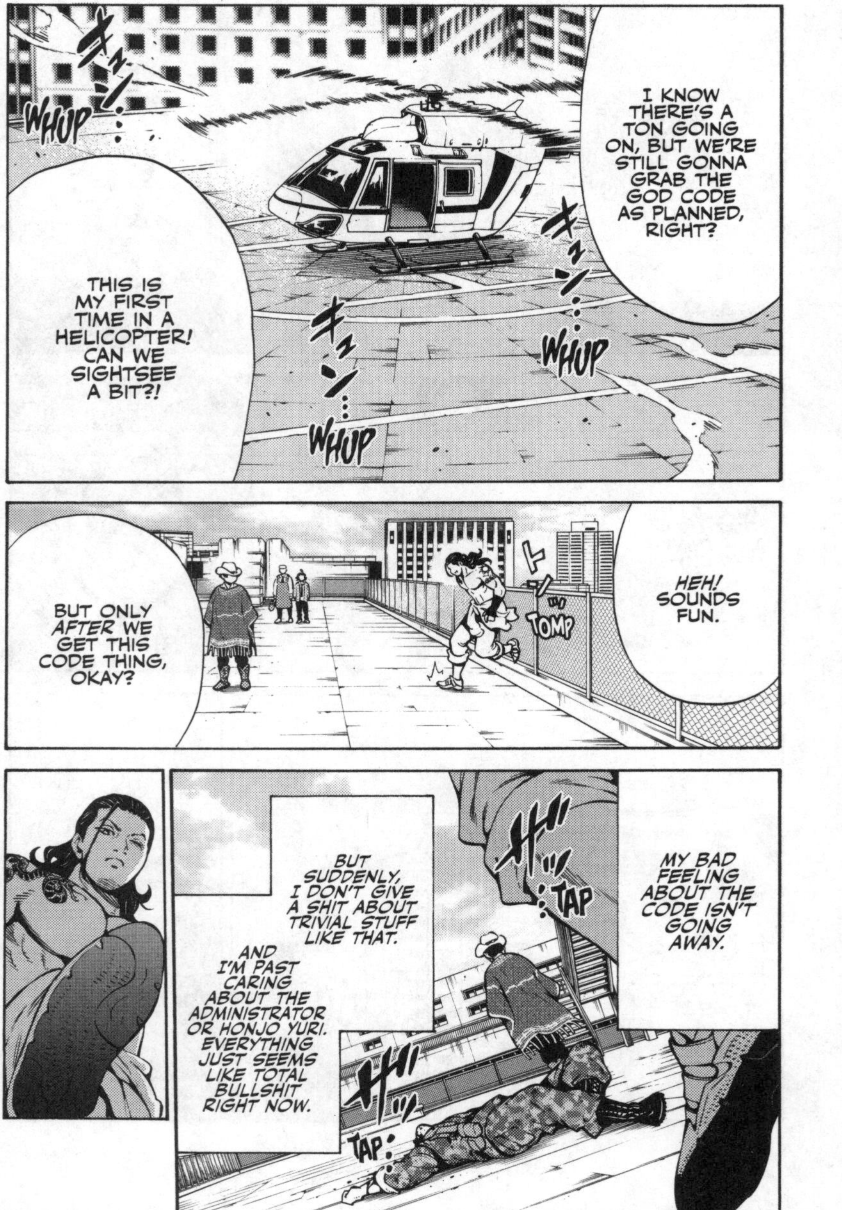
WHUP
I KNOW THERE'S A TON GOING ON, BUT WE'RE STILL GONNA GRAB THE GOD CODE AS PLANNED, RIGHT?
WHUP
THIS IS MY FIRST TIME IN A HELICOPTER! CAN WE SIGHTSEE A BIT?!
WHUP
HEH! SOUNDS FUN.
TOMP
BUT ONLY *AFTER* WE GET THIS CODE THING, OKAY?
MY BAD FEELING ABOUT THE CODE ISN'T GOING AWAY.
TAP
BUT SUDDENLY, I DON'T GIVE A SHIT ABOUT TRIVIAL STUFF LIKE THAT.
AND I'M PAST CARING ABOUT THE ADMINISTRATOR OR HONJO YURI. EVERYTHING JUST SEEMS LIKE TOTAL BULLSHIT RIGHT NOW.
TAP

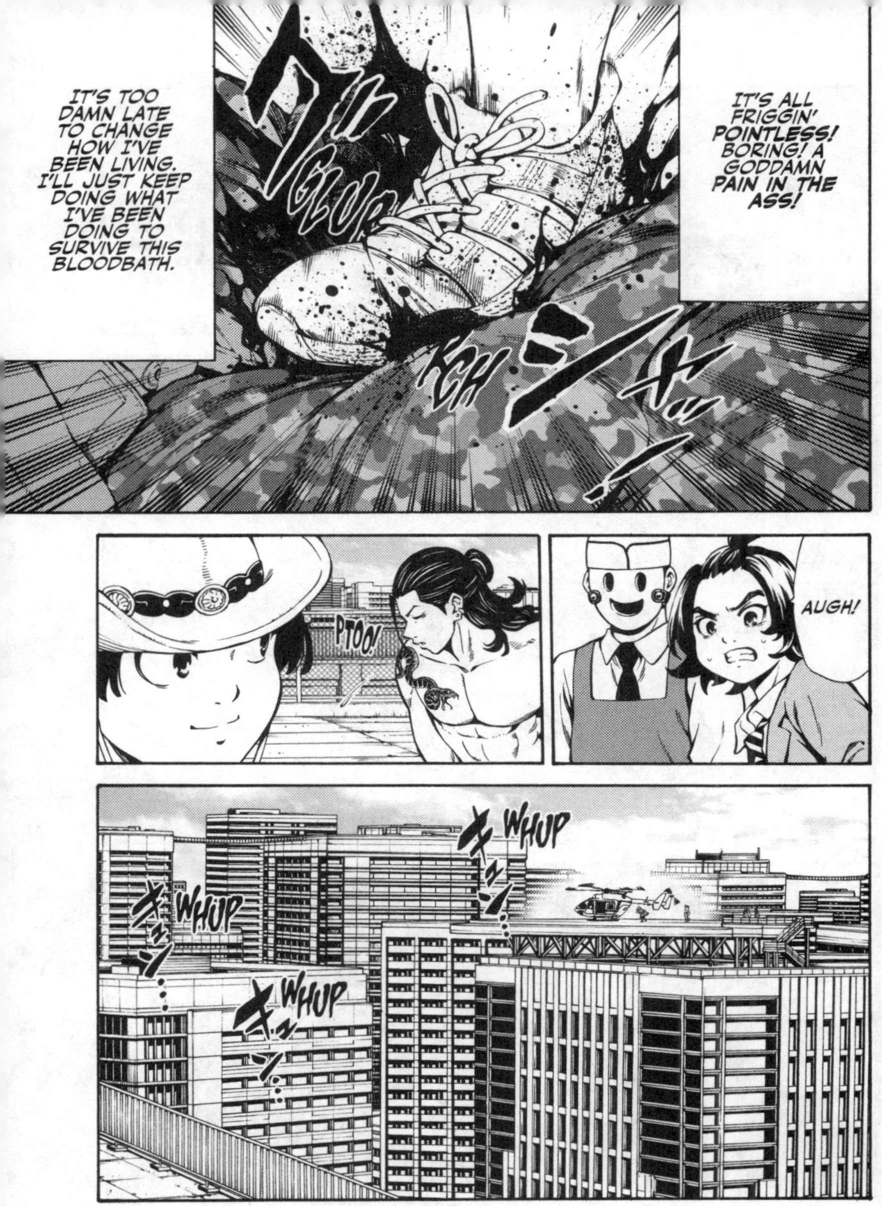
IT'S ALL FRIGGIN' POINTLESS! BORING! A GODDAMN PAIN IN THE ASS!
IT'S TOO DAMN LATE TO CHANGE HOW I'VE BEEN LIVING. I'LL JUST KEEP DOING WHAT I'VE BEEN DOING TO SURVIVE THIS BLOODBATH.
GLUP
KCH
AUGH!
PTOO!
WHUP
WHUP
WHUP

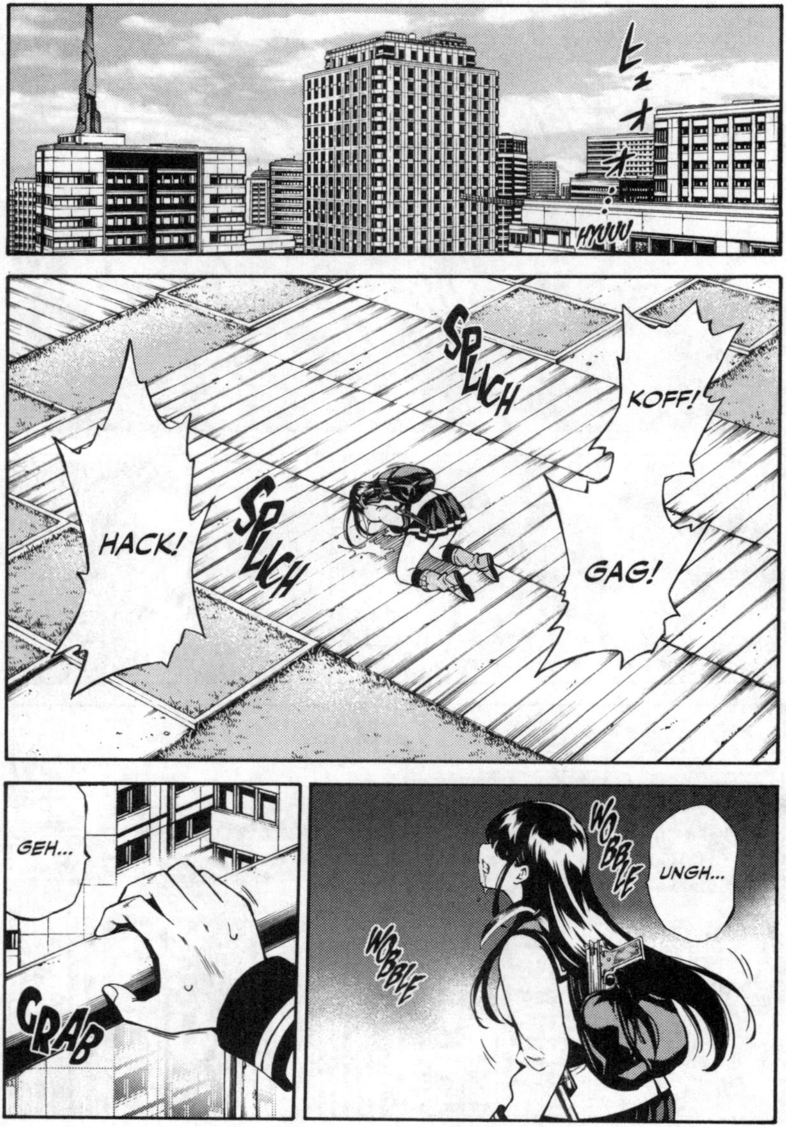

ヒュオオ…
HYUUU
KOFF!
SPLICH
GAG!
SPLICH
HACK!
WOBBLE
UNGH...
WOBBLE
GEH...
GRAB

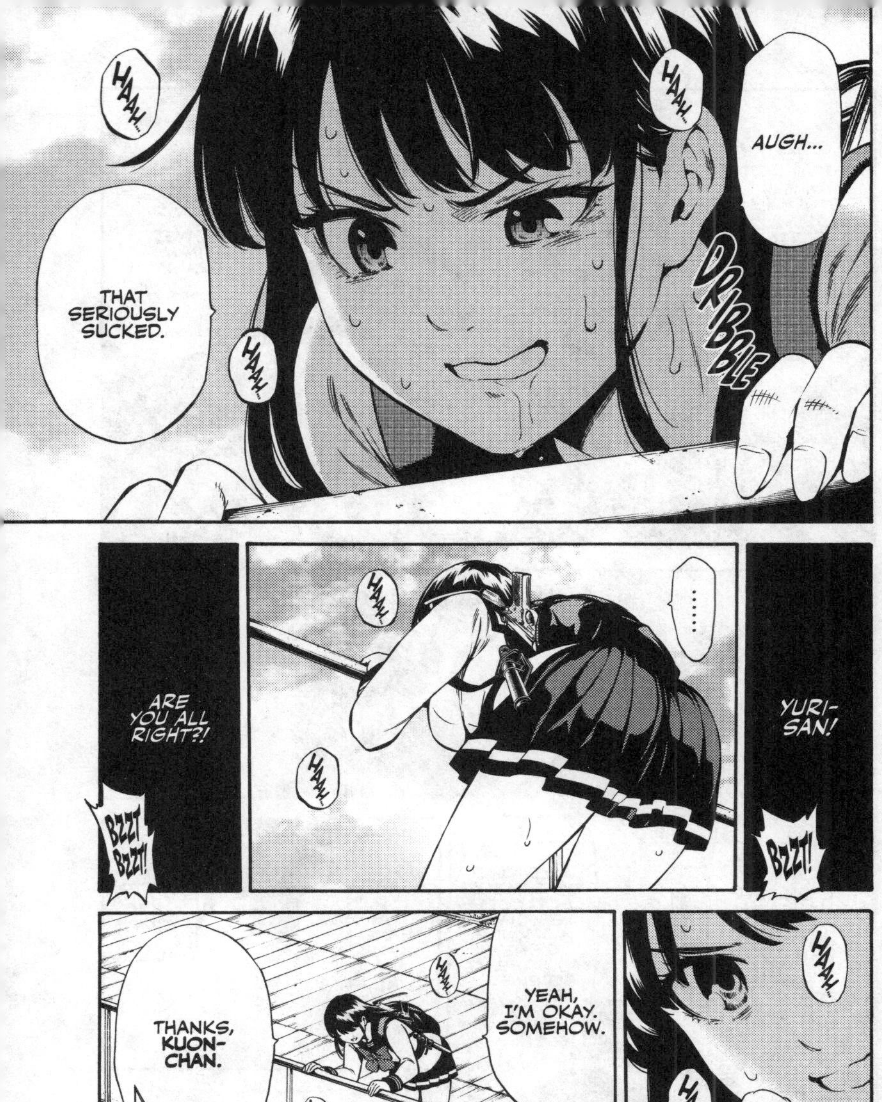
HAAAH...
AUGH...
DRIBBLE
HAAAH...
THAT SERIOUSLY SUCKED.
HAAAH...
YURI-SAN!
BZZT!
......
HAAAH...
HAAAH...
ARE YOU ALL RIGHT?!
BZZT BZZT!
HAAAH...
HAAAH...
YEAH, I'M OKAY. SOMEHOW.
HAAAH...
THANKS, KUON-CHAN.
HAAAH...
BA-DUMP!

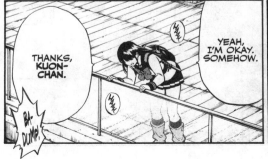

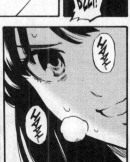

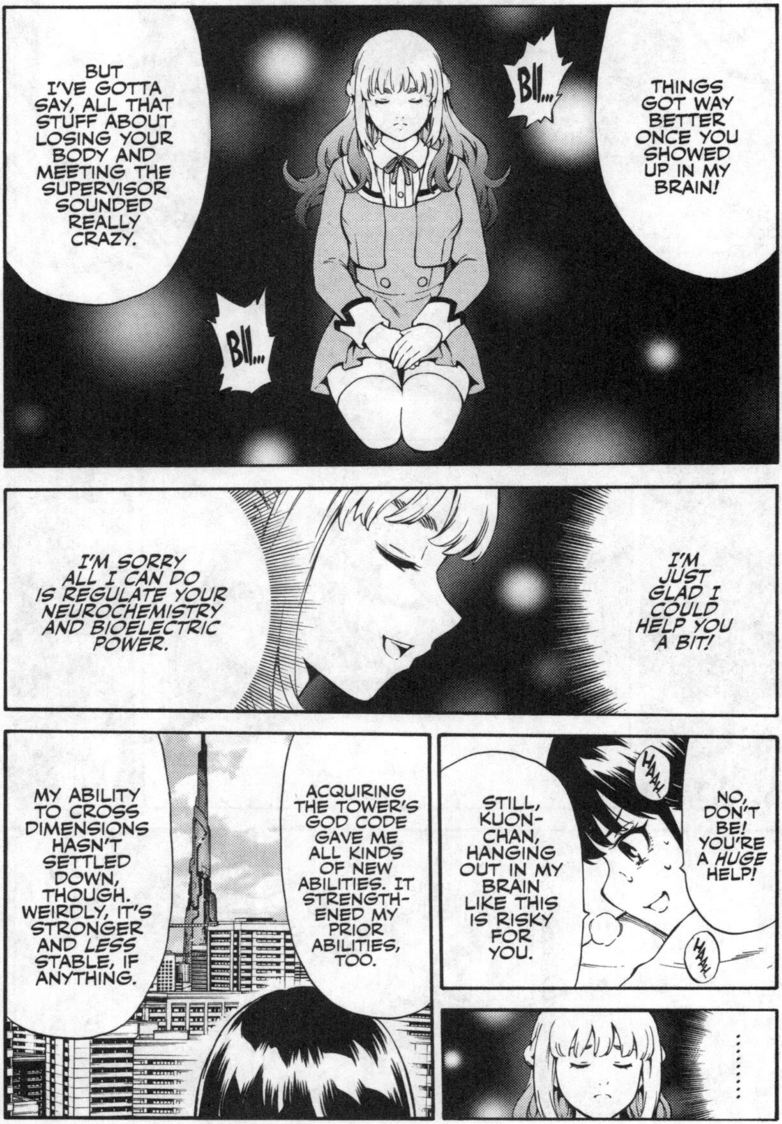
THINGS GOT WAY BETTER ONCE YOU SHOWED UP IN MY BRAIN!
BII...
BUT I'VE GOTTA SAY, ALL THAT STUFF ABOUT LOSING YOUR BODY AND MEETING THE SUPERVISOR SOUNDED REALLY CRAZY.
BII...
I'M JUST GLAD I COULD HELP YOU A BIT!
I'M SORRY ALL I CAN DO IS REGULATE YOUR NEUROCHEMISTRY AND BIOELECTRIC POWER.
HAAH
NO, DON'T BE! YOU'RE A *HUGE* HELP!
STILL, KUON-CHAN, HANGING OUT IN MY BRAIN LIKE THIS IS RISKY FOR YOU.
HAAH
......
ACQUIRING THE TOWER'S GOD CODE GAVE ME ALL KINDS OF NEW ABILITIES. IT STRENGTH-ENED MY PRIOR ABILITIES, TOO.
MY ABILITY TO CROSS DIMENSIONS HASN'T SETTLED DOWN, THOUGH. WEIRDLY, IT'S STRONGER AND *LESS* STABLE, IF ANYTHING.

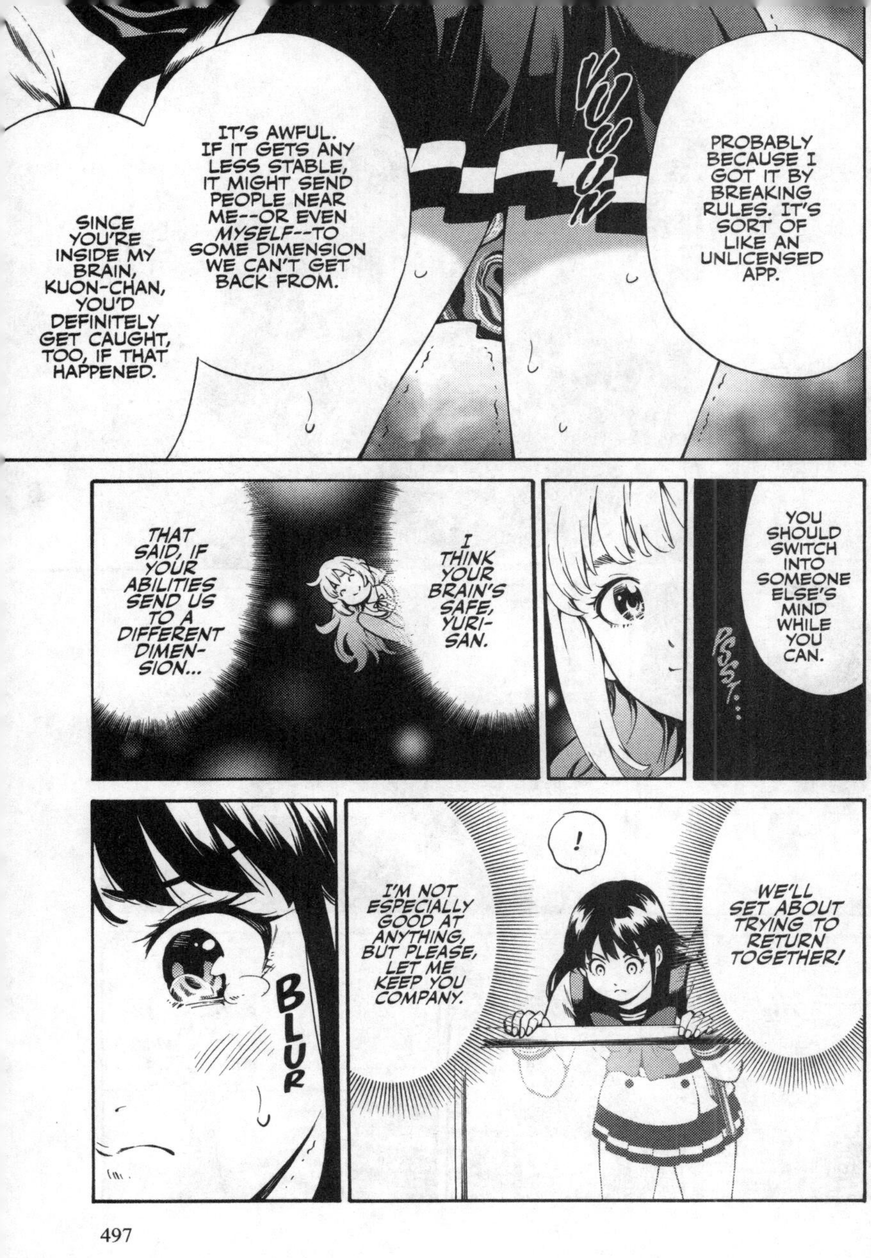
PROBABLY BECAUSE I GOT IT BY BREAKING RULES. IT'S SORT OF LIKE AN UNLICENSED APP.
VUUUN
IT'S AWFUL. IF IT GETS ANY LESS STABLE, IT MIGHT SEND PEOPLE NEAR ME--OR EVEN *MYSELF*--TO SOME DIMENSION WE CAN'T GET BACK FROM.
SINCE YOU'RE INSIDE MY BRAIN, KUON-CHAN, YOU'D DEFINITELY GET CAUGHT, TOO, IF THAT HAPPENED.
YOU SHOULD SWITCH INTO SOMEONE ELSE'S MIND WHILE YOU CAN.
PSST...
I THINK YOUR BRAIN'S SAFE, YURI-SAN.
THAT SAID, IF YOUR ABILITIES SEND US TO A DIFFERENT DIMENSION...
!
WE'LL SET ABOUT TRYING TO RETURN TOGETHER!
I'M NOT ESPECIALLY GOOD AT ANYTHING, BUT PLEASE, LET ME KEEP YOU COMPANY.
BLUR

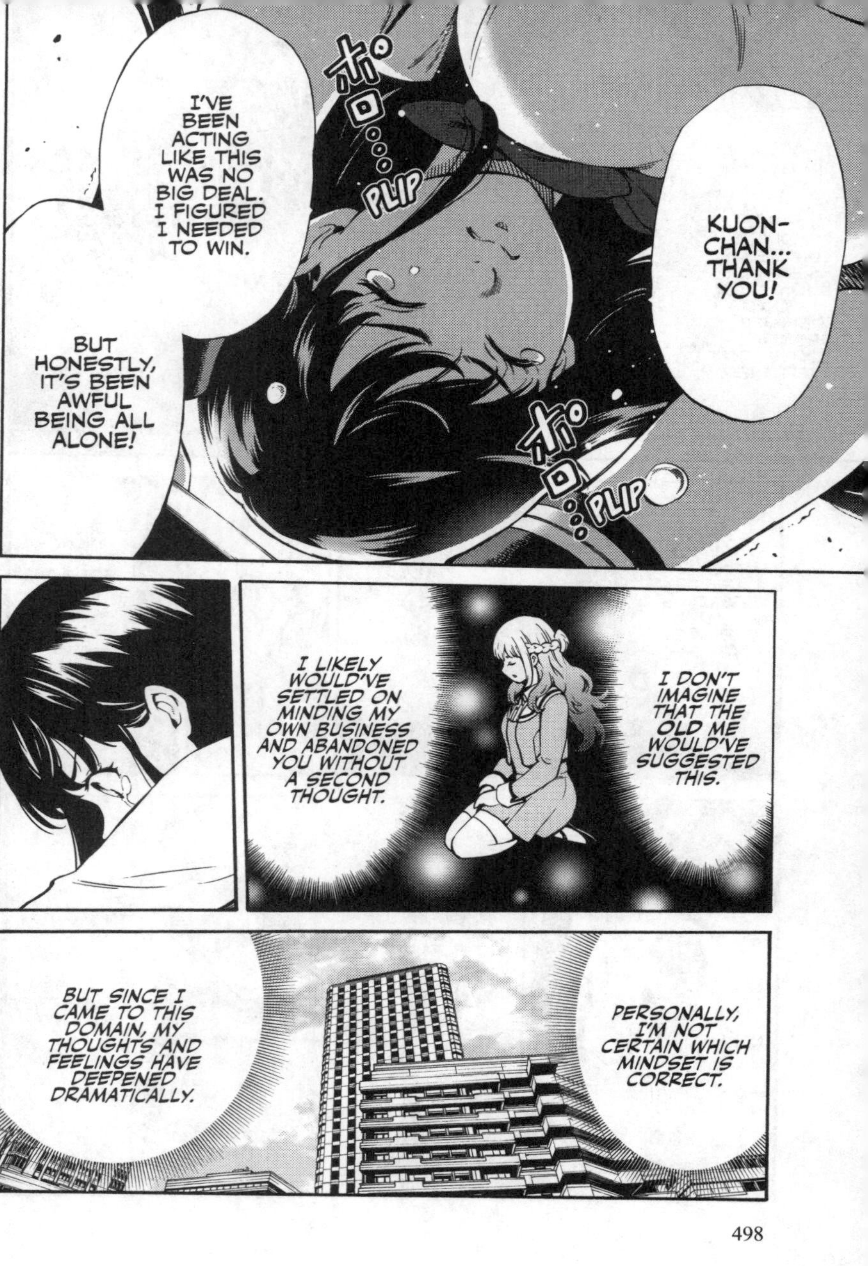
KUON-CHAN... THANK YOU!
I'VE BEEN ACTING LIKE THIS WAS NO BIG DEAL. I FIGURED I NEEDED TO WIN.
PLIP
BUT HONESTLY, IT'S BEEN AWFUL BEING ALL ALONE!
PLIP
I DON'T IMAGINE THAT THE OLD ME WOULD'VE SUGGESTED THIS.
I LIKELY WOULD'VE SETTLED ON MINDING MY OWN BUSINESS AND ABANDONED YOU WITHOUT A SECOND THOUGHT.
BUT SINCE I CAME TO THIS DOMAIN, MY THOUGHTS AND FEELINGS HAVE DEEPENED DRAMATICALLY.
PERSONALLY, I'M NOT CERTAIN WHICH MINDSET IS CORRECT.

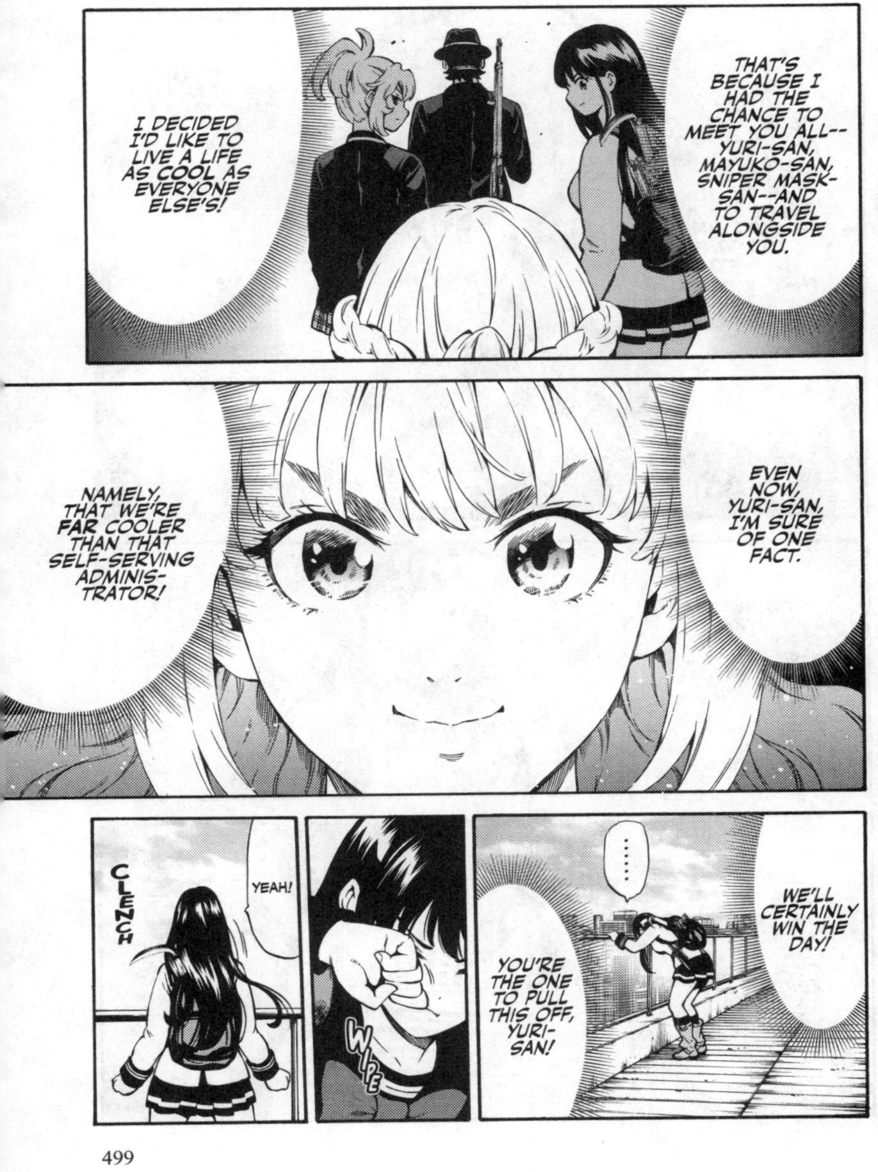
THAT'S BECAUSE I HAD THE CHANCE TO MEET YOU ALL-- YURI-SAN, MAYUKO-SAN, SNIPER MASK-SAN--AND TO TRAVEL ALONGSIDE YOU.
I DECIDED I'D LIKE TO LIVE A LIFE AS COOL AS EVERYONE ELSE'S!
EVEN NOW, YURI-SAN, I'M SURE OF ONE FACT.
NAMELY, THAT WE'RE FAR COOLER THAN THAT SELF-SERVING ADMINIS-TRATOR!
WE'LL CERTAINLY WIN THE DAY!
......
YOU'RE THE ONE TO PULL THIS OFF, YURI-SAN!
WIPE
YEAH!
CLENCH

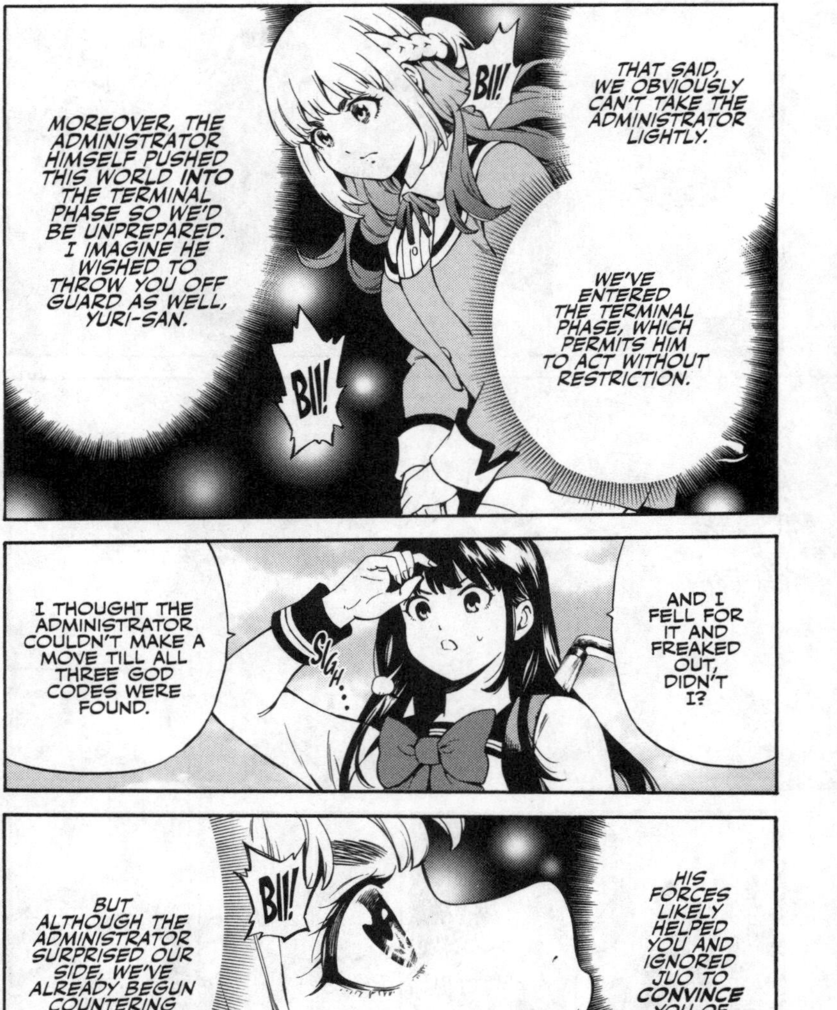
BII!
THAT SAID, WE OBVIOUSLY CAN'T TAKE THE ADMINISTRATOR LIGHTLY.
WE'VE ENTERED THE TERMINAL PHASE, WHICH PERMITS HIM TO ACT WITHOUT RESTRICTION.
MOREOVER, THE ADMINISTRATOR HIMSELF PUSHED THIS WORLD INTO THE TERMINAL PHASE SO WE'D BE UNPREPARED. I IMAGINE HE WISHED TO THROW YOU OFF GUARD AS WELL, YURI-SAN.
BII!
AND I FELL FOR IT AND FREAKED OUT, DIDN'T I?
SIGH...
I THOUGHT THE ADMINISTRATOR COULDN'T MAKE A MOVE TILL ALL THREE GOD CODES WERE FOUND.
HIS FORCES LIKELY HELPED YOU AND IGNORED JUO TO CONVINCE YOU OF THAT.
BII!
BUT ALTHOUGH THE ADMINISTRATOR SURPRISED OUR SIDE, WE'VE ALREADY BEGUN COUNTERING HIS ACTIONS.

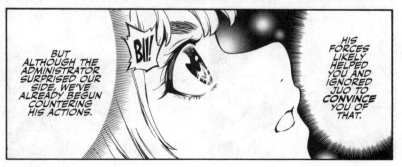

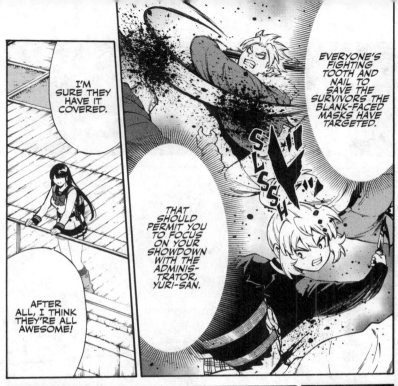

EVERYONE'S FIGHTING TOOTH AND NAIL TO SAVE THE SURVIVORS THE BLANK-FACED MASKS HAVE TARGETED.
SLSSH
THAT SHOULD PERMIT YOU TO FOCUS ON YOUR SHOWDOWN WITH THE ADMINIS-TRATOR, YURI-SAN.
I'M SURE THEY HAVE IT COVERED.
AFTER ALL, I THINK THEY'RE ALL AWESOME!
OF COURSE, THE MOST AWESOME ONE...
IS MY BROTHER!
BOUNCE

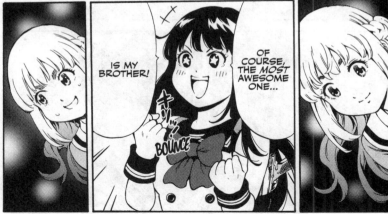

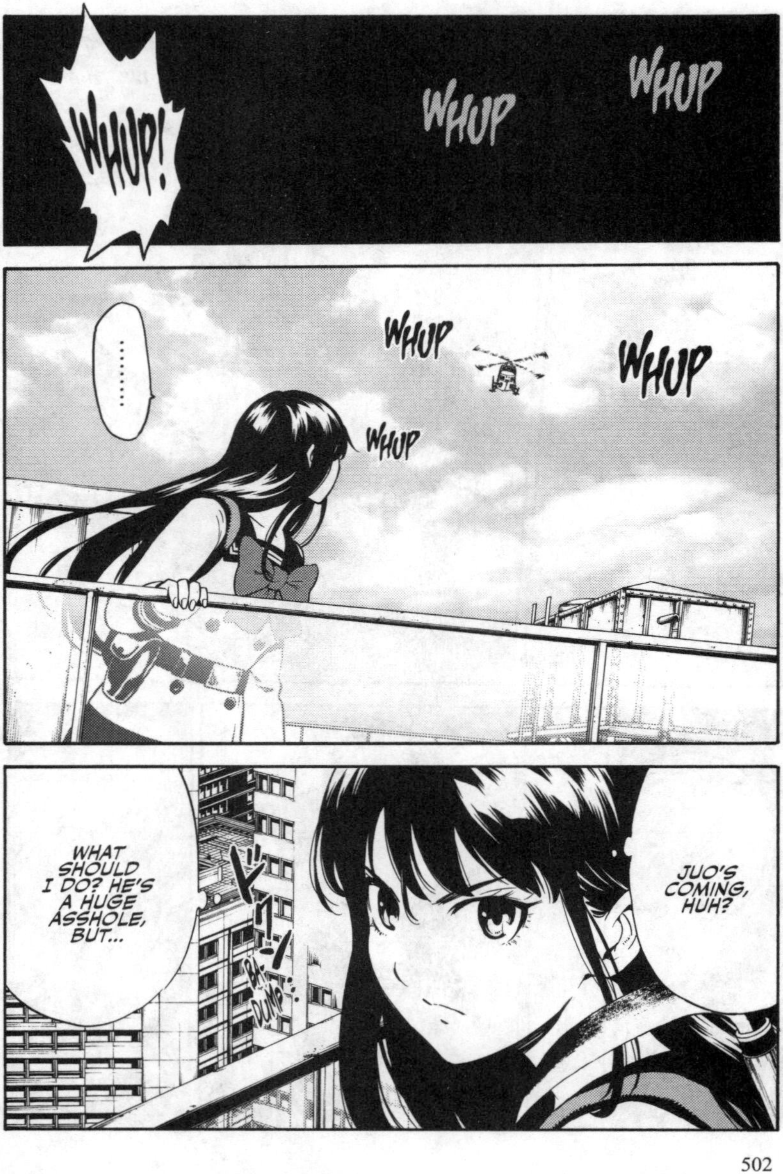
WHUP
WHUP
WHUP!
WHUP
WHUP
WHUP
......
JUO'S COMING, HUH?
WHAT SHOULD I DO? HE'S A HUGE ASSHOLE, BUT...
BA-DUMP

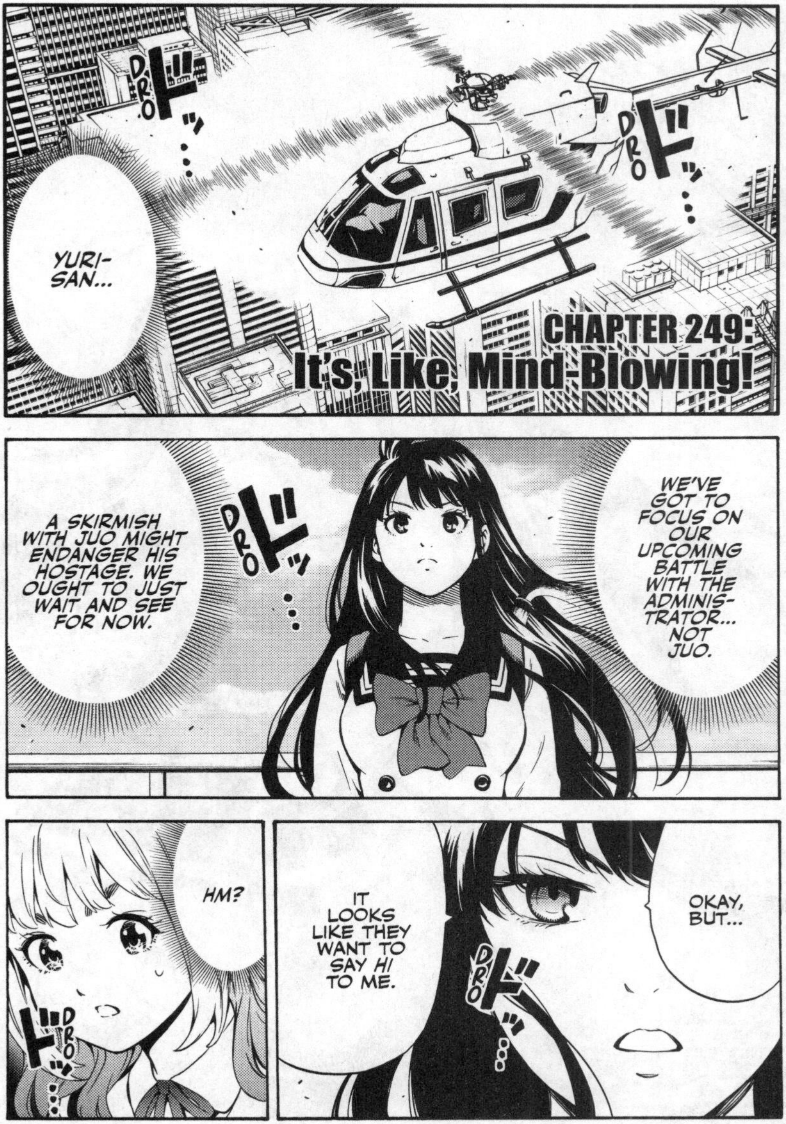
DRO
DRO
YURI-SAN...
CHAPTER 249:
It's, Like, Mind-Blowing!
WE'VE GOT TO FOCUS ON OUR UPCOMING BATTLE WITH THE ADMINISTRATOR... NOT JUO.
DRO
A SKIRMISH WITH JUO MIGHT ENDANGER HIS HOSTAGE. WE OUGHT TO JUST WAIT AND SEE FOR NOW.
OKAY, BUT...
IT LOOKS LIKE THEY WANT TO SAY HI TO ME.
DRO
HM?
DRO

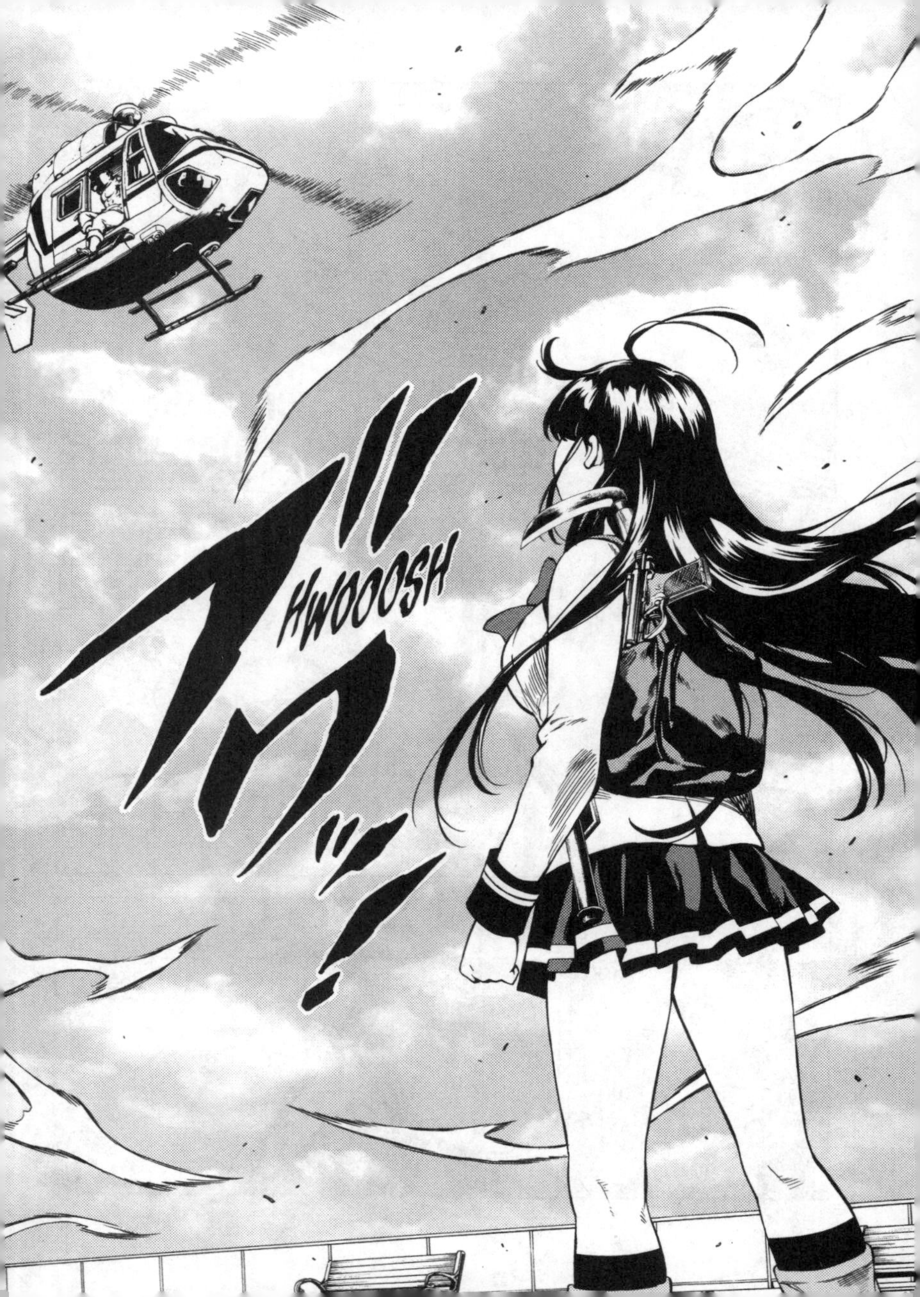
KWOOOSH

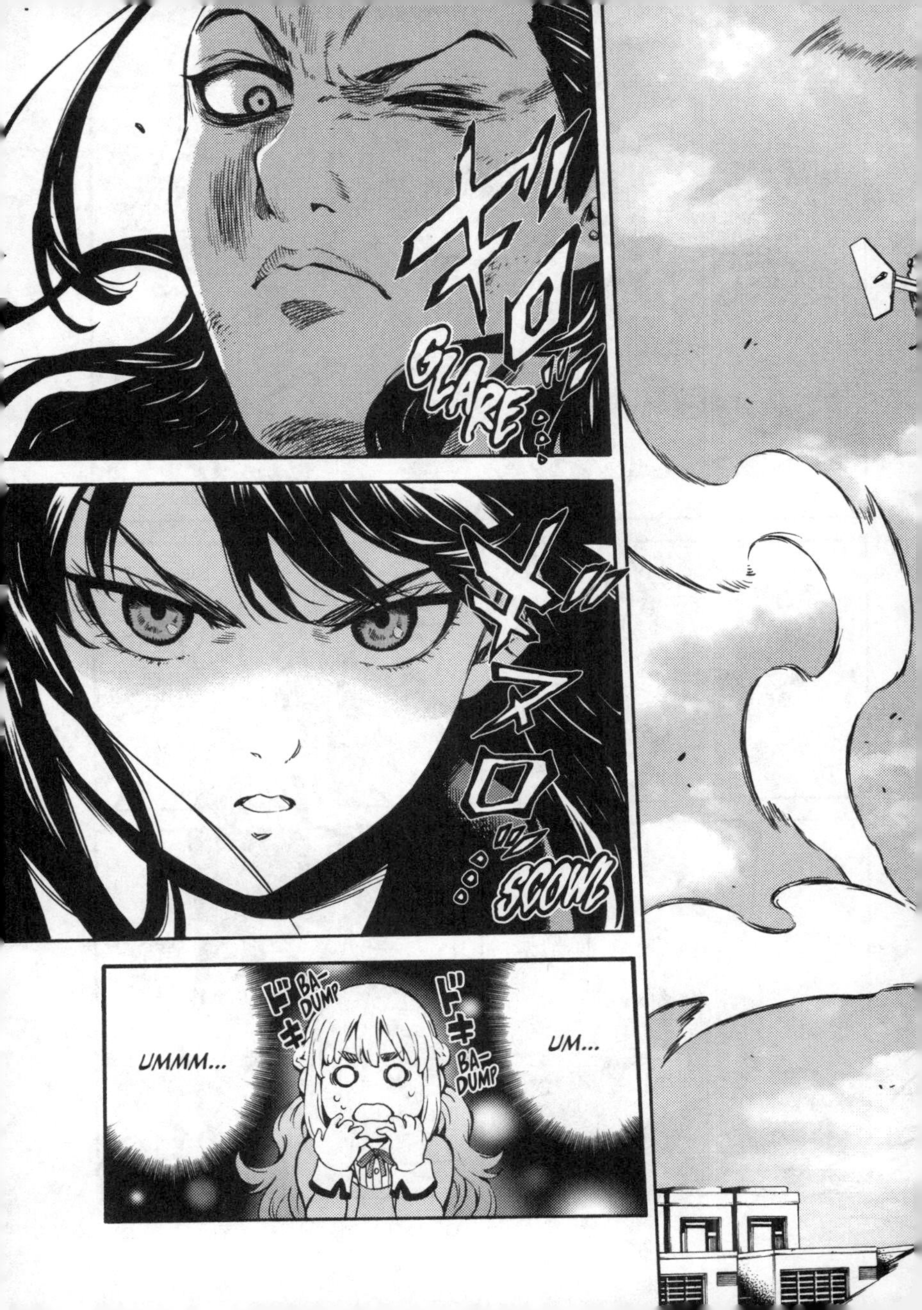

ギロ
GLARE
ギヌロ
SCOWL
UM...
ドキ
BA-DUMP
ドキ
BA-DUMP
UMMM...

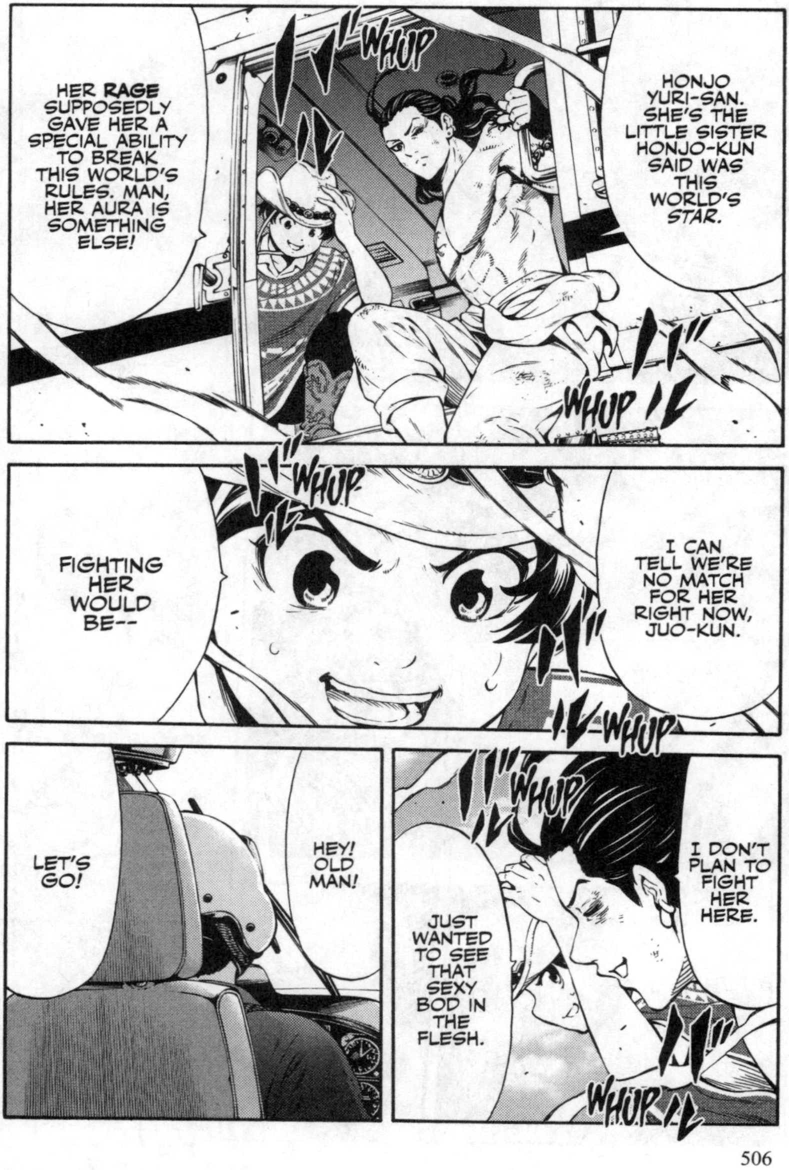
WHUP
HONJO YURI-SAN. SHE'S THE LITTLE SISTER HONJO-KUN SAID WAS THIS WORLD'S STAR.
HER RAGE SUPPOSEDLY GAVE HER A SPECIAL ABILITY TO BREAK THIS WORLD'S RULES. MAN, HER AURA IS SOMETHING ELSE!
WHUP
WHUP
I CAN TELL WE'RE NO MATCH FOR HER RIGHT NOW, JUO-KUN.
FIGHTING HER WOULD BE--
WHUP
WHUP
I DON'T PLAN TO FIGHT HER HERE.
JUST WANTED TO SEE THAT SEXY BOD IN THE FLESH.
WHUP
HEY! OLD MAN!
LET'S GO!

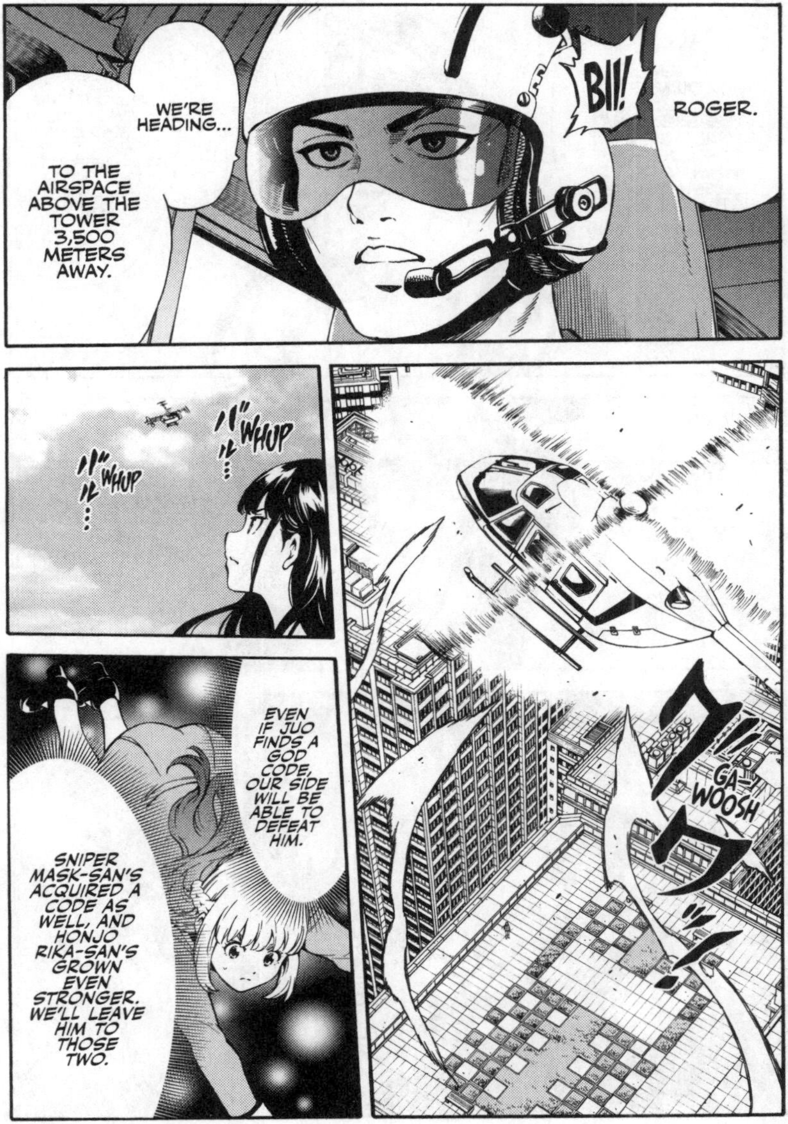
BII!
ROGER.
WE'RE HEADING...
TO THE AIRSPACE ABOVE THE TOWER 3,500 METERS AWAY.
GA-WOOSH
WHUP
WHUP
EVEN IF JUO FINDS A GOD CODE, OUR SIDE WILL BE ABLE TO DEFEAT HIM.
SNIPER MASK-SAN'S ACQUIRED A CODE AS WELL, AND HONJO RIKA-SAN'S GROWN EVEN STRONGER. WE'LL LEAVE HIM TO THOSE TWO.

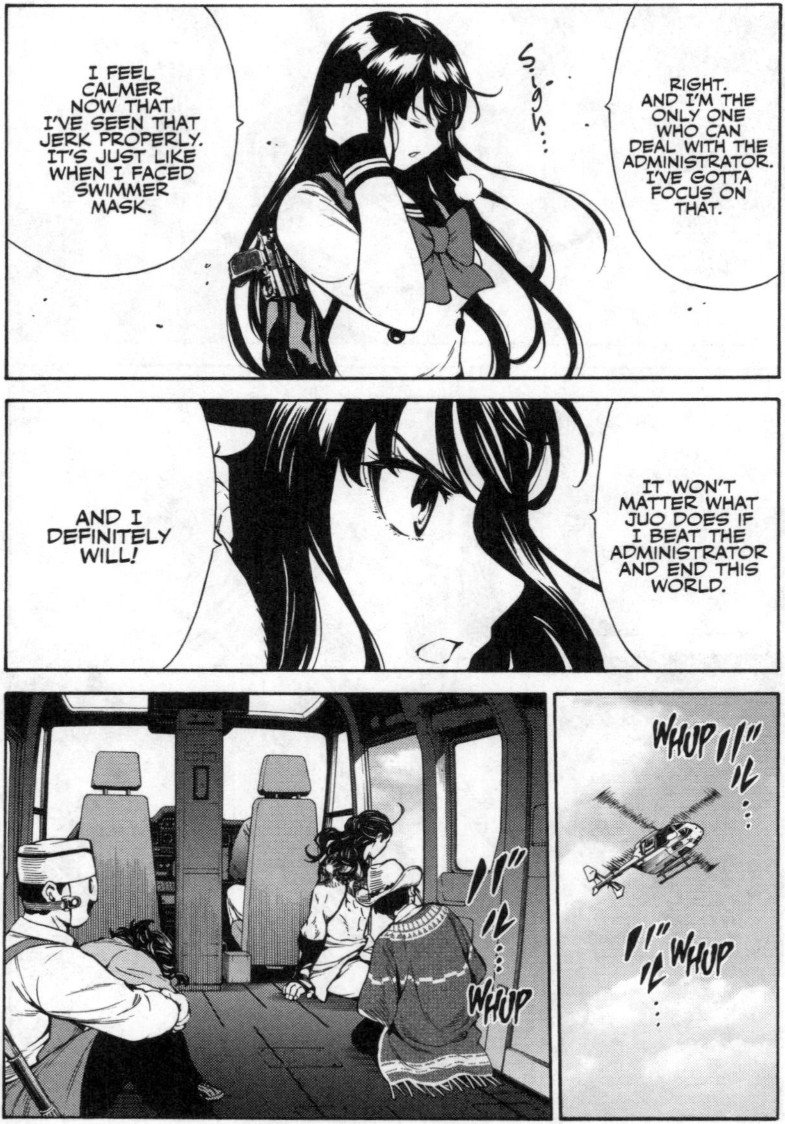
RIGHT. AND I'M THE ONLY ONE WHO CAN DEAL WITH THE ADMINISTRATOR. I'VE GOTTA FOCUS ON THAT.
Sigh...
I FEEL CALMER NOW THAT I'VE SEEN THAT JERK PROPERLY. IT'S JUST LIKE WHEN I FACED SWIMMER MASK.
IT WON'T MATTER WHAT JUO DOES IF I BEAT THE ADMINISTRATOR AND END THIS WORLD.
AND I DEFINITELY WILL!
WHUP
WHUP
WHUP

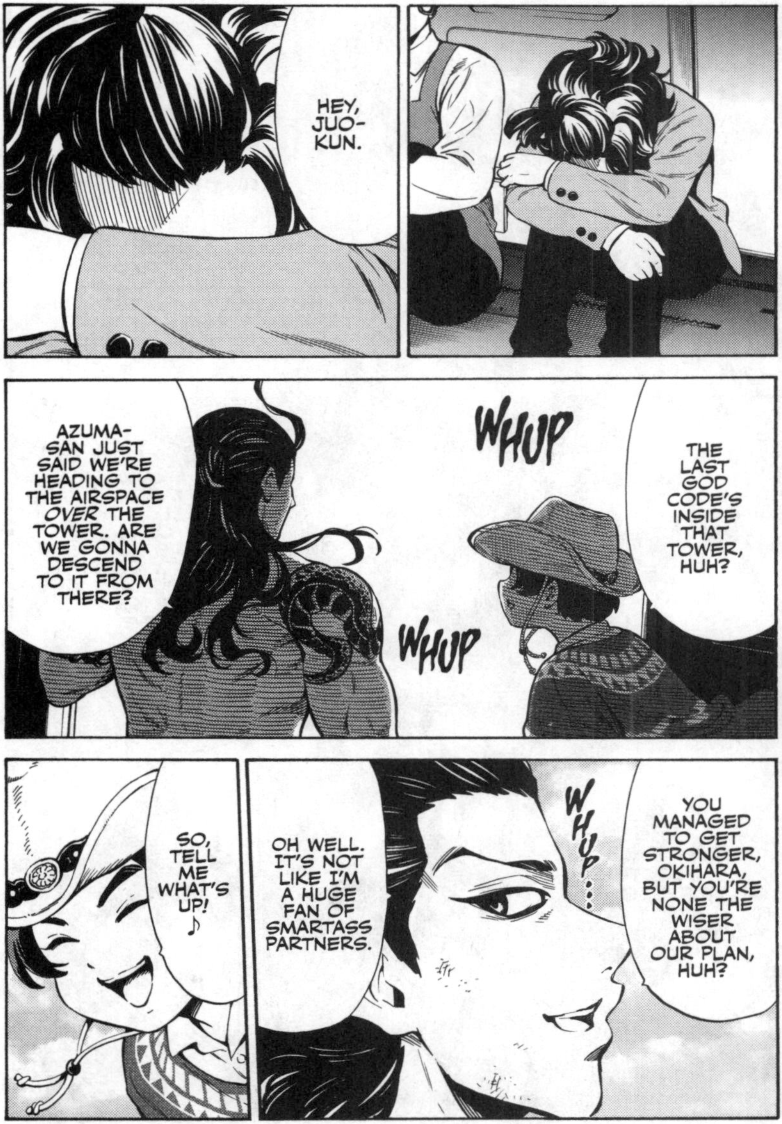
HEY, JUO-KUN.
THE LAST GOD CODE'S INSIDE THAT TOWER, HUH?
WHUP
AZUMA-SAN JUST SAID WE'RE HEADING TO THE AIRSPACE *OVER* THE TOWER. ARE WE GONNA DESCEND TO IT FROM THERE?
WHUP
YOU MANAGED TO GET STRONGER, OKIHARA, BUT YOU'RE NONE THE WISER ABOUT OUR PLAN, HUH?
WHUP...
OH WELL. IT'S NOT LIKE I'M A HUGE FAN OF SMARTASS PARTNERS.
SO, TELL ME WHAT'S UP! ♪

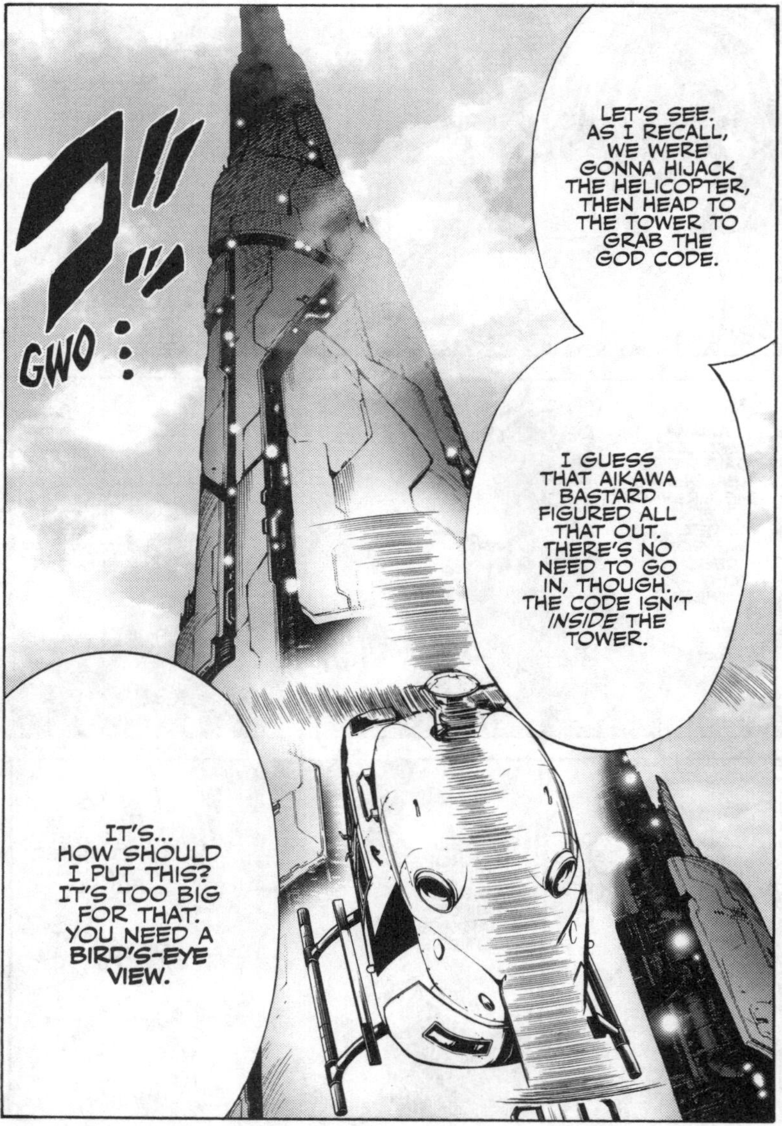
LET'S SEE. AS I RECALL, WE WERE GONNA HIJACK THE HELICOPTER, THEN HEAD TO THE TOWER TO GRAB THE GOD CODE.
GWO
I GUESS THAT AIKAWA BASTARD FIGURED ALL THAT OUT. THERE'S NO NEED TO GO IN, THOUGH. THE CODE ISN'T *INSIDE* THE TOWER.
IT'S... HOW SHOULD I PUT THIS? IT'S TOO BIG FOR THAT. YOU NEED A BIRD'S-EYE VIEW.

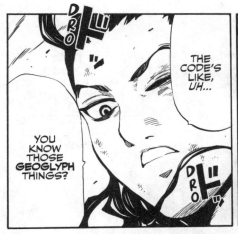

DRO
WE'RE SIXTY SECONDS FROM THE TOWER.
DRO
DRO
THE CODE'S LIKE, UH...
YOU KNOW THOSE GEOGLYPH THINGS?
DRO
GEOGLYPH THINGS?
UH... THE NAZCA ONES?
DRO
......
PEEK
WHOA! I SEE NOW.
SO, THAT'S IT, HUH? ♪
SMIRK

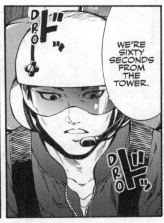

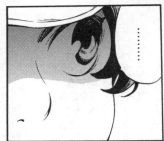

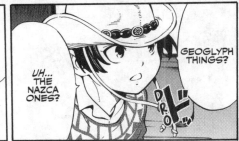

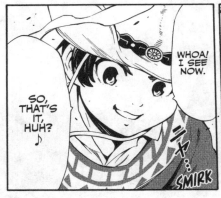

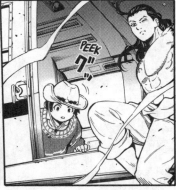

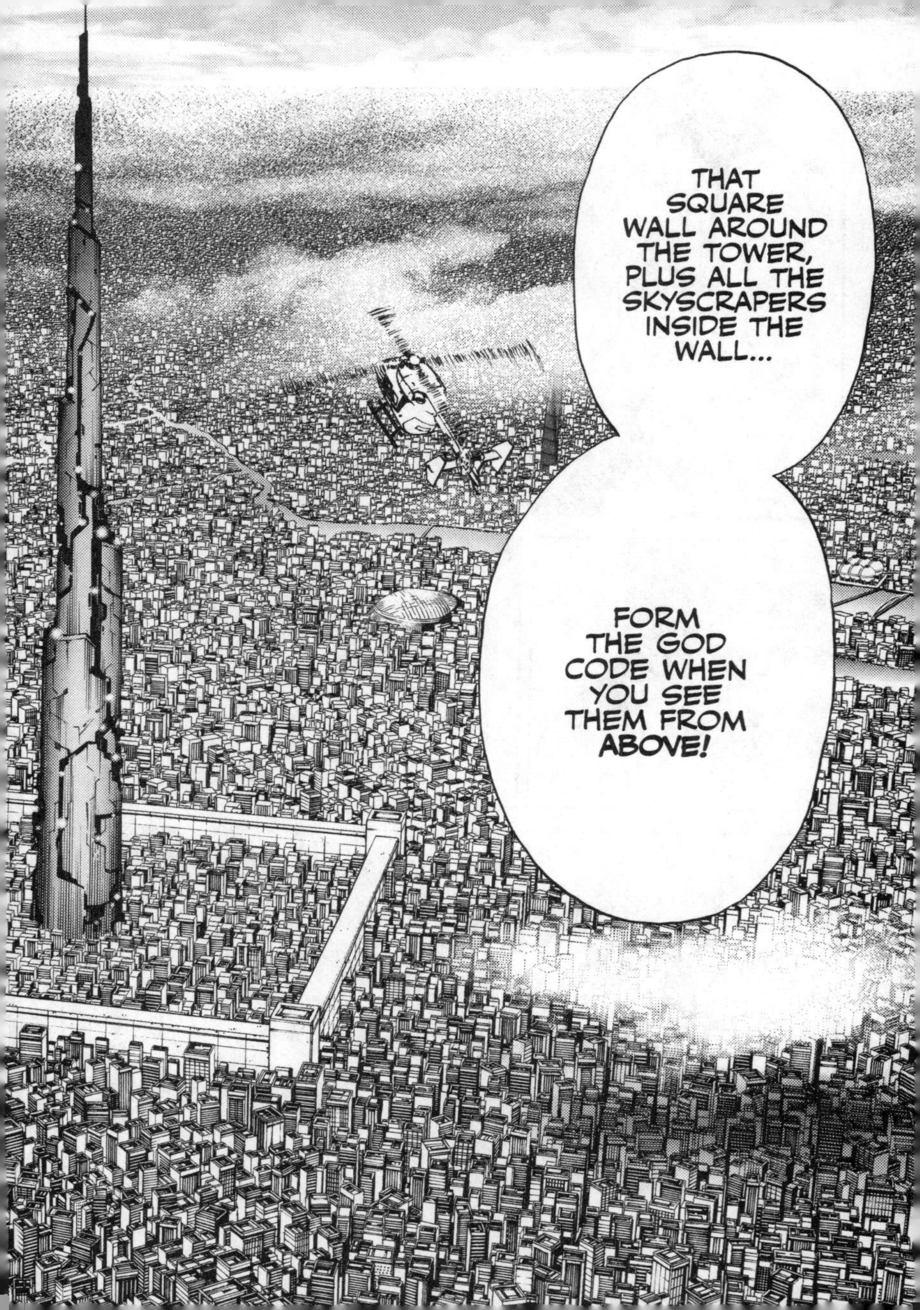
THAT SQUARE WALL AROUND THE TOWER, PLUS ALL THE SKYSCRAPERS INSIDE THE WALL...
FORM THE GOD CODE WHEN YOU SEE THEM FROM ABOVE!

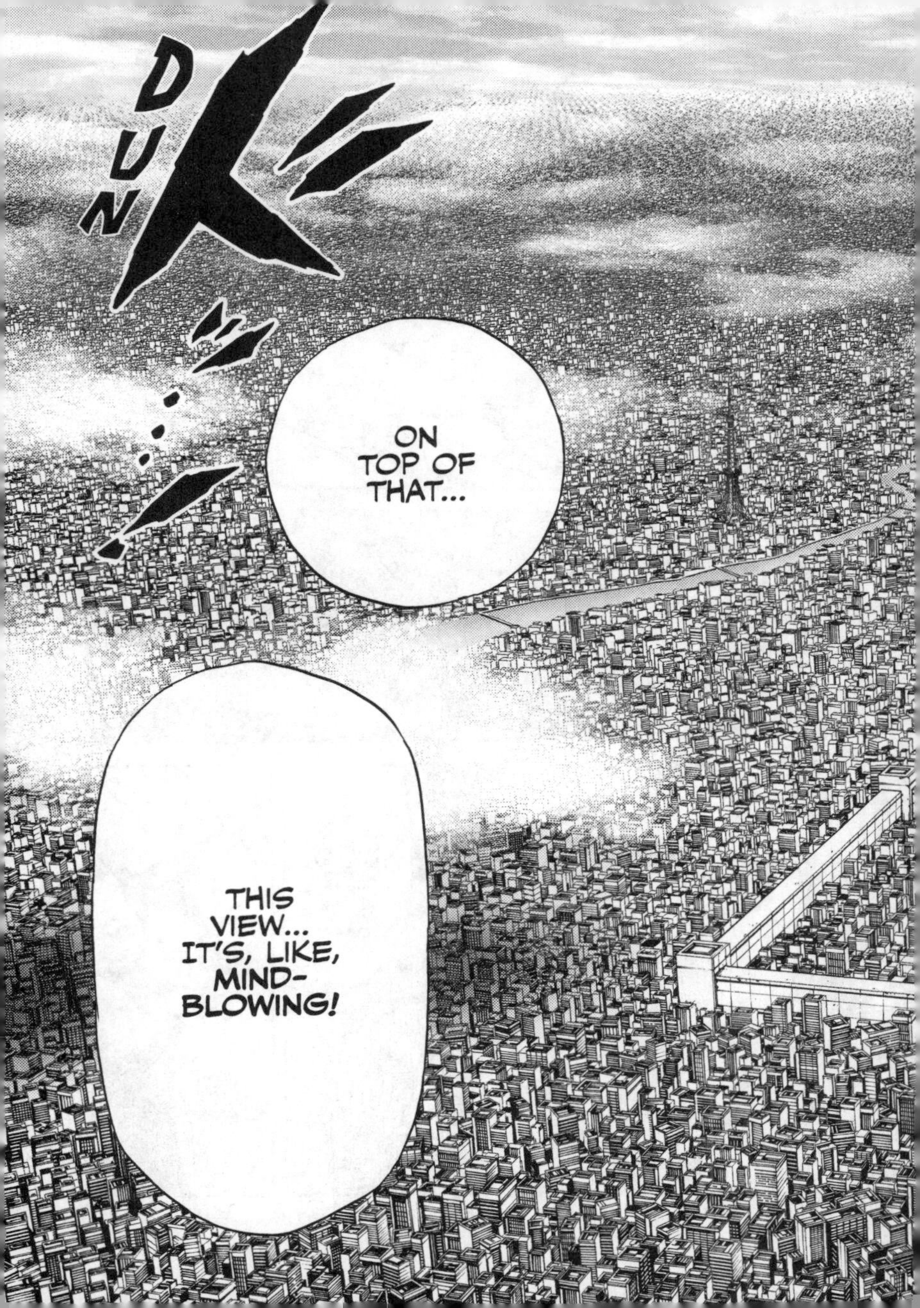
DUN
ON TOP OF THAT...
THIS VIEW... IT'S, LIKE, MIND-BLOWING!

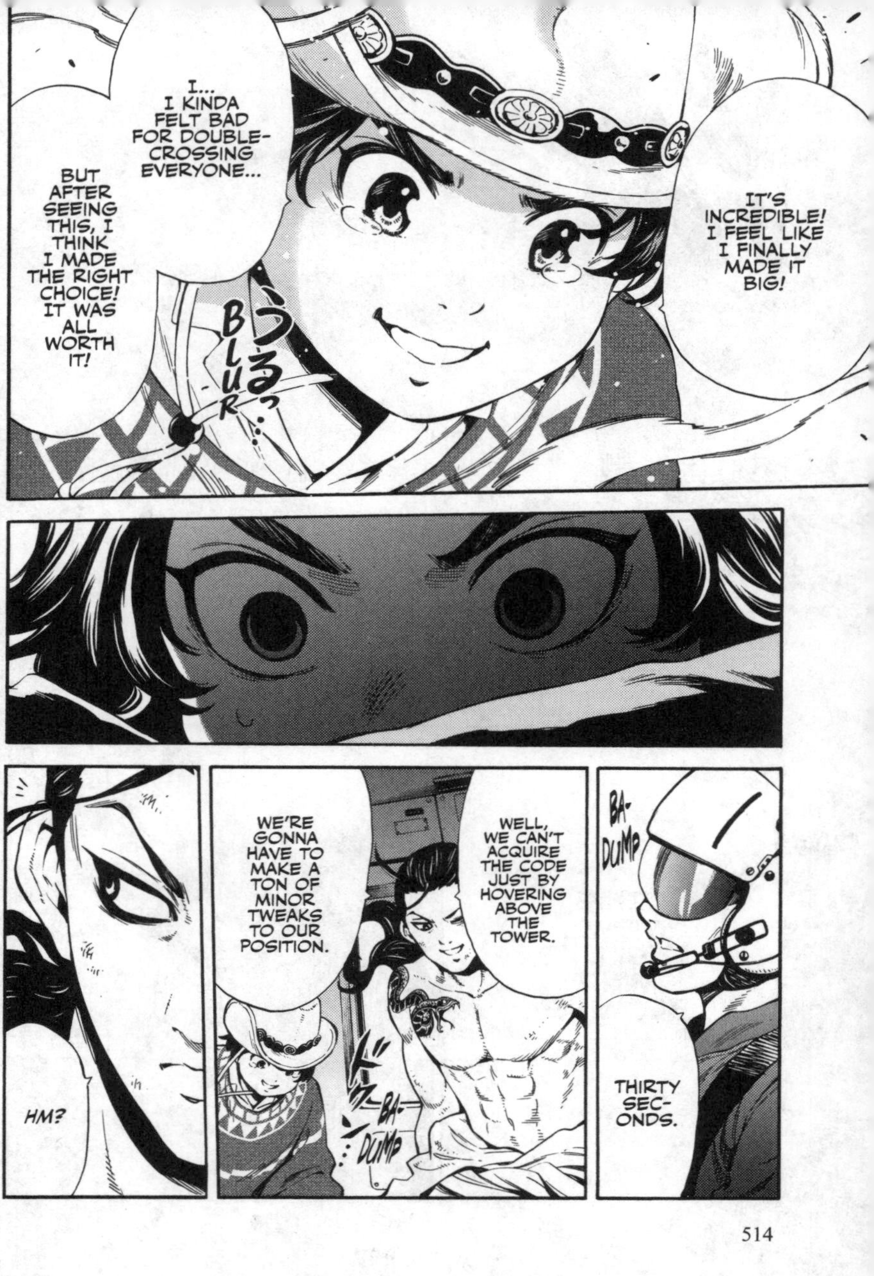
IT'S INCREDIBLE! I FEEL LIKE I FINALLY MADE IT BIG!
I... I KINDA FELT BAD FOR DOUBLE-CROSSING EVERYONE...
BUT AFTER SEEING THIS, I THINK I MADE THE RIGHT CHOICE! IT WAS ALL WORTH IT!
うるっ
BLUR
BA-DUMP
THIRTY SEC-ONDS.
WELL, WE CAN'T ACQUIRE THE CODE JUST BY HOVERING ABOVE THE TOWER.
WE'RE GONNA HAVE TO MAKE A TON OF MINOR TWEAKS TO OUR POSITION.
BA-DUMP
HM?

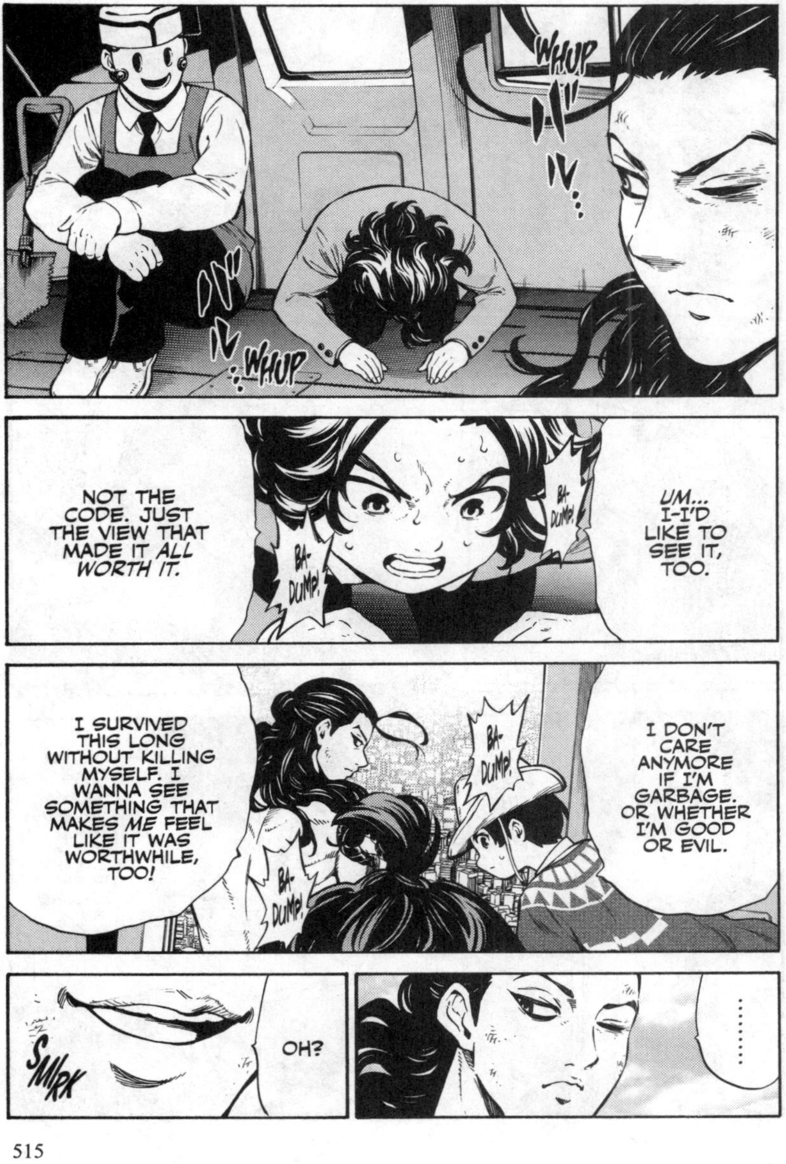
WHUP
WHUP
UM... I-I'D LIKE TO SEE IT, TOO.
BA-DUMP!
BA-DUMP!
NOT THE CODE. JUST THE VIEW THAT MADE IT *ALL WORTH IT.*
I DON'T CARE ANYMORE IF I'M GARBAGE. OR WHETHER I'M GOOD OR EVIL.
BA-DUMP!
BA-DUMP!
I SURVIVED THIS LONG WITHOUT KILLING MYSELF. I WANNA SEE SOMETHING THAT MAKES *ME* FEEL LIKE IT WAS WORTHWHILE, TOO!
......
OH?
SMIRK

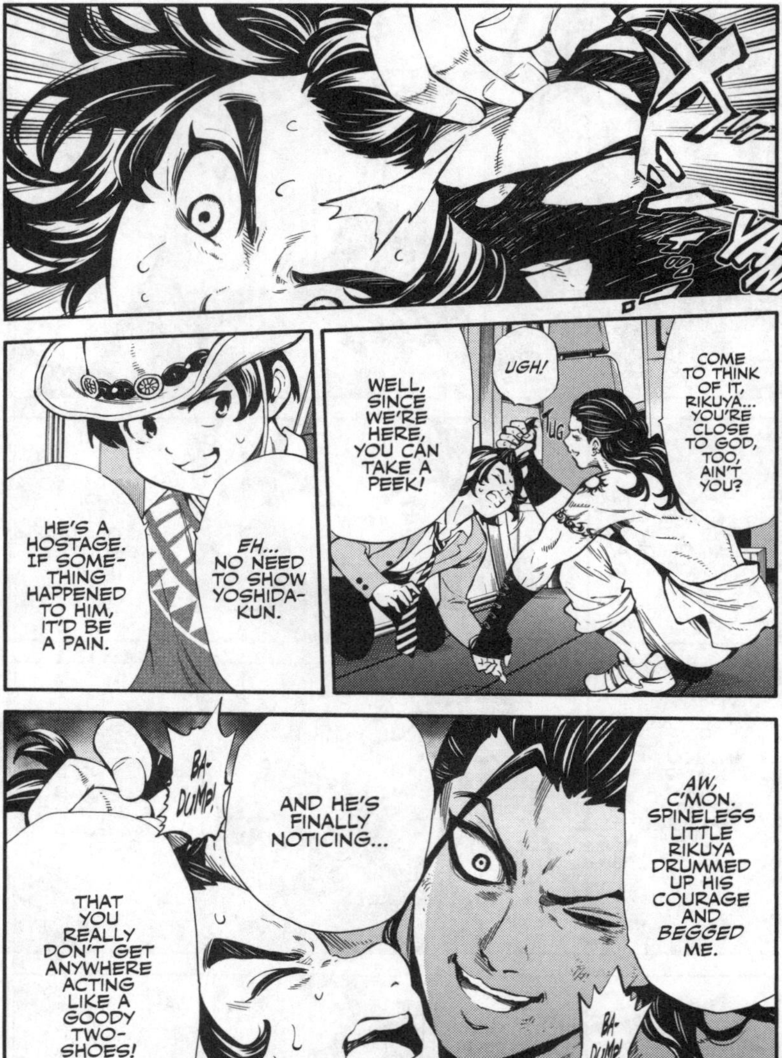
YANK
COME TO THINK OF IT, RIKUYA... YOU'RE CLOSE TO GOD, TOO, AIN'T YOU?
UGH!
TUG
WELL, SINCE WE'RE HERE, YOU CAN TAKE A PEEK!
EH... NO NEED TO SHOW YOSHIDA-KUN.
HE'S A HOSTAGE. IF SOMETHING HAPPENED TO HIM, IT'D BE A PAIN.
AW, C'MON. SPINELESS LITTLE RIKUYA DRUMMED UP HIS COURAGE AND *BEGGED* ME.
BA-DUMP!
AND HE'S FINALLY NOTICING...
BA-DUMP!
THAT YOU REALLY DON'T GET ANYWHERE ACTING LIKE A GOODY TWO-SHOES!

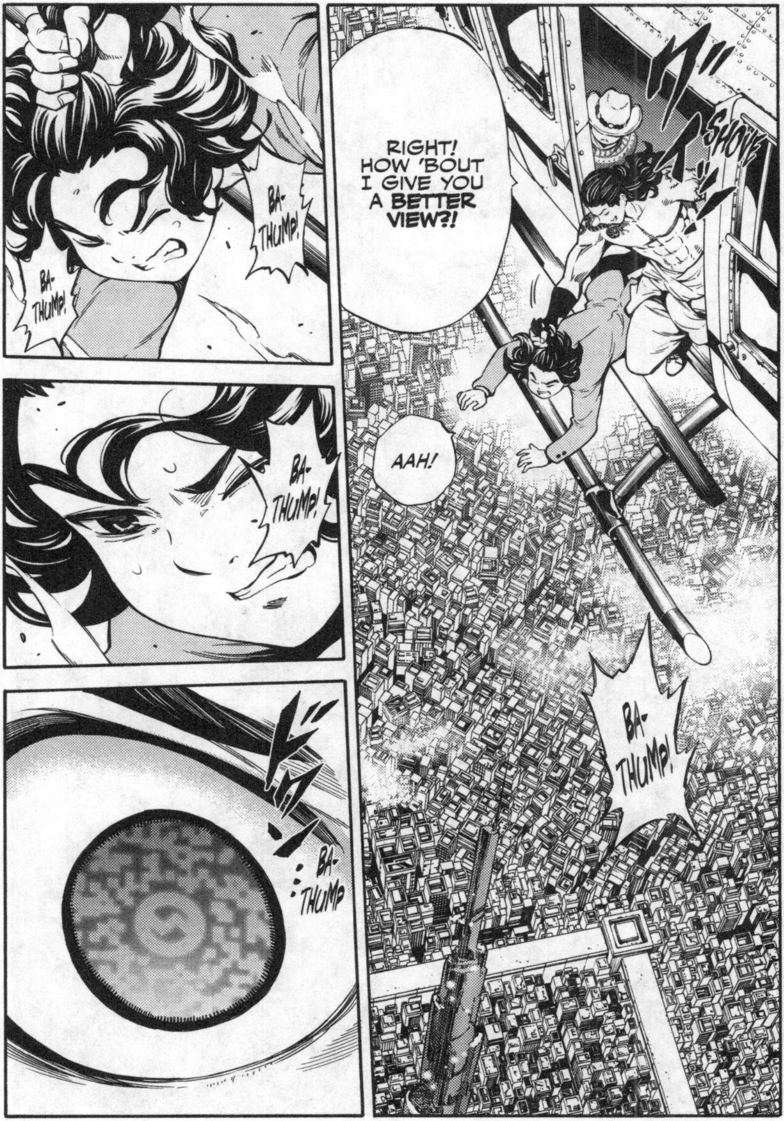
RIGHT! HOW 'BOUT I GIVE YOU A BETTER VIEW?!
SHOVE
AAH!
BA-THUMP!
BA-THUMP!
BA-THUMP!
BA-THUMP!
BA-THUMP

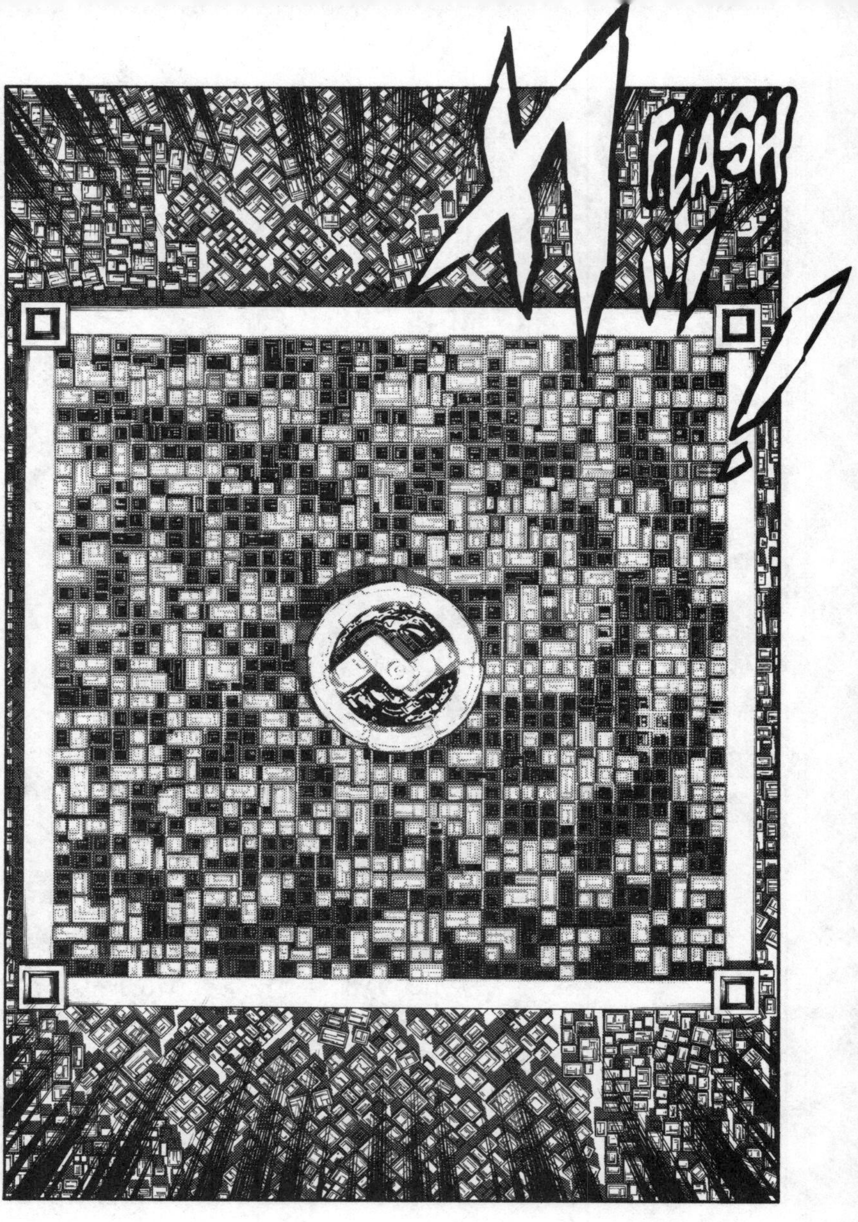
FLASH

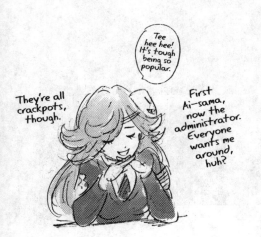

First Ai-sama, now the administrator. Everyone wants me around, huh?
Tee hee hee! It's tough being so popular.
They're all crackpots, though.

HIGH-RISE
INVASION

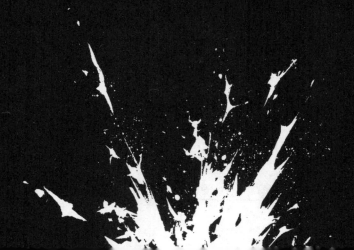

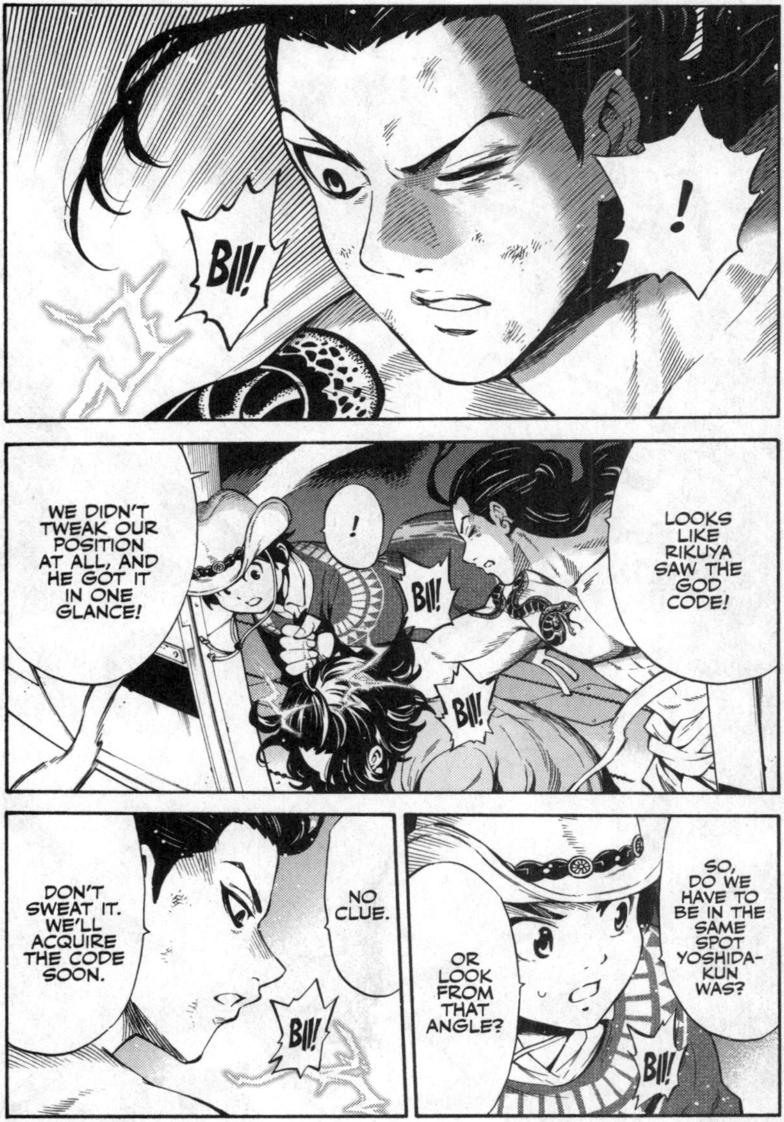
!
BII!
LOOKS LIKE RIKUYA SAW THE GOD CODE!
!
WE DIDN'T TWEAK OUR POSITION AT ALL, AND HE GOT IT IN ONE GLANCE!
BII!
BII!
SO, DO WE HAVE TO BE IN THE SAME SPOT YOSHIDA-KUN WAS?
OR LOOK FROM THAT ANGLE?
BII!
NO CLUE.
DON'T SWEAT IT. WE'LL ACQUIRE THE CODE SOON.
BII!

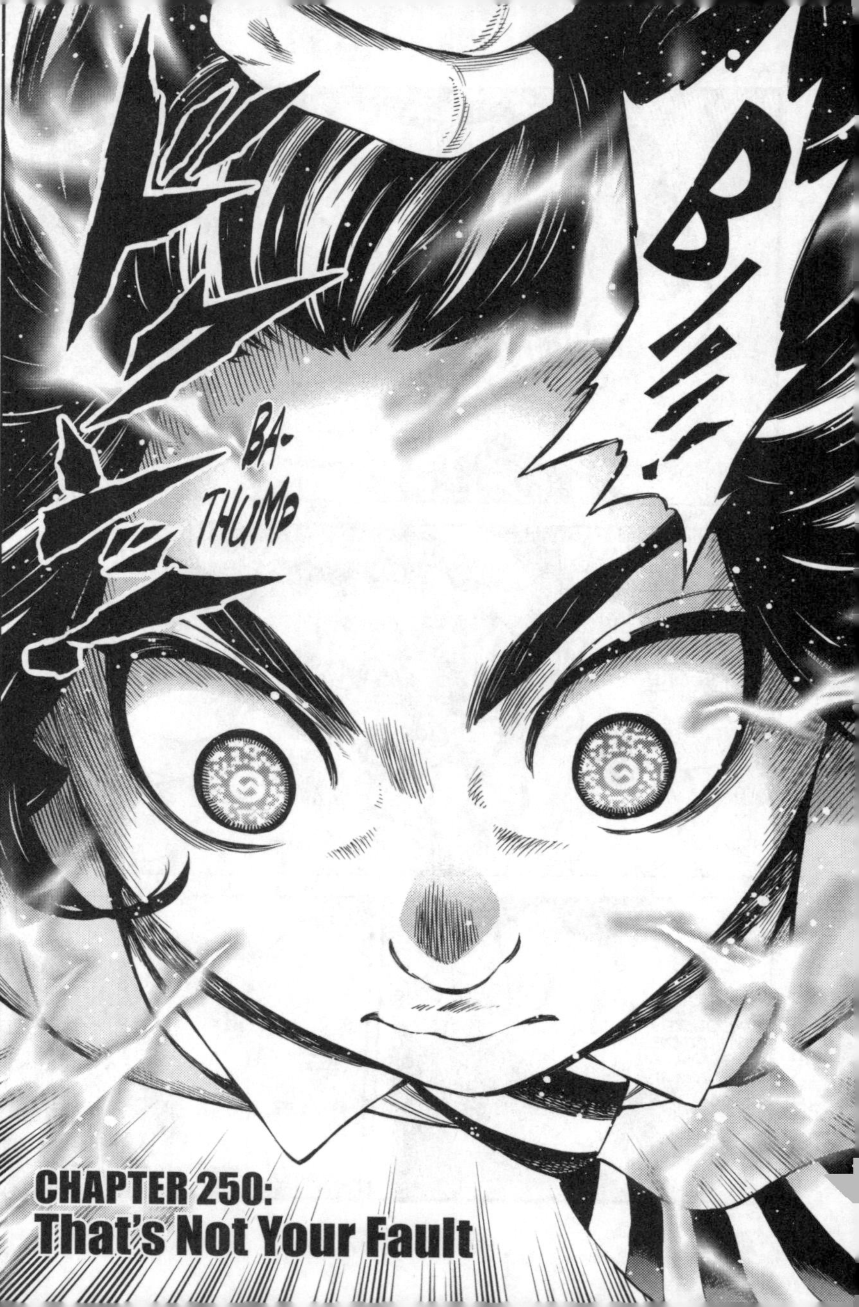
BA-
THUMP
B!!!

CHAPTER 250:
That's Not Your Fault

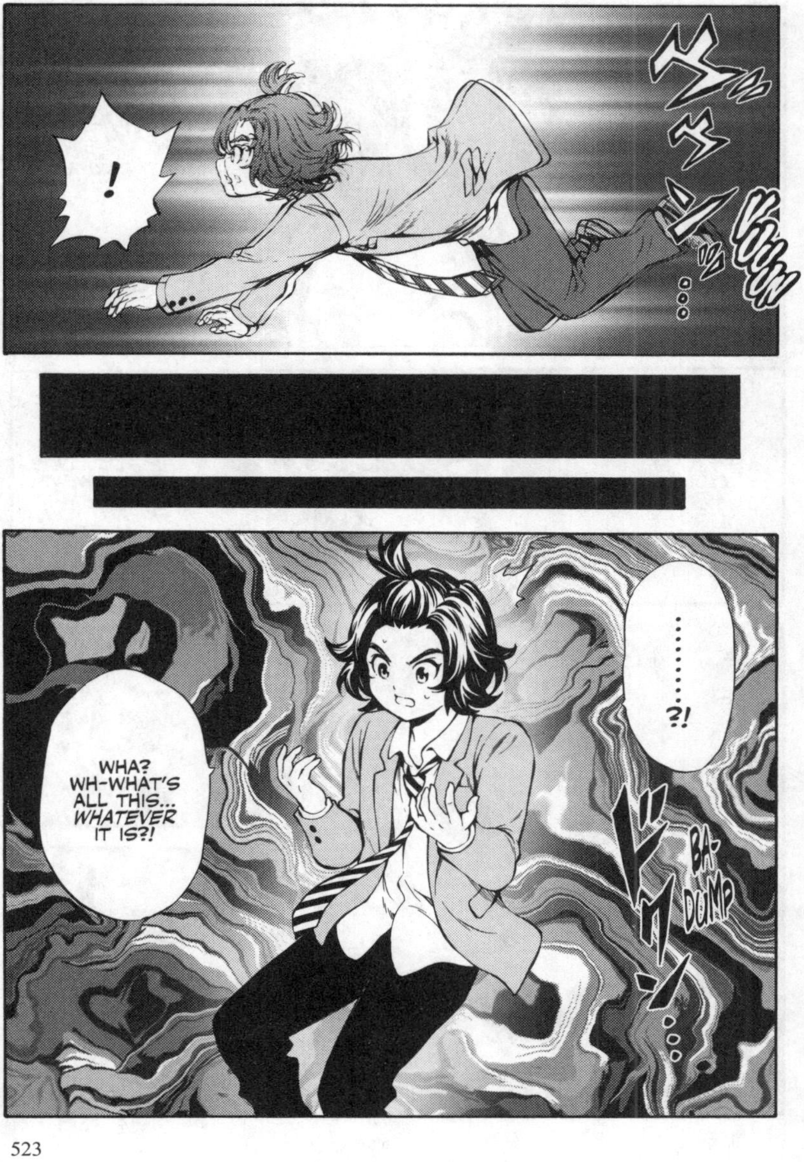

VOOOM
!
BA-DUMP
......?!
WHA? WH-WHAT'S ALL THIS... *WHATEVER* IT IS?!

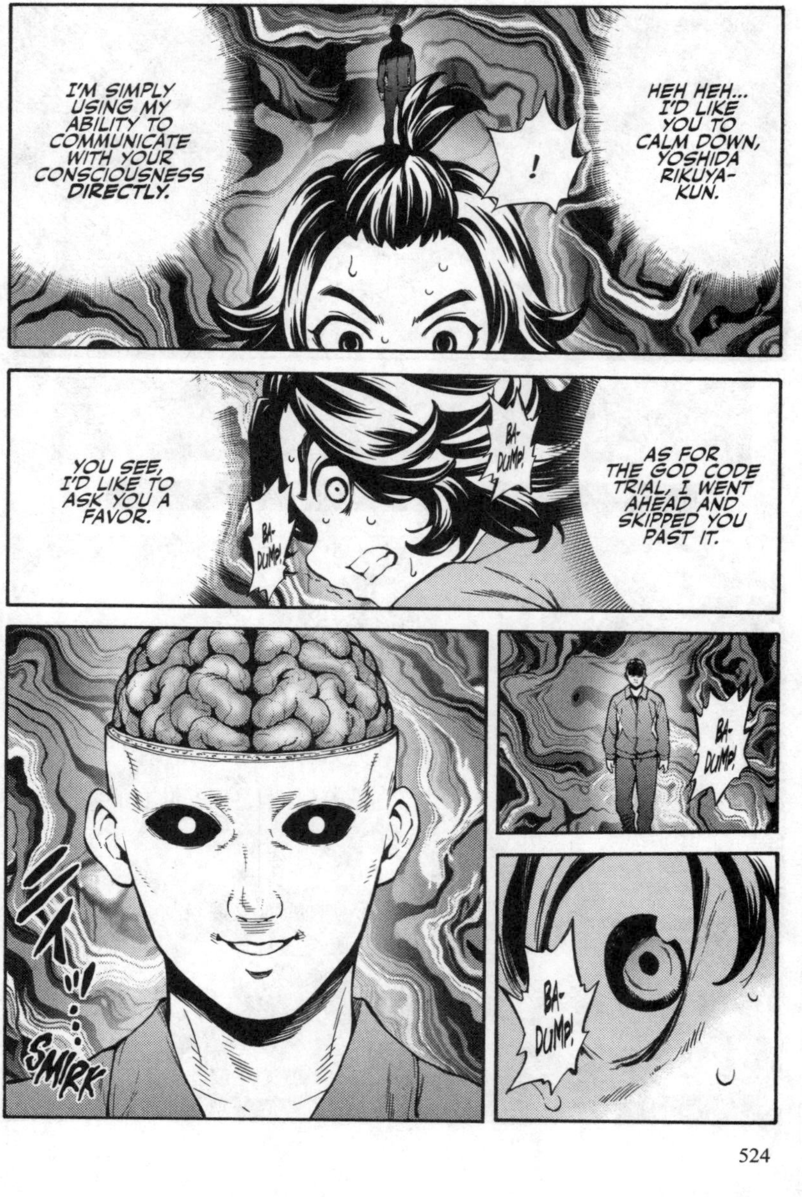
HEH HEH... I'D LIKE YOU TO CALM DOWN, YOSHIDA RIKUYA-KUN.
!
I'M SIMPLY USING MY ABILITY TO COMMUNICATE WITH YOUR CONSCIOUSNESS DIRECTLY.
AS FOR THE GOD CODE TRIAL, I WENT AHEAD AND SKIPPED YOU PAST IT.
BA-DUMP!
YOU SEE, I'D LIKE TO ASK YOU A FAVOR.
BA-DUMP!
BA-DUMP!
BA-DUMP!
SMIRK

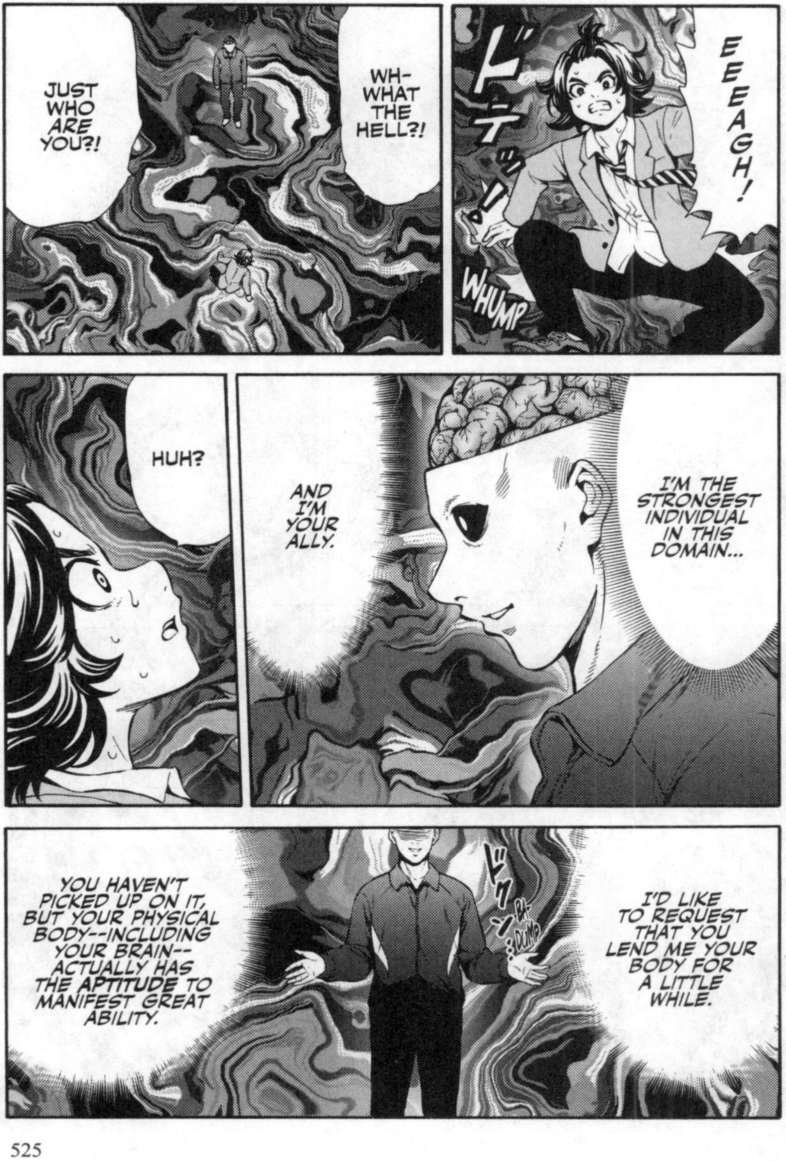
EEEAGH!
WHUMP
WH-WHAT THE HELL?!
JUST WHO ARE YOU?!
I'M THE STRONGEST INDIVIDUAL IN THIS DOMAIN...
AND I'M YOUR ALLY.
HUH?
I'D LIKE TO REQUEST THAT YOU LEND ME YOUR BODY FOR A LITTLE WHILE.
BA-DUMP
YOU HAVEN'T PICKED UP ON IT, BUT YOUR PHYSICAL BODY--INCLUDING YOUR BRAIN--ACTUALLY HAS THE APTITUDE TO MANIFEST GREAT ABILITY.

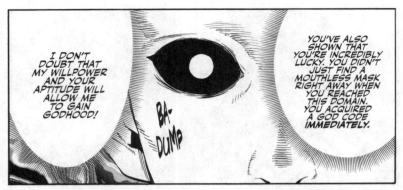

YOU'VE ALSO SHOWN THAT YOU'RE INCREDIBLY LUCKY. YOU DIDN'T JUST FIND A MOUTHLESS MASK RIGHT AWAY WHEN YOU REACHED THIS DOMAIN. YOU ACQUIRED A GOD CODE **IMMEDIATELY.**
I DON'T DOUBT THAT MY WILLPOWER AND YOUR APTITUDE WILL ALLOW ME TO GAIN GODHOOD!
BA-DUMP
GOD-HOOD?
OF COURSE, I'LL DO ALL I CAN FOR YOU.
LET'S SEE...IF YOU LEND ME YOUR BODY, I COULD START OFF BY KILLING JUO.
BA-DUMP!
I THINK HIGHLY OF YOU, YOSHIDA-KUN...
BUT YOU'RE FAR TOO PURE AND KIND TO BECOME THIS DOMAIN'S GOD.

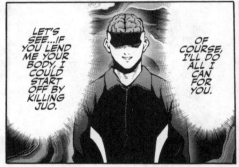

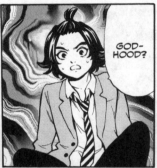

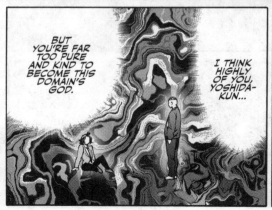

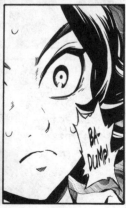

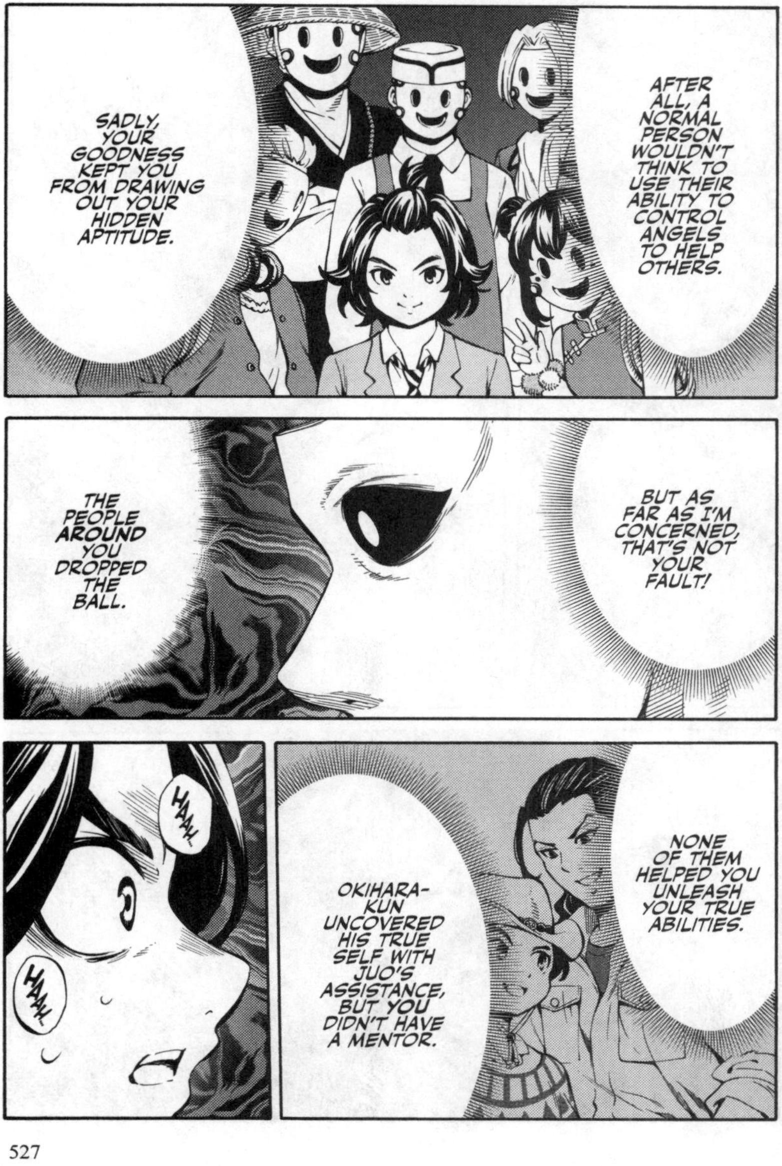
AFTER ALL, A NORMAL PERSON WOULDN'T THINK TO USE THEIR ABILITY TO CONTROL ANGELS TO HELP OTHERS.
SADLY, YOUR GOODNESS KEPT YOU FROM DRAWING OUT YOUR HIDDEN APTITUDE.
BUT AS FAR AS I'M CONCERNED, THAT'S NOT YOUR FAULT!
THE PEOPLE AROUND YOU DROPPED THE BALL.
NONE OF THEM HELPED YOU UNLEASH YOUR TRUE ABILITIES.
OKIHARA-KUN UNCOVERED HIS TRUE SELF WITH JUO'S ASSISTANCE, BUT YOU DIDN'T HAVE A MENTOR.
HAAH
HAAH

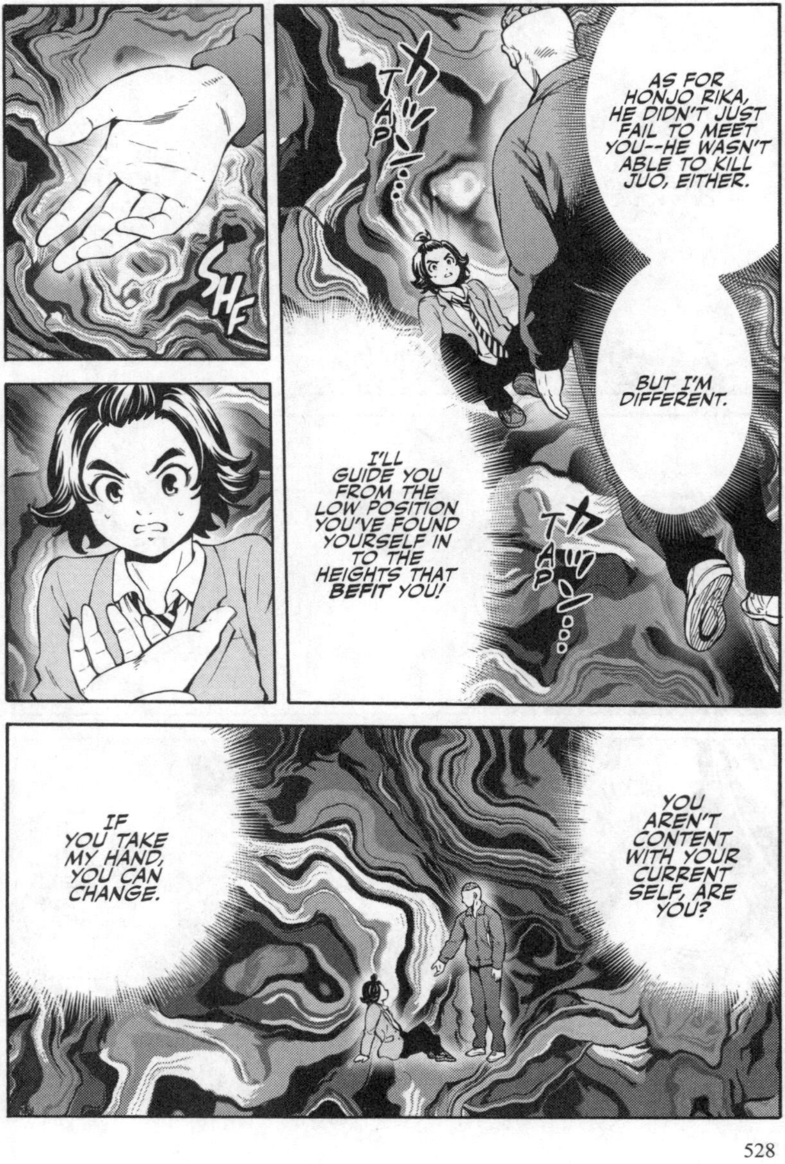
TAP
AS FOR HONJO RIKA, HE DIDN'T JUST FAIL TO MEET YOU--HE WASN'T ABLE TO KILL JUO, EITHER.
BUT I'M DIFFERENT.
I'LL GUIDE YOU FROM THE LOW POSITION YOU'VE FOUND YOURSELF IN TO THE HEIGHTS THAT BEFIT YOU!
TAP
SHF
YOU AREN'T CONTENT WITH YOUR CURRENT SELF, ARE YOU?
IF YOU TAKE MY HAND, YOU CAN CHANGE.

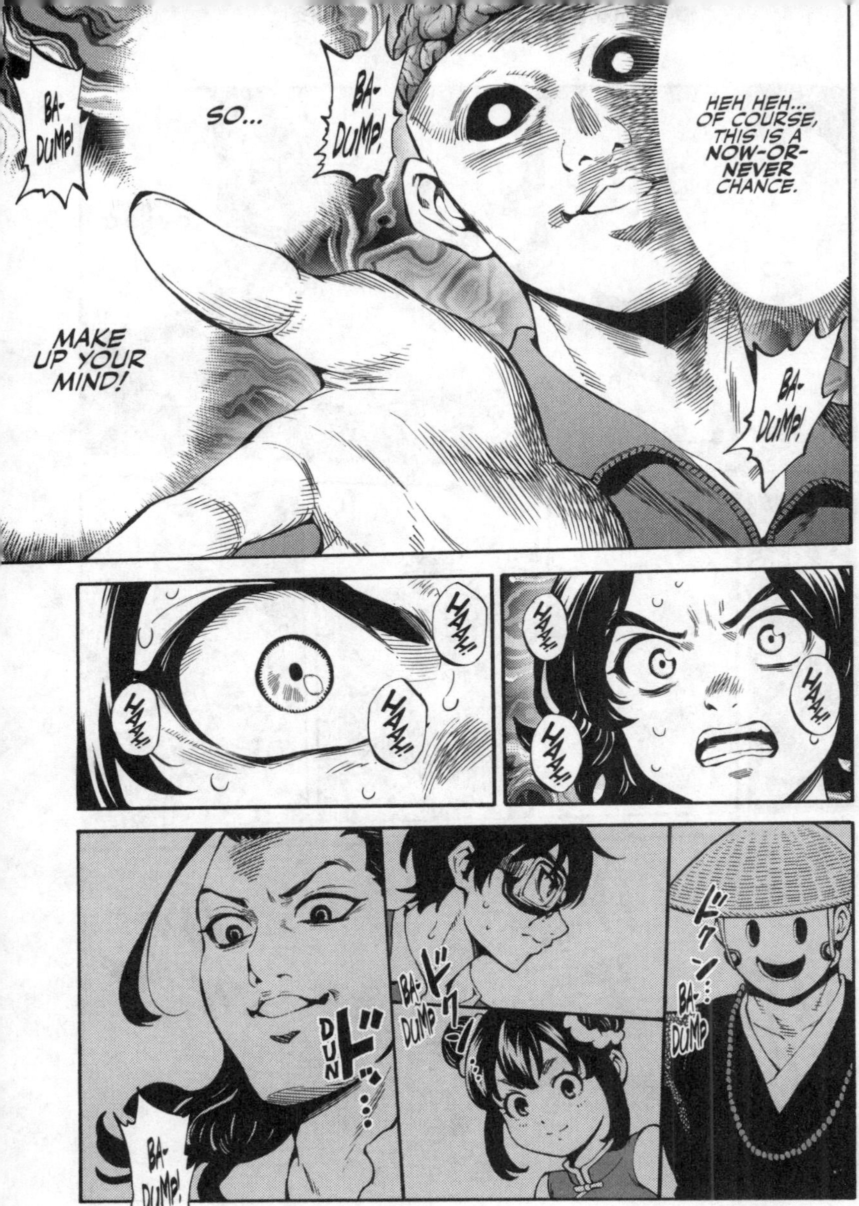
HEH HEH... OF COURSE, THIS IS A NOW-OR-NEVER CHANCE.
BA-DUMP!
SO...
BA-DUMP!
BA-DUMP!
MAKE UP YOUR MIND!
HAAH!
HAAH!
HAAH!
HAAH!
HAAH!
HAAH!
ドクン…
BA-DUMP
ドク
BA-DUMP
ド…
DUN
BA-DUMP!

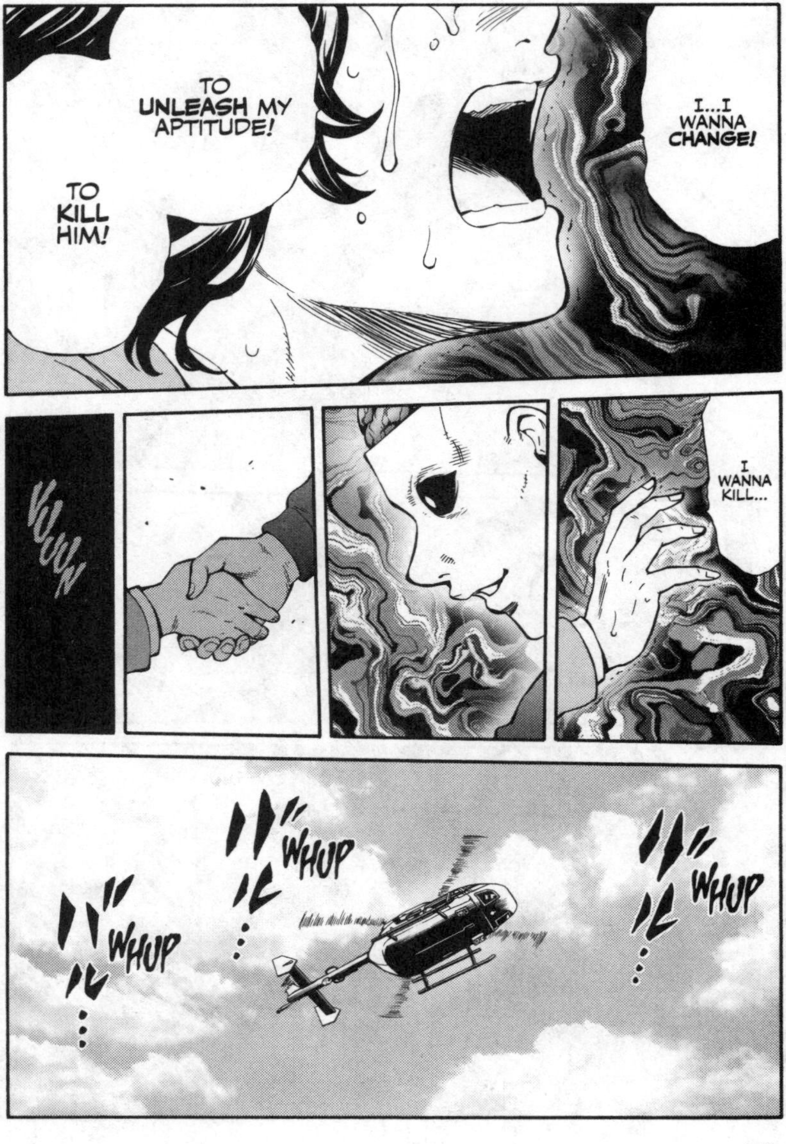
I...I WANNA CHANGE!
TO UNLEASH MY APTITUDE!
TO KILL HIM!
I WANNA KILL...
VUUUN
WHUP
WHUP
WHUP

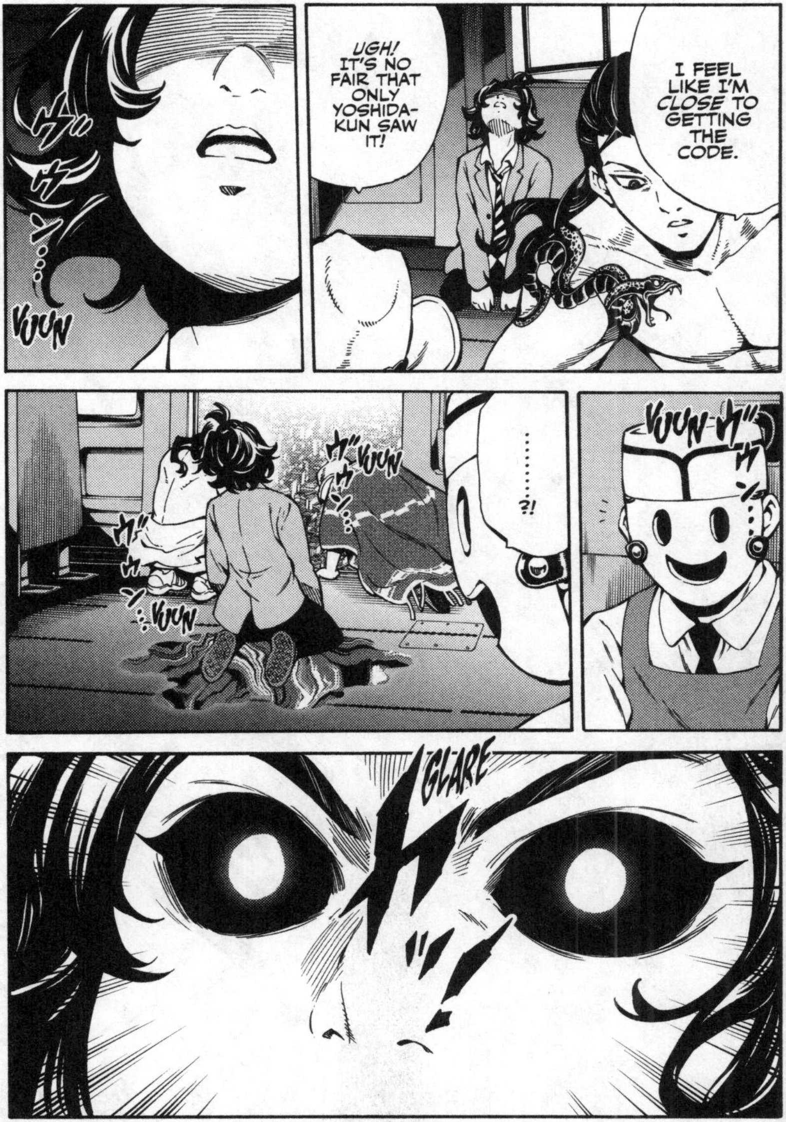

I FEEL LIKE I'M *CLOSE* TO GETTING THE CODE.
UGH! IT'S NO FAIR THAT ONLY YOSHIDA-KUN SAW IT!
VUUN
VUUN
......?!
VUUN
VUUN
GLARE

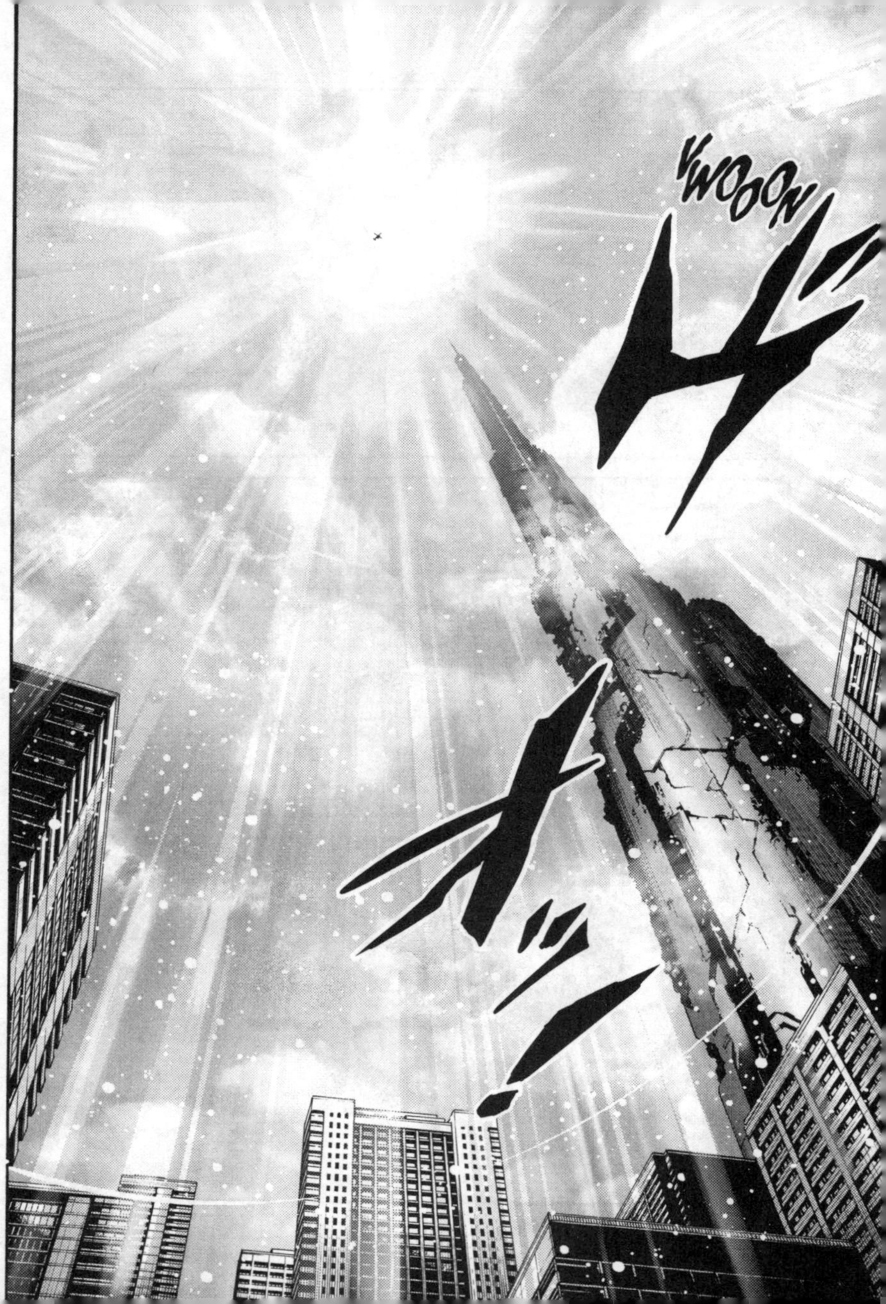
VWOOON

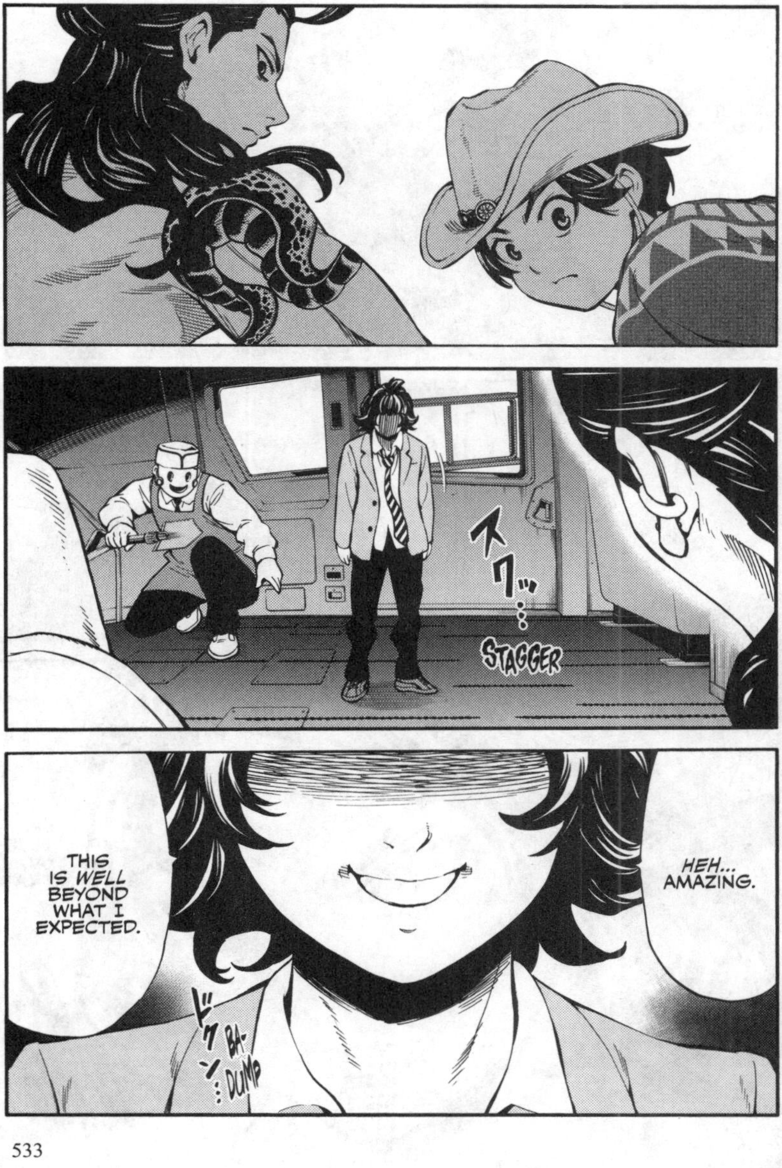
STAGGER
HEH... AMAZING.
THIS IS WELL BEYOND WHAT I EXPECTED.
BA-DUMP

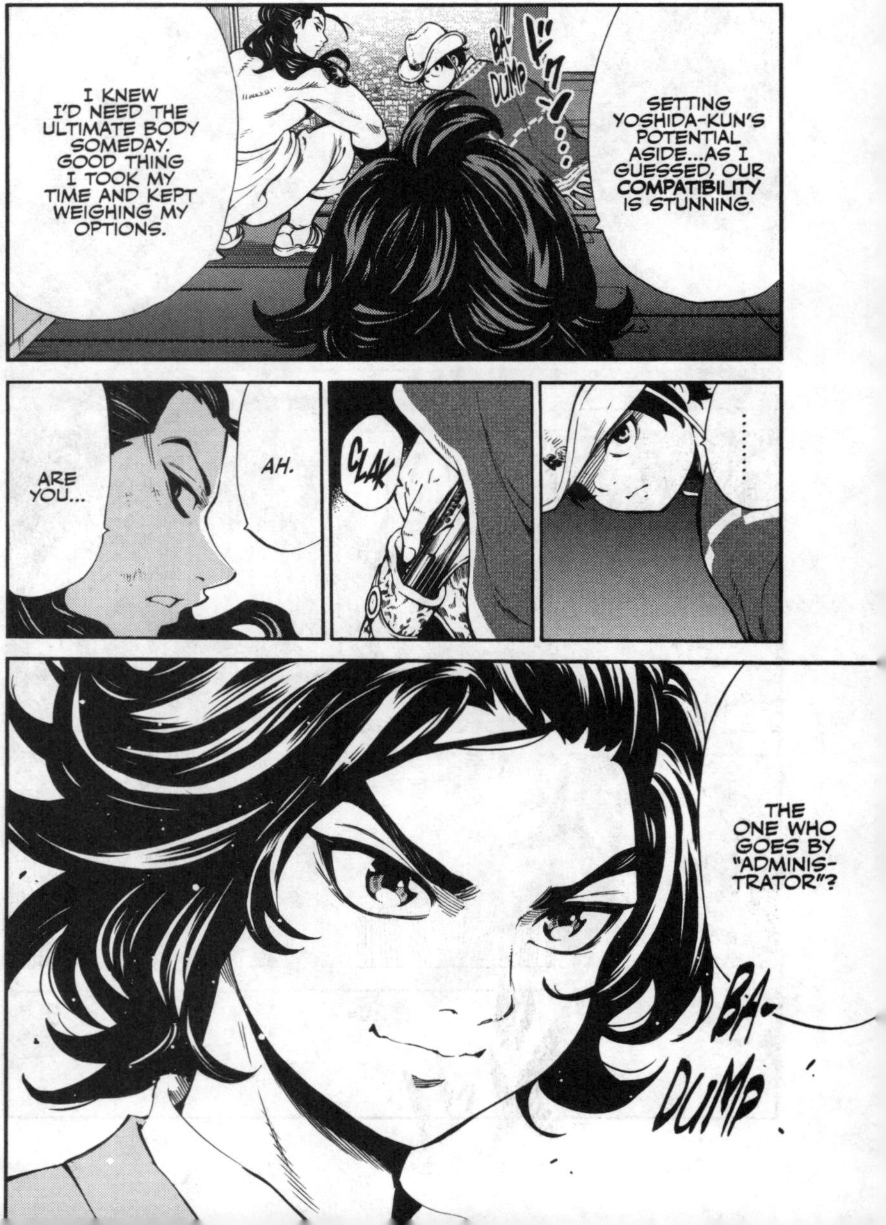
SETTING YOSHIDA-KUN'S POTENTIAL ASIDE...AS I GUESSED, OUR **COMPATIBILITY** IS STUNNING.
BA-DUMP
I KNEW I'D NEED THE ULTIMATE BODY SOMEDAY. GOOD THING I TOOK MY TIME AND KEPT WEIGHING MY OPTIONS.
......
CLAK
AH.
ARE YOU...
THE ONE WHO GOES BY "ADMINIS-TRATOR"?
BA-DUMP

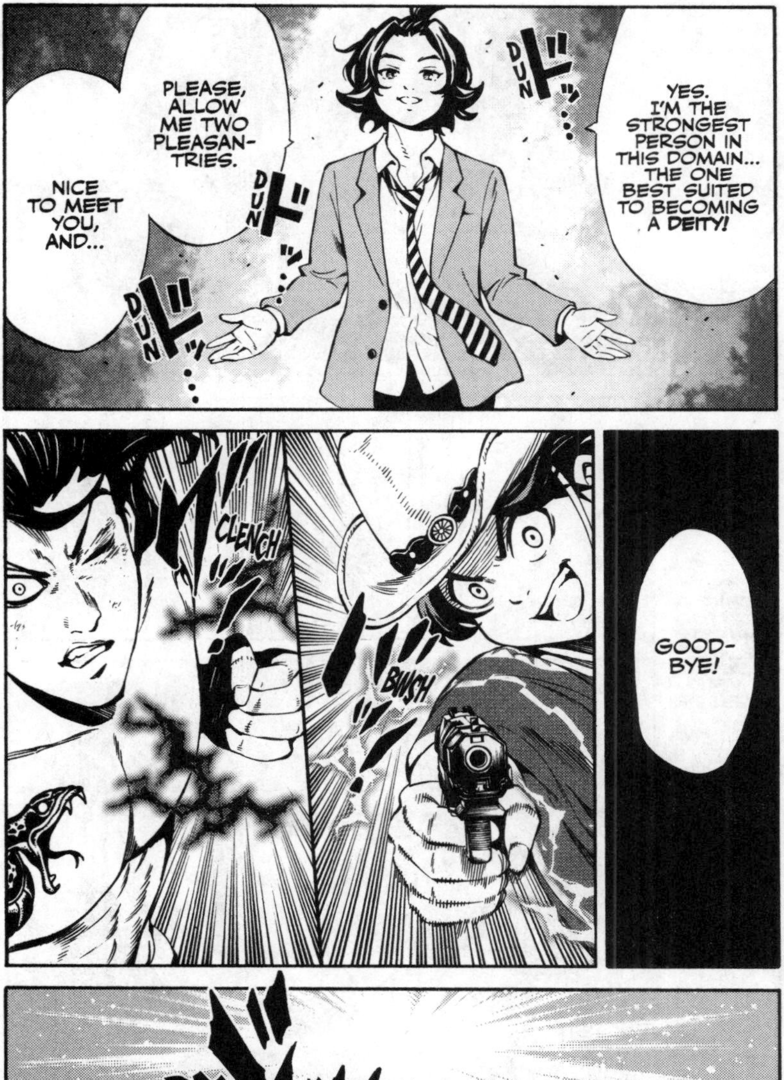
YES. I'M THE STRONGEST PERSON IN THIS DOMAIN... THE ONE BEST SUITED TO BECOMING A **DEITY**!
DUN
PLEASE, ALLOW ME TWO PLEASAN-TRIES.
DUN
NICE TO MEET YOU, AND...
DUN
GOOD-BYE!
BWSH
CLENCH
DA-DAN

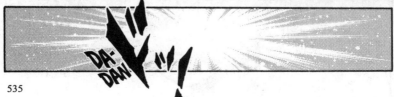

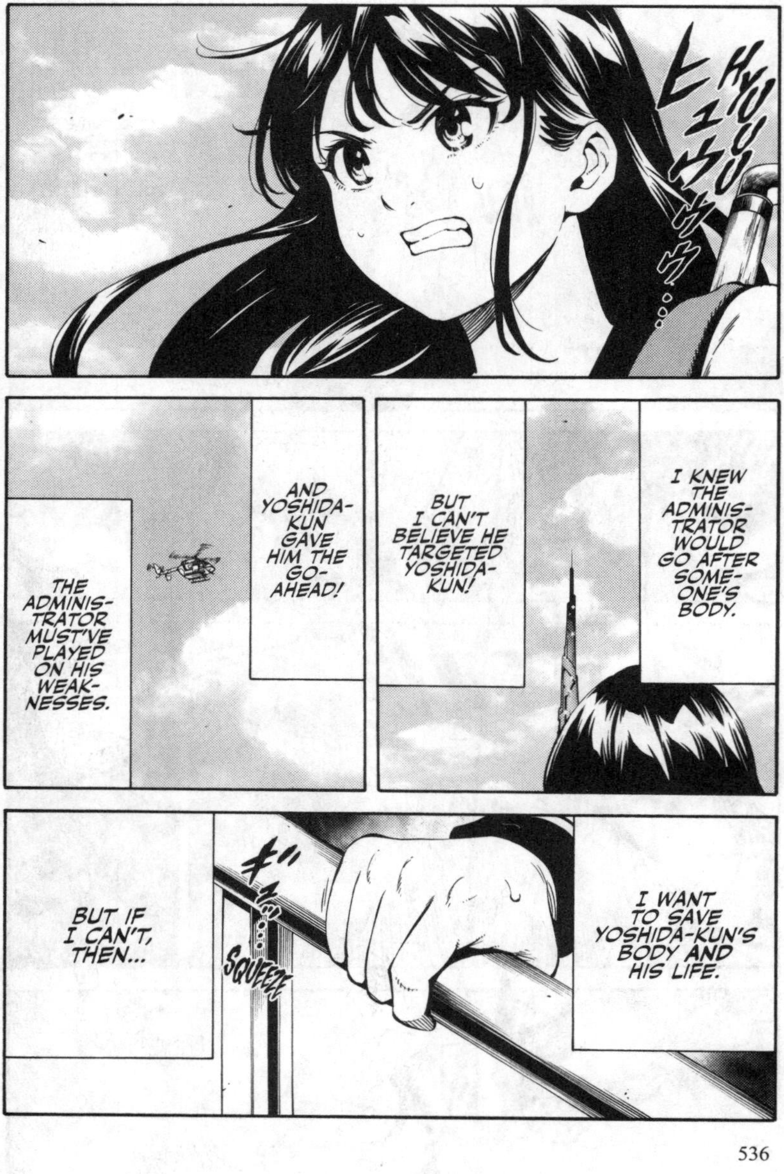

HYUUU...
I KNEW THE ADMINISTRATOR WOULD GO AFTER SOMEONE'S BODY.
BUT I CAN'T BELIEVE HE TARGETED YOSHIDA-KUN!
AND YOSHIDA-KUN GAVE HIM THE GO-AHEAD!
THE ADMINISTRATOR MUST'VE PLAYED ON HIS WEAKNESSES.
I WANT TO SAVE YOSHIDA-KUN'S BODY AND HIS LIFE.
SQUEEZE
BUT IF I CAN'T, THEN...

CHAPTER 251: Everyone Has Done That at Least Once

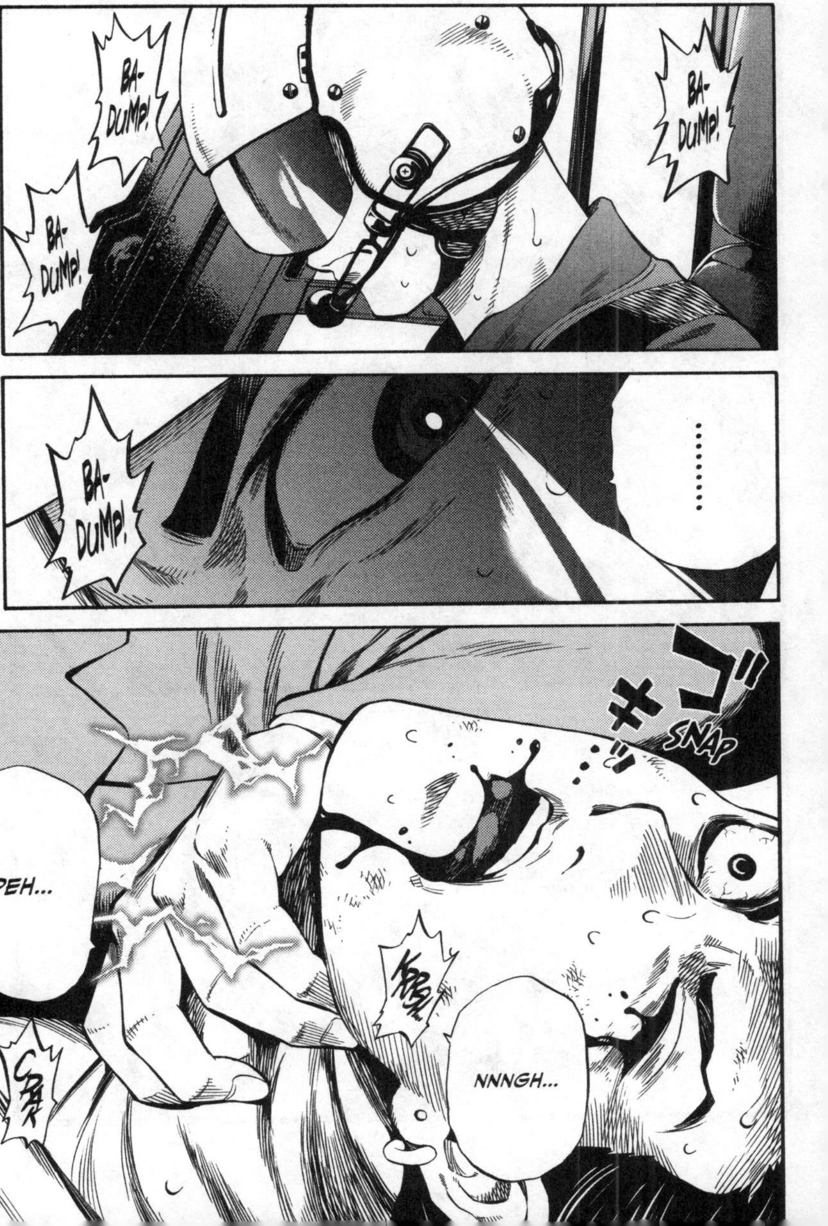
BA-DUMP!
BA-DUMP!
BA-DUMP!
......
BA-DUMP!
SNAP
KRRSH
NNNGH...
PEH...
CRAK

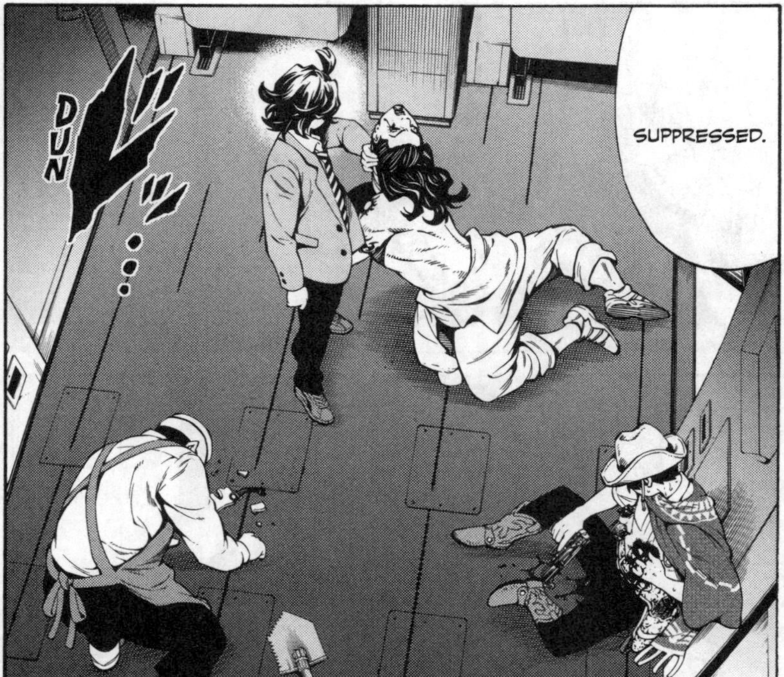
SUPPRESSED.
DUN

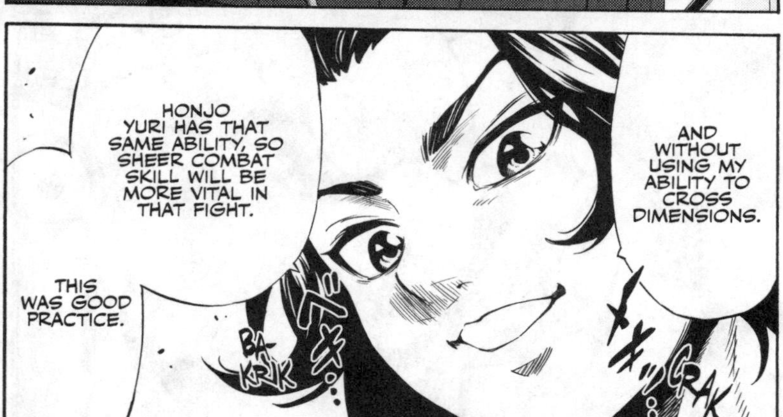
AND WITHOUT USING MY ABILITY TO CROSS DIMENSIONS.
HONJO YURI HAS THAT SAME ABILITY, SO SHEER COMBAT SKILL WILL BE MORE VITAL IN THAT FIGHT.
THIS WAS GOOD PRACTICE.
CRAK
BA-KRIK

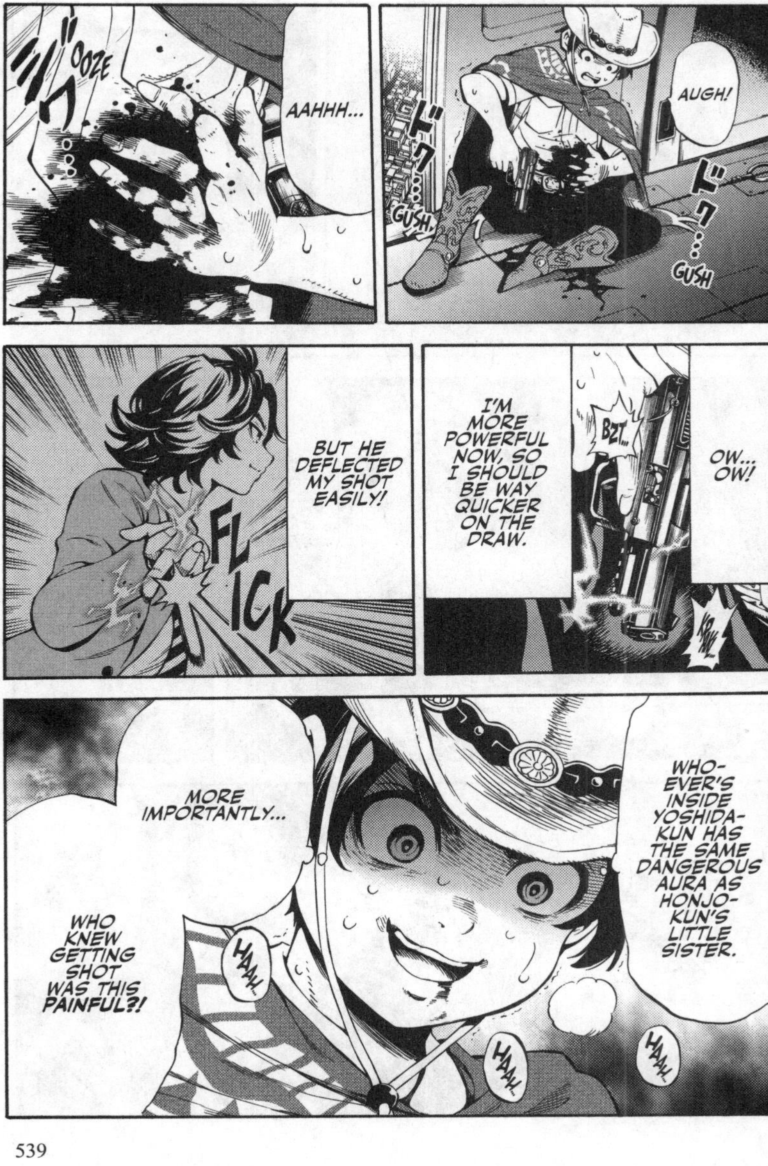
AUGH!
ドク
GUSH
ドク…
GUSH
OOZE
AAHHH…
OW… OW!
BZT…
I'M MORE POWERFUL NOW, SO I SHOULD BE WAY QUICKER ON THE DRAW.
BUT HE DEFLECTED MY SHOT EASILY!
FLICK
WHO-EVER'S INSIDE YOSHIDA-KUN HAS THE SAME DANGEROUS AURA AS HONJO-KUN'S LITTLE SISTER.
MORE IMPORTANTLY…
WHO KNEW GETTING SHOT WAS THIS PAINFUL?!
HAAH
HAAH
HAAH

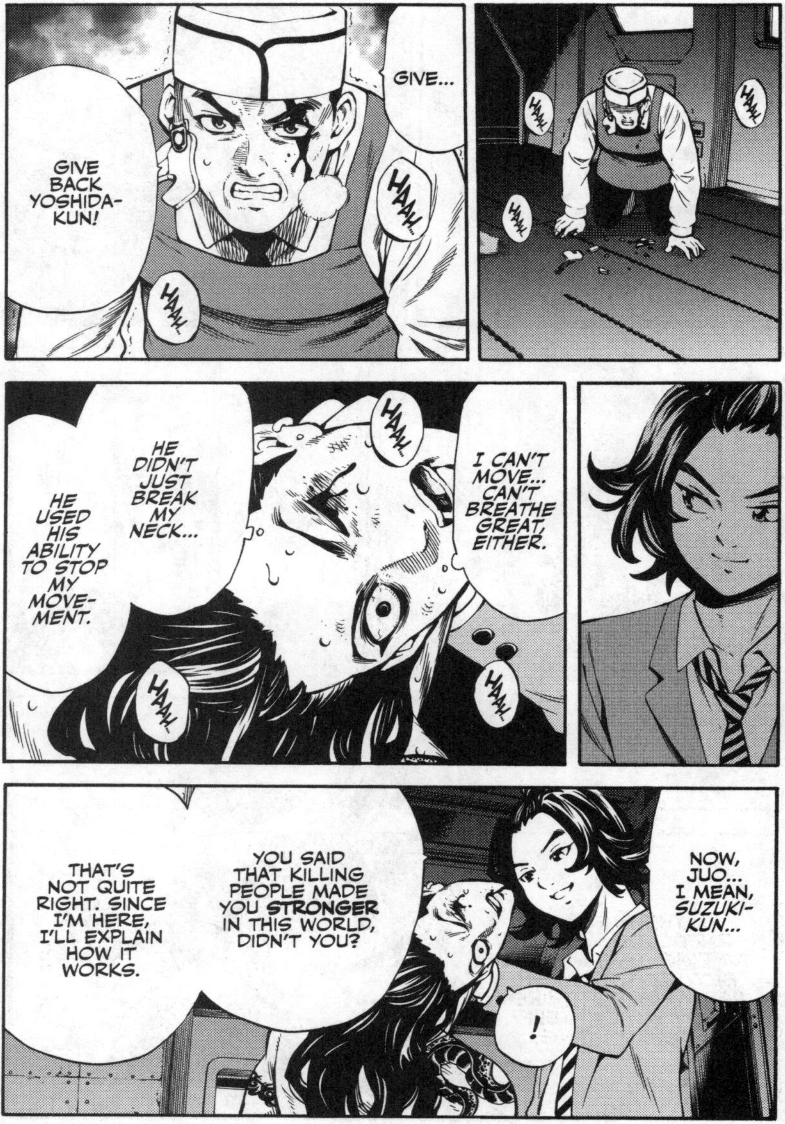
HAAH
HAAH
HAAH
GIVE...
GIVE BACK YOSHIDA-KUN!
HAAH
HAAH
HAAH
I CAN'T MOVE... CAN'T BREATHE GREAT, EITHER.
HE DIDN'T JUST BREAK MY NECK...
HE USED HIS ABILITY TO STOP MY MOVEMENT.
HAAH
HAAH
NOW, JUO... I MEAN, SUZUKI-KUN...
!
YOU SAID THAT KILLING PEOPLE MADE YOU STRONGER IN THIS WORLD, DIDN'T YOU?
THAT'S NOT QUITE RIGHT. SINCE I'M HERE, I'LL EXPLAIN HOW IT WORKS.

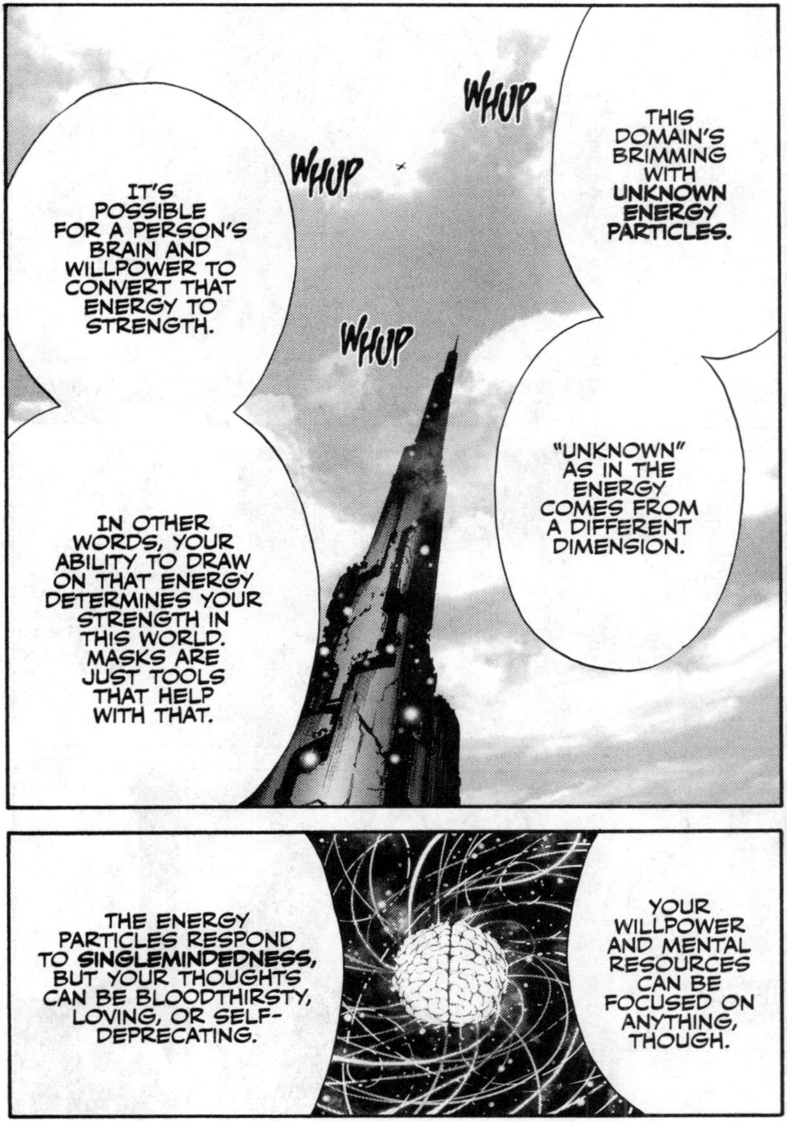
THIS DOMAIN'S BRIMMING WITH UNKNOWN ENERGY PARTICLES.
"UNKNOWN" AS IN THE ENERGY COMES FROM A DIFFERENT DIMENSION.
WHUP
WHUP
WHUP
IT'S POSSIBLE FOR A PERSON'S BRAIN AND WILLPOWER TO CONVERT THAT ENERGY TO STRENGTH.
IN OTHER WORDS, YOUR ABILITY TO DRAW ON THAT ENERGY DETERMINES YOUR STRENGTH IN THIS WORLD. MASKS ARE JUST TOOLS THAT HELP WITH THAT.
YOUR WILLPOWER AND MENTAL RESOURCES CAN BE FOCUSED ON ANYTHING, THOUGH.
THE ENERGY PARTICLES RESPOND TO SINGLEMINDEDNESS, BUT YOUR THOUGHTS CAN BE BLOODTHIRSTY, LOVING, OR SELF-DEPRECATING.

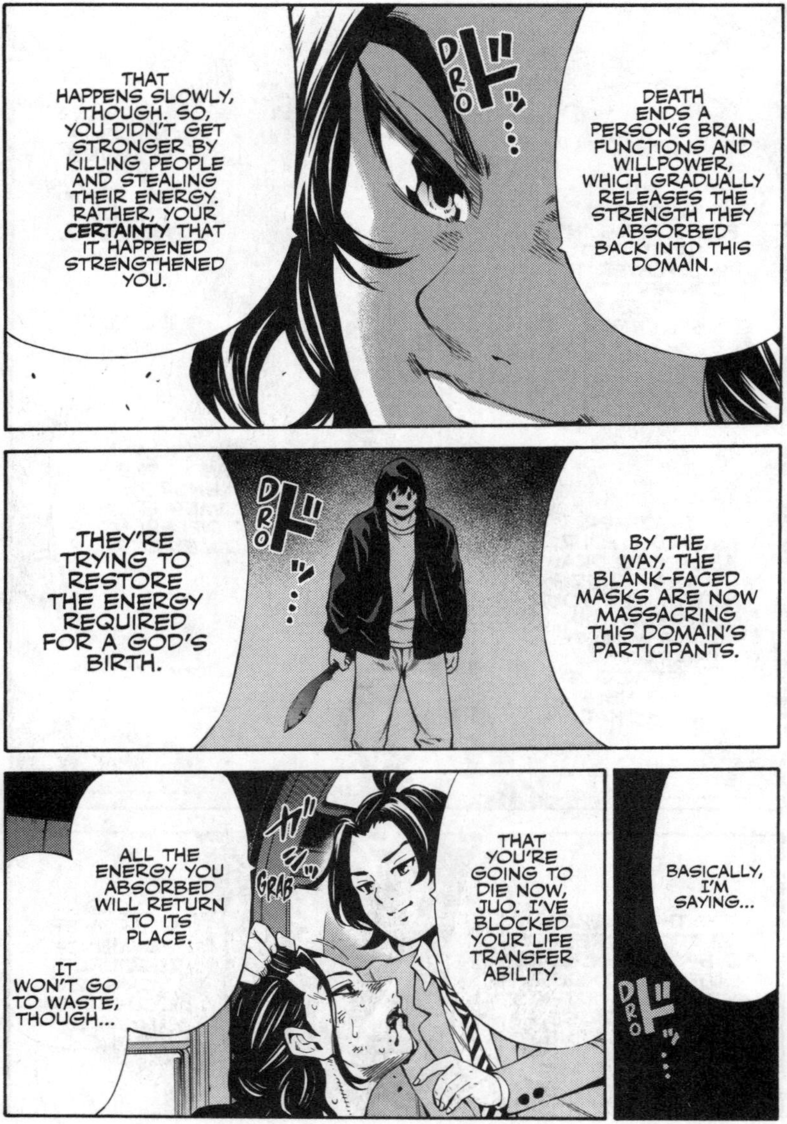
DEATH ENDS A PERSON'S BRAIN FUNCTIONS AND WILLPOWER, WHICH GRADUALLY RELEASES THE STRENGTH THEY ABSORBED BACK INTO THIS DOMAIN.
DRO
THAT HAPPENS SLOWLY, THOUGH. SO, YOU DIDN'T GET STRONGER BY KILLING PEOPLE AND STEALING THEIR ENERGY. RATHER, YOUR **CERTAINTY** THAT IT HAPPENED STRENGTHENED YOU.
BY THE WAY, THE BLANK-FACED MASKS ARE NOW MASSACRING THIS DOMAIN'S PARTICIPANTS.
DRO
THEY'RE TRYING TO RESTORE THE ENERGY REQUIRED FOR A GOD'S BIRTH.
BASICALLY, I'M SAYING...
DRO
THAT YOU'RE GOING TO DIE NOW, JUO. I'VE BLOCKED YOUR LIFE TRANSFER ABILITY.
GRAB
ALL THE ENERGY YOU ABSORBED WILL RETURN TO ITS PLACE.
IT WON'T GO TO WASTE, THOUGH...

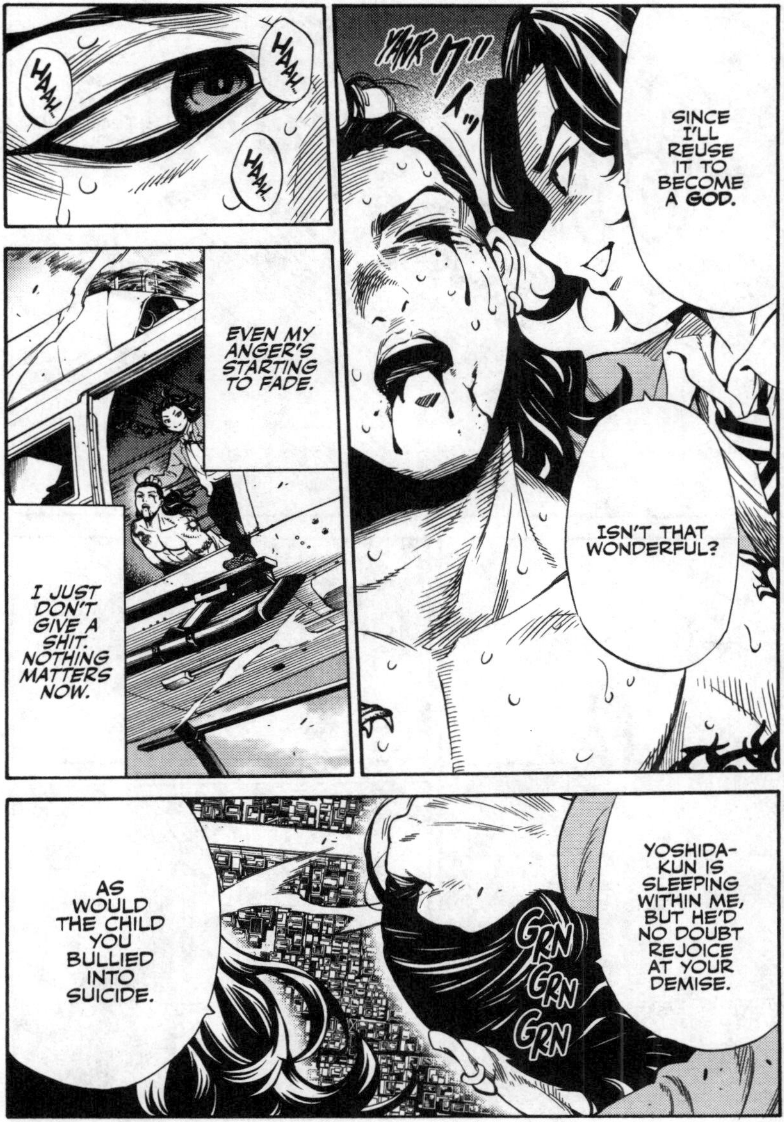
YANK
グイッ
SINCE I'LL REUSE IT TO BECOME A **GOD**.
ISN'T THAT WONDERFUL?
HAAH
HAAH
HAAH
HAAH
EVEN MY ANGER'S STARTING TO FADE.
I JUST DON'T GIVE A SHIT. NOTHING MATTERS NOW.
YOSHIDA-KUN IS SLEEPING WITHIN ME, BUT HE'D NO DOUBT REJOICE AT YOUR DEMISE.
GRN
GRN
GRN
AS WOULD THE CHILD YOU BULLIED INTO SUICIDE.

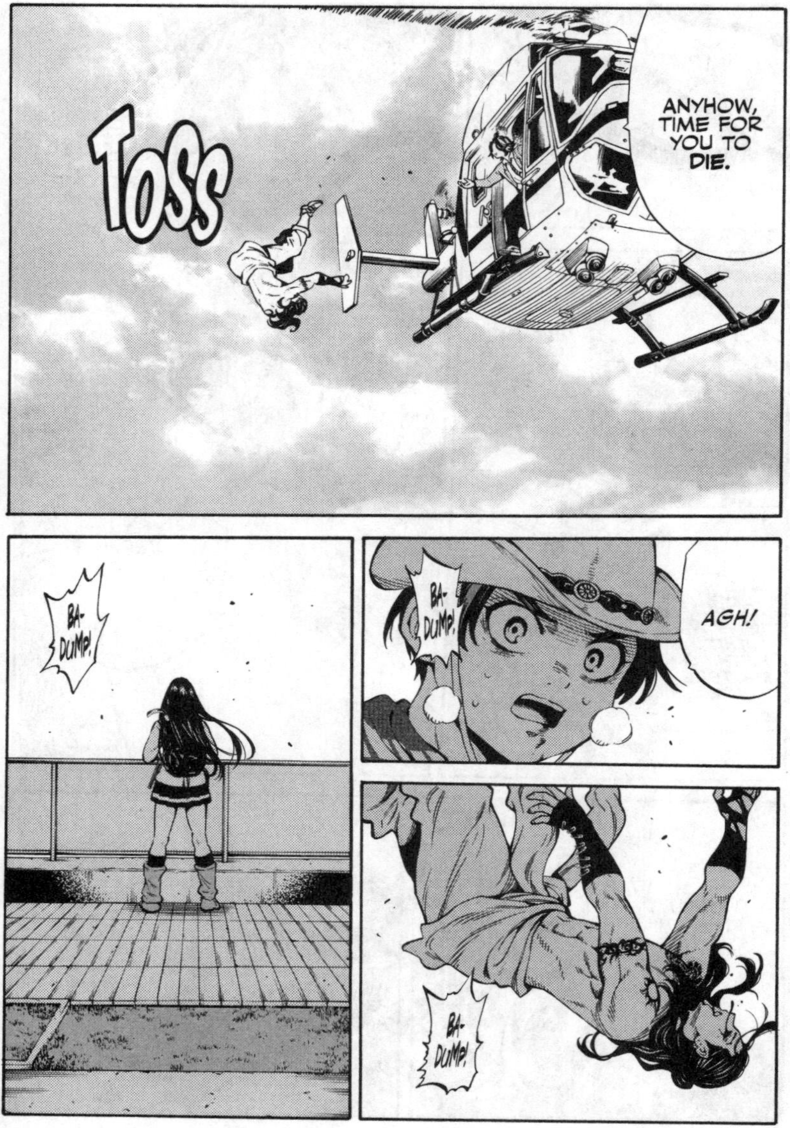
ANYHOW, TIME FOR YOU TO DIE.
TOSS
AGH!
BA-DUMP!
BA-DUMP!
BA-DUMP!

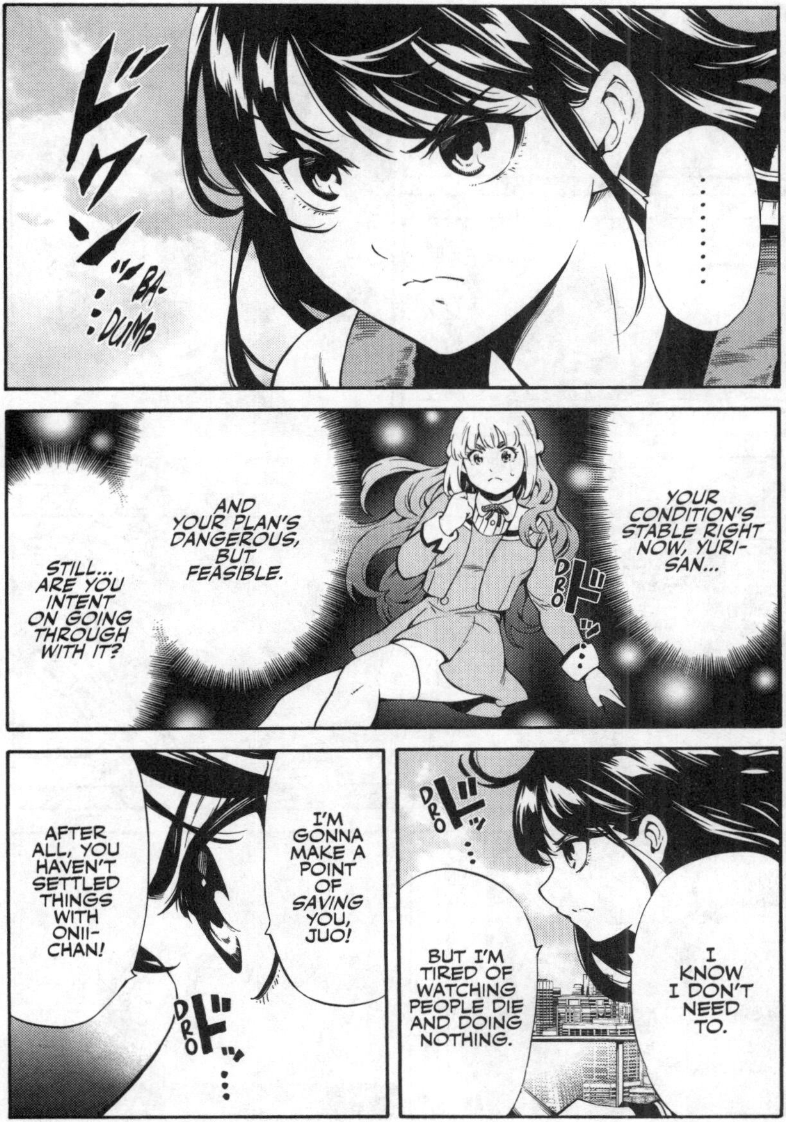
......
BA-DUMP
YOUR CONDITION'S STABLE RIGHT NOW, YURI-SAN...
DRO
AND YOUR PLAN'S DANGEROUS, BUT FEASIBLE.
STILL... ARE YOU INTENT ON GOING THROUGH WITH IT?
DRO
...
I KNOW I DON'T NEED TO.
BUT I'M TIRED OF WATCHING PEOPLE DIE AND DOING NOTHING.
I'M GONNA MAKE A POINT OF SAVING YOU, JUO!
AFTER ALL, YOU HAVEN'T SETTLED THINGS WITH ONII-CHAN!
DRO
...

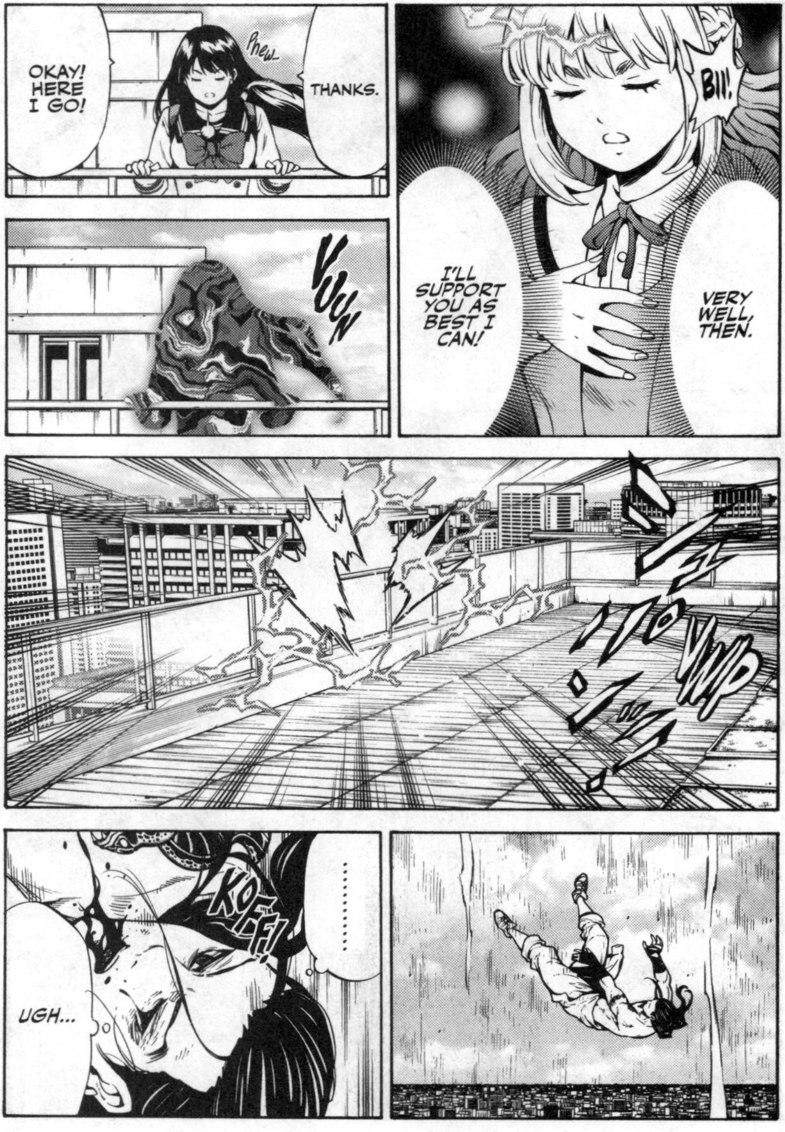
BII!
VERY WELL, THEN.
I'LL SUPPORT YOU AS BEST I CAN!
THANKS.
Phew...
OKAY! HERE I GO!
VUUN
VWIP
KOFF!
......
UGH...

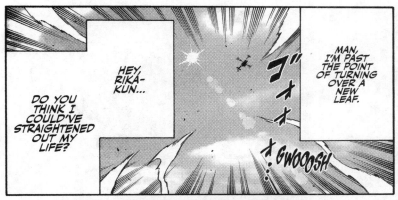

MAN, I'M PAST THE POINT OF TURNING OVER A NEW LEAF.
ゴォォォ…
GWOOOSH
HEY, RIKA-KUN...
DO YOU THINK I COULD'VE STRAIGHTENED OUT MY LIFE?
THINKING BACK ON IT, TALKING TO YOU WAS SERIOUSLY A BLAST.
NOW I CAN'T EVEN DO THAT AGAIN. AFTER ALL, I'M ABOUT TO DIE.
I'M GONNA DIE?
I CAN'T DO ANYTHING ANYMORE?
ゴォォ…
GWOOSH
I DON'T WANT TO DIE.
VOON
......?!

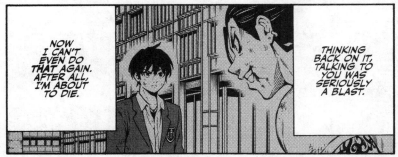

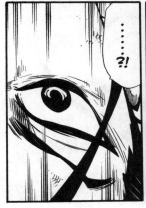

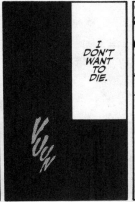

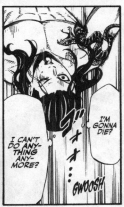

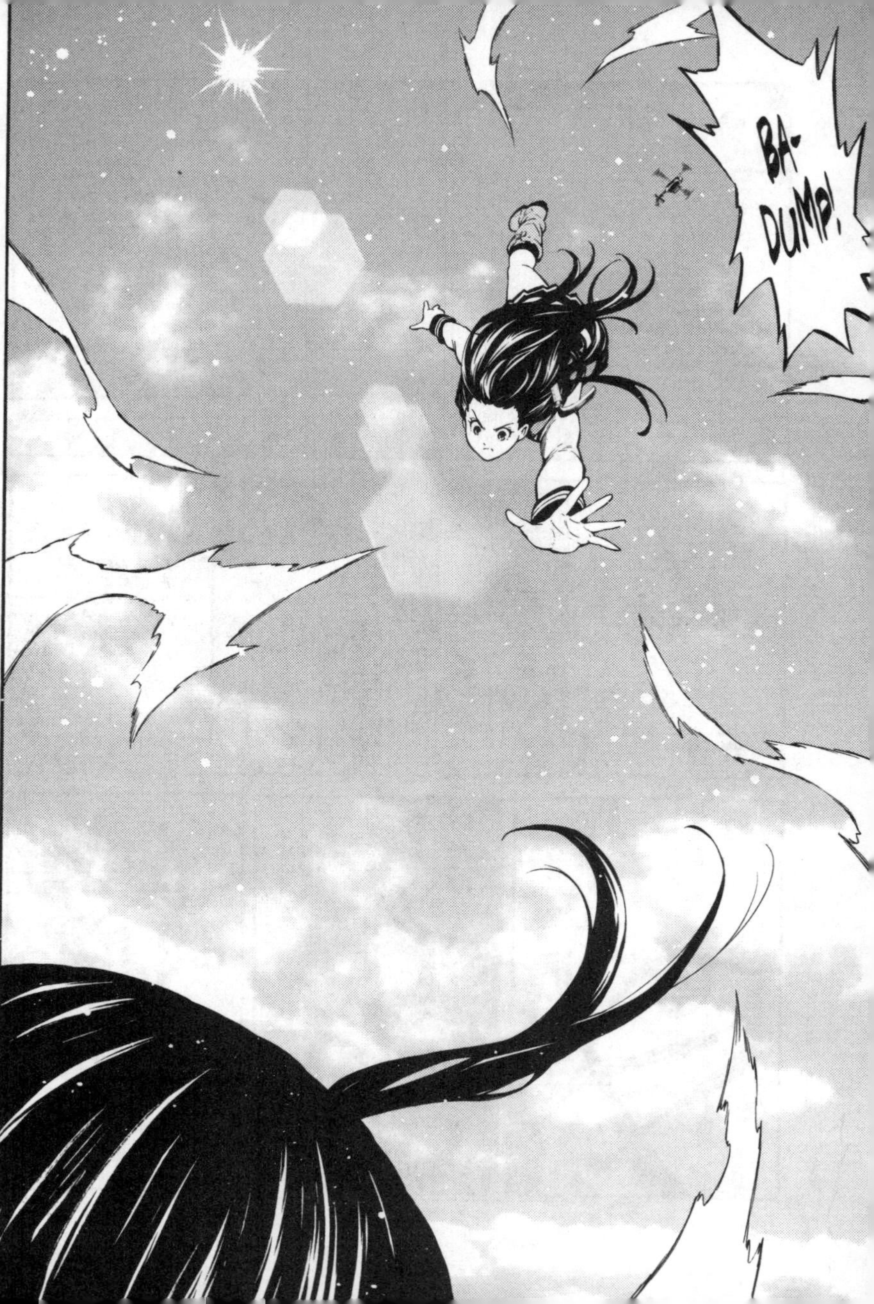
BA-DUMP!

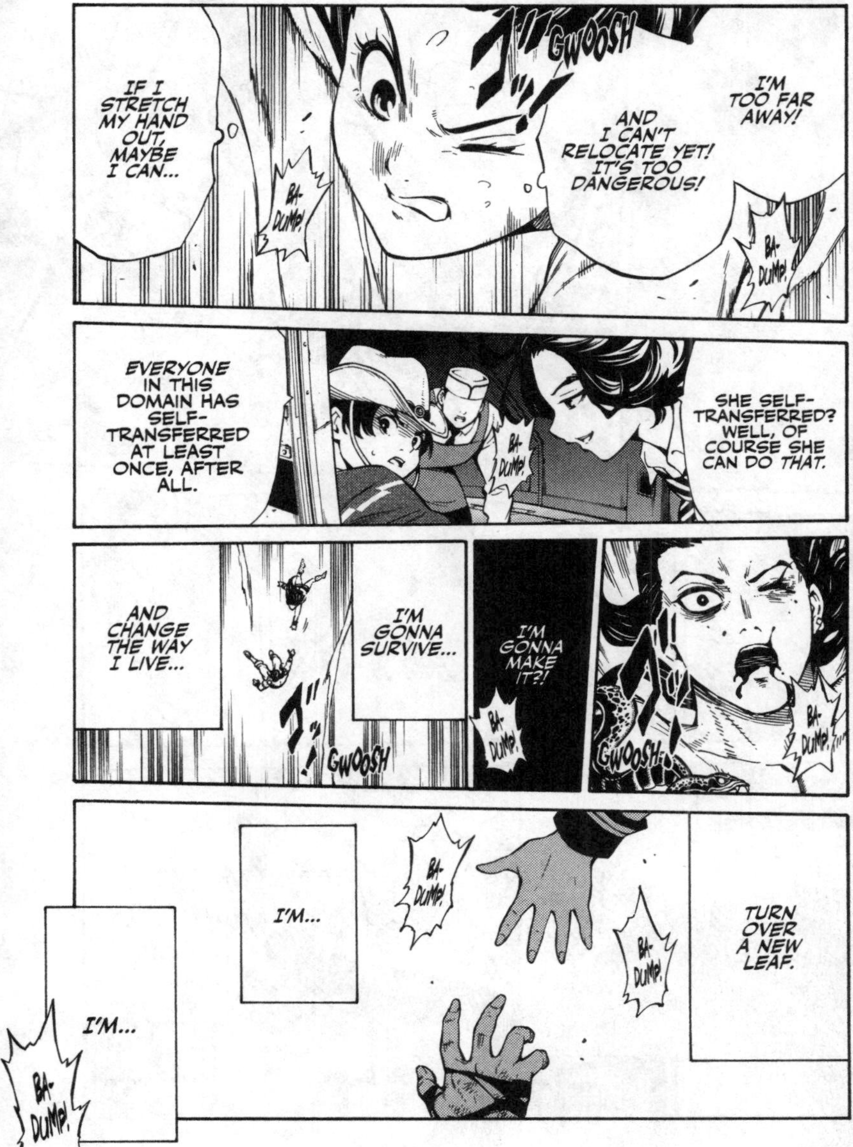
GWOOSH
I'M TOO FAR AWAY!
AND I CAN'T RELOCATE YET! IT'S TOO DANGEROUS!
IF I STRETCH MY HAND OUT, MAYBE I CAN...
BA-DUMP!
BA-DUMP!
SHE SELF-TRANSFERRED? WELL, OF COURSE SHE CAN DO *THAT.*
BA-DUMP!
EVERYONE IN THIS DOMAIN HAS SELF-TRANSFERRED AT LEAST ONCE, AFTER ALL.
BA-DUMP!
GWOOSH
I'M GONNA MAKE IT?!
BA-DUMP!
I'M GONNA SURVIVE...
AND CHANGE THE WAY I LIVE...
GWOOSH
TURN OVER A NEW LEAF.
BA-DUMP!
BA-DUMP!
I'M...
I'M...
BA-DUMP!

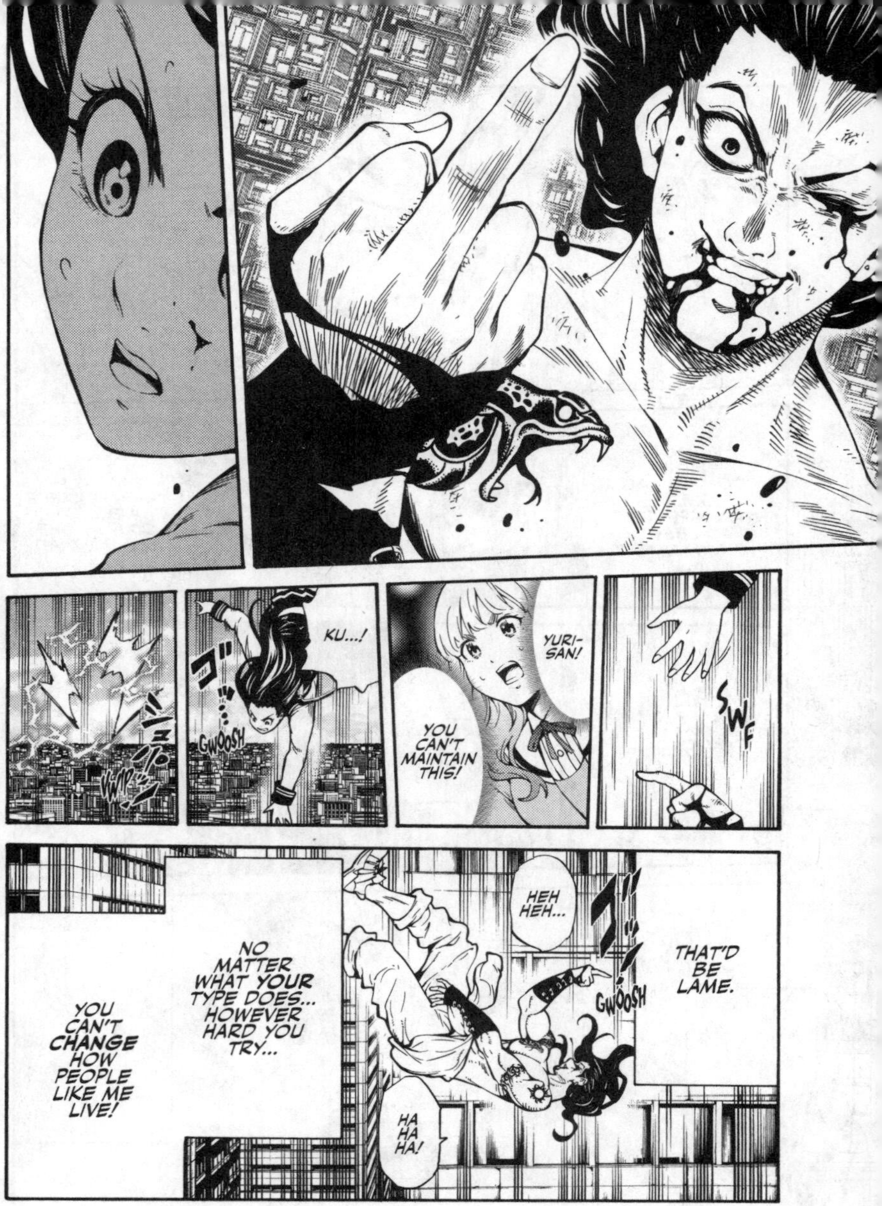
S W F
YURI-SAN!
YOU CAN'T MAINTAIN THIS!
KU...!
GWOOSH
THAT'D BE LAME.
HEH HEH...
GWOOSH
HA HA HA!
NO MATTER WHAT YOUR TYPE DOES... HOWEVER HARD YOU TRY...
YOU CAN'T CHANGE HOW PEOPLE LIKE ME LIVE!

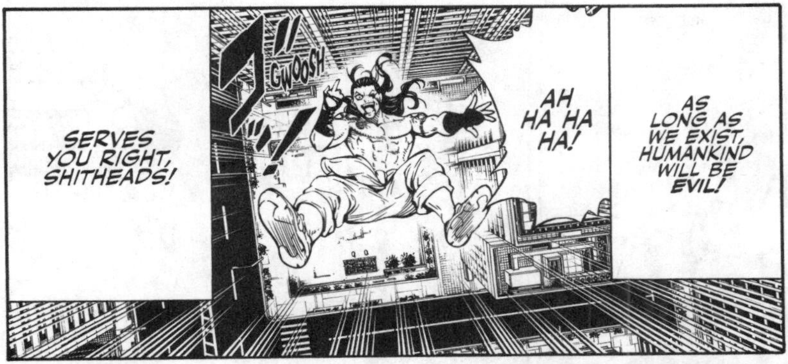
AS LONG AS WE EXIST, HUMANKIND WILL BE EVIL!
AH HA HA HA!
GWOOSH
SERVES YOU RIGHT, SHITHEADS!

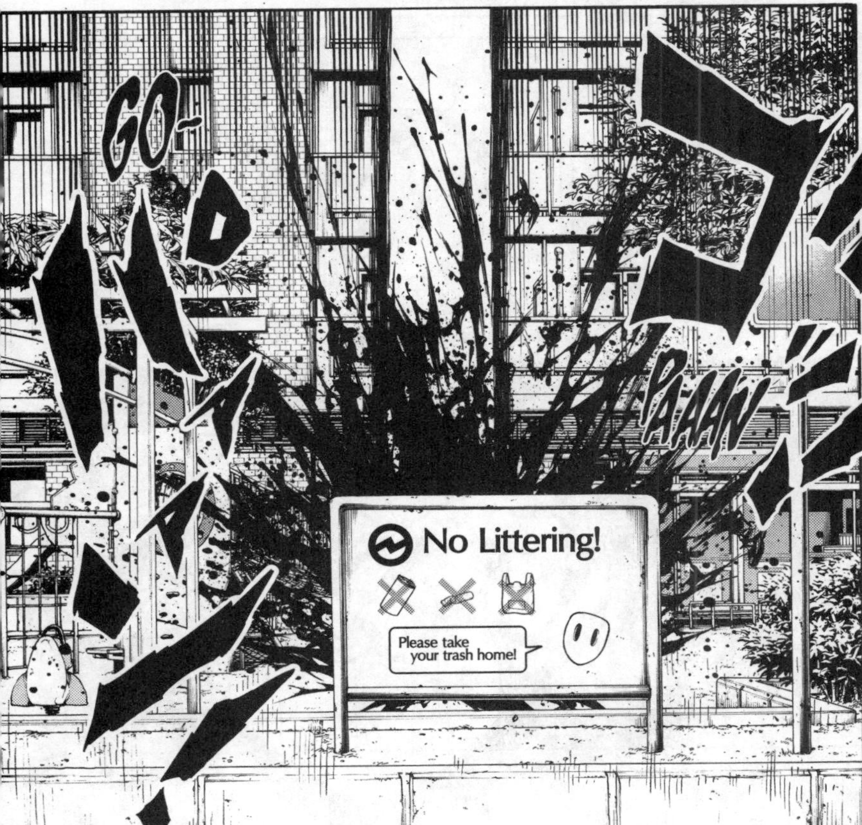
PAAAN
GO-
No Littering!
Please take your trash home!

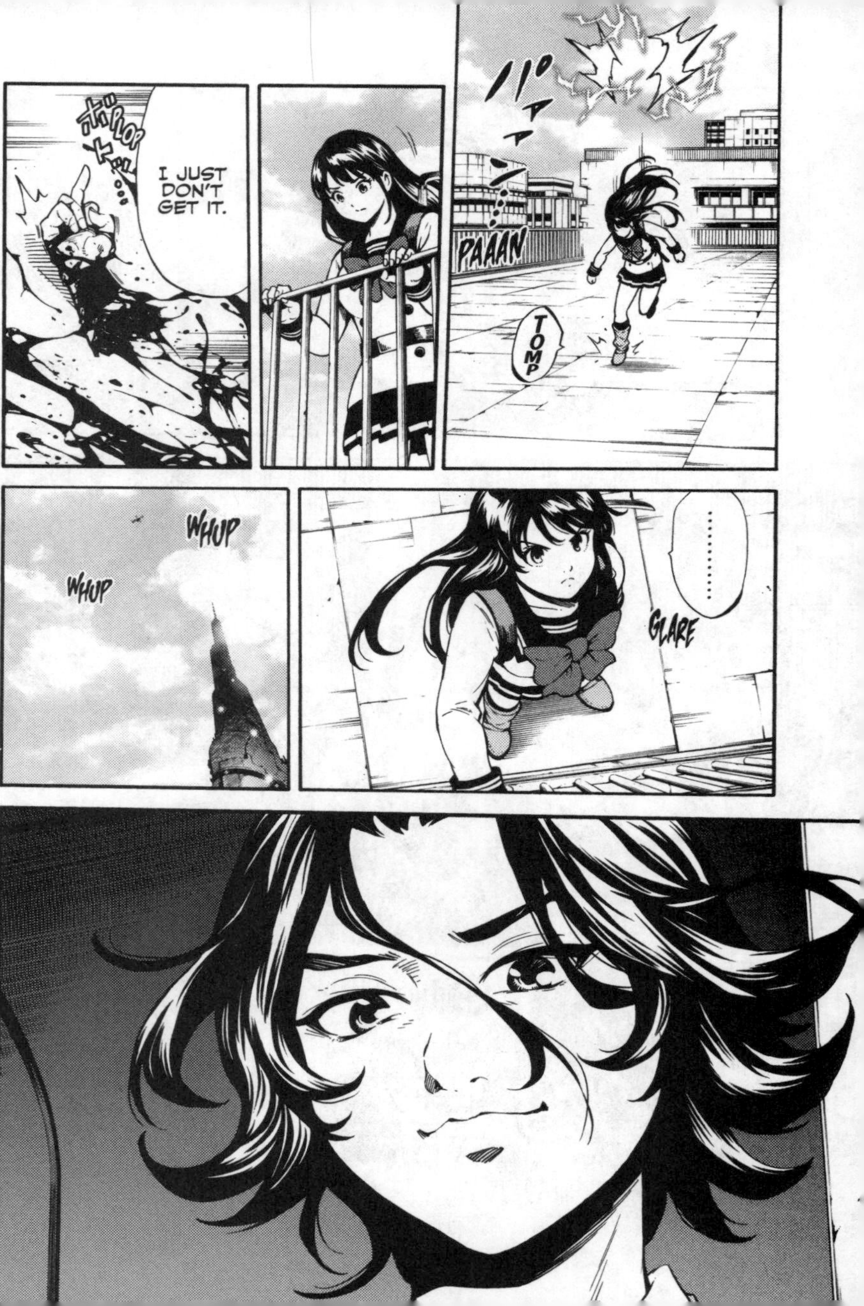
PAAAN
TOMP
PLOP
I JUST DON'T GET IT.
......
GLARE
WHUP
WHUP

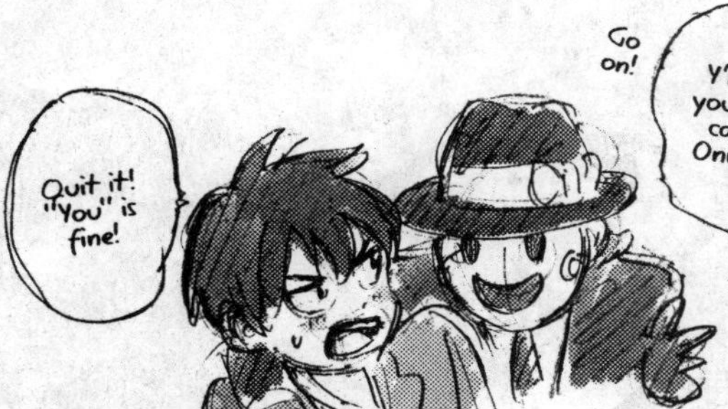
Y'know, you could call me Oniichan!
Go on!
Quit it! "You" is fine!

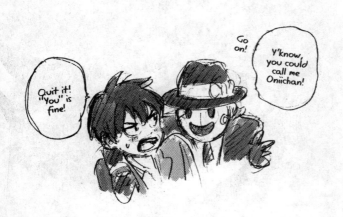

HIGH-RISE INVASION

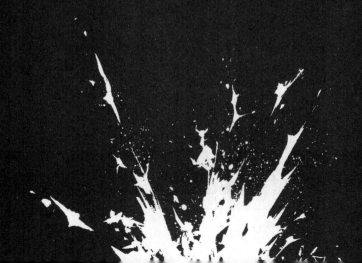

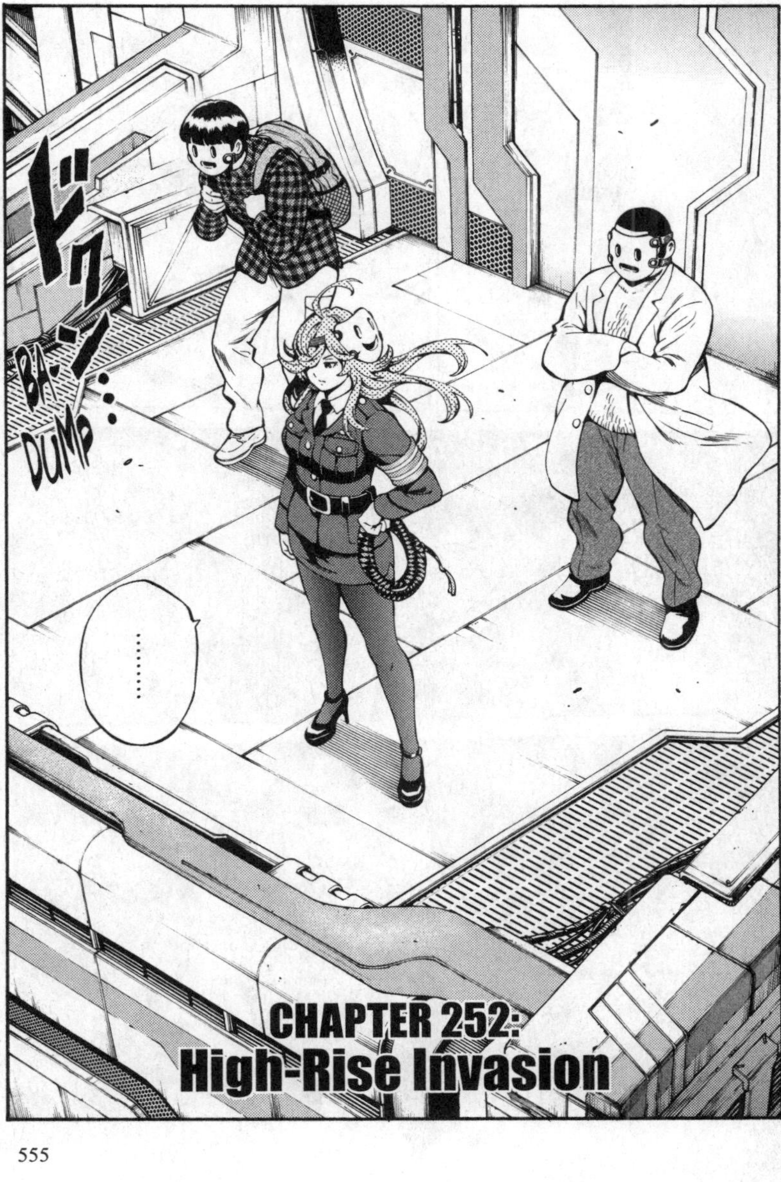
ドクン
BA-DUMP
......
CHAPTER 252:
High-Rise Invasion

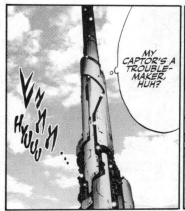

UGH...
MY CAPTOR'S A TROUBLE-MAKER, HUH?
"I'D VERY MUCH LIKE YOU TO WATCH MY BATTLE WITH HONJO YURI, KUSAKABE-SAN.
"I'M GOING TOE-TO-TOE WITH EVIL IN ORDER TO PUNISH IT. I IMAGINE THAT'LL BE VALUABLE TO YOUR APPEAL TO THE SUPERVISOR.
"AGAIN, YOU WILL TAKE MY CASE ON AND DEFEND MY CLAIM, WON'T YOU?
"I'D SAY THAT'S THE BEST WAY TO SAFEGUARD YOURSELF AND YOUR SON."

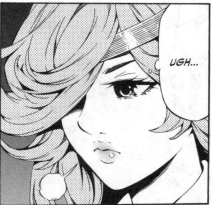

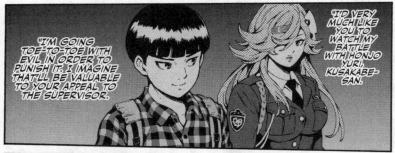

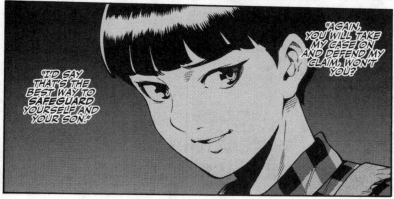

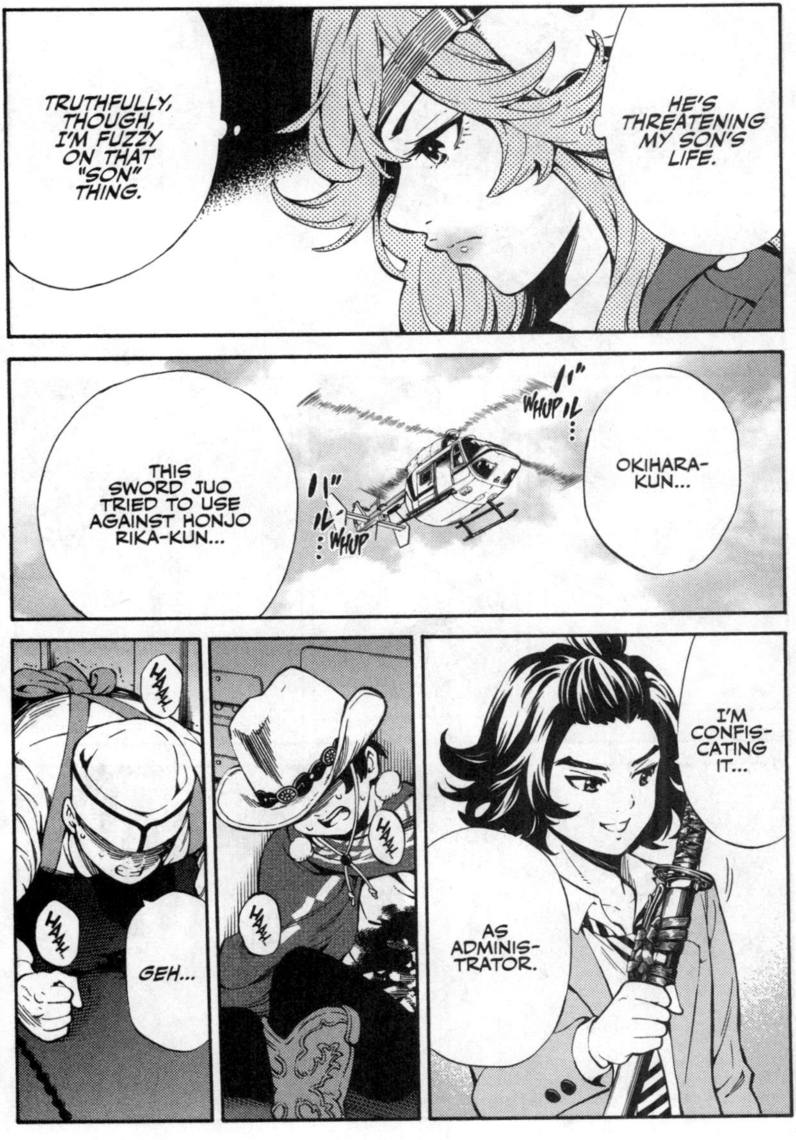
HE'S THREATENING MY SON'S LIFE.
TRUTHFULLY, THOUGH, I'M FUZZY ON THAT "SON" THING.
OKIHARA-KUN...
WHUP
THIS SWORD JUO TRIED TO USE AGAINST HONJO RIKA-KUN...
WHUP
I'M CONFISCATING IT...
AS ADMINISTRATOR.
HAAH
HAAH
HAAH
HAAH
GEH...

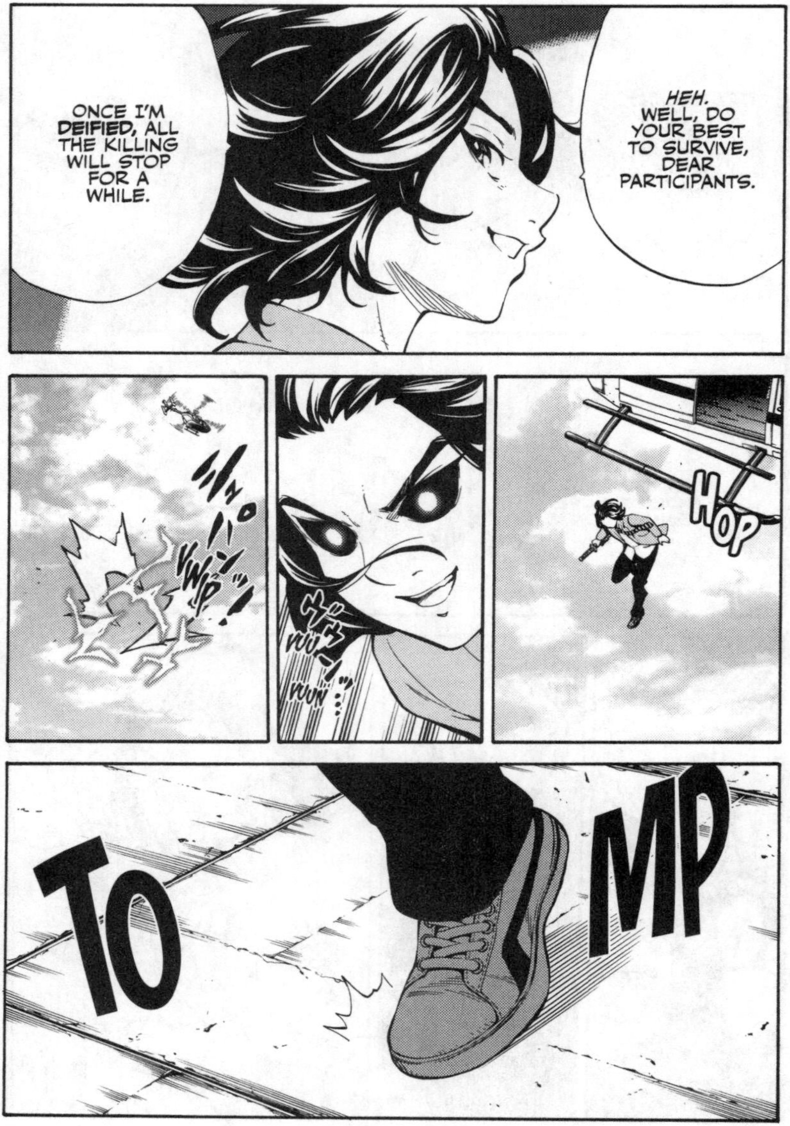
HEH. WELL, DO YOUR BEST TO SURVIVE, DEAR PARTICIPANTS.
ONCE I'M **DEIFIED**, ALL THE KILLING WILL STOP FOR A WHILE.
HOP
VUU VUUN
VWIP!
TOMP

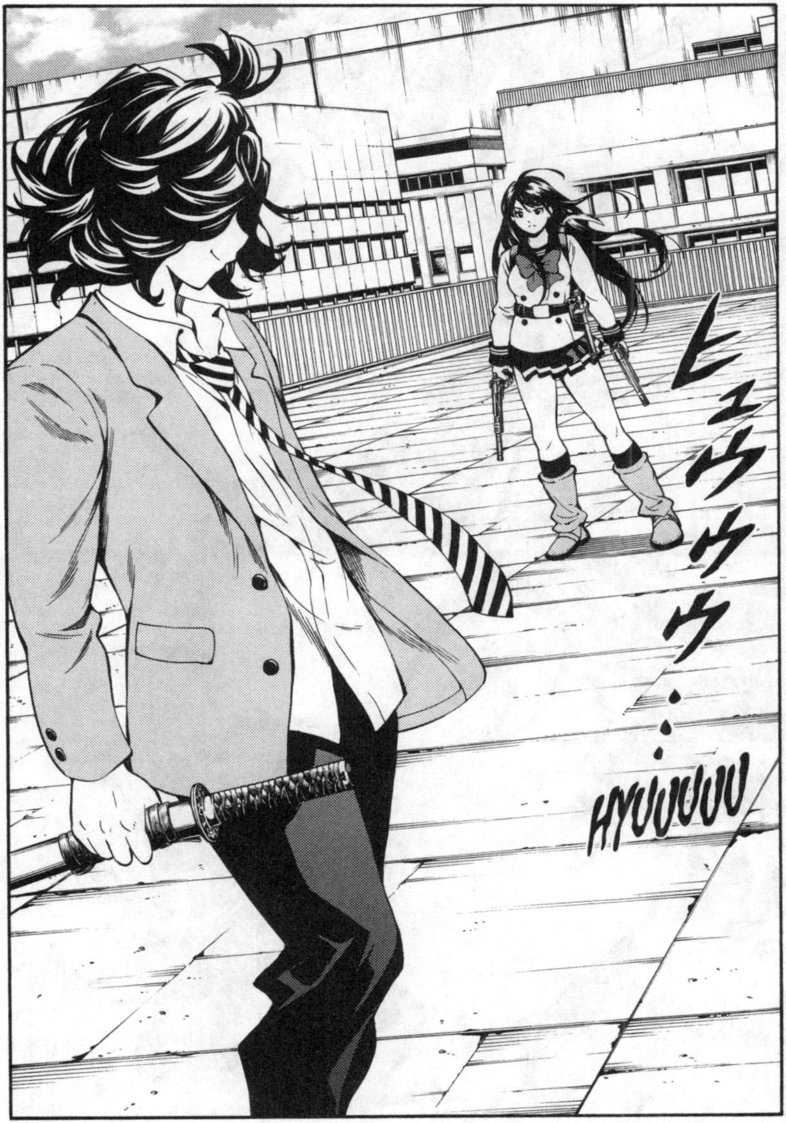
ヒュウウウ……
HYUUUUU

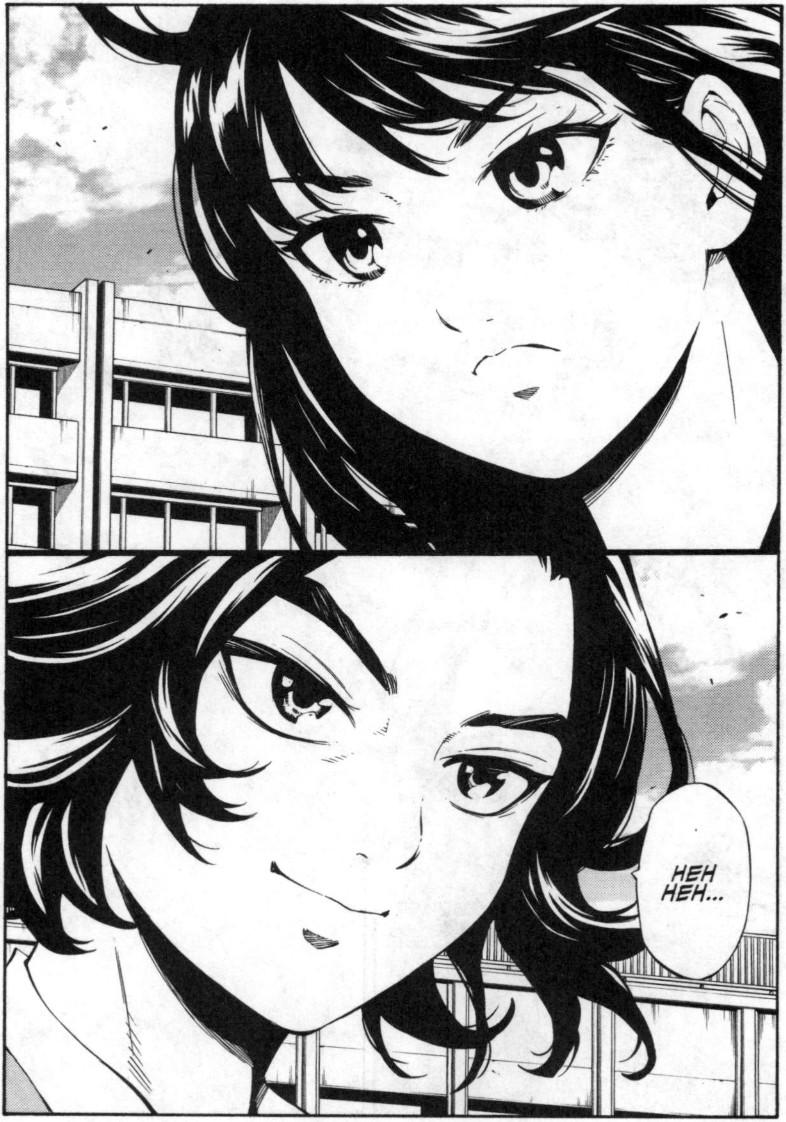
HEH HEH...

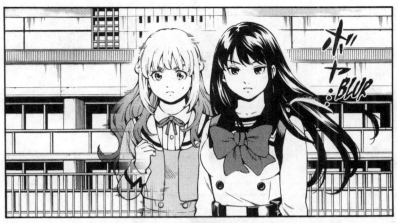

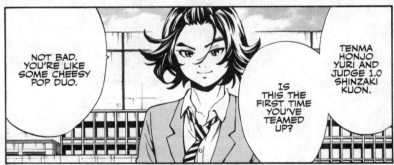

BLUR
TENMA HONJO YURI AND JUDGE 1.0 SHINZAKI KUON.
IS THIS THE FIRST TIME YOU'VE TEAMED UP?
NOT BAD. YOU'RE LIKE SOME CHEESY POP DUO.
SO, YOU CAN HEAR MY VOICE, ADMINISTRATOR-SAN?
IN THAT CASE, I'D LIKE TO ASK YOU SOMETHING.
THE SUPERVISOR INFORMED US OF ALL THE RULES YOU'VE BROKEN.
FOR ONE THING, YOU DISREGARDED THE LIMIT ON ARRIVALS TO THIS WORLD.

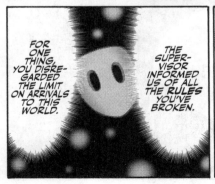

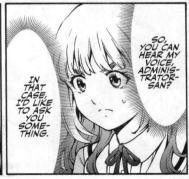

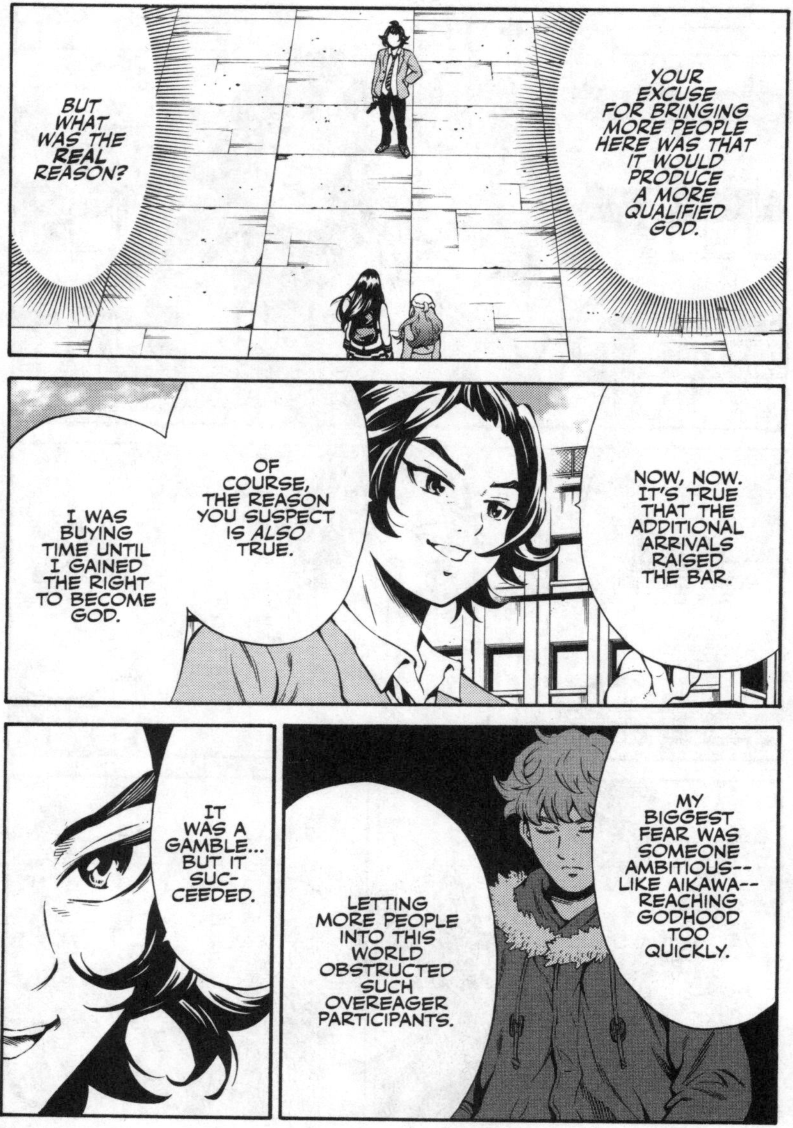
YOUR EXCUSE FOR BRINGING MORE PEOPLE HERE WAS THAT IT WOULD PRODUCE A MORE QUALIFIED GOD.
BUT WHAT WAS THE REAL REASON?
NOW, NOW. IT'S TRUE THAT THE ADDITIONAL ARRIVALS RAISED THE BAR.
OF COURSE, THE REASON YOU SUSPECT IS *ALSO* TRUE.
I WAS BUYING TIME UNTIL I GAINED THE RIGHT TO BECOME GOD.
MY BIGGEST FEAR WAS SOMEONE AMBITIOUS--LIKE AIKAWA--REACHING GODHOOD TOO QUICKLY.
LETTING MORE PEOPLE INTO THIS WORLD OBSTRUCTED SUCH OVEREAGER PARTICIPANTS.
IT WAS A GAMBLE... BUT IT SUC-CEEDED.

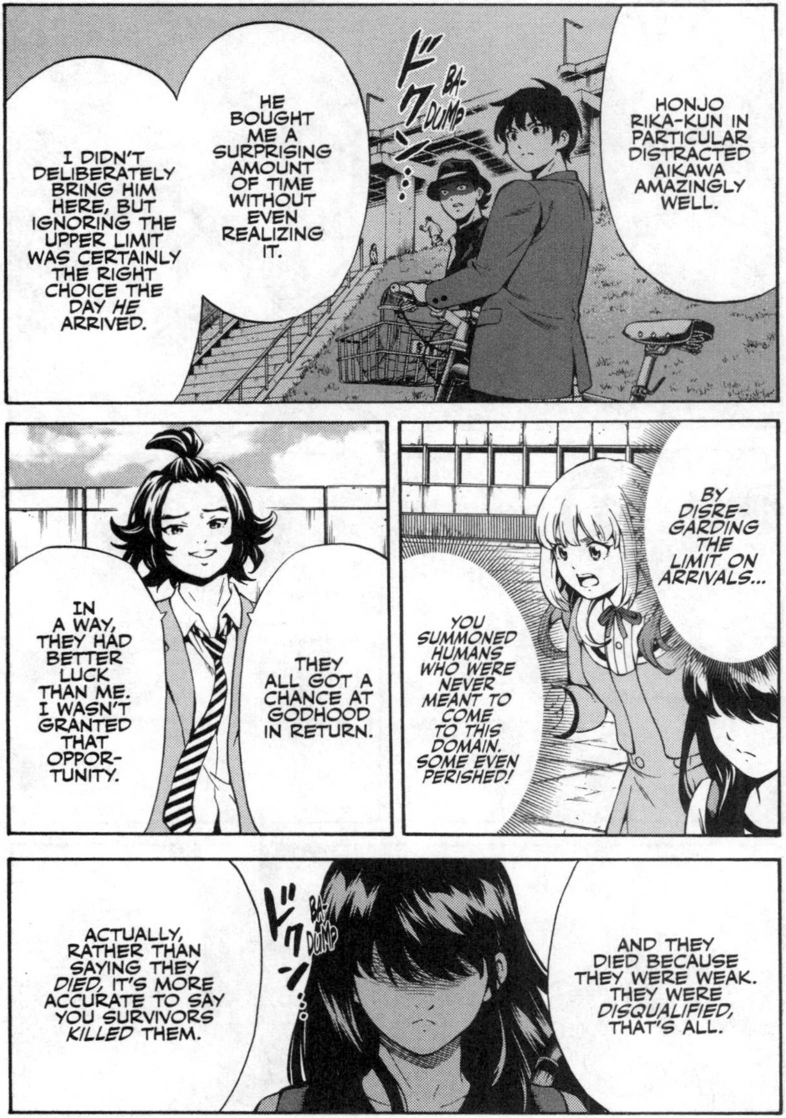
HONJO RIKA-KUN IN PARTICULAR DISTRACTED AIKAWA AMAZINGLY WELL.
BA-DUMP
HE BOUGHT ME A SURPRISING AMOUNT OF TIME WITHOUT EVEN REALIZING IT.
I DIDN'T DELIBERATELY BRING HIM HERE, BUT IGNORING THE UPPER LIMIT WAS CERTAINLY THE RIGHT CHOICE THE DAY *HE* ARRIVED.
BY DISREGARDING THE LIMIT ON ARRIVALS...
YOU SUMMONED HUMANS WHO WERE NEVER MEANT TO COME TO THIS DOMAIN. SOME EVEN PERISHED!
THEY ALL GOT A CHANCE AT GODHOOD IN RETURN.
IN A WAY, THEY HAD BETTER LUCK THAN ME. I WASN'T GRANTED THAT OPPORTUNITY.
AND THEY DIED BECAUSE THEY WERE WEAK. THEY WERE *DISQUALIFIED,* THAT'S ALL.
BA-DUMP
ACTUALLY, RATHER THAN SAYING THEY *DIED,* IT'S MORE ACCURATE TO SAY YOU SURVIVORS *KILLED* THEM.

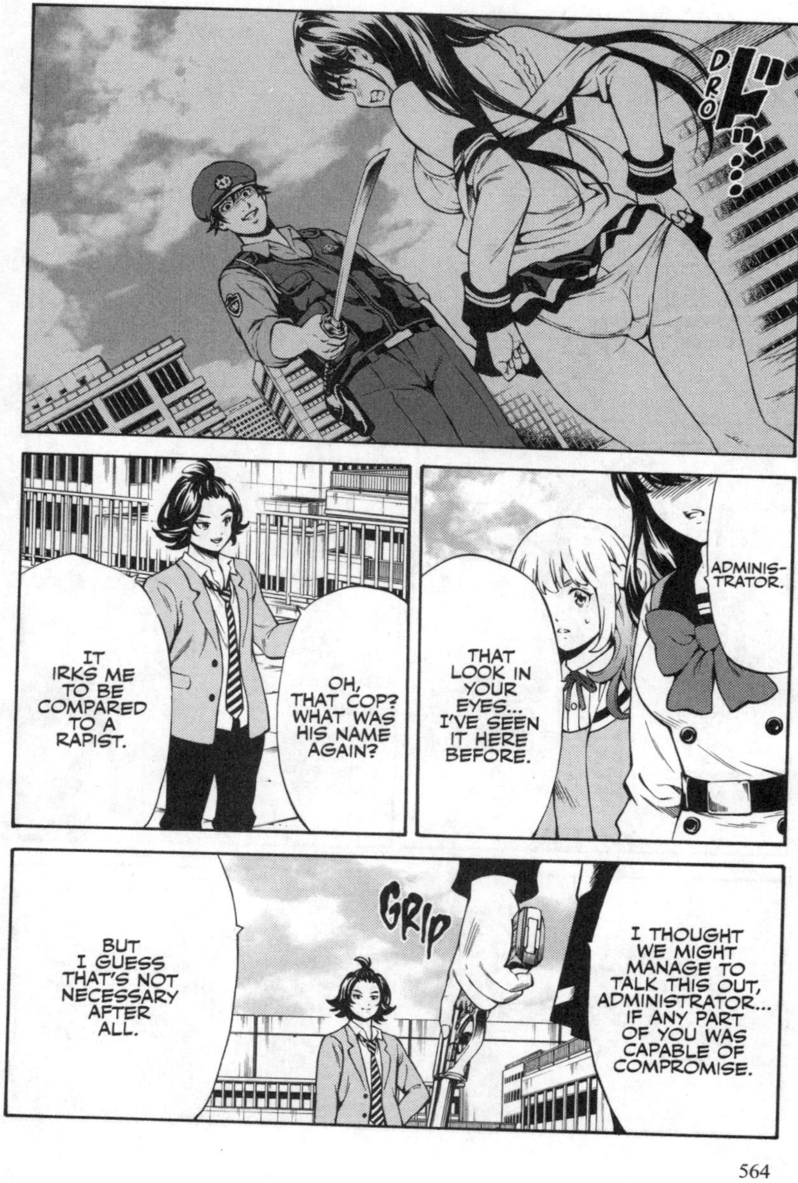
DRO
ADMINIS-TRATOR.
THAT LOOK IN YOUR EYES... I'VE SEEN IT HERE BEFORE.
OH, THAT COP? WHAT WAS HIS NAME AGAIN?
IT IRKS ME TO BE COMPARED TO A RAPIST.
I THOUGHT WE MIGHT MANAGE TO TALK THIS OUT, ADMINISTRATOR... IF ANY PART OF YOU WAS CAPABLE OF COMPROMISE.
GRIP
BUT I GUESS THAT'S NOT NECESSARY AFTER ALL.

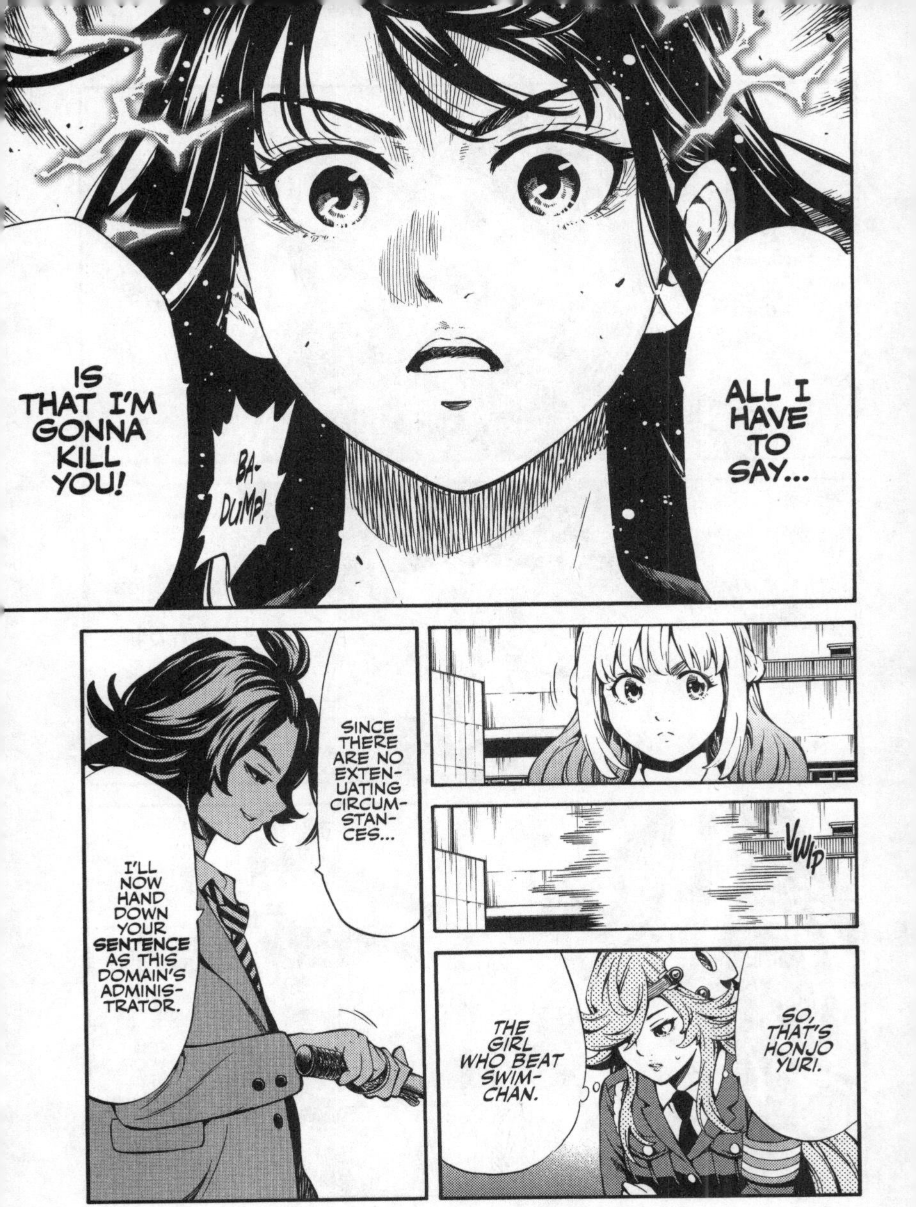

ALL I HAVE TO SAY...
BA-DUMP!
IS THAT I'M GONNA KILL YOU!
VWIP
SO, THAT'S HONJO YURI.
THE GIRL WHO BEAT SWIM-CHAN.
SINCE THERE ARE NO EXTENUATING CIRCUMSTANCES...
I'LL NOW HAND DOWN YOUR SENTENCE AS THIS DOMAIN'S ADMINISTRATOR.

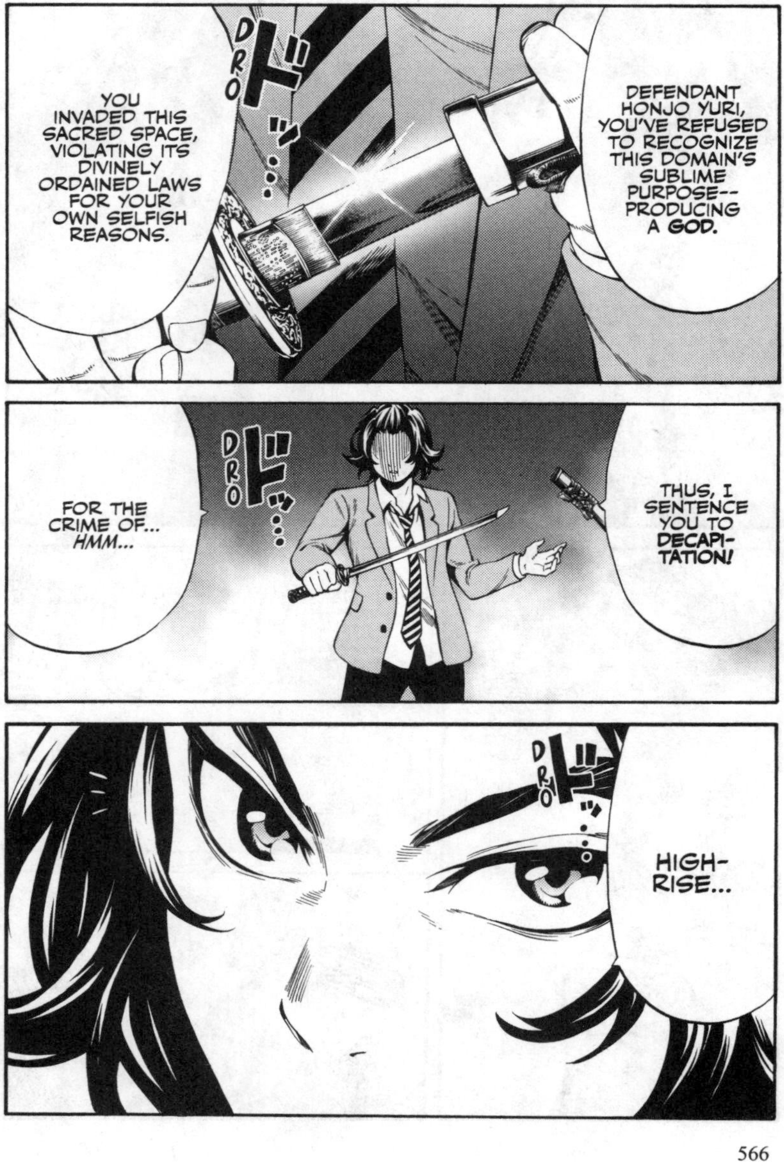
DEFENDANT HONJO YURI, YOU'VE REFUSED TO RECOGNIZE THIS DOMAIN'S SUBLIME PURPOSE-- PRODUCING A **GOD**.
DRO ド ッ...
YOU INVADED THIS SACRED SPACE, VIOLATING ITS DIVINELY ORDAINED LAWS FOR YOUR OWN SELFISH REASONS.
THUS, I SENTENCE YOU TO **DECAPI-TATION!**
DRO ド ッ...
FOR THE CRIME OF... *HMM...*
DRO ド ッ...
HIGH-RISE...

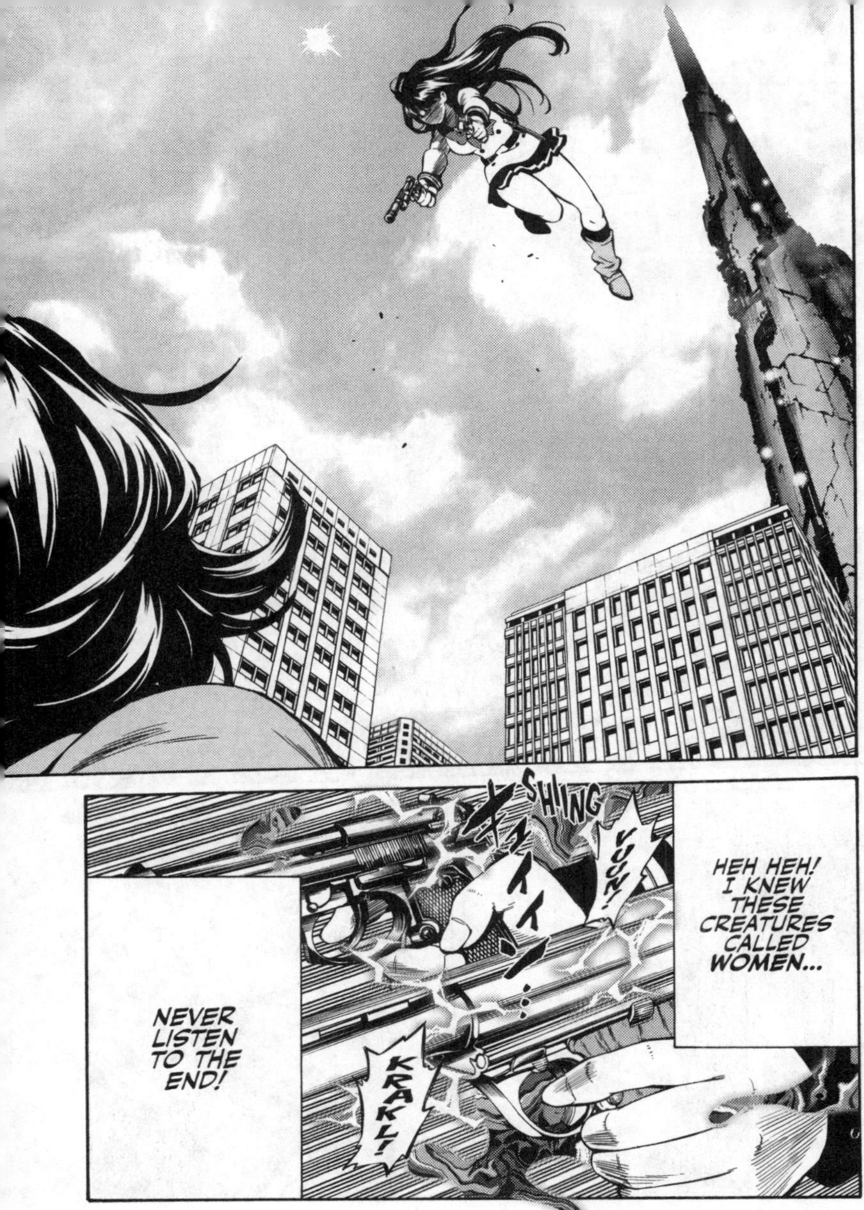
HEH HEH! I KNEW THESE CREATURES CALLED WOMEN...
SHING
VUUN!
KRAKL!
NEVER LISTEN TO THE END!

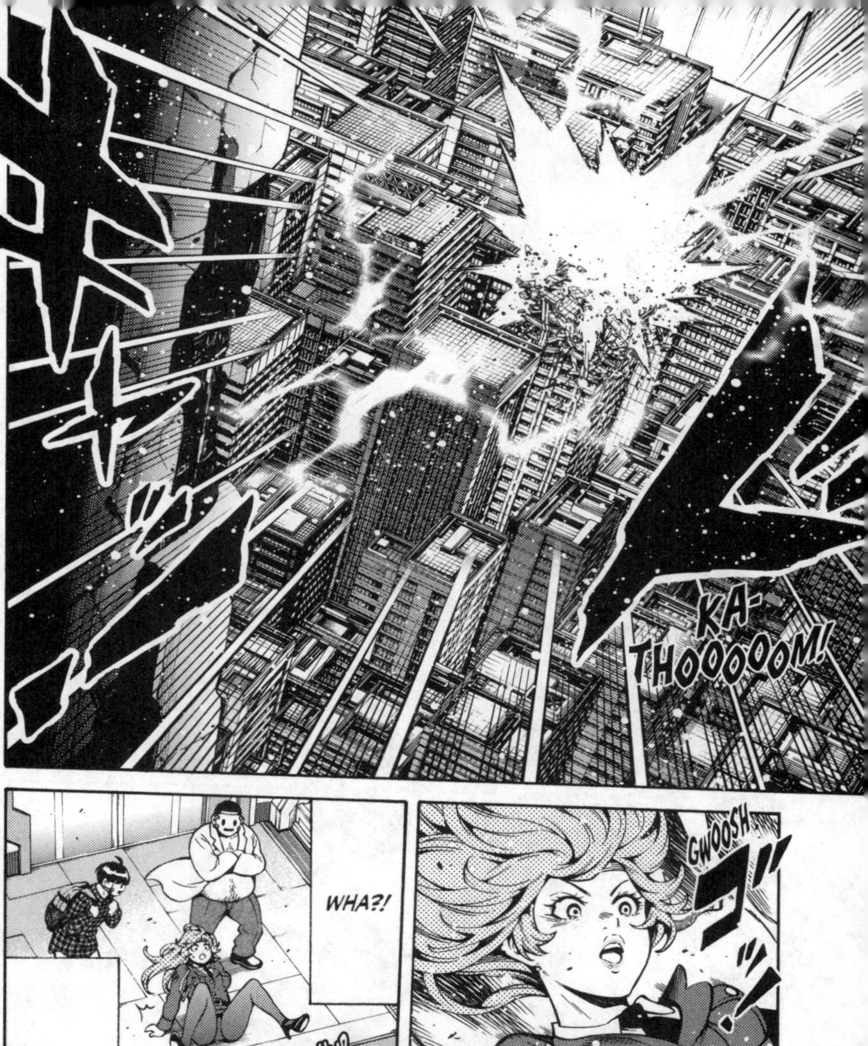
KA-THOOOOOM!
GWOOSH
WHA?!
WHAT THE HELL?!
DWUMP

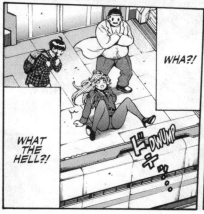

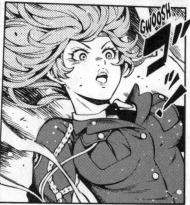

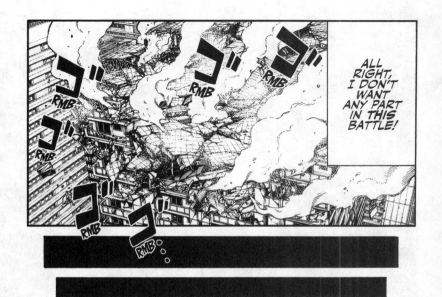

ALL RIGHT, I DON'T WANT ANY PART IN THIS BATTLE!

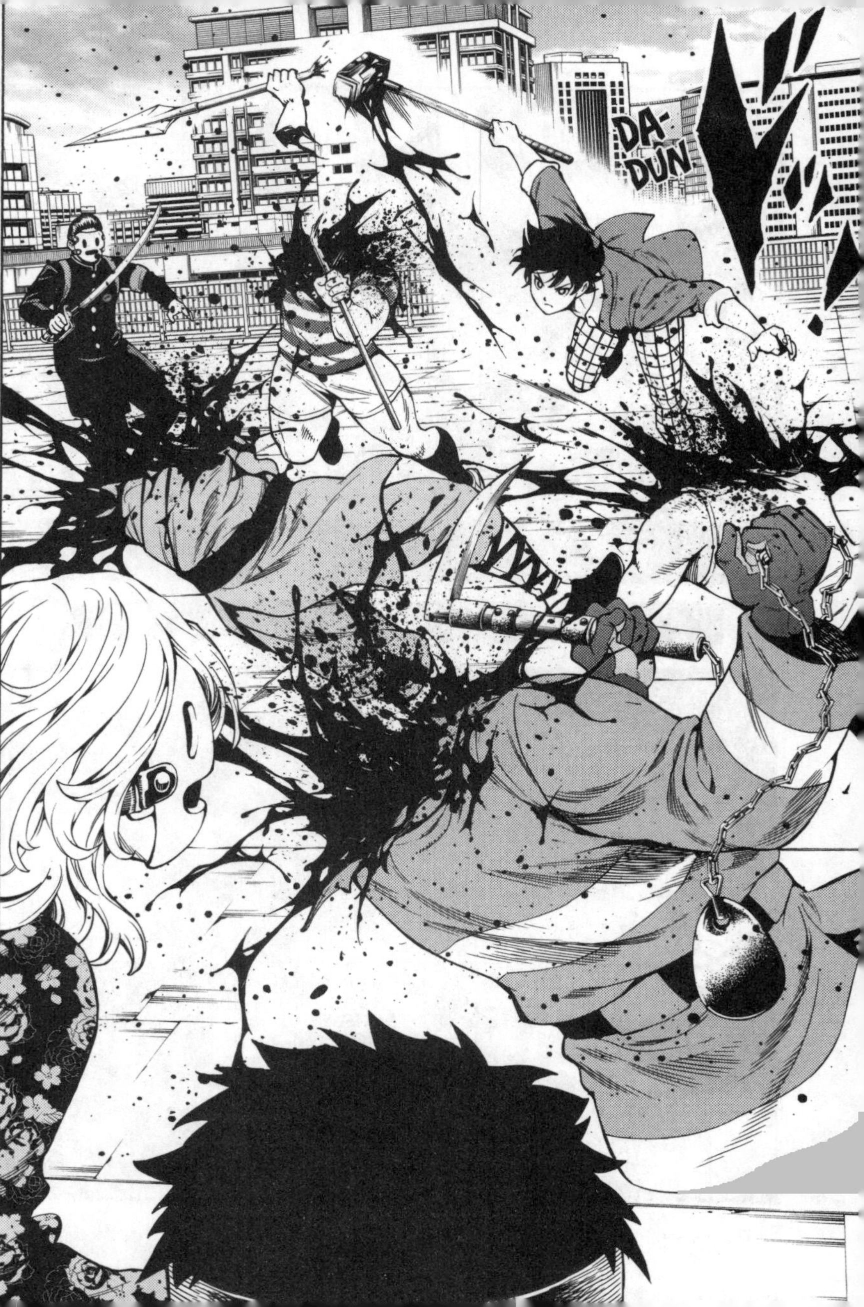
DA-DUN

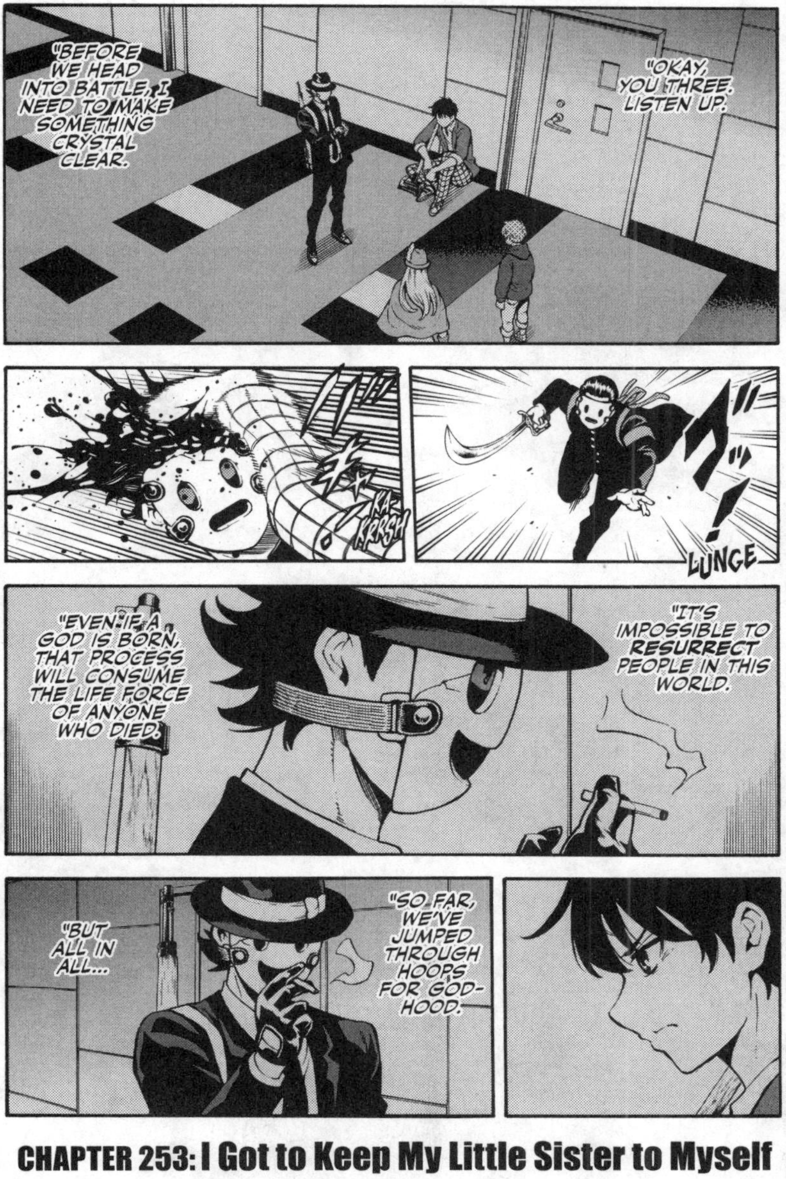
"OKAY, YOU THREE. LISTEN UP.
"BEFORE WE HEAD INTO BATTLE, I NEED TO MAKE SOMETHING CRYSTAL CLEAR.
LUNGE
KAR KRRSH
"IT'S IMPOSSIBLE TO RESURRECT PEOPLE IN THIS WORLD.
"EVEN IF A GOD IS BORN, THAT PROCESS WILL CONSUME THE LIFE FORCE OF ANYONE WHO DIED.
"SO FAR, WE'VE JUMPED THROUGH HOOPS FOR GOD-HOOD.
"BUT ALL IN ALL...

CHAPTER 253: I Got to Keep My Little Sister to Myself

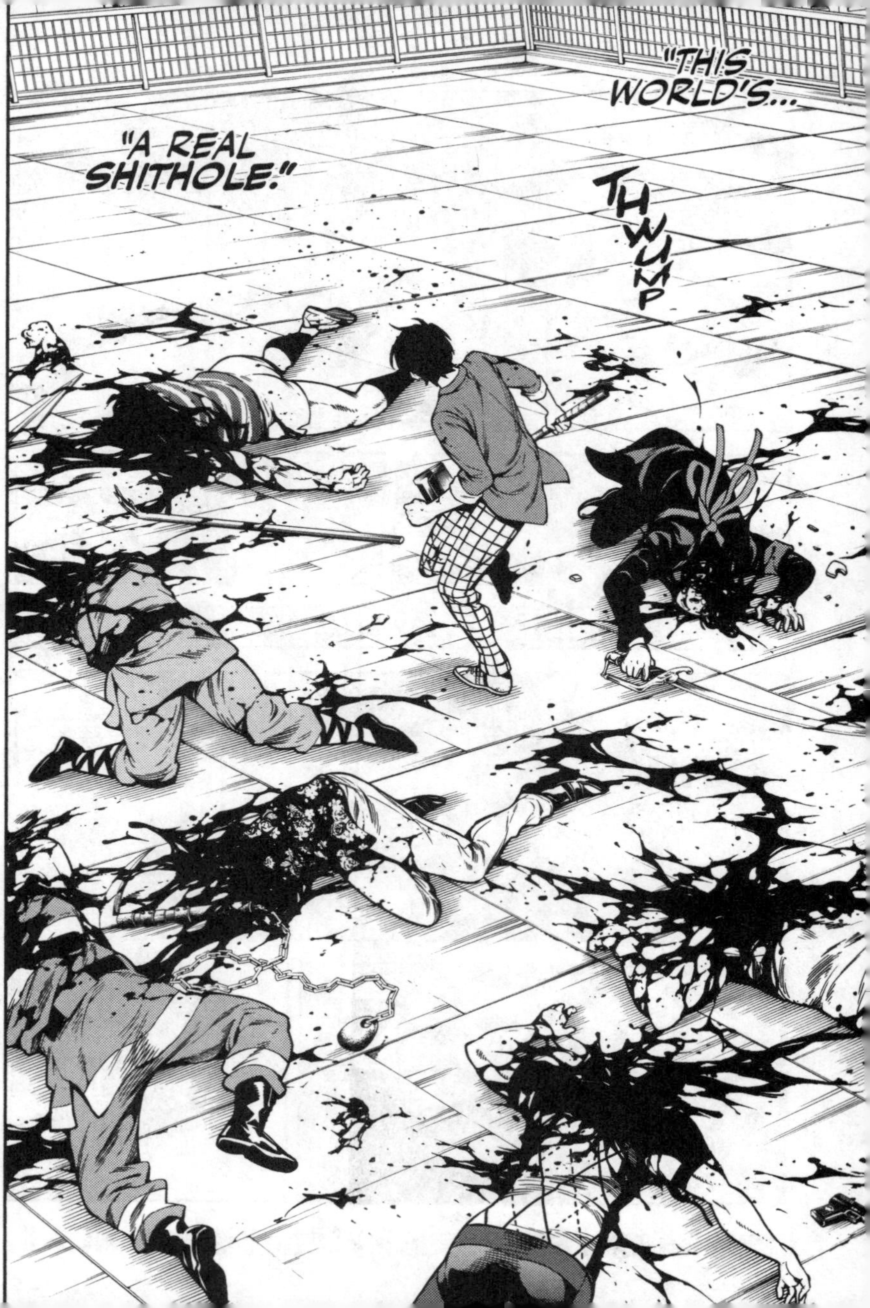

"THIS WORLD'S...
THWUMP
"A REAL SHITHOLE."

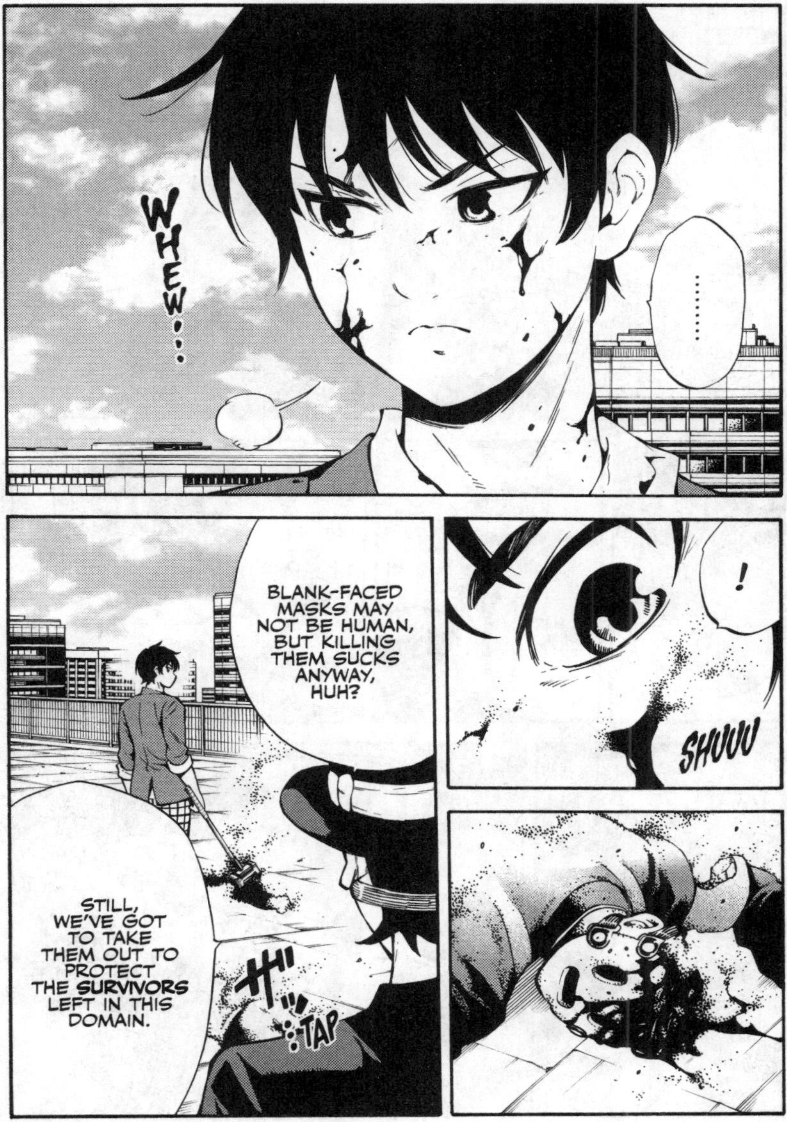
......
WHEW...
!
SHUUU
BLANK-FACED MASKS MAY NOT BE HUMAN, BUT KILLING THEM SUCKS ANYWAY, HUH?
STILL, WE'VE GOT TO TAKE THEM OUT TO PROTECT THE **SURVIVORS** LEFT IN THIS DOMAIN.
TAP

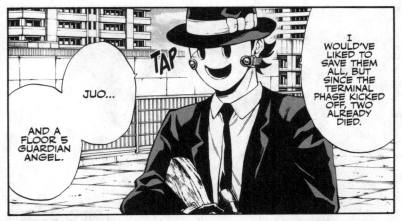

I WOULD'VE LIKED TO SAVE THEM ALL, BUT SINCE THE TERMINAL PHASE KICKED OFF, TWO ALREADY DIED.
TAP
JUO...
AND A FLOOR 5 GUARDIAN ANGEL.
JUO?
DID HE KILL THE FLOOR 5?
NO. THAT ANGEL WAS KILLED BY...
OKIHARA SHINJI.
OKIHARA? GUESS HE WASN'T BRAIN-WASHED.
SIGH...
I FEEL REALLY GUILTY ABOUT WHAT HAPPENED WITH HIM. I WISH I'D BUILT A RAPPORT.
....

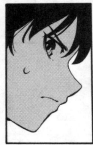

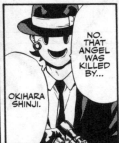

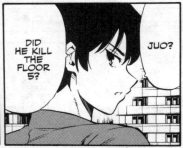

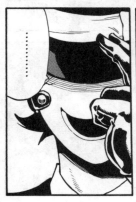

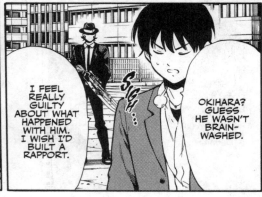

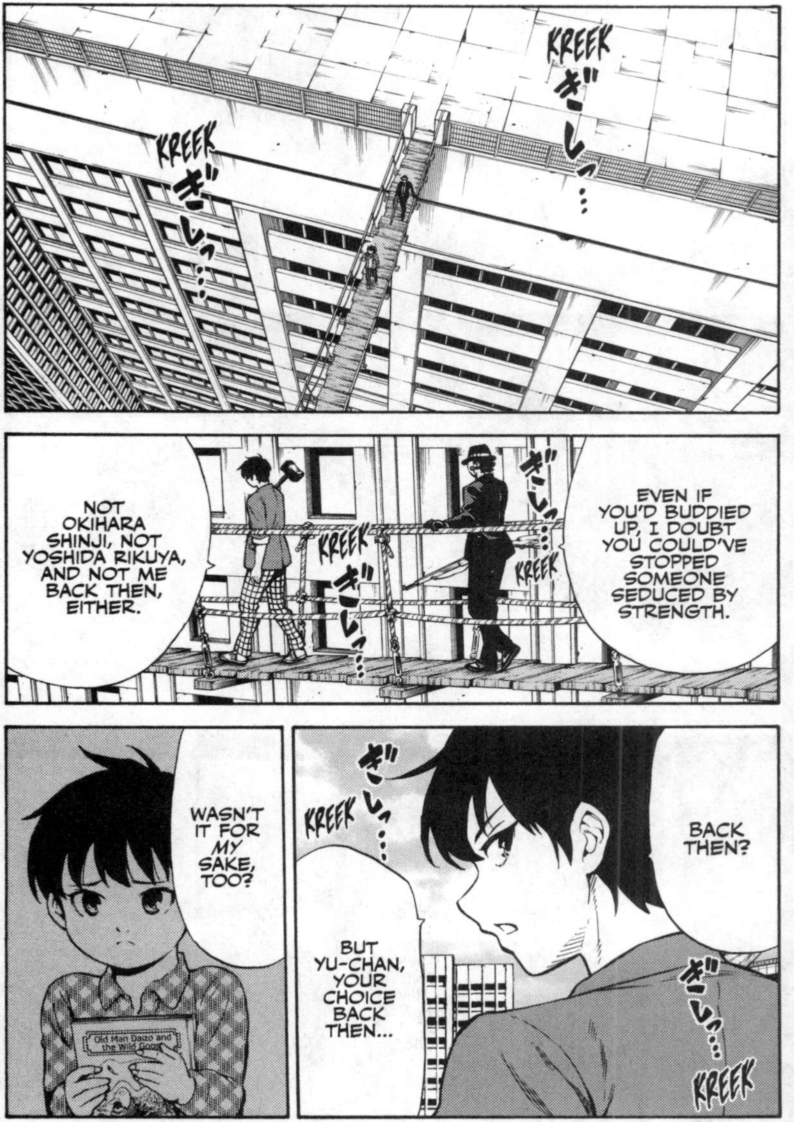
KREEK
ぎしっ…
KREEK
ぎしっ…
EVEN IF YOU'D BUDDIED UP, I DOUBT YOU COULD'VE STOPPED SOMEONE SEDUCED BY STRENGTH.
ぎしっ…
KREEK
KREEK
ぎしっ…
NOT OKIHARA SHINJI, NOT YOSHIDA RIKUYA, AND NOT ME BACK THEN, EITHER.
BACK THEN?
ぎしっ…
KREEK
KREEK
ぎしっ…
BUT YU-CHAN, YOUR CHOICE BACK THEN...
WASN'T IT FOR MY SAKE, TOO?
Old Man Daizo and the Wild Goos

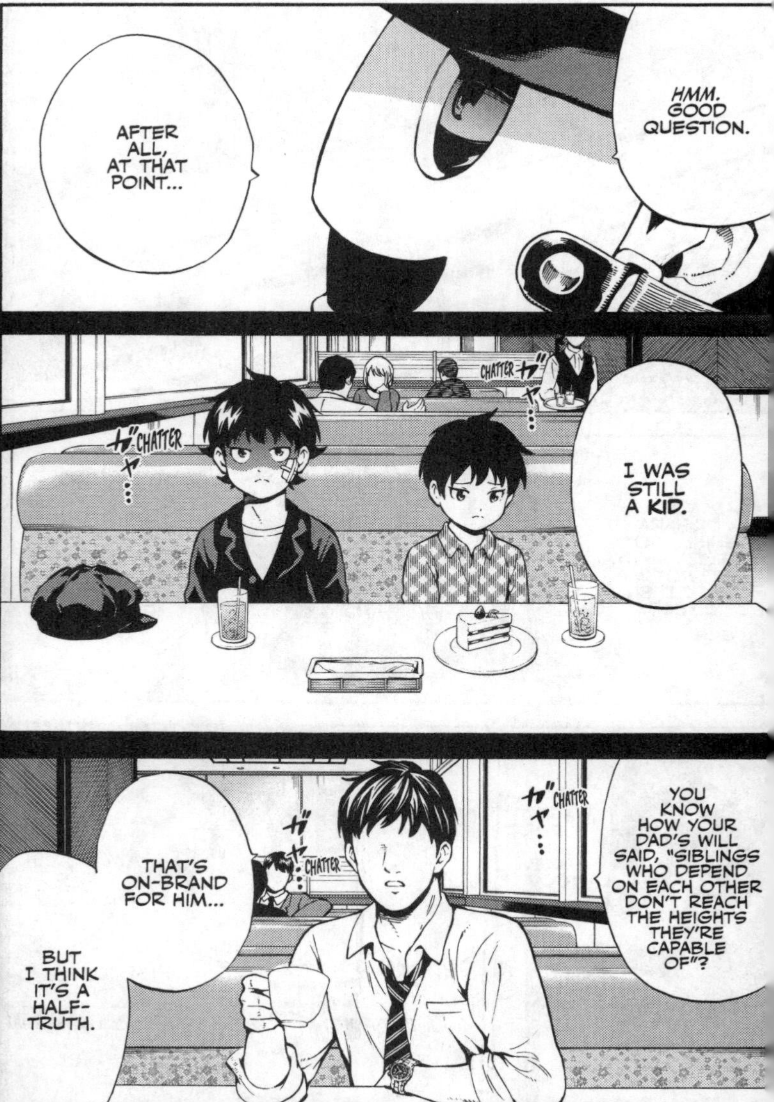
HMM. GOOD QUESTION.
AFTER ALL, AT THAT POINT...
CHATTER
I WAS STILL A **KID.**
CHATTER
YOU KNOW HOW YOUR DAD'S WILL SAID, "SIBLINGS WHO DEPEND ON EACH OTHER DON'T REACH THE HEIGHTS THEY'RE CAPABLE OF"?
CHATTER
CHATTER
THAT'S ON-BRAND FOR HIM...
BUT I THINK IT'S A HALF-TRUTH.

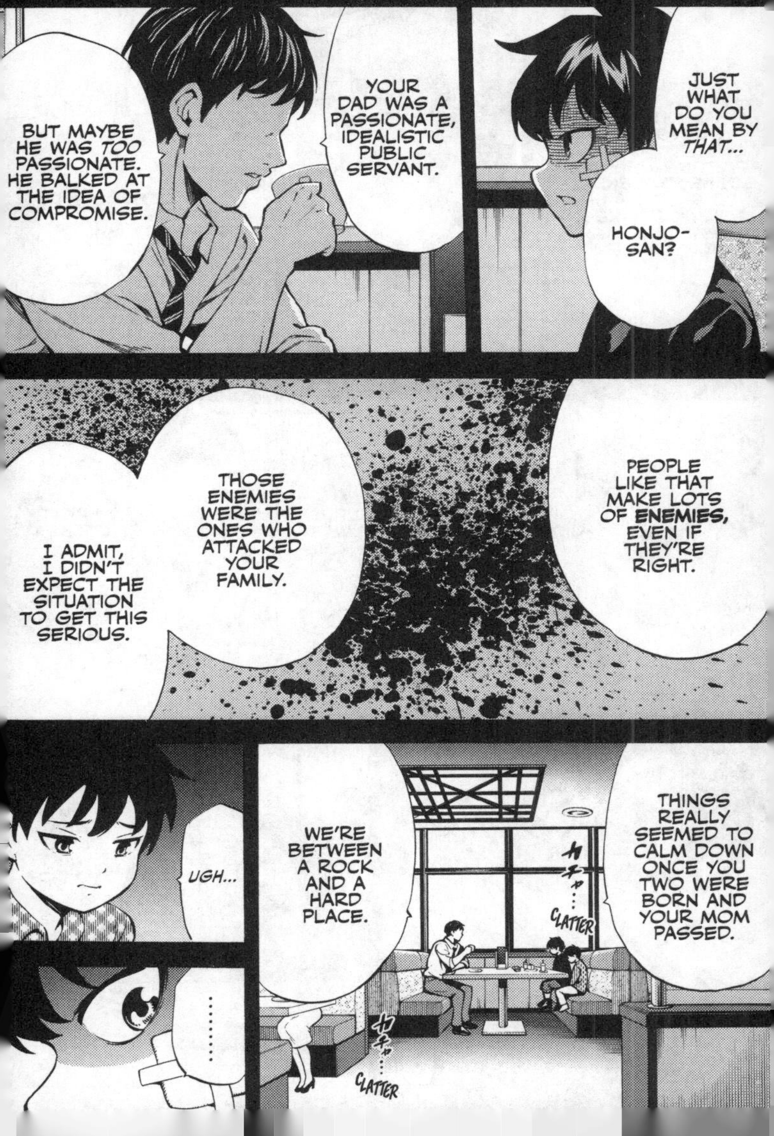
JUST WHAT DO YOU MEAN BY *THAT*...
HONJO-SAN?
YOUR DAD WAS A PASSIONATE, IDEALISTIC PUBLIC SERVANT.
BUT MAYBE HE WAS *TOO* PASSIONATE. HE BALKED AT THE IDEA OF COMPROMISE.
PEOPLE LIKE THAT MAKE LOTS OF **ENEMIES,** EVEN IF THEY'RE RIGHT.
THOSE ENEMIES WERE THE ONES WHO ATTACKED YOUR FAMILY.
I ADMIT, I DIDN'T EXPECT THE SITUATION TO GET THIS SERIOUS.
THINGS REALLY SEEMED TO CALM DOWN ONCE YOU TWO WERE BORN AND YOUR MOM PASSED.
CLATTER
WE'RE BETWEEN A ROCK AND A HARD PLACE.
CLATTER
UGH...
......

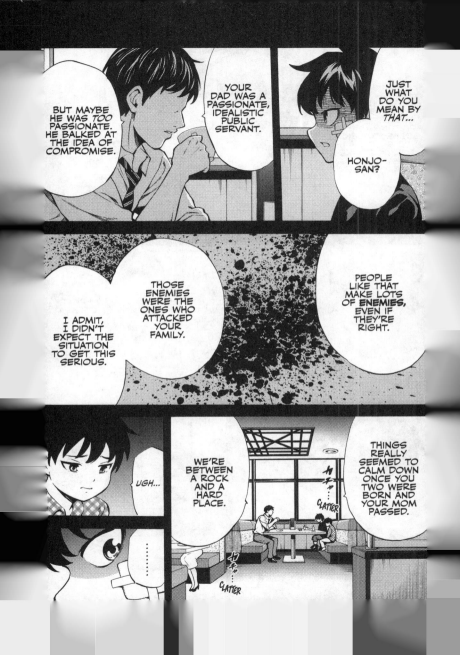

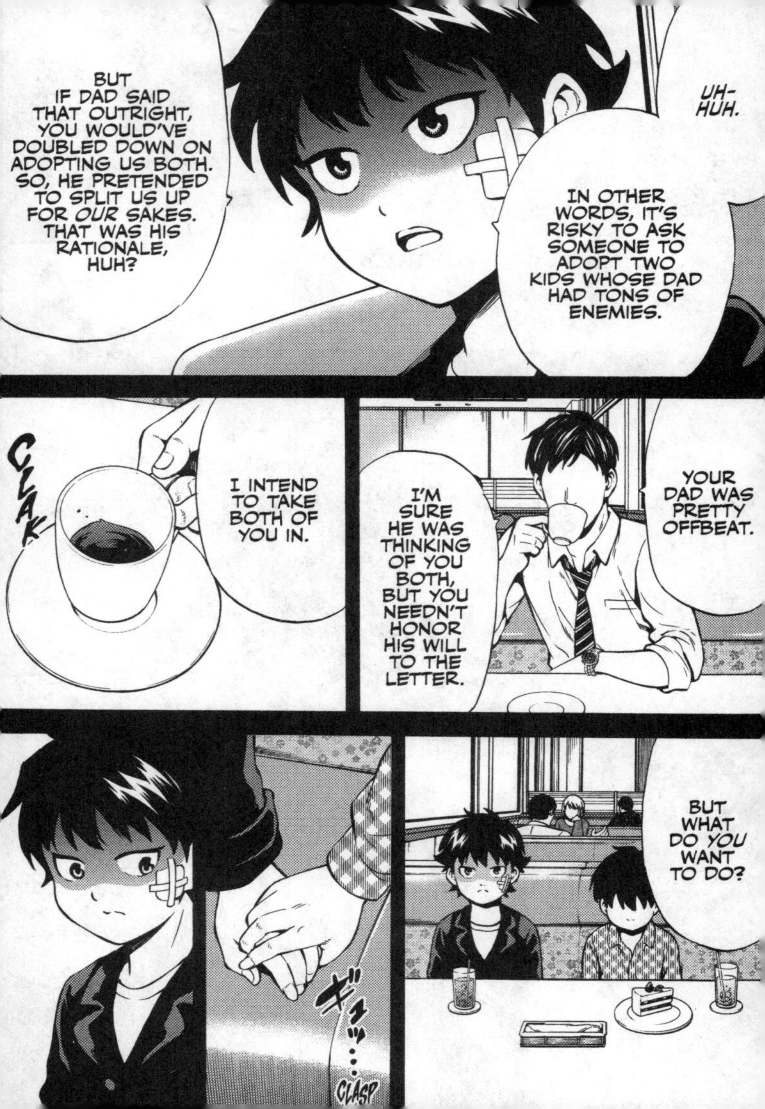
UH-HUH.
IN OTHER WORDS, IT'S RISKY TO ASK SOMEONE TO ADOPT TWO KIDS WHOSE DAD HAD TONS OF ENEMIES.
BUT IF DAD SAID THAT OUTRIGHT, YOU WOULD'VE DOUBLED DOWN ON ADOPTING US BOTH. SO, HE PRETENDED TO SPLIT US UP FOR *OUR* SAKES. THAT WAS HIS RATIONALE, HUH?
YOUR DAD WAS PRETTY OFFBEAT.
I'M SURE HE WAS THINKING OF YOU BOTH, BUT YOU NEEDN'T HONOR HIS WILL TO THE LETTER.
I INTEND TO TAKE BOTH OF YOU IN.
CLAK
BUT WHAT DO *YOU* WANT TO DO?
CLASP

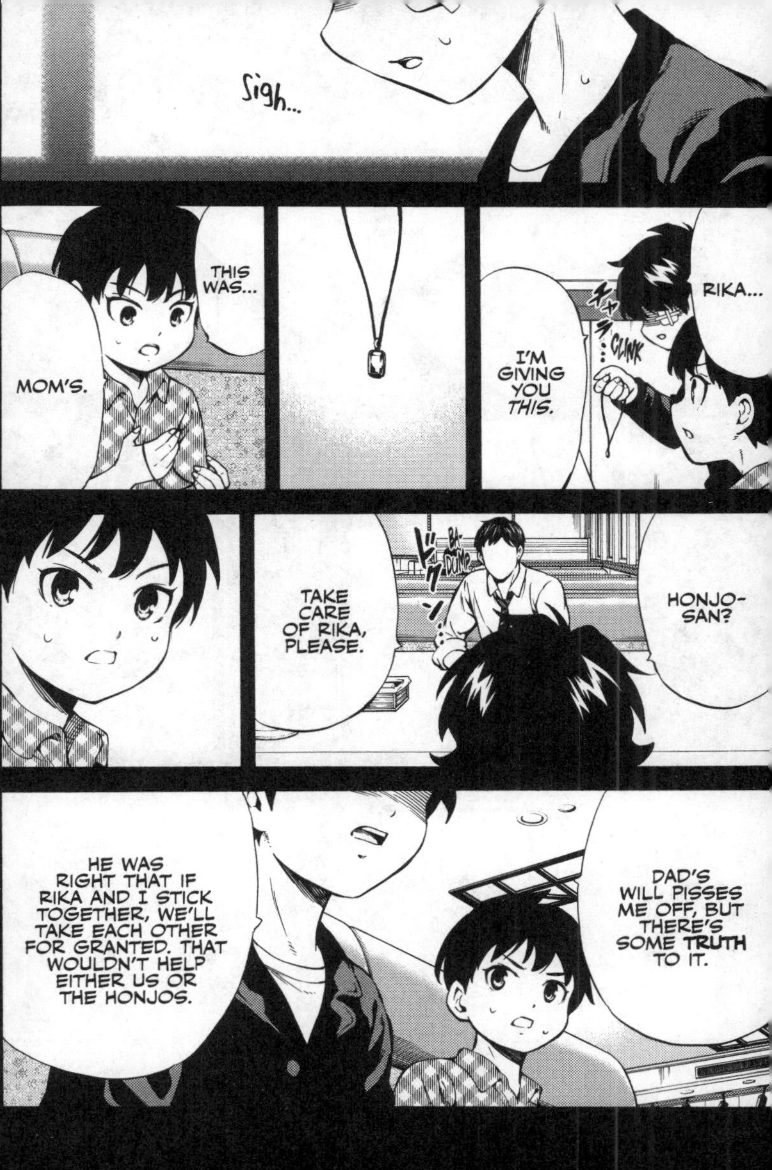
Sigh...
RIKA...
I'M GIVING YOU THIS.
CLINK
THIS WAS...
MOM'S.
HONJO-SAN?
TAKE CARE OF RIKA, PLEASE.
BA-DUMP
DAD'S WILL PISSES ME OFF, BUT THERE'S SOME TRUTH TO IT.
HE WAS RIGHT THAT IF RIKA AND I STICK TOGETHER, WE'LL TAKE EACH OTHER FOR GRANTED. THAT WOULDN'T HELP EITHER US OR THE HONJOS.

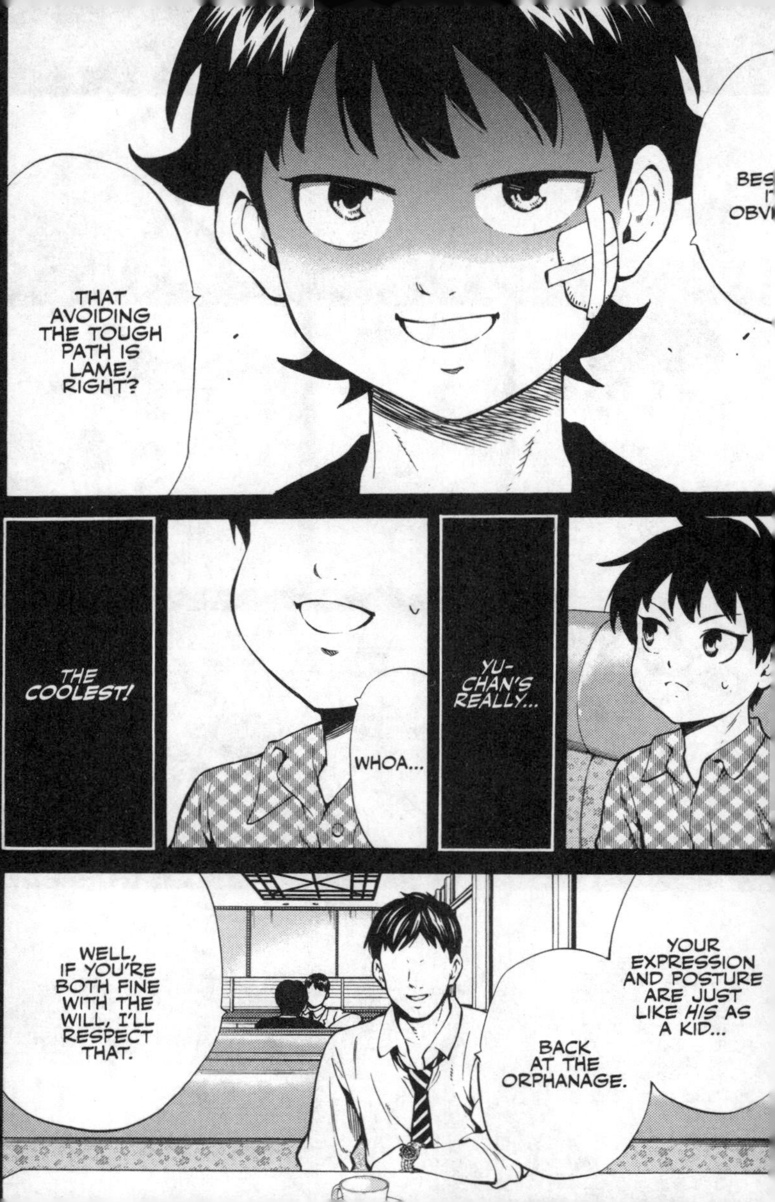
THAT AVOIDING THE TOUGH PATH IS LAME, RIGHT?
YU-CHAN'S REALLY...
WHOA...
THE COOLEST!
YOUR EXPRESSION AND POSTURE ARE JUST LIKE *HIS* AS A KID...
BACK AT THE ORPHANAGE.
WELL, IF YOU'RE BOTH FINE WITH THE WILL, I'LL RESPECT THAT.

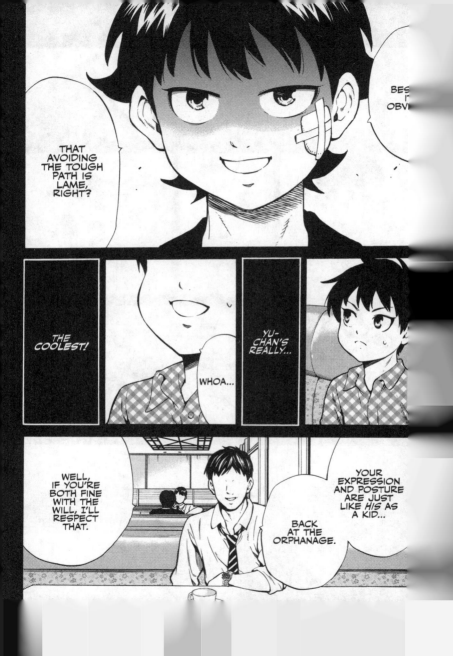

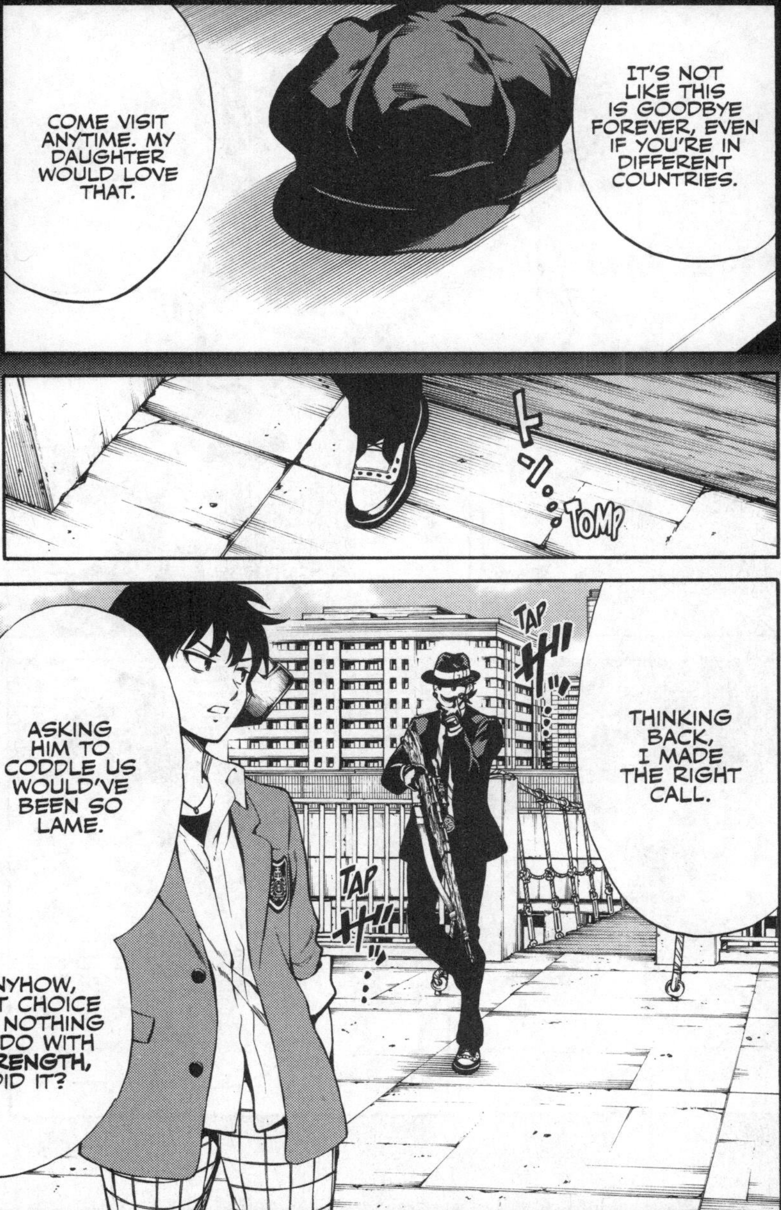
IT'S NOT LIKE THIS IS GOODBYE FOREVER, EVEN IF YOU'RE IN DIFFERENT COUNTRIES.
COME VISIT ANYTIME. MY DAUGHTER WOULD LOVE THAT.
TOMP
THINKING BACK, I MADE THE RIGHT CALL.
TAP
TAP
ASKING HIM TO CODDLE US WOULD'VE BEEN SO LAME.
ANYHOW, THAT CHOICE HAD NOTHING TO DO WITH **STRENGTH,** DID IT?

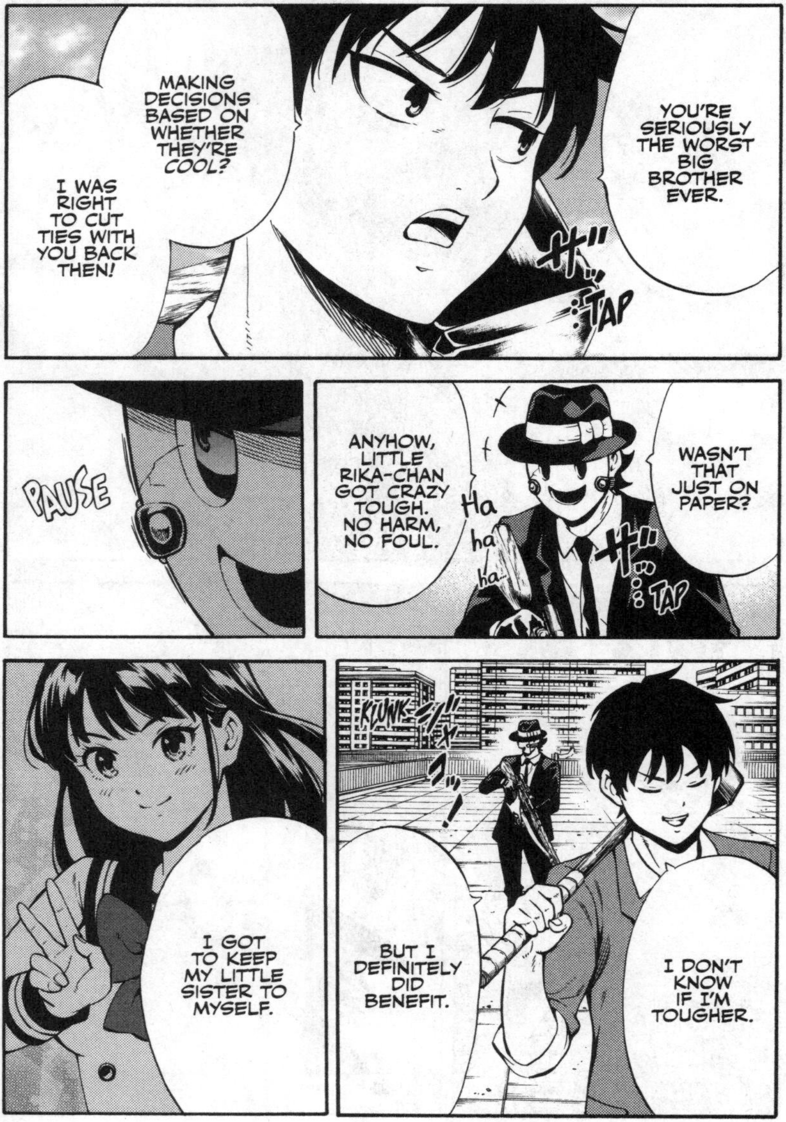
YOU'RE SERIOUSLY THE WORST BIG BROTHER EVER.
TAP
MAKING DECISIONS BASED ON WHETHER THEY'RE *COOL?*
I WAS RIGHT TO CUT TIES WITH YOU BACK THEN!
WASN'T THAT JUST ON PAPER?
TAP
ANYHOW, LITTLE RIKA-CHAN GOT CRAZY TOUGH. NO HARM, NO FOUL.
Ha ha ha...
PAUSE
KLUNK
I DON'T KNOW IF I'M TOUGHER.
BUT I DEFINITELY DID BENEFIT.
I GOT TO KEEP MY LITTLE SISTER TO MYSELF.

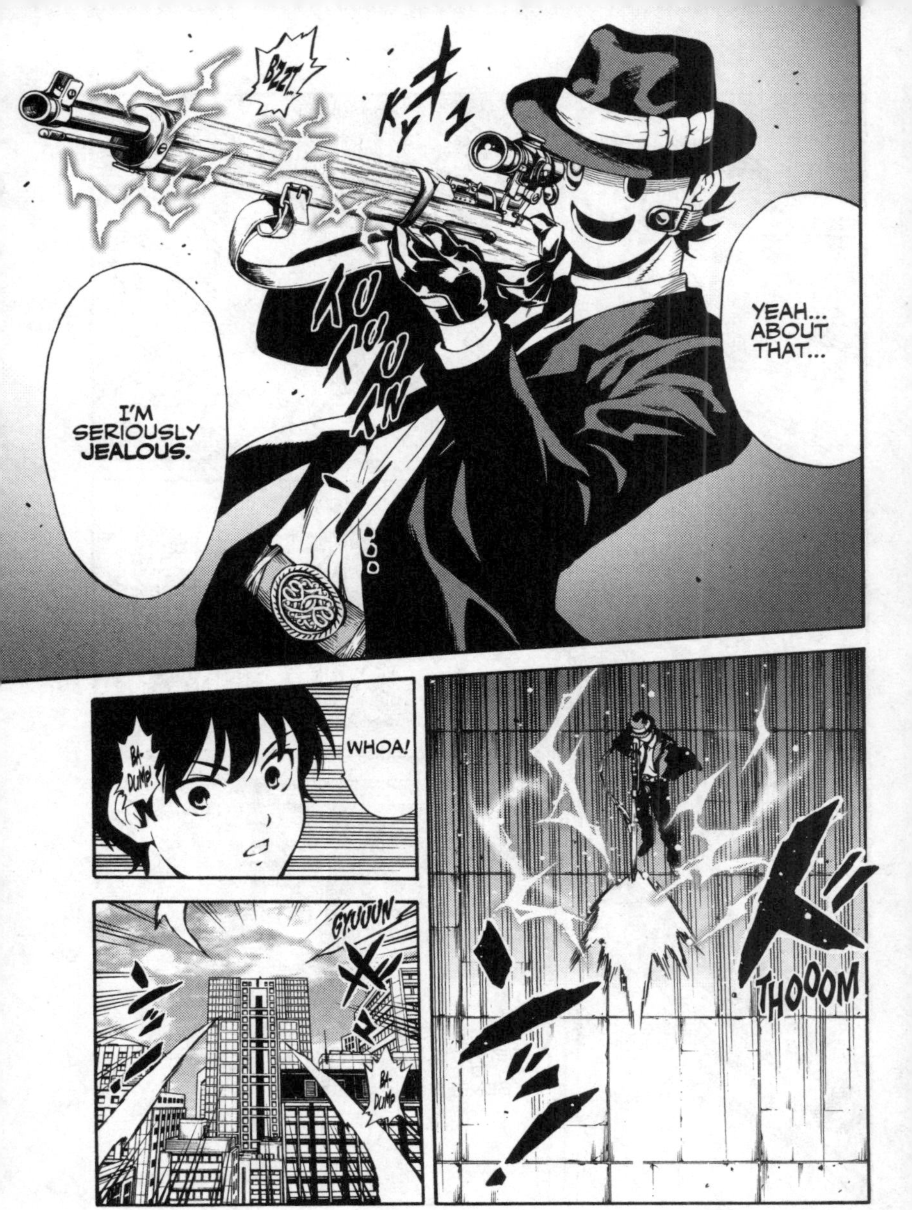
BZZT
YEAH... ABOUT THAT...
I'M SERIOUSLY JEALOUS.
THOOOM
WHOA!
BA-DUMP!
GYUUUN
BA-DUMP

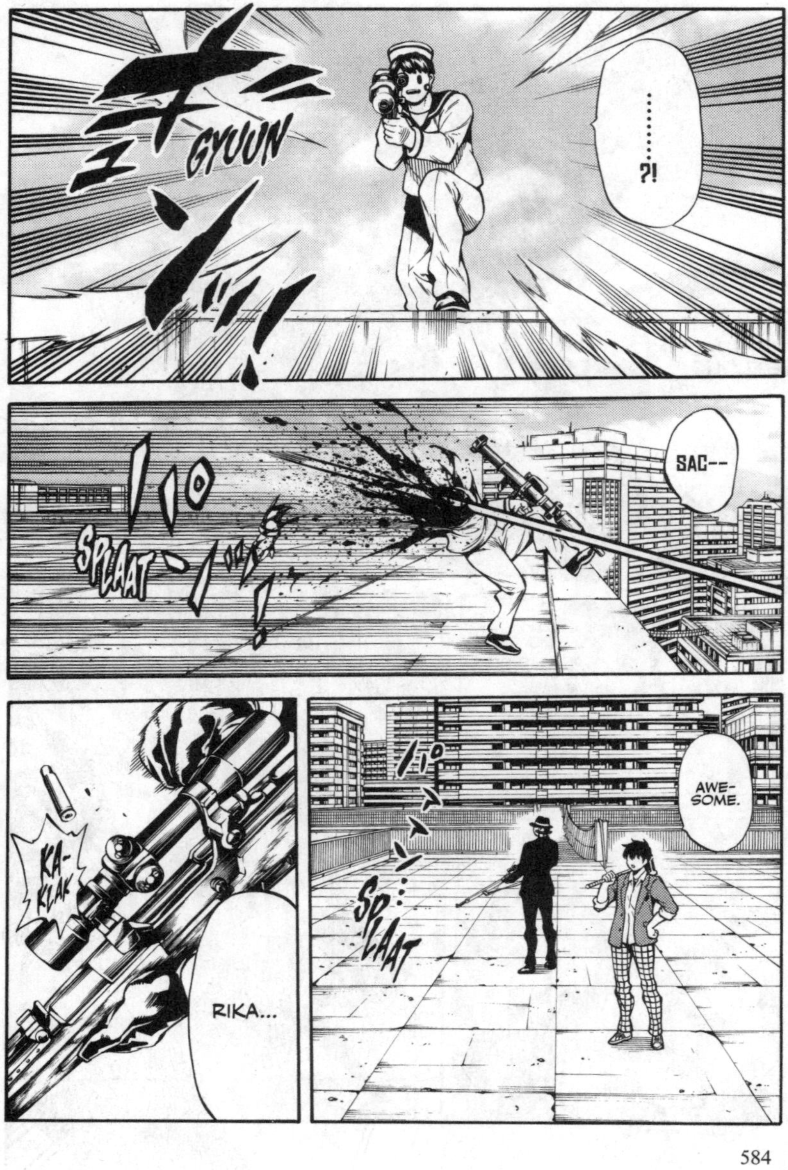
......?!
GYUUN
SAC--
SPLAAT
AWE-SOME.
SPLAAT
KA-KLAK
RIKA...

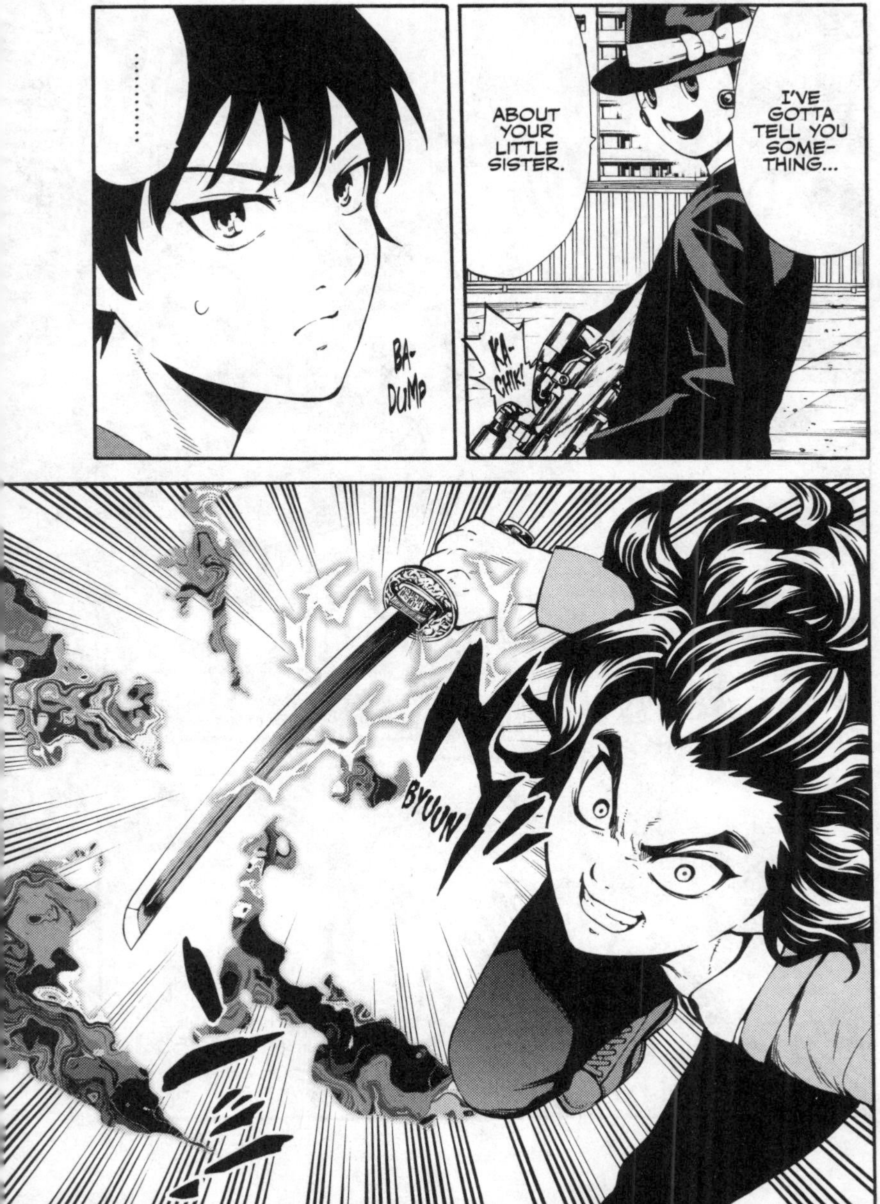
I'VE GOTTA TELL YOU SOME-THING...
ABOUT YOUR LITTLE SISTER.
KA-CHIK!
......
BA-DUMP
BYUUN

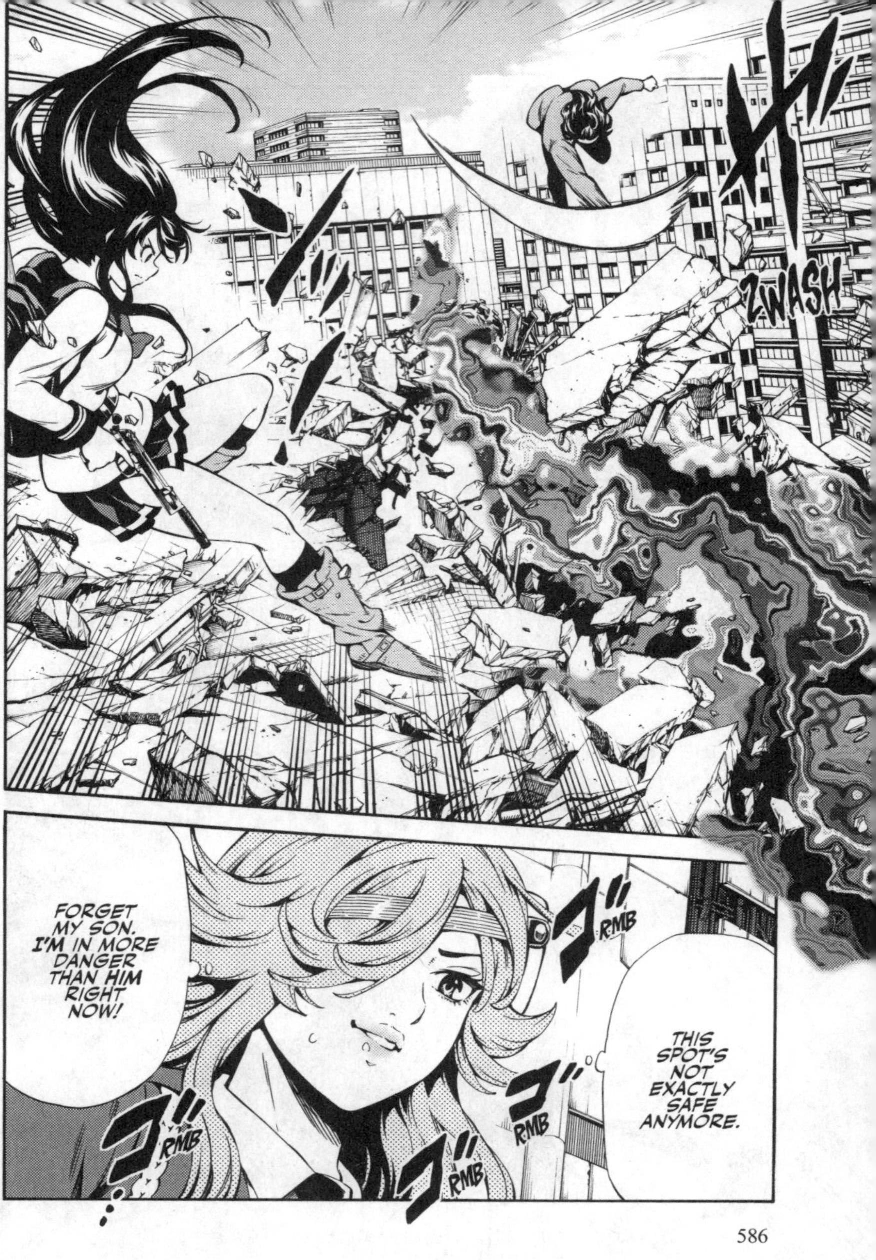
ZWASH
RMB
THIS SPOT'S NOT EXACTLY SAFE ANYMORE.
RMB
FORGET MY SON. I'M IN MORE DANGER THAN HIM RIGHT NOW!
RMB
RMB

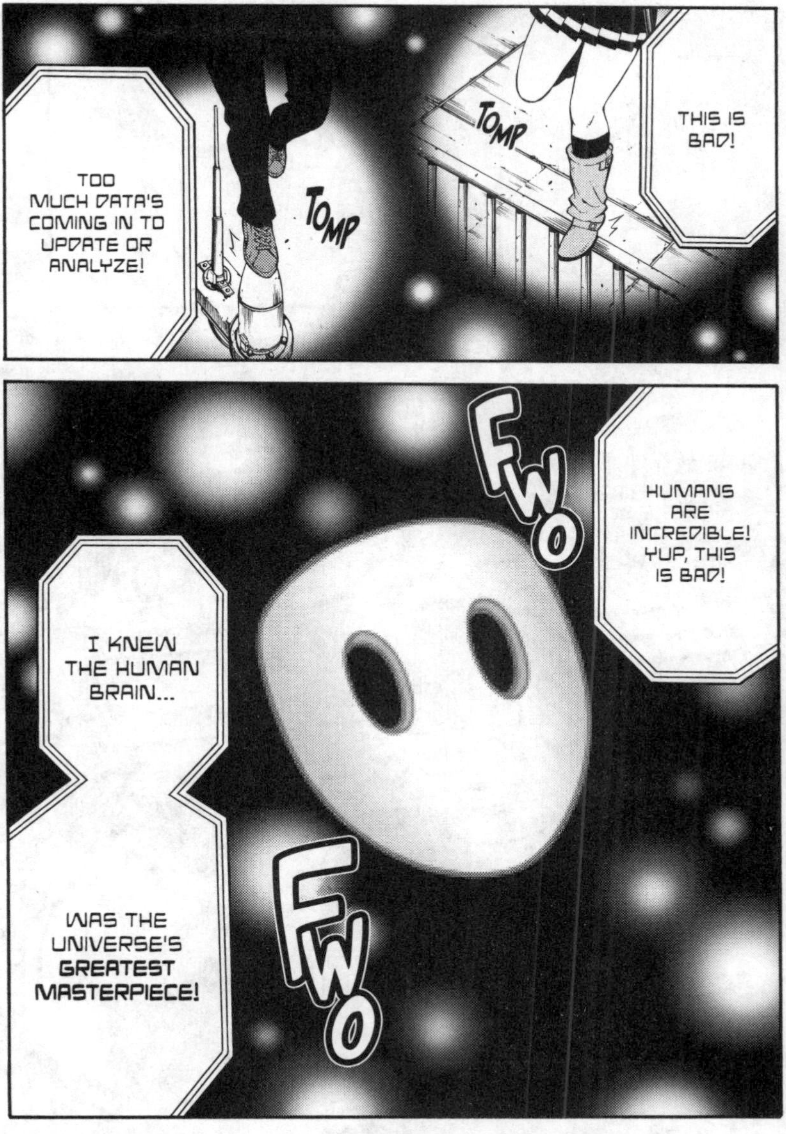
THIS IS BAD!
TOMP
TOMP
TOO MUCH DATA'S COMING IN TO UPDATE OR ANALYZE!
HUMANS ARE INCREDIBLE! YUP, THIS IS BAD!
FWO
I KNEW THE HUMAN BRAIN...
WAS THE UNIVERSE'S GREATEST MASTERPIECE!
FWO

CHAPTER 254: Hypostatic Union

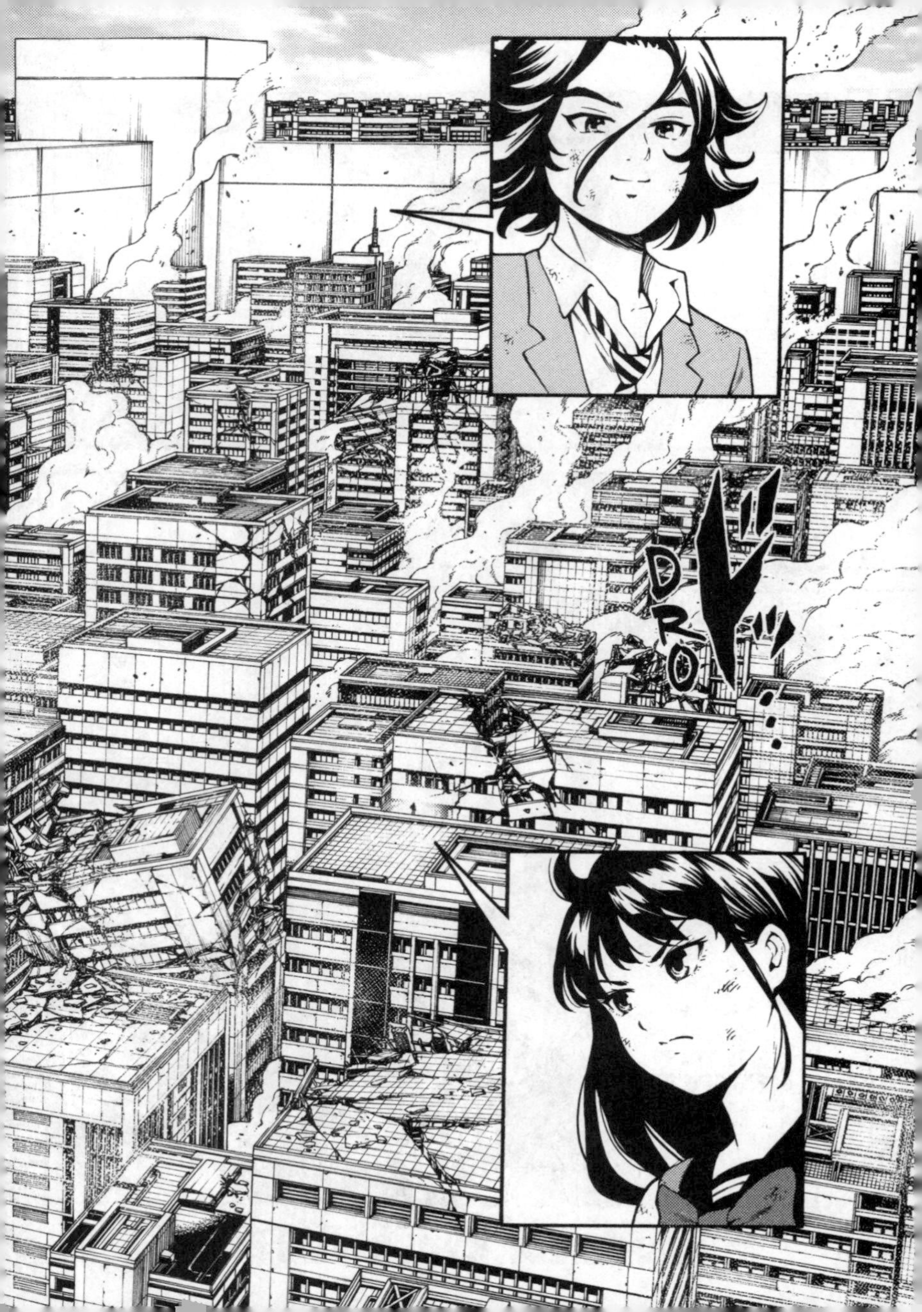
DRO

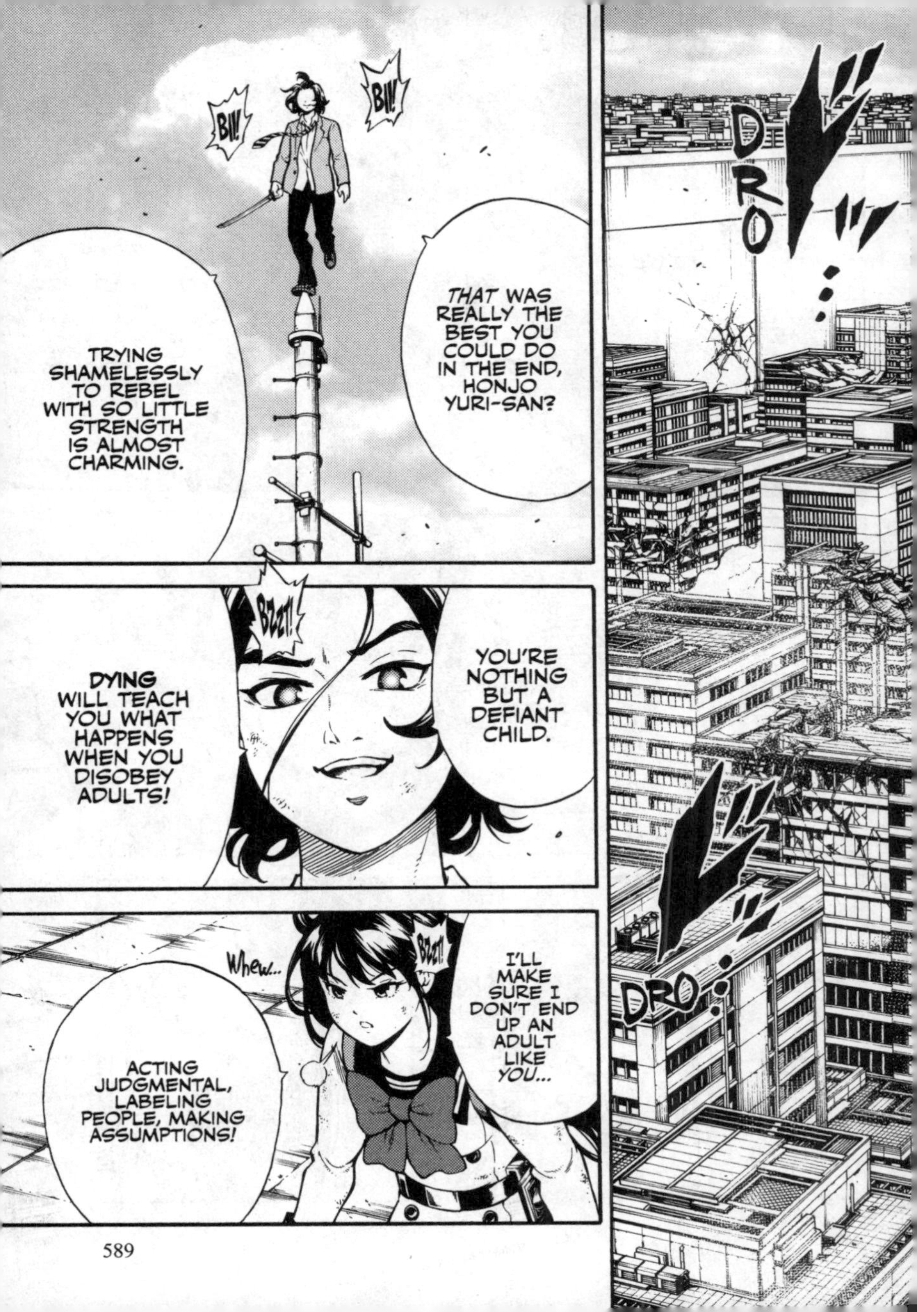
DRO
DRO...
BIV!
BIV!
THAT WAS REALLY THE BEST YOU COULD DO IN THE END, HONJO YURI-SAN?
TRYING SHAMELESSLY TO REBEL WITH SO LITTLE STRENGTH IS ALMOST CHARMING.
BZZT!
YOU'RE NOTHING BUT A DEFIANT CHILD.
DYING WILL TEACH YOU WHAT HAPPENS WHEN YOU DISOBEY ADULTS!
BZZT!
I'LL MAKE SURE I DON'T END UP AN ADULT LIKE YOU...
Whew...
ACTING JUDGMENTAL, LABELING PEOPLE, MAKING ASSUMPTIONS!

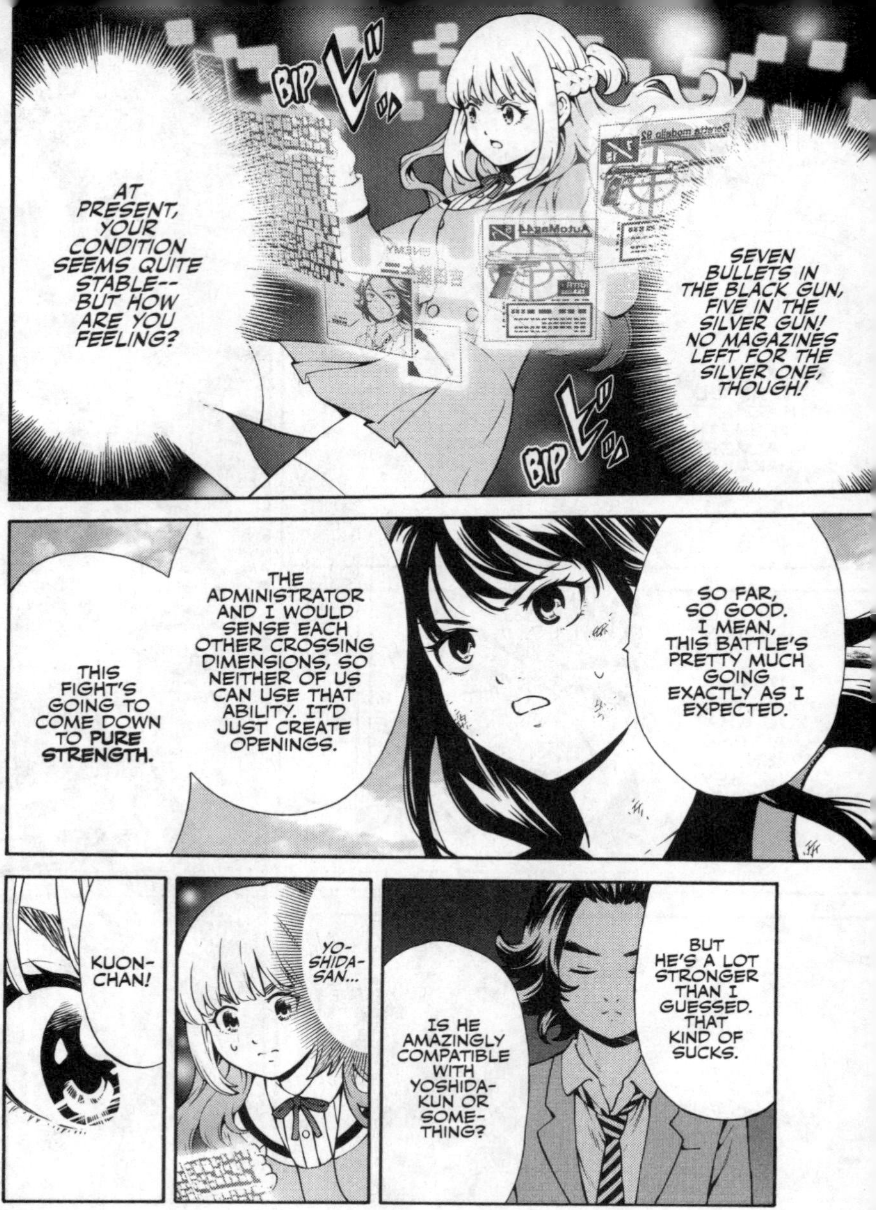
SEVEN BULLETS IN THE BLACK GUN, FIVE IN THE SILVER GUN! NO MAGAZINES LEFT FOR THE SILVER ONE, THOUGH!
BIP
AT PRESENT, YOUR CONDITION SEEMS QUITE STABLE--BUT HOW ARE YOU FEELING?
BIP
SO FAR, SO GOOD. I MEAN, THIS BATTLE'S PRETTY MUCH GOING EXACTLY AS I EXPECTED.
THE ADMINISTRATOR AND I WOULD SENSE EACH OTHER CROSSING DIMENSIONS, SO NEITHER OF US CAN USE THAT ABILITY. IT'D JUST CREATE OPENINGS.
THIS FIGHT'S GOING TO COME DOWN TO PURE STRENGTH.
BUT HE'S A LOT STRONGER THAN I GUESSED. THAT KIND OF SUCKS.
IS HE AMAZINGLY COMPATIBLE WITH YOSHIDA-KUN OR SOME-THING?
YO-SHIDA-SAN...
KUON-CHAN!

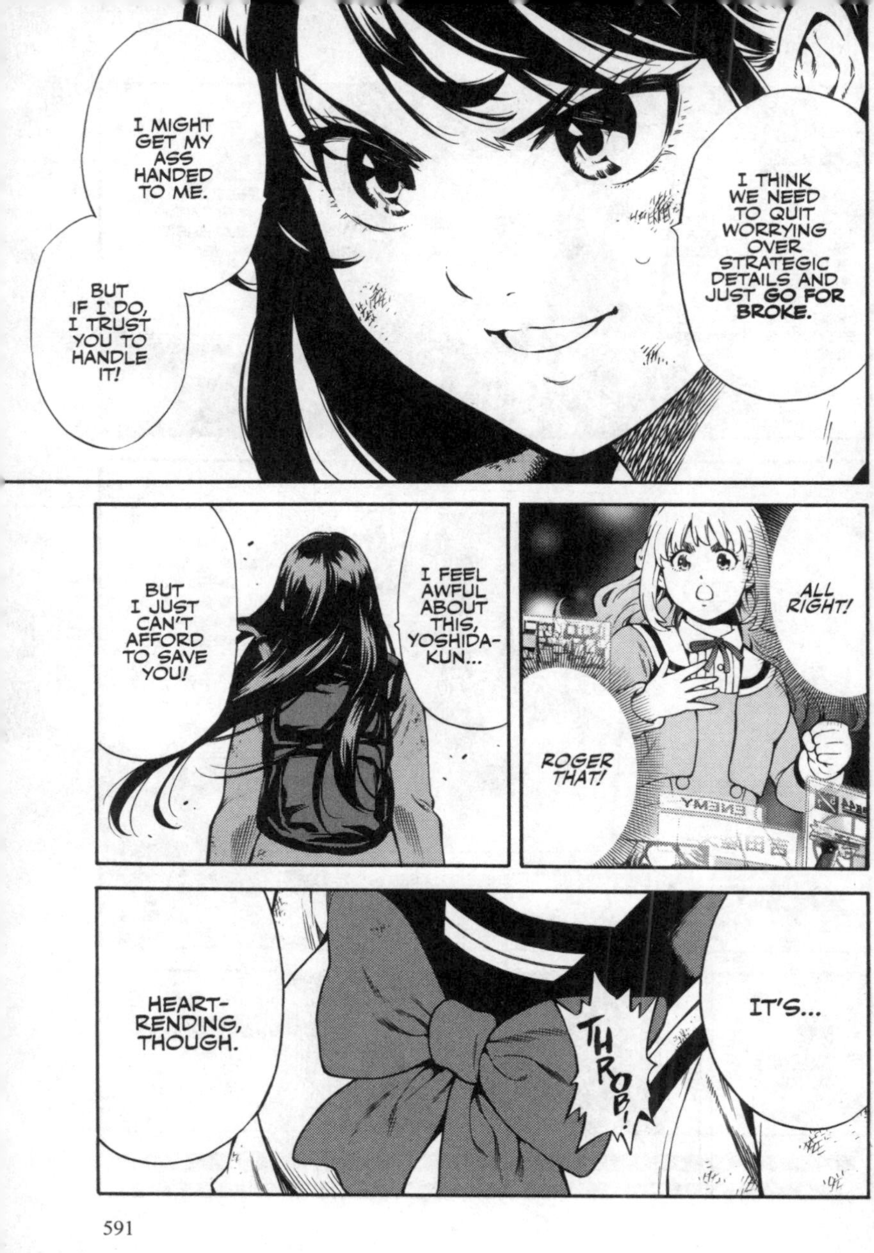
I THINK WE NEED TO QUIT WORRYING OVER STRATEGIC DETAILS AND JUST **GO FOR BROKE.**
I MIGHT GET MY ASS HANDED TO ME.
BUT IF I DO, I TRUST YOU TO HANDLE IT!
ALL RIGHT!
ROGER THAT!
I FEEL AWFUL ABOUT THIS, YOSHIDA-KUN...
BUT I JUST CAN'T AFFORD TO SAVE YOU!
IT'S...
THROB!
HEART-RENDING, THOUGH.

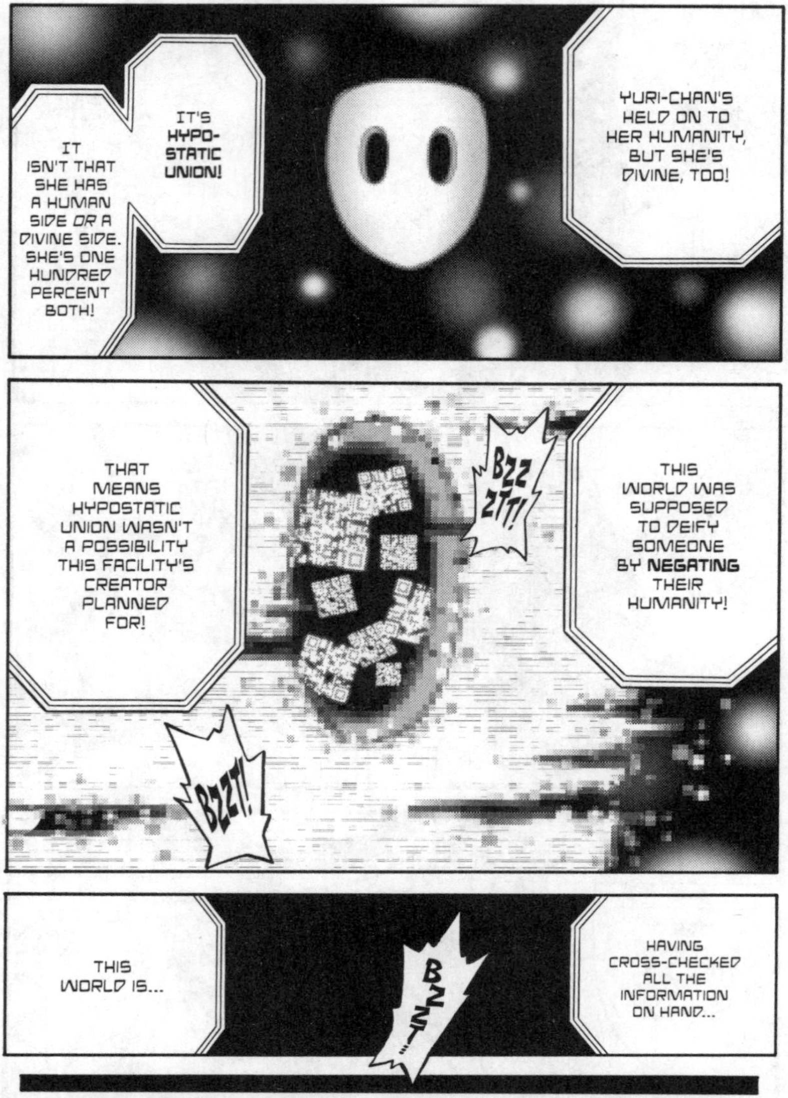
YURI-CHAN'S HELD ON TO HER HUMANITY, BUT SHE'S DIVINE, TOO!
IT'S HYPO-STATIC UNION!
IT ISN'T THAT SHE HAS A HUMAN SIDE OR A DIVINE SIDE. SHE'S ONE HUNDRED PERCENT BOTH!
THIS WORLD WAS SUPPOSED TO DEIFY SOMEONE BY NEGATING THEIR HUMANITY!
BZZ ZTT!
THAT MEANS HYPOSTATIC UNION WASN'T A POSSIBILITY THIS FACILITY'S CREATOR PLANNED FOR!
BZZT!
HAVING CROSS-CHECKED ALL THE INFORMATION ON HAND...
BZZT...
THIS WORLD IS...

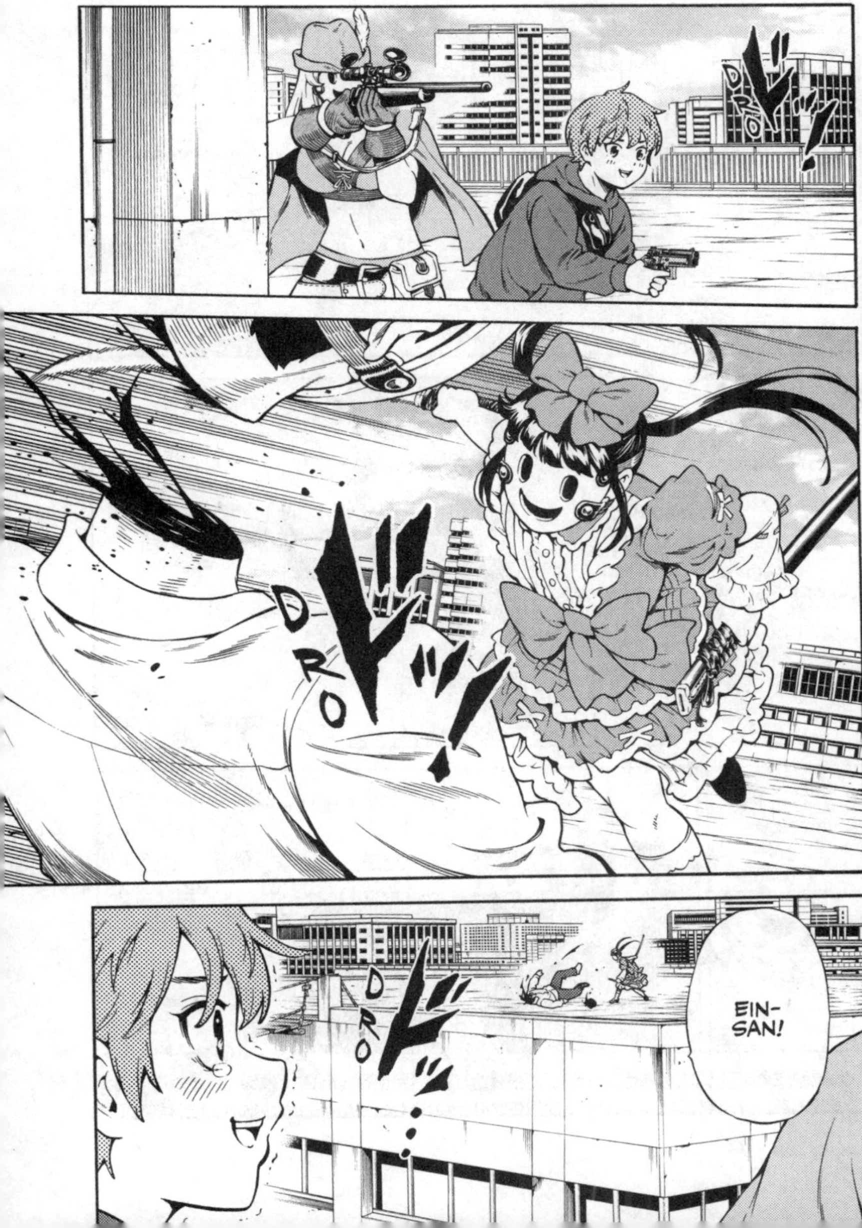
DRO!
DRO!
EIN-SAN!
DRO...

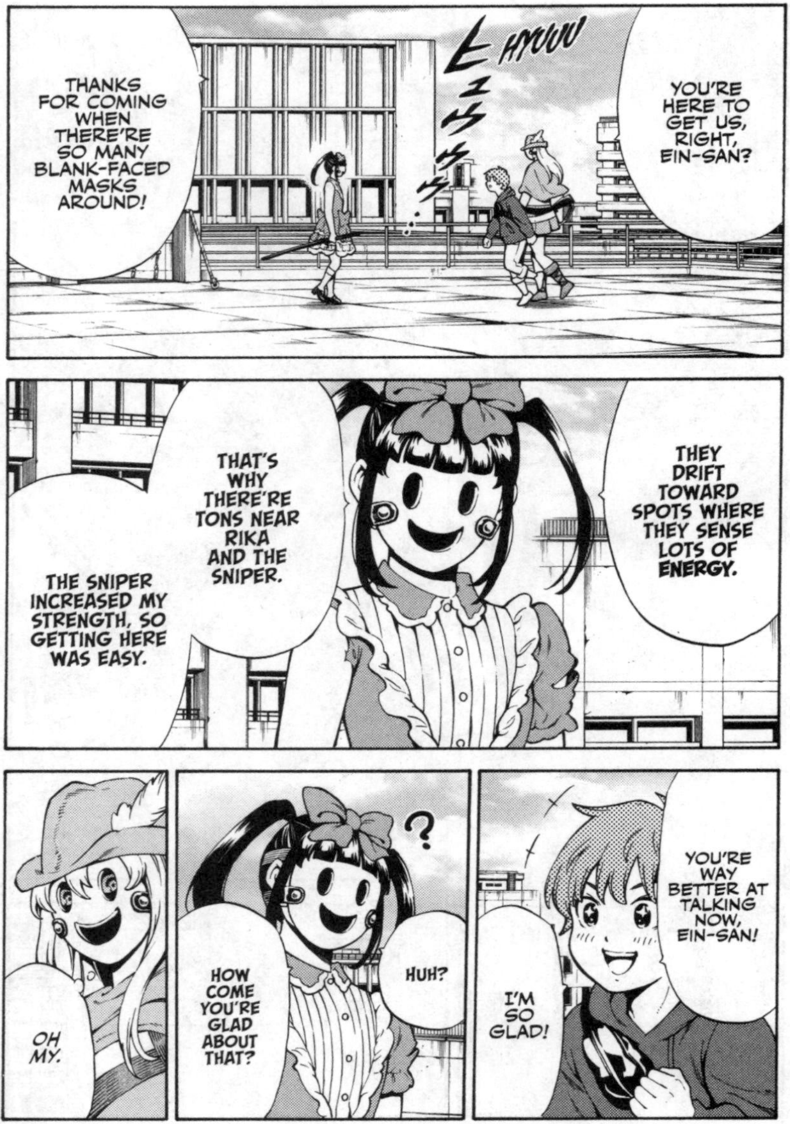
YOU'RE HERE TO GET US, RIGHT, EIN-SAN?
HYUUU
THANKS FOR COMING WHEN THERE'RE SO MANY BLANK-FACED MASKS AROUND!
THEY DRIFT TOWARD SPOTS WHERE THEY SENSE LOTS OF ENERGY.
THAT'S WHY THERE'RE TONS NEAR RIKA AND THE SNIPER.
THE SNIPER INCREASED MY STRENGTH, SO GETTING HERE WAS EASY.
YOU'RE WAY BETTER AT TALKING NOW, EIN-SAN!
I'M SO GLAD!
HUH?
HOW COME YOU'RE GLAD ABOUT THAT?
OH MY.

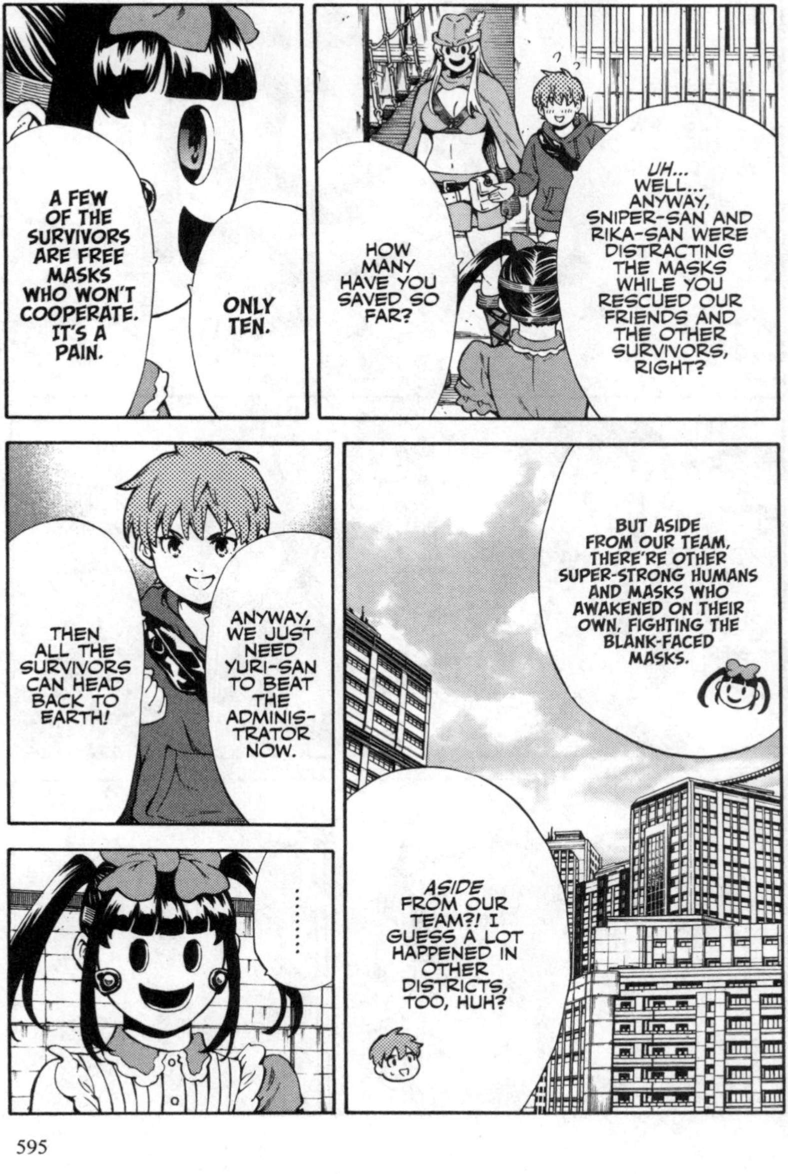
UH... WELL... ANYWAY, SNIPER-SAN AND RIKA-SAN WERE DISTRACTING THE MASKS WHILE YOU RESCUED OUR FRIENDS AND THE OTHER SURVIVORS, RIGHT?
HOW MANY HAVE YOU SAVED SO FAR?
ONLY TEN.
A FEW OF THE SURVIVORS ARE FREE MASKS WHO WON'T COOPERATE. IT'S A PAIN.
BUT ASIDE FROM OUR TEAM, THERE'RE OTHER SUPER-STRONG HUMANS AND MASKS WHO AWAKENED ON THEIR OWN, FIGHTING THE BLANK-FACED MASKS.
ASIDE FROM OUR TEAM?! I GUESS A LOT HAPPENED IN OTHER DISTRICTS, TOO, HUH?
ANYWAY, WE JUST NEED YURI-SAN TO BEAT THE ADMINIS-TRATOR NOW.
THEN ALL THE SURVIVORS CAN HEAD BACK TO EARTH!
....

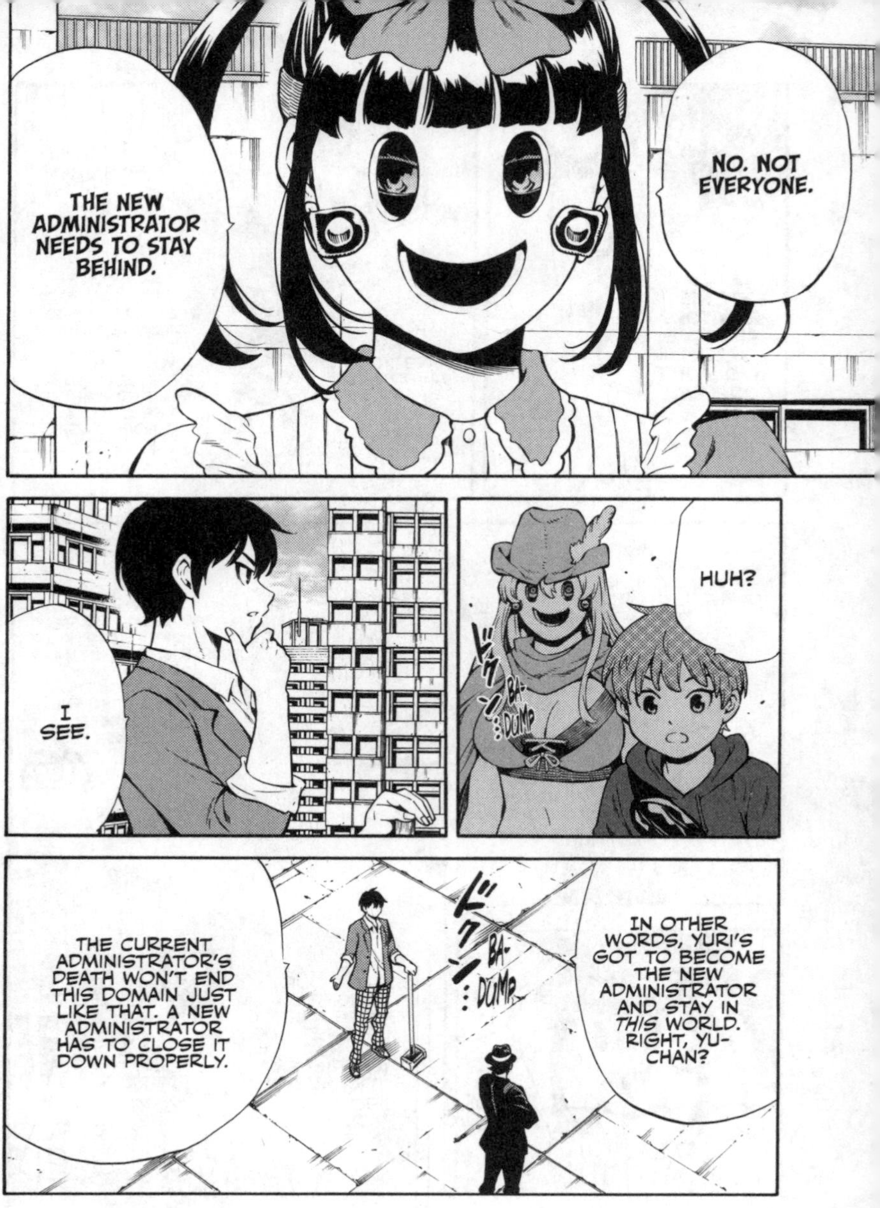
NO. NOT EVERYONE.
THE NEW ADMINISTRATOR NEEDS TO STAY BEHIND.
HUH?
BA-DUMP
I SEE.
IN OTHER WORDS, YURI'S GOT TO BECOME THE NEW ADMINISTRATOR AND STAY IN *THIS* WORLD. RIGHT, YU-CHAN?
BA-DUMP
THE CURRENT ADMINISTRATOR'S DEATH WON'T END THIS DOMAIN JUST LIKE THAT. A NEW ADMINISTRATOR HAS TO CLOSE IT DOWN PROPERLY.

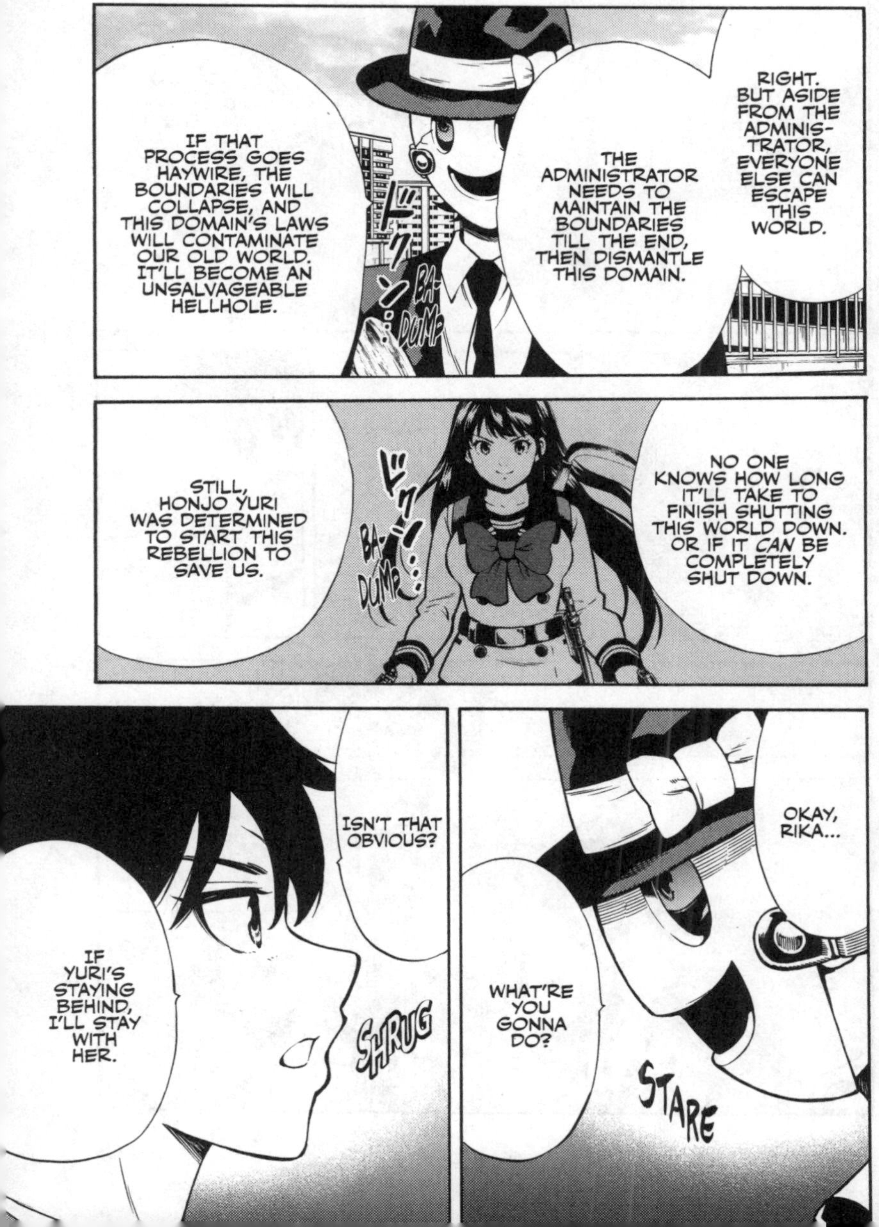
RIGHT. BUT ASIDE FROM THE ADMINISTRATOR, EVERYONE ELSE CAN ESCAPE THIS WORLD.
THE ADMINISTRATOR NEEDS TO MAINTAIN THE BOUNDARIES TILL THE END, THEN DISMANTLE THIS DOMAIN.
IF THAT PROCESS GOES HAYWIRE, THE BOUNDARIES WILL COLLAPSE, AND THIS DOMAIN'S LAWS WILL CONTAMINATE OUR OLD WORLD. IT'LL BECOME AN UNSALVAGEABLE HELLHOLE.
BA-DUMP
NO ONE KNOWS HOW LONG IT'LL TAKE TO FINISH SHUTTING THIS WORLD DOWN. OR IF IT *CAN* BE COMPLETELY SHUT DOWN.
BA-DUMP
STILL, HONJO YURI WAS DETERMINED TO START THIS REBELLION TO SAVE US.
OKAY, RIKA...
WHAT'RE YOU GONNA DO?
STARE
ISN'T THAT OBVIOUS?
SHRUG
IF YURI'S STAYING BEHIND, I'LL STAY WITH HER.

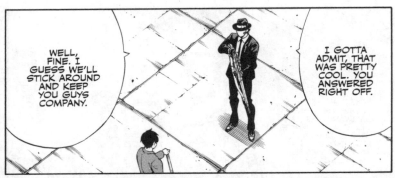

I GOTTA ADMIT, THAT WAS PRETTY COOL. YOU ANSWERED RIGHT OFF.
WELL, FINE. I GUESS WE'LL STICK AROUND AND KEEP YOU GUYS COMPANY.
ANY-HOW...
Sigh...
THAT'S ASSUMING SHE BEATS THE ADMINIS-TRATOR.
ドゴォオン…
KA-THOOOM
YURI...
YURI...

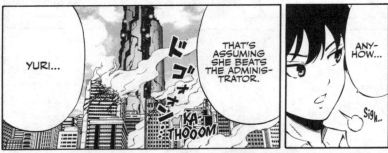

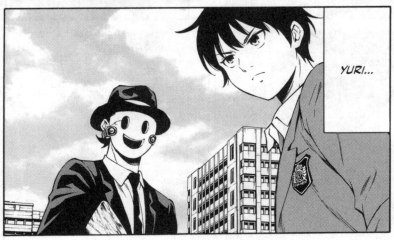

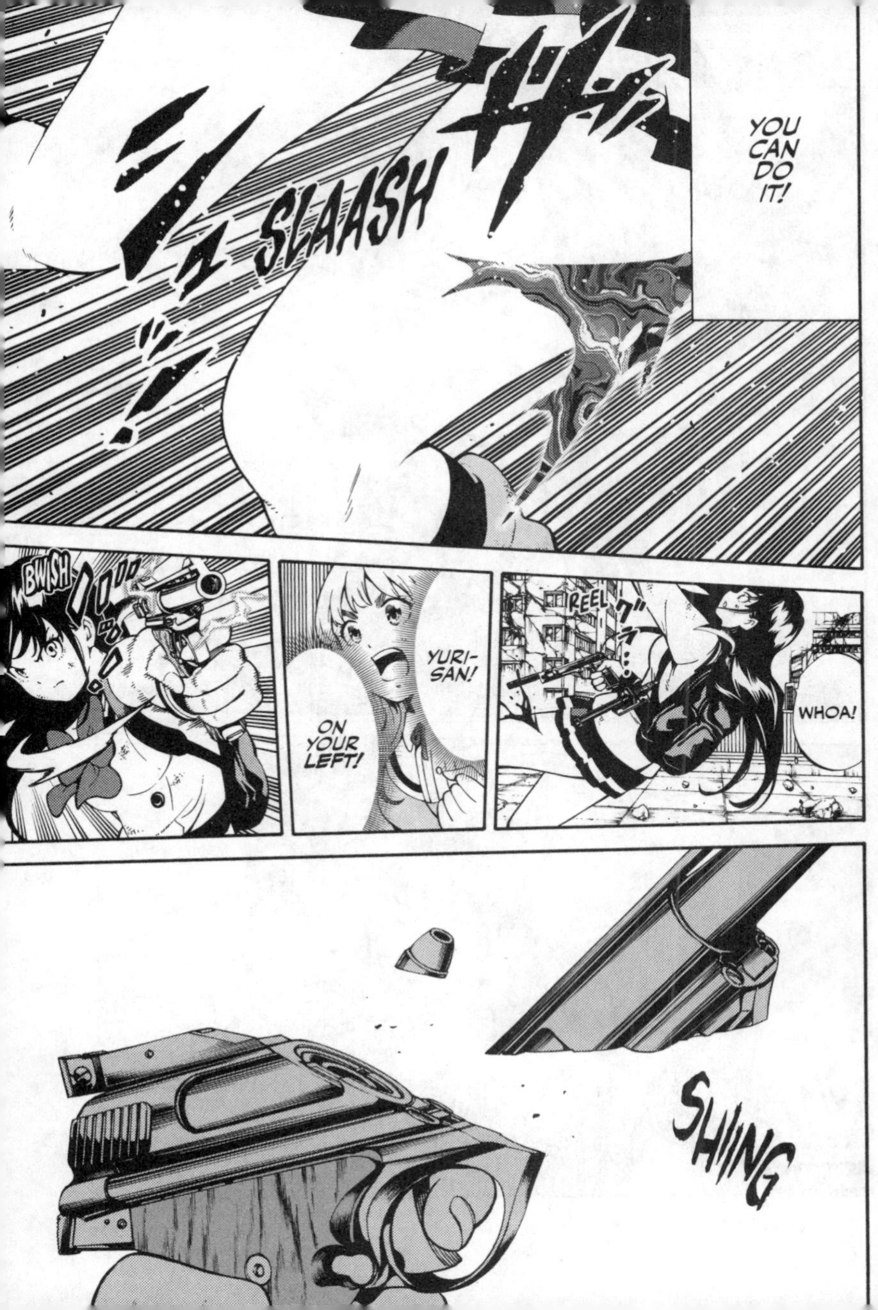
YOU CAN DO IT!
SLAASH
REEL
WHOA!
YURI-SAN!
ON YOUR LEFT!
BWISH
SHIING

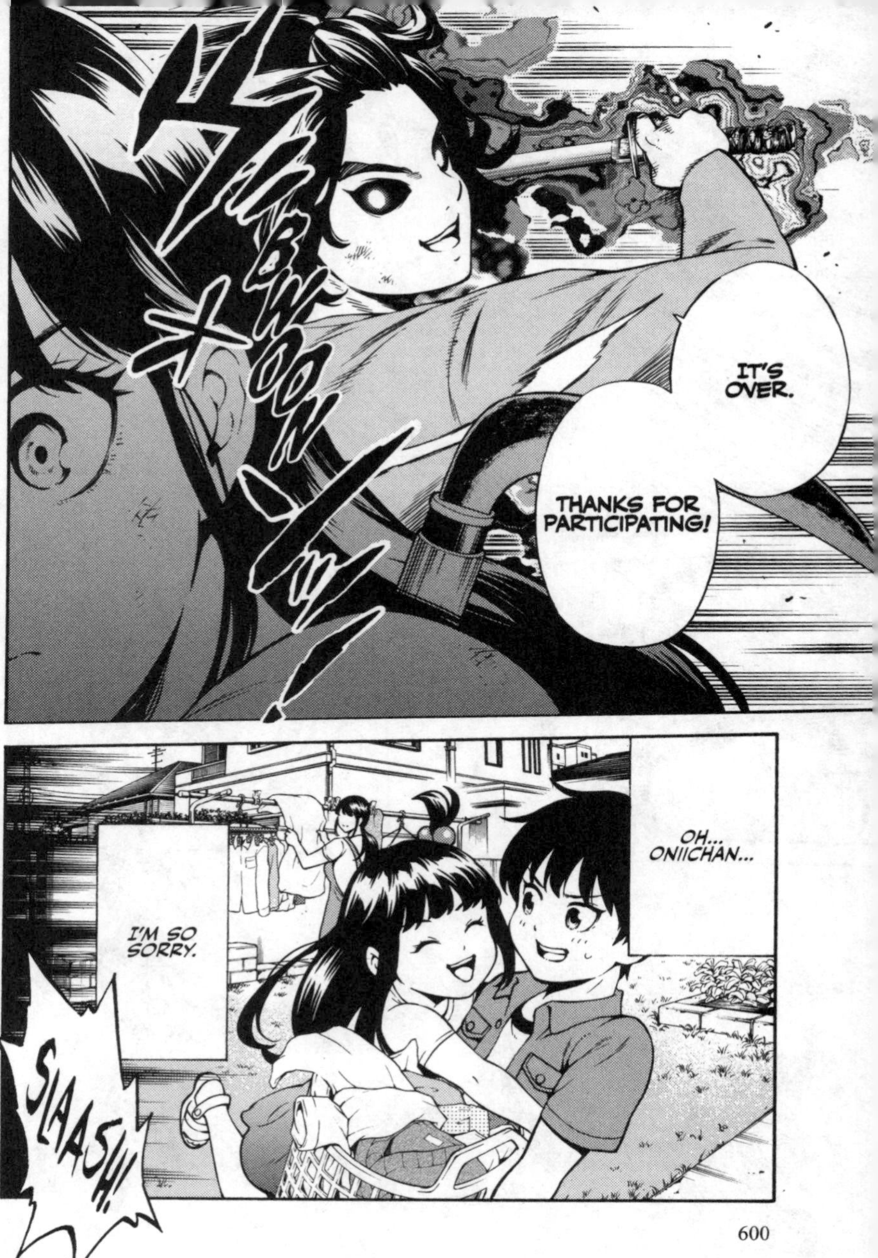
IT'S OVER.
THANKS FOR PARTICIPATING!
OH... ONIICHAN...
I'M SO SORRY.
SLAASH!

HIGH-RISE INVASION

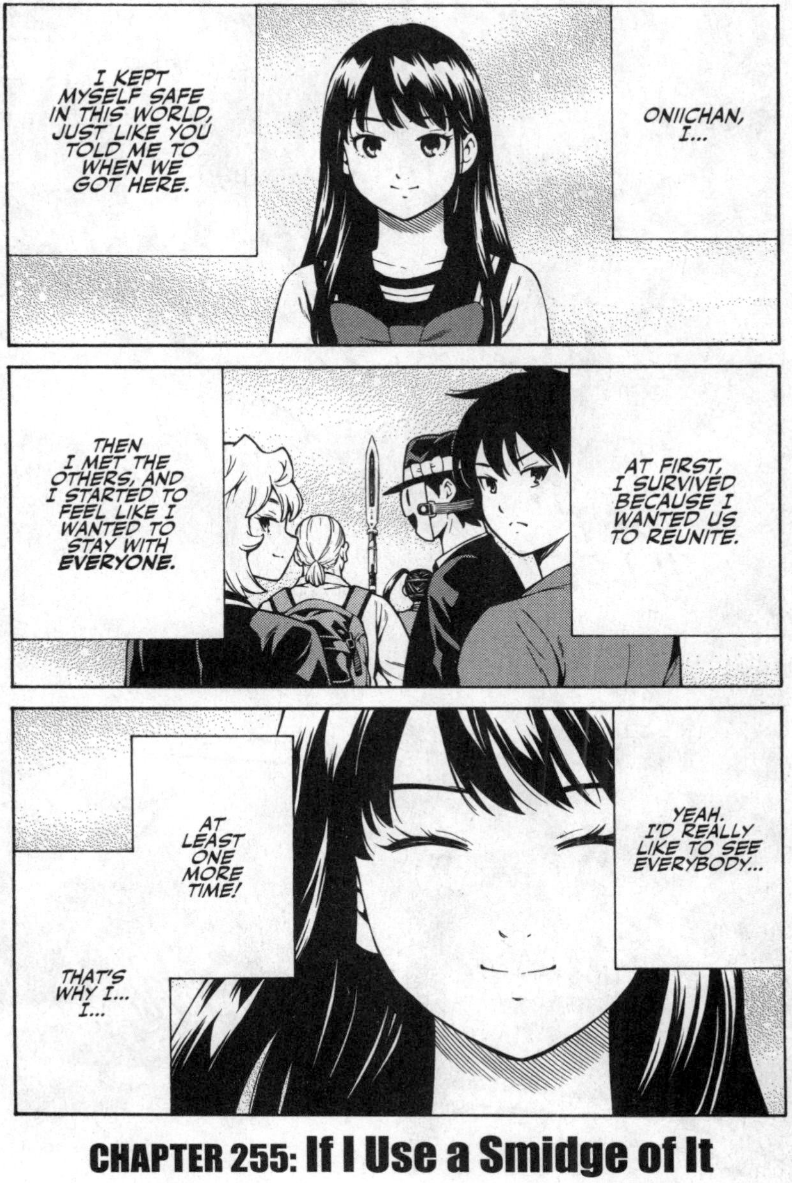
ONIICHAN, I...
I KEPT MYSELF SAFE IN THIS WORLD, JUST LIKE YOU TOLD ME TO WHEN WE GOT HERE.
AT FIRST, I SURVIVED BECAUSE I WANTED US TO REUNITE.
THEN I MET THE OTHERS, AND I STARTED TO FEEL LIKE I WANTED TO STAY WITH EVERYONE.
YEAH. I'D REALLY LIKE TO SEE EVERYBODY...
AT LEAST ONE MORE TIME!
THAT'S WHY I... I...

CHAPTER 255: If I Use a Smidge of It

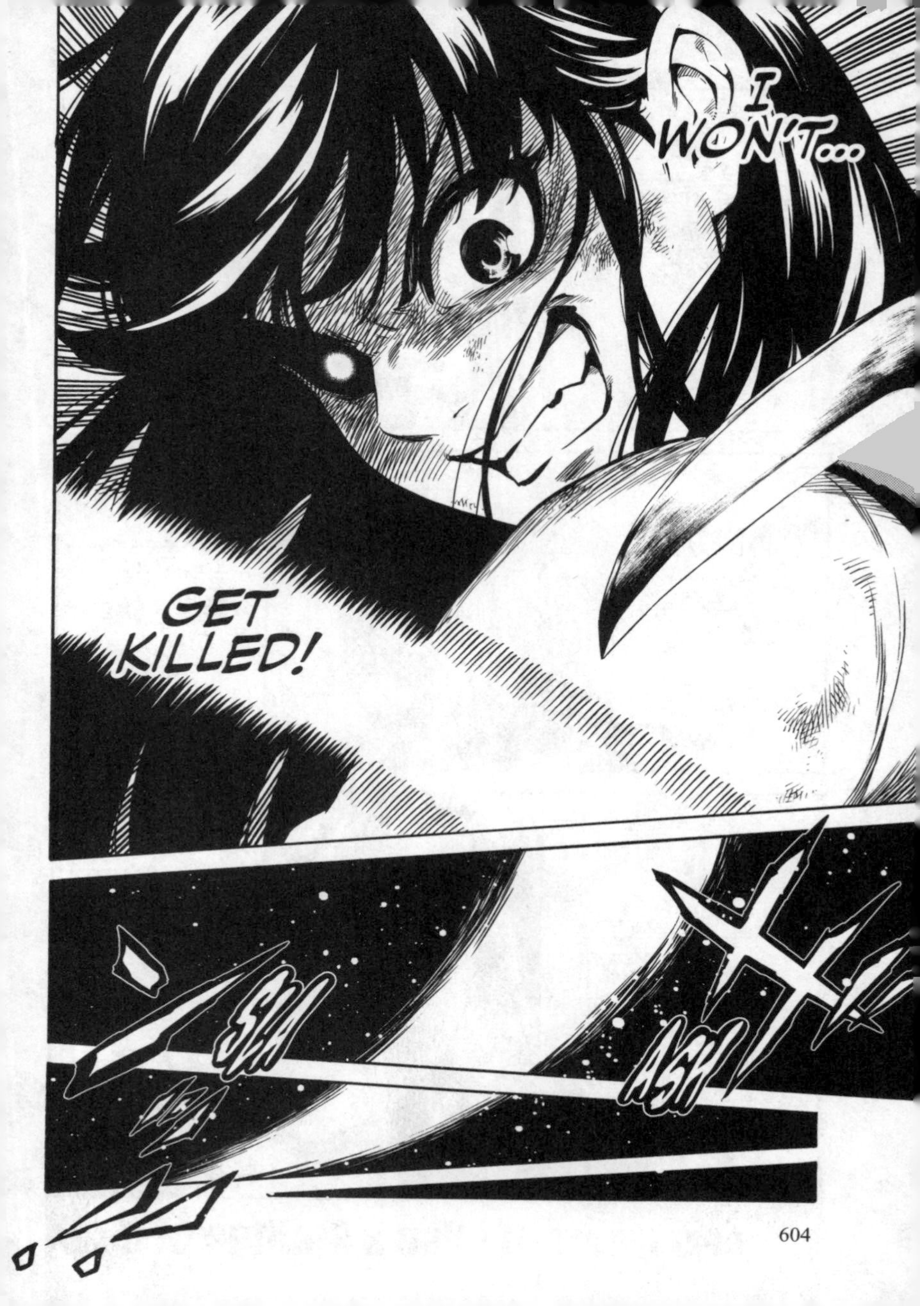
I WON'T...
GET KILLED!
SHA
ASH

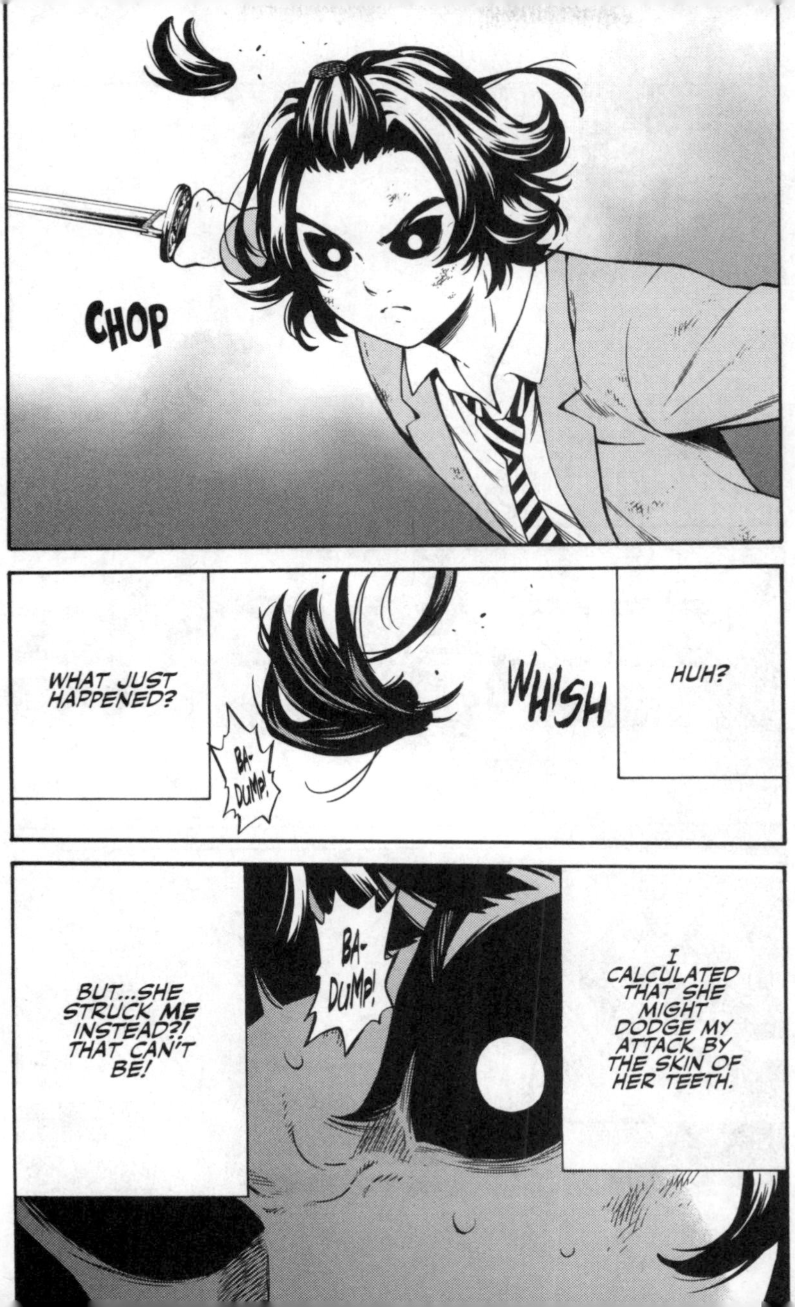
CHOP
HUH?
WHISH
BA-DUMP!
WHAT JUST HAPPENED?
I CALCULATED THAT SHE MIGHT DODGE MY ATTACK BY THE SKIN OF HER TEETH.
BA-DUMP!
BUT...SHE STRUCK ME INSTEAD?! THAT CAN'T BE!

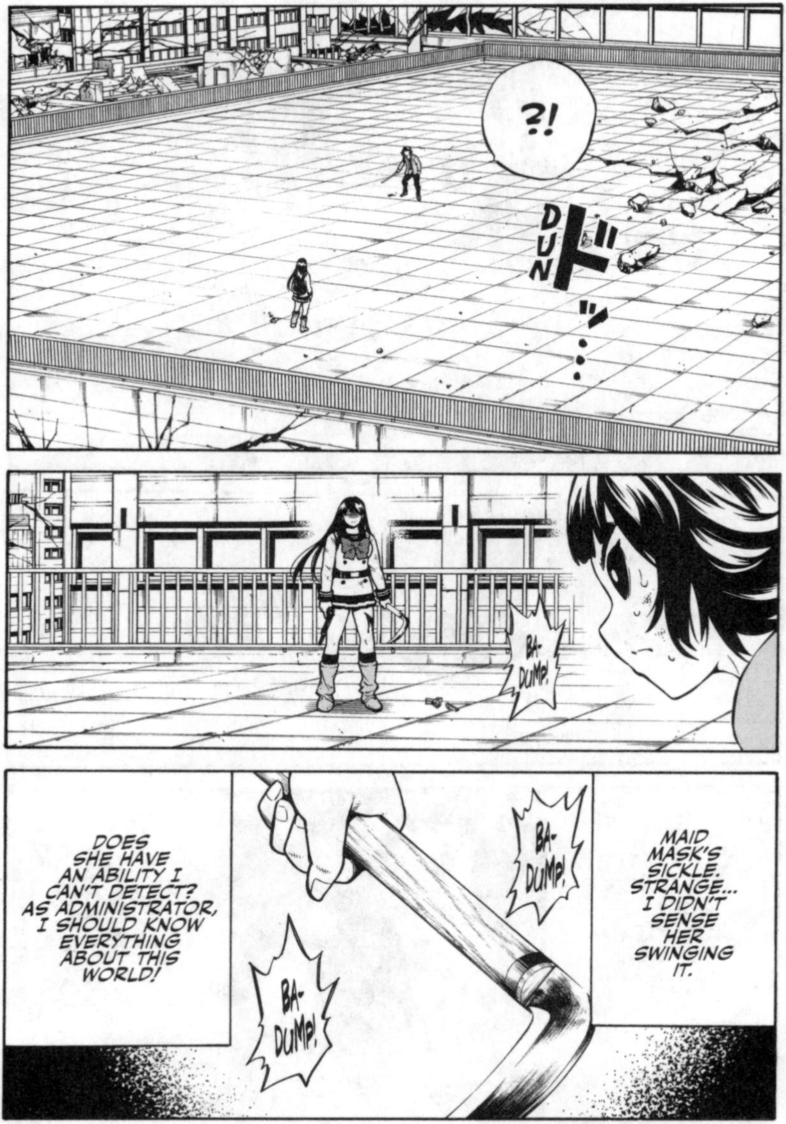
?!
DUN
BA-DUMP!
MAID MASK'S SICKLE. STRANGE... I DIDN'T SENSE HER SWINGING IT.
BA-DUMP!
BA-DUMP!
DOES SHE HAVE AN ABILITY I CAN'T DETECT? AS ADMINISTRATOR, I SHOULD KNOW EVERYTHING ABOUT THIS WORLD!

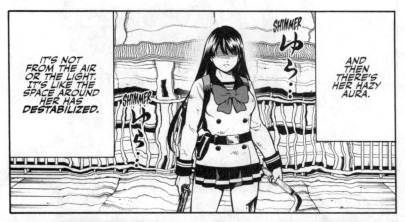

SHIMMER ゆら…
AND THEN THERE'S HER HAZY AURA.
IT'S NOT FROM THE AIR OR THE LIGHT. IT'S LIKE THE SPACE AROUND HER HAS DESTABILIZED.
SHIMMER ゆら…
YURI-SAN!
TH-THIS POWER CERTAINLY ISN'T--
BA-DUMP!
BA-DUMP!
SHIMMER ゆら…
I'M REALLY SORRY, EVERY-ONE.
I DON'T WANT TO USE THIS ABILITY, EITHER.
IT'S OBVIOUSLY DANGEROUS. PLUS, IT'LL MEAN I'M GIVING IN TO THIS WORLD A LITTLE.
BA-DUMP!
I'M PRETTY WEAK-WILLED. WHEN I REALIZED I MIGHT NOT SEE YOU GUYS AGAIN, I TAPPED INTO THIS POWER BEFORE I REALIZED WHAT I WAS DOING.
BA-DUMP!

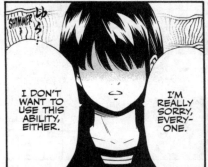

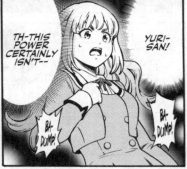

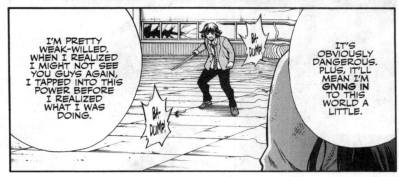

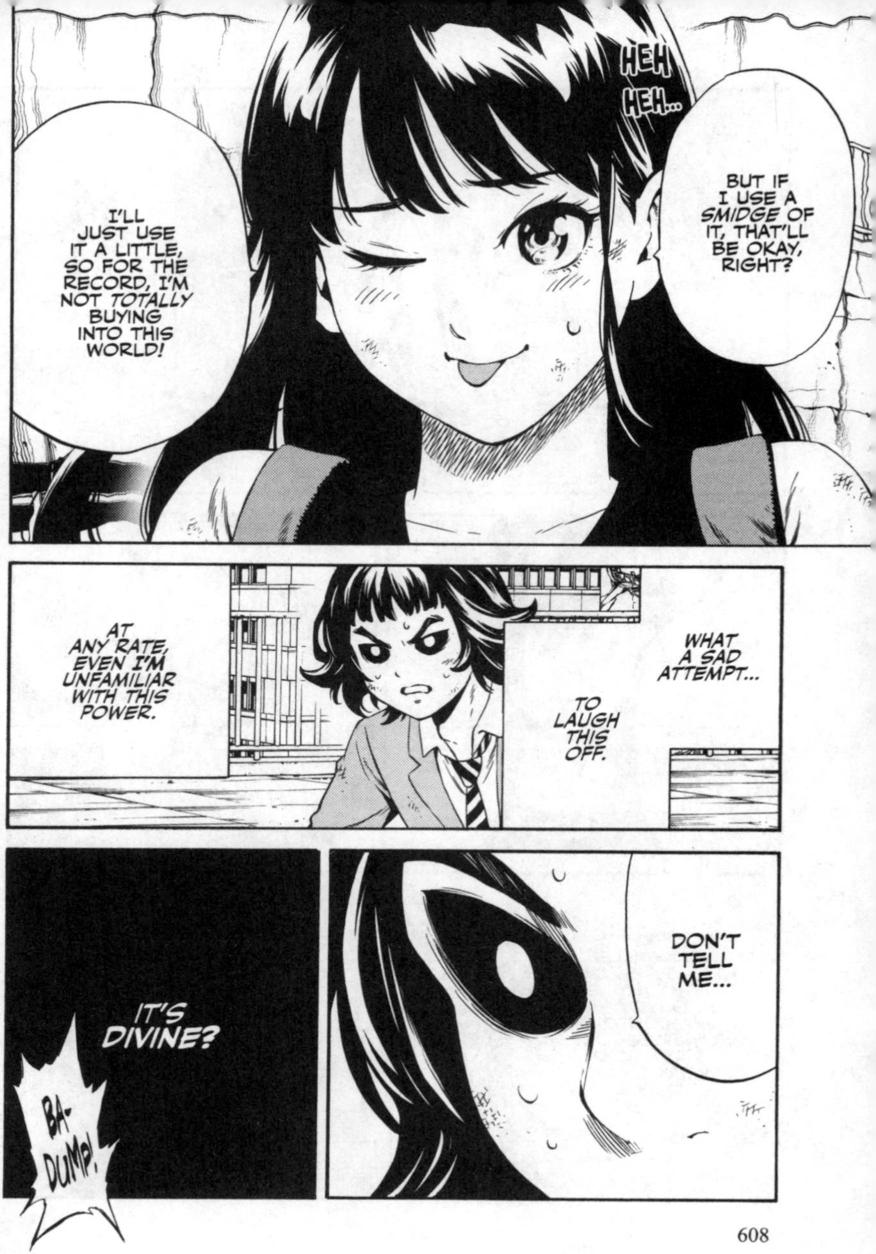
HEH HEH...
BUT IF I USE A *SMIDGE* OF IT, THAT'LL BE OKAY, RIGHT?
I'LL JUST USE IT A LITTLE, SO FOR THE RECORD, I'M NOT *TOTALLY* BUYING INTO THIS WORLD!
WHAT A SAD ATTEMPT...
TO LAUGH THIS OFF.
AT ANY RATE, EVEN I'M UNFAMILIAR WITH THIS POWER.
DON'T TELL ME...
IT'S DIVINE?
BA-DUMP!

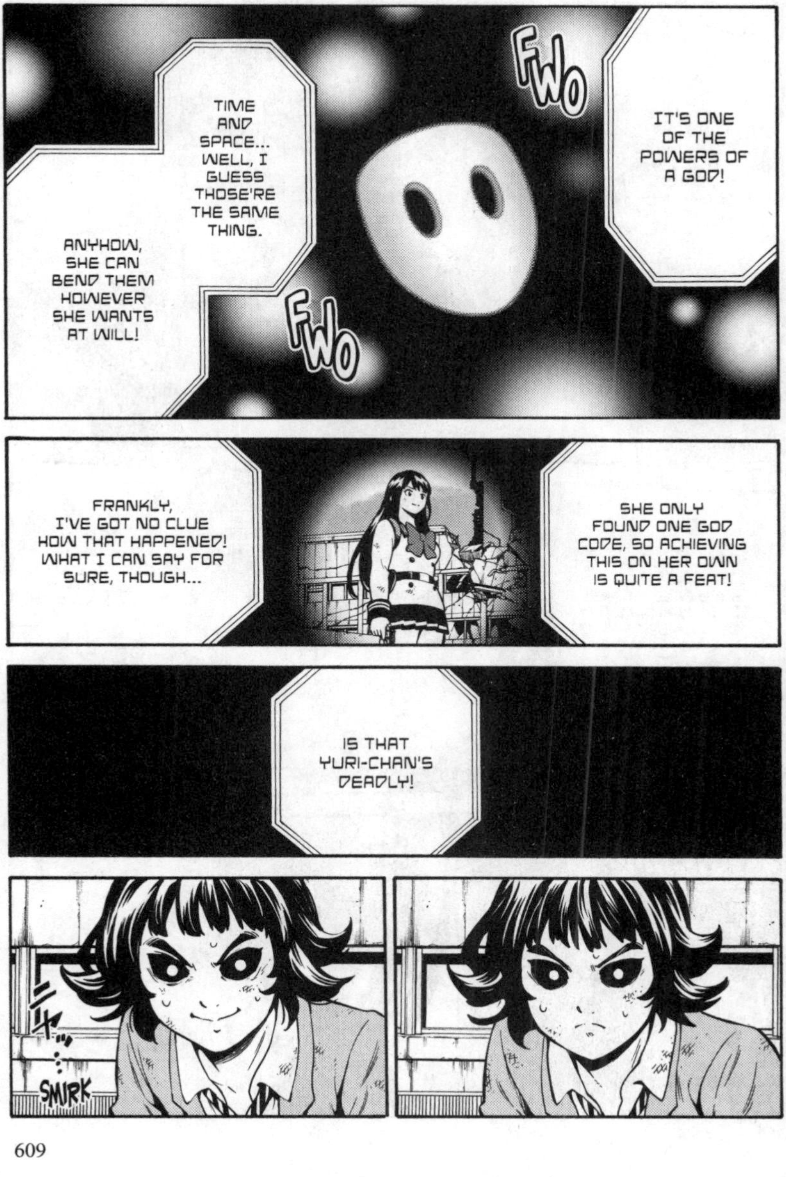
IT'S ONE OF THE POWERS OF A GOD!
FWO
TIME AND SPACE... WELL, I GUESS THOSE'RE THE SAME THING.
ANYHOW, SHE CAN BEND THEM HOWEVER SHE WANTS AT WILL!
FWO
SHE ONLY FOUND ONE GOD CODE, SO ACHIEVING THIS ON HER OWN IS QUITE A FEAT!
FRANKLY, I'VE GOT NO CLUE HOW THAT HAPPENED! WHAT I CAN SAY FOR SURE, THOUGH...
IS THAT YURI-CHAN'S DEADLY!
SMIRK

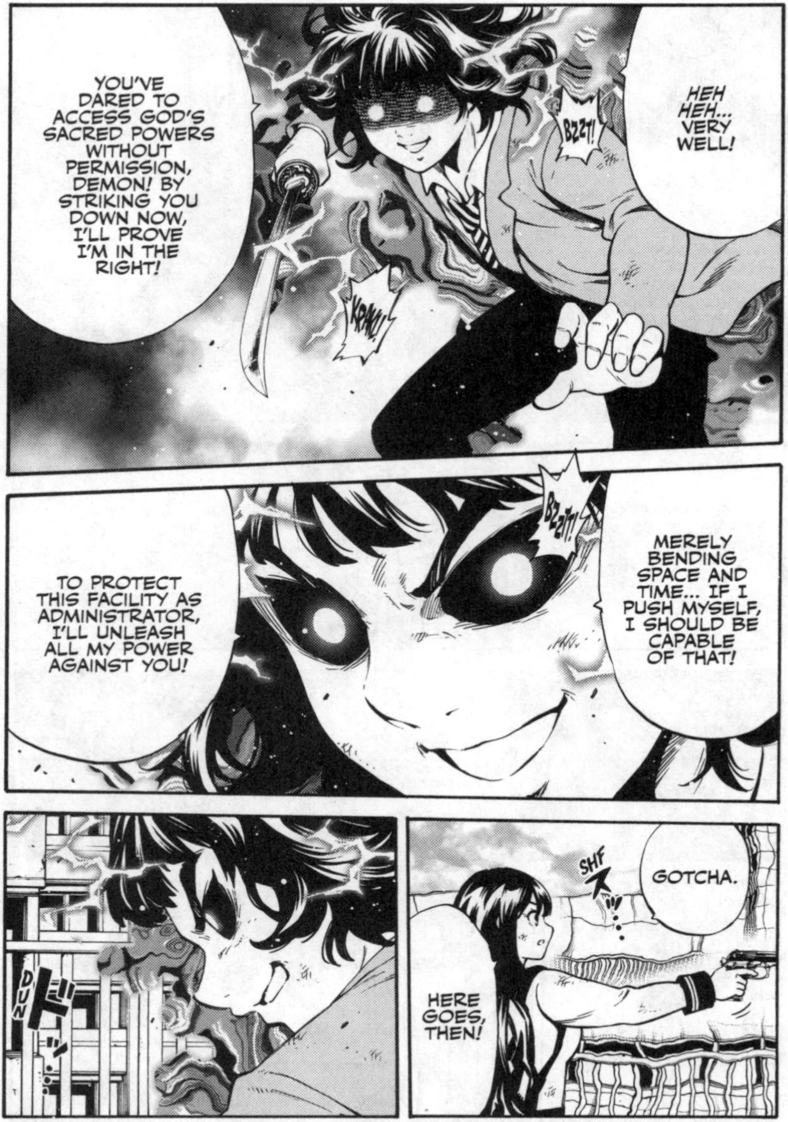
HEH HEH... VERY WELL!
BZZT!
YOU'VE DARED TO ACCESS GOD'S SACRED POWERS WITHOUT PERMISSION, DEMON! BY STRIKING YOU DOWN NOW, I'LL PROVE I'M IN THE RIGHT!
KRAKL!
BZZIT!
MERELY BENDING SPACE AND TIME... IF I PUSH MYSELF, I SHOULD BE CAPABLE OF THAT!
TO PROTECT THIS FACILITY AS ADMINISTRATOR, I'LL UNLEASH ALL MY POWER AGAINST YOU!
GOTCHA.
SHF
HERE GOES, THEN!
DUN

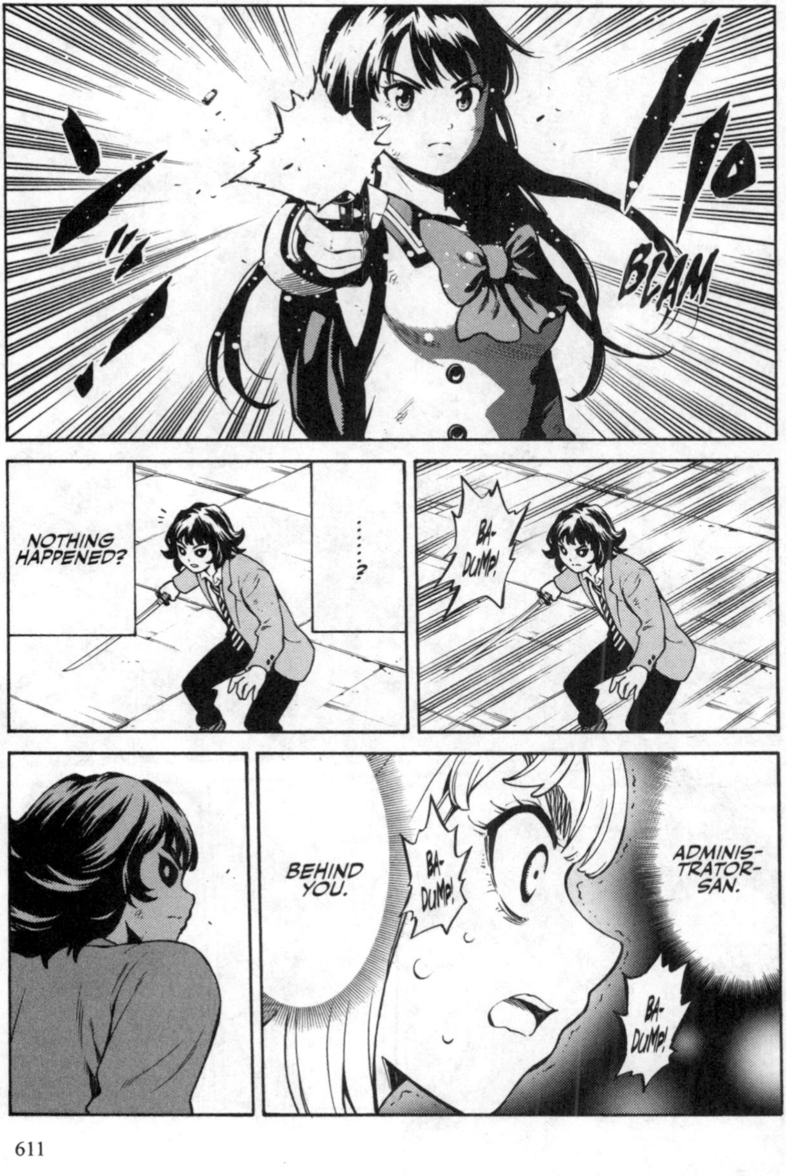
BLAM
BA-DUMP!
......?
NOTHING HAPPENED?
ADMINIS-TRATOR-SAN.
BA-DUMP!
BEHIND YOU.
BA-DUMP!

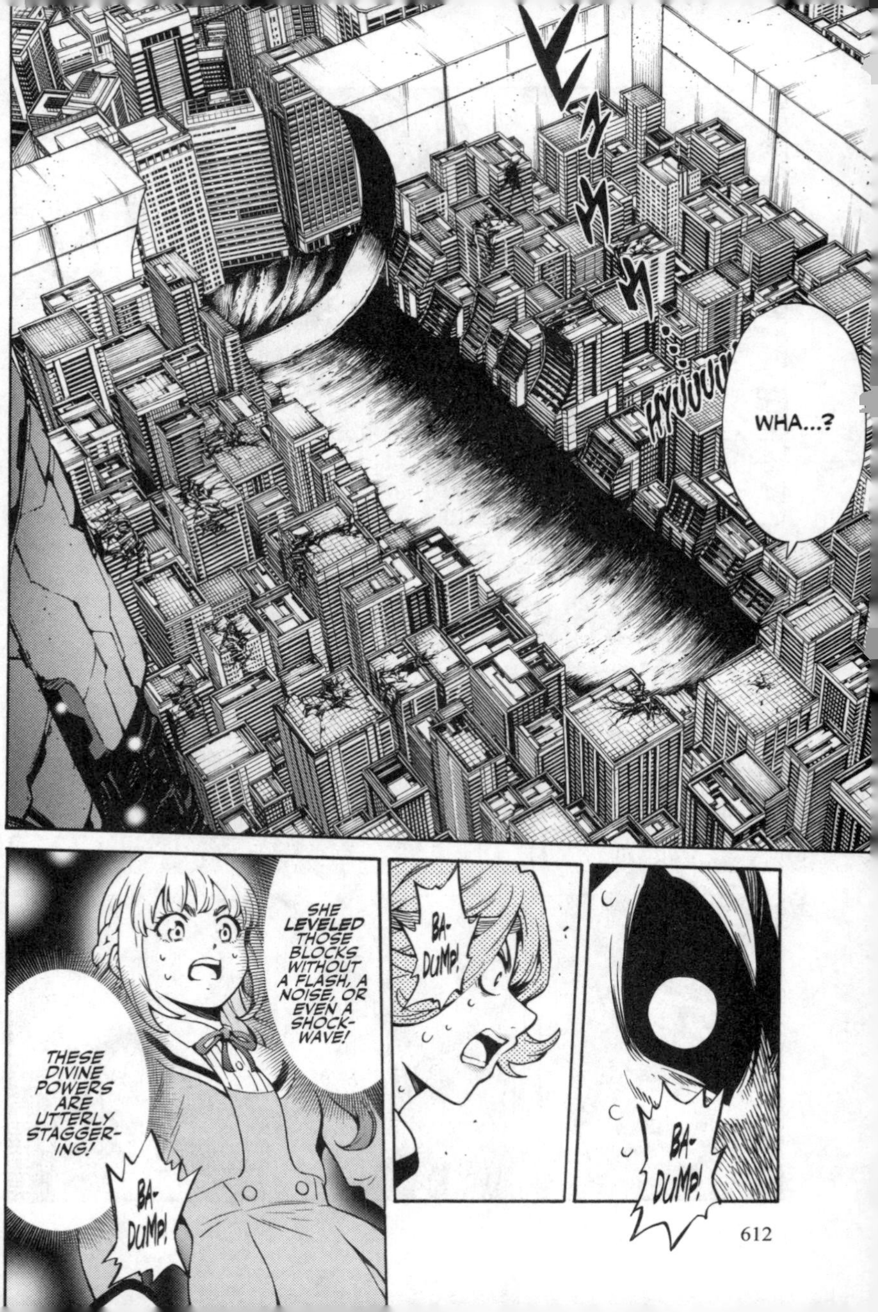
VMMM...
HYUUUU
WHA...?
BA-DUMP!
BA-DUMP!
SHE LEVELED THOSE BLOCKS WITHOUT A FLASH, A NOISE, OR EVEN A SHOCK-WAVE!
THESE DIVINE POWERS ARE UTTERLY STAGGER-ING!
BA-DUMP!

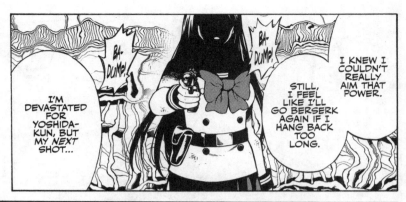

I KNEW I COULDN'T REALLY AIM THAT POWER.
STILL, I FEEL LIKE I'LL GO BERSERK AGAIN IF I HANG BACK TOO LONG.
BA-DUMP!
BA-DUMP!
I'M DEVASTATED FOR YOSHIDA-KUN, BUT MY *NEXT* SHOT...
IS GONNA END...
EVERY-THING!
BA-DUMP!
BA-DUMP
HEH HEH HEH!
HA HA HA!
HEH HEH...
DROP

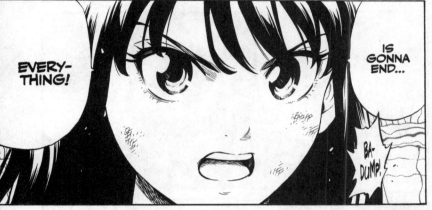

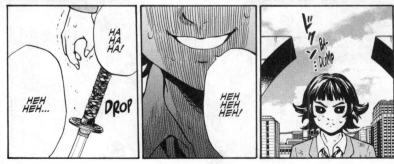

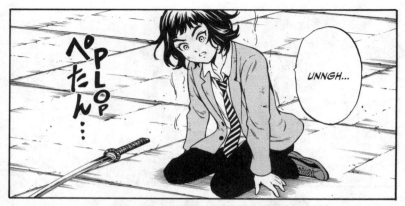

UNNGH...
ぺたん PLOP...
NO, THIS IS WRONG... WRONG, WRONG, WRONG, WRONG, WRONG!
I WAS CHOSEN. I BECAME GREATER THAN ALL OF YOU!
WHY IS THIS HAPPENING? IT ISN'T MY FAULT. SOMEONE'S SABOTAGING ME!
MMBL
MMBL
TH-THIS IS LUDICROUS!
MMBL
I JUST DON'T UNDER-STAND!
MMBL
キリッ AIM...

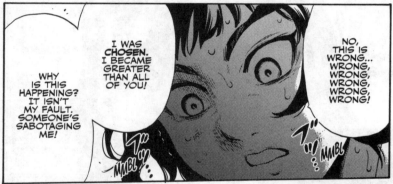

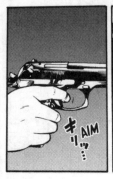

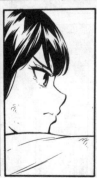

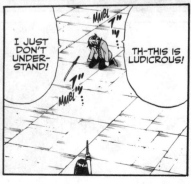

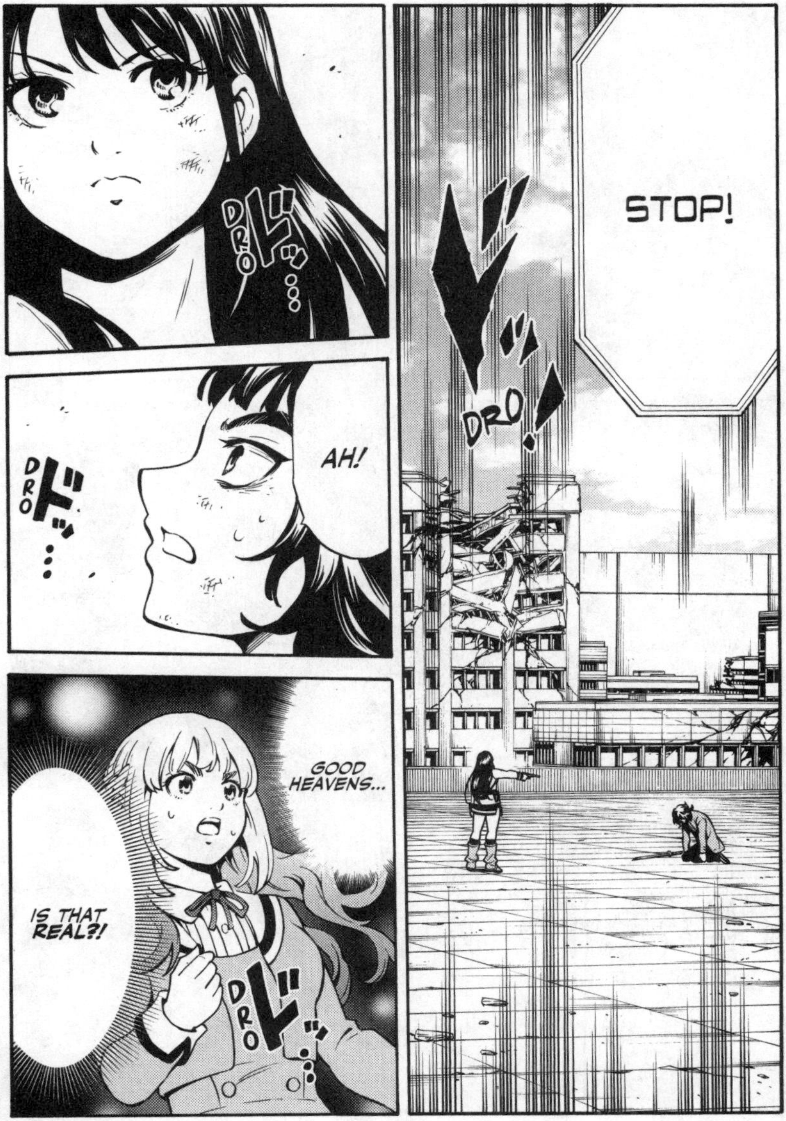
STOP!
DRO
DRO
DRO
AH!
GOOD HEAVENS...
IS THAT REAL?!
DRO

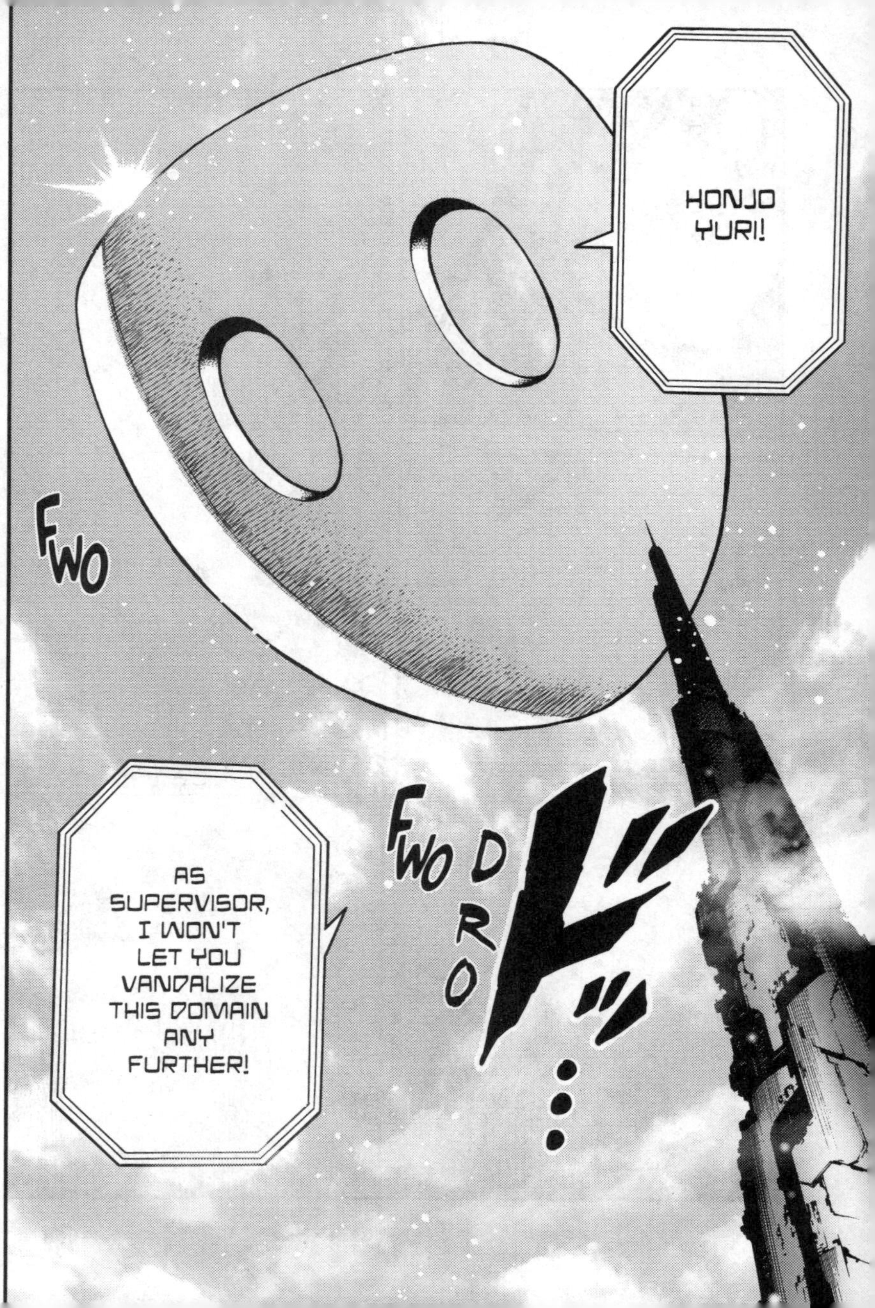
HONJO YURI!
FWO
FWO
DRO
AS SUPERVISOR, I WON'T LET YOU VANDALIZE THIS DOMAIN ANY FURTHER!

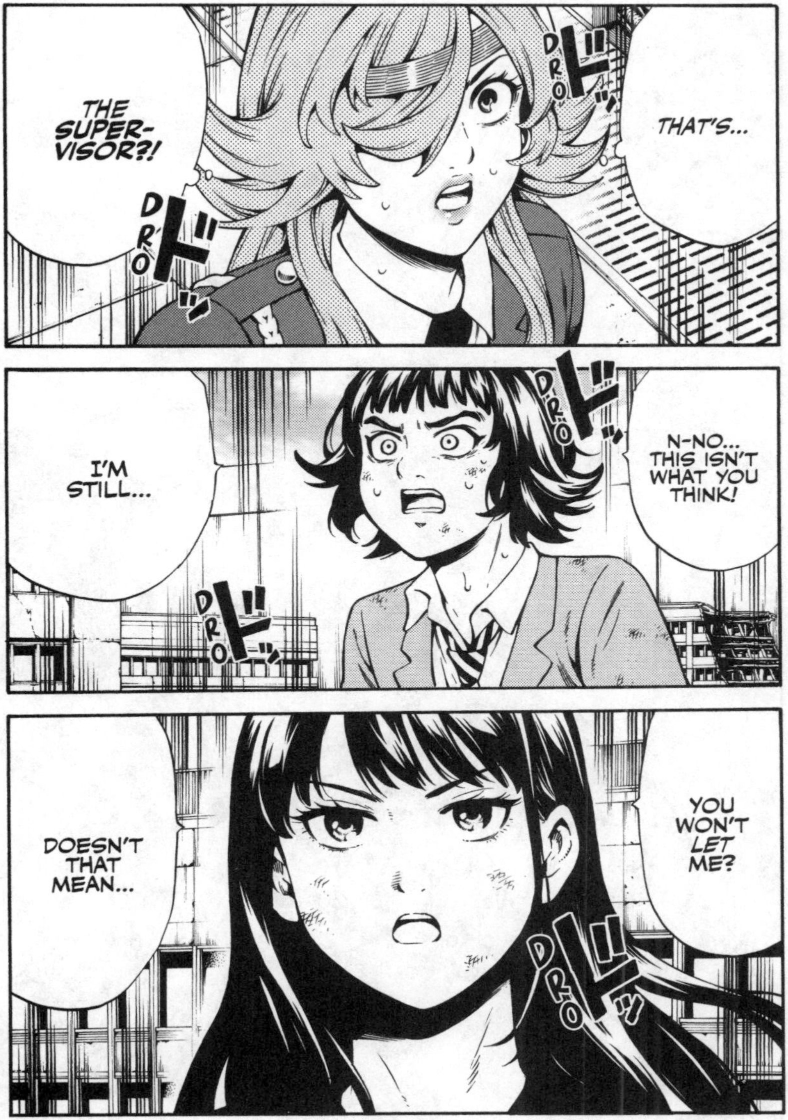
DRO
THAT'S...
THE SUPER-VISOR?!
DRO
DRO
N-NO... THIS ISN'T WHAT YOU THINK!
I'M STILL...
DRO
YOU WON'T *LET* ME?
DOESN'T THAT MEAN...
DRO

CHAPTER 256: It's Easier Just to Give Up

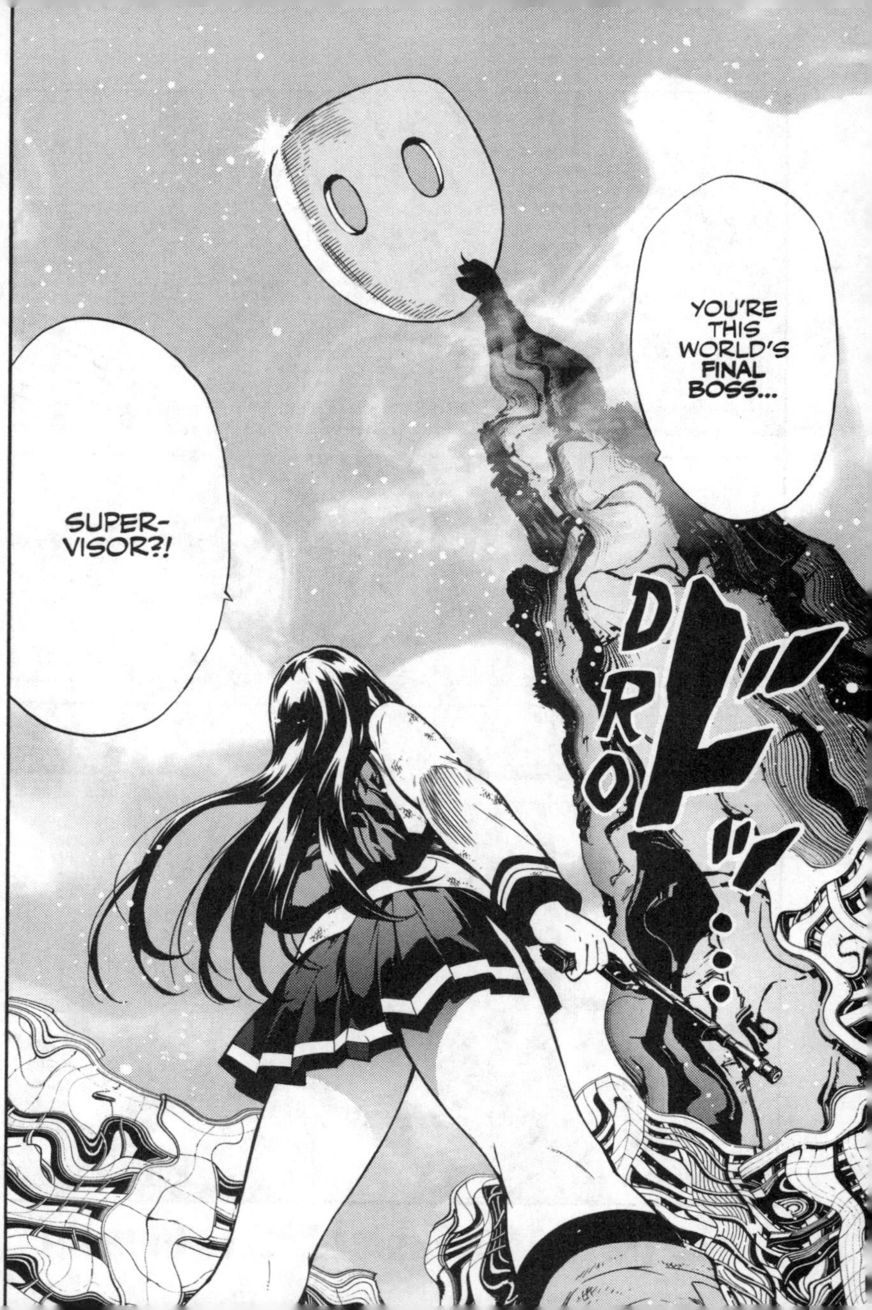
YOU'RE THIS WORLD'S FINAL BOSS...
SUPER-VISOR?!
DRO...

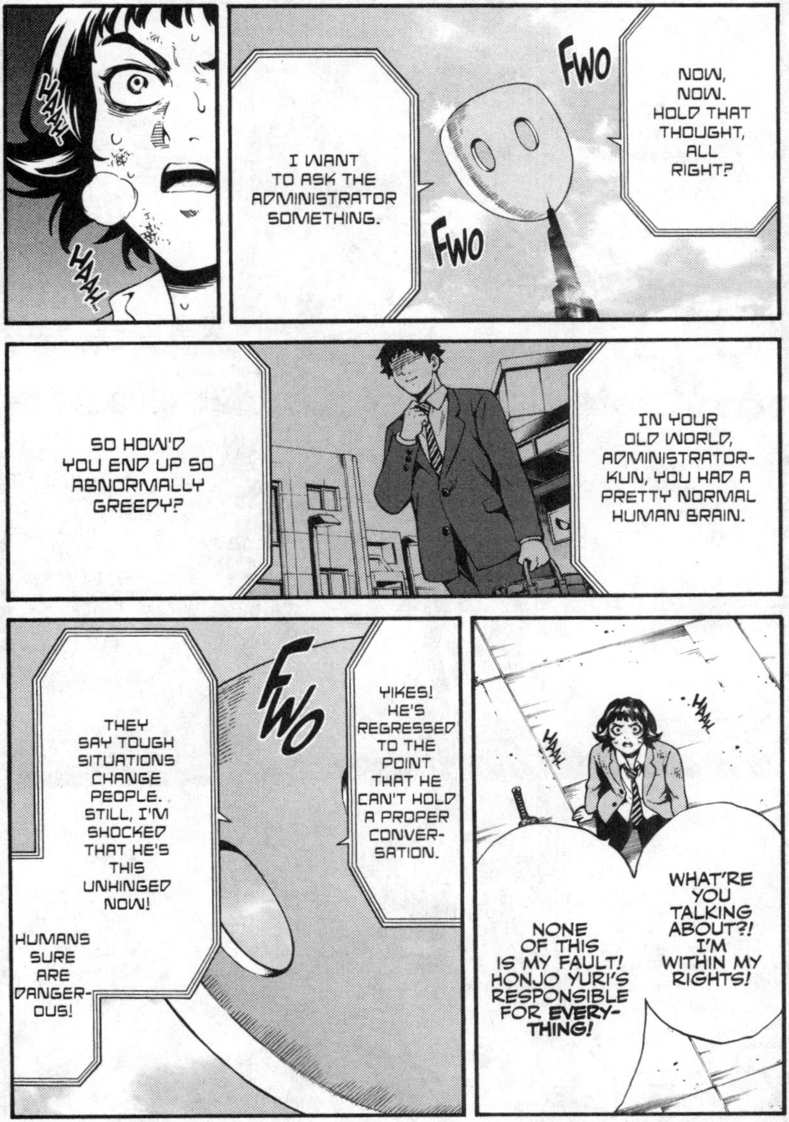
FWO
NOW, NOW. HOLD THAT THOUGHT, ALL RIGHT?
I WANT TO ASK THE ADMINISTRATOR SOMETHING.
FWO
HAAH
HAAH
IN YOUR OLD WORLD, ADMINISTRATOR-KUN, YOU HAD A PRETTY NORMAL HUMAN BRAIN.
SO HOW'D YOU END UP SO ABNORMALLY GREEDY?
HAAH
HAAH
WHAT'RE YOU TALKING ABOUT?! I'M WITHIN MY RIGHTS!
NONE OF THIS IS MY FAULT! HONJO YURI'S RESPONSIBLE FOR EVERY-THING!
FWO
YIKES! HE'S REGRESSED TO THE POINT THAT HE CAN'T HOLD A PROPER CONVER-SATION.
THEY SAY TOUGH SITUATIONS CHANGE PEOPLE. STILL, I'M SHOCKED THAT HE'S THIS UNHINGED NOW!
HUMANS SURE ARE DANGER-OUS!

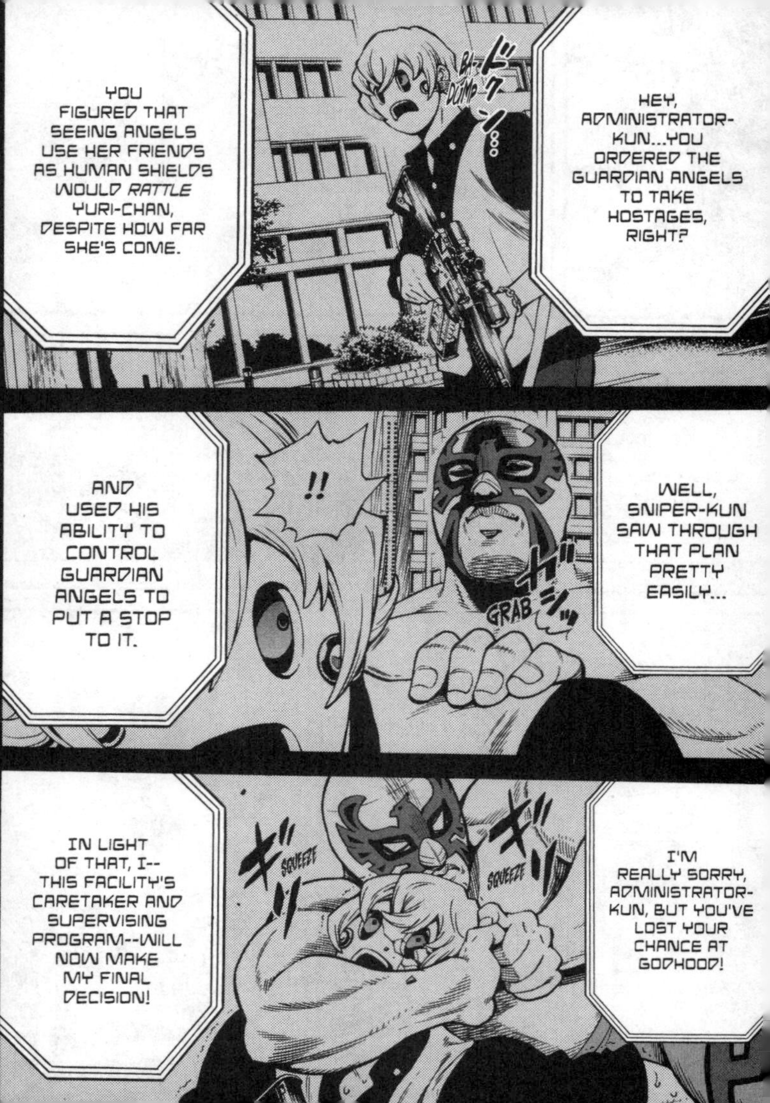
HEY, ADMINISTRATOR-KUN...YOU ORDERED THE GUARDIAN ANGELS TO TAKE HOSTAGES, RIGHT?
BA-DUMP
YOU FIGURED THAT SEEING ANGELS USE HER FRIENDS AS HUMAN SHIELDS WOULD *RATTLE* YURI-CHAN, DESPITE HOW FAR SHE'S COME.
WELL, SNIPER-KUN SAW THROUGH THAT PLAN PRETTY EASILY...
GRAB
!!
AND USED HIS ABILITY TO CONTROL GUARDIAN ANGELS TO PUT A STOP TO IT.
I'M REALLY SORRY, ADMINISTRATOR-KUN, BUT YOU'VE LOST YOUR CHANCE AT GODHOOD!
SQUEEZE
SQUEEZE
IN LIGHT OF THAT, I--THIS FACILITY'S CARETAKER AND SUPERVISING PROGRAM--WILL NOW MAKE MY FINAL DECISION!

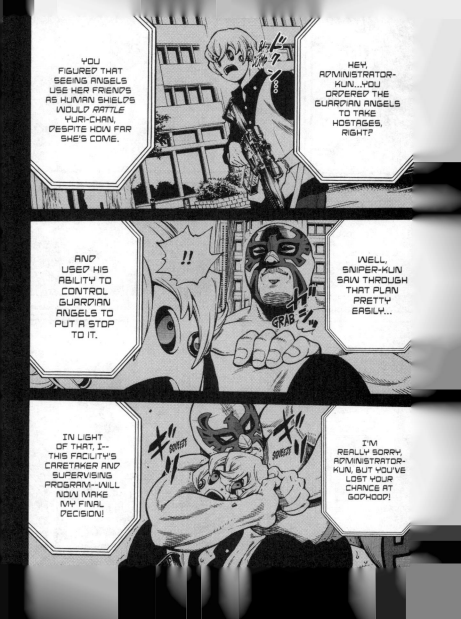

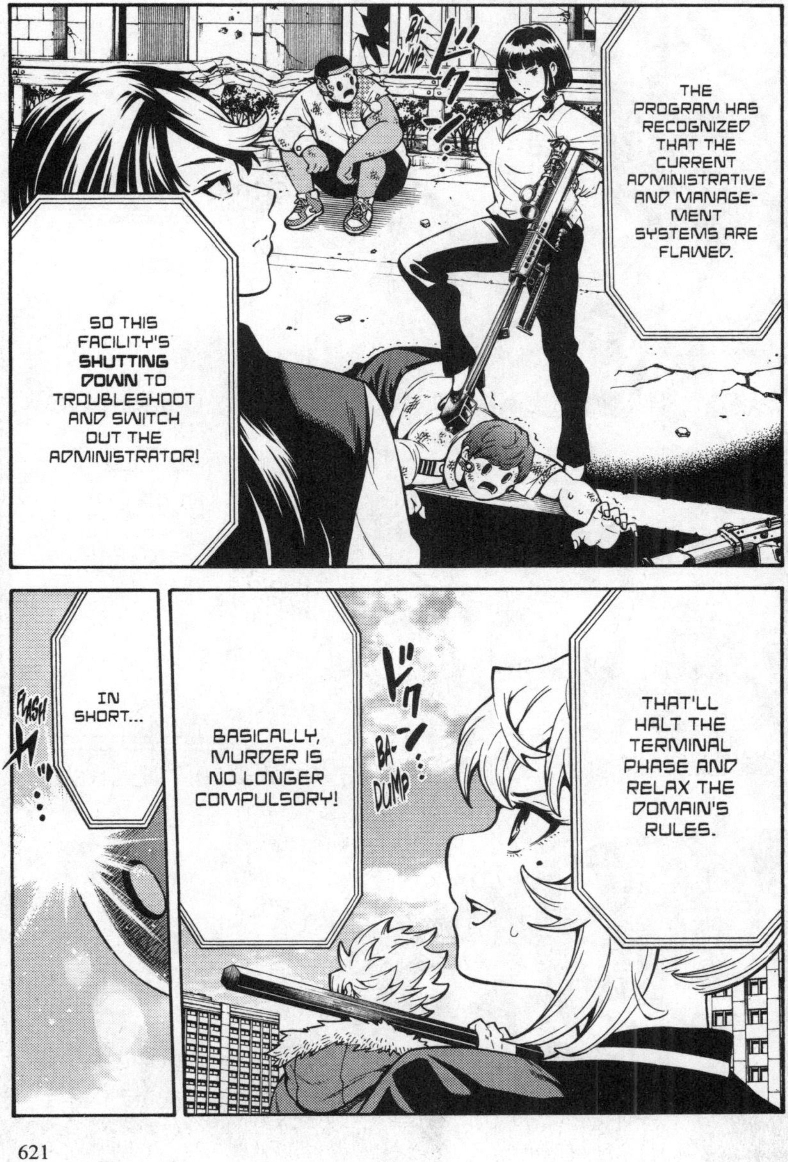
THE PROGRAM HAS RECOGNIZED THAT THE CURRENT ADMINISTRATIVE AND MANAGE-MENT SYSTEMS ARE FLAWED.
BA-DUMP
SO THIS FACILITY'S **SHUTTING DOWN** TO TROUBLESHOOT AND SWITCH OUT THE ADMINISTRATOR!
THAT'LL HALT THE TERMINAL PHASE AND RELAX THE DOMAIN'S RULES.
BA-DUMP
BASICALLY, MURDER IS NO LONGER COMPULSORY!
IN SHORT...
FLASH

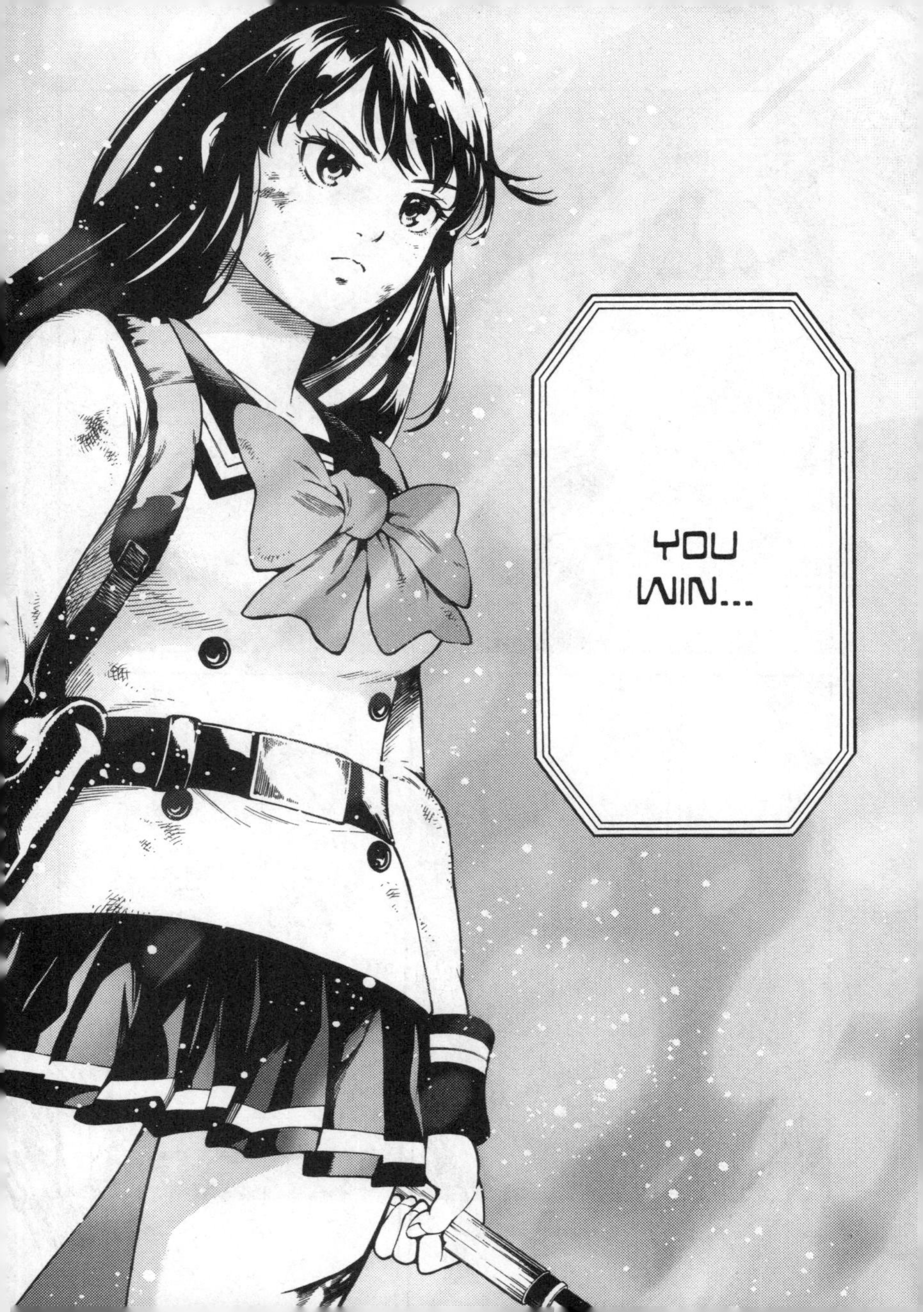
YOU WIN...

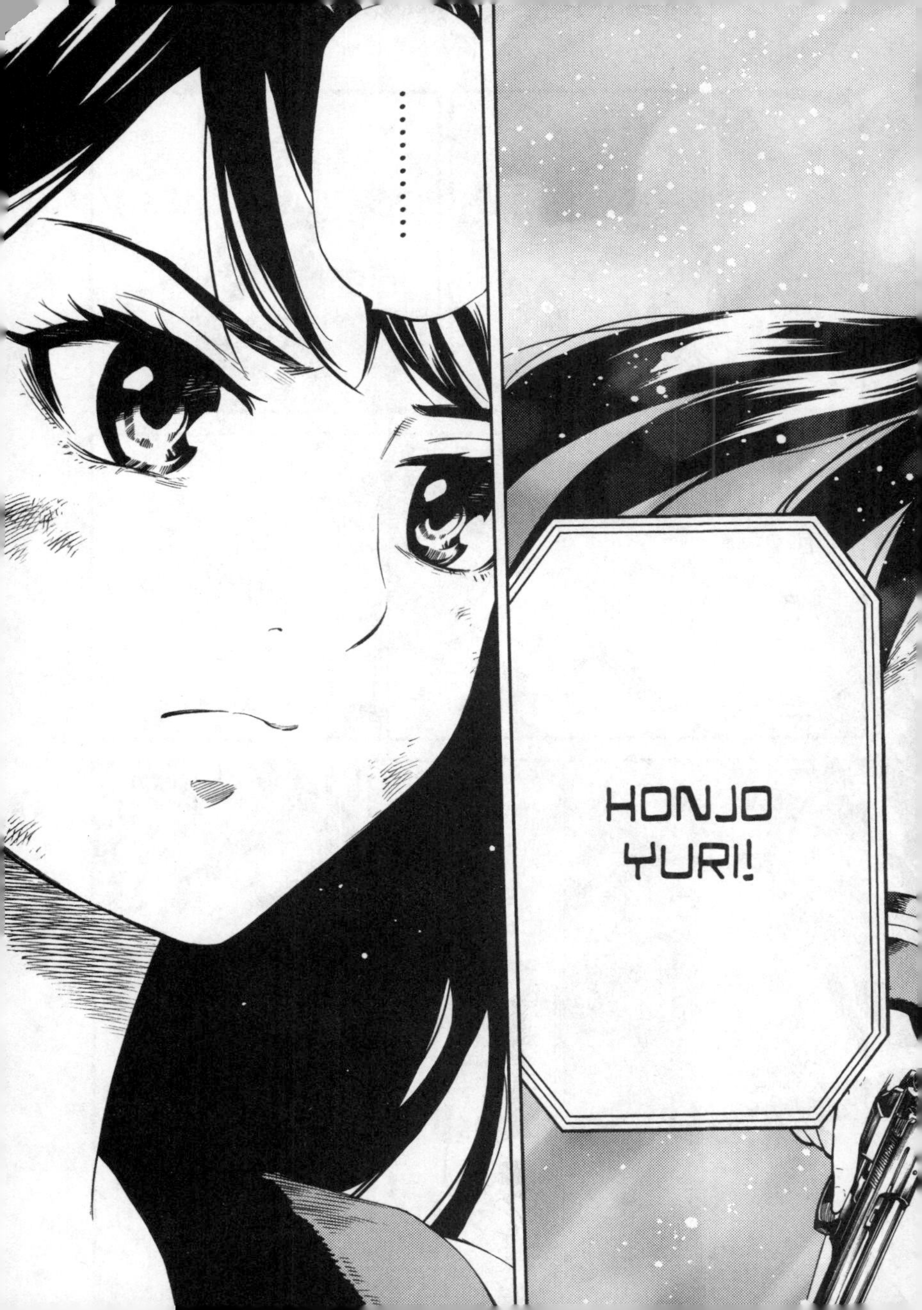
HONJO YURI!
......

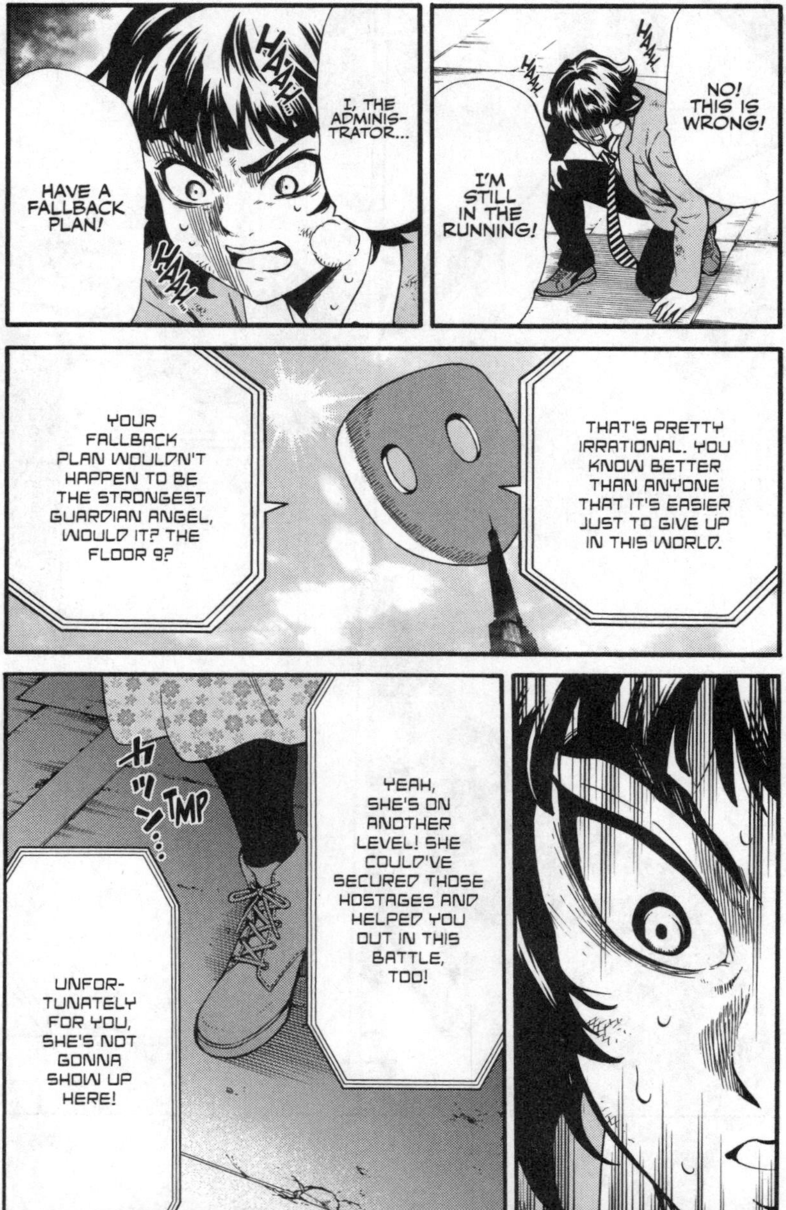
HAAH
HAAH
NO! THIS IS WRONG!
I'M STILL IN THE RUNNING!
HAAH
I, THE ADMINISTRATOR...
HAVE A FALLBACK PLAN!
HAAH
THAT'S PRETTY IRRATIONAL. YOU KNOW BETTER THAN ANYONE THAT IT'S EASIER JUST TO GIVE UP IN THIS WORLD.
YOUR FALLBACK PLAN WOULDN'T HAPPEN TO BE THE STRONGEST GUARDIAN ANGEL, WOULD IT? THE FLOOR 9?
YEAH, SHE'S ON ANOTHER LEVEL! SHE COULD'VE SECURED THOSE HOSTAGES AND HELPED YOU OUT IN THIS BATTLE, TOO!
カツン…
TMP
UNFORTUNATELY FOR YOU, SHE'S NOT GONNA SHOW UP HERE!

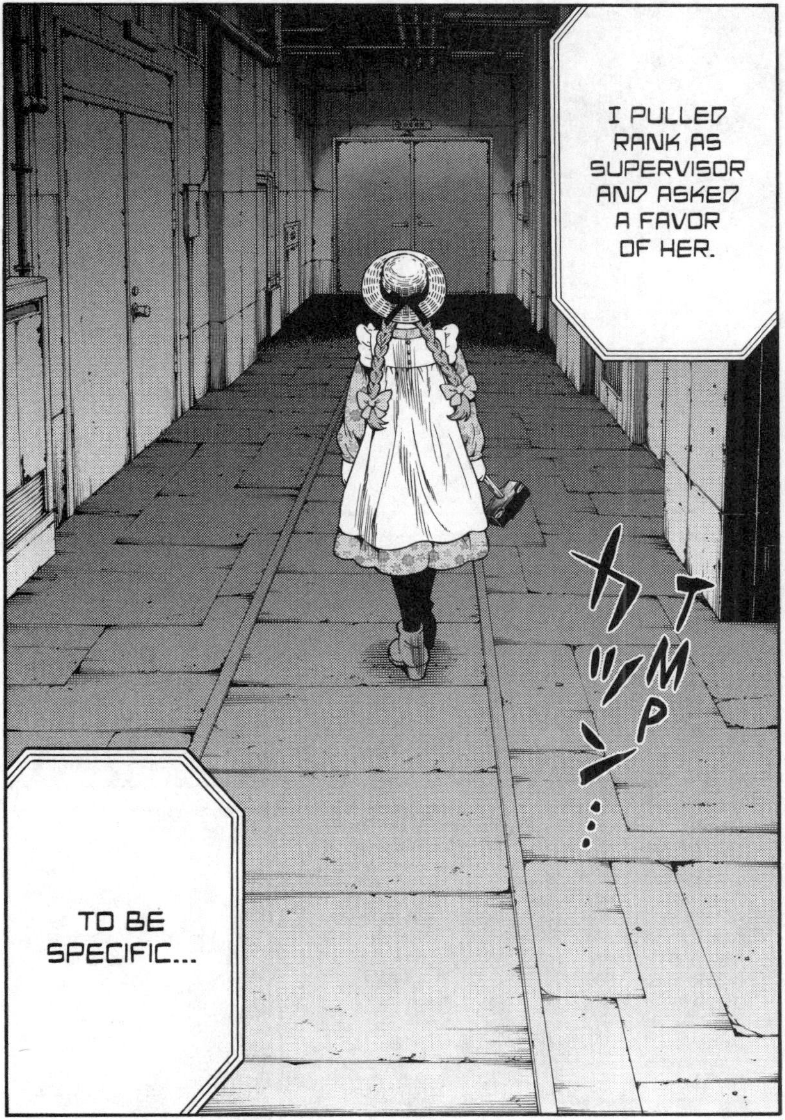
I PULLED RANK AS SUPERVISOR AND ASKED A FAVOR OF HER.
TMP...
TO BE SPECIFIC...

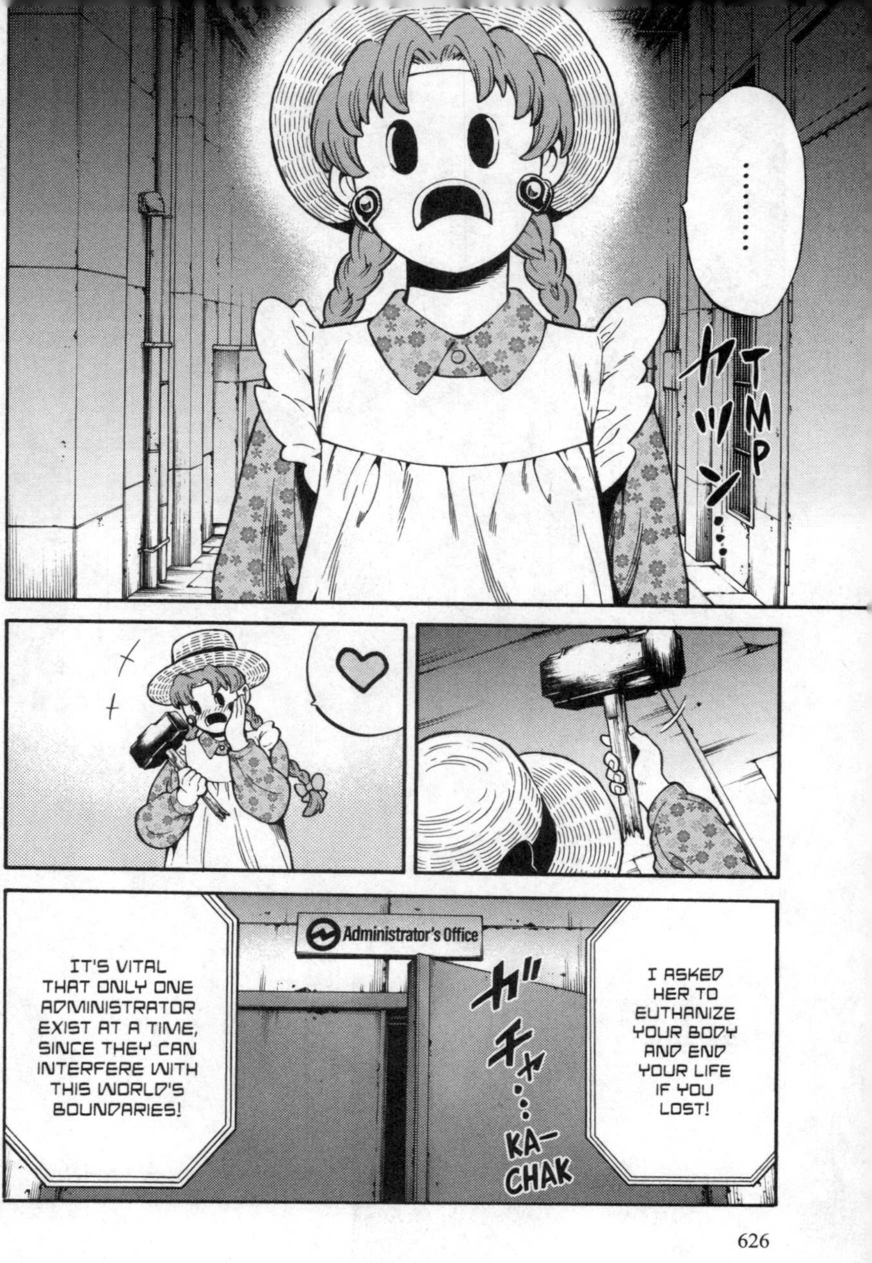
……
カツン
TMP
I ASKED HER TO EUTHANIZE YOUR BODY AND END YOUR LIFE IF YOU LOST!
ガチャ…
KA-CHAK
IT'S VITAL THAT ONLY ONE ADMINISTRATOR EXIST AT A TIME, SINCE THEY CAN INTERFERE WITH THIS WORLD'S BOUNDARIES!
Administrator's Office

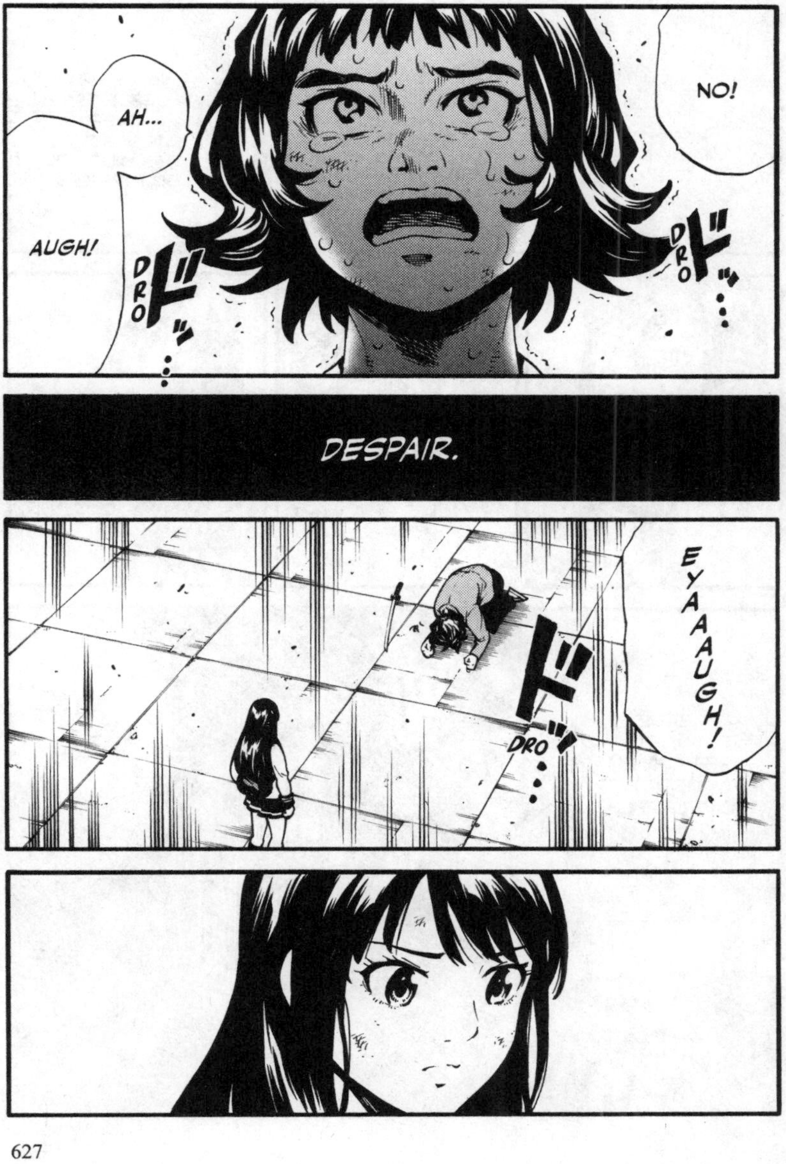
NO!
DRO
AH...
AUGH!
DRO
DESPAIR.
EYAAAUGH!
DRO

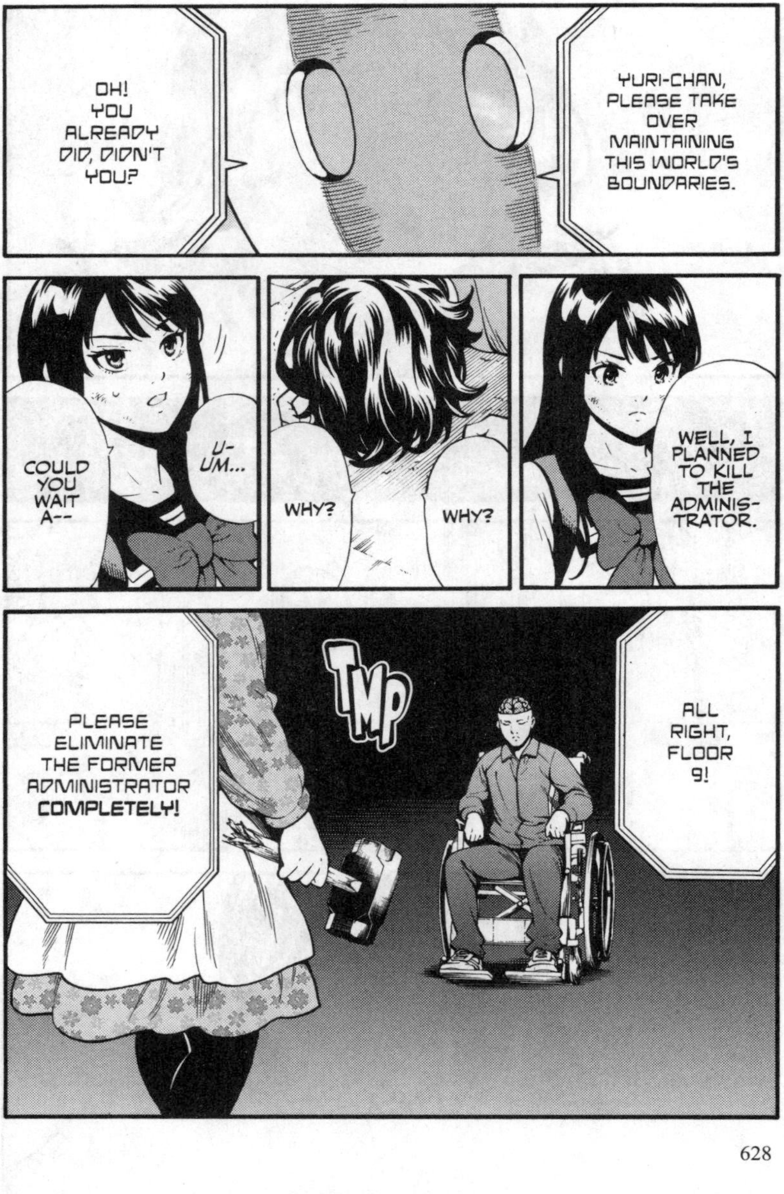
YURI-CHAN, PLEASE TAKE OVER MAINTAINING THIS WORLD'S BOUNDARIES.
OH! YOU ALREADY DID, DIDN'T YOU?
WELL, I PLANNED TO KILL THE ADMINISTRATOR.
WHY?
WHY?
U-UM...
COULD YOU WAIT A--
ALL RIGHT, FLOOR 9!
TMP
PLEASE ELIMINATE THE FORMER ADMINISTRATOR COMPLETELY!

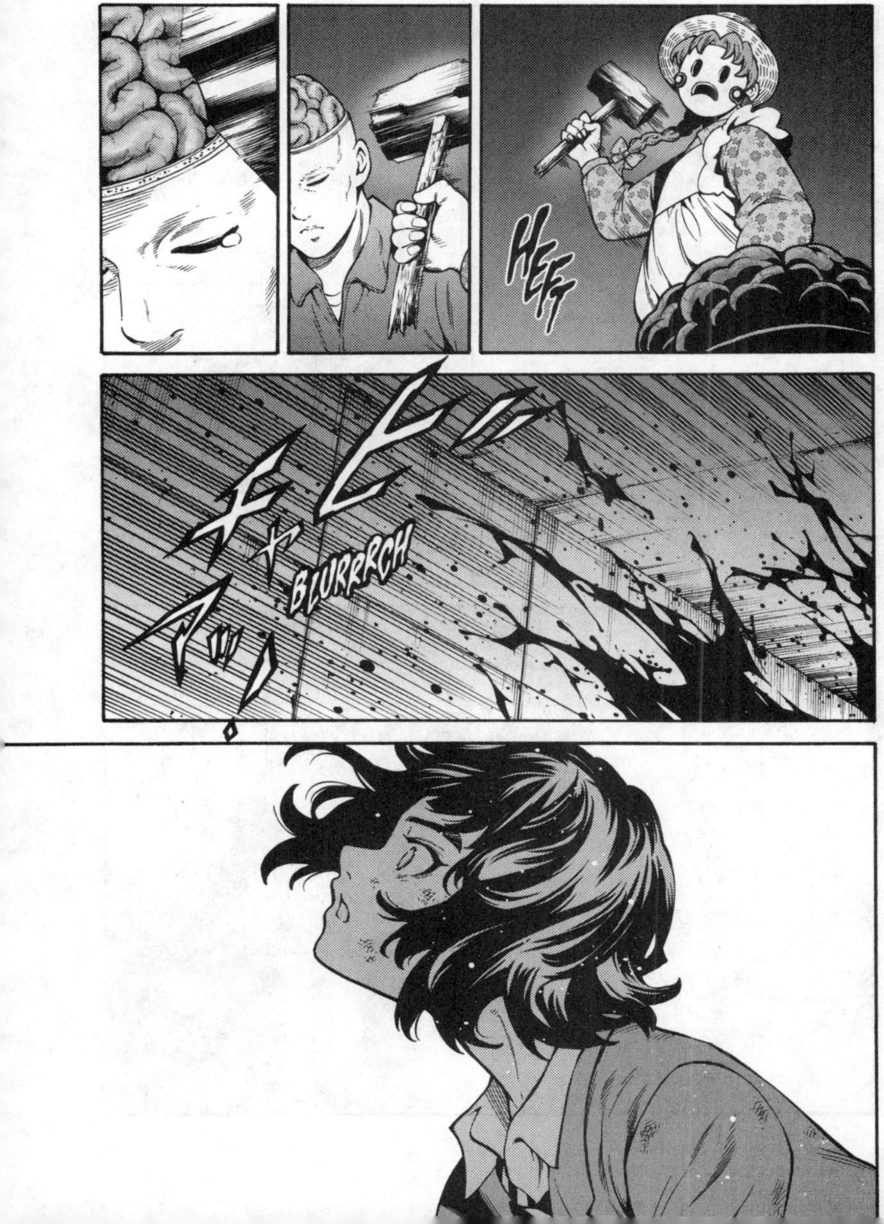
HEFT
BLURRRCH

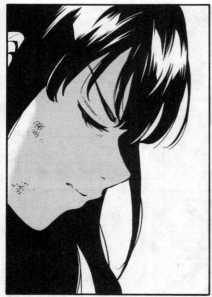

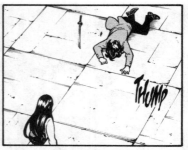

THUMP
......
ADMINIS-TRATOR-SAN WAS JUST ANOTHER VICTIM OF THIS DOMAIN.
THIS WORLD AND ITS SYSTEMS ARE AT FAULT FOR EVERY-THING.
STILL, NOW THAT THE KILLING'S ENDED, IT'LL BE PEACEFUL.

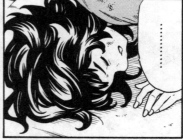

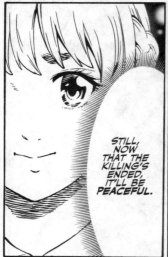

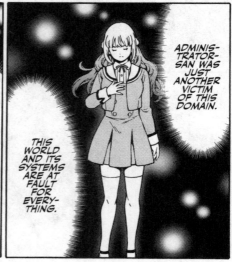

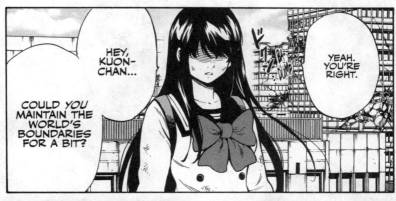

YEAH. YOU'RE RIGHT.
BA-DUMP
HEY, KUON-CHAN...
COULD YOU MAINTAIN THE WORLD'S BOUNDARIES FOR A BIT?
PARDON ME?
YOU'RE FREE TO USE MY ABILITIES AND BODY.
SWOON
SORRY... I'M...
WIPED... OUT.
THWUMP

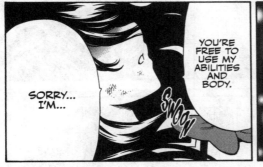

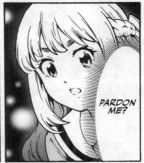

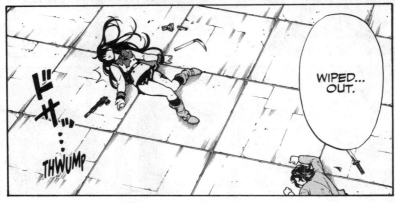

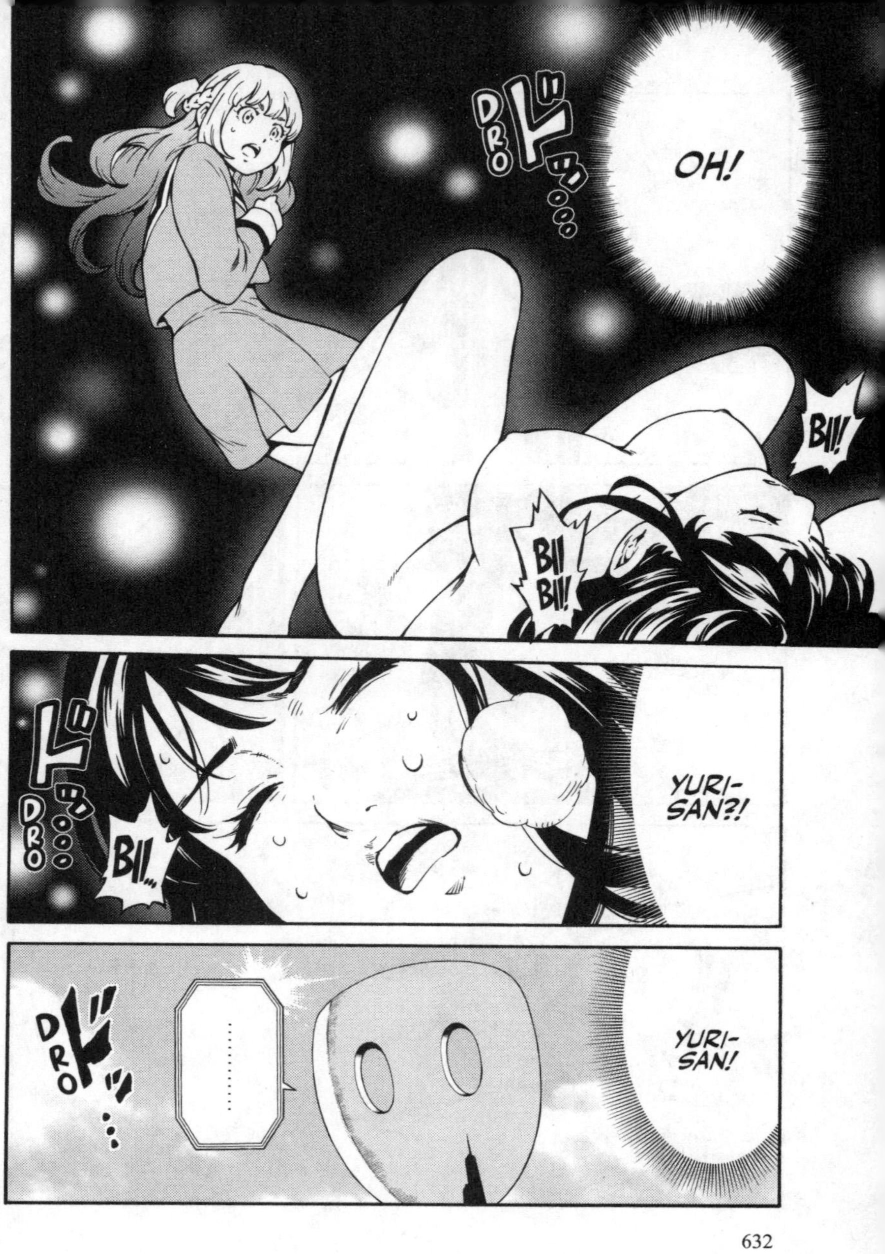

OH!
BII!
BII!
BII!
DRO...
YURI-SAN?!
BII...
DRO...
YURI-SAN!
......
DRO...

It was
always a
pain, fitting
Yoshida's
topknot
into a
panel.

HIGH-RISE INVASION

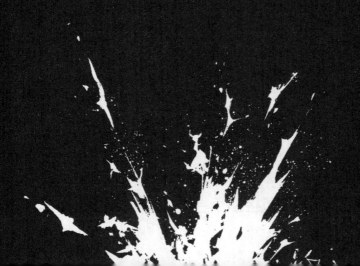

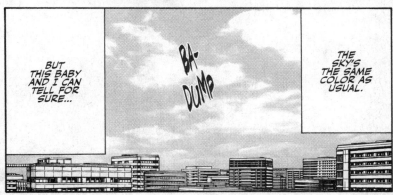

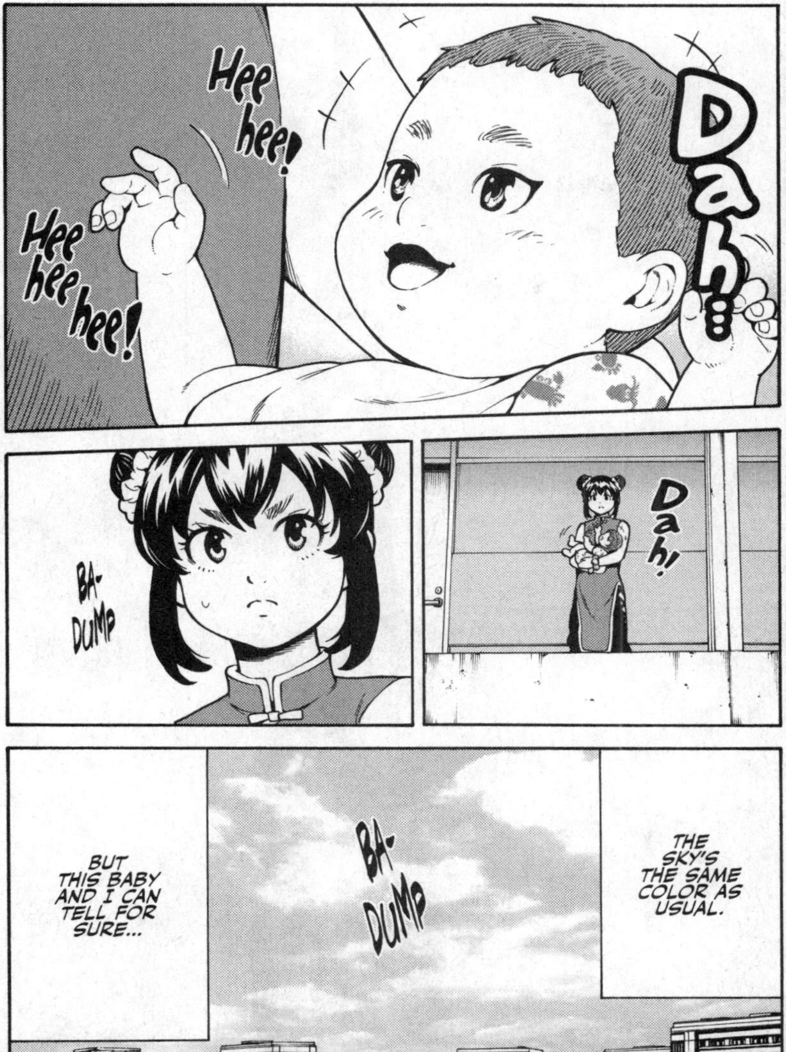
Dah...
Hee hee!
Hee hee hee hee!
Dah!
BA-DUMP
THE SKY'S THE SAME COLOR AS USUAL.
BA-DUMP
BUT THIS BABY AND I CAN TELL FOR SURE...

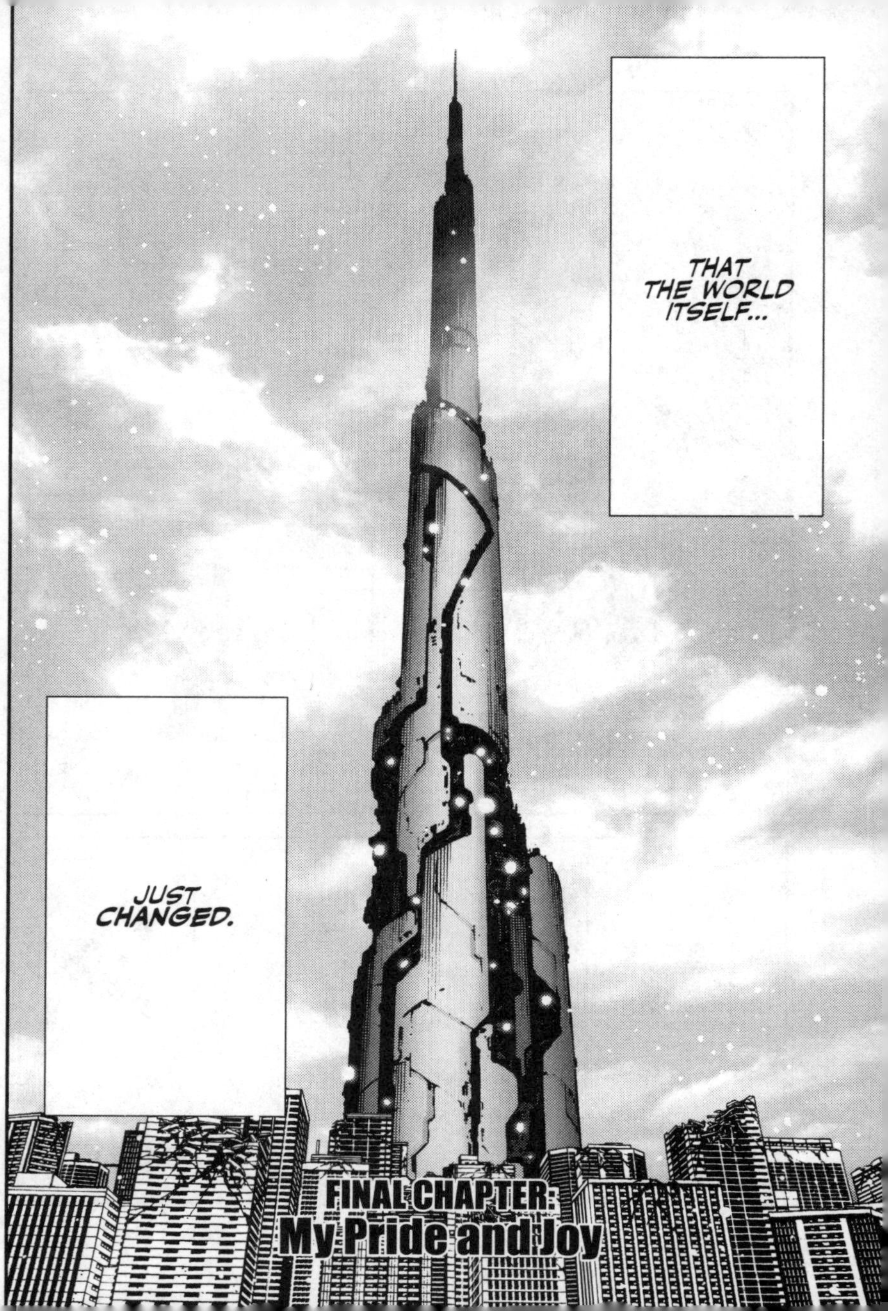
THAT THE WORLD ITSELF...
JUST CHANGED.
FINAL CHAPTER:
My Pride and Joy

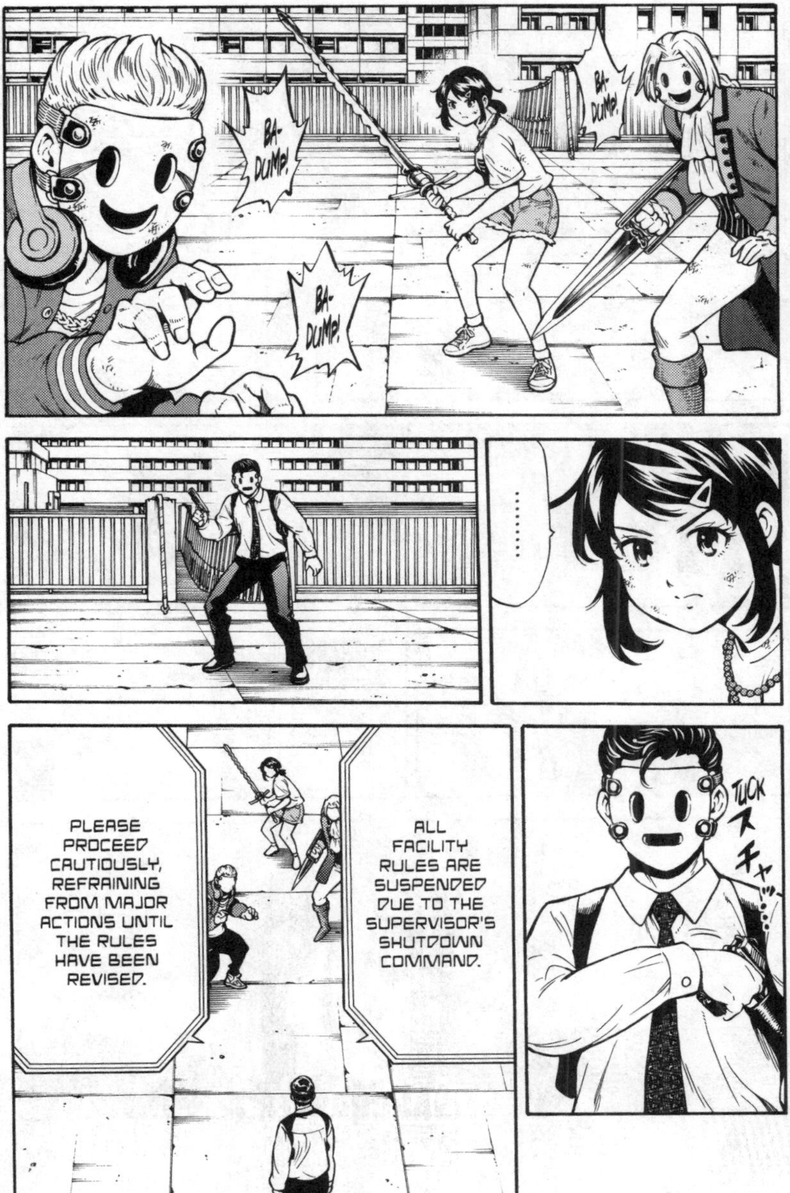

BA-DUMP!
BA-DUMP!
BA-DUMP!
......
TUCK
スチャッ…
ALL FACILITY RULES ARE SUSPENDED DUE TO THE SUPERVISOR'S SHUTDOWN COMMAND.
PLEASE PROCEED CAUTIOUSLY, REFRAINING FROM MAJOR ACTIONS UNTIL THE RULES HAVE BEEN REVISED.

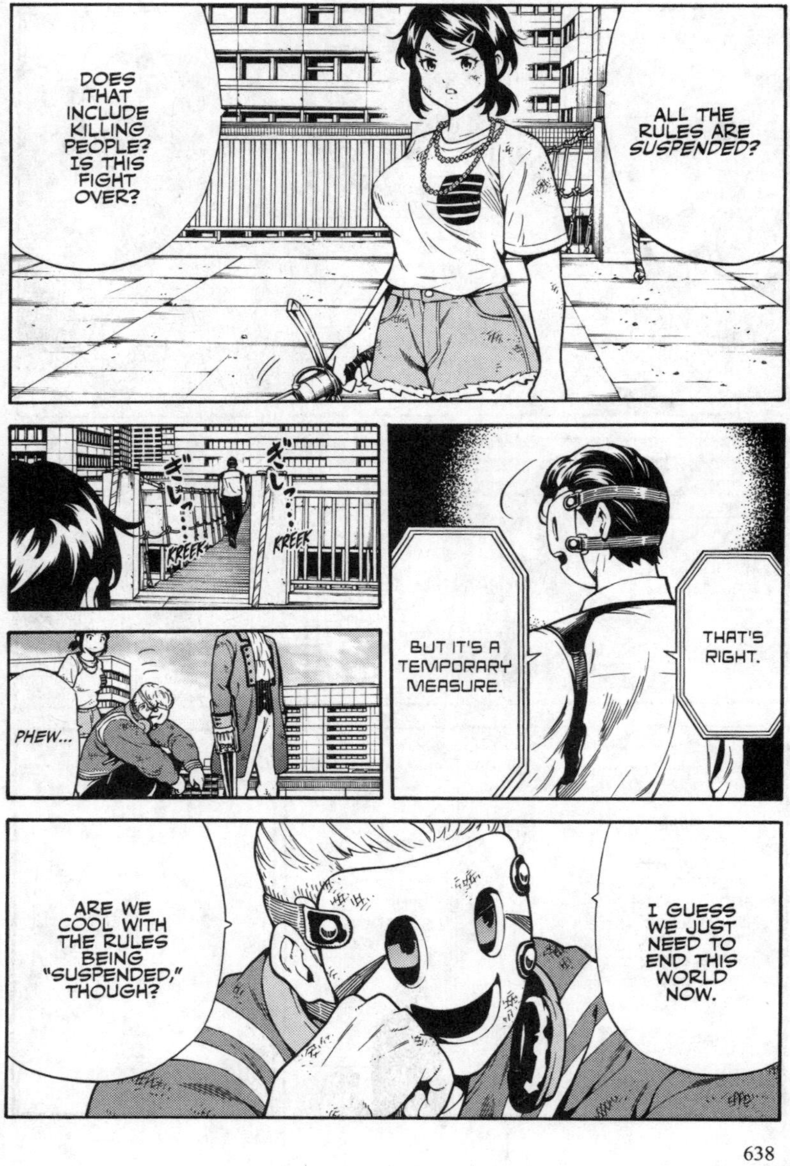
ALL THE RULES ARE *SUSPENDED?*
DOES THAT INCLUDE KILLING PEOPLE? IS THIS FIGHT OVER?
THAT'S RIGHT.
BUT IT'S A TEMPORARY MEASURE.
ぎしっ…
KREEK
ぎしっ…
KREEK
PHEW...
I GUESS WE JUST NEED TO END THIS WORLD NOW.
ARE WE COOL WITH THE RULES BEING "SUSPENDED," THOUGH?

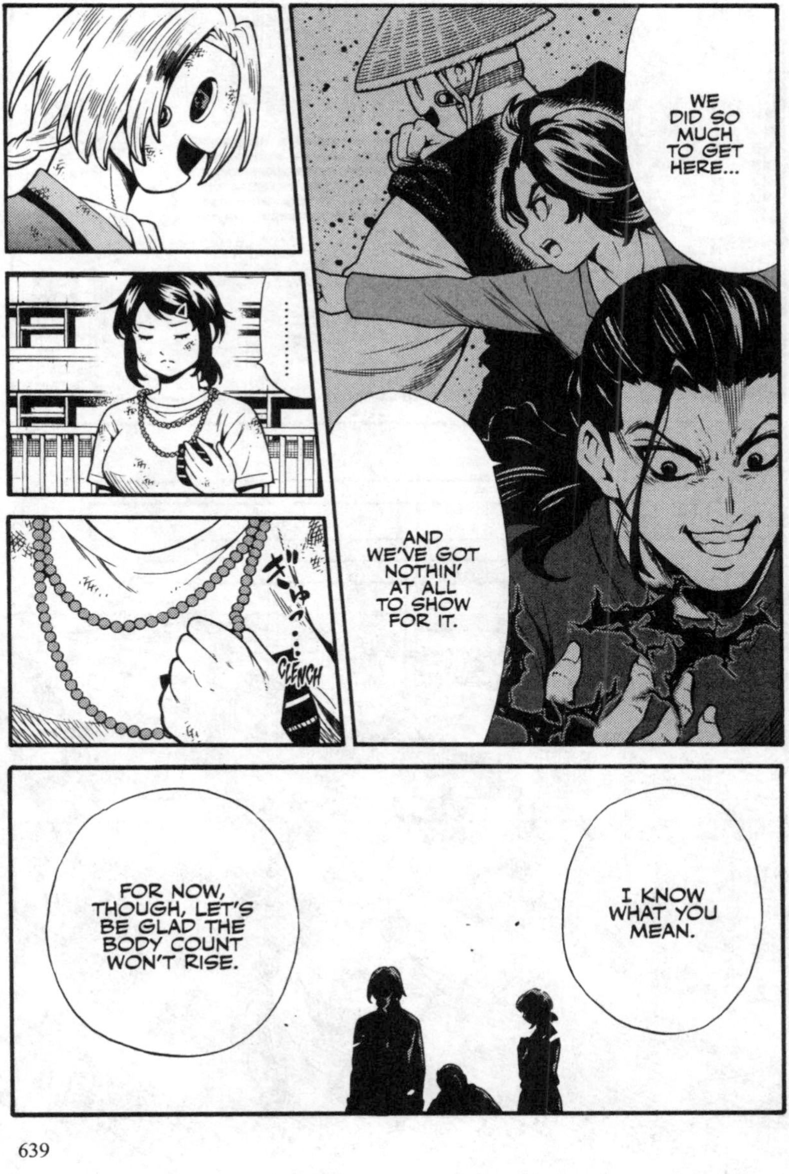
WE DID SO MUCH TO GET HERE...
AND WE'VE GOT NOTHIN' AT ALL TO SHOW FOR IT.
......
ぎゅっ...
CLENCH
I KNOW WHAT YOU MEAN.
FOR NOW, THOUGH, LET'S BE GLAD THE BODY COUNT WON'T RISE.

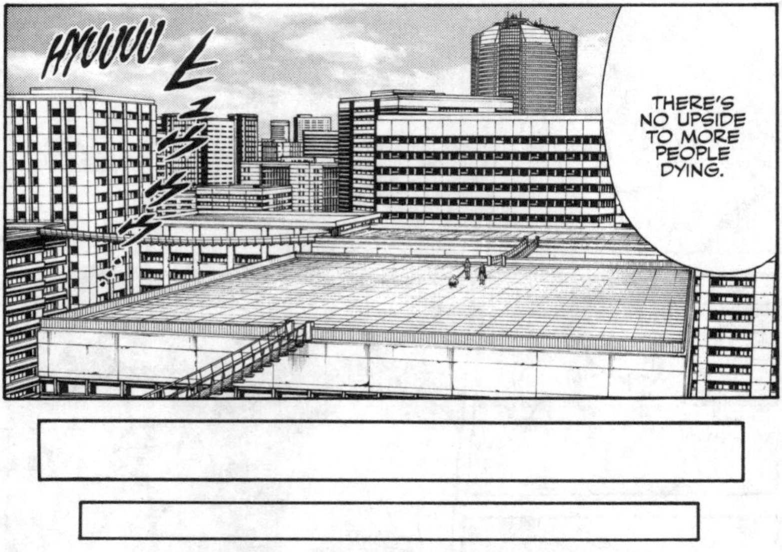
HYUUUU
THERE'S NO UPSIDE TO MORE PEOPLE DYING.

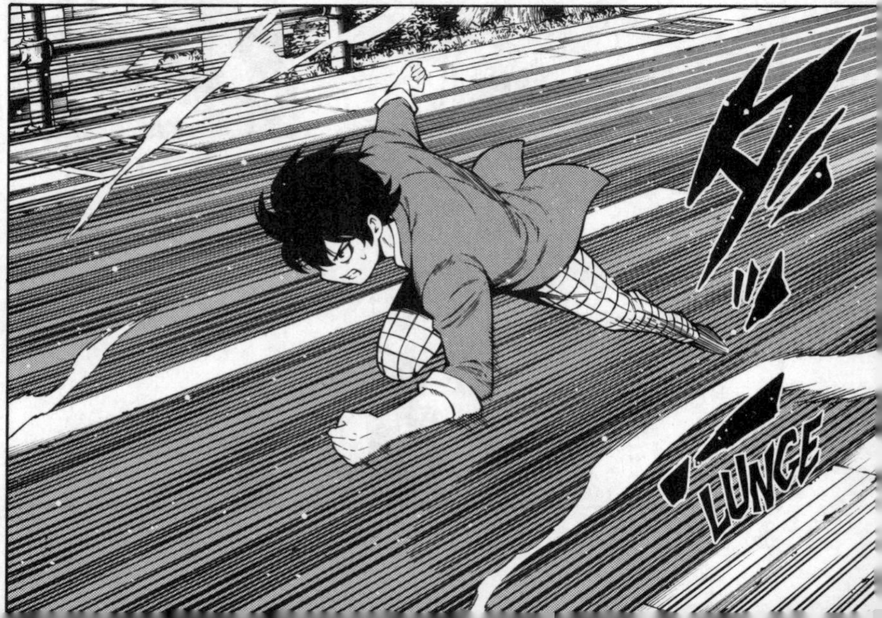
LUNGE

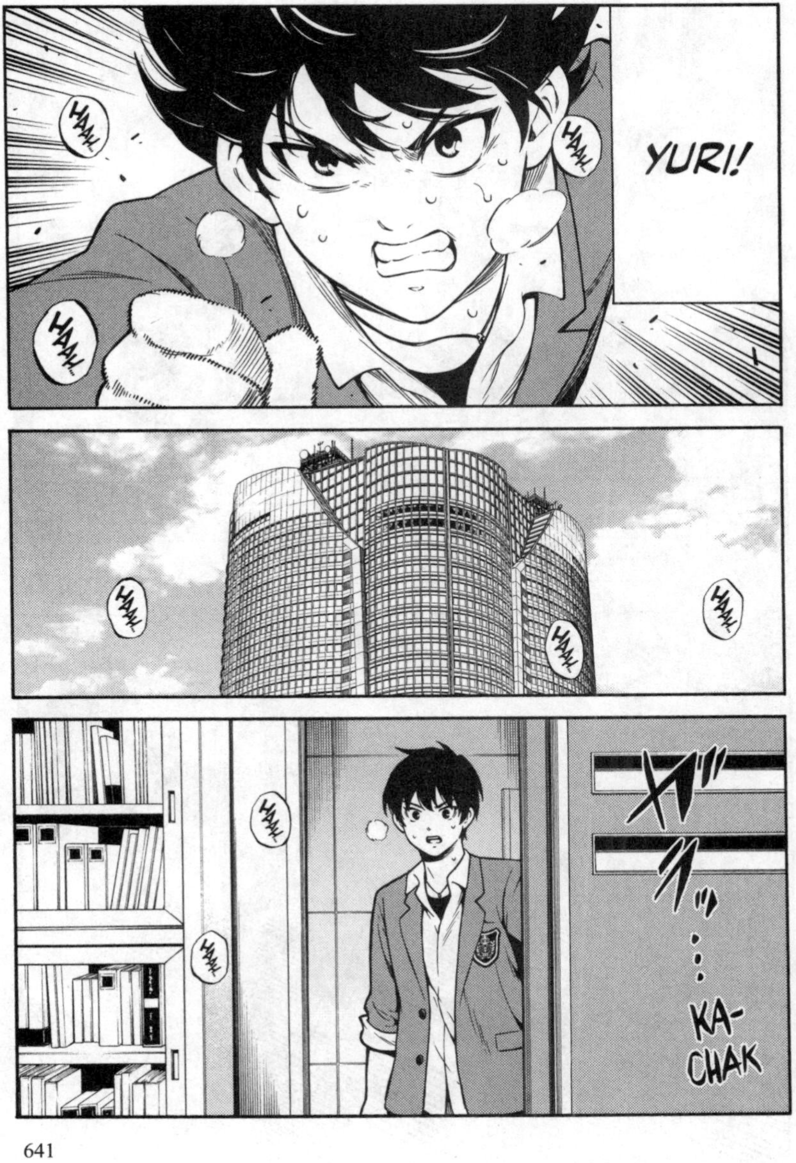
YURI!
HAAH
HAAH
HAAH
HAAH
HAAH
HAAH
KA-CHAK
HAAH
HAAH

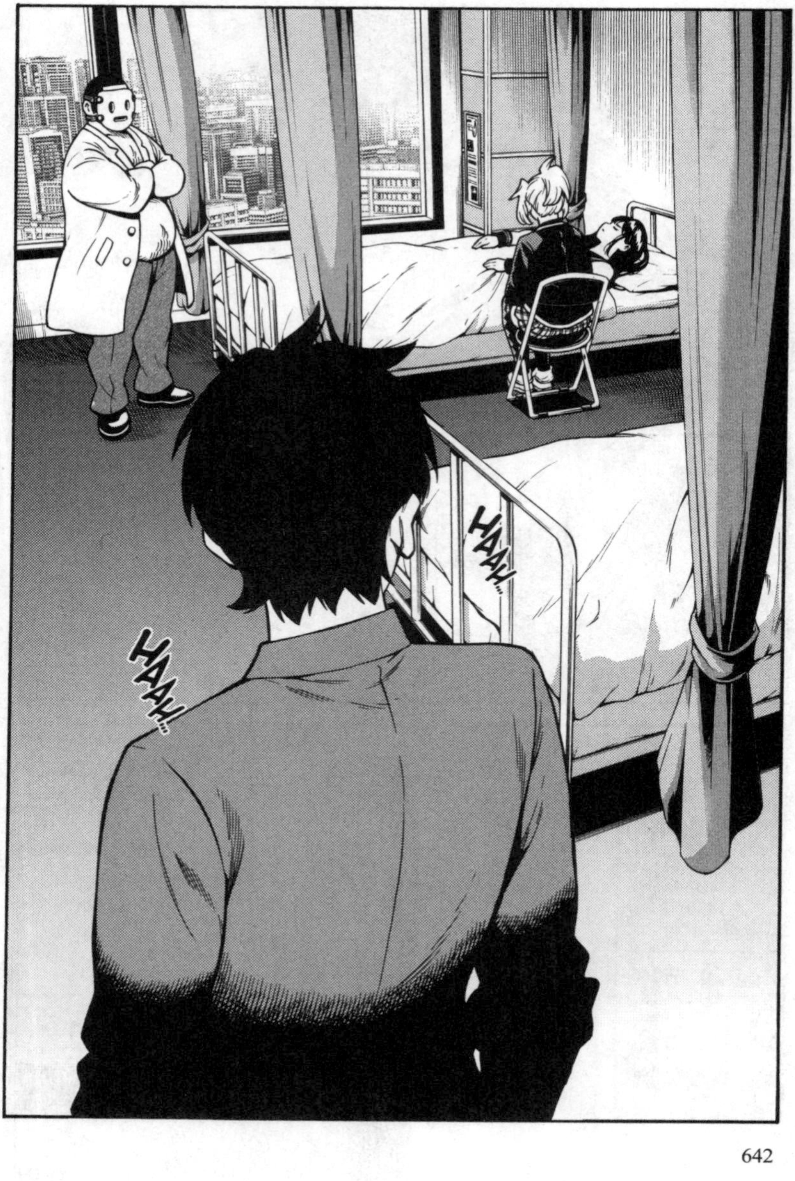
HAAH...
HAAH...

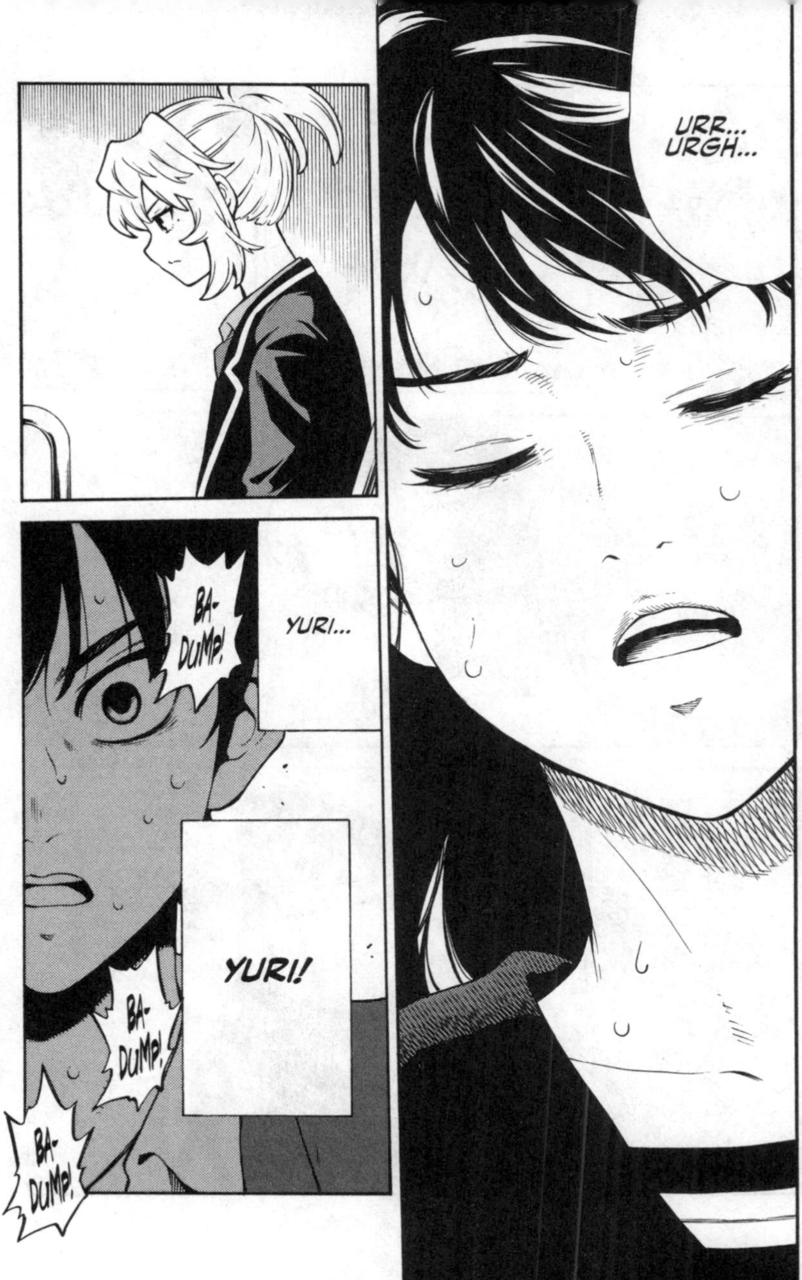
URR... URGH...
BA-DUMP!
YURI...
YURI!
BA-DUMP!
BA-DUMP!

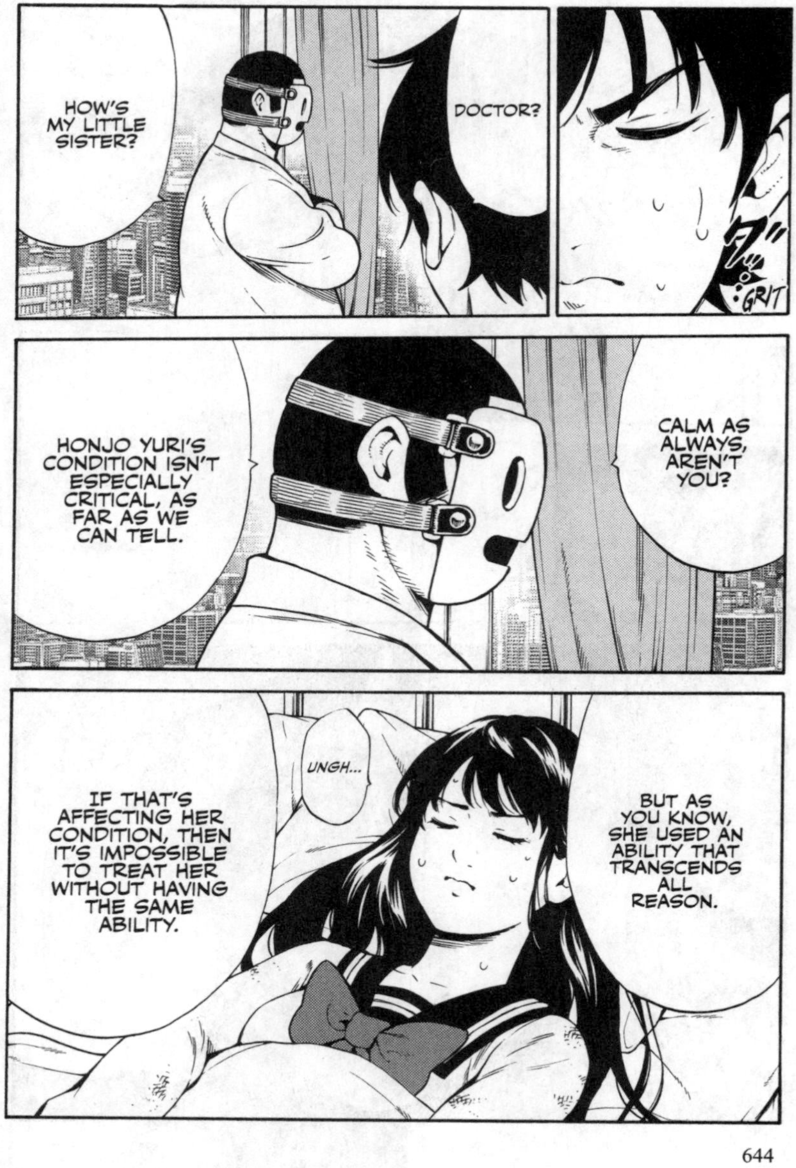
GRIT
DOCTOR?
HOW'S MY LITTLE SISTER?
CALM AS ALWAYS, AREN'T YOU?
HONJO YURI'S CONDITION ISN'T ESPECIALLY CRITICAL, AS FAR AS WE CAN TELL.
BUT AS YOU KNOW, SHE USED AN ABILITY THAT TRANSCENDS ALL REASON.
UNGH...
IF THAT'S AFFECTING HER CONDITION, THEN IT'S IMPOSSIBLE TO TREAT HER WITHOUT HAVING THE SAME ABILITY.

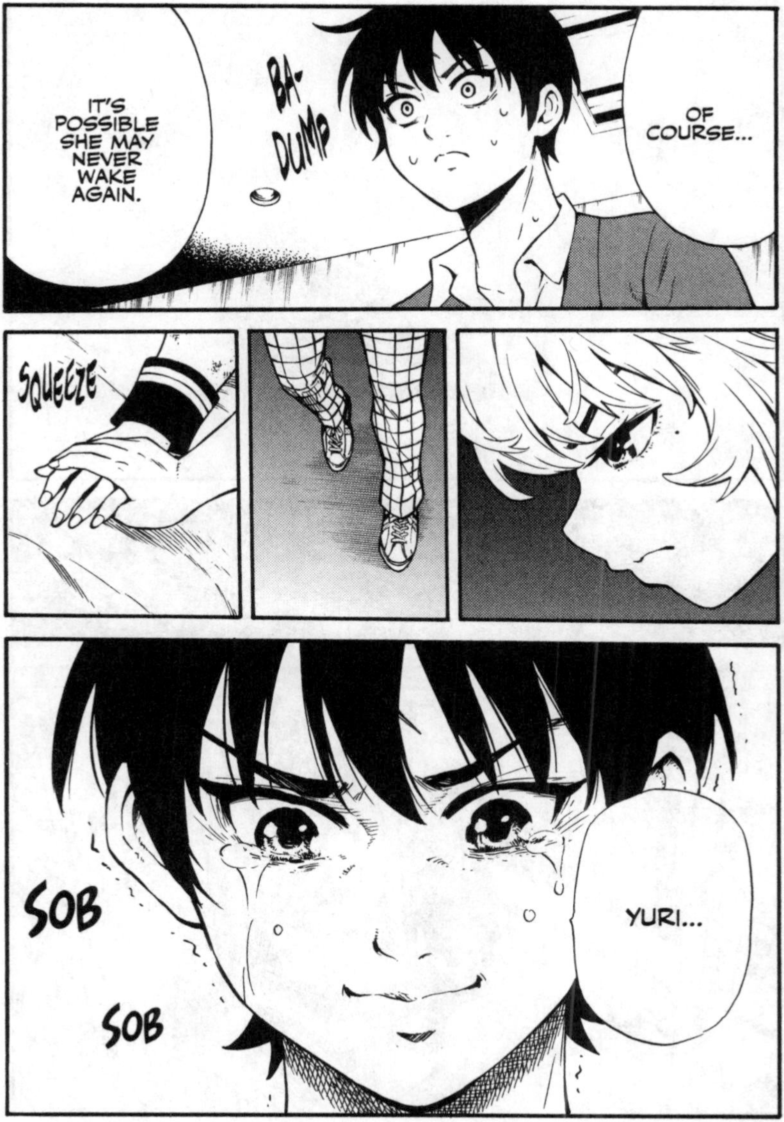
OF COURSE...
BA-DUMP
IT'S POSSIBLE SHE MAY NEVER WAKE AGAIN.
SQUEEZE
YURI...
SOB
SOB

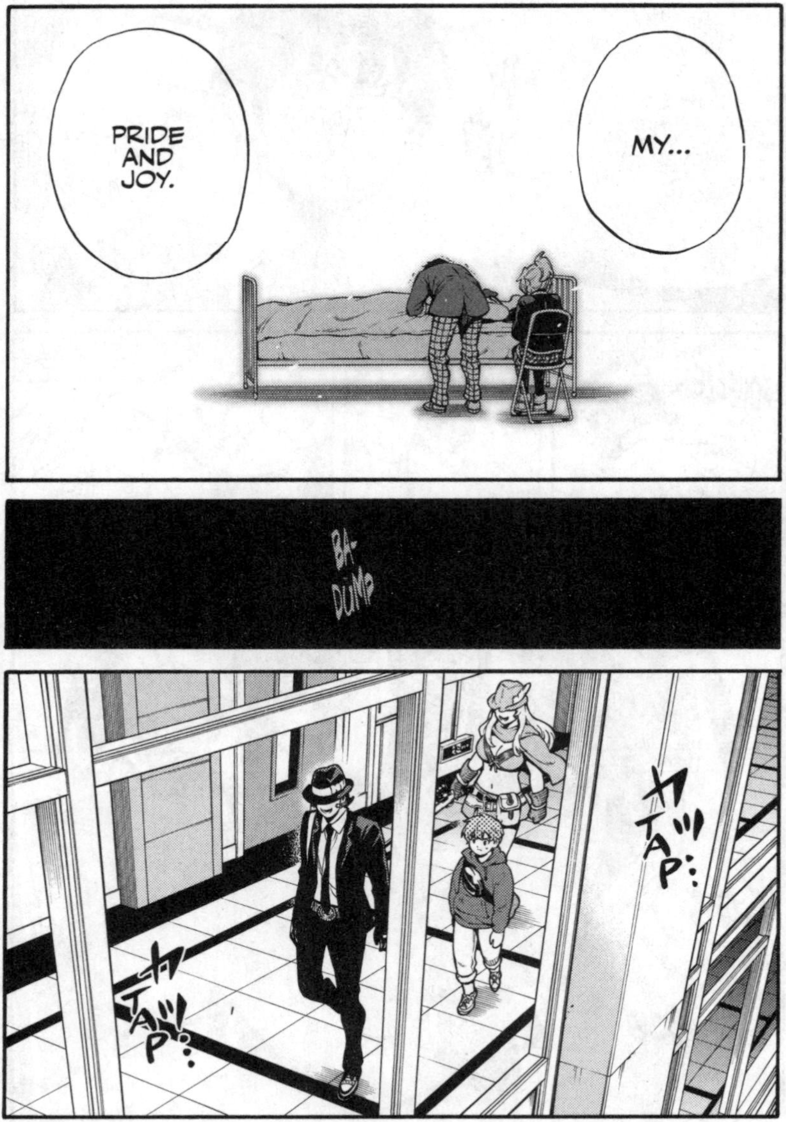
MY...
PRIDE AND JOY.
BA-DUMP
TAP
TAP

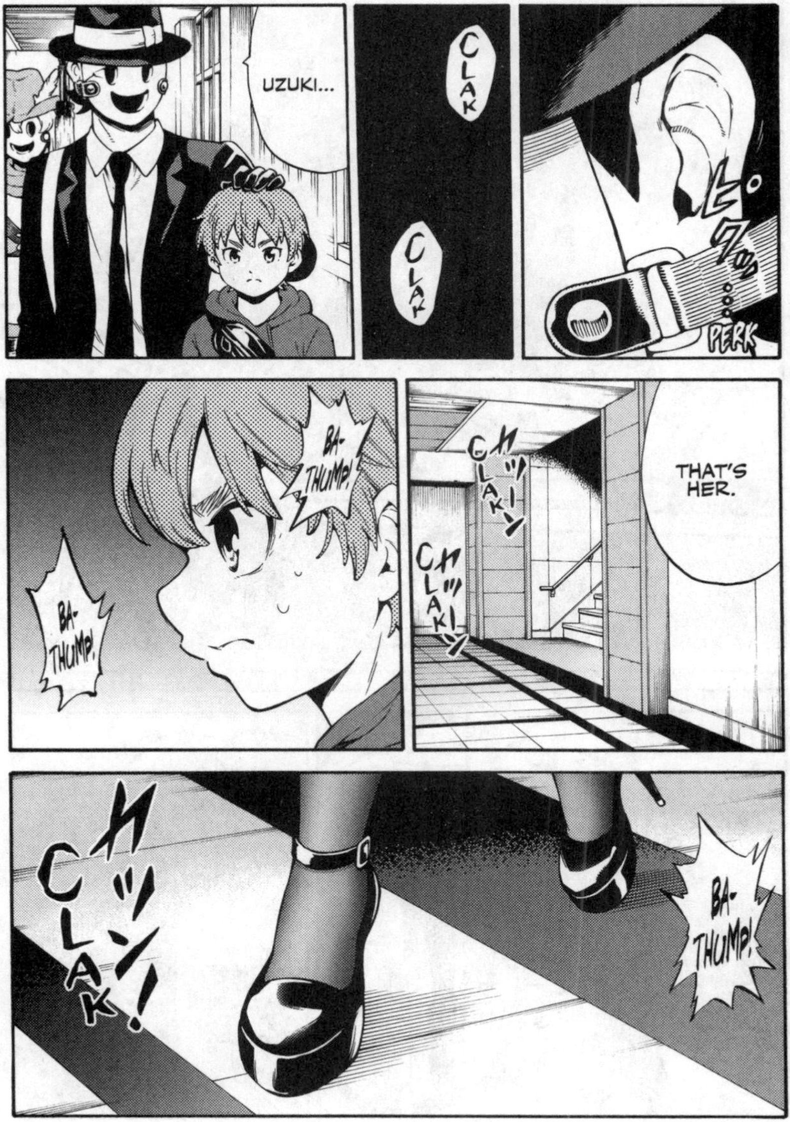
PERK
CLAK
CLAK
UZUKI...
THAT'S HER.
CLAK
CLAK
BA-THUMP!
BA-THUMP!
BA-THUMP!
CLAK!

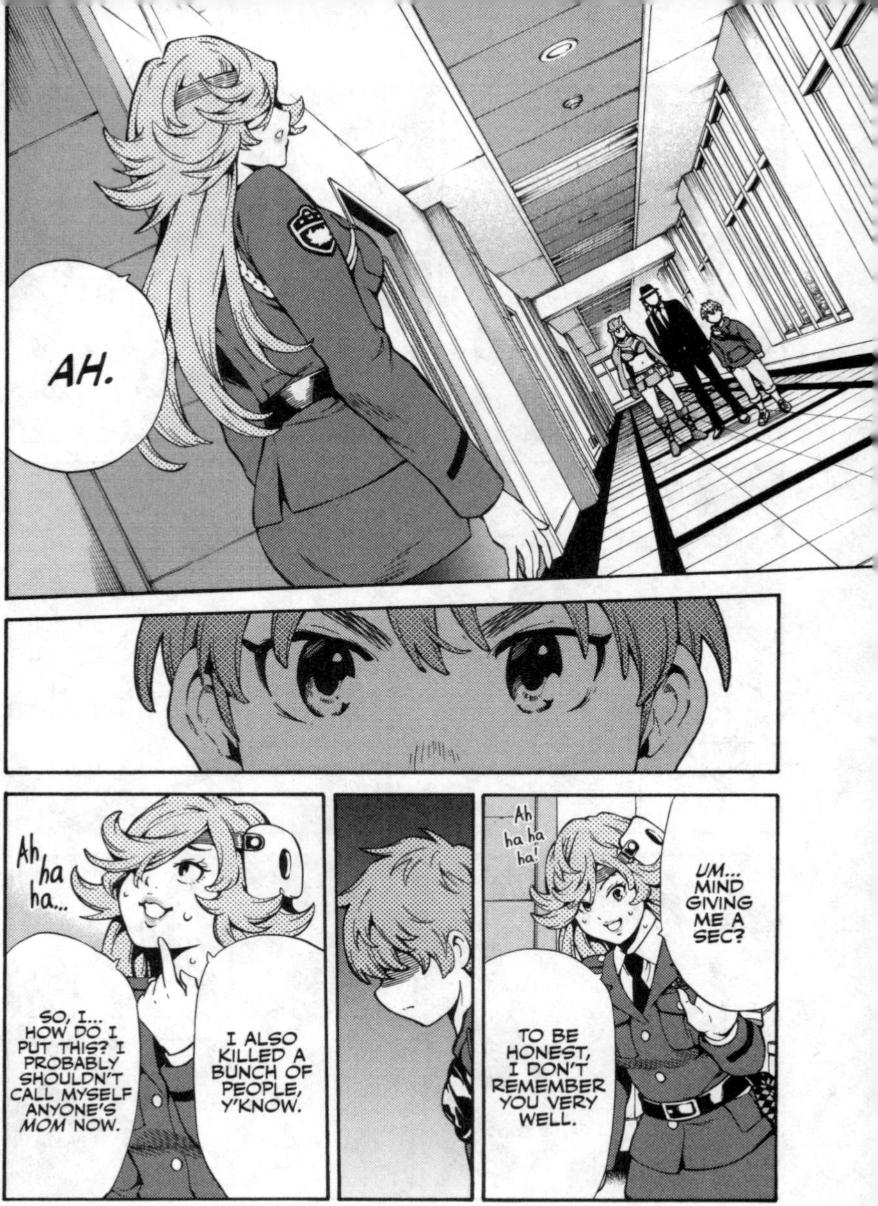
AH.
Ah ha ha ha!
UM... MIND GIVING ME A SEC?
TO BE HONEST, I DON'T REMEMBER YOU VERY WELL.
Ah ha ha...
SO, I... HOW DO I PUT THIS? I PROBABLY SHOULDN'T CALL MYSELF ANYONE'S MOM NOW.
I ALSO KILLED A BUNCH OF PEOPLE, Y'KNOW.

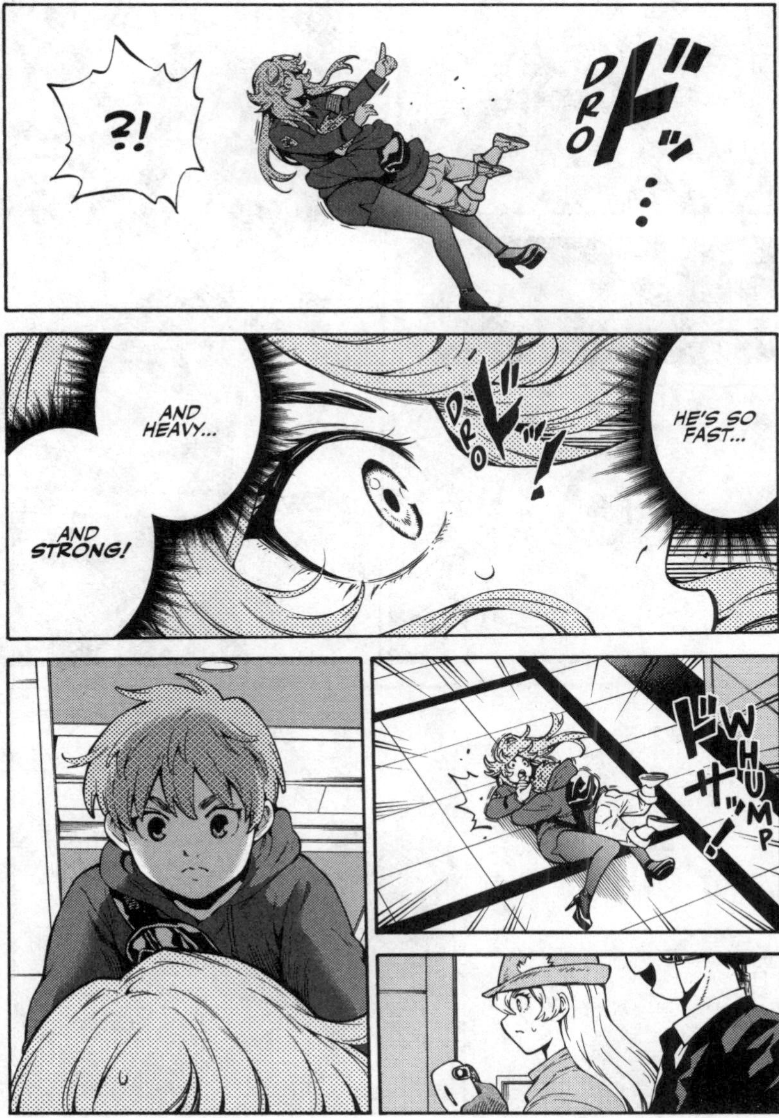
DRO ドッ...
?!
HE'S SO FAST...
DRO ドッ!
AND HEAVY...
AND STRONG!
ドサッ WHUMP!

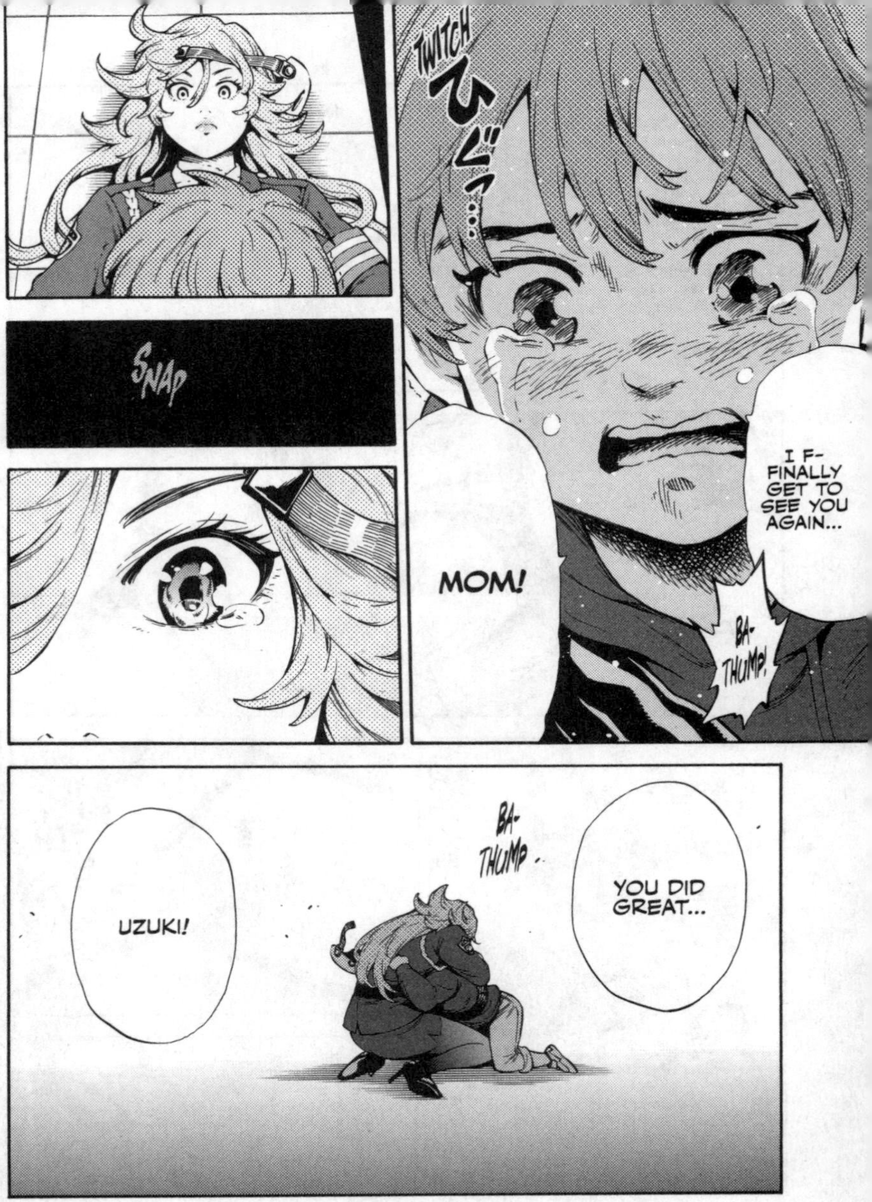
TWITCH
ひぐっ…
I F-FINALLY GET TO SEE YOU AGAIN...
MOM!
BA-THUMP!
SNAP
YOU DID GREAT...
BA-THUMP
UZUKI!

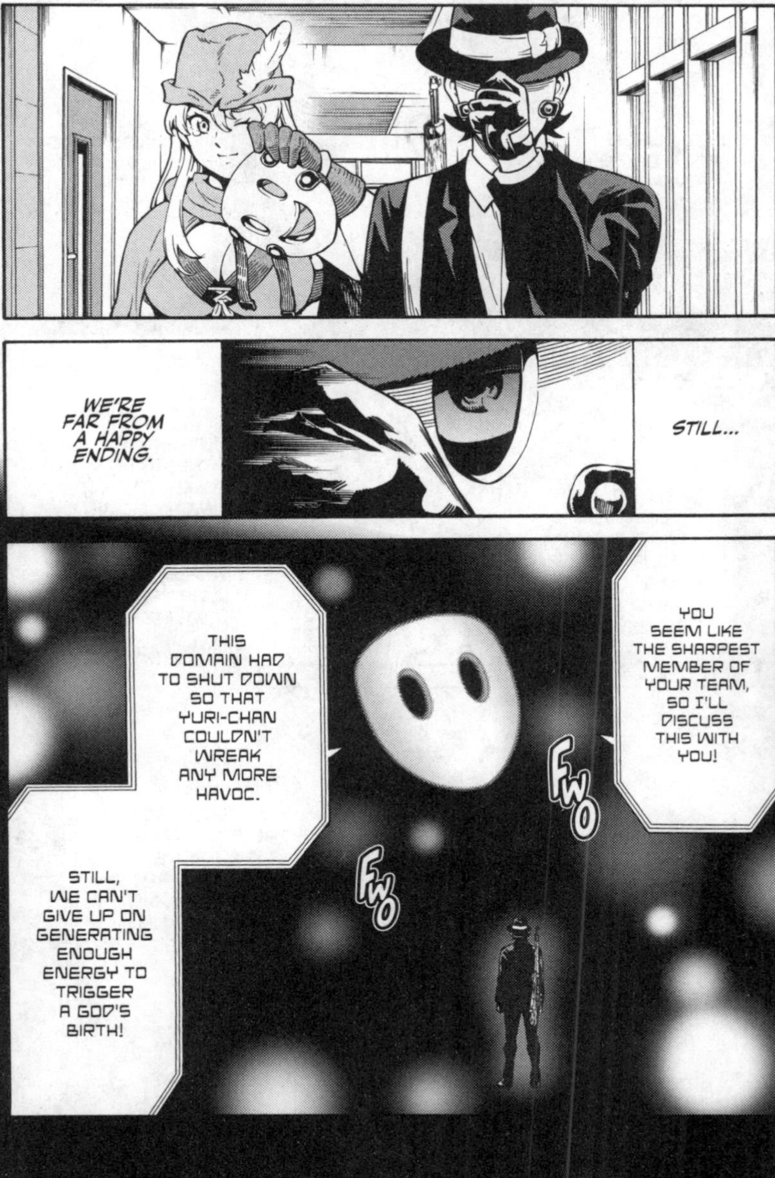
STILL...
WE'RE FAR FROM A HAPPY ENDING.
YOU SEEM LIKE THE SHARPEST MEMBER OF YOUR TEAM, SO I'LL DISCUSS THIS WITH YOU!
FWO
THIS DOMAIN HAD TO SHUT DOWN SO THAT YURI-CHAN COULDN'T WREAK ANY MORE HAVOC.
STILL, WE CAN'T GIVE UP ON GENERATING ENOUGH ENERGY TO TRIGGER A GOD'S BIRTH!
FWO

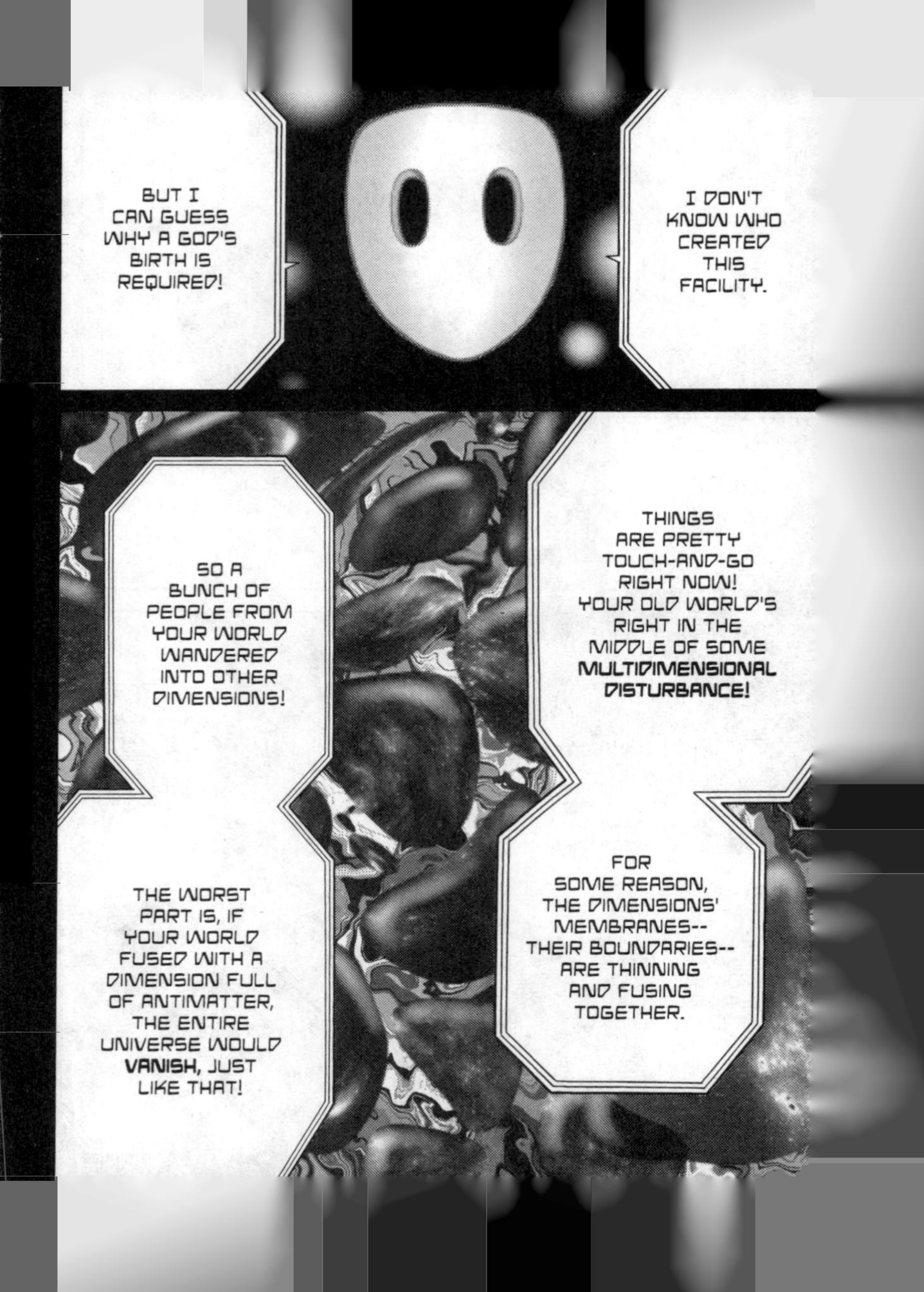
I DON'T KNOW WHO CREATED THIS FACILITY.
BUT I CAN GUESS WHY A GOD'S BIRTH IS REQUIRED!
THINGS ARE PRETTY TOUCH-AND-GO RIGHT NOW! YOUR OLD WORLD'S RIGHT IN THE MIDDLE OF SOME **MULTIDIMENSIONAL DISTURBANCE!**
SO A BUNCH OF PEOPLE FROM YOUR WORLD WANDERED INTO OTHER DIMENSIONS!
FOR SOME REASON, THE DIMENSIONS' MEMBRANES-- THEIR BOUNDARIES-- ARE THINNING AND FUSING TOGETHER.
THE WORST PART IS, IF YOUR WORLD FUSED WITH A DIMENSION FULL OF ANTIMATTER, THE ENTIRE UNIVERSE WOULD **VANISH,** JUST LIKE THAT!

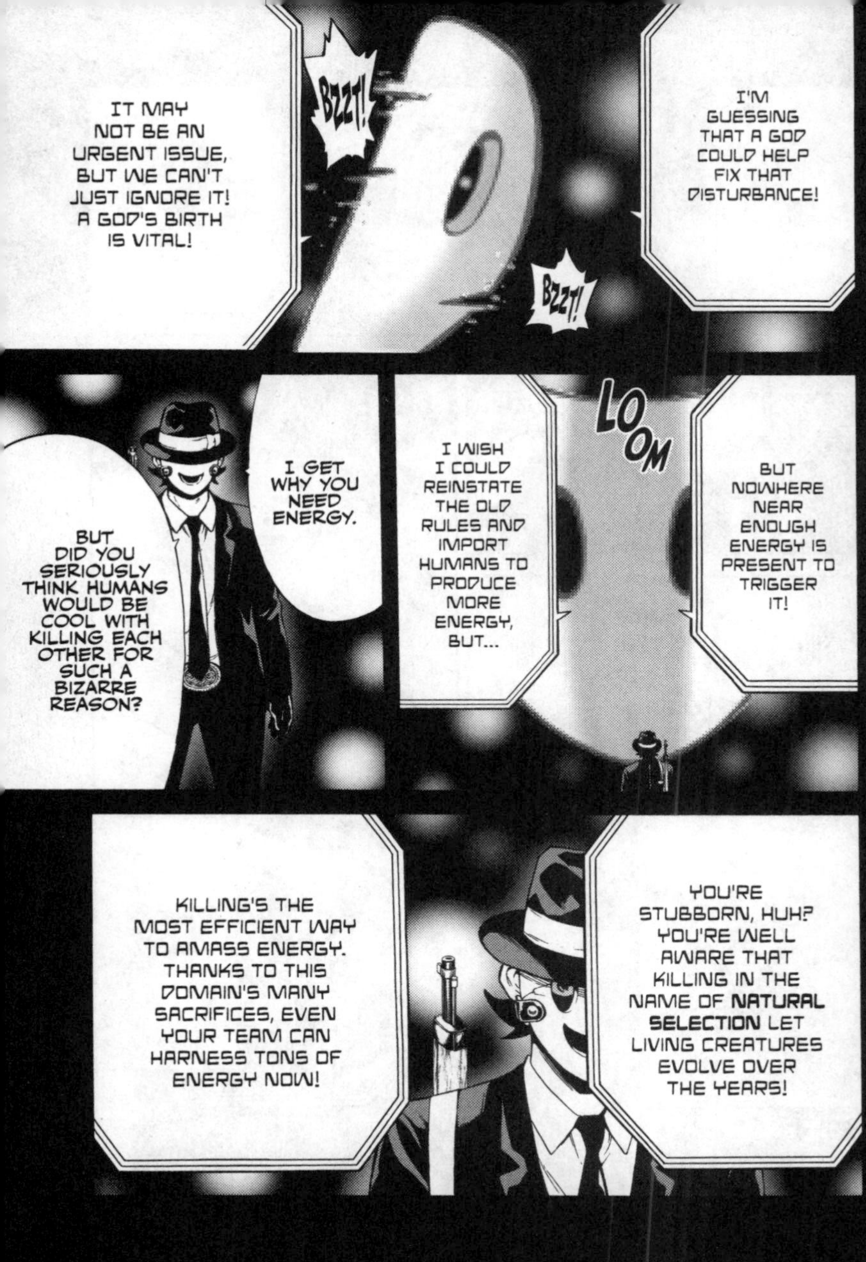
I'M GUESSING THAT A GOD COULD HELP FIX THAT DISTURBANCE!
BZZT!
IT MAY NOT BE AN URGENT ISSUE, BUT WE CAN'T JUST IGNORE IT! A GOD'S BIRTH IS VITAL!
BZZT!
BUT NOWHERE NEAR ENOUGH ENERGY IS PRESENT TO TRIGGER IT!
LOOM
I WISH I COULD REINSTATE THE OLD RULES AND IMPORT HUMANS TO PRODUCE MORE ENERGY, BUT...
I GET WHY YOU NEED ENERGY.
BUT DID YOU SERIOUSLY THINK HUMANS WOULD BE COOL WITH KILLING EACH OTHER FOR SUCH A BIZARRE REASON?
YOU'RE STUBBORN, HUH? YOU'RE WELL AWARE THAT KILLING IN THE NAME OF **NATURAL SELECTION** LET LIVING CREATURES EVOLVE OVER THE YEARS!
KILLING'S THE MOST EFFICIENT WAY TO AMASS ENERGY. THANKS TO THIS DOMAIN'S MANY SACRIFICES, EVEN YOUR TEAM CAN HARNESS TONS OF ENERGY NOW!

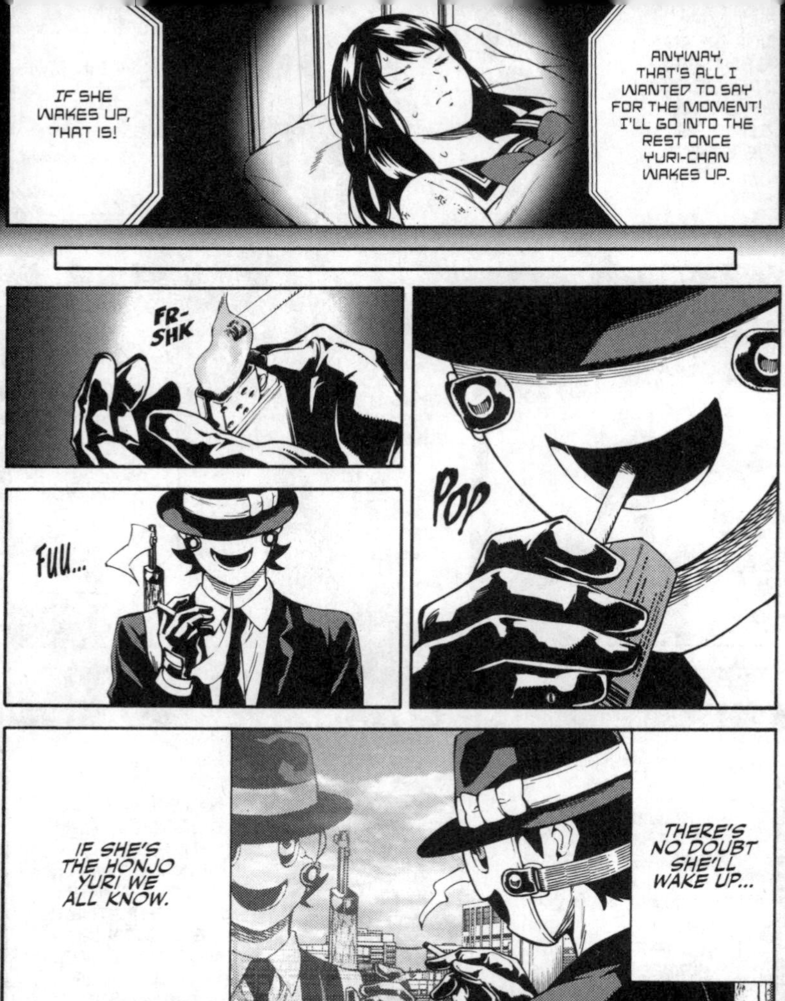
ANYWAY, THAT'S ALL I WANTED TO SAY FOR THE MOMENT! I'LL GO INTO THE REST ONCE YURI-CHAN WAKES UP.
IF SHE WAKES UP, THAT IS!
POP
FR-SHK
FUU...
THERE'S NO DOUBT SHE'LL WAKE UP...
IF SHE'S THE HONJO YURI WE ALL KNOW.

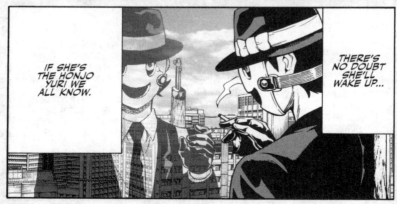

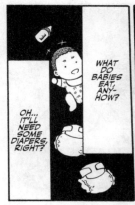

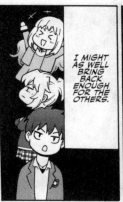

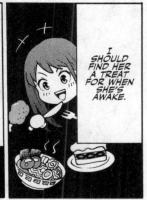

I SHOULD FIND HER A TREAT FOR WHEN SHE'S AWAKE.
I MIGHT AS WELL BRING BACK ENOUGH FOR THE OTHERS.
WHAT DO BABIES EAT, ANY-HOW?
OH... IT'LL NEED SOME DIAPERS, RIGHT?
WHAT THE HELL? WHEN DID I START THINKING LIKE A PARENT?
Sigh...
?
NGH... UNGH...

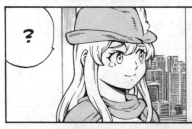

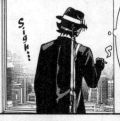

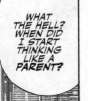

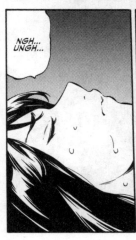

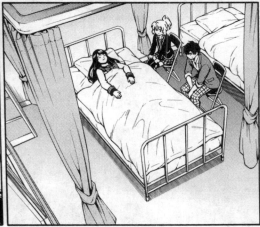

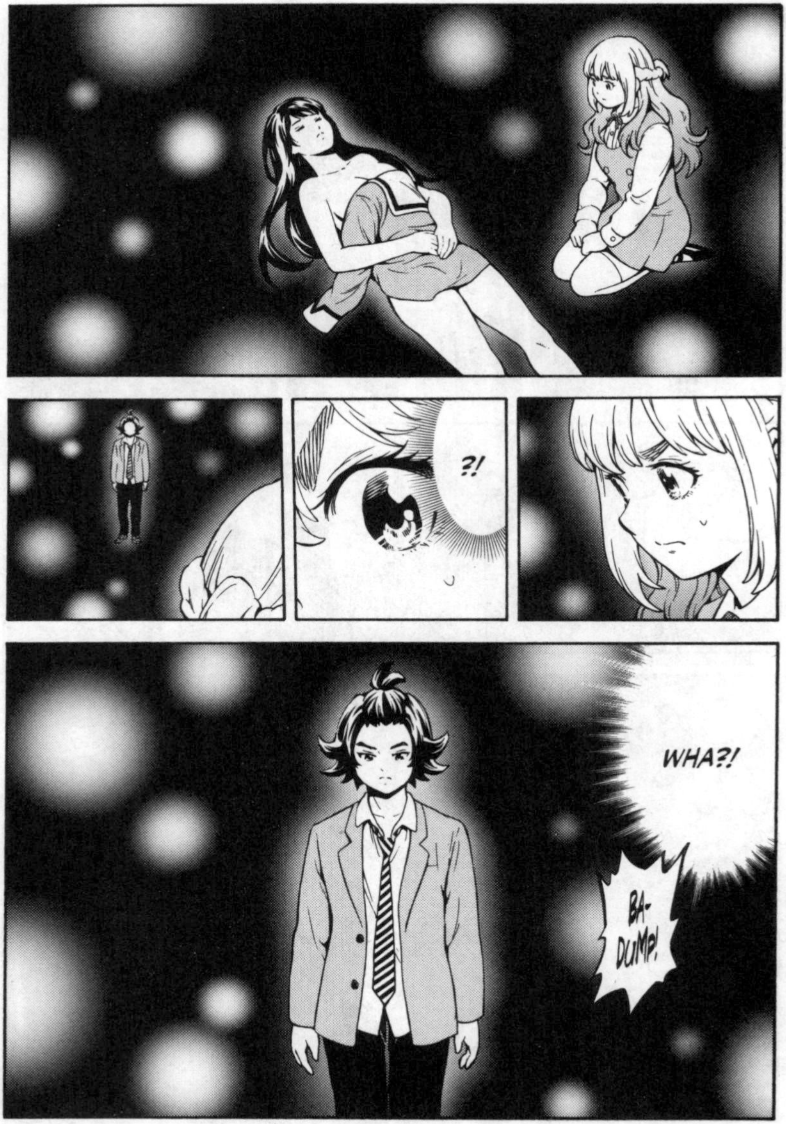
?!
WHA?!
BA-DUMP!

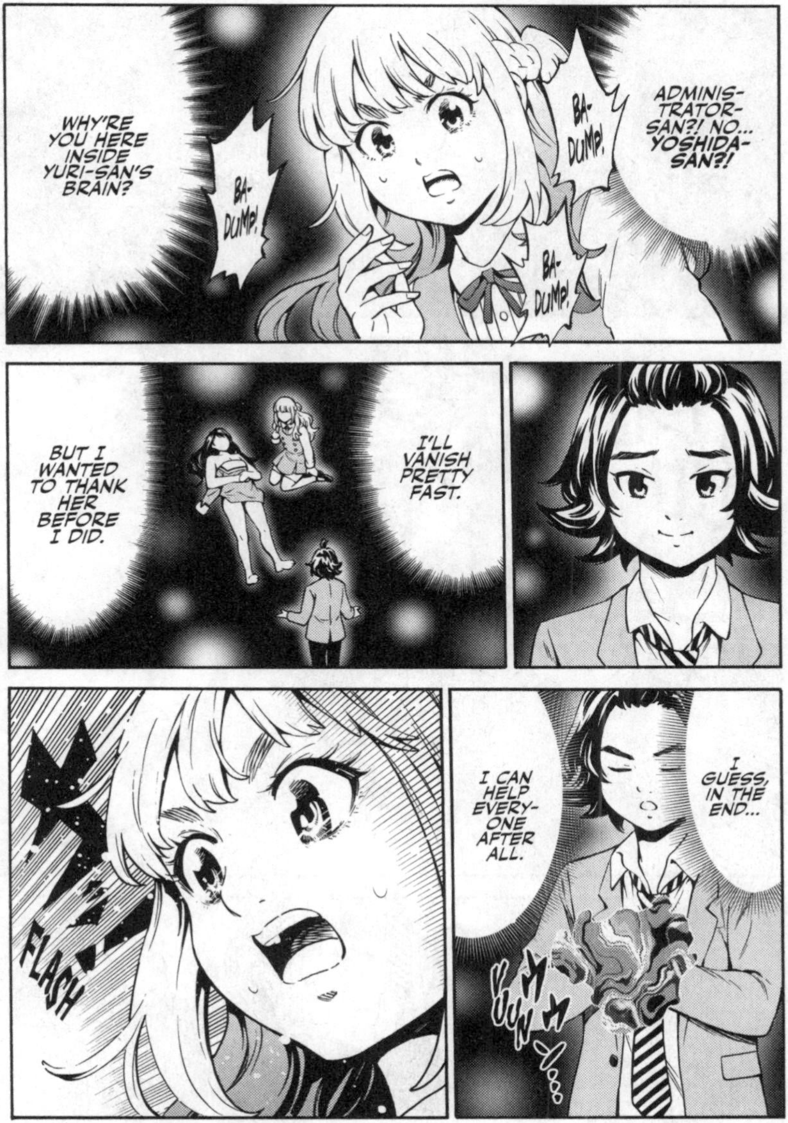
ADMINIS-TRATOR-SAN?! NO... YOSHIDA-SAN?!
BA-DUMP!
BA-DUMP!
WHY'RE YOU HERE INSIDE YURI-SAN'S BRAIN?
BA-DUMP!
I'LL VANISH PRETTY FAST.
BUT I WANTED TO THANK HER BEFORE I DID.
I GUESS, IN THE END...
I CAN HELP EVERY-ONE AFTER ALL.
FLASH

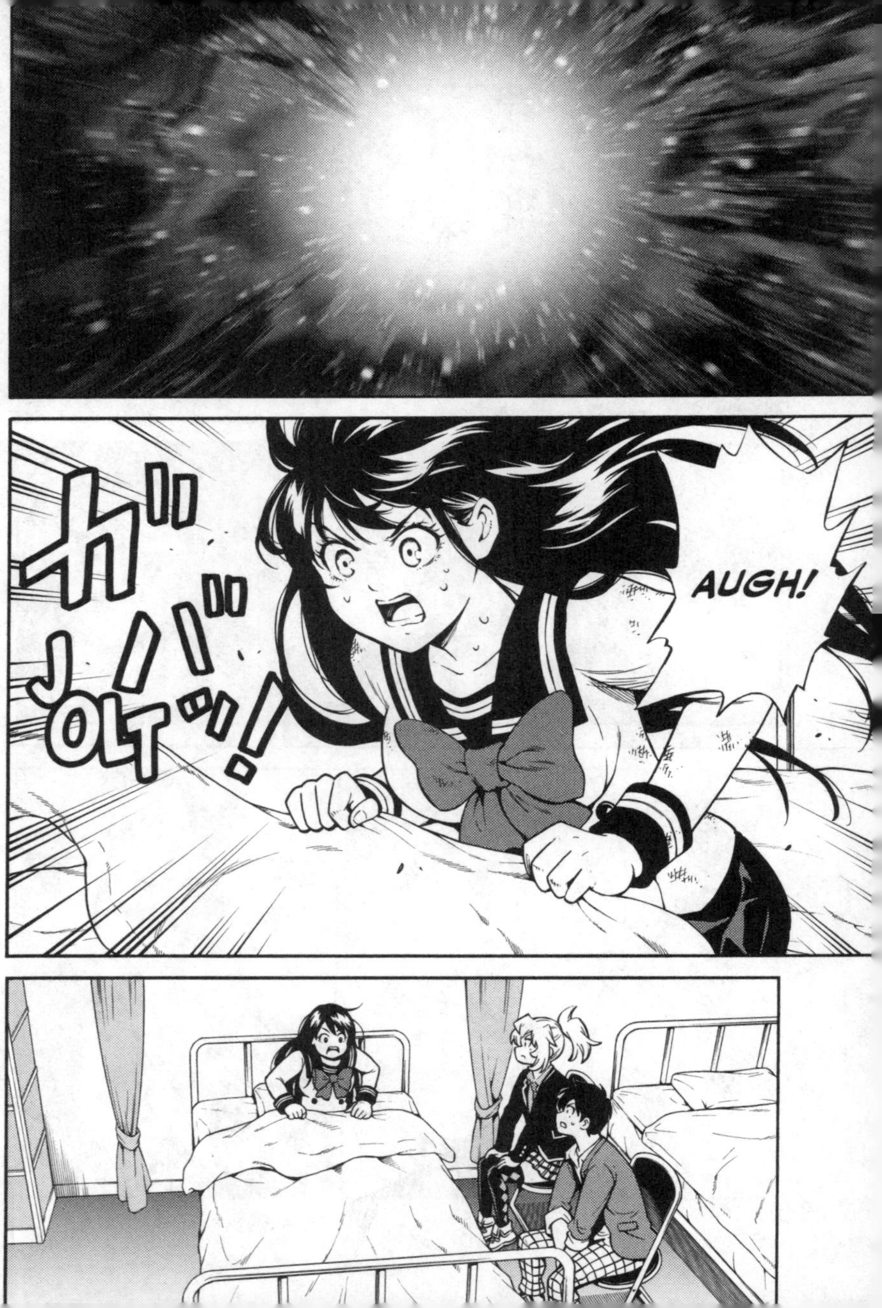
AUGH!
ガバッ
JOLT!

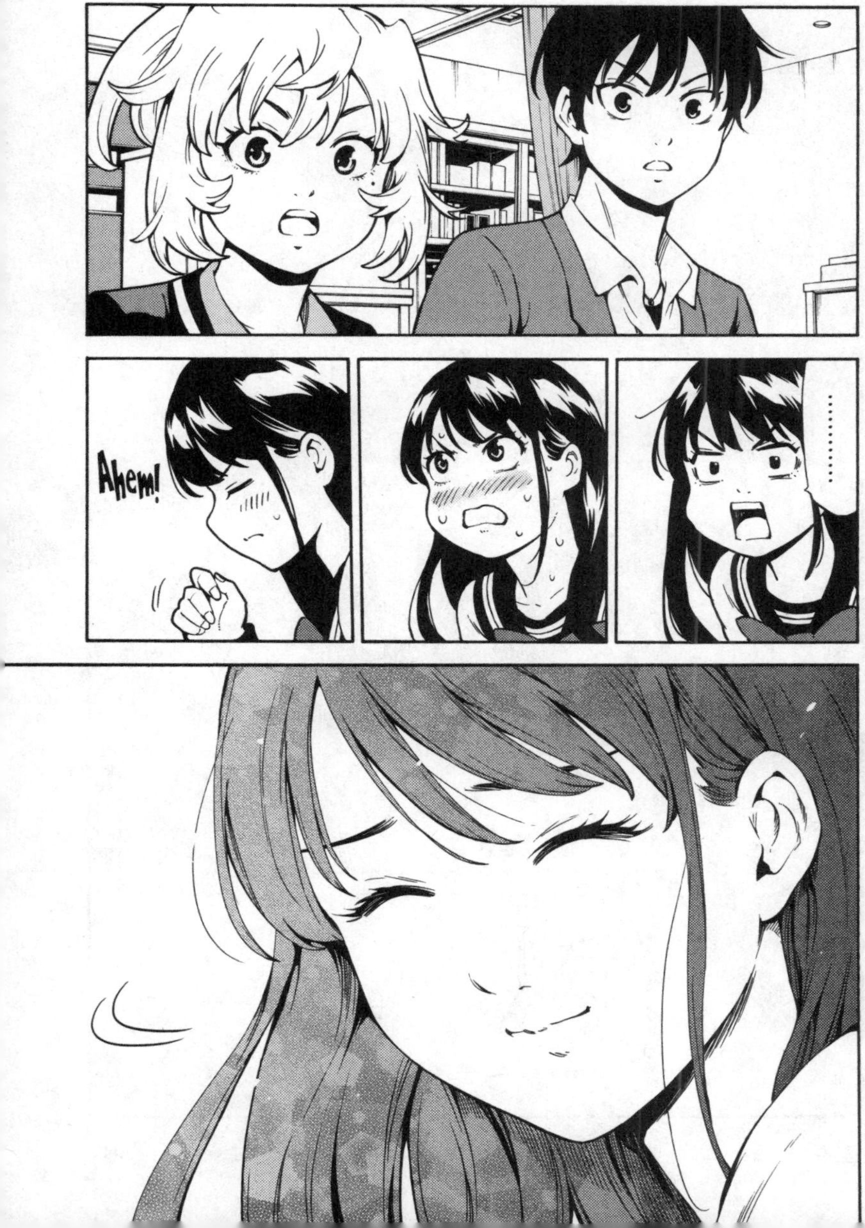
……
Ahem!

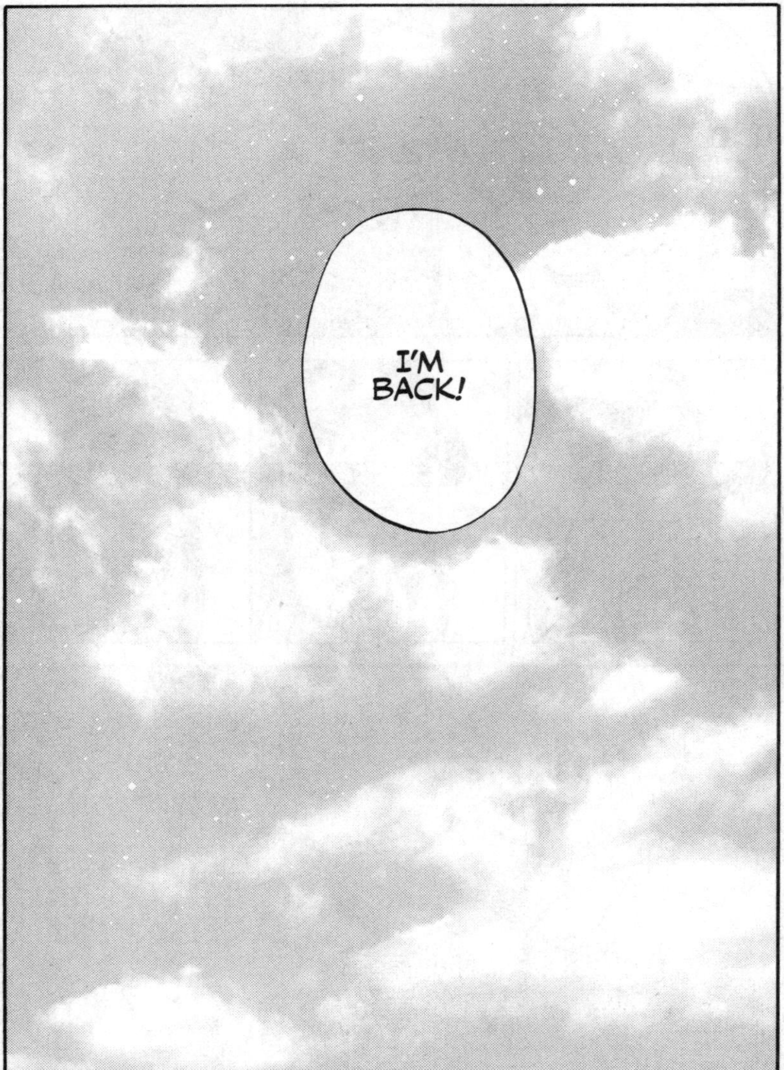
I'M BACK!

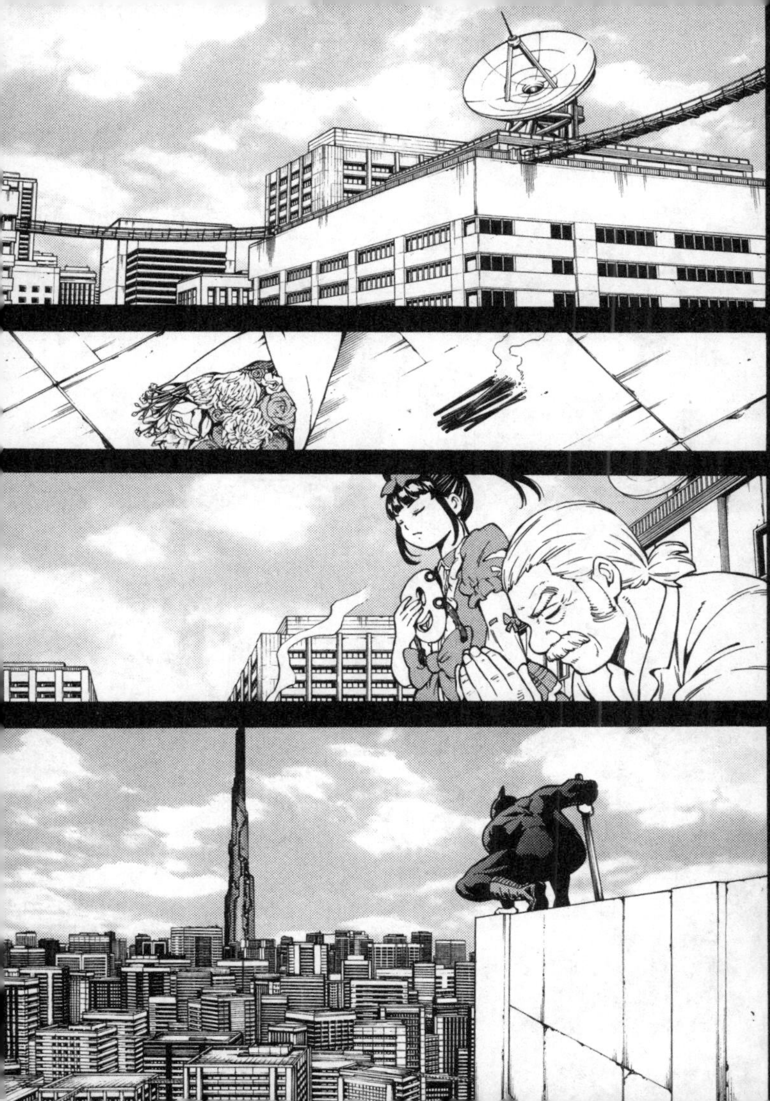

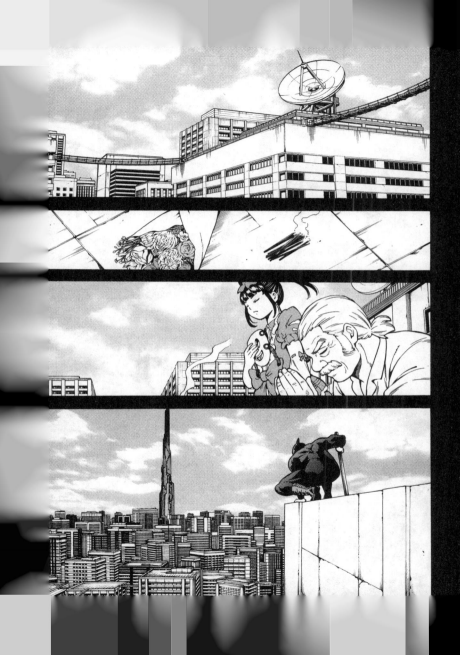

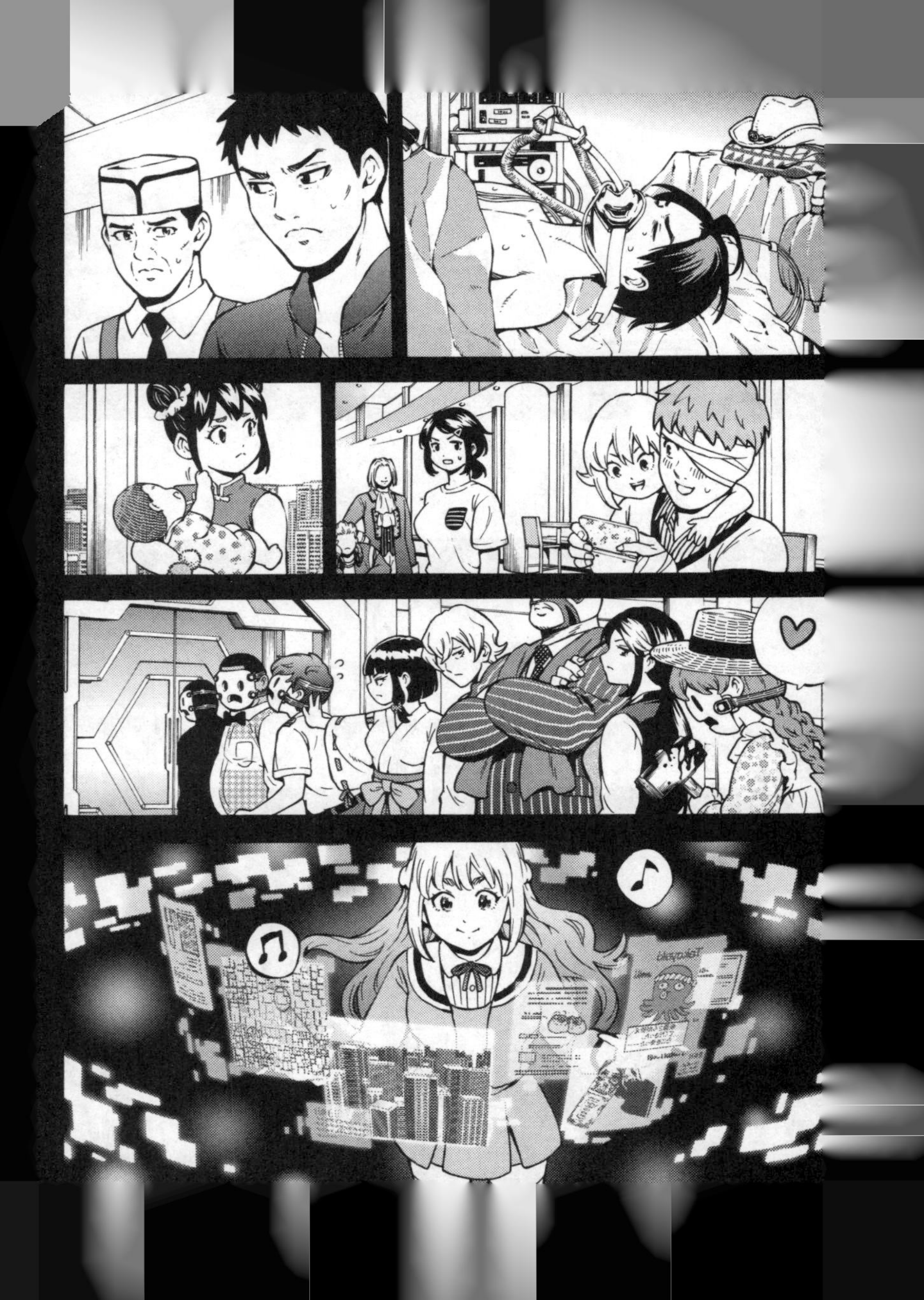

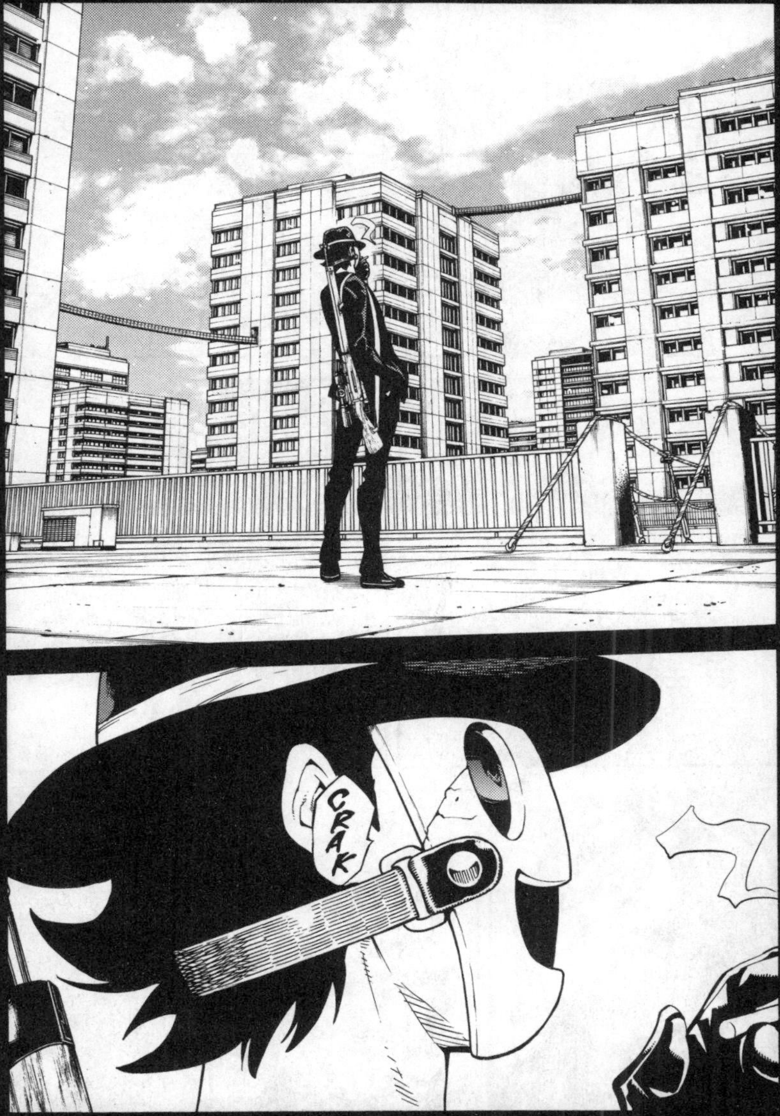
CRAK

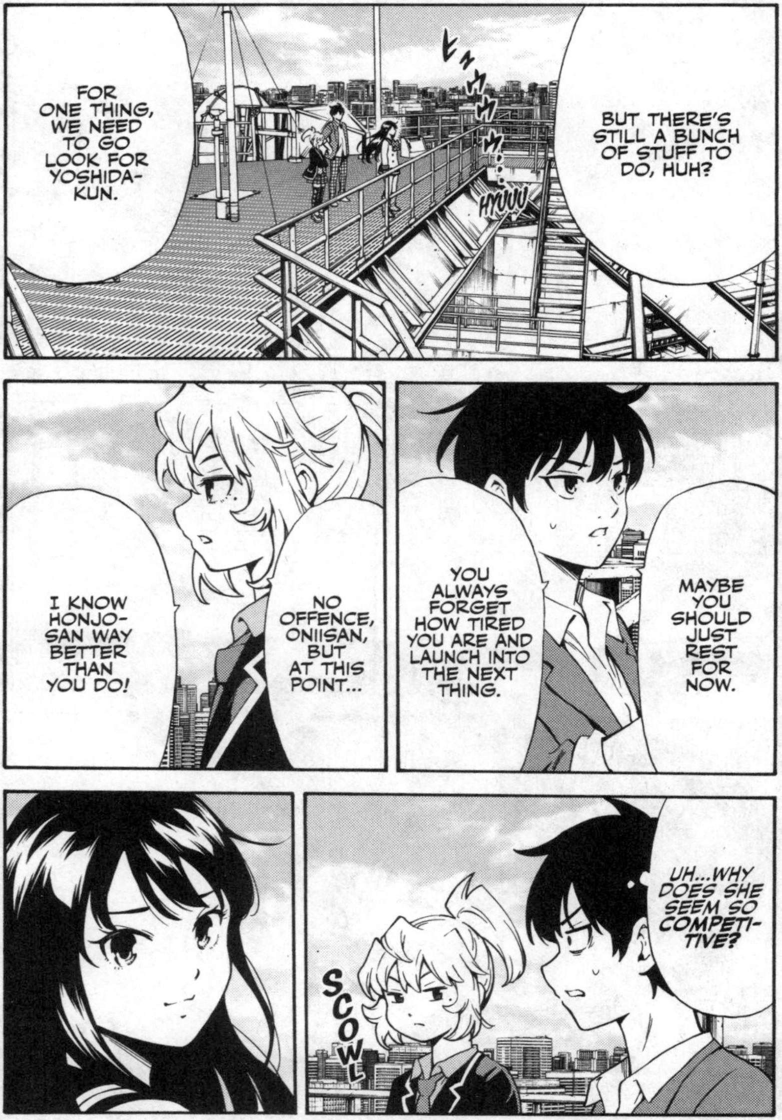
BUT THERE'S STILL A BUNCH OF STUFF TO DO, HUH?
HYUUU
FOR ONE THING, WE NEED TO GO LOOK FOR YOSHIDA-KUN.
MAYBE YOU SHOULD JUST REST FOR NOW.
YOU ALWAYS FORGET HOW TIRED YOU ARE AND LAUNCH INTO THE NEXT THING.
NO OFFENCE, ONIISAN, BUT AT THIS POINT...
I KNOW HONJO-SAN WAY BETTER THAN YOU DO!
UH...WHY DOES SHE SEEM SO COMPETITIVE?
SCOWL

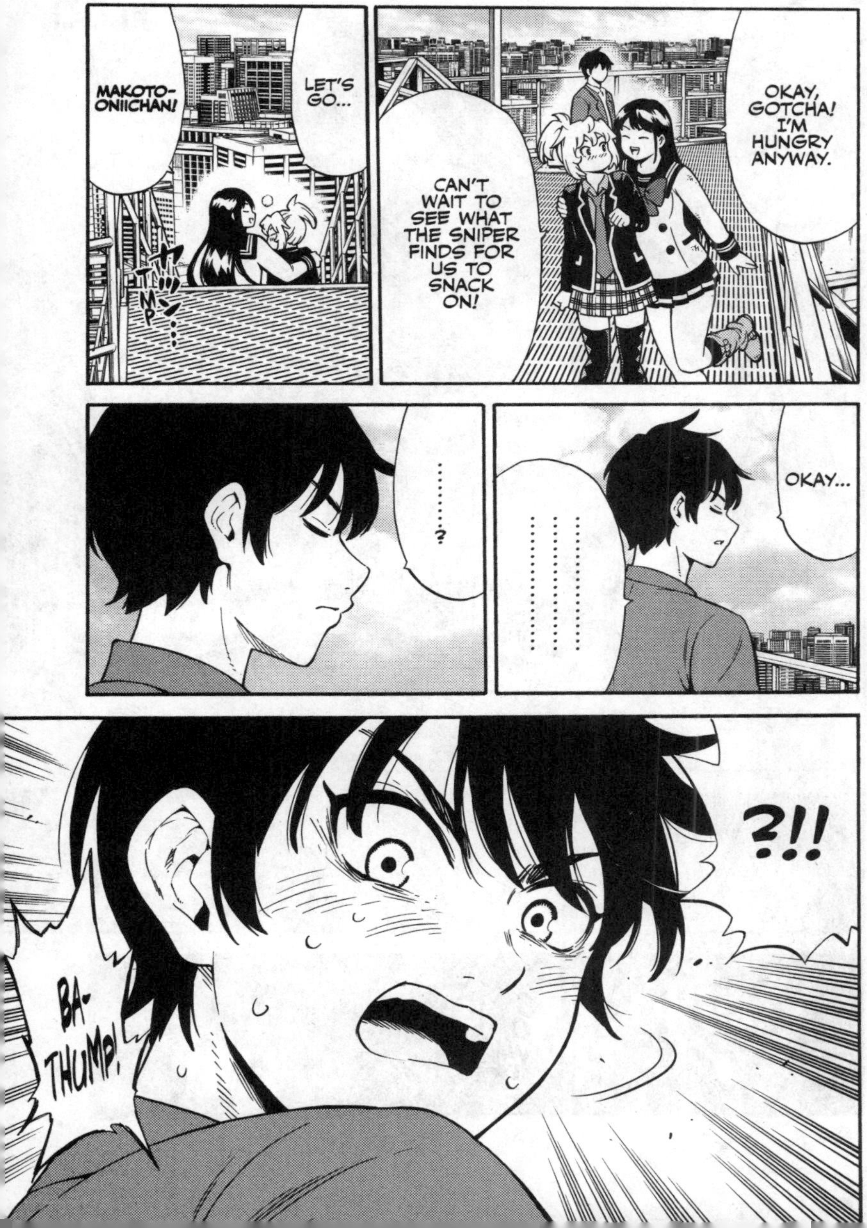
OKAY, GOTCHA! I'M HUNGRY ANYWAY.
CAN'T WAIT TO SEE WHAT THE SNIPER FINDS FOR US TO SNACK ON!
LET'S GO...
MAKOTO-ONIICHAN!
TMP...
OKAY...
......
......?
?!!
BA-THUMP!

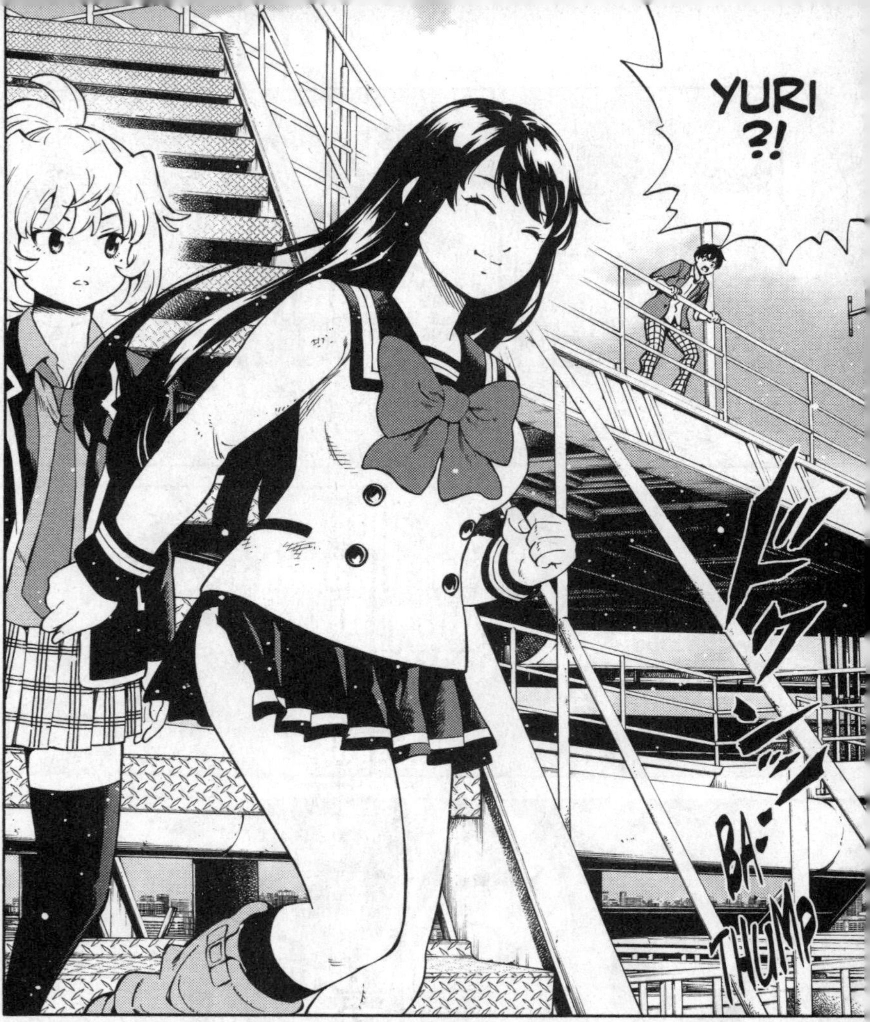
YURI ?!
BA-THUMP

HIGH-RISE INVASION

END

HIGH-RISE INVASION

STORY
Tsuina Miura

ART
Takahiro Oba

STAFF
Fukuen Kanako
Sakurai Hiroshi
Igarashi Tae

EDITORS
Uchida Tomohiro
Kohori Ryuuichi
Kayama Naoto

COMICS EDITOR
Nozawa Shinobu

COVER DESIGN
Inadome Ken

Extra pages! ☆

Epilogue and Q&A Corner!

Mouthless-kun

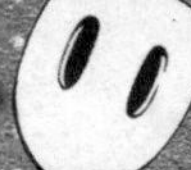

This volume went way past the page count boundary, but there was still a bunch of stuff that didn't fit! I'll go into it here instead.

~About Yuri-chan Knowing the Truth~

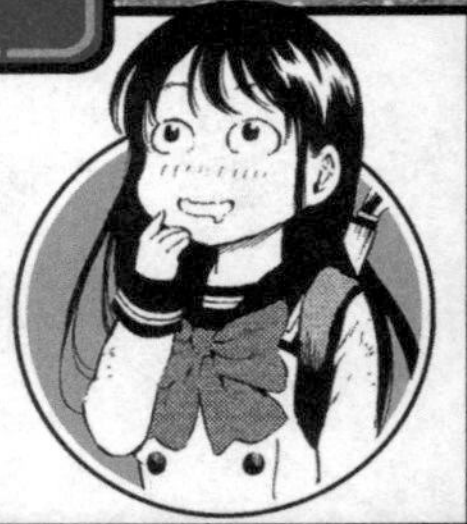

It was my job to maintain the personal records of everyone in the domain! Obviously, they're confidential, but rulebreaker Yuri-chan apparently **went ahead and accessed them**. She's known since she "awakened" that she and Rika weren't really siblings...but she kept acting pretty much the same. Kinda odd, when you think about it! Was she concentrating on the upcoming battle? Or **did she always sort of realize**? Hard to tell, since Yuri-chan's always giggling!

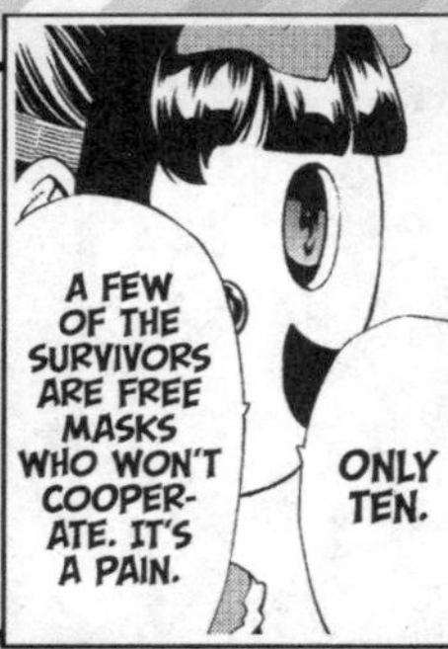
ONLY TEN.
A FEW OF THE SURVIVORS ARE FREE MASKS WHO WON'T COOPER-ATE. IT'S A PAIN.

~About the People Nise-chan and Co. Saved~

Blank-faced Masks are way stronger than normal Masks, and during the terminal phase, they attacked the domain's human inhabitants ruthlessly! (After all, those humans were supposed to be sacrifices!) But Nise-chan and the others went all-out to eliminate those blank-faced Masks, saving quite a few—but not all—of the humans. So, what's up with those other humans? Well, they do indeed exist! **We just haven't depicted them**. We didn't have enough pages! On top of that, **some of them made it through the terminal phase on their own!** Like Uzuki-kun said, "A lot happened in the other districts, too, huh?"

~For Example~

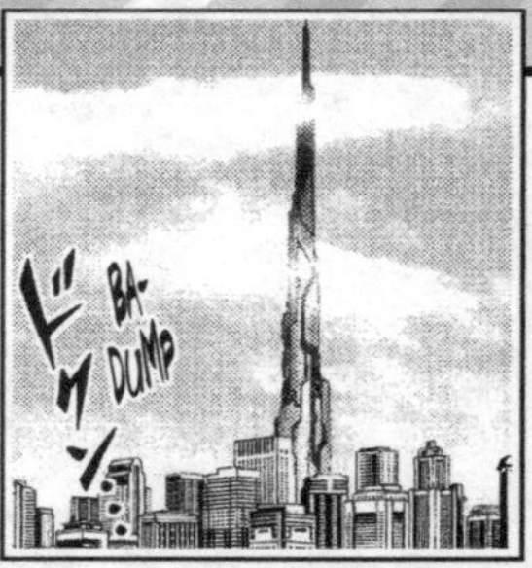
BA-DUMP

The high-rise world is huge, so lots of stuff happened beyond what you're aware of! For instance, **other folks got close to god!** One was dubbed the "Great Sage." He was quietly, carefully gunning for godhood and steadily gaining strength. When the **demonic-but-powerful Yuri-chan** showed up, though, he found himself back to square one! He's no match for Yuri and her friends in terms of strength, but he apparently hasn't thrown in the towel. Right now, he's planning his next move; helping Okihara-kun and the others was part of that plan. I'm cheering him on!

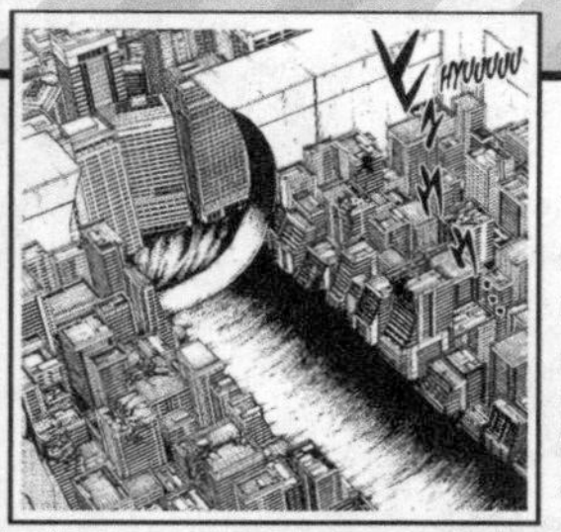

~About Yuri's Showdown with the Administrator~

Yuri-chan could've beaten the administrator if she went all-out. I guess she realized something awful would happen if she did. She was actually on thin ice! At the end of the fight, she caused massive destruction by exploiting the pressure imbalance of different dimensions, which created tons of energy. **If Yuri made one wrong move, she could've destroyed the entire domain.** So, yeah—I popped in! When she passed out, Volleyball Mask and Maid Mask carried her away.

~About Yoshida-kun's Fate~

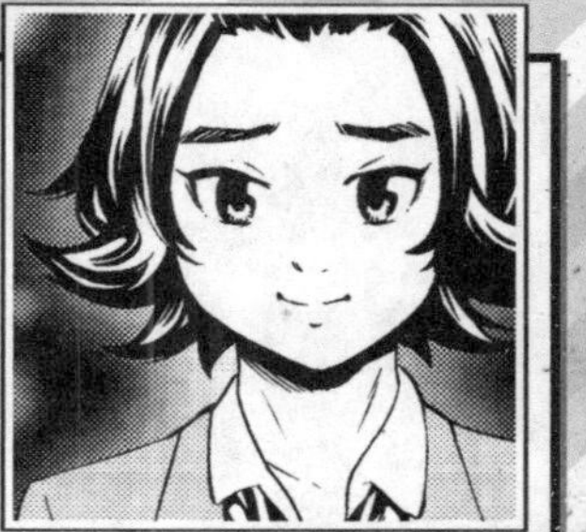

I'm not too sure myself what happened with Yoshida-kun. I guess he might've inherited some of the administrator's abilities. If so, he used them amazingly well! Frankly, although I'm the supervisor, Yoshida-kun really wasn't on my radar. Still, **this facility is partly intended to track fluctuations in humankind's will** that systems and calculations can't measure. At this point, I've figured out that Yoshida's somewhere in a nearby dimension—but since I don't supervise that dimension, I can't help!

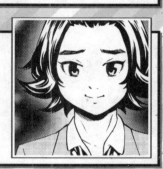

~Footnotes~

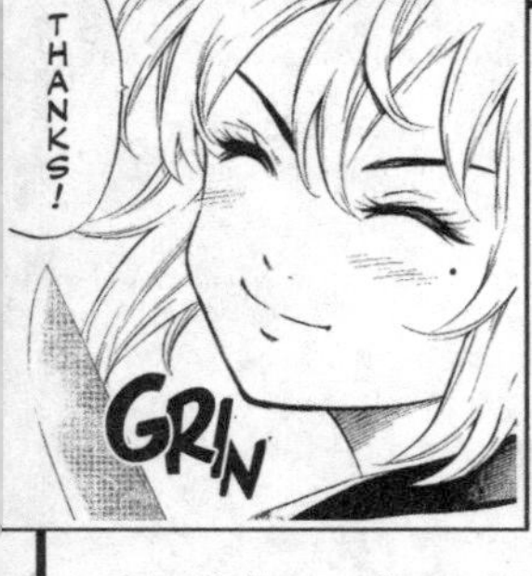
THANKS!
GRIN

· Yuri-chan isn't doing much but maintaining the domain's boundaries. **She befriended Yamanami-kun, and they hang out at an arcade in the high-rise world.** She's apparently the best gamer in the entire domain—even without using her abilities!

· Since Rika-chan learned that Yuri-chan shrugged off the truth about their family, he's privately been pretty flustered. **He's thrown himself into cooking and doing laundry to get his mind off it!**

· Nise-chan laid claim to Kijima-san's blade collection, and she's mentioned going on a journey to find every knife hidden in the domain! **Her relationship with Yuri-chan hasn't changed** at all. Cute!

· Sniper Mask's **now acting as administrator!** He consults with me, negotiates with outside forces, and leads the Free Masks, among other things. He's burning the candle at both ends! All in all, he's a good guy who gets stuff done.

· Kuon-chan's wandering from brain to brain! Is she a ghost? She could probably use a blank-faced Mask as a new body, but since I implemented a shutdown, she's holding off on major actions. Between you and me, **I really like her!**

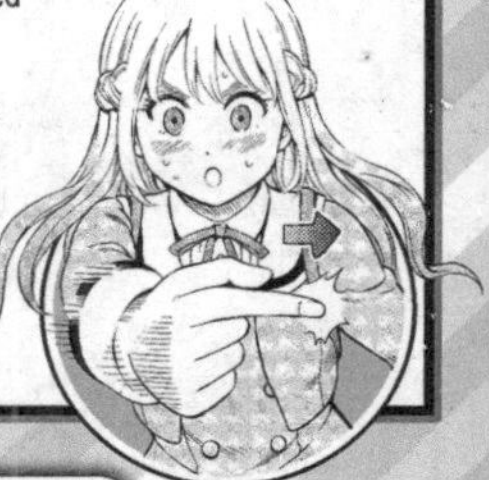

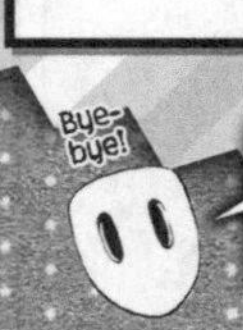
Bye-bye!

So, what exactly is the high-rise domain? And what exactly am I? Sadly, I can't answer those questions! I'm not really sure myself! I hope we find out someday, though!

Text/Tsuina Miura

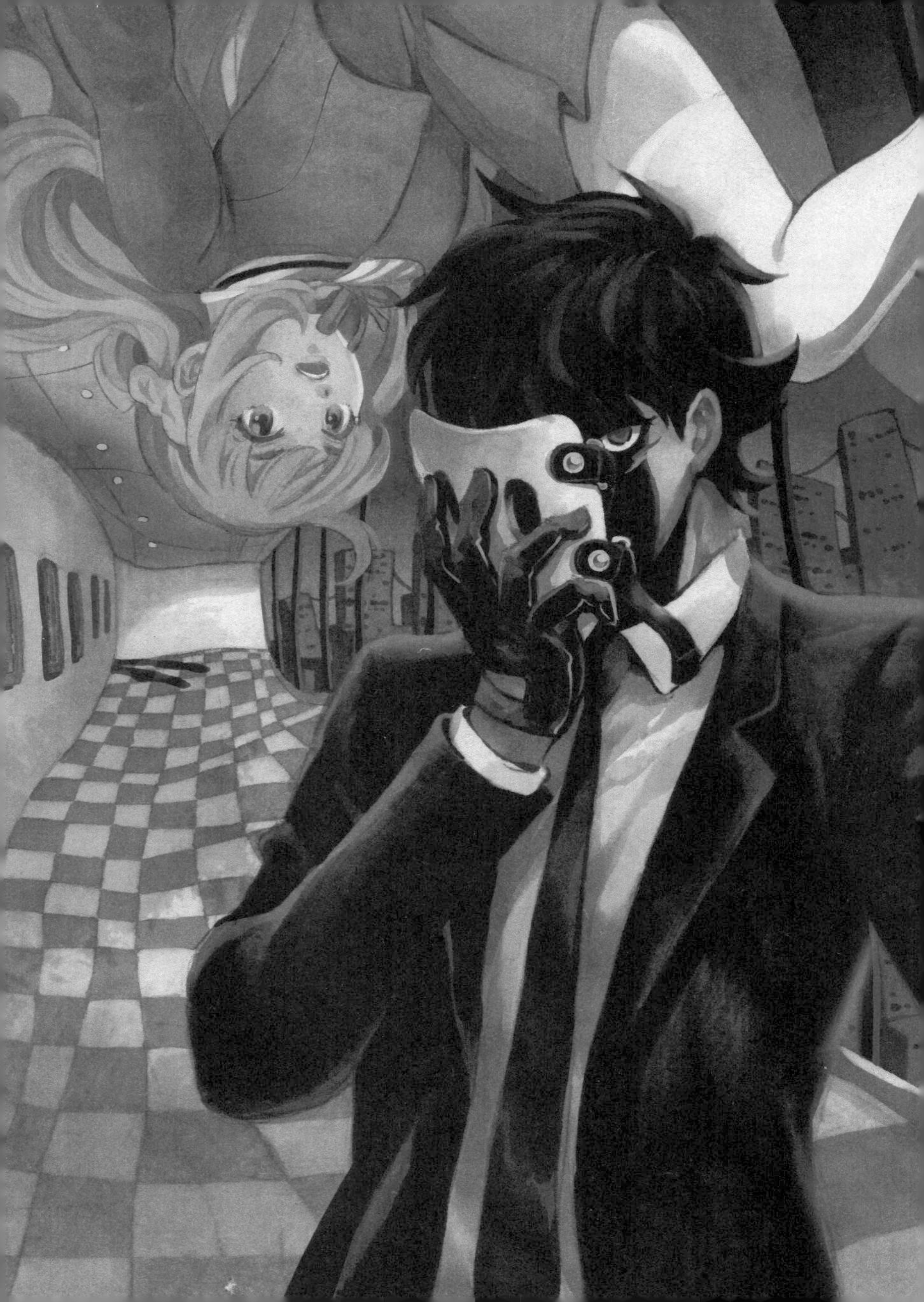

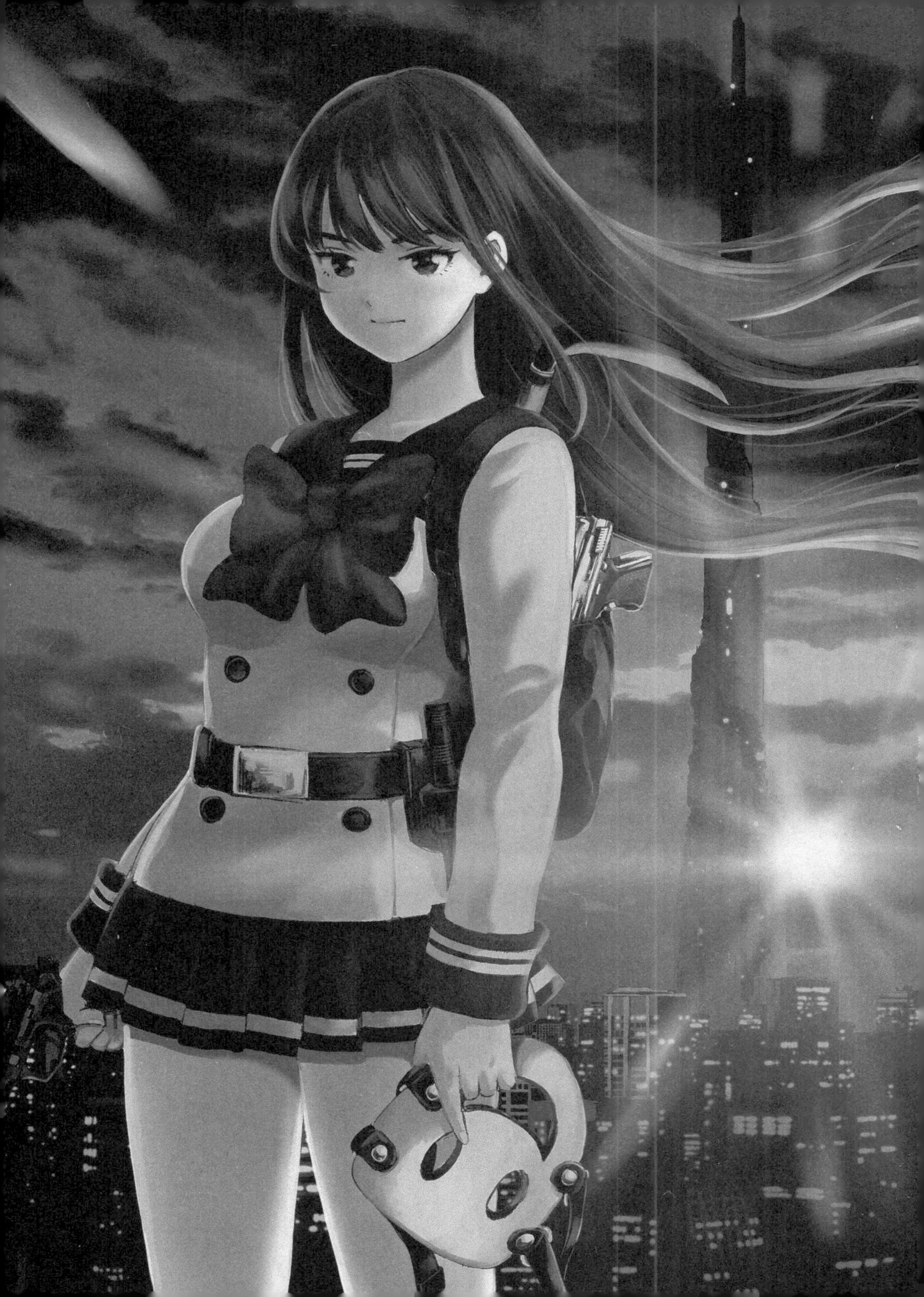

HIGH-RISE
INVASION

SEVEN SEAS ENTERTAINMENT PRESENTS

HIGH-RISE INVASION Vol. 19-21

story by TSUINA MIURA / art by TAKAHIRO OBA

TRANSLATION
Nan Rymer

ADAPTATION
Rebecca Schneidereit

LETTERING AND RETOUCH
Brendon Hull

COVER DESIGN
Kris Aubin

PROOFREADER
Dawn Davis, Janet Houck

EDITOR
Peter Adrian Behravesh

PREPRESS TECHNICIAN
Rhiannon Rasmussen-Silverstein

PRODUCTION MANAGER
Lissa Pattillo

MANAGING EDITOR
Julie Davis

ASSOCIATE PUBLISHER
Adam Arnold

PUBLISHER
Jason DeAngelis

TENKUU SHINPAN VOLUME 19-21
© Tsuina Miura 2019, © Takahiro Oba 2019
All rights reserved.
First published in Japan in 2019 by Kodansha Ltd., Tokyo.
Publication rights for this English edition arranged through Kodansha Ltd.,
Tokyo.

Seven Seas press and purchase enquiries can be sent to Marketing Manager
Lianne Sentar at press@gomanga.com. Information regarding the distribution
and purchase of digital editions is available from Digital Manager CK Russell
at digital@gomanga.com.

Seven Seas and the Seven Seas logo are trademarks of
Seven Seas Entertainment. All rights reserved.

ISBN: 978-1-64827-252-3

Printed in Canada

First Printing: September 2021

10 9 8 7 6 5 4 3 2 1

FOLLOW US ONLINE: www.sevenseasentertainment.com

READING DIRECTIONS

This book reads from *right to left*, Japanese style. If this is your first time reading manga, you start reading from the top right panel on each page and take it from there. If you get lost, just follow the numbered diagram here. It may seem backwards at first, but you'll get the hang of it! Have fun!!

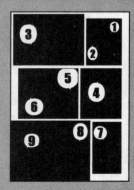